THE

ANTE-NICENE FATHERS

TRANSLATIONS OF

The Writings of the Fathers down to A.D. 325

THE REV. ALEXANDER ROBERTS, D.D.,

AND

JAMES DONALDSON, LL.D.,

EDITORS

AMERICAN REPRINT OF THE EDINBURGH EDITION

REVISED AND CHRONOLOGICALLY ARRANGED, WITH BRIEF PREFACES AND
OCCASIONAL NOTES,

BY

A. CLEVELAND COXE, D.D.

VOLUME IV

TERTULLIAN, PART FOURTH; MINUCIUS FELIX; COMMODIAN; ORIGEN, PARTS FIRST AND SECOND.

WM. B. EERDMANS PUBLISHING COMPANY
GRAND RAPIDS   MICHIGAN

ISBN 0-8028-8090

Reprinted, May 1976

PHOTOLITHOPRINTED BY CUSHING - MALLOY, INC.
ANN ARBOR, MICHIGAN, UNITED STATES OF AMERICA

FATHERS OF THE THIRD CENTURY

TERTULLIAN, PART FOURTH; MINUCIUS FELIX; COMMODIAN; ORIGEN,
PARTS FIRST AND SECOND.

AMERICAN EDITION

CHRONOLOGICALLY ARRANGED, WITH BRIEF NOTES AND PREFACES,

BY

A. CLEVELAND COXE, D.D.

Τὰ ἀρχαῖα ἔθη κρατείτω.
THE NICENE COUNCIL.

INTRODUCTORY NOTICE

[A.D. 200–250.] This fourth volume of our series is an exceptional one. It presents, under one cover, specimens of two of the noblest of the Christian Fathers; both of them exceptionally great in their influence upon the ages; both of them justly censurable for pitiable faults; each of them, in spite of such failings, endeared to the heart of Christendom by their great services to the Church; both of them geographically of Africa, but the one essentially Greek and the other a Latin; the one a builder upon the great Clementine foundations, the other himself a founder, the brilliant pioneer of Latin Christianity. The contrasts and the concurrences of such minds, and in them of the Alexandrian and Carthaginian schools, are most suggestive, and should be edifying.

The works of both, as here given, are fractional. Tertullian overflows into this volume, after filling one before; the vast proportions of Origen's labours forced the Edinburgh publishers to give specimens only.

Minucius Felix and Commodian are thrown in as a sort of appendix to Tertullian, and illustrate the school and the Church of the same country. The Italian type does not yet appear. Latin Christianity is essentially North-African, and is destined to continue such, conspicuously, till it has culminated in the genius of Augustine. From the first, the Orientals speculate concerning God; the Westerns deal with man. Both schools "contend earnestly for the faith once delivered to the saints." And, once for all, it may be said, that if their language necessarily lacks the precision of technical theology, and enables those who have little sympathy with them to set them one against another on some points, and so to impair their value as witnesses, it is quite as easy, and far more just, to show the harmony of their ideas, even when they differ in their forms of speech. This has been triumphantly done by Bull, just as the same writer harmonizes St. James and St. Paul, working down to their common base in the Rock of Ages. The test of Ante-Nicene unity is the Nicene Symbol, in which the primitive writings find their ultimate expression. That Clement and Tertullian alike would have recognised as the faith; for the earlier Fathers were, in fact, its authors. The Nicene Fathers were compilers only, and professed only to embody in the Symbol what their predecessors had established and maintained.

Let it be borne in mind that there is only one Œcumenical Symbol. The Creed called the Apostles' is unknown to the East save as an orthodox confession of their Western brethren. The "Athanasian Creed" is only a Western hymn, like the *Te Deum*, and has no œcumenical warrant as a symbol, though it embodies the common doctrine. The *Filioque*, wherever it appears, is apocryphal, and has no œcumenical force; while it is heretical (in Catholic theology) if it be held in a sense which destroys the *One Source* of divinity in the Father, its *fons et origo*. Surely, it is a noble exercise of mind and heart to see, in the splendid result of the Ante-Nicene conflicts with error, and in the enduring truth and perennial freshness of the Nicene Creed, the fulfilment of the promise of the Great Head of the Church, that the Spirit should abide with them for ever, and guide them into all truth.

The editor-in-chief, who has been forced to labour unassisted in the preceding volumes, has been so happy as to find a valued collaborator in editing the works of Origen, who has also relieved him of the task of proof-reading almost entirely throughout this volume, excepting on his own pages of prefaces or annotations. In spite of the fact that a necessity for despatch requires the printing to be done from single proofs, it is believed that this volume excels its predecessors in typographical accuracy, — a merit largely due to the eminent skill of the Boston press from which it proceeds, but primarily to the pains of the Rev. Dr. Spencer, an expert in such operations.

For the favour and generous spirit with which his Christian brethren have welcomed and encouraged this undertaking, the editor is grateful to them, and to the common Lord and Master of us all.

OCTOBER, 1885.

CONTENTS OF VOLUME IV

TERTULLIAN

PART FOURTH.

I.

ON THE PALLIUM.[1]

[TRANSLATED BY THE REV. S. THELWALL.]

CHAP. I. — TIME CHANGES NATIONS' DRESSES — AND FORTUNES.

MEN of Carthage, ever princes of Africa, ennobled by ancient memories, blest with modern felicities, I rejoice that times are so prosperous with you that you have leisure to spend and pleasure to find in criticising dress. These are the " piping times of peace " and plenty. Blessings rain from the empire and from the sky. Still, you too of old time wore your garments — your tunics — of another shape ; and indeed they were in repute for the skill of the weft, and the harmony of the hue, and the due proportion of the size, in that they were neither prodigally long across the shins, nor immodestly scanty between the knees, nor niggardly to the arms, nor tight to the hands, but, without being shadowed by even a girdle arranged to divide the folds, they stood on men's backs with quadrate symmetry. The garment of the mantle extrinsically — itself too quadrangular — thrown back on either shoulder, and meeting closely round the neck in the gripe of the buckle, used to repose on the shoulders.[2] Its counterpart is now the priestly dress, sacred to Æsculapius, whom you now call your own. So, too, in your immediate vicinity, the sister State[3] used to clothe (her citizens) ; and wherever else in Africa Tyre (has settled).[4] But when the urn of worldly[5] lots varied, and God favoured the Romans, the sister State, indeed, of her own choice hastened to effect a change ; in order that when Scipio put in at her ports she might already beforehand have greeted him in the way of dress, precocious in her Romanizing. To you, however, after the benefit in which your injury resulted, as exempting you from the infirmity of age, not (deposing you) from your height of eminence, — after Gracchus and his foul omens, after Lepidus and his rough jests, after Pompeius and his triple altars, and Cæsar and his long delays, when Statilius Taurus reared your ramparts, and Sentius Saturninus pronounced the solemn form of your inauguration, — while concord lends her aid, the *gown* is offered. Well ! what a circuit has it taken ! from Pelasgians to Lydians ;[6] from Lydians to Romans : in order that from the shoulders of the sublimer people it should descend to embrace Carthaginians ! Henceforth, finding your tunic too long, you suspend it on a dividing cincture ; and the redundancy of your now smooth *toga*[7] you support by gathering it together fold upon fold ; and, with whatever other garment social condition or dignity or season clothes you, *the mantle*, at any rate, which used to be worn by all ranks and conditions among you, you not only are unmindful of, but even deride. For my own part, I wonder not (thereat), in the face of a more ancient evidence (of your forgetfulness). For the ram withal — not that which Laberius[8] (calls)

" Back-twisted-horned, wool-skinned, stones-dragging,"

but a beam-like engine it is, which does military service in battering walls — never before poised by any, the redoubted Carthage,

" Keenest in pursuits of war,"[9]

is said to have been the first of all to have equipped for the oscillatory work of pendulous impetus ;[10] modelling the power of her engine after the choleric fury of the head-avenging beast.[11] When, however, their country's fortunes are at the last gasp, and the ram, now turned

---

[1] [Written, according to Neander, about A.D. 208.]
[2] [See Elucidation I.]
[3] Utica (Oehler).
[4] i.e., in Adrumetum (Oehler).
[5] Sæcularium.

[6] i e., Etruscans, who were supposed to be of Lydian origin.
[7] i.e., your gown.
[8] A Roman knight and mime-writer.
[9] Virg., *Æn.*, i. 14.
[10] Or, " attack."
[11] Cap*ut* vindicantis. But some read cap*ite:* " which avenges itself with its head."

Roman, is doing his deeds of daring against the ramparts which erst were his own, forthwith the Carthaginians stood dumbfounded as at a "novel" and "strange" ingenuity:

"So much doth Time's long age avail to change!"[1]

Thus, in short, it is that the mantle, too, is not recognised.

CHAP. II. — THE LAW OF CHANGE, OR MUTATION, UNIVERSAL.

Draw we now our material from some other source, lest Punichood either blush or else grieve in the midst of Romans. To change her habit is, at all events, the stated function of entire nature. The very world[2] itself (this which we inhabit) meantime discharges it. See to it Anaximander, if he thinks there are more (worlds): see to it, whoever else (thinks there exists another) anywhere at the region of the Meropes, as Silenus prates in the ears of Midas,[3] apt (as those ears are[4]), it must be admitted, for even huger fables. Nay, even if Plato thinks there exists one of which this of ours is the image, that likewise must necessarily have similarly to undergo mutation; inasmuch as, if it is a "world,"[5] it will consist of diverse substances and offices, answerable to the form of that which is here the "world:"[5] for "world" it will not be if it be not just as the "world" is. Things which, in diversity, tend to unity, are diverse *by demutation*. In short, it is their vicissitudes which federate the discord of their diversity. Thus it will be *by mutation* that every "world"[5] will exist whose corporate structure is the result of diversities, and whose attemperation is the result of vicissitudes. At all events, this hostelry of ours[6] is versiform, — a fact which is patent to eyes that are closed, or utterly Homeric.[7] Day and night revolve in turn. The sun varies by annual stations, the moon by monthly phases. The stars — distinct in their confusion — sometimes drop, sometimes resuscitate, somewhat. The circuit of the heaven is now resplendent with serenity, now dismal with cloud; or else rain-showers come rushing down, and whatever missiles (mingle) with them: thereafter (follows) a slight sprinkling, and then again brilliance. So, too, the sea has an ill repute for honesty; while at one time, the breezes equably swaying it, tranquillity gives it the semblance of probity, calm gives it the semblance of even temper; and then all of a sudden it heaves restlessly with mountain-waves. Thus, too, if you survey the

earth, loving to clothe herself seasonably, you would nearly be ready to deny her identity, when, remembering her green, you behold her yellow, and will ere long see her hoary too. Of the rest of her adornment also, what is there which is not subject to interchanging mutation — the higher ridges of her mountains by decursion, the veins of her fountains by disappearance, and the pathways of her streams by alluvial formation? There was a time when her whole orb, withal, underwent mutation, overrun by all waters. To this day marine conchs and tritons' horns sojourn as foreigners on the mountains, eager to prove to Plato that even the heights have undulated. But withal, by ebbing out, her orb again underwent a formal mutation; another, but the same. Even now her shape undergoes local mutations, when (some particular) spot is damaged; when among her islands Delos is now no more, Samos a heap of sand, and the Sibyl (is thus proved) no liar;[8] when in the Atlantic (the isle) that was equal in size to Libya or Asia is sought in vain;[9] when formerly a side of Italy, severed to the centre by the shivering shock of the Adriatic and the Tyrrhenian seas, leaves Sicily as its relics; when that total swoop of discission, whirling backwards the contentious encounters of the mains, invested the sea with a novel vice, the vice not of spuing out wrecks, but of devouring them! The continent as well suffers from heavenly or else from inherent forces. Glance at Palestine. Where Jordan's river is the arbiter of boundaries, (behold) a vast waste, and a bereaved region, and bootless land! And once (there were there) cities, and flourishing peoples, and the soil yielded its fruits.[10] Afterwards, since God is a Judge, impiety earned showers of fire: Sodom's day is over, and Gomorrah is no more; and all is ashes; and the neighbour sea no less than the soil experiences a living death! Such a cloud overcast Etruria, burning down her ancient Volsinii, to teach Campania (all the more by the ereption of her Pompeii) to look expectantly upon her own mountains. But far be (the repetition of such catastrophes)! Would that Asia, withal, were by this time without cause for anxiety about the soil's voracity! Would, too, that Africa had once for all quailed before the devouring chasm, expiated by the treacherous absorption of one single camp![11] Many other such detriments besides have made innovations upon

---

[1] See Virg., *Æn.*, iii. 415 (Oehler).
[2] Mundus.
[3] See *adv. Herm.*, c. xxv. *ad fin.* (Oehler).
[4] As being "the ears of an ass."
[5] Mundus. Oehler's pointing is disregarded.
[6] Metatio nostra, i.e., the world.
[7] i.e., blind. Cf. Milton, *P. L.*, iii. 35, with the preceding and subsequent context.

[8] Alluding to the Sibylline oracles, in which we read (l. iii.), Καὶ Σάμος ἄμμος ἔσῃ, καὶ Δῆλος ἄδηλος· and again (l. iv.), Δῆλος οὐκ ἔτι δῆλος, ἄδηλα δὲ πάντα τοῦ Δήλου (Oehler).
[9] See *Apolog.*, c. xi. *med.*; *ad Nat.*, l. i. c. ix. *med.*; Plato, *Timæus*, pp. 24, 25 (Oehler).
[10] Oehler's apt conjecture, "et solum sua dabat," is substituted for the unintelligible "et solus audiebat" of the MSS., which Rig. skilfully but ineffectually tries to explain.
[11] The "camp" of Cambyses, said by Herod. (iii. 26) to have been swallowed up in the Libyan Syrtes (Salm. in Oehler). It was one detachment of his army. Milton tells similar tales of the "Serbonian bog." *P. L.*, ii. 591-594.

the fashion of our orb, and moved (particular) spots (in it). Very great also has been the licence of wars. But it is no less irksome to recount sad details than (to recount) the vicissitudes of kingdoms, (and to show) how frequent have been *their* mutations, from Ninus, the progeny of Belus, onwards; if indeed Ninus was the first to have a kingdom, as the ancient profane authorities assert. Beyond his time the pen is not wont (to travel), in general, among you (heathens). From the Assyrians, it may be, the histories of " recorded time " [1] begin to open. We, however, who are habitual readers of *divine* histories, are masters of the subject from the nativity of the universe [2] itself. But I prefer, at the present time, *joyous* details, inasmuch as things joyous withal are subject to mutation. In short, whatever the sea has washed away, the heaven burned down, the earth undermined, the sword shorn down, reappears at some other time by the turn of compensation. [3] For in primitive days not only was the earth, for the greater part of her circuit, empty and uninhabited; but if any particular race had seized upon any part, it existed for itself alone. And so, understanding at last that all things worshipped themselves, (the earth) consulted to weed and scrape her copiousness (of inhabitants), in one place densely packed, in another abandoning their posts; in order that thence (as it were from grafts and settings) peoples from peoples, cities from cities, might be planted throughout every region of her orb. [4] Transmigrations were made by the swarms of redundant races. The exuberance of the Scythians fertilizes the Persians; the Phœnicians gush out into Africa; the Phrygians give birth to the Romans; the seed of the Chaldeans is led out into Egypt; subsequently, when transferred thence, it becomes the Jewish race. [5] So, too, the posterity of Hercules, in like wise, proceed to occupy the Peloponnesus for the behoof of Temenus. So, again, the Ionian comrades of Neleus furnish Asia with new cities: so, again, the Corinthians, with Archias, fortify Syracuse. But antiquity is by this time a vain thing (to refer to), when our own careers are before our eyes. How large a portion of our orb has the present age [6] re-formed! how many cities has the triple power of our existing empire either

produced, or else augmented, or else restored! While God favours so many Augusti unitedly, how many populations have been transferred to other localities! how many peoples reduced! how many orders restored to their ancient splendour! how many barbarians baffled! In truth, our orb is the admirably cultivated estate of this empire; every aconite of hostility eradicated; and the cactus and bramble of clandestinely crafty familiarity [7] wholly uptorn; and (the orb itself) delightsome beyond the orchard of Alcinoüs and the rosary of Midas. Praising, therefore, our *orb* in its mutations, why do you point the finger of scorn at a *man?*

CHAP. III. — BEASTS SIMILARLY SUBJECT TO THE LAW OF MUTATION.

Beasts, too, instead of a *garment*, change their *form*. And yet the peacock withal has plumage for a garment, and a garment indeed of the choicest; nay, in the bloom of his neck richer than any purple, and in the effulgence of his back more gilded than any edging, and in the sweep of his tail more flowing than any train; many-coloured, diverse-coloured, and versicoloured; never itself, ever another, albeit ever itself when other; in a word, mutable as oft as moveable. The serpent, too, deserves to be mentioned, albeit not in the same breath as the peacock; for he too wholly changes what has been allotted him — his hide and his age: if it is true, (as it is,) that when he has felt the creeping of old age throughout him, he squeezes himself into confinement; crawls into a cave and out of his skin simultaneously; and, clean shorn on the spot, immediately on crossing the threshold leaves his slough behind him then and there, and uncoils himself in a new youth: with his scales his years, too, are repudiated. The hyena, if you observe, is of an annual sex, alternately masculine and feminine. I say nothing of the stag, because himself withal, the witness of his own age, feeding on the serpent, languishes — from the effect of the poison — into youth. There is, withal,

"A tardigrade field-haunting quadruped,
Humble and rough."

The tortoise of Pacuvius, you think? No. There is another beastling which the versicle fits; in size, one of the moderate exceedingly, but a grand name. If, without previously knowing him, you hear tell of a chameleon, you will at once apprehend something yet more huge united with a lion. But when you stumble upon him, generally in a vineyard, his whole bulk sheltered beneath a vine leaf, you will forthwith laugh at the egregious audacity of the name, in-

---

[1] Ævi.

[2] Mundi.

[3] " Alias versura compensati re*dit;* " unless we may read " red*dit,*" and take " versura " as a nominative: " the turn of compensation at some other time restores."

[4] This rendering, which makes *the earth* the subject, appears to give at least an intelligible sense to this hopelessly corrupt passage. Oehler's pointing is disregarded; and his rendering not strictly adhered to, as being too forced. If for Oehler's conjectural " se demum intellegens" we might read " se *debere* demum intellegens," or simply " se *debere* intellegens," a good sense might be made, thus: " understanding at last" (or, simply, " understanding ") " that it was her duty to cultivate *all* (parts of her surface)."

[5] Comp. Gen. xi. 26–xii. 5 with Acts vii. 2–4, 15, 45, and xiii. 17–19.

[6] Sæculum.

[7] Oehler understands this of *Clodius Albinus*, and the *Augusti* mentioned above to be Severus and his two sons Antoninus and Geta. But see Kaye, pp. 36–39 (ed. 3, 1845)

asmuch as there is no moisture even in his body, though in far more minute creatures the body *is* liquefied. The chameleon is a living pellicle. His headkin begins straight from his spine, for neck he has none : and thus reflection [1] is hard for him ; but, in circumspection, his eyes are outdarting, nay, they are revolving points of light. Dull and weary, he scarce raises from the ground, but drags, his footstep amazedly, and moves forward, — he rather demonstrates, than takes, a step : ever fasting, to boot, yet never fainting ; agape he feeds ; heaving, bellowslike, he ruminates ; his food wind. Yet withal the chameleon is able to effect a total self-mutation, and that is all. For, whereas his colour is properly one, yet, whenever anything has approached him, then he blushes. To the chameleon alone has been granted — as our common saying has it — to sport with his own hide.

Much had to be said in order that, after due preparation, we might arrive at *man*. From whatever beginning you admit him as springing, naked at all events and ungarmented he came from his fashioner's hand : afterwards, at length, without waiting for permission, he possesses himself, by a premature grasp, of wisdom. Then and there hastening to forecover what, in his newly made body, it was not yet due to modesty (to forecover), he surrounds himself meantime with fig-leaves : subsequently, on being driven from the confines of his birthplace because he had sinned, he went, skinclad, to the world [2] as to a mine.[3]

But these are secrets, nor does their knowledge appertain to all. Come, let us hear from your own store — (a store) which the Egyptians narrate, and Alexander [4] digests, and his mother reads — touching the time of Osiris,[5] when Ammon, rich in sheep, comes to him out of Libya. In short, they tell us that Mercury, when among them, delighted with the softness of a ram which he had chanced to stroke, flayed a little ewe ; and, while he persistently tries and (as the pliancy of the material invited him) thins out the thread by assiduous traction, wove it into the shape of the pristine net which he had joined with strips of linen. But *you* have preferred to assign all the management of wool-work and structure of the loom to Minerva ; whereas a more diligent workshop was presided over by Arachne. Thenceforth material (was abundant). Nor do I speak of the sheep of Miletus, and Selge, and Altinum, or of those for which Taren-

tum or Bætica is famous, with nature for their dyer : but (I speak of the fact) that shrubs afford you clothing, and the grassy parts of flax, losing their greenness, turn white by washing. Nor was it enough to *plant* and *sow* your tunic, unless it had likewise fallen to your lot to *fish* for raiment. For the sea withal yields fleeces, inasmuch as the more brilliant shells of a mossy wooliness furnish a hairy stuff. Further : it is no secret that the silkworm — a species of wormling it is — presently reproduces safe and sound (the fleecy threads) which, by drawing them through the *air*, she distends more skilfully than the dial-like webs of spiders, and then devours. In like manner, if you kill it, the threads which you coil are forthwith instinct with vivid colour.

The ingenuities, therefore, of the tailoring art, superadded to, and following up, so abundant a store of materials — first with a view to covering humanity, where Necessity led the way ; and subsequently with a view to adorning withal, ay, and inflating it, where Ambition followed in the wake — have promulgated the various forms of garments. Of which forms, part are worn by particular nations, without being common to the rest ; part, on the other hand, universally, as being useful to all : as, for instance, this Mantle, albeit it is more Greek (than Latin), has yet by this time found, in speech, a home in Latium. With the word the garment entered. And accordingly the very man who used to sentence Greeks to extrusion from the city, but learned (when he was now advanced in years) their *alphabet* and *speech* — the self-same Cato, by baring his shoulder at the time of his prætorship, showed no less favour to the Greeks by his mantle-like *garb*.

CHAP. IV. — CHANGE NOT ALWAYS IMPROVEMENT.

Why, now, if the Roman fashion is (social) salvation to every one, are you nevertheless Greek to a degree, even in points not honourable ? Or else, if it is not so, whence in the world is it that provinces which have had a better training, provinces which nature adapted rather for surmounting by hard struggling the difficulties of the soil, derive the pursuits of the wrestling-ground — pursuits which fall into a sad old age [6] and labour in vain — and the unction with mud,[7] and the rolling in sand, and the dry dietary ? Whence comes it that some of our Numidians, with their long locks made longer by horsetail plumes, learn to bid the barber shave their skin close, and to exempt their crown alone from the knife ? Whence comes it tha.

---

[1] Reflecti: perhaps a play upon the word = to turn back, or (mentally) to reflect.
[2] Orbi.
[3] i.e., a place which he was to work, as condemned criminals worked mines. Comp. *de Pu.*, c. xxii. *sub init.* ; and see Gen. ii. 25 (in LXX. iii. 1), iii. 7, 21–24.
[4] Alexander Polyhistor, who dedicated his books on the affairs of the Phrygians and Egyptians to his mother (Rig. in Oehler).
[5] The Egyptian Liber, or Bacchus. See *de Cor.*, c. vii. (Rig. in Oehler).

[6] Male senescentia. Rig. (as quoted by Oehler) seems to interpret, "*which entail* a feeble old age." Oehler himself seems to take it to mean "pursuits which are growing very old, and toiling to no purpose."
[7] Or, as some take it, *with wax* (Oehler).

men shaggy and hirsute learn to teach the resin [1] to feed on their arms with such rapacity, the tweezers to weed their chin so thievishly? A prodigy it is, that all this should be done without the Mantle! To the Mantle appertains this whole Asiatic practice! What hast thou, Libya, and thou, Europe, to do with athletic refinements, which thou knowest not how to dress? For, in sooth, what kind of thing is it to practise Greekish depilation more than Greekish attire?

The transfer of dress approximates to culpability just in so far as it is not custom, but nature, which suffers the change. There is a wide enough difference between the honour due to time, and religion. Let Custom show fidelity to Time, Nature to God. To Nature, accordingly, the Larissæan hero [2] gave a shock by turning into a virgin; he who had been reared on the marrows of wild beasts (whence, too, was derived the composition of his name, because he had been a stranger with his lips to the maternal breast [3]); he who had been reared by a rocky and wood-haunting and monstrous trainer [4] in a stony school. You could bear patiently, if it were in a *boy's* case, his mother's solicitude; but he at all events was already be-haired, he at all events had already secretly given proof of his manhood to some one, [5] when he consents to wear the flowing stole, [6] to dress his hair, to cultivate his skin, to consult the mirror, to bedizen his neck; effeminated even as to his ear by boring, whereof his bust at Sigeum still retains the trace. Plainly afterwards he turned soldier: for necessity restored him his sex. The clarion had sounded of battle: nor were arms far to seek. "The steel's self," says (Homer), "attracteth the hero." [7] Else if, after that incentive as well as before, he had persevered in his maidenhood, he might withal have been married! Behold, accordingly, mutation! A monster, I call him, — a double monster: from man to woman; by and by from woman to man: whereas neither ought the truth to have been belied, nor the deception confessed. Each fashion of changing was evil: the one opposed to nature, the other contrary to safety.

Still more disgraceful was the case when lust transfigured a man in his dress, than when some maternal dread did so: and yet adoration is offered by you to me, whom you ought to blush at, — that Clubshaftandhidebearer, who exchanged for womanly attire the whole proud heritage of his name! Such licence was granted

to the secret haunts of Lydia, [8] that Hercules was prostituted in the person of Omphale, and Omphale in that of Hercules. Where were Diomed and his gory mangers? where Busiris and his funereal altars? where Geryon, triply one? The club preferred still to reek with their brains when it was being pestered with unguents! The now veteran (stain of the) Hydra's and of the Centaurs' blood upon the shafts was gradually eradicated by the pumice-stone, familiar to the hair-pin! while voluptuousness insulted over the fact that, after transfixing monsters, they should perchance sew a coronet! No sober woman even, or heroine [9] of any note, would have adventured her shoulders beneath the hide of such a beast, unless after long softening and smoothening down and deodorization (which in Omphale's house, I hope, was effected by balsam and fenugreek-salve: I suppose the mane, too, submitted to the comb) for fear of getting her tender neck imbued with lionly toughness. The yawning mouth stuffed with hair, the jaw-teeth overshadowed amid the forelocks, the whole outraged visage, would have roared had it been able. Nemea, at all events (if the spot has any presiding genius), groaned: for then she looked around, and saw that she had lost her lion. What sort of being the said Hercules was in Omphale's silk, the description of Omphale in Hercules' hide has inferentially depicted.

But, again, he who had formerly rivalled the Tirynthian [10] — the pugilist Cleomachus — subsequently, at Olympia, after losing by efflux his masculine sex by an incredible mutation — bruised within his skin and without, worthy to be wreathed among the "Fullers" even of Novius, [11] and deservedly commemorated by the mimographer Lentulus in his *Catinensians* — did, of course, not only cover with bracelets the traces left by (the bands of) the cestus, but likewise supplanted the coarse ruggedness of his athlete's cloak with some superfinely wrought tissue.

Of Physco and Sardanapalus I must be silent, whom, but for their eminence in lusts, no one would recognise as kings. But I must be silent, for fear lest even *they* set up a muttering concerning some of your Cæsars, equally lost to shame; for fear lest a mandate have been given to canine [12] constancy to point to a Cæsar impurer than Physco, softer than Sardanapalus, and indeed a second Nero. [13]

Nor less warmly does the force of *vainglory*

---

[1] Used as a depilatory.
[2] Achilles.
[3] Ἀχιλλεύς: from ἀ privative, and χεῖλος, the lip. See Oehler.
[4] The Centaur Chiron, namely.
[5] Deianira, of whom he had begotten Pyrrhus (Oehler).
[6] See the note on this word in *de Idol.*, c. xviii.
[7] Hom., *Od.*, xvi. 294 (Oehler).

[8] Jos. Mercer, quoted by Oehler, appears to take the meaning to be, "to his clandestine Lydian concubine;" but that rendering does not seem necessary.
[9] Viraginis; but perhaps = virginis. See the Vulg. in Gen. ii. 23.
[10] i.e., Hercules.
[11] Or, "which are now attributed to Novius." Novius was a writer of that kind of farce called "Atellanæ fabulæ;" and one of his farces — or one attributed to him in Tertullian's day — was called "The Fullers."
[12] i.e., cynical; comp. *de Pa.*, c. ii. *ad init.*
[13] i.e., Domitian, called by Juv. *calvum Neronem*, Sat. iv. 38.

also work for the mutation of *clothing*, even while *manhood* is preserved. Every affection is a heat : when, however, it is blown to (the flame of) *affectation*, forthwith, by the blaze of glory, it is an *ardour*. From this fuel, therefore, you see a great king [1] — inferior only to his glory — seething. He had conquered the Median race, and was conquered by Median garb. Doffing the triumphal mail, he degraded himself into the captive trousers ! The breast dissculptured with scaly bosses, by covering it with a transparent texture he bared ; panting still after the work of war, and (as it were) softening, he extinguished it with the ventilating silk ! Not sufficiently swelling of spirit was the Macedonian, unless he had likewise found delight in a highly inflated garb : only that philosophers withal (I believe) themselves affect somewhat of that kind ; for I hear that there *has* been (such a thing as) philosophizing in purple. If a philosopher (appears) in purple, why not in gilded slippers [2] too ? For a Tyrian [3] to be shod in anything but gold, is by no means consonant with Greek habits. Some one will say, " Well, but there was another [4] who wore silk indeed, and shod himself in *brazen* sandals." Worthily, indeed, in order that at the bottom of his Bacchantian raiment he might make some tinkling sound, did he walk in cymbals ! But if, at that moment, Diogenes had been barking from his tub, he would not (have trodden on him [5]) with muddy feet — as the Platonic couches testify — but would have carried Empedocles down bodily to the secret recesses of the Cloacinæ ; [6] in order that he who had madly thought himself a celestial being might, as a god, salute first his sisters, [7] and afterwards men. Such garments, therefore, as alienate from nature and modesty, let it be allowed to be just to eye fixedly and point at with the finger and expose to ridicule by a nod. Just so, if a man were to wear a dainty robe trailing on the ground with Menander-like effeminacy, he would hear applied to himself that which the comedian says, " What sort of a cloak is that maniac wasting ? " For, now that the contracted brow of censorial vigilance is long since smoothed down, so far as reprehension is concerned, promiscuous usage offers to our gaze freedmen in equestrian garb, branded slaves in that of gentlemen, the notoriously infamous in that of the freeborn, clowns in that of city-folk, buffoons in that of lawyers, rustics in regimentals ;

the corpse-bearer, the pimp, the gladiator trainer, clothe themselves as you do. Turn, again, to women. You have to behold what Cæcina Severus pressed upon the grave attention of the senate — matrons stoleless in public. In fact, the penalty inflicted by the decrees of the augur Lentulus upon any matron who had thus cashiered herself was the same as for fornication ; inasmuch as certain matrons had sedulously promoted the disuse of garments which were the evidences and guardians of dignity, as being impediments to the practising of prostitution. But now, in their self-prostitution, in order that they may the more readily be approached, they have abjured stole, and chemise, and bonnet, and cap ; yes, and even the very litters and sedans in which they used to be kept in privacy and secrecy even in public. But while one extinguishes her proper adornments, another blazes forth such as are not hers. Look at the street-walkers, the shambles of popular lusts ; also at the female self-abusers with their sex ; and, if it is better to withdraw your eyes from such shameful spectacles of publicly slaughtered chastity, yet do but look with eyes askance, (and) you will at once see (them to be) matrons ! And, while the overseer of brothels airs her swelling silk, and consoles her neck — more impure than her haunt — with necklaces, and inserts in the armlets (which even matrons themselves would, of the guerdons bestowed upon brave men, without hesitation have appropriated) hands privy to all that is shameful, (while) she fits on her impure leg the pure white or pink shoe ; why do you not stare at such garbs ? or, again, at those which falsely plead religion as the supporter of their novelty ? while for the sake of an all-white dress, and the distinction of a fillet, and the privilege of a helmet, some are initiated into (the mysteries of) Ceres ; while, on account of an opposite hankering after sombre raiment, and a gloomy woollen covering upon the head, others run mad in Bellona's temple ; while the attraction of surrounding themselves with a tunic more broadly striped with purple, and casting over their shoulders a cloak of Galatian scarlet, commends Saturn (to the affections of others). When this Mantle itself, arranged with more rigorous care, and sandals after the Greek model, serve to flatter Æsculapius, [8] how much more should you then accuse and assail it with your eyes, as being guilty of superstition — albeit superstition simple and unaffected ? Certainly, when first it clothes this wisdom [9] which renounces superstitions with all their vanities, then most assuredly is the Mantle, above all the garments in which you array your gods and goddesses, an august robe ; and, above all the caps

---

[1] Alexander.
[2] Comp. *de Idol.*, c. viii. *med.*
[3] i.e., one who affects Tyrian dress — dresses in Tyrian purple.
[4] Empedocles (Salm. in Oehler).
[5] I have adopted Oehler's suggestion, and inserted these words.
[6] i.e., of Cloacina or Cluacina (= " the Purifier," a name of Venus ; comp. White and Riddle), which Tertullian either purposely connects with " cloaca," a sewer (with which, indeed, it may be *really* connected, as coming derivatively from the same root), and takes to mean " the nymphs of the sewers " apparently.
[7] The nymphs above named (Oehler).

[8] i.e., are worn by his votaries.
[9] i.e., Christianity. Cf. 1 Cor. ii. 6, 7.

and tufts of your Salii and Flamines, a sacerdotal attire. Lower your eyes, I advise you, (and) reverence the garb, on the one ground, meantime, (without waiting for others,) of being a renouncer of your error.

CHAP. V.— VIRTUES OF THE MANTLE. IT PLEADS IN ITS OWN DEFENCE.

"Still," say you, "must we thus change from gown[1] to Mantle?" Why, what if from diadem and sceptre? Did Anacharsis change otherwise, when to the royalty of Scythia he preferred philosophy? Grant that there be no (miraculous) signs in proof of your transformation for the better: there is somewhat which this your garb can do. For, to begin with the simplicity of its uptaking: it needs no tedious arrangement. Accordingly, there is no necessity for any artist formally to dispose its wrinkled folds from the beginning a day beforehand, and then to reduce them to a more finished elegance, and to assign to the guardianship of the stretchers[2] the whole figment of the massed boss; subsequently, at daybreak, first gathering up by the aid of a girdle the tunic which it were better to have woven of more moderate length (in the first instance), and, again scrutinizing the boss, and rearranging any disarrangement, to make one part prominent on the left, but (making now an end of the folds) to draw backwards from the shoulders the circuit of it whence the hollow is formed, and, leaving the right shoulder free, heap it still upon the left, with another similar set of folds reserved for the back, and thus clothe the man with a burden! In short, I will persistently ask your own conscience, What is your first sensation in wearing your gown? Do you feel yourself clad, or laded? wearing a garment, or carrying it? If you shall answer negatively, I will follow you home; I will see what you hasten to do immediately after crossing your threshold. There is really no garment the doffing whereof congratulates a man more than the gown's does.[3] Of shoes we say nothing — implements as they are of torture proper to the gown, most uncleanly protection to the feet, yes, and false too. For who would not find it expedient, in cold and heat, to stiffen with feet bare rather than in a shoe with feet bound? A mighty munition for the tread have the Venetian shoe-factories provided in the shape of effeminate boots! Well, but, than the Mantle nothing is more expedite, even if it be double, like that of Crates.[4] Nowhere is there a compulsory waste of time in dressing yourself (in it), seeing that its whole art consists in loosely covering. That can be effected by a single circumjection, and one in no case inelegant:[5] thus it wholly covers every part of the man at once. The shoulder it either exposes or encloses:[6] in other respects it adheres to the shoulder; it has no surrounding support; it has no surrounding tie; it has no anxiety as to the fidelity with which its folds keep their place; easily it manages, easily readjusts itself: even in the doffing it is consigned to no cross until the morrow. If any shirt is worn beneath it, the torment of a girdle is superfluous: if anything in the way of shoeing is worn, it is a most cleanly work;[7] or else the feet are rather bare, — more manly, at all events, (if bare,) than in shoes. These (pleas I advance) for the Mantle in the meantime, in so far as you have defamed it by name. Now, however, it challenges you on the score of its function withal. "I," it says, "owe no duty to the forum, the election-ground, or the senate-house; I keep no obsequious vigil, preoccupy no platforms, hover about no prætorian residences; I am not odorant of the canals, am not adorant of the lattices, am no constant wearer out of benches, no wholesale router of laws, no barking pleader, no judge, no soldier, no king: I have withdrawn from the populace. My only business is with myself: except that other care I have none, save not to care. The better life you would more enjoy in seclusion than in publicity. But you will decry me as indolent. Forsooth, 'we are to live for our country, and empire, and estate.' Such used,[8] of old, to be the sentiment. None is born for another, being destined to die for himself. At all events, when we come to the Epicuri and Zenones, you give the epithet of 'sages' to the whole teacherhood of *Quietude*, who have consecrated that *Quietude* with the name of 'supreme' and 'unique' pleasure. Still, to some extent it will be allowed, even to *me*, to confer benefit on the public. From any and every boundary-stone or altar is it my wont to prescribe medicines to morals — medicines which will be more felicitous in conferring good health upon public affairs, and states, and empires, than *your* works are. Indeed, if I proceed to encounter you with naked foils, gowns have done the commonwealth more hurt than cuirasses. Moreover, I flatter no vices; I give quarter to no lethargy, no slothful encrustation. I apply

---

[1] Toga.

[2] Or, "forcipes."

[3] Of course the meaning is, "on the doffing of which a man congratulates himself more," etc.; but Tertullian as it were personifies the act of doffing, and represents it as congratulating the doffer: and I have scrupulously retained all his extravagances, believing them (in the present treatise at least) to be intentional.

[4] A Cynic philosopher.

[5] ' Inhumano;" or, perhaps, "involving superhuman effort."

[6] Oehler attempts to defend the common reading, "humerum *velans* exponit vel includit;" but the correction of Salmasius and Lud. de la Cerda which he quotes, " *vel* exponit," is followed in preference. If Oehler's reading be retained, we may render: "a covering for the shoulder, it exposes or encloses it at will."

[7] i.e., the " shoeing" appropriate to the *mantle* will consist at most of *sandals;* " *shoes* " being (as has been said) suited to the *gown.*

[8] " Erat." — Oehler, who refers to " errat" as the general reading, and (if adopted) renders: " This sentiment errs (or wanders) in all directions;" making *olim = passim.*

the cauterizing iron to the ambition which led M. Tullius to buy a circular table of citron-wood for more than £4000,[1] and Asinius Gallus to pay twice as much for an ordinary table of the same Moorish wood (Hem! at what fortunes did they value woody dapplings!), or, again, Sulla to frame dishes of an hundred pounds' weight. I fear lest that balance be small, when a Drusilla-nus (and he withal a slave of Claudius!) con-structs a tray[2] of the weight of 500 lbs.!—a tray indispensable, perchance, to the aforesaid tables, for which, if a workshop was erected,[3] there ought to have been erected a dining-room too. Equally do I plunge the scalpel into the inhumanity which led Vedius Pollio to expose slaves to fill the bellies of sea-eels. Delighted, forsooth, with his novel savagery, he kept land-monsters, toothless, clawless, hornless: it was his pleasure to turn perforce into wild beasts his fish, which (of course) were to be forthwith cooked, that in their entrails he himself withal might taste some savour of the bodies of his own slaves. I will forelop the gluttony which led Hortensius the orator to be the first to have the heart to slay a peacock for the sake of food; which led Aufidius Lurco to be the first to vitiate meat with stuffing, and by the aid of forcemeats to raise them to an adulterous[4] flavour; which led Asinius Celer to purchase the viand of a sin-gle mullet at nearly £50;[5] which led Æsopus the actor to preserve in his pantry a dish of the value of nearly £800, made up of birds of the selfsame costliness (as the mullet aforesaid), consisting of all the songsters and talkers; which led his son, after such a titbit, to have the hardi-hood to hunger after somewhat yet more sump-tuous: for he swallowed down pearls—costly even on the ground of their name—I suppose for fear he should have supped more beggarly than his father. I am silent as to the Neros and

Apicii and Rufi. I will give a cathartic to the impurity of a Scaurus, and the gambling of a Curius, and the intemperance of an Antony. And remember that these, out of the many (whom I have named), were men of the toga—such as among the men of the pallium you would not easily find. These purulencies of a state who will eliminate and exsuppurate, save a be-mantled speech?

CHAP. VI.—FURTHER DISTINCTIONS, AND CROWN-ING GLORY, OF THE PALLIUM.

"'With speech,' says (my antagonist), 'you have tried to persuade me,—a most sage medi-cament.' But, albeit utterance be mute—im-peded by infancy or else checked by bashfulness, for life is content with an even tongueless phil-osophy—my very *cut* is eloquent. A philoso-pher, in fact, is *heard* so long as he is *seen*. My very sight puts vices to the blush. Who suffers not, when he sees his own rival? Who can bear to gaze ocularly at him at whom mentally he cannot? Grand is the benefit conferred by the Mantle, at the thought whereof moral im-probity absolutely blushes. Let philosophy now see to the question of her own profitableness; for she is not the only associate whom I boast. Other scientific arts of public utility I boast. From my store are clothed the first teacher of the forms of letters, the first explainer of their sounds, the first trainer in the rudiments of arithmetic, the grammarian, the rhetorician, the sophist, the medical man, the poet, the musical timebeater, the astrologer, and the birdgazer. All that is liberal in studies is covered by my four angles. 'True; but all these rank lower than Roman knights.' Well; but your gladia-torial trainers, and all their ignominious follow-ing, are conducted into the arena in togas. This, no doubt, will be the indignity implied in 'From gown to Mantle!'" Well, so speaks the Mantle. But I confer on it likewise a fellow-ship with a divine sect and discipline. Joy, Mantle, and exult! A better philosophy has now deigned to honour thee, ever since thou hast begun to be a Christian's vesture!

---

[1] Reckoning the 1000 sesterces at their pre-Augustan value, £8, 17s. 1d.

[2] "Promulsis"—a tray on which *the first course* ("promulsis" or "antecoena") was served, otherwise called "promulsidare."

[3] As Pliny (quoted by Oehler) tells us was the case.

[4] Or, "adulterated."

[5] Reckoning the 1000 sesterces at the post-Augustan value, £7, 16s. 3d.

ELUCIDATIONS.

I.

(The garment . . . too quadrangular, p. 5.)

SPEAKING of the Greek priests of Korfou, the erudite Bishop of Lincoln, lately deceased, has remarked, "There is something very picturesque in the appearance of these persons, with their black caps resembling the *modius* seen on the heads of the ancient statues of Serapis and Osiris, their long beards and pale complexions, and their *black flowing cloak*,— a relic, no doubt, of the old ecclesiastical garment of which Tertullian wrote." These remarks [1] are illustrated by an engraving on the same page.

He thus identifies the *pallium* with the gown of Justin Martyr; [2] nor can there be any reasonable doubt that the *pallium* of the West was the counterpart of the Greek φελόνιον and of the φαιλόνη, which St. Paul left at Troas. Endearing associations have clung to it from the mention of this apostolic cloak in Holy Scripture. It doubtless influenced Justin in giving his philosopher's gown a new significance, and the modern Greeks insist that such was the apparel of the apostles. The seamless robe of Christ Himself belongs to Him only.

Tertullian rarely acknowledges his obligations to other Doctors; but Justin's example and St. Paul's cloak must have been in his thoughts when he rejected the *toga*, and claimed the *pallium*, as a Christian's attire. Our Edinburgh translator has assumed that it was the "ascetics' mantle," and perhaps it was.[3] Our author wished to make all Christians ascetics, like himself, and hence his enthusiasm for a distinctive costume. Anyhow, "the Doctor's gown" of the English universities, which is also used among the Gallicans and in Savoy, is one of the most ancient as well as dignified vestments in ecclesiastical use; and for the *prophetic* or preaching function of the clergy it is singularly appropriate.[4]

"The *pallium*," says a learned author,[5] the late Wharton B. Marriott of Oxford, "is the Greek ἱμάτιον, the outer garment or wrapper worn occasionally by *persons of all conditions of life*. It corresponded in general use to the Roman *toga*, but in the earlier Roman language, that of republican times, was as distinctively suggestive of a *Greek costume* as the *toga* of that of Rome." To Tertullian, therefore, his preference for the *pallium* was doubtless commended by all these considerations; and the distinctively Greek character of Christian theology was indicated also by his choice. He loved the learning of Alexandria, and reflected the spirit of the East.

II.

(Superstition, p. 10, near note 9.)

The *pall* afterwards imposed upon Anglican and other primates by the Court of Rome was at first a mere complimentary present from the patriarchal see of the West. It became a badge of dependence and of bondage (*obsta principiis*). Only the ornamental bordering was sent, "made of lamb's-wool and superstition," says old Fuller, for whose amusing remarks see his *Church Hist.*, vol. i. p. 179, ed. 1845. Rome gives primitive names to middle-age corruptions: needless to say the "pall" of her court is nothing like the *pallium* of our author.

---

[1] Wordsworth's *Greece*, p. 263. London, 1839.   [2] See vol. i. p. 160, this series.
[3] But it was assuming a questionable point (See Kaye, p. 49) to give it this name in the title, and I have retained it untranslated.
[4] See note on p. 160 of vol. i., this series.
[5] See his valuable and exhaustive treatise, the *Vestiarium Christianum*, especially pp. 73, 125, 233, 490. Also, for the *Gallicanum*, p. 204 and Appendix E., with pp. 210, 424. For the *Græcum*, pp. xii. (note), xv. 73, 127, 233.

II.

ON THE APPAREL OF WOMEN.[1]

[TRANSLATED BY THE REV. S. THELWALL.]

BOOK I.

CHAP. I. — INTRODUCTION. MODESTY IN APPAREL BECOMING TO WOMEN, IN MEMORY OF THE INTRODUCTION OF SIN INTO THE WORLD THROUGH A WOMAN.

IF there dwelt upon earth a faith as great as is the reward of faith which is expected in the heavens, no one of you at all, best beloved sisters, from the time that she had first "known the Lord,"[2] and learned (the truth) concerning her own (that is, woman's) condition, would have desired too gladsome (not to say too ostentatious) a style of dress; so as not rather to go about in humble garb, and rather to affect meanness of appearance, walking about as Eve mourning and repentant, in order that by every garb of penitence[3] she might the more fully expiate that which she derives from Eve, — the ignominy, I mean, of the first sin, and the odium (attaching to her as the cause) of human perdition. "In pains and in anxieties dost thou bear (children), woman; and toward thine husband (is) thy inclination, and he lords it over thee."[4] And do you not know that you are (each) an Eve? The sentence of God on this sex of yours lives in this age:[5] the guilt must of necessity live too. You are the devil's gateway: you are the unsealer[6] of that (forbidden) tree: you are the first deserter of the divine law: you are she who persuaded[7] him whom the devil was not valiant enough to attack. You destroyed so easily God's image, man. On account of your

desert — that is, death — even the Son of God had to die. And do you think about adorning yourself over and above your tunics of skins?[8] Come, now; if from the beginning of the world[9] the Milesians sheared sheep, and the Serians[10] spun trees, and the Tyrians dyed, and the Phrygians embroidered with the needle, and the Babylonians with the loom, and pearls gleamed, and onyx-stones flashed; if gold itself also had already issued, with the cupidity (which accompanies it), from the ground; if the mirror, too, already had licence to lie so largely, Eve, expelled from paradise, (Eve) already dead, would also have coveted *these* things, I imagine! No more, then, ought she *now* to crave, or be acquainted with (if she desires to live again), what, when she *was* living, she had neither had nor known. Accordingly these things are all the baggage of woman in her condemned and dead state, instituted as if to swell the pomp of her funeral.

CHAP. II. — THE ORIGIN OF FEMALE ORNAMENTATION, TRACED BACK TO THE ANGELS WHO HAD FALLEN.[11]

For they, withal, who instituted them are assigned, under condemnation, to the penalty of death, — those angels, to wit, who rushed from heaven on the daughters of men; so that this ignominy also attaches to woman. For when to an age[12] much more ignorant (than ours) they had disclosed certain well-concealed material substances, and several not well-revealed scientific arts — if it is true that they had laid bare

---

[1] [Written about A.D. 202. See Kaye, p. 56]
[2] Comp. Heb. viii. 11; Jer. xxxi. 34 (in the LXX. it is xxxviii. 34).
[3] Satisfactionis.
[4] Comp. Gen. iii. 16, in Eng. ver. and in LXX.
[5] Sæculo.
[6] Resignatrix. Comp. the phrase "*a fountain sealed*" in Cant. iv. 12.
[7] "Suasisti" is the reading of the MSS.; "persuasisti," a conjectural emendation adopted by Rig.

[8] See Gen. iii. 21.
[9] Rerum.
[10] i.e., Chinese.
[11] Comp. with this chapter, *de Idol.*, c. ix.; *de Or.*, c. xxii.; *de Cult. Fem.*, l. ii. c. x.; *de Virg. Vel.*, c. vii.
[12] Sæculo.

the operations of metallurgy, and had divulged the natural properties of herbs, and had promulgated the powers of enchantments, and had traced out every curious art,[1] even to the interpretation of the stars — they conferred properly and as it were peculiarly upon women that instrumental mean of womanly ostentation, the radiances of jewels wherewith necklaces are variegated, and the circlets of gold wherewith the arms are compressed, and the medicaments of orchil with which wools are coloured, and that black powder itself wherewith the eyelids and eyelashes are made prominent.[2] What is the quality of these things may be declared meantime, even at this point,[3] from the quality and condition of their teachers: in that sinners could never have either shown or supplied anything conducive to integrity, unlawful lovers anything conducive to chastity, renegade spirits anything conducive to the fear of God. If (these things) are to be called *teachings*, ill masters must of necessity have taught ill; if as *wages of lust*, there is nothing base of which the wages are honourable. But why was it of so much importance to show these things as well as [4] to confer them? Was it that women, without material causes of splendour, and without ingenious contrivances of grace, could not please *men*, who, while still unadorned, and uncouth, and — so to say — crude and rude, had moved (the mind of) *angels?* or was it that the lovers [5] would appear sordid and — through gratuitous use — contumelious, if they had conferred no (compensating) gift on the women who had been enticed into connubial connection with them? But these questions admit of no calculation. Women who possessed angels (as husbands) could desire nothing more; they had, forsooth, made a grand match! Assuredly they who, of course, did sometimes think whence they had fallen,[6] and, after the heated impulses of their lusts, looked up toward heaven, thus requited that very excellence of women, natural beauty, as (having proved) a cause of evil, in order that their good fortune might profit them nothing; but that, being turned from simplicity and sincerity, they, together with (the angels) themselves, might become offensive to God. Sure they were that all ostentation, and ambition, and love of pleasing by carnal means, was *dis*pleasing to God. And these are the angels whom we are destined to judge:[7] these are the angels whom in baptism we renounce:[8] these, of course, are the reasons why they have de-

served to be judged by man. What business, then, have their *things* with their *judges?* What commerce have they who are to condemn with them who are to be condemned? The same, I take it, as Christ has with Belial.[9] With what consistency do we mount that (future) judgment-seat to pronounce sentence against those whose gifts we (now) seek after? For you too, (women as you are,) have the self-same angelic nature promised [10] as your reward, the self-same sex as men: the self-same advancement to the dignity of judging, does (the Lord) promise you. Unless, then, we begin even here to *pre*-judge, by pre-condemning their *things*, which we are hereafter to condemn in *themselves, they* will rather judge and condemn *us.*

CHAP. III. — CONCERNING THE GENUINENESS OF "THE PROPHECY OF ENOCH."[11]

I am aware that the Scripture of Enoch,[12] which has assigned this order (of action) to angels, is not received by some, because it is not admitted into the Jewish canon either. I suppose they did not think that, having been published before the deluge, it could have safely survived that world-wide calamity, the abolisher of all things. If that is the reason (for rejecting it), let them recall to their memory that Noah, the survivor of the deluge, was the great-grandson of Enoch himself;[13] and he, of course, had heard and remembered, from domestic renown [14] and hereditary tradition, concerning his own great-grandfather's "grace in the sight of God,"[15] and concerning all his preachings;[16] since Enoch had given no other charge to Methuselah than that he should hand on the knowledge of them to his posterity. Noah therefore, no doubt, might have succeeded in the trusteeship of (his) preaching; or, had the case been otherwise, he would not have been silent alike concerning the disposition (of things) made by God, his Preserver, and concerning the particular glory of his own house.

If (Noah) had not had this (conservative power) by so short a route, there would (still) be this (consideration) to warrant [17] our assertion of (the genuineness of) this Scripture: he could equally have *renewed* it, under the Spirit's inspiration,[18] after it *had* been destroyed by the violence of the deluge, as, after the destruction of Jerusalem by the Babylonian storming of it,

---

1 Curiositatem. Comp. *de Idol.*, c. ix., and Acts xix. 19.
2 Quo oculorum exordia producuntur. Comp. ii. 5.
3 "Jam," i.e., without going any farther. Comp. c. iv. et seqq.
4 Sicut. But Pam. and Rig. read "sive."
5 i.e., the *angelic* lovers.
6 Comp. Rev. ii. 5.
7 See 1 Cor. vi. 3.
8 Comp. *de Idol.*, c. vi.

9 Comp. 2 Cor. vi. 14–16.
10 See Matt. xxii. 30; Mark xii. 25; Luke xx. 35, 36; and comp. Gal. iii. 28.
11 [Elucidation.]
12 Comp *de Idol.*, c. iv.
13 See Gen. v 21, 25, 28, 29.
14 "Nomine;" perhaps = "account."
15 Comp. Gen. vi. 8.
16 Prædicatis.
17 Tueretur.
18 In spiritu.

every document[1] of the Jewish literature is generally agreed to have been restored through Ezra.

But since Enoch in the same Scripture has preached likewise concerning the Lord, nothing at all must be rejected *by* us which pertains *to* us; and we read that "every Scripture suitable for edification is divinely inspired."[2] By the *Jews* it may now seem to have been rejected for that (very) reason, just like all the other (portions) nearly which tell of Christ. Nor, of course, is this fact wonderful, that they did not receive some Scriptures which spake of Him whom even in person, speaking in their presence, they were not to receive. To these considerations is added the fact that Enoch possesses a testimony in the Apostle Jude.[3]

CHAP. IV. — WAIVING THE QUESTION OF THE AUTHORS, TERTULLIAN PROPOSES TO CONSIDER THE THINGS ON THEIR OWN MERITS.

Grant now that no mark of pre-condemnation has been branded on womanly pomp by the (fact of the) fate[4] of its authors; let nothing be imputed to those angels besides their repudiation of heaven and (their) carnal marriage:[5] let us examine the qualities of the things themselves, in order that we may detect the purposes also for which they are eagerly desired.

Female habit carries with it a twofold idea — dress and ornament. By "dress" we mean what they call "womanly gracing;"[6] by "ornament," what it is suitable should be called "womanly *dis*gracing."[7] The former is accounted (to consist) in gold, and silver, and gems, and garments; the latter in care of the hair, and of the skin, and of those parts of the body which attract the eye. Against the one we lay the charge of ambition, against the other of prostitution; so that even from this early stage[8] (of our discussion) you may look forward and see what, out of (all) these, is suitable, handmaid of God, to *your* discipline, inasmuch as you are assessed on different principles (from other women), — those, namely, of humility and chastity.

CHAP. V. — GOLD AND SILVER NOT SUPERIOR IN ORIGIN OR IN UTILITY TO OTHER METALS.

Gold and silver, the principal material causes of worldly[9] splendour, must necessarily be identical (in nature) with that out of which they have their being: (they must be) earth, that is; (which earth itself is) plainly more glorious (than

they), inasmuch as it is only after it has been tearfully wrought by penal labour in the deadly laboratories of accursed mines, and there left its name of "earth" in the fire behind it, that, as a fugitive from the mine, it passes from torments to ornaments, from punishments to embellishments, from ignominies to honours. But iron, and brass, and other the vilest material substances, enjoy a parity of condition (with silver and gold), both as to earthly origin and metallurgic operation; in order that, in the estimation of nature, the substance of gold and of silver may be judged not a whit more noble (than theirs). But if it is from the quality of *utility* that gold and silver derive their glory, why, iron and brass excel them; whose usefulness is so disposed (by the Creator), that they not only discharge functions of their own more numerous and more necessary to human affairs, but do also none the less serve the turn of gold and silver, by dint of their own powers,[10] in the service of juster causes. For not only are rings made of iron, but the memory of antiquity still preserves (the fame of) certain vessels for eating and drinking made out of brass. Let the insane plenteousness of gold and silver look to it, if it serves to make utensils even for foul purposes. At all events, neither is the field tilled by means of gold, nor the ship fastened together by the strength of silver. No mattock plunges a golden edge into the ground; no nail drives a silver point into planks. I leave unnoticed the fact that the needs of our whole life are dependent upon iron and brass; whereas those rich materials themselves, requiring both to be dug up out of mines, and needing a forging process in every use (to which they are put), are helpless without the laborious vigour of iron and brass. Already, therefore, we must judge whence it is that so high dignity accrues to gold and silver, since they get precedence over material substances which are not only cousin-german to them in point of origin, but more powerful in point of usefulness.

CHAP. VI. — OF PRECIOUS STONES AND PEARLS.

But, in the next place, what am I to interpret those jewels to be which vie with gold in haughtiness, except little pebbles and stones and paltry particles of the self-same earth; but yet not necessary either for laying down foundations, or rearing party-walls, or supporting pediments, or giving density to roofs? The only edifice which they know how to rear is this silly pride of women: because they require slow rubbing that they may shine, and artful underlaying that they may show to advantage, and careful piercing that they may hang; and (because they) render to gold a mutual assistance in meretricious allure-

---

[1] Instrumentum.
[2] See 2 Tim. iij. 16.
[3] See Jude 14, 15.
[4] Exitu.
[5] Matrimonium carnis.
[6] Mundum muliebrem. Comp. Liv. xxxiv. 7.
[7] Immundum muliebrem.
[8] Jam hinc; comp. *ad. Ux.*, i. 1 *ad init.* and *ad fin.*, and 8 *ad fin.*
[9] Sæcularis.

[10] De suo. Comp. *de Bapt.*, c. xvii. *sub fin.*

ment. But whatever it is that ambition fishes up from the British or the Indian sea, it is a kind of conch not more pleasing in *savour* than — I do not say the oyster and the sea-snail, but — even the giant muscle.[1] For let me add that I know conchs (which are) sweet fruits of the sea. But if that (foreign) conch suffers from some internal pustule, that ought to be regarded rather as its defect than as its glory; and although it be called "pearl," still something else must be understood than some hard, round excrescence of the fish. Some say, too, that gems are culled from the foreheads of *dragons*, just as in the brains of fishes there is a certain stony substance. This also was wanting to the Christian woman, that she may add a grace to herself from the serpent! Is it thus that she will set her heel on the devil's head,"[2] while she heaps ornaments (taken) from his head on her own neck, or on her very head?

CHAP. VII. — RARITY THE ONLY CAUSE WHICH MAKES SUCH THINGS VALUABLE.

It is only from their rarity and outlandishness that all these things possess their grace; in short, within their own native limits they are not held of so high worth. Abundance is always contumelious toward itself. There are some barbarians with whom, because gold is indigenous and plentiful, it is customary to keep (the criminals) in their convict establishments chained with gold, and to lade the wicked with riches — the more guilty, the more wealthy. At last there has really been found a way to prevent even gold from being loved! We have also seen at Rome the nobility of gems blushing in the presence of our matrons at the contemptuous usage of the Parthians and Medes, and the rest of their own fellow-countrymen, only that (*their* gems) are not generally worn with a view to ostentation. Emeralds[3] lurk in their belts; and the sword (that hangs) below their bosom alone is witness to the cylindrical stones that decorate its hilt; and the massive single pearls on their boots are fain to get lifted out of the mud! In short, they carry nothing so richly gemmed as that which ought *not* to be gemmed if it is (either) not conspicuous, or else is conspicuous only that it may be shown to be also neglected.

CHAP. VIII. — THE SAME RULE HOLDS WITH REGARD TO COLOURS. GOD'S CREATURES GENERALLY NOT TO BE USED, EXCEPT FOR THE PURPOSES TO WHICH HE HAS APPOINTED THEM.

Similarly, too, do even the servants[4] of those barbarians cause the glory to fade from the colours of our garments (by wearing the like); nay, even their party-walls use slightingly, to supply the place of painting, the Tyrian and the violet-coloured and the grand royal hangings, which you laboriously undo and metamorphose. Purple with them is more paltry than red ochre; (and justly,) for what legitimate honour can garments derive from adulteration with illegitimate colours? That which He Himself has not produced is not pleasing to God, unless He was *unable* to order sheep to be born with purple and sky-blue fleeces! If He was *able*, then plainly He was *unwilling*: what God willed not, of course ought not to be fashioned. Those things, then, are not the best by *nature* which are not from God, the *Author* of nature. Thus they are understood to be from *the devil*, from the *corrupter* of nature: for there is no other whose they *can* be, if they are not God's; because what are not God's must necessarily be His rival's.[5] But, beside the devil and his angels, other rival of God there is none. Again, if the *material substances* are of God, it does not immediately follow that such ways of *enjoying* them among men (are so too). It is matter for inquiry not only whence come conchs,[6] but what sphere of embellishment is assigned them, and where it is that they exhibit their beauty. For all those profane pleasures of worldly[7] shows — as we have already published a volume of their own about them[8] — (ay, and) even idolatry itself, derive their material causes from the creatures[9] of God. Yet a Christian ought not to attach himself[10] to the frenzies of the racecourse, or the atrocities of the arena, or the turpitudes of the stage, simply because God has given to man the horse, and the panther, and the power of speech: just as a Christian cannot commit idolatry with impunity either, because the incense, and the wine, and the fire which feeds[11] (thereon), and the animals which are made the victims, are God's workmanship;[12] since even the material thing which is adored is God's (creature). Thus then, too, with regard to their active use, does the *origin* of the material substances, which descends from God, *excuse* (that use) as foreign to God, as guilty forsooth of worldly[13] glory!

CHAP. IX. — GOD'S DISTRIBUTION MUST REGULATE OUR DESIRES, OTHERWISE WE BECOME THE PREY OF AMBITION AND ITS ATTENDANT EVILS.

For, as some particular things distributed by God over certain individual lands, and some one

---

[1] Peloris. Comp. Hor., *S.*, ii. 4, 32, and Macleane's note there.
[2] See Gen. iii. 15.
[3] Smaragdi. Comp. Rev. iv. 3.
[4] Or, "slaves."
[5] Comp. *de Pæn.*, c. v. *med.*
[6] Comp. c. vi. above.
[7] Sæcularium.
[8] i.e , the treatise *de Spectaculis*.
[9] Rebus.
[10] "Affici" — a rare use rather of "afficere," but found in Cic.
[11] Or perhaps "is fed" thereby; for the word is "vescitur."
[12] "Conditio" — a rare use again.
[13] Sæcularis.

particular tract of sea, are mutually foreign one to the other, they are reciprocally either neglected or desired : (desired) among foreigners, as being rarities ; neglected (rightly), if anywhere, among their own compatriots, because in *them* there is no such fervid longing for a glory which, among its own home-folk, is frigid. But, however, the rareness and outlandishness which arise out of that distribution of possessions which God has ordered as He willed, ever finding favour in the eyes of strangers, excites, from the simple fact of *not* having what God has made native to other places, the concupiscence of *having* it. Hence is educed another vice — that of *immoderate* having ; because although, perhaps, *having* may be permissible, still a limit [1] is bound (to be observed). This (second vice) will be ambition ; and hence, too, its name is to be interpreted, in that from concupiscence *ambient* in the mind it is born, with a view to the desire of

glory, — a grand desire, forsooth, which (as we have said) is recommended neither by nature nor by truth, but by a vicious passion of the mind, — (namely,) concupiscence. And there are other vices connected with ambition and glory. Thus they have withal enhanced the *cost* of things, in order that (thereby) they might add fuel to themselves also ; for concupiscence becomes proportionably greater as it has set a higher value upon the thing which it has eagerly desired. From the smallest caskets is produced an ample patrimony. On a single thread is suspended a million of sesterces. One delicate neck carries about it forests and islands.[2] The slender lobes of the ears exhaust a fortune ; and the left hand, with its every finger, sports with a several money-bag. Such is the strength of ambition — (equal) to bearing on one small body, and that a woman's, the product of so copious wealth.

---

[1] Or, " moderation."

[2] " Saltus et insulæ," i.e., as much as would purchase them.

BOOK II.

CHAP. I. — INTRODUCTION. MODESTY TO BE OBSERVED NOT ONLY IN ITS ESSENCE, BUT IN ITS ACCESSORIES.

Handmaids of the living God, my fellow-servants and sisters, the right which I enjoy with you — I, the most meanest [1] in that right of fellow-servantship and brotherhood — emboldens me to address to you a discourse, not, of course, of affection, but paving the way for affection in the cause of your salvation. That salvation — and not (the salvation) of women only, but likewise of men — consists in the exhibition principally of modesty. For since, by the introduction into an appropriation [2] (in) us of the Holy Spirit, we are all " the temple of God," [3] Modesty is the sacristan and priestess of that temple, who is to suffer nothing unclean or profane to be introduced (into it), for fear that the God who inhabits it should be offended, and quite forsake the polluted abode. But on the present occasion we (are to speak) not about modesty, for the enjoining and exacting of which the divine precepts which press (upon us) on every side are sufficient ; but about the matters which pertain to it, that is, the manner in which it behoves you to walk. For most women (which very thing I trust God may permit me, with a view, of course,

to my own personal censure, to censure in all), either from simple ignorance or else from dissimulation, have the hardihood so to walk as if modesty consisted only [4] in the (bare) integrity of the flesh, and in turning away from (actual) fornication ; and there were no need for anything extrinsic to boot — in the matter (I mean) of the arrangement of dress and ornament,[5] the studied graces of form and brilliance : — wearing in their gait the self-same appearance as the women of the nations, from whom the sense of *true* modesty is absent, because in those who know not God, the Guardian and Master of truth, there is *nothing* true.[6] For if any modesty can be believed (to exist) in Gentiles, it is plain that it must be imperfect and undisciplined to such a degree that, although it be actively tenacious of itself in the *mind* up to a certain point, it yet allows itself to relax into licentious extravagances of attire ; just in accordance with Gentile perversity, in craving after that of which it carefully shuns the effect.[7] How many a one, in short, is there who does not earnestly desire even to look pleasing to strangers ? who does not on that very account take care to have herself painted out, and denies that she has (ever) been

---

[1] Postremissimus.
[2] Consecrato.
[3] See 1 Cor. iii. 16, 17, vi. 19, 20.

[4] Comp. *de Idol.*, c. ii.
[5] Cultus et ornatus. For the distinction between them, see b. i c. iv.
[6] Comp. *de Pæn.*, c. i.
[7] Or, " execution."

an object of (carnal) appetite? And yet, granting that even this is a practice familiar to Gentile modesty — (namely,) not actually to *commit* the sin, but still to be *willing* to do so; or even not to be *willing*, yet still not *quite* to refuse — what wonder? for all things which are not God's are perverse. Let those women therefore look to it, who, by not holding fast the *whole* good, easily mingle with evil even what they do hold fast. Necessary it is that *you* turn aside from them, as in all other things, so also in your gait; since you ought to be "perfect, as (is) your Father who is in the heavens." [1]

CHAP. II. — PERFECT MODESTY WILL ABSTAIN FROM WHATEVER TENDS TO SIN, AS WELL AS FROM SIN ITSELF. DIFFERENCE BETWEEN TRUST AND PRESUMPTION. IF SECURE OURSELVES, WE MUST NOT PUT TEMPTATION IN THE WAY OF OTHERS. WE MUST LOVE OUR NEIGHBOUR AS OURSELF.

You must know that in the eye of perfect, that is, Christian, modesty, (carnal) desire of one's self (on the part of others) is not only not to be desired, but even execrated, by you: first, because the study of making personal grace (which we know to be naturally the inviter of lust) a mean of pleasing does not spring from a sound conscience: why therefore excite toward yourself that evil (passion)? why invite (that) to which you profess yourself a stranger? secondly, because we ought not to open a way to temptations, which, by their instancy, sometimes achieve (a wickedness) which God expels from them who are His; (or,) at all events, put the spirit into a thorough tumult by (presenting) a stumbling-block (to it). We ought indeed to walk so holily, and with so entire substantiality [2] of faith, as to be confident and secure in regard of our own conscience, *desiring* that that (gift) may abide in us to the end, yet not *presuming* (that it will). For he who presumes feels less apprehension; he who feels less apprehension takes less precaution; he who takes less precaution runs more risk. Fear [3] is the foundation of salvation; presumption is an impediment to fear. More useful, then, is it to apprehend that we may possibly fail, than to presume that we cannot; for apprehending will lead us to fear, fearing to caution, and caution to salvation. On the other hand, if we presume, there will be neither fear nor caution to save us. He who acts securely, and not at the same time warily, possesses no safe and firm security; whereas he who is wary will be truly able to be secure. For His own servants, may the Lord by His mercy take

care that to *them* it may be lawful even to *presume* on His goodness! But why are we a (source of) danger to our neighbour? why do we import concupiscence into our neighbour? which concupiscence, if God, in "amplifying the law," [4] do not [5] dissociate in (the way of) penalty from the actual commission of fornication, [6] I know not whether He allows impunity to him who [7] has been the cause of perdition to some other. For that other, as soon as he has felt concupiscence after your beauty, and has mentally already committed (the deed) which his concupiscence pointed to, [8] perishes; and you have been made [9] the sword which destroys him: so that, albeit you be free from the (actual) crime, you are not free from the odium (attaching to it); as, when a robbery has been committed on some man's estate, the (actual) crime indeed will not be laid to the owner's charge, while yet the domain is branded with ignominy, (and) the owner himself aspersed with the infamy. Are we to paint ourselves out that our neighbours may perish? Where, then, is (the command), "Thou shalt love thy neighbour as thyself?" [10] "Care not merely about your own (things), but (about your) neighbour's?" [11] No enunciation of the Holy Spirit ought to be (confined) to the subject immediately in hand merely, and not applied and carried out with a view to *every* occasion to which its application is useful. [12] Since, therefore, both our own interest and that of others is implicated in the studious pursuit of most perilous (outward) comeliness, it is time for you to know [13] that not merely must the pageantry of fictitious and elaborate beauty be rejected by you; but that of even natural grace must be obliterated by concealment and negligence, as equally dangerous to the glances of (the beholder's) eyes. For, albeit comeliness is not to be *censured*, [14] as being a bodily happiness, as being an additional outlay of the divine plastic art, as being a kind of goodly garment [15] of the soul; yet it is to be *feared*, just on account of the injuriousness and violence of suitors: [16] which (injuriousness and violence) even the father of the faith, [17] Abraham, [18] greatly feared in regard of his own wife's grace; and Isaac, [19] by

---

[1] See Matt. v. 48.
[2] Substantia. Comp. Heb. xi. 1, ἔστι δὲ πίστις ἐλπιζομένων ὑπόστασις.
[3] Timor.

[4] Matt. v. 17. Comp. *de Or.*, c. xxii. mid.; *de Pa.*, c. vi. mid.; *de Pæn.*, c. iii. *sub fin.*
[5] The second "non," or else the first, must apparently be omitted.
[6] Matt. v. 28. See *de Idol.*, c. ii.; *de Pa.*, c. vi.; *de Pæn.*, c. iii.
[7] "Qui," Oehler; "quæ," Rig.
[8] Comp. *de Pæn.* c. iii. (latter half).
[9] Tu *facta* es.
[10] Lev. xix. 18; Matt. xix. 19, xxii. 39; Mark xii. 31; Luke x. 27; Rom. xiii. 9; Gal. v. 14; Jas. ii. 8.
[11] Comp. 1 Cor. x. 24, xiii. 5; Phil. ii. 4.
[12] Comp. 2 Pet. i. 20.
[13] Jam . . . sciatis.
[14] Accusandus.
[15] Comp. Gen. xxvii. 15.
[16] Sectatorum.
[17] Comp. Rom. iv. 11, 16.
[18] Gen. xii. 10-20, and xx.
[19] Gen. xxvi. 6-11.

falsely representing Rebecca as his sister, purchased safety by insult ! [1]

Let it now be granted that excellence of form be not to be feared, as neither troublesome to its possessors, nor destructive to its desirers, nor perilous to its compartners ; [2] let it be thought (to be) not exposed to temptations, not surrounded by stumbling-blocks : it is enough that to angels of God [3] it is not necessary. For, where modesty is, there beauty is idle ; because properly the use and fruit of beauty is voluptuousness, unless any one thinks that there is some other harvest for bodily grace to reap. [4] Are women who think that, in furnishing to their *neighbour* that which is demanded of beauty, they are furnishing it to *themselves* also, to augment that (beauty) when (naturally) given them, and to strive after it when not (thus) given? Some one will say, "Why, then, if voluptuousness be shut out and chastity let in, may (we) not enjoy the praise of beauty alone, and glory in a bodily good ? " Let whoever finds pleasure in " glorying in the flesh " [5] see to that. To us, in the first place, there is no studious pursuit of " glory," because " glory " is the essence of *exaltation*. Now *exaltation* is incongruous for professors of *humility* according to God's precepts. Secondly, if *all* " glory " is " vain " and insensate, [6] how much more (glory) *in the flesh*, especially to *us ?* For even if " glorying " is (allowable), we ought to wish our sphere of pleasing to lie in the graces [7] of the Spirit, not in the flesh ; because we are " suitors " [8] of things spiritual. In those things wherein our sphere of labour lies, let our joy lie. From the sources whence we hope for salvation, let us cull our " glory." Plainly, a Christian *will* " glory " even in the *flesh ;* but (it will be) when it has endured laceration for Christ's sake, [9] in order that the spirit may be crowned in it, not in order that it may draw the eyes and sighs of youths after it. Thus (a thing) which, from whatever point you look at it, is in *your* case superfluous, you may justly disdain if you have it not, and neglect if you have. Let a holy woman, if naturally beautiful, give none so great occasion (for carnal appetite). Certainly, if even she be so,

she ought not to set off (her beauty), but even to obscure it. [10]

As if I were speaking to Gentiles, addressing you with a Gentile precept, and (one which is) common to all, (I would say,) " You are bound to please your husbands only." [11] But you will please *them* in proportion as you take no care to please *others*. Be ye without carefulness, [12] blessed (sisters) : no wife is " ugly " to her own husband. She " pleased " him enough when she was selected (by him as his wife) ; whether commended by form or by character. Let none of you think that, if she abstain from the care of her person, [13] she will incur the hatred and aversion of husbands. Every husband is the exactor of *chastity ;* but *beauty* a believing (husband) does not require, because we are not captivated by the same graces [14] which the Gentiles think (to be) graces : [15] an *un*believing one, on the other hand, even regards with suspicion, just from that infamous opinion of us which the Gentiles have. For whom, then, is it that you cherish your beauty? If for a believer, he does not exact it : if for an *un*believer, he does not believe in it unless it be artless. [16] Why are you eager to please either one who is suspicious, or else one who desires it not?

These suggestions are not made to you, of course, to be developed into an entire crudity and wildness of appearance ; nor are we seeking to persuade you of the good of squalor and slovenliness ; but of the limit and norm and just measure of cultivation of the person. There must be no overstepping of that line to which simple and sufficient refinements limit their desires — that line which is pleasing to God. For they who rub [17] their skin with medicaments, stain their cheeks with rouge, make their eyes prominent with antimony, [18] sin against HIM. To them, I suppose, the plastic skill [19] of God is displeasing ! In their own persons, I suppose, they convict, they censure, the Artificer of all things ! For censure they do when they amend, when

---

1 " Salutem contumelia redemit ; " the ' insult " being the denial of her as his wife.
2 Conjunctis.
3 Angelis Dei. Comp. the opening sentence of the book.
4 Comp. *ad Ux.*, b. i. c. iv.
5 See Gal. vi. 13 and 1 Cor. iii. 21, v. 6.
6 Stuporata.
7 Bonis.
8 Sectatores.
9 Comp. 2 Cor. xi. 18, xii. 10 ; Phil. iii. 3, 4.

10 Non adjuvare, sed etiam impedire, debet.
11 Comp. 1 Cor. vii. 34.
12. Comp. 1 Cor. vii. 32.
13 Compositione sui.
14 Bonis.
15 Bona.
16 Simplicem.
17 Urgent. Comp. *de Pæn.*, c. xi.
18 " Fuligine," lit. " soot." Comp. b. i. c. ii.
19 See c. ii. *ad fin.*

they add to, (His work ;) taking these their additions, of course, from the adversary artificer. That adversary artificer is the devil.[1] For who would show the way to change the *body*, but he who by wickedness transfigured man's *spirit?* He it is, undoubtedly, who adapted ingenious devices of this kind ; that in your persons it may be apparent that you, in a certain sense, do violence to God. Whatever is *born* is the work of God. Whatever, then, is *plastered on*[2] (that), is the devil's work. To superinduce on a divine work Satan's ingenuities, how criminal is it ! Our servants borrow nothing from our personal enemies : soldiers eagerly desire nothing from the foes of their own general ; for, to demand for (your own) use anything from the adversary of Him in whose hand[3] you are, is a transgression. Shall a Christian be assisted in anything by that evil one? (If he do,) I know not whether this name (of " Christian ") will continue (to belong) to him ; for he will be *his* in whose lore he eagerly desires to be instructed. But how alien from *your* schoolings[4] and professions are (these things) ! How unworthy the Christian name, to wear a fictitious face, (you,) on whom simplicity in every form is enjoined ! — to lie in your appearance, (you,) to whom (lying) with the tongue is not lawful ! — to seek after what is another's, (you,) to whom is delivered (the precept of) abstinence from what is another's ! — to practise adultery in your mien,[5] (you,) who make modesty your study ! Think,[6] blessed (sisters), how will you keep God's precepts if you shall not keep in your own persons His lineaments ?

CHAP. VI. — OF DYEING THE HAIR.

I see some (women) turn (the colour of) their hair with saffron. They are ashamed even of their own nation, (ashamed) that their procreation did not assign them to Germany and to Gaul : thus, as it is, they transfer their *hair*[7] (thither) ! Ill, ay, *most* ill, do they augur for themselves with their flame-coloured head,[8] and think that graceful which (in fact) they are polluting ! Nay, moreover, the force of the cosmetics burns ruin into the hair ; and the constant application of even any *un*drugged moisture, lays up a store of harm for the head ; while the sun's warmth, too, so desirable for imparting to the hair at once growth and dryness, is hurtful. What " grace " is compatible with

" injury ? " What " beauty " with " impurities ? " Shall a Christian woman heap saffron on her head, as upon an altar ?[9] For, whatever is wont to be burned to the honour of the unclean spirit, that — unless it is applied for honest, and necessary, and salutary uses, for which God's creature was provided — may seem to be a sacrifice. But, however, God saith, " Which of you can make a white hair black, or out of a black a white ? "[10] And so they refute the Lord ! " Behold ! " say they, " instead of white or black, we make it *yellow*, — more winning in grace." [11] And yet such as repent of having lived to old age do *attempt* to change it even from white to black ! O temerity ! The age which is the object of our wishes and prayers blushes (for itself) ! a theft is effected ! youth, wherein we have sinned,[12] is sighed after ! the opportunity of sobriety is spoiled ! Far from Wisdom's daughters be folly so great ! The more old age tries to conceal itself, the more will it be detected. Here is a veritable eternity, in the (perennial) youth of your head ! Here we have an " incorruptibility " to " put on," [13] with a view to the new house of the Lord [14] which the divine monarchy promises ! Well do you speed toward the Lord ; well do you hasten to be quit of this most iniquitous world,[15] to whom it is unsightly to approach (your own) end !

CHAP. VII. — OF ELABORATE DRESSING OF THE HAIR IN OTHER WAYS, AND ITS BEARING UPON SALVATION.

What service, again, does all the labour spent in *arranging* the hair render to salvation? Why is no rest allowed to your hair, which must now be bound, now loosed, now cultivated, now thinned out? Some are anxious to force their hair into curls, some to let it hang loose and flying ; not with good simplicity : beside which, you affix I know not what enormities of subtle and textile perukes ; now, after the manner of a helmet of undressed hide, as it were a sheath for the head and a covering for the crown ; now, a mass (drawn) backward toward the neck. The wonder is, that there is no (open) contending against the Lord's prescripts ! It has been pronounced that no one can add to his own stature.[16] *You*, however, *do* add to your *weight* some kind of rolls, or shield-bosses, to be piled upon your necks ! If you feel no shame at the enormity, feel some at the pollution ; for fear you may be fitting on a holy and Christian head the slough [17]

---

1 Comp. b. i. c. viii.
2 Infingitur.
3 i.e., subject to whom.
4 Disciplinis.
5 Species.
6 Credite.
7 Jam capillos: so Oehler and Rig. But the others read *patriam capillo:* " they change their country by the instrumentality of their hair."
8 Comp. *ad Ux.*, b. i. c. vi.

9 Aram.
10 See Matt. v. 36.
11 Gratia faciliorem.
12 Comp. Ps. xxv. 7 (in LXX. xxiv. 7).
13 Comp. 1 Cor. xv. 53.
14 Comp. 2 Cor. v. 1.
15 Sæculo.
16 Mensuram. See Matt. vi. 27.
17 Exuvias.

of some one else's[1] head, unclean perchance, guilty perchance and destined to hell.[2] Nay, rather banish quite away from your "free"[3] head all this slavery of ornamentation. In vain do you labour to seem adorned : in vain do you call in the aid of all the most skilful manufacturers of false hair. God bids you "be veiled."[4] I believe (He does so) for fear the heads of some should be seen! And oh that in "that day"[5] of Christian exultation, I, most miserable (as I am), may elevate my head, even though below (the level of) your heels! I shall (then) see whether you will rise with (your) ceruse and rouge and saffron, and in all that parade of headgear :[6] whether it will be women thus tricked out whom the angels carry up to meet Christ in the air![7] If these (decorations) are *now* good, and of God, they will *then* also present themselves to the rising bodies, and will recognise their several places. But nothing can rise except flesh and spirit sole and pure.[8] Whatever, therefore, does not rise in (the form of)[9] spirit and flesh is condemned, because it is not of God. From things which are condemned abstain, even at the present day. At the present day let God see you such as He will see you *then*.

CHAP. VIII. — MEN NOT EXCLUDED FROM THESE REMARKS ON PERSONAL ADORNMENT.

Of course, now, I, a man, as being envious[10] of women, am banishing them quite from their own (domains). Are there, in our case too, some things which, in respect of the sobriety[11] we are to maintain on account of the fear[12] due to God, are disallowed?[13] If it is true, (as it is,) that in men, for the sake of women (just as in women for the sake of men), there is implanted, by a defect of nature, the will to please ; and if this sex of ours acknowledges to itself deceptive trickeries of form peculiarly its own, — (such as) to cut the beard too sharply ; to pluck it out here and there ; to shave round about (the mouth) ; to arrange the hair, and disguise its hoariness by dyes ; to remove all the incipient down all over the body ; to fix (each particular hair) in its place with (some) womanly pigment ; to smooth all the rest of the body by the aid of some rough powder or other : then, further, to take every opportunity for consulting the mirror ; to gaze anxiously into it : — while yet, when (once) the knowledge of God has put an end to all wish to please by means of voluptuous attraction, all these things are rejected as frivolous, as hostile to modesty. For where God is, there modesty is ; there is sobriety,[14] her assistant and ally. How, then, shall we practise modesty without her instrumental mean,[15] that is, without sobriety?[16] How, moreover, shall we bring sobriety[17] to bear on the discharge of (the functions of) modesty, unless seriousness in appearance and in countenance, and in the general aspect[18] of the entire man, mark our carriage?

CHAP. IX. — EXCESS IN DRESS, AS WELL AS IN PERSONAL CULTURE, TO BE SHUNNED. ARGUMENTS DRAWN FROM I COR. VII.

Wherefore, with regard to clothing also, and all the remaining lumber of your self-elaboration,[19] the like pruning off and retrenchment of too redundant splendour must be the object of your care. For what boots it to exhibit in your *face* temperance and unaffectedness, and a simplicity altogether worthy of the divine discipline, but to invest all the *other* parts of the body with the luxurious absurdities of pomps and delicacies? How intimate is the connection which these pomps have with the business of voluptuousness, and how they interfere with modesty, is easily discernible from the fact that it is by the allied aid of dress that they prostitute the grace of personal comeliness : so plain is it that if (the pomps) be wanting, they render (that grace) bootless and thankless, as if it were disarmed and wrecked. On the other hand, if natural beauty fails, the supporting aid of outward embellishment supplies a grace, as it were, from its own inherent power.[20] Those times of life, in fact, which are at last blest with quiet and withdrawn into the harbour of modesty, the splendour and dignity of dress lure away (from that rest and that harbour), and *dis*quiet seriousness by seductions of appetite, which compensate for the chill of age by the provocative charms of apparel. First, then, blessed (sisters), (take heed) that you admit not to your use meretricious and prostitutionary garbs and garments : and, in the next place, if there are any of you whom the exigencies of riches, or birth, or past dignities, compel to appear in public so gorgeously arrayed as not to appear to have attained wisdom, take heed to temper an evil of this kind ; lest, under the pretext of necessity, you give the rein without stint to the indulgence of

---

[1] "Alieni:" perhaps here = "alien," i.e., "heathen," as in other places.
[2] Gehennæ.
[3] Comp Gal iv. 31, v. 13.
[4] See 1 Cor. xi. 2–16; and comp. *de Or.*, c. xxii., and the treatise *de Virg. Vel.*
[5] Comp. *ad Ux.*, b. ii. c. iii.
[6] Ambitu (*habitu* is a conjectural emendation noticed by Oehler) capitis.
[7] See 1 Thess. iv. 13–17.
[8] Comp. 1 Cor. xv. 50 with 1 Thess. v. 23.
[9] Or, "within the limits of the flesh and the spirit."
[10] Æmulus.
[11] Gravitatis.
[12] Metus.
[13] Detrahuntur.

[14] Gravitas.
[15] Comp. *de Pa.*, c. xv. *ad fin.*
[16] Gravitate.
[17] Gravitatem.
[18] Contemplatione.
[19] Impedimenta compositionis.
[20] De suo. Comp. *de Bapt.*, c. xvii. (*sub fin.*), de *Cult. Fem.*, b. i. c. v. (*med.*).

licence. For how will you be able to fulfil (the requirements of) humility, which our (school) profess,[1] if you do not keep within bounds[2] the enjoyment of your riches and elegancies, which tend so much to "glory?" Now it has ever been the wont of glory to *exalt*, not to *humble*. "Why, shall we not use what is our own?" Who prohibits your using it? Yet (it must be) in accordance with the apostle, who warns us "to use this world[3] as if we abuse it not; for the fashion[4] of this world[5] is passing away." And "they who buy are so to act as if they possessed not."[6] Why so? Because he had laid down the premiss, saying, "The time is wound up."[7] If, then, he shows plainly that even wives themselves are so to be had as if they be *not* had,[8] on account of the straits of the times, what would be his sentiments about these vain appliances of theirs? Why, are there not many, withal, who so *do*, and seal themselves up to eunuchhood for the sake of the kingdom of God,[9] spontaneously relinquishing a pleasure so honourable,[10] and (as we know) permitted? Are there not some who prohibit to themselves (the use of) the very "creature of God,"[11] abstaining from wine and animal food, the enjoyments of which border upon no peril or solicitude; but they sacrifice to God the humility of their soul even in the chastened use of food? Sufficiently, therefore, have you, too, used your riches and your delicacies; sufficiently have you cut down the fruits of your dowries, before (receiving) the knowledge of saving disciplines. We are they "upon whom the ends of the ages have met, having ended their course."[12] We have been predestined by God, before the world[13] was, (to arise) in the extreme end of the times.[14] And so we are trained by God for the purpose of chastising, and (so to say) emasculating, the world.[15] We are the circumcision[16] — spiritual and carnal — of all things; for both in the spirit and in the flesh we circumcise worldly[17] principles.

CHAP. X. — TERTULLIAN REFERS AGAIN TO THE QUESTION OF THE ORIGIN OF ALL THESE ORNAMENTS AND EMBELLISHMENTS.[18]

It was God, no doubt, who showed the way to dye wools with the juices of herbs and the humours of conchs! It had escaped Him, when He was bidding the universe to come into being,[19] to issue a command for (the production of) purple and scarlet sheep! It was God, too, who devised by careful thought the manufactures of those very garments which, light and thin (in themselves), were to be heavy in price alone; God who produced such grand implements of gold for confining or parting the hair; God who introduced (the fashion of) finely-cut wounds for the ears, and set so high a value upon the tormenting of His own work and the tortures of innocent infancy, learning to suffer with its earliest breath, in order that from those scars of the body—born for the steel!—should hang I know not what (precious) grains, which, as we may plainly see, the Parthians insert, in place of studs, upon their very shoes! And yet even the gold itself, the "glory" of which carries you away, serves a certain race (so Gentile literature, tells us) for chains! So true is it that it is not intrinsic worth,[20] but rarity, which constitutes the goodness (of these things): the excessive labour, moreover, of working them with arts introduced by the means of the sinful angels, who were the revealers withal of the material substances themselves, joined with their rarity, excited their costliness, and hence a lust on the part of women to possess (that) costliness. But, if the self-same angels who disclosed both the material substances of this kind and their charms —of gold, I mean, and lustrous[21] stones — and taught men how to work them, and by and by instructed them, among their other (instructions), in (the virtues of) eyelid-powder and the dyeings of fleeces, have been condemned by God, as Enoch tells us, how shall we please God while we joy in the *things* of those (angels) who, on these accounts, have provoked the *anger* and the *vengeance* of God?

Now, granting that God did foresee these things; that God permitted them; that Esaias finds fault with no garment of purple,[22] represses no coif,[23] reprobates no crescent-shaped neck ornaments;[24] still let *us* not, as the Gentiles do, flatter ourselves with thinking that God is merely a Creator, not likewise a Downlooker on His own creatures. For how far more usefully and cautiously shall we act, if we hazard the presumption that all these things were indeed provided[25] at the beginning and placed in the world[26] by God, in order that there should now be means of putting to the proof the discipline of His servants, in order that the licence of *using* should

---

[1] See c. iii.
[2] Repastinantes.
[3] Mundo; κόσμῳ. See 1 Cor. vii. 31.
[4] Habitus; σχῆμα, *ib.*
[5] Κόσμου, *ib.*
[6] 1 Cor. vii. 30.
[7] 1 Cor. vii. 29.
[8] 1 Cor. vii. 29.
[9] Matt. xix. 12.
[10] Fortem.
[11] Comp. 1 Tim. iv. 4, 5.
[12] 1 Cor. x. 11, εἰς οὓς τὰ τέλη τῶν αἰώνων κατήντησεν.
[13] Mundum.
[14] In extimatione temporali. See Eph. i. 4 and 1 Pet. i. 20.
[15] Sæculo.
[16] Comp. Phil. iii. 3.
[17] Sæcularia.
[18] Comp. i. cc. ii. iii. v. vii. viii.

[19] Universa nasci.
[20] Veritate.
[21] Illustrium.
[22] De conchylio.
[23] κοσύμβους. Isa. iii. 18 (in LXX.).
[24] Lunulas = μηνίσκους, *ib.*
[25] Or, "foreseen."
[26] Sæculo.

be the means whereby the experimental trials of *continence* should be conducted? Do not wise heads of families purposely offer and permit some things to their servants [1] in order to try whether and how they will use the things thus permitted; whether (they will do so) with honesty, or with moderation? But how far more praiseworthy (the servant) who abstains entirely; who has a wholesome fear [2] even of his lord's indulgence! Thus, therefore, the apostle too: "All things," says he, "are lawful, but not all are expedient." [3] How much more easily will he fear [4] what is *unlawful* who has a reverent dread [5] of what is *lawful?*

CHAP. XI. — CHRISTIAN WOMEN, FURTHER, HAVE NOT THE SAME CAUSES FOR APPEARING IN PUBLIC, AND HENCE FOR DRESSING IN FINE ARRAY, AS GENTILES. ON THE CONTRARY, THEIR APPEARANCE SHOULD ALWAYS DISTINGUISH THEM FROM SUCH.

Moreover, what causes have you for appearing in public in excessive grandeur, removed as you are from the occasions which call for such exhibitions? For you neither make the circuit of the temples, nor demand (to be present at) public shows, nor have any acquaintance with the holy days of the Gentiles. Now it is for the sake of all these public gatherings, and of much seeing and being seen, that all pomps (of dress) are exhibited before the public eye; either for the purpose of transacting the trade of voluptuousness, or else of inflating "glory." *You*, however, have no cause of appearing in public, except such as is serious. Either some brother who is sick is visited, or else the sacrifice is offered, or else the word of God is dispensed. Whichever of these you like to name is a business of sobriety [6] and sanctity, requiring no extraordinary attire, with (studious) arrangement and (wanton) negligence. [7] And if the requirements of Gentile friendships and of kindly offices call you, why not go forth clad in your own armour; (and) all the more, in that (you have to go) to such as are strangers to the faith? so that between the handmaids of God and of the devil there may be a difference; so that you may be an example to them, and they may be edified in you; so that (as the apostle says) "God may be magnified in your body." [8] But magnified He is in the *body* through modesty: of course, too, through attire suitable to modesty. Well, but it is urged by some, "Let not the Name be blasphemed in us, [9] if we make any derogatory change from our old style and dress." Let us, then, not abolish our old vices! let us maintain the same character, if we must maintain the same appearance (as before); and then truly the nations will not blaspheme! A grand blasphemy is that by which it is said, "Ever since she became a Christian, she walks in poorer garb!" Will you fear to appear poorer, from the time that you have been made more wealthy; and *fouler*, [10] from the time when you have been made more clean? Is it according to the decree [11] of Gentiles, or according to the decree of God, that it becomes Christians to walk?

CHAP. XII. — SUCH OUTWARD ADORNMENTS MERETRICIOUS, AND THEREFORE UNSUITABLE TO MODEST WOMEN.

Let us only wish that we may be no cause for just blasphemy! But how much more provocative of blasphemy is it that you, who are called modesty's priestesses, should appear in public decked and painted out after the manner of the *im*modest? Else, (if you so do,) what inferiority would the poor unhappy victims of the public lusts have (beneath you)? whom, albeit some laws were (formerly) wont to restrain them from (the use of) matrimonial and matronly decorations, now, at all events, the daily increasing depravity of the age [12] has raised so nearly to an equality with all the most honourable women, that the difficulty is to distinguish them. And yet, even the Scriptures suggest (to us the reflection), that meretricious attractivenesses of form are invariably conjoined with and appropriate [13] to bodily prostitution. That powerful state [14] which presides over [15] the seven mountains and very many waters, has merited from the Lord the appellation of a prostitute. [16] But what kind of garb is the instrumental mean of her comparison with that appellation? She sits, to be sure, "in purple, and scarlet, and gold, and precious stone." How accursed are the things without (the aid of) which an accursed prostitute could not have been described! It was the fact that Thamar "had painted out and adorned herself" that led Judah to regard her as a harlot, [17] and thus, because she was hidden beneath her "veil," — the quality of her garb belying her as if she had been a harlot, — he judged (her to be one), and addressed and bargained with (her as such). Whence we gather an additional confirmation of the lesson, that provision must be made in every

---

[1] Or, "slaves."
[2] Timuerit.
[3] 1 Cor. x. 23.
[4] Timebit.
[5] Verebitur.
[6] Gravitatis.
[7] Et composito et soluto.
[8] See Phil. i. 20.

[9] Comp. *de Idol.*, c. xiv.
[10] Sordidior.
[11] Or "pleasure:" placitum.
[12] Sæculi.
[13] Debita.
[14] Or, "city."
[15] Or, "sits on high above."
[16] Comp. Rev. xvii.
[17] Comp. Gen. xxxviii. 12-30.

way against all immodest associations [1] and suspicions. For why is the integrity of a chaste mind defiled by its neighbour's suspicion? Why is a thing from which I am averse hoped for in me? Why does not my garb pre-announce my character, to prevent my spirit from being wounded by shamelessness through (the channel of) my ears? Grant that it be lawful to assume the appearance of a modest woman: [2] to assume that of an *im*modest is, at all events, *not* lawful.

CHAP. XIII. — IT IS NOT ENOUGH THAT GOD KNOW US TO BE CHASTE: WE MUST SEEM SO BEFORE MEN. ESPECIALLY IN THESE TIMES OF PERSECUTION WE MUST INURE OUR BODIES TO THE HARDSHIPS WHICH THEY MAY NOT IMPROBABLY BE CALLED TO SUFFER.

Perhaps some (woman) will say: "To me it is not necessary to be approved by men; for I do not require the testimony of men: [3] God is the inspector of the heart." [4] (That) we all know; provided, however, we remember what the same (God) has said through the apostle: "Let your probity appear before men." [5] For what purpose, except that malice may have no access at all to you, or that you may be an example and testimony to the evil? Else, what is (that): "Let your works shine?" [6] Why, moreover, does the Lord call us the light of the world; why has He compared us to a city built upon a mountain; [7] if we do not shine in (the midst of) darkness, and stand eminent amid them who are sunk down? If you hide your lamp beneath a bushel, [8] you must necessarily be left quite in darkness, and be run against by many. The things which make us luminaries of the world are these — our good works. What is *good*, moreover, provided it be true and full, loves not darkness: it joys in being seen, [9] and exults over the very pointings which are made at it. To Christian modesty it is not enough to *be* so, but to *seem* so too. For so great ought its

plenitude to be, that it may flow out from the mind to the garb, and burst out from the conscience to the outward appearance; so that even from the outside it may gaze, as it were, upon its own furniture, [10] — (a furniture) such as to be suited to retain faith as its inmate perpetually. For such delicacies as tend by their softness and effeminacy to unman the manliness [11] of faith are to be discarded. Otherwise, I know not whether the wrist that has been wont to be surrounded with the palmleaf-like bracelet will endure till it grow into the numb hardness of its own chain! I know not whether the leg that has rejoiced in the anklet will suffer itself to be squeezed into the gyve! I fear the neck, beset with pearl and emerald nooses, will give no room to the broadsword! Wherefore, blessed (sisters), let us meditate on hardships, and we shall not feel them; let us abandon luxuries, and we shall not regret them. Let us stand ready to endure every violence, having nothing which we may fear to leave behind. It is these things which are the bonds which retard our hope. Let us cast away earthly ornaments if we desire heavenly. Love not gold; in which (one substance) are branded all the sins of the people of Israel. You ought to *hate* what ruined your fathers; what was adored by them who were forsaking God. [12] Even *then* (we find) gold is food for the fire. [13] But Christians always, and now more than ever, pass their times not in gold but in iron: the stoles of martyrdom are (now) preparing: the angels who are to carry us are (now) being awaited! Do you go forth (to meet them) already arrayed in the cosmetics and ornaments of prophets and apostles; drawing your whiteness from simplicity, your ruddy hue from modesty; painting your eyes with bashfulness, and your mouth with silence; implanting in your ears the words of God; fitting on your necks the yoke of Christ. Submit your head to your husbands, and you will be enough adorned. Busy your hands with spinning; keep your feet at home; and you will "please" better than (by arraying yourselves) in gold. Clothe yourselves with the silk of uprightness, the fine linen of holiness, the purple of modesty. Thus painted, you will have God as your Lover!

---

[1] Congressus.
[2] Videri pudicam.
[3] Comp. John v. 34; 1 Cor. iv. 3.
[4] Comp. 1 Sam. xvi. 7; Jer. xvii. 10; Luke xvi. 15.
[5] See Phil. iv. 5, 8; Rom. xii. 17; 2 Cor. viii. 21.
[6] See Matt. v. 16; and comp. *de Idol.*, c. xv. *ad init.*
[7] Matt. v. 14.
[8] Matt. v. 15; Mark iv. 21; Luke viii. 16, xi. 33.
[9] See John iii. 21.

[10] Supellectilem.
[11] Effeminari virtus.
[12] Comp. Ex. xxxii.
[13] Ex. xxxii. 20.

ELUCIDATION.

(The Prophecy of Enoch, p. 15.)

DR. DAVIDSON is the author of a useful article on "Apocalyptic Literature," from which we extract all that is requisite to inform the reader of the *freshest* opinion as seen from his well-known point of view. He notes Archbishop Lawrence's translation into English, and that it has been rendered back again into German by Dillman (1853), as before, less accurately, by Hoffmann. Ewald, Lücke, Koestlin, and Hilgenfeld are referred to, and an article of his own in Kitto's *Cyclopædia*. We owe its re-appearance, after long neglect, to Archbishop Lawrence (1838), and its preservation to the Abyssinians. It was rescued by Bruce, the explorer, in an Æthiopic version; and the first detailed announcement of its discovery was made by De Sacy, 1800. Davidson ascribes its authorship to pre-Messianic times, but thinks it has been interpolated by a Jewish Christian. Tertullian's negative testimony points the other way: he evidently relies upon its "Christology" as genuine; and, if interpolated in his day, he could hardly have been deceived.

Its five parts are: I. The rape of women by fallen angels, and the giants that were begotten of them. The visions of Enoch begun. II. The visions continued, with views of the Messiah's kingdom. III. The physical and astronomical mysteries treated of. IV. Man's mystery revealed in dreams from the beginning to the end of the Messianic kingdom. V. The warnings of Enoch to his own family and to mankind, with appendices, which complete the book. The article in Smith's *Dictionary of the Bible* is accessible, and need only be referred to as well worth perusal; and, as it abounds in references to the entire literature of criticism respecting it, it is truly valuable. It seems to have been written by Westcott.[1]

The fact that St. Jude refers to Enoch's prophesyings no more proves that this book is other than apocryphal than St. Paul's reference to Jannes and Jambres makes Scripture of the Targum. The apostle Jude does, indeed, authenticate that particular saying by inspiration of God, and doubtless it was traditional among the Jews. St. Jerome's references to this quotation may be found textually in Lardner.[2] Although the book is referred to frequently in the *Patrologia*, Tertullian only, of the Fathers, pays it the respect due to Scripture.

---

[1] See also Pusey's reply to Dr. Farrar.   [2] *Credibility*, etc., iv. pp. 460–462.

III.

ON THE VEILING OF VIRGINS.[1]

[TRANSLATED BY THE REV. S. THELWALL.]

CHAP. I. — TRUTH RATHER TO BE APPEALED TO THAN CUSTOM, AND TRUTH PROGRESSIVE IN ITS DEVELOPMENTS.

HAVING already undergone the trouble peculiar to my opinion, I will show in Latin also that it behoves our virgins to be veiled from the time that they have passed the turning-point of their age : that this observance is exacted by truth, on which no one can impose prescription — no space of times, no influence of persons, no privilege of regions. For these, for the most part, are the sources whence, from some ignorance or simplicity, custom finds its beginning ; and then it is successively confirmed into an usage, and thus is maintained .in opposition to truth. But our Lord Christ has surnamed Himself Truth,[2] not Custom. If Christ is always, and prior to all, equally truth is a thing sempiternal and ancient. Let those therefore look to themselves, to whom that is new which is intrinsically old. It is not so much novelty as truth which convicts heresies. Whatever savours of opposition to truth, this will be heresy, even (if it be an) ancient custom. On the other hand, if any is ignorant of anything, the ignorance proceeds from his own defect. Moreover, whatever is matter of ignorance ought to have been as carefully *inquired into* as whatever is matter of acknowledgment *received*. The rule of faith, indeed, is altogether one, alone immoveable and irreformable ; the rule, to wit, of believing in one only God omnipotent, the Creator of the universe, and His Son Jesus Christ, born of the Virgin Mary, crucified under Pontius Pilate, raised again the third day from the dead, received in the heavens, sitting now at the right (hand) of the Father, destined to come to judge quick and dead through the resurrection of the flesh as well (as of the spirit). This law of faith being constant, the other succeeding points of discipline and conversation admit the "novelty" of correction ; the grace of God, to wit, operating and advancing even to the end. For what kind of (supposition) is it, that, while the devil is always operating and adding daily to the ingenuities of iniquity, the work of God should either have ceased, or else have desisted from advancing ? whereas the reason why the Lord sent the Paraclete was, that, since human mediocrity was unable to take in all things at once, discipline should, little by little, be directed, and ordained, and carried on to perfection, by that Vicar of the Lord, the Holy Spirit. "Still," He said, "I have many things to say to you, but ye are not yet able to bear them : when that Spirit of truth shall have come, He will conduct you into all truth, and will report to you the supervening (things)."[3] But above, withal, He made a declaration concerning this His work.[4] What, then, is the Paraclete's administrative office but this : the direction of discipline, the revelation of the Scriptures, the re-formation of the intellect, the advancement toward the "better things?"[5] Nothing is without stages of growth : all things await their season. In short, the preacher says, "A time to everything."[6] Look how creation itself advances little by little to fructification. First comes the grain, and from the grain arises the shoot, and from the shoot struggles out the shrub : thereafter boughs and leaves gather strength, and the whole that we call a tree expands : then follows the swelling of the germen, and from the germen bursts the flower, and from the flower the fruit opens : that fruit itself, rude for a while, and unshapely, little by little,

---

[1] [Written, possibly, as early as A.D. 204.]
[2] John xiv. 6.
[3] John xvi. 12, 13. See *de Monog.*, c. ii.
[4] See John xiv. 26.
[5] Comp. Heb. xi. 40, xii. 24.
[6] Eccles. iii. 1, briefly.

keeping the straight course of its development, is trained to the mellowness of its flavour.[1] So, too, righteousness — for the God of righteousness and of creation is the same — was first in a rudimentary state, having a natural fear of God: from that stage it advanced, through the Law and the Prophets, to infancy; from that stage it passed, through the Gospel, to the fervour of youth: now, through the Paraclete, it is settling into maturity. He will be, after Christ, the only one to be called and revered as Master;[2] for He speaks not from Himself, but what is commanded by Christ.[3] He is the only prelate, because He alone succeeds Christ. They who have received Him set truth before custom. They who have heard Him prophesying even to the present time, not of old, bid virgins be wholly covered.

CHAP. II. — BEFORE PROCEEDING FARTHER, LET THE QUESTION OF CUSTOM ITSELF BE SIFTED.

But I will not, meantime, attribute this usage to Truth. Be it, for a while, custom: that to custom I may likewise oppose custom.

Throughout Greece, and certain of its barbaric provinces, the majority of Churches keep their virgins covered. There are places, too, beneath this (African) sky, where this practice obtains; lest any ascribe the custom to Greek or barbarian Gentilehood. But I have proposed (as models) those Churches which were founded by apostles or apostolic men; and antecedently, I think, to certain (founders, who shall be nameless). Those Churches therefore, as well (as others), have the self-same authority of custom (to appeal to); in opposing phalanx they range "times" and "teachers," more than these later (Churches do). What shall we observe? What shall we choose? We cannot contemptuously reject a custom which we cannot condemn, inasmuch as it is not "strange," since it is not among "strangers" that we find it, but among those, to wit, with whom we share the law of peace and the name of brotherhood. They and we have one faith, one God, the same Christ, the same hope, the same baptismal sacraments; let me say it once for all, we are one Church.[4] Thus, whatever belongs to our brethren is ours: only, the body divides us.

Still, here (as generally happens in all cases of various practice, of doubt, and of uncertainty), examination ought to have been made to see which of two so diverse customs were the more compatible with the discipline of God. And, of course, that ought to have been chosen which keeps virgins veiled, as being known to God alone; who (besides that glory must be

sought from God, not from men[5]) ought to blush even at their own privilege. You put a virgin to the blush more by praising than by blaming her; because the front of sin is more hard, learning shamelessness from and in the sin itself. For that custom which belies virgins while it exhibits them, would never have been approved by any except by some men who must have been similar in character to the virgins themselves. Such eyes will wish that a virgin be seen as has the virgin who shall wish to be seen. The same kinds of eyes reciprocally crave after each other. Seeing and being seen belong to the self-same lust. To blush if he see a virgin is as much a mark of a chaste[6] man, as of a chaste[7] virgin if seen by a man.

CHAP. III. — GRADUAL DEVELOPMENT OF CUSTOM, AND ITS RESULTS. PASSIONATE APPEAL TO TRUTH.

But not even between customs have those most chaste[8] teachers chosen to examine. Still, until very recently, among us, either custom was, with comparative indifference, admitted to communion. The matter had been left to choice, for each virgin to veil herself or expose herself, as she might have chosen, just as (she had equal liberty) as to marrying, which itself withal is neither enforced nor prohibited. Truth had been content to make an agreement with custom, in order that under the name of custom it might enjoy itself even partially. But when the power of discerning began to advance, so that the licence granted to either fashion was becoming the mean whereby the indication of the better part emerged; immediately the great adversary of good things — and much more of good institutions — set to his own work. The virgins of men go about, in opposition to the virgins of God, with front quite bare, excited to a rash audacity; and the semblance of *virgins* is exhibited by women who have the power of asking somewhat from *husbands*,[9] not to say such a request as that (forsooth) their rivals — all the more "free" in that they are the "handmaids" of Christ alone[10] — may be surrendered to them. "We are scandalized," they say, "because others walk otherwise (than we do);" and they prefer being "scandalized" to being provoked (to modesty). A "scandal," if I mistake not, is an example not of a good thing, but of a bad, tending to sinful edification. Good things scandalize none but an evil mind. If modesty, if bashfulness, if contempt of glory, anxious to please God alone, are good things,

---

[1] Comp. Mark iv. 28.
[2] Comp. Matt. xxiii. 8.
[3] John xvi. 13.
[4] Comp. Eph. iv. 1-6.

[5] Comp. John v. 44 and xii. 43.
[6] Sancti.
[7] Sanctæ.
[8] Sanctissimi.
[9] The allusion is perhaps to 1 Cor. xiv. 35.
[10] Comp. 1 Cor. vii. 21, 22.

let women who are "scandalized" by such good learn to acknowledge their own evil. For what if the incontinent withal say they are "scandalized" by the continent? Is continence to be recalled? And, for fear the multinubists be "scandalized," is monogamy to be rejected? Why may not these latter rather complain that the petulance, the impudence, of ostentatious virginity is a "scandal" to *them?* Are therefore chaste virgins to be, for the sake of these marketable creatures, dragged into the church, blushing at being recognised in public, quaking at being unveiled, as if they had been invited as it were to rape? For they are no less unwilling to suffer even this. Every public exposure of an honourable virgin is (to her) a suffering of rape: and yet the suffering of carnal violence is the less (evil), because it comes of natural office. But when the very spirit itself is violated in a virgin by the abstraction of her covering, she has learnt to lose what she used to keep. O sacrilegious hands, which have had the hardihood to drag off a dress dedicated to God! What worse could any persecutor have done, if he had known that this (garb) had been chosen by a virgin? You have denuded a maiden in regard of her head, and forthwith she wholly ceases to be a virgin to herself; she has undergone a change! Arise, therefore, Truth; arise, and as it were burst forth from Thy patience! No *custom* do I wish Thee to defend; for by this time even that custom under which Thou didst enjoy thy own liberty is being stormed! Demonstrate that it is Thyself who art the coverer of virgins. Interpret in person Thine own Scriptures, which Custom understandeth not; for, if she had, she never would have had an existence.

CHAP. IV. — OF THE ARGUMENT DRAWN FROM I COR. XI. 5–16.

But in so far as it is the custom to argue even from the Scriptures in opposition to truth, there is immediately urged against us the fact that "no mention of virgins is made by the apostle where he is prescribing about the veil, but that 'women' only are named; whereas, if he had willed virgins as well to be covered, he would have pronounced concerning 'virgins' also together with the 'women' named; just as," says (our opponent), "in that passage where he is treating of marriage,[1] he declares likewise with regard to 'virgins' what observance is to be followed." And accordingly (it is urged) that "they are not comprised in the law of veiling the head, as not being named in this law; nay rather, that this is the origin of their being *un*-veiled, inasmuch as they who are not *named* are not *bidden*."

But we withal retort the self-same line of argument. For he who knew elsewhere how to make mention of each sex — of *virgin* I mean, and *woman,* that is, *not-virgin* — for distinction's sake; in these (passages), in which he does *not* name a *virgin,* points out (by not making the distinction) community of condition. Otherwise he could here also have marked the difference between *virgin* and *woman,* just as elsewhere he says, "Divided is the *woman* and the *virgin.*"[2] Therefore those whom, by passing them over in silence, he has not divided, he has included in the other species.

Nor yet, because in that case "divided is both *woman* and *virgin,*" will this division exert its patronizing influence in the present case as well, as some will have it. For how many sayings, uttered on another occasion, have no weight — in cases, to wit, where they are *not* uttered — unless the subject-matter be the same as on the other occasion, so that the one utterance may suffice! But the former case of *virgin* and *woman* is widely "divided" from the present question. "Divided," he says, "is the *woman* and the *virgin.*" Why? Inasmuch as "the unmarried," that is, the *virgin,* "is anxious about those (things) which are the Lord's, that she may be holy both in body and in spirit; but the married," that is, the *not-virgin,* "is anxious how she may please her husband." This will be the interpretation of that "division," having no place in this passage (now under consideration); in which pronouncement is made neither about marriage, nor about the mind and the thought of *woman* and of *virgin,* but about the veiling of the head. Of which (veiling) the Holy Spirit, willing that there should be no distinction, willed that by the one name of *woman* should likewise be understood the *virgin;* whom, by not specially naming, He has not separated from the *woman,* and, by not separating, has conjoined to her from whom He has not separated her.

Is it now, then, a "novelty" to use the primary word, and nevertheless to have the other (subordinate divisions) understood in that word, in cases where there is no necessity for individually distinguishing the (various parts of the) universal whole? Naturally, a compendious style of speech is both pleasing and necessary; inasmuch as diffuse speech is both tiresome and vain. So, too, we are content with general words, which comprehend in themselves the understanding of the specialties. Proceed we, then, to the word itself. The word (expressing the) *natural* (distinction) is *female.* Of the natural word, the *general* word is *woman.* Of the *general,* again, the *special* is *virgin,* or *wife,* or *widow,* or whatever other names, even of the

---

[1] 1 Cor. vii.   [2] 1 Cor. vii. 34.

successive stages of life, are added hereto. Subject, therefore, the *special* is to the *general* (because the general is prior); and the *succedent* to the *antecedent*, and the *partial* to the *universal:* (each) is implied in the word itself to which it is subject; and is signified in it, because contained in it. Thus neither *hand,* nor *foot,* nor any one of the *members,* requires to be signified when the *body* is named. And if you say the *universe,* therein will be both the heaven and the things that are in it, — sun and moon, and constellations and stars, — and the earth and the seas, and everything that goes to make up the list of elements. You will have named all, when you have named that which is made up of all. So, too, by naming *woman,* he has named whatever is *woman's.*

CHAP. V. — OF THE WORD WOMAN, ESPECIALLY IN CONNECTION WITH ITS APPLICATION TO EVE.

But since they use the name of *woman* in such a way as to think it inapplicable save to her alone who has known a man, the pertinence of the propriety of this word to the sex itself, not to a grade of the sex, must be proved by us; that virgins as well (as others) may be commonly comprised in it.

When this kind of second human being was made by God for man's assistance, that *female* was forthwith named *woman;* still happy, still worthy of paradise, still *virgin.* "She shall be called," said (Adam), "Woman." And accordingly you have the name, — I say, not already *common* to a *virgin,* but — *proper* (to her; a name) which from the beginning was allotted to a *virgin.* But some ingeniously will have it that it was said of the *future,* "She *shall be* called *woman,*" as if she were destined to be so when she had resigned her virginity; since he added withal: "For this cause shall a man leave father and mother, and be conglutinated to his own *woman;* and the two shall be one flesh." Let them therefore among whom that subtlety obtains show us first, if she were surnamed *woman* with a future reference, what name she meantime received. For without a name expressive of her *present* quality she cannot have been. But what kind of (hypothesis) is it that one who, with an eye to the future, was called by a definite name, at the present time should have nothing for a surname? On all animals Adam imposed names; and on none on the ground of future condition, but on the ground of the present purpose which each particular nature served; [1] called (as each nature was) by that to which from the beginning it showed a propensity. What, then, was she at that time called? Why, as often as she is named in the Scripture, she

has the appellation *woman* before she was *wedded,* and never *virgin* while she *was* a *virgin.*

This name was at that time the only one she had, and (that) when nothing was (as yet) said prophetically. For when the Scripture records that "the two were naked, Adam and his *woman,*" neither does this savour of the future, as if it said "his *woman*" as a presage of "wife;" but because his *woman* [2] was withal unwedded, as being (formed) from his own substance. "This bone," he says, "out of my bones, and flesh out of my flesh, shall be called *woman.*" Hence, then, it is from the tacit consciousness of nature that the actual divinity of the soul has educed into the ordinary usage of common speech, unawares to men, (just as *it has thus educed* many other things too which we shall elsewhere be able to show to derive from the Scriptures the origin of their doing and saying,) our fashion of calling our *wives* our *women,* however improperly withal we may in *some* instances speak. For the Greeks, too, who use the name of *woman* more (than we do) in the sense of *wife,* have other names appropriate to *wife.* But I prefer to assign this usage as a testimony to Scripture. For when two are made into one flesh through the marriage-tie, the "flesh of flesh and bone of bones" is called the *woman* of him of whose *substance* she begins to be accounted by being made his *wife.* Thus *woman* is not by nature a name of *wife,* but *wife* by condition is a name of *woman.* In fine, *woman*hood is predicable apart from *wife*hood; but *wife*hood apart from *woman*hood is not, because it cannot even exist. Having therefore settled the name of the newly-made female — which (name) is *woman* — and having explained what she formerly was, that is, having sealed the name to her, he immediately turned to the prophetic reason, so as to say, "On this account shall a man leave father and mother." The name is so truly separate from the prophecy, as far as (the prophecy) from the individual person herself, that of course it is not with reference to Eve herself that (Adam) has uttered (the prophecy), but with a view to those future females whom he has named in the maternal fount of the feminine race. Besides, Adam was not to leave "father and mother" — whom he had not — for the sake of Eve. Therefore that which was prophetically said does not apply to Eve, because it does not to Adam either. For it was predicted with regard to the condition of husbands, who were destined to leave their parents for a *woman's* sake; which could not chance to Eve, because it could not to Adam either.

If the case is so, it is apparent that she was not surnamed *woman* on account of a future

---

[1] Gen. ii. 19, 20.

[2] Mulier, throughout.

(circumstance), to whom (that) future (circumstance) did not apply.

To this is added, that (Adam) himself published the reason of the name. For, after saying, "She shall be called *woman*," he said, "inasmuch as she hath been taken out of man" — the man himself withal being still a virgin. But we will speak, too, about the name of *man*[1] in its own place. Accordingly, let none interpret with a prophetic reference a name which was deduced from another signification; especially since it is apparent when she *did* receive a name founded upon a future (circumstance) — there, namely, where she is surnamed "Eve," with a *personal* name now, because the *natural* one had gone before.[2] For if "Eve" means "the mother of the living," behold, she is surnamed from a future (circumstance)! behold, she is pre-announced to be a *wife*, and not a *virgin!* This will be the name of one who is about to wed; for of the bride (comes) the mother.

Thus in this case too it is shown, that it was not from a future (circumstance) that she was at that time named *woman*, who was shortly after to receive the name which would be proper to her future condition.

Sufficient answer has been made to this part (of the question).

CHAP. VI. — THE PARALLEL CASE OF MARY CONSIDERED.

Let us now see whether the apostle withal observes the norm of this name in accordance with Genesis, attributing it to *the sex;* calling the *virgin* Mary a *woman*, just as Genesis (does) Eve. For, writing to the Galatians, "God," he says, "sent His own Son, made of a *woman*,"[3] who, of course, is admitted to have been a *virgin*, albeit Hebion[4] resist (that doctrine). I recognise, too, the angel Gabriel as having been sent to "a *virgin*."[5] But when he is blessing her, it is "among *women*," not among *virgins*, that he ranks her: "Blessed (be) thou among *women*." The angel withal knew that even a *virgin* is called a *woman*.

But to these two (arguments), again, there is one who appears to himself to have made an ingenious answer; (to the effect that) inasmuch as Mary was "betrothed," therefore it is that both by angel and apostle she is pronounced a *woman;* for a "betrothed" is in some sense a "bride." Still, between "in some sense" and "truth" there is difference enough, at all events in the present place: for elsewhere, we grant, we must thus hold. Now, however, it is not as

being already wedded that they have pronounced Mary a *woman*, but as being none the less a *female* even if she had not been espoused; as having been called by this (name) from the beginning: for that must necessarily have a prejudicating force from which the normal type has descended. Else, as far as relates to the present passage, if Mary is here put on a level with a "betrothed," so that she is called a *woman* not on the ground of being a *female*, but on the ground of being assigned to a husband, it immediately follows that Christ was not born of a *virgin*, because (born) of one "betrothed," who by this fact will have ceased to be a *virgin*. Whereas, if He was born of a *virgin* — albeit withal "betrothed," yet intact — acknowledge that even a *virgin*, even an intact one, is called a *woman*. Here, at all events, there can be no semblance of speaking prophetically, as if the apostle should have named a *future woman*, that is, *bride*, in saying "made of a *woman*." For he could not be naming a posterior *woman*, from whom Christ had not to be born — that is, one who had known a man; but she who was then present, who was a *virgin*, was withal called a *woman* in consequence of the propriety of this name, — vindicated, in accordance with the primordial norm, (as belonging) to a *virgin*, and thus to the universal class of *women*.

CHAP. VII. — OF THE REASONS ASSIGNED BY THE APOSTLE FOR BIDDING WOMEN TO BE VEILED.

Turn we next to the examination of the reasons themselves which lead the apostle to teach that the female ought to be veiled, (to see) whether the self-same (reasons) apply to *virgins* likewise; so that hence also the community of the name between *virgins* and *not-virgins* may be established, while the self-same causes which necessitate the veil are found to exist in each case.

If "the man is head of the *woman*,"[6] of course (he is) of the *virgin* too, from whom comes the *woman* who has married; unless the *virgin* is a third generic class, some monstrosity with a head of its own. If "it is shameful for a *woman* to be shaven or shorn," of course it is so for a *virgin*. (Hence let the world, the rival of God, see to it, if it asserts that close-cut hair is graceful to a virgin in like manner as that flowing hair is to a boy.) To her, then, to whom it is equally *un*becoming to be shaven or shorn, it is equally becoming to be covered. If "the *woman* is the glory of the man," how much more the *virgin*, who is a glory withal to herself! If "the *woman* is of the man," and "for the sake of the man," that rib of Adam[7] was first a *virgin*. If "the woman ought to have

[1] Viri: so throughout.
[2] See Gen. iii. 20.
[3] Gal. iv. 4.
[4] [i.e., Ebion, founder of the Ebionites.]
[5] Luke i. 26, 27.
[6] 1 Cor. xi. 3 sqq.
[7] Gen. ii. 23.

power upon the head," [1] all the more justly ought the *virgin*, to whom pertains the essence of the cause (assigned for this assertion). For if (it is) on account of the angels — those, to wit, whom we read of as having fallen from God and heaven on account of concupiscence after females — who can presume that it was bodies already defiled, and relics of human lust, which such angels yearned after, so as not rather to have been inflamed for *virgins*, whose bloom pleads an excuse for human lust likewise? For thus does Scripture withal suggest: "And it came to pass," it says, "when men had begun to grow more numerous upon the earth, there were withal daughters born them; but the sons of God, having descried the daughters of men, that they were fair, took to themselves wives of all whom they elected." [2] For here the Greek name of *women* does seem to have the sense "*wives*," inasmuch as mention is made of marriage. When, then, it says "the *daughters* of men," it manifestly purports *virgins*, who would be still reckoned as belonging to their *parents* — for *wedded women* are called their *husbands*' — whereas it *could* have said "the *wives* of men:" in like manner not naming the angels adulterers, but husbands, while they take *unwedded* "daughters of men," who it has above said were "born," thus also signifying their *virginity:* first, "born;" but here, wedded to angels. Anything else I know not that they were except "born" and subsequently wedded. So perilous a face, then, ought to be shaded, which has cast stumbling-stones even so far as heaven: that, when standing in the presence of God, at whose bar it stands accused of the driving of the angels from their (native) confines, it may blush before the other angels as well; and may repress that former evil liberty of its head, — (a liberty) now to be exhibited not even before human eyes. But even if they were females already contaminated whom those angels had desired, so much the more "on account of the angels" would it have been the duty of *virgins* to be veiled, as it would have been the more possible for *virgins* to have been the cause of the angels' sinning. If, moreover, the apostle further adds the prejudgment of "nature," that redundancy of locks is an honour to a *woman*, because hair serves for a covering, [3] of course it is most of all to a *virgin* that this is a distinction; for their very adornment properly consists in this, that, by being massed together upon the crown, it wholly covers the very citadel of the head with an encirclement of hair.

CHAP. VIII. — THE ARGUMENT E CONTRARIO.

The contraries, at all events, of all these (considerations) effect that a *man* is *not* to cover his head: to wit, because he has not by nature been gifted with excess of hair; because to be shaven or shorn is not shameful to him; because it was not on his account that the angels transgressed; because his Head is Christ. [4] Accordingly, since the apostle is treating of *man* and *woman* — why the latter ought to be veiled, but the former not — it is apparent why he has been silent as to the *virgin;* allowing, to wit, the *virgin* to be understood in the *woman* by the self-same reason by which he forbore to name the *boy* as implied in the *man;* embracing the whole order of either sex in the names proper (to each) of *woman* and *man*. So likewise Adam, while still intact, is surnamed in Genesis *man:* [5] "She shall be called," says he, "*woman*, because she hath been taken from her own *man*." Thus was Adam a *man* before nuptial intercourse, in like manner as Eve a *woman*. On either side the apostle has made his sentence apply with sufficient plainness to the universal species of each sex; and briefly and fully, with so well-appointed a definition, he says, "*Every woman*." What is "every," but of every class, of every order, of every condition, of every dignity, of every age? — if, (as is the case), "every" means total and entire, and in none of its parts defective. But the *virgin* is withal *a part* of the *woman*. Equally, too, with regard to not veiling the *man*, he says "every." Behold two diverse names, *Man* and *Woman* — "every one" in each case: two laws, mutually distinctive; on the one hand (a law) of veiling, on the other (a law) of baring. Therefore, if the fact that it is said "every *man*" makes it plain that the name of *man* is common even to him who is *not* yet a *man*, a stripling male; (if), moreover, since the *name* is common according to nature, the law of not veiling him who among *men* is a *virgin* is common too according to discipline: why is it that it is not consequently prejudged that, *woman* being named, every *woman-virgin* is similarly comprised in the fellowship of the *name*, so as to be comprised too in the community of the *law?* If a *virgin* is not a *woman*, neither is a *stripling* a *man*. If the *virgin* is not covered on the plea that she is not a *woman*, let the *stripling* be covered on the plea that he is not a *man*. Let identity of *virginity* share equality of indulgence. As *virgins* are not compelled to be veiled, so let *boys* not be bidden to be *unveiled*. Why do we partly acknowledge the definition of the apostle, as absolute with regard to "every *man*," without entering upon disquisitions as to why he has not withal named the *boy;* but partly prevaricate, though it is equally absolute with regard to "every *woman?*" "If any," he says, "is contentious, we have not such a custom, nor

[1] 1 Cor. xi. 10.
[2] Gen. vi. 1, 2.
[3] 1 Cor. xi. 14, 15.

[4] 1 Cor. xi. 3.
[5] See Gen. ii. 23.

(has) the Church of God." [1] He shows that there had been some contention about this point; for the extinction whereof he uses the whole compendiousness (of language) : not naming the *virgin*, on the one hand, in order to show that there is to be no doubt about her veiling ; and, on the other hand, naming " every *woman*," whereas he would have named the *virgin* (had the question been confined to her). So, too, did the Corinthians themselves understand him. In fact, at this day the Corinthians do veil their *virgins*. What the apostles taught, their disciples approve.

CHAP. IX.—VEILING CONSISTENT WITH THE OTHER RULES OF DISCIPLINE OBSERVED BY VIRGINS AND WOMEN IN GENERAL.

Let us now see whether, as we have shown the arguments drawn from nature and the matter itself to be applicable to the *virgin* as well (as to other *females*), so likewise the precepts of ecclesiastical discipline concerning *women* have an eye to the *virgin*.

It is not permitted to a *woman* to speak in the church ; [2] but neither (is it permitted her) to teach, nor to baptize, nor to offer, nor to claim to herself a lot in any manly function, not to say (in any) sacerdotal office. Let us inquire whether any of these be lawful to a *virgin*. If it is *not* lawful to a *virgin*, but she is subjected on the self-same terms (as the *woman*), and the necessity for humility is assigned her together with the *woman*, whence will this one thing be lawful to *her* which is not lawful to any and every *female ?* If any is a *virgin*, and has proposed to sanctify her flesh, what prerogative does she (thereby) earn adverse to her own condition? Is the reason why it is granted her to dispense with the veil, that she may be notable and marked as she enters the church? that she may display the honour of sanctity in the liberty of her head? More worthy distinction could have been conferred on her by according her some prerogative of manly rank or office ! I know plainly, that in a certain place a virgin of less than twenty years of age has been placed in the order of *widows !* whereas if the bishop had been bound to accord her any relief, he might, of course, have done it in some other way without detriment to the respect due to discipline ; that such a miracle, not to say monster, should not be pointed at in the church, a *virgin-widow !* the more portentous indeed, that not even as a *widow* did she veil her head ; denying herself either way ; both as *virgin*, in that she is counted a *widow*, and as *widow*, in that she is styled a *virgin*. But the authority

which licenses her sitting in that seat *uncovered* is the same which allows her to sit there as a *virgin :* a seat to which (besides the " sixty years " [3]) not merely " single-husbanded " (*women*) — that is, *married women* — are at length elected, but " mothers " to boot, yes, and " educators of children ; " in order, forsooth, that their experimental training in all the affections may, on the one hand, have rendered them capable of readily aiding all others with counsel and comfort, and that, on the other, they may none the less have travelled down the whole course of probation whereby a *female* can be tested. So true is it, that, on the ground of her position, nothing in the way of public honour is permitted to a *virgin*.

CHAP. X.— IF THE FEMALE VIRGINS ARE TO BE THUS CONSPICUOUS, WHY NOT THE MALE AS WELL?

Nor, similarly, (is it permitted) on the ground of any distinctions whatever. Otherwise, it were sufficiently discourteous, that while *females*, subjected as they are throughout to men, bear in their front an honourable mark of their virginity, whereby they may be looked up to and gazed at on all sides and magnified by the brethren, so many *men-virgins*, so many voluntary eunuchs, should carry their glory in secret, carrying no token to make *them*, too, illustrious. For *they*, too, will be bound to claim some distinctions for themselves — either the feathers of the Garamantes, or else the fillets of the barbarians, or else the cicadas of the Athenians, or else the curls of the Germans, or else the tattoo-marks of the Britons ; or else let the opposite course be taken, and let them lurk in the churches with head *veiled*. Sure we are that the Holy Spirit could rather have made some such concession to *males*, if He had made it to *females ;* forasmuch as, besides the authority of sex, it would have been more becoming that *males* should have been honoured on the ground of continency itself likewise. The more their sex is eager and warm toward *females*, so much the more toil does the continence of (this) greater ardour involve ; and therefore the worthier is it of all ostentation, if ostentation of *virginity* is dignity. For is not continence withal superior to *virginity*, whether it be the continence of the widowed, or of those who, by consent, have already renounced the common disgrace (which matrimony involves) ? [4] For constancy of *virginity* is maintained by *grace ;* of *continence*, by *virtue*. For great is the struggle to overcome concupiscence when you have become accustomed to such concupiscence ; whereas a concupiscence

[1] 1 Cor. xi. 16.
[2] 1 Cor. xiv. 34, 35; 1 Tim. ii. 11, 12.
[3] 1 Tim. v. 9.
[4] See 1 Cor. vii. 5. Comp. *ad Ux.*, l. i. c. viii.: *de Ex. Cast.*, c. i.

the enjoyment whereof you have never known you will subdue easily, not having an adversary (in the shape of) the concupiscence of enjoyment.[1] How, then, would God have failed to make any such concession to *men* more (than to *women*), whether on the ground of nearer intimacy, as being "His own image," or on the ground of harder toil? But if nothing (has been thus conceded) to the *male*, much more to the *female*.

CHAP. XI. — THE RULE OF VEILING NOT APPLICABLE TO CHILDREN.

But what we intermitted above for the sake of the subsequent discussion — not to dissipate its coherence — we will now discharge by an answer. For when we joined issue about the apostle's absolute definition, that *"every woman"* must be understood (as meaning *woman*) of even *every age*, it might be replied by the opposite side, that in that case it behoved the *virgin* to be veiled from her nativity, and from the first entry of her age (upon the roll of time). But it is not so ; but from the time when she begins to be self-conscious, and to awake to the sense of her own nature, and to emerge from the *virgin's* (sense), and to experience that novel (sensation) which belongs to the succeeding age. For withal the founders of the race, Adam and Eve, so long as they were without intelligence, went "naked ;" but after they tasted of "the tree of recognition," they were first sensible of nothing more than of their cause for shame. Thus they each marked their intelligence of their own sex by a covering.[2] But even if it is "on account of the angels" that she is to be veiled,[3] doubtless the age from which the law of the veil will come into operation will be that from which "the daughters of men" were able to invite concupiscence of their persons, and to experience marriage. For a *virgin* ceases to be a *virgin* from the time that it becomes possible for her *not* to be one. And accordingly, among Israel, it is unlawful to deliver one to a husband except after the attestation by blood of her maturity ;[4] thus, before this indication, the nature is unripe. Therefore if she is a *virgin* so long as she is unripe, she ceases to be a *virgin* when she is perceived to be ripe ; and, as *not-virgin*, is now subject to the law, just as she is to marriage. And the *betrothed* indeed have the example of Rebecca, who, when she was being conducted — herself still unknown — to an unknown betrothed, as soon as she learned that he whom she had sighted from afar was the man,

awaited not the grasp of the hand, nor the meeting of the kiss, nor the interchange of salutation ; but confessing what she had felt — namely, that she had been (already) wedded in spirit — denied herself to be a *virgin* by then and there veiling herself.[5] Oh *woman* already belonging to Christ's discipline ! For she showed that marriage likewise, as fornication is, is transacted by gaze and mind ; only that a *Rebecca* likewise some do still veil. With regard to the rest, however (that is, those who are *not* betrothed), let the procrastination of their parents, arising from straitened means or scrupulosity, look (to them) ; let the vow of continence itself look (to them). In no respect does (such procrastination) pertain to an age which is already running its own assigned course, and paying its own dues to maturity. Another secret mother, Nature, and another hidden father, Time, have wedded their daughter to their own laws. Behold that *virgin-daughter* of yours already wedded — her soul by expectancy, her flesh by transformation — for whom you are preparing a second husband ! Already her voice is changed, her limbs fully formed, her "shame" everywhere clothing itself, the months paying their tributes ; and do you deny her to be a *woman* whom you assert to be undergoing *womanly* experiences ? If the contact of a *man* makes a *woman*, let there be no covering except after actual experience of marriage. Nay, but even among the heathens (the betrothed) are led *veiled* to the husband. But if it is at *betrothal* that they are veiled, because (then) both in body and in spirit they have mingled with a male, through the kiss and the right hands, through which means they first in spirit unsealed their modesty, through the common pledge of conscience whereby they mutually plighted their whole confusion ; how much more will time veil them ? — (time) without which espoused they cannot be ; and by whose urgency, without espousals, they cease to be *virgins*. Time even the heathens observe, that, in obedience to the law of nature, they may render their own rights to the (different) ages. For their *females* they despatch to their businesses from (the age of) twelve years, but the *male* from two years later ; decreeing puberty (to consist) in years, not in espousals or nuptials. "House-wife " one is called, albeit a *virgin*, and "house-father," albeit a stripling. By *us* not even natural *laws* are observed ; as if the God of nature were some other than ours !

CHAP. XII. — WOMANHOOD SELF-EVIDENT, AND NOT TO BE CONCEALED BY JUST LEAVING THE HEAD BARE.

Recognise the *woman*, ay, recognise the *wedded woman*, by the testimonies both of body

---

[1] So Oehler and others. But one MS. reads " concupiscentiæ fructum" for " concupiscentiam fructus;" which would make the sense somewhat plainer, and hence is perhaps less likely to be the genuine reading.
[2] See Gen. ii. 25, iii. 7 (in LXX. iii. 1, iii. 7).
[3] See ch. vii. above.
[4] See Deut. xxii. 13-21.

[5] Gen. xxiv. 64, 65. Comp. *de Or.*, c. xxii. *ad fin.*

and of spirit, which she experiences both in conscience and in flesh. These are the earlier tablets of *natural* espousals and nuptials. Impose a veil externally upon her who has (already) a covering internally. Let her whose lower parts are not bare have her upper likewise covered. Would you know what is the authority which age carries? Set before yourself each (of these two) ; one prematurely[1] compressed in *woman's* garb, and one who, though advanced in maturity, persists in *virginity* with its appropriate garb : the former will more easily be denied to be a *woman* than the latter believed a *virgin*. Such is, then, the honesty of age, that there is no overpowering it even by garb. What of the fact that these (*virgins*) of ours confess their change of age even *by* their garb ; and, as soon as they have understood themselves to be *women*, withdraw themselves from *virgins*, laying aside (beginning with their head itself) their former selves : dye[2] their hair ; and fasten their hair with more wanton pin ; professing manifest *womanhood* with their hair parted from the front. The next thing is, they consult the looking-glass to aid their beauty, and thin down their over-exacting face with washing, perhaps withal vamp it up with cosmetics, toss their mantle about them with an air, fit tightly the multiform shoe, carry down more ample appliances to the baths. Why should I pursue particulars? But their manifest appliances alone[3] exhibit their perfect *womanhood* : yet they wish to play the *virgin* by the sole fact of leaving their head bare — denying by one single feature what they profess by their entire deportment.

CHAP. XIII. — IF UNVEILING BE PROPER, WHY NOT PRACTISE IT ALWAYS, OUT OF THE CHURCH AS WELL AS IN IT?

If on account of men[4] they adopt a false garb, let them carry out that garb fully even for that end ;[5] and as they veil their head in presence of heathens, let them at all events *in the church* conceal their virginity, which they do veil outside the church. They fear strangers : let them stand in awe of the brethren too ; or else let them have the consistent hardihood to appear as *virgins* in the streets as well, as they have the hardihood to do in the churches. I will praise their vigour, if they succeed in selling aught of virginity among the heathens withal.[6] Identity of nature abroad as at home, identity of custom

in the presence of men as of the Lord, consists in identity of liberty. To what purpose, then, do they thrust their glory out of sight abroad, but expose it in the church? I demand a reason. Is it to please the brethren, or God Himself? If God Himself, He is as capable of beholding whatever is done in secret, as He is just to remunerate what is done for His sole honour. In fine, He enjoins us not to trumpet forth[7] any one of those things which will merit reward in His sight, nor get compensation for them from men. But if we are prohibited from letting " our left hand know " when we bestow the gift of a single halfpenny, or any eleemosynary bounty whatever, how deep should be the darkness in which we ought to enshroud ourselves when we are offering God so great an oblation of our very body and our very spirit — when we are consecrating to Him our very nature ! It follows, therefore, that what cannot appear to be done for God's sake (because God wills not that it be done in such a way) is done for the sake of men, — a thing, of course, primarily unlawful, as betraying a lust of glory. For glory is a thing unlawful to those whose probation consists in humiliation of every kind. And if it is by God that the virtue of continence is conferred, " why gloriest thou, as if thou have not received?"[8] If, however, you have *not* received it, " what hast thou which has not been given thee?" But by this very fact it is plain that it has not been given you *by God* — that it is not *to God* alone that you offer it. Let us see, then, whether what is *human* be firm and true.

CHAP. XIV. — PERILS TO THE VIRGINS THEMSELVES ATTENDANT UPON NOT-VEILING.

They report a saying uttered at one time by some one when first this question was mooted, " And how shall we invite the other (*virgins*) to similar conduct?" Forsooth, it is their numbers that will make us happy, and not the grace of God and the merits of each individual ! Is it *virgins* who (adorn or commend) the Church in the sight of God, or the Church which adorns or commends *virgins* ? (Our objector) has therefore confessed that " glory " lies at the root of the matter. Well, where glory is, there is solicitation ; where solicitation, there compulsion ; where compulsion, there necessity ; where necessity, there infirmity. Deservedly, therefore, while they do not cover their head, in order that they may be solicited for the sake of glory, they are forced to cover their bellies by the ruin resulting from infirmity. For it is emulation, not religion, which impels them. Sometimes it is that god—

---

[1] Oehler's " *immutare* " appears certainly to be a misprint for " *immature*."

[2] Vertunt: or perhaps " change the style of." But comp. (with Oehler) *de Cult. Fem.*, l. ii. c. vi.

[3] i.e., without appealing to any further proof.

[4] As distinguished from the " on account of the angels " of c. xi.

[5] i.e., for the sake of *the brethren*, who (after all) are *men*, as the *heathens* are (Oehler, after Rig.).

[6] i.e., as Rig. quoted by Oehler explains it, in inducing the heathens to practise it.

[7] See Matt. vi. 2.

[8] 1 Cor. iv. 7.

their belly ¹ — himself; because the brotherhood
readily undertakes the maintenance of *virgins*.
But, moreover, it is not merely that they are
ruined, but they draw after them "a long rope
of sins." ² For, after being brought forth into
the midst (of the church), and elated by the
public appropriation of their property,³ and
laden by the brethren with every honour and
charitable bounty, so long as they do not fall, —
when any sin has been committed, they meditate
a deed as disgraceful as the honour was high
which they had. (It is this.) If an uncovered
head is a recognised mark of virginity, (then)
if any *virgin* falls from the grace of *virginity*,
she remains permanently with head uncovered,
for fear of discovery, and walks about in a garb
which then indeed is another's. Conscious of
a now undoubted *womanhood*, they have the
audacity to draw near to God with head bare.
But the "jealous God and Lord," who has said,
"Nothing covered which shall not be revealed," ⁴
brings such in general before the public gaze;
for confess they will not, unless betrayed by the
cries of their infants themselves. But, in so far
as they are "more numerous," will you not just
have them suspected of the more crimes? I will
say (albeit I would rather not) it is a difficult
thing for one to turn *woman* once for all who
fears to do so, and who, when already so turned
(in secret), has the power of (still) falsely pretending to be a *virgin* under the eye of God.
What audacities, again, will (such an one) venture on with regard to her womb, for fear of being detected in being a *mother* as well! God
knows how many infants He has helped to perfection and through gestation till they were born
sound and whole, after being long fought against
by their mothers! Such *virgins* ever conceive
with the readiest facility, and have the happiest
deliveries, and children indeed most like to their
fathers!

These crimes does a forced and unwilling *virginity* incur. The very concupiscence of non-
concealment is not modest: it experiences
somewhat which is no mark of a *virgin*, — the
study of pleasing, of course, ay, and (of pleasing)
men. Let her strive as much as you please with
an honest mind; she must necessarily be imper-
illed by the public exhibition ⁵ of herself, while
she is penetrated by the gaze of untrustworthy
and multitudinous eyes, while she is tickled by

pointing fingers, while she is too well loved, while
she feels a warmth creep over her amid assiduous embraces and kisses. Thus the forehead
hardens; thus the sense of shame wears away;
thus it relaxes; thus is learned the desire of
pleasing in another way!

CHAP. XV. — OF FASCINATION.

Nay, but true and absolute and pure *virginity*
fears nothing more than itself. Even *female* eyes
it shrinks from encountering. Other eyes itself
has. It betakes itself for refuge to the veil of
the head as to a helmet, as to a shield, to protect its glory against the blows of temptations,
against the darts of scandals, against suspicions
and whispers and emulation; (against) envy also
itself. For there is a something even among the
heathens to be apprehended, which they call
Fascination, the too unhappy result of excessive
praise and glory. This we sometimes interpreta-
tively ascribe to the devil, for of him comes hatred
of good; sometimes we attribute it to God, for
of Him comes judgment upon haughtiness, ex-
alting, as He does, the humble, and depressing
the elated.⁶ The more holy virgin, accordingly,
will fear, even under the name of fascination, on
the one hand the adversary, on the other God, —
the envious disposition of the former, the censorial light of the latter; and will joy in being
known to herself alone and to God. But even
if she has been recognized by any other, she is
wise to have blocked up the pathway against
temptations. For who will have the audacity to
intrude with his eyes upon a shrouded face? a
face without feeling? a face, so to say, morose?
Any evil cogitation whatsoever will be broken by
the very severity. She who conceals her *virginity*, by that fact denies even her *womanhood*.

CHAP. XVI. — TERTULLIAN, HAVING SHOWN HIS DE-
FENCE TO BE CONSISTENT WITH SCRIPTURE, NA-
TURE, AND DISCIPLINE, APPEALS TO THE VIRGINS
THEMSELVES.

Herein consists the defence of our opinion, in
accordance with Scripture, in accordance with
Nature, in accordance with Discipline. Scripture
founds the law; Nature joins to attest it; Discipline exacts it. Which of these (three) does a
custom founded on (mere) opinion appear in
behalf of? or what is the colour of the opposite
view? God's is Scripture; God's is Nature;
God's is Discipline. Whatever is contrary to
these is not God's. If Scripture is uncertain,
Nature is manifest; and concerning Nature's
testimony Scripture cannot be uncertain.⁷ If
there is a doubt about Nature, Discipline points
out what is more sanctioned by God. For noth-

---

¹ Comp. Phil. iii. 19.
² See Isa. v. 18.
³ So Oehler, with Rig., seems to understand "publicato bono
suo." But it may be doubted whether the use of the singular "bono,"
and the sense in which "publicare" and "bonum" have previously
occurred in this treatise, do not warrant the rendering, "and elated
by the public announcement of their good deed" — in self-devotion.
Comp. "omnis publicatio virginis bonæ" in c. iii., and similar
phrases. Perhaps the two meanings may be intentionally implied
⁴ Matt. x. 26. Again apparently a double meaning, in the word
"*revelabitur*" = "unveiled," which (of course) is the strict sense of
"*revealed*," i e., "re-veiled."
⁵ Comp. the note above on "*publicato bono suo.*"

⁶ Comp. Ps. cxlvii. (in LXX. and Vulg. cxlvi.) 6; Luke i. 52.
⁷ See 1 Cor. xi. 14, above quoted.

ing is to Him dearer than humility; nothing more acceptable than modesty; nothing more offensive than "glory" and the study of men-pleasing. Let that, accordingly, be to you Scripture, and Nature, and Discipline, which you shall find to have been sanctioned by God; just as you are bidden to "examine all things, and diligently follow whatever is better."[1]

It remains likewise that we turn to (the *virgins*) themselves, to induce them to accept these (suggestions) the more willingly. I pray you, be you mother, or sister, or *virgin*-daughter — let me address you according to the names proper to your years — veil your head: if a mother, for your sons' sakes; if a sister, for your brethren's sakes; if a daughter for your fathers' sakes. All ages are perilled in your person. Put on the panoply of modesty; surround yourself with the stockade of bashfulness; rear a rampart for your sex, which must neither allow your own eyes egress nor ingress to other people's. Wear the full garb of *woman*, to preserve the standing of *virgin*. Belie somewhat of your inward consciousness, in order to exhibit the truth to God alone. And yet you do *not* belie yourself in appearing as a bride. For wedded you are to Christ: to Him you have surrendered your flesh; to Him you have espoused your maturity. Walk in accordance with the will of your Espoused. Christ is He who bids the espoused and wives of others veil themselves;[2] (and,) of course, much more His own.

CHAP. XVII. — AN APPEAL TO THE MARRIED WOMEN.

But we admonish you, too, *women* of the second (degree of) modesty, who have fallen into wedlock, not to outgrow so far the discipline of the veil, not even in a moment of an hour, as, because you cannot *refuse* it, to take some other means to *nullify* it, by going neither covered nor bare. For some, with their turbans and woollen bands, do not *veil* their head, but bind it up; protected, indeed, in front, but, where the head properly lies, bare. Others are to a certain extent covered over the region of the brain with linen coifs of small dimensions — I suppose for fear of pressing the head — and not reaching quite to the ears. If they are so weak in their hearing as not to be able to hear through a covering, I pity them. Let them know that the whole head constitutes "the *woman*."[3] Its limits and boundaries reach as far as the place where the robe begins. The region of the veil is co-extensive with the space covered by the hair when unbound; in order that the necks too may be encircled. For it is *they* which must be subjected, for the sake of which "power" ought to be "had on the head:" the veil is their yoke. Arabia's heathen *females* will be your judges, who cover not only the head, but the face also, so entirely, that they are content, with one eye free, to enjoy rather half the light than to prostitute the entire face. A *female* would rather see than be seen. And for this reason a certain Roman queen said that they were most unhappy, in that they could more easily fall in love than be fallen in love with; whereas thay are rather *happy* in their immunity from that second (and indeed more frequent) infelicity, that females are more apt to be fallen in love with than to fall in love. And the modesty of heathen discipline, indeed, is more simple, and, so to say, more barbaric. To *us* the Lord has, even by revelations, measured the space for the veil to extend over. For a certain sister of ours was thus addressed by an angel, beating her neck, as if in applause: "Elegant neck, and deservedly bare! it is well for thee to unveil thyself from the head right down to the loins, lest withal this freedom of thy neck profit thee not!" And, of course, what you have said to one you have said to all. But how severe a chastisement will *they* likewise deserve, who, amid (the recital of) the Psalms, and at any mention of (the name of) God, continue uncovered; (who) even when about to spend time in prayer itself, with the utmost readiness place a fringe, or a tuft, or any thread whatever, on the crown of their heads, and suppose themselves to be covered? Of so small extent do they falsely imagine their head to be! Others, who think the palm of their hand plainly greater than any fringe or thread, misuse their head no less; like a certain (creature), more beast than bird, albeit winged, with small head, long legs, and moreover of erect carriage. She, they say, when she has to hide, thrusts away into a thicket her head alone — plainly the *whole* of it, (though) — leaving all the rest of herself exposed. Thus, while she is secure in *head*, (but) bare in her larger parts, she is taken wholly, head and all. Such will be their plight withal, covered as they are less than is useful.

It is incumbent, then, at all times and in every place, to walk mindful of the law, prepared and equipped in readiness to meet every mention of God; who, if He be in the heart, will be recognised as well in the head of *females*. To such as read these (exhortations) with good will, to such as prefer Utility to Custom, may peace and grace from our Lord Jesus Christ redound: as likewise to Septimius Tertullianus, whose this tractate is.

[1] See 1 Thess. v. 21.
[2] See 1 Cor. xi.
[3] 1 Cor. xi. 6, etc.

ELUCIDATIONS.

I.

(Vicar of the Lord, p. 27.)

THE recurrence of this emphatic expression in our author is worthy of special note. He knew of no other "Vicar of Christ" than the promised Paraclete, who should bring all Christ's words to remembrance, and be "another Comforter." Let me quote from Dr. Scott[1] a very striking passage in illustration: "The Holy Ghost, after Christ's departure from the world, acted *immediately* under Christ as the supreme vicegerent of his kingdom; for next, and *immeaiately* under Christ, He authorized the bishops and governors of the Church, and constituted them *overseers of the flock* (Acts xx. 28). It was He that chose their persons, and appointed their work, and gave them their several orders and directions: in all which, it is evident that He acted under Christ as His supreme substitute. Accordingly, by Tertullian he is styled 'the Vicarious Virtue, or Power,' as He was the *Supreme Vicar* and substitute of Christ in mediating for God with men."

II.

(She shall be called woman, p. 31.)

The Vulgate reads, preserving something of the original epigrammatic force, "Vocabitur VIR-ago, quoniam de VIR-o sumpta est." The late revised English gives us, in the margin, *Isshah* and *Ish*, which marks the play upon words in the Hebrew, — " She shall be called *Isshah* because she was taken out of *Ish*." This *Epithalamium* is the earliest poem, and Adam was the first poet.

As to the argument of our author, it is quite enough to say, that, whatever we may think of his refinements upon St. Paul, he sticks to the inspired text, and enforces God's Law in the Gospel. Let us reflect, moreover, upon the awful immodesty of heathen manners (see Martial, *passim*), and the necessity of enforcing a radical reform. All that adorns the sex among Christians has sprung out of these severe and caustic criticisms of the Gentile world and its customs. And let us reflect that there is a growing licence in our age, which makes it important to revert to first principles, and to renew the apostolic injunctions, if not as Tertullian did, still as best we may, in our own times and ways.

III.

(These crimes, p. 36.)

The iniquity here pointed at has become of frightful magnitude in the United States of America. We shall hear of it again when we come to Hippolytus.[2] May the American editor be pardoned for referring to his own commonitory to his countrywomen on this awful form of murder, in *Moral Reforms*,[3] a little book upon practical subjects, addressed to his own diocese.

Hippolytus speaks of the crime which had shocked Tertullian as assuming terrible proportions at Rome in the time of Callistus[4] and under his patronage, *circa* A.D. 220. But in this case it was not so much the novelty of the evil which attracted the rebuke of the Christian moralist, but the fact that it was licensed by a bishop.

---

[1] *The Christian Life*, vol. iii. p. 64.
[2] Tertullian speaks of the heathen as "decimated by abortions." See *ad Uxor.*, p. 41, *infra.*
[3] Lippincotts, Philadelphia, 1868.
[4] Bunsen, vol. i. p. 134.

IV.

TO HIS WIFE.[1]

[TRANSLATED BY THE REV. S. THELWALL.]

BOOK I.

CHAP. I. — DESIGN OF THE TREATISE. DISAVOWAL OF PERSONAL MOTIVES IN WRITING IT.

I HAVE thought it meet, my best beloved fellow-servant in the Lord, even from this early period,[2] to provide for the course which you must pursue after my departure from the world,[3] if I shall be called before you ; (and) to entrust to your honour[4] the observance of the provision. For in things worldly[5] we are active enough, and we wish the good of each of us to be consulted. If we draw up wills for *such* matters, why ought we not much more to take forethought for our posterity[6] in things divine and heavenly, and in a sense to bequeath a legacy to be received before the inheritance be divided, — (the legacy, I mean, of) admonition and demonstration touching those (bequests) which are allotted[7] out of (our) immortal goods, and from the heritage of the heavens ? Only, that you may be able to receive in its entirety[8] this feoffment in trust[9] of my admonition, may God grant ; to whom be honour, glory, renown, dignity, and power, now and to the ages of the ages !

The precept, therefore, which I give you is, that, with all the constancy you may, you do, after our departure, renounce nuptials ; not that you will on that score confer any benefit on me, except in that you will profit yourself. But to Christians, after their departure from the world,[10]

no restoration of marriage is promised in the day of the resurrection, translated as they will be into the condition and sanctity of angels.[11] Therefore no solicitude arising from carnal jealousy will, in the day of the resurrection, even in the case of her whom they chose to represent as having been married to seven brothers successively, wound any one[12] of her so many husbands ; nor is any (husband) awaiting her to put her to confusion.[13] The question raised by the Sadducees has yielded to the Lord's sentence. Think not that it is for the sake of preserving to the end for myself the entire devotion of your flesh, that I, suspicious of the pain of (anticipated) slight, am even at this early period[14] instilling into you the counsel of (perpetual) widowhood. There will at that day be no resumption of voluptuous disgrace between us. No such frivolities, no such impurities, does God promise to His (servants). But whether to you, or to any other woman whatever who pertains to God, the advice which we are giving shall be profitable, we take leave to treat of at large.

CHAP. II. — MARRIAGE LAWFUL, BUT NOT POLYGAMY.

We do not indeed forbid the union of man and woman, blest by God as the seminary of the human race, and devised for the replenishment of the earth[15] and the furnishing of the world,[16] and therefore permitted, yet singly. For Adam was the one husband of Eve, and Eve his one wife, one woman, one rib.[17] We grant[18] that

---

1 [Written *circa* A.D. 207. Tertullian survived his wife; and we cannot date these books earlier than about the time of his writing the *De Pallio*, in the opinion of some.]
2 Jam hinc.
3 Sæculo.
4 Fidei.
5 Sæcularibus.
6 Posteritati; or, with Mr. Dodgson, " our future."
7 Deputantur.
8 Solidum; alluding to certain laws respecting a widow's power of receiving " in its entirety " her deceased husband's property.
9 Fidei commissum.
10 Sæculo.

---

11 Luke xx. 36.
12 Nulla . . . neminem — two negatives.
13 See Matt. xxii. 23–33; Mark xii. 18–27; Luke xx. 27–40.
14 Jam hinc. See beginning of chapter.
15 Orbi. Gen. i. 28.
16 Sæculo.
17 Gen. ii. 21, 22.
18 Sane.

among our ancestors, and the patriarchs themselves, it was lawful[1] not only to marry, but even
to multiply wives.[2] There were concubines, too,
(in those days.) But although the Church did
come in figuratively in the synagogue, yet (to
interpret simply) it was necessary to institute
(certain things) which should afterward deserve
to be either lopped off or modified. For the
Law was (in due time) to supervene. (Nor was
that enough :) for it was meet that causes for
making up the deficiencies of the Law should
have forerun (Him who was to supply those deficiencies). And so to the Law presently had
to succeed the Word[3] of God introducing the
spiritual circumcision.[4] Therefore, by means of
the wide licence of those days, materials for
subsequent emendations were furnished beforehand, of which materials the Lord by His Gospel, and then the apostle in the last days of the
(Jewish) age,[5] either cut off the redundancies or
regulated the disorders.

CHAP. III. — MARRIAGE GOOD : CELIBACY PREFER-
ABLE.

But let it not be thought that my reason for
premising thus much concerning the liberty
granted to the old, and the restraint imposed on
the later time, is that I may lay a foundation for
teaching that Christ's advent was intended to
dissolve wedlock, (and) to abolish marriage
unions ; as if from this period onward[6] I were
prescribing an end to marrying. Let them see
to that, who, among the rest of their perversi-
ties, teach the disjoining of the " one flesh in
twain ; "[7] denying Him who, after borrowing
the female from the male, re-combined between
themselves, in the matrimonial computation, the
two bodies taken out of the consortship of the
self-same material substance. In short, there is
no place at all where we read that nuptials are
prohibited ; of course on the ground that they
are " a good thing." What, however, is *better*
than this " good," we learn from the apostle,
who *permits* marrying indeed, but *prefers* abstinence ; the former on account of the insidious-
nesses of temptations, the latter on account of
the straits of the times.[8] Now, by looking into

the reason thus given for each proposition, it is
easily discerned that the ground on which the
power of marrying is conceded is *necessity ;* but
whatever *necessity* grants, she by her very nature
depreciates. In fact, in that it is written, " To
marry is better than to burn," what, pray, is the
nature of this " good " which is (only) commended by comparison with " evil," so that the
reason why " marrying " is *more* good is (merely)
that " burning " is *less ?* Nay, but how far better is it neither to marry nor to burn? Why,
even in persecutions it is *better* to take advantage of the permission granted, and " flee from
town to town,"[9] than, when apprehended and
racked, to deny (the faith).[10] And therefore
more blessed are they who have strength to depart (this life) in blessed confession of their
testimony.[11] I may say, What is *permitted* is not
good. For how stands the case? I must of
necessity die (if I be apprehended and confess
my faith.) If I think (that fate) deplorable,
(then flight) is good ; but if I have a fear of the
thing which is permitted, (the permitted thing)
has some suspicion attaching to the cause of its
permission. But that which is " better " no one
(ever) " permitted," as being undoubted, and
manifest by its own inherent purity. There are
some things which are not to be *desired* merely
because they are not *forbidden*, albeit they *are*
in a certain sense *forbidden* when other things
are preferred to them ; for the preference given
to the higher things is a dissuasion from the lowest. A thing is not " good " merely because it is
not " evil," nor is it " evil " merely because it
is not " harmful."[12] Further : that which is fully
" good " excels on this ground, that it is not only
not harmful, but profitable into the bargain.
For you are bound to prefer what is profitable
to what is (merely) not harmful. For the *first*
place is what every struggle aims at ; the *second*
has consolation attaching to it, but not victory.
But if we listen to the apostle, forgetting what is
behind, let us both strain after what is before,[13]
and be followers after the better rewards. Thus,
albeit he does not " cast a snare[14] upon us," he
points out what tends to utility when he says,
" The unmarried woman thinks on the things of
the Lord, that both in body and spirit she may
be holy ; but the married is solicitous how to
please her husband."[15] But he nowhere permits
marriage in such a way as not rather to wish us
to do our utmost in imitation of his own example. Happy the man who shall prove like
Paul !

---

[1] " Fas," strictly *divine* law, opp. to " jus," *human* law; thus
" lawful," as opp. to " legal."
[2] Plurifariam matrimoniis uti. The neut. pl. " matrimonia " is
sometimes used for " wives." Comp. c. v. *ad fin.* and *de Pœn.*, c. xii.
ad fin.
[3] Sermo, i.e., probably the personal Word. Comp. *de Or.*, c. i.
ad init.
[4] Rom. ii. 28, 29; Phil. iii. 3; Col. ii. 11.
[5] Sæculi. The meaning here seems clearly to be, as in the text,
" the Jewish *age* " or *dispensation ;* as in the passages referred to —
1 Cor. x. 11, where it is τὰ τέλη τῶν αἰώνων : and Heb. ix. 26, where
again it is τῶν αἰώνων, the Jewish and all preceding ages being
intended.
[6] " Jam hinc," i e., apparently from the time of Christ's advent.
[7] Matt. xix. 5, 6.
[8] 1 Cor. vii.

[9] Matt. x. 23; perhaps confused with xxiii. 34.
[10] Comp. *de Idol.*, c. xxiii., and the note there on " se negant."
[11] i.e., in martyrdom, on the ground of that open confession.
[12] Non obest.
[13] Phil. iii. 13, 14.
[14] Laqueum = βρόχον (1 Cor. vii. 35), " a noose," " lasso "
(" snare," Eng. ver.). " Laqueo trahuntur inviti " (Bengel).
[15] See note 13.

CHAP. IV. — OF THE INFIRMITY OF THE FLESH, AND SIMILAR PLEAS.

But we read "that the flesh is weak;"[1] and hence we soothe[2] ourselves in some cases. Yet we read, too, that "the spirit is strong;"[3] for each clause occurs in one and the same sentence. Flesh is an earthly, spirit a heavenly, material. Why, then, do we, too prone to self-excuse, put forward (in our defence) the weak part of us, but not look at[4] the strong? Why should not the earthly yield to the heavenly? If the spirit is stronger than the flesh, because it is withal of nobler origin, it is our own fault if we follow the weaker. Now there are two phases[5] of human weakness which make marriages[6] necessary to such as are disjoined from matrimony. The first and most powerful is that which arises from *fleshly* concupiscence; the second, from *worldly* concupiscence. But by us, who are servants of God, who renounce both voluptuousness and ambition, each is to be repudiated. Fleshly concupiscence claims the functions of adult age, craves after beauty's harvest, rejoices in its own shame, pleads the necessity of a husband to the female sex, as a source of authority and of comfort, or to render it safe from evil rumours. To meet these its counsels, do you apply the examples of sisters of ours whose names are with the Lord,[7] — who, when their husbands have preceded them (to glory), give to no opportunity of beauty or of age the precedence over holiness. They prefer to be wedded to God. To God their beauty, to God their youth (is dedicated). With Him they live; with Him they converse; Him they "handle"[8] by day and by night; *to* the Lord they assign their prayers as dowries; *from* Him, as oft as they desire it, they receive His approbation[9] as dotal gifts. Thus they have laid hold for themselves of an eternal gift of the Lord; and while on earth, by abstaining from marriage, are already counted as belonging to the angelic family. Training yourself to an emulation of (their) constancy by the examples of such women, you will by spiritual affection bury that fleshly concupiscence, in abolishing the temporal[10] and fleeting desires of beauty and youth by the compensating gain of immortal blessings.

On the other hand, this *worldly* concupiscence (to which I referred) has, as its causes, glory, cupidity, ambition, want of sufficiency; through which causes it trumps up the "necessity" for marrying, — promising itself, forsooth, heavenly things in return — to lord it, (namely,) in another's family; to roost[11] on another's wealth; to extort splendour from another's store; to lavish expenditure[12] which you do not feel! Far be all this from believers, who have no care about maintenance, unless it be that we distrust the promises of God, and (His) care and providence, who clothes with such grace the lilies of the field;[13] who, without any labour on their part, feeds the fowls of the heaven;[14] who prohibits care to be taken about to-morrow's food and clothing,[15] promising that He knows what is needful for each of His servants — not indeed ponderous necklaces, not burdensome garments, not Gallic mules nor German bearers, which all add lustre to the glory of nuptials; but "sufficiency,"[16] which is suitable to moderation and modesty. Presume, I pray you, that you have need of nothing if you "attend upon the Lord;"[17] nay, that you have all things, if you have the Lord, whose are all things. Think often[18] on things heavenly, and you will despise things earthly. To widowhood signed and sealed before the Lord nought is necessary but perseverance.

CHAP. V. — OF THE LOVE OF OFFSPRING AS A PLEA FOR MARRIAGE.

Further reasons for marriage which men allege for themselves arise from anxiety for posterity, and the bitter, bitter pleasure of children. To *us* this is idle. For why should we be eager to bear children, whom, when we have them, we desire to send before us (to glory)[19] (in respect, I mean, of the distresses that are now imminent); desirous as we are ourselves, too, to be taken out of this most wicked world,[20] and received into the Lord's presence, which was the desire even of an apostle?[21] To the servant of God, forsooth, offspring is necessary! For of our own salvation we are secure enough, so that we have leisure for children! Burdens must be sought by us for ourselves which are avoided even by the majority of the Gentiles, who are compelled by laws,[22] who are decimated[23] by

---

[1] Matt. xxvi. 41.
[2] Adulamur: "we fawn upon," or "caress," or "flatter." Comp. *de Pæn.*, c. vi. *sub init.*: "flatter their own sweetness."
[3] "Firmum," opp. to "infirmam" above. In the passage there referred to (Matt. xxvi. 41) the word is πρόθυμον.
[4] Tuemur. Mr. Dodgson renders, "guard not."
[5] Species.
[6] i e., apparently *second* marriages: "*dis*junctis a matrimonio" can scarcely include such as were never "juncti;" and comp. the "præmissis maritis" below.
[7] Comp. Phil. iv. 3; 2 Tim. ii. 19; Mal. iii. 16; and similar passages.
[8] 1 John i. 1; Luke xxiv. 39; John xx. 17.
[9] Dignationem.
[10] Or, "temporary."

[11] Incubare.
[12] Cædere sumptum.
[13] Matt. vi. 28-30.
[14] Matt. vi. 26.
[15] Matt. vi. 31, 34.
[16] Comp. Phil. iv. 19; 1 Tim. vi. 8.
[17] Comp. 1 Cor. vii. 35, esp. in Eng. ver.
[18] Recogita.
[19] Comp. c. iv. above "præmissis maritis;" "when their husbands have preceded them (to glory)."
[20] Sæculo.
[21] Phil. i. 23; comp. *de Pa.*, c. ix. *ad fin.*
[22] i.e., to get children.
[23] Expugnantur.

abortions;[1] burdens which, finally, are to *us* most of all unsuitable, as being perilous to faith! For why did the Lord foretell a "woe to them that are with child, and them that give suck,"[2] except because He testifies that in that day of disencumbrance the encumbrances of children will be an inconvenience? It is to marriage, of course, that those encumbrances appertain; but that ("woe") will not pertain to widows. (*They*) at the first trump of the angel will spring forth disencumbered — will freely bear to the end whatsoever pressure and persecution, with no burdensome fruit of marriage heaving in the womb, none in the bosom.

Therefore, whether it be for the sake of the flesh, or of the world,[3] or of posterity, that marriage is undertaken, nothing of all these "necessities" affects the servants of God, so as to prevent my deeming it enough to have once for all yielded to some one of them, and by one marriage appeased[4] all concupiscence of this kind. Let us marry daily, and in the midst of our marrying let us be overtaken, like Sodom and Gomorrah, by that day of fear![5] For *there* it was not only, of course, that they were dealing in marriage and merchandise; but when He says, "They were marrying and buying," He sets a brand[6] upon the very leading vices of the flesh and of the world,[7] which call men off the most from divine disciplines — the one through the pleasure of rioting, the other though the greed of acquiring. And yet that "blindness" *then* was felt long before "the ends of the world."[8] What, then, will the case be if God *now* keep us from the vices which *of old* were detestable before Him? "The time," says (the apostle), "is compressed.[9] It remaineth that they who have wives[10] act as if they had them not."

CHAP. VI. — EXAMPLES OF HEATHENS URGED AS COMMENDATORY OF WIDOWHOOD AND CELIBACY.

But if they who *have* (wives) are (thus) bound to consign to oblivion what they have, how much more are they who have *not*, prohibited from seeking a second time what they no longer have; so that she whose husband has departed from the world should thenceforward impose rest on her sex by abstinence from marriage — abstinence which numbers of Gentile women devote to the memory of beloved husbands! When anything seems difficult, let us survey others who cope with still greater difficulties. How many are there who from the moment of their baptism set the seal (of virginity) upon their flesh? How many, again, who by equal mutual consent cancel the debt of matrimony — voluntary eunuchs[11] for the sake of their desire after the celestial kingdom! But if, while the marriage-tie is still intact, abstinence is endured, how much more when it has been undone! For I believe it to be harder for what is intact to be quite forsaken, than for what has been lost not to be yearned after. A hard and arduous thing enough, surely, is the continence for God's sake of a holy woman after her husband's decease, when Gentiles,[12] in honour of their own Satan, endure sacerdotal offices which involve both virginity and widowhood![13] At Rome, for instance, they who have to do with the type of that "inextinguishable fire,"[14] keeping watch over the omens of their own (future) penalty, in company with the (old) dragon[15] himself, are appointed on the ground of *virginity*. To the Achæan Juno, at the town Ægium, a *virgin* is allotted; and the (priestesses) who rave at Delphi know not marriage. Moreover, we know that *widows* minister to the African Ceres; enticed away, indeed, from matrimony by a most stern oblivion: for not only do they withdraw from their still living husbands, but they even introduce other wives to them in their own room — the husbands, of course, smiling on it — all contact (with males), even as far as the kiss of their sons, being forbidden them; and yet, with enduring practice, they persevere in such a discipline of widowhood, which excludes the solace even of holy affection.[16] These precepts has the devil given to his servants, and he is heard! He challenges, forsooth, God's servants, by the continence of his own, as if on equal terms! Continent are even the priests of hell![17] For he has found a way to ruin men even in good pursuits; and with him it makes no difference to slay some by voluptuousness, some by continence.

CHAP. VII. — THE DEATH OF A HUSBAND IS GOD'S CALL TO THE WIDOW TO CONTINENCE. FURTHER EVIDENCES FROM SCRIPTURE AND FROM HEATHENISM.

To us continence has been pointed out by the Lord of salvation as an instrument for attaining

---

1 "Parricidiis." So Oehler seems to understand it.
2 Luke xxi. 23; Matt. xxiv. 19.
3 Sæculi.
4 "Expiasse" — a rare but Ciceronian use of the word.
5 Luke xvii. 28, 29.
6 Denotat.
7 Sæculi.
8 Sæculi. Comp. 1 Cor. x. 11; but the Greek there is, τὰ τέλη τῶν αἰώνων. By the "blindness," Tertullian may refer to Gen. xix. 11.
9 Or, "short" (Eng. ver.); 1 Cor. vii. 29. ὁ καιρὸς συνεσταλμένος, "in collecto."
10 "Matrimonia," neut. pl. again for the fem., the abstract for the concrete. See c. ii., " to multiply wives," and the note there. In the Greek (1 Cor. vii. 29) it is γυναῖκας: but the ensuing chapter shows that Tertullian refers the passage to women as well.

11 Comp. *de Pa.*, xiii., and Matt. xix. 12. Comp., too, *de Ex. Cast.*, c. i.
12 i.e., Gentile *women*.
13 Oehler marks this as a question.
14 Matt. iii. 12.
15 Comp. Rev. xii. 9, and *de Bapt.*, i.
16 Pietatis.
17 Gehennæ; comp. *de Pæn.*, c. xii. *ad init.*

eternity,[1] and as a testimony of (our) faith ; as a commendation of this flesh of ours, which is to be sustained for the "garment of immortality,"[2] which is one day to supervene ; for enduring, in fine, the will of God. Besides, reflect, I advise you, that there is no one who is taken out of the world[3] but by the will of God, if, (as is the case,) not even a leaf falls from off a tree without it. The same who brings us into the world,[4] must of necessity take us out of it too. Therefore when, through the will of God, the husband is deceased, the marriage likewise, by the will of God, deceases. Why should *you* restore what GOD has put an end to? Why do you, by repeating the servitude of matrimony, spurn the liberty which is offered you? "You have been bound to a wife,"[5] says the apostle ; "seek not loosing. You have been loosed from a wife ;[5] seek not binding." For even if you do not "*sin*" in re-marrying, still he says "pressure of the flesh ensues."[6] Wherefore, so far as we can, let us love the opportunity of continence ; as soon as it offers itself, let us resolve to accept it, that what we have not had strength[7] (to follow) in matrimony we may follow in widowhood. The occasion must be embraced which puts an end to that which *necessity*[8] commanded. How detrimental to faith, how obstructive to holiness, second marriages are, the discipline of the Church and the prescription of the apostle declare, when he suffers not men twice married to preside (over a Church[9]), when he would not grant a widow admittance into the order unless she had been "the wife of one man ;"[10] for it behoves God's altar[11] to be set forth pure. That whole halo[12] which encircles the Church is represented (as consisting) of holiness. Priesthood is (a function) of widowhood and of celibacies among the nations. Of course (this is) in conformity with the devil's principle of rivalry. For the king of heathendom,[13] the chief pontiff,[14] to marry a second time is unlawful. How pleasing must holiness be to God, when even His enemy affects it !—not, of course, as having any affinity with anything good, but as contumeliously affecting what is pleasing to[15] God the Lord.

---

[1] i.e., eternal life ; comp. "consecutio æternitatis," *de Bapt.*, c. ii.
[2] 1 Cor. xv. 53 ; 2 Cor. v. 4.
[3] Sæculo.
[4] Mundo.
[5] "Matrimonio," or "by matrimony." Comp. 1 Cor. vii. 27: δέδεσαι γυναικί ; μὴ ζήτει λύσιν· λέλυσαι ἀπὸ γυναικός ; μὴ ζήτει γυναῖκα. Tertullian's rendering, it will be seen, is not *verbatim*.
[6] 1 Cor. vii. 28.
[7] Or, "been able"—valuimus. But comp. c. vi.
[8] See c. iii., "quod autem *necessitas* præstat, depretiat *ipsa*," etc.
[9] 1 Tim. ii. 2 ; Tit. i. 6.
[10] 1 Tim. v. 9, 10.
[11] Aram.
[12] Comp. *de Cor.*, c. i., "et de martyrii *candida* melius coronatus," and Oehler's note.
[13] Sæculi.
[14] Or, "Pontifex maximus."
[15] Or, "has been decreed by."

CHAP. VIII. — CONCLUSION.

For, concerning the honours which widowhood enjoys in the sight of God, there is a brief summary in one saying of His through the prophet : "Do thou[16] justly to the widow and to the orphan,; and come ye,[16] let us reason, saith the LORD." These two names, left to the care of the divine mercy, in proportion as they are destitute of human aid, the Father of all undertakes to defend. Look how the widow's benefactor is put on a level with the widow herself, whose champion shall "reason with the LORD !" Not to virgins, I take it, is so great a gift given. Although in *their* case perfect integrity and entire sanctity shall have the nearest vision of the face of God, yet the *widow* has a task more toilsome, because it is easy not to crave after that which you know not, and to turn away from what you have never had to regret.[17] More glorious is the continence which is aware of its own right, which knows what it has seen. The virgin may possibly be held the happier, but the widow the more hardly tasked ; the former in that she has always kept "the good,"[18] the latter in that she has found "the good for herself." In the former it is grace, in the latter virtue, that is crowned. For some things there are which are of the divine liberality, some of our own working. The indulgences granted by the Lord are regulated by their own grace ; the things which are objects of man's striving are attained by earnest pursuit. Pursue earnestly, therefore, the virtue of continence, which is modesty's agent ; industry, which allows not women to be "wanderers ;"[19] frugality, which scorns the world.[20] Follow companies and conversations worthy of God, mindful of that short verse, sanctified by the apostle's quotation of it, "Ill interviews good morals do corrupt."[21] Talkative, idle, winebibbing, curious tent-fellows,[22] do the very greatest hurt to the purpose of widowhood. Through talkativeness there creep in words unfriendly to modesty ; through idleness they seduce one from strictness ; through winebibbing they insinuate any and every evil ; through curiosity they convey a spirit of rivalry in lust. Not one of such women knows how to speak of the good of single-husbandhood ; for their "god," as the apostle says, "is their belly ;"[23] and so, too, what is neighbour to the belly.

---

[16] So Oehler reads, with Rhenanus and the MSS. The other edd. have the plural in each case, as the LXX. in the passage referred to (Isa. i. 17, 18).
[17] Desideraveris. Oehler reads "desideres."
[18] Comp. c. iii.
[19] 1 Tim. v. 13.
[20] Sæculum.
[21] A verse said to be Menander's, quoted by St. Paul, 1 Cor. xv. 33 ; quoted again, but somewhat differently rendered, by Tertullian in b. i. c. iii.
[22] i.e., here "female companions."
[23] Phil. iii. 19.

These considerations, dearest fellow-servant, I commend to you thus early,[1] handled throughout superfluously indeed, after the apostle, but likely to prove a solace to you, in that (if so it shall turn out[2]) you will cherish my memory in them.

BOOK II.

CHAP. I. — REASONS WHICH LED TO THE WRITING OF THIS SECOND BOOK.

Very lately, best beloved fellow-servant in the Lord, I, as my ability permitted, entered for your benefit at some length into the question what course is to be followed by a holy woman when her marriage has (in whatever way) been brought to an end. Let us now turn our attention to the next best advice, in regard of human infirmity; admonished hereto by the examples of certain, who, when an opportunity for the practice of continence has been offered them, by divorce, or by the decease of the husband, have not only thrown away the opportunity of attaining so great a good, but not even in their remarriage have chosen to be mindful of the rule that "above all [1] they marry in the Lord." And thus my mind has been thrown into confusion, in the fear that, having exhorted you myself to perseverance in single husbandhood and widowhood, I may now, by the mention of precipitate [2] marriages, put "an occasion of falling"[3] in your way. But if you are perfect in wisdom, you know, of course, that the course which is the more useful is the course which you must keep. But, inasmuch as that course is difficult, and not without its embarrassments,[4] and on this account is the highest aim of (widowed) life, I have paused somewhat (in my urging you to it); nor would there have been any causes for my recurring to that point also in addressing you, had I not by this time taken up a still graver solicitude. For the nobler is the continence of the flesh which ministers to widowhood, the more pardonable a thing it seems if it be not persevered in. For it is then when things are difficult that their pardon is easy. But in as far as marrying "in the Lord" is permissible, as being within our power, so far more culpable is it *not* to observe that which you *can* observe. Add to this the fact that the apostle, with regard to widows and the unmarried, *advises* them to remain permanently in that state, when he says, "But I desire all to persevere in (imitation of) my example:"[5] but touching marrying "in the Lord," he no longer *advises*, but plainly [6] bids.[7] Therefore in this case especially, if we do not obey, we run a risk, because one may with more impunity neglect an "advice" than an "order;" in that the former springs from *counsel*, and is proposed to the *will* (for acceptance or rejection): the other descends from *authority*, and is bound to *necessity*. In the former case, to disregard appears *liberty*, in the latter, *contumacy*.

CHAP. II. — OF THE APOSTLE'S MEANING IN 1 COR. VII. 12–14.

Therefore, when in these days a certain woman removed her marriage from the pale of the Church, and united herself to a Gentile, and when I remembered that this had in days gone by been done by others: wondering at either their own waywardness or else the double-dealing[8] of their advisers, in that there is no scripture which holds forth a licence of this deed, — "I wonder," said I, "whether they flatter themselves on the ground of that passage of the first (Epistle) to the Corinthians, where it is written: 'If any of the brethren has an unbelieving wife, and she consents to the matrimony, let him not dismiss her; similarly, let not a believing woman, married to an unbeliever, if she finds her husband agreeable (to their continued union), dismiss him: for the unbelieving husband is sanctified by the believing wife, and the unbelieving wife by the believing husband; else were your children unclean.'"[9] It may be that, by understanding *generally* this monition regarding *married* believers, they think that licence is granted (thereby) to marry even *un*believers. God forbid that he who thus interprets (the passage) be *wittingly* ensnaring himself! But it is manifest that this scripture points to those believers who may have

[1] Potissimum; Gr. "μόνον," 1 Cor. vii. 39.
[2] Proclivium.
[3] Ps. lxix. 23 (according to the "Great Bible" version, ed. 1539. This is the translation found in the "Book of Common Prayer"). Comp. Rom. xiv. 13.
[4] Necessitatibus.

[5] 1 Cor. vii. 6-8.
[6] Exerte. Comp. the use of "exertus" in de Bapt., cc. xii. and xviii.
[7] 1 Cor. vii. 39, where the μόνον ἐν Κυρίῳ is on the same footing as γυνὴ δέδεται ἐφ' ὅσον χρόνον ζῇ ὁ ἀνὴρ αὐτῆς; comp. c. ix. and Rom. vii. 1 (in the Eng. ver. 2).
[8] Prævaricationem. Comp. de Pæn., c. iii.: "Dissimulator et prævaricator perspicaciæ suæ (Deus) non est."
[9] 1 Cor. vii. 12-14, in sense, not verbatim.

been found by the grace of God in (the state of) Gentile matrimony ; according to the words themselves : "If," it says, " any believer *has* an unbelieving wife ; " it does not say, " *takes* an unbelieving wife." It shows that it is the duty of one who, already living in marriage with an unbelieving woman,[1] has presently been by the grace of God converted, to continue with his wife ; for this reason, to be sure, in order that no one, after attaining to faith, should think that he must turn away from a woman[2] who is now in some sense an "alien" and "stranger."[3] Accordingly he subjoins withal a reason, that "we are called *in peace* unto the Lord God ; " and that " the unbeliever may, through the use of matrimony, *be gained* by the believer."[4] The very closing sentence of the period confirms (the supposition) that this is thus to be understood. "As each," it says, "is called by the Lord, so let him persevere."[5] But it is *Gentiles* who "are called," I take it, not *believers*. But if he had been pronouncing *absolutely*, (in the words under discussion,) touching the marriage of believers merely, (then) had he (virtually) given to saints a permission to marry promiscuously. If, however, he had given such a permission, he would never have subjoined a declaration so diverse from and contrary to his own permission, saying : "The woman, when her husband is dead, is free : let her marry whom she wishes, *only in the Lord*."[6] Here, at all events, there is no need for reconsidering ; for what there *might* have been reconsideration about, the Spirit has oracularly declared. For fear we should make an ill use of what he says, " Let her marry whom she wishes," he has added, "only in the Lord," that is, in the name of the Lord, which is, undoubtedly, "to a Christian." That " Holy Spirit,"[7] therefore, who prefers that widows and unmarried women should persevere in their integrity, who exhorts us to a copy[8] of himself, prescribes no other manner of repeating marriage except "in the Lord ; " to this condition alone does he concede the foregoing[9] of continence. "Only," he says, "in the Lord : " he has added to his law a weight — "*only*." Utter that word with what tone and manner you may, it is weighty : it both bids and advises ; both enjoins and exhorts ; both asks and threatens. It is a concise,[10] brief sentence ; and by its own very brevity, eloquent. Thus is the divine voice

wont (to speak), that you may instantly understand, instantly observe. For who but could understand that the apostle foresaw many dangers and wounds to faith in marriages of this kind, which he prohibits? and that he took precaution, in the first place, against the defilement of holy flesh in Gentile flesh? At this point some one says, "What, then, is the difference between him who is chosen by the Lord to Himself in (the state of) Gentile marriage, and him who was of old (that is, before marriage) a believer, that they should not be equally cautious for their flesh? — whereas the one is kept from marriage with an unbeliever, the other bidden to continue in it. Why, if we are defiled by a Gentile, is not the one disjoined, just as the other is not bound?" I will answer, if the Spirit give (me ability) ; alleging, before all (other arguments), that the Lord holds it more pleasing that matrimony should not be contracted, than that it should at all be dissolved : in short, divorce He prohibits, except for the cause of fornication ; but continence He commends. Let the one, therefore, have the necessity of continuing ; the other, further, even the power of not marrying. Secondly, if, according to the Scripture, they who shall be "apprehended"[11] by the faith in (the state of) Gentile marriage are not defiled (thereby) for this reason, that, together with themselves, others[12] also are sanctified : without doubt, they who have been sanctified *before* marriage, if they commingle themselves with "strange flesh,"[13] cannot sanctify that (flesh) in (union with) which they were not "apprehended." The grace of God, moreover, sanctifies that which it *finds*. Thus, what has not been able to be sanctified is unclean ; what is unclean has no part with the holy, unless to defile and slay it by its own (nature).

CHAP. III. — REMARKS ON SOME OF THE " DANGERS AND WOUNDS" REFERRED TO IN THE PRECEDING CHAPTER.

If these things are so, it is certain that believers contracting marriages with Gentiles are guilty of fornication,[14] and are to be excluded from all communication with the brotherhood, in accordance with the letter of the apostle, who says that "with persons of that kind there is to be no taking of food even."[15] Or shall we "in that day"[16] produce (our) marriage certificates before the Lord's tribunal, and allege that a marriage such as He Himself has forbidden has been duly contracted? What is prohibited (in the pas-

---

[1] Mulieris.
[2] Femina.
[3] Comp. Eph. ii. 12, 19.
[4] Comp. 1 Cor. vii. 15, 16, and Phil. iii. 8, in Vulg., for the word " lucrifieri."
[5] 1 Cor. vii. 17, inexactly given, like the two preceding citations.
[6] 1 Cor. vii. 39, not *verbatim*.
[7] i e., St. Paul, who, as inspired by the Holy Spirit, is regarded by Tertullian as merged, so to speak, in the Spirit.
[8] "Exemplum," a rarer use of the word, but found in Cic. The reference is to 1 Cor. vii. 7.
[9] Detrimenta.
[10] Districta (? = dis-stricta, " doubly strict ").

[11] Comp. Phil. iii. 12, and c. vii. *ad init.*
[12] See 1 Cor. vii. 14.
[13] Comp. Jude 7, and above, " an alien and stranger," with the reference there.
[14] Comp. *de Pa.*, c. xii. (mid.), and the note there.
[15] Comp. 1 Cor. v. 11.
[16] The translator has ventured to read " *die* illo " here, instead of Oehler's " *de* illo."

sage just referred to) is not "adultery;" it is not "fornication." The admission of a strange man (to your couch) less violates "the temple of God,"[1] less commingles "the members of Christ" with the members of an adulteress.[2] So far as I know, "we are not our own, but bought with a price;"[3] and what kind of price? The blood of God.[4] In hurting this flesh of ours, therefore, we hurt Him directly.[5] What did that man mean who said that "to wed a 'stranger' was indeed a sin, but a very small one?" whereas in other cases (setting aside the injury done to the flesh which pertains to the Lord) *every* voluntary sin against the Lord is *great*. For, in as far as there was a power of avoiding it, in so far is it burdened with the charge of contumacy.

Let us now recount the other dangers or wounds (as I have said) to faith, foreseen by the apostle; most grievous not to the flesh merely, but likewise to the spirit too. For who would doubt that faith undergoes a daily process of obliteration by unbelieving intercourse? "Evil confabulations corrupt good morals;"[6] how much more fellowship of life, and indivisible intimacy! Any and every believing woman must of necessity obey God. And how can she serve two lords[7] — the Lord, and her husband — a Gentile to boot? For in obeying a Gentile she will carry out Gentile practices, — personal attractiveness, dressing of the head, worldly[8] elegancies, baser blandishments, the very secrets even of matrimony tainted: not, as among the saints, where the duties of the sex are discharged with honour (shown) to the very necessity (which makes them incumbent), with modesty and temperance, as beneath the eyes of God.

CHAP. IV. — OF THE HINDRANCES WHICH AN UN-
BELIEVING HUSBAND PUTS IN HIS WIFE'S WAY.

But let her see to (the question) how she discharges her duties to her husband. To the Lord, at all events, she is unable to give satisfaction according to the requirements of discipline; having at her side a servant of the devil, *his* lord's agent for hindering the pursuits and duties of believers: so that if a station[9] is to be kept, the husband at daybreak makes an appointment with his wife to meet him at the baths; if there are fasts to be observed, the husband

that same day holds a convivial banquet; if a charitable expedition has to be made, never is family business more urgent. For who would suffer his wife, for the sake of visiting the brethren, to go round from street to street to other men's, and indeed to all the poorer, cottages? Who will willingly bear her being taken from his side by nocturnal convocations, if need so be? Who, finally, will without anxiety endure her absence all the night long at the paschal solemnities? Who will, without some suspicion of his own, dismiss her to attend that Lord's Supper which they defame? Who will suffer her to creep into prison to kiss a martyr's bonds? nay, truly, to meet any one of the brethren to exchange the kiss? to offer water for the saints' feet?[10] to snatch (somewhat for them) from her food, from her cup? to yearn (after them)? to have (them) in her mind? If a pilgrim brother arrive, what hospitality for him in an alien home? If bounty is to be distributed to any, the granaries, the storehouses, are foreclosed.

CHAP. V. — OF SIN AND DANGER INCURRED EVEN
WITH A "TOLERANT" HUSBAND.

"But some husband does endure our (practices), and not annoy us." *Here*, therefore, there is a sin; in that Gentiles *know* our (practices); in that we are subject to the privity of the unjust; in that it is thanks to them that we do any (good) work. He who "endures" (a thing) cannot be ignorant of it; or else, if he is kept in ignorance because he does *not* endure (it), he is feared. But since Scripture commands each of two things — namely, that we work for the Lord without the privity of any second person,[11] and without pressure upon ourselves, it matters not in which quarter you sin; whether in regard to your husband's privity, if he be tolerant, or else in regard of your own affliction in avoiding his *in*tolerance. "Cast not," saith He, "your pearls to swine, lest they trample them to pieces, and turn round and overturn you also."[12] "Your pearls" are the distinctive marks[13] of even your daily conversation. The more care you take to conceal them, the more liable to suspicion you will make them, and the more exposed to the grasp of Gentile curiosity. Shall you escape notice when you sign your bed, (or) your body; when you blow away some impurity;[14] when even by night you rise to pray? Will you not be thought to be engaged in some work of magic? Will not your husband know what it is which you secretly

[1] 1 Cor. iii. 16, comp. vi. 19.
[2] 1 Cor. vi. 15.
[3] 1 Cor. vi. 19, 20.
[4] See the last reference, and Acts xx. 28, where the MSS. vary between Θεοῦ and Κυρίου.
[5] De proximo. Comp. *de. Pa.*, cc. v. and vii. "Deo *de proximo* amicus;" "*de proximo* in Deum peccat."
[6] Comp. b. i. c. viii. *sub. fin.*, where Tertullian quotes the same passage, but renders it somewhat differently.
[7] Comp. Matt. vi. 24; Luke xvi. 13.
[8] Sæculares.
[9] For the meaning of "statio," see *de Or.*, c. xix.

[10] 1 Tim. v. 10.
[11] Comp. Matt. vi. 1-4.
[12] Matt. vii. 6.
[13] Insignia.
[14] Comp. *de Idol.*, c. xi. *sub fin.*

taste before (taking) any food? and if he knows it to be bread, does he not believe it to be *that* (bread) which it is *said* to be? And will every (husband), ignorant of the reason of these things, simply endure them, without murmuring, without suspicion whether it be bread or poison? Some, (it is true,) *do* endure (them); but it is that they may trample· on, that they may make sport of such women; whose secrets they keep in reserve against the danger which they believe in, in case they ever chance to be hurt: they do endure (wives), whose dowries, by casting in their teeth their (Christian) name, they make the wages of silence; while they threaten them, forsooth, with a suit before some spy [1] as arbitrator! which most women, not foreseeing, have been wont to discover either by the extortion of their property, or else by the loss of their faith.

CHAP. VI. — DANGER OF HAVING TO TAKE PART IN HEATHENISH RITES AND REVELS.

The handmaid of God [2] dwells amid alien labours; and among these (labours), on all the memorial days [3] of demons, at all solemnities of kings, at the beginning of the year, at the beginning of the month, she will be agitated by the odour of incense. And she will have to go forth (from her house) by a gate wreathed with laurel, and hung with lanterns, as from some new consistory of public lusts; she will have to sit with her husband ofttimes in club meetings, ofttimes in taverns; and, wont as she was formerly to minister to the "saints," will sometimes have to minister to the "unjust." [4] And will she not hence recognise a prejudgment of her own damnation, in that she *tends* them whom (formerly) she was expecting to *judge?* [5] whose hand will she yearn after? of whose cup will she partake? What will her husband sing [6] to her, or she to her husband? From the tavern, I suppose, she who sups upon God [7] will hear somewhat! From hell what mention of God (arises)? what invocation of Christ? Where are the fosterings of faith by the interspersion of the Scriptures (in conversation)? Where the Spirit? where refreshment? where the divine benediction? All things are strange, all inimical, all condemned; aimed by the Evil One for the attrition of salvation!

CHAP. VII. — THE CASE OF A HEATHEN WHOSE WIFE IS CONVERTED AFTER MARRIAGE WITH HIM VERY DIFFERENT, AND MUCH MORE HOPEFUL.

If these things may happen to those women also who, having attained the faith while in (the state of) Gentile matrimony, continue in that state, still they are excused, as having been "apprehended by God" [8] in these very circumstances; and they are *bidden* to persevere in their married state, and are sanctified, and have hope of "making a gain" [9] held out to them. "If, then, a marriage of this kind (contracted *before* conversion) stands ratified before God, why should not (one contracted *after* conversion) too go prosperously forward, so as not to be thus harassed by pressures, and straits, and hindrances, and defilements, having already (as it has) the partial sanction of divine grace?" Because, on the one hand, the wife [10] in the former case, called *from among* the Gentiles to the exercise of some eminent heavenly virtue, is, by the visible proofs of some marked (divine) regard, a terror to her Gentile husband, so as to make him less ready to annoy her, less active in laying snares for her, less diligent in playing the spy over her. He has felt "mighty works;" [11] he has seen experimental evidences; he knows her changed for the better: thus even he himself is, by his fear, [12] a candidate for God. [13] Thus men of this kind, with regard to whom the grace of God has established a familiar intimacy, are more easily "gained." But, on the other hand, to descend into forbidden ground unsolicited and spontaneously, is (quite) another thing. Things which are not pleasing to the Lord, of course offend the Lord, are of course introduced by the Evil One. A sign hereof is this fact, that it is *wooers* only who find the Christian name pleasing; and, accordingly, some heathen men are found not to shrink in horror from Christian women, just in order to exterminate them, to wrest them away, to exclude them from the faith. So long as marriage of this kind is procured by the Evil One, but condemned by God, you have a reason why you need not doubt that it can in no case be carried to a prosperous end.

CHAP. VIII. — ARGUMENTS DRAWN EVEN FROM HEATHENISH LAWS TO DISCOUNTENANCE MARRIAGE WITH UNBELIEVERS. THE HAPPINESS OF UNION BETWEEN PARTNERS IN THE FAITH ENLARGED ON IN CONCLUSION.

Let us further inquire, as if we were in very deed inquisitors of divine sentences, whether

---

[1] "Speculatorem;" also = an executioner. Comp. Mark vi. 27.
[2] Comp. Luke i. 38, and *de Cult. Fem.*, b. ii. c. i. *ad init.*
[3] Nominibus; al. honoribus.
[4] Sanctis — iniquis. Comp. St. Paul's antithesis of ἀδίκων and ἁγίων in 1 Cor. vi. 1.
[5] See 1 Cor. vi. 2, 3.
[6] See Eph. v. 19.
[7] So Oehler understands (apparently) the meaning to be. The translator is inclined to think that,·adopting Oehler's reading, we may perhaps take the "Dei" with "aliquid," ánd the "coenans" absolutely, and render, "From the tavern, no doubt, while supping, she will hear some (strain) of God," in allusion to the former sentence, and to such passages as Ps. cxxxvii. 4 (in the LXX. it is cxxxvi. 4).

[8] Comp. Phil. iii. 12, and c. ii. *sub fin.*
[9] Comp. 1 Cor. vii. 16, and 1 Pet. iii. 1.
[10] Tertullian here and in other places appears, as the best editors maintain, to use the masculine gender for the feminine.
[11] Magnalia. Comp. 2 Cor. xii. 12.
[12] Timore.
[13] Comp. *de Or.*, c. iii. (*med.*), "angelorum candidati;" and *de Bapt.*, c. x. *sub fin.*, "candidatus remissionis,"

they be lawfully (thus condemned). Even among the nations, do not all the strictest lords and most tenacious of discipline interdict their own slaves from marrying out of their own house?—in order, of course, that they may not run into lascivious excess, desert their duties, purvey their lords' goods to strangers. Yet, further, have not (the nations) decided that such women as have, after their lords'[1] formal warning, persisted in intercourse with other men's slaves, may be claimed as slaves? Shall earthly disciplines be held more strict than heavenly prescripts; so that *Gentile* women, if united to strangers, lose their liberty; *ours* conjoin to themselves the devil's slaves, and continue in their (former) position? Forsooth, they will deny that any formal warning has been given them by the Lord through His own apostle![2]

What am I to fasten on as the cause of this madness, except the weakness of faith, ever prone to the concupiscences of worldly[3] joys? —which, indeed, is chiefly found among the wealthier; for the more any is rich, and inflated with the name of "matron," the more capacious house does she require for her burdens, as it were a field wherein ambition may run its course. To such the churches look paltry. A rich man is a difficult thing (to find) in the house of God;[4] and if such an one is (found there), difficult (is it to find such) unmarried. What, then, are they to do? Whence but from the devil are they to seek a husband apt for maintaining their sedan, and their mules, and their hair-curlers of outlandish stature? A Christian, even although rich, would perhaps not afford (all) these. Set before yourself, I beg of you, the examples of Gentiles. Most Gentile women, noble in extraction and wealthy in property, unite themselves indiscriminately with the ignoble and the mean, sought out for themselves for luxurious, or mutilated for licentious, purposes. Some take up with their own freedmen and slaves, despising public opinion, provided they may but have (husbands) from whom to fear no impediment to their own liberty. To a Christian believer it is irksome to wed a believer inferior to herself in estate, destined as she will

be to have her wealth augmented in the person of a poor husband! For if it is "the poor," not the rich, "whose are the kingdoms of the heavens,"[5] the rich will find more in the poor (than she brings him, or than she would in the rich). She will be dowered with an ampler dowry from the goods of him who is rich in God. Let her be on an equality with him on earth, who in the heavens will perhaps not be so. Is there need for doubt, and inquiry, and repeated deliberation, whether he whom God has entrusted with His own property[6] is fit for dotal endowments?[7] Whence are we to find (words) enough fully to tell the happiness of that marriage which the Church cements, and the oblation confirms, and the benediction signs and seals; (which) angels carry back the news of (to heaven), (which) the Father holds for ratified? For even on earth children[8] do not rightly and lawfully wed without their fathers' consent. What kind of yoke is that of two believers, (partakers) of one hope, one desire,[9] one discipline, one and the same service? Both (are) brethren, both fellow servants, no difference of spirit or of flesh; nay, (they are) truly "two in one flesh."[10] Where the flesh is one, one is the spirit too. Together they pray, together prostrate themselves, together perform their fasts; mutually teaching, mutually exhorting,[11] mutually sustaining. Equally (are they) both (found) in the Church of God; equally at the banquet of God; equally in straits, in persecutions, in refreshments. Neither hides (ought) from the other; neither shuns the other; neither is troublesome to the other. The sick is visited, the indigent relieved, with freedom. Alms (are given) without (danger of ensuing) torment; sacrifices (attended) without scruple; daily diligence (discharged) without impediment: (there is) no stealthy signing, no trembling greeting, no mute benediction. Between the two echo psalms and hymns;[12] and they mutually challenge each other which shall better chant to their Lord. Such things when Christ sees and hears, He joys. To these He sends His own peace.[13] Where two (are), there withal (is) He Himself.[14] Where He (is), there the Evil One is not.

These are the things which that utterance of

[1] Oehler refers us to Tac., *Ann.*, xii. 53, and the notes on that passage. (Consult especially Orelli's edition.)
[2] The translator inclines to think that Tertullian, desiring to keep up the parallelism of the last-mentioned case, in which (see note 1) the *slave's* master had to give the "warning," means by "domino" here, *not* "the Lord," who on his hypothesis is the *woman's* Master, not the *slave's*, but the "lord" of the "unbeliever," i.e., the devil: so that the meaning would be (with a bitter irony, especially if we compare the end of the last chapter, where "the Evil One" is said to "procure" these marriages, so far is he from "condemning" them): "Forsooth, they" (i.e., the Christian women) "will deny that a formal warning has been given them by the lord" (of the unbelievers, i.e., the Evil One) "through an apostle of his!" If the other interpretation be correct, the reference will be to c. ii. above.
[3] Sæcularium.
[4] Matt. xix. 23, 24; Mark x. 23, 24; Luke xviii. 24, 25; 1 Cor. i. 26, 27.

[5] Matt. v. 3; but Tertullian has omitted "spiritu," which he inserts in *de Pa.*, c. xi., where he refers to the same passage. In Luke vi. 20 there is no τῷ πνεύματι.
[6] Censum.
[7] Invecta. Comp. *de Pa.*, c. xiii. *ad init.*
[8] Filii.
[9] Comp. *de Or.*, c. v. *ad fin.*; *de Pa.*, c. ix. *ad fin.*; *ad Ux.*, i. c. v. *ad init.*
[10] Gen. ii. 24; Matt. xix. 5; Mark x. 8; Eph. v. 31.
[11] Col. iii. 16.
[12] Eph. v. 19; Col. iii. 16.
[13] Comp. John xiv. 27.
[14] Matt. xviii. 20.

the apostle has, beneath its brevity, left to be understood by us. These things, if need shall be, suggest to your own mind. By these turn yourself away from the examples of some. To marry *otherwise* is, to believers, not "lawful;" is not "expedient." [1]

[1] Comp. 1 Cor. x. 23.

ELUCIDATION.

(Marriage lawful, p. 39.)

St. Peter was a married apostle, and the traditions of his wife which connect her married life with Rome itself render it most surprising that those who claim to be St. Peter's successors should denounce the marriage of the clergy as if it were crime. The touching story, borrowed from Clement of Alexandria, is related by Eusebius. "And will they," says Clement, "reject even the apostles? Peter and Philip, indeed, had children; Philip also gave his daughters in marriage to husbands; and Paul does not demur, in a certain Epistle, to mention his own wife, whom he did not take about with him, in order to expedite his ministry the better." Of St. Peter and his wife, Eusebius subjoins, "Such was the marriage of these blessed ones, and such was their perfect affection." [1]

The Easterns to this day perpetuate the marriage of the clergy, and enjoin it; but unmarried men only are chosen to be bishops. Even Rome relaxes her discipline for the *Uniats*, and hundreds of her priesthood, therefore, live in honourable marriage. Thousands live in secret marriage, but their wives are dishonoured as "concubines." It was not till the eleventh century that the celibate was enforced. In England it was *never* successfully imposed; and, though the "priest's *leman*" was not called his *wife* (to the disgrace of the whole system), she was yet honoured (see Chaucer), and often carried herself too proudly.

The enormous evils of an enforced celibacy need not here be remarked upon. The history of *Sacerdotal Celibacy*, by Henry C. Lea [2] of Philadelphia, is compendious, and can be readily procured by all who wish to understand what it is that this treatise of Tertullian's orthodoxy may best be used to teach; viz., that we must not be wiser than God, even in our zeal for His service.

[1] Eccl. Hist., Book III. cap. xxx.   [2] Boston: Houghton, Mifflin, & Co., second edition, enlarged, 1884.

V.

ON EXHORTATION TO CHASTITY.[1]

[TRANSLATED BY THE REV. S. THELWALL.]

CHAP. I. — INTRODUCTION. VIRGINITY CLASSIFIED UNDER THREE SEVERAL SPECIES.

I DOUBT not, brother, that after the premission in peace of your wife, you, being wholly bent upon the composing of your mind (to a right frame), are seriously thinking about the end of your lone life, and of course are standing in need of counsel. Although, in cases of this kind, each individual ought to hold colloquy with his own faith, and consult its strength; still, inasmuch as, in this (particular) species (of trial), the *necessity of the flesh* (which generally is faith's antagonist at the bar of the same inner consciousness, to which I have alluded) sets cogitation astir, faith has need of counsel from without, as an advocate, as it were, to oppose the *necessities of the flesh :* which necessity, indeed, may very easily be circumscribed, if the *will* rather than the *indulgence* of God be considered. No one deserves (favour) by availing himself of the indulgence, but by rendering a prompt obedience to the will, (of his master).[2] The will of God is our sanctification,[3] for He wishes His " image " — us — to become likewise His " likeness ; "[4] that we may be " holy " just as Himself is " holy."[5] That good — sanctification, I mean — I distribute into several species, that in some one of those species we may be found. The first species is, virginity from one's birth : the second, virginity from one's *second* birth, that is, from the font ; which (second virginity) either in the marriage state keeps (its subject) pure by mutual compact,[6] or else perseveres in widowhood from choice : a third grade remains, monogamy, when, after the interception of a marriage once contracted, there is there-after a renunciation of sexual connection. The first virginity is (the virginity) of happiness, (and consists in) total ignorance of that from which you will afterwards wish to be freed : the second, of virtue, (and consists in) contemning that the power of which you know full well : the remaining species, (that) of marrying no more after the disjunction of matrimony by death, besides being the glory of virtue, is (the glory) of moderation likewise ;[7] for moderation is the not regretting a thing which has been taken away, and taken away by the Lord God,[8] without whose will neither does a leaf glide down from a tree, nor a sparrow of one farthing's worth fall to the earth.[9]

CHAP. II. — THE BLAME OF OUR MISDEEDS NOT TO BE CAST UPON GOD. THE ONE POWER WHICH RESTS WITH MAN IS THE POWER OF VOLITION.

What moderation, in short, is there in that utterance, "The Lord gave, the Lord hath taken away ; as seemed (good) to the Lord, so hath it been done ! "[10] And accordingly, if we renew nuptials which have been taken away, doubtless we strive against the will of God, willing to have over again a thing which He has not willed us to have. For had He willed (that we should), He would not have taken it away ; unless we interpret this, too, to be the will of God, as if He again willed us to have what He just now did not will. It is not the part of good and solid faith to refer all things to the will of God in such a manner as that ; and that each individual should so flatter[11] himself by saying that " nothing is done without His permission," as to make us fail to understand that there is a something

1 [Written, possibly, *circa* A.D. 204.]
2 Comp. c. iii. and the references there.
3 1 Thess. iv. 3.
4 Comp. 1 Cor. xi. 7, where the Greek is εἰκὼν καὶ δόξα.
5 Lev. xi. 44 ; 1 Pet. i. 16.
6 Comp. 1 Cor. vii. 5 ; and *ad Ux.*, b. i. c. vi.
7 Comp. *ad Ux.*, b. i. c. viii.
8 Comp. Job i. 21.
9 Comp. Matt. x. 29.
10 Job i. 21 (in LXX. and Vulg.).
11 Adulari. Comp. *de Pæn.*, c. vi. *sub init.;* ad Ux., b. i. c. iv. *ad init.*

in our own power. Else every sin will be excused if we persist in contending that nothing is done by us without the will of God; and that definition will go to the destruction of (our) whole discipline, (nay), even of God Himself; if either He produce by [1] His own will things which He wills not, or else (if) there is nothing which God wills not. But as there are some things which He forbids, against which He denounces even eternal punishment — for, of course, things which He *forbids*, and by which withal He is *offended*, He does not *will* — so, too, on the contrary, what He *does* will, He enjoins and sets down as acceptable, and repays with the reward of eternity.[2] And so, when we have learnt from His precepts each (class of actions), what He does not will and what He does, we still have a volition and an arbitrating power of electing the one ; just as it is written, " Behold, I have set before thee good and evil : for thou hast tasted of the tree of knowledge." And accordingly we ought not to lay to the account of the Lord's will that which lies subject to our own choice ; (on the hypothesis) that He does not will, or else (positively) nills what is good, who does nill what is evil. Thus, it is a volition of our own when we will what is evil, in antagonism to God's will, who wills what is good. Further, if you inquire whence comes that volition whereby we will anything in antagonism to the will of God, I shall say, It has its source in ourselves. And I shall not make the assertion rashly — for you must needs correspond to the seed whence you spring — if indeed it be true, (as it is), that the originator of our race and our sin, Adam,[3] willed the sin which he committed. For the devil did not impose upon him the volition to sin, but subministered material to the volition. On the other hand, the will of God had come to be a question of obedience.[4] In like manner you, too, if you fail to obey God, who has trained you by setting before you the precept of free action, will, through the liberty of your will, willingly turn into the downward course of doing what God nills : and thus you think yourself to have been subverted by the devil ; who, albeit he does *will* that you should will something which God nills, still does not *make* you will it, inasmuch as he did not *reduce* those our protoplasts to the volition of sin ; nay, nor (did *reduce* them at all) against their will, or in ignorance as to what God nilled. For, of course, He nilled (a thing) to be done when He made death the destined consequence of its commission. Thus the work of the devil is one : to make trial whether you do will that

which it rests with you to will. But when you *have* willed, it follows that he subjects you to himself ; not by having *wrought* volition in you, but by having found a favourable opportunity in your volition. Therefore, since the only thing which is in our power is volition — and it is herein that our mind toward God is put to proof, whether we will the things which coincide with His will — deeply and anxiously must the will of God be pondered again and again, I say, (to see) what even in *secret* He may will.

CHAP. III. — OF INDULGENCE AND PURE VOLITION. THE QUESTION ILLUSTRATED.[5]

For what things are *manifest* we all know ; and *in what sense* these very things are manifest must be thoroughly examined. For, albeit some things seem to savour of " the will of God," seeing that they are *allowed* by Him, it does not forthwith follow that everything which is *permitted* proceeds out of the mere and absolute will of him who permits. *Indulgence* is the source of all *permission*. And albeit indulgence is not independent of volition, still, inasmuch as it has its *cause* in him to whom the indulgence is granted, it comes (as it were) from *unwilling* volition, having experienced a producing cause of itself which *constrains* volition. See what is the nature of a volition of which some second party is the cause. There is, again, a second species of *pure* volition to be considered. God wills us to do some acts pleasing to [6] Himself, in which it is not indulgence which patronizes, but discipline which lords it. If, however, He has given a preference over these to some other acts — (acts), of course, which He *more* wills — is there a doubt that the acts which we are to pursue are those which He *more* wills ; since those which He *less* wills (because He wills others *more*) are to be similarly regarded as if He did *not* will them ? For, by showing what He *more* wills, He has effaced the lesser volition by the greater. And in as far as He has proposed each (volition) to your knowledge, in so far has He defined it to be your duty to pursue that which He has declared that He *more* wills. Then, if the object of His declaring has been that you may pursue that which He *more* wills ; doubtless, unless you do so, you savour of contrariety to His volition, by savouring of contrariety to His *superior* volition ; and you rather offend than merit reward, by doing what He wills indeed, and rejecting what He *more* wills. Partly, you sin ; partly, if you sin not, still you deserve no reward. Moreover, is not even the unwillingness to deserve reward a sin?

If, therefore, second marriage finds the source of its allowance in that " will of God " which is

---

[1] Or, " from " — *de*.
[2] i.e., eternal *life :* as in *de Bapt.*, c. ii.; *ad Ux.*, b. i. c. vii. *ad init.*
[3] *De Pæn.*, c. xii. *ad fin.*
[4] In obaudientiam venerat.

[5] From 1 Cor. vii.
[6] Or, " decreed by."

called indulgence, we shall deny that that which has indulgence for its cause is volition pure ; if in that to which some other — that, namely, which regards continence as more desirable — is preferred as superior, we shall have learned (by what has been argued above), that the not-superior is rescinded by the superior.

Suffer me to have touched upon these considerations, in order that I may now follow the course of the apostle's words. But, in the first place, I shall not be thought irreligious if I remark on what he himself professes ; (namely), that he has introduced all *indulgence* in regard to marriage from his own (judgment) — that is, from human sense, not from divine prescript. For, withal, when he has laid down the definitive rule with reference to "the widowed and the unwedded," that they are to "marry if they cannot contain," because "better it is to marry than to burn,"[1] he turns round to the other class, and says : "But to the wedded I make official declaration — not indeed I, but the Lord." Thus he shows, by the transfer of his own personality to the Lord, that what he had said above he had pronounced not in the Lord's person, but in his own : "Better it is to marry than to burn." Now, although that expression pertain to such as *are "apprehended" by the faith* in an unwedded or widowed condition, still, inasmuch as *all* cling to it with a view to licence in the way of marrying, I should wish to give a thorough treatment to the inquiry what kind of good he is pointing out which is "better than" a penalty ; which cannot seem good but by comparison with something very bad ; so that the reason why "marrying" is good, is that "burning" is worse. "Good" is worthy of the name if it continue to keep that name without comparison, I say not with evil, but even with some second good ; so that, even if it *is* compared to some other good, and is by some other cast into the shade, it do nevertheless remain in possession of the name "good." If, however, it is the nature of an *evil* which is the means which compels the predicating "good," it is not so much "good" as a species of inferior evil, which by being obscured by a superior evil is driven to the name of good. Take away, in short, the condition of comparison, so as not to say, "Better it is to marry than to burn ;" and I question whether you will have the hardihood to say, "Better it is to marry," not adding what that is which is better. Therefore what is not *better*, of course is not *good* either ; inasmuch as you have taken away and removed the condition of comparison, which, while it makes the thing "better," so compels it to be regarded as "good." "Better it is to marry than to burn" is to be understood in the

same way as, "Better it is to lack one eye than two :" if, however, you withdraw from the comparison, it will not be "better" to have one eye, inasmuch as it is not "good" either. Let none therefore catch at a defence (of marriage) from this paragraph, which properly refers to "the unmarried and widows," for whom no (matrimonial) conjunction is yet reckoned : although I hope I have shown that even such must understand the nature of the *permission*.

CHAP. IV. — FURTHER REMARKS UPON THE APOSTLE'S LANGUAGE.

However, touching second marriage, we know plainly that the apostle has pronounced : "Thou hast been loosed from a wife ; seek not a wife. But if thou shalt marry, thou wilt not sin."[2] Still, as in the former case, he has introduced the order of this discourse too from his personal suggestion, not from a divine precept. But there is a wide difference between a precept of God and a suggestion of man. "Precept of the Lord," says he, "I have not ; but I give advice, as having obtained mercy of the Lord to be faithful."[3] In fact, neither in the Gospel nor in Paul's own Epistles will you find a precept of God as the source whence repetition of marriage is permitted. Whence the doctrine that unity (of marriage) must be observed derives confirmation ; inasmuch as that which is not found to be *permitted* by the Lord is acknowledged to be *forbidden*. Add (to this consideration) the fact, that even this very introduction of human advice, as if already beginning to reflect upon its own extravagance, immediately restrains and recalls itself, while it subjoins, "However, such shall have pressure of the flesh ;" while he says that he "spares them ;" while he adds that "the time is wound up," so that "it behoves even such as have wives to act as if they had not ;" while he compares the solicitude of the wedded and of the unwedded : for, in teaching, by means of these considerations, the reasons why marrying is not expedient, he dissuades from that to which he had above granted indulgence. And this is the case with regard to first marriage : how much more with regard to second ! When, however, he exhorts us to the imitation of his own example, of course, in showing what he *does* wish us to be ; that is, continent ; he equally declares what he does *not* wish us to be, that is, *incontinent*. Thus he, too, while he *wills* one thing, gives no spontaneous or true permission to that which he nills. For had he willed, he would not have *permitted ;* nay, rather, he would have *commanded*. "But see again : a woman when her husband is dead, he says, can marry, if she wish

[1] 1 Cor. vii. 8, 9.

[2] 1 Cor. vii. 27, 28.
[3] Or, "to be a believer ;" ver. 25.

to marry any one, only 'in the Lord.'" Ah! but "happier will she be," he says, "if she shall remain permanently as she is, according to my opinion. I think, moreover, I too have the Spirit of God." We see two advices: that whereby, above, he grants the indulgence of marrying; and that whereby, just afterwards, he teaches continence with regard to marrying. "To which, then," you say, "shall we assent?" Look at them carefully, and choose. In granting indulgence, he alleges the advice of a prudent *man;* in enjoining continence, he affirms the advice of the HOLY SPIRIT. Follow the admonition which has divinity for its patron. It is true that believers likewise "have the Spirit of God;" but not all believers are apostles. When, then, he who had called himself a "believer," added thereafter that he "had the Spirit of God," which no one would doubt even in the case of an (ordinary) believer; his reason for saying so was, that he might re-assert for himself apostolic dignity. For apostles have the Holy Spirit properly, who have Him fully, in the operations of prophecy, and the efficacy of (healing) virtues, and the evidences of tongues; not partially, as all others have. Thus he attached the Holy Spirit's authority to that form (of advice) to which he willed us rather to attend; and forthwith it became not an *advice* of the Holy Spirit, but, in consideration of His majesty, a *precept.*

CHAP. V. — UNITY OF MARRIAGE TAUGHT BY ITS FIRST INSTITUTION, AND BY THE APOSTLE'S APPLICATION OF THAT PRIMAL TYPE TO CHRIST AND THE CHURCH.

For the laying down [1] of the law of once marrying, the very origin of the human race is our authority; witnessing as it emphatically does what God constituted in the beginning for a type to be examined with care by posterity. For when He had moulded man, and had foreseen that a peer was necessary for him, He borrowed from his ribs one, and fashioned for him one woman; [2] whereas, of course, neither the Artificer nor the material would have been insufficient (for the creation of more). There were more ribs in Adam, and hands that knew no weariness in God; but not more wives [3] in the eye of God. [4] And accordingly the man of God, Adam, and the woman of God, Eve, discharging mutually (the duties of) one marriage, sanctioned for mankind a type by (the considerations of) the authoritative precedent of their origin and the primal will of God. Finally, "there shall be," said He, "two in one flesh," [5] not three nor

four. On any other hypothesis, there would no longer be "one flesh," nor "two (joined) into one flesh." These will be so, if the conjunction and the growing together in unity take place *once for all.* If, however, (it take place) a second time, or oftener, immediately (the flesh) ceases to be "one," and there will not be "two (joined) into one flesh," but plainly one rib (divided) into more. But when the apostle interprets, "The two shall be (joined) into one flesh," [6] of the Church and Christ, according to the spiritual nuptials of the Church and Christ (for Christ is one, and one is His Church), we are bound to recognise a duplication and additional enforcement for *us* of the law of unity of marriage, not only in accordance with the foundation of our race, but in accordance with the sacrament of Christ. From one marriage do we derive our origin in each case; carnally in Adam, spiritually in Christ. The two births combine in laying down one prescriptive rule of monogamy. In regard of each of the two, is he degenerate who transgresses the limit of monogamy. Plurality of marriage began with an accursed man. Lamech was the first who, by marrying himself to two women, caused *three* to be (joined) "into one flesh." [7]

CHAP. VI. — THE OBJECTION FROM THE POLYGAMY OF THE PATRIARCHS ANSWERED.

"But withal the blessed patriarchs," you say, "made mingled alliances not only with more wives (than one), but with concubines likewise." Shall that, then, make it lawful for us also to marry without limit? I grant that it will, if there still remain types — sacraments of something future — for your nuptials to figure; or if even now there is room for that command, "Grow and multiply;" [8] that is, if no other command has yet supervened: "The time is already wound up; it remains that both they who have wives act as if they had not:" for, of course, by enjoining continence, and restraining concubitance, the seminary of our race, (this latter command) has abolished that "Grow and multiply." As I think, moreover, each pronouncement and arrangement is (the act) of one and the same God; who did then indeed, in the beginning, send forth a sowing of the race by an indulgent laxity granted to the reins of connubial alliances, until the world should be replenished, until the material of the new discipline should attain to forwardness: now, however, at the extreme boundaries of the times, has checked (the command) which He had sent out, and recalled the indulgence which He had granted; not without a reasonable ground

---

[1] Dirigendam.
[2] Gen. ii. 21, 22.
[3] Or, "but no plurality of wives."
[4] Apud Deum.
[5] Gen. ii. 24.

[6] Eph. v. 31.
[7] Gen. iv. 18, 19.
[8] Gen. i. 28.

for the extension (of that indulgence) in the beginning, and the limitation [1] of it in the end. Laxity is always allowed to the beginning (of things). The reason why any one plants a wood and lets it grow, is that at his own time he may cut it. The wood was the old order, which is being pruned down by the new Gospel, in which withal "the axe has been laid at the roots." [2] So, too, "Eye for eye, and tooth for tooth," [3] has now grown old, ever since " Let none render evil for evil " [4] grew young. I think, moreover, that even with a view to *human* institutions and decrees, things later prevail over things primitive.

CHAP. VII. — EVEN THE OLD DISCIPLINE WAS NOT WITHOUT PRECEDENTS TO ENFORCE MONOGAMY. BUT IN THIS AS IN OTHER RESPECTS, THE NEW HAS BROUGHT IN A HIGHER PERFECTION.

Why, moreover, should we not rather recognise, from among (the store of) primitive precedents, those which communicate with the later (order of things) in respect of discipline, and transmit to novelty the typical form of antiquity? For look, in the old law I find the pruning-knife .applied to the licence of repeated marriage. There is a caution in Leviticus : " My priests shall not pluralize marriages." [5] I may affirm even that that is plural which is not once for all. That which is not unity is number. In short, after unity begins number. Unity, moreover, is everything which is once for all. But for Christ was reserved, as in all other points so in this also, the " fulfilling of the law." [6] Thence, therefore, among *us* the prescript is more fully and more carefully laid down, that they who are chosen into the sacerdotal order must be men of one marriage ; [7] which rule is so rigidly observed, that I remember some removed from their office for digamy. But you will say, " Then all others may (marry more than once), whom he excepts." Vain shall we be if we think that what is not lawful for priests [8] is lawful for laics. Are not even we laics priests? It is written : " A kingdom also, and priests to His God and Father, hath He made us." [9] It is the authority of the Church, and the honour which has acquired sanctity through the joint session of the Order, which has established the difference between the Order and the laity. Accordingly, where there is no joint session of the ecclesiastical Order,

you offer, and baptize, and are priest, alone for yourself. But where three are, a church is, albeit they be laics. For each individual lives by his own faith, [10] nor is there exception of persons with God ; since it is not hearers of the law who are justified by the Lord, but doers, according to what the apostle withal says. [11] Therefore, if you have the *right* of a priest in your own person, in cases of necessity, it behoves you to have likewise the *discipline* of a priest whenever it may be necessary to have the right of a priest. If you are a digamist, do you baptize? If you are a digamist, do you offer? How much more capital (a crime) is it for a digamist laic to act as a priest, when the priest himself, if he turn digamist, is deprived of the power of acting the priest ! " But to necessity," you say, " indulgence is granted." No necessity is excusable which is avoidable. In a word, shun to be found guilty of digamy, and you do not expose yourself to the necessity of administering what a digamist may not lawfully administer. God wills us all to be so conditioned, as to be ready at all times and places to undertake (the duties of) His sacraments. There is " one God, one faith," [12] one discipline too. So truly is this the case, that unless the laics as well observe the rules which are to guide the choice of presbyters, how will there be presbyters at all, who are chosen to that office from among the laics? Hence we are bound to contend that the command to abstain from second marriage relates *first* to the laic ; so long as no other can be a presbyter than a laic, provided he have been *once for all* a husband.

CHAP. VIII. — IF IT BE GRANTED THAT SECOND MARRIAGE IS LAWFUL, YET ALL THINGS LAWFUL ARE NOT EXPEDIENT.

Let it now be granted that repetition of marriage is lawful, if everything which is lawful is good. The same apostle exclaims : " All things are lawful, but all are not profitable." [13] Pray, can what is " not profitable " be called good? If even things which do not make for salvation are " lawful," it follows that even things which are not good are " lawful." But what will it be your duty rather to choose ; that which is good because it is " lawful," or that which is so because it is " profitable? " A wide difference I take to exist between " licence " and salvation. Concerning the " good " it is not said " it is lawful ; " inasmuch as " good " does not expect to be permitted, but to be assumed. But that is " permitted " about which a doubt exists whether it be " good ; " which may likewise *not* be per-

---

[1] Repastinationis. Comp. *de Cult. Fem.*, l. ii. c. ix., *repastinantes.*
[2] Comp. Matt. iii. 10.
[3] Ex. xxi. 24; Lev. xxiv. 20; Deut. xix. 21; Matt. v. 38.
[4] See Rom. xii. 17; Matt. v. 39; 1 Thess. v. 16.
[5] I cannot find any such passage. Oehler refers to Lev. xxi. 14; but neither the Septuagint nor the Vulgate has any such prohibition there.
[6] Matt. v. 17, very often referred to by Tertullian.
[7] Comp. 1 Tim. iii. 1, 2; Tit. i. 5, 6; and Ellicott's *Commentary.*
[8] Sacerdotibus.
[9] Rev. i. 6.

[10] See Hab. ii. 4; Rom. i. 17; Gal. iii. 11; Heb. x. 38.
[11] Rom. ii. 13; Eph. vi. 9; Col. iii. 25; 1 Pet. i. 17; Deut. x. 17.
[12] Eph. iv. 5, 6.
[13] 1 Cor. x. 23.

mitted, if it have not some first (extrinsic) cause of its being : — inasmuch as it is *on account of the danger of incontinence* that second marriage, (for instance), is permitted : — because, unless the "licence" of some not (absolutely) good thing were subject (to our choice), there were no means of proving who rendered a willing obedience to the Divine will, and who to his own power ; which of us follows presentiality, and which embraces the opportunity of licence. "Licence," for the most part, is a trial of discipline ; since it is through trial that discipline is proved, and through "licence" that trial operates. Thus it comes to pass that "all things are lawful, but not all are expedient," so long as (it remains true that) whoever has a "permission" granted is (thereby) tried, and is (consequently) judged during the process of trial in (the case of the particular) "permission." Apostles, withal, had a "licence" to marry, and lead wives about (with them [1]). They had a "licence," too, to "live by the Gospel." [2] But he who, when occasion required,[3] "did not use this right," provokes us to imitate his own example ; teaching us that our probation consists in that wherein "licence" has laid the groundwork for the experimental proof of abstinence.

CHAP. IX. — SECOND MARRIAGE A SPECIES OF ADULTERY. MARRIAGE ITSELF IMPUGNED, AS AKIN TO ADULTERY.

If we look deeply into his meanings, and interpret them, second marriage will have to be termed no other than a species of fornication. For, since he says that married persons make this their solicitude, "how to please one another" [4] (not, of course, *morally*, for a good solicitude he would not impugn) ; and (since), he wishes them to be understood to be solicitous about dress, and ornament, and every kind of personal attraction, with a view to increasing their power of allurement ; (since), moreover, to please by personal beauty and dress is the genius of carnal concupiscence, which again is the cause of fornication : pray, does second marriage seem to you to border upon fornication, since in it are detected those ingredients which are appropriate to fornication? The Lord Himself said, "Whoever has seen a woman with a view to concupiscence has already violated her in his heart." [5] But has he who has seen her with a view to marriage done so less or more? What if he have even married her? — which he would not do had he not desired her with a view to marriage, and seen her with a view to concupiscence ; unless it is possible for

a wife to be married whom you have not seen or desired. I grant it makes a wide difference whether a married man or an unmarried desire another woman. Every woman, (however), even to an unmarried man, is "another," so long as she belongs to some one else ; nor yet is the mean through which she becomes a married woman any other than that through which withal (she becomes) an adulteress. It is laws which seem to make the difference between marriage and fornication ; through diversity of illicitness, not through the nature of the thing itself. Besides, what is the thing which takes place in all men and women to produce marriage and fornication? Commixture of the flesh, of course ; the concupiscence whereof the Lord put on the same footing with fornication. "Then," says (some one), "are you by this time destroying first — that is, single — marriage too?" And (if so) not without reason ; inasmuch as it, too, consists of that which is the essence of fornication.[6] Accordingly, the best thing for a man is not to touch a woman ; and accordingly the virgin's is the principal sanctity,[7] because it is free from affinity with fornication. And since these considerations may be advanced, even in the case of first and single marriage, to forward the cause of continence, how much more will they afford a prejudgment for refusing second marriage? Be thankful if God has once for all granted you indulgence to marry. Thankful, moreover, you will be if you know not that He has granted you that indulgence a second time. But you abuse indulgence if you avail yourself of it without moderation. Moderation is understood (to be derived) from *modus*, a limit. It does not suffice you to have fallen back, by marrying, from that highest grade of immaculate virginity ; but you roll yourself down into yet a third, and into a fourth, and perhaps into more, after you have failed to be continent in the second stage ; inasmuch as he who has treated about contracting second marriages has not willed to prohibit even more. Marry we, therefore, daily.[8] And marrying, let us be overtaken by the last day, like Sodom and Gomorrah ; that day when the "woe" pronounced over "such as are with child and giving suck" shall be fulfilled, that is, over the married and the incontinent : for from marriage result wombs, and breasts, and infants. And when an end of marrying? I believe after the end of living !

CHAP. X. — APPLICATION OF THE SUBJECT. ADVANTAGES OF WIDOWHOOD.

Renounce we things carnal, that we may at length bear fruits spiritual. Seize the opportu-

---

[1] See 1 Cor. ix. 5.
[2] See vers. 4, 9–18.
[3] In occasionem.
[4] Sibi, "themselves," i.e., mutually. See 1 Cor. vii. 32–35.
[5] Matt. v. 28. See *de Idol.*, cc. ii. xxiii.; *de Pœn.*, c. iii.; *de Cult. Fem.*, l. ii. c. ii. ; *de Pa.*, c. vi.

[6] But compare, or rather contrast, herewith, *ad Ux.*, l. i. cc. ii. iii.
[7] Comp. *ad Ux.*, l. i. c. viii.; c. i. above; and *de Virg. Vel.*, c. x.
[8] Comp. *ad Ux.*, l. i. c. v. *ad fin.*

nity — albeit not earnestly desired, yet favourable — of not having any one to whom to pay a debt, and by whom to be (yourself) repaid ! You have ceased to be a debtor. Happy man ! You have released [1] your debtor ; sustain the loss. What if you come to feel that what we have called a loss is a gain? For continence will be a mean whereby you will traffic in [2] a mighty substance of sanctity : by parsimony of the flesh you will gain the Spirit. For let us ponder over our conscience itself, (to see) how different a man feels himself when he chances to be deprived of his wife. He savours spiritually. If he is making prayer to the Lord, he is near heaven. If he is bending over the Scriptures, he is "wholly in them." [3] If he is singing a psalm, he satisfies himself.[4] If he is adjuring a demon, he is confident in himself. Accordingly, the apostle added (the recommendation of) a temporary abstinence for the sake of adding an efficacy to prayers,[5] that we might know that what is profitable "for a time" should be always practised by us, that it may be always profitable. Daily, every moment, prayer is necessary to men ; of course continence (is so) too, since prayer is necessary. Prayer proceeds from conscience. If the conscience blush, prayer blushes. It is the spirit which conducts prayer to God. If the spirit be self-accused of a blushing [6] conscience, how will it have the hardihood to conduct prayer to the altar ; seeing that, if prayer blush, the holy minister (of prayer) itself is suffused too? For there is a prophetic utterance of the Old Testament : "Holy shall ye be, because God is holy ;" [7] and again : "With the holy thou shalt be sanctified ; and with the innocent man thou shalt be innocent ; and with the elect, elect." [8] For it is our duty so to walk in the Lord's discipline as is "worthy," [9] not according to the filthy concupiscences of the flesh. For so, too, does the apostle say, that "to savour according to the flesh is death, but to savour according to the spirit is life eternal in Jesus Christ our Lord." [10] Again, through the holy prophetess Prisca [11] the Gospel is thus preached : that "the holy minister knows how to minister sanctity." "For purity," says she, "is harmonious, and they see visions ; and, turning their face downward, they even hear manifest voices, as salutary as they are withal secret." If this dulling (of the spiritual faculties), even when the carnal nature is allowed room for exercise in first marriage,

averts the Holy Spirit ; how much more when it is brought into play in second marriage !

CHAP. XI. — THE MORE THE WIVES, THE GREATER THE DISTRACTION OF THE SPIRIT.

For (in that case) the shame is double ; inasmuch as, in second marriage, two wives beset the same husband — one in spirit, one in flesh. For the first wife you cannot hate, for whom you retain an even more religious affection, as being already received into the Lord's presence ; for whose spirit you make request ; for whom you render annual oblations. Will you stand, then, before the Lord with as many wives as you commemorate in prayer ; and will you offer for two ; and will you commend those two (to God) by the ministry of a priest ordained (to his sacred office) on the score of monogamy, or else consecrated (thereto) on the score even of virginity, surrounded by widows married but to one husband? And will your sacrifice ascend with unabashed front, and — among all the other (graces) of a good mind — will you request for yourself and for your wife chastity ?

CHAP. XII. — EXCUSES COMMONLY URGED IN DEFENCE OF SECOND MARRIAGE. THEIR FUTILITY, ESPECIALLY IN THE CASE OF CHRISTIANS, POINTED OUT.

I am aware of the excuses by which we colour our insatiable carnal appetite.[12] Our pretexts are : the necessities of props to lean on ; a house to be managed ; a family to be governed ; chests [13] and keys to be guarded ; the wool-spinning to be dispensed ; food to be attended to ; cares to be generally lessened. Of course the houses of none but married men fare well ! The families of celibates, the estates of eunuchs, the fortunes of military men, or of such as travel without wives, have gone to rack and ruin ! For are not we, too, soldiers? Soldiers, indeed, subject to all the stricter discipline, that we are subject to so great a General? [14] Are not we, too, travellers in this world? [15] Why moreover, Christian, are you so conditioned, that you cannot (so travel) without a wife? "In my present (widowed) state, too, a consort in domestic works is necessary." (Then) take some spiritual wife. Take to yourself from among the widows one fair in faith, dowered with poverty, sealed with age. You will (thus) make a good marriage. A plurality of *such* wives is pleasing to God. "But Christians concern themselves about posterity " — to whom there is no to-morrow ! [16] Shall the servant of God yearn after heirs, who has disinherited himself from the

---

[1] *Dimisisti,* al. *amisisti* = "you have lost."
[2] Or, "amass" — negotiaberis. See Luke xix. 15.
[3] Comp. 1 Tim. iv. 15.
[4] Placet sibi.
[5] See 1 Cor. vii. 5.
[6] i.e., guilty.
[7] See Lev. xi. 44, 45, xix. 2, xx. 7, LXX. and Vulg.
[8] See Ps. xviii. 25, 26, esp. in Vulg. and LXX., where it is xvii. 26, 27.
[9] See Eph. iv. 1; Col. i. 10; 1 Thess. ii. 12.
[10] See Rom. viii. 5, 6, esp. in Vulg.
[11] A Marcionite prophetess, also called Priscilla.

[12] Comp. herewith, *ad Ux.*, l. i. c. iv.
[13] Or "purses."
[14] Comp. 2 Tim. ii. 3, 4; Heb. ii. 10.
[15] Or "age" — sæculo. Comp. Ps. xxxix. 12 (in LXX. xxxviii. 13, as in Vulg.) and Heb. xi. 13.
[16] Comp. Matt vi. 34; Jas. iv. 13-15.

world? And is it to be a reason for a man to repeat marriage, if from his first (marriage) he have no children? And shall he thus have, as the first benefit (resulting therefrom), this, that he should desire longer life, when the apostle himself is in haste to be "with the Lord?"[1] Assuredly, most free will he be from encumbrance in persecutions, most constant in martyrdoms, most prompt in distributions of his goods, most temperate in acquisitions; lastly, undistracted by cares will he die, when he has left children behind him — perhaps to perform the last rites over his grave! Is it then, perchance, in forecast for the commonwealth that such (marriages) are contracted? for fear the states fail, if no rising generations be trained up? for fear the rights of law, for fear the branches of commerce, sink quite into decay? for fear the temples be quite forsaken? for fear there be none to raise the acclaim, "The lion for the Christians?" — for these are the acclaims which they desire to hear who go in quest of offspring! Let the well-known burdensomeness of children — especially in *our* case — suffice to counsel widowhood: (children) whom men are compelled by laws to undertake (the charge of); because no wise man would ever willingly have desired sons! What, then, will you do if you succeed in filling your new wife with your own conscientious scruples? Are you to dissolve the conception by aid of drugs? I think to *us* it is no more lawful to hurt (a child) in process of birth, than one (already) born. But perhaps at that time of your wife's pregnancy you will have the hardihood to beg from God a remedy for so grave a solicitude, which, when it lay in your own power, you refused? Some (naturally) barren woman, I suppose, or (some woman) of an age already feeling the chill of years, will be the object of your forecasting search. A course prudent enough, and, above all, worthy of a believer! For there is no woman whom we have believed to have borne (a child) when barren or old, when God so willed! which he is all the more likely to do if any one, by the presumption of this foresight of his own, provoke emulation on the part of God. In fine, we know a case among our brethren, in which one of them took a barren woman in second marriage for his daughter's sake, and became as well for the second time a father as for the second time a husband.

CHAP. XIII. — EXAMPLES FROM AMONG THE HEATHEN, AS WELL AS FROM THE CHURCH, TO ENFORCE THE FOREGOING EXHORTATION.

To this my exhortation, best beloved brother, there are added even heathenish examples;

which have often been set by ourselves as well (as by others) in evidence, when anything good and pleasing to God is, even among "strangers," recognised and honoured with a testimony. In short, monogamy among the heathen is so held in highest honour, that even virgins, when legitimately marrying, have a woman never married but once appointed them as brideswoman; and if *you say that* "this is for the sake of the omen," of course it is for the sake of a *good* omen; again, that in some solemnities and official functions, single-husbandhood takes the precedence: at all events, the wife of a Flamen must be but once married, which is the law of the Flamen (himself) too. For the fact that the chief pontiff himself must not iterate marriage is, of course, a glory to monogamy. When, however, Satan affects God's sacraments, it is a challenge to us; nay, rather, a cause for blushing, if we are slow to exhibit to God a continence which some render to the devil, by perpetuity sometimes of virginity, sometimes of widowhood. We have heard of Vesta's virgins, and Juno's at the town[2] of Achaia, and Apollo's among the Delphians, and Minerva's and Diana's in some places. We have heard, too, of continent *men*, and (among others) the priests of the famous Egyptian bull: women, moreover, (dedicated) to the African Ceres, in whose honour they even spontaneously abdicate matrimony, and so live to old age, shunning thenceforward all contact with males, even so much as the kisses of their sons. The devil, forsooth, has discovered, after voluptuousness, even a chastity which shall work perdition; that the guilt may be all the deeper of the Christian who refuses the chastity which helps to salvation! A testimony to us shall be, too, some of heathendom's women, who have won renown for their obstinate persistence in single-husbandhood: some Dido,[3] (for instance), who, refugee as she was on alien soil, when she ought rather to have desired, without any external solicitation, marriage with a king, did yet, for fear of experiencing a second union, prefer, contrariwise, to "burn" rather than to "marry;" or the famous Lucretia, who, albeit it was but once, by force, and against her will, that she had suffered a strange man, washed her stained flesh in her own blood, lest she should live, when no longer single-husbanded in her own esteem! A little more care will furnish you with more examples from our own (sisters); and *those* indeed, superior to the others, inasmuch as it is a greater thing to live in chastity than to die for it. Easier it is to lay down your life because you have lost a blessing, than to

---

[1] Comp. Phil. i. 23.

[2] Ægium (Jos. Scaliger, in Oehler).
[3] But Tertullian overlooks the fact that both Ovid and Virgil represent her as more than willing to marry Æneas. [Why should he note the fables of poets? This testimony of a Carthaginian is historic evidence of the fact.]

keep by living that for which you would rather die outright. How many men, therefore, and how many women, in Ecclesiastical Orders, owe their position to continence, who have preferred to be wedded to God; who have restored the honour of their flesh, and who have already dedicated themselves as sons of that (future) age, by slaying in themselves the concupiscence of lust, and that whole (propensity) which could not be admitted within Paradise! [1] Whence it is presumable that such as shall wish to be received within Paradise, ought at last to begin to cease from that thing from which Paradise is intact.

[1] Comp. Matt. xxii. 29, 30; Mark xii. 24, 25; Luke xx. 34-36.

ELUCIDATION.

(Albeit they be laics, p. 54.)

IN the tract on *Baptism* [1] Tertullian uses language implying that three persons compose a Church. But here we find it much more strongly pronounced,—*Ubi tres, Ecclesia est, licet Laici.* The question of lay-baptism we may leave till we come to Cyprian, only noting here, that, while Cyprian abjures his "master" on this point, his adversary, the Bishop of Rome, adopts Tertullian's principle in so far. But, in view of Matt. xviii. 20, surely we may all allow that three are a *quorum* when so "gathered together in Christ's name," albeit not for all purposes. Three women may claim the Saviour's promise when lawfully met together for social devotions, nor can it be denied that they have a share in the priesthood of the "peculiar people." So, too, even of three pious children. But it does not follow that they are a church *for all purposes*, — preaching, celebrating sacraments, ordaining, and the like. The late Dean Stanley was fond of this passage of Tertullian, but obviously it might be abused to encourage a state of things which all orderly and organized systems of religion must necessarily discard. [2] On p. 58 there is a reference, apparently, to *deaconesses* as "women in Ecclesiastical Orders."

[1] Chap. vi. vol. iii. p. 672, this series.   [2] Hooker, *Eccl. Polity*, b. iii. cap. i. 14.

VI.

ON MONOGAMY.[1]

[TRANSLATED BY THE REV. S. THELWALL.]

CHAP. I. — DIFFERENT VIEWS IN REGARD TO MARRIAGE HELD BY HERETICS, PSYCHICS, AND SPIRITUALISTS.

HERETICS do away with marriages; Psychics accumulate them. The former marry not *even* once; the latter not *only* once. What dost thou, Law of the Creator? Between alien eunuchs and thine own grooms, thou complainest as much of the over-obedience of thine own household as of the contempt of strangers. They who abuse thee, do thee equal hurt with them who use thee not. In fact, neither is such continence laudable because it is heretical, nor such licence defensible because it is psychical. The former is blasphemous, the latter wanton; the former destroys the God of marriages, the latter puts Him to the blush. Among *us*, however, whom the recognition of spiritual gifts entitles to be deservedly called Spiritual, continence is as religious as licence is modest; since both the one and the other are in harmony with the Creator. Continence honours the law of marriage, licence tempers it; the former is not forced, the latter is regulated; the former recognises the power of free choice, the latter recognises a limit. We admit one marriage, just as we do one God. The law of marriage reaps an accession of honour where it is associated with shamefastness. But to the Psychics, since they receive not the Spirit, the things which are the Spirit's are not pleasing. Thus, so long as the things which are the Spirit's please them not, the things which are of the flesh will please, as being the contraries of the Spirit. "The flesh," saith (the apostle), "lusteth against the Spirit, and the Spirit against the flesh."[2] But what will the flesh "lust" after, except what is more *of* the flesh? For which reason withal, in the beginning, it became estranged from the Spirit. "My Spirit," saith (God), "shall not permanently abide in these men eternally,[3] for that they are flesh."[4]

CHAP. II. — THE SPIRITUALISTS VINDICATED FROM THE CHARGE OF NOVELTY.

And so they upbraid the discipline of monogamy with being a heresy; nor is there any other cause whence they find themselves compelled to deny the Paraclete more than the fact that they esteem Him to be the institutor of a novel discipline, and a discipline which they find most harsh: so that this is already the first ground on which we must join issue in a general handling (of the subject), whether there is room for maintaining that the Paraclete has taught any such thing as can either be charged with novelty, in opposition to catholic tradition,[5] or with burdensomeness, in opposition to the "light burden"[6] of the Lord.

Now concerning each point the Lord Himself has pronounced. For in saying, "I still have many things to say unto you, but ye are not yet able to bear them: when the Holy Spirit shall be come, He will lead you into all truth,"[7] He sufficiently, of course, sets before us that He will bring such (teachings) as may be esteemed alike *novel*, as having never before been published, and finally *burdensome*, as if that were the reason why they were not published. "It follows," you say, "that by this line of argument, anything you please which is novel and burdensome may be ascribed to the Paraclete, even if it have come from the adversary spirit." No, of course. For the adversary spirit would be apparent from the diversity of his preaching, beginning by adulter-

---

ating the rule of faith, and so (going on to) adulterating the order of discipline ; because the corruption of that which holds the first grade, (that is, of faith, which is prior to discipline,) comes first. A man must of necessity hold heretical views of God first, and then of His institution. But the Paraclete, having many things to teach fully which the Lord deferred till He came, (according to the pre-definition,) will begin by bearing emphatic witness to Christ, (as being) such as we believe (Him to be), together with the whole order of God the Creator, and will glorify Him,[1] and will "bring to remembrance" concerning Him. And when He has thus been recognised (as the promised Comforter), on the ground of the cardinal rule, He will reveal those "many things" which appertain to disciplines ; while the integrity of His preaching commands credit for these (revelations), albeit they be "novel," inasmuch as they are now in course of revelation, albeit they be "burdensome," inasmuch as not even *now* are they found bearable : (revelations), however, of none other Christ than (the One) who said that He had withal "other many things" which were to be fully taught by the Paraclete, no less burdensome to men of our own day than to them, by whom they were then "not yet able to be borne."

CHAP. III. — THE QUESTION OF NOVELTY FURTHER CONSIDERED IN CONNECTION WITH THE WORDS OF THE LORD AND HIS APOSTLES.

But (as for the question) whether monogamy be "burdensome," let the still shameless "infirmity of the flesh" look to that : let us meantime come to an agreement as to whether it be "novel." This (even) broader assertion we make : that even if the Paraclete had in this our day definitely prescribed a virginity or continence total and absolute, so as not to permit the heat of the flesh to foam itself down even in single marriage, even thus He would seem to be introducing nothing of "novelty ;" seeing that the Lord Himself opens "the kingdoms of the heavens" to "eunuchs,"[2] as being Himself, withal, a virgin ; to whom looking, the apostle also — himself too for this reason abstinent — gives the preference to continence.[3] ("Yes"), you say, "but saving the law of marriage." Saving it, plainly, and we will see under what limitations ; nevertheless already destroying it, in so far as he gives the preference to continence. "Good," he says, "(it is) for a man not to have contact with a woman." It follows that it is evil to have contact with her ; for nothing is contrary to good except evil. And accordingly (he says), "It

remains, that both they who have wives so be as if they have not,"[4] that it may be the more binding on them who have not to abstain from having them. He renders reasons, likewise, for so advising : that the unmarried think about God, but the married about how, in (their) marriage, each may please his (partner).[5] And I may contend, that what is *permitted* is not absolutely good.[6] For what is absolutely good is not *permitted*, but needs no asking to make it lawful. Permission has its cause sometimes even in *necessity*. Finally, in this case, there is no *volition* on the part of him who permits marriage. For his *volition* points another way. "I *will*," he says, "that you all so be as I too (am)."[7] And when he shows that (so to abide) is "better," what, pray, does he demonstrate himself to "will," but what he has premised is "better?" And thus, if he *permits* something other than whât he has "willed" — permitted not voluntarily, but of necessity — he shows that what he has unwillingly granted as an indulgence is not absolutely good. Finally, when he says, "Better it is to marry than to burn," what sort of good must that be understood to be which is better than a penalty? which cannot seem "better" except when compared to a thing very bad? "Good" is that which keeps this name *per se* ; without comparison — I say not with an evil, but even — with some other good : so that, even if it be compared to and overshadowed by another good, it nevertheless remains in (possession of) the name of good. If, on the other hand, comparison with evil is the mean which obliges it to be called good ; it is not so much "good" as a species of inferior evil, which, when obscured by a higher evil, is driven to the name of good. Take away, in short, the condition, so as not to say, "Better it is to marry than to burn ;" and I question whether you will have the hardihood to say, "Better (it is) to marry," not adding *than what* it is better. This done, then, it becomes *not* "better ;" and while not "better," not "good" either, the condition being taken away which, while making it "better" than another thing, in that sense obliges it to be considered "good." Better it is to lose one eye than two. If, however, you withdraw from the comparison of either evil, it will not be better to have one eye, because it is not even good. What, now, if he accommodatingly grants all indulgence to marry on the ground of his own (that is, of human) sense, out of the necessity which we have mentioned, inasmuch as "better it is to marry than to burn?" In fact, when he

---

[1] See John xvi. 14.
[2] See Matt. xix. 12. Comp. *de. Pa.*, c. xiii.; *de. Cult. Fem.*, l. ii. c. ix.
[3] See 1 Cor. vii. 1, 7, 37, 40; and comp. *de Ex. Cast.*, c. iv.

[4] 1 Cor. vii. 29.
[5] 1 Cor. vii. 32–34.
[6] Comp. *ad Ux.*, l. i. c. iii.; *de Cult. Fem.*, l. ii. c. x. *sub fin.*; and *de Ex. Cast.*, c. iii , which agrees nearly verbatim with what follows.
[7] 1 Cor. vii. 7, only the Greek is θέλω, not βούλομαι.

turns to the second case, by saying, "But to the married I officially announce — not I, but the Lord" — he shows that those things which he had said above had not been (the dictates) of the Lord's authority, but of human judgment. When, however, he turns their minds back to continence, ("But I will you all so to be,") "I think, moreover," he says, "I too have the Spirit of God;" in order that, if he had granted any indulgence out of necessity, that, by the Holy Spirit's authority, he might recall. But John, too, when advising us that "we ought so to walk as the Lord withal did," [1] of course admonished us to walk as well in accordance with sanctity of the flesh (as in accordance with His example in other respects). Accordingly he says more manifestly: "And every (man) who hath this hope in Him maketh himself chaste, just as Himself withal is chaste." [2] For elsewhere, again, (we read): "Be ye holy, just as He withal was holy" [3] — in the flesh, namely. For of the Spirit he would not have said (that), inasmuch as the Spirit is without any external influence recognised as "holy;" nor does He wait to be admonished to sanctity, which is His proper nature. But the flesh *is taught* sanctity; and that withal, in Christ, was holy.

Therefore, if all these (considerations) obliterate the licence of marrying, whether we look into the condition on which the licence is granted, or the preference of continence which is imposed, why, after the apostles, could not the same Spirit, supervening for the purpose of conducting disciplehood [4] into "all truth" through the gradations of the times (according to what the preacher says, "A time to everything" [5]), impose by this time a final bridle upon the flesh, no longer obliquely calling us away from marriage, but openly; since now more (than ever) "the time is become wound up," [6] — about 160 years having elapsed since then? Would you not spontaneously ponder (thus) in your own mind: "This discipline is old, shown beforehand, even at that early date, in the Lord's flesh and will, (and) successively thereafter in both the counsels and the examples of His apostles? Of old we were destined to this sanctity. Nothing of novelty is the Paraclete introducing. What He premonished, He is (now) definitively appointing; what He deferred, He is (now) exacting." And presently, by revolving these thoughts, you will easily persuade yourself that it was much more competent to the Paraclete to preach unity of marriage, who could withal have preached its annulling; and that it is more

credible that He should have tempered what it would have become Him even to have abolished, if you understand what Christ's "will" is. Herein also you ought to recognise the Paraclete in His character of Comforter, in that He excuses your infirmity [7] from (the stringency of) an absolute continence.

CHAP. IV. — WAIVING ALLUSION TO THE PARACLETE, TERTULLIAN COMES TO THE CONSIDERATION OF THE ANCIENT SCRIPTURES, AND THEIR TESTIMONY ON THE SUBJECT IN HAND.

Waiving, now, the mention of the Paraclete, as of some authority of our own, evolve we the common instruments of the primitive Scriptures. This very thing is demonstrable by us: that the rule of monogamy is neither novel nor strange, nay rather, is both ancient, and proper to Christians; so that you may be sensible that the Paraclete is rather its *re*stitutor than *in*stitutor. As for what pertains to antiquity, what more ancient formal type can be brought forward, than the very original fount of the human race? One female did God fashion for the male, culling one rib of his, and (of course) (one) out of a plurality. But, moreover, in the introductory speech which preceded the work itself, He said, "It is not good for the man that he be alone; let us make an help-meet for him." For He would have said "helpers" if He had destined him to have more wives (than one). He added, too, a law concerning the future; if, that is, (the words) "And two shall be (made) into one flesh" — not three, nor more; else they would be no more "two" if (there were) more — were prophetically uttered. The law stood (firm). In short, the unity of marriage lasted to the very end in the case of the authors of our race; not because there were no other women, but because the reason *why* there were none was that the first-fruits of the race might not be contaminated by a double marriage. Otherwise, had God (so) willed, there *could* withal have been (others); at all events, he might have taken from the abundance of his own daughters — having no less an Eve (taken) out of his own bones and flesh — if piety had allowed it to be done. But where the first crime (is found) — homicide, inaugurated in fratricide — no crime was so worthy of the second place as a double marriage. For it makes no difference whether a man have had two wives singly, or whether individuals (taken) at the same time have made two. The number of (the individuals) conjoined and separate is the same. Still, God's institution, after once for all suffering violence through Lamech, remained firm to the very end of that race. Second Lamech there arose none, in the

---

[1] I John ii. 6.
[2] I John iii. 3.
[3] There is no such passage in any Epistle of St. John. There is one similar in 1 Pet. i. 15.
[4] Disciplinam.
[5] Eccles. iii. I.
[6] I Cor. vii. 29.

[7] Comp. Rom. viii. 26.

way of being husband to two wives. What Scripture does not note, it denies. Other iniquities provoke the deluge : (iniquities) once for all avenged, whatever was their nature ; not, however, "seventy-seven times," [1] which (is the vengeance which) double marriages have deserved.

But again : the re-formation of the second human race is traced from monogamy as its mother. Once more, "two (joined) into one flesh" undertake (the duty of) "growing and multiplying," — Noah, (namely), and his wife, and their sons, in single marriage. [2] Even in the very animals monogamy is recognised, for fear that even beasts should be born of adultery. "Out of all beasts," said (God), [3] "out of all flesh, two shalt thou lead into the ark, that they may live with thee, male and female : they shall be (taken) from all flying animals according to (their) kind, and from all creepers of the earth according to their kind ; two out of all shall enter unto thee, male and female." In the same formula, too, He orders sets of sevens, made up of pairs, to be gathered to him, consisting of male and female — one male and one female. [4] What more shall I say ? Even unclean birds were not allowed to enter with two females each.

CHAP. V. — CONNECTION OF THESE PRIMEVAL TESTIMONIES WITH CHRIST.

Thus far for the testimony of things primordial, and the sanction of our origin, and the pre-judgment of the divine institution, which of course is a law, not (merely) a memorial ; inasmuch as, if it was "so done from the beginning," we find ourselves directed to the beginning by Christ : just as, in the question of divorce, by saying that that had been permitted by Moses on account of their hard-heartedness, but from the beginning it had not been so, He doubtless recalls to "the beginning" the (law of) the individuity of marriage. And accordingly, those whom God "from the beginning" conjoined, "two into one flesh," man shall not at the present day separate. [5] The apostle, too, writing to the Ephesians, says that God "had proposed in Himself, at the dispensation of the fulfilment of the times, to recall to the head" (that is, to the beginning) "things universal in Christ, which are above the heavens and above the earth in Him." [6] So, too, the two letters of Greece, the first and the last, the Lord assumes to Himself, as figures of the beginning and end which concur in Himself : so that, just as Alpha rolls on till it reaches Omega, and again Omega rolls back till it reaches Alpha, in the same way He might show that in Himself is both the downward course of the beginning on to the end, and the backward course of the end up to the beginning ; so that every economy, ending in Him through whom it began, — through the Word of God, that is, who was made flesh, [7] — may have an end correspondent to its beginning. And so truly in Christ are all things recalled to "the beginning," that even faith returns from circumcision to the integrity of that (original) flesh, as "it was from the beginning ;" and freedom of meats and abstinence from blood alone, as "it was from the beginning ;" and the individuality of marriage, as "it was from the beginning ;" and the restriction of divorce, which *was not* "from the beginning ;" and lastly, the whole man into Paradise, where he was "from the beginning." Why, then, ought He not to restore Adam thither at least as a monogamist, who cannot present him in so entire perfection as he was when dismissed thence ? Accordingly, so far as pertains to the restitution of the beginning, the logic both of the dispensation you live under, and of your hope, exact this from you, that what was "from the beginning" (should be) in accordance with "the beginning ;" which (beginning) you find counted in Adam, and recounted in Noah. Make your election, in which of the twain you account your "beginning." In both, the censorial power of monogamy claims you for itself. But again : if the beginning passes on to the end (as Alpha to Omega), as the end passes back to the beginning (as Omega to Alpha), and thus our origin is transferred to Christ, the animal to the spiritual — inasmuch as "(that was) not first which is spiritual, but (that) which (is) animal ; then what (is) spiritual," [8] — let us, in like manner (as before), see whether you owe this very (same) thing to this second origin also : whether the last Adam also meet you in the selfsame form as the first ; since the last Adam (that is, Christ) was entirely unwedded, as was even the first Adam before his exile. But, presenting to your weakness the gift of the example of His own flesh, the more perfect Adam — that is, Christ, more perfect on this account as well (as on others), that He was more entirely pure — stands before you, if you are willing (to copy Him), as a voluntary celibate in the flesh. If, however, you are unequal (to that perfection), He stands before you a monogamist in spirit, having one Church as His spouse, according to the figure of Adam and of Eve, which (figure) the apostle interprets of that great sacrament of Christ and the Church, (teaching that), through the spiritual, it was analogous to the carnal

---

[1] Septuagies septies. See Gen. iv. 19-24.
[2] Comp. Gen. vii. 7 with 1 Pet. iii. 20 *ad fin.*
[3] Comp. Gen. vi. 19, 20.
[4] See Gen. vii. 3.
[5] See Matt. xix. 6.
[6] Eph. i. 9, 10. The Latin of Tertullian deserves careful comparison with the original Greek of St. Paul.

[7] See John i. 1-14.
[8] 1 Cor. xv. 46.

monogamy. You see, therefore, after what manner, renewing your origin even in Christ, you cannot trace down that (origin) without the profession of monogamy; unless, (that is), you be in flesh what He is in spirit; albeit withal, what He was in flesh, you equally ought to have been.

CHAP. VI. — THE CASE OF ABRAHAM, AND ITS BEARING ON THE PRESENT QUESTION.

But let us proceed with our inquiry into some eminent chief fathers of our origin : for there are some to whom our monogamist parents Adam and Noah are not pleasing, nor perhaps Christ either. To Abraham, in fine, they appeal ; prohibited though they are to acknowledge any other father than God.[1] Grant, now, that Abraham is our father ; grant, too, that Paul is. "In the Gospel," says he, "I have begotten you."[2] Show yourself a son even of Abraham. For your origin in him, you must know, is not referable to every period of his life : there is a definite time at which he is your father. For if "faith" is the source whence we are reckoned to Abraham as his "sons" (as the apostle teaches, saying to the Galatians, "You know, consequently, that (they) who are of faith, these are sons of Abraham"[3]), *when* did Abraham "believe God, and it was accounted to him for righteousness?" I suppose when still in monogamy, since (he was) not yet in circumcision. But if afterwards he changed to either (opposite) — to digamy through cohabitation with his handmaid, and to circumcision through the seal of the testament — you cannot acknowledge him as your father except at that time when he "believed God," if it is true that it is according to *faith* that you are his son, not according to *flesh*. Else, if it be the later Abraham whom you follow as your father — that is, the digamist (Abraham) — receive him withal in his circumcision. If you reject his circumcision, it follows that you will refuse his digamy too. Two characters of his, mutually diverse in two several ways, you will not be able to blend. His digamy began with circumcision, his monogamy with uncircumcision.[4] You receive digamy ; admit circumcision too. You retain uncircumcision ; you are bound to monogamy too. Moreover, so true is it that it is of the monogamist Abraham that you are the son, just as of the uncircumcised, that if you be circumcised you immediately cease to be his son, inasmuch as you will not be "of faith," but of the *seal* of a faith which had been justified in uncircumcision. You have the apostle : learn (of him), together with the Galatians.[5] In like

manner, too, if you have involved yourself in digamy, you are not the son of that Abraham whose "faith" preceded in monogamy. For albeit it is subsequently that he is called "a father of many nations,"[6] still it is of *those* (nations) who, as the fruit of the "faith" which precedes digamy, had to be accounted "sons of Abraham."[7]

Thenceforward let matters see to themselves. Figures are one thing ; laws another. Images are one thing ; statutes another. Images pass away when fulfilled : statutes remain permanently to be fulfilled. Images prophesy : statutes govern. What that digamy of Abraham portends, the same apostle fully teaches,[8] the interpreter of each testament, just as he likewise lays it down that our "seed" is called in Isaac.[9] If you are "of the free woman," and belong to Isaac, he, at all events, maintained unity of marriage to the last.

These accordingly, I suppose, are they in whom my origin is counted. All others I ignore. And if I glance around at their examples — (examples) of some David heaping up marriages for himself even through sanguinary means, of some Solomon rich in wives as well as in other riches — you are bidden to "follow the better things;"[10] and you have withal Joseph but once wedded, and on this score I venture to say better than his father; you have Moses, the intimate eyewitness of God;[11] you have Aaron the chief priest. The second Moses, also, of the second People, who led our representatives into the (possession of) the promise of God, in whom the Name (of JESUS) was first inaugurated, was no digamist.

CHAP. VII. — FROM PATRIARCHAL, TERTULLIAN COMES TO LEGAL, PRECEDENTS.

After the ancient examples of the patriarchs, let us equally pass on to the ancient documents of the legal Scriptures, that we may treat in order of all our canon. And since there are some who sometimes assert that they have nothing to do with the law (which Christ has not dissolved, but fulfilled),[12] sometimes catch at such parts of the law as they choose ; plainly do we too assert that the law has deceased in this sense, that its burdens — according to the sentence of the apostles — which not even the fathers were able to sustain,[13] have wholly ceased : such (parts), however, as relate to righteousness not only permanently remain reserved, but

---

1 See Matt. xxiii. 9.
2 1 Cor. iv. 15, where it is διὰ τοῦ εὐαγγελίου.
3 Gal. iii. 7.
4 This is an error. Comp. Gen. xvi. with Gen. xvii.
5 See Gal. iii. iv. and comp. Rom. iv.
6 See Gen. xvii. 5.
7 See Rom. iv. 11, 12, Gal. iii. 7; and comp. Matt. iii. 9, John viii. 39.
8 See Gal. iv. 21–31.
9 See vers. 28, 31.
10 See Ps. xxxvii. 27 (in LXX. xxxvi. 27); 1 Pet. iii. 11; 3 John 11.
11 Dei de proximo arbitrum. See Num. xii. 6–8; Deut. xxxiv. 10.
12 See Matt. v. 17.
13 See Acts xv. 10.

even amplified ; in order, to be sure, that our righteousness may be able to redound above the righteousness of the scribes and of the Pharisees.[1] If "righteousness" must, of course chastity must too. If, then, forasmuch as there is in the law a precept that a man is to take in marriage the wife of his brother if he have died without children,[2] for the purpose of raising up seed to his brother ; and this may happen repeatedly to the same person, according to that crafty question of the Sadducees ;[3] men for that reason think that frequency of marriage is permitted in other cases as well : it will be their duty to understand first the reason of the precept itself ; and thus they will come to know that that reason, now ceasing, is among those parts of the law which have been cancelled. Necessary it was that there should be a succession to the marriage of a brother if he died childless : first, because that ancient benediction, "Grow and multiply,"[4] had still to run its course ; secondly, because the sins of the fathers used to be exacted even from the sons ;[5] thirdly, because eunuchs and barren persons used to be regarded as ignominious. And thus, for fear that such as had died childless, not from natural inability, but from being prematurely overtaken by death, should be judged equally accursed (with the other class) ; for this reason a vicarious and (so to say) posthumous offspring used to be supplied them. But (now), when the "extremity of the times" has cancelled (the command) "Grow and multiply," since the apostle superinduces (another command), "It remaineth, that both they who have wives so be as if they have not," because "the time is compressed ;[6] and "the sour grape" chewed by "the fathers" has ceased "to set the sons' teeth on edge,"[7] for, "each one shall die in his own sin ; " and "eunuchs" not only have lost ignominy, but have even deserved grace, being invited into "the kingdoms of the heavens : "[8] the law of succeeding to the wife of a brother being buried, its contrary has obtained — that of *not* succeeding to the wife of a brother. And thus, as we have said before, what has ceased to be valid, on the cessation of its reason, cannot furnish a ground of argument to another. Therefore a wife, when her husband is dead, will not marry ; for if she marry, she will of course be marrying (his) brother : for "all we are brethren."[9] Again, the woman, if intending to marry,

has to marry "in the Lord ; "[10] that is, not to an heathen, but to a brother, inasmuch as even the ancient law forbids[11] marriage with members of another tribe. Since, moreover, even in Leviticus there is a caution, "Whoever shall have taken (his) brother's wife, (it) is uncleanness — turpitude ; without children shall (he) die ; "[12] beyond doubt, while the man is prohibited from marrying a second time, the woman is prohibited too, having no one to marry except a brother. In what way, then, an agreement shall be established between the apostle and the Law (which he is not impugning in its entirety), shall be shown when we shall have come to his own epistle. Meantime, so far as pertains to the law, the lines of argument drawn from it are more suitable for us (than for our opponents). In short, the same (law) prohibits priests from marrying a second time. The daughter also of a priest it bids, if widowed or repudiated, if she have had no seed, to return into her father's home and be nourished from his bread.[13] The reason why (it is said), "If she have had no seed," is not that if she have she may marry again — for how much more will she abstain from marrying if she have sons? — but that, if she have, she may be "nourished" by her son rather than by her father ; in order that the son, too, may carry out the precept of God, "Honour father and mother."[14] Us, moreover, Jesus, the Father's Highest and Great Priest,[15] clothing us from His own store[16] — inasmuch as they "who are baptized in Christ[17] have put on Christ " — has made "priests to God His Father,"[18] according to John. For the reason why He recalls that young man who was hastening to his father's obsequies,[19] is that He may show that we are called priests by Him ; (priests) whom the Law used to forbid to be present at the sepulture of parents :[20] "Over every dead soul," it says, "the priest shall not enter, and over his own father and over his own mother he shall not be contaminated." "Does it follow that we too are bound to observe *this* prohibition?" No, of course. For our one Father, God, *lives*, and our mother, the Church ; and neither are we dead who live to God, nor do we bury our dead, inasmuch as they too are living in Christ. At all

---

[1] See Matt. v. 20.
[2] Deut xxv. 5, 6.
[3] See Matt. xxii. 23-33; Mark xii. 18-27; Luke xx. 26-38. Comp. *ad Ux.*, l. i.
[4] Gen. i. 28. Comp. *de Ex. Cast.*, c. vi.
[5] See Ex. xx. 5; and therefore there must be sons begotten from whom to exact them.
[6] Comp. *de Ex. Cast.*, c. vi.
[7] See Jer. xxxi. 29, 30 (in LXX. xxxviii. 29, 30); Ezek. xviii. 1-4.
[8] Matt. xix. 12, often quoted.
[9] Matt. xxiii. 8.

[10] 1 Cor. vii. 39.
[11] "Adimit; " but the two MSS. extant of this treatise read "admittit " = admits.
[12] Lev. xx. 21, not exactly given.
[13] Lev. xxii. 13, where there is no *command* to her to return, in the Eng. ver.: in the LXX. there is.
[14] Ex. xx. 12 in brief.
[15] Summus sacerdos et magnus patris. But Oehler notices a conjecture of Jos. Scaliger, "agnus patris," when we must unite "the High Priest and Lamb of the Father."
[16] De suo. Comp. *de Bapt.*, c. xvii. *ad fin.*; *de Cult. Fem.*, l. i. c. v., l. ii. c. ix.; *de Ex. Cast.*, c. iii. *med.*; and for the ref. see Rev. iii. 18.
[17] Gal. iii. 27; where it is εἰς Χριστόν, however.
[18] See Rev. i. 6.
[19] Matt. viii. 21, 22; Luke ix. 59, 60.
[20] Lev. xxi. 11.

events, priests we are called by Christ; debtors to monogamy, in accordance with the pristine Law of God, which prophesied at that time of us in its own priests.

CHAP. VIII. — FROM THE LAW TERTULLIAN COMES TO THE GOSPEL. HE BEGINS WITH EXAMPLES BEFORE PROCEEDING TO DOGMAS.

Turning now to the law, which is properly ours — that is, to the Gospel — by what kind of examples are we met, until we come to definite dogmas? Behold, there immediately present themselves to us, on the threshold as it were, the two priestesses of Christian sanctity, Monogamy and Continence : one modest, in Zechariah the priest ; one absolute, in John the forerunner: one appeasing God ; one preaching Christ: one proclaiming a perfect priest; one exhibiting "more than a prophet," [1] — him, namely, who has not only preached or personally pointed out, but even baptized Christ. For who was more worthily to perform the initiatory rite on the body of the Lord, than flesh similar in kind to that which conceived and gave birth to that (body)? And indeed it was a virgin, about to marry once for all after her delivery, who gave birth to Christ, in order that each title of sanctity might be fulfilled in Christ's parentage, by means of a mother who was both virgin, and wife of one husband. Again, when He is presented as an infant in the temple, who is it who receives Him into his hands? who is the first to recognise Him in spirit? A man "just and circumspect," and of course no digamist, (which is plain) even (from this consideration), lest (otherwise) Christ should presently be more worthily preached by a woman, an aged widow, and "the wife of one man;" who, living devoted to the temple, was (already) giving in her own person a sufficient token what sort of persons ought to be the adherents to the spiritual temple, — that is, the Church. Such eye-witnesses the Lord in infancy found ; no different ones had He in adult age. Peter alone do I find — through (the mention of) his "mother-in-law" [2] — to have been married. Monogamist I am led to presume him by consideration of the Church, which, built upon him, [3] was destined to appoint every grade of her Order from monogamists. The rest, while I do not find them married, I must of necessity understand to have been either eunuchs or continent. Nor indeed, if, among the Greeks, in accordance with the carelessness of custom, women and wives are classed under a common name — however, there is a name proper to *wives* — shall we therefore so interpret Paul as if he demonstrates the apostles to have had wives? [4]

For if he were disputing about marriages, as he does in the sequel, where the apostle could better have named some particular example, it would appear right for him to say, "For have we not the power of leading about *wives*, like the other apostles and Cephas?" But when he subjoins those (expressions) which show his abstinence from (insisting on) the supply of maintenance, saying, "For have we not the power of eating and drinking?" he does not demonstrate that "wives" were led about by the apostles, whom even such as have not still have the power of eating and drinking ; but simply "women," who used to minister to them in the same way (as they did) when accompanying the Lord. [5] But further, if Christ reproves the scribes and Pharisees, sitting in the official chair of Moses, but not doing what they taught, [6] what kind of (supposition) is it that He Himself withal should set upon His own official chair men who were mindful rather to enjoin — (but) not likewise to practise — sanctity of the flesh, which (sanctity) He had in all ways recommended to their teaching and practising? — first by His own example, then by all other arguments ; while He tells (them) that "the kingdom of heavens" is "children's ;" [7] while He associates with these (children) others who, after marriage, remained (or became) virgins ;" [8] while He calls (them) to (copy) the simplicity of the dove, a bird not merely innocuous, but modest too, and whereof one male knows one female ; while He denies the Samaritan woman's (partner to be) a husband, that He may show that manifold husbandry is adultery ; [9] while, in the revelation of His own glory, He prefers, from among so many saints and prophets, to have with him Moses and Elias [10] — the one a monogamist, the other a voluntary celibate (for Elias was nothing else than John, who came "in the power and spirit of Elias" [11]) ; while that "man gluttonous and toping," the "frequenter of luncheons and suppers, in the company of publicans and sinners," [12] sups once for all at a single marriage, [13] though, of course, many were marrying (around Him) ; for He willed to *attend* (marriages) only so often as (He willed) them to *be*.

CHAP. IX. — FROM EXAMPLES TERTULLIAN PASSES TO DIRECT DOGMATIC TEACHINGS. HE BEGINS WITH THE LORD'S TEACHING.

But grant that these argumentations may be thought to be forced and founded on con-

---

[1] See Matt. xi. 9; Luke vii. 26.
[2] See Mark i. 29, 30.
[3] See Matt. xvi. 13-19. Comp. *de Pu.*, c. xxi.
[4] See 1 Cor. ix. 1-5.

[5] See Luke viii. 1-3; Matt. xxvii. 55, 56.
[6] Matt. xxiii. 1-3.
[7] See Matt. xviii. 1-4, xix. 13-15; Mark x. 13-15.
[8] Alios post nuptias pueros. The reference seems to be to Matt. xix. 12.
[9] See John iv. 16-18.
[10] See Matt. xvii. 1-8; Mark ix. 2-9; Luke ix. 28-36.
[11] See Luke i. 17.
[12] See Matt. xi. 19; Luke vii. 34.
[13] See John ii. 1-11.

jectures, if no dogmatic teachings have stood parallel with them which the Lord uttered in treating of divorce, which, permitted formerly, He now prohibits, first because "from the beginning it was not so," like plurality of marriage; secondly, because "What God hath conjoined, man shall not separate," [1] — for fear, namely, that he contravene the Lord: for He alone shall "separate" who has "conjoined" (separate, moreover, not through the harshness of divorce, which (harshness) He censures and restrains, but through the debt of death) if, indeed, "one of two sparrows falleth not on the ground without the Father's will." [2] Therefore, if those whom God has conjoined man shall not separate by divorce, it is equally congruous that those whom God has separated by death man is not to conjoin by marriage; the joining of the separation will be just as contrary to God's will as would have been the separation of the conjunction.

So far as regards the non-*de*struction of the will of God, and the *re*struction of the law of "the beginning." But another reason, too, conspires; nay, not another, but (one) which imposed the law of "the beginning," and moved the will of God to prohibit divorce: the fact that (he) who shall have dismissed his wife, except on the ground of adultery, makes her commit adultery; and (he) who shall have married a (woman) dismissed by her husband, of course commits adultery.[3] A divorced woman cannot even marry legitimately; and if she commit any such act without the name of marriage, does it not fall under the category of adultery, in that adultery is crime in the way of marriage? Such is God's verdict, within straiter limits than men's, that universally, whether through marriage or promiscuously, the admission of a second man (to intercourse) is pronounced adultery by Him. For let us see what marriage is in the eye of God; and thus we shall learn what adultery equally is. Marriage is (this): when God joins "two into one flesh;" or else, finding (them already) joined in the same flesh, has given His seal to the conjunction. Adultery is (this): when, the two having been — in whatsoever way — *dis*joined, other — nay, rather alien — flesh is mingled (with either): flesh concerning which it cannot be affirmed, "This is flesh out of my flesh, and this bone out of my bones." [4] For this, once for all done and pronounced, as from the beginning, so now too, cannot apply to "other" flesh. Accordingly, it will be without cause that you will say that God wills not a divorced woman to be joined to another man

"while her husband liveth," as if He do will it "when he is dead;" [5] whereas if she is not bound to him when dead, no more is she when living. "Alike when divorce dissevers marriage as when death does, she will not be bound to him by whom the binding medium has been broken off." To whom, then, will she be bound? In the eye of God, it matters nought whether she marry during her husband's life or after his death. For it is not against him that she sins, but against herself. "Any sin which a man may have committed is external to the body; but (he) who commits adultery sins against his own body." But — as we have previously laid down above — whoever shall intermingle with himself "other" flesh, over and above that pristine flesh which God either conjoined into two or else found (already) conjoined, commits adultery. And the reason why He has abolished divorce, which "was not from the beginning," is, that He may strengthen that which "was from the beginning" — the permanent conjunction, (namely), of "two into one flesh:" for fear that necessity or opportunity for a *third* union of flesh may make an irruption (into His dominion); permitting divorce to no cause but one — if, (that is), the (evil) against which precaution is taken chance to have occurred beforehand. So true, moreover, is it that divorce "was not from the beginning," that among the Romans it is not till after the six hundredth year from the building of the city that this kind of "hardheartedness" [6] is set down as having been committed. But *they* indulge in promiscuous adulteries, even without divorcing (their partners): to *us*, even if we do divorce them, even marriage will not be lawful.

CHAP. X. — ST. PAUL'S TEACHING ON THE SUBJECT.

From this point I see that we are challenged by an appeal to the apostle; for the more easy apprehension of whose meaning we must all the more earnestly inculcate (the assertion), that a woman is more bound when her husband is dead not to admit (to marriage) another husband. For let us reflect that divorce either is caused by discord, or else causes discord; whereas death is an event resulting from the law of God, not from an offence of man; and that it is a debt which all owe, even the unmarried. Therefore, if a divorced woman, who has been separated (from her husband) in soul as well as body, through discord, anger, hatred, and the causes of these — injury, or contumely, or whatsoever cause of complaint — is bound to a personal enemy, not to say a husband, how much more will one who, neither by her own nor her hus-

---

[1] See Matt. xix. 3–8, where, however, Tertullian's order is reversed. Comp. with this chapter, c. v. above.
[2] See Matt. x. 29. Comp. *de Ex. Cast.*, c. i. *ad fin.*
[3] See Matt. v. 32.
[4] Gen. ii. 23, in reversed order again.

[5] Comp. Rom. vii. 1–3.
[6] Comp. Matt. xix. 8; Mark x 5.

band's fault, but by an event resulting from the Lord's law, has been — not separated from, but left behind by — her consort, be his, even when dead, to whom, even when dead, she owes (the debt of) concord? From him from whom she has heard no (word of) divorce she does not turn away; with him she is, to whom she has written no (document of) divorce; him whom she was unwilling to have lost, she retains. She has within her the licence of the mind, which represents to a man, in imaginary enjoyment, all things which he has not. In short, I ask the woman herself, "Tell me, sister, have you sent your husband before you (to his rest) in peace?" What will she answer? (Will she say), "In discord?" In that case she is the more bound to him with whom she has a cause (to plead) at the bar of God. She who is bound (to another) has not departed (from him). But (will she say), "In peace?" In that case, she must necessarily persevere in that (peace) with him whom she will no longer have the power to divorce; not that she would, even if she had been able to divorce him, have been marriageable. Indeed, she prays for his soul, and requests refreshment for him meanwhile, and fellowship (with him) in the first resurrection; and she offers (her sacrifice) on the anniversaries of his falling asleep. For, unless she does these deeds, she has in the true sense divorced him, so far as in her lies; and indeed the more iniquitously — inasmuch as (she did it) as far as *was* in her power — because she had *no* power (to do it); and with the more indignity, inasmuch as it *is* with more indignity if (her reason for doing it is) because he did *not* deserve it. Or else shall we, pray, cease to be after death, according to (the teaching of) some Epicurus, and not according to (that of) Christ? But if we believe the resurrection of the dead, of course we shall be bound to them with whom we are destined to rise, to render an account the one of the other. "But if 'in that age they will neither marry nor be given in marriage, but will be equal to angels,'[1] is not the fact that there will be no restitution of the conjugal relation a reason why we shall *not* be bound to our departed consorts?" Nay, but the more shall we *be* bound (to them), because we are destined to a better estate — destined (as we are) to rise to a spiritual consortship, to recognise as well our own selves as them who are ours. Else how shall we sing thanks to God to eternity, if there shall remain in us no sense and memory of this debt; if we shall be *re*-formed in substance, not in consciousness? Consequently, we who shall be with God shall be together; since we shall all be with the one God — albeit the wages be various,[2]

albeit there be "many mansions" in the house of the same Father[3] — having laboured for the "one penny"[4] of the self-same hire, that is, of eternal life; in which (eternal life) God will still less separate them whom He has conjoined, than in this lesser life He forbids them to be separated.

Since this is so, how will a woman have room for another husband, who is, even to futurity, in the possession of her own? (Moreover, we speak to each sex, even if our discourse address itself but to the one; inasmuch as one discipline is incumbent [on both].) She will have one in spirit, one in flesh. This will be adultery, the conscious affection of one woman for two men. If the one has been disjoined from her flesh, but remains in her heart — in that place where even cogitation without carnal contact achieves beforehand both adultery by concupiscence, and matrimony by volition — he is to this hour her husband, possessing the very thing which is the mean whereby he became so — her mind, namely, in which withal, if another shall find a habitation, this will be a crime. Besides, excluded he is not, if he *has* withdrawn from viler carnal commerce. A more honourable husband is he, in proportion as he is become more pure.

CHAP. XI. — FURTHER REMARKS UPON ST. PAUL'S TEACHING.

Grant, now, that you marry "in the Lord," in accordance with the law and the apostle — if, notwithstanding, you care even about this — with what face do you request (the solemnizing of) a matrimony which is unlawful to those of whom you request it; of a monogamist bishop, of presbyters and deacons bound by the same solemn engagement, of widows whose Order you have in your own person refused? And they, plainly, will give husbands and wives as they would morsels of bread; for this is their rendering of "To every one who asketh thee thou shalt give!"[5] And they will join you together in a virgin church, the one betrothed of the one Christ! And you will pray for your *husbands*, the new and the old. Make your election, to which of the twain you will play the adulteress. I think, to both. But if you have any wisdom, be silent on behalf of the dead one. Let your silence be to him a divorce, already endorsed in the dotal gifts of another. In this way you will earn the new husband's favour, if you forget the old. You ought to take more pains to please him for whose sake you have not preferred to please God! Such (conduct) the Psychics will have it the apostle approved, or else totally failed to think about, when he wrote: "The woman is

---

[1] See Matt. xxii. 30; Mark xii. 25; Luke xx. 35, 36.
[2] Comp. 1 Cor. iii. 8.
[3] Comp. John xiv. 2.
[4] Matt. xx. 1-16.
[5] See Matt. v. 42; Luke vi. 30. Comp. *de Bapt.*, c. xviii.

bound for such length of time as her husband
liveth; but if he shall have died, she is free;
whom she will let her marry, only in the Lord." [1]
For it is out of this passage that they draw their
defence of the licence of second marriage; nay,
even of (marriages) to any amount, if of second
(marriage): for that which has ceased to be *once
for all*, is open to *any and every number*. But
the sense in which the apostle did write will be
apparent, if first an agreement be come to that
he did *not* write it in the sense of which the
Psychics avail themselves. Such an agreement,
moreover, will be come to if one first recall to
mind those (passages) which are diverse from
the passage in question, when tried by the standard of doctrine, of volition, and of Paul's own
discipline. For, if he permits second nuptials,
which were *not* "from the beginning," how does
he affirm that all things are being re-collected *to*
the beginning in Christ? [2] If he wills us to iterate conjugal connections, how does he maintain
that "our seed is called" in the but once married Isaac as its author? How does he make
monogamy the base of his disposition of the
whole Ecclesiastical Order, if this rule does not
antecedently hold good in the case of laics, from
whose ranks the Ecclesiastical Order proceeds? [3]
How does he call away from the enjoyment of
marriage such as are still in the married position,
saying that "the time is wound up," if he calls
back again into marriage such as through death
had escaped from marriage? If these (passages) are diverse from that one about which
the present question is, it will be agreed (as we
have said) that he did not write in that sense of
which the Psychics avail themselves; inasmuch
as it is easier (of belief) that that one passage
should have some explanation agreeable with the
others, than that an apostle should seem to have
taught (principles) mutually diverse. That explanation we shall be able to discover in the
subject-matter itself. What was the subject-
matter which led the apostle to write such
(words)? The inexperience of a new and just
rising Church, which he was rearing, to wit,
"with milk," not yet with the "solid food" [4] of
stronger doctrine; inexperience so great, that
that infancy of faith prevented them from yet
knowing what they were to do in regard of carnal and sexual necessity. The very phases themselves of this (inexperience) are intelligible from
(the apostle's) rescripts, when he says: [5] "But
concerning these (things) which ye write; good
it is for a man not to touch a woman; but, on
account of fornications, let each one have his
own wife." He shows that there were who, having been "apprehended by the faith" in (the
state of) marriage, were apprehensive that it
might not be lawful for them thenceforward to
enjoy their marriage, because they had believed
on the holy flesh of Christ. And yet it is "by
way of allowance" that he makes the concession,
"not by way of command;" that is, indulging,
not enjoining, the practice. On the other hand,
he "willed rather" that all should be what he
himself was. Similarly, too, in sending a rescript
on (the subject of) divorce, he demonstrates
that some had been thinking over that also,
chiefly because withal they did not suppose that
they were to persevere, after faith, in heathen
marriages. They sought counsel, further, "concerning virgins" — for "precept of the Lord"
there was none — (and were told) that "it is
good for a man if he so remain permanently;"
("so"), of course, as he may have been found
by the faith. "Thou hast been bound to a wife,
seek not loosing; thou hast been loosed from a
wife, seek not a wife." "But if thou shalt have
taken to (thyself) a wife, thou hast not sinned;"
because to one who, before believing, had been
"loosed from a wife," she will not be counted a
second wife who, subsequently to believing, is
the *first*: for it is from (the time of our) believing that our life itself dates its origin. But here
he says that he "is sparing them;" else "pressure of the flesh" would shortly follow, in consequence of the straits of the times, which
shunned the encumbrances of marriage: yea,
rather solicitude must be felt about earning the
Lord's favour than a husband's. And thus he
recalls his permission. So, then, in the very
same passage in which he definitely rules that
"each one ought permanently to remain in that
calling in which he shall be called;" adding,
"A woman is bound so long as her husband
liveth; but if he shall have fallen asleep, she is
free: whom she shall wish let her marry, only in
the Lord," he hence also demonstrates that such
a woman is to be understood as has withal herself been "found" (by the faith) "loosed from
a husband," similarly as the husband "loosed
from a wife" — the "loosing" having taken
place through death, of course, not through divorce; inasmuch as to the *divorced* he would
grant no permission to marry, in the teeth of the
primary precept. And so "a woman, if she shall
have married, will not sin;" because he will not
be reckoned a second husband who is, subsequently to her believing, the first, any more (than
a wife thus taken will be counted a second wife).
And so truly is this the case, that he *therefore*
adds, "only in the Lord;" because the question
in agitation was about her who had had a *heathen*
(husband), and had believed *subsequently to losing him*: for fear, to wit, that she might presume
herself able to marry a heathen even *after* believ-

---

[1] 1 Cor. vii. 39, not rendered with very strict accuracy.
[2] See c. v. above.
[3] See *de Ex. Cast.*, c. vii.
[4] Comp. 1 Cor iii. 2 with Heb. v. 11-14.
[5] 1 Cor. vii. 1, 2.

ing; albeit not even *this* is an object of care to the Psychics. Let us plainly know that, in the Greek original, it does not stand in the form which (through the either crafty or simple alteration of two syllables) has gone out into common use, "But if her husband *shall have* fallen asleep," as if it were speaking of the future, and thereby seemed to pertain to her who has lost her husband when already in a believing state. If this indeed had been so, licence let loose without limit would have granted a (fresh) husband as often as one had been lost, without any such modesty in marrying as is congruous even to heathens. But even if it had been so, as if referring to future time, "If any (woman's) husband *shall have* died," even the future would just as much pertain to her whose husband shall die before she believed. Take it which way you will, provided you do not overturn the rest. For since these (other passages) agree to the sense (given above): "Thou hast been called (as) a slave; care not:" "Thou hast been called in uncircumcision; be not circumcised:" "Thou hast been called in circumcision; become not uncircumcised:" with which concurs, "Thou hast been bound to a wife; seek not loosing: thou hast been loosed from a wife; seek not a wife,"—manifest enough it is that these passages pertain to such as, finding themselves in a new and recent "calling," were consulting (the apostle) on the subject of those (circumstantial conditions) in which they had been "apprehended" by the faith.

This will be the interpretation of that passage, to be examined as to whether it be congruous with the time and the occasion, and with the examples and arguments preceding as well as with the sentences and senses succeeding, and primarily with the individual advice and practice of the apostle himself: for nothing is so much to be guarded as (the care) that no one be found self-contradictory.

CHAP. XII. — THE EXPLANATION OF THE ABOVE PASSAGE OFFERED BY THE PSYCHICS CONSIDERED.

Listen, withal, to the very subtle argumentation on the contrary side. "So true is it," say (our opponents), "that the apostle has permitted the iteration of marriage, that it is only such as are in the Clerical Order that he has stringently bound to the yoke of monogamy. For that which he prescribes to certain (individuals) he does not prescribe to all." Does it then follow, too, that to bishops alone he does *not* prescribe what he does enjoin upon all; if what he does prescribe to bishops he does *not* enjoin upon all? or is it *therefore* to all *because* to bishops? and *therefore* to bishops *because* to all? For whence is it that the bishops and clergy come? Is it not from *all?* If *all* are not bound to monogamy,

whence are monogamists (to be taken) into the clerical rank? Will some separate order of monogamists have to be instituted, from which to make selection for the clerical body? (No); but when we are extolling and inflating ourselves in opposition to the clergy, then "we are all one:" then "we are all priests, because He hath made us priests to (His) God and Father." When we are challenged to a thorough equalization with the sacerdotal discipline, we lay down the (priestly) fillets, and (still) are on a par! The question in hand (when the apostle was writing), was with reference to Ecclesiastical Orders—what sort of men ought to be ordained. It was therefore fitting that all the form of the common discipline should be set forth on its fore-front, as an edict to be in a certain sense universally and carefully attended to, that the laity might the better know that they must themselves observe that order which was indispensable to their overseers; and that even the office of honour itself might not flatter itself in anything tending to licence, as if on the ground of privilege of position. The Holy Spirit foresaw that some would say, "All things are lawful to bishops;" just as that bishop of Utina of yours feared not even the Scantinian law. Why, how many digamists, too, preside in your churches; insulting the apostle, of course: at all events, not blushing when these passages are read under their presidency!

Come, now, you who think that an exceptional law of monogamy is made with reference to bishops, abandon withal your remaining disciplinary titles, which, together with monogamy, are ascribed to bishops.[1] Refuse to be "irreprehensible, sober, of good morals, orderly, hospitable, easy to be taught;" nay, indeed, (be) "given to wine, prompt with the hand to strike, combative, money-loving, not ruling your house, nor caring for your children's discipline,"—no, nor "courting good renown even from strangers." For if bishops have a law of their own teaching monogamy, the other (characteristics) likewise, which will be the fitting concomitants of monogamy, will have been written (exclusively) for bishops. With laics, however, to whom monogamy is not suitable, the other (characteristics) also have nothing to do. (Thus), Psychic, you have (if you please) evaded the bonds of discipline in its entirety! Be consistent in prescribing, that "what is enjoined upon certain (individuals) is not enjoined upon all;" or else, if the other (characteristics) indeed are common, but monogamy is imposed upon bishops alone, (tell me), pray, whether *they* alone are to be pronounced *Christians* upon whom is conferred the entirety of discipline?

---

[1] See 1 Tim. iii. 1-7; Tit. i. 6-9.

CHAP. XIII. — FURTHER OBJECTIONS FROM ST. PAUL
ANSWERED.

"But again, writing to Timotheus, he 'wills
the very young (women) to marry, bear children, act the housewife.'"[1] He is (here) directing (his speech) to such as he denotes
above — "very young widows," who, after being
"apprehended" in widowhood, and (subsequently) wooed for some length of time, after
they have had Christ in their affections, "wish to
marry, having judgment, because they have rescinded the first faith," — that (faith), to wit, by
which they were "found" in widowhood, and,
after professing it, do not persevere. For which
reason he "wills" them to "marry," for fear of
their subsequently rescinding the first faith of
professed widowhood; not to sanction their marrying as often as ever they may refuse to persevere in a widowhood plied with temptation —
nay, rather, spent in indulgence.

"We read him withal writing to the Romans:
'But the woman who is under an husband, is bound
to her husband (while) living; but if he shall
have died, she has been emancipated from the
law of the husband.' Doubtless, then, the husband living, she will be thought to commit adultery if she shall have been joined to a second
husband. If, however, the husband shall have
died, she has been freed from (his) law, (so)
that she is not an adulteress if made (wife) to
another husband."[2] But read the sequel as well,
in order that this sense, which flatters you, may
evade (your grasp). "And so," he says, "my
brethren, be ye too made dead to the law through
the body of Christ, that ye may be made (subject) to a second, — to Him, namely, who hath
risen from the dead, that we may bear fruit to
God. For when we were in the flesh, the passions of sin, which (passions) used to be effi-
ciently caused through the law, (wrought) in our
members unto the bearing of fruit to death; but
now we have been emancipated from the law,
being dead (to that) in which we used to be
held,[3] unto the serving of God in newness of
spirit, and not in oldness of letter." Therefore,
if he bids us "be made dead to the law through
the body of Christ," (which is the Church,[4]
which consists in the spirit of newness,) not
"through the letter of oldness," (that is, of the
law,) — taking you away from the law, which
does not keep a wife, when her husband is dead,
from becoming (wife) to another husband — he
reduces you to (subjection to) the contrary condition, that you are *not* to marry when you have
lost your husband; and in as far as you would
not be accounted an adulteress if you became

(wife) to a second husband after the death of
your (first) husband, if you were still bound to
act in (subjection to) the law, in so far as a result of the diversity of (your) condition, he *does*
prejudge you (guilty) of adultery if, after the
death of your husband, you do marry another:
inasmuch as you have now been made dead to
the law, it cannot be lawful for you, now that
you have withdrawn from that (law) in the eye
of which it *was* lawful for you.

CHAP. XIV. — EVEN IF THE PERMISSION HAD BEEN
GIVEN BY ST. PAUL IN THE SENSE WHICH THE
PSYCHICS ALLEGE, IT WAS MERELY LIKE THE
MOSAIC PERMISSION OF DIVORCE — A CONDESCEN-
SION TO HUMAN HARD-HEARTEDNESS.

Now, if the apostle had even absolutely permitted marriage when one's partner has been
lost *subsequently to* (conversion to) the faith, he
would have done (it), just as (he did) the other
(actions) which he did adversely to the (strict)
letter of his own rule, to suit the circumstances
of the times: circumcising Timotheus[5] on account of "supposititious false brethren;" and
leading certain "shaven men" into the temple[6]
on account of the observant watchfulness of the
Jews — he who chastises the Galatians when they
desire to live in (observance of) the law.[7] But
so did circumstances require him to "become all
things to all, in order to gain all;"[8] "travailing
in birth with them until Christ should be formed
in them;"[9] and "cherishing, as it were a nurse,"
the little ones of faith, by teaching them some
things "by way of indulgence, not by way of
command" — for it is one thing to *indulge*, another to *bid* — permitting a temporary licence
of re-marriage on account of the "weakness of
the flesh," just as Moses of divorcing on account
of "the hardness of the heart."

And here, accordingly, we will render the sup-
plement of this (his) meaning. For if Christ
abrogated what Moses enjoined, because "from
the beginning (it) was not so;" and (if) — this
being so — Christ will not therefore be reputed
to have come from some other Power; why may
not the Paraclete, too, have abrogated an indulgence which Paul granted — because second
marriage withal "was not from the beginning"
— without deserving on this account to be regarded with suspicion, as if he were an alien
spirit, provided only that the superinduction be
worthy of God and of Christ? If it was worthy
of God and of Christ to check "hard-heartedness" when the time (for its indulgence) was

---

[1] 1 Tim. v. 14.
[2] Rom. vii. 2, 3, not exactly rendered.
[3] Comp. the marginal reading in the Eng. ver., Pom. vii. 6.
[4] Comp. Eph. i. 23, and the references there.

[5] Acts xvi. 3; see Gal. iii. iv.
[6] Comp. Acts xxi. 20-26.
[7] See Gal. iii. iv.
[8] See 1 Cor. ix. 22.
[9] Gal. iv. 19.

fully expired, why should it not be *more* worthy both of God and of Christ to shake off "infirmity of the flesh" when "the time" is already *more* "wound up?" If it is just that marriage be not severed, it is, of course, honourable too that it be not iterated. In short, in the estimation of the world, each is accounted a mark of good discipline : one under the name of concord ; one, of modesty. "Hardness of heart" reigned till Christ's time ; let "infirmity of the flesh" (be content to) have reigned till the time of the Paraclete. The New Law abrogated divorce — it had (somewhat) to abrogate ; the New Prophecy (abrogates) second marriage, (which is) no less a divorce of the former (marriage). But the "hardness of heart" yielded to Christ more readily than the "infirmity of the flesh." The latter claims Paul in its own support more than the former Moses ; if, indeed, it is claiming him in its support when it catches at his indulgence, (but) refuses his prescript — eluding his more deliberate opinions and his constant "wills," not suffering us to render to the apostle the (obedience) which he "prefers."

And how long will this most shameless "infirmity" persevere in waging a war of extermination against the "better things?" The time for its indulgence was (the interval) until the Paraclete began His operations, to whose coming were deferred by the Lord (the things) which in His day "could not be endured;" which it is now no longer competent for any one to be unable to endure, seeing that He through whom the power of enduring is granted is not wanting. How long shall we allege "the flesh," because the Lord said, "the flesh is weak?"[1] But He has withal premised that "the Spirit is prompt," in order that the Spirit may vanquish the flesh — that the weak may yield to the stronger. For again He says, "Let him who is able to receive, receive (it) ;"[2] that is, let him who is *not* able go his way. That rich man *did* go his way who had not "received" the precept of dividing his substance to the needy, and was abandoned by the Lord to his own opinion.[3] Nor will "harshness" be on this account imputed to Christ, on the ground of the vicious action of each individual free-will. "Behold," saith He, "I have set before thee good and evil."[4] Choose that which is good : if you cannot, because you will not — for that you can if you will He has shown, because He has proposed each to your free-will — you ought to depart from Him whose will you do not.

[1] Matt. xxvi. 41.
[2] Matt. xix. 12.
[3] See Matt. xix. 16-26; Mark x. 17-27; Luke xviii. 18-27.
[4] See Deut. xxx. 1, 15, 19, and xi. 26. See, too, *de Ex Cast.*, c. ii.

CHAP. XV. — UNFAIRNESS OF CHARGING THE DISCIPLES OF THE NEW PROPHECY WITH HARSHNESS. THE CHARGE RATHER TO BE RETORTED UPON THE PSYCHICS.

What harshness, therefore, is here on our part, if we renounce (communion with) such as do not the will of God? What heresy, if we judge second marriage, as being unlawful, akin to adultery? For what is adultery but unlawful marriage? The apostle sets a brand upon those who were wont entirely to forbid marriage, who were wont at the same time to lay an interdict on meats which God has created.[5] We, however, no more do away with marriage if we abjure its repetition, than we reprobate meats if we fast oftener (than others). It is one thing to do away with, another to regulate ; it is one thing to lay down a law of not marrying, is another to fix a limit to marrying. To speak plainly, if they who reproach us with harshness, or esteem heresy (to exist) in this (our) cause, foster the "infirmity of the flesh" to such a degree as to think it must have support accorded to it in frequency of marriage ; why do they in another case neither accord it support nor foster it with indulgence — when, (namely), torments have reduced it to a denial (of the faith)? For, of course, that (infirmity) is more capable of excuse which has fallen in battle, than (that) which (has fallen) in the bed-chamber; (that) which has succumbed on the rack, than (that) which (has succumbed) on the bridal bed; (that) which has yielded to cruelty, than (that) which (has yielded) to appetite ; that which has been overcome groaning, than (that) which (has been overcome) in heat. But the former they excommunicate, because it has not "endured unto the end :"[6] the latter they prop up, as if withal it has "endured unto the end." Propose (the question) why each has not "endured unto the end;" and you will find the cause of that (infirmity) to be more honourable which has been unable to sustain savagery, than (of that) which (has been unable to sustain) modesty. And yet not even a bloodwrung — not to say an immodest — defection does the "infirmity of the flesh" excuse !

CHAP. XVI. — WEAKNESS OF THE PLEAS URGED IN DEFENCE OF SECOND MARRIAGE.

But I smile when (the plea of) "infirmity of the flesh" is advanced in opposition (to us : infirmity) which is (rather) to be called the height of strength. Iteration of marriage is an affair of strength : to rise again from the ease of continence to the works of the flesh, is (a thing requiring) substantial reins. Such "infirmity" is

[5] See 1 Tim. iv. 1-3.
[6] See Matt. xxiv. 13, and the references there.

equal, to a third, and a fourth, and even (perhaps) a seventh marriage; as (being a thing) which increases its strength as often as its weakness; which will no longer have (the support of) an apostle's authority, but of some Hermogenes — wont to marry more women than he paints. For in him matter is abundant: whence he presumes that even the soul is material; and therefore much more (than other men) he has *not* the Spirit from God, being no longer even a Psychic, because even his psychic element is not derived from God's afflatus! What if a man allege "indigence," so as to profess that his flesh is openly prostituted, and given in marriage for the sake of maintenance; forgetting that there is to be no careful thought about food and clothing?[1] He has God (to look to), the Foster-father even of ravens, the Rearer even of flowers. What if he plead the loneliness of his home? as if one woman afforded company to a man ever on the eve of flight! He has, of course, a widow (at hand), whom it will be lawful for him to take. Not one such wife, but even a plurality, it is permitted to have. What if a man thinks on posterity, with thoughts like the eyes of Lot's wife; so that a man is to make the fact that from his former marriage he has had no children a reason for repeating marriage? A Christian, forsooth, will seek heirs, disinherited as he is from the entire world! He has "brethren;" he has the Church as his mother. The case is different if men believe that, at the bar of Christ as well (as of Rome), action is taken on the principle of the Julian laws; and imagine that the unmarried and childless cannot receive their portion in full, in accordance with the testament of God. Let such (as thus think), then, marry to the very end; that in this confusion of flesh they, like Sodom and Gomorrah, and the day of the deluge, may be overtaken by the fated final end of the world. A third saying let them add, "Let us eat, and drink, *and marry*, for to-morrow we shall die;"[2] not reflecting that the "woe" (denounced) "on such as are with child, and are giving suck,"[3] will fall far more heavily and bitterly in the "universal shaking"[4] of the entire world[5] than it did in the devastation of one fraction of Judæa. Let them accumulate by their iterated marriages fruits right seasonable for the last times — breasts heaving, and wombs qualmish, and infants whimpering. Let them prepare for Antichrist (children) upon whom he may more passionately (than Pharaoh) spend his savagery. He will lead to them murderous midwives.[6]

CHAP. XVII. — HEATHEN EXAMPLES CRY SHAME UPON THIS "INFIRMITY OF THE FLESH."[7]

They will have plainly a specious privilege to plead before Christ — the everlasting "infirmity of the flesh!" But upon this (infirmity) will sit in judgment no longer an Isaac, our monogamist father; or a John, a noted voluntary celibate[8] of Christ's; or a Judith, daughter of Merari; or so many other examples of saints. Heathens are wont to be destined our judges. There will arise a queen of Carthage, and give sentence upon the Christians, who, refugee as she was, living on alien soil, and at that very time the originator of so mighty a state, whereas she ought unasked to have craved royal nuptials, yet, for fear she should experience a second marriage, preferred on the contrary rather to "burn" than to "marry." Her assessor will be the Roman matron who, having — albeit it was through noctural violence, nevertheless — known another man, washed away with blood the stain of her flesh, that she might avenge upon her own person (the honour of) monogamy. There have been, too, who preferred to die for their husbands rather than marry after their husbands' death. To idols, at all events, both monogamy and widowhood serve as apparitors. On Fortuna Muliebris, as on Mother Matuta, none but a once wedded woman hangs the wreath. Once for all do the Pontifex Maximus and the wife of a Flamen marry. The priestesses of Ceres, even during the lifetime and with the consent of their husbands, are widowed by amicable separation. There are, too, who may judge us on the ground of absolute continence: the virgins of Vesta, and of the Achaian Juno, and of the Scythian Diana, and of the Pythian Apollo. On the ground of continence the priests likewise of the famous Egyptian bull will judge the "infirmity" of Christians. Blush, O flesh, who hast "put on"[9] Christ! Suffice it thee once for all to marry, whereto "from the beginning" thou wast created, whereto by "the end" thou art being recalled! Return at least to the former Adam, if to the last thou canst not! Once for all did he taste of the tree; once for all felt concupiscence; once for all veiled his shame; once for all blushed in the presence of God; once for all concealed his guilty hue; once for all was exiled from the paradise of holiness;[10] once for all thenceforward married. If you were "in him,"[11] you have your norm; if you have passed over "into Christ,"[12] you will be bound to be (yet) better. Exhibit (to us) a third Adam, and him a digamist; and then you will be able to be what, between the two, you cannot.

---

[1] See Matt. vi. 25-34.
[2] See 1 Cor. xv. 32.
[3] Matt. xxiv. 19; Luke xxi. 23. Comp. *ad Ux.*, l. i. c. v.
[4] Concussione. Comp. Hag. ii. 6, 7; Heb. xii. 26, 27.
[5] Mundi.
[6] Comp. Ex. i. 8-16.

[7] Spado.
[8] Comp. *ad Ux.*, l. i. cc. vi. vii.; and *de Ex. Cast.*, c. xiii.
[9] See Rom. xiii. 14; Gal. iii. 27.
[10] Or "chastity."
[11] Comp. 1 Cor. xv. 22, ἐν τῷ Ἀδάμ.
[12] See Rom. vi. 3.

ELUCIDATIONS.

I.

(About 160 years having elapsed, pp. 59, 61.)

IF the First Epistle to the Corinthians was written A.D. 57, and if our author speaks with designed precision, and not in round numbers, the date of this treatise should be A.D. 217, — a date which I should prefer to accept. Bishop Kaye,[1] however, instances capp. 7 and 9 in the *Ad Nationes* as proving his disposition to give his numbers in loose rhetoric, and not with arithmetical accuracy. Pamelius, on the other hand, gives A.D. 213.

On the general subject Kaye bids us read cap. 3, with cap. 14, to grasp the argument of our enthusiast.[2] In few words, our author holds that St. Paul condescends to human infirmity in permitting any marriage whatever, pointing to a better way.[3] The apostle himself says, "The time is short;" but a hundred and sixty years have passed since then, and why may not the Spirit of truth and righteousness now, after so long a time, be given to animate the adult Church to that which is pronounced the better way in Scripture itself ?

Our author seems struggling here, according to my view, with his own rule of *prescription*. He would free the doctrine from the charge of novelty by pointing it out in the Scripture of a hundred and sixty years before. But how instinctively the Church ruled against this sophistry, condemning in advance that whole system of " development " which a modern Tertullian defends on grounds quite as specious, under a Montanistic subjection that makes a Priscilla of the Roman pontiff. Let me commend the reader to the remarks upon Tertullian of the "judicious Hooker," in book ii. capp. v. 5, 6 ; also book iv. cap. vii. 4, 5, and elsewhere.

II.

(Abrogated indulgence (comp. capp. 2 and 3), p. 70.)

Poor Tertullian is at war with himself in all the works which he indites against Catholic orthodoxy. In the tract *De Exhort. Castitatis* he gives one construction to 1 Cor. ix. 5, which in this he explains away ;[4] and now he patches up his conclusion by referring to his Montanistic " Paraclete." In fighting Marcion, how thoroughly he agrees with Clement of Alexandria as to the sanctity of marriage. In the second epistle to his wife, how beautiful his tribute to the married state, blessed by the Church, and enjoyed in chastity. But here[5] how fanatically he would make out that marriage is but tolerated adultery ! From Tertullian himself we may prove the marriage of the clergy, and that (*de Exhort. Cast.*, last chapter) abstinence was voluntary and exceptional, however praiseworthy. Also, if he here urges that (cap. 12) even laymen should abstain from second marriages, he allows the liberty of the clergy to marry once. He admits St. Peter's marriage. Eusebius proves the marriage of St. Jude. Concerning " the grave dignity " of a single marriage, we may concede that Tertullian proves his point, but no further.

In England the principles of the *Monogamia* were revived by the eccentric Whiston (*circa* A.D. 1750), and attracted considerable attention among the orthodox, — a fact pleasantly satirized by Goldsmith in his *Vicar of Wakefield*.

On the general subject comp. Chrysost., tom. iii. p. 226 : " Laus Maximi, et quales ducendæ sint uxores."

---

[1] P. 40, Kaye's *Tertullian*.   [2] P. 24, Kaye's *Tertullian*.
[3] Comp. Bacon, *Essays*, No. viii., Of Marriage and Single Life.
[4] Comp. *Ex. Cast.*, cap. viii. p. 55, *supra*, with the *Monogam.*, cap. viii. p. 65, *supra*.
[5] Comp. Apparel of Women, ii. cap. ix. p. 23, *supra*.

VII.

ON MODESTY.[1]

[TRANSLATED BY THE REV. S. THELWALL.]

MODESTY, the flower of manners, the honour of our bodies, the grace of the sexes, the integrity of the blood, the guarantee of our race, the basis of sanctity, the pre-indication of every good disposition; rare though it is, and not easily perfected, and scarce ever retained in perpetuity, will yet up to a certain point linger in the world, if nature shall have laid the preliminary groundwork of it, discipline persuaded to it, censorial rigour curbed its excesses — on the hypothesis, that is, that every mental good quality is the result either of birth, or else of training, or else of external compulsion.

But as the conquering power of things evil is on the increase — which is the characteristic of the last times[2] — things good are now not allowed either to be born, so corrupted are the seminal principles; or to be trained, so deserted are studies; nor to be enforced, so disarmed are the laws. In fact, (the modesty) of which we are now beginning (to treat) is by this time grown so obsolete, that it is not the abjuration but the moderation of the appetites which modesty is believed to be; and he is held to be chaste *enough* who has not been *too* chaste. But let the world's[3] modesty see to itself, together with the world[4] itself: together with its inherent nature, if it was wont to originate in birth; its study, if in training; its servitude, if in compulsion: except that it had been even more unhappy if it had remained only to prove fruitless, in that it had not been in God's household that its activities had been exercised. I should prefer no good to a vain good: what profits it that that should exist whose existence profits not? It is *our own* good things whose position is now sinking; it is the system of *Christian* modesty which is being shaken to its foundation — (Christian modesty), which derives its all from heaven; its nature, "through the laver of regeneration;"[5] its discipline, through the instrumentality of preaching; its censorial rigour, through the judgments which each Testament exhibits; and is subject to a more constant external compulsion, arising from the apprehension or the desire of the eternal fire or kingdom.[6]

In opposition to this (modesty), could I not have acted the dissembler? I hear that there has even been an edict set forth, and a peremptory one too. The *Pontifex Maximus*[7] — that is, the bishop of bishops[8] — issues an edict: "I remit, to such as have discharged (the requirements of) repentance, the sins both of adultery and of fornication." O edict, on which cannot be inscribed, "Good deed!" And where shall this liberality be posted up? On the very spot, I suppose, on the very gates of the sensual appetites, beneath the very titles of the sensual appetites. There is the place for promulgating such repentance, where the delinquency itself shall haunt. There is the place to read the pardon, where entrance shall be made under the hope thereof. But it is in the church that this (edict) is read, and in the church that it is pronounced; and (the church) is a virgin! Far, far from Christ's betrothed be such a proclamation! She, the true, the modest, the saintly, shall be free from stain even of her ears. She has none to whom to make such a promise; and if she have had, she does not make it; since

---

[1] [Written not earlier than A.D. 208; probably very much later. See Bp. Kaye's very important remarks on this treatise, p. 224.]
[2] Comp. 2 Tim. iii. 1–5; Matt. xxiv. 12.
[3] Sæculi.
[4] Sæculo.

[5] Tit. iii. 5.
[6] Comp. Matt. xxv. 46.
[7] [This is irony; a heathen epithet applied to Victor (or his successor), ironically, because he seemed ambitious of superiority over other bishops.]
[8] Zephyrinus (de Genoude): Zephyrinus or (his predecessor) Victor. J. B. Lightfoot, *Ep. ad Phil.*, 221, 222, ed. 1, 1868. [See also Robertson, *Ch. Hist.*, p. 121. S.]

even the earthly temple of God can sooner have been called by the Lord a "den of robbers,"[1] than of adulterers and fornicators.

This too, therefore, shall be a count in my indictment against the Psychics; against the fellowship of sentiment also which I myself formerly maintained with them; in order that they may the more cast this in my teeth for a mark of fickleness. Repudiation of fellowship is never a pre-indication of sin. As if it were not easier to err with the majority, when it is in the company of the few that truth is loved! But, however, a profitable fickleness shall no more be a disgrace to me, than I should wish a hurtful one to be an ornament. I blush not at an error which I have ceased to hold, because I am delighted at having ceased to hold it, because I recognise myself to be better and more modest. No one blushes at his own improvement. Even in Christ, knowledge had its stages of growth;[2] through which stages the apostle, too, passed. "When I was a child," he says, "as a child I spake, as a child I understood; but when I became a man, those (things) which had been the child's I abandoned:"[3] so truly did he turn away from his early opinions: nor did he sin by becoming an emulator not of ancestral but of Christian traditions,[4] wishing even the præ-cision of them who advised the retention of circumcision.[5] And would that the same fate might befall those, too, who obtruncate the pure and true integrity of the flesh; amputating not the extremest superficies, but the inmost image of modesty itself, while they promise pardon to adulterers and fornicators, in the teeth of the primary discipline of the Christian Name; a discipline to which heathendom itself bears such emphatic witness, that it strives to punish that discipline in the persons of our females rather by defilements of the flesh than tortures; wishing to wrest from them that which they hold dearer than life! But now this glory is being extinguished, and that by means of those who ought with all the more constancy to refuse concession of any pardon to defilements of this kind, that they make the fear of succumbing to adultery and fornication their reason for marrying as often as they please — since "better it is to marry than to burn."[6] No doubt it is for continence sake that incontinence is necessary — the "burning" will be extinguished by "fires!" Why, then, do they withal grant indulgence, under the name of repentance, to crimes for which they furnish remedies by their law of multinuptialism? For remedies will be idle while crimes are indulged, and crimes will remain if remedies are idle. And so, either way, they trifle with solicitude and negligence; by taking emptiest precaution against (crimes) to which they grant quarter, and granting absurdest quarter to (crimes) against which they take precaution: whereas either precaution is not to be taken where quarter is given, or quarter not given where precaution is taken; for they take precaution, as if they were unwilling that something should be committed; but grant indulgence, as if they were willing it should be committed: whereas, if they be unwilling it should be committed, they ought not to grant indulgence; if they be willing to grant indulgence, they ought not to take precaution. For, again, adultery and fornication will not be ranked at the same time among the moderate and among the greatest sins, so that each course may be equally open with regard to them — the solicitude which takes precaution, and the security which grants indulgence. But since they are such as to hold the culminating place among crimes, there is no room at once for their indulgence as if they were moderate, and for their precaution as if they were greatest. But by *us* precaution is thus also taken against the greatest, or, (if you will), *highest* (crimes, viz.,) in that it is not permitted, after believing, to know even a second marriage, differentiated though it be, to be sure, from the work of adultery and fornication by the nuptial and dotal tablets: and accordingly, with the utmost strictness, we excommunicate digamists, as bringing infamy upon the Paraclete by the irregularity of their discipline. The self-same liminal limit we fix for adulterers also and fornicators; dooming them to pour forth tears barren of peace, and to regain from the Church no ampler return than the publication of their disgrace.

CHAP. II. — GOD JUST AS WELL AS MERCIFUL; ACCORDINGLY, MERCY MUST NOT BE INDISCRIMINATE.

"But," say they, "God is 'good,' and 'most good,'[7] and 'pitiful-hearted,' and 'a pitier,' and 'abundant in pitiful-heartedness,'[8] which He holds 'dearer than all sacrifice,'[9] 'not thinking the sinner's death of so much worth as his repentance,'[10] 'a Saviour of all men, most of all of believers.'[11] And so it will be becoming for 'the sons of God'[12] too to be 'pitiful-hearted'[13] and 'peacemakers;'[14] 'giving in their turn just as

---

1 Matt. xxi. 13; Mark xi. 17; Luke xix. 46; Jer. vii. 11.
2 See Luke ii. 52.
3 1 Cor. xiii. 11, one clause omitted.
4 Comp. Gal. i. 14 with 2 Thess. ii. 15.
5 See Gal. v. 12.
6 1 Cor. vii. 9, repeatedly quoted.

7 See Matt. xix. 17; Mark x. 18; Luke xviii. 19.
8 See Ex. xxxiv. 6, 7.
9 Hos. vi. 6; Mic. vi. 8; Matt. ix. 13, xii. 7.
10 Ezek. xviii. 23, 32, xxxiii. 11.
11 1 Tim. iv. 10.
12 1 John iii. 1, 2.
13 Luke vi. 36.
14 Matt. v. 9.

Christ withal hath given to us;' [1] 'not judging, that we be not judged.' [2] For 'to his own lord a man standeth or falleth; who art thou, to judge another's servant?' [3] ' Remit, and remission shall be made to thee.'" [4] Such and so great futilities of theirs wherewith they flatter God and pander to themselves, effeminating rather than invigorating discipline, with how cogent and contrary (arguments) are we for our part able to rebut, — (arguments) which set before us warningly the " severity " [5] of God, and provoke our own constancy? Because, albeit God is by nature good, still He is " just " [6] too. For, from the nature of the case, just as He knows how to " heal," so does He withal know how to " smite; " [7] " making peace," but withal " creating evils; " [8] preferring repentance, but withal commanding Jeremiah not to pray for the aversion of ills on behalf of the sinful People, — " since, if they shall have fasted," saith He, " I will not listen to their entreaty." [9] And again: " And pray not thou unto (me) on behalf of the People, and request not on their behalf in prayer and supplication, since I will not listen to (them) in the time wherein they shall have invoked me, in the time of their affliction." [10] And further, above, the same preferrer of mercy above sacrifice (says): " And pray not thou unto (me) on behalf of this People, and request not that they may obtain mercy, and approach not on their behalf unto me, since I will not listen to (them)" [11] — of course when they sue for mercy, when out of repentance they weep and fast, and when they offer their self-affliction to God. For God is " jealous," [12] and is One who is not contemptuously derided [13] — derided, namely, by such as flatter His goodness — and who, albeit " patient," [14] yet threatens, through Isaiah, an end of (His) patience. " I have held my peace; shall I withal always hold my peace and endure? I have been quiet as (a woman) in birth-throes; I will arise, and will make (them) to grow arid." [15] For " a fire shall proceed before His face, and shall utterly burn His enemies; " [16] striking down not the body only, but the souls too, into hell. [17] Besides, the Lord Himself demonstrates the

manner in which He threatens such as judge: " For with what judgment ye judge, judgment shall be given on you." [18] Thus He has not prohibited judging, but taught (how to do it). Whence the apostle withal judges, and that in a case of fornication, [19] that " such a man must be surrendered to Satan for the destruction of the flesh; " [20] chiding them likewise because " brethren " were not " judged at the bar of the saints: " [21] for he goes on and says, " To what (purpose is it) for me to judge those who are without?" " But you remit, in order that remission may be granted you by God." The sins which are (thus) cleansed are such as a man may have committed against his brother, not against God. We profess, in short, in our prayer, that we will grant remission to our debtors; [22] but it is not becoming to distend further, on the ground of the authority of such Scriptures, the cable of contention with alternate pull into diverse directions; so that one (Scripture) may seem to draw tight, another to relax, the reins of discipline — in uncertainty, as it were, — and the latter to debase the remedial aid of repentance through lenity, the former to refuse it through austerity. Further: the authority of Scripture will stand within its own limits, without reciprocal opposition. The remedial aid of repentance is determined by its own conditions, without unlimited concession; and the causes of it themselves are anteriorly distinguished without confusion in the proposition. We agree that the causes of repentance are sins. These we divide into two issues: some will be remissible, some irremissible: in accordance wherewith it will be doubtful to no one that some deserve chastisement, some condemnation. Every sin is dischargeable either by pardon or else by penalty: by pardon as the result of chastisement, by penalty as the result of condemnation. Touching this difference, we have not only already premised certain antithetical passages of the Scriptures, on one hand retaining, on the other remitting, sins; [23] but John, too, will teach us: " If any knoweth his brother to be sinning a sin not unto death, he shall request, and life shall be given to him; " because he is not " sinning unto death," this will be remissible. " (There) is a sin unto death; not for this do I say that any is to request " [24] — this will be irremissible. So, where there is the efficacious power of " making request," there likewise is that of remission: where there is no (efficacious power) of " making request," there equally is none of remission either. According to this

---

[1] Comp. Matt. x. 8; but the reference seems to be to Eph. iv. 32, where the Vulgate reads almost as Tertullian does, " donantes invicem, sicut et Deus in Christo donavit vobis."
[2] Matt. vii. 1; Luke vi. 37.
[3] Comp. Rom. xiv. 4.
[4] Comp. Luke vi. 37.
[5] See Rom. xi. 22.
[6] Comp. Isa. xlv. 21; Rom. iii. 26.
[7] Comp. Job v. 18; Deut. xxxii. 39.
[8] Isa. xlv. 7.
[9] Jer. xiv. 11, 12, vii. 16, xi. 14.
[10] Jer. xi 14.
[11] Jer. vii. 16.
[12] Comp. Ex. xx. 5, xxxiv. 14; Deut. iv. 24, v. 9, vi. 15; Josh. xxiv. 19; Nahum i. 2.
[13] Gal. vi. 7.
[14] Comp. Rom. xv. 5; Ps. vii. 12 (in LXX.).
[15] Isa. xlii. 14.
[16] Comp. Ps. xcvii. 3.
[17] Comp. Matt. x. 28; Luke xii. 4, 5.

[18] Matt. vii. 2; Luke vi. 37.
[19] Or rather incest, as appears by 1 Cor. v. 1.
[20] 1 Cor. v. 5.
[21] See 1 Cor. vi. 1–6, v. 12.
[22] Luke xi. 4.
[23] Comp. John xx. 23.
[24] 1 John v. 16, not quite *verbatim.*

difference of sins, the condition of repentance also is discriminated. There will be a condition which may possibly obtain pardon, — in the case, namely, of a remissible sin : there will be a condition which can by no means obtain it, — in the case, namely, of an irremissible sin. And it remains to examine specially, with regard to the position of adultery and fornication, to which class of sins they ought to be assigned.

CHAP. III. — AN OBJECTION ANTICIPATED BEFORE THE DISCUSSION ABOVE PROMISED IS COMMENCED.

But before doing this, I will make short work with an answer which meets us from the opposite side, in reference to that species of repentance which we are just defining as being without pardon. "Why, if," say they, "there is a repentance which lacks pardon, it immediately follows that such repentance must withal be wholly unpractised by you. For nothing is to be done in vain. Now repentance will be practised in vain, if it is without pardon. But *all* repentance *is* to be practised. Therefore let (us allow that) *all* obtains pardon, that it may not be practised in vain ; because it will not be to be practised, if it be practised in vain. Now, in vain it *is* practised, if it shall lack pardon." Justly, then, do they allege (this argument) against us ; since they have usurpingly kept in their own power the fruit of this as of other repentance — that is, pardon ; for, so far as *they* are concerned, at whose hands (repentance) obtains *man's* peace, (it *is* in vain). As regards *us*, however, who remember that the Lord alone concedes (the pardon of) sins, (and of course of *mortal* ones,) it will *not* be practised in vain. For (the repentance) being referred back to the Lord, and thenceforward lying prostrate before Him, will by this very fact the rather avail to win pardon, that it gains it by entreaty *from God alone*, that it believes not that *man's* peace is adequate to its guilt, that as far as regards the Church it prefers the blush of shame to the privilege of communion. For before her doors it stands, and by the example of its own stigma admonishes all others, and calls at the same time to its own aid the brethren's tears, and returns with an even richer merchandise — their compassion, namely — than their communion. And if it reaps not the harvest of peace here, yet it sows the seed of it with the Lord ; nor does it lose, but prepares, its fruit. It will not fail of emolument if it do not fail in duty. Thus, neither is such repentance vain, nor such discipline harsh. Both honour God. The former, by laying no flattering unction to itself, will more readily win success ; the latter, by assuming nothing to itself, will more fully aid.

CHAP. IV. — ADULTERY AND FORNICATION SYNONYMOUS.

Having defined the distinction (between the kinds) of repentance, we are by this time, then, able to return to the assessment of the sins — whether they be such as can obtain pardon at the hand of men. In the first place, (as for the fact) that we call adultery likewise fornication, usage requires (us so to do). "Faith," withal, has a familiar acquaintance with sundry appellations. So, in every one of our little works, we carefully guard usage. Besides, if I shall say "adulterium," and if "stuprum," the indictment of contamination of the flesh will be one and the same. For it makes no difference whether a man assault another's bride or widow, provided it be not his own "female ;" just as there is no difference made by places — whether it be in chambers or in towers that modesty is massacred. Every homicide, even outside a wood, is banditry. So, too, whoever enjoys any other than nuptial intercourse, in whatever place, and in the person of whatever woman, makes himself guilty of adultery and fornication. Accordingly, among *us*, secret connections as well — connections, that is, not first professed in presence of the Church — run risk of being judged akin to adultery and fornication ; nor must we let them, if thereafter woven together by the covering of marriage, elude the charge. But all the other frenzies of passions — impious both toward the bodies and toward the sexes — beyond the laws of nature, we banish not only from the threshold, but from all shelter of the Church, because they are not sins, but monstrosities.

CHAP. V. — OF THE PROHIBITION OF ADULTERY IN THE DECALOGUE.

Of how deep guilt, then, adultery — which is likewise a matter of fornication, in accordance with its criminal function — is to be accounted, the Law of God first comes to hand to show us ; if it is true, (as it is), that after interdicting the superstitious service of alien gods, and the making of idols themselves, after commending (to religious observance) the veneration of the Sabbath, after commanding a religious regard toward parents second (only to that) toward God, (that Law) laid, as the next substratum in strengthening and fortifying such counts, no other precept than "Thou shalt not commit adultery." For after spiritual chastity and sanctity followed corporeal integrity. And this (the Law) accordingly fortified, by immediately prohibiting its foe, adultery. Understand, consequently, what kind of sin (that must be), the repression of which (the Law) ordained next to (that of) idolatry. Nothing that is a second is remote from the first ; nothing is so close to the first as the second. That which results from the first is (in a sense) another first. And so adultery is bordering on idolatry. For idolatry withal, often cast as a reproach upon the People under the name of adultery and fornication, will be alike conjoined therewith in fate as in following — will be alike co-heir therewith in condemnation as in co-ordination. Yet further: premising "Thou shalt not commit adultery," (the Law) adjoins, "Thou shalt not kill." It honoured adultery, of course, to which it gives the precedence over murder, in the very fore-front of the most holy law, among the primary counts of the celestial edict, marking it with the inscription of the very principal sins. From its place you may discern the measure, from its rank the station, from its neighbourhood the merit, of each thing. Even evil has a dignity, consisting in being stationed at the summit, or else in the centre, of the superlatively bad. I behold a certain pomp and circumstance of adultery: on the one side, Idolatry goes before and leads the way; on the other, Murder follows in company. Worthily, without doubt, has she taken her seat between the two most conspicuous eminences of misdeeds, and has completely filled the vacant space, as it were, in their midst, with an equal majesty of crime. Enclosed by such flanks, encircled and supported by such ribs, who shall dislocate her from the corporate mass of coherencies, from the bond of neighbour crimes, from the embrace of kindred wickednesses, so as to set apart her alone for the enjoyment of repentance? Will not on one side Idolatry, on the other Murder, detain her, and (if they have any voice) reclaim: "This is our wedge, this our compacting power? By (the standard of) Idolatry we are measured; by her disjunctive intervention we are conjoined; to her, outjutting from our midst, we are united; the Divine Scripture has made us concorporate; the very letters are our glue; herself can no longer exist without us. 'Many and many a time do I, Idolatry, subminister occasion to Adultery; witness my groves and my mounts, and the living waters, and the very temples in cities, what mighty agents we are for overthrowing modesty.' 'I also, Murder, sometimes exert myself on behalf of Adultery. To omit tragedies, witness nowadays the poisoners, witness the magicians, how many seductions I avenge, how many rivalries I revenge; how many guards, how many informers, how many accomplices, I make away with. Witness the midwives likewise, how many adulterous conceptions are slaughtered.' Even among Christians there is no adultery without us. Wherever the business of the unclean spirit is, there are idolatries; wherever a man, by being polluted, is slain, there too is murder. Therefore the remedial aids of repentance will not be suitable to *them*, or else they will likewise be to *us*. We either detain Adultery, or else follow her." These words the sins themselves do speak. If the *sins* are deficient in speech, hard by (the door of the church) stands an idolater, hard by stands a murderer; in their midst stands, too, an adulterer. Alike, as the duty of repentance bids, they sit in sackcloth and bristle in ashes; with the self-same weeping they groan; with the self-same prayers they make their circuits; with the self-same knees they supplicate; the self-same mother they invoke. What doest thou, gentlest and humanest Discipline? Either to *all* these will it be thy duty so to be, for "blessed are the peacemakers;"[1] or else, if not to *all*, it will be thy duty to range thyself on our side. Dost thou once for all condemn the idolater and the murderer, but take the adulterer out from their midst? — (the adulterer), the successor of the idolater, the predecessor of the murderer, the colleague of each? It is "an accepting of person:"[2] the more pitiable repentances thou hast left (unpitied) behind!

CHAP. VI. — EXAMPLES OF SUCH OFFENCES UNDER THE OLD DISPENSATION NO PATTERN FOR THE DISCIPLES OF THE NEW. BUT EVEN THE OLD HAS EXAMPLES OF VENGEANCE UPON SUCH OFFENCES.

Plainly, if you show by what patronages of heavenly precedents and precepts it is that you open to adultery alone — and therein to fornication also — the gate of repentance, at this very line our hostile encounter will forthwith cross swords. Yet I must necessarily prescribe you a law, not to stretch out your hand after the old things,[3] not to look backwards:[4] for "the old things are passed away,"[5] according to Isaiah; and "a renewing hath been renewed,"[6] according to Jeremiah; and "forgetful of former things, we are reaching forward,"[7] according to the apostle; and "the law and the prophets (were) until John,"[8] according to the Lord. For even if we are just now beginning with the Law in demonstrating (the nature of) adultery, it is justly with that phase of the law which Christ has "not dissolved, but fulfilled."[9] For it is the "burdens" of the law which were "until John," not the remedial virtues. It is the "yokes" of "works" that have been rejected, not those

---

[1] Matt. v. 9.
[2] Job xxxii. 21, Lev. xix. 15, and the references there.
[3] Comp. Isa. xliii. 18.
[4] Comp. Luke ix. 62.
[5] There is no passage, so far as I am aware, in Isaiah containing this distinct assertion. We have almost the exact words in Rev. xxi. 4. The reference may be to Isa. xlii. 9: but there the Eng. ver. reads, "are come to pass," and the LXX. have τὰ ἀπ' ἀρχῆς ἰδοὺ ἥκασι.
[6] Comp. Jer. iv. 3 in LXX.
[7] Comp. Phil. iii. 13.
[8] Comp. Matt. xi. 13; Luke xvi. 16.
[9] See Matt. v. 17.

of disciplines.[1] " Liberty in Christ "[2] has done no injury to innocence. The law of piety, sanctity, humanity, truth, chastity, justice, mercy, benevolence, modesty, remains in its entirety ; in which law " blessed (is) the man who shall meditate by day and by night."[3] About that (law) the same David (says) again : " The law of the Lord (is) unblameable,[4] converting souls ; the statutes of the Lord (are) direct, delighting hearts ; the precept of the Lord far-shining, enlightening eyes." Thus, too, the apostle : " And so the law indeed is holy, and the precept holy and most good "[5] — " Thou shalt not commit adultery," of course. But he had withal said above : " Are we, then, making void the law through faith ? Far be it ; but we are establishing the law "[6] — forsooth in those (points) which, being even now interdicted by the New Testament, are prohibited by an even more emphatic precept : instead of, " Thou shalt not commit adultery," " Whoever shall have seen with a view to concupiscence, hath already committed adultery in his own heart ; "[7] and instead of, " Thou shalt not kill," " Whoever shall have said to his brother, Racha, shall be in danger of hell."[8] Ask (yourself) whether the law of not committing adultery be still in force, to which has been added that of not indulging concupiscence. Besides, if any precedents (taken from the Old Dispensation) shall favour you in (the secrecy of) your bosom, they shall not be set in opposition to this discipline which we are maintaining. For it is in vain that an additional law has been reared, condemning the *origin* even of sins — that is, concupiscences and wills — no less than the actual deeds ; if the fact that pardon was of old in some cases conceded to adultery is to be a reason why it shall be conceded at the present day. " What will be the reward attaching to the restrictions imposed upon the more fully developed discipline of the present day, except that the elder (discipline) may be made the agent for granting indulgence to your prostitution ? " In that case, you will grant pardon to the idolater too, and to every apostate, because we find the People itself, so often guilty of these crimes, as often reinstated in their former privileges. You will maintain communion, too, with the murderer : because Ahab, by deprecation, washed away (the guilt of) Naboth's blood ;[9] and David, by confession, purged Uriah's slaughter, together with its cause — adultery.[10] That done, you will condone incests, too, for Lot's sake ;[11] and fornications combined with incest, for Judah's sake ;[12] and base marriages with prostitutes, for Hosea's sake ;[13] and not only the frequent repetition of marriage, but its simultaneous plurality, for our fathers' sakes : for, of course, it is meet that there should also be a perfect equality of grace in regard of *all* deeds to which indulgence was in days bygone granted, if on the ground of some pristine precedent pardon is claimed for *adultery.* We, too, indeed have precedents in the self-same antiquity on the side of our opinion, — (precedents) of judgment not merely not waived, but even summarily executed upon fornication. And of course it is a sufficient one, that so vast a number — (the number) of 24,000 — of the People, when they committed fornication with the daughters of Madian, fell in one plague.[14] But, with an eye to the glory of Christ, I prefer to derive (my) discipline from Christ. Grant that the pristine days may have had — if the Psychics please — even a *right* of (indulging) every immodesty ; grant that, before Christ, the flesh may have disported itself, nay, may have *perished* before its Lord went to seek and bring it back : not yet was it worthy of the gift of salvation ; not yet apt for the office of sanctity. It was still, up to that time, accounted as being *in Adam*, with its own vicious nature, easily indulging concupiscence after whatever it had seen to be " attractive to the sight,"[15] and looking back at the lower things, and checking its itching with fig-leaves.[16] Universally inherent was the virus of lust — the dregs which are formed out of milk contain it — (dregs) fitted (for so doing), in that even the waters themselves had not yet been bathed. But when the Word of God descended into flesh, — (flesh) not unsealed even by marriage, — and " the Word was made flesh,"[17] — (flesh) never to be unsealed by marriage, — which was to find its way to the tree not of incontinence, but of endurance ; which was to taste from that tree not anything sweet, but something bitter ; which was to pertain not to the infernal regions, but to heaven ; which was to be precinct not with the leaves of lasciviousness, but the flowers of holiness ;[18] which was to impart to the waters its own purities — thenceforth, whatever flesh (is) " in Christ "[19] has lost its pristine soils, is now a thing different, emerges in a new state, no longer (generated) of the slime of natural seed, nor of the grime of concupiscence, but of " pure water " and a " clean

1 See Acts xv. 10.
2 See Gal. ii. 4, v. 1, 13.
3 Ps. i. 1, briefly.
4 Ps. xix. 7: " perfect," Eng. ver. In LXX. it is xviii. 8.
5 Rom. vii. 12, not literally.
6 Rom. iii. 31.
7 Matt. v. 27, 28.
8 Matt. v. 21, 22.
9 See 1 Kings xxi. (in LXX. 3 Kings xx.).
10 See 2 Sam. xi., xii. 1-13.

11 See Gen. xix. 30-38.
12 See Gen. xxxviii.
13 See Hos. i. 2, 3, iii. 1-3.
14 See Num. xxv. 1-9 ; 1 Cor. x 8.
15 See Gen. iii. 6; and comp. 1 John ii. 16.
16 See Gen. iii. 7.
17 John i. 14.
18 Or, " chastity."
19 Comp. 2 Cor. v. 17.

Spirit." And, accordingly, why excuse it on the ground of pristine precedent? It did not bear the names of "body of Christ,"[1] of "members of Christ,"[2] of "temple of God,"[3] at the time when it used to obtain pardon for adultery. And thus if, from the moment when it changed its condition, and "having been baptized into Christ put on Christ,"[4] and was "redeemed with a great price"—"the blood," to wit, "of the Lord and Lamb"[5]—you take hold of any one precedent (be it precept, or law, or sentence,) of indulgence granted, or to be granted, to adultery and fornication,—you have likewise at our hands a definition of the time from which the age of the question dates.

CHAP. VII.—OF THE PARABLES OF THE LOST EWE AND THE LOST DRACHMA.

You shall have leave to begin with the parables, where you have the lost ewe re-sought by the Lord, and carried back on His shoulders.[6] Let the very paintings upon your cups come forward to show whether even in them the figurative meaning of that sheep will shine through (the outward semblance, to teach) whether a Christian or heathen sinner be the object it aims at in the matter of restoration. For we put in a demurrer arising out of the teaching of nature, out of the law of ear and tongue, out of the soundness of the mental faculty, to the effect that such answers are always given as are called forth (by the question,—answers), that is, to the (questions) which call them forth. That which was calling forth (an answer in the present case) was, I take it, the fact that the Pharisees were muttering in indignation at the Lord's admitting to His society heathen publicans and sinners, and communicating with them in food. When, in reply to this, the Lord had figured the restoration of the lost ewe, to whom else is it credible that he configured it but to the lost *heathen*, about whom the question was then in hand,—not about a *Christian*, who up to that time had no existence? Else, what kind of (hypothesis) is it that the Lord, like a quibbler in answering, omitting the present subject-matter which it was His duty to refute, should spend His labour about one yet future? "But a 'sheep' properly means a Christian,[7] and the Lord's 'flock' is the people of the Church,[8] and the 'good shepherd' is Christ;[9] and hence in the 'sheep' we must understand a Christian who has erred from the Church's 'flock.'" In that case, you make the Lord to have given no answer to

the Pharisees' muttering, but to your presumption. And yet you will be bound so to defend that presumption, as to deny that the (points) which you think applicable to Christians are referable to a heathen. Tell me, is not all mankind one flock of God? Is not the same God both Lord and Shepherd of the universal nations?[10] Who more "perishes" from God than the heathen, so long as he "errs?" Who is more "re-sought" by God than the heathen, when he is recalled by Christ? In fact, it is among heathens that this order finds antecedent place; if, that is, Christians are not otherwise made out of heathens than by being first "lost," and "re-sought" by God, and "carried back" by Christ. So likewise ought this order to be kept, that we may interpret any such (figure) with reference to those in whom it finds prior place. But you, I take it, would wish this: that He should represent the ewe as lost not from a flock, but from an ark or a chest! In like manner, albeit He calls the remaining number of the heathens "righteous," it does not follow that He shows them to be *Christians;* dealing as He is with *Jews*, and at that very moment refuting them, because they were indignant at the hope of the heathens. But in order to express, in opposition to the Pharisees' envy, His own grace and goodwill even in regard of one heathen, He preferred the salvation of one sinner by repentance to theirs by righteousness; or else, pray, were the Jews *not* "righteous," and such as "had no need of repentance," having, as they had, as pilotages of discipline and instruments of fear, "the Law and the Prophets?" He set them therefore in the parable—and if not such as they were, yet such as they ought to have been—that they migh blush the more when they heard that repentance was necessary to others, and not to themselves.

Similarly, the parable of the drachma,[11] as being called forth out of the same subject-matter, we equally interpret with reference to a heathen; albeit it had been "lost" in a house, as it were in the church; albeit "found" by aid of a "lamp," as it were by aid of God's word.[12] Nay, but this whole world is the one house of all; in which world it is more the heathen, who is found in darkness, whom the grace of God enlightens, than the Christian, who is already in God's light.[13] Finally, it is *one* "straying" which is ascribed to the ewe and the drachma: (and this is an evidence in my favour); for if the parables had been composed with a view to a *Christian* sinner, after the loss of his faith, a *second* loss and restoration of them would have been noted.

---

1 1 Cor. xii. 27.
2 *Ib*. and vi. 15.
3 1 Cor. iii. 16, vi. 19.
4 Gal. iii. 27.
5 Comp. 1 Cor. vi. 20, and the references there.
6 Luke xv. 3–7.
7 Comp. John x. 27.
8 Comp. Acts xx. 28.
9 Comp. John x. 11.

10 Comp. Rom. iii. 29.
11 Luke xv. 8–10.
12 Comp. Ps. cxix. 105 (in LXX. cxviii. 105).
13 Comp. 1 John i. 5–7, ii. 8; also Rom. xiii. 12, 13; 1 Thess. v. 4, 5.

I will now withdraw for a short time from this position ; in order that I may, even by withdrawing, the more recommend it, when I shall have succeeded even thus also in confuting the presumption of the opposite side. I admit that the sinner portrayed in each parable is one who is already a Christian ; yet not that on this account must he be affirmed to be such an one as can be restored, through repentance, from the crime of adultery and fornication. For although he be said to "have perished," there will be the *kind* of perdition to treat of ; inasmuch as the "ewe" "perished" not by dying, but by straying ; and the "drachma" not by being destroyed, but by being hidden. In this sense, a thing which is safe may be said to "have perished." Therefore the believer, too, "perishes," by lapsing out of (the right path) into a public exhibition of charioteering frenzy, or gladiatorial gore, or scenic foulness, or athletic vanity ; or else if he has lent the aid of any special "arts of curiosity" to sports, to the convivialities of heathen solemnity, to official exigence, to the ministry of another's idolatry ; if he has impaled himself upon some word of ambiguous denial, or else of blasphemy. For some such cause he has been driven outside the flock ; or even himself, perhaps, by anger, by pride, by jealousy, (or) — as, in fact, often happens — by disdaining to submit to chastisement, has broken away (from it). He ought to be re-sought and recalled. That which can be recovered does not "perish," unless it persist in remaining outside. You will well interpret the parable by recalling the sinner *while he is still living*. But, for the adulterer and fornicator, who is there who has not pronounced him to be *dead* immediately upon commission of the crime ? With what face will you restore to the flock one who is dead, on the authority of that parable which recalls a sheep *not* dead ?

Finally, if you are mindful of the prophets, when they are chiding the shepherds, there is a word — I think it is Ezekiel's : "Shepherds, behold, ye devour the milk, and clothe you with the fleeces : what is strong ye have slain ; what is weak ye have not tended ; what is shattered ye have not bound ; what has been driven out ye have not brought back ; what has perished ye have not re-sought."[1] Pray, does he withal upbraid them at all concerning that which is *dead*, that they have taken no care to restore that too to the flock ? Plainly, he makes it an additional reproach that they have caused the sheep to perish, and to be eaten up by the beasts of the field ; nor can they either " perish mortally," or be " eaten up," if they are left remaining. " Is it not possible — (granting) that ewes which have been mortally lost, and eaten up, are re-

covered — that (in accordance also with the example of the drachma (lost and found again) even within the house of God, the Church) there may be some sins of a moderate character, proportionable to the small size and the weight of a drachma, which, lurking in the same Church, and by and by in the same discovered, forthwith are brought to an end in the same with the joy of amendment?" But of adultery and fornication it is not a drachma, but a talent, (which is the measure) ; and for searching them out there is need not of the javelin-light of a lamp, but of the spear-like ray of the entire sun. No sooner has (such a) man made his appearance than he is expelled from the Church ; nor does he remain there ; nor does he cause joy to the Church which discovers him, but grief ; nor does he invite the congratulation of her neighbours, but the fellowship in sadness of the surrounding fraternities.

By comparison, even in this way, of this our interpretation with theirs, the arguments of both the ewe and the drachma will all the more refer to the heathen, that they cannot possibly apply to the Christian guilty of the sin for the sake of which they are wrested into a forced application to the Christian on the opposite side.

CHAP. VIII. — OF THE PRODIGAL SON.

But, however, the majority of interpreters of the parables are deceived by the self-same result as is of very frequent occurrence in the case of embroidering garments with purple. When you think that you have judiciously harmonized the proportions of the hues, and believe yourself to have succeeded in skilfully giving vividness to their mutual combination ; presently, when each body (of colour) and (the various) lights are fully developed, the convicted diversity will expose all the error. In the self-same darkness, accordingly, with regard to the parable of the two sons also, they are led by some figures (occurring in it), which harmonize in hue with the present (state of things), to wander out of the path of the true light of that comparison which the subject-matter of the parable presents. For they set down, as represented in the two sons, two peoples — the elder the Jewish, the younger the Christian : for they cannot in the sequel arrange for the Christian sinner, in the person of the younger son, to obtain pardon, unless in the person of the elder they first portray the Jewish. Now, if I shall succeed in showing that the Jewish fails to suit the comparison of the elder son, the consequence of course will be, that the Christian will not be admissible (as represented) by the joint figure of the younger son. For although the Jew withal be called " a son," and an " elder one," inasmuch as he had priority in adoption ;[2]

---

[1] See Ezek. xxxiv. 1-4.

[2] See Ex. iv. 22; Rom. ix. 4.

although, too, he envy the Christian the reconciliation of God the Father, — a point which the opposite side most eagerly catches at, — still it will be no speech of a Jew to the Father : " Behold, in how many years do I serve Thee, and Thy precept have I never transgressed." For when has the Jew *not* been a transgressor of the law ; hearing with the ear, and not hearing ;[1] holding in hatred him who reproveth in the gates,[2] and in scorn holy speech?[3] So, too, it will be no speech of the Father to the Jew : " Thou art always with Me, and all Mine are thine." For the Jews are pronounced "apostate sons, begotten indeed and raised on high, but who have not understood the Lord, and who have quite forsaken the LORD, and have provoked unto anger the Holy One of Israel."[4] That all things, plainly, were *conceded* to the Jew, we shall admit ; but he has likewise had every more savoury morsel torn from his throat,[5] not to say the very land of paternal promise. And accordingly the Jew at the present day, no less than the younger son, having squandered God's substance, is a beggar in alien territory, serving even until now its princes, that is, the princes of this world.[6] Seek, therefore, the Christians some other as their brother ; for the Jew the parable does not admit. Much more aptly would they have matched the Christian with the elder, and the Jew with the younger son, "according to the analogy of faith,"[7] if the order of each people as intimated from Rebecca's womb[8] permitted the inversion : only that (in that case) the concluding paragraph would oppose them ; for it will be fitting for the Christian to rejoice, and not to grieve, at the restoration of Israel, if it be true, (as it is), that the whole of our hope is intimately united with the remaining expectation of Israel.[9] Thus, even if some (features in the parable) are favourable, yet by others of a contrary significance the thorough carrying out of this comparison is destroyed ; although (albeit all points be capable of corresponding with mirror-like accuracy) there be one cardinal danger in interpretations — the danger lest the felicity of our comparisons be tempered with a different aim from that which the subject-matter of each particular parable has bidden us (temper it). For we remember (to have seen) actors withal, while accommodating allegorical gestures to their ditties, giving expression to such as are far different from the immediate plot, and scene, and character, and yet *with the utmost congruity*. But

away with extraordinary ingenuity, for it has nothing to do with our subject. Thus heretics, too, apply the self-same parables where they list, and exclude them (in other cases) — not where they *ought* — with the utmost aptitude. Why the utmost aptitude? Because from the very beginning they have moulded together the very subject-matters of their doctrines in accordance with the opportune incidences of the parables. Loosed as they are from the constraints of the rule of truth, they have had leisure, of course, to search into and put together those things of which the parables seem (to be symbolical).

CHAP. IX. — CERTAIN GENERAL PRINCIPLES OF PARABOLIC INTERPRETATION. THESE APPLIED TO THE PARABLES NOW UNDER CONSIDERATION, ESPECIALLY TO THAT OF THE PRODIGAL SON.

We, however, who do not make the parables the sources whence we devise our subject-matters, but the subject-matters the sources whence we interpret the parables, do not labour hard, either, to twist all things (into shape) in the exposition, while we take care to avoid all contradictions. Why " an hundred sheep?" and why, to be sure, " ten drachmas?" And what is that " besom?" Necessary it was that He who was desiring to express the extreme pleasure which the salvation of *one* sinner gives to God, should name some special quantity of a numerical whole from which to describe that "one" had perished. Necessary it was that the style of one engaged in searching for a " drachma " in a " house," should be aptly fitted with the helpful accompaniment of a " besom " as well as of a " lamp." For curious niceties of this kind not only render some things suspected, but, by the subtlety of forced explanations, generally lead away from the truth. There are, moreover, some points which are just simply introduced with a view to the structure and disposition and texture of the parable, in order that they may be worked up throughout to the end for which the typical example is being provided. Now, of course the (parable of) the two sons will point to the same end as (those of) the drachma and the ewe : for it has the self-same cause (to call it forth) as those to which it coheres, and the selfsame " muttering," of course, of the Pharisees at the intercourse between the Lord and heathens. Or else, if any doubts that in the land of Judea, subjugated as it had been long since by the hand of Pompey and of Lucullus, the publicans were heathens, let him read Deuteronomy : " There shall be no tribute-weigher of the sons of Israel."[10] Nor would the name of publicans have been so execrable in the eyes of the Lord, unless as being

---

[1] Comp. Isa. vi. 9.
[2] Comp. Isa. xxix. 21.
[3] Comp. Jer. xx. 7, 8.
[4] Comp. Isa. i. 2–4.
[5] See Ps. lxxviii. 30, 31 (in LXX. it is lxxvii. 30, 31).
[6] Or "age"—sæculi. Comp. 1 Cor. ii. 6.
[7] Comp. Rom. xii. 6.
[8] Comp. Rom. ix. 10–13; Gen. xxv. 21–24.
[9] Comp. Rom. xi. 11–36.

[10] Oehler refers to Deut. xxiii. 19; but the ref. is not satisfactory.

a "strange"[1] name, — a (name) of such as put up the pathways of the very sky, and earth, and sea, for sale. Moreover, when (the writer) adjoins "sinners" to "publicans,"[2] it does not follow that he shows them to have been Jews, albeit some may possibly have been so; but by placing on a par the one *genus* of heathens — some sinners by office, that is, publicans; some by nature, that is, not publicans — he has drawn a distinction between them. Besides, the Lord would not have been censured for partaking of food with Jews, but with heathens, from whose board the Jewish discipline excludes (its disciples).[3]

Now we must proceed, in the case of the prodigal son, to consider first that which is more useful; for no adjustment of examples, albeit in the most nicely-poised balance, shall be admitted if it shall prove to be most hurtful to salvation. But the whole system of salvation, as it is comprised in the maintenance of discipline, we see is being subverted by that interpretation which is affected by the opposite side. For if it is a *Christian* who, after wandering far from his Father, squanders, by living heathenishly, the "substance" received from God his Father, — (the substance), of course, of baptism — (the substance), of course, of the Holy Spirit, and (in consequence) of eternal hope; if, stripped of his mental "goods," he has even handed his service over to the prince of the world[4] — who else but the devil? — and by him being appointed over the business of "feeding swine" — of tending unclean spirits, to wit — has recovered his senses so as to return to his Father, — the result will be, that, not adulterers and fornicators, but idolaters, and blasphemers, and renegades, and every class of apostates, will by this parable make satisfaction to the Father; and in this way (it may) rather (be said that) the whole "substance" of the sacrament is most truly wasted away. For who will fear to squander what he has the power of afterwards recovering? Who will be careful to preserve to perpetuity what he will be able to lose *not* to perpetuity? Security in sin is likewise an appetite for it. Therefore the apostate withal will recover his former "garment," the robe of the Holy Spirit; and a renewal of the "ring," the sign and seal of baptism; and Christ will again be "slaughtered;"[5] and he will recline on that couch from which such as are *unworthily clad* are wont to be lifted by the torturers, and cast

away into darkness,[6] — much more such as have been *stripped*. It is therefore a further step if it is not *expedient*, (any more than *reasonable*), that the story of the prodigal son should apply to a Christian. Wherefore, if the image of a "son" is not entirely suitable to a Jew either, our interpretation shall be simply governed with an eye to the object the Lord had in view. The Lord had come, of course, to save that which "had perished;"[7] "a Physician" necessary to "the sick" "more than to the whole."[8] This fact He was in the habit both of typifying in parables and preaching in direct statements. Who among men "perishes," who falls from health, but he who knows not the Lord? Who is "safe and sound," but he who knows the Lord? These two classes — "brothers" by birth — this parable also will signify. See whether the heathen have in God the Father the "substance" of origin, and wisdom, and natural power of Godward recognition; by means of which power the apostle withal notes that "in the wisdom of God, the world through wisdom knew not God,"[9] — (wisdom) which, of course, it had received originally from God. This ("substance"), accordingly, he "squandered;" having been cast by his moral habits far from the Lord, amid the errors and allurements and appetites of the world,[10] where, compelled by hunger after truth,[11] he handed himself over to the prince of this age. He set him over "swine," to feed that flock familiar to demons,[12] where he would not be master of a supply of vital food, and at the same time would see others (engaged) in a divine work, having abundance of heavenly bread. He remembers his Father, God; he returns to Him when he has been satisfied; he receives again the pristine "garment," — the condition, to wit, which Adam by transgression had lost. The "ring" also he is then wont to receive for the first time, wherewith, after being interrogated,[13] he publicly seals the agreement of faith, and thus thenceforward feeds upon the "fatness" of the Lord's body, — the Eucharist, to wit. This will be the prodigal son, who never in days bygone was thrifty; who was from the first prodigal, because *not* from the first a Christian. Him withal, returning from the world to the Father's embraces, the Pharisees mourned over, in the persons of the "publicans and sinners." And accordingly to this point alone the elder brother's envy is adapted: not because the Jews were innocent, and obedient to God, but because they envied the nation salvation; being plainly

---

[1] Extraneum. Comp. such phrases as "*strange* children," Ps. cxliv. 7, 11 (cxliii. 7, 11, in LXX.), and Hos. v. 7; "*strange* gods," etc.
[2] See Luke xv. 1, 2; Matt. ix. 10, 11, xi. 19; Mark ii. 15, 16; Luke v. 29, 30.
[3] See Acts x. 28, xi. 3.
[4] Sæculi. Comp. 1 Cor. ii. 8; 2 Cor. iv. 4.
[5] Besides the reference to Luke xv. 23, there may be a reference to Heb. vi. 6.

[6] See Matt. xxii. 11-14.
[7] See Matt. xviii. 11.
[8] Matt. ix. 12; Mark ix. 17; Luke v. 21.
[9] 1 Cor. i. 21.
[10] Sæculi.
[11] Amos viii. 11.
[12] See Matt. viii. 30-34; Mark v. 11-14; Luke viii. 32, 33.
[13] Comp. 1 Pet. iii. 21; and Hooker, *Eccl. Pol.*, v. 63, 3.

they who *ought* to have been "ever with" the Father. And of course it is immediately over the *first* calling of the Christian that the Jew groans, not over his *second* restoration : for the former reflects its rays even upon the heathen ; but the latter, which takes place in the churches, is not known even to the Jews. I think that I have advanced interpretations more consonant with the subject-matter of the parables, and the congruity of things, and the preservation of disciplines. But if the view with which the opposite party is eager to mould the ewe, and the drachma, and the voluptuousness of the son to the shape of the Christian sinner, is that they may endow adultery and fornication with (the gift of) repentance ; it will be fitting either that all other crimes equally capital should be conceded remissible, or else that their peers, adultery and fornication, should be retained inconcessible.

But it is more (to the point) that it is not lawful to draw conclusions about anything else than the subject which was immediately in hand. In short, if it were lawful to transfer the parables to other ends (than they were originally intended for), it would be rather to *martyrdom* that we would direct the hope drawn from those now in question ; for that is the only thing which, after all his substance has been squandered, will be able to restore the son ; and will joyfully proclaim that the drachma has been found, albeit among all (rubbish) on a dungheap ; and will carry back into the flock on the shoulders of the Lord Himself the ewe, fugitive though she have been over all that is rough and rugged. But we prefer, if it must be so, to be *less* wise *in* the Scriptures, than to be wise *against* them. We are as much bound to keep the *sense* of the Lord as His *precept.* Transgression in interpretation is not lighter than in conversation.

CHAP. X. — REPENTANCE MORE COMPETENT TO HEATHENS THAN TO CHRISTIANS.

When, therefore, the yoke which forbade the discussion of these parables with a view to the heathens has been shaken off, and the necessity once for all discerned or admitted of not interpreting otherwise than is (suitable to) the subject-matter of the proposition ; they contend in the next place, that the official proclamation of repentance is not even applicable to heathens, since their sins are not even amenable to it, imputable as they are to ignorance, which nature alone renders culpable before God. Hence the remedies are unintelligible to such to whom the perils themselves are unintelligible : whereas the principle of repentance finds there its corresponding place where sin is committed with conscience and will, where both the fault and the favour are intelligible ; that he who mourns, he who pros-

trates himself, is he who knows both what he has lost and what he will recover if he makes to God the offering of his repentance — to God who, of course, offers that repentance rather to sons than to strangers.

Was that, then, the reason why Jonah thought not repentance necessary to the heathen Ninevites, when he tergiversated in the duty of preaching? or did he rather, foreseeing the mercy of God poured forth even upon strangers, fear that that mercy would, as it were, destroy (the credit of) his proclamation? and accordingly, for the sake of a profane city, not yet possessed of a knowledge of God, still sinning in ignorance, did the prophet well-nigh perish?[1] except that he suffered a typical example of the Lord's passion, which was to redeem heathens as well (as others) on their repentance. It is enough for me that even John, when "strewing the Lord's ways,"[2] was the herald of repentance no less to such as were on military service and to publicans, than to the sons of Abraham.[3] The Lord Himself presumed repentance on the part of the Sidonians and Tyrians if they had seen the evidences of His "miracles."[4]

Nay, but I will even contend that repentance is *more* competent to natural sinners than to voluntary. For he will merit its fruit who has not yet *used* more than he who has already withal *abused* it ; and remedies will be more effective on their first application than when outworn. No doubt the Lord is "kind" to "the unthankful,"[5] rather than to the ignorant! and "merciful" to the "reprobates" sooner than to such as have yet had no probation! so that insults offered to His clemency do not rather incur His *anger* than His *caresses!* and He does not more willingly impart to strangers that (clemency) which, in the case of His own sons, He has lost, seeing that He has thus adopted the Gentiles while the Jews make sport of His patience! But what the Psychics mean is this — that God, the Judge of righteousness, prefers the repentance to the death of that sinner who has preferred death to repentance! If this is so, it is by sinning that we merit favour.

Come, you rope-walker upon modesty, and chastity, and every kind of sexual sanctity, who, by the instrumentality of a discipline of this nature remote from the path of truth, mount with uncertain footstep upon a most slender thread, balancing flesh with spirit, moderating your animal principle by faith, tempering your eye by fear ; why are you thus wholly engaged in a single step? Go on, if you succeed in finding power and will, while you are so secure, and

[1] Comp. Jonah i. iv.
[2] See Luke i. 76.
[3] See Luke iii. 8, 12, 14.
[4] Matt. xi. 21 ; Luke x. 13.
[5] Comp. Luke vi. 35.

as it were upon solid ground. For if any wavering of the flesh, any distraction of the mind, any wandering of the eye, shall chance to shake you down from your equipoise, "God is good." To His own (children), not to heathens, He opens His bosom : a second repentance will await you ; you will again, from being an adulterer, be a Christian ! These (pleas) you (will urge) to me, most benignant interpreter of God. But I would yield my ground to you, if the scripture of "the Shepherd," [1] which is the only one which favours adulterers, had deserved to find a place in the Divine canon ; if it had not been habitually judged by every council of Churches (even of your own) among apocryphal and false (writings) ; itself adulterous, and hence a patroness of its comrades ; from which in other respects, too, you derive initiation ; to which, perchance, that "Shepherd ' will play the patron whom you depict upon your (sacramental) chalice, (depict, I say, as) himself withal a prostitutor of the Christian sacrament, (and hence) worthily both the idol of drunkenness, and the brize of adultery by which the chalice will quickly be followed, (a chalice) from which you sip nothing more readily than (the flavour of) the "ewe" of (your) second repentance ! I, however, imbibe the Scriptures of that Shepherd who cannot be broken. Him John forthwith offers me, together with the laver and duty of repentance ; (and offers Him as) saying, "Bear worthy fruits of repentance : and say not, We have Abraham (as our) father " — for fear, to wit, lest they should again take flattering unctions for delinquency from the grace shown to the fathers — " for God is able from these stones to raise sons to Abraham." Thus it follows that we too (must judge) such as "sin no more" (as) "bearing worthy fruits of repentance." For what more ripens as the fruit of repentance than the achievement of emendation ? But even if *pardon* is rather the " fruit of repentance," even pardon cannot co-exist without the cessation from sin. So is the cessation from sin the root of pardon, that pardon may be the fruit of repentance.

CHAP. XI. — FROM PARABLES TERTULLIAN COMES TO CONSIDER DEFINITE ACTS OF THE LORD.

From the side of its pertinence to the Gospel, the question of the parables indeed has by this time been disposed of. If, however, the Lord, by His *deeds* withal, issued any such proclamation in favour of sinners ; as when He permitted contact even with his own body to the " woman, a sinner," — washing, as she did, His feet with tears, and wiping them with her hair, and inaugurating His sepulture with ointment ; as when

to the Samaritaness — not an adulteress by her now sixth marriage, but a prostitute — He showed (what He did show readily to any one) who He was ; [2] — no benefit is hence conferred upon our adversaries, even if it had been to such as were already Christians that He (in these several cases) granted pardon. For we now affirm : This is lawful to the Lord alone : may the power of His indulgence be operative at the present day ! [3] At those times, however, in which He lived on earth we lay this down definitively, that it is no prejudgment against us if pardon used to be conferred on sinners — even Jewish ones. For Christian discipline dates from the renewing of the Testament, [4] and (as we have premised) from the redemption of flesh — that is, the Lord's passion. None was perfect before the discovery of the order of faith ; none a Christian before the resumption of Christ to heaven ; none holy before the manifestation of the Holy Spirit from heaven, the Determiner of discipline itself.

CHAP. XII.— OF THE VERDICT OF THE APOSTLES, ASSEMBLED IN COUNCIL, UPON THE SUBJECT OF ADULTERY.

Accordingly, these who have received "another Paraclete " in and through the apostles, — (a Paraclete) whom, not recognising Him even in His special prophets, they no longer possess in the apostles either ; — come, now, let them, even from the apostolic instrument, teach us the possibility that the stains of a flesh which after baptism has been repolluted, can by repentance be washed away. Do we not, in the apostles also, recognise the form of the Old Law with regard to the demonstration of adultery, how great (a crime) it is ; lest perchance it be esteemed more trivial in the new stage of disciplines than in the old? When first the Gospel thundered and shook the old system to its base, when dispute was being held on the question of retaining or not the Law ; this is the first rule which the apostles, on the authority of the Holy Spirit, send out to those who were already beginning to be gathered to their side out of the nations : " It has seemed (good)," say they, "to the Holy Spirit and to us to cast upon you no ampler weight than (that) of those (things) from which it is necessary that abstinence be observed ; from sacrifices, and from fornications, and from blood : [5] by abstaining from which ye act rightly, the Holy Spirit carrying you." Sufficient it is, that in this place withal there has been preserved to adultery and fornication the post of their own honour between idolatry and mur-

---

[1] i.e., the "Shepherd " of Hermas. See *de Or.*, c. xvi.

[2] John iv. 1–25.
[3] Comp. c iii. above.
[4] Comp. Matt. xxvi. 28, Mark xiv. 24, Luke xxii. 21, with Heb. ix. 11–20.
[5] See Acts xv. 28, 29.

der : for the interdict upon "blood" we shall understand to be (an interdict) much more upon *human* blood. Well, then, in what light do the apostles will those crimes to appear which alone they select, in the way of careful guarding against, from the pristine Law? which alone they prescribe as necessarily to be abstained from? Not that they permit others ; but that these alone they put in the foremost rank, of course as not remissible ; (they,) who, for the heathens' sake, made the other burdens of the law remissible. Why, then, do they release our neck from so heavy a yoke, except to place forever upon those (necks) these compendia of discipline? Why do they indulgently relax so many bonds, except that they may wholly bind us in perpetuity to such as are more necessary? They loosed us from the more numerous, that we might be bound up to abstinence from the more noxious. The matter has been settled by compensation : we have gained much, in order that we may render somewhat. But the compensation is not revocable ; if, that is, it will be revoked by iteration — (iteration) of adultery, of course, and blood and idolatry : for it will follow that the (burden of) the whole law will be incurred, if the condition of pardon shall be violated. But it is not lightly that the Holy Spirit has come to an agreement with us — coming to this agreement even without our asking ; whence He is the more to be honoured. His engagement none but an ungrateful man will dissolve. In that event, He will neither accept back what He has discarded, nor discard what He has retained. Of the latest Testament the condition is ever immutable ; and, of course, the public recitation of that decree,[1] and the counsel embodied therein, will cease (only) with the world.[2] He has definitely enough refused pardon to those crimes the careful avoidance whereof He selectively enjoined ; He has claimed whatever He has not inferentially conceded. Hence it is that there is no restoration of peace granted by the Churches to "idolatry" or to "blood." From which final decision of theirs that the apostles should have departed, is (I think) not lawful to believe ; or else, if some find it possible to believe so, they will be bound to prove it.

CHAP. XIII. — OF ST. PAUL, AND THE PERSON WHOM HE URGES THE CORINTHIANS TO FORGIVE.

We know plainly at this point, too, the suspicions which they raise. For, in fact, they suspect the Apostle Paul of having, in the second (Epistle) to the Corinthians, granted pardon to the self-same fornicator whom in the first he has publicly sentenced to be "surrendered to Satan,

for the destruction of the flesh,"[3]—impious heir as he was to his father's wedlock ; as if he subsequently erased his own words, writing : "But if any hath wholly saddened, he hath not wholly saddened *me*, but in part, lest I burden you all. Sufficient is such a chiding which is given by many ; so that, on the contrary, ye should prefer to forgive and console, lest, perhaps, by more abundant sadness, such an one be devoured. For which reason, I pray you, confirm toward him affection. For to this end withal have I written, that I may learn a proof of you, that in all (things) ye are obedient to me. But if ye shall have forgiven any, so (do) I ; for I, too, if I have forgiven ought, have forgiven in the person of Christ, lest we be overreached by Satan, since we are not ignorant of his injections."[4] What (reference) is understood here to the fornicator? what to the contaminator of his father's bed?[5] what to the Christian who had overstepped the shamelessness of heathens?—since, of course, he would have absolved by a special pardon one whom he had condemned by a special anger. He is more obscure in his pity than in his indignation. He is more open in his austerity than in his lenity. And yet, (generally), anger is more readily indirect than indulgence. Things of a sadder are more wont to hesitate than things of a more joyous cast. Of course the question in hand concerned some *moderate* indulgence ; which (moderation in the indulgence) was now, if ever, to be divined, when it is usual for all the *greatest* indulgences not to be granted without public proclamation, so far (are they from being granted) without particularization. Why, do you yourself, when introducing into the church, for the purpose of melting the brotherhood by his prayers, the repentant adulterer, lead into the midst and prostrate him, all in haircloth and ashes, a compound of disgrace and horror, before the widows, before the elders, suing for the tears of all, licking the footprints of all, clasping the knees of all? And do you, good shepherd and blessed father that you are, to bring about the (desired) end of the man, grace your harangue with all the allurements of mercy in your power, and under the parable of the "ewe" go in quest of your goats?[6] do you, for fear lest your "ewe" again take a leap out from the flock — as if that were no more lawful for the future which was not even once lawful—fill all the rest likewise full of apprehension at the very moment of granting indulgence? And would the apostle so carelessly have granted indulgence to the atrocious licentiousness of fornication burdened with incest, as not at least to have exacted from

---

[1] See Acts xv. 30 and xvi. 4.
[2] Sæculo.

[3] See 1 Cor. v. 5.
[4] See 2 Cor. ii. 5–11.
[5] Comp. Gen. xlix. 4.
[6] Comp. Matt. xxv. 32, 33.

the criminal even this legally established garb of repentance which you ought to have learned from him? as to have uttered no commination on the past? no allocution touching the future? Nay, more; he goes further, and beseeches that they "would confirm toward him affection," as if he were making satisfaction to him, not as if he were granting an indulgence! And yet I hear (him speak of) "affection," not "communion;" as (he writes) withal to the Thessalonians: "But if any obey not our word through the epistle, him mark; and associate not with him, that he may feel awed; not regarding (him) as an enemy, but rebuking as a brother." [1] Accordingly, he could have said that to a fornicator, too, "affection" only was conceded, not "communion" as well; to an incestuous man, however, not even "affection;" whom he would, to be sure, have bidden to be banished from their *midst* [2] — much more, of course, from their *mind*. "But he was apprehensive lest they should be 'overreached by Satan' with regard to the loss of that person whom himself had cast forth to Satan; or else lest, 'by abundance of mourning, he should be devoured' whom he had sentenced to 'destruction of the flesh.'" Here they go so far as to interpret "destruction of the flesh" of the office of repentance; in that by fasts, and squalor, and every species of neglect and studious ill-treatment devoted to the extermination of the flesh, it seems to make satisfaction to God; so that they argue that that fornicator — that incestuous person rather — having been delivered by the apostle to Satan, not with a view to "perdition," but with a view to "emendation," on the hypothesis that subsequently he would, on account of the "destruction" (that is, the general affliction) "of the flesh," attain pardon, therefore did actually attain it. Plainly, the self-same apostle delivered to Satan Hymenæus and Alexander, "that they might be emended into not blaspheming," [3] as he writes to his Timotheus. "But withal himself says that 'a stake [4] was given him, an angel of Satan,' by which he was to be buffeted, lest he should exalt himself." If they touch upon this (instance) withal, in order to lead us to understand that such as were "delivered to Satan" by him (were so delivered) with a view to emendation, not to perdition; what similarity is there between blasphemy and incest, and a soul entirely free from these, — nay, rather elated from no other source than the highest sanctity and all innocence; which (elation of soul) was being restrained in the apostle by "buffets," if you will, by means (as they say) of pain in the ear or head? In-

cest, however, and blasphemy, deserved to have delivered the entire persons of men to Satan himself for a possession, not to "an angel" of his. And (there is yet another point): for about this it makes a difference, nay, rather withal in regard to this it is of the utmost consequence, that we find those men delivered by the apostle to Satan, but to the apostle himself an angel of Satan given. Lastly, when Paul is praying the Lord for its removal, what does he hear? "Hold my grace sufficient; for virtue is perfected in infirmity." [5] This they who are surrendered to Satan cannot hear. Moreover, if the crime of Hymenæus and Alexander — blasphemy, to wit — is irremissible in this and in the future age, [6] of course the apostle would not, in opposition to the determinate decision of the Lord, have given to Satan, *under a hope of pardon*, men already sunken from the faith into blasphemy; whence, too, he pronounced them "shipwrecked with regard to faith," [7] having no longer the solace of the ship, the Church. For to those who, after believing, have struck upon (the rock of) blasphemy, pardon is denied; on the other hand, *heathens* and *heretics* are daily emerging *out of* blasphemy. But even if he did say, "I delivered them to Satan, that they might receive the discipline of not blaspheming," he said it of the rest, who, by *their* deliverance to Satan — that is, their projection outside the Church — had to be trained in the knowledge that there must be no blaspheming. So, therefore, the incestuous fornicator, too, he delivered, not with a view to emendation, but with a view to perdition, to Satan, to whom he had already, by sinning above an heathen, gone over; that they might learn there must be no fornicating. Finally, he says, "for the *destruction* of the flesh," not its "*torture*" — condemning the actual substance through which he had fallen out (of the faith), which substance had already perished immediately on the loss of baptism — "in order that the spirit," he says, "may be saved in the day of the Lord." And (here, again, is a difficulty): for let this point be inquired into, whether *the man's own spirit* will be saved. In that case, a spirit polluted with so great a wickedness will be saved; the object of the perdition of the flesh being, that the spirit may be saved *in penalty*. In that case, the interpretation which is contrary to ours will recognise a penalty *without the flesh*, if we lose the resurrection of the flesh. It remains, therefore, that his meaning was, that *that* spirit which is accounted to exist *in the Church* must be presented "saved," that is, untainted by the contagion of impurities in the day of the Lord, by the ejection of the incestuous fornicator; if,

---

[1] 2 Thess. iii. 14, 15.
[2] Comp. 1 Cor. v. 2.
[3] 1 Tim. i. 20.
[4] 2 Cor. xii. 7-10.

[5] 2 Cor. xii. 9, not very exactly rendered.
[6] Ævo. Comp. Matt. xii. 32.
[7] 1 Tim. i. 19.

that is, he subjoins : " Know ye not, that a little leaven spoileth the savour of the whole lump?" [1] And yet incestuous fornication was not a little, but a large, leaven.

CHAP. XIV. — THE SAME SUBJECT CONTINUED.

And — these intervening points having accordingly been got rid of — I return to the second of Corinthians ; in order to prove that this saying also of the apostle, "Sufficient to such a man be *this rebuke* which (is administered) by many," is not suitable to the person of the fornicator. For if he had sentenced him " to be surrendered to Satan for the destruction of the flesh," of course he had *condemned* rather than *rebuked* him. Some other, then, it was to whom he willed the " rebuke " to be sufficient ; if, that is, the fornicator had incurred not " rebuke " from his sentence, but " condemnation." For I offer you withal, for your investigation, this very question : Whether there were in the first Epistle others, too, who " wholly saddened " the apostle by " acting disorderly," [2] and " were wholly saddened " by him, through incurring (his) " rebuke," according to the sense of the second Epistle ; of whom some particular one may in that (second Epistle) have received pardon. Direct we, moreover, our attention to the entire first Epistle, written (that I may so say) as a whole, not with ink, but with gall ; swelling, indignant, disdainful, comminatory, invidious, and shaped through (a series of) individual charges, with an eye to certain individuals who were, as it were, the proprietors of those charges? For so had schisms, and emulations, and discussions, and presumptions, and elations, and contentions required, that they should be laden with invidiousness, and rebuffed with curt reproof, and filed down by haughtiness, and deterred by austerity. And what kind of invidiousness is the pungency of humility? " To God I give thanks that I have baptized none of you, except Crispus and Gaius, lest any say that I have baptized in mine own name." [3] " For neither did I judge to know anything among you but Jesus Christ, and Him crucified." [4] And, "(I think) God hath selected us the apostles (as) hindmost, like men appointed to fight with wild beasts ; since we have been made a spectacle to this world, both to angels and to men : " And, " We have been made the offscourings of this world, the refuse of all : " And, " Am I not free? am I not an apostle? have I not seen Christ Jesus our Lord?" [5] With what kind of superciliousness, on the contrary, was he compelled to declare, " But to me

it is of small moment that I be interrogated by you, or by a human court-day ; for neither am I conscious to myself (of any guilt) ; " and, " My glory none shall make empty." [6] " Know ye not that we are to judge angels?" [7] Again, of how open censure (does) the free expression (find utterance), how manifest the edge of the spiritual sword, (in words like these) : " Ye are already enriched ! ye are already satiated ! ye are already reigning ! " [8] and, " If any thinks himself to know, he knoweth not yet how it behoves him to know ! " [9] Is he not even then " smiting some one's face," [10] in saying, " For who maketh *thee* to differ? What, moreover, hast thou which thou hast not received? Why gloriest thou as if thou have not received?" [11] Is he not withal " smiting them upon the mouth," [12] (in saying) : " But some, in (their) conscience, even until now eat (it) as if (it were) an idol-sacrifice. But, so sinning, by shocking the weak consciences of the brethren thoroughly, they will sin against Christ." [13] By this time, indeed, (he mentions individuals) by name : " Or have we not a power of eating, and of drinking, and of leading about women, just as the other apostles withal, and the bretnren of the Lord, and Cephas?" and, " If others attain to (a share) in power over you, (may) not we rather?" In like manner he pricks *them*, too, with an individualizing pen : " Wherefore, let *him* who thinketh himself to be standing, see lest he fall ;" and, " If *any seemeth* to be contentious, we have not such a custom, nor (has) the Church of the Lord." With such a final clause (as the following), wound up with a malediction, " If *any loveth not* the Lord Jesus, be he anathema maranatha," he is, of course, striking *some particular individual* through.

But I will rather take my stand at that point where the apostle is more fervent, where the fornicator himself has troubled others also. " As if I be not about to come unto you, some are inflated. But I will come with more speed, if the Lord shall have permitted, and will learn not the speech of those who are inflated, but the power. For the kingdom of God is not in speech, but in power. And what will ye? shall I come unto you in a rod, or in a spirit of lenity?" For what was to succeed? " There is heard among you generally fornication, and such fornication as (is) not (heard) even among the Gentiles, that one should have his own father's wife. And are ye inflated, and have ye not rather mourned, that he who hath committed

---

[1] 1 Cor. v. 6, where Tertullian appears to have used δολοῖ, not ζυμοῖ.
[2] Comp. 2 Thess. iii. 6, 11.
[3] 1 Cor. i. 14, 15; but the Greek is, εἰς τὸ ἐμὸν ὄνομα.
[4] 1 Cor. ii. 2.
[5] 1 Cor. ix. 1.

[6] Comp. 1 Cor. ix. 15.
[7] 1 Cor. vi. 3.
[8] 1 Cor. iv. 8, inaccurately.
[9] 1 Cor. viii. 2, inaccurately.
[10] See 2 Cor. xi. 20.
[11] 1 Cor. iv. 7, with some words omitted.
[12] Comp. Acts xxiii. 2.
[13] 1 Cor. viii. 7, 12, inaccurately.

such a deed may be taken away from the midst of you?" *For* whom were they to "mourn?" Of course, for one dead. *To* whom were they to mourn? Of course, to the Lord, in order that in some way or other he may be "taken away from the midst of them;" not, of course, in order that he may be put outside the Church. For a thing would not have been requested of God which came within the official province of the president (of the Church); but (what would be requested of Him was), that through death — not only this death common to all, but one specially appropriate to that very flesh which was already a corpse, a tomb leprous with irremediable uncleanness — he might more fully (than by simple excommunication) incur the penalty of being "taken away" from the Church. And accordingly, in so far as it was meantime possible for him to be "taken away," he "adjudged such an one to be surrendered to Satan for the destruction of the flesh." For it followed that flesh which was being cast forth to the devil should be accursed, in order that it might be discarded from the sacrament of blessing, never to return into the camp of the Church.

And thus we see in this place the apostle's severity divided, against one who was "inflated," and one who was "incestuous:" (we see the apostle) armed against the one with "a rod," against the other with a sentence, — a "rod," which he was threatening; a sentence, which he was executing: the former (we see) still brandishing, the latter instantaneously hurtling; (the one) wherewith he was rebuking, and (the other) wherewith he was condemning. And certain it is, that forthwith thereafter the rebuked one indeed trembled beneath the menace of the uplifted rod, but the condemned perished under the instant infliction of the penalty. Immediately the former retreated fearing the blow, the latter paying the penalty. When a letter of the self-same apostle is sent a second time to the Corinthians, pardon is granted plainly; but it is uncertain *to whom*, because neither person nor cause is advertised. I will compare the cases with the senses. If the "incestuous" man is set before us, on the same platform will be the "inflated" man too. Surely the analogy of the case is sufficiently maintained, when the "inflated" is rebuked, but the "incestuous" is condemned. To the "inflated" pardon is granted, but after rebuke; to the "incestuous" no pardon seems to have been granted, as under condemnation. If it was to him for whom it was feared that he might be "devoured by mourning" that pardon was being granted, the "rebuked" one was still in danger of being devoured, losing heart on account of the commination, and mourning on account of the rebuke. The "condemned" one, however, was perma-

nently accounted as already devoured, alike by his fault and by his sentence; (accounted, that is, as one) who had not to "mourn," but to *suffer* that which, before suffering it, he might have mourned. If the reason why pardon was being granted was "lest we should be defrauded by Satan," the loss against which precaution was being taken had to do with that which had not yet perished. No precaution is taken in the case of a thing finally despatched, but in the case of a thing still safe. But the condemned one — condemned, too, to the possession of Satan — had already perished *from the Church* at the moment when he had committed such a deed, not to say withal at the moment of being forsworn by the Church itself. How should (the Church) fear to suffer a fraudulent loss of him whom she had already lost on his ereption, and whom, after condemnation, she could not have held? Lastly, to what will it be becoming for a judge to grant indulgence? to that which by a formal pronouncement he has decisively settled, or to that which by an interlocutory sentence he has left in suspense? And, of course, (I am speaking of) *that* judge who is not wont "to rebuild those things which he has destroyed, lest he be held a transgressor."[1]

Come, now, if he had not "wholly saddened" so many persons in the first Epistle; if he had "rebuked" none, had "terrified"[2] none; if he had "smitten" the incestuous man alone; if, for his cause, he had sent none into panic, had struck (no) "inflated" one with consternation, — would it not be better for you to suspect, and more believing for you to argue, that rather some one far different had been in the same predicament at that time among the Corinthians; so that, rebuked, and terrified, and already wounded with mourning, he therefore — the moderate nature of his fault permitting it — subsequently received pardon, than that you should interpret that (pardon as granted) to an incestuous fornicator? For this you had been bound to read, even if not in an Epistle, yet impressed upon the very character of the apostle, by (his) modesty more clearly than by the instrumentality of a pen: not to steep, to wit, Paul, the "apostle of Christ,"[3] the "teacher of the nations in faith and verity,"[4] the "vessel of election,"[5] the founder of Churches, the censor of discipline, (in the guilt of) levity so great as that he should either have condemned rashly one whom he was presently to absolve, or else rashly absolved one whom he had not rashly condemned, albeit on the ground of that fornication which is the result of simple immodesty, not to say on the ground

[1] Comp. Gal. ii. 18.
[2] Comp. 2 Cor. x. 9.
[3] Comp. Rom. i. 1, and the beginnings of his Epp. *passim.*
[4] 1 Tim. ii. 7.
[5] Acts ix. 15.

of incestuous nuptials and impious voluptuousness and parricidal lust, — (lust) which he had
refused to compare even with (the lusts of) the
nations, for fear it should be set down to the
account of custom ; (lust) on which he would
sit in judgment though absent, for fear the culprit should " gain the time ; " [1] (lust) which he
had condemned after calling to his aid even
" the Lord's power," for fear the sentence should
seem human. Therefore he has trifled both
with his own " spirit," [2] and with " the angel
of the Church," [3] and with " the power of the
Lord," if he rescinded what by their counsel he
had formally pronounced.

CHAP. XV. — THE SAME SUBJECT CONTINUED.

If you hammer out the sequel of that Epistle
to illustrate the meaning of the apostle, neither
will that sequel be found to square with the obliteration of incest ; lest even here the apostle
be put to the blush by the incongruity of his
later meanings. For what kind (of hypothesis)
is it, that the very moment after making a largess
of restoration to the privileges of ecclesiastical
peace to an incestuous fornicator, he should
forthwith have proceeded to accumulate exhortations about turning away from impurities, about
pruning away of blemishes, about exhortations
to deeds of sanctity, as if he had decreed nothing of a contrary nature just before? Compare,
in short, (and see) whether it be his province
to say, " Wherefore, having this ministration, in
accordance with (the fact) that we have obtained
mercy, we faint not ; but renounce the secret
things of disgrace," [4] who has just released from
condemnation one manifestly convicted of, not
"disgrace" merely, but crime too : whether it be
his province, again, to excuse a conspicuous
immodesty, who, among the counts of his own
labours, after " straits and pressures," after " fasts
and vigils," has named "chastity" also : [5] whether
it be, once more, his province to receive back
into communion whatsoever reprobates, who
writes, " For what society (is there) between
righteousness and iniquity? what communion,
moreover, between light and darkness? what con-
sonance between Christ and Belial? or what part
for a believer with an unbeliever? or what agreement between the temple of God and idols?"
Will he not deserve to hear constantly (the reply) : "And in what manner do you make a
separation between things which, in the former
part of your Epistle, by restitution of the incestuous one, you have joined? For by his restoration
to concorporate unity with the Church, righteousness is made to have fellowship with iniquity,

darkness has communion with light, Belial is
consonant with Christ, and believer shares the
sacraments with unbeliever. And idols may see
to themselves : the very vitiator of the temple
of God is converted into a temple of God : for
here, too, he says, ' For ye are a temple of the
living God. For He saith, That I will dwell in
you, and will walk in (you), and will be their
God, and they shall be to Me a people. Wherefore depart from the midst of them, be separate,
and touch not the unclean.' [6] This (thread of
discourse) also you spin out, O apostle, when at
the very moment you yourself are offering your
hand to so huge a whirlpool of impurities ; nay,
you superadd yet further, ' Having therefore this
promise, beloved, cleanse we ourselves out from
every defilement of flesh and spirit, perfecting
chastity in God's fear.' " [7] I pray you, had he
who fixes such (exhortations) in our minds
been recalling some notorious fornicator into the
Church? or is his reason for writing it, to prevent himself from appearing to you in the present
day to have so recalled him? These (words of
his) will be in duty bound alike to serve as a
prescriptive rule for the foregone, and a prejudgment for the following, (parts of the Epistle).
For in saying, toward the end of the Epistle,
" Lest, when I shall have come, God humble
me, and I bewail many of those who have formerly sinned, and have not repented of the
impurity which they have committed, the fornication, and the vileness," [8] he did not, of course,
determine that they were to be received back
(by him *into* the Church) if they should have
entered (the path of) repentance, whom he was
to find *in* the Church, but that they were to be
bewailed, and indubitably ejected, that they
might lose (the benefit of) repentance. And,
besides, it is not congruous that he, who had
above asserted that there was no communion
between light and darkness, righteousness and
iniquity, should in this place have been indicating somewhat touching communion. But all
such are ignorant of the apostle as understand
anything in a sense contrary to the nature and
design of the man himself, contrary to the norm
and rule of his docrines ; so as to presume that
he, a teacher of every sanctity, even by his own
example, an execrator and expiator of every impurity, and universally consistent with himself in
these points, restored ecclesiastical privileges to
an incestuous person sooner than to some more
mild offender.

CHAP. XVI. — GENERAL CONSISTENCY OF THE APOSTLE.

Necessary it is, therefore, that the (character
of the) apostle should be continuously pointed

---

[1] Comp. Dan. ii. 8.
[2] Comp. 1 Cor. v. 3.
[3] Comp. Rev. i. 20, ii. 1, 8, 12, 18, iii. 1, 7, 14.
[4] 2 Cor. iv. 1, 2.
[5] *Ib.* vi. 5, 6.

[6] 2 Cor. vi. 16–18.
[7] 2 Cor. vii. 1, not accurately given.
[8] 2 Cor. xii. 21, again inexactly given.

out to them; whom I will maintain to be such in the second of Corinthians withal, as I know (him to be) in all his letters. (He it is) who even in the first (Epistle) was the first of all (the apostles) to dedicate the temple of God: "Know ye not that ye are the temple of God, and that in you the Lord dwells?"[1] — who likewise, for the consecrating and purifying (of) that temple, wrote the law pertaining to the temple-keepers: "If any shall have marred the temple of God, him shall God mar; for the temple of God is holy, which (temple) are ye."[2] Come, now; who in the world has (ever) redintegrated one who has been "marred" by God (that is, delivered to Satan with a view to destruction of the flesh), after subjoining for that reason, "Let none seduce himself;"[3] that is, let none presume that one "marred" by God can possibly be redintegrated anew? Just as, again, among all other crimes — nay, even *before* all others — when affirming that "adulterers, and fornicators, and effeminates, and cohabitors with males, will not attain the kingdom of God," he premised, "Do not err"[4] — to wit, if you think they will attain it. But to them from whom "the kingdom" is taken away, of course the life which exists in the kingdom is not permitted either. Moreover, by superadding, "But such indeed ye have been; but ye have received ablution, but ye have been sanctified, in the Name of the Lord Jesus Christ, and in the Spirit of our God;"[5] in as far as he puts on the paid side of the account such sins *before* baptism, in so far *after* baptism he determines them irremissible, if it is true, (as it is), that they are not allowed to "receive ablution" anew. Recognise, too, in what follows, Paul (in the character of) an immoveable column of discipline and its rules: "Meats for the belly, and the belly for meats: God maketh a full end both of the one and of the others; but the body (is) not for fornication, but for God:"[6] for "Let Us make man," said God, "(conformable) to Our image and likeness." "And God made man; (conformable) to the image and likeness of God made He him."[7] "The Lord for the body:" yes; for "the Word was made flesh."[8] "Moreover, God both raised up the Lord, and will raise up us through His own power;"[9] on account, to wit, of the union of our body with Him. And accordingly, "Know ye not your bodies (to be) members of Christ?" because Christ, too, is God's temple. "Overturn this temple, and I

will in three days' space resuscitate it."[10] "Taking away the members of Christ, shall I make (them) members of an harlot? Know ye not, that whoever is agglutinated to an harlot is made one body? (for the two shall be (made) into one flesh): but whoever is agglutinated to the Lord is one spirit? Flee fornication."[11] If revocable by pardon, in what sense am I to flee it, to turn adulterer anew? I shall gain nothing if I do flee it: I shall be "one body," to which by communion I shall be agglutinated. "Every sin which a human being may have committed is extraneous to the body; but whoever fornicateth, sinneth against his own body."[12] And, for fear you should fly to that statement for a licence to fornication, on the ground that you will be sinning against a thing which is yours, not the Lord's, he takes you away from yourself, and awards you, according to his previous disposition, to Christ: "And ye are not your own;" immediately opposing (thereto), "for bought ye are with a price" — the blood, to wit, of the Lord:[13] "glorify and extol the Lord in your body."[14] See whether he who gives this injunction be likely to have pardoned one who has disgraced the Lord, and who has cast Him down from (the empire of) his body, and this indeed through incest. If you wish to imbibe to the utmost all knowledge of the apostle, in order to understand with what an axe of censorship he lops, and eradicates, and extirpates, every forest of lusts, for fear of permitting aught to regain strength and sprout again; behold him desiring souls to keep a fast from the legitimate fruit of nature — the apple, I mean, of marriage: "But with regard to what ye wrote, good it is for a man to have no contact with a woman; but, on account of fornication, let each one have his own wife: let husband to wife, and wife to husband, render what is due."[15] Who but must know that it was against his will that he relaxed the bond of this "good," in order to prevent fornication? But if he either has granted, or does grant, indulgence to fornication, of course he has frustrated the design of his own remedy, and will be bound forthwith to put the curb upon the nuptials of continence, if the fornication for the sake of which those nuptials are permitted shall cease to be feared. For (a fornication) which has indulgence granted it will not be feared. And yet he professes that he has granted the use of marriage "by way of indulgence, not of command."[16] For he "*wills*" all to be on a level with himself. But when things

[1] 1 Cor. iii. 16, inexactly.
[2] Ver. 17, not quite correctly.
[3] Ver. 18.
[4] 1 Cor. vi. 9, 10.
[5] Ver. 11, inexactly.
[6] Ver. 13.
[7] Comp. Gen. i. 26, 27.
[8] John i. 14.
[9] 1 Cor. vi. 14.

[10] John ii. 19.
[11] 1 Cor. vi. 15-17.
[12] 1 Cor. vi. 18.
[13] Comp. 1 Pet. i. 19; and c. vi. above, *ad fin.*
[14] 1 Cor. vi. 19, 20, not exactly.
[15] 1 Cor. vii. 1-3.
[16] *Ib.*, ver. 6.

lawful are (only) granted by way of indulgence, who hope for things unlawful? "To the un-married" also, "and widows," he says, "It is good, by his example, to persevere" (in their present state) ; "but if they were too weak, to marry ; because it is preferable to marry than to burn." [1] With what fires, I pray you, is it preferable to "burn" — (the fires) of concupiscence, or (the fires) of penalty? Nay, but if fornication is pardonable, it will not be an object of *concupiscence*. But it is more (the manner) of an apostle to take forethought for the fires of *penalty*. Wherefore, if it is *penalty* which "burns," it follows that fornication, which *penalty* awaits, is not pardonable. Meantime withal, while prohibiting divorce, he uses the Lord's precept against adultery as an instrument for providing, in place of divorce, either perseverance in widowhood, or else a reconciliation of peace : inasmuch as "whoever shall have dismissed a wife (for any cause) except the cause of adultery, maketh her commit adultery ; and he who marrieth one dismissed by a husband committeth adultery." [2] What powerful remedies does the Holy Spirit furnish, to prevent, to wit, the commission anew of that which He wills not should anew be pardoned !

Now, if in all cases he says it is best for a man thus to be ; "Thou art joined to a wife, seek not loosing" (that you may give no occasion to adultery) ; "thou art loosed from a wife, seek not a wife," that you may reserve an opportunity for yourself : "but withal, if thou shalt have married a wife, and if a virgin shall have married, she sinneth not ; pressure, however, of the flesh such shall have," — even here he is granting a permission by way of "sparing them." [3] On the other hand, he lays it down that "the time is wound up," in order that even "they who have wives may be as if they had them not." "For the fashion of this world is passing away," — (this world) no longer, to wit, requiring (the command), "Grow and multiply." Thus he wills us to pass our life "without anxiety," because "the unmarried care about the Lord, how they may please God ; the married, however, muse about the world,[4] how they may please their spouse." [5] Thus he pronounces that the "preserver of a virgin" doeth "better" than her "giver in marriage." [6] Thus, too, he discriminatingly judges her to be more blessed, who, after losing her husband subsequently to her entrance into the faith, lovingly embraces the opportunity of widowhood.[7] Thus he com-

mends as Divine all these counsels of continence : "I think," [8] he says, "I too have the Spirit of God." [9]

Who is this your most audacious asserter of all immodesty, plainly a "most faithful" advocate of the adulterous, and fornicators, and incestuous, in whose honour he has undertaken this cause against the Holy Spirit, so that he recites a false testimony from (the writings of) His apostle? No such indulgence granted Paul, who endeavours to obliterate "necessity of the flesh" wholly from (the list of) even honourable pretexts (for marriage unions). He does grant "indulgence," I allow ; — not to adulteries, but to nuptials. He does "spare," I allow ; — marriages, not harlotries. He tries to avoid giving pardon even to nature, for fear he may flatter guilt. He is studious to put restraints upon the union which is heir to blessing, for fear that which is heir to curse be excused. This (one possibility) was left him — to purge the flesh from (natural) dregs, for (cleanse it) from (foul) stains he cannot. But this is the usual way with perverse and ignorant heretics ; yes, and by this time even with Psychics universally : to arm themselves with the opportune support of some one ambiguous passage, in opposition to the disciplined host of sentences of the entire document.

CHAP. XVII. — CONSISTENCY OF THE APOSTLE IN HIS OTHER EPISTLES.

Challenge me to front the apostolic line of battle ; look at his Epistles : they all keep guard in defence of modesty, of chastity, of sanctity ; they all aim their missiles against the interests of luxury, and lasciviousness, and lust. What, in short, does he write to the Thessalonians withal? "For our consolation [10] (originated) not of seduction, nor of impurity : " and, "This is the will of God, your sanctification, that ye abstain from fornication ; that each one know how to possess his vessel in sanctification and honour, not in the lust of concupiscence, as (do) the nations which are ignorant of God." [11] What do the Galatians read? "Manifest are the works of the flesh." What are these? Among the first he has set "fornication, impurity, lasciviousness : " "(concerning) which I foretell you, as I have foretold, that whoever do such acts are not to attain by inheritance the kingdom of God." [12] The Romans, moreover, — what learning is more impressed upon them than that there must be no dereliction of the Lord after believing? "What, then, say we? Do we persevere in sin, in order that grace may superabound? Far be

1 1 Cor. vii. 8, 9.
2 Matt. v. 32.
3 1 Cor. vii. 26-28, constantly quoted in previous treatises.
4 Mundo.
5 Vers. 32, 33, loosely.
6 1 Cor. vii. 38.
7 Vers. 39, 40.

8 Puto: Gr. δοκῶ.
9 Ver. 40 *ad fin.*
10 1 Thess. ii. 3, omitting the last clause.
11 1 Thess. iv. 3-5.
12 Gal. v. 19-21.

it. We, who are dead to sin, how shall we live in it still? Are ye ignorant that we who have been baptized in Christ have been baptized into His death? Buried with Him, then, we have been, through the baptism into the death, in order that, as Christ hath risen again from the dead, so we too may walk in newness of life. For if we have been buried together in the likeness of His death, why, we shall be (in that) of (His) resurrection too; knowing this, that our old man hath been crucified together with Him. But if we died with Christ, we believe that we shall live, too, with Him; knowing that Christ, having been raised from the dead, no more dieth, (that) death no more hath domination over Him. For in that He died to sin, He died once for all; but in that He liveth, to God He liveth. Thus, too, repute ye yourselves dead indeed to sin, but living to God through Christ Jesus." [1] Therefore, Christ being *once for all* dead, none who, subsequently to Christ, has died, can live again to sin, and especially to so heinous a sin. Else, if fornication and adultery may by possibility be anew admissible, Christ withal will be able anew to die. Moreover, the apostle is urgent in prohibiting "sin from reigning in our mortal body," [2] whose "infirmity of the flesh" he knew. "For as ye have tendered your members to servile impurity and iniquity, so too now tender them servants to righteousness unto holiness." For even if he has affirmed that "good dwelleth not in his flesh," [3] yet (he means) according to the law of the letter," [4] in which he "was:" but according to "the law of the Spirit," [5] to which he annexes us, he frees us from the "infirmity of the flesh." "For the law," he says, "of the Spirit of life hath manumitted thee from the law of sin and of death." [6] For albeit he may appear to be partly disputing from the standpoint of Judaism, yet it is to us that he is directing the integrity and plenitude of the rules of discipline, — (us), for whose sake soever, labouring (as we were) in the law, "God hath sent, through flesh, His own Son, in similitude of flesh of sin; and, because of sin, hath condemned sin in the flesh; in order that the righteousness of the law," he says, "might be fulfilled in us, who walk not according to flesh, but according to (the) Spirit. For they who walk according to flesh are sensible as to those things which are the flesh's, and they who (walk) according to (the) Spirit those which (are) the Spirit's." [7] Moreover, he has affirmed the "sense of the flesh" to be "death;" [8] hence,

too, "enmity," and enmity *toward God;* [9] and that "they who are in the flesh," that is, in the *sense* of the flesh, "cannot please God:" [10] and, "If ye live according to flesh," he says, "it will come to pass that ye die." [11] But what do we understand "the sense of the flesh" and "the life of the flesh" (to mean), except whatever "it shames (one) to pronounce?" [12] for the other (works) of the flesh even an apostle would have named. [13] Similarly, too, (when writing) to the Ephesians, while recalling past (deeds), he warns (them) concerning the future: "In which we too had our conversation, doing the concupiscences and pleasures of the flesh." [14] Branding, in fine, such as had denied themselves — Christians, to wit — on the score of having "delivered themselves up to the working of every impurity," [15] "But ye," he says, "not so have learnt Christ." And again he says thus: "Let him who was wont to steal, steal no more." [16] But, similarly, let him who was wont to commit adultery hitherto, not commit adultery; and he who was wont to fornicate hitherto, not fornicate: for he would have added these (admonitions) too, had he been in the habit of extending pardon to such, or at all willed it to be extended — (he) who, not willing pollution to be contracted even by a word, says, "Let no base speech proceed out of your mouth." [17] Again: "But let fornication and every impurity not be even named among you, as becometh saints," [18] — so far is it from being excused, — "knowing this, that every fornicator or impure (person) hath not God's kingdom. Let none seduce you with empty words: on this account cometh the wrath of God upon the sons of unbelief." [19] Who "seduces with empty words" but he who states in a public harangue that adultery is remissible? not seeing into the fact that its very foundations have been dug out by the apostle, when he puts restraints upon drunkennesses and revellings, as withal here: "And be not inebriated with wine, in which is voluptuousness." [20] He demonstrates, too, to the Colossians what "members" they are to "mortify" upon earth: "fornication, impurity, lust, evil concupiscence," and "base talk." [21] Yield up, by this time, to so many and such sentences, the one (passage) to which you cling. Paucity is cast into the shade by multitude, doubt by certainty, obscurity by plainness. Even if, for certain, the apostle had granted pardon

---

[1] Rom. vi. 1-11.
[2] Ver. 12.
[3] See Rom. vii. 18.
[4] This exact expression does not occur; but comp. 2 Cor. iii. 6.
[5] Comp. the last reference and Rom. viii. 2.
[6] Rom. viii. 2, omitting ἐν Χριστῷ Ἰησοῦ, and substituting (unless it be a misprint) "te" for μέ.
[7] Rom. viii. 3-5.
[8] Ver. 6.

[9] Ver. 7.
[10] Ver. 8.
[11] Ver. 12.
[12] See Eph. v. 12.
[13] As he did to the Galatians: see Gal. v. 19-21.
[14] Eph. ii. 3, briefly, and not literally.
[15] Eph. iv. 17-20.
[16] Ver. 28.
[17] Ver. 29 *ad init.*
[18] Eph. v. 3.
[19] Vers. 5, 6, not accurately.
[20] Ver. 18.
[21] See Col. iii. 5, 8.

of fornication to that Corinthian, it would be another instance of his once for all contravening his own practice to meet the requirement of the time. He circumcised Timotheus alone, and yet did away with circumcision.[1]

CHAP. XVIII. — ANSWER TO A PSYCHICAL OBJECTION.

"But these (passages)," says (our opponent), "will pertain to the interdiction of all immodesty, and the enforcing of all modesty, yet without prejudice to the place of pardon; which (pardon) is not forthwith quite denied when sins are condemned, since the time of the pardon is concurrent with the condemnation which it excludes."

This piece of shrewdness on the part of the Psychics was (naturally) sequent; and accordingly we have reserved for this place the cautions which, even in the times of antiquity, were openly taken with a view to the refusing of ecclesiastical communion to cases of this kind.

For even in the Proverbs, which we call Parœmiæ, Solomon specially (treats) of the adulterer (as being) nowhere admissible to expiation. "But the adulterer," he says, "through indigence of senses acquireth perdition to his own soul; sustaineth dolors and disgraces. His ignominy, moreover, shall not be wiped away for the age. For indignation, full of jealousy, will not spare the man in the day of judgment."[2] If you think this said about a heathen, at all events about believers you have already heard (it said) through Isaïah: "Go out from the midst of them, and be separate, and touch not the impure."[3] You have at the very outset of the Psalms, "Blessed the man who hath not gone astray in the counsel of the impious, nor stood in the way of sinners, and sat in the state-chair of pestilence;"[4] whose voice,[5] withal, (is heard) subsequently: "I have not sat with the conclave of vanity; and with them who act iniquitously will I not enter"—this (has to do) with "*the church*" of such as act ill—"and with the impious will I not sit;"[6] and, "I will wash with the innocent mine hands, and Thine altar will I surround, LORD"[7]—as being "a host in himself"—inasmuch as indeed "With an holy (man), holy Thou wilt be; and with an innocent man, innocent Thou wilt be; and with an elect, elect Thou wilt be; and with a perverse, perverse Thou wilt be."[8] And elsewhere: "But to the sinner saith the Lord, Why expoundest thou my righteous acts, and takest up my testament through thy mouth? If thou sawest a thief, thou rannest with him; and with adulterers thy portion thou madest."[9] Deriving his instructions, therefore, from hence, the apostle too says: "I wrote to you in the Epistle, not to be mingled up with fornicators: not, of course, with the fornicators of this world"—and so forth—"else it behoved you to go out from the world. But now I write to you, if any is named a brother among you, (being) a fornicator, or an idolater" (for what so intimately joined?), "or a defrauder" (for what so near akin?), and so on, "with such to take no food even,"[10] not to say the Eucharist: because, to wit, withal "a little leaven spoileth the flavour of the whole lump."[11] Again to Timotheus: "Lay hands on no one hastily, nor communicate with others' sins."[12] Again to the Ephesians: "Be not, then, partners with them: for ye were at one time darkness."[13] And yet more earnestly: "Communicate not with the unfruitful works of darkness; nay rather withal convict them. For (the things) which are done by them in secrecy it is disgraceful even to utter."[14] What more disgraceful than immodesties? If, moreover, even from a "brother" who "walketh idly"[15] he warns the Thessalonians to withdraw themselves, how much more withal from a fornicator! For these are the deliberate judgments of Christ, "loving the Church," who "hath delivered self up for her, that He may sanctify her (purifying her utterly by the laver of water) in the word, that He may present the Church to Himself glorious, not having stain or wrinkle"—of course *after* the laver—"but (that) she may be holy and without reproach;"[16] thereafter, to wit, being "without wrinkle" as a virgin, "without stain" (of fornication) as a spouse, "without disgrace" (of vileness), as having been "utterly purified."

What if, even here, you should conceive to reply that communion is indeed denied to sinners, very especially such as had been "polluted by the flesh,"[17] but (only) for the present; to be restored, to wit, as the result of penitential suing: in accordance with that clemency of God which prefers a sinner's repentance to his death?[18]—for this fundamental ground of your opinion must be universally attacked. We say, accordingly, that if it had been competent to the Divine clemency to have guaranteed the demonstration of itself even to the post-baptismally lapsed, the apostle would have said thus: "Communicate not with the works of darkness, *unless they shall*

---

[1] Comp. Acts xvi. 1-3 with Gal. v. 2-6, and similar passages.
[2] Prov. vi. 32-34.
[3] Isa. lii. 11, quoted in 2 Cor. vi. 17.
[4] Ps. i. 1 in LXX.
[5] i.e., the voice of this "blessed man," this true "Asher."
[6] Ps. xxvi. 4, 5 (in LXX. xxv. 4, 5).
[7] Ps. xxvi. (xxv. in LXX.) 6, not quite exactly.
[8] Ps. xviii. 25, 26 (in LXX. Ps. xviii. 26, 27), nearly.
[9] Ps. l. (xlix. in LXX.) 16, 18.
[10] 1 Cor. v. 9-11.
[11] Ver. 6.
[12] 1 Tim. v. 22.
[13] Eph. v. 7, 8 *ad init.*
[14] Vers. 11, 12.
[15] 2 Thess. iii. 6.
[16] Eph. v. 26, 27.
[17] Comp. Jude 23 *ad fin.*
[18] Comp. Ezek. xxxiii. 11, etc.; and see cc. ii., x., xxii.

have repented;" and, "With such take not food even, *unless after they shall have wiped, with rolling at their feet, the shoes of the brethren;*" and, "Him who shall have marred the temple of God, shall God mar, *unless he shall have shaken off from his head in the church the ashes of all hearths.*" For it had been his duty, in the case of those things which he had condemned, to have equally determined the extent to which he had (and that conditionally) condemned them, — whether he had condemned them with a temporary and conditional, and not a perpetual, severity. However, since in all Epistles he both prohibits such a character, (so sinning) after believing, from being admitted (to the society of believers) ; and, if admitted, detrudes him from communion, without hope of any condition or time ; he sides more with *our* opinion, pointing out that the repentance which the Lord prefers is that which *before* believing, *before* baptism, is esteemed better than the death of the sinner, — (the sinner, I say,) once for all to be washed through the grace of Christ, who once for all has suffered death for our sins. For this (rule), even in his own person, the apostle has laid down. For, when affirming that Christ came for this end, that He might save sinners,[1] of whom himself had been the "first," what does he add? "And I obtained mercy, because I did (so) ignorantly in unbelief."[2] Thus that clemency of God, preferring the repentance of a sinner to his death, looks at such as are ignorant still, and still unbelieving, for the sake of whose liberation Christ came ; not (at such) as already know God, and have learnt the sacrament of the faith. But if the clemency of God is applicable to such as are ignorant still, and unbelieving, of course it follows that repentance invites clemency to itself ; without prejudice to that species of repentance *after* believing, which either, for lighter sins, will be able to obtain pardon from the bishop, or else, for greater and irremissible ones, from God only.[3]

CHAP. XIX. — OBJECTIONS FROM THE REVELATION AND THE FIRST EPISTLE OF ST. JOHN REFUTED.

But how far (are we to treat) of Paul ; since even John appears to give some secret countenance to the opposite side? as if in the Apocalypse he has manifestly assigned to fornication the auxiliary aid of repentance, where, to the angel of the Thyatirenes, the Spirit sends a message that He "hath against him that he kept (in communion) the woman Jezebel, who calleth herself a prophet, and teacheth,[4] and seduceth my servants unto fornicating and eating of idol-

sacrifices. And I gave her bounteously a space of time, that she might enter upon repentance ; nor is she willing to enter upon it on the count of fornication. Behold, I will give her into a bed, and her adulterers with herself into greatest pressure, unless they shall have repented of her works."[5] I am content with the fact that, between apostles, there is a common agreement in rules of faith and of discipline. For, "Whether (it be) I," says (Paul), "or they, thus we preach."[6] Accordingly, it is material to the interest of the whole sacrament to believe nothing conceded by John, which has been flatly refused by Paul. This harmony of the Holy Spirit whoever observes, shall by Him be conducted into His meanings. For (the angel of the Thyatirene Church) was secretly introducing into the Church, and urging justly to repentance, an heretical woman, who had taken upon herself to teach what she had learnt from the Nicolaitans. For who has a doubt that an heretic, deceived by (a spurious baptismal) rite, upon discovering his mischance, and expiating it by repentance, both attains pardon and is restored to the bosom of the Church? Whence even among us, as being on a par with an heathen, nay even more than heathen, an heretic likewise, (such an one) is purged through the baptism of truth from each character,[7] and admitted (to the Church). Or else, if you are certain that that woman had, after a living faith, subsequently expired, and turned heretic, in order that you may claim pardon as the result of repentance, not as it were for an heretical, but as it were for a believing, sinner : let her, I grant, repent ; but with the view of ceasing from adultery, not however in the prospect of restoration (to Church-fellowship) as well. For this will be a repentance which we, too, acknowledge to be due much more (than you do) ; but which we reserve, for pardon, to God.[8]

In short, this Apocalypse, in its later passages, has assigned "the infamous and fornicators," as well as "the cowardly, and unbelieving, and murderers, and sorcerers, and idolaters," who have been guilty of any such crime while professing the faith, to "the lake of fire,"[9] without any *conditional* condemnation. For it will not appear to savour of (a bearing upon) *heathens,* since it has (just) pronounced with regard to *believers,* "They who shall have conquered shall have this inheritance ; and I will be to them a God, and they to me for sons ;" and so has subjoined : "But to the cowardly, and unbelieving, and infamous, and fornicators, and murderers, and sorcerers, and idolaters, (shall be) a

---

[1] See 1 Tim. i. 15.
[2] 1 Tim. i. 13, 16.
[3] See cc. iii. and xi., above.
[4] Or, " saith and teacheth that she is a prophet."

[5] Rev. ii. 18, 20–22.
[6] 1 Cor. xv. 11.
[7] i.e., of *heathen* and *heretic.*
[8] See the end of the foregoing chapter.
[9] Rev. xxi. 8.

share in the lake of fire and sulphur, which (lake) is the second death." Thus, too, again: "Blessed they who act according to the precepts, that they may have•power over the tree of life, and over the gates, for entering into the holy city. Dogs, sorcerers, fornicators, murderers, out!"[1] — of course, such as do *not* act according to the precepts; for *to be sent out* is the portion of those *who have been within.* Moreover, "What have I to do to judge them who are without?"[2] had preceded (the sentences now in question).

From the Epistle also of John they forthwith cull (a proof). It is said: "The blood of His Son purifieth us utterly from every sin."[3] Always then, and in every form, we will sin, if always and from every sin He utterly purifies us; or else, if not *always*, not again after believing; and if not from sin, not again from fornication. But what is the point whence (John) has started? He had predicated "God" to be "Light," and that "darkness is not in Him," and that "we lie if we say that we have communion with Him, and walk in darkness."[4] "If, however," he says, "we walk in the light, we shall have communion with Him, and the blood of Jesus Christ our Lord purifieth us utterly from every sin."[5] Walking, then, in the light, do we sin? and, sinning in the light, shall we be utterly purified? By no means. For he who sins is not in the light, but in darkness. Whence, too, he points out the mode in which we shall be utterly purified from sin — (by) "walking in the light," in which sin cannot be committed. Accordingly, the sense in which he says we "are utterly purified" is, not in so far as we sin, but in so far as we do *not* sin. For, "walking in the light," but not having communion with darkness, we shall act as they that are "utterly purified;" sin not being quite laid down, but not being wittingly committed. For this is the virtue of the Lord's blood, that such as it has already purified from sin, and thenceforward has set "in the light," it renders thenceforward pure, if they shall continue to persevere walking in the light. "But he subjoins," you say, "'If we say that we have not sin, we are seducing ourselves, and the truth is not in us. If we confess our sins, faithful and just is He to remit them to us, and utterly purify us from every unrighteousness.'"[6] Does he say "from impurity?" (No): or else, if that is so, then (He "utterly purifies" us) from "idolatry" too. But there is a difference in the sense. For see yet again: "If we say," he says, "that we have not sinned, we make Him a liar, and His

word is not in us."[7] All the more fully: "Little children, these things have I written to you, lest ye sin; and if ye shall have sinned, an Advocate we have with God the Father, Jesus Christ the righteous; and He is the propitiation for our sins."[8] "According to these words," you say, "it will be admitted both that we sin, and that we have pardon." What, then, will become (of your theory), when, proceeding (with the Epistle), I find something different? For he affirms that *we do not sin at all;* and to this end he treats at large, that he may make no such concession; setting forth that sins have been once for all deleted by Christ, not subsequently to obtain pardon; in which statement the sense requires us (to apply the statement) to an admonition to *chastity.* "Every one," he says, "who hath this hope, maketh himself chaste, because He too is chaste. Every one who doeth sin, doeth withal iniquity;[9] and sin is iniquity.[10] And ye know that He hath been manifested to take away sins" — henceforth, of course, to be no more incurred, if it is true, (as it is,) that he subjoins, "Every one who abideth in Him sinneth not; every one who sinneth neither hath seen nor knoweth Him. Little children, let none seduce you. Every one who doeth righteousness is righteous, as He withal is righteous. He who doeth sin is of the devil, inasmuch as the devil sinneth from the beginning. For unto this end was manifested the Son of God, to undo the works of the devil:[11] for He has "undone" them withal, by setting man free through baptism, the "handwriting of death" having been "made a gift of" to him: and accordingly, "he who is being born of God doeth not sin, because the seed of God abideth in him; and he cannot sin, because he hath been born of God. Herein are manifest the sons of God and the sons of the devil."[12] *Where*in? except it be (thus): the former by not sinning, from the time that they were born from God; the latter by sinning, because they are from the devil, just as if they never were born from God? But if he says, "He who is not *righteous* is not of God,"[13] how shall he who is not *modest* again become (a son) of God, who has already ceased to be so?

"It is therefore nearly equivalent to saying that John has forgotten himself; asserting, in the former part of his Epistle, that we are not without sin, but now prescribing that we do not sin at all: and in the one case flattering us somewhat with hope of pardon, but in the other as

---

[1] Rev. xxii. 14, 15.
[2] 1 Cor. v. 12 *ad init.*
[3] 1 John i. 7 *ad fin.*
[4] Vers. 5, 6.
[5] Ver. 8, incorrectly.
[6] 1 John i. 8, 9.

[7] 1 John i. 9.
[8] 1 John ii. 1, 2.
[9] Iniquitatem = ἀνομίαν.
[10] Iniquitas; ἀνομία = "lawlessness."
[11] See Col. ii. 13, 14.
[12] 1 John iii. 3-10.
[13] 1 John iii. 10.

serting with all stringency, that whoever may have sinned are no sons of God." But away with (the thought) : for not even we ourselves forget the distinction between sins, which was the starting-point of our digression. And (a right distinction it was) ; for John has here sanctioned it ; in that there are some sins of daily committal, to which we all are liable : for who will be free from the accident of either being angry unjustly, and retaining his anger beyond sunset ;[1] or else even using manual violence ; or else carelessly speaking evil ; or else rashly swearing ; or else forfeiting his plighted word ; or else lying, from bashfulness or "necessity?" In businesses, in official duties, in trade, in food, in sight, in hearing, by how great temptations are we plied ! So that, if there were no pardon for such sins as these, salvation would be unattainable to any. Of these, then, there will be pardon, through the successful Suppliant of the Father, Christ. But there are, too, the contraries of these ; as the graver and destructive ones, such as are incapable of pardon — murder, idolatry, fraud, apostasy, blasphemy ; (and), of course, too, adultery and fornication ; and if there be any other "violation of the temple of God." For these Christ will no more be the successful Pleader : these will not at all be incurred by one who has been born of God, who will cease to be the son of God if he do incur them.

Thus John's rule of diversity will be established ; arranging as he does a distinction of sins, while he now admits and now denies that the sons of God sin. For (in making these assertions) he was looking forward to the final clause of his letter, and for that (final clause) he was laying his preliminary bases ; intending to say, in the end, more manifestly : "If any knoweth his brother to be sinning a sin not unto death, he shall make request, and the Lord shall give life to him who sinneth not unto death. For there is a sin unto death : not concerning that do I say that one should make request."[2] He, too, (as I have been), was mindful that Jeremiah had been prohibited by God to deprecate (Him) on behalf of a people which was committing mortal sins. "Every unrighteousness is sin ; and there is a sin unto death.[3] But we know that every one who hath been born of God sinneth not"[4] — to wit, the sin which is unto death. Thus there is no course left for you, but either to deny that adultery and fornication are mortal sins ; or else to confess them irremissible, for which it is not permitted even to make successful intercession.

CHAP. XX. — FROM APOSTOLIC TEACHING TERTULLIAN TURNS TO THAT OF COMPANIONS OF THE APOSTLES, AND OF THE LAW.

The discipline, therefore, of the apostles properly (so called), indeed, instructs and determinately directs, as a principal point, the overseer of all sanctity as regards the temple of God to the universal eradication of every sacrilegious outrage upon modesty, without any mention of restoration. I wish, however, redundantly to superadd the testimony likewise of one particular comrade of the apostles, — (a testimony) aptly suited for confirming, by most proximate right, the discipline of his masters. For there is extant withal an Epistle to the Hebrews under the name of Barnabas — a man sufficiently accredited by God, as being one whom Paul has stationed next to himself in the uninterrupted observance of abstinence : "Or else, I alone and Barnabas, have not we the power of working?"[5] And, of course, the Epistle of Barnabas is more generally received among the Churches than that apocryphal "Shepherd" of adulterers. Warning, accordingly, the disciples to omit all first principles, and strive rather after perfection, and not lay again the foundations of repentance from the works of the dead, he says : "For impossible it is that they who have once been illuminated, and have tasted the heavenly gift, and have participated in the Holy Spirit, and have tasted the word of God and found it sweet, when they shall — their age already setting — have fallen away, should be again recalled unto repentance, crucifying again for themselves the Son of God, and dishonouring Him."[6] "For the earth which hath drunk the rain often descending upon it, and hath borne grass apt for them on whose account it is tilled withal, attaineth God's blessing ; but if it bring forth thorns, it is reprobate, and nighest to cursing, whose end is (doomed) unto utter burning."[7] He who learnt this *from* apostles, and taught it *with* apostles, never knew of any "second repentance" promised by apostles to the adulterer and fornicator.

For excellently was he wont to interpret the law, and keep its figures even in (the dispensation of) the Truth itself. It was with a reference, in short, to this species of discipline that the caution was taken in the case of the leper : "But if the speckled appearance shall have become efflorescent over the skin, and shall have covered the whole skin from the head even unto the feet through all the visible surface, then the priest, when he shall have seen, shall utterly cleanse him : since he hath wholly turned into white he is clean. But on the day that there

---

[1] Eph. iv. 26.
[2] 1 John v. 16. But Tertullian has rendered αἰτεῖν and ἐρωτᾶν by the one word *postulare*. See Trench, *N. T. Synonyms*, pp. 169-173. ed. 4, 1858.
[3] So Oehler; but it appears that a " non " must have been omitted.
[4] Vers. 17, 18.
[5] 1 Cor. ix. 6; but our copies read, τοῦ μὴ ἐργάζεσθαι.
[6] Comp. Heb. vi. 1, 4-6.
[7] Vers. 7, 8.

shall have been seen in such an one quick colour, he is defiled."[1] (The Law) would have the man who is wholly turned from the pristine habit of the flesh to the whiteness of faith—which (faith) is esteemed a defect and blemish in (the eyes of) the world[2]—and is wholly made new, to be understood to be "clean;" as being no longer "speckled," no longer dappled with the pristine and the new (intermixt). If, however, after the reversal (of the sentence of uncleanness), ought of the old nature shall have revived with its tendencies, that which was beginning to be thought utterly dead to sin in his flesh must again be judged unclean, and must no more be expiated by the priest. Thus adultery, sprouting again from the pristine stock, and wholly blemishing the unity of the new colour from which it had been excluded, is a defect that admits of no cleansing. Again, in the case of a house: if any spots and cavities in the party-walls had been reported to the priest, before he entered to inspect that house he bids all (its contents) be taken away from it; thus the belongings of the house would not be unclean. Then the priest, if, upon entering, he had found greenish or reddish cavities, and their appearance to the sight deeper down within the body of the party-wall, was to go out to the gate, and separate the house for a period within seven days. Then, upon returning on the seventh day, if he should have perceived the taint to have become diffused in the party-walls, he was to order those stones in which the taint of the leprosy had been to be extracted and cast away outside the city into an unclean place; and other stones, polished and sound, to be taken and replaced in the stead of the first, and the house to be plastered with other mortar.[3] For, in coming to the High Priest of the Father—Christ—all impediments must first be taken away, in the space of a week, that the house which remains, the flesh and the soul, may be clean; and when the Word of God has entered it, and has found "stains of red and green," forthwith must the deadly and sanguinary passions "be extracted" and "cast away" out of doors—for the Apocalypse withal has set "death" upon a "green horse," but a "warrior" upon a "red"[4]—and in their stead must be under-strewn stones polished and apt for conjunction, and firm,—such as are made (by God) into (sons) of Abraham,[5]—that thus the man may be fit for God. But if, after the recovery and reformation, the priest again perceived in the same house ought of the pristine disorders and blemishes, he pronounced it unclean, and bade the timbers, and the stones, and all the

structure of it, to be pulled down, and cast away into an unclean place.[6] This will be the man—flesh and soul—who, subsequently to reformation, after baptism and the entrance of the priests, again resumes the scabs and stains of the flesh, and "is cast away outside the city into an unclean place,"—"surrendered," to wit, "to Satan for the destruction of the flesh,"—and is no more rebuilt in the Church after his ruin. So, too, with regard to lying with a female slave who had been betrothed to an husband, but not yet redeemed, not yet set free: "provision," say (the Law), shall be made for her, and she shall not die, because she was not yet manumitted for him for whom she was being kept.[7] For flesh not yet manumitted to Christ, for whom it was being kept,[8] used to be contaminated with impunity: so now, after manumission, it no more receives pardon.

CHAP. XXI.—OF THE DIFFERENCE BETWEEN DISCIPLINE AND POWER, AND OF THE POWER OF THE KEYS.

If the apostles understood these (figurative meanings of the Law) better, of course they were more careful (with regard to them than even apostolic men). But I will descend even to this point of contest now, making a separation between the *doctrine* of apostles and their *power*. Discipline governs a man, power sets a seal upon him; apart from the fact that power is the Spirit, but the Spirit is God. What, moreover, used (the Spirit) to teach? That there must be no communicating with the works of darkness.[9] Observe what He bids. Who, moreover, was able to forgive sins? This is His alone prerogative; for "who remitteth sins but God alone?"[10] and of course, (who but He can remit) *mortal* sins such as have been committed against Himself, and against His temple? For, as far as you are concerned, such as are chargeable with offence against you personally, you are commanded, in the person of Peter, to forgive even seventy times sevenfold.[12] And so, if it were agreed that even the blessed apostles had granted any such indulgence (to any crime) the pardon of which (comes from God, not from man, it would be competent (for them) to have done so, not in the exercise of discipline, but of power. For they both raised the dead,[13] which God alone (can do), and restored the debilitated to their integrity, which none but Christ (can do); nay, they inflicted plagues too, which Christ would not do

---

[1] See Lev. xiii. 12–14 (in LXX.).
[2] Sæculo.
[3] See Lev. xiv. 33–42.
[4] See Rev. vi. 4, 8.
[5] Comp. Matt. iii. 9; Luke iii. 8.

[6] Lev. xiv. 43–45.
[7] See Lev. xix. 20.
[8] Comp. 2 Cor. xi. 2.
[9] Eph. v. 11. See ch. xviii. above.
[10] Mark ii. 7; Luke v. 21.
[11] Comp. Ps. li. 4 (in LXX. Ps, l. 6).
[12] Matt. xviii. 22.
[13] Comp. Acts ix. 36–43, xx. 9–12.
[14] Comp. Acts iii. 1–11, v. 13–16.

For it did not beseem Him to be severe who had come to suffer. Smitten were both Ananias[1] and Elymas[2] — Ananias with death, Elymas with blindness — in order that by this very fact it might be proved that Christ had *had the power* of doing even *such* (miracles). So, too, had the prophets (of old) granted to the repentant the *pardon* of murder, and therewith of adultery, inasmuch as they gave, at the same time, manifest proofs of *severity*.[3] Exhibit therefore even now to me,[4] apostolic sir, prophetic evidences, that I may recognise your divine virtue, and vindicate to yourself the *power* of remitting such sins ! If, however, you have had the functions of *discipline* alone allotted you, and (the duty) of presiding not imperially, but ministerially ;[5] who or how great are you, that you should grant indulgence, who, by exhibiting neither the prophetic nor the apostolic character, lack that virtue whose property it is to indulge ?

"But," you say, " *the Church* has the power of forgiving sins." This I acknowledge and adjudge more (than you ; I) who have the Paraclete Himself in the persons of the new prophets, saying, "The Church has the power to forgive sins ; but I will not do it, lest they commit others withal." " What if a pseudo-prophetic spirit has made that declaration ? " Nay, but it would have been more the part of a subverter on the one hand to commend himself on the score of clemency, and on the other to influence all others to sin. Or if, again, (the pseudo-prophetic spirit) has been eager to affect this (sentiment) in accordance with " the Spirit of truth,"[6] it follows that " the Spirit of truth " has indeed the *power* of indulgently granting pardon to fornicators, but *wills* not to do it if it involve evil to the majority.

I now inquire into your opinion, (to see) from what source you usurp this right to "the Church."

If, because the Lord has said to Peter, "Upon this rock will I build My Church,"[7] " to thee have I given the keys of the heavenly kingdom ;"[8] or, " Whatsoever thou shalt have bound or loosed in earth, shall be bound or loosed in the heavens,"[9] you therefore presume that the power of binding and loosing has derived to you, that is, to every Church akin to Peter, what sort of man are you, subverting and wholly changing the manifest intention of the Lord, conferring (as that intention did) this (gift) personally upon Peter? " *On thee*," He says, " will I build My Church ; " and, " I will give *to thee* the keys,"

not *to the Church ;* and, "Whatsoever *thou shalt have loosed or bound*," not what *they* shall have loosed or bound. For so withal the result teaches. In (Peter) himself the Church was reared ; that is, *through* (Peter) himself ; (Peter) himself essayed the key ; you see *what* (key) : " Men of Israel, let what I say sink into your ears : Jesus the Nazarene, a man destined by God for you," and so forth.[10] (Peter) himself, therefore, was the first to unbar, in Christ's baptism, the entrance to the heavenly kingdom, in which (kingdom) are " loosed " the sins that were beforetime " bound ; " and those which have not been " loosed " are " bound," in accordance with true salvation ; and Ananias he " bound " with the bond of death, and the weak in his feet he " absolved " from his defect of health. Moreover, in that dispute about the observance or non-observance of the Law, Peter was the first of all to be endued with the Spirit, and, after making preface touching the calling of the nations, to say, " And now why are ye tempting the Lord, concerning the imposition upon the brethren of a yoke which neither we nor our fathers were able to support? But however, through the grace of Jesus we believe that we shall be saved in the same way as they."[11] This sentence both " loosed " those parts of the law which were abandoned, and " bound " those which were reserved. Hence the power of loosing and of binding committed to Peter had nothing to do with the capital sins of believers ; and if the Lord had given him a precept that he must grant pardon to a brother sinning against *him* even " seventy times sevenfold," of course He would have commanded him to " bind " — that is, to " retain "[12] — *nothing* subsequently, unless perchance such (sins) as one may have committed against *the Lord*, not against a *brother*. For the forgiveness of (sins) committed in the case of a *man* is a prejudgment against the remission of sins against *God*.

What, now, (has this to do) with the Church, and *your* (church), indeed, Psychic? For, in accordance with the person of Peter, it is to *spiritual* men that this power will correspondently appertain, either to an apostle or else to a prophet. For the very Church itself is, properly and principally, the Spirit Himself, in whom is the Trinity of the One Divinity — Father, Son, and Holy Spirit.[13] (The Spirit) combines that Church which the Lord has made to consist in " three." And thus, from that time forward,[14] every number (of persons) who may have combined together into this faith is accounted " a Church," from the Author and Consecrator (of

---

[1] Acts v. 1-6.
[2] Acts xiii. 6-12.
[3] Comp. 2 Sam. xii. 1-14, etc.
[4] Kaye suggests " apostolica et prophetica " — " apostolic and prophetic evidences ; " which is very probable.
[5] Comp. 1 Pet. v. 1-4.
[6] Comp. John xv. 26.
[7] Matt. xvi. 18.
[8] Matt. xvi. 19 *ad init.*, incorrectly.
[9] Matt. xvi. 19.

[10] Acts ii. 22 et seqq.
[11] See Acts xv 7-11.
[12] Comp. John xx. 23.
[13] See *de Or.*, c. ii.
[14] See Matt. xviii. 20.

the Church). And accordingly "the Church," it is true, will forgive sins : but (it will be) the Church of the Spirit, by means of a spiritual man ; not the Church which consists of a number of bishops. For the right and arbitrament is the Lord's, not the servant's ; God's Himself, not the priest's.

CHAP. XXII. — OF MARTYRS, AND THEIR INTERCESSION ON BEHALF OF SCANDALOUS OFFENDERS.

But you go so far as to lavish this "power" upon martyrs withal! No sooner has any one, acting on a preconceived arrangement, put on the bonds — (bonds), moreover, which, in the nominal custody now in vogue,[1] are soft ones — than adulterers beset him, fornicators gain access to him ; instantly prayers echo around him ; instantly pools of tears (from the eyes) of all the polluted surround him ; nor are there any who are more diligent in purchasing entrance into the prison than they who have lost (the fellowship of) the Church! Men and women are violated in the darkness with which the habitual indulgence of lusts has plainly familiarized them ; and they seek peace at the hands of those who are risking their own! Others betake them to the mines, and return, in the character of communicants, from thence, where by this time another "martyrdom" is necessary for sins committed *after* "martyrdom." "Well, who on earth and in the flesh is faultless?" What "martyr" (continues to be) an inhabitant of the world[2] supplicating? pence in hand? subject to physician and usurer? Suppose, now, (your "martyr") beneath the glaive, with head already steadily poised ; suppose him on the cross, with body already outstretched ; suppose him at the stake, with the lion already let loose ; suppose him on the axle, with the fire already heaped ; in the very certainty, I say, and possession of martyrdom : who permits *man* to condone (offences) which are to be reserved for *God*, by whom those (offences) have been condemned without discharge, which not even apostles (so far as I know) — martyrs withal themselves — have judged condonable? In short, Paul had already "fought with beasts at Ephesus," when he decreed "destruction" to the incestuous person.[3] Let it suffice to the martyr to have purged his own sins : it is the part of ingratitude or of pride to lavish upon others also what one has obtained at a high price.[4] Who has redeemed another's death by his own, but the Son of God alone? For even in His very passion He set the robber free.[5] For to this end had He come, that, being

Himself pure from sin,[6] and in all respects holy,[7] He might undergo death on behalf of sinners.[8] Similarly, you who emulate Him in condoning sins, if you yourself have done no sin, plainly suffer in my stead. If, however, you are a sinner, how will the oil of your puny torch be able to suffice for you and for me?[9]

I have, even now, a test whereby to prove (the presence of) Christ (in you). If Christ is in the martyr for this reason, that the martyr may absolve adulterers and fornicators, let Him tell publicly the secrets of the heart, that He may thus concede (pardon to) sins ; and He is Christ. For thus it was that the Lord Jesus Christ showed His power : "Why think ye evil in your hearts? For which is easier, to say to the paralytic, Thy sins are remitted thee ; or, Rise and walk? Therefore, that ye may know the Son of man to have the power upon earth of remitting sins, I say to thee, paralytic, Rise, and walk."[10] If the Lord set so much store by the proof of His power as to reveal thoughts, and so impart health by His command, lest He should not be believed to have the power of remitting sins ; it is not lawful for me to believe the same power (to reside) in any one, whoever he be, without the same proofs. In the act, however, of urgently entreating from a martyr pardon for adulterers and fornicators, you yourself confess that crimes of that nature are not to be washed away except by the martyrdom of the criminal himself, while you presume (they can be washed away) by another's. If this is so, then martyrdom will be another baptism. For "I have withal," saith He, "another baptism."[11] Whence, too, it was that there flowed out of the wound in the Lord's side water and blood, the materials of either baptism.[12] I ought, then, by the *first* baptism too to (have the right of) setting another free if I can by the *second :* and we must necessarily force upon the mind (of our opponents this conclusion) : Whatever authority, whatever reason, restores ecclesiastical peace to the adulterer and fornicator, the same will be bound to come to the aid of the murderer and idolater in their repentance, — at all events, of the apostate, and of course of him whom, in the battle of his confession, after hard struggling with torments, savagery has overthrown. Besides, it were unworthy of God and of His mercy, who prefers the repentance of a sinner to his death, that they should have easier return into (the bosom of) the Church who have fallen in heat of passion, than they who have fallen in hand-to-

---

[1] Comp. *de Je.*, c. xii.
[2] *Sæculi.*
[3] See 1 Cor. xv. 32.
[4] See Acts xxii. 28.
[5] Luke xxiii. 39–43.

[6] See 1 John iii. v.
[7] See Heb. vii. 26–viii. 1.
[8] See 1 Pet. iii. 18.
[9] See Matt. xxv. 8, 9.
[10] See Mark ii. 9–11.
[11] Luke xii. 50.
[12] John xix. 33, 34.

hand combat.[1] Indignation urges us to speak. Contaminated bodies you will recall rather than gory ones ! Which repentance is more pitiable — that which prostrates tickled flesh, or lacerated? Which pardon is, in all causes, more justly concessible — that which a voluntary, or that which an involuntary, sinner implores? No one is compelled *with* his will to apostatize ; no one *against* his will commits fornication. Lust is exposed to no violence, except itself : it knows no coercion whatever. Apostasy, on the contrary, what ingenuities of butchery and tribes of penal inflictions enforce ! Which has more truly apostatized — he who has lost Christ amid

<hr>

[1] Comp. *de Monog.*, c. xv.

agonies, or (he who has done so) amid delights? he who when losing Him grieved, or he who when losing Him sported? And yet those scars graven on the Christian combatant — scars, of course, enviable in the eyes of Christ, because they yearned after conquest, and thus also glorious, because failing to conquer they yielded ; (scars) after which even the devil himself yet sighs ; (scars) with an infelicity of their own, but a chaste one, with a repentance that mourns, but blushes not, to the Lord for pardon — will anew be remitted to such, because their apostasy was expiable ! In their case alone is the "flesh weak." Nay, no flesh so strong as that which crushes out the Spirit !

ELUCIDATIONS.

I.

(The Shepherd of Hermas, p. 85.)

HERE, and in chap. xx. below, Tertullian's rabid utterances against the *Shepherd* may be balanced by what he had said, less unreasonably, in his better mood.[1] Now he refers to the *Shepherd's* (ii. 1)[2] view of pardon, even to adulterers. But surely it might be objected even more plausibly against "the Shepherd," whom he prefers, in common with all Christians, as see John viii. 1–11, which I take to be canonical Scripture. A curious question is suggested by what he says of the figure of the Good Shepherd portrayed on the chalice : Is this *irony*, as if the figure so familiar from illustrations of the catacombs must be meant for the *Shepherd* of Hermas? Regarding all pictures as idolatrous, he may intend to intimate that adultery (= idolatry) was thus symbolized.

II.

(Clasping the knees of all, p. 86.)

Here is a portrait of the early penitential discipline sufficiently terrible, and it conforms to the apostolic pictures of the same. "Tell it unto the Church," says our Lord (St. Matt. xviii. 17). In 1 Cor. v. 4 the apostle ("present in spirit") gives judgment, but the whole Church is "gathered together." In St. James v. 16 the "confession to *one another*" seems to refer to this public discipline, as also the prayer for *healing* enjoined on one another. St. Chrysostom, however, reflecting the discipline of his day, in which great changes were made, says, on Matt. xviii. 17, unless it be a gloss, "*Dic Ecclesiæ* id est *Præsidibus* = προεδρευούσιν." (Tom. vii. p. 536, ed. Migne.)

III.

(Remedial discipline, p. 87.)

Powerfully as Tertullian states his view of this apostolic "delivering unto Satan" as for final perdition, it is not to be gainsaid that (1 Cor. v. 5) the object was salvation and hope, "that the spirit may be saved in the day of the Lord Jesus." Thus, the power of Satan to inflict bodily suffering (Job ii. 6), when divinely permitted, is recognised under the Gospel (Luke xiii. 16 ; 2 Cor. xii. 7). The remedial mercy of trials and sufferings may be inferred when providentially occurring.

IV.

(Personally upon Peter, p. 99.)

See what has been said before. But note our author (now writing against the Church, and as a Montanist) has no idea that the *personal* prerogative of St. Peter had descended to any bishop. More when we come to Cyprian, and see vol. iii. p. 630, this series.

<hr>

[1] *On Prayer*, vol. iii. cap. xvi p. 686, *supra*, where he speaks respectfully.   [2] Vol. ii. p. 22 (also p. 43), this series.

VIII.

ON FASTING.[1]

IN OPPOSITION TO THE PSYCHICS.

[TRANSLATED BY THE REV. S. THELWALL.]

CHAP. I. — CONNECTION OF GLUTTONY AND LUST. GROUNDS OF PSYCHICAL OBJECTIONS AGAINST THE MONTANISTS.

I SHOULD wonder at the Psychics, if they were enthralled to voluptuousness alone, which leads them to repeated marriages, if they were not likewise bursting with gluttony, which leads them to hate fasts. Lust without voracity would certainly be considered a monstrous phenomenon; since these two are so united and concrete, that, had there been any possibility of disjoining them, the pudenda would not have been affixed to the belly itself rather than elsewhere. Look at the body : the region (of these members) is one and the same. In short, the order of the vices is proportionate to the arrangement of the members. First, the belly; and then immediately the materials of all other species of lasciviousness are laid subordinately to daintiness : through love of eating, love of impurity finds passage. I recognise, therefore, *animal*[2] faith by its care of the flesh (of which it wholly consists) — as prone to manifold feeding as to manifold marrying — so that it deservedly accuses the *spiritual* discipline, which according to its ability opposes it, in this species of continence as well; imposing, as it does, reins upon the appetite, through taking, sometimes no meals, or late meals, or dry meals, just as upon lust, through allowing but one marriage.

It is really irksome to engage with such : one is really ashamed to wrangle about subjects the very defence of which is offensive to modesty. For how am I to protect chastity and sobriety without taxing their adversaries? What those adversaries are I will once for all mention : they are the exterior and interior *botuli* of the Psychics. It is these which raise controversy with the Paraclete; it is on this account that the New Prophecies are rejected : not that Montanus and Priscilla and Maximilla preach another God, nor that they disjoin Jesus Christ (from God), nor that they overturn any particular rule of faith or hope, but that they plainly teach more frequent fasting than marrying. Concerning the limit of marrying, we have already published a defence of monogamy.[3] Now our battle is the battle of the secondary (or rather the primary) continence, in regard of the chastisement of diet. They charge us with keeping fasts of our own; with prolonging our Stations generally into the evening; with observing xerophagies likewise, keeping our food unmoistened by any flesh, and by any juiciness, and by any kind of specially succulent fruit; and with not eating or drinking anything with a winey flavour; also with abstinence from the bath, congruent with our dry diet. They are therefore constantly reproaching us with NOVELTY; concerning the unlawfulness of which they lay down a prescriptive rule, that either it must be adjudged *heresy*, if (the point in dispute) is a human presumption; or else pronounced *pseudo-prophecy*, if it is a spiritual declaration; provided that, either way, we who reclaim hear (sentence of) anathema.

CHAP. II. — ARGUMENTS OF THE PSYCHICS, DRAWN FROM THE LAW, THE GOSPEL, THE ACTS, THE EPISTLES, AND HEATHENISH PRACTICES.

For, so far as pertains to fasts, they oppose to us the definite days appointed by God : as when, in Leviticus, the Lord enjoins upon Moses the tenth day of the seventh month (as) a day of

---

[3] [Which is a note of time, not unimportant.]

atonement, saying, " Holy shall be to you the day, and ye shall vex your souls ; and every soul which shall not have been vexed in that day shall be exterminated from his people." [1] At all events, in the Gospel they think that those days were definitely appointed for fasts in which "the Bridegroom was taken away ; " [2] and that these are now the only legitimate days for Christian fasts, the legal and prophetical antiquities having been abolished : for wherever it suits their wishes, they recognise what is the meaning of " the Law and the prophets until John." [3] Accordingly, (they think) that, with regard to the future, fasting was to be indifferently observed, by the New Discipline, of choice, not of command, according to the times and needs of each individual : that this, withal, had been the observance of the apostles, imposing (as they did) no other yoke of definite fasts to be observed by all generally, nor similarly of Stations either, which (they think) have withal days of their own (the fourth and sixth days of the week), but yet take a wide range according to individual judgment, neither subject to the law of a given precept, nor (to be protracted) beyond the last hour of the day, since even prayers the ninth hour generally concludes, after Peter's example, which is recorded in the Acts. Xerophagies, however, (they consider) the novel name of a studied duty, and very much akin to heathenish superstition, like the abstemious rigours which purify an Apis, an Isis, and a Magna Mater, by a restriction laid upon certain kinds of food ; whereas faith, free in Christ, [4] owes no abstinence from particular meats to the Jewish Law even, admitted as it has been by the apostle once for all to the whole range of the meat-market [5] — (the apostle, I say), that detester of such as, in like manner as they prohibit marrying, so bid us abstain from meats created by God. [6] And accordingly (they think) *us* to have been even then prenoted as " in the latest times departing from the faith, giving heed to spirits which seduce the world, having a conscience inburnt with doctrines of liars." [7] (Inburnt?) With what fires, prithee? The fires, I ween, which lead us to repeated contracting of nuptials and daily cooking of dinners ! Thus, too, they affirm that we share with the Galatians the piercing rebuke (of the apostle), as " observers of days, and of months, and of years." [8] Meantime they hurl in our teeth the fact that Isaiah withal has authoritatively declared, " Not such a fast hath the Lord elected," that is, not abstinence from food, but the

works of righteousness, which he there appends : [9] and that the Lord Himself in the Gospel has given a compendious answer to every kind of scrupulousness in regard to food ; " that not by such things as are introduced into the mouth is a man defiled, but by such as are produced out of the mouth ; " [10] while Himself withal was wont to eat and drink till He made Himself noted thus ; " Behold, a gormandizer and a drinker : " [11] (finally), that so, too, does the apostle teach that " food commendeth us not to God ; since we neither abound if we eat, nor lack if we eat not." [12]

By the instrumentalities of these and similar passages, they subtlely tend at last to such a point, that every one who is somewhat prone to appetite finds it possible to regard as superfluous, and not so very necessary, the duties of abstinence from, or diminution or delay of, food, since " God," forsooth, " prefers the works of justice and of innocence." And we know the quality of the hortatory addresses of carnal conveniences, how easy it is to say, " I must believe with my whole heart ; [13] I must love God, and my neighbour as myself : [14] for ' on these two precepts the whole Law hangeth, and the prophets,' not on the emptiness of my lungs and intestines."

CHAP. III. — THE PRINCIPLE OF FASTING TRACED BACK TO ITS EARLIEST SOURCE.

Accordingly we are bound to affirm, before proceeding further, this (principle), which is in danger of being secretly subverted ; (namely), of what value in the sight of God this " emptiness " you speak of is : and, first of all, whence has proceeded the rationale itself of earning the favour of God in this way. For the necessity of the observance will then be acknowledged, when the authority of a rationale, to be dated back from the very beginning, shall have shone out to view.

Adam had received from God the law of not tasting " of the tree of recognition of good and evil," with the doom of death to ensue upon tasting. [15] However, even (Adam) himself at that time, reverting to the condition of a Psychic after the spiritual ecstasy in which he had prophetically interpreted that " great sacrament " [16] with reference to Christ and the Church, and no longer being " capable of the things which were the Spirit's," [17] yielded more readily to his belly than to God, heeded the meat rather than the mandate, and sold salvation for his gullet ! He

---

[1] Lev. xvi. 29, xxiii. 26–29.
[2] Matt. ix. 14, 15; Mark ii. 18–20; Luke v. 33–35.
[3] Luke xvi. 16; Matt. xi. 13.
[4] Comp. Gal. v. 1.
[5] Comp. 1 Cor. x. 25.
[6] Comp. 1 Tim. iv. 3.
[7] So Oehler punctuates. The reference is to 1 Tim. iv. 1, 2.
[8] See Gal. iv. 10; the words καὶ καιρούς Tertullian omits.
[9] See Isa. lviii. 3–7.
[10] See Matt. xv. 11; Mark vii. 15.
[11] Matt. xi 19; Luke vii. 34.
[12] 1 Cor. viii. 8.
[13] Rom. x. 10.
[14] Comp. Matt. xxii. 37–40, and the parallel passages.
[15] See Gen. ii. 16, 17.
[16] Comp. Eph. v. 32 with Gen. ii. 23, 24.
[17] See 1 Cor. ii. 14.

ate, in short, and perished; saved (as he would) else (have been), if he had preferred to fast from one little tree: so that, even from this early date, *animal faith* may recognise its own seed, deducing from thence onward its appetite for carnalities and rejection of spiritualities. I hold, therefore, that from the very beginning the murderous gullet was to be punished with the torments and penalties of hunger. Even if God had enjoined no preceptive fasts, still, by pointing out the source whence Adam was slain, He who had demonstrated the offence had left to my intelligence the remedies for the offence. Unbidden, I would, in such ways and at such times as I might have been able, have habitually accounted food as poison, and taken the antidote, hunger; through which to purge the primordial cause of death — a cause transmitted to me also, concurrently with my very generation; certain that God willed that whereof He nilled the contrary, and confident enough that the care of continence will be pleasing to Him by whom I should have understood that the crime of *incontinence* had been condemned. Further: since He Himself both commands fasting, and calls "a soul [1] wholly shattered" — properly, of course, by straits of diet — "a sacrifice;" who will any longer doubt that of all dietary macerations the rationale has been this, that by a renewed interdiction of food and observation of precept the primordial sin might now be expiated, in order that man may make God satisfaction through the self-same causative material through which he had offended, that is, through interdiction of food; and thus, in emulous wise, hunger might rekindle, just as satiety had extinguished, salvation, contemning for the sake of one *un*lawful more lawful (gratifications)?

CHAP. IV. — THE OBJECTION IS RAISED, WHY, THEN, WAS THE LIMIT OF LAWFUL FOOD EXTENDED AFTER THE FLOOD? THE ANSWER TO IT.

This rationale was constantly kept in the eye of the providence of God — modulating all things, as He does, to suit the exigencies of the times — lest any from the opposite side, with the view of demolishing our proposition, should say: "Why, in that case, did not God forthwith institute some definite restriction upon food? nay, rather, why did He withal enlarge His permission? For, at the beginning indeed, it had only been the food of herbs and trees which He had assigned to man: 'Behold, I have given you all grass fit for sowing, seeding seed, which is upon the earth; and every tree which hath in itself the fruit of seed fit for sowing shall be to you for food.' [2] Afterwards, however, after enumerating to Noah the subjection (to him) of 'all

beasts of the earth, and fowls of the heaven, and things moving on earth, and the fish of the sea, and every creeping thing,' He says, 'They shall be to you for food: just like grassy vegetables have I given (them) you universally: but flesh in the blood of its own soul shall ye not eat.' [3] For even by this very fact, that He exempts from eating that flesh only the 'soul' of which is not out-shed through 'blood,' it is manifest that He has conceded the use of all other flesh." To this we reply, that it was not suitable for man to be burdened with any further special law of abstinence, who so recently showed himself unable to tolerate so light an interdiction — of one single fruit, to wit; that, accordingly, having had the rein relaxed, he was to be strengthened by his very liberty; that equally after the deluge, in the *re*formation of the human race, (as before it), *one* law — of abstaining from blood — was sufficient, the use of all things else being allowed. For the Lord had already shown His judgment through the deluge; had, moreover, likewise issued a comminatory warning through the "requisition of blood from the hand of a brother, and from the hand of every beast." [4] And thus, preministering the justice of judgment, He issued the materials of liberty; preparing through allowance an undergrowth of discipline; permitting all things, with a view to take some away; meaning to "exact more" if He had "committed more;" [5] to command abstinence since He had foresent indulgence: in order that (as we have said) the primordial sin might be the more expiated by the operation of a greater abstinence in the (midst of the) opportunity of a greater licence.

CHAP. V. — PROCEEDING TO THE HISTORY OF ISRAEL, TERTULLIAN SHOWS THAT APPETITE WAS AS CONSPICUOUS AMONG THEIR SINS AS IN ADAM'S CASE. THEREFORE THE RESTRAINTS OF THE LEVITICAL LAW WERE IMPOSED.

At length, when a familiar people began to be chosen by God to Himself, and the restoration of man was able to be essayed, then all the laws and disciplines were imposed, even such as curtailed food; certain things being prohibited as unclean, in order that man, by observing a perpetual abstinence in certain particulars, might at last the more easily tolerate absolute fasts. For the first People had withal reproduced the first man's crime, being found more prone to their belly than to God, when, plucked out from the harshness of Egyptian servitude "by the mighty hand and sublime arm" [6] of God, they were seen to be its lord, destined to the "land flowing with

---

[1] The reference is to Ps. li. 17 (in LXX. Ps. l. 19).
[2] Gen. i. 29.

[3] See Gen. ix. 2-5 (in LXX.).
[4] See Gen. ix. 5, 6.
[5] See Luke xii. 48.
[6] Comp. Ps. cxxxvi. 12 (in LXX. cxxxv. 12).

milk and honey ;[1] but forthwith, stumbled at the surrounding spectacle of an incopious desert, sighing after the lost enjoyments of Egyptian satiety, they murmured against Moses and Aaron : "Would that we had been smitten to the heart by the Lord, and perished in the land of Egypt, when we were wont to sit over our jars of flesh and eat bread unto the full ! How leddest thou us out into these deserts, to kill this assembly by famine ?"[2] From the self-same belly-preference were they destined (at last) to deplore[3] (the fate of) the self-same leaders of their own and eye-witnesses of (the power of) God, whom, by their regretful hankering after flesh, and their recollection of their Egyptian plenties, they were ever exacerbating : "Who shall feed us with flesh? there have come into our mind the fish which in Egypt we were wont to eat freely, and the cucumbers, and the melons, and the leeks, and the onions, and the garlic. But now our soul is arid : nought save manna do our eyes see !"[4] Thus used they, too, (like the Psychics), to find the angelic bread[5] of xerophagy displeasing : they preferred the fragrance of garlic and onion to that of heaven. And therefore from men so ungrateful all that was more pleasing and appetizing was withdrawn, for the sake at once of punishing gluttony and exercising continence, that the former might be condemned, the latter practically learned.

CHAP. VI. — THE PHYSICAL TENDENCIES OF FASTING AND FEEDING CONSIDERED. THE CASES OF MOSES AND ELIJAH.

Now, if there has been temerity in our retracing to primordial experiences the reasons for God's having laid, and our duty (for the sake of God) to lay, restrictions upon food, let us consult common conscience. Nature herself will plainly tell with what qualities she is ever wont to find us endowed when she sets us, *before* taking food and drink, with our saliva still in a virgin state, to the transaction of matters, by the sense especially whereby things divine are handled ; whether (it be not) with a mind much more vigorous, with a heart much more alive, than when that whole habitation of our interior man, stuffed with meats, inundated with wines, fermenting for the purpose of excremental secretion, is already being turned into a premeditatory of privies, (a premeditatory) where, plainly, nothing is so proximately supersequent as the savouring of lasciviousness. "The people did eat and drink, and they arose to play."[6] Understand the modest language of Holy Scripture :

"play," unless it had been immodest, it would not have reprehended. On the other hand, how many are there who are mindful of religion, when the seats of the memory are occupied, the limbs of wisdom impeded ? No one will suitably, fitly, usefully, remember God at that time when it is customary for a man to forget his own self. All discipline food either slays or else wounds. I am a liar, if the Lord Himself, when upbraiding Israel with forgetfulness, does not impute the cause to "fulness : " " (My) beloved is waxen thick, and fat, and distent, and hath quite forsaken God, who made him, and hath gone away from the Lord his Saviour."[7] In short, in the self-same Deuteronomy, when bidding precaution to be taken against the self-same cause, He says : "Lest, when thou shalt have eaten, and drunken, and built excellent houses, thy sheep and oxen being multiplied, and (thy) silver and gold, thy heart be elated, and thou be forgetful of the Lord thy God."[8] To the corrupting power of riches He made the enormity of edacity antecedent, for which riches themselves are the procuring agents.[9] Through them, to wit, had "the heart of the People been made thick, lest they should see with the eyes, and hear with the ears, and understand with a heart "[10] obstructed by the "fats " of which He had expressly forbidden the eating,[11] teaching man not to be studious of the stomach.[12]

On the other hand, he whose "heart " was habitually found "lifted up "[13] rather than fattened up, who in forty days and as many nights maintained a fast above the power of human nature, while spiritual faith subministered strength (to his body),[14] both saw with his eyes God's glory, and heard with his ears God's voice, and understood with his heart God's law : while He taught him even then (by experience) that man liveth not upon bread alone, but upon every word of God ; in that the People, though fatter than he, could not constantly contemplate even Moses himself, fed as he had been upon God, nor his leanness, sated as it had been with His glory ![15] Deservedly, therefore, even while in the flesh, did the Lord show Himself to him, the colleague of His own fasts, no less than to Elijah.[16] For Elijah withal had, by this fact primarily, that he had imprecated a famine,[17] already sufficiently devoted himself to fasts : "The Lord liveth," he said, "before whom I am standing in His

---

[1] See Ex. iii. 8.
[2] See Ex. xvi. 1-3.
[3] Comp. Num. xx. 1-12 with Ps. cvi. 31-33 (in LXX. cv. 31-33).
[4] See Num. xi. 1-6.
[5] See Ps. lxxviii. 25 (in LXX. lxxvii. 25).
[6] Comp. 1 Cor x. 7 with Ex. xxxii. 6.

[7] See Deut. xxxii. 15.
[8] See Deut. viii. 12-14.
[9] Comp. Eccles. vi. 7; Prov. xvi. 26. (The LXX. render the latter quotation very differently from the Eng. ver. or the Vulg.)
[10] See Isa. vi. 10; John xii. 40; Acts xxviii. 26, 27.
[11] See Lev. iii. 17.
[12] See Deut. viii. 3; Matt. iv. 4; Luke iv. 4.
[13] See Ps. lxxxvi. 4 (in LXX. lxxxv. 4); Lam. iii. 41 (in LXX. iii. 40).
[14] Twice over. See Ex. xxiv. 18 and xxxiv. 28; Deut. ix. 11, 25.
[15] See Ex. xxxiii. 18, 19, with xxxiv. 4-9, 29-35.
[16] See Matt. xvii. 1-13; Mark ix. 1-13; Luke ix. 28-36.
[17] See Jas. v. 17.

sight, if there shall be dew in these years, and rain-shower." [1] Subsequently, fleeing from threatening Jezebel, after one single (meal of) food and drink, which he had found on being awakened by an angel, he too himself, in a space of forty days and nights, his belly empty, his mouth dry, arrived at Mount Horeb; where, when he had made a cave his inn, with how familiar a meeting with God was he received! [2] "What (doest) thou, Elijah, here?" [3] Much more friendly was this voice than, "Adam, where art thou?" [4] For the latter voice was uttering a threat to a fed man, the former soothing a fasting one. Such is the prerogative of circumscribed food, that it makes God tent-fellow [5] with man—peer, in truth, with peer! For if the eternal God will not hunger, as He testifies through Isaiah, [6] this will be the time for man to be made equal with God, when he lives without food.

CHAP. VII. — FURTHER EXAMPLES FROM THE OLD TESTAMENT IN FAVOUR OF FASTING.

And thus we have already proceeded to examples, in order that, by its profitable efficacy, we may unfold the powers of this duty which reconciles God, even when angered, to man.

Israel, before their gathering together by Samuel on occasion of the drawing of water at Mizpeh, had sinned; but so immediately do they wash away the sin by a fast, that the peril of battle is dispersed by them simultaneously (with the water on the ground). At the very moment when Samuel was offering the holocaust (in no way do we learn that the clemency of God was more procured than by the *abstinence* of the people), and the aliens were advancing to battle, then and there "the Lord thundered with a mighty voice upon the aliens, and they were thrown into confusion, and fell in a mass in the sight of Israel; and the men of Israel went forth out of Mizpeh, and pursued the aliens, and smote them unto Bethor," — the unfed (chasing) the fed, the unarmed the armed. Such will be the strength of them who "fast to God." [7] For such, Heaven fights. You have (before you) a condition upon which (divine) defence will be granted, necessary even to spiritual wars.

Similarly, when the king of the Assyrians, Sennacherib, after already taking several cities, was volleying blasphemies and menaces against Israel through Rabshakeh, nothing else (but fasting) diverted him from his purpose, and sent him into the Ethiopias. After that, what else swept away by the hand of the angel an hundred eighty and four thousand from his army than Hezekiah the king's humiliation? if it is true, (as it is), that on hearing the announcement of the harshness of the foe, he rent his garment, put on sackcloth, and bade the elders of the priests, similarly habited, approach God through Isaiah — fasting being, of course, the escorting attendant of their prayers. [8] For peril has no time for food, nor sackcloth any care for satiety's refinements. Hunger is ever the attendant of mourning, just as gladness is an accessory of fulness.

Through this attendant of mourning, and (this) hunger, even that sinful state, Nineveh, is freed from the predicted ruin. For repentance for sins had sufficiently commended the fast, keeping it up in a space of three days, starving out even the cattle with which God was not angry. [9] Sodom also, and Gomorrah, would have escaped if they had fasted. [10] This remedy even Ahab acknowledges. When, after his transgression and idolatry, and the slaughter of Naboth, slain by Jezebel on account of his vineyard, Elijah had upbraided him, "How hast thou killed, and possessed the inheritance? In the place where dogs had licked up the blood of Naboth, thine also shall they lick up," — he "abandoned himself, and put sackcloth upon his flesh, and fasted, and slept in sackcloth. And then (came) the word of the Lord unto Elijah, Thou hast seen how Ahab hath shrunk in awe from my face: for that he hath shrunk in awe I will not bring the hurt upon (him) in his own days; but in the days of his son I will bring it upon (him)" — (his son), who was not to fast. [11] Thus a Godward fast is a work of reverential awe: and by its means also Hannah the wife of Elkanah making suit, barren as she had been beforetime, easily obtained from God the filling of her belly, empty of food, with a son, ay, and a prophet. [12]

Nor is it merely change of nature, or aversion of perils, or obliteration of sins, but likewise the recognition of mysteries, which fasts will merit from God. Look at Daniel's example. About the dream of the King of Babylon all the sophists are troubled: they affirm that, without external aid, it cannot be discovered by human skill. Daniel alone, trusting to God, and knowing what would tend to the deserving of God's favour, requires a space of three days, fasts with his fraternity, and — his prayers thus commended — is instructed throughout as to the order and signification of the dream; quarter is granted to the tyrant's sophists; God is glorified; Daniel is honoured; destined as he was to receive, even subsequently also, no less a favour of God in the first year of King Darius, when, after care-

---

[1] See 1 Kings xvii. 1 (in LXX. 3 Kings *ib.*).
[2] See 1 Kings xix. 1–8. But he took *two* meals: see vers. 6, 7, 8.
[3] Vers. 9, 13.
[4] Gen. iii. 9 (in LXX.).
[5] Comp. Matt. xvii. 4; Mark ix. 5; Luke ix. 33.
[6] See Ps. xl. 28 in LXX. In E. V., "fainteth not."
[7] See Zech. vii. 5.

[8] See 2 Kings xviii. xix.; 2 Chron. xxxii.; Isa. xxxvi. xxxvii.
[9] See Jonah iii. Comp. *de Pa.*, c. x.
[10] See Ezek. xvi. 49; Matt. xi. 23, 24; Luke x. 12–14.
[11] See 1 Kings xxi. (in the LXX. it is 3 Kings xx.).
[12] See 1 Sam. i. 1, 2, 7–20, iii. 20 (in LXX. 1 Kings).

ful and repeated meditation upon the times predicted by Jeremiah, he set his face to God in fasts, and sackcloth, and ashes. For the angel, withal, sent to him, immediately professed this to be the cause of the Divine approbation: "I am come," he said, "to demonstrate to thee, since thou art pitiable"[1] — by fasting, to wit. If to God he was "pitiable," to the lions in the den he was formidable, where, six days fasting, he had breakfast provided him by an angel.[2]

CHAP. VIII. — EXAMPLES OF A SIMILAR KIND FROM THE NEW.

We produce, too, our remaining (evidences). For we now hasten to modern proofs.

On the threshold of the Gospel,[3] Anna the prophetess, daughter of Phanuel, "who both recognised the infant Lord, and preached many things about Him to such as were expecting the redemption of Israel," after the pre-eminent distinction of long-continued and single-husbanded widowhood, is additionally graced with the testimony of "fastings" also; pointing out, as she does, what the duties are which should characterize attendants of the Church, and (pointing out, too, the fact) that Christ is understood by none more than by the once married and often fasting.

By and by the Lord Himself consecrated His own baptism (and, in His own, that of all) by fasts;[4] having (the power) to make "loaves out of stones,"[5] ay, to make Jordan flow with wine perchance, if He had been such a "glutton and toper."[6] Nay, rather, by the virtue of contemning food He was initiating "the new man" into "a severe handling" of "the old,"[7] that He might show that (new man) to the devil, again seeking to tempt him by means of *food*, (to be) too strong for the whole power of hunger.

Thereafter He prescribed to fasts a law — that they are to be performed "without sadness:"[8] for why should what is salutary be sad? He taught likewise that fasts are to be the weapons for battling with the more direful demons:[9] for what wonder if the same operation is the instrument of the iniquitous spirit's egress as of the Holy Spirit's ingress? Finally, granting that upon the centurion Cornelius, even *before baptism*, the honourable gift of the Holy Spirit, together with the gift of prophecy besides, had hastened to descend, we see that *his fasts* had been heard.[10] I think, moreover, that the apostle too, in the Second of Corinthians, among his labours, and perils, and hardships, after "hunger and thirst," enumerates "fasts" also "very many."[11]

CHAP. IX. — FROM FASTS ABSOLUTE (JEJUNIA) TERTULLIAN COMES TO PARTIAL ONES AND XEROPHAGIES.

This principal species in the category of dietary restriction may already afford a prejudgment concerning the inferior operations of abstinence also, as being themselves too, in proportion to their measure, useful or necessary. For the exception of certain kinds from use of food is a partial fast. Let us therefore look into the question of the novelty or vanity of xerophagies, to see whether in them too we do not find an operation alike of most ancient as of most efficacious religion.

I return to Daniel and his brethren, preferring as they did a diet of vegetables and the beverage of water to the royal dishes and decanters, and being found as they were therefore "more handsome" (lest any be apprehensive on the score of his paltry body, to boot!), besides being spiritually cultured into the bargain.[12] For God gave to the young men knowledge and understanding in every kind of literature, and to Daniel in every word, and in dreams, and in every kind of wisdom; which (wisdom) was to make him wise in this very thing also, — namely, by what means the recognition of mysteries was to be obtained from God. Finally, in the third year of Cyrus king of the Persians, when he had fallen into careful and repeated meditation on a vision, he provided another form of humiliation. "In those days," he says, "I Daniel was mourning during three weeks: pleasant bread I ate not; flesh and wine entered not into my mouth; with oil I was not anointed; until three weeks were consummated:" which being elapsed, an angel was sent out (from God), addressing him on this wise: "Daniel, thou art a man pitiable; fear not: since, from the first day on which thou gavest thy soul to recogitation and to humiliation before God, thy word hath been heard, and I am entered at thy word."[13] Thus the "pitiable" spectacle and the humiliation of xerophagies expel fear, and attract the ears of God, and make men masters of secrets.

I return likewise to Elijah. When the ravens had been wont to satisfy him with "bread and

---

[1] Dan. ix. 23, x. 11.
[2] See Bel and the Dragon (in LXX.) vers. 31–39. "Pitiable" appears to be Tertullian's rendering of what in the E. V. is rendered "greatly beloved." Rig. (in Oehler) renders: "of how great compassion thou hast attained the favour;" but surely that overlooks the fact that the Latin is "*miserabilis es*," not "*sis*."
[3] See Luke ii. 36–38. See *de Monog.*, c. viii.
[4] Matt. iv. 12; Luke iv. 1, 2; comp. *de Bapt.*, c. xx.
[5] See Matt. iv. 3; Luke iv. 3.
[6] See c. ii.
[7] Comp. Eph. iv. 22, 23; and, for the meaning of *sugillationem* ("severe handling"), comp. 1 Cor. ix. 27, where St. Paul's word ὑπωπιάζω (= "I smite under the eye," Eng. ver. "I keep under") is perhaps exactly equivalent in meaning.
[8] Matt. vi. 16–18.
[9] See Matt. xvii. 21; Mark ix. 29.

[10] See Acts x. 44–46, 1–4. and 30.
[11] 2 Cor. xi. 27.
[12] Dan. i.
[13] See Dan. x. 1–3, 5, 12.

flesh,"[1] why was it that afterwards, at Beersheba of Judea, that certain angel, after rousing him from sleep, offered him, beyond doubt, bread *alone*, and water?[2] Had ravens been wanting, to feed him more liberally? or had it been difficult to the "angel" to carry away from some part of the banquet-room of the king some attendant with his amply-furnished waiter, and transfer him to Elijah, just as the breakfast of the reapers was carried into the den of lions and presented to Daniel in his hunger? But it behoved that an example should be set, teaching us that, at a time of pressure and persecution and whatsoever difficulty, we must live on xerophagies. With such food did David express his own exomologesis; "eating ashes indeed as it were bread," that is, bread dry and foul like ashes: "mingling, moreover, his drink with weeping"—of course, instead of wine.[3] For *abstinence from wine* withal has honourable badges of its own: (an abstinence) which had dedicated Samuel, and consecrated Aaron, to God. For of Samuel his mother said: "And wine and that which is intoxicating shall he not drink:"[4] for such was her condition withal when praying to God.[5] And the I ord said to Aaron: "Wine and spirituous liquor shall ye not drink, thou and thy son after thee, whenever ye shall enter the tabernacle, or ascend unto the sacrificial altar; and ye shall not die."[6] So true is it, that such as shall have ministered in the Church, being not sober, shall "die." Thus, too, in recent times He upbraids Israel: "And ye used to give my sanctified ones wine to drink." And, moreover, this limitation upon drink is the portion of xerophagy. Anyhow, wherever abstinence from wine is either exacted by God or vowed by man, there let there be understood likewise a restriction of *food* forefurnishing a formal type to *drink*. For the quality of the drink is correspondent to that of the eating. It is not probable that a man should sacrifice to God *half* his appetite; temperate in waters, and intemperate in meats. Whether, moreover, the apostle had any acquaintance with xerophagies—(the apostle) who had repeatedly practised greater rigours, "hunger, and thirst, and fasts many," who had forbidden "drunkennesses and revellings"[7]—we have a sufficient evidence even from the case of his disciple Timotheus; whom when he admonishes, "for the sake of his stomach and constant weaknesses," to use "a little wine,"[8] from which he was abstaining not from rule, but from devotion

—else the custom would rather have been beneficial to his stomach—by this very fact he has advised abstinence from wine as "worthy of God," which, on a ground of *necessity*, he has *dis*suaded.

CHAP. X.—OF STATIONS, AND OF THE HOURS OF PRAYER.

In like manner they censure on the count of novelty our Stations as being *enjoined;* some, moreover, (censure them) too as being prolonged habitually too late, saying that this duty also ought to be observed of free choice, and not continued beyond the ninth hour,—(deriving their rule), of course, from their own practice. Well: as to that which pertains to the question of *injunction*, I will once for all give a reply to suit all causes. Now, (turning) to the point which is proper to this particular cause—concerning the limit of time, I mean—I must first demand from themselves whence they derive this prescriptive law for concluding Stations at the ninth hour. If it is from the fact that we read that Peter and he who was with him entered the temple "at the ninth (hour), the hour of prayer," who will prove to me that they had that day been performing a Station, so as to interpret the ninth hour as the hour for the conclusion and discharge of the Station? Nay, but you would more easily find that Peter at the *sixth* hour had, for the sake of taking food, gone up first on the roof to pray;[9] so that the *sixth* hour of the day may the rather be made the limit to this duty, which (in Peter's case) was apparently to finish that duty, after prayer. Further: since in the self-same commentary of Luke the *third* hour is demonstrated as an hour of prayer, about which hour it was that they who had received the initiatory gift of the Holy Spirit were held for drunkards;[10] and the *sixth*, at which Peter went up on the roof; and the *ninth*, at which they entered the temple: why should we not understand that, with absolutely perfect indifference, we must pray[11] always, and everywhere, and at every time; yet still that these three hours, as being more marked in things human—(hours) which divide the day, which distinguish businesses, which re-echo in the public ear—have likewise ever been of special solemnity in divine prayers? A persuasion which is sanctioned also by the corroborative fact of Daniel praying thrice in the day;[12] of course, through exception of certain stated hours, no other, moreover, than the more marked and subsequently apostolic (hours)—the third, the sixth, the ninth. And hence, accordingly, I shall affirm that Peter too had been led rather

---

[1] See 1 Kings xvii. (in LXX. 3 Kings xvii.) 1-6.
[2] 1 Kings xix. 3-7.
[3] See Ps. cii. (in LXX. ci.) 9.
[4] 1 Sam. (in LXX. 1 Kings) i. 11.
[5] 1 Sam. i. 15.
[6] See Lev. x. 9.
[7] See Rom. xiii. 13.
[8] 1 Tim. v. 23.

[9] See Acts x. 9.
[10] Acts ii. 1-4. 13, 15.
[11] The reference is to Eph. vi. 18 ; Col. iv. 2 ; 1 Thess. v. 17 ; Luke xviii. 1.
[12] See Dan. vi. 10.

by ancient usage to the observance of the ninth hour, praying at the third specific interval, (the interval) of final prayer.

These (arguments), moreover, (we have advanced) for their sakes who think that they are acting in conformity with Peter's model, (a model) of which they are ignorant : not as if we slighted the ninth hour, (an hour) which, on the fourth and sixth days of the week, we most highly honour ; but because, of those things which are observed on the ground of tradition, we are bound to adduce so much the more worthy reason, that they lack the authority of Scripture, until by some signal celestial gift they be either confirmed or else corrected. "And if," says (the apostle), "there are matters which ye are ignorant about, the Lord will reveal to you."[1] Accordingly, setting out of the question the confirmer of all such things, the Paraclete, the guide of universal truth,[2] inquire whether there be not a worthier reason adduced among *us* for the observing of the ninth hour ; so that this reason (of ours) must be attributed even to Peter if he observed a Station at the time in question. For (the practice) comes from the death of the Lord ; which death albeit it behoves to be commemorated always, without difference of hours ; yet are we at that time more impressively commended to its commemoration, according to the actual (meaning of the) name of Station. For even soldiers, though never unmindful of their military oath, yet pay a greater deference to Stations. And so the "pressure" must be maintained up to that hour in which the orb — involved from the sixth hour in a general darkness — performed for its dead Lord a sorrowful act of duty ; so that we too may then return to enjoyment when the universe regained its sunshine.[3] If this savours more of the spirit of Christian religion, while it celebrates more the glory of Christ, I am equally able, from the self-same order of events, to fix the condition of *late protraction of the Station ;* (namely), that we are to fast till a late hour, awaiting the time of the Lord's sepulture, when Joseph took down and entombed the body which he had requested. Thence (it follows) that it is even irreligious for the flesh of the servants to take refreshment before their Lord did.

But let it suffice to have thus far joined issue on the *argumentative* challenge ; rebutting, as I have done, conjectures by conjectures, and yet (as I think) by conjectures more worthy of a believer. Let us see whether any such (principle) drawn from the ancient times takes us under its patronage.

In Exodus, was not that position of Moses,

battling against Amalek by prayers, maintained as it was perseveringly even till "sunset," a "late Station?"[4] Think we that Joshua the son of Nun, when warring down the Amorites, had breakfasted on that day on which he ordered the very elements to keep a Station?[5] The sun "stood" in Gibeon, and the moon in Ajalon ; the sun and the moon "stood in station until the People was avenged of his enemies, and the sun stood in the mid heaven." When, moreover, (the sun) did draw toward his setting and the end of the one day, there was no such day beforetime and in the latest time (of course, (no day) so *long*), "that God," says (the writer), "should hear a man" — (a man,) to be sure, the sun's peer, so long persistent in his duty — a Station longer even than *late*.

At all events, Saul himself, when engaged in battle, manifestly *enjoined* this duty : "Cursed (be) the man who shall have eaten bread until evening, until I avenge me on mine enemy ;" and his whole people tasted not (food), and (yet) the whole earth was breakfasting ! So solemn a sanction, moreover, did God confer on the edict which enjoined that Station, that Jonathan the son of Saul, although it had been in ignorance of the fast having been appointed till a late hour that he had allowed himself a taste of honey, was both presently convicted, by lot, of sin, and with difficulty exempted from punishment through the prayer of the People :[6] for he had been convicted of gluttony, although of a simple kind. But withal Daniel, in the first year of King Darius, when, fasting in sackcloth and ashes, he was doing exomologesis to God, said : "And while I was still speaking in prayer, behold, the man whom I had seen in dreams at the beginning, swiftly flying, approached me, as it were, at the hour of the evening sacrifice."[7] This will be a "late" Station which, fasting *until the evening*, sacrifices a fatter (victim of) prayer to God ![8]

CHAP XI. — OF THE RESPECT DUE TO "HUMAN AUTHORITY ;" AND OF THE CHARGES OF "HERESY" AND "PSEUDO-PROPHECY."

But all these (instances) I believe to be unknown to those who are in a state of agitation at our proceedings ; or else known by the reading alone, not by careful study as well ; in accordance with the greater bulk of "the unskilled"[9] among the overboastful multitude, to wit, of the Psychics. This is why we have steered our course straight through the different individual species of fastings, of xerophagies, of stations :

---

[1] See Phil. iii. 15.
[2] John xiv. 26, xvi. 13.
[3] See Matt. xxvii. 45-54 ; Mark xvi. 33-39 ; Luke xxiii. 44-47.

[4] See Ex. xvii. 8-12.
[5] See Josh. x. 12-14.
[6] See 1 Sam. (in LXX. 1 Kings) xiv. 24-45.
[7] See Dan. ix. 1, 3, 4, 20, 21.
[8] Comp. *de Or.*, c. xxviii.
[9] Comp 2 Pet. iii. 16.

in order that, while we recount, according to the materials which we find in either Testament, the advantages which the dutiful observances of abstinence from, or curtailment or deferment of, food confer, we may refute those who invalidate these things as empty observances; and again, while we similarly point out in what rank of religious duty they have always had place, may confute those who accuse them as novelties: for neither is that novel which has always been, nor that empty which is useful.

The question, however, still lies before us, that some of these observances, having been commanded by God to man, have constituted this practice legally binding; some, offered by man to God, have discharged some votive obligation. Still, even a vow, when it has been accepted by God, constitutes a law for the time to come, owing to the authority of the Acceptor; for he who has given his approbation to a deed, when done, has given a mandate for its doing thenceforward. And so from this consideration, again, the wrangling of the opposite party is silenced, while they say: "It is either a pseudo-prophecy, if it is a spiritual voice which institutes these your solemnities; or else a heresy, if it is a human presumption which devises them." For, while censuring that form in which the ancient economies ran their course, and at the same time drawing out of that form arguments to hurl back (upon us) which the very adversaries of the ancient economies will in their turn be able to retort, they will be bound either to reject those arguments, or else to undertake these proven duties (which they impugn): necessarily so; chiefly because these very duties (which they impugn), from whatsoever institutor they are, be he a spiritual man or merely an ordinary believer, direct their course to the honour of the same God as the ancient economies. For, indubitably, both heresy and pseudo-prophecy will, in the eyes of us who are all priests of one only God the Creator and of His Christ, be judged by diversity of divinity: and so far forth I defend this side indifferently, offering my opponents to join issue on whatever ground they choose. "It is the spirit of the devil," you say, O Psychic. And how is it that he enjoins duties which belong to our God, and enjoins them to be offered to none other than our God? Either contend that the devil works with our God, or else let the Paraclete be held to be Satan. But you affirm it is "a human Antichrist:" for by this name heretics are called in John.[1] And how is it that, whoever he is, he has in (the name of) our Christ directed these duties toward our Lord; whereas withal antichrists have (ever) gone forth (professedly teaching) towards God, (but) in

opposition to our Christ? On which side, then, do you think the Spirit is confirmed as existing among us; when He commands, or when He approves, what our God has always both commanded and approved? But you again set up boundary-posts to God, as with regard to grace, so with regard to discipline; as with regard to gifts, so, too, with regard to solemnities: so that our observances are supposed to have ceased in like manner as His benefits; and you thus deny that He still continues to impose duties, because, in this case again, "the Law and the prophets (were) until John." It remains for you to banish Him wholly, being, as He is, so far as lies in *you*, so otiose.

CHAP. XII. — OF THE NEED FOR SOME PROTEST AGAINST THE PSYCHICS AND THEIR SELF-INDULGENCE.

For, by this time, in this respect as well as others, "you are reigning in wealth and satiety"[2] — not making inroads upon such sins as fasts diminish, nor feeling need of such revelations as xerophagies extort, nor apprehending such wars of your own as Stations dispel. Grant that from the time of John the Paraclete had grown mute; we ourselves would have arisen as prophets to ourselves, for this cause chiefly: I say not now to bring down by our prayers God's anger, nor to obtain his protection or grace; but to secure by premunition the moral position of the "latest times;"[3] enjoining every species of ταπεινοφρό-νησις, since the prison must be familiarized to us, and hunger and thirst practised, and capacity of enduring as well the absence of food as anxiety about it acquired: in order that the Christian may enter into prison in like condition as if he had (just) come forth of it, — to suffer there not penalty, but discipline, and not the world's tortures, but his own habitual observances; and to go forth out of custody to (the final) conflict with all the more confidence, having nothing of sinful false care of the flesh about him, so that the tortures may not even have material to work on, since he is cuirassed in a mere dry skin, and cased in horn to meet the claws, the succulence of his blood already sent on (heavenward) before him, the baggage as it were of his soul, — the soul herself withal now hastening (after it), having already, by frequent fasting, gained a most intimate knowledge of death!

Plainly, *your* habit is to furnish cookshops in the prisons to untrustworthy martyrs, for fear they should miss their accustomed usages, grow weary of life, (and) be stumbled at the novel discipline of abstinence; (a discipline) which not even the well-known Pristinus — *your* martyr,

---

[1] See I John ii. 18, 29; 2 John 7-10.

[2] I Cor. iv. 8.
[3] See the Vulg. in I Tim. iv. 1, 2 Tim. iii. 1; and comp. therewith the Greek in both places.

no *Christian* martyr—had ever come in contact with: he whom—stuffed as he had long been, thanks to the facilities afforded by the "free custody" (now in vogue, and) under an obligation, I suppose, to all the baths (as if they were better than baptism!), and to all the retreats of voluptuousness (as if they were more secret than those of the Church!), and to all the allurements of this life (as if they were of more worth than those of life eternal!), not to be willing to die —on the very last day of trial, at high noon, you premedicated with drugged wine as an antidote, and so completely enervated, that on being tickled—for his intoxication made it feel like tickling—with a few claws, he was unable any more to make answer to the presiding officer interrogating him "whom he confessed to be Lord;" and, being now put on the rack for this silence, when he could utter nothing but hiccoughs and belchings, died in the very act of apostasy! This is why they who preach sobriety are "false prophets;" this why they who practise it are "heretics!" Why then hesitate to believe that the Paraclete, whom you deny in a Montanus, exists in an Apicius?

CHAP. XIII. — OF THE INCONSISTENCIES OF THE PSYCHICS.

You lay down a prescription that this faith has its solemnities "appointed" by the Scriptures or the tradition of the ancestors; and that no further addition in the way of observance must be added, on account of the unlawfulness of innovation. Stand on that ground, if you can. For, behold, I impeach you of fasting besides on the Paschal-day, beyond the limits of those days in which "the Bridegroom was taken away;" and interposing the half-fasts of Stations; and you, (I find), sometimes living on bread and water, when it has seemed meet to each (so to do). In short, you answer that "these things are to be done of choice, not of command." You have changed your ground, therefore, by exceeding tradition, in undertaking observances which have not been "appointed." But what kind of deed is it, to permit to your own choice what you grant not to the command of God? Shall human volition have more licence than Divine power? I am mindful that I am free from *the world*,[1] not from God. Thus it is my part to perform, without external suggestion thereto, an act of respect to my Lord, it is His to enjoin. I ought not merely to pay a willing obedience to Him, but withal to court Him; for the former I render to His command, the latter to my own choice.

But it is enough for me that it is a customary practice for the bishops withal to issue mandates for fasts to the universal commonalty of the Church; I do not mean for the special purpose of collecting contributions of alms, as your beggarly fashion has it, but sometimes too from some particular cause of ecclesiastical solicitude. And accordingly, if you practise ταπεινοφρόνησις at the bidding of a man's edict, and all unitedly, how is it that in our case you set a brand upon the very unity also of our fastings, and xerophagies, and Stations?—unless, perhaps, it is against the decrees of the senate and the mandates of the emperors which are opposed to "meetings" that we are sinning! The Holy Spirit, when He was preaching in whatsoever lands He chose, and through whomsoever He chose, was wont, from foresight of the imminence either of temptations to befall the Church, or of plagues to befall the world, in His character of Paraclete (that is, Advocate for the purpose of winning over the judge by prayers), to issue mandates for observances of this nature; for instance, at the present time, with the view of practising the discipline of sobriety and abstinence: we, who receive Him, must necessarily observe also the appointments which He then made. Look at the Jewish calendar, and you will find it nothing novel that all succeeding posterity guards with hereditary scrupulousness the precepts given to the fathers. Besides, throughout the provinces of Greece there are held in definite localities those councils gathered out of the universal Churches, by whose means not only all the deeper questions are handled for the common benefit, but the actual representation of the whole Christian-name is celebrated with great veneration. (And how worthy a thing is this, that, under the auspices of faith, men should congregate from all quarters to Christ! "See, how good and how enjoyable for brethren to dwell in unity!"[2] This psalm *you* know not easily how to sing, except when you are supping with a goodly company!) But those conclaves first, by the operations of Stations and fastings, know what it is "to grieve with the grieving," and thus at last "to rejoice in company with the rejoicing."[3] If we also, in our diverse provinces, (but) present mutually in spirit,[4] observe those very solemnities, whose then celebration our present discourse has been defending, that is the sacramental law.

CHAP. XIV.— REPLY TO THE CHARGE OF "GALATICISM."

Being, therefore, observers of "seasons" for these things, and of "days, and months, and years,"[5] we *Galaticize*. Plainly we do, if we are

---

[1] 1 Cor. ix. 19; sæculo.

[2] Ps. cxxxiii. (in LXX. and Vulg. cxxxii.).
[3] See Rom. xii. 15.
[4] Comp. 1 Cor. v. 3; Col. ii. 5.
[5] Comp. Gal. iv. 10.

observers of *Jewish* ceremonies, of *legal* solemnities : for *those* the apostle unteaches, suppressing the continuance of the Old Testament which has been buried in Christ, and establishing that of the New. But if there is a new creation in Christ,[1] our solemnities too will be bound to be new : else, if the apostle has erased *all* devotion absolutely " of seasons, and days, and months, and years," why do we celebrate the passover by an *annual* rotation in the *first month?* Why in the *fifty* ensuing *days* do we spend our time in all exultation? Why do we devote to Stations the *fourth* and *sixth days* of the week, and to fasts the *"preparation-day ?"* [2] Anyhow, *you* sometimes continue your Station even over the Sabbath, — a day never to be kept as a fast except at the passover season, according to a reason elsewhere given. With us, at all events, *every* day likewise is celebrated by an ordinary consecration. And it will not, then, be, in the eyes of the apostle, the *differentiating principle* — distinguishing (as he is doing) " things new and old " [3] — which will be ridiculous ; but (in this case too) it will be your own unfairness, while you taunt us with the *form* of *antiquity* all the while you are laying against us the *charge* of *novelty.*

CHAP. XV. — OF THE APOSTLE'S LANGUAGE CONCERNING FOOD.

The apostle reprobates likewise such as " bid to abstain from meats ; but he does so from the foresight of the Holy Spirit, precondemning already the heretics who would enjoin *perpetual* abstinence to the extent of destroying and despising the works of the Creator ; such as I may find in the person of a Marcion, a Tatian, or a Jupiter, the Pythagorean heretic of to-day ; not in the person of the Paraclete. For how limited is the extent of *our* " interdiction of meats ! " Two weeks of xerophagies in the year (and not the whole of these, — the Sabbaths, to wit, and the Lord's days, being excepted) we offer to God ; abstaining from things which we do not *reject*, but *defer*. But further : when writing to the Romans, the apostle now gives *you* a home-thrust, detractors as you are of this observance : " Do not for the sake of food," he says, " undo [4] the work of God." What " work ? " That about which he says,[5] " It is good not to eat flesh, and not to drink wine : " " for he who in these points doeth service, is pleasing and propitiable to our God." " One believeth that all things may be eaten ; but another, being weak, feedeth on vegetables. Let not him who eateth lightly esteem him who eateth not. Who art thou, who judgest

another's servant ? " " Both he who eateth, and he who eateth not, giveth God thanks." But, since he forbids *human* choice to be made matter of controversy, how much more *Divine !* Thus he knew how to chide certain restricters and interdicters of food, such as abstained from it of contempt, not of duty ; but to approve such as did so to the honour, not the insult, of the Creator. And if he has " delivered you the keys of the meat-market," permitting the eating of " all things " with a view to establishing the exception of " things offered to idols ; " still he has not included the kingdom of God in the meat-market : " For," he says, " the kingdom of God is neither meat nor drink ; " [6] and, " Food commendeth us not to God " — not that you may think this said about *dry* diet, but rather about rich and carefully prepared, if, when he subjoins, " Neither, if we shall have eaten, shall we abound ; nor, if we shall not have eaten, shall we be deficient," the ring of his words suits, (as it does), you rather (than us), who think that you do " abound " if you eat, and are " deficient " if you eat not ; and for this reason disparage these observances.

How unworthy, also, is the way in which you interpret to the favour of your own lust the fact that the Lord " ate and drank " promiscuously ! But I think that He must have likewise " fasted," inasmuch as He has pronounced, not " the full," but " the hungry and thirsty, blessed : " [7] (He) who was wont to profess " food " to be, not that which His disciples had supposed, but " the thorough doing of the Father's work ; " [8] teaching " to labour for the meat which is permanent unto life eternal ; " [9] in our ordinary prayer likewise commanding us to request " bread," [10] not the wealth of Attalus [11] therewithal. Thus, too, Isaiah has not denied that God " hath chosen " a " fast ; " but has particularized in detail the *kind* of fast which He has *not* chosen : " for in the days," he says, " of your fasts your own wills are found (indulged), and all who are subject to you ye stealthily sting ; or else ye fast with a view to abuse and strifes, and ye smite with the fists. Not *such* a fast have I elected ; " [12] but such an one as He has subjoined, and by subjoining has not abolished, but confirmed.

CHAP. XVI. — INSTANCES FROM SCRIPTURE OF DIVINE JUDGMENTS UPON THE SELF-INDULGENT ; AND APPEALS TO THE PRACTICES OF HEATHENS.

For even if He does *prefer* " the works of righteousness," still not without a sacrifice, which

---

[1] Comp. Luke xxii. 20; 2 Cor. v. 17, etc.
[2] Comp. Mark xv. 42.
[3] Comp. Matt. xiii. 52 *ad fin.*
[4] Rom. xiv. 20.
[5] Ver. 21.

[6] Rom. xiv. 17.
[7] Comp. Luke vi. 21 with 25, and Matt. v. 6.
[8] John iv. 31–34.
[9] John vi. 27.
[10] Matt. vi. 11; Luke xi. 3.
[11] See Hor., *Od.*, i. 1, 12, and Macleane's note there.
[12] See Isa. lviii. 3, 4, 5, briefly, and more like the LXX. than the Vulg. or the Eng. ver.

is a soul afflicted with fasts.[1] He, at all events, is the God to whom neither a· People incontinent of appetite, nor a priest, nor a prophet, was pleasing. To this day the "monuments of concupiscence" remain, where the People, greedy of "flesh," till, by devouring without digesting the quails, they brought on cholera, were buried. Eli breaks his neck before the temple doors,[2] his sons fall in battle, his daughter-in-law expires in child-birth:[3] for such was the blow which had been deserved at the hand of God by the shameless house, the defrauder of the fleshly sacrifices.[4] Sameas, a "man of God," after prophesying the issue of the idolatry introduced by King Jeroboam — after the drying up and immediate restoration of that king's hand — after the rending in twain of the sacrificial altar, — being on account of these signs invited (home) by the king by way of recompense, plainly declined (for he had been prohibited by God) to touch food at all in that place; but having presently afterwards rashly taken food from another old man, who lyingly professed himself a prophet, he was deprived, in accordance with the word of God then and there uttered over the table, of burial in his fathers' sepulchres. For he was prostrated by the rushing of a lion upon him in the way, and was buried among strangers; and thus paid the penalty of his breach of fast.[5]

These will be warnings both to people and to bishops, even spiritual ones, in case they may ever have been guilty of incontinence of appetite. Nay, even in Hades the admonition has not ceased to speak; where we find in the person of the rich feaster, convivialities tortured; in that of the pauper, fasts refreshed; having — (as convivialities and fasts alike had) — as preceptors "Moses and the prophets."[6] For Joel withal exclaimed: "Sanctify a fast, and a religious service;"[7] foreseeing even then that other apostles and prophets would sanction fasts, and would preach observances of special service to God. Whence it is that even they who court their *idols* by dressing them, and by adorning them in their sanctuary, and by saluting them at each particular hour, are said to do them *service*. But, more than that, the heathens recognise every form of ταπεινοφρόνησις. When the heaven is rigid and the year arid, barefooted processions are enjoined by public proclamation; the magistrates lay aside their purple, reverse the fasces, utter prayer, offer a victim. There are, moreover, some colonies where, besides (these extraordinary solemnities, the inhabitants), by an annual rite, clad in sackcloth and besprent with ashes, present a suppliant importunity to their idols, (while) baths and shops are kept shut till the ninth hour. They have one single fire in public — on the altars; no water even in their platters. There is, I believe, a Ninevitan suspension of business! A Jewish fast, at all events, is universally celebrated; while, neglecting the temples, throughout all the shore, in every open place, they continue long to send prayer up to heaven. And, albeit by the dress and ornamentation of mourning they disgrace the duty, still they do affect a faith in abstinence, and sigh for the arrival of the long-lingering evening star to sanction (their feeding). But it is enough for me that you, by heaping blasphemies upon *our* xerophagies, put them on a level with the chastity of an Isis and a Cybele. I admit the comparison in the way of evidence. Hence (our xerophagy) will be proved divine, which the devil, the emulator of things divine, imitates. It is out of truth that falsehood is built; out of religion that superstition is compacted. Hence *you* are more irreligious, in proportion as a heathen is more conformable. He, in short, sacrifices his appetite to an idol-god; *you* to (the true) God will not. For to you your belly is god, and your lungs a temple, and your paunch a sacrificial altar, and your cook the priest, and your fragrant smell the Holy Spirit, and your condiments spiritual gifts, and your belching prophecy.

CHAP. XVII. — CONCLUSION.

"Old" you are, if we will say the truth, you who are so indulgent to appetite, and justly do you vaunt your "priority:" always do I recognise the savour of Esau, the hunter of wild beasts: so unlimitedly studious are you of catching fieldfares, so do you come from "the field" of your most lax discipline, so faint are you in spirit.[8] If I offer you a paltry lentile dyed red with must well boiled down, forthwith you will sell all your "primacies:" with you "love" shows its fervour in sauce-pans, "faith" its warmth in kitchens, "hope" its anchorage in waiters; but of greater account is "love," because that is the means whereby your young men sleep with their sisters! Appendages, as we all know, of appetite are lasciviousness and voluptuousness. Which alliance the apostle withal was aware of; and hence, after premising, "Not in drunkenness and revels," he adjoined, "nor in couches and lusts."[9]

To the indictment of your appetite pertains (the charge) that "double honour" is with you

[1] See Ps. li. (l. in LXX. and Vulg.) 18, 19; see c. iii. above.
[2] This seems an oversight; see 1 Sam. (in LXX. and Vulg. 1 Kings) iv. 13.
[3] 1 Sam. iv. 17-21.
[4] 1 Sam. ii. 12-17, 22-25.
[5] See 1 Kings (in LXX. and Vulg. 3 Kings) xiii.
[6] Luke xvi. 19-31.
[7] Joel ii. 15.

[8] Comp. Gen. xxiii. 2, 3, 4, 31, and xxv. 27-34.
[9] Rom. xiii. 13.

assigned to your presiding (elders) by double shares (of meat and drink) ; whereas the apostle has given them "double honour" as being both *brethren* and *officers*.[1] Who, among you, is superior in holiness, except him who is more frequent in banqueting, more sumptuous in catering, more learned in cups? Men of soul and flesh alone as you are, justly do you reject things spiritual. If the prophets were pleasing to *such*, my (prophets) they were not. Why, then, do not you constantly preach, "Let us eat and drink, for to-morrow we shall die?"[2] just as *we* do not hesitate manfully to command, "Let us fast, brethren and sisters, lest to-morrow perchance we die." Openly let us vindicate our disciplines. Sure we are that "they who are in the flesh cannot please God;"[3] not, of course, those who are in the *substance* of the flesh, but in the *care*, the *affection*, the *work*, the *will*, of it. Emaciation displeases not us; for it is not by weight that God bestows flesh, any more than

He does "the Spirit by measure."[4] More easiiy, it may be, through the "strait gate"[5] of salvation will slenderer flesh enter; more speedily will lighter flesh rise; longer in the sepulchre will drier flesh retain its firmness. Let Olympic cestus-players and boxers cram themselves to satiety. To them bodily ambition is suitable to whom bodily strength is necessary; and yet they also strengthen themselves by xerophagies. But ours are other thews and other sinews, just as our contests withal are other; we whose "wrestling is not against flesh and blood, but against the world's[6] power, against the spiritualities of malice." Against these it is not by robustness of flesh and blood, but of faith and spirit, that it behoves us to make our antagonistic stand. On the other hand, an over-fed Christian will be more necessary to bears and lions, perchance, than to God; only that, even to encounter beasts, it will be his duty to practise emaciation.

---

[1] 1 Tim. v. 17.
[2] Isa. xxii. 13; 1 Cor. xv. 32.
[3] Rom. viii. 8.

[4] John iii. 34.
[5] Matt. vii. 13, 14; Luke xiii. 24.
[6] Mundi: cf. κοσμοκράτορας, Eph. vi. 12.

ELUCIDATIONS.

I.

(Greater licence, p. 104.)

IN this treatise, which is designed to justify the extremes of Montanistic fasts, Tertullian's genius often surprises us by his ingenuity. This is one of the instances where the forensic orator comes out, trying to outflank and turn the position of an antagonist who has gained an advantage. The fallacy is obvious. Kaye cites, in comparison, a passage[1] from "The Apparel of Women," and another[2] from "The Exhortation to Chastity." He remarks, "Were we required to produce an instance [i.e. to prove the tendency of mankind to run into extremes], we should without hesitation refer the reader to this treatise."

Fasting was ordained of Christ Himself as a means to an end. It is here reduced from its instrumental character, and made an excuse for dividing the household of faith, and for cruel accusations against brethren.

In our age of an entire relaxation of discipline, the enthusiast may nevertheless awaken us, perhaps, to honest self-examination as to our manner of life, in view of the example of Christ and His apostles, and their holy precepts.

II.

(Provinces of Greece, p. 111.)

We have here an interesting hint as to the ἀρχαῖα ἔθη to which the Council of Nice[3] refers in one of her most important canons. Provinces, synods, and the charges or pastoral letters of the bishops are referred to as established institutions. And note the emphasis given to "Greece" as

---

[1] II. cap. 10, p. 23, *supra*.   [2] Cap. 8, p. 55, *supra*.   [3] See our minor titlepage.

the mother of churches, and of laws and customs. He looks Eastward, and not by any means to the West, for high examples of the Catholic usages by which he was endeavouring to justify his own.

III.

(An over-fed Christian, p. 114.)

" Are we not carnal " (psychics) in our days? May not the very excesses of Tertullian sting and reproach us with the charge of excessive indulgence (Matt. ix. 15)? The " over-fed Christians " whom he here reproaches are proved by this very treatise to have observed a system of fasting which is little practised anywhere in our times — for a mere change to luxurious fish-diet is the very mockery of fasting. We learn that the customary fasts of these *psychics* were as follows: (1) the annual Paschal fast,[1] from Friday till Easter-Day; (2) Wednesdays and Fridays (stationary days[2]) every week; and (3) the " dry-food days,"[3] — abstinence from " pleasant bread " (Dan. x. 2), — though some Catholics objected to these voluntary abstinences.

IV.

(Practise emaciation, p. 114.)

Think of our Master's fast among the wild beasts! Let us condescend to go back to Clement, to Origen, and to Tertullian to learn the practical laws of the Gospel against avarice, luxury, and " the deceitfulness of sin." I am emboldened to say this by some remarkable words which I find, to my surprise, thrown out *in a scientific work*[4] proceeding from Harvard University. It is with exceeding gratitude that I quote as follows: " *It is well to go away at times, that we may see another aspect of human life* which still survives in the East, and to feel that influence which led even the Christ into the wilderness to prepare for the struggle with the animal nature of man.[5] We need something of the experience of the Anchorites of Egypt, to impress us with the great truth that the distinction between the spiritual and the material remains broad and clear, even if with the scalpel of our modern philosophy we cannot completely dissect the two ; and this experience will give us courage to cherish our aspirations, keep bright our hopes, and hold fast our Christian faith until the consummation comes."

---

[1] Capp. 2, 13, 14, *supra*.
[2] Cap. 14. See *De Orat.*, cap. 19, p. 687.
[3] The *Xerophagiæ*, cap. 2, p. 103.
[4] *Scientific Culture*, by J. P. Cooke, professor of chemistry, etc. New York, 1884.
[5] This is ambiguous, but I merely note it. Heb. iv. 15.

DE FUGA IN PERSECUTIONE.[1]

[TRANSLATED BY THE REV. S. THELWALL.]

1. My brother Fabius, you very lately asked, because some news or other were communicated, whether or not we ought to flee in persecution. For my part, having on the spot made some observations in the negative suited to the place and time, I also, owing to the rudeness of some persons, took away with me the subject but half treated, meaning to set it forth now more fully by my pen ; for your inquiry had interested me in it, and the state of the times had already on its own account pressed it upon me. As persecutions in increasing number threaten us, so the more are we called on to give earnest thought to the question of how faith ought to receive them, and the duty of carefully considering it concerns you no less, who no doubt, by not accepting the Comforter, the guide to all truth, have, as was natural, opposed us hitherto in regard to other questions also. We have therefore applied a methodical treatment, too, to your inquiry, as we see that we must first come to a decision as to how the matter stands in regard to persecution itself, whether it comes on us from God or from the devil, that with the less difficulty we may get on firm ground as to our duty to meet it ; for of everything one's knowledge is clearer when it is known from whom it has its origin. It is enough indeed to lay it down, (in bar of all besides,) that nothing happens without the will of God. But lest we be diverted from the point before us, we shall not by this deliverance at once give occasion to the other discussions if one make answer — Therefore evil and sin are both from God ; the devil henceforth, and even we ourselves, are entirely free. The question in hand is persecution. With respect to this, let me in the meantime say, that nothing happens without God's will; on the ground that persecution is especially worthy of God, and, so to speak, requisite, for the approving, to wit, or if you will, the rejection of His professing servants. For what is the issue of persecution, what other result comes of it, but the approving and rejecting of faith, in regard to which the Lord will certainly sift His people? Persecution, by means of which one is declared either approved or rejected, is just the judgment of the Lord. But the judging properly belongs to God alone. This is that fan which even now cleanses the Lord's threshing-floor — the Church, I mean — winnowing the mixed heap of believers, and separating the grain[2] of the martyrs from the chaff of the deniers ; and this is also the ladder[3] of which Jacob dreams, on which are seen, some mounting up to higher places, and others going down to lower. So, too, persecution may be viewed as a contest. By whom is the conflict proclaimed, but by Him by whom the crown and the rewards are offered? You find in the Revelation its edict, setting forth the rewards by which He incites to victory — those, above all, whose is the distinction of conquering in persecution, in very deed contending in their victorious struggle not against flesh and blood, but against spirits of wickedness. So, too, you will see that the adjudging of the contest belongs to the same glorious One, as umpire, who calls us to the prize. The one great thing in persecution is the promotion of the glory of God, as He tries and casts away, lays on and takes off. But what concerns the glory of God will surely come to pass by His will. And when is trust in God more strong, than when there is a greater fear of Him, and when persecution breaks out? The Church is awe-struck. Then is faith both more zealous in preparation, and better disciplined in fasts, and meetings, and prayers, and lowliness, in brotherly-kindness and love, in holiness and temperance. There is no room, in fact, for

[2] Matt. iii. 12.
[3] Gen. xxviii. 12.

ought but fear and hope. So even by this very thing we have it clearly proved that persecution, improving as it does the servants of God, cannot be imputed to the devil.

2. If, because injustice is not from God, but from the devil, and persecution consists of injustice (for what more unjust than that the bishops of the true God, that all the followers of the truth, should be dealt with after the manner of the vilest criminals?), persecution therefore seems to proceed from the devil, by whom the injustice which constitutes persecution is perpetrated, we ought to know, as you have neither persecution without the injustice of the devil, nor the trial of faith without persecution, that the injustice necessary for the trial of faith does not give a warrant for persecution, but supplies an agency; that in reality, in reference to the trial of faith, which is the reason of persecution, the will of God goes first, but that as the instrument of persecution, which is the way of trial, the injustice of the devil follows. For in other respects, too, injustice in proportion to the enmity it displays against righteousness affords occasion for attestations of that to which it is opposed as an enemy, that so righteousness may be perfected in injustice, as strength is perfected in weakness.[1] For the weak things of the world have been chosen by God to confound the strong, and the foolish things of the world to confound its wisdom.[2] Thus even injustice is employed, that righteousness may be approved in putting unrighteousness to shame. Therefore, since the service is not of free-will, but of subjection (for persecution is the appointment of the Lord for the trial of faith, but its ministry is the injustice of the devil, supplied that persecution may be got up), we believe that persecution comes to pass, no question, by the devil's agency, but not by the devil's origination. Satan will not be at liberty to do anything against the servants of the living God unless the Lord grant leave, either that He may overthrow Satan himself by the faith of the elect which proves victorious in the trial, or in the face of the world show that apostatizers to the devil's cause have been in reality His servants. You have the case of Job, whom the devil, unless he had received authority from God, could not have visited with trial, not even, in fact, in his property, unless the Lord had said, "Behold, all that he has I put at your disposal; but do not stretch out your hand against himself."[3] In short, he would not even have stretched it out, unless afterwards, at his request, the Lord had granted him this permission also, saying, "Behold, I deliver him to you; only preserve his life." So he asked in the case of the

apostles likewise an opportunity to tempt them, having it only by special allowance, since the Lord in the Gospel says to Peter, "Behold, Satan asked that he might sift you as grain; but I have prayed for you that your faith fail not;"[4] that is, that the devil should not have power granted him sufficient to endanger his faith. Whence it is manifest that both things belong to God, the shaking of faith as well as the shielding of it, when both are sought from Him — the shaking by the devil, the shielding by the Son. And certainly, when the Son of God has faith's protection absolutely committed to Him, beseeching it of the Father, from whom He receives all power in heaven and on earth, how entirely out of the question is it that the devil should have the assailing of it in *his* own power! But in the prayer prescribed to us, when we say to our Father, "Lead us not into temptation"[5] (now what greater temptation is there than persecution?), we acknowledge that that comes to pass by His will whom we beseech to exempt us from it. For this is what follows, "But deliver us from the wicked one," that is, do not lead us into temptation by giving us up to the wicked one, for then are we delivered from the power of the devil, when we are not handed over to him to be tempted. Nor would the devil's legion have had power over the herd of swine[6] unless they had got it from God; so far are they from having power over the sheep of God. I may say that the bristles of the swine, too, were then counted by God, not to speak of the hairs of holy men. The devil, it must be owned, seems indeed to have power — in this case really his own — over those who do not belong to God, the nations being once for all counted by God as a drop of the bucket, and as the dust of the threshing-floor, and as the spittle of the mouth, and so thrown open to the devil as, in a sense, a free possession. But against those who belong to the household of God he may not do ought as by any right of his own, because the cases marked out in Scripture show when — that is, for what reasons — he may touch them. For either, with a view to their being approved, the power of trial is granted to him, challenged or challenging, as in the instances already referred to, or, to secure an opposite result, the sinner is handed over to him, as though he were an executioner to whom belonged the inflicting of punishment, as in the case of Saul. "And the Spirit of the LORD," says Scripture, "departed from Saul, and an evil spirit from the LORD troubled and stifled him;"[7] or the design is to humble, as the apostle tells us, that there was given him

---

[1] 2 Cor xii. 9.
[2] 1 Cor. i. 27, 28.
[3] Job i. 12.

[4] Luke xxii. 31, 32.
[5] Matt. vi. 13.
[6] Mark v. 11.
[7] 1 Sam. xvi. 14.

a stake, the messenger of Satan, to buffet him ;[1] and even this sort of thing is not permitted in the case of holy men, unless it be that at the same time strength of endurance may be perfected in weakness. For the apostle likewise delivered Phygellus and Hermogenes over to Satan, that by chastening they might be taught not to blaspheme.[2] You see, then, that the devil receives more suitably power even from the servants of God ; so far is he from having it by any right of his own.

3. Seeing therefore, too, these cases occur in persecutions more than at other times, as there is then among us more of proving or rejecting, more of abasing or punishing, it must be that their general occurrence is permitted or commanded by Him at whose will they happen even partially ; by Him, I mean, who says, " I am He who make peace and create evil,"[3] — that is, war, for that is the antithesis of peace. But what other war has our peace than persecution? If in its issues persecution emphatically brings either life or death, either wounds or healing, you have the author, too, of this. " I will smite and heal, I will make alive and put to death."[4] " I will burn them," He says, " as gold is burned ; and I will try them," He says, " as silver is tried,"[5] for when the flame of persecution is consuming us, then the stedfastness of our faith is proved. These will be the fiery darts of the devil, by which faith gets a ministry of burning and kindling ; yet by the will of God. As to this I know not who can doubt, unless it be persons with frivolous and frigid faith, which seizes upon those who with trembling assemble together in the church. For you say, seeing we assemble without order, and assemble at the same time, and flock in large numbers to the church, the heathen are led to make inquiry about us, and we are alarmed lest we awaken their anxieties. Do ye not know that God is Lord of all? And if it is God's will, then you shall suffer persecution ; but if it is not, the heathen will be still. Believe it most surely, if indeed you believe in that God without whose will not even the sparrow, a penny can buy, falls to the ground.[6] But we, I think, are better than many sparrows.

4. Well, then, if it is evident from whom persecution proceeds, we are able at once to satisfy your doubts, and to decide from these introductory remarks alone, that men should not flee in it. For if persecution proceeds from God, in no way will it be our duty to flee from what has God as its author ; a twofold reason opposing : for what proceeds from God ought not on the one hand to be avoided, and it cannot be evaded on the other. It ought not to be avoided, because it is good ; for everything must be good on which God has cast His eye. And with this idea has perhaps this statement been made in Genesis, " And God saw because it is good ; " not that He would have been ignorant of its goodness unless He had seen it, but to indicate by this expression that it was good because it was viewed by God. There are many events indeed happening by the will of God, and happening to somebody's harm. Yet for all that, a thing is therefore good because it is of God, as divine, as reasonable ; for what is divine, and not reasonable and good? What is good, yet not divine? But if to the universal apprehension of mankind this seems to be the case, in judging, man's faculty of apprehension does not predetermine the nature of things, but the nature of things his power of apprehension. For every several nature is a certain definite reality, and it lays it on the perceptive power to perceive it just as it exists. Now, if that which comes from God is good indeed in its natural state (for there is nothing from God which is not good, because it is divine, and reasonable), but seems evil only to the human faculty, all will be right in regard to the former ; with the latter the fault will lie. In its real nature a very good thing is chastity, and so is truth, and righteousness ; and yet they are distasteful to many. Is perhaps the real nature on this account sacrificed to the sense of perception? Thus persecution in its own nature too is good, because it is a divine and reasonable appointment ; but those to whom it comes as a punishment do not feel it to be pleasant. You see that as proceeding from Him, even that evil has a reasonable ground, when one in persecution is cast out of a state of salvation, just as you see that you have a reasonable ground for the good also, when one by persecution has his salvation made more secure. Unless, as it depends on the Lord, one either perishes irrationally, or is irrationally saved, he will not be able to speak of persecution as an evil, which, while it is under the direction of reason, is, even in respect of its evil, good. So, if persecution is in every way a good, because it has a natural basis, we on valid grounds lay it down, that what is good ought not to be shunned by us, because it is a sin to refuse what is good ; besides that, what has been looked upon by God can no longer indeed be avoided, proceeding as it does from God, from whose will escape will not be possible. Therefore those who think that they should flee, either reproach God with doing what is evil, if they flee from persecution as an evil (for no one avoids what is good) ; or they count themselves stronger than God : so they think, who imagine it possible to escape when it is God's pleasure that such events should occur.

---

[1] 2 Cor. xii. 7.
[2] 2 Tim. i. 15 ; see 1 Tim. i. 20.
[3] Isa. xlv. 7.
[4] Deut. xxxii. 39.
[5] Zech. xiii. 9.
[6] Matt. x. 29.

5. But, says some one, 1 flee, the thing it belongs to me to do, that I may not perish, if I deny; it is for Him on His part, if He chooses, to bring me, when I flee, back before the tribunal. First answer me this: Are you sure you will deny if you do not flee, or are you not sure? For if you are sure, you have denied already, because by presupposing that you will deny, you have given yourself up to that about which you have made such a presupposition; and now it is vain for you to think of flight, that you may avoid denying, when in intention you have denied already. But if you are doubtful on that point, why do you not, in the incertitude of your fear wavering between the two different issues, presume that you are able rather to act a confessor's part, and so add to your safety, that you may not flee, just as you presuppose denial to send you off a fugitive? The matter stands thus — we have either both things in our own power, or they wholly lie with God. If it is ours to confess or to deny, why do we not anticipate the nobler thing, that is, that we shall confess? If you are not willing to confess, you are not willing to suffer; and to be unwilling to confess is to deny. But if the matter is wholly in God's hand, why do we not leave it to His will, recognising His might and power in that, just as He can bring us back to trial when we flee, so is He able to screen us when we do not flee; yes, and even living in the very heart of the people? Strange conduct, is it not, to honour God in the matter of flight from persecution, because He can bring you back from your flight to stand before the judgment-seat; but in regard of witness-bearing, to do Him high dishonour by despairing of power at His hands to shield you from danger? Why do you not rather on this, the side of constancy and trust in God, say, I do my part; I depart not; God, if He choose, will Himself be my protector? It beseems us better to retain our position in submission to the will of God, than to flee at our own will. Rutilius, a saintly martyr, after having ofttimes fled from persecution from place to place, nay, having bought security from danger, as he thought, by money, was, notwithstanding the complete security he had, as he thought, provided for himself, at last unexpectedly seized, and being brought before the magistrate, was put to the torture and cruelly mangled, — a punishment, I believe, for his fleeing, — and thereafter he was consigned to the flames, and thus paid to the mercy of God the suffering which he had shunned. What else did the Lord mean to show us by this example, but that we ought not to flee from persecution because it avails us nothing if God disapproves?

6. Nay, says some one, he fulfilled the command, when he fled from city to city. For so a certain individual, but a fugitive likewise, has chosen to maintain, and others have done the same who are unwilling to understand the meaning of that declaration of the Lord, that they may use it as a cloak for their cowardice, although it has had its persons as well as its times and reasons to which it specially applies. "When they begin," He says, "to persecute you, flee from city to city."[1] We maintain that this belongs specially to the persons of the apostles, and to their times and circumstances, as the following sentences will show, which are suitable only to the apostles: "Do not go into the way of the Gentiles, and into a city of the Samaritans do not enter: but go rather to the lost sheep of the house of Israel."[2] But to us the way of the Gentiles is also open, as in it we in fact were found, and to the very last we walk; and no city has been excepted. So we preach throughout all the world; nay, no special care even for Israel has been laid upon us, save as also we are bound to preach to all nations. Yes, and if we are apprehended, we shall not be brought into Jewish councils, nor scourged in Jewish synagogues, but we shall certainly be cited before Roman magistrates and judgment-seats.[3] So, then, the circumstances of the apostles even required the injunction to flee, their mission being to preach first to the lost sheep of the house of Israel. That, therefore, this preaching might be fully accomplished in the case of those among whom this behoved first of all to be carried out — that the sons might receive bread before the dogs, for that reason He commanded them to flee then for a time — not with the object of eluding danger, under the plea strictly speaking which persecution urges (rather He was in the habit of proclaiming that they would suffer persecutions, and of teaching that these must be endured); but in order to further the proclamation of the Gospel message, lest by their being at once put down, the diffusion of the Gospel too might be prevented. Neither were they to flee to any city as if by stealth, but as if everywhere about to proclaim their message; and for this, everywhere about to undergo persecutions, until they should fulfil their teaching. Accordingly the Saviour says, "Ye will not go over all the cities of Israel."[4] So the command to flee was restricted to the limits of Judea. But no command that shows Judea to be specially the sphere for preaching applies to us, now that the Holy Spirit has been poured out upon all flesh. Therefore Paul and the apostles themselves, mindful of the precept of the Lord, bear this solemn testimony before Israel, which they had now filled with their doctrine — saying, "It was

[1] Matt. x. 23.
[2] Matt. x. 5.
[3] Matt. x. 17.
[4] Matt. x. 23.

necessary that the word of God should have been first delivered to you; but seeing ye have rejected it, and have not thought yourselves worthy of eternal life, lo, we turn to the Gentiles."[1] And from that time they turned their steps away, as those who went before them had laid it down, and departed into the way of the Gentiles, and entered into the cities of the Samaritans; so that, in very deed, their sound went forth into all the earth, and their words to the end of the world.[2] If, therefore, the prohibition against setting foot in the way of the Gentiles, and entering into the cities of the Samaritans, has come to an end, why should not the command to flee, which was issued at the same time, have come also to an end? Accordingly, from the time when, Israel having had its full measure, the apostles went over to the Gentiles, they neither fled from city to city, nor hesitated to suffer. Nay, Paul too, who had submitted to deliverance from persecution by being let down from the wall, as to do so was at this time a matter of command, refused in like manner now at the close of his ministry, and after the injunction had come to an end, to give in to the anxieties of the disciples, eagerly entreating him that he would not risk himself at Jerusalem, because of the sufferings in store for him which Agabus had foretold; but doing the very opposite, it is thus he speaks, "What do ye, weeping and disquieting my heart? For I could wish not only to suffer bonds, but also to die at Jerusalem, for the name of my Lord Jesus Christ."[3] And so they all said, "Let the will of the Lord be done." What was the will of the Lord? Certainly no longer to flee from persecution. Otherwise they who had wished him rather to avoid persecution, might also have adduced that prior will of the Lord, in which He had commanded flight. Therefore, seeing even in the days of the apostles themselves, the command to flee was temporary, as were those also relating to the other things at the same time enjoined, that [command] cannot continue with us which ceased with our teachers, even although it had not been issued specially for them; or if the Lord wished it to continue, the apostles did wrong who were not careful to keep fleeing to the last.

7. Let us now see whether also the rest of our Lord's ordinances accord with a lasting command of flight. In the first place, indeed, if persecution is from God, what are we to think of our being ordered to take ourselves out of its way, by the very party who brings it on us? For if He wanted it to be evaded, He had better not have sent it, that there might not be the appear-

ance of His will being thwarted by another will. For He wished us either to suffer persecution or to flee from it. If to flee, how to suffer? If to suffer, how to flee? In fact, what utter inconsistency in the decrees of One who commands to flee, and yet urges to suffer, which is the very opposite! "Him who will confess Me, I also will confess before My Father."[4] How will he confess, fleeing? How flee, confessing? "Of him who shall be ashamed of Me, will I also be ashamed before My Father."[5] If I avoid suffering, I am ashamed to confess. "Happy they who suffer persecution for My name's sake."[6] Unhappy, therefore, they who, by running away, will not suffer according to the divine command. "He who shall endure to the end shall be saved."[7] How then, when you bid me flee, do you wish me to endure to the end? If views so opposed to each other do not comport with the divine dignity, they clearly prove that the command to flee had, at the time it was given, a reason of its own, which we have pointed out. But it is said, the Lord, providing for the weakness of some of His people, nevertheless, in His kindness, suggested also the haven of flight to them. For He was not able even without flight — a protection so base, and unworthy, and servile — to preserve in persecution such as He knew to be weak! Whereas in fact He does not cherish, but ever rejects the weak, teaching first, not that we are to fly from our persecutors, but rather that we are not to fear them. "Fear not them who are able to kill the body, but are unable to do ought against the soul; but fear Him who can destroy both body and soul in hell."[8] And then what does He allot to the fearful? "He who will value his life more than Me, is not worthy of Me; and he who takes not up his cross and follows Me, cannot be My disciple."[9] Last of all, in the Revelation, He does not propose flight to the "fearful,"[10] but a miserable portion among the rest of the outcast, in the lake of brimstone and fire, which is the second death.

8. He sometimes also fled from violence Himself, but for the same reason as had led Him to command the apostles to do so: that is, He wanted to fulfil His ministry of teaching; and when it was finished, I do not say He stood firm, but He had no desire even to get from His Father the aid of hosts of angels: finding fault, too, with Peter's sword. He likewise acknowledged, it is true, that His "soul was troubled, even unto death,"[11] and the flesh weak; with the

[1] Acts xiii. 46.
[2] Ps. xix. 4.
[3] Acts xxi. 13.

[4] Matt. x. 32, 33.
[5] Mark viii. 38; Luke ix. 26.
[6] Matt. v. 11.
[7] Matt. x. 22.
[8] Matt. x. 28.
[9] Matt. x. 37, 38.
[10] Rev. xxi. 8.
[11] Matt. xxvi. 38.

design, (however,) first of all, that by having, as His own, trouble of soul and weakness of the flesh, He might show you that both the substances in Him were truly human ; lest, as certain persons have now brought it in, you might be led to think either the flesh or the soul of Christ different from ours ; and then, that, by an exhibition of their states, you might be convinced that they have no power at all of themselves without the spirit. And for this reason He puts first " the willing spirit," [1] that, looking to the natures respectively of both the substances, you may see that you have in you the spirit's strength as well as the flesh's weakness ; and even from this may learn what to do, and by what means to do it, and what to bring under what, — the weak, namely, under the strong, that you may not, as is now your fashion, make excuses on the ground of the weakness of the flesh, forsooth, but put out of sight the strength of the spirit. He also asked of His Father, that if it might be, the cup of suffering should pass from Him.[2] So ask you the like favour ; but as He did, holding your position, — merely offering supplication, and adding, too, the other words : " but not what I will, but what Thou wilt." But when you run away, how will you make this request ? taking, in that case, into your own hands the removal of the cup from you, and instead of doing what your Father wishes, doing what you wish yourself.

9. The teaching of the apostles was surely in everything according to the mind of God : they forgot and omitted nothing of the Gospel. Where, then, do you show that they renewed the command to flee from city to city ? In fact, it was utterly impossible that they should have laid down anything so utterly opposed to their own examples as a command to flee, while it was just from bonds, or the islands in which, for confessing, not fleeing from the Christian name, they were confined, they wrote their letters to the Churches. Paul [3] bids us support the weak, but most certainly it is not when they flee. For how can the absent be supported by you ? By bearing with them ? Well, he says that people must be supported, if anywhere they have committed a fault through the weakness of their faith, just as (he enjoins) that we should comfort the fainthearted ; he does not say, however, that they should be sent into exile. But when he urges us not to give place to evil,[4] he does not offer the suggestion that we should take to our heels, he only teaches that passion should be kept under restraint ; and if he says that the time must be redeemed, because the days are evil,[5] he wishes us to gain a lengthening of life, not

by flight, but by wisdom. Besides, he who bids us shine as sons of light,[6] does not bid us hide away out of sight as sons of darkness. He commands us to stand stedfast,[7] certainly not to act an opposite part by fleeing ; and to be girt, not to play the fugitive or oppose the Gospel. He points out weapons, too, which persons who intend to run away would not require. And among these he notes the shield [8] too, that ye may be able to quench the darts of the devil, when doubtless ye resist him, and sustain his assaults in their utmost force. Accordingly John also teaches that we must lay down our lives for the brethren ; [9] much more, then, we must do it for the Lord. This cannot be fulfilled by those who flee. Finally, mindful of his own Revelation, in which he had heard the doom of the fearful, (and so) speaking from personal knowledge, he warns us that fear must be put away. " There is no fear," says he, " in love ; but perfect love casteth out fear ; because fear has torment " — the fire of the lake, no doubt. " He that feareth is not perfect in love " [10] — to wit, the love of God. And yet who will flee from persecution, but he who fears ? Who will fear, but he who has not loved ? Yes ; and if you ask counsel of the Spirit, what does He approve more than that utterance of the Spirit ? For, indeed, it incites all almost to go and offer themselves in martyrdom, not to flee from it ; so that we also make mention of it. If you are exposed to public infamy, says he, it is for your good ; for he who is not exposed to dishonour among men is sure to be so before the Lord. Do not be ashamed ; righteousness brings you forth into the public gaze. Why should you be ashamed of gaining glory ? The opportunity is given you when you are before the eyes of men. So also elsewhere : seek not to die on bridal beds, nor in miscarriages, nor in soft fevers, but to die the martyr's death, that He may be glorified who has suffered for you.

10. But some, paying no attention to the exhortations of God, are readier to apply to themselves that Greek versicle of worldly wisdom, " He who fled will fight again ; " perhaps also in the battle to flee again. And when will he who, as a fugitive, is a defeated man, be conqueror ? A worthy soldier he furnishes to his commander Christ, who, so amply armed by the apostle, as soon as he hears persecution's trumpet, runs off from the day of persecution. I also will produce in answer a quotation taken from the world : " Is it a thing so very sad to die ? " [11] He must die, in whatever way of it, either as

---

[1] Matt. xxvi. 41.
[2] Matt. xxvi. 39.
[3] 1 Thess. v. 14.
[4] Eph. iv. 27.
[5] Eph. v. 16.

[6] 1 Thess. v. 5.
[7] 1 Cor. xv. 58.
[8] Eph. vi. 16.
[9] 1 John iii. 16.
[10] 1 John iv. 18.
[11] Æneid, xii. 646.

conquered or as conqueror. But although he has succumbed in denying, he has yet faced and battled with the torture. I had rather be one to be pitied than to be blushed for. More glorious is the soldier pierced with a javelin in battle, than he who has a safe skin as a fugitive. Do you fear man, O Christian?— you who ought to be feared by the angels, since you are to judge angels; who ought to be feared by evil spirits, since you have received power also over evil spirits; who ought to be feared by the whole world, since by you, too, the world is judged. You are Christ-clothed, you who flee before the devil, since into Christ you have been baptized. Christ, who is in you, is treated as of small account when you give yourself back to the devil, by becoming a fugitive before him. But, seeing it is from the Lord you flee, you taunt all runaways with the futility of their purpose. A certain bold prophet also had fled from the Lord, he had crossed over from Joppa in the direction of Tarsus, as if he could as easily transport himself away from God; but I find him, I do not say in the sea and on the land, but, in fact, in the belly even of a beast, in which he was confined for the space of three days, unable either to find death or even thus escape from God. How much better the conduct of the man who, though he fears the enemy of God, does not flee from, but rather despises him, relying on the protection of the Lord; or, if you will, having an awe of God all the greater, the more that he has stood in His presence, says, "It is the Lord, He is mighty. All things belong to Him; wherever I am, I am in His hand: let Him do as He wills, I go not away; and if it be His pleasure that I die, let Him destroy me Himself, while I save myself for Him. I had rather bring odium upon Him by dying by His will, than by escaping through my own anger."

11. Thus ought every servant of God to feel and act, even one in an inferior place, that he may come to have a more important one, if he has made some upward step by his endurance of persecution. But when persons in authority themselves — I mean the very deacons, and presbyters, and bishops — take to flight, how will a layman be able to see with what view it was said, Flee from city to city? Thus, too, with the leaders turning their backs, who of the common rank will hope to persuade men to stand firm in the battle? Most assuredly a good shepherd lays down his life for the sheep, according to the word of Moses, when the Lord Christ had not as yet been revealed, but was already shadowed forth in himself: "If you destroy this people," he says, "destroy me also along with it."[1] But Christ, confirming these foreshadowings Himself, adds: "The bad shepherd is he who, on seeing the wolf, flees, and leaves the sheep to be torn in pieces."[2] Why, a shepherd like this will be turned off from the farm; the wages to have been given him at the time of his discharge will be kept from him as compensation; nay, even from his former savings a restoration of the master's loss will be required; for "to him who hath shall be given, but from him who hath not shall be taken away even that which he seemeth to have."[3] Thus Zechariah threatens: "Arise, O sword, against the shepherds, and pluck ye out the sheep; and I will turn my hand against the shepherds."[4] And against them both Ezekiel and Jeremiah declaim with kindred threatenings, for their not only wickedly eating of the sheep, — they feeding themselves rather than those committed to their charge, — but also scattering the flock, and giving it over, shepherdless, a prey to all the beasts of the field. And this never happens more than when in persecution the Church is abandoned by the clergy. If any one recognises the Spirit also, he will hear him branding the runaways. But if it does not become the keepers of the flock to flee when the wolves invade it — nay, if that is absolutely unlawful (for He who has declared a shepherd of this sort a bad one has certainly condemned him; and whatever is condemned has, without doubt, become unlawful) — on this ground it will not be the duty of those who have been set over the Church to flee in the time of persecution. But otherwise, if the flock should flee, the overseer of the flock would have no call to hold his ground, as his doing so in that case would be, without good reason, to give to the flock protection, which it would not require in consequence of its liberty, forsooth, to flee.

12. So far, my brother, as the question proposed by you is concerned, you have our opinion in answer and encouragement. But he who inquires whether persecution ought to be shunned by us must now be prepared to consider the following question also: Whether, if we should not flee from it, we should at least buy ourselves off from it. Going further than you expected, therefore, I will also on this point give you my advice, distinctly affirming that persecution, from which it is evident we must not flee, must in like manner not even be bought off. The difference lies in the payment; but as flight is a buying off without money, so buying off is money-flight. Assuredly you have here too the counselling of fear. Because you fear, you buy yourself off; and so you flee. As regards your feet, you have stood; in respect of the money you have paid,

---

[1] Ex. xxxii. 32.

[2] John x. 12.
[3] Luke viii. 18.
[4] Zech. xiii. 7.

you have run away. Why, in this very standing of yours there was a fleeing from persecution, in the release from persecution which you bought ; but that you should ransom with money a man whom Christ has ransomed with His blood, how unworthy is it of God and His ways of acting, who spared not His own Son for you, that He might be made a curse for us, because cursed is he that hangeth on a tree,[1] — Him who was led as a sheep to be a sacrifice, and just as a lamb before its shearer, so opened He not His mouth ;[2] but gave His back to the scourges, nay, His cheeks to the hands of the smiter, and turned not away His face from spitting, and, being numbered with the transgressors, was delivered up to death, nay, the death of the cross. All this took place that He might redeem us from our sins. The sun ceded to us the day of our redemption ; hell re-transferred the right it had in us, and our covenant is in heaven ; the ever-lasting gates were lifted up, that the King of Glory, the Lord of might, might enter in,[3] after having redeemed man from earth, nay, from hell, that he might attain to heaven. What, now, are we to think of the man who strives against that glorious One, nay, slights and defiles His goods, obtained at so great a ransom — no less, in truth, than His most precious blood? It appears, then, that it is better to flee than to fall in value, if a man will not lay out for himself as much as he cost Christ. And the Lord indeed ransomed him from the angelic powers which rule the world — from the spirits of wickedness, from the darkness of this life, from eternal judgment, from everlasting death. But *you* bargain for him with an informer, or a soldier, or some paltry thief of a ruler — under, as they say, the folds of the tunic — as if *he* were stolen goods whom Christ purchased in the face of the whole world, yes, and set at liberty. Will you value, then, this free man at any price, and possess him at any price, but the one, as we have said, it cost the Lord, — namely, His own blood? (And if not,) why then do you purchase Christ in the man in whom He dwells, as though He were some human property? No otherwise did Simon even try to do, when he offered the apostles money for the Spirit of Christ. Therefore this man also, who in buying himself has bought the Spirit of Christ, will hear that word, "Your money perish with you, since you have thought that the grace of God is to be had at a price !"[4] Yet who will despise him for being (what he is), a denier? For what says that extorter? Give me money : assuredly that he may not deliver him up, since he tries to sell you nothing else than that which he is going to give you for

money. When you put that into his hands, it is certainly your wish *not* to be delivered up. But not delivered up, had you to be held up to public ridicule? While, then, in being unwilling to be delivered up, you are not willing to be thus exposed ; by this unwillingness of yours you have denied that you are what you have been unwilling to have it made public that you are. Nay, you say, While I am unwilling to be held up to the public as being what I am, I have acknowledged that I am what I am unwilling to be so held up as being, that is, a Christian. Can Christ, therefore, claim that you, as a witness for Him, have stedfastly shown Him forth? He who buys himself off does nothing in that way. Before *one* it might, I doubt not, be said, You have confessed Him ; so also, on the account of your unwillingness to confess Him before many you have denied Him. A man's very safety will pronounce that he has fallen while getting out of persecution's way. He has fallen, therefore, whose desire has been to escape. The refusal of martyrdom is denial. A Christian is preserved by his wealth, and for this end has his treasures, that he may not suffer, while he will be rich toward God. But it is the case that Christ was rich in blood for him. Blessed therefore are the poor, because, He says, the kingdom of heaven is theirs who have the soul only treasured up.[5] If we cannot serve God and mammon, can we be redeemed both by God and by mammon? For who will serve mammon more than the man whom mammon has ransomed? Finally, of what example do you avail yourself to warrant your averting by money the giving of you up? When did the apostles, dealing with the matter, in any time of persecution trouble, extricate themselves by money? And money they certainly had from the prices of lands which were laid down at their feet,[6] there being, without a doubt, many of the rich among those who believed — men, and also women, who were wont, too, to minister to their comfort. When did Onesimus, or Aquila, or Stephen,[7] give them aid of this kind when they were persecuted? Paul indeed, when Felix the governor hoped that he should receive money for him from the disciples,[8] about which matter he also dealt with the apostle in private, certainly neither paid it himself, nor did the disciples for him. Those disciples, at any rate, who wept because he was equally persistent in his determination to go to Jerusalem, and neglectful of all means to secure himself from the persecutions which had been foretold as about to occur there, at last say, "Let the will of the Lord be done." What was that will? No doubt that he should suffer for the name of the Lord, not

---

[1] Rom. viii. 32 ; Gal. iii. 13.
[2] Isa. liii. 7.
[3] Ps. xxiv. 7.
[4] Acts viii. 20.

[5] Matt. v. 3.
[6] Acts iv. 34, 35.
[7] Stephanas is perhaps intended. — Tr.
[8] Acts xxiv. 26.

that he should be bought off. For as Christ laid down His life for us, so, too, we should do for Him ; and not only for the Lord Himself, nay, but likewise for our brethren on His account. This, too, is the teaching of John when he declares, not that we should pay for our brethren, but rather that we should die for them. It makes no difference whether the thing not to be done by you is to buy *off* a Christian, or to *buy* one. And so the will of God accords with this. Look at the condition — certainly of God's ordaining, in whose hand the king's heart is — of kingdoms and empires. For increasing the treasury there are daily provided so many appliances — registerings of property, taxes in kind, benevolences, taxes in money ; but never up to this time has ought of the kind been provided by bringing Christians under some purchase-money for the person and the sect, although enormous gains could be reaped from numbers too great for any to be ignorant of them. Bought with blood, paid for with blood, we owe no money for our head, because Christ is our Head. It is not fit that Christ should cost us money. How could martyrdoms, too, take place to the glory of the Lord, if by tribute we should pay for the liberty of our sect? And so he who stipulates to have it at a price, opposes the divine appointment. Since, therefore, Cæsar has imposed nothing on us after this fashion of a tributary sect — in fact, such an imposition never can be made, — with Antichrist now close at hand, and gaping for the blood, not for the money of Christians — how can it be pointed out to me that there is the command, " Render to Cæsar the things which are Cæsar's ? " [1] A soldier, be he an informer or an enemy, extorts money from me by threats, exacting nothing on Cæsar's behalf ; nay, doing the very opposite, when for a bribe he lets me go — Christian as I am, and by the laws of man a criminal. Of another sort is the *denarius* which I owe to Cæsar, a thing belonging to him, about which the question then was started, it being a tribute coin due indeed by those subject to tribute, not by children. Or how shall I render to God the things which are God's, — certainly, therefore, His own likeness and money inscribed with His name, that is, a Christian man? But what do I owe God, as I do Cæsar the *denarius*, but the blood which His own Son shed for me? Now if I owe God, indeed, a human being and my own blood ; but I am now in this juncture, that a demand is made upon me for the payment of that debt, I am undoubtedly guilty of cheating God if I do my best to withhold payment. I have well kept the commandment, if, rendering to Cæsar the things which

are Cæsar's, I refuse to God the things which are God's !

13. But also to every one who asks me I will give on the plea of charity, not under any intimidation. Who asks? [2] He says. But he who uses intimidation does not ask. One who threatens if he does not receive, does not crave, but compels. It is not alms he looks for, who comes not to be pitied, but to be feared. I will give, therefore, because I pity, not because I fear, when the recipient honours God and returns me his blessing ; not when rather he both believes that he has conferred a favour on me, and, beholding his plunder, says, " Guilt money." Shall I be angry even with an enemy? But enmities have also other grounds. Yet withal he did not say a, betrayer, or persecutor, or one seeking to terrify you by his threats. For how much more shall I heap coals upon the head of a man of this sort, if I do not redeem myself by money? " In like manner," says Jesus, " to him who has taken away your coat, grant even your cloak also." But that refers to him who has sought to take away my property, not my faith. The cloak, too, I will grant, if I am not threatened with betrayal. If he threatens, I will demand even my coat back again. Even now, the declarations of the Lord have reasons and laws of their own. They are not of unlimited or universal application. And so He commands us to give to every one who asks, yet He Himself does not give to those who ask a sign. Otherwise, if you think that we should give indiscriminately to all who ask, that seems to me to mean that you would give, I say not wine to him who has a fever, but even poison or a sword to him who longs for death. But how we are to understand, " Make to yourselves friends of mammon," [3] let the previous parable teach you. The saying was addressed to the Jewish people ; inasmuch as, having managed ill the business of the Lord which had been entrusted to them, they ought to have provided for themselves out of the men of mammon, which we then were, friends rather than enemies, and to have delivered us from the dues of sins which kept us from God, if they bestowed the blessing upon us, for the reason given by the Lord, that when grace began to depart from them, they, betaking themselves to our faith, might be admitted into everlasting habitations. Hold now any other explanation of this parable and saying you like, if only you clearly see that there is no likelihood of our opposers, should we make them friends with mammon, then receiving us into everlasting abodes. But of what will not cowardice convince men? As if Scripture both allowed them to flee, and commanded them to

---

[1] Matt. xxii. 21.

[2] Matt. v. 42.
[3] Luke xvi. 9.

buy off! Finally, it is not enough if one or another is so rescued. Whole Churches have imposed tribute *en masse* on themselves. I know not whether it is matter for grief or shame when, among hucksters, and pickpockets, and bath-thieves, and gamesters, and pimps, Christians too are included as taxpayers in the lists of free soldiers and spies. Did the apostles, with so much foresight, make the office of overseer of this type, that the occupants might be able to enjoy their rule free from anxiety, under colour of providing (a like freedom for their flocks)? For such a peace, forsooth, Christ, returning to His Father, commanded to be bought from the soldiers by gifts like those you have in the Saturnalia!

14. But how shall we assemble together? say you; how shall we observe the ordinances of the Lord? To be sure, just as the apostles also did, who were protected by faith, not by money; which faith, if it can remove a mountain, can much more remove a soldier. Be your safe-guard wisdom, not a bribe. For you will not have at once complete security from the people also, should you buy off the interference of the soldiers. Therefore all you need for your protection is to have both faith and wisdom: if you do not make use of these, you may lose even the deliverance which you have purchased for yourself; while, if you do employ them, you can have no need of any ransoming. Lastly, if you can-

not assemble by day, you have the night, the light of Christ luminous against its darkness. You cannot run about among them one after another. Be content with a church of threes. It is better that you sometimes should not see your crowds, than subject yourselves (to a tribute bondage). Keep pure for Christ His betrothed virgin; let no one make gain of her. These things, my brother, seem to you perhaps harsh and not to be endured; but recall that God has said, "He who receives it, let him receive it," [1] that is, let him who does not receive it go his way. He who fears to suffer, cannot belong to Him who suffered. But the man who does not fear to suffer, he will be perfect in love — in the love, it is meant, of God; "for perfect love casteth out fear." [2] "And therefore many are called, but few chosen." [3] It is not asked who is ready to follow the broad way, but who the narrow. And therefore the Comforter is requisite, who guides into all truth, and animates to all endurance. And they who have received Him will neither stoop to flee from persecution nor to buy it off, for they have the Lord Himself, One who will stand by us to aid us in suffering, as well as to be our mouth when we are put to the question.

[1] Matt. xix. 12.
[2] 1 John iv. 18.
[3] Matt. xxii. 14.

ELUCIDATIONS.

I.

(Persecutions threaten, p. 116.)

WE have reserved this heroic tract to close our series of the ascetic essays of our author because it places even his sophistical enthusiasm in a light which shows much to admire. Strange that this defiant hero should have died (as we may infer) in his bed, and in extreme old age. Great man, how much, alike for weal and woe, the ages have been taught by thee!

This is the place for a tabular view of the *ten persecutions* of the Ante-Nicene Church. They are commonly enumerated as follows: [1] —

I.	Under Nero	A.D. 64.
II.	Under Trajan	A.D. 95.
III.	Under Trajan	A.D. 107.
IV.	Under Hadrian (A.D. 118 and)	A.D. 134.
V.	Under Aurelius (A.D. 177) and Severus	A.D. 202.
VI.	Under Maximin	A.D. 235.
VII.	Under Decius	A.D. 250.
VIII.	Under Valerian	A.D. 254.
IX.	Under Aurelian	A.D. 270.
X.	Under Diocletian (A.D. 284 and)	A.D. 303.

[1] See what Gibbon can say to *minimize* the matter (in cap. xvi. 4, vol. ii. p. 45, New York).

Periods of Comparative Rest.

I.   Under Antoninus Pius . . . . A.D. 151.
II. Under Commodus . . . . A.D. 185.
III. Under Alexander Severus. . . . . A.D. 223.
IV. Under Philip . . . . A.D. 248.
V.   Under Diocletian . . . . A.D. 284 till A.D. 303.

In thus chastising and sifting his Church in the years of her gradual growth " from the smallest of all seeds," we see illustrations of the Lord's Epistles to the seven churches of the Apocalypse. Who can doubt that Tertullian's writings prepared the North-African Church for the Decian furnace, and all believers for the " seven times hotter " fires of Diocletian?

(To the fearful, p. 120.)

In the *Patientia* [1] Tertullian reflects the views of Catholics, and seems to allow those " persecuted in one city to flee to another." So also in the *Ad Uxorem,* [2] as instanced by Kaye. [3] In the *Fuga* we have the enthusiast, but not as Gibbon will have it, [4] the most wild and fanatical of declaimers. On the whole subject we again refer our readers to the solid and sober comments of Kaye on the martyrdoms and persecutions of the early faithful, and on the patristic views of the same.

II.

(Enormous gains from numbers, p. 124.)

Christians were now counted by millions. The following tabular view of the Christian population of the world from the beginning has been attributed to *Sharon Turner.* I do not find it in any of his works with which I am familiar. The *nineteenth century* is certainly credited too low, according to the modern computists ; but I insert it merely for the centuries we are now considering.

GROWTH OF THE CHURCH IN NUMBERS.

First	century	500,000
Second	"	2,000,000
Third	"	5,000,000
Fourth	"	10,000,000
Fifth	"	15,000,000
Sixth	"	20,000,000
Seventh	"	24,000,000
Eighth	"	30,000,000
Ninth	"	40,000,000
Tenth	"	50,000,000
Eleventh	"	70,000,000
Twelfth	"	80,000,000
Thirteenth	"	75,000,000
Fourteenth	"	80,000,000
Fifteenth	"	100,000,000
Sixteenth	"	125,000,000
Seventeenth	"	155,000,000
Eighteenth	"	200,000,000
Nineteenth	"	400,000,000

[1] Cap. xiii.   [2] I. cap. iii.   [3] pp. 46, 138.   [4] In his disgraceful chap. xvi.

APPENDIX.[1]

[TRANSLATED BY THE REV. S. THELWALL.]

I. A STRAIN OF JONAH THE PROPHET.

AFTER the living, aye-enduring death
Of Sodom and Gomorrah; after fires
Penal, attested by time-frosted plains
Of ashes; after fruitless apple-growths,
5 Born but to feed the eye; after the death
Of sea and brine, both in like fate involved;
While whatsoe'er is human still retains
In change corporeal its penal badge:[2]
A city — Nineveh — by stepping o'er
10 The path of justice and of equity,
On her own head had well-nigh shaken down
More fires of rain supernal. For what dread[3]
Dwells in a mind subverted? Commonly
Tokens of penal visitations prove
15 All vain where error holds possession. Still,
Kindly and patient of our waywardness,
And slow to punish, the Almighty Lord
Will launch no shaft of wrath, unless He first
Admonish and knock oft at hardened hearts,
20 Rousing with mind august presaging seers.
For to the merits of the Ninevites
The Lord had bidden Jonah to foretell
Destruction; but he, conscious that He spares
The subject, and remits to suppliants
25 The dues of penalty, and is to good
Ever inclinable, was loth to face
That errand; lest he sing his seerly strain
In vain, and peaceful issue of his threats
Ensue. His counsel presently is flight:
30 (If, howsoe'er, there is at all the power
God to avoid, and shun the Lord's right hand,
'Neath whom the whole orb trembles and is held
In check: but is there reason in the act

Which in[4] his saintly heart the prophet
dares?)
35 On the beach-lip, over against the shores
Of the Cilicians, is a city poised,[5]
Far-famed for trusty port — Joppa her name.
Thence therefore Jonah speeding in a barque
Seeks Tarsus,[6] through the signal providence
40 Of the same God;[7] nor marvel is't, I ween,
If, fleeing from the Lord upon the lands,
He found Him in the waves. For suddenly
A little cloud had stained the lower air
With fleecy wrack sulphureous, itself[8]
45 By the wind's seed excited: by degrees,
Bearing a brood globose, it with the sun
Cohered, and with a train caliginous
Shut in the cheated day. The main becomes
The mirror of the sky; the waves are dyed
50 With black encirclement; the upper air
Down rushes into darkness, and the sea
Uprises; nought of middle space is left;
While the clouds touch the waves, and the
waves all
Are mingled by the bluster of the winds
55 In whirling eddy. 'Gainst the renegade,
'Gainst Jonah, diverse frenzy joined to rave,
While one sole barque did all the struggle
breed
'Twixt sky and surge. From this side and
from that
Pounded she reels; 'neath each wave-break-
ing blow
60 The forest of her tackling trembles all;

---

[1] [Elucidation.]
[2] These two lines, if this be their true sense, seem to refer to Lot's wife. But the grammar and meaning of this introduction are alike obscure.
[3] "Metus;" used, as in other places, of *godly* fear.
[4] Lit. "from," i.e., which, *urged by* a heart which is that of a saint, even though on this occasion it failed, the prophet dared.
[5] Libratur.
[6] "Tarshish," Eng. ver.; perhaps Tartessus in Spain. For this question, and the "trustiness" of Joppa (now Jaffa) as a port, see Pusey on Jonah i. 3.
[7] Ejusdem per signa Dei.
[8] i.e., the cloud.

127

As, underneath, her spinal length of keel,
Staggered by shock on shock, all palpitates;
And, from on high, her labouring mass of yard
Creaks shuddering; and the tree-like mast itself
65 Bends to the gale, misdoubting to be riven.
Meantime the rising [1] clamour of the crew
Tries every chance for barque's and dear life's sake:
To pass from hand to hand [2] the tardy coils
To tighten the girth's noose: straitly to bind
70 The tiller's struggles; or, with breast opposed,
T' impel reluctant curves. Part, turn by turn,
With foremost haste outbale the reeking well
Of inward sea. The wares and cargo all
They then cast headlong, and with losses seek
75 Their perils to subdue. At every crash
Of the wild deep rise piteous cries; and out
They stretch their hands to majesties of gods,
Which gods are none; whom might of sea and sky
Fears not, nor yet the less from off their poops
80 With angry eddy sweeping sinks them down.
Unconscious of all this, the guilty one
'Neath the poop's hollow arch was making sleep
Re-echo stertorous with nostril wide
Inflated: whom, so soon as he who guides
85 The functions of the wave-dividing prow
Saw him sleep-bound in placid peace, and proud
In his repose, he, standing o'er him, shook,
And said, "Why sing'st, with vocal nostril, dreams,
In such a crisis? In so wild a whirl,
90 Why keep'st thou only harbour? Lo! the wave
Whelms us, and our one hope is in the gods.
Thou also, whosoever is thy god,
Make vows, and, pouring prayers on bended knee,
Win o'er thy country's Sovran!"
            Then they vote
95 To learn by lot who is the culprit, who
The cause of storm; nor does the lot belie
Jonah: whom then they ask, and ask again,
"Who? whence? who in the world? from what abode,

What people, hail'st thou?" He avows himself
100 A servant, and an over-timid one,
Of God, who raised aloft the sky, who based
The earth, who corporally fused the whole:
A renegade from Him he owns himself,
And tells the reason. Rigid turned they all
105 With dread. "What grudge, then, ow'st thou us? What now
Will follow? By what deed shall we appease
The main?" For more and far more swelling grew
The savage surges. Then the seer begins
Words prompted by the Spirit of the Lord: [3]
110 "Lo! I your tempest am; I am the sum
Of the world's [4] madness: 'tis in me," he says,
"That the sea rises, and the upper air
Down rushes; land in me is far, death near,
And hope in God is none! Come, headlong hurl
115 Your cause of bane: lighten your ship, and cast
This single mighty burden to the main,
A willing prey!" But they — all vainly! — strive
Homeward to turn their course; for helm refused
To suffer turning, and the yard's stiff poise
120 Willed not to change. At last unto the Lord
They cry: "For one soul's sake give us not o'er
Unto death's maw, nor let us be besprent
With righteous blood, if thus Thine own right hand
Leadeth." And from the eddy's depth a whale
125 Outrising on the spot, scaly with shells, [5]
Unravelling his body's train, 'gan urge
More near the waves, shocking the gleaming brine,
Seizing — at God's command — the prey; which, rolled
From the poop's summit prone, with slimy jaws
130 He sucked; and into his long belly sped
The living feast; and swallowed, with the man,
The rage of sky and main. The billowy waste
Grows level, and the ether's gloom dissolves;
The waves on this side, and the blasts on that,

---

[1] Ge*nit*us (Oehler); ge*min*us (Migne) = "twin clamour," which is not inapt.
[2] Mandare (Oehler). If this be the true reading, the rendering in the text seems to represent the meaning; for "mandare" with an *accusative*, in the sense of "to *bid* the tardy coils tighten the girth's noose," seems almost too gross a solecism for even so lax a Latinist as our present writer. Migne, however, reads m*und*are = *to* "*clear* the tardy coils," i.e., probably from the wash and weed with which the gale was cloying them.

[3] Tunc Domini vates ingesta Spiritus infit. Of course it is a gross offence against quantity to make a genitive in "us" short, as the rendering in the text does. But a writer who makes the first syllable in "clamor" and the last syllable of gerunds in *do* short, would scarcely be likely to hesitate about taking similar liberties with a genitive of the so-called fourth declension. It is possible, it is true, to take "vates" and "Spiritus" as in apposition, and render, "Then the seer-Spirit of the Lord begins to utter words inspired," or, "Then the seer-Spirit begins to utter the promptings of the Lord." But these renderings seem to accord less well with the ensuing words.
[4] Mundi.
[5] i.e., apparently with shells which had gathered about him as he lay in the deep.

135 Are to their friendly mood restored; and,
    where
The placid keel marks out a path secure,
White traces in the emerald furrow bloom.
The sailor then does to the reverend Lord
Of death make grateful offering of his fear;[1]
140 Then enters friendly ports.
                    Jonah the seer
The while is voyaging, in other craft
Embarked, and cleaving 'neath the lowest
    waves

A wave: his sails the intestines of the fish,
Inspired with breath ferine; himself, shut in
145 By waters, yet untouched; in the sea's heart,
And yet beyond its reach; 'mid wrecks of
    fleets
Half-eaten, and men's carcasses dissolved
In putrid disintegrity: in life
Learning the process of his death; but still —
150 To be a sign hereafter of the Lord[2] —
A witness was he (in his very self),[3]
Not of destruction, but of death's repulse.

[1] This seems to be the sense of Oehler's "Nauta at tum Domino leti venerando timorem Sacrificat grates"—"grates" being in apposition with "timorem." But Migne reads: "Nautæ tum Domino læti venerando timorem Sacrificant grates:"—

    "The sailors then do to the reverend Lord
       Gladly make grateful sacrifice of fear:"
and I do not see that Oehler's reading is much better.

[2] Comp. Matt. xii. 38–41; Luke xi. 29, 30.
[3] These words are not in the original, but are inserted (I confess) to fill up the line, and avoid ending with an incomplete verse. If, however, any one is curious enough to compare the translation, with all its defects, with the Latin, he may be somewhat surprised to find how very little alteration or adaptation is necessary in turning verse into verse.

---

2. A STRAIN OF SODOM.

(AUTHOR UNCERTAIN.)

Already had Almighty God wiped off
By vengeful flood (with waters all conjoined
Which heaven discharged on earth and the
    sea's plain[1]
Outspued) the times of the primeval age:
5 Had pledged Himself, while nether air should
    bring
The winters in their course, ne'er to decree,
By *liquid* ruin, retribution's due;
And had assigned, to curb the rains, the bow
Of many hues, sealing the clouds with band
10 Of purple and of green, Iris its name,
The rain-clouds' proper baldric.[2]
                But alike
With mankind's second race impiety
Revives, and a new age of ill once more
Shoots forth; allotted now no more to *showers*
15 For ruin, but to *fires:* thus did the land
Of SODOM earn to be by glowing dews
Upburnt, and typically thus portend
The future end.[3] There wild voluptuousness
(Modesty's foe) stood in the room of law;
20 Which prescient guest would shun, and sooner
    choose
At Scythian or Busirian altar's foot
'Mid sacred rites to die, and, slaughtered, pour
His blood to Bebryx, or to satiate
Libyan palæstras, or assume new forms
25 By virtue of Circæan cups, than lose
His outraged sex in Sodom.

[1] Maris æquor.
[2] See Gen. ix. 21, 22, x. 8–17.
[3] Comp. 2 Pet. iii. 5–14.

                    At heaven's gate
There knocked for vengeance marriages com-
    mixt
With equal incest common 'mong a race
By nature rebels 'gainst themselves;[4] and
    hurts
30 Done to man's name and person equally.
But God, forewatching all things, at fix'd time
Doth judge the unjust; with patience tarrying
The hour when crime's ripe age — not any
    force
Of wrath impetuous — shall have circum-
    scribed
35 The space for waiting.[5]
               Now at length the day
Of vengeance was at hand. Sent from the
    host
Angelical, two, youths in form, who both
Were ministering spirits,[6] carrying
The Lord's divine commissions, come beneath
40 The walls of Sodom. There was dwelling Lot,
A transplantation from a pious stock;

[4] The expression, "sinners against their own souls," in Num. xvi. 38 — where, however, the LXX. have a very different version — may be compared with this; as likewise Prov. viii. 36.
[5] Whether the above be the sense of this most obscure triplet I will not presume to determine. It is at least (I hope) *intelligible* sense. But that the reader may judge for himself whether he can offer any better, I subjoin the lines, which form a sentence alone, and therefore can be judged of without their context: —

    "Tempore sed certo Deus omnia prospectulatus,
      Judicat injustos, patiens ubi criminis ætas
      Cessandi spatium vis nulla coëgerit iræ."

[6] Comp. Heb. i. 14. It may be as well here to inform the reader once for all that prosody as well as syntax is repeatedly set at defiance in these metrical fragments; and hence, of course, arise some of the chief difficulties in dealing with them.

Wise, and a practiser of righteousness,
He was the only one to think on God :
As oft a fruitful tree is wont to lurk,
45 Guest-like, in forests wild.   He, sitting then
Before the gate (for the celestials scarce
Had reached the ramparts), though he knew
    not them
Divine,[1] accosts them unsolicited,
Invites, and with ancestral honour greets ;
50 And offers them, preparing to abide
Abroad, a hospice.   By repeated prayers
He wins them ; and then ranges studiously
The sacred pledges[2] on his board,[3] and quits[4]
His friends with courteous offices.   The night
55 Had brought repose : alternate[5] dawn had
    chased
The night, and Sodom with her shameful law
Makes uproar at the doors.   Lot, suppliant-
    wise,
Withstands : "Young men, let not your new-
    fed lust
Enkindle you to violate this youth ![6]
60 Whither is passion's seed inviting you?
To what vain end your lust?   For such an end
No creaturès wed : not such as haunt the fens ;
Not stall-fed cattle ; not the gaping brood
Subaqueous ; nor they which, modulant
65 On pinions, hang suspended near the clouds ;
Nor they which with forth-stretchèd body
    creep
Over earth's face.   To conjugal delight
Each kind its kind doth owe : but female still
To all is wife ; nor is there one that has
70 A mother save a female one.   Yet now,
If youthful vigour holds it right[7] to waste
The flower of modesty, I have within
Two daughters of a nuptial age, in whom
Virginity is swelling in its bloom,
75 Already ripe for harvest — a desire
Worthy of men — which let your pleasure
    reap !
Myself their sire, I yield them ; and will pay,
For my guests' sake, the forfeit of my grief !"
Answered the mob insane : "And who art
    thou?
80 And what? and whence? to lord it over us,
And to expound us laws?   Shall foreigner

Rule Sodom, and hurl threats?   Now, then,
    thyself
For daughters and for guests shalt sate our
    greed !
One shall suffice for all ! "   So said, so done :
85 The frantic mob delays not.   As, whene'er
A turbid torrent rolls with wintry tide,
And rushes at one speed through countless
    streams
Of rivers, if, just where it forks, some tree
Meets the swift waves (not long to stand,
    save while
90 By her root's force she shall avail to oppose
Her tufty obstacles), when gradually
Her hold upon the underminèd soil
Is failing, with her barèd stem she hangs,
And, with uncertain heavings to and fro,
95 Defers her certain fall ; not otherwise
Lot in the mid-whirl of the dizzy mob
Kept nodding, now almost o'ercome.   But
    power
Divine brings succour : the angelic youths,
Snatching him from the threshold, to his roof
100 Restore him ; but upon the spot they mulct
Of sight the mob insane in open day, —
Fit augury of coming penalties !
Then they unlock the just decrees of God :
That penalty condign from heaven will fall
105 On Sodom ; that himself had merited
Safety upon the count of righteousness.
"Gird thee, then, up to hasten hence thy
    flight,
And with thee to lead out what family
Thou hast : already we are bringing on
110 Destruction o'er the city."   Lot with speed
Speaks to his sons-in-law ; but their hard heart
Scorned to believe the warning, and at fear
Laughed.   At what time the light attempts
    to climb
The darkness, and heaven's face wears double
    hue
115 From night and day, the youthful visitants
Were instant to outlead from Sodoma
The race Chaldæan,[8] and the righteous house
Consign to safety : " Ho ! come, Lot ! arise,
And take thy yokefellow and daughters twain,
120 And hence, beyond the boundaries be gone,
Preventing[9] Sodom's penalties ! "   And eke
With friendly hands they lead them trembling
    forth,
And then their final mandates give : " Save,
    Lot,
Thy life, lest thou perchance should will to
    turn
125 Thy retroverted gaze behind, or stay
The step once taken : to the mountain speed ! "

---

1 " Divinos; " i.e., apparently " superhuman," as everything *heavenly* is.
2 Of hospitality — bread and salt, etc.
3 " Mens*a ;* " but perhaps " mensæ " may be suggested — " the sacred pledges *of the board.*"
4 " Dispungit," which is the only verb in the sentence, and refers both to *pia pignora* and to *amicos.* I use " quit " in the sense in which we speak of " quitting a debtor," i.e., giving him his full due; but the two lines are very hard, and present (as in the case of those before quoted) a jumble of words without grammar: " pia pignora mensa Officiisque probis studio dispungit amicos; " which may be somewhat more literally rendered than in our text, thus: " he zealously discharges " (i.e., fulfils) " his sacred pledges " (i.e., the promised hospitality which he had offered them) " with (a generous) board, and discharges " (i.e., fulfils his obligations to) " his friends with honourable courtesies."
5 Àltera = alterna.   But the statement differs from Gen. xix. 4.
6 " Istam juventam," i.e., the two " juvenes " (ver. 31) within.
7 " Fas " = ὅσιον, *morally* right; distinct from " jus " or " licitum."

8 i.e., Lot's race or family, which had come from " Ur of the Chaldees."   See Gen. xi. 26, 27, 28.
9 I use " preventing " in its now unusual sense of " anticipating the arrival of."

Lot feared to creep the heights with tardy step,
Lest the celestial wrath-fires should o'ertake
And whelm him : therefore he essays to crave
130 Some other ports ; a city small, to wit,
Which opposite he had espied.   " Hereto,"
He said, " I speed my flight : scarce with its
  walls
'Tis visible ; nor is it far, nor great."
They, favouring his prayer, safety assured
135 To him and to the city ; whence the spot
Is known in speech barbaric by the name
Segor.[1]   Lot enters Segor while the sun
Is rising,[2] the last sun, which glowing bears
To Sodom conflagration ; for his rays
140 He had armed all with fire : beneath him
  spreads
An emulous gloom, which seeks to intercept
The light ; and clouds combine to interweave
Their smoky globes with the confusèd sky :
Down pours a novel shower : the ether seethes
145 With sulphur mixt with blazing flames :[3] the
  air
Crackles with liquid heats exust.   From
  hence
The fable has an echo of the truth
Amid its false, that the sun's progeny
Would drive his father's team ; but nought
  availed
150 The giddy boy to curb the haughty steeds
Of fire : so blazed our orb : then lightning
  reft
The lawless charioteer, and bitter plaint
Transformed his sisters.   Let Eridanus
See to it, if one poplar on his banks
155 Whitens, or any bird dons plumage there
Whose note old age makes mellow ![4]
            Here they mourn
O'er miracles of metamorphosis
Of other sort.   For, partner of Lot's flight,
His wife (ah me, for woman ! even then[5]
160 Intolerant of law !) alone turned back
At the unearthly murmurs of the sky)
Her daring eyes, but bootlessly : not doomed
To utter what she saw ! and then and there
Changed into brittle salt, herself her tomb
165 She stood, herself an image of herself,
Keeping an incorporeal form : and still

In her unsheltered station 'neath the heaven
Dures she, by rains unmelted, by decay
And winds unwasted ; nay, if some strange
  hand
170 Deface her form, forthwith from her own
  store
Her wounds she doth repair.   Still is she
  said
To live, and, 'mid her corporal change, discharge
With wonted blood her sex's monthly dues.

Gone are the men of Sodom ; gone the glare
175 Of their unhallowed ramparts ; all the house
Inhospitable, with its lords, is gone :
The champaign is one pyre ; here embers
  rough
And black, here ash-heaps with hoar mould,
  mark out
The conflagration's course : evanishèd
180 Is all that old fertility[6] which Lot,
Seeing outspread before him, . . .

. . . .

No ploughman spends his fruitless toil on
  glebes
Pitchy with soot : or if some acres there,
But half consumed, still strive to emulate
185 Autumn's glad wealth, pears, peaches, and
  all fruits
Promise themselves full easely[7] to the eye
In fairest bloom, until the plucker's hand
Is on them : then forthwith the seeming
  fruit
Crumbles to dust 'neath the bewraying touch,
190 And turns to embers vain.
            Thus, therefore (sky
And earth entombed alike), not e'en the sea
Lives there : the quiet of that quiet sea
Is death ![8] — a sea which no wave animates
Through its anhealant volumes ; which be-
  neath

---

[1] Σηγώρ in the LXX., " Zoar " in Eng. ver.
[2] " *Simul exoritur* sol."   But both the LXX. and the Eng. ver. say the sun *was risen* when Lot entered the city.
[3] So Oehler and Migne.   But perhaps we may alter the pointing slightly, and read : —
  " Down pours a novel shower, sulphur mixt
  With blazing flames : the ether seethes : the air
  Crackles with liquid heats exust."
[4] The story of Phaëthon and his fate is told in Ov., *Met.*, ii. 1-399, which may be compared with the present piece.   His two sisters were transformed into white poplars, according to some ; alders, according to others.   See Virg., *Æn.*, x. 190 sqq., *Ec.*, vi. 62 sqq.   His half-brother (Cycnus or Cygnus) was turned into a swan : and the scene of these transformations is laid by Ovid on the banks of the Eridanus (the Po).   But the fable is variously told : and it has been suggested that the groundwork of it is to be found rather in the still-standing of the sun recorded in Joshua.
[5] i.e., as she had been before in the case of Eve.   See Gen. iii. 1 sqq.

[6] I have hazarded the bold conjecture — which I see others (Pamelius at all events) had hazarded before me — that " feritas " is used by our author as = " fertilitas."   The word, of course, is very incorrectly formed etymologically ; but etymology is not our author's *forte* apparently.   It will also be seen that there is seemingly a gap at this point, or else some enormous mistake, in the mss.   An attempt has been made (see Migne) to correct it, but not a very satisfactory one.   For the common reading, which gives two lines,
  " Occidit illa prior feritas, quam prospiciens Loth
  Nullus arat frustra piceas fuligine glebas,"
which are evidently entirely unconnected with one another, it is proposed to read,
  " Occidit illa prior feritas, quam prospiciens Loth,
  Deseruisse pii fertur commercia fratris.
  Nullus arat," etc.
This use of " fratris " in a wide sense may be justified from Gen. xiii. 8 (to which passage, with its immediate context, there seems to be a reference, whether we adopt the proposed correction or no), and similar passages in Holy Writ.   But the transition is still abrupt to the " nullus arat," etc., and I prefer to leave the passage as it is, without attempting to supply the hiatus.
[7] This use of " easely " as a dissyllable is justifiable from Spenser.
[8] This seems to be the sense, but the Latin is somewhat strange : " mors est maris illa quieti," i.e., illa (quies) maris quieti mors est. The opening lines of " Jonah " (above) should be compared with this passage and its context.

195 Its native Auster sighs not anywhere ;
Which cannot from its depths one scaly
race,
Or with smooth skin or cork-like fence en-
cased,
Produce, or curlèd shell in single valve
Or double fold enclosed.   Bitumen there
200 (The sooty reek of sea exust) alone,
With its own crop, a spurious harvest yields ;
Which 'neath the stagnant surface vivid heat
From seething mass of sulphur and of brine
Maturing tempers, making earth cohere
205 Into a pitch marine.[1]   At season due
The heated water's fatty ooze is borne
Up to the surface ; and with foamy flakes
Over the level top a tawny skin
Is woven.   They whose function is to catch
210 That ware put to, tilting their smooth skin
down
With balance of their sides, to teach the
film,
Once o'er the gunnel, to float in : for, lo !
Raising itself spontaneous, it will swim
Up to the edge of the unmoving craft ;

215 And will, when pressed,[2] for guerdon large,
ensure
Immunity from the defiling touch
Of weft which female monthly efflux clothes.
Behold another portent notable,
Fruit of that sea's disaster : all things cast
220 Therein do swim : gone is its native power
For sinking bodies : if, in fine, you launch
A torch's lightsome[3] hull (where spirit serves
For fire) therein, the apex of the flame
Will act as sail ; put out the flame, and 'neath
225 The waters will the light's wreckt ruin go !

Such Sodom's and Gomorrah's penalties,
For ages sealed as signs before the eyes
Of unjust nations, whose obdurate hearts
God's fear have quite forsaken,[4] will them
teach
230 To reverence heaven-sanctioned rights,[5] and
lift
Their gaze unto one only Lord of all.

---

[1] Inque picem dat terræ hærere marinam.

[2] "Pressum" (Oehler); "pretium" (Migne) : "it will yield a
prize, namely, that," etc.
[3] Luciferam.
[4] Oehler's pointing is disregarded.
[5] "De cælo jura tueri ; " possibly "to look for laws from heaven."

3. GENESIS.

(AUTHOR UNCERTAIN.)

In the beginning did the Lord create
The heaven and earth :[1] for formless was the
land,[2]
And hidden by the wave, and God immense[3]
O'er the vast watery plains was hovering,
5 While chaos and black darkness shrouded all :
Which darkness, when God bade be from the
pole[4]
Disjoined, He speaks, " Let there be light ; "
and all
In the clear world[5] was bright.   Then, when
the Lord
The first day's work had finishèd, He formed
10 Heaven's axis white with nascent clouds : the
deep
Immense receives its wandering[6] shores, and
draws

The rivers manifold with mighty trains.
The third dun light unveiled earth's[7] face,
and soon
(Its name assigned[8]) the dry land's story
'gins :
15 Together on the windy champaigns rise
The flowery seeds, and simultaneously
Fruit-bearing boughs put forth procurvant
arms.
The fourth day, with[9] the sun's lamp gen-
erates
The moon, and moulds the stars with trem-
ulous light
20 Radiant : these elements it[10] gave as signs
To th' underlying world,[11] to teach the times
Which, through their rise and setting, were
to change.
Then, on the fifth, the liquid[12] streams receive
Their fish, and birds poise in the lower air
25 Their pinions many-hued.   The sixth, again,

---

[1] Terram.
[2] Tellus.
[3] Immensus.   See note on the word in the fragment " Concerning
the Cursing of the Heathen's Gods."
[4] Cardine.
[5] Mundo.
[6] "Errantia ; " so called, probably, either because they appear to
move as ships pass them, or because they may be said to "wander"
by reason of the constant change which they undergo from the action
of the sea, and because of the shifting nature of their sands.

[7] Terrarum.
[8] "God called the dry land Earth : " Gen. i. 10.
[9] i.e., "together with ; " it begets both sun and moon.
[10] i.e., "the fourth day."
[11] Mundo.
[12] Or, "lucid"—liquentia.

Supples the ice-cold snakes into their coils,
And over the whole fields diffuses herds
Of quadrupeds ; and mandate gave that all
Should grow with multiplying seed, and roam
30 And feed in earth's immensity.
                                    All these
When power divine by mere command ar-
  ranged,
Observing that things mundane still would
  lack
A ruler, thus It [1] speaks : " With utmost care,
Assimilated to our own aspèct,[2]
35 Make We a man to reign in the whole orb."
And him, although He with a single word [3]
Could have compounded, yet Himself did
  deign
To shape him with His sacred own right
  hand,
Inspiring his dull breast from breast divine.
40 Whom when He saw formed in a likeness
  such
As is His own, He measures how he broods
Alone on gnawing cares. Straightway his
  eyes
With sleep irriguous He doth perfuse ;
That from his left rib woman softlier
45 May formèd be, and that by mixture twin
His substance may add firmness to her limbs.
To her the name of " Life " — which is
  called " Eve " [4] —
Is given : wherefore sons, as custom is,
Their parents leave, and, with a settled home,
50 Cleave to their wives.
                        The seventh came, when God
At His works' end did rest, decreeing it
Sacred unto the coming ages' joys.
Straightway — the crowds of living things
  deployed
Before him — Adam's cunning skill (the gift
55 Of the good Lord) gives severally to all
The name which still is permanent. Himself,
And, joined with him, his Eve, God deigns
  address
" Grow, for the times to come, with manifold
Increase, that with your seed the pole and
  earth [5]
60 Be filled ; and, as Mine heirs, the varied
  fruits
Pluck ye, which groves and champaigns ren-
  der you,
From their rich turf." Thus after He dis-
  coursed,
In gladsome court [6] a paradise is strewn,
And looks towàrds the rays of th' early sun.[7]

65 These joys among, a tree with deadly fruits,
Breeding, conjoined, the taste of life and
  death,
Arises. In the midst of the demesne [8]
Flows with pure tide a stream, which irrigates
Fair offsprings from its liquid waves, and cuts
70 Quadrified paths from out its bubbling fount.
Here wealthy Phison, with auriferous waves,
Swells, and with hoarse tide wears [9] conspicu-
  ous gems,
This prasinus,[10] that glowing carbuncle,[11]
By name ; and laves, transparent in its shoals,
75 The margin of the land of Havilath.
Next Gihon, gliding by the Æthiops,
Enriches them. The Tigris is the third,
Adjoined to fair Euphrates, furrowing
Disjunctively with rapid flood the land
80 Of Asshur. Adam, with his faithful wife,
Placed here as guard and workman, is in-
  formed
By such the Thunderer's [12] speech : " Tremble
  ye not
To pluck together the permitted fruits
Which, with its leafy bough, the unshorn
  grove
85 Hath furnished ; anxious only lest perchance
Ye cull the hurtful apple,[13] which is green
With a twin juice for functions several."
And, no less blind meantime than Night her-
  self,
Deep night 'gan hold them, nor had e'en a
  robe
90 Covered their new-formed limbs.
                                    Amid these haunts,
And on mild berries reared, a foamy snake,
Surpassing living things in sense astute,
Was creeping silently with chilly coils.
He, brooding over envious lies instinct
95 With gnawing sense, tempts the soft heart
  beneath
The woman's breast : " Tell me, why shouldst
  thou dread
The apple's [14] happy seeds ? Why, hath not
  God
All known fruits hallowed ? [15] Whence if thou
  be prompt
To cull the honeyed fruits, the golden world [16]
100 Will on its starry pole return." [17] But she
Refuses, and the boughs forbidden fears
To touch. But yet her breast 'gins be o'er-
  come

---

[1] i.e., " Power Divine."
[2] So Milton and Shakespeare.
[3] As (see above, l. 31) He had all other things.
[4] See Gen. iii. 20, with the LXX., and the marg. in the Eng. ver
[5] Terræ.
[6] The " gladsome court " — " læta aula " — seems to mean *Eden*,
in which the garden is said to have been planted. See Gen. ii. 8.
[7] i.e., eastward. See the last reference.

[8] Ædibus in mediis.
[9] Terit. So Job (xiv. 19), " The waters *wear* the stones."
[10] " Onyx," Eng. ver. See the following piece, l. 277.
[11] " Bdellium," Eng. Ver.; ἄνθραξ, LXX.
[12] Comp. Ps. xxix. 3, especially in " Great Bible " (xxviii. 3 in
LXX.).
[13] Malum.
[14] Mali.
[15] " Numquid poma Deus non omnia nota sacravit ? "
[16] Mundus.
[17] The writer, supposing it to be night (see 88, 89), seems to mean
that the serpent hinted that the fruit would instantly dispel night and
restore day. Compare the ensuing lines.

With sense infirm. Straightway, as she at
  length
With snowy tooth the dainty morsels bit,
105 Stained with no cloud the sky serene up-lit !
Then taste, instilling lure in honeyed jaws,
To her yet uninitiated lord
Constrained her to present the gift ; which he
No sooner took, than — night effaced ! —
  their eyes
110 Shone out serene in the resplendent world.[1]
When, then, they each their body bare
  espied,
And when their shameful parts they see, with
  leaves
Of fig they shadow them.
                          By chance, beneath
The sun's now setting light, they recognise
115 The sound of the Lord's voice, and, trem-
  bling, haste
To bypaths.   Then the Lord of heaven
  accosts
The mournful Adam : "Say, where now thou
  art."
Who suppliant thus answers : "Thine address,
O Lord, O Mighty One, I tremble at,
120 Beneath my fearful heart ; and, being bare,
I faint with chilly dread."   Then said the
  Lord :
"Who hath the hurtful fruits, then, given
  you ? "
" This woman, while she tells me how her
  eyes
With brilliant day promptly perfusèd were,
125 And on her dawned the liquid sky serene,
And heaven's sun and stars, o'ergave them
  me ! "
Forthwith God's anger frights perturbèd Eve,
While the Most High inquires the authorship
Of the forbidden act.   Hereon she opes
130 Her tale : "The speaking serpent's suasive
  words
I harboured, while the guile and bland re-
  quest
Misled me : for, with venoms viperous
His words inweaving, stories told he me
Of those delights which should all fruits
  excel."
135 Straightway the Omnipotent the dragon's
  deeds
Condemns, and bids him be to all a sight
Unsightly, monstrous ; bids him presently
With grovelling beast to crawl ; and then to
  bite
And chew the soil ; while war should to all
  time
140 'Twixt human senses and his tottering self
Be waged, that he might creep, crestfallen,
  prone,

Behind the legs of men,[2] — that while he
  glides
Close on their heels they may down-trample
  him.
The woman, sadly caught by guileful words,
145 Is bidden yield her fruit with struggle hard,
And bear her husband's yoke with patien:
  zeal.[3]
"But thou, to whom the sentence[4] of tl
  wife
(Who, vanquished, to the dragon pitiless
Yielded) seemed true, shalt through long
  times deplore
150 Thy labour sad ; for thou shalt see, instead
Of wheaten harvest's seed, the thistle rise,
And the thorn plenteously with pointed
  spines :
So that, with weary heart and mournful
  breast,
Full many sighs shall furnish anxious food ;[5]
155 Till, in the setting hour of coming death,
To level earth, whence thou thy body draw'st,
Thou be restored."   This done, the Lord
  bestows
Upon the trembling pair a tedious life ;
And from the sacred gardens far removes
160 Them downcast, and locates them opposite,
And from the threshold bars them by mid
  fire,
Wherein from out the swift heat is evolved
A cherubim,[6] while fierce the hot point
  glows,
And rolls enfolding flames.   And lest their
  limbs
165 With sluggish cold should be benumbed, the
  Lord
Hides flayed from cattle's flesh together sews,
With vestures warm their bare limbs cover-
  ing.
When, therefore, Adam — now believing —
  felt
(By wedlock taught) his manhood, he confers
170 On his loved wife the mother's name ; and,
  made
Successively by scions twain a sire,
Gives names to stocks[7] divèrse : Caïn the first
Hath for his name, to whom is Abel joined.
The latter's care tended the harmless sheep ;
175 The other turned the earth with curvèd
  plough.

---

[1] Mundo.

[2] Virorum.
[3] " Servitiumque sui studio perferre mariti ; " or, perhaps, " and
drudge in patience at her husband's beck."
[4] " Sententia : " her sentence, or opinion, as to the fruit and its
effects.
[5] Or,
    " That with heart-weariness and mournful breast
    Full many sighs may furnish anxious food."
[6] The writer makes " cherubim " — or " cherubin " — singular. I
have therefore retained his mistake.   What the " hot point " — " cali-
dus apex " — is, is not clear.   It may be an allusion to the " flaming
sword " (see Gen. iii. 24) ; or it may mean the top of the flame.
[7] Or, " origins " — " orsis " — because Cain and Abel were original types, as it were, of two separate classes of men.

These, when in course of time [1] they brought
their gifts
To Him who thunders, offered — as their
sense
Prompted them — fruits unlike. The elder
one
Offered the first-fruits [2] of the fertile glebes :
180 The other pays his vows with gentle lamb,
Bearing in hand the entrails pure, and fat
Snow-white ; and to the Lord, who pious vows
Beholds, is instantly accèptable.
Wherefore with anger cold did Caïn glow ; [3]
185 With whom God deigns to talk, and thus
begins :
" Tell Me, if thou live rightly, and discern
Things hurtful, couldst thou not then pass
thine age
Pure from contracted guilt ? Cease to essay

With gnawing sense thy brother's ruin, who,
190 Subject to thee as lord, his neck shall yield."
Not e'en thus softened, he unto the fields
Conducts his brother ; whom when overta'en
In lonely mead he saw, with his twin palms
Bruising his pious throat, he crushed life out.
195 Which deed the Lord espying from high
heaven,
Straitly demands " where Abel is on earth ? "
He says " he will not as his brother's guard
Be set." Then God outspeaks to him again :
" Doth not the sound of his blood's voice,
sent up
200 To Me, ascend unto heaven's lofty pole ?
Learn, therefore, for so great a crime what
doom
Shall wait thee. Earth, which with thy kins-
man's blood
Hath reeked but now, shall to thy hateful
hand
Refuse to render back the cursèd seeds
205 Entrusted her ; nor shall, if set with herbs,
Produce her fruit : that, torpid, thou shalt
dash
Thy limbs against each other with much
fear." . . . . . .

---

[1] " Perpetuo ; " " in process of time," Eng. ver.; μεθ' ἡμέρας, LXX. in Gen. iv. 3.
[2] Quæ prosata fuerant. But, as Wordsworth remarks on Gen. iv., we do not read that Caïn's offerings were first-fruits even.
[3] Quod propter gelida Caïn incanduit ira. If this, which is Oehler's and Migne's reading, be correct, the words *gelida* and *incanduit* seem to be intentionally contrasted, unless *incandescere* be used here in a supposed sense of " growing white," " turning pale." *Urere* is used in Latin of heat and cold indifferently. *Calida* would, of course, be a ready emendation ; but *gelida* has the advantage of being far more startling.

---

4. A STRAIN OF THE JUDGMENT OF THE LORD.

(AUTHOR UNCERTAIN.)[1]

Who will for me in fitting strain adapt
Field-haunting muses ? and with flowers will
grace
The spring-tide's rosy gales ? And who will
give
The summer harvest's heavy stalks mature ?
5 And to the autumn's vines their swollen
grapes ?
Or who in winter's honour will commend
The olives, ever-peaceful ? and will ope
Waters renewed, even at their fountainheads ?
And cut from waving grass the leafy flowers ?
10 Forthwith the breezes of celestial light
I will attune. Now be it granted me
To meet the lightsome [2] muses ! to disclose
The secret rivers on the fluvial top
Of Helicon,[3] and gladsome woods that grow
15 'Neath other star.[4] And simultaneously

I will attune in song the eternal flames ;
Whence the sea fluctuates with wave immense ;
What power [5] moves the solid lands to quake ;
And whence the golden light first shot its
rays
20 On the new world ; or who from gladsome
clay
Could man have moulded ; whence in empty
world [6]
Our race could have upgrown ; and what the
greed
Of living which each people so inspires ;
What things for ill created are ; or what
25 Death's propagation ; whence have rosy
wreaths
Sweet smell and ruddy hue ; what makes the
vine
Ferment in gladsome grapes away ; and
makes
Full granaries by fruit of slender stalks
distended be ; or makes the tree grow ripe

---

[1] The reader is requested to bear in mind, in reading this piece, tedious in its elaborate struggles after effect, that the constant repetitions of words and expressions with which his patience will be tried, are due to the original. It was irksome to reproduce them ; but fidelity is a translator's first law.
[2] Luciferas.
[3] Helicon is not named in the original, but it seems to be meant.
[4] i.e., in another clime or continent. The writer is (or feigns to be) an African. Helicon, of course, is in Europe.

[5] Virtus.
[6] Sæculo.

30 'Mid ice, with olives black; who gives to
    seeds
Their increments of vigour various;
And with her young's soft shadowings pro-
    tects
The mother.   Good it is all things to know
Which wondrous are in nature, that it may
35 Be granted us to recognise through all
The true Lord, who light, seas, sky, earth
    prepared,
And decked with varied star the new-made
    world;[1]
And first bade beasts and birds to issue forth;
And gave the ocean's waters to be stocked
40 With fish; and gathered in a mass the sands,
With living creatures fertilized.   Such strains
With stately[2] muses will I spin, and waves
Healthful will from their fountainheads dis-
    close:
And may this strain of mine the gladsome
    shower
45 Catch, which from placid clouds doth come,
    and flows
Deeply and all unsought into men's souls,
And guide it into our new-turnèd lands
In copious rills.[3]
                    Now come: if any one
Still ignorant of God, and knowing naught
50 Of life to come,[4] would fain attain to touch
The care-effacing living nymph, and through
The swift waves' virtue his lost life repair,
And 'scape the penalties of flame eterne,[5]
And rather win the guerdons of the life
55 To come, let such remember GOD is ONE,
Alone the object of our prayers; who 'neath
His threshold hath the whole world poised;
    Himself
Eternally abiding, and to be
Alway for aye; holding the ages[6] all;
60 Alone, before all ages;[6] unbegotten,
Limitless God; who holds alone His seat
Supernal; supereminent alone;
Above high heavens; omnipotent alone;
Whom all things do obey; who for Himself
65 Formed, when it pleased Him, man for aye;
    and gave
Him to be pastor of beasts tame, and lord
Of wild; who by a word[7] could stretch forth
    heaven;
And with a word could solid earth suspend;

And quicklier than word[8] had the seas wave
70 Disjoined;[9] and man's dear form with His
    own hands
Did love to mould; and furthermore did
    will
His own fair likeness[10] to exist in him;
And by His Spirit on his countenance
The breath[11] of life did breathe.
                    Unmindful he
75 Of God, such guilt rashly t' incur!   Beyond
The warning's range he was not ought to
    touch.[12]
One fruit illicit, whence he was to know
Forthwith how to discriminate alike
Evil and equity, God him forbade
80 To touch.   What functions of the world[13] did
    God
Permit to man, and sealed the sweet sweet
    pledge
Of His own love! and jurisdiction gave
O'er birds, and granted him both deep and
    soil
To tame, and mandates useful did impart
85 Of dear salvation!   'Neath his sway He gave
The lands, the souls of flying things, the race
Feathered, and every race, or tame or wild,
Of beasts, and the sea's race, and monster-
    forms
Shapeless of swimming things.   But since so
    soon
90 The primal man by primal crime transgressed
The law, and left the mandates of the Lord
(Led by a wife who counselled all the ills),
By death he 'gan to perish.   Woman 'twas
Who sin's first ill committed, and (the law
95 Transgressed) deceived her husband.   Eve,
    induced
By guile, the thresholds oped to death, and
    proved
To her own self, with her whole race as
    well,
A procreatrix of funereal woes.
Hence unanticipated wickedness,
100 Hence death, like seed, for aye, is scattered.
    Then
More frequent grew atrocious deed; and toil
More savage set the corrupt orb astir:
(This lure the crafty serpent spread, inspired
By envy's self:) then peoples more invent
105 Practices of ill deeds; and by ill deeds
Gave birth to seeds of wickedness.
                    And so
The only Lord, whose is the power supreme,

---

[1] Mundum.
[2] Compositis.
[3] I have endeavoured to give some intelligible sense to these
lines: but the absence of syntax in the original, as it now stands,
makes it necessary to guess at the meaning as best one may.
[4] Venturi ævi.
[5] "But in them nature's copy's not *eterne*."—Shakespeare,
Macbeth, act iii. scene 2.
[6] Sæcula.
[7] *Sermone tenus:* i.e., the exertion (so to speak) needed to do
such mighty works only extended to the uttering of a speech; no
more was requisite.   See for a similar allusion to the contrast between the making of other things and the making of man, the
"Genesis," 30-39.

[8] Dicto.
[9] i.e., from the solid mass of earth.   See Gen. i. 9, 10.
[10] Faciem.
[11] "Auram," or "breeze."
[12] "Immemor ille Dei temere committere tale!
        Non ultra monitum quidquam contingeret."
    Whether I have hit the sense here I know not.   In this and in
other passages I have punctuated for myself.
[13] Munera mundi.

Who o'er the heights the summits holds of
heaven
Supreme, and in exalted regions dwells
110 In lofty light for ages, mindful too
Of present time, and of futurity
Prescient beforehand, keeps the progeny
Of ill-desert, and all the souls which move
By reason's force much-erring man—nor less
115 Their tardy bodies governs He—against
The age decreed, so soon as, stretched in
death,
Men lay aside their ponderous limbs, and,
light
As air, shall go, their earthly bonds undone,
And take in diverse parts their proper spheres.
120 (But some He bids be forthwith by glad gales
Recalled to life, and be in secret kept
To wait the decreed law's awards, until
Their bodies with resuscitated limbs
Revive.[1]) Then shall men 'gin to weigh the
awards
125 Of their first life, and on their crime and faults
To think, and keep them for their penalties
Which will be far from death; and mindful
grow
Of pious duties, by God's judgments taught;
To wait expectant for their penalty
130 And their descendants', fruit of their own
crime;
Or else to live wholly the life of sheep,[2]
Without a name; and in God's ear, now deaf,
Pour unavailing weeping.
                                Shall not God
Almighty, 'neath whose law are all things
ruled,
135 Be able after death life to restore?
Or is there ought which the creation's Lord
Unable seems to do? If, darkness chased,
He could outstretch the light, and could
compound
All the world's mass by a word suddenly,
140 And raise by potent voice all things from
nought,
Why out of *somewhat*[3] could He not com-
pound
The well-known shape which erst had been,
which He
Had moulded formerly; and bid the form
Arise assimilated to Himself
145 Again? Since God's are all things, earth the
more

Gives Him all back; for she will, when He
bids,
Unweave whate'er she woven had before.
If one, perhaps, laid on sepulchral pyre,
The flame consumed; or one in its blind
waves
150 The ocean have dismembered; if of one
The entrails have, in hunger, satisfied
The fishes; or on any's limbs wild beasts
Have fastened cruel death; or any's blood,
His body reft by birds, unhid have lain:
155 Yet shall they not wrest from the mighty Lord
His latest dues. Need is that men appear
Quickened from death 'fore God, and at His
bar
Stand in their shapes resumed. Thus arid
seeds
Are dropt into the vacant lands, and deep
160 In the fixt furrows die and rot: and hence
Is not their surface[4] animated soon
With stalks repaired? and do they[5] not grow
strong
And yellow with the living grains? and, rich
With various usury,[6] new harvests rise
165 In mass? The stars all set, and, born again,
Renew their sheen; and day dies with its
light
Lost in dense night; and now night wanes
herself
As light unveils creation presently;
And now another and another day
170 Rises from its own stars; and the sun sets,
Bright as it is with splendour-bearing light;
Light perishes when by the coming eve
The world[7] is shaded; and the phœnix lives
By her own soot[8] renewed, and presently
175 Rises, again a bird, O wondrous sight!
After her burnings! The bare tree in time
Shoots with her leaves; and once more are
her boughs
Curved by the germen of the fruits.
                                While then
The world[9] throughout is trembling at God's
voice,
180 And deeply movèd are the high air's powers,[10]
Then comes a crash unwonted, then ensue
Heaven's mightiest murmurs, on the ap-
proach of God,
The whole world's[11] Judge! His countless
ministers
Forthwith conjoin their rushing march, and
God

---

[1] These lines, again, are but a guess at the meaning of the original, which is as obscure as defiance of grammar can well make it.
The sense seems to be, in brief, that while the vast majority are, immediately on their death, shut up in Hades to await the "decreed
age," i.e., the day of judgment, some, like the children raised by
Elijah and Elisha, the man who revived on touching Elisha's bones,
and the like, are raised *to die again*. Lower down it will be seen
that the writer believes that the saints who came out of their graves
after our Lord's resurrection (see Matt. xxvii. 51–54) did *not* die
again.
[2] Cf. Ps. xlix. 14 (xlviii. 15 in LXX.).
[3] i.e., the dust into which our bodies turn.

[4] i.e., the surface or ridge of the furrows.
[5] i.e., the furrows.
[6] "Some thirty-fold, some sixty-fold, some an hundred-fold." See
the parable of the sower.
[7] Mundo.
[8] Fuligine.
[9] Mundo.
[10] Virtutibus. Perhaps the allusion is to Eph. ii. 2, Matt. xxiv.
29, Luke xxi. 26.
[11] Mundi.

185 With majesty supernal fence around.
Angelic bands will from the heaven descend
To earth ; all, God's host, whose is faculty
Divine ; in form and visage spirits all
Of virtue : in them fiery vigour is ;
190 Rutilant are their bodies ; heaven's might
Divine about them flashes ; the whole orb
Hence murmurs ; and earth, trembling to
　　her depths
(Or whatsoe'er her bulk is [1]), echoes back
The roar, parturient of men, whom she,
195 Being bidden, will with grief upyield.[2] All
　　stand
In wonderment. At last disturbèd are
The clouds, and the stars move and quake
　　from height
Of sudden power.[3] When thus God comes,
　　with voice
Of potent sound, at once throughout all
　　realms
200 The sepulchres are burst, and every ground
Outpours bones from wide chasms, and open-
　　ing sand
Outbelches living peoples ; to the hair [4]
The members cleave ; the bones inwoven are
With marrow ; the entwinèd sinews rule
205 The breathing bodies ; and the veins 'gin
　　throb
With simultaneously infusèd blood :
And, from their caves dismissed, to open day
Souls are restored, and seek to find again
Each its own organs, as at their own place
210 They rise. O wondrous faith ! Hence every
　　age
Shoots forth ; forth shoots from ancient dust
　　the host
Of dead. Regaining light, there rise again
Mothers, and sires, and high-souled youths,
　　and boys,
And maids unwedded ; and deceased old men
215 Stand by with living souls ; and with the cries
Of babes the groaning orb resounds.[5] Then
　　tribes
Various from their lowest seats will come :
Bands of the Easterns ; those which earth's
　　extreme

Sees ; those which dwell in the downsloping
　　clime
220 Of the mid-world, and hold the frosty star's
Riphæan citadels. Every colonist
Of every land stands frighted here : the
　　boor ;
The son of Atreus [6] with his diadem
Of royalty put off ; the rich man mixt
225 Coequally in line with pauper peers.
Deep tremor everywhere : then groans the
　　orb
With prayers ; and peoples stretching forth
　　their hands
Grow stupid with the din !
　　　　　　　　The Lord Himself
Seated, is bright with light sublime ; and fire
230 Potent in all the Virtues [7] flashing shines.
And on His high-raised throne the Heavenly
　　One
Coruscates from His seat ; with martyrs
　　hemmed
(A dazzling troop of men), and by His seers
Elect accompanied (whose bodies bright
235 Effulgent are with snowy stoles), He towers
Above them. And now priests in lustrous
　　robes
Attend, who wear upon their markèd [8] front
Wreaths golden-red ; and all submissive
　　kneel
And reverently adore. The cry of all
240 Is one : "O Holy, Holy, Holy, God ! "
To these [9] the Lord will mandate give, to
　　range
The people in twin lines ; and orders them
To set apart by number the depraved ;
While such as have His biddings followèd
245 With placid words He calls, and bids them,
　　clad
With vigour — death quite conquered — ever
　　dwell
Amid light's inextinguishable airs,
Stroll through the ancients' ever blooming
　　realm,
Through promised wealth, through ever sunny
　　swards,
250 And in bright body spend perpetual life.
　　　　　A place there is, belovèd of the Lord,
In Eastern coasts, where light is bright and
　　clear,
And healthier blows the breeze ; day is
　　eterne,
Time changeless : 'tis a region set apart
255 By God, most rich in plains, and passing
　　blest,

---

[1] Vel quanta est. If this be the right sense, the words are probably inserted, because the conflagration of "the earth and the works
that are therein" predicted in 2 Pet. iii. 10, and referred to lower
down in this piece, is supposed to have begun, and thus the "depths"
of the earth are supposed to be already diminishing.
[2] I have ventured to alter one letter of the Latin; and for "quos
reddere jussa do*c*ebit," read "quos reddere jussa do*l*ebit." If the
common reading be retained, the only possible meaning seems to be
"whom she will teach to render (to God) His commands," i.e., to
render obedience to them; or else, "to render (to God) what they
are bidden to render," i.e., an account of themselves; and earth, as
their mother, giving them birth out of her womb, is said to teach them
to do this. But the emendation, which is at all events simple, seems
to give a better sense: "being bidden to render the dead, whom she
is keeping, up, earth will grieve at the throes it causes her, but will
do it."
[3] Subitæ virtutis ab alto.
[4] Comis, here "the heads."
[5] This passage is imitated from Virgil, *Æn.*, vi. 305 sqq.; *Georg.*,
iv. 475 sqq.

[6] i.e., "the king." The "Atridæ" of Homer are referred to,—
Agamemnon "king of men," and Menelaus.
[7] Or, "Powers."
[8] Insigni. The allusion seems to be to Ezek. ix. 4, 6, Rev. vii. 3 et
seqq., xx. 3, 4, and to the inscribed mitre of the Jewish high priest,
see Ex. xxviii. 36, xxxix. 30.
[9] I have corrected "*his*" for "*hic*." If the latter be retained,
it would seem to mean "hereon."

In the meridian [1] of His cloudless seat.
There gladsome is the air, and is in light
Ever to be ; soft is the wind, and breathes
Life-giving blasts ; earth, fruitful with a soil
260 Luxuriant, bears all things ; in the meads
Flowers shed their fragrance ; and upon the
　　plains
The purple — not in envy — mingles all
With golden-ruddy light.　One gladsome
　　flower,
With its own lustre clad, another clothes ;
265 And here with many a seed the dewy fields
Are dappled, and the snowy tilths are crisped
With rosy flowers.　No region happier
Is known in other spots ; none which in look
Is fairer, or in honour more excels.
270 Never in flowery gardens are there born
Such lilies, nor do such upon our plains
Outbloom ; nor does the rose so blush, what
　　time,
New-born, 'tis opened by the breeze ; nor is
The purple with such hue by Tyrian dye
275 Imbued.　With coloured pebbles beauteous
　　gleams
The gem : here shines the prasinus ; [2] there
　　glows
The carbuncle ; and giant-emerald
Is green with grassy light.　Here too are
　　born
The cinnamons, with odoriferous twigs ;
280 And with dense leaf gladsome amomum
　　joins
Its fragrance.　Here, a native, lies the gold
Of radiant sheen ; and lofty groves reach
　　heaven
In blooming time, and germens fruitfullest
Burden the living boughs.　No glades like
　　these
285 Hath Ind herself forth-stretcht ; no tops so
　　dense
Rears on her mount the pine ; nor with a
　　shade
So lofty-leavèd is her cypress crisped ;
Nor better in its season blooms her bough
In spring-tide.　Here black firs on lofty peak
290 Bloom ; and the only woods that know no
　　hail
Are green eternally : no foliage falls ;
At no time fails the flower.　There, too, there
　　blooms
A flower as red as Tarsine purple is :
A rose, I ween, it is (red hue it has,
295 An odour keen) ; such aspect on its leaves
It wears, such odour breathes.　A tree it [3]
　　stands,
With a new flower, fairest in fruits ; a crop

Life-giving, dense, its happy strength does
　　yield.
Rich honies with green cane their fragrance
　　join,
300 And milk flows potable in runnels full ;
And with whate'er that sacred earth is green,
It all breathes life ; and there Crete's healing
　　gift [4]
Is sweetly redolent.　There, with smooth
　　tide,
Flows in the placid plains a fount : four
　　floods
305 Thence water parted lands. [5]　The garden
　　robed
With flowers, I wot, keeps ever spring ; no
　　cold
Of wintry star varies the breeze ; and earth,
After her birth-throes, with a kindlier blast
Repairs.　Night there is none ; the stars
　　maintain
310 Their darkness ; angers, envies, and dire
　　greed
Are absent ; and out-shut is fear, and cares
Driven from the threshold.　Here the Evil
　　One
Is homeless ; he is into worthy courts
Out-gone, nor is't e'er granted him to touch
315 The glades forbidden.　But here ancient
　　faith
Rests in elect abode ; and life here treads,
Joying in an eternal covenant ;
And health [6] without a care is gladsome here
In placid tilths, ever to live and be
320 Ever in light.
　　　　　　　Here whosoe'er hath lived
Pious, and cultivant of equity
And goodness ; who hath feared the thun-
　　dering God
With mind sincere ; with sacred duteousness
Tended his parents ; and his other life [7]
325 Spent ever crimeless ; or who hath consoled
With faithful help a friend in indigence ;
Succoured the over-toiling needy one,
As orphans' patron, and the poor man's aid ;
Rescued the innocent, and succoured them
330 When prest with accusation ; hath to guests
His ample table's pledges given ; hath done
All things divinely ; pious offices
Enjoined ; done hurt to none ; ne'er coveted
Another's : such as these, exulting all
335 In divine praises, and themselves at once
Exhorting, raise their voices to the stars ;
Thanksgivings to the Lord in joyous wise
They psalming celebrate ; and they shall go

---

[1] Cardine, i.e., the *hinge* as it were upon which the sun turns in his course.
[2] See the " Genesis," 73.
[3] Or, " there."　The question is, whether a different tree is meant, or the rose just spoken of.

[4] This seems to be *marshmallows.*
[5] Here again it is plain that the writer is drawing his description from what we read of the garden of Eden.
[6] " Salus," health (probably) in its widest sense, both bodily and mental ; or perhaps " safety," " salvation."
[7] Reliquam vitam, i.e., apparently his life in all other relations ; unless it mean his life *after his parents' death*, which seems less likely.

Their harmless way with comrade messengers.

340 When ended hath the Lord these happy gifts,
And likewise sent away to realms eterne
The just, then comes a pitiable crowd
Wailing its crimes; with parching tears it pours
All groans effusely, and attests [1] in acts
345 With frequent ululations. At the sight
Of flames, their merit's due, and stagnant pools
Of fire, wrath's weapons, they 'gin tremble all.[2]
Them an angelic host, upsnatching them,
Forbids to pray, forbids to pour their cries
350 (Too late!) with clamour loud: pardon withheld,
Into the lowest bottom they are hurled!
O miserable men! how oft to you
Hath Majesty divine made itself known!
The sounds of heaven ye have heard; have seen
355 Its lightnings; have experienced its rains
Assiduous; its ires of winds and hail!
How often nights and days serene do make
Your seasons — God's gifts — fruitful with fair yields!
Roses were vernal; the grain's summer-tide
360 Failed not; the autumn variously poured
Its mellow fruits; the rugged winter brake
The olives, icy though they were: 'twas God
Who granted all, nor did His goodness fail.
At God earth trembled; on His voice the deep
365 Hung, and the rivers trembling fled and left
Sands dry; and every creature everywhere
Confesses God! Ye (miserable men!)
Have heaven's Lord and earth's denied; and oft
(Horrible!) have God's heralds put to flight;[3]
370 And rather slain the just with slaughter fell;
And, after crime, fraud ever hath in you
Inhered. Ye then shall reap the natural fruit
Of your iniquitous sowing. That God is
Ye know; yet are ye wont to laugh at Him.
375 Into deep darkness ye shall go of fire
And brimstone; doomed to suffer glowing ires
In torments just.[4] God bids your bones descend
To [5] penalty eternal; go beneath

The ardour of an endless raging hell;[6]
380 Be urged, a seething mass, through rotant pools
Of flame; and into threatening flame He bids
The elements convert; and all heaven's fire
Descend in clouds.
Then greedy Tartarus
With rapid fire enclosèd is; and flame
385 Is fluctuant within with tempest waves;
And the whole earth her whirling embers blends!
There is a flamy furrow; teeth acute
Are turned to plough it, and for all the years [7]
The fiery torrent will be armed: with force
390 Tartarean will the conflagrations gnash
Their teeth upon the world.[8] There are they scorched
In seething tide with course precipitate;
Hence flee; thence back are borne in sharp career;
The savage flame's ire meets them fugitive!
395 And now at length they own the penalty
Their own, the natural issue of their crime.
And now the reeling earth, by not a swain
Possest, is by the sea's profundity
Prest, at her farthest limit, where the sun
400 (His ray out-measurèd) divides the orb,
And where, when traversed is the world,[8] the stars
Are hidden. Ether thickens. O'er the light
Spreads sable darkness; and the latest flames
Stagnate in secret rills. A place there is
405 Whose nature is with sealèd penalties
Fiery, and a dreadful marsh white-hot
With heats infernal, where, in furnaces
Horrific, penal deed roars loud, and seethes,
And, rushing into torments, is up-caught
410 By the flame's vortex wide; by savage wave
And surge the turbid sand all mingled is
With miry bottom. Hither will be sent,
Groaning, the captive crowd of evil ones,
And wickedness (the sinful body's train),
415 To burn! Great is the beating there of breasts,
By bellowing of grief accompanied;
Wild is the hissing of the flames, and thence
The ululation of the sufferers!
And flames, and limbs sonorous,[9] will outrise
420 Afar: more fierce will the fire burn; and up
To th' upper air the groaning will be borne.
Then human progeny its bygone deeds
Of ill will weigh; and will begin to stretch
Heavenward its palms; and then will wish to know

---

[1] i.e., "appeals to." So Burke: "I *attest* the former, I *attest* the coming generations." This "attesting of its acts" seems to refer to Matt. xxv. 44 It appeals to them in hope of mitigating its doom.
[2] This seems to be the sense. The Latin stands thus: "Flammas pro meritis, stagnantia tela tremiscunt."
[3] Or, "banished."
[4] I adopt the correction (suggested in Migne) of just*is* for just*as*.
[5] This is an extraordinary use for the Latin dative; and even if the meaning be "*for* (i.e., to suffer) penalty eternal," it is scarcely less so.

[6] Gehennæ.
[7] Or, "*in* all the years:" but see note 5 on this page.
[8] Mundo.
[9] "Artusque sonori," i.e., probably the arms and hands with which (as has been suggested just before) the sufferers beat their unhappy breasts.

425 The Lord, whom erst it would not know, what time
To know Him had proved useful to them. There,
His life's excesses, handiworks unjust,
And crimes of savage mind, each will confess,
And at the knowledge of the impious deeds
430 Of his own life will shudder. And now first,
Whoe'er erewhile cherished ill thoughts of God ;
Had worshipped stones unsteady, lyingly
Pretending to divinity ; hath e'er
Made sacred to gore-stainèd images
435 Altars ; hath voiceless pictured figures feared ;
Hath slender shades of false divinity
Revered ; whome'er ill error onward hath
Seduced ; whoe'er was an adulterer,
Or with the sword had slain his sons ; whoe'er
440 Had stalked in robbery ; whoe'er by fraud
His clients had deferred ; whoe'er with mind
Unfriendly had behaved himself, or stained
His palms with blood of men, or poison mixt
Wherein death lurked, or robed with wicked guise
445 His breast, or at his neighbour's ill, or gain
Iniquitous, was wont to joy ; whoe'er
Committed whatsoever wickedness
Of evil deeds : him mighty heat shall rack,
And bitter fire ; and these all shall endure,
450 In passing painful death, their punishment.
Thus shall the vast crowd lie of mourning men !
          This oft as holy prophets sang of old,
And (by God's inspiration warned) oft told
The future, none ('tis pity !) none (alas !)
455 Did lend his ears. But God Almighty willed
His guerdons to be known, and His law's threats
'Mid multitudes of such like signs promulged.
He 'stablished them [1] by sending prophets more,
These likewise uttering words divine ; and some,
460 Roused from their sleep, He bids go from their tombs
Forth with Himself, when He, His own tomb burst,
Had risen. Many 'wildered were, indeed,
To see the tombs agape, and in clear light
Corpses long dead appear ; and, wondering
465 At their discourses pious, dulcet words !
Starward they stretch their palms at the mere sound,[2]
And offer God and so-victorious Christ
Their gratulating homage. Certain 'tis
That these no more re-sought their silent graves,

470 Nor were retained within earth's bowels shut ; [3]
But the remaining host reposes now
In lowliest beds, until — time's circuit run —
That great day do arrive.
          Now all of you
Own the true Lord, who alone makes this soul
475 Of ours to see His light,[4] and can the same
(To Tartarus sent) subject to penalties ;
And to whom all the power of life and death
Is open. Learn that God can do whate'er
He list ; for 'tis enough for Him to will,
480 And by mere speaking He achieves the deed ;
And Him nought plainly, by withstanding, checks.
He is my God alone, to whom I trust
With deepest senses. But, since death concludes
Every career, let whoe'er is to-day
485 Bethink him over all things in his mind.
And thus, while life remains, while 'tis allowed
To see the light and change your life, before
The limit of allotted age o'ertake
You unawares, and that last day, which [5] is
490 By death's law fixt, your senseless eyes do glaze,
Seek what remains worth seeking : watchful be
For dear salvation ; and run down with ease
And certainty the good course. Wipe away
By pious sacred rites your past misdeeds
495 Which expiation need ; and shun the storms,
The too uncertain tempests, of the world.[6]
Then turn to right paths, and keep sanctities.
Hence from your gladsome minds depravèd crime
Quite banish ; and let long-inveterate fault
500 Be washed forth from your breast ; and do away
Wicked ill-stains contracted ; and appease
Dread God by prayers eternal ; and let all
Most evil mortal things to living good
Give way : and now at once a new life keep
505 Without a crime ; and let your minds begin
To use themselves to good things and to true :
And render ready voices to God's praise.
Thus shall your piety find better things
All growing to a flame ; thus shall ye, too,
510 Receive the gifts of the celestial life ;[7]
And, to long age, shall ever live with God,
Seeing the starry kingdom's golden joys.

---

[1] i.e., the "guerdons" and the "threats."
[2] "Ipsa voce," unless it mean "voice and all," i.e., and their voice as well as their palms.

[3] See note 1, p. 137.
[4] Here again a correction suggested in Migne's ed., of "suam lucem" for "sua luce," is adopted.
[5] "Qui" is read here, after Migne's suggestion, for "quia ;" and Oehler's and Migne's punctuation both are set aside.
[6] Mundi.
[7] Or, "assume the functions of the heavenly life."

5. FIVE BOOKS IN REPLY TO MARCION.

(AUTHOR UNCERTAIN.)

BOOK I.

OF THE DIVINE UNITY, AND THE RESURREC-
TION OF THE FLESH.

PART I. — OF THE DIVINE UNITY.

AFTER the Evil One's impiety
Profound, and his life-grudging mind, en-
trapped
Seducèd men with empty hope, it laid
Them bare, by impious suasion to false trust
5 In him, — not with impunity, indeed ;
For he forthwith, as guilty of the deed,
And author rash of such a wickedness,
Received deservèd maledictions. Thus,
Thereafter, maddened, he, most desperate
foe,
10 Did more assail and instigate men's minds
In darkness sunk. He taught them to forget
The Lord, and leave sure hope, and idols
vain
Follow, and shape themselves a crowd of
gods,
Lots, auguries, false names of stars, the show
15 Of being able to o'errule the births
Of embryos by inspecting entrails, and
Expecting things to come, by hardihood
Of dreadful magic's renegadoes led,
Wondering at a mass of feignèd lore ;
20 And he impelled them headlong to spurn
life,
Sunk in a criminal insanity ;
To joy in blood ; to threaten murders fell ;
To love the wound, then, in their neighbour's
flesh ;
Or, burning, and by pleasure's heat entrapped,
25 To transgress nature's covenants, and stain
Pure bodies, manly sex, with an embrace
Unnameable, and uses feminine
Mingled in common contact lawlessly ;
Urging embraces chaste, and dedicate
30 To generative duties, to be held
For intercourse obscene for passion's sake.
Such in time past his deeds, assaulting men,
Through the soul's lurking-places, with a flow
Of scorpion-venom, — not that men would
blame
35 Him, for they followed of their own accord :
His suasion was in guile ; in freedom man
Performed it.
        Whileas the perfidious one
Continuously through the centuries [1]

Is breathing such ill fumes, and into hearts
40 Seduced injecting his own counselling,
And hoping in his folly (alas !) to find
Forgiveness of his wickedness, unware
What sentence on his deed is waiting him ;
With words of wisdom's weaving,[2] and a voice
45 Presaging from God's Spirit, speak a host
Of prophets. Publicly he [3] does not dare
Nakedly to speak evil of the Lord,
Hoping by secret ingenuity
He possibly may lurk unseen. At length
50 The soul's Light [4] as the thrall of flesh is held ;
The hope of the despairing, mightier
Than foe, enters the lists ; the Fashioner,
The Renovator, of the body He ;
True Glory of the Father ; Son of God ;
55 Author unique ; a Judge and Lord He came,
The orb's renownèd King ; to the opprest
Prompt to give pardon, and to loose the
bound ;
Whose friendly aid and penal suffering
Blend God and renewed man in one. With
child
60 Is holy virgin : life's new gate opes ; words
Of prophets find their proof, fulfilled by facts ;
Priests [5] leave their temples, and — a star
their guide —
Wonder the Lord so mean a birth should
choose.
Waters — sight memorable ! — turn to wine ;
65 Eyes are restored to blind ; fiends trembling
cry,
Outdriven by His bidding, and own Christ !
All limbs, already rotting, by a word
Are healed ; now walks the lame ; the deaf
forthwith
Hears hope ; the maimed extends his hand ;
the dumb
70 Speaks mighty words : sea at His bidding
calms,
Winds drop ; and all things recognise the
Lord :
Confounded is the foe, and yields, though
fierce,
Now triumphed over, to unequal [6] arms !
        When all his enterprises now revoked
75 He [7] sees ; the flesh, once into ruin sunk,

---

[1] Sæcula.

[2] The "*tectis*" of the edd. I have ventured to alter to "*textis*,"
which gives (as in my text) a far better sense.
[3] i.e., the Evil One.
[4] i.e., the Son of God.
[5] i.e., the Magi.
[6] i.e., arms which *seemed* unequal : for the cross, in which Christ
seemed to be vanquished, was the very means of His triumph. See
Col. ii. 14, 15.
[7] i.e., the Enemy.

Now rising ; man — death vanquisht quite
  — to heavens
Soaring ; the peoples sealed with holy pledge
Outpoured ;[1] the work and envied deeds of
  might
Marvellous ;[2] and hears, too, of penalties
80 Extreme, and of perpetual dark, prepared
For himself by the Lord by God's decree
Irrevocable ; naked and unarmed,
Damned, vanquisht, doomed to perish in a
  death
Perennial, guilty now, and sure that he
85 No pardon has, a last impiety
Forthwith he dares, — to scatter everywhere
A word for ears to shudder at, nor meet
For voice to speak. Accosting men cast off
From God's community,[3] men wandering
90 Without the light, found mindless, following
Things earthly, them he teaches to become
Depravèd teachers of depravity.
    By [4] them he preaches that there are
  two Sires,
And realms divided : ill's cause is the Lord [5]
95 Who built the orb, fashioned breath-quick-
  ened flesh,
And gave the law, and by the seers' voice
  spake.
Him he affirms not *good*, but owns Him *just;*
Hard, cruel, taking pleasure fell in war ;
In judgment dreadful, pliant to no prayers.
100 His suasion tells of other one, to none
E'er known, who nowhere is, a deity
False, nameless, constituting nought, and
  who
Hath spoken precepts none. Him he calls
  good,
Who judges none, but spares all equally,
105 And grudges life to none. No judgment
  waits
The guilty ; so he says, bearing about
A gory poison with sweet honey mixt
For wretched men. That flesh can rise —
  to which
Himself was cause of ruin, which he spoiled
110 Iniquitously with contempt (whence,[6] cursed,

He hath grief without end), its ever-foe, —
He doth deny ; because with various wound
Life to expel and the salvation whence
He fell he strives : and therefore says that
  Christ
115 Came suddenly to earth,[7] but was not made,
By any compact, partner of the flesh ;
But Spirit-form, and body feigned beneath
A shape imaginary, seeks to mock
Men with a semblance that what is not is.
120 Does this, then, become God, to sport with
  men
By darkness led? to act an impious lie?
Or falsely call Himself a man? He walks,
Is carried, clothed, takes due rest, handled
  is,
Suffers, is hung and buried : man's are all
125 Deeds which, in holy body conversant,
But sent by God the Father, who hath all
Created, He did perfect properly,
Reclaiming not another's but His own ;
Discernible to peoples who of old
130 Were hoping for Him by His very work,
And through the prophets' voice to the round
  world [8]
Best known : and now they seek an un-
  known Lord,
Wandering in death's threshold manifest,
And leave behind the known. False is their
  faith,
135 False is their God, deceptive their reward,
False is their resurrection, death's defeat
False, vain their martyrdoms, and e'en
  Christ's name
An empty sound : whom, teaching that He
  came
Like magic mist, they (quite demented) own
140 To be the actor of a lie, and make
His passion bootless, and the populace [9]
(A feigned one !) without crime ! Is God
  thus true?
Are *such* the honours rendered to the Lord?
Ah ! wretched men ! gratuitously lost
145 In death ungrateful ! Who, by blind guide
  led,
Have headlong rushed into the ditch ![10] and
  as
In dreams the fancied rich man in his store
Of treasure doth exult, and with his hands
Grasps it, the sport of empty hope, so ye
150 Deceived, are hoping for a shadow vain
Of guerdon !
      Ah ! ye silent laughingstocks,
Or doomed prey, of the dragon, do ye hope,

---

[1] i.e., with the Holy Spirit, the "Pledge" or "Promise" of the Father (see Acts i. 4, 5), "outpoured" upon "the peoples"—both Jewish and Gentile—on the day of Pentecost and many subsequent occasions; see, for instances, Acts x. and xix.

[2] The "mirandæ virtutis opus, invisaque facta," I take to be the miracles wrought by the apostles through the might (virtus) of the Spirit, as we read in the Acts. These were objects of "envy" to the Enemy, and to such as—like Simon Magus, of whom we find record—were his servants.

[3] i.e., excommunicated, as Marcion was. The "last impiety" '*extremum nefas*), or "last atrocity" (*extremum facinus*),— see 218, lower down—seems to mean the introduction of *heretical teaching*.

[4] This use of the ablative, though quite against classical usage, is apparently admissible in late Latinity. It seems to me that the "his" *is* an ablative here, the men being regarded for the moment as merely *instruments*, not *agents ;* but it *may* be a dative = "to these he preaches," etc., i.e., he dictates *to* them what they afterwards are to teach in public.

[5] It must be borne in mind that "Dominus" (the Lord), and "Deus" (God), are kept as distinct terms throughout this piece.

[6] i.e., for which reason.

[7] i.e., as Marcion is stated by some to have taught, in the fifteenth year of Tiberius; founding his statement upon a perverted reading of Luke iii. 1. It will be remembered that Marcion only used St. Luke's Gospel, and that in a mutilated and corrupted form.

[8] Orbi.

[9] i.e., of the Jews.

[10] "In fossa," i e., as Fabricius (quoted in Migne's ed.) explains it, "in *de*fossa." It is the past part. of *fodio.*

Stern men, for death in room of gentle peace?[1]
Dare ye blame GOD, who hath created works
155 So great? in whose earth, 'mid profuse dis-
plays
Of His exceeding parent-care, His gifts
(Unmindful of Himself!) ye largely praise,
Rushing to ruin! do ye reprobate —
Approving of the works — the Maker's self,
160 The world's[2] Artificer, whose work withal
Ye are yourselves? Who gave those little
selves
Great honours; sowed your crops; made all
the brutes[3]
Your subjects; makes the seasons of the year
Fruitful with stated months; grants sweet-
nesses,
165 Drinks various, rich odours, jocund flowers,
And the groves' grateful bowers; to growing
herbs
Grants wondrous juices; founts and streams
dispreads
With sweet waves, and illumes with stars the
sky
And the whole orb: the infinite sole LORD,
170 Both JUST and GOOD; known by His work;
to none
By aspect known; whom nations, flourishing
In wealth, but foolish, wrapped in error's
shroud,
(Albeit 'tis beneath an alien name
They praise Him, yet) their Maker knowing,
dread
175 To blame: nor e'en one[4] — save you, hell's
new gate! —
Thankless, ye choose to speak ill of your
Lord!
These cruel deadly gifts the Renegade
Terrible has bestowed, through Marcion —
thanks
To Cerdo's mastership — on you; nor comes
180 The thought into your mind that, from Christ's
name
Seducèd, Marcion's name has carried you
To lowest depths.[5] Say of His many acts

What one displeases you? or what hath God
Done which is not to be extolled with praise?
185 Is it that He permits you, all too long,
(Unworthy of His patience large,) to see
Sweet light? you, who read truths,[6] and,
docking them,
Teach these your falsehoods, and approve as
past
Things which are yet to be?[7] What hinders,
else,
190 That we believe your God incredible?[8]
Nor marvel is't if, practised as he[9] is,
He captived you unarmed, persuading you
There are two Fathers (being damned by
One),
And all, whom he had erst seduced, are
gods;
195 And after that dispread a pest, which ran
With multiplying wound, and cureless crime,
To many. Men unworthy to be named,
Full of all magic's madness, he induced
To call themselves "Virtue Supreme;" and
feign
200 (With harlot comrade) fresh impiety;
To roam, to fly.[10] He is the insane god
Of Valentine, and to his Æonage
Assigned heavens thirty, and Profundity
Their sire.[11] He taught two baptisms, and
led
205 The body through the flame. That there
are gods
So many as the year hath days, he bade
A Basilides to believe, and worlds
As many. Marcus, shrewdly arguing
Through numbers, taught to violate chaste
form
210 'Mid magic's arts; taught, too, that the
Lord's cup
Is an oblation, and by prayers is turned
To blood. His[12] suasion prompted Hebion
To teach that Christ was born from human
seed;

---

[1] If this line be correct, — "Speratis pro pace truces homicidia blanda," — though I cannot see the propriety of the "truces" in it, it seems to mean, "Do ye hope or expect that the master you are serving will, instead of the gentle peace he promises you, prove a murderer and lead you to death? No, you do not expect it; but so it is."

[2] Mundi.

[3] Animalia.

[4] The sentence breaks off abruptly, and the verb which should apparently have gone with "e'en one" is joined to the "ye" in the next line.

[5] The Latin is: —

"Nec venit in mentem quod vos, a nomine Christi
Seductos, ad Marcionis tulit infima nomen."

The rendering in my text, I admit, involves an exceedingly harsh construction of the Latin, but I see not how it is to be avoided; unless either (1) we take nomen absolutely, and "ad Marcionis infima" together, and translate, "A name has carried you to Marcion's lowest depths;" in which case the question arises, What name is meant? can it be the name "Electi"? Or else (2) we take "tulit" as referring to the "terrible renegade," i.e., the arch-fiend, and "infima" as in appo-sition with "ad Marcionis nomen," and translate, "He has carried you to the name of Marcion — deepest degradation."

[6] i.e., the Gospels and other parts of Holy Scripture.

[7] i.e., I take it, the resurrection. Cf. 2 Tim. ii. 17, 18.

[8] Whether this be the sense (i.e., "either tell us what it is which displeases you in our God, whether it be His too great patience in bearing with you, or what; or else tell us what is to hinder us from believing your God to be an incredible being") of this passage, I will not venture to determine. The last line in the edd. previous to Oehler's ran: "Aut incredibile quid differt credere vestrum?" Oehler reads "incredibilem" (sc. Deum), which I have followed; but he suggests, "Aut incredibilem qui differt cædere vestrum?" Which may mean "or else" — i e., if it were not for his "too great patience" — "why" — "qui" — "does He delay to smite your incredible god?" and thus challenge a contest and prove His own superiority.

[9] i.e., the "terrible renegade."

[10] The reference here is to Simon Magus; for a brief account of whom, and of the other heretics in this list, down to Hebion inclusive, the reader is referred to the Adv. omn. Hær., above. The words "to roam, to fly," refer to the alleged wanderings of Simon with his para-mour Helen, and his reported attempt (at Rome, in the presence of St. Peter) to fly. The tale is doubtful.

[11] The Latin runs thus: —
"Et ævo
Triginta tribuit cælos, patremque Profundum."
But there seems a confusion between Valentine and his æons and Basilides and his heavens. See the Adv. omn. Hær., above.

[12] i.e., the Evil One's, as before.

He taught, too, circumcision, and that room
215 Is still left for the Law, and, though Law's founts
Are lost,[1] its elements must be resumed.
Unwilling am I to protract in words
His last atrocity, or to tell all
The causes, or the names at length.   Enough
220 It is to note his many cruelties
Briefly, and the unmentionable men,
The dragon's organs fell, through whom he now,
Speaking so much profaneness, ever toils
To blame the Maker of the world.[2]   But come ;
225 Recall your foot from savage Bandit's cave,
While space is granted, and to wretched men
God, patient in perennial parent-love,
Condones all deeds through error done !   Believe
Truly in the true SIRE, who built the orb ;
230 Who, on behalf of men incapable
To bear the law, sunk in sin's whirlpool, sent
The true LORD to repair the ruin wrought,
And bring them the salvation promisèd
Of old through seers.   He who the mandates gave
235 Remits sins too.   Somewhat, deservèdly,
Doth He exact, because He formerly
Entrusted somewhat ; or else bounteously,
As Lord, condones as it were debts to slaves :
Finally, peoples shut up 'neath the curse,
240 And meriting the penalty, Himself
Deleting the indictment, bids be washed !

PART II. — OF THE RESURRECTION OF THE FLESH.

The *whole* man, then, believes ; the *whole* is washed ;
Abstains from sin, or truly suffers wounds
For Christ's name's sake : he rises a true[3] man,
245 Death, truly vanquisht, shall be mute.   But not
Part of the man, — his *soul*, — her own part[4] left
Behind, will win the palm which, labouring
And wrestling in the course, combinèdly
And simultaneously with *flesh*, she earns.
250 Great crime it were for two in chains to bear
A weight, of whom the one were affluent
The other needy, and the wretched one
Be spurned, and guerdons to the happy one
Rendered.   Not so the Just — fair Renderer
255 Of wages — deals, both good and just, whom we
Believe Almighty : to the thankless kind,

Full is His will of pity.   Nay, whate'er
He who hath greater mortal need[5] doth need[6]
That, by advancement, to his comrade he
260 May equalled be, that will the affluent
Bestow the rather unsolicited :
So are we bidden to believe, and not
Be willing to cast blame unlawfully
On the Lord in our teaching, as if He
265 Were one to raise the *soul*, as having met
With ruin, and to set her free from death,
So that the granted faculty of life
Upon the ground of sole desert (because
She bravely acted), should abide with her ;[7]
270 While she who ever shared the common lot
Of toil, the *flesh*, should to the earth be left,
The prey of a perennial death.   Has, then,
The *soul* pleased God by acts of fortitude ?
By no means could she Him have pleased alone
275 Without the *flesh*.   Hath she borne penal bonds ?[8]
The *flesh* sustained upon her limbs the bonds.
Contemned she death ?   But she hath left the *flesh*
Behind in death.   Groaned she in pain ?   The *flesh*
Is slain and vanquisht by the wound.   Repose
280 Seeks she ?   The *flesh*, spilt by the sword in dust,
Is left behind to fishes, birds, decay,
And ashes ; torn she is, unhappy one !
And broken ; scatterèd, she melts away.
Hath she not earned to rise ? for what could she
285 Have e'er committed, lifeless and alone ?
What so life-grudging[9] cause impedes, or else
Forbids, the *flesh* to take God's gifts, and live
Ever, conjoinèd with her comrade *soul*,
And see what she hath been, when formerly
290 Converted into dust ?[10]   After, renewed,
Bear she to God deservèd meeds of praise,
Not ignorant of herself, frail, mortal, sick.[11]
Contend ye as to what the living might[12]

---

[1] i.e., probably Jerusalem and the temple there.
[2] Mundi.
[3] Oehler's "versus" (="changed the man rises") is set aside for Migne's "verus." Indeed it is probably a misprint.
[4] i.e., her own dwelling or "quarters," — the body, to wit, if the reading "sua parte" be correct.

[5] Egestas.
[6] Eget.
[7] I have ventured to alter the "*et viventi*" of Oehler and Migne into "*ut vivendi*," which seems to improve the sense.
[8] It seems to me that these ideas should all be expressed interrogatively, and I have therefore so expressed them in my text.
[9] See line 2.
[10] "Cernere quid fuerit conversa in pulvere quondam." Whether the meaning be that, as the *soul* will be able (as it should seem) to retrace all that she has experienced since she left the body, so the *body*, when revived, will be able as it were to look back upon all that has happened to her since the soul left her, — something after the manner in which Hamlet traces the imaginary vicissitudes of Cæsar's dust, — or whether there be some great error in the Latin, I leave the reader to judge.
[11] i.e., apparently remembering that she *was so before*.
[12] Vivida virtus.

Of the great God can do ; who, good alike
295 And potent, grudges life to none? Was this
Death's captive?[1] shall this perish vanquishèd,
Which the Lord hath with wondrous wisdom
made,
And art? This by His virtue wonderful
Himself upraises ; this our Leader's self
300 Recalls, and this with His own glory clothes.
God's art and wisdom, then, our body shaped.
What can by these be made, how faileth it
To be by virtue reproduced?[2] No cause
Can holy parent-love withstand ; (lest else
305 Ill's cause[3] should mightier prove than Power
Supreme ;)
That man even now saved by God's gift, may
learn[4]
(Mortal before, now robed in light immense,
Inviolable, wholly quickened,[5] soul
And body) God, in virtue infinite,
310 In parent-love perennial, through His King
Christ, through whom opened is light's way ;
and now,
Standing in new light, filled now with each
gift,[6]
Glad with fair fruits of living Paradise,
May praise and laud Him to eternity,[7]
315 Rich in the wealth of the celestial hall.

BOOK II.

OF THE HARMONY OF THE OLD AND NEW LAWS.[8]

After the faith was broken by the dint
Of the foe's breathing renegades,[9] and swoln
With wiles the hidden pest[10] emerged ; with
lies
Self-prompted, scornful of the Deity
5 That underlies the sense, he did his plagues
Concoct : skilled in guile's path, he mixed
his own
Words impious with the sayings of the saints,

And on the good seed sowed his wretched
tares,
Thence willing that foul ruin's every cause
10 Should grow combined ; to wit, that with
more speed
His own iniquitous deeds he may assign
To God clandestinely, and may impale
On penalties such as his suasion led ;
False with true veiling, turning rough with
smooth,
15 And, (masking his spear's point with rosy
wreaths,)
Slaying the unwary unforeseen with death
Supreme. His supreme wickedness is this :
That men, to such a depth of madness sunk !
Off-broken boughs ![11] should into parts divide
20 The endlessly-dread Deity ; Christ's deeds
Sublime should follow with false praise, and
blame
The former acts,[12] God's countless miracles,
Ne'er seen before, nor heard, nor in a heart
Conceived ;[13] and should so rashly frame in
words
25 The impermissible impiety
Of wishing by " wide dissimilitude
Of sense " to prove that the two Testa-
ments
Sound adverse each to other, and the Lord's
Oppose the prophets' words ; of drawing
down
30 All the Law's cause to infamy ; and eke
Of reprobating holy fathers' life
Of old, whom into friendship, and to share
His gifts, God chose. Without beginning,
one
Is, for its lesser part, accepted.[14] Though
35 Of one are four, of four one,[15] yet to them
One part is pleasing, three they (in a word)
Reprobate : and they seize, in many ways,
On Paul as their own author ; yet was he
Urged by a frenzied impulse of his own
40 To his last words :[16] all whatsoe'er he spake
Of the old covenant[17] seems hard to them,

---

[1] I rather incline to read for "hæc captiva fu*it* mortis," "hæc captiva fu*at* mortis "=
"Is this
To be death's thrall?"
" This" is, of course, the flesh.
[2] For "Quod c*a*pit his fieri, deest hoc virtute reduci," I venture to read, " Quod c*a*pit," etc., taking " capit " as = " capax est." " By these," of course, is by wisdom and art ; and " virtue " = " power."
[3] i.e., the Evil One.
[4] i.e., may learn *to know.*
[5] Oehler's " visus " seems to be a mistake for ,"vi*v*us," which is Migne's reading ; as in the fragment " De exsecrandis gentium diis," we saw (*sub fin.*) " vi*d*entem " to be a probable misprint for " vi*v*entem." If, however, it is to be retained, it must mean " appearing " (i.e., in presence of God) " wholly," in body as well as soul.
[6] i.e., the double gift of a saved soul and a saved body.
[7] In æternum.
[8] I have so frequently had to construct my own text (by altering the reading or the punctuation of the Latin) in this book, that, for brevity's sake, I must ask the reader to be content with this statement once for all, and not expect each case to be separately noted.
[9] The " foe," as before, is Satan ; his " breathing instruments" are the men whom he uses (cf. Shakespeare's " *no breather* "=no man, in the dialogue between Orlando and Jacques, *As you Like it,* act iii. sc. 2) ; and they are called " renegades," like the Evil One himself, because they have deserted from their allegiance to God in Christ.
[10] Heresy.

[11] Cf. John xv. 2, 4, 5, 6 ; Rom. xi. 17–20. The writer simply calls them " abruptos homines;" and he seems to mean *excommunicated,* like Marcion.
[12] i.e., those recorded in the Old Testament.
[13] I have followed Migne's suggestion here, and transposed one line of the original. The reference seems to be to Isa. lxiv. 4, quoted in 1 Cor. ii. 9, where the Greek differs somewhat remarkably from the LXX.
[14] Unless some line has dropped out here, the construction, harsh enough in my English, is yet harsher in the Latin. " Accipitur " has no subject of any kind, and one can only guess from what has gone before, and what follows, that it must mean " *one Testament.*"
[15] Harsh still. It must refer to the four Gospels — the " coat without seam " — in their quadrate unity : Marcion receiving but one — St Luke's — and that without St. Luke's name, and also in a mutilated and interpolated form.
[16] This seems to be the sense. The allusion is to the fact that Marcion and his sect accepted but *ten* of St. Paul's Epistles : leaving out entirely those to Timothy and Titus, and *all* the other books, except his one Gospel.
[17] It seems to me that the reference here must evidently be to the Epistle to the Hebrews, which treats specially of the old covenant. If so, we have some indication as to the authorship, if not the date, of the book ; for Tertullian himself, though he frequently cites the Epistle, appears to hesitate (to say the least) as to ascribing it to St. Paul.

Because, deservedly, "made gross in heart." [1]
Weight apostolic, grace of beaming word,
Dazzles their mind, nor can they possibly
45 Discern the Spirit's drift. Dull as they are,
Seek they congenial animals !
                But ye
Who have not yet, (false deity your guide,
Reprobate in your very mind,[2]) to death's
Inmost caves penetrated, learn there flows
50 A stream perennial from its fount, which
    feeds
A tree, (twice sixfold are the fruits, its grace !)
And into earth and to the orb's four winds
Goes out : into so many parts doth flow
The fount's one hue and savour.[3] Thus,
    withal,
55 From apostolic word descends the Church,
Out of Christ's womb, with glory of His Sire
All filled, to wash off filth, and vivify
Dead fates.[4] The Gospel, four in number,
    one
In its diffusion 'mid the Gentiles, this,
60 By faith elect accepted, Paul hands down
(Excellent doctor !) pure, without a crime ;
And from it he forbade Galatian saints
To turn aside withal ; whom " brethren false,"
(Urging them on to circumcise themselves,
65 And follow " elements," leaving behind
Their novel " freedom,") to " a shadow old
Of things to be " were teaching to be slaves.
These were the causes which Paul had to
    write
To the Galatians : not that they took out
70 One small part of the Gospel, and held that
For the whole bulk, leaving the greater part
Behind. And hence 'tis no words of a book,
But Christ Himself, Christ sent into the orb,
Who is the gospel, if ye will discern ;
75 Who from the Father came, sole Carrier
Of tidings good ; whose glory vast completes
The early testimonies ; by His work
Showing how great the orb's Creator is :
Whose deeds, conjoined at the same time
    with words,
80 Those faithful ones, Matthew, Mark, Luke,
    and John,
Recorded unalloyed (not speaking words
External), sanctioned by God's Spirit, 'neath
So great a Master's eye !
           This paschal Lamb
Is hung, a victim, on the tree : Him Paul,

85 Writing decrees to Corinth, with his torch,[5]
Hands down as slain, the future life and God
Promisèd to the fathers, whom before
He had attracted.
           See what virtue, see
What power, the paschal image[6] has ; ye thus
90 Will able be to see what power there is
In the true Passover.
          Lest well-earned love
Should tempt the faithful sire and seer, [7] to
    whom
His pledge and heir [8] was dear, whom God
    by chance [9]
Had given him, to offer him to God
95 (A mighty execution !), there is shown
To him a lamb entangled by the head
In thorns ; a holy victim — holy blood
For blood — to God. From whose piacular
    death,
That to the wasted race [10] it might be sign
100 And pledge of safety, signèd are with blood
Their posts and thresholds many : [11] — aid
    immense ! —
The flesh (a witness credible) is given
For food. The Jordan crossed, the land
    possessed,
Joshua by law kept passover with joy,
105 And immolates a lamb ; and the great kings
And holy prophets that were after him,
Not ignorant of the good promises
Of sure salvation ; full of godly fear
The great Law to transgress, (that mass of
    types
110 In image of the Supreme Virtue once
To come,) did celebrate in order due
The mirrorly-inspected passover.[12]

---

[1] Comp. Isa. vi. 9, 10, with Acts xxviii. 17–29.
[2] The reference seems to be to Rom. i. 28; comp., too, Tit. i.
15, 16.
[3] The reference is to Gen. ii. 9–14.
[4] Fata mortua. This extraordinary expression appears to mean
"dead *men;*" men who, through Adam, are *fated,* so to speak, to
die, and are under the sad *fate* of being "*dead* in trespasses and
sins." See Eph. ii. 1. As far as *quantity* is concerned, it might as
well be "*facta mortua,*" "*dead works,*" such as we read of in Heb.
vi. 1, ix. 14. It is true *these* works cannot strictly be said to be ever
vivified; but a very similar inaccuracy seems to be committed by
our author lower down in this same book.

[5] I have followed Oehler's " face " for the common " phase; " but
what the meaning is I will not venture to decide. It may probably
mean one of two things: (*a*) that Paul wrote *by torchlight ;* (*b*) that
the *light* which Paul holds forth in his life and writings, is a *torch* to
show the Corinthians and others Christ.
[6] i.e., the legal passover, " image " or type of " the true Passover," Christ. See 1 Cor. v. 6–9.
[7] Abraham. See Gen. xxii. 1–19.
[8] Isaac, a pledge to Abraham of all God's other promises.
[9] Forte. I suppose this means out of the ordinary course of
nature; but it is a strange word to use.
[10] Israel, wasted by the severities of their Egyptian captivity.
[11] "Mu*lta ;*" but "mu*ta*" = " mute " has been suggested, and is
not inapt.
[12] I have given what appears to be a possible sense for these almost
unintelligible lines. They run as follows in Oehler: —

    " Et reliqui magni reges sanctique prophetæ,
    Non ignorantes certæ promissa salutis,
    Ingentemque metu pleni transcendere legem,
    Venturam summæ virtutis imagine molem,
    Inspectam e speculo celebrarunt ordine pascham."
I rather incline to alter them somehow thus: —

    " Ingentemque metu plen*is* transcendere legem,
    Ventur*um* i*n* summæ virtutis imagine, — *solem*
    Inspect*um* e speculo, — celebrarunt ordine pascham; "
connecting these three lines with " non ignorantes," and rendering: —

    " Not ignorant of the good promises
    Of sure salvation; and that One would come,
    For such as fillèd are with godly fear
    The law to overstep, a mighty One,
    In Highest Virtue's image, — the Sun seen
    In mirror: — did in order celebrate
    The passover."
That is, in brief, they all, in celebrating the type, looked forward to
the Antitype to come.

In short, if thou recur with rapid mind
To times primordial, thou wilt find results
115 Too fatal following impious words. That
    man
Easily credulous, alas ! and stripped
Of life's own covering, might covered be
With skins, a lamb is hung : the wound slays
    sins,
Or death by blood effaces, or enshrouds
120 Or cherishes the naked with its fleece.
Is sheep's blood of more worth than human
    blood,
That, offered up for sins, it should quench
    wrath?
Or is a lamb (as if he were more dear !)
Of more worth than much people's? aid
    immense!
125 As safeguard of so great salvation, could
A lamb, if offered, have been price enough
For the redeemed? Nay: but Almighty
    God,
The heaven's and earth's Creator, infinite,[1]
Living, and perfect, and perennially
130 Dwelling in light, is not appeased by these,
Nor joys in cattle's blood. Slain be all
    flocks ;
Be every herd upburnèd into smoke ;
That expiatively 't may pardon win
Of but one sin : in vain at so vile price
135 Will the stained figure of the Lord — foul
    flesh —
Prepare, if wise, such honours :[2] but the
    hope
And faith to mortals promisèd of old —
Great Reason's counterpart [3] — hath wrought
    to bring
These boons premeditated and prepared
140 Erst by the Father's passing parent-love ;
That Christ should come to earth, and be a
    man !
Whom when John saw, baptism's first open-
    er, John,
Comrade of seers, apostle great, and sent
As sure forerunner, witness faithful ; John,
145 August in life, and marked with praise sub-
    lime,[4]
He shows, to such as sought of olden time
God's very Paschal Lamb, that He is come
At last, the expiation of misdeed,
To undo many's sins by His own blood,
150 In place of reprobates the Proven One,
In place of vile the dear ; in body, man ;
And, in life, God : that He, as the slain
    Lamb,

Might us accept,[5] and for us might outpour
Himself. Thus hath it pleased the Lord to
    spoil
155 Proud death : thus wretched man will able be
To hope salvation. This slain paschal Lamb
Paul preaches : nor does a phantasmal shape
Of the sublime Lord (one consimilar
To Isaac's silly sheep [6]) the passion bear,
160 Wherefore He is called Lamb : but 'tis
    because,
As wool, He these renewèd bodies clothes,
Giving to many covering, yet Himself
Never deficient. Thus does the Lord shroud
In His Sire's virtue, those whom, disarrayed
165 Of their own light, He by His death re-
    deemed,
Virtue which ever is in Him. So, then,
The Shepherd who hath lost the sheep Him-
    self
Re-seeks it. He, prepared to tread the
    strength
Of the vine, and its thorns, or to o'ercome
170 The wolf's rage, and regain the cattle lost,
And brave to snatch them out, the Lion He
In sheepskin-guise, unasked presents Him-
    self
To the contemned [7] teeth, baffling by His
    garb
The robber's bloody jaws.
                            Thus everywhere
175 Christ seeks force-captured Adam ; treads
    the path
Himself where death wrought ruin ; per-
    meates
All the old heroes' monuments ;[8] inspects
Each one ; the One of whom all types were
    full ;
Begins e'en from the womb to expel the
    death
180 Conceivèd simultaneously with seed
Of flesh within the bosom ; purging all
Life's stages with a silent wisdom ; debts
Assuming ;[9] ready to cleanse all, and give
Their Maker back the many whom the one [10]
185 Had scattered. And, because one direful
    man
Down-sunk in pit iniquitous did fall,
By dragon-subdued virgin's [11] suasion led ;
Because he pleased her wittingly ;[12] because
He left his heavenly covering [13] behind ;

[1] Immensus.
[2] This, again, seems to be the meaning, unless the passage (which
is not improbable) be corrupt. The flesh, "foul" now with sin, is
called the "stained image of the Lord," as having been originally in
His image, but being now stained by guilt.
[3] Faith is called so, as being the reflection of divine reason.
[4] i.e., the praise of Christ Himself. See Matt. xi. 7-15, with the
parallel passage, Luke vii. 24-30; comp. also John v. 33-35.

[5] i.e., perhaps "render acceptable."
[6] See above, 91-99.
[7] i.e., teeth which He contemned, for His people's sake: not that
they are to us contemptible.
[8] i.e., perhaps permeating, by the influence of His death, the
tombs of all the old saints.
[9] i.e., undertaking our debts in our stead.
[10] Adam. See Rom. v., passim
[11] It is an idea of the genuine Tertullian, apparently, that Eve
was a "virgin" all the time she was with Adam in Paradise. A similar idea appears in the "Genesis" above.
[12] Consilio. Comp. 1 Tim. ii. 14, "Adam was not deceived."
[13] Called "life's own covering" (i.e., apparently his innocence) in
117, above.

190 Because the "tree" their nakedness did
prove;
Because dark death coerced them: in like
wise
Out of the self-same mass [1] re-made returns,
Renewèd now, — the flower of flesh, and
host
Of peace, — a flesh from espoused virgin
born,
195 Not of man's seed; conjoinèd to its own
Artificer; without the debt of death.
These mandates of the Father through bright
stars
An angel carries down, that angel-fame
The tidings may accredit; telling how
200 "A virgin's debts a virgin, flesh's flesh,
Should pay." Thus introduced, the Giant-
Babe,
The Elder-Boy, the Stripling-Man, pursues
Death's trail. Thereafter, when completed
was
The ripe age of man's strength, when man
is wont
205 To see the lives that were his fellows drop
By slow degrees away, and to be changed
In mien to wrinkles foul and limbs inert,
While blood forsakes his veins, his course he
stayed,
And suffered not his fleshly garb to age.
210   Upon what day or in what place did fall
Most famous Adam, or outstretched his hand
Rashly to touch the tree, on that same day,
Returning as the years revolve, within
The stadium of the "tree" the brave Athlete,
215 'Countering, outstretched His hands, and,
penalty
For praise pursuing,[2] quite did vanquish
death,
Because He left death of His own accord
Behind, disrobing Him of fleshly slough,
And of death's dues; and to the "tree"
affixed
220 The serpent's spoil — "the world's [3] prince"
vanquisht quite! —
Grand trophy of the renegades: for sign
Whereof had Moses hung the snake, that all,
Who had by many serpents stricken been,
Might gaze upon the dragon's self, and see
225 Him vanquisht and transfixt.
                When, afterwards,
He reached the infernal region's secret
waves,
And, as a victor, by the light which aye
Attended Him, revealed His captive thrall,
And by His virtue thoroughly fulfilled
230 The Father's bidding, He Himself re-took

The body which, spontaneous, He had left:
This was the cause of death: this same was
made
Salvation's path: a messenger of guile
The former was; the latter messenger
235 Of peace: a spouse her man [4] did slay; a
spouse
Did bear a lion: [5] hurtful to her man [6]
A virgin [7] proved; a man [8] from virgin born
Proved victor: for a type whereof, while
sleep
His [9] body wrapped, out of his side is ta'en
240 A woman,[10] who is her lord's [11] rib; whom he,
Awaking, called "flesh from his flesh, and
bones
From his own bones;" with a presaging mind
Speaking. Faith wondrous! Paul, deserv-
èdly,
(Most certain author!) teaches Christ to be
245 "The Second Adam from the heavens." [12]
Truth,
Using her own examples, doth refulge;
Nor covets out of alien source to show
Her paces keen: [13] this is a pauper's work,
Needy of virtue of his own! Great Paul
250 These mysteries — taught to him — did teach;
to wit,
Discerning that in Christ thy glory is,
O Church! from His side, hanging on high
"tree,"
His lifeless body's "blood and humour"
flowed.
The blood the woman [14] was; the waters
were
255 The new gifts of the font: [15] this is the
Church,
True mother of a living people; flesh
New from Christ's flesh, and from His bones
a bone.
A spot there is called Golgotha, — of old
The fathers' earlier tongue thus called its
name, —
260 "The skull-pan of a head:" here is earth's
midst;
Here victory's sign; here, have our elders
taught,
There was a great head [16] found; here the
first man,

---

[1] Or, "ore."
[2] Comp. Heb. xii. 2, "Who, for the joy that was set before
Him" — ὃς ἀντὶ τῆς προκειμένης αὐτῷ χαρᾶς.
[3] Mundi. See John xiv. 30.

[4] Virum.
[5] "The Lion of the tribe of Juda." Rev. v. 5.
[6] Viro. This use of "man" may be justified, to say nothing of
other arguments, from Jer. xliv. 19, where "our men" seem plainly
="our husbands." See marg.
[7] Virgo: a play on the word in connection with the "viro" and
what follows.
[8] Vir.
[9] i.e., Adam's. The constructions, as will be seen, are oddly confused throughout, and I rather suspect some transposition of lines.
[10] Mulier.
[11] Mariti.
[12] See 1 Cor. xv. 22 sqq., especially 45, 47.
[13] Acres gressus.
[14] Femina.
[15] Lavacri.
[16] "Os;" lit., "face" or "mouth."

We have been taught, was buried ; here the
    Christ
Suffers ; with sacred blood the earth [1] grows
    moist.
265 That the old Adam's dust may able be,
Commingled with Christ's blood, to be up-
    raised
By dripping water's virtue.   The "one ewe"
That is, which, during Sabbath-hours, alive
The Shepherd did resolve that He would
    draw
270 Out of th' infernal pit.   This was the cause
Why, on the Sabbaths, He was wont to cure
The prematurely dead limbs of all flesh ;
Or perfected for sight the eyes of him
Blind from his birth — eyes which He had
    not erst
275 Given ; or, in presence of the multitude,
Called, during Sabbath-hours, one wholly dead
To life, e'en from the sepulchre.[2]   Himself
The new man's Maker, the Repairer good
Of th' old, supplying what did lack, or else
280 Restoring what was lost.   About to do —
When dawns " the holy day " — these works,
    for such
As hope in Him, in plenitude, (to keep
His plighted word,) He taught men thus
    His power
To do them.
           What ?   If flesh dies, and no hope
285 Is given of salvation, say, what grounds
Christ had to feign Himself a man, and heal
Men, or have care for flesh ?   If He recalls [3]
Some few, why shall He not withal recall
All ?   Can corruption's power liquefy
290 The body and undo it, and shall not
The virtue of the Lord be powerful
The undone to recall ?
              They, who believe
Their bodies are *not* loosed from death, do not
Believe the Lord, who wills to raise His own
295 Works sunken ; or else say they that the Good
Wills not, and that the Potent hath not
    power,—
Ignorant from how great a crime they suck
Their milk, in daring to set things infirm
Above the Strong.[4]   In the grain lurks the
    tree ;
300 And if this [5] rot not, buried in the earth,
It yields not tree-graced fruits.[6]   Soon bound
    will be

The liquid waters : 'neath the whistling cold
They will become, and ever will be, stones,
Unless a mighty power, by leading on
305 Soft-breathing warmth, undo them.   The great
    bunch
Lurks in the tendril's slender body : if
Thou seek it, it is not ; when God doth will,
'Tis seen to be.   On trees their leaves, on
    thorns
The rose, the seeds on plains, are dead and
    fail,
310 And rise again, new living.   For man's use
These things doth God before his eyes recall
And form anew — man's, for whose sake at
    first [7]
The wealthy One made all things bounteously.
All naked fall ; with its own body each
315 He clothes.   Why man alone, on whom He
    showered
Such honours, should He not recall in all
His first perfection [8] to Himself ? man, whom
He set o'er all ?
           Flesh, then, and blood are said
To be not worthy of God's realm, as if
320 Paul spake of flesh *materially*.   He
Indeed taught mighty truths ; but hearts inane
Think he used carnal speech : for *pristine
    deeds*
He meant beneath the name of " flesh and
    blood ; "
Remembering, heavenly home-slave that he
    is,
325 His heavenly Master's words ; who gave the
    name
Of His own honour to men born from Him
Through water, and from His own Spirit
    poured
A pledge ; [9] that, by whose virtue men had
    been
Redeemed, His name of honour they withal
330 Might, when renewed, receive.   Because,
    then, He
Refused, on the old score, the heavenly
    realm
To peoples not yet from His fount re-born,
Still with their ancient sordid raiment clad —
These are " the dues of death " — saying
    that that
335 Which human is must needs be born again, —
" What hath been born of flesh is flesh ; and
    what
From Spirit, life ; " [10] and that the body,
    washed,
Changing with glory its old root's new seeds,[11]

---

[1] Terra.
[2] This would seem to refer to Lazarus : but it seems to be an assumption that his raising took place on a Sabbath.
[3] i.e., to life.
[4] I have ventured to alter the " *Morti*," of the edd. into " *Forti* ; "
and " causas " (as we have seen) seems, in this late Latin, nearly =
" res."
[5] i.e., the grain.
[6] This may seem an unusual expression, as it is more common to
regard the fruit as gracing the tree, than the tree the fruit.   But, in
point of fact, the tree, with its graceful form and foliage, may be said
to give a grace to the fruit ; and so our author puts it here : " decora-
tos arbore fructus."

[7] I read " prim*um* " here for " prim*us*."
[8] " Tantum " = " tantum quantum primo fuerat," i.e., with a body
as well as a spirit.
[9] Pignus : " the *promise* of the Father " (Acts i. 4) ; " the
earnest of the Spirit " (2 Cor. i. 22 ; v. 5).   See, too, Eph. i. 13, 14 ;
Rom. viii. 23.
[10] The reference is to John iii. 6, but it is not quite correctly given.
[11] See note on 245, above.

Is no more called " from flesh : " Paul follows
this ;
340 Thus did he speak of " flesh." In fine, he
said [1]
This frail garb with a robe must be o'erclad,
This mortal form be wholly coverèd ;
Not that another body must be given,
But that the former one, dismantled,[2] must
345 Be with God's kingdom wholly on all sides
Surrounded : " In the moment of a glance,"
He says, " it shall be changed : " as, on the
blade,
Dispreads the red corn's [3] face, and changes
'neath
The sun's glare its own hue ; so the same
flesh,
350 From " the effulgent glory " [4] borrowing,
Shall ever joy, and joying,[5] shall lack death ;
Exclaiming that " the body's cruel foe
Is vanquisht quite ; death, by the victory
Of the brave Christ, is swallowed ; " [6] praises
high
355 Bearing to God, unto the highest stars.

BOOK III.

OF THE HARMONY OF THE FATHERS OF THE
OLD AND NEW TESTAMENTS.

Now hath the mother, formerly surnamed
Barren, giv'n birth : [7] now a new people, born
From the free woman,[8] joys : (the slave ex-
pelled,
Deservedly, with her proud progeny ;
5 Who also leaves ungratefully behind
The waters of the living fount,[9] and drinks —
Errant on heated plains — 'neath glowing
star : [10])
Now can the Gentiles as their parent claim
Abraham ; who, the Lord's voice following,
10 Like him, have all things left,[11] life's pil-
grimage
To enter. " Be glad, barren one ; " conceive
The promised people ; " break thou out, and
cry,"
Who with no progeny wert blest ; of whom
Spake, through the seers, the Spirit of old
time :
15 She hath borne, out of many nations, one ;

With whose beginning are her pious limbs
Ever in labour.
Hers " just ABEL " [12] was,
A pastor and a cattle-master he ;
Whom violence of brother's right hand slew
20 Of old. Her ENOCH, signal ornament,
Limb from her body sprung, by counsel strove
To recall peoples gone astray from God
And following misdeed, (while raves on earth
The horde of robber-renegades,[13]) to flee
25 The giants' sacrilegious cruel race ;
Faithful in all himself. With groaning deep [14]
Did he please God, and by deservèd toil
Translated [15] is reservèd as a pledge,
With honour high. Perfect in praise, and
found
30 Faultless, and just — God witnessing [16] the
fact —
In an adulterous people, NOAH (he
Who in twice fifty years [17] the ark did weave)
By deeds and voice the coming ruin told.
Favour he won, snatched out of so great waves
35 Of death, and, with his progeny, preserved.
Then, in the generation [18] following,
Is ABRAHAM, whose sons ye do deny
Yourselves to be ; who first — race, country,
sire,
All left behind — at suasion of God's voice
40 Withdrew to realms extern : such honours he
At God's sublime hand worthily deserved
As to be father to believing tribes
And peoples. JACOB with the patriarchs
(Himself their patriarch) through all his own
45 Life's space the gladdest times of Christ fore-
sang
By words, act, virtue, toil.
Him follows — free
From foul youth's stain — JOSEPH, by slander
feigned,
Doomed to hard penalty and gaol : his groans
Glory succeeds, and the realm's second
crown,
50 And in dearth's time large power of fur-
nishing
Bread : so appropriate a type of Christ,
So lightsome type of Light, is manifest
To all whose mind hath eyes, that they may
see
In a face-mirror [19] their sure hope.
Himself
55 The patriarch JUDAH, see ; the origin

[1] See 2 Cor. v. 1 sqq.
[2] I read " inerm*um* " — a very rare form — here for " inerm*em*."
But there seems a confusion in the text, which here, as elsewhere, is
probably corrupt.
[3] " Cer*æ*," which seems senseless here, I have changed to
cer*eris*."
[4] There seems to be a reference to 2 Pet. i. 17.
[5] Here again I have altered the punctuation by a very simple
change.
[6] See 1 Cor. xv. 54 ; Isa. xxv. 8 (where the LXX. have a strange
reading).
[7] Isa. liv. 1 ; Gal iv. 27.
[8] Gal. iv. 19-31.
[9] The Jewish people leaving Christ, " the fountain of living
waters " (Jer. ii. 13 ; John vii. 37-39), is compared to Hagar leaving
the well, which was, we may well believe, close to Abraham's tent.
[10] Et tepidis errans ardenti sidere potat. See Gen. xxi. 12-20.
[11] See Matt. xix. 27 ; Mark x. 28 ; Luke xviii. 28.

[12] See Matt. xxiii. 35.
[13] i.e., apparently the " giants ; " see Gen. vi. 4 ; but there is no
mention of them in Enoch's time (Migne).
[14] i.e., over the general sinfulness.
[15] I suggest " translat*us* " for " translat*um* " here.
[16] See Gen. vii. 1.
[17] Loosely ; 120 years is the number in Gen. vi. 3.
[18] Gente.
[19] Speculo vultus. The two words seem to *me* to go together,
and, unless the second be indeed redundant, to mean perhaps a small
hand-mirror, which affords more facilities for minute examination
of the face than a larger fixed one.

Of royal line,[1] whence leaders rose, nor kings
Failed ever from his seed, until the Power
To come, by Gentiles looked for, promised
long,
Came.
      MOSES, leader of the People, (he
60 Who, spurning briefly-blooming riches, left
The royal thresholds,) rather chose to bear
His people's toils, afflicted, with bowed
nec..,
By no threats daunted, than to gain himself
Enjoyments, and of many penalties
65 Remission : admirable for such faith
And love, he, with God's virtue armed,
achieved
Great exploits : smote the nation through
with plagues ;
And left their land behind, and their hard
king
Confounds, and leads the People back ; trod
waves ;
70 Sunk the foes down in waters ; through a
"tree"[2]
Made ever-bitter waters sweet ; spake much
(Manifestly to the People) with the Christ,[3]
From whose face light and brilliance in his
own
Reflected shone ; dashed on the ground the
law
75 Accepted through some few,[4] — implicit type,
And sure, of his own toils ! — smote through
the rock ;
And, being bidden, shed forth streams ; and
stretched
His hands that, by a sign,[5] he vanquish might
The foe ; of Christ all *severally*, all [6]

80 *Combined through* Christ, do speak. Great
and approved,
He [7] rests with praise and peace.
           But JOSHUA,
The son of Nun, erst called OSHEA — this
man
The Holy Spirit to Himself did join
As partner in His name : [8] hence did he
cleave
85 The flood ; constrained the People to pass
o'er ;
Freely distributed the land — the prize
Promised the fathers ! — stayed both sun and
moon
While vanquishing the foe ; races extern
And giants' progeny outdrave ; razed groves ;
90 Altars and temples levelled ; and with mind
Loyal [9] performed all due solemnities :
Type of Christ's name ; his virtue's image.
            What
Touching the People's Judges shall I say
Singly ? whose virtues,[10] it unitedly
95 Recorded, fill whole volumes numerous
With space of words. But yet the order due
Of filling out the body of my words,
Demands that, out of many, I should tell
The life of few.
        Of whom when GIDEON, guide
100 Of martial band, keen to attack the foe,
(Not keen to gain for his own family,
By virtue,[11] tutelary dignity,[12])
And needing to be strengthened [13] in the faith
Excited in his mind, seeks for a sign
105 Whereby he either could not, or could, wage
Victorious war ; to wit, that with the dew
A fleece, exposèd for the night, should be
Moistened, and all the ground lie dry around
(By this to show that, with the world,[14] should
dry [15]
110 The enemies' palm) ; and then again, the
fleece
Alone remaining dry, the earth by night
Should with the self-same [16] moisture be be-
dewed :

---

[1] "Sortis ;" lit. "lot," here = "the line or family chosen *by lot*. Compare the similar derivation of "clergy."

[2] Lignum.

[3] I have ventured to substitute "Christ*o*" for "Christ*i* ; and thus, for

    "Cum Christ*i* populo manifeste multa locutus,"
read,
    "Cum Christo (populo manifeste) multa locutus."
The reference is to the fact, on which such special stress is laid, of the Lord's "speaking to Moses *face to face, as a man speaketh with his friend.*" See especially Num. xii. 5-8, Deut. xxxiv. 9-12, with Deut. xviii. 17-19, Acts iii. 22, 23, vii. 37.

[4] The Latin in Oehler and Migne is thus:
    "Acceptam legem per paucos fudit in orbem ;"
and the reference seems to me to be to Ex. xxxii. 15-20, though the use of "orbem" for "ground" is perhaps strange ; but "humum" would have been against the metre, if that argument be of any weight in the case of a writer so prolific of false quantities. Possibly the lines may mean that "he diffused through some few" — i.e., through the Jews, "few" as compared with the total inhabitants of the orb — "the Law which he had received ;" but then the following line seems rather to favour the former view, because the tables of the Law — called briefly "the Law" — broken by Moses so soon after he had received them, were typical of the inefficacy of all Moses' own toils, which, after all, ended in disappointment, as he was forbidden, on account of a sin committed in the very last of the forty years, to lead the people into "the land," as 'he had fondly hoped to do. Only I suspect some error in "per paucos ;" unless it be lawful to supply "dies," and take it to mean "received during but few days," i.e., "with*in* few days," "only a few days before," and "accepted" or "kep*t* by the People "during but a few days." Would it be lawful to conjecture "perpa*ucis*" as one word, with "ante diebus" to be understood?

[5] i.e., the sign of the cross. See Tertullian, *adv. Marc.*, l. iii. c. xviii. *sub. fin.;* also *adv. Jud.*, c. x. *med.*

[6] i.e., all the acts and the experiences of Moses.

[7] Moses.

[8] See Ex. xxiii. 20-23 ; and comp, *adv. Marc.*, l. iii. c. xvi.

[9] Legitima, i.e., reverent of law.

[10] i.e., virtuous acts.

[11] Or, "valour."

[12] The Latin runs thus :
        "Acer in hostem,
Non virtute su*æ* tutelam acquirere genti."
I have ventured to read "su*æ*," and connect it with "genti ;" and thus have obtained what seems to me a probable sense. See Judg. viii. 22, 23.

[13] I read "firm*andus*" for "firm*atus*."

[14] Mundo.

[15] I have again ventured a correction, "coa*rescere*" for "coa*lescere.*" It makes at least *some* sense out of an otherwise (to *me*) unintelligible passage, the "palm" being taken as the well-known symbol of bloom and triumph. So David in Ps. xcii. 12 (xci. 13 in LXX.), "The righteous shall *flourish* like the *palm-tree.*" To "dry" here is, of course, neuter, and means to "wither."

[16] I have changed "*eadem*" — which must agree with "nocte," and hence give a false sense ; for it was not, of course, on "*the same night,*" but on the next, that this second sign was given — into "*eodem,*" to agree with "liquore," which gives a true one, as the "moisture," of course, *was* the same, — dew, namely.

For by this sign he prostrated the heaps
Of bandits ; with Christ's People 'countering
them
115 Without much soldiery, with cavalry [1]
Three hundred — the Greek letter Tau, in
• truth,
That number is [2] — with torches armed, and
horns
Of blowers with the mouth : then [3] was the
fleece,
The people of Christ's sheep,. from holy seed
120 Born (for the *earth* means nations various,
And scattered through the orb), which fleece
the word
Nourishes ; *night* death's image ; *Tau* the sign
Of the dear cross ; the *horn* the heraldings
Of life ; the *torches* shining in their stand [4]
125 The glowing Spirit : and this *testing*, too,
Forsooth, an image of Christ's virtue was : [5]
To teach that death's fierce battles should
not be
By trump angelic vanquishèd before
Th' indocile People be deservèdly
130 By their own fault left desolate behind,
And Gentiles, flourishing in faith, received
In praise.
      Yea, DEBORAH, a woman far
Above all fame, appears ; who, having braced
Herself for warlike toil, for country's sake,
135 Beneath the palm-tree sang how victory
Had crowned her People ; thanks to whom
it was
That the foes, vanquisht, turned at once their
backs,
And Sisera their leader fled ; whose flight
No man, nor any band, arrested : him,
140 Suddenly renegade, a woman's hand —
JAEL'S [6] — with wooden weapon vanquished
quite,
For token of Christ's victory.
                  With firm faith
JEPHTHAH appears, who a deep-wounding
vow
Dared make — to promise God a grand re-
ward
145 Of war : him [7] then, because he senselessly
Had promised what the Lord not wills, first
meets
The pledge [8] dear to his heart ; who suddenly

Fell by a lot unhoped by any.   He,
To keep his promise, broke the sacred laws
150 Of parenthood : the shade of mighty fear
Did in his violent mind cover his vow
Of sin : as solace of his widowed life
For [9] wickedness, renown, and, for crime,
praise,
He won.
            Nor SAMSON's strength, all corporal
might
155 Passing, must we forget ; the Spirit's gift
Was this ; the power was granted to his head. [10]
Alone he for his People, daggerless,
Armless, an ass-jaw grasping, prostrated
A thousand corpses ; and no bonds could
keep
160 The hero bound : but after his shorn pride
Forsook him thralled, he fell, and, by his
death, —
Though vanquisht, — bought his foes back
'neath his power.
Marvellous SAMUEL, who first received
The precept to anoint kings, to give chrism
165 And show men-Christs, [11] so acted laudably
In life's space as, e'en after his repose,
To keep prophetic rights. [12]
                        Psalmographist
DAVID, great king and prophet, with a voice
Submiss was wont Christ's future suffering
170 To sing : which prophecy spontaneously
His thankless lawless People did perform :
Whom [13] God had promised that in time to
come,
Fruit of his womb, [14] a holy progeny,
He would on his sublime throne set : the
Lord's
175 Fixt faith did all that He had promisèd.
Corrector of an inert People rose
Emulous [15] HEZEKIAH ; who restored
Iniquitous forgetful men the Law : [16]
All these God's mandates of old time he first
180 Bade men observe, who ended war by
prayers, [17]
Not by steel's point : he, dying, had a grant
Of years and times of life made to his tears :
Deservèdly such honour his career
Obtained.
            With zeal immense, JOSIAH, prince
185 Himself withal, in like wise acted : none
So much, before or after ! — Idols he
Dethroned ; destroyed unhallowed temples ;
burned

[1] Equite. It appears to be used loosely for " men of war " gener-
rally.
[2] Which is taken, from its form, as a sign of the cross: see below.
[3] Refers to the " when " in 99, above.
[4] Lychno. The "*faces*" are probably the *wicks*.
[5] " Scilicet hoc testamen erat virtutis imago."
[6] The text as it stands is, in Oehler : —
      . . . " Hic Baal Christi victoria signo
          Extemplo refugam devicit femina ligno; "
which I would read : —
      . . . " Hunc Jael, Christi victoriæ signo,
          Extemplo," etc.
[7] For " *hic* " I would incline to read " *huic*."
[8] i.e., child.

[9] i.e., instead of.
[10] i.e., to his unshorn Nazarite locks.
[11] Viros ostendere Christos.
[12] See I Sam. xxviii. (in LXX. I Kings) 11-19.
[13] i.e., *to* whom, to *David*.
[14] " Ex utero:" a curious expression for a man; but so it is.
[15] i.e., emulous of David's virtues.
[16] Comp. especially 2 Chron. xxix. xxx. xxxi.
[17] Our author is quite correct in his order. A comparison of dates
as given in the Scripture history shows us that his reforms preceded
his war with Sennacherib.

With fire priests on their altars ; all the bones
Of prophets false updug ; the altars burned,
190 The carcases to be consumed did serve
For fuel !
        To the praise of signal faith,
Noble ELIJAH, (memorable fact !)
Was rapt ;[1] who hath not tasted yet death's
dues ;
Since to the orb he is to come again.
195 His faith unbroken, then, chastening with
stripes
People and frenzied king, (who did desert
The Lord's best service), and with bitter flames
The foes, shut up the stars ; kept in the clouds
The rain ; showed all collectively that God
200 Is ; made their error patent ; — for a flame,
Coming with force from heaven at his prayers,
Ate up the victim's parts, dripping with flood,
Upon the altar :[2] — often as he willed,
So often from on high rushed fire ;[3] the
stream
205 Dividing, he made pathless passable ;[4]
And, in a chariot raised aloft, was borne
To paradise's hall.
        Disciple his
ELISHA was, succeeding to his lot :[5]
Who begged to take to him Elijah's lot[6]
210 In double measure ; so, with forceful stripe,
The People to chastise :[7] such and so great
A love for the Lord's cause he breathed.
He smote
Through Jordan ; made his feet a way, and
crossed
Again ; raised with a twig the axe down-sunk
215 Beneath the stream ; changed into vital meat
The deathful food ; detained a second time,
Double in length,[8] the rains ; cleansed lep-
rosies ;[9]
Entangled foes in darkness ; and when one
Offcast and dead, by bandits' slaughter slain,
220 His limbs, after his death, already hid
In sepulchre, did touch, he — light recalled —
Revived.
     ISAIAH, wealthy seer, to whom
The fount was oped, — so manifest his
faith ! —

---

[1] The " tactus " of the Latin is without sense, unless indeed it
refer to his being twice " touched " by an angel. See 1 Kings (in
LXX. 3 Kings) xix. 1-8. I have therefore substituted " raptus,"
there being no mention of the angel in the Latin.
[2] " Aras " should probably be " aram."
[3] See 2 Kings (in LXX. 4 Kings) i. 9-12.
[4] For " transgressas et avia fecit," I read " transgressus avia
fecit," taking " transgressus " as a subst.
[5] Sortis.
[6] Sortem.
[7] Our author has somewhat mistaken Elisha's mission apparently;
for as there is a significant difference in the meaning of their respective names, so there is in their works: Elijah's miracles being rather
miracles of judgment, it has been remarked; Elisha's, of mercy.
[8] The reference is to a famine in Elisha's days, which — 2 Kings
(in LXX. 4 Kings) viii. i. — was to last seven years ; whereas that
for which Elijah prayed, as we learn in Jas. v. 17, lasted three and
six months. But it is not said that Elisha prayed for that famine.
[9] We only read of one leprosy which Elisha cleansed — Naaman's.
He inflicted leprosy on Gehazi, which was " to cleave to him and to
his seed for ever."

Poured from his mouth God's word forth.
Promised was
225 The Father's will, bounteous through Christ ;
through him
It testified before the way of life,
And was approved :[10] but him, though stain-
less found,
And undeserving, the mad People cut
With wooden saw in twain, and took away
230 With cruel death.
        The holy JEREMY
Followed ; whom the Eternal's Virtue bade
Be prophet to the Gentiles, and him told
The future : who, because he brooded o'er
His People's deeds illaudable, and said
235 (Speaking with voice presaging) that, unless
They had repented of betaking them
To deeds iniquitous against their slaves,[11]
They should be captived, bore hard bonds,
shut up
In squalid gaol ; and, in the miry pit,
240 Hunger exhausted his decaying limbs.
But, after he did prove what they to hear
Had been unwilling, and the foes did lead
The People bound in their triumphal trains,
Hardly at length his wrinkled right hand lost
245 Its chains : it is agreed that by no death
Nor slaughter was the hero ta'en away.
     Faithful EZEKIEL, to whom granted
was
Rich grace of speech, saw sinners' secrets ;
wailed
His own afflictions ; prayed for pardon ; saw
250 The vengeance of the saints, which is to be
By slaughter ; and, in Spirit wrapt, the place
Of the saints' realm, its steps and accesses,
And the salvation of the flesh, he saw.
     HOSEA, AMOS, MICAH, JOEL, too,
255 With OBADIAH, JONAH, NAHUM, come ;
HABAKKUK, ZEPHANIAH, HAGGAI,
And ZECHARIAH who did violence
Suffer, and MALACHI — angel himself ! —
Are here : these are the Lord's seers ; and
their choir,
260 As still they sing, is heard ; and equally
Their proper wreath of praise they all have
earned.
      How great was DANIEL ! What a
man !
      What power !
Who by their own mouth did false witnesses
Bewray, and saved a soul on a false charge
265 Condemned ;[12] and, before that, by mouth
resolved

---

[10] Prætestata viam vitæ atque probata per ipsam est. I suspect
we should read " via," quantity being of no importance with our
author, and take " prætestata " as passive: " The way of life was
testified before, and proved, through him."
[11] This seems to be the meaning, and the reference will then be to
Jer. xxxiv. 8-22 (in LXX. xli. 8-22) ; but the punctuation both in
Oehler and Migne makes nonsense, and I have therefore altered it.
[12] See the apocryphal " Susanna."

The king's so secret dreams; foresaw how
    Christ
Dissolves the limbs of kingdoms; was ac-
    cused
For his Lord's sake; was made the lions'
    prey;
And, openly preserved [1] before all eyes,
270 Rested in peace.
        His THREE COMPANIONS, scarce
With due praise to be sung, did piously
Contemn the king's iniquitous decree,
Out of so great a number : to the flames
Their bodies given were ; but they preferred,
275 For the Great Name, to yield to penalties
Themselves, than to an image stretch their
    palms
On bended knees. Now their o'erbrilliant
    faith,
Now hope outshining all things, the wild
    fires
Hath quencht, and vanquisht the iniquitous !
280   EZRA the seer, doctor of Law, and
    priest
Himself (who, after full times, back did lead
The captive People), with the Spirit filled
Of memory, restored by word of mouth
All the seers' volumes, by the fires and mould [2]
285 Consumèd.
        Great above all born from seed
Is JOHN : whose praises hardly shall we skill
To tell : the washer [3] of the flesh : the Lord's
Open forerunner ; washer, [3] too, of Christ,
Himself first born again from Him : the first
290 Of the new convenant, last of the old,
Was he ; and for the True Way's sake he
    died,
The first slain victim.
        See GOD-CHRIST ! behold
Alike, His TWELVE-FOLD WARRIOR-YOUTH ! [4]
    in all
One faith, one love, one power ; the flower
    of men ;
295 Lightening the world [5] with light ; comrades
    of Christ
And apostolic men ; who, speaking truth,
Heard with their ears Salvation, [6] with their
    eyes
Saw It, and handled with their hand the late
From death recovered body, [7] and partook

300 As fellow-guests of food therewith, as they
    Themselves bear witness.
        Him did PAUL as well
(Forechosen apostle, and in due time sent),
When rapt into the heavens, [8] behold : and
    sent
By Him, he, with his comrade BARNABAS,
305 And with the earlier associates
Joined in one league together, everywhere
Among the Gentiles hands the doctrine
    down
That Christ is Head, whose members are
    the Church,
He the salvation of the body, He
310 The members' life perennial ; He, made
    flesh,
He, ta'en away for all, Himself first rose
Again, salvation's only hope ; and gave
The norm to His disciples : they at once
All variously suffered, for His Name,
315 Unworthy penalties.
        Such members bears
With beauteous body the free mother, since
She never her Lord's precepts left behind,
And in His home hath grown old, to her
    Lord
Ever most choice, having for His Name's
    sake
320 Penalties suffered. For since, barren once,
Not yet secure of her futurity,
She hath outgiven a people born of seed
Celestial, and [9] been spurned, and borne the
    spleen [10]
Of her own handmaid ; now 'tis time to see
325 This former-barren mother have a son
The heir of her own liberty ; not like
The *handmaid's* heir, yoked in *estate* to *her*,
Although she bare him from celestial seed
Conceived. Far be it that ye should with
    words
330 Unlawful, with rash voice, collectively
Without distinction, give men exemplary
(Heaven's glowing constellations, to the mass
Of men conjoined by seed alone or blood),
The rugged bondman's [11] name ; or that one
    think
335 That he may speak in servile style about
A People who the mandates followèd
Of the Lord's Law. No : but we mean the
    troop
Of sinners, empty, mindless, who have placed
God's promises in a mistrustful heart ;

---

[1] For "servat*is*que palam cunctis in pace quievit," which the edd. give, I suggest "servat*us*que," etc., and take "palam" for governing "cunctis."

[2] Ignibus et *multa* consumpta volumina vatum. *Multa* must, apparently, be an error for some word signifying "mould" or the like ; unless, with the disregard of construction and quantity observable in this author, it be an *acc. pl.* to agree with *volumina*, so that we must take "*omnia multa volumina*" together, which would alter the whole construction of the context.

[3] Ablutor.

[4] Juventus.

[5] Mundo.

[6] Salutem = Christum. So Simeon, "Mine eyes have seen *Thy salvation*," where the Greek word should be noted and compared with its usage in the LXX., especially in the Psalms. See Luke ii. 30.

[7] Comp. 1 John i. 1, 2.

---

[8] See 2 Cor. xii. 1 sqq.

[9] The common reading is, "Atque suæ famulæ porta*vit* spretæ dolorem," for which Oehler reads "porta*rit* ;" but I incline rather to suggest that "porta*vit*" be retained, but that the "a*t*que" be changed into "a*e*que," thus : "A*e*que suæ famulæ porta*vit* spretæ dolorem ; " i.e., Since, like Sarah, the once barren Christian church-mother hath had children, *equally*, like Sarah, hath she had to bear scorn and spleen at her handmaid's — the Jewish church-mother's — hands.

[10] Dolorem.

[11] i.e., Ishmael's.

340 Men vanquisht by the miserable sweet
Of present life : that troop would have been
bound
Capital slavery to undergo,
By their own fault, if sin's cause shall impose
Law's yoke upon the mass. For to serve
God,
345 And be whole-heartedly intent thereon,
Untainted faith, and freedom, is thereto
Prepared spontaneous.
The just fathers, then,
And holy stainless prophets, many, sang
The future advent of the Lord ; and they
350 Faithfully testify what Heaven bids
To men profane : with them the giants,[1] men
With Christ's own glory satiated, made
The consorts of His virtue, filling up
The hallowed words, have stablishèd our
faith ;
355 By facts predictions proving.
Of these men
Disciples who succeeded them throughout
The orb, men wholly filled with virtue's
breath,
And our own masters, have assigned to us
Honours conjoined with works.
Of whom the first
360 Whom PETER bade to take his place and sit
Upon this chair in mightiest Rome where he
Himself had sat,[2] was LINUS, great, elect,
And by the mass approved. And after him
CLETUS himself the fold's flock undertook ;
365 As his successor ANACLETUS was
By lot located : CLEMENT follows him ;
Well known was he to apostolic men :[3]
Next EVARISTUS ruled without a crime
The law.[4] To SIXTUS SEXTUS ALEXANDER
370 Commends the fold : who, after he had filled
His lustral times up, to TELESPHORUS
Hands it in order : excellent was he,
And martyr faithful. After him succeeds
A comrade in the law,[5] and master sure :
375 When lo ! the comrade of your wickedness,
Its author and forerunner — Cerdo hight —
Arrived at Rome, smarting with recent
wounds :
Detected, for that he was scattering
Voices and words of venom stealthily :
380 For which cause, driven from the band, he
bore
This sacrilegious brood, the dragon's breath

Engendering it. Blooming in piety
United stood the Church of Rome, compact
By PETER : whose successor, too, himself,
385 And now in the ninth place, HYGINUS was,
The burden undertaking of his chair.
After him followed PIUS — HERMAS his
Own brother[6] was ; angelic " Pastor " he,
Because he spake the words delivered him :[7]
390 And ANICETUS[8] the allotted post
In pious order undertook. 'Neath whom
Marcion here coming, the new Pontic pest,
(The secret daring deed in his own heart
Not yet disclosed,) went, speaking commonly,
395 In all directions, in his perfidy,
With lurking art. But after he began
His deadly arrows to produce, cast off
Deservedly (as author of a crime
So savage), reprobated by the saints,
400 He burst, a wondrous monster ! on our view.

BOOK IV.

OF MARCION'S ANTITHESES.[9]

What the Inviolable Power bids
The youthful people,[10] which, rich, free, and
heir,
Possesses an eternal hope of praise
(By right assigned) is this : that with great
zeal
5 Burning, armed with the love of peace — yet
not
As teachers (Christ alone doth all things
teach[11]),
But as Christ's household-servants — o'er the
earth
They should conduct a massive war ;[12] should
raze
The wicked's lofty towers, savage walls,
10 And threats which 'gainst the holy people's
bands
Rise, and dissolve such empty sounds in air.
Wherefore we, justly speaking emulous words,[13]
Out of his[14] own words even strive to express
The meaning of salvation's records,[15] which
15 Large grace hath poured profusely ; and to
ope

---

1 " Immanes," if it be the true reading.
2 This is the way Oehler's punctuation reads. Migne's reads as
follows : —
. . . " Of whom the first
Whom mightiest Rome bade take his place and sit
Upon the chair where Peter's self had sat," etc.
3 " Is apostolicis bene notus." This may mean, (a) as in our
text ; (b) by his apostolically-minded writings — writings like an
apostle's ; or (c) by the apostolic writings, i.e., by the mention made
of him, supposing him to be the same, in Phil. iv. 3.
4 Legem.
5 Legis.

6 Germine frater.
7 An allusion to the well-known Pastor or Shepherd of Hermas.
8 Our author makes the name Anicētus. Rig. (as quoted by
Oehler) observes that a comparison of the list of bishops of Rome
here given with that given by Tertullian in de Præscr., c. xxxii.,
seems to show that this metrical piece cannot be his.
9 The state of the text in some parts of this book is frightful. It
has been almost hopeless to extract any sense whatever out of the
Latin in many passages — indeed, the renderings are in these cases
little better than guess-work — and the confusion of images, ideas,
and quotations is extraordinary.
10 See the preceding book.
11 I have changed the unintelligible " daret " of the edd into
" docet." The reference seems to be to Matt. xxiii. 8 ; Jas. iii. 1 ;
1 Pet. v. 2, 3.
12 Molem belli deducere terræ.
13 Æmulamenta. Migne seems to think the word refers to Marcion's " Antitheses."
14 i.e., apparently Marcion's.
15 Monumenta.

To the saints' eyes the Bandit's [1] covert
  plague :
Lest any untrained, daring, ignorant,
Fall therein unawares, and (being caught)
Forfeit celestial gifts.
             GOD, then, is ONE
20 To mortals all and everywhere ; a Realm
Eternal, Origin of light profound ;
Life's Fount ; a Draught fraught [2] with all
  wisdom. HE
Produced the orb whose bosom all things
  girds ;
HIM not a region, not a place, includes
25 In circuit : matter none perennial is, [3]
So as to be self-made, or to have been
Ever, created by no Maker : heaven's,
Earth's, sea's, and the abyss's [4] Settler [5] is
The Spirit ; air's Divider, Builder, Author,
30 Sole God perpetual, Power immense, is He. [6]
HIM had the Law the People [7] shown to be
ONE GOD, [8] whose mighty voice to Moses
  spake
Upon the mount. Him this His Virtue, too,
His Wisdom, Glory, Word, and Son, this
  Light
35 Begotten from the Light immense, [9] proclaims
Through the seers' voices, to be One : and
  Paul, [10]
Taking the theme in order up, thus too
Himself delivers ; " Father there is One [11]
Through whom were all things made : Christ
  One, through whom
40 God all things made ; " [12] to whom he plainly
  owns
That every knee doth bow itself ; [13] of whom
Is every fatherhood [14] in heaven and earth
Called : who is zealous with the highest love
Of parent-care His people-ward ; and wills
45 All flesh to live in holy wise, and wills
His people to appear before Him pure
Without a crime. With such zeal, by a law [15]
Guards He our safety ; warns us *loyal* be ;
Chastens ; is instant. So, too, has the same
50 Apostle (when Galatian brethren

Chiding)—Paul—written that such zeal hath
  he. [16]
The fathers' sins God freely rendered, then,
Slaying in whelming deluge utterly
Parents alike with progeny, and e'en
55 Grandchildren in " fourth generation " [17] now
Descended from the parent-stock, when He
Has then for nearly these nine hundred years
Assisted them. Hard does the judgment
  seem ?
The sentence savage ? And in Sodom, too,
60 That the still guiltless little one unarmed
And tender should lose life : for what had e'er
The infant sinned ? What cruel thou mayst
  think,
Is parent-care's true duty. Lest misdeed
Should further grow, crime's authors He did
  quench,
65 And sinful parents' brood. But, with his sires,
The harmless infant pays not penalties
Perpetual, ignorant and not advanced
In crime : but lest he partner should become
Of adult age's guilt, death immature
70 Undid spontaneous future ills.
                Why, then,
Bids God libation to be poured to Him
With blood of sheep ? and takes so stringent
  means
By Law, that, in the People, none transgress
Erringly, threatening them with instant death
75 By stoning ? and why reprobates, again,
These gifts of theirs, and says they are to
  Him
Unwelcome, while He chides a People prest
With swarm of sin ? [18] Does He, the truthful,
  bid,
And He, the just, at the same time repel ?
80 The causes if thou seekst, cease to be moved
Erringly : for faith's cause is weightier
Than fancied reason. [19] Through a mirror [20]—
  shade
Of fulgent light ! — behold what the calf's
  blood,
The heifer's ashes, and each goat, do mean :
85 The one dismissed goes off, the other falls
A victim at the temple.
              With calf's blood
With water mixt the seer [21] (thus from on high
Bidden) besprinkled People, vessels all,
Priests, and the written volumes of the Law.
90 See here not their true hope, nor yet a mere
Semblance devoid of virtue ; [22] but behold

---

[1] See the opening of the preceding book.
[2] "Conditus;" i.e., probably (in violation of quantity) the past part. of " condio" = flavoured, seasoned.
[3] I have altered the punctuation here.
[4] Inferni.
[5] Locator.
[6] These lines are capable, according to their punctuation, of various renderings, which for brevity's sake I must be content to omit.
[7] i.e., the People of Israel. See the *de Idol.*, p. 148, c. v. note 1.
[8] See Deut. vi. 3, 4, quoted in Mark xii. 29, 30.
[9] This savours of the Nicene Creed.
[10] Migne's pointing is followed, in preference to Oehler's.
[11] "Unum hunc esse Patrem;" i.e., "that *this One* (God) is the Father." But I rather incline to read, " un*umque* esse; " or we may render, " This One is the Sire."
[12] See 1 Cor. viii. 5, 6 (but notice the prepositions in the Greek; our author is not accurate in rendering them); Eph. iv. 4, 5, 6.
[13] Se curvare se curvabo genu plane omne fatetur. The reference is to Phil. ii. 10; but our author is careless in using the present tense, " se curvare."
[14] The reference is to Eph. iii. 14, 15; but here again our author seems in error, as he refers the words to *Christ*, whereas the meaning of the apostle appears clearly to refer them to *the Father*.
[15] Legitimos. See book iv. 91.

[16] See Gal. iii. 20. But here, again, "Galatas" seems rather like an error; for in speaking to the *Corinthians* St. Paul uses an expression more like our author's: see 2 Cor. xi. 2. The Latin, too, is faulty: " Talem *se* Paulus zelum *se* scripsit habere," where, perhaps, for the first " se" we should read " *sic*."
[17] Comp. Ex. xx. 5; Deut. v. 9.
[18] See Isa. i. 10-15; Jer. vi. 20.
[19] Causa etenim fidei rationis imagine major.
[20] Comp. 1 Cor. xiii. 12; Heb. x. 1.
[21] Moses. See Heb. ix. 19-22, and the references there.
[22] Comp. Heb. ix. 13.

In the calf's type CHRIST destined *bodily*
To suffer; who upon His shoulders bare
The plough-beam's hard yokes,[1] and with fortitude
95 Brake His own heart with the steel share, and poured
Into the furrows water of His own
Life's blood. For these "temple-vessels" do
Denote our bodies: God's true temple[2] He,
Not dedicated erst; for to Himself
100 He by His blood associated men,
And willed them be His body's priests, Himself
The Supreme Father's perfect Priest by right.
Hearing, sight, step inert, He cleansed; and, for a "book,"[3]
Sprinkled, by speaking[4] words of presage, those
105 His witnesses: demonstrating the Law
Bound by His holy blood.
This cause withal
Our victim through "*the heifer*" manifests
From whose blood taking for the People's sake
Piacular drops, them the first Levite[5] bare
110 Within the veil; and, by God's bidding, burned
Her corse without the camp's gates; with whose ash
He cleansed lapsed bodies.
Thus our Lord (who us
By His own death redeemed), without the camp[6]
Willingly suffering the violence
115 Of an iniquitous People, did fulfil
The Law, by facts predictions proving;[7] who
A people of contamination full
Doth truly cleanse, conceding all things, as
The body's Author rich; within heaven's veil
120 Gone with the blood which. — One for many's deaths —
He hath outpoured.
A holy victim, then,
Is meet for a great priest; which worthily
He, being perfect, may be proved to have,
And offer. He *a body* hath: this is
125 For mortals a live victim; worthy this

Of great price did He offer, One for all.
The [8] semblance of the "goats" teaches that they
Are men exiled out of the "peoples twain"[9]
As barren;[10] fruitless both; (of whom the Lord
130 Spake also, in the Gospel, telling how
The kids are severed from the sheep, and stand
On the left hand[11]) : that some indeed there are
Who for the Lord's Name's sake have suffered: thus
That fruit has veiled their former barrenness:
135 And such, the prophet teaches, on the ground
Of that their final merit worthy are
Of the Lord's altar: others, cast away
(As was th' iniquitous rich man, we read,
By Lazarus[12]), are such as have remained
140 Exiled, persistent in their stubbornness.
Now a veil, hanging in the midst, did both
Dissever,[13] and had into portions twain
Divided the one shrine.[14] The inner parts
Were called "Holies of holies." Stationed there
145 An altar shone, noble with gold; and there,
At the same time, the testaments and ark
Of the Law's tablets; covered wholly o'er
With lambs' skins[15] dyed with heaven's hue; within
Gold-clad;[16] and all between of wood. Here are
150 The tablets of the Law; here is the urn
Replete with manna; here is Aaron's rod
Which puts forth germens of the cross[17] — unlike

---

[1] Alluding probably to our Lord's bearing of the *cross-beam* of His *cross* — the beam being the "yokes," and the upright stem of the cross the "plough-beam" — on His shoulders. — See John xix. 17.

[2] Templum. Comp. John ii. 19-22; Col. ii. 9.

[3] Libro. The reference is to the preceding lines, especially 89, and Heb. ix. 19, αὐτὸ τὸ βιβλίον. The use of "libro" is curious, as it seems to be used partly as if it would be equivalent to *pro libro*, "in the place of a book," partly in a more truly dative sense, "to serve the purposes of a book;" and our "for" is capable of the two senses.

[4] For this comparison of "speaking" to "sprinkling," comp. Deut. xxxii. 2, "My *doctrine shall drop as the rain; my speech shall distil as the dew*," etc.; Job xxix. 22, "My *speech dropped* upon them;" with Eph. v. 26, and with our Lord's significant action (recorded in the passage here alluded to, John xx. 22) of "*breathing on*" (ἐνεφύσησεν) His disciples. Comp., too, for the "witnesses" and "words of presage," Luke xxiv. 48, 49; Acts i. 6-8.

[5] i.e., the chief of the Levites, the high priest.

[6] Comp. Heb. xiii. 12, 13; John xix. 19, 20.

[7] Comp. the preceding book, 355.

[8] The passage which follows is almost unintelligible. The sense which I have offered in my text is so offered with great diffidence, as I am far from certain of having hit the meaning; indeed, the state of the text is such, that *any* meaning must be a matter of some uncertainty.

[9] i.e., perhaps the Jewish and Christian peoples. Comp. *adv. Jud.*, c. 1.

[10] i.e., "barren" of faith and good works The "goats" being but "kids" (see Lev. xvi. 8), would, of course, be barren. "Exiled" seems to mean "excommunicated." But the comparison of the sacrificed goat to a penitent, and of the scapegoat to an impenitent, excommunicate, is extravagant. Yet I see no other sense.

[11] See Matt. xxv. 31-33.

[12] i e., Lazarus was not allowed to help him. In that sense he may be said to have been "cast away;" but it is Abraham, not Lazarus, who pronounces his doom. See Luke xvi. 19-31.

[13] i.e., in that the blood of the one was brought within the veil; the other was not.

[14] Ædem.

[15] The meaning seems to be, that *the ark*, when it had to be removed from place to place, had (as we learn from Num. iv. 5) to be covered with "the second veil" (as it is called in Heb. ix. 3), which was "of blue," etc. But that this veil was made "of lambs' skins" does not appear; on the contrary, it was made of "linen." The *outer* veil, indeed (not the out*most*, which was of "badgers' skins," according to the Eng. ver.; but of "ὑακίνθινα δέρματα" — of what material is not said — according to the LXX.), *was* made "of rams' skins;" but then they were "dyed *red*" (ἠρυθροδανωμένα, LXX.), not "*blue*." So there is some confusion in our author.

[16] The ark was overlaid with gold *without* as well as within. (See Ex. xxv. 10, 11, xxxvii. 1, 2; and this is referred to in Heb. ix. 3, 4 — κιβωτὸν . . . περικεκαλυμμένην πάντοθεν χρυσίῳ — where our Eng. ver. rendering is defective, and in the context as well.) This, however, may be said to be implied in the following words: "and *all between*," i.e., between the layers above and beneath, "of wood."

[17] Migne supposes some error in these words. Certainly the sense is dark enough; but see lower down.

The cross itself, yet born of storax-tree [1] —
And over it — in uniformity
155 Fourfold — the cherubim their pinions spread,
And the inviolable sanctities [2]
Covered obediently.[3]   Without the veil
Part of the shrine stood open : facing it,
Heavy with broad brass, did an altar stand ;
160 And with two triple sets (on each side one)
Of branches woven with the central stem,
A lampstand, and as many [4] lamps :
The golden substance wholly filled with light
The temple.[5]
                 Thus the temple's outer face,
165 Common and open, does the ritual
Denote, then, of a people lingering
Beneath the Law ; amid whose [6] gloom there
shone
The Holy Spirit's sevenfold unity
Ever, the People sheltering.[7]   And thus
170 The Lampstand True and living Lamps do
shine
Persistently throughout the Law and Seers
On men subdued in heart.   And for a type
Of earth,[8] the altar — so tradition says —
Was made.   Here constantly, in open space,
175 Before all eyes were visible of old
The People's "works," [9] which ever — "not
without
Blood" [10] — it did offer, shedding out the gore
Of lawless life.[11]   There, too, the Lord —
Himself
Made victim on behalf of all — denotes
180 The whole earth [12] — altar in specific sense.
Hence likewise that new covenant author,
whom
No language can describe, Disciple John,
Testifies that beneath such altar he
Saw souls which had for Christ's name suf-
ferèd,
185 Praying the vengeance of the mighty God
Upon their slaughter.[13]   There,[14] meantime, is
rest.
   In some unknown part there exists a spot
Open, enjoying its own light ; 'tis called
"Abraham's bosom ; " high above the
glooms,[15]

190 And far removed from fire, yet 'neath the
earth.[16]
The brazen altar this is called, whereon
(We have recorded) was a dusky veil.[17]
This veil divides both parts, and leaves the
one
Open, from the eternal one distinct
195 In worship and time's usage.   To itself
'Tis not unfriendly, though of fainter love,
By time and space divided, and yet linked
By reason.   'Tis one house, though by a veil
Parted it seems : and thus (when the veil
burst,
200 On the Lord's passion) heavenly regions
oped
And holy vaults,[18] and what was double erst
Became one house perennial.
                                 Order due
Traditionally has interpreted
The inner temple of the people called
205 After Christ's Name, with worship heavenly,
God's actual mandates following ; (no
"shade " . .
Is herein bound, but persons real ; [19]) com-
plete
By the arrival of the "perfect things." [20]
The ark beneath a type points out to us
210 Christ's venerable body, joined, through
"wood," [21]
With sacred Spirit : the aërial [22] skins
Are flesh not born of seed, outstretcht on
"wood ; " [23]
At the same time, with golden semblance
fused,[24]
Within, the glowing Spirit joinèd is
215 Thereto ; that, with peace [25] granted, flesh
might bloom
With Spirit mixt.   Of the Lord's flesh, again,
The urn, golden and full, a type doth bear.
Itself denotes that the new covenant's Lord
Is manna ; in that He, true heavenly Bread,
220 Is, and hath by the Father been transfused [26]
Into that bread which He hath to His saints

---

1 It yielded "almonds," according to the Eng. ver. (Num. xvii. 8).   But see the LXX.
2 Sagmina.   But the word is a very strange one to use indeed. See the Latin Lexicons, s.v.
3 It might be questionable whether "jussa" refers to "cherubim" or to "sagmina."
4 i.e., twice three+the central one=7.
5 Our author persists in calling the tabernacle temple.
6 i.e., the Law's.
7 "Tegebat," i.e., with the "fiery-cloudy pillar," unless it be an error for "regebat," which still might apply to the pillar.
8 Terræ.
9 "Operæ," i.e., sacrifices.   The Latin is a hopeless jumble of words without grammatical sequence, and any rendering is mere guess-work.
10 Heb. ix. 7.
11 i.e., of animals which, as irrational, were "without the Law."
12 Terram.
13 Rev. vi. 9, 10.
14 i.e., beneath the altar.   See the 11th verse ib.
15 Or possibly, "deeper than the glooms : " "altior a tenebris."

16 Terra.
17 See 141, 142, above.
18 Cælataque sancta.   We might conjecture "celataque sancta," == " and the sanctuaries formerly hidden."
19 This sense appears intelligible, as the writer's aim seems to be to distinguish between the "actual" commands of God, i.e., the spiritual, essential ones, which the spiritual people "follow," and which " bind " — not the ceremonial observance of a "shadow of the future blessings" (see Heb. x. 1), but "real persons," i.e., living souls.   But, as Migne has said, the passage is probably faulty and mutilated.
20 Comp. Heb. vii. 19, x. 1, ix. 11, 12.
21 "Lignum : " here probably = " the flesh," which He took from Mary ; the "rod" (according to our author) which Isaiah had foretold.
22 Aërial, i.e., as he said above, "dyed with heaven's hue."
23 "Ligno," i.e., "the cross," represented by the "wood" of which the tabernacle's boards, on which the coverings were stretched (but comp. 147-8, above), were made.
24 As the flame of the lamps appeared to grow out of and be fused with the "golden semblance " or "form" of the lampstand or candle-stick.
25 Of which the olive — of which the pure oil for the lamps was to be made : Ex. xxvii. 20 ; Lev. xxiv. 2 — is a type.   "Peace" is granted to "the flesh" through Christ's work and death in flesh.
26 Traditus.

Assignèd for a pledge : this Bread will He
Give perfectly to them who (of good works
The lovers ever) have the bonds of peace
225 Kept.   And *the double tablets of the Law
Written all over*, these, at the same time,
Signify that that Law was ever hid
In Christ, who mandate old and new ful-
    filled,
Ark of the Supreme Father as He is,
230 Through whom He, being rich, hath all things
    given.
The *storax-rod*, too, nut's fruit bare itself ;
(The virgin's semblance this, who bare in
    blood
A body :) on the " wood " [1] conjoined 'twill
    lull
Death's bitter, which within sweet fruit doth
    lurk,
235 By virtue of the Holy Spirit's grace :
Just as Isaiah did predict " a rod "
From Jesse's seed [2] — Mary — from which a
    flower
Issues into the orb.
                    The *altar bright with gold*
Denotes the heaven on high, whither ascend
240 Prayers holy, sent up without crime : the
    Lord
This " altar " spake of, where if one doth gifts
Offer, he must first reconciliate
Peace with his brother : [3] thus at length his
    prayers
Can flame unto the stars.   Christ, Victor sole
245 And foremost [4] Priest, thus offered *incense*
    born
Not of a *tree*, but prayers.[5]
                    The *cherubim* [6]
Being, with twice two countenances, one,
And are the one word through fourfold order
    led ; [7]
The hopèd comforts of life's mandate new,
250 Which in their plenitude Christ bare Himself
Unto us from the Father.   But the *wings*
In number *four times six*,[8] the heraldings
Of the old world denote, witnessing things
Which, we are taught, were after done.   On
    these [9]
255 The heavenly words fly through the orb :
    with these

Christ's blood is likewise held contèxt, so
    told
Obscurely by the seers' presaging mouth.
The *number* of the wings doth set a seal
Upon the ancient volumes ; teaching us
260 Those *twenty-four* have certainly enough
Which sang the Lord's ways and the times
    of peace :
These all, we see, with the new covenant
Cohere.   Thus also John ; the Spirit thus
To him reveals that in that number stand
265 The enthroned elders white [10] and crowned,
    who (as
With girding-rope) all things surround, be-
    fore
The Lord's throne, and upon the glassy sea
Subigneous : and four living creatures, winged
And full of eyes within and outwardly,
270 Do signify that hidden things are oped,
And all things shut are at the same time seen,
In the word's eye.   The glassy flame-mixt
    sea
Means that the laver's gifts, with Spirit fused
Therein, upon believers are conferred.
275 Who could e'en tell what the Lord's parent-
    care
Before His judgment-seat, before His bar,
Preparèd hath ? that such as willing be
His forum and His judgment for themselves
To antedate, should 'scape ! that who thus
    hastes
280 Might find abundant opportunity !
        Thus   therefore   Law   and   wondrous
        prophets sang ;
Thus all parts of the covenant old and new,
Those sacred rights and pregnant utterances
Of words, conjoined, do flourish.   Thus
    withal,
285 Apostles' voices witness everywhere ;
Nor aught of old, in fine, but to the new
Is joined.
            Thus err they, and thus facts retort
Their sayings, who to false ways have de-
    clined ;
And from the Lord and God, eternal King,
290 Who such an orb produced, detract, and
    seek
Some other deity 'neath feignèd name,
Bereft of minds, which (frenzied) they have
    lost ;
Willing to affirm that Christ a stranger is
To the Law ; nor is the world's [11] Lord ; nor
    doth will
295 Salvation of the flesh ; nor was Himself
The body's Maker, by the Father's power.[12]

---

[1] In ligno.   The passage is again in an almost desperate state.
[2] Isa. xi. 1, 2.
[3] Matt. v. 23, 24.
[4] Primus.
[5] See Rev. viii. 3, 4.
[6] Here ensues a confused medley of all the cherubic figures of
Moses, Ezekiel, and St. John.
[7] i.e., by the four evangelists.
[8] The cherubim, (or " seraphim" rather,) of Isa. vi. have each
six wings. Ezekiel mentions *four* cherubim, or " living creatures."
St. John likewise mentions *four* " living creatures." Our author,
combining the passages, and thrusting them into the subject of the
Mosaic cherubim, multiplies the *six* (wings) by the *four* (cherubs),
and so attains his end — the desired number " *twenty-four* " — to
represent the books of the Old Testament, which (by combining
certain books) may be reckoned to be *twenty-four* in number.
[9] These wings.

[10] There is again some great confusion in the text. The elders
could not " *stand enthroned :*" nor do they stand " *over*," but
" *around*" God's throne; so that the " insuper solio " could not apply
to that.
[11] Mundi.
[12] Virtute.

Them must we flee, stopping (unasked) our
    ears ;
Lest with their speech they stain innoxious
    hearts.
Let therefore us, whom so great grace [1] of
    God
300 Hath penetrated, and the true celestial words
Of the great Master-Teacher in good ways
Have trained, and given us right monu-
    ments ; [2]
Pay honour ever to the Lord, and sing
Endlessly, joying in pure faith, and sure
305 Salvation. Born of the true God, with bread
Perennial are we nourishèd, and hope
With our whole heart after eternal life.

BOOK V.

GENERAL REPLY TO SUNDRY OF MARCION'S HERESIES.[3]

The *first* Book did the enemy's words recall
In order, which the senseless renegade
Composed and put forth lawlessly ; hence,
    too,
Touched briefly flesh's hope, Christ's victory,
5 And false ways' speciousness. The *next* doth
    teach
The Law's conjoinèd mysteries, and what
In the new covenant the one God hath
Delivered. The *third* shows the race, create
From freeborn mother, to be ministers
10 Sacred to seers and patriarchs ; [4] whom Thou,
O Christ, in number twice six out of all,[5]
Chosest ; and, with their names, the lustral [6]
    times
Of our own elders noted, (times preserved
On record,) showing in whose days appeared
15 The author [7] of this wickedness, unknown,
Lawless, and roaming, cast forth [8] with his
    brood.
The *fourth*, too, the piacular rites recalls
Of the old Law themselves, and shows them
    types
In which the Victim True appeared, by saints
20 Expected long since, with the holy Seed.
This *fifth* doth many twists and knots untie,
Rolls wholly into sight what ills soe'er

Were lurking ; drawing arguments, but not
Without attesting prophet.
                 And although
25 With strong arms fortified we vanquish foes,
Yet hath the serpent mingled so at once
All things polluted, impious, unallowed,
Commaculate, — the blind's path without
    light !
A voice contaminant ! — that, all the while
30 We are contending the world's Maker is
Himself sole God, who also spake by voice
Of seers, and proving that there is none else
Unknown ; and, while pursuing Him with
    praise,
Who is by various endearment [9] known,
35 Are blaming — among other fallacies —
The Unknown's tardy times : our subject's
    fault
Will scarce keep pure our tongue. Yet, for
    all that,
Guile's many hidden venoms us enforce
(Although with double risk [10]) to ope our
    words.
40 Who, then, the God whom ye say is the true,
Unknown to peoples, alien, in a word,
To all the world ? [11] Him whom none knew
    before ?
Came he from high ? If 'tis his own [12] he
    seeks,
Why seek so late ? If not his own, why rob
45 Bandit-like ? and why ply with words un-
    known
So oft throughout Law's rein a People still
Lingering 'neath the Law ? If, too, he comes
To pity and to succour all combined,
And to re-elevate men vanquisht quite
50 By death's funereal weight, and to release
Spirit from flesh's bond obscene, whereby
The inner man (iniquitously dwarfed)
Is held in check ; why, then, so late appear
His ever-kindness, duteous vigilance ?
55 How comes it that he ne'er at all before
Offered himself to any, but let slip
Poor souls in numbers ? [13] and then with his
    mouth
Seeks to regain another's subjects : ne'er
Expected ; not known ; sent into the orb.
60 Seeking the " ewe " he had not lost before,
The Shepherd ought [14] to have disrobed him-
    self
Of flesh, as if his victor-self withal
Had ever been a spirit, and as such [15]
Willèd to rescue all expellèd souls,

---

[1] Honestas.
[2] Or, " records:" " monumenta," i.e., the written word, according to the canon.
[3] I make no apology for the ruggedness of the versification and the obscurity of the sense in this book, further than to say that the state of the Latin text is such as to render it almost impossible to find any sense at all in many places, while the grammar and metre are not reducible to any known laws. It is about the hardest and most uninteresting book of the five.
[4] Or, " consecrated by seers and patriarchs."
[5] i.e., all the number of Thy disciples.
[6] Tempora lustri, i.e., apparently the times during which these "elders " (i.e., the bishops, of whom a list is given at the end of book iii.) held office. " Lustrum " is used of other periods than it strictly implies, and this seems to give some sense to this difficult passage.
[7] i.e., Marcion.
[8] i.e., excommunicated.

[9] Complexu vario.
[10] Ancipiti quamquam cum crimine. The last word seems almost = "*dis*crimine;" just as our author uses " cerno " = " *dis*cerno."
[11] Mundo.
[12] Cf. John i. 11, and see the Greek.
[13] Whether this be the sense I know not. The passage is a mass of confusion.
[14] i.e., according to Marcion's *view*.
[15] i.e, as spirits, like himself.

65 Without a body, everywhere, and leave
   The spoilèd flesh to earth ; wholly to fill
   The world[1] on one day equally with corpses
   To leave the orb void ; and to raise the souls
   To heaven.   Then would human progeny
70 At once have ceasèd to be born ; nor had
   Thereafter any scion of *your*[2] kith
   Been born, or spread a new pest[3] o'er the orb.
   Or (since at that time[4] none of all these
       things
   Is shown to have been done) he should have
       set
75 A bound to future race ; with solid heart
   Nuptial embraces would he, in that case,
   Have sated quite ;[5] made men grow torpid,
       reft
   Of fruitful seed ; made irksome intercourse
   With female sex ; and closed up inwardly
80 The flesh's organs genital : our mind
   Had had no will, no potent faculty
   Our body : after this the " inner man "
   Could withal, joined with blood,[6] have been
       infused
   And cleaved to flesh, and would have ever
       been
85 Perishing.   Ever perishes the " ewe : "
   And is there then no power of saving her ?
   Since man is ever being born beneath
   Death's doom, what is the Shepherd's work,
       if thus
   The " ewe " is stated[7] to be found ?   *Un-
       sought,*
90 In that case, but not *rescued,* she is proved.
   But now choice is allowed of entering
   Wedlock, as hath been ever ; and that choice
   Sure progeny hath yoked : nations are born
   And folk scarce numerable, at whose birth
95 Their souls by living bodies are received ;
   Nor was it meet that Paul (though, for the
       time,
   He did exhort some few, discerning well
   The many pressures of a straitened time)
   To counsel men in like case to abide
100 As he himself :[8] for elsewhere he has bidden

The tender ages marry, nor defraud
Each other, but their compact's dues dis-
    charge.
But say, whose suasion hath, with fraud astute,
Made you " abide," and in divided love
105 Of offspring live secure, and commit crime
Adulterous, and lose your life ? and, though
'Tis perishing, belie (by verbal name)
That fact.   For which cause all the so sweet
    sounds
Of his voice pours he forth, that " you must
    do,
110 Undaunted, whatsoever pleases you ; "
Outwardly chaste, stealthily stained with
    crime !
Of honourable wedlock, by this plea,[9]
He hath deprived you.   But why more ?   'Tis
    well
(Forsooth) to be disjoined ! for the world,
    too,
115 Expedient 'tis ! lest any of *your* seed
Be born !   Then will death's organs [10] cease
    at length !
   The while you hope salvation to retain,
Your " total man " quite loses part of man,
With mind profane : but neither is man said
120 To be *sole spirit,* nor the *flesh* is called
" The old man ; " nor unfriendly are the flesh
And spirit, the *true man* combined in one,
The *inner,* and he whom you call " *old
    foe ;* " [11]
Nor are they seen to have each his own set
125 Of senses.   One is ruled ; the other rules,
Groans, joys, grieves, loves ; himself [12] to his
    own flesh
Most dear, too ; *through* which [13] his human-
    ity
Is visible, *with* which commixt he is
Held ever : to its wounds he care applies ;
130 And pours forth tears ; and nutriments of
    food
Takes, through its limbs, often and eagerly :
This hopes he to have ever with himself
Immortal ; o'er its fracture doth he groan ;
And grieves to quit it limb by limb : fixt time
135 Death lords it o'er the unhappy flesh ; that
    so
From light dust it may be renewed, and
    death
Unfriendly fail at length, when flesh, released,
Rises again.   This will that victory be
Supreme and long expected, wrought by
    Him,
140 The aye-to-be-revered, who did become

---

[1] Mundum.
[2] i.e., Marcionite.
[3] See book ii. 3.
[4] i.e., apparently on the day of Christ's resurrection.
[5] Rep*l*esset, i.e., replevisset.   If this be the right reading, the meaning would seem to be, " would have taken away all further desire for" them, as satiety or *repletion* takes away all appetite for food.   One is almost inclined to hazard the suggestion " rep*r*esset," i.e., repressisset, " he would have *repressed,*" but that such a contraction would be irregular.   Yet, with an author who takes such liberties as the present one, perhaps that might not be a decisive objection.
[6] " Junct*us,*" for the edd.'s " junct*is,*" which, if retained, will mean " in the case of beings still joined with (or to) blood."
[7] " Doc*e*tur," for the edd.'s " doc*e*ntur."   The sense seems to be, if there be any, exceedingly obscure; but for the idea of a half-salvation — the salvation of the " inner man " without the outer — being no salvation at all, and unworthy of " the Good Shepherd " and His work, we may compare the very difficult passage in the *de Pudic.,* c. xiii. *ad fin.*
[8] This sense, which I deduce from a transposition of one line and the supplying of the words " *he did exhort,*" which are not expressed, but seem necessary, in the original, agrees well with 1 Cor. vii., which is plainly the passage referred to.

[9] " Causa; " or perhaps " *means.*"   It is, of course, the French " chose."
[10] i.e., you and your like, through whom sin, and in consequence death, is disseminated.
[11] Here, again, for the sake of the sense, I have transposed a line.
[12] i.e., " the other," the " inner man," or spirit.
[13] i.e., through flesh.

True man ; and by His Father's virtue won :
Who man's redeemed limbs unto the heavens
Hath raised,[1] and richly opened access up
Thither in hope, first to His nation ; then
145 To those among all tongues in whom His work
Is ever doing : Minister imbued
With His Sire's parent-care, seen by the eye
Of the Illimitable, He performed,
By suffering, His missions.[2]
　　　　　　　　What say now
150 The impious voices ? what th' abandoned crew?
If He Himself, God the Creator's self,
Gave not the Law,[3] He who from Egypt's vale[4]
Paved in the waves a path, and freely gave
The seats which He had said of old, why comes
155 He in that very People and that land
Aforesaid? and why rather sought He not
Some other[5] peoples or some rival[6] realms?
Why, further, did He teach that, through the seers,
(With Name foretold in full, yet not His own,)
160 He had been often sung of ? Whence, again,
Could He have issued baptism's kindly gifts,
Promised by some one else, as His own works?
These gifts men who God's mandates had transgressed,
And hence were found polluted, longed for,
165 And begged a pardoning rescue from fierce death.
Expected long, they[7] came : but that to those
Who recognised them when erst heard, and now
Have recognised them, when in due time found,
Christ's true hand is to give them, this, with voice
170 Paternal, the Creator-Sire Himself
Warns ever from eternity, and claims ;
And thus the work of virtue which He framed,
And still frames, arms, and fosters, and doth now
Victorious look down on and reclothe
175 With His own light, should with perennial praise
Abide.[8]

What[9] hath the Living Power done
To make men recognise what God can give
And man can suffer, and thus live ?[10] But since
Neither predictions earlier nor facts
180 The latest can suade senseless frantic[11] men
That God became a man, and (after He
Had suffered and been buried) rose ; that they
May credit those so many witnesses
Harmonious,[12] who of old did cry aloud
185 With heavenly word, let them both[13] learn to trust
At least terrestrial reason.
　　　　　　　　When the Lord
Christ came to be, as flesh, born into the orb
In time of king Augustus' reign at Rome,
First, by decree, the nations numbered are
190 By census everywhere : this measure, then,
This same king chanced to pass, because the Will
Supreme, in whose high reigning hand doth lie
The king's heart, had impelled him :[14] he was first
To do it, and the enrolment was reduced
195 To orderly arrangement.　Joseph then
Likewise, with his but just delivered wife
Mary,[15] with her celestial Son alike,
Themselves withal are numbered.　Let, then, such
As trust to instruments of human skill,
200 Who may (approving of applying them
As attestators of the holy word)
Inquire into this census, if it be
But found so as we say, then afterwards
Repent they and seek pardon while time still
205 Is had.[16]

[1] i.e., in His own person.
[2] I hope I have succeeded in giving some intelligible sense; but the passage as it stands in the Latin is nearly hopeless.
[3] I read "lege*m*" for "leges."
[4] I read "*valle*" for "*calle*."
[5] Alios.
[6] Altera.
[7] i.e., "the gifts of baptism."
[8] This seems to give sense to a very obscure passage, in which I have been guided more by Migne's pointing than by Oehler's.

[9] I read here "qu*i*d" for "qu*o*d."
[10] i.e., to make men live by recognising that. Comp. the Psalmist's prayer: "Give me *understanding* and I shall *live*" (Ps. cxix. 144; in LXX., Ps. cxviii. 144).
[11] The "*furentes*" of Pam. and Rig. is preferred to Oehler's "*ferentes*."
[12] "Complexis," lit. "embracing."
[13] i.e., both Jews and Gentile heretics, the "senseless frantic men" just referred to probably: or possibly the "ambo" may mean "*both sects*," viz., the Marcionites and Manichees, against whom the writer whom Oehler supposes to be the probable author of these "Five Books," Victorinus, a rhetorician of Marseilles, directed his efforts. But it may again be the acc. neut. pl., and mean "let them"—i.e., the "senseless frantic men"—"learn to believe *as to both facts*," i.e., the incarnation and the resurrection; (see vers. 179, 180;) "the testimony at least of human reason."
[14] I would suggest here, for
　　　　" . . . quia summa voluntas
　　In cujus manu regnantis cor *legibus esset*,"
something like this,
　　　　　" . . . quia summa voluntas,
　　In cujus manu regnantis cor *regis, egisset*,"
which would only add one more to our author's false quantities. "Regum egisset" would avoid even that, while it would give some sense. Comp. Prov. xxi. 1.
[15] Maria cum conjuge feta. What follows seems to decide the meaning of "feta," as a child could hardly be included in a census before birth.
[16] Again I have had to attempt to amend the text of the Latin, in order to extract any sense, and am far from sure that I have extracted the right one.

The Jews, who own [1] to having wrought
A grave crime, while in our disparagement
They glow, and do resist us, neither call
Christ's family unknown, nor can [2] affirm
They hanged a man, who spake truth, on a
tree : [3]
210 Ignorant that the Lord's flesh which they
bound [4]
Was not seed-gendered. But, while partially
They keep a reticence, so partially
They triumph ; for they strive to represent
God to the peoples commonly as man.
215 Behold the error which o'ercomes you both ! [5]
This error will our cause assist, the while,
We prove to you those things which certain
are.
They do deny Him God ; you falsely call
Him man, a body bodiless ! and ah !
220 A various insanity of mind
Sinks you ; which him who hath presumed to
hint
You both do, sinking, sprinkle : [6] for His deeds
Will then approve Him man alike and God
Commingled, and the world [7] will furnish signs
225 No few.
            While then the Son Himself of God
Is seeking to regain the flesh's limbs, [8]
Already robed as King, He doth sustain
Blows from rude palms ; with spitting covered
is
His face ; a thorn-inwoven crown His head
230 Pierces all round ; and to the tree [9] Himself
Is fixed ; wine drugged with myrrh, [10] is drunk,
and gall [11]
Is mixt with vinegar ; parted His robe, [12]
And in it [13] lots are cast ; what for himself
Each one hath seized he keeps ; in murky
gloom,
235 As God from fleshly body silently
Outbreathes His soul, in darkness trembling
day
Took refuge with the sun ; twice dawned one
day ;

Its centre black night covered : from their base
Mounts move in circle, wholly moved was
earth,
240 Saints' sepulchres stood ope, and all things
joined
In fear to see His passion whom they knew !
His lifeless side a soldier with bare spear
Pierces, and forth flows blood, nor water less
Thence followed. These facts they [14] agree
to hide,
245 And are unwilling the misdeed to own,
Willing to blink the crime.
                          Can spirit, then,
Without a body wear a robe ? or is't
Susceptible of penalty ? the wound
Of violence does it bear ? or die ? or rise ?
250 Is blood thence poured ? from what flesh,
since ye say
He had none ? or else, rather, feigned He ? if
'Tis safe for you to say so ; though you do
(Headlong) so say, by passing over more
In silence. Is not, then, faith manifest ?
255 And are not all things fixed ? The day before
He then [15] should suffer, keeping Passover,
And handing down a memorable rite [16]
To His disciples, taking bread alike
And the vine's juice, " My body, and My
blood
260 Which is poured [17] for you, this is," did He
say ;
And bade it ever afterward be done.
Of what created elements were made,
Think ye, the bread and wine which were
(He said)
His body with its blood ? and what must be
265 Confessèd ? Proved He not Himself the
world's [18]
Maker, through deeds ? and that He bore at
once
A body formed from flesh and blood ?
                              This God,
This true Man, too, the Father's Virtue 'neath
An Image, [19] with the Father ever was,
270 United both in glory and in age ; [20]
Because alone He ministers the words
Of the All-Holder ; whom He [21] upon earth
Accepts ; [22] through whom He all things did
create :
God's Son, God's dearest Minister, is He !
275 Hence hath He generation, hence Name too,
Hence, finally, a kingdom ; Lord from Lord ;
Stream from perennial Fount ! He, He it was

---

1 " Fatentur," unless our author use it passively = " are confessed."
2 " Possunt," i.e., probably " have the hardihood."
3 Because Christ plainly, as they understood Him, " made Himself the Son of God ; " and hence, if they confessed that He had said
the truth, and yet that they hanged Him on a tree, they would be
pronouncing their own condemnation.
4 " Vinctam " for " victam " I read here.
5 i.e., you and the Jews. See above on 185.
6 Quod qui præsumpsit mergentes spargitis ambo. What the
meaning is I know not, unless it be this: if any one hints to you that
you are in an error which is sinking you into perdition, you both join
in trying to sink him (if " mergentes " be active; or " while you are
sinking," if neuter), and in sprinkling him with your doctrine (or be-
sprinkling him with abuse).
7 Mundus.
8 " Dum carnis membra requirit," i.e., seeking to regain for God
all the limbs of the flesh as His instruments. Comp. Rom. vi. 13, 19.
9 Ligno.
10 " Scriblita," a curious word.
11 Fel miscetur aceto. The reading may have arisen — and it is
not confined to our author — from confounding ὄξος with οἶνος.
Comp. Matt. xxvii. 33 with Mark xv. 23.
12 This is an error, if the " coat " be meant.
13 Perhaps for " in illa " we should read " in illam " — " on it," for
" in it."

14 The Jews.
15 For " ante diem quam cum pateretur " I have read " qua tum."
16 Or, " deed " — " factum."
17 Or, " is being poured " — " funditur."
18 Mundi.
19 I read with Migne, " Patris sub imagine virtus," in preference
to the conjecture which Oehler follows, " Christi sub imagine virtus."
The reference seems clearly to be to Heb. i. 3.
20 Ævo. Perhaps here = " eternity."
21 i.e., " The All-Holder."
22 Capit.

Who to the holy fathers (whosoe'er
Among them doth profess to have "seen
God" [1])—
280 God is our witness — since the origin
Of this our world,[2] appearing, opened up
The Father's words of promise and of charge
From heaven high : He led the People out ;
Smote through th' iniquitous nation ; was
Himself
285 The column both of light and of cloud's
shade ;
And dried the sea ; and bids the People go
Right through the waves, the foe therein in-
volved
And covered with the flood and surge : a way
Through deserts made He for the followers
290 Of His high biddings ; sent down bread in
showers [3]
From heaven for the People ; brake the rock ;
Bedewed with wave the thirsty ;[4] and from
God
The mandate of the Law to Moses spake
With thunder, trumpet-sound, and flamey
column
295 Terrible to the sight, while men's hearts
shook.
After twice twenty years, with months com-
plete,
Jordan was parted ; a way oped ; the wave
Stood in a mass ; and the tribes shared the
land,
Their fathers' promised boons ! The Father's
word,
300 Speaking Himself by prophets' mouth, that
He [5]
Would come to earth and be a man, He did
Predict ; Christ manifestly to the earth
Foretelling.
            Then, expected for our aid,
Life's only Hope, the Cleanser of our flesh,[6]
305 Death's Router, from th' Almighty Sire's
empire
At length He came, and with our human
limbs
He clothed Him.   Adam — virgin — dragon
— tree,[7]

The cause of ruin, and the way whereby
Rash death us all had vanquisht ! by the same
310 Our Shepherd treading, seeking to regain
His sheep — with angel — virgin — His own
flesh —
And the "tree's" remedy ;[8] whence van-
quisht man
And doomed to perish was aye wont to go
To meet his vanquisht peers ; hence, inter-
posed,
315 ONE in all captives' room, He did sustain
In body the unfriendly penalty
With patience ; by His own death spoiling
death ;
Becomes salvation's cause ; and, having paid
Throughly our debts by throughly suffering
320 On earth, in holy body, everything,
Seeks the infern ! here souls, bound for their
crime,
Which shut up all together by Law's weight,
Without a guard,[9] were asking for the boons
Promised of old, hoped for, and tardy, He
325 To the saints' rest admitted, and, with light,
Brought back.   For on the third day mount-
ing up,[10]
A victor, with His body, by His Sire's
Virtue immense, (salvation's pathway made,)
And bearing God and man is form create,
330 He clomb the heavens, leading back with Him
Captivity's first-fruits (a welcome gift
And a dear figure [11] to the Lord), and took
His seat beside light's Father, and resumed
The virtue and the glory of which, while
335 He was engaged in vanquishing the foe,
He had been stripped ;[12] conjoined with
Spirit ; bound
With flesh, on our part.   Him, Lord, Christ,
King, God,
Judgment and kingdom given to His hand,
The father is to send unto the orb.

(N.B. — It has been impossible to note the
changes which I have had to make in the text
of the Latin.   In some cases they will suggest
themselves to any scholar who may compare the
translation with the original ; and in others I
must be content to await a more fitting opportunity, if such ever arise, for discussing them.)

---

[1] Cf. Jacob's words in Gen. xxxii. 30; Manoah's in Judg. xiii.
22; etc.
[2] Mundi.
[3] For "*di*misit in *u*mbris" I read here "*de*misit in *im*bris." If
we retain the former reading, it will then mean, "dispersed during the
shades of night," during which it was that the manna seems always to
have fallen.
[4] "Sitient*is*" in Oehler must be a misprint for "sitient*es*."
[5] There ought to be a "se" in the Latin if this be the meaning.
[6] For "Mundator carnis *seræ*" = "the Cleanser of *late* flesh"
(which would seem, if it mean anything, to mean that the flesh had
to wait long for its cleansing), I have read "carnis *nostræ*."
[7] Lignum.

[8] I have followed the disjointed style of the Latin as closely as I
could here.
[9] Here we seem to see the idea of the "limbus patrum."
[10] "Subiens" = "going beneath," i.e., apparently coming beneath
the walls of heaven.
[11] i.e., a figure of the future harvest.
[12] I have hazarded the conjecture "m*i*nutus" here for the edd.'s
"m*u*nitus."   It add's one more, it is true, to our author's false quantities, but that is a minor difficulty, while it improves (to my mind)
the sense vastly.

ELUCIDATIONS.

I.

(Appendix, p. 127.)

ABOUT these versifications, which are " poems " only as mules are horses, it is enough to say of them, with Dupin, " They are no more Tertullian's than they are Virgil's or Homer's. The poem called *Genesis* seems to be that which Gennadius attributes to Salvian, Bishop of Marseilles. That concerning the *Judgment of God* was, perhaps, composed by Verecundus, an African bishop. In the books *Against Marcion* there are some opinions different from those of Tertullian. There is likewise a poem *To a Senator* in Pamelius' edition, one of *Sodom*, and in the *Bibliotheca Patrum* one of *Jonas and Nineve;* the first of which is ancient, and the other two seem to be by the same author."

It is worth while to observe that this rhymester makes two bishops out of one.[1] Cletus and Anacletus he supposes different persons, which brings Clement into the fourth place in the see of Rome. Our author elsewhere makes St. Clement the immediate successor of the apostles.[2]

II.

(Or is there ought, etc., l. 136, p. 137.)

In taking leave of Tertullian, it may be well to say a word of his famous saying, *Certum est quia impossibile est.* It occurs in the tract *De Carne Christi,*[3] and is one of those startling epigrammatic dicta of our author which is no more to be pressed in argument than any other *bon-mot* of a wit or a poet. It is evidently designed as a rhetorical climax, to enforce the same idea which we find in the hymn of Aquinas : —

> " Et si sensus deficit,
> Ad firmandum cor sincerum
> Sola fides sufficit."

As Jeremy Taylor[4] argues, the condition is, that holy Scripture affirms it. If that be the case, then " all things are possible with God : " I believe ; but I do not argue, for it is impossible with men. This is the plain sense of the great Carthaginian doctor's pithy rhetoric. But Dr. Bunsen sets it on all-fours, and treats it as if it were soberly designed to defy reason, — that reason to which Tertullian constantly makes his appeal against Marcion, and in many of his sayings[5] hardly less witty. Speaking of Hippolytus, that writer remarks,[6] " He might have said on some points, *Credibile licet ineptum :* he would never have exclaimed with Tertullian, ' Credibile *quia* ineptum.' " Why attempt to prove the absurdity of such a reflection? As well attempt to defend St. John's hyperbole[7] against a mind incapable of comprehending a figure of speech.

---

[1] See p. 156, *supra.*
[2] See *De Præscrip.*, cap. xxxii. vol. iii. p. 258.
[3] Cap. v. vol. iii. p. 525.

[4] *Christ in the Holy Sacrament*, § xi. 6.
[5] *De Anima*, cap. xvii.
[6] Vol. i. p. 304.

[7] Chap. xxi. verse 25.

MINUCIUS FELIX.

[TRANSLATED BY THE REV. ROBERT ERNEST WALLIS, Ph.D.]

INTRODUCTORY NOTE

TO

MINUCIUS FELIX.

[A.D. 210.]   Though Tertullian is the founder of Latin Christianity, his contemporary Minucius Felix gives to Christian thought its earliest clothing in Latinity.   The harshness and provincialism, with the *Græcisms*, if not the mere *Tertullianism*, of Tertullian, deprive him of high claims to be classed among Latin writers, as such; but in Minucius we find, at the very fountain-head of Christian Latinity, a disciple of Cicero and a precursor of Lactantius in the graces of style.   The question of his originality is earnestly debated among moderns, as it was in some degree with the ancients.   It turns upon the doubt as to his place with respect to Tertullian, whose *Apology* he seems to quote, or rather to abridge.   But to me it seems evident that his argument reflects so strikingly that of Tertullian's *Testimony of the Soul*, coincident though it be with portions of the *Apology*, that we must make the date of the *Testimony* the pivot of our inquiry concerning Minucius.   Now, Tertullian's *Apology* preceded the *Testimony*, and the latter preceded the essay on the *Flesh of Christ*.   If the *Testimony* was quoted or employed by Minucius, therefore, he could not have written before [1] A.D. 205; and the statement of Jerome is confirmed, which makes our author, and not Tertullian, the copyist.   The modern discussion of the matter is an interesting literary controversy; not yet settled, perhaps, though the dip of the balance just now sustains my own impressions.[2]   But it is a very unimportant matter in itself, the primary place in Latin Christianity being necessarily adjudged to the commanding genius and fertile mind of Tertullian, while it is no discredit to assign to Minucius his proper but secondary credit, of showing, at the very outset of the literature of Western Christianity, that believers were not all illiterate men, nor destitute of polite erudition, and that the language of the Tusculan philosopher was not degraded by its new destination to the higher and holier service of the faith.

Like Tertullian, our author appears to have been a jurisconsult, at Rome, at some period of his history.   Beautiful glimpses of his life and character and surroundings are gained from his own pages, and nearly all we know about him is to be found therein.   So far, he is his own biographer.   He probably continued a layman, and may have lived, as some suppose, till the middle of the third century.

It is not unimportant to note that we are still dealing with "the North-African school," and that Rome has nothing to do with the birth of Latin Christianity, as such.   We have entered upon the third Christian century, and as yet the venerable apostolic see of the West has made no movement whatever towards the creation of a Latin literature among Christians.   So far from being "the mother and mistress" of the churches, she is yet voiceless in Christendom; while

---

[1] Possibly as late as A.D. 230.   Comp. Wordsworth, *Hippol.*, p. 126.
[2] A condensed and valuable view of this matter may be seen in Dr. Schaff's *History*, etc., vol. iii. pp. 834–841.

Africa holds the mastery of Christian thought alike in her schools of Alexandria and Carthage. This, although it is our fourth volume, contains nothing to modify this fact; and yet the whole literature of early Christianity is contained in our series. Well said Æneas Sylvius, who afterwards became Pope Pius the Second, "Verily, before the Council of Nice, some regard there was unto the Bishops of Rome, *although but small*." Holy men as most of them were, they are invisible and unfelt in the formation of Christian theology.[1]

In our author's style and thought there is a charm and a fragrance which associate him, in my mind, with the pure spirit of "Mathetes," with whose *Epistle to Diognetus*, written nearly a hundred years before, it may be profitably compared. See also my prefatory remarks to Mathetes, and the reference to Bunsen which I have suffixed to the Notice of the Edinburgh editors.[2]

In the Edinburgh series, Minucius comes into view after Cyprian, and not till the end of the thirteenth volume of that edition. It will gratify the scholar to find it here where it belongs, and not less to note that it has an index of its own, while in the Edinburgh edition its contents are indexed with those of Cyprian. Consequently, the joint index is rendered nearly worthless, and the injury and confusion resulting to the Contents of Cyprian are not inconsiderable.

Here follows the valuable PREFATORY NOTICE of Dr. Wallis:—

MINUCIUS FELIX is said by Jerome[3] to have been an advocate at Rome prior to his conversion to Christianity.[4] Very little else is known, however, of his history; and of his writings nothing with any certainty, except the following dialogue; although Jerome speaks of another tract as having, probably without reason, been ascribed to him.

The *Octavius*, which is here translated, is a supposed argument between the heathen Cæcilius and the Christian Octavius — the writer being requested to arbitrate between the disputants. The date of its composition is still a matter of keen dispute. The settlement of the point hinges upon the answer to the question — Whether, in the numerous passages which are strikingly similar, occurring in the *Apologeticus* and the *Octavius*, Tertullian borrowed from Minucius, or Minucius borrowed from Tertullian? If Minucius borrowed from Tertullian, he must have flourished in the commencement of the third century, as the *Apologeticus* was written about the year 198 A.D. If, on the other hand, Tertullian borrowed from Minucius, the *Octavius* was written probably about the year 166, and Minucius flourished in the reign of Marcus Aurelius. The later date was the one adopted by earlier critics, and the reasons for it are well given by Mr. Holden in his introduction. The earlier date was suggested by Rösler, maintained by Niebuhr, and elaborately defended by Muralto. An exhaustive exhibition of arguments in favour of the earlier date has been given by Adolf Ebert in his paper, *Tertullian's Verhältniss zu Minucius Felix*, Leipzig, 1868.

Of the literary character of the dialogue, it is sufficient to quote the testimony of the late Dean Milman: "Perhaps no late work, either Pagan or Christian, reminds us of the golden days of Latin prose so much as the *Octavius* of Minucius Felix."[5]

In considering the claim of the dialogue to such praise as this, it must be borne in mind that the text as we have it is very uncertain, and often certainly corrupt; so that many passages seem to us confused, and some hopelessly obscure. Only one manuscript of the work has come down to us, which is now in the Imperial Library in Paris. It is beautifully written. Some editors have spoken of two other MSS.; but it is now known that they were wrong. They supposed that the first edition was taken from a different MS. than the Codex Regius, and they were not aware that a codex in Brussels was merely a transcript of the one in Paris.

The *Octavius* appears in the MS. as the eighth book of Arnobius, and at first it was published as such. To Franciscus Balduinus (1560) is due the merit of having discovered the real author.

1 See Bishop Jewell, *Works*, vol. i. pp. 386, 441. Cambridge, 1845.
2 Vol. I. of this series, pp. 23, 24. See also Bunsen, *Hippol.*, i. p. 244.   3 *De Viris Illustribus*, c. 58.
4 [His connection with the Roman courts is inferred from cap. ii. *infra*.]
5 Milman's *Hist. of Christianity*, vol. iii. book iv. ch. iii.

There are very many editions of the *Octavius*. Among the earlier, those of Gronovius (1709) and Davies (1712) are valuable. Among the later, Lindner (1760), Eduard de Muralto (1836), and Oehler (1847) may be mentioned. There is a very good English edition by the Rev. H. A. Holden, M.A., Cambridge, 1853. The most recent edition is that of Carl Halm, published under the auspices of the Imperial Academy of Letters in Vienna ; Vindobonæ, 1867. Both Holden and Halm give new recensions of the Codex Regius.[1]

---

1 [Dr. Wallis, the learned translator of the *Octavius*, is described in the Edinburgh edition as " Senior Priest-Vicar of Wells Cathedral, and incumbent of Christ Church, Coxley, Somerset."]

THE OCTAVIUS OF MINUCIUS FELIX.

CHAP. I. — ARGUMENT : MINUCIUS RELATES HOW DELIGHTFUL TO HIM IS THE RECOLLECTION OF THE THINGS THAT HAD HAPPENED TO HIM WITH OCTAVIUS WHILE HE WAS ASSOCIATED WITH HIM AT ROME, AND ESPECIALLY OF THIS DISPUTATION.

WHEN I consider and mentally review my remembrance of Octavius, my excellent and most faithful companion, the sweetness and charm of the man so clings to me, that I appear to myself in some sort as if I were returning to past times, and not merely recalling in my recollection things which have long since happened and gone by. Thus, in the degree in which the actual contemplation of him is withdrawn from my eyes, it is bound up in my heart and in my most intimate feelings. And it was not without reason that that remarkable and holy man, when he departed *this life*, left to me an unbounded regret for him, especially since he himself also glowed with such a love for me at all times, that, whether in matters of amusement or of business, he agreed with me in similarity of will, in either liking or disliking the same things.[1] You would think that one mind had been shared between us two. Thus he alone was my confidant in my loves, my companion in my mistakes ; and when, after the gloom had been dispersed, I emerged from the abyss of darkness into the light of wisdom and truth, he did not cast off his associate, but — what is more glorious still — he outstripped him. And thus, when my thoughts were traversing the entire period of our intimacy and friendship, the direction of my mind fixed itself chiefly on that discourse of his, wherein by very weighty arguments he converted Cæcilius, who was still cleaving to superstitious vanities, to the true religion.[2]

CHAP. II. — ARGUMENT : THE ARRIVAL OF OCTAVIUS AT ROME DURING THE TIME OF THE PUBLIC HOLIDAYS WAS VERY AGREEABLE TO MINUCIUS. BOTH OF THEM WERE DESIROUS OF GOING TO THE MARINE BATHS OF OSTIA, WITH CÆCILIUS ASSOCIATED WITH THEM AS A COMPANION OF MINUCIUS. ON THEIR WAY TOGETHER TO THE SEA, CÆCILIUS, SEEING AN IMAGE OF SERAPIS, RAISES HIS HAND TO HIS MOUTH, AND WORSHIPS IT.

For, for the sake of business and of visiting me, Octavius had hastened to Rome, having left his home, his wife, his children, and that which is most attractive in children, while yet their innocent years are attempting only half-uttered words, — a language all the sweeter for the very imperfection of the faltering tongue. And at this his arrival I cannot express in words with how great and with how impatient a joy I exulted, since the unexpected presence of a man so very dear to me greatly enhanced my gladness. Therefore, after one or two days, when the frequent enjoyment of our continual association had satisfied the craving of affection, and when we had ascertained by mutual narrative all that we were ignorant of about one another by reason of our separation, we agreed to go to that very pleasant city Ostia, that my body might have a soothing and appropriate remedy for drying its humours from the marine bathing, especially as the holidays of the courts at the vintage-time had released me from my cares. For at that time, after the summer days, the autumn season was tending to a milder temperature. And thus, when in the early morning we were going towards the sea along the shore (of the Tiber), that both the breathing air might gently refresh our limbs, and that the yielding sand might sink down under our easy footsteps with excessive pleasure ; Cæcilius, observing an image of Serapis, raised his hand to his mouth, as is the custom of the superstitious common people, and pressed a kiss on it with his lips.

CHAP. III. — ARGUMENT : OCTAVIUS, DISPLEASED AT THE ACT OF THIS SUPERSTITIOUS MAN, SHARPLY REPROACHES MINUCIUS, ON THE GROUND THAT THE DISGRACE OF THIS WICKED DEED IS REFLECTED NOT LESS ON HIMSELF, AS CÆCILIUS' HOST, THAN ON CÆCILIUS.

Then Octavius said : " It is not the part of a good man, my brother Marcus, so to desert a

---

[1] [Sallust, *Catiline*, " Idem facere atque sentire," etc. Also, Catiline's speech, p. 6 of *The Conspiracy*.]
[2] [Beautiful tribute to Christian friendship, in a primitive example. We must bear in mind that the story is of an earlier period than that of the work itself, written at Cirta.]

man who abides by your side at home and abroad, in this blindness of vulgar ignorance, as that you should suffer him in such broad daylight as this to give himself up to stones, however they may be carved into images, anointed and crowned ; since you know that the disgrace of this his error redounds in no less degree to your discredit than to his own." With this discourse of his we passed over the distance between the city and the sea, and we were now walking on the broad and open shore. There the gently rippling wave was smoothing the outside sands, as if it would level them for a promenade ; and as the sea is always restless, even when the winds are lulled, it came up on the shore, although not with waves crested and foaming, yet with waves crisped and curling. Just then we were excessively delighted at its vagaries, as on the very threshold of the water we were wetting the soles of our feet, and it now by turns approaching broke upon our feet, and now the wave retiring and retracing its course, sucked itself back into itself. And thus, slowly and quietly going along, we tracked the coast of the gently bending shore, beguiling the way with stories. These stories were related by Octavius, who was discoursing on navigation. But when we had occupied a sufficiently reasonable time of our walk with discourse, retracing the same way again, we trod the path with reverted footsteps. And when we came to that place where the little ships, drawn up on an oaken framework, were lying at rest supported above the (risk of) ground-rot, we saw some boys eagerly gesticulating as they played at throwing shells into the sea. This play is : To choose a shell from the shore, rubbed and made smooth by the tossing of the waves ; to take hold of the shell in a horizontal position with the fingers ; to whirl it along sloping and as low down as possible upon the waves, that when thrown it may either skim the back of the wave, or may swim as it glides along with a smooth impulse, or may spring up as it cleaves the top of the waves, and rise as if lifted up with repeated springs. That boy claimed to be conqueror whose shell both went out furthest, and leaped up most frequently.

CHAP. IV. — ARGUMENT : CÆCILIUS, SOMEWHAT GRIEVED AT THIS KIND OF REBUKE WHICH FOR HIS SAKE MINUCIUS HAD HAD TO BEAR FROM OCTAVIUS, BEGS TO ARGUE WITH OCTAVIUS ON THE TRUTH OF HIS RELIGION. OCTAVIUS WITH HIS COMPANION CONSENTS, AND MINUCIUS SITS IN THE MIDDLE BETWEEN CÆCILIUS AND OCTAVIUS.

And thus, while we were all engaged in the enjoyment of this spectacle, Cæcilius was paying no attention, nor laughing at the contest ; but silent, uneasy, standing apart, confessed by his countenance that he was grieving for I knew not what. To whom I said : " What is the matter ? Wherefore do I not recognise, Cæcilius, your usual liveliness ? and why do I seek vainly for that joyousness which is characteristic of your glances even in serious matters ? " Then said he : " For some time our friend Octavius' speech has bitterly vexed and worried me, in which he, attacking you, reproached you with negligence, that he might under cover of that charge more seriously condemn me for ignorance. Therefore I shall proceed further : the matter is now wholly and entirely between me and Octavius. If he is willing that I, a man of that form of opinion, should argue with him, he will now at once perceive that it is easier to hold an argument among his comrades, than to engage in close conflict after the manner of the philosophers. Let us be seated on those rocky barriers that are cast there for the protection of the baths, and that run far out into the deep, that we may be able both to rest after our journey, and to argue with more attention." And at his word we sat down, so that, by covering me on either side, they sheltered me in the midst of the three.[1] Nor was this a matter of observance, or of rank, or of honour, because friendship always either receives or makes equals ; but that, as an arbitrator, and being near to both, I might give my attention, and being in the middle, I might separate the two. Then Cæcilius began thus : —

CHAP. V. — ARGUMENT : CÆCILIUS BEGINS HIS ARGUMENT FIRST OF ALL BY REMINDING THEM THAT IN HUMAN AFFAIRS ALL THINGS ARE DOUBTFUL AND UNCERTAIN, AND THAT THEREFORE IT IS TO BE LAMENTED THAT CHRISTIANS, WHO FOR THE MOST PART ARE UNTRAINED AND ILLITERATE PERSONS, SHOULD DARE TO DETERMINE ON ANYTHING WITH CERTAINTY CONCERNING THE CHIEF OF THINGS AND THE DIVINE MAJESTY : HENCE HE ARGUES THAT THE WORLD IS GOVERNED BY NO PROVIDENCE, AND CONCLUDES THAT IT IS BETTER TO ABIDE BY THE RECEIVED FORMS OF RELIGION.

" Although to you, Marcus my brother, the subject on which especially we are inquiring is not in doubt, inasmuch as, being carefully informed in both kinds of life, you have rejected the one and assented to the other, yet in the present case your mind must be so fashioned that you may hold the balance of a most just judge, nor lean with a disposition to one side (more than another), lest your decision may seem not to arise so much from our arguments, as to be originated from your own perceptions.

---

[1] " Ita ut me ex tribus medium lateris ambitione protegerent."

Accordingly, if you sit in judgment on me, as a person who is new, and as one ignorant of either side, there is no difficulty in making plain that all things in human affairs are doubtful, uncertain, and unsettled, and that all things are rather probable than true. Wherefore it is the less[1] wonderful that some, from the weariness of thoroughly investigating truth, should rashly succumb to any sort of opinion rather than persevere in exploring it with persistent diligence. And thus all men must be indignant, all men must feel pain,[2] that certain persons — and these unskilled in learning, strangers to literature, without knowledge even[3] of sordid arts — should dare to determine on any certainty concerning the nature at large, and the (divine) majesty, of which so many of the multitude of sects in all ages (still doubt), and philosophy itself deliberates still. Nor without reason; since the mediocrity of human intelligence is so far from (the capacity of) divine investigation, that neither is it given us to know, nor is it permitted to search, nor is it religious to ravish,[4] the things that are supported in suspense in the heaven above us, nor the things which are deeply submerged below the earth; and we may rightly seem sufficiently happy and sufficiently prudent, if, according to that ancient oracle of the sage, we should know ourselves intimately. But even if we indulge in a senseless and useless labour, and wander away beyond the limits proper to our humility, and though, inclined towards the earth, we transcend with daring ambition heaven itself, and the very stars, let us at least not entangle this error with vain and fearful opinions. Let the seeds of all things have been in the beginning condensed by a nature combining them in itself — what God is the author here? Let the members of the whole world be by fortuitous concurrences united, digested, fashioned — what God is the contriver? Although fire may have lit up the stars; although (the lightness of) its own material may have suspended the heaven; although its own material may have established the earth by its weight;[5] and although the sea may have flowed in from moisture,[6] whence is this religion? Whence this fear? What is this superstition? Man, and every animal which is born, inspired with life, and nourished,[7] is as a voluntary concretion of the elements, into which again man and every

animal is divided, resolved, and dissipated. So all things flow back again into their source, and are turned again into themselves, without any artificer, or judge, or creator. Thus the seeds of fires, being gathered together, cause other suns, and again others, always to shine forth. Thus the vapours of the earth, being exhaled, cause the mists always to grow, which being condensed and collected, cause the clouds to rise higher; and when they fall, cause the rains to flow, the winds to blow, the hail to rattle down; or when the clouds clash together, they cause the thunder to bellow, the lightnings to grow red, the thunderbolts to gleam forth. Therefore they fall everywhere, they rush on the mountains, they strike the trees; without any choice,[8] they blast places sacred and profane; they smite mischievous men, and often, too, religious men. Why should I speak of tempests, various and uncertain, wherein the attack upon all things is tossed about without any order or discrimination? — in shipwrecks, that the fates of good and bad men are jumbled together, their deserts confounded? — in conflagrations, that the destruction of innocent and guilty is united? — and when with the plague-taint of the sky a region is stained, that all perish without distinction? — and when the heat of war is raging, that it is the better men who generally fall? In peace also, not only is wickedness put on the same level with (the lot of) those who are better, but it is also regarded in such esteem,[9] that, in the case of many people, you know not whether their depravity is most to be detested, or their felicity to be desired. But if the world were governed by divine providence and by the authority of any deity, Phalaris and Dionysius would never have deserved to reign, Rutilius and Camillus would never have merited banishment, Socrates would never have merited the poison. Behold the fruit-bearing trees, behold the harvest already white, the vintage, already dropping, is destroyed by the rain, is beaten down by the hail. Thus either an uncertain truth is hidden from us, and kept back; or, which is rather to be believed, in these various and wayward chances, fortune, unrestrained by laws, is ruling over us.

CHAP. VI. — ARGUMENT: THE OBJECT OF ALL NATIONS, AND ESPECIALLY OF THE ROMANS, IN WORSHIPPING THEIR DIVINITIES, HAS BEEN TO ATTAIN FOR THEIR WORSHIP THE SUPREME DOMINION OVER THE WHOLE EARTH.

"Since, then, either fortune is certain or nature is uncertain, how much more reverential and

---

[1] The MS. and first edition read "more;" Ursinus suggested *minus* instead of *magis*.
[2] This clause is otherwise read: "Therefore we must be indignant, nay, must be grieved."
[3] Otherwise for "even," "except."
[4] The reading of the MS. is "stuprari," as above. "Scrutari," "sciari," or "lustrare" and "suspicari," are proposed emendations.
[5] Or, "although its weight may have established the earth."
[6] Or, "although the moisture may have flowed into the sea."
[7] Variously read, "is raised up," or "and is raised up." The MS. has "attollitur," which by some is amended into "et alitur," or "et tollitur."

[8] Either "delectu" or "dilectu."
[9] Or, "it is extolled."

better it is, as the high priests of truth, to receive the teaching of your ancestors, to cultivate the religions handed down to you, to adore the gods whom you were first trained by your parents to fear rather than to know [1] with familiarity; not to assert an opinion concerning the deities, but to believe your forefathers, who, while the age was still untrained in the birth-times of the world itself, deserved to have gods either propitious to them, or as their kings.[2] Thence, therefore, we see through all empires, and provinces, and cities, that each people has its national rites of worship, and adores its local gods : as the Eleusinians worship Ceres; the Phrygians, Mater;[3] the Epidaurians, Æsculapius; the Chaldæans, Belus; the Syrians, Astarte; the Taurians, Diana; the Gauls, Mercurius; the Romans, all divinities. Thus their power and authority has occupied the circuit of the whole world: thus it has propagated its empire beyond the paths of the sun, and the bounds of the ocean itself; in that in their arms they practise a religious valour; in that they fortify their city with the religions of sacred rites, with chaste virgins, with many honours, and the names of priests; in that, when besieged and taken, all but the Capitol alone, they worship the gods which when angry any other people would have despised;[4] and through the lines of the Gauls, marvelling at the audacity of their superstition, they move unarmed with weapons, but armed with the worship of their religion; while in the city of an enemy, when taken while still in the fury of victory, they venerate the conquered deities; while in all directions they seek for the gods of the strangers, and make them their own; while they build altars even to unknown divinities, and to the Manes. Thus, in that they acknowledge the sacred institutions of all nations, they have also deserved their dominion. Hence the perpetual course of their veneration has continued, which is not weakened by the long lapse of time, but increased, because antiquity has been accustomed to attribute to ceremonies and temples so much of sanctity as it has ascribed of age.

CHAP. VII. — ARGUMENT : THAT THE ROMAN AUSPICES AND AUGURIES HAVE BEEN NEGLECTED WITH ILL CONSEQUENCES, BUT HAVE BEEN OBSERVED WITH GOOD FORTUNE.

"Nor yet by chance (for I would venture in the meantime even to take for granted *the point in debate*, and so to err on the safe side) have our ancestors succeeded in their undertakings either by the observance of auguries, or by consulting the entrails, or by the institution of sacred rites, or by the dedication of temples. Consider what is the record of books. You will at once discover that they have inaugurated the rites of all kinds of religions, either that the divine indulgence might be rewarded, or that the threatening anger might be averted, or that the wrath already swelling and raging might be appeased. Witness the Idæan mother,[5] who at her arrival both approved the chastity of the matron, and delivered the city from the fear of the enemy. Witness the statues of the equestrian brothers,[6] consecrated even as they had showed themselves on the lake, who, with horses breathless,[7] foaming, and smoking, announced the victory over the Persian on the same day on which they had gained it. Witness the renewal of the games of the offended Jupiter,[8] on account of the dream of a man of the people. And an acknowledged witness is the devotion of the Decii. Witness also Curtius, who filled up the opening of the profound chasm either with the mass, or with the glory of his knighthood. Moreover, more frequently than we wished have the auguries, when despised, borne witness to the presence of the gods: thus Allia is an unlucky name; thus the battle of Claudius and Junius is not a battle against the Carthaginians, but a fatal shipwreck. Thus, that Thrasymenus might be both swollen and discoloured with the blood of the Romans, Flaminius despised the auguries; and that we might again demand our standards from the Parthians, Crassus both deserved and scoffed at the imprecations of the terrible sisters. I omit the old stories, which are many, and I pass by the songs of the poets about the births, and the gifts, and the rewards of the gods. Moreover, I hasten over the fates predicted by the oracles, lest antiquity should appear to you excessively fabulous. Look at the temples and fanes of the gods by which the Roman city is both protected and armed: they are more august by the deities which are their inhabitants, who are present and constantly dwelling in them, than opulent by the ensigns and gifts of worship. Thence therefore the prophets, filled with the god, and mingled with him, collect futurity beforehand, give caution for dangers, medicine for diseases, hope for the afflicted, help to the wretched, solace to calamities, alleviation to labours. Even in our repose we see, we hear, we acknowledge the gods, whom in the day-time we impiously deny, refuse, and abjure.

---

[1] "To think of rather than to know" in some texts.
[2] Neander quotes this passage as illustrating the dissatisfied state of the pagan mind with the prevailing infidelity at that time.
[3] Or, "the great mother" [i.e., Cybele. S.].
[4] Or, "which another people, when angry, would have despised."

[5] Otherwise, "the goddess mother."
[6] *Scil.* Castor and Pollux.
[7] Otherwise, "who breathless with horses foaming," etc.
[8] Otherwise, "the offence of Jupiter, the renewal of the games," etc.

CHAP. VIII. — ARGUMENT: THE IMPIOUS TEMERITY OF THEODORUS, DIAGORAS, AND PROTAGORAS IS NOT AT ALL TO BE ACQUIESCED IN, WHO WISHED EITHER ALTOGETHER TO GET RID OF THE RELIGION OF THE GODS, OR AT LEAST TO WEAKEN IT. BUT INFINITELY LESS TO BE ENDURED IS THAT SKULKING AND LIGHT-SHUNNING PEOPLE OF THE CHRISTIANS, WHO REJECT THE GODS, AND WHO, FEARING TO DIE AFTER DEATH, DO NOT IN THE MEANTIME FEAR TO DIE.

"Therefore, since the consent of all nations concerning the existence of the immortal gods remains established, although their nature or their origin remains uncertain, I suffer nobody swelling with such boldness, and with I know not what irreligious wisdom, who would strive to undermine or weaken this religion, so ancient, so useful, so wholesome, even although he may be Theodorus of Cyrene, or one who is before him, Diagoras the Melian,[1] to whom antiquity applied the surname of Atheist, — both of whom, by asseverating that there were no gods, took away all the fear by which humanity is ruled, and all veneration absolutely; yet never will they prevail in this discipline of impiety, under the name and authority of their pretended philosophy. When the men of Athens both expelled Protagoras of Abdera, and in public assembly burnt his writings, because he disputed deliberately[2] rather than profanely concerning the divinity, why is it not a thing to be lamented, that men (for you will bear with my making use pretty freely of the force of the plea that I have undertaken) — that men, I say, of a reprobate, unlawful, and desperate faction, should rage against the gods? who, having gathered together from the lowest dregs the more unskilled, and women, credulous and, by the facility of their sex, yielding, establish a herd of a profane conspiracy, which is leagued together by nightly meetings, and solemn fasts, and inhuman meats — not by any sacred rite, but by that which requires expiation — a people skulking and shunning the light, silent in public, but garrulous in corners. They despise the temples as dead-houses, they reject the gods, they laugh at sacred things; wretched, they pity, if they are allowed, the priests; half naked themselves, they despise honours and purple robes. Oh, wondrous folly and incredible audacity! they despise present torments, although they fear those which are uncertain and future; and while they fear to die after death, they do not fear to die for the present: so does a deceit-ful hope soothe their fear with the solace of a revival.[3]

CHAP. IX. — ARGUMENT: THE RELIGION OF THE CHRISTIANS IS FOOLISH, INASMUCH AS THEY WORSHIP A CRUCIFIED MAN, AND EVEN THE INSTRUMENT ITSELF OF HIS PUNISHMENT. THEY ARE SAID TO WORSHIP THE HEAD OF AN ASS, AND EVEN THE NATURE OF THEIR FATHER. THEY ARE INITIATED BY THE SLAUGHTER AND THE BLOOD OF AN INFANT, AND IN SHAMELESS DARKNESS THEY ARE ALL MIXED UP IN AN UNCERTAIN MEDLEY.

"And now, as wickeder things advance more fruitfully, and abandoned manners creep on day by day, those abominable shrines of an impious assembly are maturing themselves throughout the whole world. Assuredly this confederacy ought to be rooted out and execrated. They know one another by secret marks and insignia, and they love one another almost before they know one another. Everywhere also there is mingled among them a certain religion of lust, and they call one another promiscuously brothers and sisters, that even a not unusual debauchery may by the intervention of that sacred name become incestuous: it is thus that their vain and senseless superstition glories in crimes. Nor, concerning these things, would intelligent report speak of things so great and various,[4] and requiring to be prefaced by an apology, unless truth were at the bottom of it. I hear that they adore the head of an ass, that basest of creatures, consecrated by I know not what silly persuasion, — a worthy and appropriate religion for such manners. Some say that they worship the *virilia* of their pontiff and priest,[5] and adore the nature, as it were, of their common parent. I know not whether these things are false; certainly suspicion is applicable to secret and nocturnal rites; and he who explains their ceremonies by reference to a man punished by extreme suffering for his wickedness, and to the deadly wood of the cross, appropriates fitting altars for reprobate and wicked men, that they may worship what they deserve. Now the story about the initiation of young novices is as much to be detested as it is well known. An infant covered over with meal, that it may deceive the unwary, is placed before him who is to be stained with their rites: this infant is slain by the young pupil, who has been urged on as if to harmless blows on the surface of the meal, with dark and secret wounds.

---

[1] According to the codex, "the Milesian." [See note in Reeves's *Apologies of Justin Martyr, Tertullian,* and *Minucius Felix,* vol. ii. p. 59. S.]

[2] Some have corrected this word, reading "without consideration," *scil.* "inconsulte;" and the four first editions omit the subsequent words, "concerning the divinity."

[3] There are various emendations of this passage, but their meaning is somewhat obscure. One is elaborately ingenious: "Ita illis pavorum fallax spes solatio redivivo blanditur," which is said to imply, "Thus the hope that deceives their fears, soothes them with the hope of living again."

[4] Otherwise read "abominable."

[5] This charge, as Oehler thinks, refers apparently to the kneeling posture in which penitents made confession before their bishop.

Thirstily — O horror ! — they lick up its blood ; eagerly they divide its limbs. By this victim they are pledged together ; with this consciousness of wickedness they are covenanted to mutual silence.[1] Such sacred rites as these are more foul than any sacrileges. And of their banqueting it is well known all men speak of it everywhere ; even the speech of our Cirtensian[2] testifies to it. On a solemn day they assemble at the feast, with all their children, sisters, mothers, people of every sex and of every age. There, after much feasting, when the fellowship has grown warm, and the fervour of incestuous lust has grown hot with drunkenness, a dog that has been tied to the chandelier is provoked, by throwing a small piece of offal beyond the length of a line by which he is bound, to rush and spring ; and thus the conscious light being overturned and extinguished in the shameless darkness, the connections of abominable lust involve them in the uncertainty of fate. Although not all in fact, yet in consciousness all are alike incestuous, since by the desire of all of them everything is sought for which can happen in the act of each individual.

CHAP. X. — ARGUMENT : WHATEVER THE CHRISTIANS WORSHIP, THEY STRIVE IN EVERY WAY TO CONCEAL : THEY HAVE NO ALTARS, NO TEMPLES, NO ACKNOWLEDGED IMAGES. THEIR GOD, LIKE THAT OF THE JEWS, IS SAID TO BE ONE, WHOM, ALTHOUGH THEY ARE NEITHER ABLE TO SEE NOR TO SHOW, THEY THINK NEVERTHELESS TO BE MISCHIEVOUS, RESTLESS, AND UNSEASONABLY INQUISITIVE.

" I purposely pass over many things, for those that I have mentioned are already too many ; and that all these, or the greater part of them, are true, the obscurity of their vile religion declares. For why do they endeavour with such pains to conceal and to cloak whatever they worship, since honourable things always rejoice in publicity, while crimes are kept secret ? Why have they no altars, no temples, no acknowledged images ?[3] Why do they never speak openly, never congregate freely, unless for the reason that what they adore and conceal is either worthy of punishment, or something to be ashamed of ? Moreover, whence or who is he, or where is the *one* God, solitary, desolate, whom no free people, no kingdoms, and not even Roman superstition, have known ? The lonely and miserable nationality of the Jews worshipped one God, and one peculiar to itself ; but they worshipped him open-

ly, with temples, with altars, with victims, and with ceremonies ; and he has so little force or power, that he is enslaved, with his own special nation, to the Roman deities. But the Christians, moreover, what wonders, what monstrosities do they feign ! — that he who is their God, whom they can neither show nor behold, inquires diligently into the character of all, the acts of all, and, in fine, into their words and secret thoughts ; that he runs about everywhere, and is everywhere present : they make him out to be troublesome, restless, even shamelessly inquisitive, since he is present at everything that is done, wanders in and out in all places, although, being occupied with the whole, he cannot give attention to particulars, nor can he be sufficient for the whole while he is busied with particulars. What ! because they threaten conflagration to the whole world, and to the universe itself, with all its stars, are they meditating its destruction ? — as if either the eternal order constituted by the divine laws of nature would be disturbed, or the league of all the elements would be broken up, and the heavenly structure dissolved, and that fabric in which it is contained and bound together[4] would be overthrown.[5]

CHAP. XI. — ARGUMENT : BESIDES ASSERTING THE FUTURE CONFLAGRATION OF THE WHOLE WORLD, THEY PROMISE AFTERWARDS THE RESURRECTION OF OUR BODIES : AND TO THE RIGHTEOUS AN ETERNITY OF MOST BLESSED LIFE ; TO THE UNRIGHTEOUS, OF EXTREME PUNISHMENT.

" And, not content with this wild opinion, they add to it and associate with it old women's fables :[6] they say that they will rise again after death, and ashes, and dust ; and with I know not what confidence, they believe by turns in one another's lies : you would think that they had already lived again. It is a double evil and a twofold madness to denounce destruction to the heaven and the stars, which we leave just as we find them, and to promise eternity to ourselves, who are dead and extinct — who, as we are born, so also perish ! It is for this cause, doubtless, also that they execrate our funeral piles, and condemn our burials by fire, as if every body, even although it be withdrawn from the flames, were not, nevertheless, resolved into the earth by lapse of years and ages, and as if it mattered not whether wild beasts tore the body to pieces, or seas consumed it, or the ground covered it, or the flames carried it away ; since for the carcases every mode of sepulture is a penalty if they feel it ; if they feel it not,

---

[1] This calumny seems to have originated from the sacrament of the Eucharist.

[2] *Scil.* Fronto of Cirta, spoken of again in ch. xxxi. [A recent very interesting discovery goes to show that our author was the chief magistrate of Cirta, in Algeria, from A.D. 210 to 217. See Schaff, vol. iii. p. 841.]

[3] Otherwise, " no consecrated images."

[4] Otherwise, " we are contained and bound together."

[5] [These very accusations, reduced back to Christian language, show that much of the Creed was, in fact, known to the heathen at this period.]

[6] [1 Tim. iv. 7.]

in the very quickness of their destruction there is relief. Deceived by this error, they promise to themselves, as being good, a blessed and perpetual life after their death; to others, as being unrighteous, eternal punishment. Many things occur to me to say in addition, if the limits of my discourse did not hasten me. I have already shown, and take no more pains to prove,[1] that they themselves are unrighteous; although, even if I should allow them to be righteous, yet your agreement also concurs with the opinions of many, that guilt and innocence are attributed by fate. For whatever we do, as some ascribe it to fate, so you refer it to God: thus it is according to your sect to believe that men will, not of their own accord, but as elected to will. Therefore you feign an iniquitous judge, who punishes in men, not their will, but their destiny. Yet I should be glad to be informed whether or no you rise again with bodies;[2] and if so, with what bodies — whether with the same or with renewed bodies? Without a body? Then, as far as I know, there will neither be mind, nor soul, nor life. With the same body? But this has already been previously destroyed. With another body? Then it is a new man who is born, not the former one restored; and yet so long a time has passed away, innumerable ages have flowed by, and what single individual has returned from the dead either by the fate of Protesilaus, with permission to sojourn even for a few hours, or that we might believe it for an example? All such figments of an unhealthy belief, and vain sources of comfort, with which deceiving poets have trifled in the sweetness of their verse, have been disgracefully remoulded by you, believing undoubtingly[3] on your God.

CHAP. XII. — ARGUMENT: MOREOVER, WHAT WILL HAPPEN TO THE CHRISTIANS THEMSELVES AFTER DEATH, MAY BE ANTICIPATED FROM THE FACT THAT EVEN NOW THEY ARE DESTITUTE OF ALL MEANS, AND ARE AFFLICTED WITH THE HEAVIEST CALAMITIES AND MISERIES.

"Neither do you at least take experience from things present, how the fruitless expectations of vain promise deceive you. Consider, wretched creatures, (from your lot) while you are yet living, what is threatening you after death.[4] Behold, a portion of you — and, as you declare, the larger and better portion — are in want, are cold, are labouring in hard work and hunger; and God suffers it, He feigns; He either is not willing or not able to assist His people; and thus He is either weak or inequitable.

Thou, who dreamest over a posthumous immortality, when thou art shaken by danger,[5] when thou art consumed with fever, when thou art torn with pain, dost thou not then feel thy real condition? Dost thou not then acknowledge thy frailty? Poor wretch, art thou unwillingly convinced of thine infirmity, and wilt not confess it? But I omit matters that are common to all alike. Lo, for you there are threats, punishments, tortures, and crosses; and that no longer as objects of adoration, but as tortures to be undergone; fires also, which you both predict and fear. Where is that God who is able to help you when you come to life again, since he cannot help you while you are in this life? Do not the Romans, without any help from your God, govern, reign, have the enjoyment of the whole world, and have dominion over you? But you in the meantime, in suspense and anxiety, are abstaining from respectable enjoyments. You do not visit exhibitions; you have no concern in public displays; you reject the public banquets, and abhor the sacred contests; the meats previously tasted by, and the drinks made a libation of upon, the altars. Thus you stand in dread of the gods whom you deny. You do not wreath your heads with flowers; you do not grace your bodies with odours; you reserve unguents for funeral rites; you even refuse garlands to your sepulchres — pallid, trembling beings, worthy of the pity even of our gods! Thus, wretched as you are, you neither rise again, nor do you live in the meanwhile. Therefore, if you have any wisdom or modesty, cease from prying into the regions of the sky, and the destinies and secrets of the world: it is sufficient to look before your feet, especially for untaught, uncultivated, boorish, rustic people: they who have no capacity for understanding civil matters, are much more denied the ability to discuss divine.

CHAP. XIII. — ARGUMENT: CÆCILIUS AT LENGTH CONCLUDES THAT THE NEW RELIGION IS TO BE REPUDIATED; AND THAT WE MUST NOT RASHLY PRONOUNCE UPON DOUBTFUL MATTERS.

"However, if you have a desire to philosophize, let any one of you who is sufficiently great, imitate, if he can, Socrates the prince of wisdom. The answer of that man, whenever he was asked about celestial matters, is well known: '*What is above us is nothing to us.*' Well, therefore, did he deserve from the oracle the testimony of singular wisdom, which oracle he himself had a presentiment of, that he had been preferred to all men for the reason, not that he had discovered all things, but because he had learnt that he knew nothing. And thus the confession

---

[1] "And I have already shown, without any trouble," is another reading.
[2] Otherwise, "without a body or with."
[3] Otherwise, "too credulous."
[4] Otherwise, "while you consider, while you are yet alive, poor wretches, what is threatening after death."

[5] Some read, "with shivering."

of ignorance is the height of wisdom. From this source flowed the safe doubting of Arcesilas, and long after of Carneades, and of very many of the Academics,[1] in questions of the highest moment, in which species of philosophy the unlearned can do much with caution, and the learned can do gloriously. What! is not the hesitation of Simonides the lyric poet to be admired and followed by all? Which Simonides, when he was asked by Hiero the tyrant what, and what like he thought the gods to be, asked first of all for a day to deliberate; then postponed his reply for two days; and then, when pressed, he added only another; and finally, when the tyrant inquired into the causes of such a long delay, he replied that, the longer his research continued, the obscurer the truth became to him.[2] In my opinion also, things which are uncertain ought to be left as they are. Nor, while so many and so great men are deliberating, should we rashly and boldly give an opinion in another direction, lest either a childish superstition should be introduced, or all religion should be overthrown."

CHAP. XIV. — ARGUMENT: WITH SOMETHING OF THE PRIDE OF SELF-SATISFACTION, CÆCILIUS URGES OCTAVIUS TO REPLY TO HIS ARGUMENTS; AND MINUCIUS WITH MODESTY ANSWERS HIM, THAT HE MUST NOT EXULT AT HIS OWN BY NO MEANS ORDINARY ELOQUENCE, AND AT THE HARMONIOUS VARIETY OF HIS ADDRESS.

Thus far Cæcilius; and smiling cheerfully (for the vehemence of his prolonged discourse had relaxed the ardour of his indignation), he added: "And what does Octavius venture to reply to this, a man of the race of Plautus,[3] who, while he was chief among the millers, was still the lowest of philosophers?" "Restrain," said I, "your self-approval against him; for it is not worthy of you to exult at the harmony of your discourse, before the subject shall have been more fully argued on both sides; especially since your reasoning is striving after truth, not praise. And in however great a degree your discourse has delighted me by its subtle variety, yet I am very deeply moved, not concerning the present discussion, but concerning the entire kind of disputation — that for the most part the condition of truth should be changed according to the powers of discussion, and even the faculty of perspicuous eloquence. This is very well known to occur by reason of the facility of the hearers,

who, being distracted by the allurement of words from attention to things, assent without distinction to everything that is said, and do not separate falsehood from truth; unaware that even in that which is incredible there is often truth, and in verisimilitude falsehood. Therefore the oftener they believe bold assertions, the more frequently they are convinced by those who are more clever, and thus are continually deceived by their temerity. They transfer the blame of the judge to the complaint of uncertainty; so that, everything being condemned, they would rather that all things should be left in suspense, than that they should decide about matters of doubt. Therefore we must take care that we do not in such sort suffer from the hatred at once of all discourses, even as very many of the more simple kind are led to execration and hatred of men in general. For those who are carelessly credulous are deceived by those whom they thought worthy; and by and by, by a kindred error, they begin to suspect every one as wicked, and dread even those whom they might have regarded as excellent. Now therefore we are anxious — because in everything there may be argument on both sides; and on the one hand, the truth is for the most part obscure; and on the other side there is a marvellous subtlety, which sometimes by its abundance of words imitates the confidence of acknowledged proof — as carefully as possible to weigh each particular, that we may, while ready to applaud acuteness, yet elect, approve, and adopt those things which are right."

CHAP. XV. — ARGUMENT: CÆCILIUS RETORTS UPON MINUCIUS, WITH SOME LITTLE APPEARANCE OF BEING HURT, THAT HE IS FOREGOING THE OFFICE OF A RELIGIOUS UMPIRE, WHEN HE IS WEAKENING THE FORCE OF HIS ARGUMENT. HE SAYS THAT IT SHOULD BE LEFT TO OCTAVIUS TO CONFUTE ALL THAT HE HAD ADVANCED.

"You are withdrawing," says Cæcilius, "from the office of a religious judge; for it is very unfair for you to weaken the force of my pleading by the interpolation of a very important argument, since Octavius has before him each thing that I have said, sound and unimpaired, if he can refute it." "What you are reproving," said I, "unless I am mistaken, I have brought forward for the common advantage, so that by a scrupulous examination we might weigh our decision, not by the pompous style of the eloquence, but by the solid character of the matter itself. Nor must our attention, as you complain, be any longer called away, but with absolute silence let us listen to the reply of our friend Januarius,[4] who is now beckoning to us."

---

[1] This is otherwise read, "Academic Pyrrhonists."

[2] Cicero, de Natura Deorum, i. 22.

[3] "Plautinæ prosapiæ." The expression is intended as a reproach against the humble occupations of many of the Christian professors. Plautus is said, when in need, to have laboured at a baker's hand-mill. Cæcilius tells Octavius that he may be the first among the millers, but he is the last among the philosophers. Stieber proposes "Christianorum" instead of "pistorum" — "Christians" instead of "millers."

[4] Scil. "Octavius."

CHAP. XVI. — ARGUMENT : OCTAVIUS ARRANGES HIS REPLY, AND TRUSTS THAT HE SHALL BE ABLE TO DILUTE THE BITTERNESS OF REPROACH WITH THE RIVER OF TRUTHFUL WORDS. HE PROCEEDS TO WEAKEN THE INDIVIDUAL ARGUMENTS OF CÆCILIUS. NOBODY NEED COMPLAIN THAT THE CHRISTIANS, UNLEARNED THOUGH THEY MAY BE, DISPUTE ABOUT HEAVENLY THINGS, BECAUSE IT IS NOT THE AUTHORITY OF HIM WHO ARGUES, BUT THE TRUTH OF THE ARGUMENT ITSELF, THAT SHOULD BE CONSIDERED.

And thus Octavius began : " I will indeed speak as I shall be able to the best of my powers, and you must endeavour with me to dilute the very offensive strain of recriminations in the river [1] of veracious words. Nor will I disguise in the outset, that the opinion of my friend Natalis [2] has swayed to and fro in such an erratic, vague, and slippery manner, that we are compelled to doubt whether your [3] information was confused, or whether it wavered backwards and forwards [4] by mere mistake. For he varied at one time from believing the gods, at another time to being in a state of hesitation on the subject ; so that the direct purpose of my reply was established with the greater uncertainty,[5] by reason of the uncertainty of his proposition. But in my friend Natalis — I will not allow, I do not believe in, any chicanery — far from his simplicity is crafty trickery.[6] What then ? As he who knows not the right way, when as it happens one road is separated into many, because he knows not the way, remains in anxiety, and dares neither make choice of particular roads, nor try them all ; so, if a man has no stedfast judgment of truth, even as his unbelieving suspicion is scattered, so his doubting opinion is unsettled. It is therefore no wonder if Cæcilius in the same way is cast about by the tide, and tossed hither and thither among things contrary and repugnant to one another ; but that this may no longer be the case, I will convict and refute all that has been said, however diverse, confirming and approving the truth alone ; and for the future he must neither doubt nor waver. And since my brother broke out in such expressions as these, that he was grieved, that he was vexed, that he was indignant, that he regretted that illiterate, poor, unskilled people should dispute about heavenly things ; let him know that all men are begotten alike, with a capacity and ability of reasoning and feeling, without preference of age, sex, or dignity. Nor do they obtain wisdom by

fortune, but have it implanted by nature ; moreover, the very philosophers themselves, or any others who have gone forth unto celebrity as discoverers of arts, before they attained an illustrious name by their mental skill, were esteemed plebeian, untaught, half-naked. Thus it is, that rich men, attached to their means, have been accustomed to gaze more upon their gold than upon heaven, while our sort of people, though poor, have both discovered wisdom, and have delivered their teaching to others ; whence it appears that intelligence is not given to wealth, nor is gotten by study, but is begotten with the very formation of the mind. Therefore it is nothing to be angry or to be grieved about, though any one should inquire, should think, should utter his thoughts about divine things ; since what is wanted is not the authority of the arguer, but the truth of the argument itself : and even the more unskilled the discourse, the more evident the reasoning, since it is not coloured by the pomp of eloquence and grace ; but as it is, it is sustained by the rule of right.

CHAP. XVII. — ARGUMENT : MAN OUGHT INDEED TO KNOW HIMSELF, BUT THIS KNOWLEDGE CANNOT BE ATTAINED BY HIM UNLESS HE FIRST OF ALL ACKNOWLEDGES THE ENTIRE SCOPE OF THINGS, AND GOD HIMSELF. AND FROM THE CONSTITUTION AND FURNITURE OF THE WORLD ITSELF, EVERY ONE ENDOWED WITH REASON HOLDS THAT IT WAS ESTABLISHED BY GOD, AND IS GOVERNED AND ADMINISTERED BY HIM.

" Neither do I refuse to admit what Cæcilius earnestly endeavoured to maintain among the chief matters, that man ought to know himself, and to look around and see what he is, whence he is, why he is ; whether collected together from the elements, or harmoniously formed of atoms, or rather made, formed, and animated by God. And it is this very thing which we cannot seek out and investigate without inquiry into the universe ; since things are so coherent, so linked and associated together, that unless you diligently examine into the nature of divinity, you must be ignorant of that of humanity. Nor can you well perform your social duty unless you know that community of the world which is common to all, especially since in this respect we differ from the wild beasts, that while they are prone and tending to the earth, and are born to look upon nothing but their food, we, whose countenance is erect, whose look is turned towards heaven, as is our converse and reason, whereby we recognise, feel, and imitate God,[7] have neither right nor reason to be ignorant of the celestial glory which forms itself into our eyes and senses. For it is as bad as the grossest sacrilege even,

---

[1] Some read, " in the light."
[2] Cæcilius.
[3] Otherwise " his."
[4] Some read " cavillaverit " instead of " vacillaverit," which would give the sense, " make captious objections."
[5] This is otherwise given " certainty," which helps the meaning of the passage.
[6] Otherwise, " Far from his guileless subtlety is so crafty a trickery." But the readings are very unsettled.

[7] Some read, " the Lord God."

to seek on the ground for what you ought to find on high. Wherefore the rather, they who deny that this furniture of the whole world was perfected by the divine reason, and assert that it was heaped together by certain fragments [1] casually adhering to each other, seem to me not to have either mind or sense, or, in fact, even sight itself. For what can possibly be so manifest, so confessed, and so evident, when you lift your eyes up to heaven, and look into the things which are below and around, than that there is some Deity of most excellent intelligence, by whom all nature is inspired, is moved, is nourished, is governed? Behold the heaven itself, how broadly it is expanded, how rapidly it is whirled around, either as it is distinguished in the night by its stars, or as it is lightened in the day by the sun, and you will know at once how the marvellous and divine balance of the Supreme Governor is engaged therein. Look also on the year, how it is made by the circuit of the sun ; and look on the month, how the moon drives it around in her increase, her decline, and decay. What shall I say of the recurring changes of darkness and light ; how there is thus provided for us an alternate restoration of labour and rest? Truly a more prolix discourse concerning the stars must be left to astronomers, whether as to how they govern the course of navigation, or bring on [2] the season of ploughing or of reaping, each of which things not only needed a Supreme Artist and a perfect intelligence, nor only to create, to construct, and to arrange ; but, moreover, they cannot be felt, peceived and understood without the highest intelligence and reason. What ! when the order of the seasons and of the harvests is distinguished by stedfast variety, does it not attest its Author and Parent? As well the spring with its flowers, and the summer with its harvests, and the grateful maturity of autumn, and the wintry olive-gathering,[3] are needful ; and this order would easily be disturbed unless it were established by the highest intelligence. Now, how great is the providence needed, lest there should be nothing but winter to blast with its frost, or nothing but summer to scorch with its heat, to interpose the moderate temperature of autumn and spring, so that the unseen and harmless transitions of the year returning on its footsteps may glide by ! Look attentively at the sea ; it is bound by the law of its shore. Wherever there are trees, look how they are animated from the bowels of the earth ! Consider the ocean ; it ebbs and flows with alternate tides. Look at the fountains, how they gush in perpetual streams ! Gaze on the rivers ; they always roll on in regular courses. Why

should I speak of the aptly ordered peaks of the mountains, the slopes of the hills, the expanses of the plains? Wherefore should I speak of the multiform protection provided by animated creatures against one another? — some armed with horns, some hedged with teeth, and shod with claws, and barbed with stings, or with freedom obtained by swiftness of feet, or by the capacity of soaring furnished by wings? The very beauty of our own figure especially confesses God to be its artificer : our upright stature, our uplooking countenance, our eyes placed at the top, as it were, for outlook ; and all the rest of our senses as if arranged in a citadel.

CHAP. XVIII. — ARGUMENT : MOREOVER, GOD NOT ONLY TAKES CARE OF THE UNIVERSAL WORLD, BUT OF ITS INDIVIDUAL PARTS. THAT BY THE DECREE OF THE ONE GOD ALL THINGS ARE GOVERNED, IS PROVED BY THE ILLUSTRATION OF EARTHLY EMPIRES. BUT ALTHOUGH HE, BEING INFINITE AND IMMENSE — AND HOW GREAT HE IS, IS KNOWN TO HIMSELF ALONE — CANNOT EITHER BE SEEN OR NAMED BY US, YET HIS GLORY IS BEHELD MOST CLEARLY WHEN THE USE OF ALL TITLES IS LAID ASIDE.

" It would be a long matter to go through particular instances. There is no member in man which is not calculated both for the sake of necessity and of ornament ; and what is more wonderful still, all have the same form, but each has certain lineaments modified, and thus we are each found to be unlike to one another, while we all appear to be like in general. What is the reason of our being born? what means the desire of begetting? Is it not given by God, and that the breasts should become full of milk as the offspring grows to maturity, and that the tender progeny should grow up by the nourishment afforded by the abundance of the milky moisture? Neither does God have care alone for the universe as a whole, but also for its parts. Britain is deficient in sunshine, but it is refreshed by the warmth of the sea that flows around it. The river Nile tempers the dryness of Egypt ; the Euphrates cultivates Mesopotamia ; the river Indus makes up for the want of rains, and is said both to sow and to water the East. Now if, on entering any house, you should behold everything refined, well arranged, and adorned, assuredly you would believe that a master presided over it, and that he himself was much better than all those excellent things. So in this house of the world, when you look upon the heaven and the earth, its providence, its ordering, its law, believe that there is a Lord and Parent of the universe far more glorious than the stars themselves, and the parts of the whole world. Unless, perchance — since there is no doubt as to the ex-

---

[1] *Scil.* "atoms."
[2] According to some, "point out" or "indicate."
[3] Olives ripen in the month of December.

istence of providence — you think that it is a subject of inquiry, whether the celestial kingdom is governed by the power of one or by the rule of many ; and this matter itself does not involve much trouble in opening out, to one who considers earthly empires, for which the examples certainly are taken from heaven. When at any time was there an alliance in royal authority which either began with good faith or ceased without bloodshed ? I pass over the Persians, who gathered the augury for their chieftainship from the neighing of horses ;[1] and I do not quote that absolutely dead fable of the Theban brothers.[2] The story about the twins (Romulus and Remus), in respect of the dominion of shepherds, and of a cottage, is very well known. The wars of the son-in-law and the father-in-law[3] were scattered over the whole world ; and the fortune[4] of so great an empire could not receive two rulers. Look at other matters. The bees have one king ; the flocks one leader ; among the herds there is one ruler. Canst thou believe that in heaven there is a division of the supreme power, and that the whole authority of that true and divine empire is sundered, when it is manifest that God, the Parent of all, has neither beginning nor end — that He who gives birth to all gives perpetuity to Himself — that He who was before the world, was Himself to Himself instead of the world ? He orders everything, whatever it is, by a word ; arranges it by His wisdom ; perfects it by His power. He can neither be seen — He is brighter than light ; nor can be grasped — He is purer than touch ;[5] nor estimated ; He is greater than all perceptions ; infinite, immense, and how great is known to Himself alone. But our heart is too limited to understand Him, and therefore we are then worthily estimating Him when we say that He is beyond estimation. I will speak out in what manner I feel. He who thinks that he knows the magnitude of God, is diminishing it ; he who desires not to lessen it, knows it not. Neither must you ask a name for God. God is His name. We have need of names when a multitude is to be separated into individuals by the special characteristics of names ; to God, who is alone, the name God is the whole. If I were to call Him Father, you would judge Him to be earthly ; if a King, you would suspect Him to be carnal ; if a Lord, you will certainly understand Him to be mortal. Take away the additions of names, and you will behold His glory. What ! is it not true that I have in this matter the consent of all men ? I hear the common people, when they lift their hands to heaven, say

nothing else but *Oh God*, and *God is great*, and *God is true*, and *if God shall permit*. Is this the natural discourse of the common people, or is it the prayer of a confessing Christian ? And they who speak of Jupiter as the chief, are mistaken in the name indeed, but they are in agreement about the unity of the power.

CHAP. XIX. — ARGUMENT : MOREOVER, THE POETS HAVE CALLED HIM THE PARENT OF GODS AND MEN, THE CREATOR OF ALL THINGS, AND THEIR MIND AND SPIRIT. AND, BESIDES, EVEN THE MORE EXCELLENT PHILOSOPHERS HAVE COME ALMOST TO THE SAME CONCLUSION AS THE CHRISTIANS ABOUT THE UNITY OF GOD.

" I hear the poets also announcing ' the One Father of gods and men ; ' and that such is the mind of mortal men as the Parent of all has appointed His day.[6] What says the Mantuan Maro ? Is it not even more plain, more apposite, more true ? ' In the beginning,' says he, ' the spirit within nourishes, and the mind infused stirs the heaven and the earth,' and the other members ' of the world. Thence arises the race of men and of cattle,'[7] and every other kind of animal. The same poet in another place calls that mind and spirit God. For these are his words :[8] ' For that God pervades all the lands, and the tracts of the sea, and the profound heaven, from whom are men and cattle ; from whom are rain and fire.'[9] What else also is God announced to be by us, but mind, and reason, and spirit ? Let us review, if it is agreeable, the teaching of philosophers. Although in varied kinds of discourse, yet in these matters you will find them concur and agree in this one opinion. I pass over those untrained and ancient ones who deserved to be called wise men for their sayings. Let Thales the Milesian be the first of all, for he first of all disputed about heavenly things. That same Thales the Milesian said that water was the beginning of things, but that God was that mind which from water formed all things. Ah ! a higher and nobler account of water and spirit than to have ever been discovered by man. It was delivered to him by God. You see that the opinion of this original philosopher absolutely agrees with ours. Afterwards Anaximenes, and then Diogenes of Apollonia, decide that the air, infinite and unmeasured, is God. The agreement of these also as to the Divinity is like ours. But the description of Anaxagoras also is, that God is said to be the motion of an infinite mind ; and the God of Pythagoras is the soul passing to and fro and intent, throughout the universal nature of things, from whom also

---

[1] [In the case of Darius Hystaspes.]
[2] Eteocles and Polynices.
[3] Pompey and Cæsar.
[4] According to some, " one fate."
[5] These words are omitted by some editors.

[6] Homer, *Odyss.*, xviii. 136, 137.
[7] Virgil, *Æneid*, vi. 724.
[8] Some read, " For these things are true."
[9] Virgil, *Georgics*, iv. 221 ; *Æneid*, i. 743.

the life of all animals is received. It is a known fact, that Xenophanes delivered that God was all infinity with a mind ; and Antisthenes, that there are many gods of the people, but that one God of Nature was the chief of all ; that Xeuxippus [1] acknowledged as God a natural animal force, whereby all things are governed. What says Democritus? Although the first discoverer of atoms, does not he especially speak of nature, which is the basis of forms, and intelligence, as God? Strato also himself says that God is nature. Moreover, Epicurus, the man who feigns either otiose gods or none at all, still places above all, Nature. Aristotle varies, but nevertheless assigns a unity of power : for at one time he says that Mind, at another the World, is God ; at another time he sets God above the world.[2] Heraclides of Pontus also ascribes, although in various ways, a divine mind to God. Theophrastus, and Zeno, and Chrysippus, and Cleanthes are indeed themselves of many forms of opinion ; but they are all brought back to the one fact of the unity of providence. For Cleanthes discoursed of God as of a mind, now of a soul, now of air, but for the most part of reason. Zeno, his master, will have the law of nature and of God, and sometimes the air, and sometimes reason, to be the beginning of all things. Moreover, by interpreting Juno to be the air, Jupiter the heaven, Neptune the sea, Vulcan to be fire, and in like manner by showing the other gods of the common people to be elements, he forcibly denounces and overcomes the public error. Chrysippus says almost the same. He believes that a divine force, a rational nature, and sometimes the world, and a fatal necessity, is God ; and he follows the example of Zeno in his physiological interpretation of the poems of Hesiod, of Homer, and of Orpheus. Moreover, the teaching of Diogenes of Babylon is that of expounding and arguing that the birth of Jupiter, and the origin of Minerva, and this kind, are names for other things, not for gods. For Xenophon the Socratic says that the form of the true God cannot be seen, and therefore ought not to be inquired after. Aristo the Stoic [3] says that He cannot at all be comprehended. And both of them were sensible of the majesty of God, while they despaired of understanding Him. Plato has a clearer discourse about God, both in the matters themselves and in the names by which he expresses them ; and his discourse would be altogether heavenly, if it were not occasionally fouled by a mixture of merely civil belief. Therefore in his *Timæus* Plato's God is by His

very name the parent of the world, the artificer of the soul, the fabricator of heavenly and earthly things, whom both to discover he declares is difficult, on account of His excessive and incredible power ; and when you have discovered Him, impossible to speak of in public. The same almost are the opinions also which are ours. For we both know and speak of a God who is parent of all, and never speak of Him in public unless we are interrogated.[4]

CHAP. XX. — ARGUMENT : BUT IF THE WORLD IS RULED BY PROVIDENCE AND GOVERNED BY THE WILL OF ONE GOD, AN IGNORANT ANTIPATHY OUGHT NOT TO CARRY US AWAY INTO THE ERROR OF AGREEMENT WITH IT : ALTHOUGH DELIGHTED WITH ITS OWN FABLES, IT HAS BROUGHT IN RIDICULOUS TRADITIONS. NOR IS IT SHOWN LESS PLAINLY THAT THE WORSHIP OF THE GODS HAS ALWAYS BEEN SILLY AND IMPIOUS, IN THAT THE MOST ANCIENT OF MEN HAVE VENERATED THEIR KINGS, THEIR ILLUSTRIOUS GENERALS, AND INVENTORS OF ARTS, ON ACCOUNT OF THEIR REMARKABLE DEEDS, NO OTHERWISE THAN AS GODS.

" I have set forth the opinions almost of all the philosophers whose more illustrious glory it is to have pointed out that there is one God, although with many names ; so that any one might think either that Christians are now philosophers, or that philosophers were then already Christians. But if the world is governed by providence, and directed by the will of one God, antiquity of unskilled people ought not, however delighted and charmed with its own fables, to carry us away into the mistake of a mutual agreement, when it is rebutted by the opinions of its own philosophers, who are supported by the authority both of reason and of antiquity. For our ancestors had such an easy faith in falsehoods, that they rashly believed even other monstrosities as marvellous wonders ; [5] a manifold Scylla, a Chimæra of many forms, and a Hydra rising again from its auspicious wounds, and Centaurs, horses entwined with their riders ; and whatever Report was allowed [6] to feign, they were entirely willing to listen to. Why should I refer to those old wives' fables, that men were changed from men into birds and beasts, and from men into trees and flowers? — which things, if they had happened at all, would happen again ; and because they cannot happen now, therefore never happened at all. In like manner with respect to the gods too, our ancestors believed carelessly, credulously, with untrained simplicity , while worshipping their kings religiously, desiring

---

[1] Otherwise, " Speusippus."
[2] The MS. here inserts, " Aristoteles of Pontus varies, at one time attributing the supremacy to the world, at another to the divine mind." Some think that this is an interpolation, others transfer the words to Theophrastus below.
[3] Otherwise, " Aristo the Chian."

[4] [See note on Plato, chap. xxvi.]
[5] Some editors read, " mere wonders," apparently on conjecture only.
[6] Otherwise, " was pleased."

to look upon them when dead in outward forms, anxious to preserve their memories in statues,[1] those things became sacred which had been taken up merely as consolations. Thereupon, and before the world was opened up by commerce, and before the nations confounded their rites and customs, each particular nation venerated its Founder, or illustrious Leader, or modest Queen braver than her sex, or the discoverer of any sort of faculty or art, as a citizen of worthy memory; and thus a reward was given to the deceased, and an example to those who were to follow.

CHAP. XXI. — ARGUMENT: OCTAVIUS ATTESTS THE FACT THAT MEN WERE ADOPTED AS GODS, BY THE TESTIMONY OF EUHEMERUS, PRODICUS, PERSÆUS, AND ALEXANDER THE GREAT, WHO ENUMERATE THE COUNTRY, THE BIRTHDAYS, AND THE BURIAL-PLACES OF THE GODS. MOREOVER HE SETS FORTH THE MOURNFUL ENDINGS, MISFORTUNES, AND DEATHS OF THE GODS. AND, IN ADDITION, HE LAUGHS AT THE RIDICULOUS AND DISGUSTING ABSURDITIES WHICH THE HEATHENS CONTINUALLY ALLEGE ABOUT THE FORM AND APPEARANCE OF THEIR GODS.

"Read the writings of the Stoics,[2] or the writings of wise men, you will acknowledge these facts with me. On account of the merits of their virtue or of some gift, Euhemerus asserts that they were esteemed gods; and he enumerates their birthdays, their countries, their places of sepulture, and throughout various provinces points out these circumstances of the Dictæan Jupiter, and of the Delphic Apollo, and of the Pharian Isis, and of the Eleusinian Ceres. Prodicus speaks of men who were taken up among the gods, because they were helpful to the uses of men in their wanderings, by the discovery of new kinds of produce. Persæus philosophizes also to the same result; and he adds thereto, that the fruits discovered, and the discoverers of those same fruits, were called by the same names; as the passage of the comic writer runs, that Venus freezes without Bacchus and Ceres. Alexander the Great, the celebrated Macedonian, wrote in a remarkable document[3] addressed to his mother, that under fear of his power there had been betrayed to him by the priest the secret of the gods having been men: to her he makes Vulcan the original of all, and then the race of Jupiter. And you behold the swallow and the cymbal of Isis,[4] and the tomb of your Serapis or Osiris empty, with his limbs scattered

about. Then consider the sacred rites themselves, and their very mysteries: you will find mournful deaths, misfortunes, and funerals, and the griefs and wailings of the miserable gods. Isis bewails, laments, and seeks after her lost son, with her Cynocephalus and her bald priests; and the wretched Isiacs beat their breasts, and imitate the grief of the most unhappy mother. By and by, when the little boy is found, Isis rejoices, and the priests exult, Cynocephalus the discoverer boasts, and they do not cease year by year either to lose what they find, or to find what they lose. Is it not ridiculous either to grieve for what you worship, or to worship that over which you grieve? Yet these were formerly Egyptian rites, and now are Roman ones. Ceres with her torches lighted, and surrounded[5] with a serpent, with anxiety and solicitude tracks the footsteps of Proserpine, stolen away in her wandering, and corrupted. These are the Eleusinian mysteries. And what are the sacred rites of Jupiter? His nurse is a she-goat, and as an infant he is taken away from his greedy father, lest he should be devoured; and clanging uproar[6] is dashed out of the cymbals of the Corybantes, lest the father should hear the infant's wailing. Cybele of Dindymus — I am ashamed to speak of it — who could not entice her adulterous lover, who unhappily was pleasing to her, to lewdness, because she herself, as being the mother of many gods, was ugly and old, mutilated him, doubtless that she might make a god of the eunuch. On account of this story, the Galli also worship her by the punishment of their emasculated body. Now certainly these things are not sacred rites, but tortures. What are the very forms and appearances (of the gods)? do they not argue the contemptible and disgraceful characters of your gods?[7] Vulcan is a lame god, and crippled; Apollo, smooth-faced after so many ages; Æsculapius well bearded, notwithstanding that he is the son of the ever youthful Apollo; Neptune with sea-green eyes; Minerva with eyes bluish grey; Juno with ox-eyes; Mercury with winged feet; Pan with hoofed feet; Saturn with feet in fetters; Janus, indeed, wears two faces, as if that he might walk with looks turned back; Diana sometimes is a huntress, with her robe girded up high; and as the Ephesian she has many and fruitful breasts; and when exaggerated as Trivia, she is horrible with three heads and with many hands. What is your Jupiter himself? Now he is represented in a statue as beardless, now he is set up as bearded; and when he is called Hammon, he has horns; and when Capitolinus, then he wields

---

[1] Four early editions read "instantius" for "in statuis," making the meaning probably, "more keenly," "more directly."
[2] Otherwise, according to some, "of the historians."
[3] This treatise is mentioned by Athenagoras, *Legat. pro Christ.*, ch. xxviii. [See vol. ii. p. 143, this series.] Also by Augustine, *de Civ. Dei*, lib. viii. ch. iii. and xxvii. In the fifth chapter Augustine calls the priest by the name of Leo.
[4] This passage is very doubtful both in its text and its meaning.

[5] Otherwise, "carried about."
[6] Otherwise, "his approach is drowned."
[7] Otherwise, "do they not show what are the sports and the honours of your gods?"

the thunderbolts; and when Latiaris, he is sprinkled with gore; and when Feretrius, he is not approached;[1] and not to mention any further the multitude of Jupiters, the monstrous appearances of Jupiter are as numerous as his names. Erigone was hanged from a noose, that as a virgin she might be glowing[2] among the stars. The Castors die by turns, that they may live. Æsculapius, that he may rise into a god, is struck with a thunderbolt. Hercules, that he may put off humanity, is burnt up by the fires of Œta.[3]

CHAP. XXII. — ARGUMENT: MOREOVER, THESE FABLES, WHICH AT FIRST WERE INVENTED BY IGNORANT MEN, WERE AFTERWARDS CELEBRATED BY OTHERS, AND CHIEFLY BY POETS, WHO DID NO LITTLE MISCHIEF TO THE TRUTH BY THEIR AUTHORITY. BY FICTIONS OF THIS KIND, AND BY FALSEHOODS OF A YET MORE ATTRACTIVE NATURE, THE MINDS OF YOUNG PEOPLE ARE CORRUPTED, AND THENCE THEY MISERABLY GROW OLD IN THESE BELIEFS, ALTHOUGH, ON THE OTHER HAND, THE TRUTH IS OBVIOUS TO THEM IF THEY WILL ONLY SEEK AFTER IT.

"These fables and errors we both learn from ignorant parents, and, what is more serious still, we elaborate them in our very studies and instructions, especially in the verses of the poets, who as much as possible have prejudiced[4] the truth[5] by their authority. And for this reason Plato rightly expelled from the state which he had founded in his discourse, the illustrious Homer whom he had praised and crowned.[6] For it was he especially who in the Trojan war allowed your gods, although he made jests of them, still to interfere in the affairs and doings of men: he brought them together in contest; he wounded Venus; he bound, wounded, and drove away Mars. He relates that Jupiter was set free by Briareus, so as not to be bound fast by the rest of the gods; and that he bewailed in showers of blood his son Sarpedon, because he could not snatch him from death; and that, enticed by the girdle of Venus, he lay more eagerly with his wife Juno than he was accustomed to do with his adulterous loves. Elsewhere Hercules threw out dung, and Apollo is feeding cattle for Admetus. Neptune, however, builds walls for Laomedon, and the unfortunate builder did not receive the wages for his work. Then Jupiter's thunderbolt is fabricated[7] on the anvil with the arms of Æneas, although there were heaven, and thunderbolts, and lightnings long before Jupiter was born in Crete; and neither could the Cyclops imitate, nor Jupiter himself help fearing, the flames of the real thunderbolt. Why should I speak of the detected adultery of Mars and Venus, and of the violence of Jupiter against Ganymede, — a deed consecrated, (as you say,) in heaven? And all these things have been put forward with this view, that a certain authority might be gained for the vices[8] of men. By these fictions, and such as these, and by lies of a more attractive kind, the minds of boys are corrupted; and with the same fables clinging to them, they grow up even to the strength of mature age; and, poor wretches, they grow old in the same beliefs, although the truth is plain, if they will only seek after it. For all the writers of antiquity, both Greek and Roman, have set forth that Saturn, the beginner of this race and multitude, was a man. Nepos knows this, and Cassius in his history; and Thallus and Diodorus speak the same thing. This Saturn then, driven from Crete by the fear of his raging son, had come to Italy, and, received by the hospitality of Janus, taught those unskilled and rustic men many things, — as, being something of a Greek, and polished, — to print letters for instance, to coin money, to make instruments. Therefore he preferred that his hiding-place, because he had been safely hidden (latent) there, should be called Latium; and he gave a city, from his own name, the name of Saturnia, and Janus, Janiculum, so that each of them left their names to the memory of posterity. Therefore it was certainly a man that fled, certainly a man who was concealed, and the father of a man, and sprung from a man. He was declared, however, to be the son of earth or of heaven, because among the Italians he was of unknown parents; as even to this day we call those who appear unexpectedly, sent from heaven, those who are ignoble and unknown, sons of the earth. His son Jupiter reigned at Crete after his father was driven out. There he died, there he had sons. To this day the cave of Jupiter is visited, and his sepulchre is shown, and he is convicted of being human by those very sacred rites of his.

CHAP. XXIII. — ARGUMENT: ALTHOUGH THE HEATHENS ACKNOWLEDGE THEIR KINGS TO BE MORTAL, YET THEY FEIGN THAT THEY ARE GODS EVEN AGAINST THEIR OWN WILL, NOT BECAUSE OF THEIR BELIEF IN THEIR DIVINITY, BUT IN HONOUR OF THE POWER THAT THEY HAVE EXERTED.

---

[1] These words are very variously read. Davis conjectures that they should be, "When Feretrius, he does not hear," and explains the allusion as follows: that Jupiter Feretrius could only be approached with the *spolia opima;* and Minucius is covertly ridiculing the Romans, because, not having taken *spolia opima* for so long a time, they could not approach Feretrius.
[2] Otherwise, "pointed out," or "designated."
[3] Otherwise corrupted into Ætna.
[4] Some read, "and it is marvellous how these have prejudiced," etc.
[5] Some read, "the truth itself."
[6] Plat., *de Rep*, lib. iii.

[7] Otherwise, "Then Vulcan fabricates," etc.
[8] Otherwise, "judgments."

YET A TRUE GOD HAS NEITHER RISING NOR SET-
TING. THENCE OCTAVIUS CRITICISES THE IMAGES
AND SHRINES OF THE GODS.

" It is needless to go through each individual
case, and to develope the entire series of that
race, since in its first parents their mortality is
proved, and must have flowed down into the
rest by the very law of their succession, unless
perhaps you fancy that they were gods after
death ; as by the perjury of Proculus, Romulus
became a god ; and by the good-will of the
Mauritanians, Juba is a god ; and other kings
are divine who are consecrated, not in the faith
of their divinity, but in honour of the power that
they exercised. Moreover, this name is ascribed
to those who are unwilling to bear it. They
desire to persevere in their human condition.
They fear that they may be made gods ; although they are already old men, they do not
wish it. Therefore neither are gods made from
dead people, since a god cannot die ; nor of
people that are born, since everything which is
born dies. But that is divine which has neither
rising nor setting. For why, if they were born,
are they not born in the present day also ? —
unless, perchance, Jupiter has already grown
old, and child-bearing has failed in Juno, and
Minerva has grown grey before she has borne
children. Or has that process of generation
ceased, for the reason that no assent is any
longer yielded to fables of this kind ? Besides,
if the gods could create,[1] they could not perish :
we should have more gods than all men together ;
so that now, neither would the heaven contain
them, nor the air receive them, nor the earth
bear them. Whence it is manifest, that those
were men whom we both read of as having been
born, and know to have died. Who therefore
doubts that the common people pray to and
publicly worship the consecrated images of these
men ; in that the belief and mind of the ignorant
is deceived by the perfection of art, is blinded
by the glitter of gold, is dimmed with the shining
of silver and the whiteness of ivory ? But if any
one were to present to his mind with what instruments and with what machinery every image
is formed, he would blush that he had feared
matter, treated after his fancy by the artificer to
make a god.[2] For a god of wood, a portion
perhaps of a pile, or of an unlucky log, is hung
up, is cut, is hewn, is planed ; and a god of
brass or of silver, often from an impure vessel,
as was done by the Egyptian king,[3] is fused, is
beaten with hammers and forged on anvils ; and
the god of stone is cut, is sculptured, and is

polished by some abandoned man, nor feels the
injury done to him in his nativity, any more than
afterwards it feels the worship flowing from your
veneration ; unless perhaps the stone, or the
wood, or the silver is not yet a god. When,
therefore, does the god begin his existence ?
Lo, it is melted, it is wrought, it is sculptured —
it is not yet a god ; lo, it is soldered, it is built
together — it is set up, and even yet it is not a
god ; lo, it is adorned, it is consecrated, it is
prayed to — then at length it is a god, when
man has chosen it to be so, and for the purpose
has dedicated it.

CHAP. XXIV. — ARGUMENT : HE BRIEFLY SHOWS,
MOREOVER, WHAT RIDICULOUS, OBSCENE, AND
CRUEL RITES WERE OBSERVED IN CELEBRATING
THE MYSTERIES OF CERTAIN GODS.

" How much more truly do dumb animals
naturally judge concerning your gods ? Mice,
swallows, kites, know that they have no feeling :
they gnaw them, they trample on them, they sit
upon them ; and unless you drive them off, they
build their nests in the very mouth of your god.
Spiders, indeed, weave their webs over his face,
and suspend their threads from his very head.
You wipe, cleanse, scrape, and you protect and
fear those whom you make ; while not one of
you thinks that he ought to know God before
he worships Him ; desiring without consideration to obey their ancestors, choosing rather to
become an addition to the error of others, than
to trust themselves ; in that they know nothing
of what they fear. Thus avarice has been consecrated in gold and silver ; thus the form of
empty statues has been established ; thus has
arisen Roman superstition. And if you recon-
sider the rites of these gods, how many things
are laughable, and how many also pitiable !
Naked people run about in the raw winter ;
some walk bonneted, and carry around old
bucklers, or beat drums, or lead their gods
a-begging through the streets. Some fanes it
is permitted to approach once a year, some it is
forbidden to visit at all. There is one place
where a man may not go, and there are some
that are sacred from women : it is a crime needing atonement for a slave even to be present
at some ceremonies. Some sacred places are
crowned by a woman having one husband, some
by a woman with many ; and she who can reckon
up most adulteries is sought after with most religious zeal. What ! would not a man who makes
libations of his own blood, and supplicates (his
god) by his own wounds, be better if he were
altogether profane, than religious in such a way
as this ? And he whose shameful parts are cut
off, how greatly does he wrong God in seeking
to propitiate Him in this manner ! since, if God

---

[1] " Be created" is a more probable reading.
[2] Otherwise, " that he had rashly been so deceived by the artificer
in the material, as to make a god."
[3] [Footbaths. See vol. ii., *Theophilus*, p. 92, and *Athenagoras*,
p. 143.]

wished for eunuchs, He could bring them as such into existence, and would not make them so afterwards. Who does not perceive that people of unsound mind, and of weak and degraded apprehension, are foolish in these things, and that the very multitude of those who err affords to each of them mutual patronage? Here the defence of the general madness is the multitude of the mad people.

CHAP. XXV.—ARGUMENT : THEN HE SHOWS THAT CÆCILIUS HAD BEEN WRONG IN ASSERTING THAT THE ROMANS HAD GAINED THEIR POWER OVER THE WHOLE WORLD BY MEANS OF THE DUE OBSERVANCE OF SUPERSTITIONS OF THIS KIND. RATHER THE ROMANS IN THEIR ORIGIN WERE COLLECTED BY CRIME, AND GREW BY THE TERRORS OF THEIR FEROCITY. AND THEREFORE THE ROMANS WERE NOT SO GREAT BECAUSE THEY WERE RELIGIOUS, BUT BECAUSE THEY WERE SACRILEGIOUS WITH IMPUNITY.

" Nevertheless, you will say that that very superstition itself gave, increased, and established their empire for the Romans, since they prevailed not so much by their valour as by their religion and piety. Doubtless the illustrious and noble justice of the Romans had its beginning from the very cradle of the growing empire. Did they not in their origin, when gathered together and fortified by crime, grow by the terror of their own fierceness? For the first people were assembled together as to an asylum. Abandoned people, profligate, incestuous, assassins, traitors, had flocked together; and in order that Romulus himself, their commander and governor, might excel his people in guilt, he committed fratricide.[1] These are the first auspices of the religious state ! By and by they carried off, violated, and ruined foreign virgins, already betrothed, already destined for husbands, and even some young women from their marriage vows — a thing unexampled [2] — and then engaged in war with their parents, that is, with their fathers-in-law, and shed the blood of their kindred. What more irreligious, what more audacious, what could be safer than the very confidence of crime? Now, to drive their neighbours from the land, to overthrow the nearest cities, with their temples and altars, to drive them into captivity, to grow up by the losses of others and by their own crimes, is the course of training common to the rest of the kings and the latest leaders with Romulus. Thus, whatever the Romans hold, cultivate, possess, is the spoil of their audacity. All their temples are built from the spoils of violence, that is, from the ruins of cities, from the spoils

of the gods, from the murders of priests. This is to insult and scorn, to yield to conquered religions, to adore them when captive, after having vanquished them. For to adore what you have taken by force, is to consecrate sacrilege, not divinities. As often, therefore, as the Romans triumphed, so often they were polluted ; and as many trophies as they gained from the nations, so many spoils did they take from the gods. Therefore the Romans were not so great because they were religious, but because they were sacrilegious with impunity. For neither were they able in the wars themselves to have the help of the gods against whom they took up arms ; and they began to worship those when they were triumphed over, whom they had previously challenged. But what avail such gods as those on behalf of the Romans, who had had no power on behalf of their own worshippers against the Roman arms? For we know the indigenous gods of the Romans — Romulus, Picus, Tiberinus, and Consus, and Pilumnus, and Picumnus. Tatius both discovered and worshipped Cloacina ; Hostilius, Fear and Pallor. Subsequently Fever was dedicated by I know not whom : such was the superstition that nourished that city, — diseases and ill states of health. Assuredly also Acca Laurentia, and Flora, infamous harlots, must be reckoned among the diseases [3] and the gods of the Romans. Such as these doubtless enlarged the dominion of the Romans, in opposition to others who were worshipped by the nations : for against their own people neither did the Thracian Mars, nor the Cretan Jupiter, nor Juno, now of Argos, now of Samos, now of Carthage, nor Diana of Tauris, nor the Idæan Mother, nor those Egyptian — not deities, but monstrosities — assist them ; unless perchance among the Romans the chastity of virgins was greater, or the religion of the priests more holy : though absolutely among very many of the virgins unchastity was punished, in that they, doubtless without the knowledge of Vesta, had intercourse too carelessly with men ; and for the rest their impunity arose not from the better protection of their chastity, but from the better fortune of their immodesty. And where are adulteries better arranged by the priests than among the very altars and shrines? where are more panderings debated, or more acts of violence concerted? Finally, burning lust is more frequently gratified in the little chambers of the keepers of the temple, than in the brothels themselves. And still, long before the Romans, by the ordering of God, the Assyrians held dominion, the Medes, the Persians, the Greeks also, and the Egyptians, although they had not any Pontiffs, nor Arvales, nor Salii, nor Vestals,

---

[1] Parricidium.
[2] Virg., Æneid, viii. 635.

[3] Some read " probra " for " morbos," scil. " reproaches."

nor Augurs, nor chickens shut up in a coop, by whose feeding or abstinence the highest concerns of the state were to be governed.

CHAP. XXVI. — ARGUMENT: THE WEAPON THAT CÆCILIUS HAD SLIGHTLY BRANDISHED AGAINST HIM, TAKEN FROM THE AUSPICES AND AUGURIES OF BIRDS, OCTAVIUS RETORTS BY INSTANCING THE CASES OF REGULUS, MANCINUS, PAULUS, AND CÆSAR. AND HE SHOWS BY OTHER EXAMPLES, THAT THE ARGUMENT FROM THE ORACLES IS OF NO GREATER FORCE THAN THE OTHERS.

" And now I come to those Roman auspices and auguries which you have collected with extreme pains, and have borne testimony that they were both neglected with ill consequences, and observed with good fortune. Certainly Clodius, and Flaminius, and Junius lost their armies on this account, because they did not judge it well to wait for the very solemn omen given by the greedy pecking of the chickens. But what of Regulus? Did he not observe the auguries, and was taken captive? Mancinus maintained his religious duty, and was sent under the yoke, and was given up. Paulus also had greedy chickens at Cannæ, yet he was overthrown with the greater part of the republic.[1] Caius Cæsar despised the auguries and auspices that resisted his making his voyage into Africa before the winter, and thus the more easily he both sailed and conquered. But what and how much shall I go on to say about oracles? After his death Amphiaraus answered as to things to come, though he knew not (while living) that he should be betrayed by his wife on account of a bracelet. The blind Tiresias saw the future, although he did not see the present. Ennius invented the replies of the Pythian Apollo concerning Pyrrhus, although Apollo had already ceased to make verses; and that cautious and ambiguous oracle of his, failed just at the time when men began to be at once more cultivated and less credulous. And Demosthenes, because he knew that the answers were feigned, complained that the Pythia *philippized.* But sometimes, it is true, even auspices or oracles have touched the truth. Although among many falsehoods chance might appear as if it imitated forethought; yet I will approach the very source of error and perverseness, whence all that obscurity has flowed, and both dig into it more deeply, and lay it open more manifestly. There are some insincere and vagrant spirits degraded from their heavenly vigour by earthly stains and lusts. Now these spirits, after having lost the simplicity of their nature by being weighed down and immersed in vices, for a solace of their calamity,

cease not, now that they are ruined themselves, to ruin others; and being depraved themselves, to infuse into others the error of their depravity; and being themselves alienated from God, to separate others from God by the introduction of degraded superstitions. The poets know that those spirits are demons; the philosophers discourse of them; Socrates knew it, who, at the nod and decision of a demon that was at his side, either declined or undertook affairs. The Magi, also, not only know that there are demons, but, moreover, whatever miracle they affect to perform, do it by means of demons; by their aspirations and communications they show their wondrous tricks, making either those things appear which are not, or those things not to appear which are. Of those magicians, the first both in eloquence and in deed, Sosthenes,[2] not only describes the true God with fitting majesty, but the angels that are the ministers and messengers of God, even the true God. And he knew that it enhanced His veneration, that in awe of the very nod and glance of their Lord they should tremble. The same man also declared that demons were earthly, wandering, hostile to humanity. What said Plato,[3] who believed that it was a hard thing to find out God? Does not he also, without hesitation, tell of both angels and demons? And in his *Symposium* also, does not he endeavour to explain the nature of demons? For he will have it to be a substance between mortal and immortal — that is, mediate between body and spirit, compounded by a mingling of earthly weight and heavenly lightness; whence also he warns us of the desire of love,[4] and he says that it is moulded and glides into the human breast, and stirs the senses, and moulds the affections, and infuses the ardour of lust.

CHAP. XXVII. — ARGUMENT: RECAPITULATION. DOUBTLESS HERE IS A SOURCE OF ERROR: DEMONS LURK UNDER THE STATUES AND IMAGES, THEY HAUNT THE FANES, THEY ANIMATE THE FIBRES OF THE ENTRAILS, DIRECT THE FLIGHTS OF BIRDS, GOVERN THE LOTS, POUR FORTH ORACLES INVOLVED IN FALSE RESPONSES. THESE THINGS NOT FROM GOD; BUT THEY ARE CONSTRAINED TO CONFESS WHEN THEY ARE ADJURED IN THE NAME OF THE TRUE GOD, AND ARE DRIVEN FROM THE POSSESSED BODIES. HENCE THEY FLEE HASTILY FROM THE NEIGHBOURHOOD OF CHRISTIANS, AND STIR UP A HATRED AGAINST THEM IN THE MINDS OF THE GENTILES WHO BEGIN TO HATE THEM BEFORE THEY KNOW THEM.

" These impure spirits, therefore — the demons — as is shown by the Magi, by the philos-

---

[1] Reipublicæ; but it is shrewdly conjectured that the passage was written, " cum majore R. P. parte " — " with the greater part of the Roman people," and the mistake made by the transcriber of the MS.

[2] Otherwise Hostanes.

[3] [Octavius and Minucius had but one mind (see cap. i. *supra*), and both were philosophers of the Attic Academy reflecting Cicero. See my remarks on Athenagoras, vol. ii. p. 126, this series.]

[4] According to some editors, " warns us that the desire of love is received."

ophers, and by Plato, consecrated under statues and images, lurk there, and by their afflatus attain the authority as of a present deity ; while in the meantime they are breathed into the prophets, while they dwell in the shrines, while sometimes they animate the fibres of the entrails, control the flights of birds, direct the lots, are the cause of oracles involved in many falsehoods. For they are both deceived, and they deceive ; inasmuch as they are both ignorant of the simple truth, and for their own ruin they confess not that which they know. Thus they weigh men downwards from heaven, and call them away from the true God to material things : they disturb the life, render all men [1] unquiet ; creeping also secretly into human bodies, with subtlety, as being spirits, they feign diseases, alarm the minds, wrench about the limbs ; that they may constrain men to worship them, being gorged with the fumes of altars or the sacrifices of cattle, that, by remitting what they had bound, they may seem to have cured it. These raging maniacs also, whom you see rush about in public, are moreover themselves prophets without a temple ; thus they rage, thus they rave, thus they are whirled around. In them also there is a like instigation of the demon, but there is a dissimilar occasion for their madness. From the same causes also arise those things which were spoken of a little time ago by you, that Jupiter demanded the restoration of his games in a dream, that the Castors appeared with horses, and that a small ship was following the leading of the matron's girdle. A great many, even some of your own people, know all those things that the demons themselves confess concerning themselves, as often as they are driven by us from bodies by the torments of our words and by the fires of our prayers. Saturn himself, and Serapis, and Jupiter, and whatever demons you worship, overcome by pain, speak out what they are ; and assuredly they do not lie to their own discredit, especially when any of you are standing by. Since they themselves are the witnesses that they are demons, believe them when they confess the truth of themselves ; for when abjured by the only and true God, unwillingly the wretched beings shudder in [2] their bodies, and either at once leap forth, or vanish by degrees, as the faith of the sufferer assists or the grace of the healer inspires. Thus they fly from Christians when near at hand, whom at a distance they harassed by your means in their assemblies. And thus, introduced into the minds of the ignorant, they secretly sow there a hatred of us by means of fear. For it is natural both to hate one whom you fear, and to injure one

whom you have feared, if you can. Thus they take possession of the minds and obstruct the hearts, that men may begin to hate us before they know us ; lest, if known, they should either imitate us, or not be able to condemn us.

CHAP. XXVIII. — ARGUMENT : NOR IS IT ONLY HATRED THAT THEY AROUSE AGAINST THE CHRISTIANS, BUT THEY CHARGE AGAINST THEM HORRID CRIMES, WHICH UP TO THIS TIME HAVE BEEN PROVED BY NOBODY. THIS IS THE WORK OF DEMONS. FOR BY THEM A FALSE REPORT IS BOTH SET ON FOOT AND PROPAGATED. THE CHRISTIANS ARE FALSELY ACCUSED OF SACRILEGE, OF INCEST, OF ADULTERY, OF PARRICIDE ; AND, MOREOVER, IT IS CERTAIN AND TRUE THAT THE VERY SAME CRIMES, OR CRIMES LIKE TO OR GREATER THAN THESE, ARE IN FACT COMMITTED BY THE GENTILES THEMSELVES.

" BUT how unjust it is,[3] to form a judgment on things unknown and unexamined, as you do ! Believe us ourselves when penitent, for we also were the same as you, and formerly, while yet blind and obtuse, thought the same things as you ; to wit, that the Christians worshipped monsters, devoured infants, mingled in incestuous banquets. And we did not perceive that such fables as these were always set afloat by those (newsmongers), and were never either inquired into nor proved ; and that in so long a time no one had appeared to betray (their doings), to obtain not only pardon for their crime, but also favour for its discovery : moreover, that it was to this extent not evil, that a Christian, when accused, neither blushed nor feared, and that he only repented that he had not been one before. We, however, when we undertook to defend and protect some sacrilegious and incestuous persons, and even parricides, did not think that these (Christians) were to be heard at all. Sometimes even, when we affected to pity them, we were more cruelly violent against them, so as to torture them [4] when they confessed, that they might deny, to wit, that they might not perish ; making use of a perverse inquisition against them, not to elicit the truth, but to compel a falsehood. And if any one, by reason of greater weakness, overcome with suffering, and conquered, should deny that he was a Christian, we showed favour to him, as if by forswearing that name he had at once atoned for all his deeds by that simple denial. Do not you acknowledge that we felt and did the same as you feel and do ? when, if reason and not the instigation of a demon were to judge, they should rather have been pressed not to disavow themselves Christians, but to confess themselves guilty of incests, of

---

[1] Some read "slumbers" for "all men."
[2] "Cling to" is another reading.

[3] Otherwise read, "But how great a fault it is."
[4] "To urge them" is the reading in some text.

abominations, of sacred rites polluted, of infants immolated. For with these and such as these stories, did those same demons fill up the ears of the ignorant against us, to the horror of their execration. Nor yet was it wonderful, since the common report of men,[1] which is always fed by the scattering of falsehoods, is wasted away when the truth is brought to light. Thus this is the business of demons, for by them false rumours are both sown and cherished. Thence arises what you say that you hear, that an ass's head is esteemed among us a divine thing. Who is such a fool as to worship this? Who is so much more foolish as to believe that it is an object of worship? unless that you even consecrate whole asses in your stables, together with your Epona,[2] and religiously devour[3] those same asses with Isis. Also you offer up and worship the heads of oxen and of wethers, and you dedicate gods mingled also of a goat and a man, and gods with the faces of dogs and lions. Do you not adore and feed Apis the ox, with the Egyptians? And you do not condemn their sacred rites instituted in honour of serpents, and crocodiles, and other beasts, and birds, and fishes, of which if any one were to kill one of these gods, he is even punished with death. These same Egyptians, together with very many of you, are not more afraid of Isis than they are of the pungency of onions, nor of Serapis more than they tremble at the basest noises produced by the foulness of their bodies. He also who fables against us about our adoration of the members of the priest, tries to confer upon us what belongs really to himself. (Ista enim impudicitiæ eorum forsitan sacra sint, apud quos sexus omnis membris omnibus prostat, apud quos tota impudicitia vocatur urbanitas ; qui scortorum licentiæ invident, qui medios viros lambunt, libidinoso ore inguinibus inhærescunt, homines malæ linguæ etiam si tacerent, quos prius tædescit impudicitiæ suæ quam pudescit.) Abomination ! they suffer on themselves such evil deeds, as no age is so effeminate as to be able to bear, and no slavery so cruel as to be compelled to endure.

CHAP. XXIX. — ARGUMENT : NOR IS IT MORE TRUE THAT A MAN FASTENED TO A CROSS ON ACCOUNT OF HIS CRIMES IS WORSHIPPED BY CHRISTIANS, FOR THEY BELIEVE NOT ONLY THAT HE WAS INNOCENT, BUT WITH REASON THAT HE WAS GOD. BUT, ON THE OTHER HAND, THE HEATHENS INVOKE THE DIVINE POWERS OF KINGS RAISED INTO GODS BY THEMSELVES ; THEY PRAY TO IMAGES, AND BESEECH THEIR GENII.

"These, and such as these infamous things, we are not at liberty even to hear ; it is even disgraceful with any more words to defend our-

selves from such charges. For you pretend that those things are done by chaste and modest persons, which we should not believe to be done at all, unless you proved that they were true concerning yourselves. For in that you attribute to our religion the worship of a criminal and his cross,[4] you wander far from the neighbourhood of the truth, in thinking either that a criminal deserved, or that an earthly being was able, to be believed God. Miserable indeed is that man whose whole hope is dependent on mortal man, for all his help is put an end to with the extinction of the man.[5] The Egyptians certainly choose out a man for themselves whom they may worship ; him alone they propitiate ; him they consult about all things ; to him they slaughter victims ; and he who to others is a god, to himself is certainly a man whether he will or no, for he does not deceive his own consciousness, if he deceives that of others. Moreover, a false flattery disgracefully caresses princes and kings, not as great and chosen men, as is just, but as gods ; whereas honour is more truly rendered to an illustrious man, and love is more pleasantly given to a very good man. Thus they invoke their deity, they supplicate their images, they implore their Genius, that is, their demon ; and it is safer to swear falsely by the genius of Jupiter than by that of a king. Crosses, moreover, we neither worship nor wish for.[6] You, indeed, who consecrate gods of wood, adore wooden crosses perhaps as parts of your gods. For your very standards, as well as your banners; and flags of your camp, what else are they but crosses gilded and adorned? Your victorious trophies not only imitate the appearance of a simple cross, but also that of a man affixed to it. We assuredly see the sign of a cross,[7] naturally, in the ship when it is carried along with swelling sails, when it glides forward with expanded oars ; and when the military yoke is lifted up, it is the sign of a cross ; and when a man adores God with a pure mind, with hands outstretched. Thus the sign of the cross either is sustained by a natural reason, or your own religion is formed with respect to it.

CHAP. XXX. — ARGUMENT : THE STORY ABOUT CHRISTIANS DRINKING THE BLOOD OF AN INFANT THAT THEY HAVE MURDERED, IS A BAREFACED CALUMNY. BUT THE GENTILES, BOTH CRUELLY EXPOSE THEIR CHILDREN NEWLY BORN, AND BEFORE THEY ARE BORN DESTROY THEM BY A CRUEL ABORTION. CHRISTIANS ARE NEITHER ALLOWED TO SEE NOR TO HEAR OF MANSLAUGHTER.

"And now I should wish to meet him who says or believes that we are initiated by the

---

[1] "Of all men" is another reading.
[2] Otherwise, "Hippona."
[3] Otherwise, "devote," and other readings.

[4] [A reverent allusion to the Crucified, believed in and worshipped as God.]
[5] [Jer. xvii 5-7.]
[6] [See Justin Martyr's *Dialogue with Trypho*, chap. lxxxix. et seqq. vol. i. p. 244. S.]
[7] [See Reeves's *Apologies* (ut supra), vol. ii. p. 144, note. S.]

slaughter and blood of an infant. Think you that it can be possible for so tender, so little a body to receive those fatal wounds ; for any one to shed, pour forth, and drain that new blood of a youngling, and of a man scarcely come into existence? No one can believe this, except one who can dare to do it. And I see that you at one time expose your begotten children to wild beasts and to birds ; at another, that you crush them when strangled with a miserable kind of death. There are some women who, by drinking medical preparations,[1] extinguish the source of the future man in their very bowels, and thus commit a parricide before they bring forth. And these things assuredly come down from the teaching of your gods. For Saturn did not expose his children, but devoured them. With reason were infants sacrificed to him by parents in some parts of Africa, caresses and kisses repressing their crying, that a weeping victim might not be sacrificed. Moreover, among the Tauri of Pontus, and to the Egyptian Busiris, it was a sacred rite to immolate their guests, and for the Galli to slaughter to Mercury human, or rather inhuman, sacrifices. The Roman sacrificers buried living a Greek man and a Greek woman, a Gallic man and a Gallic woman ; and to this day, Jupiter Latiaris is worshipped by them with murder ; and, what is worthy of the son of Saturn, he is gorged with the blood of an evil and criminal man. I believe that he himself taught Catiline to conspire under a compact of blood, and Bellona to steep her sacred rites with a draught of human gore, and taught men to heal epilepsy with the blood of a man, that is, with a worse disease. They also are not unlike to him who devour the wild beasts from the arena, besmeared and stained with blood, or fattened with the limbs or the entrails of men. To us it is not lawful either to see or to hear of homicide ; and so much do we shrink from human blood, that we do not use the blood even of eatable animals in our food.

CHAP. XXXI. — ARGUMENT : THE CHARGE OF OUR ENTERTAINMENTS BEING POLLUTED WITH INCEST, IS ENTIRELY OPPOSED TO ALL PROBABILITY, WHILE IT IS PLAIN THAT GENTILES ARE ACTUALLY GUILTY OF INCEST. THE BANQUETS OF CHRISTIANS ARE NOT ONLY MODEST, BUT TEMPERATE. IN FACT, INCESTUOUS LUST IS SO UNHEARD OF, THAT WITH MANY EVEN THE MODEST ASSOCIATION OF THE SEXES GIVES RISE TO A BLUSH.

"And of the incestuous banqueting, the plotting of demons has falsely devised an enormous fable against us, to stain the glory of our modesty, by the loathing excited by an outrageous infamy, that before inquiring into the truth it might turn men away from us by the terror of an abominable charge. It was thus your own Fronto[2] acted in this respect : he did not produce testimony, as one who alleged a charge, but he scattered reproaches as a rhetorician. For these things have rather originated from your own nations. Among the Persians, a promiscuous association between sons and mothers is allowed. Marriages with sisters are legitimate among the Egyptians and in Athens. Your records and your tragedies, which you both read and hear with pleasure, glory in incests : thus also you worship incestuous gods, who have intercourse with mothers, with daughters, with sisters. With reason, therefore, is incest frequently detected among you, and is continually permitted. Miserable men, you may even, without knowing it, rush into what is unlawful : since you scatter your lusts promiscuously, since you everywhere beget children, since you frequently expose even those who are born at home to the mercy of others, it is inevitable that you must come back to your own children, and stray to your own offspring. Thus you continue the story of incest, even although you have no consciousness of your crime. But we maintain our modesty not in appearance, but in our heart we gladly abide by the bond of a single marriage ; in the desire of procreating, we know either one wife, or none at all. We practise sharing in banquets, which are not only modest, but also sober : for we do not indulge in entertainments nor prolong our feasts with wine ; but we temper our joyousness with gravity, with chaste discourse, and with body even more chaste (divers of us unviolated) enjoy rather than make a boast of a perpetual virginity of a body. So far, in fact, are they from indulging in incestuous desire, that with some even the (idea of a) modest intercourse of the sexes causes a blush. Neither do we at once stand on the level of the lowest of the people, if we refuse your honours and purple robes ; and we are not fastidious, if we all have a discernment of one good, but are assembled together with the same quietness with which we live as individuals ; and we are not garrulous in corners, although you either blush or are afraid to hear us in public. And that day by day the number of us is increased, is not a ground for a charge of error, but is a testimony which claims praise ; for, in a fair mode of life, our actual number both continues and abides undiminished, and strangers increase it. Thus, in short, we do not distinguish our people by some small bodily mark, as you suppose, but easily enough by the sign of innocency and modesty. Thus

---

[1] By medicaments and drinks.

[2] [Fronto is called "*our* Cirtensian" in cap. ix. *supra ;* and this suggests that the *Octavius* was probably written in Cirta, *circa* A.D. 210. See *supra*, p. 178.]

we love one another, to your regret, with a mutual love, because we do not know how to hate. Thus we call one another, to your envy, brethren, as being men born of one God and Parent, and companions in faith, and as fellow-heirs in hope. You, however, do not recognise one another, and you are cruel in your mutual hatreds; nor do you acknowledge one another as brethren, unless indeed for the purpose of fratricide.

CHAP. XXXII. — ARGUMENT: NOR CAN IT BE SAID THAT THE CHRISTIANS CONCEAL WHAT THEY WORSHIP BECAUSE THEY HAVE NO TEMPLES AND NO ALTARS, INASMUCH AS THEY ARE PERSUADED THAT GOD CAN BE CIRCUMSCRIBED BY NO TEMPLE, AND THAT NO LIKENESS OF HIM CAN BE MADE. BUT HE IS EVERYWHERE PRESENT, SEES ALL THINGS, EVEN THE MOST SECRET THOUGHTS OF OUR HEARTS; AND WE LIVE NEAR TO HIM, AND IN HIS PROTECTION.

"But do you think that we conceal what we worship, if we have not temples and altars? And yet what image of God shall I make, since, if you think rightly, man himself is the image of God? What temple shall I build to Him, when this whole world fashioned by His work cannot receive Him? And when I, a man, dwell far and wide, shall I shut up the might of so great majesty within one little building? Were it not better that He should be dedicated in our mind, consecrated in our inmost heart? Shall I offer victims and sacrifices to the Lord, such as He has produced for my use, that I should throw back to Him His own gift? It is ungrateful when the victim fit for sacrifice is a good disposition, and a pure mind, and a sincere judgment.[1] Therefore he who cultivates innocence supplicates God; he who cultivates justice makes offerings to God; he who abstains from fraudulent practices propitiates God; he who snatches man from danger slaughters the most acceptable victim. These are our sacrifices, these are our rites of God's worship; thus, among us, he who is most just is he who is most religious. But certainly the God whom we worship we neither show nor see. Verily for this reason we believe Him to be God, that we can be conscious of Him, but cannot see Him; for in His works, and in all the movements of the world, we behold His power ever present when He thunders, lightens, darts His bolts, or when He makes all bright again. Nor should you wonder if you do not see God. By the wind and by the blasts of the storm all things are ·driven on and shaken, are agitated, and yet neither wind nor tempest comes under our eyesight. Thus we cannot look upon the sun, which is the cause of seeing to all creatures: the pupil of the eye is with-

drawn from his rays, the gaze of the beholder is dimmed; and if you look too long, all power of sight is extinguished. What! can you sustain the Architect of the sun Himself, the very source of light, when you turn yourself away from His lightnings, and hide yourself from His thunderbolts? Do you wish to see God with your carnal eyes, when you are neither able to behold nor to grasp your own soul itself, by which you are enlivened and speak? But, moreover, it is said that God is ignorant of man's doings; and being established in heaven, He can neither survey all nor know individuals. Thou errest, O man, and art deceived; for from where is God afar off, when all things heavenly and earthly, and which are beyond this province of the universe, are known to God, are full of God? Everywhere He is not only very near to us, but He is infused into us. Therefore once more look upon the sun: it is fixed fast in the heaven, yet it is diffused over all lands equally; present everywhere, it is associated and mingled with all things; its brightness is never violated. How much more God, who has made all things, and looks upon all things, from whom there can be nothing secret, is present in the darkness, is present in our thoughts, as if in the deep darkness. Not only do we act in Him, but also, I had almost said, we live with Him.

CHAP. XXXIII. — ARGUMENT: THAT EVEN IF GOD BE SAID TO HAVE NOTHING AVAILED THE JEWS, CERTAINLY THE WRITERS OF THE JEWISH ANNALS ARE THE MOST SUFFICIENT WITNESSES THAT THEY FORSOOK GOD BEFORE THEY WERE FORSAKEN BY HIM.

"Neither let us flatter ourselves concerning our multitude. We seem many to ourselves, but to God we are very few. We distinguish peoples and nations; to God this whole world is one family. Kings only know all the matters of their kingdom by the ministrations of their servants: God has no need of information. We not only live in His eyes, but also in His bosom. But it is objected that it availed the Jews nothing that they themselves worshipped the one God with altars and temples, with the greatest superstition. You are guilty of ignorance if you are recalling later events while you are forgetful or unconscious of former ones. For they themselves also, as long as they worshipped our God — and He is the same God of all — with chastity, innocency, and religion, as long as they obeyed His wholesome precepts, from a few became innumerable, from poor became rich, from being servants became kings · a few overwhelmed many; unarmed men overwhelmed armed ones as they fled from them, following them up by God's command, and with the elements striving on their behalf. Carefully read over their Scrip-

---

[1] According to some editions, "conscience."

tures, or if you are better pleased with the Roman writings,[1] inquire concerning the Jews in the books (to say nothing of ancient documents) of Flavius Josephus[2] or Antoninus Julianus, and you shall know that by their wickedness they deserved this fortune, and that nothing happened which had not before been predicted to them, if they should persevere in their obstinacy. Therefore you will understand that they forsook before they were forsaken, and that they were not, as you impiously say, taken captive with their God, but they were given up by God as deserters from His discipline.

CHAP. XXXIV. — ARGUMENT : MOREOVER, IT IS NOT AT ALL TO BE WONDERED AT IF THIS WORLD IS TO BE CONSUMED BY FIRE, SINCE EVERYTHING WHICH HAS A BEGINNING HAS ALSO AN END. AND THE ANCIENT PHILOSOPHERS ARE NOT AVERSE FROM THE OPINION OF THE PROBABLE BURNING UP OF THE WORLD. YET IT IS EVIDENT THAT GOD, HAVING MADE MAN FROM NOTHING, CAN RAISE HIM UP FROM DEATH INTO LIFE. AND ALL NATURE SUGGESTS A FUTURE RESURRECTION.

" Further, in respect of the burning up of the world, it is a vulgar error not to believe either that fire will fall upon it in an unforeseen way, or that the world will be destroyed by it.[3] For who of wise men doubts, who is ignorant, that all things which have had a beginning perish, all things which are made come to an end? The heaven also, with all things which are contained in heaven, will cease even as it began. The nourishment of the seas by the sweet waters of the springs shall pass away into the power of fire.[4] The Stoics have a constant belief that, the moisture being dried up, all this world will take fire ; and the Epicureans have the very same opinion concerning the conflagration of the elements and the destruction of the world. Plato speaks, saying that parts of the world are now inundated, and are now burnt up by alternate changes ; and although he says that the world itself is constructed perpetual and indissoluble, yet he adds that to God Himself, the only artificer,[5] it is both dissoluble and mortal. Thus it is no wonder if that mass be destroyed by Him by whom it was reared. You observe that philosophers dispute of the same things that we are saying, not that we are following up their tracks, but that they, from the divine announce-

ments of the prophets, imitated the shadow of the corrupted truth. Thus also the most illustrious of the wise men, Pythagoras first, and Plato chiefly, have delivered the doctrine of resurrection with a corrupt and divided faith ; for they will have it, that the bodies being dissolved, the souls alone both abide for ever, and very often pass into other new bodies. To these things they add also this, by way of misrepresenting the truth, that the souls of men return into cattle, birds, and beasts. Assuredly such an opinion as that is not worthy of a philosopher's inquiry, but of the ribaldry of a buffoon.[6] But for our argument it is sufficient, that even in this your wise men do in some measure harmonize with us. But who is so foolish or so brutish as to dare to deny that man, as he could first of all be formed by God, so can again be re-formed ; that he is nothing after death, and that he was nothing before he began to exist ; and as from nothing it was possible for him to be born, so from nothing it may be possible for him to be restored? Moreover, it is more difficult to begin that which is not, than to repeat that which has been. Do you think that, if anything is withdrawn from our feeble eyes, it perishes to God? Every body, whether it is dried up into dust, or is dissolved into moisture, or is compressed into ashes, or is attenuated into smoke, is withdrawn from us, but it is reserved for God in the custody of the elements. Nor, as you believe, do we fear any loss from sepulture,[7] but we adopt the ancient and better custom of burying in the earth. See, therefore, how for our consolation all nature suggests a future resurrection. The sun sinks down and arises, the stars pass away and return, the flowers die and revive again, after their wintry decay the shrubs resume their leaves, seeds do not flourish again unless they are rotted :[8] thus the body in the sepulchre is like the trees which in winter hide their verdure with a deceptive dryness. Why are you in haste for it to revive and return, while the winter is still raw? We must wait also for the spring-time of the body. And I am not ignorant that many, in the consciousness of what they deserve, rather desire than believe that they shall be nothing after death ; for they would prefer to be altogether extinguished, rather than to be restored for the purpose of punishment. And their error also is enhanced, both by the liberty granted them in this life, and by God's very great patience, whose judgment, the more tardy it is, is so much the more just.

CHAP. XXXV. — ARGUMENT : RIGHTEOUS AND PIOUS MEN SHALL BE REWARDED WITH NEVER-ENDING

1 [Minucius is blamed for not introducing more Scripture! He relates his friend's argument with a scoffing Pagan. How could Octavius have used the Scriptures with such an antagonist?]
2 [Wars of the Jews, b. v. cap. 9, etc.]
3 This passage is very indefinite, and probably corrupt ; the meaning is anything but satisfactory. The general meaning is given freely thus : " Further, it is a vulgar error to doubt or disbelieve a future conflagration of the world."
4 This passage is very variously read, without substantial alteration of the sense.
5 Otherwise, " to God Himself alone, the artificer."

6 This is otherwise read, " the work of the mimic or buffoon."
7 Scil. " by burning."
8 [1 Cor. xv. 36, Job xiv. 7-15.]

FELICITY, BUT UNRIGHTEOUS MEN SHALL BE VISITED WITH ETERNAL PUNISHMENT.   THE MORALS OF CHRISTIANS ARE FAR MORE HOLY THAN THOSE OF THE GENTILES.

"And yet men are admonished in the books and poems of the most learned poets of that fiery river, and of the heat flowing in manifold turns from the Stygian marsh, — things which, prepared for eternal torments, and known to them by the information of demons and from the oracles of their prophets, they have delivered to us. And therefore among them also even king Jupiter himself swears religiously by the parching banks and the black abyss; for, with foreknowledge of the punishment destined to him, with his worshippers, he shudders. Nor is there either measure or termination to these torments. There the intelligent fire [1] burns the limbs and restores them, feeds on them and nourishes them. As the fires of the thunderbolts strike upon the bodies, and do not consume them; as the fires of Mount Ætna and of Mount Vesuvius, and of burning lands everywhere, glow, but are not wasted; so that penal fire is not fed by the waste of those who burn, but is nourished by the unexhausted eating away of their bodies. But that they who know not God are deservedly tormented as impious, as unrighteous persons, no one except a profane man hesitates to believe, since it is not less wicked to be ignorant of, than to offend the Parent of all, and the Lord of all. And although ignorance of God is sufficient for punishment, even as knowledge of Him is of avail for pardon, yet if we Christians be compared with you, although in some things our discipline is inferior, yet we shall be found much better than you. For you forbid, and yet commit, adulteries; we are born [2] *men* only for our own wives: you punish crimes when committed; with us, even to think of crimes is to sin: you are afraid of those who are aware of what you do; we are even afraid of our own conscience alone, without which we cannot exist: finally, from your numbers the prison boils over; but there is no Christian there, unless he is accused on account of his religion, or a deserter.

CHAP. XXXVI. — ARGUMENT: FATE IS NOTHING, EXCEPT SO FAR AS FATE IS GOD.   MAN'S MIND IS FREE, AND THEREFORE SO IS HIS ACTION: HIS BIRTH IS NOT BROUGHT INTO JUDGMENT.   IT IS NOT A MATTER OF INFAMY, BUT OF GLORY, THAT CHRISTIANS ARE REPROACHED FOR THEIR POVERTY; AND THE FACT THAT THEY SUFFER BODILY EVILS IS NOT AS A PENALTY, BUT AS A DISCIPLINE.

"Neither let any one either take comfort from, or apologize for what happens from fate. Let what happens be of the disposition of fortune, yet the mind is free; and therefore man's doing, not his dignity, is judged. For what else is fate than what God has spoken [3] of each one of us? who, since He can foresee our constitution, determines also the fates for us, according to the deserts and the qualities of individuals. Thus in our case it is not the star under which we are born that is punished, but the particular nature of our disposition is blamed. And about fate enough is said; or if, in consideration of the time, we have spoken too little, we shall argue the matter at another time more abundantly [4] and more fully. But that many of us are called poor, this is not our disgrace, but our glory; for as our mind is relaxed by luxury, so it is strengthened by frugality. And yet who can be poor if he does not want, if he does not crave for the possessions of others, if he is rich towards God? He rather is poor, who, although he has much, desires more. Yet I will speak [5] according as I feel. No one can be so poor as he is born. Birds live without any patrimony, and day by day the cattle are fed; and yet these creatures are born for us — all of which things, if we do not lust after, we possess. Therefore, as he who treads a road is the happier the lighter he walks, so happier is he in this journey of life who lifts himself along in poverty, and does not breathe heavily under the burden of riches. And yet even if we thought wealth useful to us, we should ask it of God. Assuredly He might be able to indulge us in some measure, whose is the whole; but we would rather despise riches than possess them: [6] we desire rather innocency, we rather entreat for patience, we prefer being good to being prodigal; and that we feel and suffer the human mischiefs of the body is not punishment — it is warfare. For fortitude is strengthened by infirmities, and calamity is very often the discipline of virtue; in addition, strength both of mind and of body grows torpid without the exercise of labour. Therefore all your mighty men whom you announce as an example have flourished illustriously by their afflictions. And thus God is neither unable to aid us, nor does He despise us, since He is both the ruler of all men and the lover of His own people. But in adversity He looks into and searches out each one; He weighs the disposition of every indi-

---

[1] πῦρ σωφρονοῦν is an expression of Clemens Alexandrinus, so that there is no need for the emendation of "rapiens" instead of "sapiens," suggested by one editor.
[2] "Are known as" is another reading.

[3] Fatus.
[4] Otherwise read, "both more truly."
[5] Some read, "I will speak at length."
[6] Probably a better reading is "strive for them."

vidual in dangers, even to death at last; He investigates the will of man, certain that to Him nothing can perish. Therefore, as gold by the fires, so are we declared by critical moments.

CHAP. XXXVII. — ARGUMENT : TORTURES MOST UN-JUSTLY INFLICTED FOR THE CONFESSION OF CHRIST'S NAME ARE SPECTACLES WORTHY OF GOD. A COMPARISON INSTITUTED BETWEEN SOME OF THE BRAVEST OF THE HEATHENS AND THE HOLY MARTYRS. HE DECLARES THAT CHRISTIANS DO NOT PRESENT THEMSELVES AT PUBLIC SHOWS AND PROCESSIONS, BECAUSE THEY KNOW THEM, WITH THE GREATEST CERTAINTY, TO BE NO LESS IMPIOUS THAN CRUEL.

" How beautiful is the spectacle to God when a Christian does battle with pain ; when he is drawn up against threats, and punishments, and tortures ; when, mocking [1] the noise of death, he treads under foot the horror of the executioner ; when he raises up his liberty against kings and princes, and yields to God alone, whose he is ; when, triumphant and victorious, he tramples upon the very man who has pronounced sentence against him ! For he has conquered who has obtained that for which he contends. What soldier would not provoke peril with greater boldness under the eyes of his general? For no one receives a reward before his trial, and yet the general does not give what he has not : he cannot preserve life, but he can make the warfare glorious. But God's soldier is neither forsaken in suffering, nor is brought to an end by death. Thus the Christian may seem to be miserable ; he cannot be really found to be so. You your-selves extol unfortunate men to the skies ; Mucius Scævola, for instance, who, when he had failed in his attempt against the king, would have per-ished among the enemies unless he had sacrificed his right hand. And how many of our people have borne that not their right hand only, but their whole body, should be burned — burned up without any cries of pain, especially when they had it in their power to be sent away ! Do I compare men with Mucius or Aquilius, or with Regulus? Yet boys and young women among us treat with contempt crosses and tortures, wild beasts, and all the bugbears of punishments, with the inspired [2] patience of suffering. And do you not perceive, O wretched men, that there is no-body who either is willing without reason to undergo punishment, or is able without God to bear tortures? Unless, perhaps, the fact has deceived you, that those who know not God abound in riches, flourish in honours, and excel in power. Miserable men! in this respect they are lifted up the higher, that they may fall down lower. For these are fattened as victims for punishment, as sacrifices they are crowned for the slaughter. Thus in this respect some are lifted up to empires and dominations, that the unrestrained exercise of power might make a market of their spirit to the unbridled licence that is characteristic of a ruined soul.[3] For, apart from the knowledge of God, what solid happiness can there be, since death must come ? Like a dream, happiness slips away before it is grasped. Are you a king? Yet you fear as much as you are feared ; and however you may be surrounded with abundant followers, yet you are alone in the presence of danger. Are you rich? But fortune is ill trusted ; and with a large travelling equipage the brief journey of life is not furnished, but burdened. Do you boast of the fasces and the magisterial robes? It is a vain mistake of man, and an empty worship of dig-nity, to glitter in purple and to be sordid in mind. Are you elevated by nobility of birth? do you praise your parents? Yet we are all born with one lot; it is only by virtue that we are distinguished. We therefore, who are estimated by our character and our modesty, reasonably abstain from evil pleasures, and from your pomps and exhibitions, the origin of which in connec-tion with sacred things we know, and condemn their mischievous enticements. For in the char-iot games who does not shudder at the madness of the people brawling among themselves? or at the teaching of murder in the gladiatorial games? In the scenic games also the madness is not less, but the debauchery is more prolonged : for now a mimic either expounds or shows forth adul-teries ; now a nerveless player, while he feigns lust, suggests it ; the same actor disgraces your gods by attributing to them adulteries, sighs, hatreds ; the same provokes your tears with pre-tended sufferings, with vain gestures and expres-sions. Thus you demand murder, in fact, while you weep at it in fiction.

CHAP. XXXVIII. — ARGUMENT : CHRISTIANS ABSTAIN FROM THINGS CONNECTED WITH IDOL SACRI-FICES, LEST ANY ONE SHOULD THINK EITHER THAT THEY YIELD TO DEMONS, OR THAT THEY ARE ASHAMED OF THEIR RELIGION. THEY DO NOT INDEED DESPISE ALL THE COLOUR AND SCENT OF FLOWERS, FOR THEY ARE ACCUSTOMED TO USE THEM SCATTERED ABOUT LOOSELY AND NEGLIGENTLY, AS WELL AS TO ENTWINE THEIR NECKS WITH GARLANDS ; BUT TO CROWN THE HEAD OF A CORPSE THEY THINK SUPERFLUOUS AND USELESS. MOREOVER, WITH THE SAME

---

[1] " Arridens," but otherwise " arripiens," scil. " snatching at," suggesting possibly the idea of the martyrs chiding the delays of the executioners, or provoking the rush of the wild beasts.

[2] Otherwise, " unhoped-for." [This chapter has been supposed to indicate that the work was written in a time of persecution. Faint tokens of the same have been imagined also, in capp. 29 and 33, supra.]

[3] This passage is peculiar ; the original is, " Ut ingenium eorum perditæ mentis licentiæ potestatis liberæ nundinentur," with various modifications of reading.

TRANQUILLITY WITH WHICH THEY LIVE THEY BURY THEIR DEAD, WAITING WITH A VERY CERTAIN HOPE THE CROWN OF ETERNAL FELICITY. THEREFORE THEIR RELIGION, REJECTING ALL THE SUPERSTITIONS OF THE GENTILES, SHOULD BE ADOPTED AS TRUE BY ALL MEN.

"But that we despise the leavings of sacrifices, and the cups out of which libations have been poured, is not a confession of fear, but an assertion of our true liberty. For although nothing which comes into existence as an inviolable gift of God is corrupted by any agency, yet we abstain, lest any should think either that we are submitting to demons, to whom libation has been made, or that we are ashamed of our religion. But who is he who doubts of our indulging ourselves in spring flowers, when we gather both the rose of spring and the lily, and whatever else is of agreeable colour and odour among the flowers? For these we both use scattered loose and free, and we twine our necks with them in garlands. Pardon us, forsooth, that we do not crown our heads; we are accustomed to receive the scent of a sweet flower in our nostrils, not to inhale it with the back of our head or with our hair. Nor do we crown the dead. And in this respect I the more wonder at you, in the way in which you apply to a lifeless person, or to one who does not feel, a torch; or a garland[1] to one who does not smell it, when either as blessed he does not want, or, being miserable, he has no pleasure in, flowers. Still we adorn our obsequies with the same tranquillity with which we live; and we do not bind to us a withering garland, but we wear one living with eternal flowers from God, since we, being both moderate and secure in the liberality of our God, are animated to the hope of future felicity by the confidence of His present majesty. Thus we both rise again in blessedness, and are already living in contemplation of the future. Then let Socrates the Athenian buffoon see to it, confessing that he knew nothing, although boastful in the testimony of a most deceitful demon; let Arcesilaus also, and Carneades, and Pyrrho, and all the multitude of the Academic philosophers, deliberate; let Simonides also for ever put off the decision of his opinion. We despise the bent brows of the philosophers, whom we know to be corrupters, and adulterers, and tyrants, and ever eloquent against their own vices. We who[2] bear wisdom not in our dress, but in our mind, we do not speak great things, but we live them; we boast that we have attained what they have sought for with the utmost eagerness, and have not been able to find. Why are we ungrateful?

why do we grudge if the truth of divinity has ripened in the age of our time? Let us enjoy our benefits, and let us in rectitude moderate our judgments; let superstition be restrained; let impiety be expiated; let true religion be preserved.

CHAP. XXXIX. — ARGUMENT: WHEN OCTAVIUS HAD FINISHED THIS ADDRESS, MINUCIUS AND CÆCILIUS SATE FOR SOME TIME IN ATTENTIVE AND SILENT WONDER. AND MINUCIUS INDEED KEPT SILENCE IN ADMIRATION OF OCTAVIUS, SILENTLY REVOLVING WHAT HE HAD HEARD.

When Octavius had brought his speech to a close, for some time we were struck into silence, and held our countenances fixed in attention; and as for me, I was lost in the greatness of my admiration, that he had so adorned those things which it is easier to feel than to say, both by arguments and by examples, and by authorities derived from reading; and that he had repelled the malevolent objectors with the very weapons of the philosophers with which they are armed, and had moreover shown the truth not only as easy, but also as agreeable.

CHAP. XL. — ARGUMENT: THEN CÆCILIUS EXCLAIMS THAT HE IS VANQUISHED BY OCTAVIUS; AND THAT, BEING NOW CONQUEROR OVER ERROR, HE PROFESSES THE CHRISTIAN RELIGION. HE POSTPONES, HOWEVER, TILL THE MORROW HIS TRAINING IN THE FULLER BELIEF OF ITS MYSTERIES.

While, therefore, I was silently turning over these things in my own mind, Cæcilius broke forth: "I congratulate as well my Octavius as myself, as much as possible on that tranquillity in which we live, and I do not wait for the decision. Even thus we have conquered: not unjustly do I assume to myself the victory. For even as he is my conqueror, so I am triumphant over error. Therefore, in what belongs to the substance of the question, I both confess concerning providence, and I yield to God;[3] and I agree concerning the sincerity of the way of life which is now mine. Yet even still some things remain in my mind, not as resisting the truth, but as necessary to a perfect training;[4] of which on the morrow, as the sun is already sloping to his setting, we shall inquire at length in a more fitting and ready manner."

CHAP. XLI. — ARGUMENT: FINALLY, ALL ARE PLEASED, AND JOYFULLY DEPART: CÆCILIUS, THAT HE HAD BELIEVED; OCTAVIUS, THAT HE HAD CONQUERED; AND MINUCIUS, THAT THE FORMER HAD BELIEVED, AND THE LATTER HAD CONQUERED.

"But for myself," said I, "I rejoice more fully on behalf of all of us; because also Octa-

---

[1] The probable reading here is, "You apply to a lifeless person, either if he has feeling, a torch; or, if he feels not, a garland."
[2] "We who do not," etc., is a conjectural reading, omitting the subsequent "we."

[3] Otherwise read, "and I believe concerning Cod."
[4] [i e., he will become a *catechumen* on the morrow.]

vius has conquered for me, in that the very great invidiousness of judging is taken away from me. Nor can I acknowledge by my praises the merit of his words : the testimony both of man, and of one man only, is weak. He has an illustrious reward from God, inspired by whom he has pleaded, and aided by whom he has gained the victory."

After these things we departed, glad and cheerful : Cæcilius, to rejoice that he had believed ; Octavius, that he had succeeded ; and I, that the one had believed, and the other had conquered.

ELUCIDATIONS.

I.

(Editions, p. 171.)

FOR an interesting account of the bibliographical history of this work, see Dupin. It passed for the Eight Book of Arnobius until A.D. 1560, and was first printed in its true character at Heidelberg in that year, with a learned preface by Balduinus, who restored it to its true author.

II.

(The neighing of horses, note 1, p. 183.)

It strikes me as singular that the Edinburgh edition, which gives a note to each of the instances that follow, should have left me to supply this reference to the case of Darius Hystaspes. The story is told, as will be remembered by all who have ever read it, by Herodotus, and is certainly one of the most extraordinary in history, when one reflects that a horse elected a great monarch, and one whose life not a little affected the fortunes of mankind. A knavish groom was indeed the engineer of this election, as often, in such events, the secret springs of history are hidden ; but, if the story is not wholly a fable, the coincidence of thunder in the heavens is most noteworthy. It seemed to signify the overruling of Providence, and the power of God to turn the folly, not less than the wrath, of men, to God's praise. See Herod., book iii. cap. lxxxvi.

III.

(From nothing, p. 194.)

From this chapter, if not from others, it had been rashly affirmed that our author imagined that the soul perishes with the body, and is to be renewed out of nothing. The argument is wholly *ad hominem*, and asserts nothing from the author's own point of view, as I understand it. He gives what is "sufficient for his argument," and professes nothing more. He was not a clergyman, nor is his work a sermon to the faithful. He defies any one to deny, that, if God could form man out of nothing, He can make him anew out of nothing. The residue of the argument is a brilliant assertion of the imperishability of matter, in terms which might satisfy modern science ; and the implication is, that the soul no more perishes to the sight of God than does the body vaporized and reserved in the custody of the elements.

COMMODIANUS.

[TRANSLATED BY THE REV. ROBERT ERNEST WALLIS, Ph. D.]

INTRODUCTORY NOTE

TO THE

INSTRUCTIONS OF COMMODIANUS.

[A.D. 240.]   Our author seems to have been a North-African bishop, of whom little is known save what we learn from his own writings.   He has been supposed to incline to some ideas of Praxeas, and also to the Millenarians, but perhaps on insufficient grounds.   His Millenarianism reflects the views of a very primitive age, and that without the corrupt Chiliasm of a later period, which brought about a practical repudiation of the whole system.[1]   Of his writings, two poems only remain, and of these the second, a very recent discovery, has no place in the Edinburgh series.   I greatly regret that it cannot be included in ours.

As a poetical work the following prose version probably does it no injustice.   His versification is pronounced very crabbed, and his diction is the wretched *patois* of North Africa.   But the piety and earnestness of a practical Christian seem everywhere conspicuous in this fragment of antiquity.

---

[1] He gives us a painful picture of the decline of godliness in his days ; of which see Wordsworth's *Hippolytus*, p. 140.

THE INSTRUCTIONS OF COMMODIANUS

IN FAVOUR OF

CHRISTIAN DISCIPLINE,

AGAINST THE GODS OF THE HEATHENS.

(EXPRESSED IN ACROSTICS.)

I. PREFACE.

My preface sets forth the way to the wanderer, and a good visitation when the goal of life shall have come, that he may become eternal — a thing which ignorant hearts disbelieve. I in like manner have wandered for a long time, by giving attendance upon *heathen* fanes, my parents themselves being ignorant.[1] Thence at length I withdrew myself by reading concerning the law. I bear witness to the Lord; I grieve: alas, the crowd of citizens! ignorant of what it loses in going to seek vain gods. Thoroughly taught by these things, I instruct the ignorant in the truth.

II. GOD'S INDIGNATION.

In the law, the Lord of heaven, and earth, and sea has commanded, saying, Worship not vain gods made by your own hands out of wood or gold, lest my wrath destroy you for such things. The people before Moses, unskilled, abiding without law, and ignorant of God, prayed to gods that perished, after the likenesses of which they fashioned vain idols. The Lord having brought the Jews out of the land of Egypt, subsequently imposed on them a law; and the Omnipotent enjoined these things, that they should serve Him alone, and not those idols. Moreover, in that law is taught concerning the resurrection, and the hope of living in happiness again in the world, if vain idols be forsaken and not worshipped.

III. THE WORSHIP OF DEMONS.

When Almighty God, to beautify the nature of the world, willed that that earth should be visited by angels, when they were sent down they despised His laws. Such was the beauty of women, that it turned them aside; so that, being contaminated, they could not return to heaven. Rebels from God, they uttered words against Him. Then the Highest uttered His judgment against them; and from their seed giants are said to have been born. By them arts were made known in the earth, and they taught the dyeing of wool, and everything which is done; and to them, when they died, men erected images. But the Almighty, because they were of an evil seed, did not approve that, when dead, they should be brought back from death. Whence wandering they now subvert many bodies, and it is such as these especially that ye this day worship and pray to as gods.

IV. SATURN.

And Saturn the old, if he is a god, how does he grow old? Or if he was a god, why was he driven by his terrors to devour his children? But because he was not a god, he consumed the bowels of his sons in a monstrous madness. He was a king upon earth, born in the mount Olympus; and he was not divine, but called himself a god. He fell into weakness of mind, and swallowed a stone for his son. Thus he became a god; of late he is called Jupiter.

V. JUPITER.

This Jupiter was born to Saturn in the island of Breta; and when he was grown up, he deprived his father of the kingdom. He then deluded the wives and sisters of the nobles. Moreover, Pyracmon, a smith, had made for him a sceptre. In the beginning God made the heaven, the

---

[1] [Sufficient evidence of his heathen origin.]

earth, and the sea. But that frightful creature, born in the midst of time, went forth as a youth from a cave, and was nourished by stealth. Behold, that God is the author of all things, not that Jupiter.

VI. OF THE SAME JUPITER'S THUNDERBOLT.

Ye say, O fools, Jupiter thunders. It is he that hurls thunderbolts; and if it was childishness that thought thus, why for two hundred years have ye been babies?[1] And will ye still be so always? Infancy is passed into maturity, old age does not enjoy trifles, the age of boyhood has departed; let the mind of youth in like manner depart. Your thoughts ought to belong to the character of men. Thou art then a fool, to believe that it is Jupiter that thunders. He, born on the earth, is nourished with goats' milk. Therefore if Saturn had devoured him, who was it in those times that sent rain when he was dead? Especially, if a god may be thought to be born of a mortal father, Saturn grew old on the earth, and on the earth he died. There was none that predicted his previous birth. Or if he thunders, the law would have been given by him. The stories that the poets feign seduce you. He, however, reigned in Crete, and there died. He who to you is the Almighty became Alcmena's lover; he himself would in like manner be in love with living men now if he were alive. Ye pray to unclean gods, and ye call them heavenly who are born of mortal seed from those giants. Ye hear and ye read that he was born in the earth: whence was it that that corrupter so well deserved to ascend into heaven? And the Cyclopes are said to have forged him a thunderbolt; for though he was immortal, he received arms from mortals. Ye have conveyed to heaven by your authority one guilty of so many crimes, and, moreover, a parricide of his own relations.

VII. OF THE SEPTIZONIUM AND THE STARS.

Your want of intelligence deceives you concerning the circle of the zone, and perchance from that you find out that you must pray to Jupiter. Saturn is told of there, but it is as a star, for he was driven forth by Jupiter, or let Jupiter be believed to be in the star. He who controlled the constellations of the pole, and the sower of the soil; he who made war with the Trojans, he loved the beautiful Venus. Or among the stars themselves Mars was caught with her by married jealousy: he is called the youthful god. Oh excessively foolish, to think that those who are born of Maia rule from the stars, or that they rule the entire nature of the world! Subjected to wounds, and themselves living under the dominion of the fates, obscene, inquisitive, warriors of an impious life; and they made sons, equally mortal with themselves, and were all terrible, foolish, strong, in the sevenfold girdle. If ye worship the stars, worship also the twelve signs *of the zodiac*, as well the ram, the bull, the twins, as the fierce lion; and finally, they go on into fishes, — cook them and you will prove them. A law without law is your refuge: what wishes to be, will prevail. A woman desires to be wanton; she seeks to live without restraint. Ye yourselves will be what ye wish for, and pray to as gods and goddesses. Thus I worshipped while I went astray, and now I condemn it.

VIII. OF THE SUN AND MOON.

Concerning the Sun and Moon ye are in error, although they are in our immediate presence; in that ye, as I formerly did, think that you must pray to them. They, indeed, are among the stars; but they do not run of their own accord. The Omnipotent, when He established all things at first, placed them there with the stars, on the fourth day. . . . And, indeed, He commanded in the law that none should worship them. Ye worship so many gods who promise nothing concerning life, whose law is not on the earth, nor are they themselves foretold. But a few priests seduce you, who say that any deity destined to die can be of service. Draw near now, read, and learn the truth.

IX. MERCURY.

Let your Mercury be depicted with a Saraballum, and with wings on his helmet or his cap, and in other respects naked. I see a marvellous thing, a god flying with a little satchel. Run, poor creatures, with your lap spread open when he flies, that he may empty his satchel: do ye from thence be prepared. Look on the painted one, since he will thus cast you money from on high: then dance ye securely. Vain man, art thou not mad, to worship painted gods in heaven? If thou knowest not how to live, continue to dwell with the beasts.

X. NEPTUNE.

Ye make Neptune a god descended from Saturn; and he wields a trident that he may spear the fishes. It is plain by his being thus provided that he is a sea-god. Did not he himself with Apollo raise up walls for the Trojans? How did that poor stone-mason become a god? Did not he beget the cyclops-monster? And was he himself when dead unable to live again,. though his structure admitted of this?[2] Thus begotten, he begot who was already once dead.

---

[1] [An index of time. He writes, therefore, in the third century.]

[2] We have changed *marhus et* into *mortuus*, and *de suo* into *denuo*.

XI. APOLLO THE SOOTHSAYING AND FALSE.

Ye make Apollo a player on the cithara, and divine. Born at first of Maia, in the isle of Delos, subsequently, for offered wages, a builder, obeying the king Laomedon, he reared the walls of the Trojans. And he established himself, and ye are seduced into thinking him a god, in whose bones the love of Cassandra burned, whom the virgin craftily sported with, and, though a divine being, he is deceived. By his office of augur he was able to know the double-hearted one. Moreover rejected, he, though divine, departed thence. Him the virgin burnt up with her beauty, whom he ought to have burnt up; while she ought first of all to have loved the god who thus lustfully began to love Daphne, and still follows her up, wishing to violate the maid. The fool loves in vain. Nor can he obtain her by running. Surely, if he were a god, he would come up with her through the air. She first came under the roof, and the divine being remained outside. The race of men deceive you, for they were of a sad way of life. Moreover, he is said to have fed the cattle of Admetus. While in imposed sports he threw the quoit into the air, he could not restrain it as it fell, and it killed his friend. That was the last day of his companion Hyacinthus. Had he been divine, he would have foreknown the death of his friend.

XII. FATHER LIBER — BACCHUS.

Ye yourselves say that Father Liber was assuredly twice begotten. First of all he was born in India of Proserpine and Jupiter, and waging war against the Titans, when his blood was shed, he expired even as one of mortal men. Again restored from his death, in another womb Semele conceived him again of Jupiter, a second Maia, whose womb being divided, he is taken away near to birth from his dead mother, and as a nursling is given to be nourished to Nisus. From this being twice born he is called Dionysus; and his religion is falsely observed in vanity; and they celebrate his orgies such that now they themselves seem to be either foolhardy or burlesquers of Mimnermomerus. They conspire in evil; they practise beforehand with pretended heat, that they may deceive others into saying that a deity is present. Hence you manifestly see men living a life like his, violently excited with the wine which he himself had pressed out; they have given him divine honour in the midst of their drunken excess.

XIII. THE UNCONQUERED ONE.

The unconquered one was born from a rock, if he is regarded as a god. Now tell us, then, on the other hand, which is the first of these two. The rock has overcome the god: then the creator of the rock has to be sought after.

Moreover, you still depict him also as a thief; although, if he were a god, he certainly did not live by theft. Assuredly he was of earth, and of a monstrous nature. And he turned other people's oxen into his caves; just as did Cacus, that son of Vulcan.

XIV. SYLVANUS.

Whence, again, has Sylvanus appeared to be a god? Perhaps it is agreeable *so to call him* from this, that the pipe sings sweetly because he bestows the wood; for, perhaps, it might not be so. Thou hast bought a venal master, when thou shalt have bought from him. Behold the wood fails! What is due to him? Art thou not ashamed, O fool, to adore such pictures? Seek one God who will allow you to live after death. Depart from such as have become dead in life.

XV. HERCULES.

Hercules, because he destroyed the monster of the Aventine Mount, who had been wont to steal the herds of Evander, *is a god:* the rustic mind of men, untaught also, when they wished to return thanks instead of praise to the absent thunderer, senselessly vowed victims as to a god to be besought, they made milky altars as a memorial to themselves. Thence it arises that he is worshipped in the ancient manner. But he is no god, although he was strong in arms.

XVI. OF THE GODS AND GODDESSES.

Ye say that they are gods who are plainly cruel, and ye say that genesis assigns the fates to you. Now, then, say to whom first of all sacred rites are paid. Between the ways on either side immature death is straying. If the fates give the generations, why do you pray to the god? Thou art vainly deceived who art seeking to beseech the manes, and thou namest them to be lords over thee who are fabricated. Or, moreover, I know not what women you pray to as goddesses — Bellona and Nemesis the goddesses, together with the celestial Fury, the Virgins and Venus, for whom your wives are weak in the loins. Besides, there are in the fanes other demons which are not as yet numbered, and are worn on the neck, so that they themselves cannot give to themselves an account. Plagues ought rather to be exported to the ends of the earth.

XVII. OF THEIR IMAGES.

A few wicked and empty poets delude you; while they seek with difficulty to procure their living, they adorn falsehood to be for others under the guise of mystery. Thence feigning to be smitten by some deity, they sing of his majesty, and weary themselves under his form. Ye have often seen the Dindymarii, with what a din they enter upon luxuries while they seek to feign the furies, or when they strike their backs with the filthy axe, although with their teaching they keep what they heal by their blood. Behold in what name they do not compel those who first of all unite themselves to them with a sound mind. But that they may take away a gift, they seek such minds. Thence see how all things are feigned. They cast a shadow over a simple people, lest they should believe, while they perish, the thing once for all proceeded in vanity from antiquity, that a prophet who uttered false things might be believed; but their majesty has spoken nought.

XVIII. OF AMMYDATES AND THE GREAT GOD.

We have already said many things of an abominable superstition, and yet we follow up the subject, lest we should be said to have passed anything over. And the worshippers worshipped their Ammydates after their manner. He was great to them when there was gold in the temple. They placed their heads under his power, as if he were present. It came to the highest point that Cæsar took away the gold. The deity failed, or fled, or passed away into fire. The author of this wickedness is manifest who formed this same god, and falsely prophesying seduces so many and so great men, and only was silent about Him who was accustomed to be divine. For voices broke forth, as if with a changed mind, as if the wooden god were speaking into his ear. Say now yourselves if they are not false deities? From that prodigy how many has that prophet destroyed? He forgot to prophesy who before was accustomed to prophesy; so those prodigies are feigned among those who are greedy of wine, whose damnable audacity feigns deities, for they were carried about, and such an image was dried up. For both he himself is silent, and no one prophesies concerning him at all. But ye wish to ruin yourselves.

XIX. OF THE VAIN NEMESIACI.

Is it not ignominy, that a prudent man should be seduced and worship such a one, or say that a log is Diana? You trust a man who in the morning is drunk, costive, and ready to perish, who by art speaks falsely what is seen by him. While he lives strictly, he feeds on his own bowels. A detestable one defiles all the citizens; and he has attached to himself — a similar gathering being made — those with whom he feigns the history, that he may adorn a god. He is ignorant how to prophesy for himself; for others he dares it. He places it on his shoulder when he pleases, and again he places it down. Whirling round, he is turned by himself with the tree of the two-forked one, as if you would think that he was inspired with the deity of the wood. Ye do not worship the gods whom they themselves falsely announce; ye worship the priests themselves, fearing them vainly. But if thou art strong in heart, flee at once from the shrines of death.

XX. THE TITANS.

Ye say that the Titans are to you *Tutans*. Ye ask that these fierce ones should be silent under your roof, as so many Lares, shrines, images made like to a Titan. For ye foolishly adore those who have died by an evil death, not reading their own law. They themselves speak not, and ye dare to call them gods who are melted out of a brazen vessel; ye should rather melt them into little vessels for yourselves.

XXI. THE MONTESIANI.

Ye call the mountains also gods. Let them rule in gold, darkened by evil, and aiding with an averted mind. For if a pure spirit and a serene mind remained to you, thou thyself ought to examine for thyself concerning them. Thou art become senseless as a man, if thou thinkest that these can save thee, whether they rule or whether they cease. If thou seekest anything healthy, seek rather the righteousness of the law, that brings the help of salvation, and says that you are becoming eternal. For what you shall follow in vanity rejoices you for a time. Thou art glad for a brief space, and afterwards bewailest in the depths. Withdraw thyself from these, if thou wilt rise again with Christ.

XXII. THE DULNESS OF THE AGE.

Alas, I grieve, citizens, that ye are thus blinded by the world. One runs to the lot; another gazes on the birds; another, having shed the blood of bleating animals, calls forth the manes, and credulously desires to hear vain responses. When so many leaders and kings have taken counsel concerning life, what benefit has it been to them to have known even its portents? Learn, I beg you, citizens, what is good; beware of idolfanes. Seek, indeed, all of you, in the law of the Omnipotent. Thus it has pleased the Lord of lords Himself in the heavens, that demons should wander in the world for our discipline. And yet, on the other hand, He has sent out His mandates, that they who forsake their altars shall become inhabitants of heaven. Whence I am not careful to argue this in a small treatise. The law teaches; it calls on you in your midst. Consider for yourselves. Ye have entered upon two roads; decide upon the right one.[1]

XXIII. OF THOSE WHO ARE EVERYWHERE READY.

While thou obeyest the belly, thou sayest that thou art innocent; and, as if courteously, makest thyself everywhere ready. Woe to thee, foolish man! thou thyself lookest around upon death.

---

[1] [He defers to the Canon Law and notes the *Duæ Viæ*.]

Thou seekest in a barbarous fashion to live without law. Thou thyself hymnest thyself also to play upon a word, who feignest thyself simple. I live in simplicity with such a one. Thou believest that thou livest, whilst thou desirest to fill thy belly. To sit down disgracefully of no account in thy house, ready for feasting, and to run away from precepts. Or because thou believest not that God will judge the dead, thou foolishly makest thyself ruler of heaven instead of Him. Thou regardest thy belly as if thou canst provide for it. Thou seemest at one time to be profane, at another to be holy. Thou appearest as a suppliant of God, under the aspect of a tyrant. Thou shalt feel in thy fates by whose law thou art aided.

XXIV. OF THOSE WHO LIVE BETWEEN THE TWO.

Thou who thinkest that, by living doubtfully between the two, thou art on thy guard, goest on thy way stript of law, broken down by luxury. Thou art looking forward vainly to so many things, why seekest thou unjust things? And whatever thou hast done shall there remain to thee when dead. Consider, thou foolish one, thou wast not, and lo, thou art seen. Thou knowest not whence thou hast proceeded, nor whence thou art nourished. Thou avoidest the excellent and benignant God of thy life, and thy Governor, who would rather wish thee to live. Thou turnest thyself to thyself, and givest thy back to God. Thou drownest thyself in darkness, whilst thou thinkest thou art abiding in light. Why runnest thou in the synagogue to the Pharisees, that He may become merciful to thee, whom thou of thy own accord deniest? Thence thou goest abroad again; thou seekest healthful things. Thou wishest to live between both ways, but thence thou shalt perish. And, moreover, thou sayest, Who is He who has redeemed from death, that we may believe in Him, since there punishments are awarded? Ah! not thus, O malignant man, shall it be as thou thinkest. For to him who has lived well there is advantage after death. Thou, however, when one day thou diest, shalt be taken away in an evil place. But they who believe in Christ shall be led into a good place, and those to whom that delight is given are caressed; but to you who are of a double mind, against you is punishment without the body. The course of the tormentor stirs you up to cry out against your brother.

XXV. THEY WHO FEAR AND WILL NOT BELIEVE.

How long, O foolish man, wilt thou not acknowledge Christ? Thou avoidest the fertile field, and castest thy seeds on the sterile one. Thou seekest to abide in the wood where the thief is delaying. Thou sayest, I also am of God; and thou wanderest out of doors. Now at length, after so many invitations, enter within the palace. Now is the harvest ripe, and the time so many times prepared. Lo, now reap! What! dost thou not repent? Thence now, if thou hast not, gather the seasonable wines. The time of believing to life is present in the time of death. The first law of God is the foundation of the subsequent law. Thee, indeed, it assigned to believe in the second law. Nor are threats from Himself, but from it, powerful over thee. Now astounded, swear that thou wilt believe in Christ; for the Old Testament proclaims concerning Him. For it is needful only to believe in Him who was dead, to be able to rise again to live for all time. Therefore, if thou art one who disbelievest that these things shall be, at length he shall be overcome in his guilt in the second death. I will declare things to come in few words in this little treatise. In it can be known when hope must be preferred. Still I exhort you as quickly as possible to believe in Christ.

XXVI. TO THOSE WHO RESIST THE LAW OF CHRIST THE LIVING GOD.

Thou rejectest, unhappy one, the advantage of heavenly discipline, and rushest into death while wishing to stray without a bridle. Luxury and the shortlived joys of the world are ruining thee, whence thou shalt be tormented in hell for all time. They are vain joys with which thou art foolishly delighted. Do not these make thee to be a man dead? Cannot thirty years at length make thee a wise man? Ignorant how thou hast first strayed, look upon ancient time, thou thinkest now to enjoy here a joyous life in the midst of wrongs. These are the ruins of thy friends, wars, or wicked frauds, thefts with bloodshed: the body is vexed with sores, and groaning and wailing is indulged; whether a slight disease invade thee, or thou art held down by long sickness, or thou art bereaved of thy children, or thou mournest over a lost wife. All is a wilderness: alas, dignities are hurried down from their height by vices and poverty; doubly so, assuredly, if thou languishest long. And callest thou it life when this life of glass is mortal? Consider now at length that this time is of no avail, but in the future you have hope without the craft of living. Certainly the little children which have been snatched away desired to live. Moreover, the young men who have been deprived of life, perchance were preparing to grow old, and they themselves were making ready to enjoy joyful days; and yet we unwillingly lay aside all things in the world. I have delayed with a perverse mind, and I have thought that the life of this world was a true one; and I judged that death would come in like manner as ye did—that when once life had departed, the soul also was dead and perished. These things, however, are not so; but the Founder and Author of the world has certainly required the brother slain by a brother. Impious man, say, said He, where is thy brother? and he denied. For the blood of thy brother has cried aloud to Me to heaven. Thou art tormented, I see, when thou thoughtest to feel nothing; but he lives and occupies the place on the right hand. He enjoys delights which thou, O wicked one, hast lost; and when thou hast called back the world, he also has gone before, and will be immortal: for thou shalt wail in hell. Certainly God lives, who makes the dead to live, that He may give worthy rewards to the innocent and to the good; but to the fierce and impious, cruel hell. Commence, O thou who art led away, to perceive the judgments of God.

XXVII. O FOOL, THOU DOST NOT DIE TO GOD.

O fool, thou dost not absolutely die; nor, when dead, dost thou escape the lofty One. Although thou shouldst arrange that when dead thou perceivest nothing, thou shalt foolishly be overcome. God the Creator of the world liveth, whose laws cry out that the dead are in existence. But thou, whilst recklessly thou seekest to live without God, judgest that in death is extinction, and thinkest that it is absolute. God has not ordered it as thou thinkest, that the dead are forgetful of what they have previously done. Now has the governor made for us receptacles of death, and after our ashes we shall behold them. Thou art stripped, O foolish one, who thinkest that by death thou art not, and hast made thy Ruler and Lord to be able to do nothing. But death is not a mere vacuity, if thou reconsiderest in thine heart. Thou mayest know that He is to be desired, for late thou shalt perceive Him. Thou wast the ruler of the flesh; certainly flesh ruled not thee. Freed from it, the former is buried; thou art here. Rightly is mortal man separated from the flesh. Therefore mortal eyes will not be able to be equalled (to divine things). Thus our depth keeps us from the secret of God. Give thou now, whilst in weakness thou art dying, the honour to God, and believe that Christ will bring thee back living from the dead. Thou oughtest to give praises in the church to the omnipotent One.

XXVIII. THE RIGHTEOUS RISE AGAIN.

Righteousness and goodness, peace and true patience, and care concerning one's deeds, make to live after death. But a crafty mind, mischievous, perfidious, evil, destroys itself by degrees, and delays in a cruel death. O wicked man, hear now what thou gainest by thy evil deeds. Look on the judges of earth, who now in the body torture with terrible punishments; either chastisements are prepared for the deserving by the sword, or to weep in a long imprisonment. Dost thou, last of all, hope to laugh at the God of heaven and the Ruler of the sky, by whom all things were made? Thou ragest, thou art mad, and now thou takest away the name of God, from whom, moreover, thou shalt not escape; and He will award punishments according to your deeds. Now I would have you be cautious that thou come not to the burning of fire. Give thyself up at once to Christ, that goodness may attend thee.

XXIX. TO THE WICKED AND UNBELIEVING RICH MAN.

Thou wilt, O rich man, by insatiably looking too much to all thy wealth, squander those things to which thou art still seeking to cling. Thou sayest, I do not hope when dead to live after such things as these. O ungrateful to the great God, who thus judgest thyself to be a god; to Him who, when thou knewest nothing of it, brought thee forth, and then nourished thee. He governs thy meadows; He, thy vineyards; He, thy herd of cattle; and He, whatever thou possessest. Nor dost thou give heed to these things; or thou, perchance, rulest all things. He who made the sky, and the earth, and the salt seas, decreed to give us back again ourselves in a golden age. And only if thou believest, thou livest in the secret of God. Learn God, O foolish man, who wishes thee to be immortal, that thou mayest give Him eternal thanks in thy struggle. His own law teaches thee; but since thou seekest to wander, thou disbelievest all things, and thence thou shalt go into hell. By and by thou givest up thy life; thou shalt be taken where it grieveth thee to be: there the spiritual punishment, which is eternal, is undergone; there are always wailings: nor dost thou absolutely die therein—there at length too late proclaiming the omnipotent God.

XXX. RICH MEN, BE HUMBLE.

Learn, O thou who art about to die, to show thyself good to all. Why, in the midst of the people, makest thou thyself to be another *than thou art?* Thou goest where thou knowest not, and ignorantly thence thou departest. Thou managest wickedly with thy very body; thou thirstest always after riches. Thou exaltest thyself too much on high; and thou bearest pride, and dost not willingly look on the poor. Now ye do not even feed your parents themselves when placed under you. Ah, wretched men, let ordinary men flee far from you. He lived, and I have destroyed him; the poor man cries out εὕρηκα. By and by thou shalt be driven with the furies of Charybdis, when thou thyself dost perish. Thus ye rich men are undisciplined, ye give a law to those, ye yourselves not being prepared. Strip thyself, O rich man turned away from God, of such evils, if assuredly, perchance, what thou hast seen done may aid thee. Be ye the attendant of God while ye have time. Even as the elm loves the vine, so love ye people of no account. Observe now, O barren one, the law which is terrible to the evil, and equally benignant to the good; be humble in prosperity. Take away, O rich men, hearts of fraud, and take up hearts of peace. And look upon your evil-doing. Do ye do good? I am here.

XXXI. TO JUDGES.

Consider the sayings of Solomon, all ye judges; in what way, with one word of his, he disparages you. How gifts and presents corrupt the judges, thence, thence follows the law. Ye always love givers; and when there shall be a cause, the unjust cause carries off the victory. Thus I am innocent; nor do I, a man of no account, accuse you, because Solomon openly raises the blasphemy. But your god is your belly, and rewards are your laws. Paul the apostle suggests this, I am not deceitful.

XXXII. TO SELF-PLEASERS.

If place or time is favourable, or the person has advanced, let there be a new judge. Why now art thou lifted up thence? Untaught, thou blasphemest Him of whose liberality thou livest. In such weakness thou dost not ever regard Him. Throughout advances and profits thou greedily presumest on fortune. There is no law to thee, nor dost thou discern thyself in prosperity. Although they may be counted of gold, let the strains of the pipe always be raving. If thou hast not adored the crucifixion of the Lord, thou hast perished.[1] Both place and occasion and person are now given to thee, if, however, thou believest; but if not, thou shalt fear before Him. Bring thyself into obedience to Christ, and place thy neck under Him. To Him remains the honour and all the confidence of things. When the time flatters thee, be more cautious. Not foreseeing, as it behoves thee, the final awards of fate, thou art not able ever to live again without Christ.

XXXIII. TO THE GENTILES.

O people, ferocious, without a shepherd, now at length wander not. For I also who admonish you was the same, ignorant, wandering. Now, therefore, take the likeness of your Lord. Raise upward your wild and roughened hearts. Enter stedfastly into the fold of your sylvan Shepherd, remaining safe from robbers under the royal roof. In the wood are wolves; therefore take refuge in the cave. Thou warrest, thou art mad; nor dost thou behold where thou abidest. Believe in the one God, that when dead thou mayest live, and mayest rise in His kingdom, when there shall be the resurrection to the just.

XXXIV. MOREOVER, TO IGNORANT GENTILES.

The unsubdued neck refuses to bear the yoke of labour. Then it delights to be satisfied with herbs in the rich plains. And still unwillingly is subdued the useful mare, and it is made to be less fierce when it is first brought into subjection. O people, O man, thou brother, do not be a brutal flock. Pluck thyself forth at length, and thyself withdraw thyself. Assuredly thou art not cattle, thou art not a beast, but thou art born a man. Do thou thyself wisely subdue thyself, and enter under arms. Thou who followest idols art nothing but the vanity of the age. Your trifling hearts destroy you when almost set free. There gold, garments, silver is brought to the elbows; there war is made; there love is sung of instead of psalms. Dost thou think it to be life, when thou playest or lookest forward to such things as these? Thou choosest, O ignorant one, things that are extinct; thou seekest golden things. Thence thou shalt not escape the plague, although thyself art divine. Thou seekest not that grace which God sent to be read of in the earth, but thus as a beast thou wanderest. The golden age before spoken of shall come to thee if thou believest, and again thou shalt begin to live always an immortal life. That also is permitted to know what thou wast before. Give thyself as a subject to God, who governs all things.[2]

XXXV. OF THE TREE OF LIFE AND DEATH.

Adam was the first who fell, and that he might shun the precepts of God, Belial was his tempter by the lust of the palm tree. And he conferred on us also what he did, whether of good or of evil, as being the chief of all that was born from him; and thence we die by his means, as he himself, receding from the divine, became an outcast from the Word. We shall be immortal when six thousand years are accomplished. The tree of the apple being tasted, death has entered into the world. By this tree of death we are born to the life to come. On the tree depends the life that bears fruits — precepts. Now, therefore, pluck[3] believingly the fruits of life. A law was given from the tree to be feared by the primitive man, whence comes death by the neglect of the law of the beginning. Now stretch forth your hand, and take of the tree of life.

---

[1] [This is not Patripassianism. Nor does the "one God" of the next chapter involve this heresy.]

[2] [Here ends the apologetic portion.]

[3] *Scil.* "capite," conjectural for "cavete."

The excellent law of the Lord which follows has issued from the tree. The first law is lost; man eats whence he can, who adores the forbidden gods, the evil joys of life. Reject this partaking; it will suffice you to know what it should be. If you wish to live, surrender yourselves to the second law. Avoid the worship of temples, the oracles of demons; turn yourselves to Christ, and ye shall be associates with God. Holy is God's law, which teaches the dead to live. God alone has commanded us to offer to Him the hymn of praise. All of you shun absolutely the law of the devil.

XXXVI. OF THE FOOLISHNESS OF THE CROSS.

I have spoken of the twofold sign whence death proceeded, and again I have said that thence life frequently proceeds; but the cross has become foolishness to an adulterous people. The awful King of eternity shadows forth *these things* by the cross, that they may now believe on Him.[1] O fools, that live in death! Cain slew his younger brother by the invention of wickedness. Thence the sons of Enoch[2] are said to be the race of Cain. Then the evil people increased in the world, which never transfers souls to God. To believe the cross came to be a dread, and they say that they live righteously. The first law was in the tree; and thence, too, the second. And thence the second law first of all overcame the terrible law with peace.[3] Lifted up, they have rushed into vain prevarications. They are unwilling to acknowledge the Lord pierced with nails; but when His judgment shall come, they will then discern Him. But the race of Abel already believes on a merciful Christ.

XXXVII. THE FANATICS WHO JUDAIZE.

What! art thou half a Jew? wilt thou be half profane? Whence thou shalt not when dead escape the judgment of Christ. Thou thyself blindly wanderest, and foolishly goest in among the blind. And thus the blind leadeth the blind into the ditch. Thou goest whither thou knowest not, and thence ignorantly withdrawest. Let them who are learning go to the learned, and let the learned depart. But thou goest to those from whom thou canst learn nothing. Thou goest forth before the doors, and thence also thou goest to the idols. Ask first of all what is commanded in the law. Let them tell thee if it be commanded to adore the gods; for they are ignored in respect of that which they are especially able to do. But because they are guilty of that very crime, they relate nothing concerning the commandments of God save what is

marvellous. Then, however, they blindly lead you with them into the ditch. There are deaths too well known by them to relate, or because the heaping up of the plough closes up the field. The Almighty would not have them understand their King. Why such a wickedness? He Himself took refuge from those bloody men. He gave Himself to us by a superadded law. Thence now they lie concealed with us, deserted by their King. But if you think that in them there is hope, you are altogether in error if you worship God and heathen temples.

XXXVIII. TO THE JEWS.

Evil always, and recalcitrant, with a stiff neck ye wish not that ye should be overcome; thus ye will be heirs. Isaiah said that ye were of hardened heart. Ye look upon the law which Moses in wrath dashed to pieces; and the same Lord gave to him a second law. In that he placed his hope; but ye, half healed, reject it, and therefore ye shall not be worthy of the kingdom of heaven.

XXXIX. ALSO TO THE JEWS.

Look upon Leah, that was a type of the synagogue, which Jacob received as a sign, with eyes so weak; and yet he served again for the younger one beloved: a true mystery, and a type of our Church. Consider what was abundantly said of Rebecca from heaven; whence, imitating the alien, ye may believe in Christ. Thence come to Tamar and the offspring of twins. Look to Cain, the first tiller of the earth, and Abel the shepherd, who was an unspotted offerer in the ruin of his brother, and was slain by his brother. Thus therefore perceive, that the younger are approved by Christ.

XL. AGAIN TO THE SAME.

There is not an unbelieving people such as yours. O evil men! in so many places, and so often rebuked by the law of those who cry aloud. And the lofty One despises your Sabbaths, and altogether rejects your universal monthly feasts according to law, that ye should not make to Him the commanded sacrifices; who told you to throw a stone for your offence. If any should not believe that He had perished by an unjust death, and that those who were beloved were saved by other laws, thence that life was suspended on the tree, and believe not on Him. God Himself is the life; He Himself was suspended for us. But ye with indurated heart insult Him.

XLI. OF THE TIME OF ANTICHRIST.[4]

Isaiah said: This is the man who moveth the world and so many kings, and under whom

---

[1] [Or, "shadows forth *Himself.*"]
[2] "Eusebius tells of another Enoch, who was not translated without seeing death." — RIG. [See Gen. iv. 17, 18. S.]
[3] Et inde secunda terribilem legem primo cum pace revincit. — DAVIS, conjecturally.

[4] [See Elucidation at end.]

the land shall become desert. Hear ye how the prophet foretold concerning him. I have said nothing elaborately, but negligently. Then, doubtless, the world shall be finished when he shall appear. He himself shall divide the globe into three ruling powers, when, moreover, Nero shall be raised up from hell, Elias shall first come to seal the beloved ones; at which things the region of Africa and the northern nation, the whole earth on all sides, for seven years shall tremble. But Elias shall occupy the half of the time, Nero shall occupy half. Then the whore Babylon, being reduced to ashes, its embers shall thence advance to Jerusalem; and the Latin conqueror shall then say, I am Christ, whom ye always pray to; and, indeed, the original ones who were deceived combine to praise him. He does many wonders, since his is the false prophet. Especially that they may believe him, his image shall speak. The Almighty has given it power to appear such. The Jews, recapitulating Scriptures from him, exclaim at the same time to the Highest that they have been deceived.

XLII. OF THE HIDDEN AND HOLY PEOPLE OF THE ALMIGHTY CHRIST, THE LIVING GOD.

Let the hidden, the final, the holy people be longed for; and, indeed, let it be unknown by us where it abides, acting by nine of the tribes and a half . . . ; and he has bidden to live by the former law. Now let us all live: the tradition of the law is new, as the law itself teaches, I point out to you more plainly. Two of the tribes and a half are left: wherefore is the half of the tribes *separated* from them? That they might be martyrs, when He should bring war on His elected ones into the world; or certainly the choir of the holy prophets would rise together upon the people who should impose a check upon them whom the obscene horses have slaughtered with kicking heel; nor would the band hurry rashly at any time to *the gift of* peace. Those of the tribes are withdrawn, and all the mysteries of Christ are fulfilled by them throughout the whole age. Moreover, they have arisen from the crime of two brothers, by whose auspices they have followed crime. Not undeservedly are these bloody ones thus scattered: they shall again assemble on behalf of the mysteries of Christ. But then the things told of in the law are hastening to their completion. The Almighty Christ descends to His elect, who have been darkened from our view for so long a time — they have become so many thousands — that is the true heavenly people. The son does not die before his father, then; nor do they feel pains in their bodies, nor polypus in their nostrils. They who cease depart in ripe years in their bed, fulfilling all the things of the law, and

therefore they are protected. They are bidden to pass on the right side of their Lord; and when they have passed over as before, He dries up the river. Nor less does the Lord Himself also proceed with them. He has passed over to our side, they come with the King of heaven; and in their journey, what shall I speak of which God will bring to pass? Mountains subside before them, and fountains break forth. The creation rejoices to see the heavenly people. Here, however, they hasten to defend the captive matron. But the wicked king who possesses her, when he hears, flies into the parts of the north, and collects all *his followers*. Moreover, when the tyrant shall dash himself against the army of God, his soldiery are overthrown by the celestial terror; the false prophet himself is seized with the wicked one, by the decree of the Lord; they are handed over alive to Gehenna. From him chiefs and leaders are bidden to obey; then will the holy ones enter into the breasts of their ancient mother, that, moreover, they also may be refreshed whom he has evil persuaded. With various punishments he will torment those who trust in him; they come to the end, whereby offences are taken away from the world. The Lord will begin to give judgment by fire.

XLIII. — OF THE END OF THIS AGE.

The trumpet gives the sign in heaven, the lion being taken away, and suddenly there is darkness with the din of heaven. The Lord casts down His eyes, so that the earth trembles. He cries out, so that all may hear throughout the world: Behold, long have I been silent while I bore your doings in such a time. They cry out together, complaining and groaning too late. They howl, they bewail; nor is there room found for the wicked. What shall the mother do for the sucking child, when she herself is burnt up? In the flame of fire the Lord will judge the wicked. But the fire shall not touch the just, but shall by all means lick them up.[1] In one place they delay, but a part has wept at the judgment. Such will be the heat, that the stones themselves shall melt. The winds assemble into lightnings, the heavenly wrath rages; and wherever the wicked man fleeth, he is seized upon by this fire. There will be no succour nor ship of the sea. Amen[2] flames on the nations, and the Medes and Parthians burn for a thousand years, as the hidden words of John declare. For then after a thousand years they are delivered over to Gehenna; and he whose work they were, with them are burnt up.

---

[1] [The translator here inserts a mark of interrogation. The meaning is: lick up them (the wicked) who have persecuted them. Dan. iii. 22.]
[2] [Rev. iii. 14.]

XLIV. OF THE FIRST RESURRECTION.

From heaven will descend the city in the first resurrection ; this is what we may tell of such a celestial fabric. We shall arise again to Him, who have been devoted to Him. And they shall be incorruptible, even already living without death. And neither will there be any grief nor any groaning in that city. They shall come also who overcame cruel martydom under Antichrist, and they themselves live for the whole time, and receive blessings because they have suffered evil things ; and they themselves marrying, beget for a thousand years. There are prepared all the revenues of the earth, because the earth renewed without end pours forth abundantly. Therein are no rains ; no cold comes into the golden camp. No sieges as now, nor rapines, nor does that city crave the light of a lamp. It shines from its Founder. Moreover, Him it obeys ; in breadth 12,000 furlongs, and length and depth. It levels its foundation in the earth, but it raises its head to heaven. In the city before the doors, moreover, sun and moon shall shine ; he who is evil is hedged up in torment, for the sake of the nourishment of the righteous. But from the thousand years God will destroy all those evils.

XLV. OF THE DAY OF JUDGMENT.

I add something, on account of unbelievers, of the day of judgment. Again, the fire of the Lord sent forth shall be appointed. The earth gives a true groan ; then those who are making their journey in the last end, and then all unbelievers, *groan*. The whole of nature is converted in flame, which yet avoids the camp of His saints. The earth is burned up from its foundations, and the mountains melt. Of the sea nothing remains : it is overcome by the powerful fire. This sky perishes, and the stars and these things are changed. Another newness of sky and of everlasting earth is arranged. Thence they who deserve it are sent away in a second death, but the righteous are placed in inner dwelling-places.

XLVI. TO CATECHUMENS.

In few words, I admonish all believers in Christ, who have forsaken idols, for your salvation. In the first times, if in any way thou fallest into error, still, when entreated, do thou leave all things for Christ ; and since thou hast known God, be a recruit good and approved, and let virgin modesty dwell with thee in purity. Let the mind be watchful for good things. Beware that thou fall not into former sins. In baptism the coarse dress of thy birth is washed. For if any sinful catechumen is marked with punishment, let him live in the signs of *Christian-*

ity, although not without loss.[1] The whole of the matter for thee is this, Do thou ever shun great sins.

XLVII. TO THE FAITHFUL.

I admonish the faithful not to hold their brethren in hatred. Hatreds are accounted impious by martyrs for the flame. The martyr is destroyed whose confession is of such kind ; nor is it taught that the evil is expiated by the shedding of blood. A law is given to the unjust man that he may restrain himself. Thence he ought to be free from craft ; so also oughtest thou. Twice dost thou sin against God, if thou extendest strifes to thy brother ; whence thou shalt not avoid sin following thy former courses. Thou hast once been washed : shalt thou be able to be immersed again?

XLVIII. O FAITHFUL, BEWARE OF EVIL.

The birds are deceived, and the beasts of the woods in the woods, by those very charms by which their ruin is ever accomplished, and caves as well as food deceive them as they follow ; and they know not how to shun evil, nor are they restrained by law. Law is given to man, and a doctrine of life to be chosen, from which he remembers that he may be able to live carefully, and recalls his own place, and takes away those things which belong to death. He severely condemns himself who forsakes rule ; either bound with iron, or cast down from his degree ; or deprived of life, he loses what he ought to enjoy. Warned by example, do not sin gravely ; translated by the laver, rather have charity ; flee far from the bait of the mouse-trap, where there is death. Many are the martyrdoms which are made without shedding of blood. Not to desire other men's goods ; to wish to have the benefit of martyrdom ; to bridle the tongue, thou oughtest to make thyself humble ; not willingly to use force, nor to return force used against thee, thou wilt be a patient mind, understand that thou art a martyr.

XLIX. TO PENITENTS.

Thou art become a penitent ; pray night and day ; yet from thy Mother *the Church* do not far depart, and the Highest will be able to be merciful to thee. The confession of thy fault shall not be in vain. Equally in thy state of accusation learn to weep manifestly. Then, if thou hast a wound, seek herbs and a physician ; and yet in thy punishments thou shalt be able to mitigate thy sufferings. For I will even confess that I alone of you am here, and that terror must be foregone. I have myself felt the destruction ; and therefore I warn those who are

[1] [Catechumens falling away before baptism must not despair, but persevere and remain under discipline.]

wounded to walk more cautiously, to put thy hair and thy beard in the dust of the earth, and to be clothed in sackcloth, and to entreat from the highest King will aid thee, that thou perish not perchance from among the people.

L. WHO HAVE APOSTATIZED FROM GOD.

Moreover, when war is waged, or an enemy attacks, if one be able either to conquer or to be hidden, they are great trophies; but unhappy will he be who shall be taken by them. He loses country and king who has been unwilling to fight worthily for the truth, for his country, or for life. He ought to die rather than go under a barbarian king; and let him seek slavery who is willing to transfer himself to enemies without law. Then, if in warring thou shouldst die for thy king, thou hast conquered, or if thou hast given thy hands, thou hast perished uninjured by law. The enemy crosses the river; do thou hide under thy lurking-place; or, if he can enter or not, do not linger. Everywhere make thyself safe, and thy friends also; thou hast conquered. And take watchful care lest any one enter in that lurking-place. It will be an infamous thing if any one declares himself to the enemy. He who knows not how to conquer, and runs to deliver himself up, has weakly foregone praise for neither his own nor his country's good. Then he was unwilling to live, since life itself will perish. If any one is without God, or profane from the enemy, they are become as sounding brass, or deaf as adders: such men ought abundantly to pray or to hide themselves.

LI. OF INFANTS.

The enemy has suddenly come flooding us over with war; and before they could flee, he has seized upon the helpless children. They cannot be reproached, although they are seen to be taken captive; nor, indeed, do I excuse them. Perhaps they have deserved it on account of the faults of their parents; therefore God has given them up. However, I exhort the adults that they run to arms, and that they should be born again, as it were, to their Mother from the womb. Let them avoid a law that is terrible, and always bloody, impious, intractable, living with the life of the beasts; for when another war by chance should be to be waged, he who should be able to conquer or even rightly to know how to beware . . .

LII. DESERTERS.

For deserters are not called so as all of one kind. One is wicked, another partially withdraws; but yet true judgments are decreed for both. So Christ is fought against, even as Cæsar is obeyed. Seek the refuge of the king, if thou hast been a delinquent. Do thou implore of Him; do thou prostrate confess to Him: He will grant all things whose also are all our things. The camp being replaced, beware of sinning further; do not wander long as a soldier through caves of the wild beasts. Let it be sin to thee to cease from unmeasured doing.

LIII. TO THE SOLDIERS OF CHRIST.

When thou hast given thy name to the warfare, thou art held by a bridle. Therefore begin thou to put away thy former doings. Shun luxuries, since labour is threatening arms. With all thy virtue thou must obey the king's command, if thou wishest to attain the last times in-gladness. He is a good soldier, always wait for things to be enjoyed. Be unwilling to flatter thyself; absolutely put away sloth, that thou mayest daily be ready for what is set before thee. Be careful beforehand; in the morning revisit the standards. When thou seest the war, take the nearest contest. This is the king's glory, to see the soldiery prepared. The king is present; desire that ye may fight beyond his hope. He makes ready gifts. He gladly looks for the victory, and assigns you to be a fit follower. Do thou be unwilling to spare thyself besides for Belial; be thou rather diligent, that he may give fame for your death.

LIV. OF FUGITIVES.

The souls of those that are lost deservedly of themselves separate themselves. Begotten of him, they again recur to those things which are his. The root of Cain, the accursed seed, breaks forth and takes refuge in the servile nation under a barbarian king; and there the eternal flame will torment on the day decreed. The fugitive will wander vaguely without discipline, loosed from law to go about through the defiles of the ways. These, therefore, are such whom no penalty has restrained. If they will not live, they ought to be seen by the idols.

LV. OF THE SEED OF THE TARES.

Of the seed of the tares, who stand mingled in the Church. When the times of the harvest are filled up, the tares that have sprung up are separated from the fruit, because God had not sent them. The husbandman separates all those collected tares. The law is our field; whoever does good in it, assuredly the Ruler Himself will afford a true repose, for the tares are burned with fire. If, therefore, you think that under one they are delaying, you are wrong. I designate you as barren Christians; cursed was the fig-tree without fruit in the word of the Lord, and immediately it withered away. Ye do not works; ye prepare no gift for the treasury, and yet ye thus vainly think to deserve well of the Lord.

LVI. TO THE DISSEMBLER.

Dost thou dissemble with the law that was given with such public announcement, crying out in the heavenly word of so many prophets? If a prophet had only cried out to the clouds,[1] the word of the Lord uttered by him would surely suffice. The law of the Lord proclaims itself into so many volumes of prophets; none of them excuses wickedness; thus even thou wishest from the heart to see good things; thou art also seeking to live by deceits. Why, then, has the law itself gone forth with so much pains? Thou abusest the commands of the Lord, and yet thou callest thyself His son. Thou art seen, if thou wilt be such without reason. I say, the Almighty seeks the meek to be His sons, those who are upright with a good heart, those who are devoted to the divine law; but ye know already where He has plunged the wicked.

LVII. THAT WORLDLY THINGS ARE ABSOLUTELY TO BE AVOIDED.

If certain teachers, while looking for your gifts or fearing your persons, relax individual things to you, not only do I not grieve, but I am compelled to speak the truth. Thou art going to vain shows with the crowd of the evil one, where Satan is at work in the circus with din. Thou persuadest thyself that everything that shall please thee is lawful. Thou art the offspring of the Highest, mingled with the sons of the devil. Dost thou wish to see the former things which thou hast renounced? Art thou again conversant with them? What shall the Anointed One profit thee? Or if it is permitted, on account of weakness, that thou foolishly profane . . . Love not the world, nor its contents. Such is God's word, and it seems good to thee. Thou observest man's command, and shunnest God's. Thou trustedst to the gift whereby the teachers shut up their mouths, that they may be silent, and not tell thee the divine commands; while I speak the truth, as thou art bound look to the Highest. Assign thyself as a follower to Him whose son thou wast. If thou seekest to live, being a believing man, as do the Gentiles, the joys of the world remove thee from the grace of Christ. With an undisciplined mind thou seekest what thou presumest to be easily lawful, both thy dear actors and their musical strains; nor carest thou that the offspring of such an one should babble follies. While thou thinkest that thou art enjoying life, thou art improvidently erring. The Highest commands, and thou shunnest His righteous precepts.

LVIII. THAT THE CHRISTIAN SHOULD BE SUCH.

When the Lord says that man should eat bread with groaning, here what art thou now doing, who desirest to live with joy? Thou seekest to rescind the judgment uttered by the highest God when He first formed man; thou wishest to abandon the curb of the law. If the Almighty God have bidden thee live with sweat, thou who art living in pleasure wilt already be a stranger to Him. The Scripture saith that the Lord was angry with the Jews. Their sons, refreshed with food, rose up to play. Now, therefore, why do we follow these circumcised men?[2] In what respect they perished, we ought to beware; the greatest part of you, surrendered to luxuries, obey them. Thou transgressest the law in staining thyself with dyes; against thee the apostle cries out; yea, God cries out by him. Your dissoluteness, says he, in itself ruins[3] you. Be, then, such as Christ wishes you to be, gentle, and in Him joyful, for in the world you are sad. Run, labour, sweat, fight with sadness. Hope comes with labour, and the palm is given to victory. If thou wishest to be refreshed, give help and encouragement to the martyr. Wait for the repose to come in the passage of death.

LIX. TO THE MATRONS OF THE CHURCH OF THE LIVING GOD.

Thou wishest, O Christian woman, that the matrons should be as the ladies of the world. Thou surroundest thyself with gold, or with the modest silken garment. Thou givest the terror of the law from thy ears to the wind. Thou affectest vanity with all the pomp of the devil. Thou art adorned at the looking-glass with thy curled hair turned back from thy brow. And moreover, with evil purposes, thou puttest on false medicaments, on thy pure eyes the stibium, with painted beauty, or thou dyest thy hair that it may be always black. God is the overlooker, who dives into each heart. But these things are not necessary for modest women. Pierce thy breast with chaste and modest feeling. The law of God bears witness that such laws fail from the heart which believes; to a wife approved of her husband, let it suffice that she is so, not by her dress, but by her good disposition. To put on clothes which the cold and the heat or too much sun demands, only that thou mayest be approved modest, and show forth the gifts of thy capacity among the people of God. Thou who wast formerly most illustrious, givest to thyself the guise of one who is contemptible. She who lay without life, was raised by the prayers of the widows. She deserved this, that she should be raised from death, not by her costly dress, but by her gifts. Do ye, O good matrons, flee from the adornment of vanity; such attire is fitting for women who haunt the brothels. Overcome the evil one, O modest women of Christ. Show forth all your wealth in giving.

---

[1] Or, "If one prophet only had cried out to the world."

[2] Sponte profectos.
[3] Deperdunt.

LX. TO THE SAME AGAIN.

Hear my voice, thou who wishest to remain a Christian woman, in what way the blessed Paul commands you to be adorned. Isaiah, moreover, the teacher and author that spoke from heaven, for he detests those who follow the wickedness of the world, says: The daughters of Zion that are lifted up shall be brought low. It is not right in God that a faithful Christian woman should be adorned. Dost thou seek to go forth after the fashion of the Gentiles, O thou who art consecrated to God? God's heralds, crying aloud in the law, condemn such to be unrighteous women, who in such wise adorn themselves. Ye stain your hair; ye paint the opening of your eyes with black; ye lift up your pretty hair one by one on your painted brow; ye anoint your cheeks with some sort of ruddy colour laid on; and, moreover, ear-rings hang down with very heavy weight. Ye bury your neck with necklaces; with gems and gold ye bind hands worthy of God with an evil presage. Why should I tell of your dresses, or of the whole pomp of the devil? Ye are rejecting the law when ye wish to please the world. Ye dance in your houses; instead of psalms, ye sing love songs. Thou, although thou mayest be chaste, dost not prove thyself so by following evil things. Christ therefore makes you, such as you are, equal with the Gentiles. Be pleasing to the hymned chorus, and to an appeased Christ with ardent love fervently offer your savour to Christ.

LXI. IN THE CHURCH TO ALL THE PEOPLE OF GOD.

I, brethren, am not righteous who am lifted up out of the filth, nor do I exalt myself; but I grieve for you, as seeing that out of so great a people, none is crowned in the contest; certainly, even if he does not himself fight, yet let him suggest encouragement to others. Ye rebuke calamity; O belly, stuff yourself out with luxury. The brother labours in arms with a world opposed to him; and dost thou, stuffed with wealth, neither fight, nor place thyself by his side when he is fighting? O fool, dost not thou perceive that one is warring on behalf of many? The whole Church is suspended on such a one if he conquers. Thou seest that thy brother is withheld, and that he fights with the enemy. Thou desirest peace in the camp, he outside rejects it. Be pitiful, that thou mayest be before all things saved. Neither dost thou fear the Lord, who cries aloud with such an utterance; even He who commands us to give food even to our enemies. Look forward to thy meals from that Tobias who always on every day shared them entirely with the poor man. Thou seekest to feed him, O fool, who feedeth thee again. Dost thou wish that he should prepare for me, who is

setting before him his burial? The brother oppressed with want, nearly languishing away, cries out at the splendidly fed, and with distended belly. What sayest thou of the Lord's day? If he have not placed himself before, call forth a poor man from the crowd whom thou mayest take to thy dinner. In the tablets is your hope from a Christ refreshed.

LXII. TO HIM WHO WISHES FOR MARTYRDOM.

Since, O son, thou desirest martyrdom, hear. Be thou such as Abel was, or such as Isaac himself, or Stephen, who chose for himself on the way the righteous life. Thou indeed desirest that which is a matter suited for the blessed. First of all, overcome the evil one with thy good acts by living well; and when He thy King shall see thee, be thou secure. It is His own time, and we are living for both; so that if war fails, the martyrs shall go in peace. Many indeed err who say, With our blood we have overcome the wicked one; and if he remains, they are unwilling to overcome. He perishes by lying in wait, and the wicked thus feels it; but he that is lawful does not feel the punishments applied. With exclamation and with eagerness beat thy breast with thy fists. Even now, if thou hast conquered by good deeds, thou art a martyr in Him. Thou, therefore, who seekest to extol martyrdom with thy word, in peace clothe thyself with good deeds, and be secure.[1]

LXIII. THE DAILY WAR.

Thou seekest to wage war, O fool, as if wars were at peace. From the first formed day in the end you fight. Lust precipitates you, there is war; fight with it. Luxury persuades, neglect it; thou hast overcome the war. Be sparing of abundance of wine, lest by means of it thou shouldest go wrong. Restrain thy tongue from cursing, because with it thou adorest the Lord. Repress rage. Make thyself peaceable to all. Beware of trampling on thy inferiors when weighed down with miseries. Lend thyself as a protector only, and do no hurt. Lead yourselves in a righteous path, unstained by jealousy. In thy riches make thyself gentle to those that are of little account. Give of thy labour, clothe the naked. Thus shalt thou conquer. Lay snares for no man, since thou servest God. Look to the beginning, whence the envious enemy has perished. I am not a teacher, but the law itself teaches by its proclamation. Thou wearest such great words vainly, who in one moment seekest without labour to raise a martyrdom to Christ.

LXIV. OF THE ZEAL OF CONCUPISCENCE.

In desiring, thence thou perishest, whilst thou art burning with envy of thy neighbour. Thou

---

[1] [Compare Clement's reproof, vol. ii. p. 423, this series.]

extinguishest thyself, when thou inflamest thyself within. Thou art jealous, O envious man, of another who is struggling with evil, and desirest that thou mayest become equally the possessor of so much wealth. The law does not thus behold him when thou seekest to fall upon him. Depending on all things, thou livest in the lust of gain ; and although thou art guilty to thyself, thou condemnest thyself by thy own judgment. The greedy survey of the eyes is never satisfied. Now, therefore, if thou mayest return and consider, lust is vain . . . whence God cries out, Thou fool, this night thou art summoned. Death rushes after thee. Whose, then, shall be those talents? By hiding the unrighteous gains in the concealed treasury, when the Lord shall supply to every one his daily life. Let another accumulate ; do thou seek to live well. And when thy heart is conscious of God, thou shalt be victor over all things ; yet I do not say that thou shouldest boast thyself in public, when thou art watching for thy day by living without fraud. The bird perishes in the midst of food, or carelessly sticks fast in the bird-lime. Think that in thy simplicity thou hast much to beware of. Let others trangress these bounds. Do thou always look forward.

LXV. THEY WHO GIVE FROM EVIL.

Why dost thou senselessly feign thyself good by the wound of another? Whence thou bestowest, another is daily weeping. Dost not thou believe that the Lord sees those things from heaven? The Highest says, He. does not approve of the gifts of the wicked. Thou shalt break forth upon the wretched when thou shalt have gained a place. One gives gifts that he may make another of no account ; or if thou hast lent on usury, taking twenty-four per cent, thou wishest to bestow charity that thou mayest purge thyself, as being evil, with that which is evil. The Almighty absolutely rejects such works as these. Thou hast given *that which has been wrung* from tears ; that candidate, oppressed with ungrateful usuries, and become needy, deplores it. Besides having obtained an opportunity for the exactors, thy enemy for the present is the people ; thou consecrated, hast become wicked for reward. Also thou wishest to atone for thyself by the gain of wages. O wicked one, thou deceivest thyself, but none else.

LXVI. OF A DECEITFUL PEACE.

The arranged time comes to our people ; there is peace in the world ; and, at the same time, ruin is weighing us down from the enticement of the world, (the destruction) of the reckless people whom ye have rent into schism. Either obey the law of the city, or depart from it. Ye behold the mote sticking in our eyes, and will not see the beam in your own. A treacherous peace is coming to you ; persecution is rife ; the wounds do not appear ; and thus, without slaughter, ye are destroyed. War is waged in secret, because, in the midst of peace itself, scarcely one of you has behaved himself with caution. O badly fortified, and foretold for slaughter, ye praise a treacherous peace, — a peace that is mischievous to you. Having become the soldiers of another than Christ, ye have perished.

LXVII. TO THE READERS.

I warn certain readers only to consider, and to give material to others by an example of life, to avoid strife, and to shun so many quarrels ; to repress terror, and never to be proud ; moreover, denounce the righteous obedience of wicked men. Make yourselves like to Christ your Master, O little ones. Be among the lilies of the field by your benefits ; ye have become blessed when ye bear the edicts ; ye are flowers in the congregation ; ye are Christ's lanterns. Keep what ye are, and ye shall be able to tell it.

LXVIII. TO MINISTERS.

Exercise the mystery of Christ, O deacons, with purity ; therefore, O ministers, do the commands of your Master ; do not play the person of a righteous judge ; strengthen your office by all things, as learned men, looking upwards, always devoted to the Supreme God. Render the faithful sacred ministries of the altar to God, prepared in divine matters to set an example ; yourselves incline your head to the pastors, so shall it come to pass that ye may be approved of Christ.

LXIX. TO GOD'S SHEPHERDS.

A shepherd, if he shall have confessed, has doubled his conflict. Moreover, the apostle bids that such should be teachers. Let him be a patient ruler ; let him know when he may relax the reins ; let him terrify at first, and then anoint with honey ; and let him first observe to do himself what he says. The shepherd who minds worldly things is esteemed in fault, against whose countenance thou mightest dare to say anything. Gehenna itself bubbles up in hell with rumours. Woe to the wretched people which wavers with doubtful brow ! if such a shepherd shall be present to it, it is almost ruined. But a devout man restrains it, governing rightly. The swarms are rejoiced under suitable kings ; in such there is hope, and the entire Church lives.

LXX. I SPEAK TO THE ELDER-BORN.

The time demands that I alone should speak to you truth.

He is often admonished by one word which

many refuse. I wish you to turn your hatred against me alone, that the hearts of all may tremble at the tempter. Look to the saying that truly begets hatred, (and consider) how many things I have lately indeed foretold concerning a delusive peace, while, alas, the enticing seducer has come upon you unawares, and because ye have not known how that his wiles were imminent, ye have perished; ye work absolutely bitter things, but that is itself the characteristic of the world; not any one for whom ye intercede acts for nothing. He who takes refuge from your fire, plunges in the whirlpool. Then the wretch, stripped naked, seeks assistance from you. The judges themselves shudder at your frauds . . . . of a shorter title, I should not labour at so many lines. Ye who teach, look upon those to whom ye willingly tend, when for yourselves ye both receive banquets and feed upon them. For those things are ye already almost entering the foundations of the earth.

LXXI. TO VISIT THE SICK.

If thy brother should be weak — I speak of the poor man — do not empty-handed visit such an one as he lies ill. Do good under God; pay your obedience by your money. Thence he shall be restored; or if he should perish, let a poor man be refreshed, who has nothing wherewith to pay you, but the Founder and Author of the world on his behalf. Or if it should displease thee to go to the poor man, always hateful, send money, and something 'whence he may recover himself. And, similarly, if thy poor sister lies upon a sick-bed, let your matrons begin to bear her victuals. God Himself cries out, Break thy bread to the needy. There is no need to visit with words, but with benefits. It is wicked that thy brother should be sick through want of food. Satisfy him not with words. He needs meat and drink. Look upon such assuredly weakened, who are not able to act for themselves. Give to them at once. I pledge my word that fourfold shall be given you by God.

LXXII. TO THE POOR IN HEALTH.

What can healthful poverty do, unless wealth be present? Assuredly, if thou hast the means, at once communicate also to thy brother. Be responsible to thyself for one, lest thou shouldst be said to be proud. I promise that thou shalt live more secure than the rich man. Receive into thy ears the teaching of the great Solomon: God hates the poor man to be a pleader on high.[1] Therefore submit thyself, and give honour to Him that is powerful; for the soft speech — thou knowest the proverb — melts.[2] One is

conquered by service, even although there be an ancient anger. If the tongue be silent, thou hast found nothing better. If there should not wholesomely be an art whereby life may be governed, either give aid or direction by the command of Him that is mighty. Let it not shame or grieve you that a healthy man should have faith. In the treasury, besides, thou oughtest to give of thy labour, even as that widow whom the Anointed One preferred.[3]

LXXIII. THAT SONS ARE NOT TO BE BEWAILED.

Although the death of sons leaves grief for the heart, yet it is not right either to go forth in black garments, or to bewail them. The Lord prudently says that ye must grieve with the mind, not with outward show, which is finished in the week. In the book of Solomon the promises of the Lord concerning the resurrection are forgotten if thou wouldest make thy sons martyrs, and thus with thy voice will bewail them. Art thou not ashamed without restraint to lament thy sons, like the Gentiles? Thou tearest thy face, thou beatest thy breast, thou takest off thy garments; and dost thou not fear the Lord, whose kingdom thou desirest to behold? Mourn as it is right, but do not do wrong on their behalf. Ye therefore are such. What less than Gentiles are ye? Ye do as the crowds that are descended from the diabolical stock. Ye cry that they are extinct. With what advantage, O false one, thou hast perished! The father has not led his son with grief to be slain at the altar, nor has the prophet mourned over a deceased son with grief, nor even has a weeping parent. But one devoted to God was hastily dying.

LXXIV. OF FUNERAL POMP.

Thou who seekest to be careful of the pomp of death art in error. As a servant of God, thou oughtest even in death to please Him. Alas that the lifeless body should be adorned in death! O true vanity, to desire honour for the dead! A mind enchained to the world; not even in death devoted to Christ. Thou knowest the proverbs. He wished to be carried through the forum. Thus ye, who are like to him, and living with untrained mind, wish to have a happy and blessed day at your death, that the people may come together, and that you may see praise with mourning. Thou dost not foresee whither thou mayest deserve to go when dead. Lo, they are following thee; and thou, perchance, art already burning, being driven to punishment. What will the pomp benefit the dead man? Thou shalt be accused, who seekest them on account of those gatherings. Thou desirest to live under idols. Thou deceivest thyself.

---

[1] [Prov. xxiii. 11.]
[2] [Prov. xv. 1.]

[3] [Mark xii. 42; Luke xxi. 2.]

LXXV. TO THE CLERKS.

They will assemble together at Easter, that day of ours most blessed; and let them rejoice, who ask for divine entertainments. Let what is sufficient be expended upon them, wine and food. Look back at the source whence these things may be told on your behalf. Ye are wanting in a gift to Christ, in moderate expenditure. Since ye yourselves do it not, in what manner can ye persuade the righteousness of the law to such people, even once in the year? Thus often blasphemy suggests to many concerning you.

LXXVI. OF THOSE WHO GOSSIP, AND OF SILENCE.

When a thing appears to anybody of no consequence, and is not shunned, and it rushes forth, as if easy, whilst thou abusest it. Fables assist it when thou comest to pour out prayers, or to beat thy breast for thy daily sin. The trumpet of the heralds sounds forth, while the reader is reading, that the ears may be open, and thou rather impedest them. Thou art luxurious with thy lips, with which thou oughtest to groan. Shut up thy breast to evils, or loose them in thy breast. But since the possession of money gives barefacedness to the wealthy, thence every one perishes when they are most trusting to themselves. Thus, moreover, the women assemble, as if they would enter the bath. They press closely, and make of God's house as if it were a fair. Certainly the Lord frightened the house of prayer. The Lord's priest commanded with "sursum corda," when prayer was to be made, that your silence should be made. Thou answerest fluently, and moreover abstainest not from promises. He entreats the Highest on behalf of a devoted people, lest any one should perish, and thou turnest thyself to fables. Thou mockest at him, or detractest from thy neighbour's reputation. Thou speakest in an undisciplined manner, as if God were absent — as if He who made all things neither hears nor sees.

LXXVII. TO THE DRUNKARDS.

I place no limit to a drunkard; but I prefer a beast. From those who are proud in drinking thou withdrawest in thine inner mind, holding the power of the ruler, O fool, among Cyclopes. Thence in the histories thou criest, While I am dead I drink not. Be it mine to drink the best things, and to be wise in heart. Rather give assistance (what more seekest thou to abuse?) to the lowest pauper, and ye shall both be refreshed. If thou doest such things, thou extinguishest Gehenna for thyself.

LXXVIII. TO THE PASTORS.

Thou who seekest to feed others, and hast prepared what thou couldest by assiduously feeding, hast done rightly. But still look after the poor man, who cannot feed thee again: then will thy table be approved by the one God. The Almighty has bidden such even especially to be fed. Consider, when thou feedest the sick, thou art also lending to the High One. In that thing the Lord has wished that you should stand before Him approved.

LXXIX. TO THE PETITIONERS.

If thou desirest, when praying, to be heard from heaven, break the chains from the lurking-places of wickedness; or if, pitying the poor, thou prayest by thy benefits, doubt not but what thou shalt have asked may be given to the petitioner. Then truly, if void of benefits, thou adorest God, do not thus at all make thy prayers vainly.

LXXX. THE NAME OF THE MAN OF GAZA.

Ye who are to be inhabitants of the heavens with God-Christ, hold fast the beginning, look at all things from heaven. Let simplicity, let meekness dwell in your body. Be not angry with thy devout brother without a cause, for ye shall receive whatever ye may have done from him. This has pleased Christ, that the dead should rise again, yea, with their bodies; and those, too, whom in this world the fire has burned, when six thousand years are completed, and the world has come to an end. The heaven in the meantime is changed with an altered course, for then the wicked are burnt up with divine fire. The creature with groaning burns with the anger of the highest God. Those who are more worthy, and who are begotten of an illustrious stem, and the men of nobility under the conquered Antichrist, according to God's command living again in the world for a thousand years, indeed, that they may serve the saints, and the High One, under a servile yoke, that they may bear victuals on their neck. Moreover, that they may be judged again when the reign is finished. They who make God of no account when the thousandth year is finished shall perish by fire, when they themselves shall speak to the mountains. All flesh in the monuments and tombs is restored according to its deed: they are plunged in hell; they bear their punishments in the world; they are shown to them, and they read the things transacted from heaven; the reward according to one's deeds in a perpetual tyranny. I cannot comprehend all things in a little treatise; the curiosity of the learned men shall find my name in this.[1]

---

[1] [Dr. Schaff says this *Nomen Gazæi* may indicate his possession of the wealth of truth, etc. But, if we read the acrostical initials of the verses *backwards*, we find the name *Commodianus Mendicus Christi*, which betokens his poverty also, in the spirit of St. Paul (2 Cor. vi. 10; also, Rev. ii. 9), which our author would naturally make emphatic here.]

ELUCIDATION.

I KNOW nothing of the second poem of our author, and am indebted for the following particulars to Dr. Schaff.[1]

It is an *apologetic poem* against Jews and Gentiles, written in uncouth hexameters, and discusses in forty-seven sections the doctrine concerning God and the Redeemer and mankind. It treats of the names of Son and Father; and here, probably, he lays himself open to the charge of Patripassian heresy. He passes to the obstacles encountered by the Gospel, warns the Jews and the Gentiles to forsake their unprofitable devotions, and enlarges on the eschatology, as he conceives of it. Let me now quote textually, as follows:—

"The most interesting part of the second poem is the conclusion. It contains a fuller description of Antichrist than the first poem. The author expects that the end of the world will come with the seventh persecution. The Goths will conquer Rome and redeem the Christians; but then Nero will appear as the heathen Antichrist, reconquer Rome, and rage against the Christians three years and a half. He will be conquered in turn by the Jewish and real Antichrist from the East, who, after the defeat of Nero and the burning of Rome, will return to Judea, perform false miracles, and be worshipped by the Jews. At last Christ appears, that is, God himself (from the *Monarchian* stand-point of the author) with the lost Twelve Tribes [?] as his army, which had lived beyond Persia in happy simplicity and virtue. Under astounding phenomena of nature he will conquer Antichrist and his host, convert all nations, and take possession of the holy city of Jerusalem."

This idea of a double Antichrist re-appears in Lactantius, *Inst. Div.*, vii. 16 seqq.

This second poem was discovered by Cardinal Pitra in 1852. The two poems were edited by E. Ludwig, Leipzig, 1877 and 1878.

---

[1] *Hist.*, vol. ii. 855.

ORIGEN.

[TRANSLATED BY THE REV. FREDERICK CROMBIE, D.D.]

INTRODUCTORY NOTE

TO THE

WORKS OF ORIGEN.

[A.D. 185–230–254.] The reader will remember the rise and rapid development of the great Alexandrian school, and the predominance which was imparted to it by the genius of the illustrious Clement.[1] But in Origen, his pupil, who succeeded him at the surprising age of eighteen, a new sun was to rise upon its noontide. Truly was Alexandria "the mother and mistress of churches" in the benign sense of a nurse and instructress of Christendom, not its arrogant and usurping imperatrix.

The full details of Origen's troubled but glorious career are given by Dr. Crombie, who in my opinion deserves thanks for the kind and apologetic temper of his estimate of the man and the sublime doctor, as well as of the period of his life. Upon the fervid spirit of a confessor in an age of cruelty, lust, and heathenism, what right have we to sit in judgment? Of one whose very errors were virtues at their source, how can a Christian of our self-indulgent times presume to speak in censure? Well might the Psalmist exclaim,[2] "Let us fall now into the hand of the Lord; for His mercies are great: let me not fall into the hand of man."

Justly has it been urged that to those whose colossal labours during the ante-Nicene period exposed them to hasty judgment, and led them into mistakes, much indulgence must be shown. The language of theology was but assuming shape under their processes, and we owe them an incalculable debt of gratitude: but it was not yet moulded into precision; nor had great councils, presided over by the Holy Ghost, as yet afforded those safeguards to freedom of thought which gradually defined the limits of orthodoxy. To no single teacher did the Church defer. Holy Scripture and the *quod ab omnibus* were the grand *prescription*, against which no individual prelate or doctor could prevail, against which no see could uplift a voice, without chastisement and subjection. Over and over again were the bishops of patriarchal and apostolic sees, including Rome, adjudged heretics, and anathematized by the inexorable law of truth, and of "the faith once delivered to the saints," which not even "an angel from heaven" might presume to change or to enlarge. But before the great Synodical period (A.D. 325 to 451), while orthodoxy is marvellously maintained and witnessed to by Origen and Tertullian themselves, their errors, however serious, have never separated them from the grateful and loving regard of those upon whom their lives of heroic sorrow and suffering have conferred blessings unspeakable. The Church cannot leave their errors uncorrected. Their persons she leaves to the Master's award: their characters she cherishes, while their faults she deplores.

The great feature of the ante-Nicene theology, even in the mistakes of the writers, is its reliance on the Holy Scripture. What wealth of Scripture they lavish in their pages! We identify the Scriptures by their aid; but, were they lost in other forms, we might almost restore them from

---

[1] Vol. ii. p. 105, this series. [2] 2 Sam. xxiv. 14.

their pages. And forever is the Church indebted to Origen for the patient and encyclopedic labour and learning which he bestowed on the Scriptures in producing his *Hexapla*. Would that, in his interpretations of the inspired text, he had more strictly adhered to the counsels of Leonides, who was of Bacon's opinion, that the meanings which flow naturally from the holy text are sweetest and best, even as that wine is best which is not crushed out and extorted from the grape, but which trickles of itself from the ripe and luscious cluster in all its purity and natural flavour. So Hooker remarks; and his view is commonly accepted by critics, that the interpretation of a text which departeth most from its natural rendering is commonly the worst.

It is too striking an illustration of the childlike simplicity of the primitive faithful to be passed by, in Origen's history, that anecdote of his father, Leonides, who was himself a confessor and martyr: how he used to strip the bosom of his almost inspired boy as he lay asleep, and imprint kisses on his naked breast, "the temple of the Holy Ghost." That blessed Spirit, he believed, was near to his own lips when he thus saluted a Christian child, "for of such is the kingdom of heaven." From a child, this other Timothy "knew the Scriptures" indeed. His own doting father imbued him with the literature of the Greeks: but, far better, he taught him to love the lively oracles of the Lord of glory; and in these he became so proficient, even from tender years, that he puzzled his parent with his "understanding and answers," like the holy Child of Nazareth when He heard the doctors in the Temple, and also "asked them questions." In will he was also a martyr from his youth, and to the genuine spirit of martyrdom we must attribute that heroic fault of his youth which he lived to condemn in riper years, and which, evil and rash as it was, enabled the Church, once and for all, to give an authoritative interpretation to the language of the Saviour, and to guard her children thenceforth from similar exploits of pious mistake. None can doubt the purity of the motive. Few draw the important inference of the nature of the Church's conflict with that intolerable prevalence of sensuality and shameless vice which so impressed her children with the import of Christ's words, "Blessed are the pure in heart: for they shall see God."

Here follows the very full account of the life of Origen by Dr. Crombie, professor of biblical criticism in St. Mary's College, St. Andrews:—

ORIGEN, surnamed ADAMANTINUS, was born in all probability at Alexandria, about the year 185 A.D.[1] Notwithstanding that his name is derived from that of an Egyptian deity,[2] there seems no reason to doubt that his parents were Christian at the time of his birth. His father Leonides was probably, as has been conjectured,[3] one of the many teachers of rhetoric or grammar who abounded in that city of Grecian culture, and appears to have been a man of decided piety. Under his superintendence, the youthful Origen was not only educated in the various branches of Grecian learning, but was also required daily to commit to memory and to repeat portions of Scripture prescribed him by his father; and while under this training, the spirit of inquiry into the meaning of Scripture, which afterwards formed so striking a feature in the literary character of the great Alexandrine, began to display itself. Eusebius[4] relates that he was not satisfied with the plain and obvious meaning of the text, but sought to penetrate into its deeper signification, and caused his father trouble by the questions which he put to him regarding the sense of particular passages of Holy Writ. Leonides, like many parents, assumed the appearance of rebuking the curiosity of the boy for inquiring into things which were beyond his youthful capacity, and recommended him to be satisfied with the simple and apparent meaning of Scripture, while he is

---

[1] Cf. Redepenning's *Origenes*, vol. i. pp. 417–420 (Erste Beilage: über Origenes Geburtsjahr und den Ort, wo er geboren wurde). [His surname denotes the strength, clearness, and point of his mind and methods. It is generally given ADAMANTIUS.]

[2] Horus *vel* Or. Cf. *Ibid.* (Zweite Beilage: über Namen und Beinamen der Origenes). [But compare Cave, vol. i. p. 322. *Lives of the Fathers*, Oxford, 1840.]

[3] *Encyclopaedie der Katholischen Theologie*, s.v. Origenes.

[4] *Hist. Eccles.*, b. vi. c. ii. § 9.

described as inwardly rejoicing at the signs of genius exhibited by his son, and as giving thanks to God for having made him the parent of such a child.[1]　But this state of things was not to last; for in the year 202, when Origen was about seventeen years of age, the great persecution of the Christians under Septimius Severus broke out, and among the victims was his father Leonides, who was apprehended and put in prison.　Origen wished to share the fate of his father, but was prevented from quitting his home by the artifice of his mother, who was obliged to conceal his clothes to prevent him from carrying out his purpose.　He wrote to his father, however, a letter, exhorting him to constancy under his trials, and entreating him not to change his convictions for the sake of his family.[2]　By the death of his father, whose property was confiscated to the imperial treasury, Origen was left, with his mother and six younger brothers dependent upon him for support.　At this juncture, a wealthy and benevolent lady of Alexandria opened to him her house, of which he became an inmate for a short time.　The society, however, which he found there was far from agreeable to the feelings of the youth.　The lady had adopted as her son one Paul of Antioch, whom Eusebius terms an "advocate of the heretics then existing at Alexandria." The eloquence of the man drew crowds to hear him, although Origen could never be induced to regard him with any favour, nor even to join with him in any act of worship, giving then, as Eusebius remarks, "unmistakeable specimens of the orthodoxy of his faith."[3]

Finding his position in his household so uncomfortable, he resolved to enter upon the career of a teacher of grammar, and to support himself by his own exertions.　As he had been carefully instructed by his father in Grecian literature, and had devoted himself to study after his death, he was enabled successfully to carry out his intention.　And now begins the second stadium of his career.

The diligence and ability with which Origen prosecuted his profession speedily attracted attention and brought him many pupils.　Among others who sought to avail themselves of his instructions in the principles of the Christian religion, were two young men, who afterwards became distinguished in the history of the Church, — Plutarch, who died the death of martyrdom, and Heraclas, who afterwards became bishop of Alexandria.　It was not, however, merely by his success as a teacher that Origen gained a reputation.　The brotherly kindness and unwearied affection which he displayed to all the victims of the persecution, which at that time was raging with peculiar severity at Alexandria under the prefect Aquila, and in which many of his old pupils and friends were martyred, are described as being so marked and conspicuous, as to draw down upon him the fury of the mob, so that he was obliged on several occasions to flee from house to house to escape instant death.　It is easy to understand that services of this kind could not fail to attract the attention of the heads of the Christian community at Alexandria ; and partly, no doubt, because of these, but chiefly on account of his high literary reputation, Bishop Demetrius appointed him to the office of master in the Catechetical School, which was at that time vacant (by the departure of Clement, who had quitted the city on the outbreak of the persecution), although he was still a layman, and had not passed his eighteenth year.　The choice of Demetrius was amply justified by the result.　Origen discontinued his instructions in literature, in order to devote himself exclusively to the work of teaching in the Catechetical School.　For his labours he refused all remuneration.　He sold the books which he possessed, — many of them manuscripts which he himself had copied, — on condition of receiving from the purchaser four obols [4] a day ; and on this scanty pittance he subsisted, leading for many years a life of the greatest asceticism and devotion to study.　After a day of labour in the school, he used to devote the greater part of the night to the investigation of Scripture, sleeping on the bare ground, and keeping frequent fasts.　He carried out literally the command of the Saviour, not to possess two coats, nor wear shoes.　He consummated his work of mortification of the flesh by an act of self-

---

[1] *Hist. Eccles.*, b. vi. c. ii. §§ 10, 11.
[2] Eusebius, *Hist. Eccles.*, b. vi. c. ii.: Επεχε, μὴ δι' ἡμᾶς ἄλλο τι φρονήσης.
[3] τῆς ἐξ ἐκείνου περὶ τὴν πίστιν ὀρθοδοξίας ἐναργῆ παρείχετο δείγματα.
[4] The obol was about three-halfpence of English money.

mutilation, springing from a perverted interpretation of our Lord's words in Matt. xix. 12, and the desire to place himself beyond the reach of temptation in the intercourse which he necessarily had to hold with youthful female catechumens.[1] This act was destined to exercise a baneful influence upon his subsequent career in the Church.

During the episcopate of Zephyrinus (201–218) Origen visited Rome,[2] and on his return again resumed his duties in the Catechetical School, transferring the care of the younger catechumens to his friend and former pupil Heraclas, that he might devote himself with less distraction to the instruction of the more advanced, and to the more thorough investigation and exposition of Scripture. With a view to accomplish this more successfully, it is probable that about this time he set himself to acquire a knowledge of the Hebrew language, the fruit of which may be seen in the fragments which remain to us of his *magnum opus*, the *Hexapla ;* and as many among the more cultured heathens, attracted by his reputation, seem to have attended his lectures, he felt it necessary to make himself more extensively acquainted with the doctrines of the Grecian schools, that he might meet his opponents upon their own ground, and for this purpose he attended the prelections of Ammonius Saccas, at that time in high repute at Alexandria as an expounder of the Neo-Platonic philosophy, of which school he has generally been considered the founder. The influence which the study of philosophical speculations exerted upon the mind of Origen may be traced in the whole course of his after development, and proved the fruitful source of many of those errors which were afterwards laid to his charge, and the controversies arising out of which disturbed the peace of the Church during the two following centuries. As was to be expected, the fame of the great Alexandrine teacher was not confined to his native city, but spread far and wide ; and an evidence of this was the request made by the Roman governor of the province of Arabia to Demetrius and to the prefect of Egypt, that they would send Origen to him that he might hold an interview with one whose reputation was so great. We have no details of this visit, for all that Eusebius relates is that, " having accomplished the objects of his journey, he again returned to Alexandria."[3] It was in the year 216 that the Emperor Caracalla visited Alexandria, and directed a bloody persecution against its inhabitants, especially the literary members of the community, in revenge for the sarcastic verses which had been composed against him for the murder of his brother Geta, a crime which he had perpetrated under circumstances of the basest treachery and cruelty.

Origen occupied too prominent a position in the literary society of the city to be able to remain with safety, and therefore withdrew to Palestine to his friend Bishop Alexander of Jerusalem, and afterwards to Cæsarea, where he received an honourable welcome from Bishop Theoctistus. This step proved the beginning of his after troubles. These two men, filled with becoming admiration for the most learned teacher in the Church, requested him to expound the Scriptures in their presence in a public assembly of the Christians. Origen, although still a layman, and without any sacerdotal dignity in the Church, complied with the request. When this proceeding reached the ears of Demetrius, he was filled with the utmost indignation. " Such an act was never either heard or done before, that laymen should deliver discourses in the presence of the bishops,"[4] was his indignant remonstrance to the two offending bishops, and Origen received a command to return immediately to Alexandria. He obeyed, and for some years appears to have devoted himself solely to his studies in his usual spirit of self-abnegation.

It was probably during this period that the commencement of his friendship with Ambrosius is to be dated. Little is known of this individual. Eusebius[5] states that he had formerly been

[1] For a full discussion of the doubts which have been thrown upon the credibility of Eusebius in this matter by Schnitzer and Baur. cf. Redepenning, *Origenes*, vol. i. pp. 444–458, and Hefele, *Encyclopaedie der Katholischen Theologie*, s.v. Origenes.

[2] [Where he met with Hippolytus, and heard him preach, according to St. Jerome.]

[3] Euseb., *Hist. Eccles.*, b. vi. c. 19, § 16.

[4] *Ibid.*, b. vi. c. 19.

[5] *Ibid.*, b. vi. c. 18.

an adherent of the Valentinian heresy, but had been converted by the arguments and eloquence of Origen to the orthodox faith of the Church. They became intimate friends; and as Ambrose seems to have been possessed of large means, and entertained an unbounded admiration of the learning and abilities of his friend, it was his delight to bear the expenses attending the transcription and publication of the many works which he persuaded him to give to the world. He furnished him "with more than seven amanuenses, who relieved each other at stated times, and with an equal number of transcribers, along with young girls who had been practised in calligraphy," [1] to make fair copies for publication of the works dictated by Origen. The literary activity of these years must have been prodigious, and probably they were among the happiest which Origen ever enjoyed. Engaged in his favourite studies, surrounded by many friends, adding yearly to his own stores of learning, and enriching the literature of the Church with treatises of the highest value in the department of sacred criticism and exegesis, it is difficult to conceive a condition of things more congenial to the mind of a true scholar. Only one incident of any importance seems to have taken place during these peaceful years, — his visit to Julia Mammæa, the pious mother of Alexander Severus. This noble lady had heard of the fame of Origen, and invited him to visit her at Antioch, sending a military escort to conduct him from Alexandria to the Syrian capital. He remained with her some time, "exhibiting innumerable illustrations of the glory of the Lord, and of the excellence of divine instruction, and then hastened back to his accustomed studies." [2]

These happy years, however, were soon to end. Origen was called to Greece, probably about the year 228,[3] upon what Eusebius vaguely calls "the pressing need of ecclesiastical affairs." [4] But, this has generally been understood [5] to refer to the prevalence of heretical views in the Church there, for the eradication of which the assistance of Origen was invoked. Before entering on this journey, he obtained letters of recommendation from his bishop.[6] He passed through Palestine on his way to Greece, and at Cæsarea received at the hands of his friends Alexander and Theoctistus ordination to the office of presbyter, — an honour which proved to him afterwards the source of much persecution and annoyance. No doubt the motives of his friends were of the highest kind, and among them may have been the desire to take away the ground of objection formerly raised by Demetrius against the public preaching of a mere layman in the presence of a bishop. But they little dreamed of the storm which this act of theirs was to raise, and of the consequences which it was to bring upon the head of him whom they had sought to honour. After completing his journey through Greece, Origen returned to Alexandria about the year 230. He there found his bishop greatly incensed against him for what had taken place at Cæsarea. Nor did his anger expend itself in mere objurgations and rebukes. In the year 231 a synod was summoned by Demetrius, composed of Egyptian bishops and Alexandrian presbyters, who declared Origen unworthy to hold the office of teacher, and excommunicated him from the fellowship of the Church of Alexandria. Even this did not satisfy the vindictive feeling of Demetrius. He summoned a second synod, in which the bishops alone were permitted to vote, and by their suffrages Origen was degraded from the office of presbyter, and intimation of this sentence was ordered to be made by encyclical letter to the various Churches. The validity of the sentence was recognised by all of them, with the exception of those in Palestine, Phœnicia, Arabia, and Achaia; a remarkable proof of the position of influence which was at that time held by the Church of Alexandria. Origen appears to have quitted the city before the bursting of the storm, and betook himself to Cæsarea, which henceforth became his home, and the seat of his labours for a period of nearly a quarter of a century. The motives which impelled Demetrius to this

---

[1] Euseb., *Hist. Eccles.*, b. vi. c. 23.

[2] Euseb., *Hist. Eccles.*, b. vi. c. 21: παρ' ᾗ χρόνον διατρίψας, πλεῖστά τε ὅσα εἰς τὴν τοῦ Κυρίου δόξαν καὶ τῆς τοῦ θείου διδασκαλείου ἀρετῆς ἐπιδειξάμενος, ἐπὶ τὰς συνήθεις ἔσπευδε διατριβάς.

[3] Cf. Hefele, *Encyclopaedie*, etc., s.v. Origenes.

[4] Ἐπειγούσης χρείας ἐκκλησιαστικῶν ἕνεκα πραγμάτων.

[5] Cf. Redepenning, vol. i. p. 406, etc.

[6] Cf. *ibid*.

treatment of Origen have been variously stated and variously criticised.   Eusebius [1] refers his
readers for a full account of all the matters involved to the treatise which he and Pamphilus composed in his defence ; but this work has not come down to us,[2] although we possess a brief notice
of it in the *Bibliotheca* of Photius,[3] from which we derive our knowledge of the proceedings of
the two synods.   There seems little reason to doubt that jealousy of interference on the part of the
bishops of another diocese was one main cause of the resentment displayed by Demetrius ; while
it is also possible that another alleged cause, the heterodox character of some of Origen's opinions,
as made known in his already published works, among which were his *Stromata* and *De Principiis*,[4]
may have produced some effect upon the minds of the hostile bishops.   Hefele [5] asserts that the
act of the Palestinian bishops was contrary to the Church law of the time, and that Demetrius
was justified on that ground for his procedure against him.   But it may well be doubted whether
there was any generally understood law or practice existing at so early a period of the Church's
history.   If so, it is difficult to understand how it should have been unknown to the Palestinian
bishops ; or, on the supposition of any such existing law or usage, it is equally difficult to conceive that either they themselves or Origen should have agreed to disregard it, knowing as they
did the jealous temper of Demetrius, displayed on the occasion of Origen's preaching at Cæsarea
already referred to.   This had drawn from the Alexandrine bishop an indignant remonstrance, in
which he had asserted that such an act was " quite unheard of before ; " [6] but, to this statement
the Cæsarean bishops replied in a letter, in which they enumerated several instances of laymen
who had addressed the congregation.[7]   The probabilities, therefore, are in favour of there being
no generally understood law or practice on the subject, and that the procedure, therefore, was
dictated by hierarchical jealousy on the part of Demetrius.   According to Eusebius,[8] indeed, the
act of mutilation already referred to was made a ground of accusation against Origen ; and there
seems no doubt that there existed an old canon of the Church,[9] based upon the words in Deut.
xxiii. 1, which rendered one who had committed such an act ineligible for office in the Church.
But there is no trace of this act, as disqualifying Origen for the office of presbyter, having been
urged by Demetrius, so far as can be discovered from the notices of the two synods which have
been preserved by Rufinus and Photius.   And it seems extremely probable, as Redepenning
remarks,[10] that if Demetrius were acquainted with this act of Origen, as Eusebius says he was,[11]
he made no public mention of it, far less that he made it a pretence for his deposition.

Demetrius did not long survive the execution of his vengeance against his unfortunate cate-
chist.   He died about a year afterwards, and was succeeded by Heraclas, the friend and former
pupil of Origen.   It does not, however, appear that Heraclas made any effort to have the sentence against Origen recalled, so that he might return to the early seat of his labours.   Origen
devoted himself at Cæsarea chiefly to exegetical studies upon the books of Scripture, enjoying the
countenance and friendship of the two bishops Alexander and Theoctistus, who are said by Eusebius " to have attended him the whole time as pupils do their master."   He speedily raised the
theological school of that city to a degree of reputation which attracted many pupils.   Among
those who placed themselves under his instructions were two young Cappadocians, who had come
to Cæsarea with other intentions, but who were so attracted by the whole character and personality of Origen, that they immediately became his pupils.   The former of these, afterwards Gregory

---

[1] *Hist. Eccles.*, b. vi. c. 22 and c. 33.
[2] With the exception of the first book; cf. Migne, vol. ix. pp. 542–632.
[3] Cf. Photii *Bibliotheca*, ed. Hoeschel, p. 298.
[4] Eusebius expressly mentions that both these works, among others, were published before he left Alexandria. — *Hist. Eccles.*, b. vi. c. 24.
[5] s.v. Origenes.
[6] *Hist. Eccles.*, b. vi. c. 19.
[7] *Ibid.*
[8] *Ibid.*, b. vi. c. 8.
[9] ὁ ἀκρωτηριάσας ἑαυτὸν μὴ γενέσθω κληρικός.   Cf. Redepenning, vol. i. pp 208, 216, 218.
[10] Cf. Redepenning, vol. i. p. 409, note 2.
[11] *Hist. Eccles.*, b. vi. c. 8.

Thaumaturgus, Bishop of New Cæsarea, has left us, in the panegyric which he wrote after a discipleship of five years, a full and admiring account of the method of his great master.

The persecution under the Emperor Maximin obliged Origen to take refuge in Cæsarea in Cappadocia, where he remained in concealment about two years in the house of a Christian lady named Juliana, who was the heiress of Symmachus, the Ebionite translator of the Septuagint, and from whom he obtained several MSS. which had belonged to Symmachus. Here, also, he composed his *Exhortation to Martyrdom*, which was expressly written for the sake of his friends Ambrosius and Protoctetus, who had been imprisoned on account of their Christian profession, but who recovered their freedom after the death of Maximin, — an event which allowed Origen to return to the Palestinian Cæsarea and to the prosecution of his labours. A visit to Athens, where he seems to have remained some time, and to Bostra in Arabia, in order to bring back to the true faith Bishop Beryllus, who had expressed heterodox opinions upon the subject of the divinity of Christ, (in which attempt he proved successful,) were the chief events of his life during the next five years. On the outbreak of the Decian persecution, however, in 249, he was imprisoned at Tyre, to which city he had gone from Cæsarea for some unknown reason, and was made to suffer great cruelties by his persecutors. The effect of these upon a frame worn out by ascetic labours may be easily conceived. Although he survived his imprisonment, his body was so weakened by his sufferings, that he died at Tyre in 254, in the seventieth year of his age.

The character of Origen is singularly pure and noble ; for his moral qualities are as remarkable as his intellectual gifts. The history of the Church records the names of few whose patience and meekness under unmerited suffering were more conspicuous than his. How very differently would Jerome have acted under circumstances like those which led to Origen's banishment from Alexandria ! And what a favourable contrast is presented by the self-denying asceticism of his whole life, to the sins which stained the early years of Augustine, prior to his conversion ! The impression which his whole personality made upon those who came within the sphere of his influence is evidenced in a remarkable degree by the admiring affection displayed towards him by his friend Ambrose and his pupil Gregory. Nor was it friends alone that he so impressed. To him belongs the rare honour of convincing heretics of their errors, and of leading them back to the Church ; a result which must have been due as much to the gentleness and earnestness of his Christian character, as to the prodigious learning, marvellous acuteness, and logical power, which entitle him to be regarded as the greatest of the Fathers. It is singular, indeed, that a charge of heresy should have been brought, not only after his death, but even during his life, against one who rendered such eminent services to the cause of orthodox Christianity. But this charge must be considered in reference to the times when he lived and wrote. No General Council had yet been held to settle authoritatively the doctrine of the Church upon any of those great questions, the discussion of which convulsed the Christian world during the two following centuries ; and in these circumstances greater latitude was naturally permissible than would have been justifiable at a later period. Moreover, a mind so speculative as that of Origen, and so engrossed with the deepest and most difficult problems of human thought, must sometimes have expressed itself in a way liable to be misunderstood. But no doubt the chief cause of his being regarded as a heretic is to be found in the haste with which he allowed many of his writings to be published. Had he considered more carefully what he intended to bring before the public eye, less occasion would have been furnished to objectors, and the memory of one of the greatest scholars and most devoted Christians that the world has ever seen would have been freed, to a great extent at least, from the reproach of heresy.

Origen was a very voluminous author. Jerome says that he wrote more than any individual could read ; and Epiphanius [1] relates that his writings amounted to 6,000 volumes, by which statement we are probably to understand that every individual treatise, large or small, including each of the numerous homilies, was counted as a separate volume. The admiration entertained

---

[1] *Hæres.*, lxiv. 63.

for him by his friend Ambrosius, and the readiness with which the latter bore all the expenses of transcription and publication, led Origen to give to the world much which otherwise would never have seen the light.

The works of the great Adamantinus may be classed under the following divisions:—

(1) EXEGETICAL WORKS.

These comprise Σχόλια, brief notes on Scripture, of which only fragments remain: Τόμοι, Commentaries, lengthened expositions, of which we possess considerable portions, including those on Matthew, John, and Epistle to the Romans; and about 200 Homilies, upon the principal books of the Old and New Testaments, a full list of which may be seen in Migne's edition. In these works his peculiar system of interpretation found ample scope for exercise; and although he carried out his principle of allegorizing many things, which in their historical and literal signification offended his exegetical sense, he nevertheless maintains that "the passages which hold good in their historical acceptation are much more numerous than those which contain a purely spiritual meaning." [1] The student will find much that is striking and suggestive in his remarks upon the various passages which he brings under review. For an account of his method of interpreting Scripture, and the grounds on which he based it, the reader may consult the fourth book of the treatise On the Principles.

(2) CRITICAL WORKS.

The great critical work of Origen was the Hexapla or Six-columned Bible; an attempt to provide a revised text of the Septuagint translation of Old Testament Scripture. On this undertaking he is said to have spent eight-and-twenty years of his life, and to have acquired a knowledge of Hebrew in order to qualify himself for the task. Each page of this work consisted, with the exception to be noticed immediately, of six columns. In the first was placed the current Hebrew text; in the second, the same represented in Greek letters; in the third, the version of Aquila; in the fourth, that of Symmachus; in the fifth, the text of the LXX., as it existed at the time; and in the sixth, the version of Theodotion. Having come into possession also of certain other Greek translations of some of the books of Scripture, he added these in their appropriate place, so that the work presented in some parts the appearance of seven, eight, or nine columns, and was termed Heptapla, Octopla, or Enneapla, in consequence. He inserted critical marks in the text of the LXX., an asterisk to denote what ought to be added, and an obelus to denote what ought to be omitted; taking the additions chiefly from the version of Theodotion. The work, with the omission of the Hebrew column, and that representing the Hebrew in Greek letters, was termed Tetrapla; and with regard to it, it is uncertain whether it is to be considered a preliminary work on the part of Origen, undertaken by way of preparation for the larger, or merely as an excerpt from the latter. The whole extended, it is said, to nearly fifty volumes, and was, of course, far too bulky for common use, and too costly for transcription. It was placed in some repository in the city of Tyre, from which it was removed after Origen's death to the library at Cæsarea, founded by Pamphilus, the friend of Eusebius. It is supposed to have been burnt at the capture of Cæsarea by the Arabs in 653 A.D. The column, however, containing the version of the LXX. had been copied by Pamphilus and Eusebius, along with the critical marks of Origen, although, owing to carelessness on the part of subsequent transcribers, the text was soon again corrupted. The remains of this work were published by Montfaucon at Paris, 1713, 2 vols. folio; by Bahrdt at Leipsic in 1769; and is at present again in course of publication from the Clarendon press, Oxford, under the editorship of Mr. Field, who has made use of the Syriac-Hexaplar version, and has added various fragments not contained in prior editions. (For a full and critical account of this work, the English reader is referred to Dr. Sam. Davidson's Biblical Criticism, vol. i. ch. xii., which has been made use of for the above notice.)

---

[1] [De Princip., B. IV. i. 19. S.]

(3) APOLOGETICAL WORKS.

His great apologetical work was the treatise undertaken at the special request of his friend Ambrosius, in answer to the attack of the heathen philosopher Celsus on the Christian religion, in a work which he entitled Λόγος ἀληθής, or *A True Discourse*. Origen states that he had heard that there were two individuals of this name, both of them Epicureans, the earlier of the two having lived in the time of Nero, and the other in the time of Adrian, or later.[1] Redepenning is of opinion that Celsus must have composed his work in the time of Marcus Aurelius (161–180 A.D.), on account of his supposed mention of the Marcionites (whose leader did not make his appearance at Rome before 142 A.D.), and of the Marcellians (followers of the Carpocratian Marcellina), a sect which was founded after the year 155 A.D. under Bishop Anicetus.[2] Origen believed his opponent to be an Epicurean, but to have adopted other doctrines than those of Epicurus, because he thought that by so doing he could assail Christianity to greater advantage.[3] The work which Origen composed in answer to the so-styled *True Discourse* consists of eight books, and belongs to the latest years of his life. It has always been regarded as the great apologetic work of antiquity; and no one can peruse it without being struck by the multifarious reading, wonderful acuteness, and rare subtlety of mind which it displays. But the rule which Origen prescribed to himself, of not allowing a single objection of his opponent to remain unanswered, leads him into a minuteness of detail, and into numerous repetitions, which fatigue the reader, and detract from the interest and unity of the work. He himself confesses that he began it on one plan, and carried it out on another.[4] No doubt, had he lived to re-write and condense it, it would have been more worthy of his reputation. But with all its defects, it is a great work, and well deserves the notice of the students of Apologetics. The table of contents subjoined to the translation will convey a better idea of its nature than any description which our limits would permit us to give.

(4) DOGMATIC WORKS.

These include the Στρωματεῖς, a work composed in imitation of the treatise of Clement of the same name, and consisting originally of ten books, of which only three fragments exist in a Latin version by Jerome;[5] a treatise on the Resurrection, of which four fragments remain;[6] and the treatise Περὶ Ἀρχῶν, *De Principiis*, which contains Origen's views on various questions of systematic theology. The work has come down to us in the Latin translation of his admirer Rufinus; but, from a comparison of the few fragments of the original Greek which have been preserved, we see that Rufinus was justly chargeable with altering many of Origen's expressions, in order to bring his doctrine on certain points more into harmony with the orthodox views of the time. The *De Principiis* consists of four books, and is the first of the works of Origen in this series, to which we refer the reader.

(5) PRACTICAL WORKS.

Under this head we place the little treatise Περὶ Εὐχῆς, *On Prayer*, written at the instance of his friend Ambrose, and which contains an exposition of the Lord's Prayer; the Λόγος προτρεπτικὸς εἰς μαρτύριον, *Exhortation to Martyrdom*, composed at the outbreak of the persecution by Maximian, when his friends Ambrose and Protoctetus were imprisoned. Of his numerous letters only two have come down entire, viz., that which was addressed to Julius Africanus, who had questioned the genuineness of the history of Susanna in the apocryphal additions to the book of Daniel, and that to Gregory Thaumaturgus on the use of Greek philosophy in the explanation of Scripture, although, from the brevity of the latter, it is questionable whether it is more than a

---

[1] Cf. *Contra Celsum*, I. c. viii. *ad fin.*
[2] Cf. Redepenning, vol. ii. p. 131, note 2.
[3] *Contra Celsum*, I. ch. viii.
[4] Preface, b. i. § 6.
[5] Migne, vol. i. pp. 102–107.
[6] Migne, vol. i. pp. 91–100.

fragment of the original.[1] The Φιλοκαλία, *Philocalia*, was a compilation from the writings of Origen, intended to explain the difficult passages of Scripture, and executed by Basil the Great and Gregory of Nazianzum ; large extracts of which have been preserved, especially of that part which was taken from the treatise against Celsus. The remains were first printed at Paris in 1618, and again at Cambridge in 1676, in the reprint of Spencer's edition of the *Contra Celsum*. In the Benedictine edition, and in Migne's reprint, the various portions are quoted in foot-notes under the respective passages of Origen's writings.

(6) EDITIONS OF ORIGEN.[2]

The first published works of Origen were his Homilies, which appeared in 1475, although neither the name of the publisher nor the place of publication is given. These were followed by the treatise against Celsus in the translation of Christopher Persana, which appeared at Rome in 1481 ; and this, again, by an edition of the Homilies at Venice in 1503, containing those on the first four books of Moses, Joshua, and Judges. The first collective edition of the whole works was given to the world in a Latin translation by James Merlin, and was published in two folio volumes, first at Paris in 1512 and 1519, and afterwards at Paris in 1522 and 1530. A revision of Merlin's edition was begun by Erasmus, and completed, after his death, by Beatus Rhenanus. This appeared at Basle in 1536 in two folio volumes, and again in 1557 and 1571. A much better and more complete edition was undertaken by the Benedictine Gilbertus Genebrardus, which was published also in two volumes folio at Paris in 1574, and again in 1604 and 1619. Hoeschel published the treatise against Celsus at Augsburg in 1605 ; Spencer, at Cambridge in 1658 and 1677, to which was added the *Philocalia*, which had first appeared in a Latin translation by Genebrardus, and afterwards in Greek by Tarinus at Paris in 1618 and 1624, in quarto. Huet, Bishop of Avranches, published the exegetical writings in Greek, including the Commentaries on Matthew and John, in two volumes folio, of which the one appeared at Rouen in 1668, and the other at Paris in 1679. The great edition by the two learned Benedictines of St. Maur — Charles de la Rue, and his nephew Vincent de la Rue — was published at Paris between the years 1733 and 1759. This is a work of immense industry and labour, and remains the standard to the present time. It has been reprinted by Migne in his series of the Greek Fathers, in nine volumes, large 8vo. In Oberthür's series of the Greek Fathers, seven volumes contain the chief portion of Origen's writings ; while Lommatzsch has published the whole in twenty-five small volumes, Berlin, 1831–48, containing the Greek text alone.

For further information upon the life and opinions of Origen, the reader may consult Redepenning's *Origenes*, 2 vols., Bonn, 1841, 1846 ; the articles in Herzog's *Encyclopädie* and Wetzer's and Wette's *Kirchen-Lexikon*, by Kling and Hefele respectively ; the brilliant sketch by Pressensé in his *Martyrs and Apologists ;* [3] and the learned compilation of Huet, entitled *Origeniana*, to be found in the ninth volume of Migne's edition.

[In the Edinburgh series the foregoing Life was delayed till the appearance of the second volume. The earlier volume appeared with a preface, as follows :] —

THE name of the illustrious Origen comes before us in this series in connection with his works *De Principiis, Epistola ad Africanum, Epistola ad Gregorium,*[4] and the treatise *Contra Celsum.*[5]

It is in his treatise Περὶ Ἀρχῶν, or, as it is commonly known under the Latin title, *De Princi-*

---

[1] Both of these are translated in the first volume of Origen's works in this series.
[2] Abridged from Redepenning.
[3] Harwood's translation.
[4] i.e., Thaumaturgus.
[5] [The Messrs. Clark announced, in their original plan, that, of the manifold works of this great Father, only these specimens could be given.]

piis, that Origen most fully develops his system, and brings out his peculiar principles. None of his works exposed him to so much animadversion in the ancient Church as this. On it chiefly was based the charge of heresy which some vehemently pressed against him, — a charge from which even his firmest friends felt it no easy matter absolutely to defend him. The points on which it was held that he had plainly departed from the orthodox faith, were the four following: *First*, That the souls of men had existed in a previous state, and that their imprisonment in material bodies was a punishment for sins which they had then committed. *Second*, That the human soul of Christ had also previously existed, and been united to the Divine nature before that incarnation of the Son of God which is related in the Gospels. *Third*, That our material bodies shall be transformed into absolutely ethereal ones at the resurrection; and *Fourth*, That all men, and even devils, shall be finally restored through the mediation of Christ. His principles of interpreting Scripture are also brought out in this treatise; and while not a little ingenuity is displayed in illustrating and maintaining them, the serious errors into which they might too easily lead will be at once perceived by the reader.

It is much to be regretted that the original Greek of the *De Principiis* has for the most part perished. We possess it chiefly in a Latin translation by Rufinus. And there can be no doubt that he often took great liberties with his author. So much was this felt to be the case, that Jerome undertook a new translation of the work; but only small portions of his version have reached our day. He strongly accuses Rufinus of unfaithfulness as an interpreter, while he also inveighs bitterly against Origen himself, as having departed from the Catholic Faith, specially in regard to the doctrine of the Trinity. There seems, however, after all, no adequate reason to doubt the substantial orthodoxy of our author, although the bent of his mind and the nature of his studies led him to indulge in many vain and unauthorized speculations.

The *Epistle to Africanus* was drawn forth by a letter which that learned writer had addressed to Origen respecting the story of Susanna appended to the book of Daniel. Africanus had grave doubts as to the canonical authority of the account. Origen replies to his objections, and seeks to uphold the story as both useful in itself, and a genuine portion of the ancient prophetical writings.

The treatise of Origen *Against Celsus* is, of all his works, the most interesting to the modern reader. It is a defence of Christianity in opposition to a Greek philosopher named Celsus, who had attacked it in a work entitled Ἀληθὴς Λόγος, that is, *The True Word*, or *The True Discourse*. Of this work we know nothing, except from the quotations contained in the answer given to it by Origen. Nor has anything very certain been ascertained respecting its author. According to Origen, he was a follower of Epicurus, but others have regarded him as a Platonist. If we may judge of the work by those specimens of it preserved in the reply of Origen, it was little better than a compound of sophistry and slander. But there is reason to be grateful for it, as having called forth the admirable answer of Origen. This work was written in the old age of our author, and is composed with great care; while it abounds with proofs of the widest erudition. It is also perfectly orthodox; and, as Bishop Bull has remarked, it is only fair that we should judge from a work written with the view of being considered by the world at large, and with the most elaborate care, as to the mature and finally accepted views of the author.

The best edition of Origen's works is that superintended by Charles and Charles Vincent de la Rue, Paris, 1783, 4 vols. fol., which is reprinted by Migne. There is also an edition in 25 volumes, based upon that of De la Rue, but without the Latin translation, by Lommatzsch, Berlin, 1831–1848. The *De Principiis* has been separately edited by Redepenning, Leipzig, 1836. Spencer edited the *Contra Celsum*, Cambridge, 1677.

[Professor Crombie was assisted in the *Contra Celsum* by the Rev. W. H. Cairns, M.A., Rector of the Dumfries Academy. Mr. Cairns (since deceased) was the translator of Books VII. and VIII. of that work.]

[The Works of Origen included in this volume having been placed in my hands by the Right Reverend Editor of the present series (who restricts himself to a limited task of supervision), I have endeavoured to do for them that which seemed needful in the circumstances. The temptation was strong to enter upon annotations, for which no one of the authors among the Ante-Nicene Fathers offers larger room, and to insert corrections of various sorts, based upon modern progress and research. But, in accordance with the plan of this series, I have been forced to resist this temptation, and have striven only to be useful in matters which, though of great moment, are toilsome, and in no wise flattering to editorial vanity or conceit.

I have silently corrected numerous typographical errors which exist in the Edinburgh edition, and have sought to secure uniformity in the details of reproducing the work, and, above all, accuracy in all its parts. Particularly, I may mention that the Scripture references needed correction to the extent of more than a hundred places, and that references to classical and other writers were often quite astray. A very few notes, enclosed in brackets, are all that I have deemed it expedient or proper, on my part, to add.

While no one who is aware of human infirmity will ever dare to claim perfection in the typography of a book which has passed through the press under his hands, yet in the present case I venture to assure the student and reader that no pains or effort have been spared in order to make the volume as accurate as possible in this respect. Much experience and training incline me to hope and believe that success has attended my efforts. S.]

PREFATORY NOTICE TO ORIGEN'S WORKS.

[THE great biblical scholar and critic of the first half of the third century deserves a more cordial recognition and appreciation than have always been accorded to him. While it is true that in various matters he has strange, even wild, fancies, and gives utterance to expressions which can hardly, if at all, be justified; while it is also true that he indulges beyond all reason (as it appears to us of the present age) in utterly useless speculations, and carries to excess his great love of allegorizing, — yet these are rather of the nature of possible guesses and surmises on numerous topics, of more or less interest, than deliberate, systematic teaching as matters of faith. He frequently speaks of them in this wise, and does not claim for these guesses and speculations any more credit than they may appear to his readers to be worth. In the great fundamentals of the Christian creed Origen is unquestionably sound and true. He does not always express himself in accordance with the exact definitions which the Church Catholic secured in the century after his decease, as a necessary result of the struggle with Arian and other deadly heresies; but surely, in fairness, he is not to be too severely judged for this. Some writers (e.g., J. M. Neale, in his *History of the Patriarchate of Alexandria*) give an unfavorable and condemnatory view of Origen and his career, but I am of opinion that Neale and others push their objections much too far. I hold that Bishop Bull, and men like him, are nearer to truth and justice in defending Origen and his lifelong labors in the cause of the Master.

The Περὶ Ἀρχῶν, which has come to us through the professedly paraphrastic but really unsatisfactory version of Rufinus, is the work which has given chief offence, and brought much odium upon Origen; but as this was written in early life, and it is doubtful in how far Origen is responsible for many things that are in it, it is only fair and just to judge him by such works as the Κατὰ Κέλσον and his valuable *Homilies* on various books of Holy Scripture.[1] These go far to prove clearly that he, whom Dr. Barrow designates as "the father of interpreters," is worthy the high estimate which ancient as well as modern defenders of his good name have fully set forth, and to justify the conviction, that, if we possessed more out of the numerous works of his which have entirely perished, we should rank him even more highly than is done by Bishop Bull in his *Defensio Fidei Nicenæ*.[2]

In conclusion, I give a paragraph from the very valuable *Introduction to the Criticism of the New Testament*, by Dr. F. H. Scrivener,[3] one of the ablest of living biblical scholars and critics:—

"Origen is the most celebrated biblical critic of antiquity. His is the highest name among the critics and expositors of the early Church. He is perpetually engaged in the discussion of various readings of the New Testament, and employs language, in describing the then existing state of the text, which would be deemed strong if applied even to its present condition, after the changes which sixteen more centuries must needs have produced. . . . Seldom have such warmth of fancy and so bold a grasp of mind been united with the lifelong, patient industry which procured for this famous man the honourable appellation of *Adamantius*." S.]

---

[1] It is matter of deep regret that the proposal of the Edinburgh publishers, to include in Origen's works a translation of his *Homilies*, did not meet with sufficient encouragement to warrant them in adding these to the present series.

[2] Book II. cap. ix.

[3] Third edition, Cambridge, 1883, pp. 418, 509.

PROLOGUE OF RUFINUS.

I KNOW that very many of the brethren, induced by their thirst for a knowledge of the Scriptures, have requested some distinguished men, well versed in Greek learning, to translate Origen into Latin, and so make him accessible to Roman readers. Among these, when our brother and colleague [1] had, at the earnest entreaty of Bishop Damasus, translated two of the Homilies on the Song of Songs out of Greek into Latin, he prefixed so elegant and noble a preface to that work, as to inspire every one with a most eager desire to read and study Origen, saying that the expression, "The King hath brought me into his chamber," [2] was appropriate to his feelings, and declaring that while Origen in his other works surpassed all writers, he in the Song of Songs surpassed even himself. He promises, indeed, in that very preface, that he will present the books on the Song of Songs, and numerous others of the works of Origen, in a Latin translation, to Roman readers. But he, finding greater pleasure in compositions of his own, pursues an end that is attended with greater fame, viz., in being the author rather than the translator of works. Accordingly we enter upon the undertaking, which was thus begun and approved of by him, although we cannot compose in a style of elegance equal to that of a man of such distinguished eloquence; and therefore I am afraid lest, through my fault, the result should follow, that that man, whom he deservedly esteems as the second teacher of knowledge and wisdom in the Church after the apostles, should, through the poverty of my language, appear far inferior to what he is. And this consideration, which frequently recurred to my mind, kept me silent, and prevented me from yielding to the numerous entreaties of my brethren, until your influence, my very faithful brother Macarius, which is so great, rendered it impossible for my unskilfulness any longer to offer resistance. And therefore, that I might not find you too grievous an exactor, I gave way, even contrary to my resolution; on the condition and arrangement, how-

ever, that in my translation I should follow as far as possible the rule observed by my predecessors, and especially by that distinguished man whom I have mentioned above, who, after translating into Latin more than seventy of those treatises of Origen which are styled *Homilies*, and a considerable number also of his writings on the apostles, in which a good many "stumbling-blocks" are found in the original Greek, so smoothed and corrected them in his translation, that a Latin reader would meet with nothing which could appear discordant with our belief. His example, therefore, we follow, to the best of our ability; if not with equal power of eloquence, yet at least with the same strictness of rule, taking care not to reproduce those expressions occurring in the works of Origen which are inconsistent with and opposed to each other. The cause of these variations we have explained more freely in the *Apologeticus*, which Pamphilus wrote in defence of the works of Origen, where we added a brief tract, in which we showed, I think, by unmistakeable proofs, that his books had been corrupted in numerous places by heretics and malevolent persons, and especially those books of which you now require me to undertake the translation, i.e., the books which may be entitled *De Principiis* or *De Principatibus*, and which are indeed in other respects full of obscurities and difficulties. For he there discusses those subjects with respect to which philosophers, after spending all their lives upon them, have been unable to discover anything. But here our author strove, as much as in him lay, to turn to the service of religion the belief in a Creator, and the rational nature of created beings, which the latter had degraded to purposes of wickedness. If, therefore, we have found anywhere in his writings, any statement opposed to that view, which elsewhere in his works he had himself piously laid down regarding the Trinity, we have either omitted it, as being corrupt, and not the composition of Origen, or we have brought it forward, agreeably to the rule which we frequently find affirmed by himself. If, indeed, in his desire to pass rapidly

---

[1] Jerome is the person alluded to.
[2] Cant. i. 4.

on, he has, as speaking to persons of skill and knowledge, sometimes expressed himself obscurely, we have, in order that the passage might be clearer, added what we had read more fully stated on the same subject in his other works, keeping explanation in view, but adding nothing of our own, but simply restoring to him what was his, although occurring in other portions of his writings.

These remarks, therefore, by way of admonition, I have made in the preface, lest slanderous individuals perhaps should think that they had a second time discovered matter of accusation. But let perverse and disputatious men have a care what they are about. For we have in the meantime undertaken this heavy labour, if God should aid your prayers, not to shut the mouths of slanderers (which is impossible, although God perhaps will do it), but to afford material to those who desire to advance in the knowledge of these things. And, verily, in the presence of God the Father, and of the Son, and of the Holy Spirit, I adjure and beseech every one, who may either transcribe or read these books, by his belief in the kingdom to come, by the mystery of the resurrection from the dead, and by that everlasting fire prepared for the devil and his angels, that, as he would not possess for an eternal inheritance that place where there is weeping and gnashing of teeth, and where their fire is not quenched and their worm dieth not, he add nothing to Scripture, and take nothing away from it, and make no insertion or alteration, but that he compare his transcript with the copies from which he made it, and make the emendations and distinctions according to the letter, and not have his manuscript incorrect or indistinct, lest the difficulty of ascertaining the sense, from the indistinctness of the copy, should cause greater difficulties to the readers.

ORIGEN DE PRINCIPIIS.

PREFACE.

1. ALL who believe and are assured that grace and truth were obtained through Jesus Christ, and who know Christ to be the truth, agreeably to His own declaration, "I am the truth,"[1] derive the knowledge which incites men to a good and happy life from no other source than from the very words and teaching of Christ. And by the words of Christ we do not mean those only which He spake when He became man and tabernacled in the flesh; for before that time, Christ, the Word of God, was in Moses and the prophets. For without the Word of God, how could they have been able to prophesy of Christ? And were it not our purpose to confine the present treatise within the limits of all attainable brevity, it would not be difficult to show, in proof of this statement, out of the Holy Scriptures, how Moses or the prophets both spake and performed all they did through being filled with the Spirit of Christ. And therefore I think it sufficient to quote this one testimony of Paul from the Epistle to the Hebrews,[2] in which he says: "By faith Moses, when he was come to years, refused to be called the son of Pharaoh's daughter; choosing rather to suffer affliction with the people of God, than to enjoy the pleasures of sin for a season; esteeming the reproach of Christ greater riches than the treasures of the Egyptians."[3] Moreover, that after His ascension into heaven He spake in His apostles, is shown by Paul in these words: "Or do you seek a proof of Christ, who speaketh in me?"[4]

2. Since many, however, of those who profess to believe in Christ differ from each other, not only in small and trifling matters, but also on subjects of the highest importance, as, e.g., regarding God, or the Lord Jesus Christ, or the Holy Spirit; and not only regarding these, but also regarding others which are created existences, viz., the powers[5] and the holy virtues;[6] it seems on that account necessary first of all to fix a definite limit and to lay down an unmistakeable rule regarding each one of these, and then to pass to the investigation of other points. For as we ceased to seek for truth (notwithstanding the professions of many among Greeks and Barbarians to make it known) among all who claimed it for erroneous opinions, after we had come to believe that Christ was the Son of God, and were persuaded that we must learn it from Himself; so, seeing there are many who think they hold the opinions of Christ, and yet some of these think differently from their predecessors, yet as the teaching of the Church, transmitted in orderly succession from the apostles, and remaining in the Churches to the present day, is still preserved, that alone is to be accepted as truth which differs in no respect from ecclesiastical and apostolical tradition.

3. Now it ought to be known that the holy apostles, in preaching the faith of Christ, delivered themselves with the utmost clearness on certain points which they believed to be necessary to every one, even to those who seemed somewhat dull in the investigation of divine knowledge; leaving, however, the grounds of their statements to be examined into by those who should deserve the excellent gifts of the Spirit, and who, especially by means of the Holy Spirit Himself, should obtain the gift of language, of wisdom, and of knowledge: while on other subjects they merely stated the fact that things were so, keeping silence as to the manner or origin of their existence; clearly in order that the more zealous of their successors, who should be lovers of wisdom, might have a subject of exercise on which to display the fruit of their talents, — those persons, I mean, who should prepare themselves to be fit and worthy receivers of wisdom.

---

[1] John xiv. 6.
[2] [Here, and frequently elsewhere (some two hundred times in all), Origen, in his extant works, ascribes the authorship of the Epistle to the Hebrews to St. Paul. Eusebius (*Ecclesiastical History*, vi. 25) quotes Origen as saying, "My opinion is this: the thoughts are the apostle's; but the diction and phraseology belong to some one who has recorded what the apostle said, and as one who noted down what his master dictated. If, then, any Church considers this Epistle as coming from Paul, let it be commended for this; for neither did those ancient men deliver it as such without cause. But who it was that committed the Epistle to writing, is known only to God." S.]
[3] Heb. xi. 24–26.
[4] 2 Cor. xiii. 3.

[5] Dominationes.
[6] Virtutes.

4. The particular points [1] clearly delivered in the teaching of the apostles are as follow : —

First, That there is one God, who created and arranged all things, and who, when nothing existed, called all things into being — God from the first creation and foundation of the world — the God of all just men, of Adam, Abel, Seth, Enos, Enoch, Noe, Sem, Abraham, Isaac, Jacob, the twelve patriarchs, Moses, and the prophets ; and that this God in the last days, as He had announced beforehand by His prophets, sent our Lord Jesus Christ to call in the first place Israel to Himself, and in the second place the Gentiles, after the unfaithfulness of the people of Israel. This just and good God, the Father of our Lord Jesus Christ, Himself gave the law, and the prophets, and the Gospels, being also the God of the apostles and of the Old and New Testaments.

Secondly, That Jesus Christ Himself, who came (into the world), was born of the Father before all creatures ; that, after He had been the servant of the Father in the creation of all things — " For by Him were all things made " [2] — He in the last times, divesting Himself (of His glory), became a man, and was incarnate although God, and while made a man remained the God which He was ; that He assumed a body like to our own, differing in this respect only, that it was born of a virgin and of the Holy Spirit : that this Jesus Christ was truly born, and did truly suffer, and did not endure this death common (to man) in appearance only, but did truly die ; that He did truly rise from the dead ; and that after His resurrection He conversed with His disciples, and was taken up (into heaven).

Then, *Thirdly*, the apostles related that the Holy Spirit was associated in honour and dignity with the Father and the Son. But in His case it is not clearly distinguished whether He is to be regarded as born or innate,[3] or also as a Son of God or not : for these are points which have to be inquired into out of sacred Scripture according to the best of our ability, and which demand careful investigation. And that this Spirit inspired each one of the saints, whether prophets or apostles ; and that there was not one Spirit in the men of the old dispensation, and another in those who were inspired at the advent of Christ, is most clearly taught throughout the Churches.

5. After these points, also, the apostolic teaching is that the soul, having a substance [4] and life of its own, shall, after its departure from the world, be rewarded according to its deserts, being destined to obtain either an inheritance of eternal life and blessedness, if its actions shall have procured this for it, or to be delivered up to eternal fire and punishments, if the guilt of its crimes shall have brought it down to this : and also, that there is to be a time of resurrection from the dead, when this body, which now " is sown in corruption, shall rise in incorruption," and that which " is sown in dishonour will rise in glory." [5] This also is clearly defined in the teaching of the Church, that every rational soul is possessed of free-will and volition ; that it has a struggle to maintain with the devil and his angels, and opposing influences,[6] because they strive to burden it with sins ; but if we live rightly and wisely, we should endeavour to shake ourselves free of a burden of that kind. From which it follows, also, that we understand ourselves not to be subject to necessity, so as to be compelled by all means, even against our will, to do either good or evil. For if we are our own masters, some influences perhaps may impel us to sin, and others help us to salvation ; we are not forced, however, by any necessity either to act rightly or wrongly, which those persons think is the case who say that the courses and movements of the stars are the cause of human actions, not only of those which take place beyond the influence of the freedom of the will, but also of those which are placed within our own power. But with respect to the soul, whether it is derived from the seed by a process of traducianism, so that the reason or substance of it may be considered as placed in the seminal particles of the body themselves, or whether it has any other beginning ; and this beginning itself, whether it be by birth or not, or whether bestowed upon the body from without or no, is not distinguished with sufficient clearness in the teaching of the Church.

6. Regarding the devil and his angels, and the opposing influences, the teaching of the Church has laid down that these beings exist indeed ; but what they are, or how they exist, it has not explained with sufficient clearness. This opinion, however, is held by most, that the devil was an angel, and that, having become an apostate, he induced as many of the angels as possible to fall away with himself, and these up to the present time are called his angels.

7. This also is a part of the Church's teaching, that the world was made and took its beginning at a certain time, and is to be destroyed on account of its wickedness. But what existed

---

[1] Species.
[2] John i. 3.
[3] Innatus. The words which Rufinus has rendered "natus an innatus" are rendered by Jerome in his *Epistle to Avitus* (94 *alias* 59), " factus an infectus." Criticising the errors in the first book of the *Principles*, he says: " Origen declares the Holy Spirit to be third in dignity and honour after the Father and the Son; and although professing ignorance whether he were created or not (factus an infectus), he indicated afterwards his opinion regarding him, maintaining that nothing was uncreated except God the Father." Jerome, no doubt, read γενητὸς ἢ ἀγένητος, and Rufinus γεννητὸς ἢ ἀγέννητος. — R.

[4] Substantia.
[5] 1 Cor. xv. 42, 43.
[6] Virtutes.

before this world, or what will exist after it, has not become certainly known to the many, for there is no clear statement regarding it in the teaching of the Church.

8. Then, finally, that the Scriptures were written by the Spirit of God, and have a meaning, not such only as is apparent at first sight, but also another, which escapes the notice of most. For those (words) which are written are the forms of certain mysteries,[1] and the images of divine things. Respecting which there is one opinion throughout the whole Church, that the whole law is indeed spiritual; but that the spiritual meaning which the law conveys is not known to all, but to those only on whom the grace of the Holy Spirit is bestowed in the word of wisdom and knowledge.

The term ἀσώματον, i.e., incorporeal, is disused and unknown, not only in many other writings, but also in our own Scriptures. And if any one should quote it to us out of the little treatise entitled *The Doctrine of Peter*,[2] in which the Saviour seems to say to His disciples, " I am not an incorporeal demon,"[3] I have to reply, in the first place, that that work is not included among ecclesiastical books ; for we can show that it was not composed either by Peter or by any other person inspired by the Spirit of God. But even if the point were to be conceded, the word ἀσώματον there does not convey the same meaning as is intended by Greek and Gentile authors when incorporeal nature is discussed by philosophers. For in the little treatise referred to he used the phrase " incorporeal demon" to denote that that form or outline of demoniacal body, whatever it is, does not resemble this gross and visible body of ours ; but, agreeably to the intention of the author of the treatise, it must be understood to mean that He had not such a body as demons have, which is naturally fine,[4]

and thin as if formed of air (and for this reason is either considered or called by many incorporeal), but that He had a solid and palpable body. Now, according to human custom, everything which is not of that nature is called by the simple or ignorant incorporeal ; as if one were to say that the air which we breathe was incorporeal, because it is not a body of such a nature as can be grasped and held, or can offer resistance to pressure.

9. We shall inquire, however, whether the thing which Greek philosophers call ἀσώματον, or " incorporeal," is found in holy Scripture under another name. For it is also to be a subject of investigation how God himself is to be understood, — whether as corporeal, and formed according to some shape, or of a different nature from bodies, — a point which is not clearly indicated in our teaching. And the same inquiries have to be made regarding Christ and the Holy Spirit, as well as respecting every soul, and everything possessed of a rational nature.

10. This also is a part of the teaching of the Church, that there are certain angels of God, and certain good influences, which are His servants in accomplishing the salvation of men. When these, however, were created, or of what nature they are, or how they exist, is not clearly stated. Regarding the sun, moon, and stars, whether they are living beings or without life, there is no distinct deliverance.[5]

Every one, therefore, must make use of elements and foundations of this sort, according to the precept, " Enlighten yourselves with the light of knowledge,"[6] if he would desire to form a connected series and body of truths agreeably to the reason of all these things, that by clear and necessary statements he may ascertain the truth regarding each individual topic, and form, as we have said, one body of doctrine, by means of illustrations and arguments, — either those which he has discovered in holy Scripture, or which he has deduced by closely tracing out the consequences and following a correct method.

---

[1] Sacramentorum.
[2] Eusebius (*Eccles. Hist.*, iii. c. 36), treating of Ignatius, quotes from his Epistle to the Church of Smyrna as follows: " Writing to the Smyrnæans, he (Ignatius) has also employed words respecting Jesus, I know not whence they are taken, to the following effect: ' But I know and believe that He was seen after the resurrection; and when He came to Peter and his companions, He said to them, Take and handle Me, and see that I am not an incorporeal spirit.' " Jerome, in his catalogue of ecclesiastical writers, says the words are a quotation from the Gospel of the Nazarenes, a work which he had recently translated. Origen here quotes them, however, from *The Doctrine of Peter*, on which Ruæus remarks that the words might be contained in both of these apocryphal works.
[3] Dæmonium.
[4] Subtile.

[5] [See note, *infra*, at end of cap. vi. S.]
[6] Hos. x. 12. The words in the text are not the rendering of the Authorized Version, but that of the Septuagint, which has φωτίσατε ἑαυτοῖς φῶς γνώσεως. Where the Masoretic text has דָּעַת (*et tempus*) Origen evidently read דֵּעָה (*scientia*), the similarity of *Vau* and *Daleth* accounting for the error of the transcriber.

BOOK I.

CHAP. I. — ON GOD.

1. I know that some will attempt to say that, even according to the declarations of our own Scriptures, God is a body, because in the writings of Moses they find it said, that "our God is a consuming fire;"[1] and in the Gospel according to John, that "God is a Spirit, and they who worship Him must worship Him in spirit and in truth."[2] Fire and spirit, according to them, are to be regarded as nothing else than a body. Now, I should like to ask these persons what they have to say respecting that passage where it is declared that God is light; as John writes in his Epistle, "God is light, and in Him there is no darkness at all."[3] Truly He is that light which illuminates the whole understanding of those who are capable of receiving truth, as is said in the thirty-sixth Psalm, "In Thy light we shall see light."[4] For what other light of God can be named, "in which any one sees light," save an influence of God, by which a man, being enlightened, either thoroughly sees the truth of all things, or comes to know God Himself, who is called the truth? Such is the meaning of the expression, "In Thy light we shall see light;" i.e., in Thy word and wisdom, which is Thy Son, in Himself we shall see Thee the Father. Because He is called light, shall He be supposed to have any resemblance to the light of the sun? Or how should there be the slightest ground for imagining, that from that corporeal light any one could derive the cause of knowledge, and come to the understanding of the truth?

2. If, then, they acquiesce in our assertion, which reason itself has demonstrated, regarding the nature of light, and acknowledge that God cannot be understood to be a body in the sense that light is, similar reasoning will hold true of the expression "a consuming fire." For what will God consume in respect of His being fire? Shall He be thought to consume material substance, as wood, or hay, or stubble? And what in this view can be called worthy of the glory of God, if He be a fire, consuming materials of that kind? But let us reflect that God does indeed consume and utterly destroy; that He consumes evil thoughts, wicked actions, and sinful desires, when they find their way into the minds of believers; and that, inhabiting along with His Son those souls which are rendered capable of receiving His word and wisdom, according to His own declaration, "I and the Father shall come, and We shall make our abode with him,"[5] He makes them, after all their vices and passions have been consumed, a holy temple, worthy of Himself. Those, moreover, who, on account of the expression "God is a Spirit," think that He is a body, are to be answered, I think, in the following manner. It is the custom of sacred Scripture, when it wishes to designate anything opposed to this gross and solid body, to call it spirit, as in the expression, "The letter killeth, but the spirit giveth life,"[6] where there can be no doubt that by "letter" are meant bodily things, and by "spirit" intellectual things, which we also term "spiritual." The apostle, moreover, says, "Even unto this day, when Moses is read, the veil is upon their heart: nevertheless, when it shall turn to the Lord, the veil shall be taken away: and where the Spirit of the Lord is, there is liberty."[7] For so long as any one is not converted to a spiritual understanding, a veil is placed over his heart, with which veil, i.e., a gross understanding, Scripture itself is said or thought to be covered: and this is the meaning of the statement that a veil was placed over the countenance of Moses when he spoke to the people, i.e., when the law was publicly read aloud. But if we turn to the Lord, where also is the word of God, and where the Holy Spirit reveals spiritual knowledge, then the veil is taken away, and with unveiled face we shall behold the glory of the Lord in the holy Scriptures.

3. And since many saints participate in the Holy Spirit, He cannot therefore be understood to be a body, which being divided into corporeal parts, is partaken of by each one of the saints; but He is manifestly a sanctifying power, in which all are said to have a share who have deserved to be sanctified by His grace. And in order that what we say may be more easily understood, let us take an illustration from things very dissimilar. There are many persons who take a part in the science[8] or art of medicine: are we therefore to suppose that those who do so take to themselves the particles of some body called medicine, which is placed before them, and in this way participate in the same? Or must we not rather understand that all who with quick and trained minds come to understand the art and discipline itself, may be said to be par-

---

[1] Deut. iv. 24.
[2] John iv. 24.
[3] 1 John i. 5.
[4] Ps. xxxvi. 9.

[5] John xiv. 23.
[6] 2 Cor. iii. 6.
[7] 2 Cor. iii. 15-17.
[8] Disciplina.

takers of the art of healing? But these are not to be deemed altogether parallel instances in a comparison of medicine to the Holy Spirit, as they have been adduced only to establish that that is not necessarily to be considered a body, a share in which is possessed by many individuals. For the Holy Spirit differs widely from the method or science of medicine, in respect that the Holy Spirit is an intellectual existence,[1] and subsists and exists in a peculiar manner, whereas medicine is not at all of that nature.

4. But we must pass on to the language of the Gospel itself, in which it is declared that "God is a Spirit," and where we have to show how that is to be understood agreeably to what we have stated. For let us inquire on what occasion these words were spoken by the Saviour, before whom He uttered them, and what was the subject of investigation. We find, without any doubt, that He spoke these words to the Samaritan woman, saying to her, who thought, agreeably to the Samaritan view, that God ought to be worshipped on Mount Gerizim, that "God is a Spirit." For the Samaritan woman, believing Him to be a Jew, was inquiring of Him whether God ought to be worshipped in Jerusalem or on this mountain; and her words were, "All our fathers worshipped on this mountain, and ye say that in Jerusalem is the place where we ought to worship."[2] To this opinion of the Samaritan woman, therefore, who imagined that God was less rightly or duly worshipped, according to the privileges of the different localities, either by the Jews in Jerusalem or by the Samaritans on Mount Gerizim, the Saviour answered that he who would follow the Lord must lay aside all preference for particular places, and thus expressed Himself: "The hour is coming when neither in Jerusalem nor on this mountain shall the true worshippers worship the Father. God is a Spirit, and they who worship Him must worship Him in spirit and in truth."[3] And observe how logically He has joined together the spirit and the truth: He called God a Spirit, that He might distinguish Him from bodies; and He named Him the truth, to distinguish Him from a shadow or an image. For they who worshipped in Jerusalem worshipped God neither in truth nor in spirit, being in subjection to the shadow or image of heavenly things; and such also was the case with those who worshipped on Mount Gerizim.

5. Having refuted, then, as well as we could, every notion which might suggest that we were to think of God as in any degree corporeal, we go on to say that, according to strict truth, God is incomprehensible, and incapable of being measured.[4] For whatever be the knowledge which we are able to obtain of God, either by perception or reflection, we must of necessity believe that He is by many degrees far better than what we perceive Him to be. For, as if we were to see any one unable to bear a spark of light, or the flame of a very small lamp, and were desirous to acquaint such a one, whose vision could not admit a greater degree of light than what we have stated, with the brightness and splendour of the sun, would it not be necessary to tell him that the splendour of the sun was unspeakably and incalculably better and more glorious than all this light which he saw? So our understanding, when shut in by the fetters of flesh and blood, and rendered, on account of its participation in such material substances, duller and more obtuse, although, in comparison with our bodily nature, it is esteemed to be far superior, yet, in its efforts to examine and behold incorporeal things, scarcely holds the place of a spark or lamp. But among all intelligent, that is, incorporeal beings, what is so superior to all others — so unspeakably and incalculably superior — as God, whose nature cannot be grasped or seen by the power of any human understanding, even the purest and brightest?

6. But it will not appear absurd if we employ another similitude to make the matter clearer. Our eyes frequently cannot look upon the nature of the light itself — that is, upon the substance of the sun; but when we behold his splendour or his rays pouring in, perhaps, through windows or some small openings to admit the light, we can reflect how great is the supply and source of the light of the body. So, in like manner, the works of Divine Providence and the plan of this whole world are a sort of rays, as it were, of the nature of God, in comparison with His real substance and being. As, therefore, our understanding is unable of itself to behold God Himself as He is, it knows the Father of the world from the beauty of His works and the comeliness of His creatures. God, therefore, is not to be thought of as being either a body or as existing in a body, but as an uncompounded intellectual nature,[5] admitting within Himself no addition of any kind; so that He cannot be believed to have within him a greater and a less, but is such that He is in all parts Μονάς, and, so to speak, Ἑνάς, and is the mind and source from which all intellectual nature or mind takes its beginning. But mind, for its movements or operations, needs no physical space, nor sensible magnitude, nor bodily shape, nor colour, nor any other of those adjuncts which are the properties of body or matter. Wherefore that simple and

---

[1] Subsistentia.
[2] John iv. 20.
[3] John. iv. 23, 24.

[4] "Inæstimabilem."
[5] "Simplex intellectualis natura."

wholly intellectual nature [1] can admit of no delay or hesitation in its movements or operations, lest the simplicity of the divine nature should appear to be circumscribed or in some degree hampered by such adjuncts, and lest that which is the beginning of all things should be found composite and differing, and that which ought to be free from all bodily intermixture, in virtue of being the one sole species of Deity, so to speak, should prove, instead of being one, to consist of many things. That mind, moreover, does not require space in order to carry on its movements agreeably to its nature, is certain from observation of our own mind. For if the mind abide within its own limits, and sustain no injury from any cause, it will never, from diversity of situation, be retarded in the discharge of its functions ; nor, on the other hand, does it gain any addition or increase of mobility from the nature of particular places. And here, if any one were to object, for example, that among those who are at sea, and tossed by its waves, the mind is considerably less vigorous than it is wont to be on land, we are to believe that it is in this state, not from diversity of situation, but from the commotion or disturbance of the body to which the mind is joined or attached. For it seems to be contrary to nature, as it were, for a human body to live at sea ; and for that reason it appears, by a sort of inequality of its own, to enter upon its mental operations in a slovenly and irregular manner, and to perform the acts of the intellect with a duller sense, in as great degree as those who on land are prostrated with fever ; with respect to whom it is certain, that if the mind do not discharge its functions as well as before, in consequence of the attack of disease, the blame is to be laid not upon the place, but upon the bodily malady, by which the body, being disturbed and disordered, renders to the mind its customary services under by no means the well-known and natural conditions : for we human beings are animals composed of a union of body and soul, and in this way (only) was it possible for us to live upon the earth. But God, who is the beginning of all things, is not to be regarded as a composite being, lest perchance there should be found to exist elements prior to the beginning itself, out of which everything is composed, whatever that be which is called composite. Neither does the mind require bodily magnitude in order to perform any act or movement ; as when the eye by gazing upon bodies of larger size is dilated, but is compressed and contracted in order to see smaller objects. The mind, indeed, requires magnitude of an intellectual kind, because it grows, not after the fashion of a body, but after that of intelligence.

For the mind is not enlarged, together with the body, by means of corporal additions, up to the twentieth or thirtieth year of life ; but the intellect is sharpened by exercises of learning, and the powers implanted within it for intelligent purposes are called forth ; and it is rendered capable of greater intellectual efforts, not being increased by bodily additions, but carefully polished by learned exercises. But these it cannot receive immediately from boyhood, or from birth, because the framework of limbs which the mind employs as organs for exercising itself is weak and feeble ; and it is unable to bear the weight of its own operations, or to exhibit a capacity for receiving training.

7. If there are any now who think that the mind itself and the soul is a body, I wish they would tell me by way of answer how it receives reasons and assertions on subjects of such importance — of such difficulty and such subtlety ; Whence does it derive the power of memory ; and whence comes the contemplation of invisible [2] things ? How does the body possess the faculty of understanding incorporeal existences ; How does a bodily nature investigate the processes of the various arts, and contemplate the reasons of things ? How, also, is it able to perceive and understand divine truths, which are manifestly incorporeal ? Unless, indeed, some should happen to be of opinion, that as the very bodily shape and form of the ears or eyes contributes something to hearing and to sight, and as the individual members, formed by God, have some adaptation, even from the very quality of their form, to the end for which they were naturally appointed ; so also he may think that the shape of the soul or mind is to be understood as if created purposely and designedly for perceiving and understanding individual things, and for being set in motion by vital movements. do not perceive, however, who shall be able to describe or state what is the colour of the mind, in respect of its being mind, and acting as an intelligent existence. Moreover, in confirmation and explanation of what we have already advanced regarding the mind or soul—to the effect that it is better than the whole bodily nature—the following remarks may be added. There underlies every bodily sense a certain peculiar sensible substance,[3] on which the bodily sense exerts itself. For example, colours, form, size, underlie vision ; voices and sound, the sense of hearing ; odours, good or bad, that of smell ; savours, that of taste ; heat or cold, hardness or softness, roughness or smoothness, that of touch. Now, of those senses enumerated above, it is manifest to all that the sense of mind is much the best. How then, should it not appear absurd, that under

---

[1] " Natura illa simplex et tota mens."

[2] Some read " visible."
[3] " Substantia quædam sensibilis propria."

those senses which are inferior, substances should have been placed on which to exert their powers, but that under this power, which is far better than any other, i.e., the sense of mind, nothing at all of the nature of a substance should be placed, but that a power of an intellectual nature should be an accident, or consequent upon bodies? Those who assert this, doubtless do so to the disparagement of that better substance which is within them; nay, by so doing, they even do wrong to God Himself, when they imagine He may be understood by means of a bodily nature, so that according to their view He is a body, and that which may be understood or perceived by means of a body; and they are unwilling to have it understood that the mind bears a certain relationship to God, of whom the mind itself is an intellectual image, and that by means of this it may come to some knowledge of the nature of divinity, especially if it be purified and separated from bodily matter.

8. But perhaps these declarations may seem to have less weight with those who wish to be instructed in divine things out of the holy Scriptures, and who seek to have it proved to them from that source how the nature of God surpasses the nature of bodies. See, therefore, if the apostle does not say the same thing, when, speaking of Christ, he declares, that "He is the image of the invisible God, the first-born of every creature." [1] Not, as some suppose, that the nature of God is visible to some and invisible to others: for the apostle does not say "the image of God invisible" to men or "invisible" to sinners, but with unvarying constancy pronounces on the nature of God in these words: "the image of the invisible God." Moreover, John, in his Gospel, when asserting that "no one hath seen God at any time," [2] manifestly declares to all who are capable of understanding, that there is no nature to which God is visible: not as if He were a being who was visible by nature, and merely escaped or baffled the view of a frailer creature, but because by the *nature* of His being it is impossible for Him to be seen. And if you should ask of me what is my opinion regarding the Only-begotten Himself, whether the nature of God, which is naturally invisible, be not visible even to Him, let not such a question appear to you at once to be either absurd or impious, because we shall give you a logical reason. It is one thing to see, and another to know: to see and to be seen is a property of bodies; to know and to be known, an attribute of intellectual being. Whatever, therefore, is a property of bodies, cannot be predicated either of the Father or of the Son; but what belongs to the nature

of deity is common to the Father and the Son. [3] Finally, even He Himself, in the Gospel, did not say that no one has *seen* the Father, save the Son, nor any one the Son, save the Father; but His words are: "No one *knoweth* the Son, save the Father; nor any one the Father, save the Son." [4] By which it is clearly shown, that whatever among bodily natures is called seeing and being seen, is termed, between the Father and the Son, a knowing and being known, by means of the power of knowledge, not by the frailness of the sense of sight. Because, then, neither seeing nor being seen can be properly applied to an incorporeal and invisible nature, neither is the Father, in the Gospel, said to be seen by the Son, nor the Son by the Father, but the one is said to be known by the other.

9. Here, if any one lay before us the passage where it is said, "Blessed are the pure in heart, for they shall see God," [5] from that very passage, in my opinion, will our position derive additional strength; for what else is seeing God in heart, but, according to our exposition as above, understanding and knowing Him with the mind? For the names of the organs of sense are frequently applied to the soul, so that it may be said to see with the eyes of the heart, i.e., to perform an intellectual act by means of the power of intelligence. So also it is said to hear with the ears when it perceives the deeper meaning of a statement. So also we say that it makes use of teeth, when it chews and eats the bread of life which cometh down from heaven. In like manner, also, it is said to employ the services of other members, which are transferred from their bodily appellations, and applied to the powers of the soul, according to the words of Solomon, "You will find a divine sense." [6] For he knew that there were within us two kinds of senses: the one mortal, corruptible, human; the other immortal and intellectual, which he now termed divine. By this divine sense, therefore, not of the eyes, but of a pure heart, which is the mind, God may be seen by those who are worthy. For you will certainly find in all the Scriptures, both old and new, the term "heart" repeatedly used instead of "mind," i.e., intellectual power. In this manner, therefore, although far below the dignity of the subject, have we spoken of the nature of God, as those who understand it under the limitation of the human understanding. In the next place, let us see what is meant by the name of Christ.

CHAP. II. — ON CHRIST.

1. In the first place, we must note that the nature of that deity which is in Christ in respect

---

[1] Col. i. 15.
[2] John i. 18.

[3] "Constat inter Patrem et Filium."
[4] Matt. xi. 27.
[5] Matt. v. 8.
[6] Cf. Prov. ii. 5.

of His being the only-begotten Son of God is one thing, and that human nature which He assumed in these last times for the purposes of the dispensation (of grace) is another. And therefore we have first to ascertain what the only-begotten Son of God is, seeing He is called by many different names, according to the circumstances and views of individuals. For He is termed Wisdom, according to the expression of Solomon : "The Lord created me — the beginning of His ways, and among His works, before He made any other thing ; He founded me before the ages. In the beginning, before He formed the earth, before He brought forth the fountains of waters, before the mountains were made strong, before all the hills, He brought me forth." [1] He is also styled First-born, as the apostle has declared : "who is the first-born of every creature." [2] The first-born, however, is not by nature a different person from the Wisdom, but one and the same. Finally, the Apostle Paul says that "Christ (is) the power of God and the wisdom of God." [3]

2. Let no one, however, imagine that we mean anything impersonal [4] when we call Him the wisdom of God ; or suppose, for example, that we understand Him to be, not a living being endowed with wisdom, but something which makes men wise, giving itself to, and implanting itself in, the minds of those who are made capable of receiving His virtues and intelligence. If, then, it is once rightly understood that the only-begotten Son of God is His wisdom hypostatically [5] existing, I know not whether our curiosity ought to advance beyond this, or entertain any suspicion that that ὑπόστασις or substantia contains anything of a bodily nature, since everything that is corporeal is distinguished either by form, or colour, or magnitude. And who in his sound senses ever sought for form, or colour, or size, in wisdom, in respect of its being wisdom? And who that is capable of entertaining reverential thoughts or feelings regarding God, can suppose or believe that God the Father ever existed, even for a moment of time, [6] without having generated this Wisdom? For in that case he must say either that God was unable to generate Wisdom before He produced her, so that He afterwards called into being her who formerly did not exist, or that He possessed the power indeed, but — what cannot be said of God without impiety — was unwilling to use it ; both of which suppositions, it is patent to all, are alike absurd and impious : for they amount to this, either that

God advanced from a condition of inability to one of ability, or that, although possessed of the power, He concealed it, and delayed the generation of Wisdom. Wherefore we have always held that God is the Father of His only-begotten Son, who was born indeed of Him, and derives from Him what He is, but without any beginning, not only such as may be measured by any divisions of time, but even that which the mind alone can contemplate within itself, or behold, so to speak, with the naked powers of the understanding. And therefore we must believe that Wisdom was generated before any beginning that can be either comprehended or expressed. And since all the creative power of the coming creation [7] was included in this very existence of Wisdom (whether of those things which have an original or of those which have a derived existence), having been formed beforehand and arranged by the power of foreknowledge ; on account of these very creatures which had been described, as it were, and prefigured in Wisdom herself, does Wisdom say, in the words of Solomon, that she was created the beginning of the ways of God, inasmuch as she contained within herself either the beginnings, or forms, or species of all creation.

3. Now, in the same way in which we have understood that Wisdom was the beginning of the ways of God, and is said to be created, forming beforehand and containing within herself the species and beginnings of all creatures, must we understand her to be the Word of God, because of her disclosing to all other beings, i.e., to universal creation, the nature of the mysteries and secrets which are contained within the divine wisdom ; and on this account she is called the Word, because she is, as it were, the interpreter of the secrets of the mind. And therefore that language which is found in the Acts of Paul,[8] where it is said that "here is the Word a living being," appears to me to be rightly used. John, however, with more sublimity and propriety, says in the beginning of his Gospel, when defining God by a special definition to be the Word, "And God was the Word,[9] and this was in the beginning with God." Let him, then, who assigns a beginning to the Word or Wisdom of God, take care that he be not guilty of impiety against the unbegotten Father Himself, seeing he denies that He had always been a Father, and had generated the Word, and had possessed wisdom in all preceding periods, whether they

[1] Prov. viii. 22-25. The reading in the text differs considerably from that of the Vulgate.
[2] Col. i. 15.
[3] 1 Cor. i. 24.
[4] Aliquid insubstantivum.
[5] Substantialiter.
[6] Ad punctum alicujus momenti.

[7] Omnis virtus ac deformatio futuræ creaturæ.
[8] This work is mentioned by Eusebius, Hist. Eccles., iii. c. 3 and 25, as among the spurious writings current in the Church. The Acts of Paul and Thecla was a different work from the Acts of Paul. The words quoted, " Hic est verbum animal vivens," seem to be a corruption from Heb. iv. 12, ζῶν γὰρ ὁ λόγος τοῦ Θεοῦ. [Jones on the Canon, vol. ii. pp. 353-411, as to Paul and Thecla. As to this quotation of our author, see Lardner, Credib., ii. p. 539.]
[9] Or, " and the Word was God."

be called times or ages, or anything else that can be so entitled.

4. This Son, accordingly, is also the truth and life of all things which exist. And with reason. For how could those things which were created live, unless they derived their being from life? or how could those things which are, truly exist, unless they came down from the truth? or how could rational beings exist, unless the Word or reason had previously existed? or how could they be wise, unless there were wisdom? But since it was to come to pass that some also should fall away from life, and bring death upon themselves by their declension — for death is nothing else than a departure from life — and as it was not to follow that those beings which had once been created by God for the enjoyment of life should utterly perish, it was necessary that, before death, there should be in existence such a power as would destroy the coming death, and that there should be a resurrection, the type of which was in our Lord and Saviour, and that this resurrection should have its ground in the wisdom and word and life of God. And then, in the next place, since some of those who were created were not to be always willing to remain unchangeable and unalterable in the calm and moderate enjoyment of the blessings which they possessed, but, in consequence of the good which was in them being theirs not by nature or essence, but by accident, were to be perverted and changed, and to fall away from their position, therefore was the Word and Wisdom of God made the Way. And it was so termed because it leads to the Father those who walk along it.

Whatever, therefore, we have predicated of the wisdom of God, will be appropriately applied and understood of the Son of God, in virtue of His being the Life, and the Word, and the Truth, and the Resurrection : for all these titles are derived from His power and operations, and in none of them is there the slightest ground for understanding anything of a corporeal nature which might seem to denote either size, or form, or colour ; for those children of men which appear among us, or those descendants of other living beings, correspond to the seed of those by whom they were begotten, or derive from those mothers, in whose wombs they are formed and nourished, whatever that is, which they bring into this life, and carry with them when they are born.[1] But it is monstrous and unlawful to compare God the Father, in the generation of His only-begotten Son, and in the substance[2] of the same, to

any man or other living thing engaged in such an act ; for we must of necessity hold that there is something exceptional and worthy of God which does not admit of any comparison at all, not merely in things, but which cannot even be conceived by thought or discovered by perception, so that a human mind should be able to apprehend how the unbegotten God is made the Father of the only-begotten Son. Because His generation is as eternal and everlasting as the brilliancy which is produced from the sun. For it is not by receiving the[3] breath of life that He is made a Son, by *any outward act*, but by His own nature.

5. Let us now ascertain how those statements which we have advanced are supported by the authority of holy Scripture. The Apostle Paul says, that the only-begotten Son is the "image of the invisible God," and "the first-born of every creature."[4] And when writing to the Hebrews, he says of Him that He is "the brightness of His glory, and the express image of His person."[5] Now, we find in the treatise called the Wisdom of Solomon the following description of the wisdom of God : "For she is the breath of the power of God, and the purest efflux[6] of the glory of the Almighty."[7] Nothing that is polluted can therefore come upon her. For she is the splendour of the eternal light, and the stainless mirror of God's working, and the image of His goodness. Now we say, as before, that Wisdom has her existence nowhere else save in Him who is the beginning of all things : from whom also is derived everything that is wise, because He Himself is the only one who is by nature a Son, and is therefore termed the Only-begotten.

6. Let us now see how we are to understand the expression "invisible image," that we may in this way perceive how God is rightly called the Father of His Son ; and let us, in the first place, draw our conclusions from what are customarily called images among men. That is sometimes called an image which is painted or sculptured on some material substance, such as wood or stone ; and sometimes a child is called the image of his parent, when the features of the child in no respect belie their resemblance to the father. I think, therefore, that that man who was formed after the image and likeness of God may be fittingly compared to the first illustration. Respecting him, however, we shall see more precisely, God willing, when we come to expound the passage in Genesis. But the image

---

[1] "Quoniam hi qui videntur apud nos hominum filii, vel ceterorum animalium, semini eorum a quibus seminati sunt respondent, vel earum quarum in utero formantur ac nutriuntur, habent ex his quidquid illud est quod in lucem hanc assumunt, ac deferunt processuri." Probably the last two words should be "deferunt processuris" — "and hand it over to those who are destined to come forth from them," i.e., to their descendants.

[2] Subsistentia. Some would read here, "substantia."

[3] Per adoptionem Spiritus. The original words here were probably εἰσποίησις τοῦ πνεύματος, and Rufinus seems to have mistaken the allusion to Gen. ii. 7. To "adoption," in the technical theological sense, the words in the text cannot have any reference. — SCHNITZER.

[4] Col. i. 15.

[5] Heb. i. 3.

[6] ἀπόρροια.

[7] Wisd. vii. 25.

of the Son of God, of whom we are now speaking, may be compared to the second of the above examples, even in respect of this, that He is the invisible image of the invisible God, in the same manner as we say, according to the sacred history, that the image of Adam is his son Seth. The words are, " And Adam begat Seth in his own likeness, and after his own image." [1] Now this image contains the unity of nature and substance belonging to Father and Son. For if the Son do, in like manner, all those things which the Father doth, then, in virtue of the Son doing all things like the Father, is the image of the Father formed in the Son, who is born of Him, like an act of His will proceeding from the mind. And I am therefore of opinion that the will of the Father ought alone to be sufficient for the existence of that which He wishes to exist. For in the exercise of His will He employs no other way than that which is made known by the counsel of His will. And thus also the existence [2] of the Son is generated by Him. For this point must above all others be maintained by those who allow nothing to be unbegotten, i.e., unborn, save God the Father only. And we must be careful not to fall into the absurdities of those who picture to themselves certain emanations, so as to divide the divine nature into parts, and who divide God the Father as far as they can, since even to entertain the remotest suspicion of such a thing regarding an incorporeal being is not only the height of impiety, but a mark of the greatest folly, it being most remote from any intelligent conception that there should be any physical division of any incorporeal nature. Rather, therefore, as an act of the will proceeds from the understanding, and neither cuts off any part nor is separated or divided from it, so after some such fashion is the Father to be supposed as having begotten the Son, His own image; namely, so that, as He is Himself invisible by nature, He also begat an image that was invisible. For the Son is the Word, and therefore we are not to understand that anything in Him is cognisable by the senses. He is wisdom, and in wisdom there can be no suspicion of anything corporeal. He is the true light, which enlightens every man that cometh into this world ; but He has nothing in common with the light of this sun. Our Saviour, therefore, is the image of the invisible God, inasmuch as compared with the Father Himself He is the truth : and as compared with us, to whom He reveals the Father, He is the image by which we come to the knowledge of the Father, whom no one knows save the Son, and he to whom the Son is pleased to reveal Him. And the method of revealing Him is through the understanding. For He by whom the Son Himself is understood, understands, as a consequence, the Father also, according to His own words : " He that hath seen Me, hath seen the Father also." [3]

7. But since we quoted the language of Paul regarding Christ, where He says of Him that He is " the brightness of the glory of God, and the express figure of His person," [4] let us see what idea we are to form of this. According to John, " God is light." The only-begotten Son, therefore, is the glory of this light, proceeding inseparably from (God) Himself, as brightness does from light, and illuminating the whole of creation. For, agreeably to what we have already explained as to the manner in which He is the Way, and conducts to the Father ; and in which He is the Word, interpreting the secrets of wisdom, and the mysteries of knowledge, making them known to the rational creation ; and is also the Truth, and the Life, and the Resurrection, — in the same way ought we to understand also the meaning of His being the brightness : for it is by its splendour that we understand and feel what light itself is. And this splendour, presenting itself gently and softly to the frail and weak eyes of mortals, and gradually training, as it were, and accustoming them to bear the brightness of the light, when it has put away from them every hindrance and obstruction to vision, according to the Lord's own precept, " Cast forth the beam out of thine eye," [5] renders them capable of enduring the splendour of the light, being made in this respect also a sort of mediator between men and the light.

8. But since He is called by the apostle not only the brightness of His glory, but also the express figure of His person or *subsistence*, [6] it does not seem idle to inquire how there can be said to be another figure of that person besides the person of God Himself, whatever be the meaning of person and subsistence. Consider, then, whether the Son of God, seeing He is His Word and Wisdom, and alone knows the Father, and reveals Him to whom He will (i.e., to those who are capable of receiving His word and wisdom), may not, in regard of this very point of making God to be understood and acknowledged, be called the figure of His person and subsistence ; that is, when that Wisdom, which desires to make known to others the means by which God is acknowledged and understood by them, describes Himself first of all, it may by so doing be called the express figure of the person of God. In order, however, to arrive at a fuller understanding of the manner in which the Saviour is the figure of the person or subsistence

---

[1] Gen. v. 3.
[2] Subsistentia.
[3] John xiv. 9.
[4] Heb. i. 3.
[5] Luke vi. 42.
[6] Heb. i. 3. Substantiæ vel subsistentiæ.

of God, let us take an instance, which, although it does not describe the subject of which we are treating either fully or appropriately, may nevertheless be seen to be employed for this purpose only, to show that the Son of God, who was in the form of God, divesting Himself (of His glory), makes it His object, by this very divesting of Himself, to demonstrate to us the fulness of His deity. For instance, suppose that there were a statue of so enormous a size as to fill the whole world, and which on that account could be seen by no one; and that another statue were formed altogether resembling it in the shape of the limbs, and in the features of the countenance, and in form and material, but without the same immensity of size, so that those who were unable to behold the one of enormous proportions, should, on seeing the latter, acknowledge that they had seen the former, because it preserved all the features of its limbs and countenance, and even the very form and material, so closely, as to be altogether undistinguishable from it; by some such similitude, the Son of God, divesting Himself of His equality with the Father, and showing to us the way to the knowledge of Him, is made the express image of His person: so that we, who were unable to look upon the glory of that marvellous light when placed in the greatness of His Godhead, may, by His being made to us brightness, obtain the means of beholding the divine light by looking upon the brightness. This comparison, of course, of statues, as belonging to material things, is employed for no other purpose than to show that the Son of God, though placed in the very insignificant form of a human body, in consequence of the resemblance of His works and power to the Father, showed that there was in Him an immense and invisible greatness, inasmuch as He said to His disciples, "He who sees Me, sees the Father also;" and, "I and the Father are one." And to these belong also the similar expression, "The Father is in Me, and I in the Father."

9. Let us see now what is the meaning of the expression which is found in the Wisdom of Solomon, where it is said of Wisdom that "it is a kind of breath of the power of God, and the purest efflux of the glory of the Omnipotent, and the splendour of eternal light, and the spotless mirror of the working or power of God, and the image of His goodness."[1] These, then, are the definitions which he gives of God, pointing out by each one of them certain attributes which belong to the Wisdom of God, calling wisdom the power, and the glory, and the everlasting light, and the working, and the goodness of God. He does not say, however, that wisdom is the breath of the glory of the Almighty, nor of the everlasting light, nor of the working of the Father, nor of His goodness, for it was not appropriate that breath should be ascribed to any one of these; but, with all propriety, he says that wisdom is the breath of the power of God. Now, by the power of God is to be understood that by which He is strong; by which He appoints, restrains, and governs all things visible and invisible; which is sufficient for all those things which He rules over in His providence; among all which He is present, as if one individual. And although the breath of all this mighty and immeasurable power, and the vigour itself produced, so to speak, by its own existence, proceed from the power itself, as the will does from the mind, yet even this will of God is nevertheless made to become the power of God.[2]

Another power accordingly is produced, which exists with properties of its own,— a kind of breath, as Scripture says, of the primal and unbegotten power of God, deriving from Him its being, and never at any time non-existent. For if any one were to assert that it did not formerly exist, but came afterwards into existence, let him explain the reason why the Father, who gave it being, did not do so before. And if he shall grant that there was once a beginning, when that breath proceeded from the power of God, we shall ask him again, why not even before the beginning, which he has allowed; and in this way, ever demanding an earlier date, and going upwards with our interrogations, we shall arrive at this conclusion, that as God was always possessed of power and will, there never was any reason of propriety or otherwise, why He may not have always possessed that blessing which He desired. By which it is shown that that breath of God's power always existed, having no beginning save God Himself. Nor was it fitting that there should be any other beginning save God Himself, from whom it derives its birth. And according to the expression of the apostle, that Christ "is the power of God,"[3] it ought to be termed not only the breath of the power of God, but power out of power.

10. Let us now examine the expression, "Wisdom is the purest efflux of the glory of the Almighty;" and let us first consider what the glory of the omnipotent God is, and then we shall also understand what is its efflux. As no one can be a father without having a son, nor a master without possessing a servant, so even God cannot be called omnipotent unless there exist those over whom He may exercise His power; and therefore, that God may be shown to be almighty, it

---

[1] Wisd. vii. 25, 26.

[2] "Hujus ergo totius virtutis tantæ et tam immensæ vapor, et, ut ita dicam, vigor ipse in propriâ subsistentiâ effectus, quamvis ex ipsa virtute velut voluntas ex mente procedat, tamen et ipsa voluntas Dei nihilominus Dei virtus efficitur."

[3] 1 Cor. i. 24.

is necessary that all things should exist. For if any one would have some ages or portions of time, or whatever else he likes to call them, to have passed away, while those things which were afterwards made did not yet exist, he would undoubtedly show that during those ages or periods God was not omnipotent, but became so afterwards, viz., from the time that He began to have persons over whom to exercise power; and in this way He will appear to have received a certain increase, and to have risen from a lower to a higher condition; since there can be no doubt that it is better for Him to be omnipotent than not to be so. And now how can it appear otherwise than absurd, that when God possessed none of those things which it was befitting for Him to possess, He should afterwards, by a kind of progress, come into the possession of them? But if there never was a time when He was not omnipotent, of necessity those things by which He receives that title must also exist; and He must always have had those over whom He exercised power, and which were governed by Him either as king or prince, of which we shall speak more fully in the proper place, when we come to discuss the subject of the creatures. But even now I think it necessary to drop a word, although cursorily, of warning, since the question before us is, how wisdom is the purest efflux of the glory of the Almighty, lest any one should think that the title of Omnipotent was anterior in God to the birth of Wisdom, through whom He is called Father, seeing that Wisdom, which is the Son of God, is the purest efflux of the glory of the Almighty. Let him who is inclined to entertain this suspicion hear the undoubted declaration of Scripture pronouncing, "In wisdom hast Thou made them all,"[1] and the teaching of the Gospel, that "by Him were all things made, and without Him nothing was made;"[2] and let him understand from this that the title of Omnipotent in God cannot be older than that of Father; for it is through the Son that the Father is almighty. But from the expression "glory of the Almighty," of which glory Wisdom is the efflux, this is to be understood, that Wisdom, through which God is called omnipotent, has a share in the glory of the Almighty. For through Wisdom, which is Christ, God has power over all things, not only by the authority of a ruler, but also by the voluntary obedience of subjects. And that you may understand that the omnipotence of Father and Son is one and the same, as God and the Lord are one and the same with the Father, listen to the manner in which John speaks in the Apocalypse: "Thus saith the Lord God, which is, and which was, and which is to come, the

Almighty."[3] For who else was "He which is to come" than Christ? And as no one ought to be offended, seeing God is the Father, that the Saviour is also God; so also, since the Father is called omnipotent, no one ought to be offended that the Son of God is also called omnipotent. For in this way will that saying be true which He utters to the Father, "All Mine are Thine, and Thine are Mine, and I am glorified in them."[4] Now, if all things which are the Father's are also Christ's, certainly among those things which exist is the omnipotence of the Father; and doubtless the only-begotten Son ought to be omnipotent, that the Son also may have all things which the Father possesses. "And I am glorified in them," He declares. For "at the name of Jesus every knee shall bow, of things in heaven, and things in earth, and things under the earth; and every tongue shall confess that the Lord Jesus is in the glory of God the Father."[5] Therefore He is the efflux of the glory of God in this respect, that He is omnipotent — the pure and limpid Wisdom herself — glorified as the efflux of omnipotence or of glory. And that it may be more clearly understood what the glory of omnipotence is, we shall add the following. God the Father is omnipotent, because He has power over all things, i.e., over heaven and earth, sun, moon, and stars, and all things in them. And He exercises His power over them by means of His Word, because at the name of Jesus every knee shall bow, both of things in heaven, and things on earth, and things under the earth. And if every knee is bent to Jesus, then, without doubt, it is Jesus to whom all things are subject, and He it is who exercises power over all things, and through whom all things are subject to the Father; for through wisdom, i.e., by word and reason, not by force and necessity, are all things subject. And therefore His glory consists in this very thing, that He possesses all things, and this is the purest and most limpid glory of omnipotence, that by reason and wisdom, not by force and necessity, all things are subject. Now the purest and most limpid glory of wisdom is a convenient expression to distinguish it from that glory which cannot be called pure and sincere. But every nature which is convertible and changeable, although glorified in the works of righteousness or wisdom, yet by the fact that righteousness or wisdom are accidental qualities, and because that which is accidental may also fall away, its glory cannot be called sincere and pure. But the Wisdom of God, which is His only-begotten Son, being in all respects incapable of change or alteration, and every good quality in Him

---

[1] Ps. civ. 24.
[2] John i. 3.

[3] Rev. i. 8.
[4] John xvii. 10.
[5] Phil. ii. 10, 11.

being essential, and such as cannot be changed and converted, His glory is therefore declared to be pure and sincere.

11. In the third place, wisdom is called the splendour of eternal light. The force of this expression we have explained in the preceding pages, when we introduced the similitude of the sun and the splendour of its rays, and showed to the best of our power how this should be understood. To what we then said we shall add only the following remark. That is properly termed everlasting or eternal which neither had a beginning of existence, nor can ever cease to be what it is. And this is the idea conveyed by John when he says that "God is light." Now His wisdom is the splendour of that light, not only in respect of its being light, but also of being everlasting light, so that His wisdom is eternal and everlasting splendour. If this be fully understood, it clearly shows that the existence of the Son is derived from the Father, but 'not in time, nor from any other beginning, except, as we have said, from God Himself.

12. But wisdom is also called the stainless mirror of the ἐνέργεια or working of God. We must first understand, then, what the working of the power of God is. It is a sort of vigour, so to speak, by which God operates either in creation, or in providence, or in judgment, or in the disposal and arrangement of individual things, each in its season. For as the image formed in a mirror unerringly reflects all the acts and movements of him who gazes on it, so would Wisdom have herself to be understood when she is called the stainless mirror of the power and working of the Father: as the Lord Jesus Christ also, who is the Wisdom of God, declares of Himself when He says, "The works which the Father doeth, these also doeth the Son likewise."[1] And again He says, that the Son cannot do anything of Himself, save what He sees the Father do. As therefore the Son in no respect differs from the Father in the power of His works, and the work of the Son is not a different thing from that of the Father, but one and the same movement, so to speak, is in all things, He therefore named Him a stainless mirror, that by such an expression it might be understood that there is no dissimilarity whatever between the Son and the Father. How, indeed, can those things which are said by some to be done after the manner in which a disciple resembles or imitates his master, or according to the view that those things are made by the Son in bodily material which were first formed by the Father in their spiritual essence, agree with the declarations of Scripture, seeing in the Gospel the Son is said to do not similar things, but the *same* things in a similar manner?

13. It remains that we inquire what is the "image of His goodness;" and here, I think, we must understand the same thing which we expressed a little ago, in speaking of the image formed by the mirror. For He is the primal goodness, doubtless, out of which the Son is born, who, being in all respects the image of the Father, may certainly also be called with propriety the image of His goodness. For there is no other second goodness existing in the Son, save that which is in the Father. And therefore also the Saviour Himself rightly says in the Gospel, "There is none good save one only, God the Father,"[2] that by such an expression it may be understood that the Son is not of a different goodness, but of that only which exists in the Father, of whom He is rightly termed the image, because He proceeds from no other source but from that primal goodness, lest there might appear to be in the Son a different goodness from that which is in the Father. Nor is there any dissimilarity or difference of goodness in the Son. And therefore it is not to be imagined that there is a kind of blasphemy, as it were, in the words, "There is none good save one only, God the Father," as if thereby it may be supposed to be denied that either Christ or the Holy Spirit was good. But, as we have already said, the primal goodness is to be understood as residing in God the Father, from whom both the Son is born and the Holy Spirit proceeds, retaining within them, without any doubt, the nature of that goodness which is in the source whence they are derived. And if there be any other things which in Scripture are called good, whether angel, or man, or servant, or treasure, or a good heart, or a good tree, all these are so termed catachrestically,[3] having in them an accidental, not an essential goodness. But it would require both much time and labour to collect together all the titles of the Son of God, such, e.g., as the true light, or the door, or the righteousness, or the sanctification, or the redemption, and countless others; and to show for what reasons each one of them is so given. Satisfied, therefore, with what we have already advanced, we go on with our inquiries into those other matters which follow.

CHAP. III. — ON THE HOLY SPIRIT.

1. The next point is to investigate as briefly as possible the subject of the Holy Spirit. All who perceive, in whatever manner, the existence of Providence, confess that God, who created and disposed all things, is unbegotten, and rec-

---

[1] John v. 19.

[2] [Luke xviii. 19.]
[3] Abusive [= improperly used. S.]

ognise Him as the parent of the universe. Now, that to Him belongs a Son, is a statement not made by us only; although it may seem a sufficiently marvellous and incredible assertion to those who have a reputation as philosophers among Greeks and Barbarians, by some of whom, however, an idea of His existence seems to have been entertained, in their acknowledging that all things were created by the word or reason of God. We, however, in conformity with our belief in that doctrine, which we assuredly hold to be divinely inspired, believe that it is possible in no other way to explain and bring within the reach of human knowledge this higher and diviner reason as the Son of God, than by means of those Scriptures alone which were inspired by the Holy Spirit, i.e., the Gospels and Epistles, and the law and the prophets, according to the declaration of Christ Himself. Of the existence of the Holy Spirit no one indeed could entertain any suspicion, save those who were familiar with the law and the prophets, or those who profess a belief in Christ. For although no one is able to speak with certainty of God the Father, it is nevertheless possible for some knowledge of Him to be gained by means of the visible creation and the natural feelings of the human mind; and it is possible, moreover, for such knowledge to be confirmed from the sacred Scriptures. But with respect to the Son of God, although no one knoweth the Son save the Father, yet it is from sacred Scripture also that the human mind is taught how to think of the Son; and that not only from the New, but also from the Old Testament, by means of those things which, although done by the saints, are figuratively referred to Christ, and from which both His divine nature, and that human nature which was assumed by Him, may be discovered.

2. Now, what the Holy Spirit is, we are taught in many passages of Scripture, as by David in the fifty-first Psalm, when he says, "And take not Thy Holy Spirit from me;"[1] and by Daniel, where it is said, "The Holy Spirit which is in thee."[2] And in the New Testament we have abundant testimonies, as when the Holy Spirit is described as having descended upon Christ, and when the Lord breathed upon His apostles after His resurrection, saying, "Receive the Holy Spirit;"[3] and the saying of the angel to Mary, "The Holy Spirit will come upon thee;"[4] the declaration by Paul, that no one can call Jesus Lord, save by the Holy Spirit.[5] In the Acts of the Apostles, the Holy Spirit was given by the imposition of the apostles' hands in baptism.[6]

From all which we learn that the person of the Holy Spirit was of such authority and dignity, that saving baptism was not complete except by the authority of the most excellent Trinity of them all, i.e., by the naming of Father, Son, and Holy Spirit, and by joining to the unbegotten God the Father, and to His only-begotten Son, the name also of the Holy Spirit. Who, then, is not amazed at the exceeding majesty of the Holy Spirit, when he hears that he who speaks a word against the Son of man may hope for forgiveness; but that he who is guilty of blasphemy against the Holy Spirit has not forgiveness, either in the present world or in that which is to come!?[7]

3. That all things were created by God, and that there is no creature which exists but has derived from Him its being, is established from many declarations of Scripture; those assertions being refuted and rejected which are falsely alleged by some respecting the existence either of a matter co-eternal with God, or of unbegotten souls, in which they would have it that God implanted not so much the power of existence, as equality and order. For even in that little treatise called *The Pastor or Angel of Repentance*, composed by Hermas, we have the following: "First of all, believe that there is one God who created and arranged all things; who, when nothing formerly existed, caused all things to be; who Himself contains all things, but Himself is contained by none."[8] And in the book of Enoch also we have similar descriptions. But up to the present time we have been able to find no statement in holy Scripture in which the Holy Spirit could be said to be made or created,[9] not even in the way in which we have shown above that the divine wisdom is spoken of by Solomon, or in which those expressions which we have discussed are to be understood of the life, or the word, or the other appellations of the Son of God. The Spirit of God, therefore, which was borne upon the waters, as is written in the beginning of the creation of the world, is, I am of opinion, no other than the Holy Spirit, so far as I can understand; as indeed we have shown in our exposition of the passages themselves, not according to the historical, but according to the spiritual method of interpretation.

4. Some indeed of our predecessors have observed, that in the New Testament, whenever the Spirit is named without that adjunct which denotes quality, the Holy Spirit is to be understood; as e.g., in the expression, "Now the fruit of the Spirit is love, joy, and peace;"[10] and, "Seeing ye began in the Spirit, are ye now made

---

[1] Ps. li. 11.
[2] Dan. iv. 8.
[3] John xx. 22.
[4] Luke i. 35.
[5] 1 Cor. xii. 3.
[6] Acts viii. 18.

[7] Cf. Matt. xii. 32 and Luke xii. 10.
[8] Cf. *Hermæ Past.*, Vision v. Mandat. 1. [See vol. ii. p. 20.]
[9] Per quem Spiritus Sanctus factura esse vel creatura diceretur.
[10] Gal. v. 22.

perfect in the flesh?"[1] We are of opinion that this distinction may be observed in the Old Testament also, as when it is said, "He that giveth His Spirit to the people who are upon the earth, and Spirit to them who walk thereon."[2] For, without doubt, every one who walks upon the earth (i.e., earthly and corporeal beings) is a partaker also of the Holy Spirit, receiving it from God. My Hebrew master also used to say that those two seraphim in Isaiah, which are described as having each six wings, and calling to one another, and saying, "Holy, holy, holy, is the LORD God of hosts,"[3] were to be understood of the only-begotten Son of God and of the Holy Spirit. And we think that that expression also which occurs in the hymn of Habakkuk, "In the midst either of the two living things, or of the two lives, Thou wilt be known,"[4] ought to be understood of Christ and of the Holy Spirit. For all knowledge of the Father is obtained by revelation of the Son through the Holy Spirit, so that both of these beings which, according to the prophet, are called either "living things" or "lives," exist as the ground of the knowledge of God the Father. For as it is said of the Son, that "no one knoweth the Father but the Son, and he to whom the Son will reveal Him,"[5] the same also is said by the apostle of the Holy Spirit, when He declares, "God hath revealed them to us by His Holy Spirit; for the Spirit searcheth all things, even the deep things of God;"[6] and again in the Gospel, when the Saviour, speaking of the divine and profounder parts of His teaching, which His disciples were not yet able to receive, thus addresses them: "I have yet many things to say unto you, but ye cannot bear them now; but when the Holy Spirit, the Comforter, is come, He will teach you all things, and will bring all things to your remembrance, whatsoever I have said unto you."[7] We must understand, therefore, that as the Son, who alone knows the Father, reveals Him to whom He will, so the Holy Spirit, who alone searches the deep things of God, reveals God to whom He will: "For the Spirit bloweth where He listeth."[8] We are not, however, to suppose that the Spirit derives His knowledge through revelation from the Son. For if the Holy Spirit knows the Father through the Son's revelation, He passes from a state of ignorance into one of knowledge; but it is alike impious and foolish to confess the Holy Spirit, and yet to ascribe to Him ignorance. For even although something else existed before the Holy Spirit, it was not by

progressive advancement that He came to be the Holy Spirit; as if any one should venture to say, that at the time when He was not yet the Holy Spirit He was ignorant of the Father, but that after He had received knowledge He was made the Holy Spirit. For if this were the case, the Holy Spirit would never be reckoned in the Unity of the Trinity, i.e., along with the unchangeable Father and His Son, unless He had always been the Holy Spirit. When we use, indeed, such terms as "always" or "was," or any other designation of time, they are not to be taken absolutely, but with due allowance; for while the significations of these words relate to time, and those subjects of which we speak are spoken of by a stretch of language as existing in time, they nevertheless surpass in their real nature all conception of the finite understanding.

5. Nevertheless it seems proper to inquire what is the reason why he who is regenerated by God unto salvation has to do both with Father and Son and Holy Spirit, and does not obtain salvation unless with the co-operation of the entire Trinity; and why it is impossible to become partaker of the Father or the Son without the Holy Spirit. And in discussing these subjects, it will undoubtedly be necessary to describe the special working of the Holy Spirit, and of the Father and the Son. I am of opinion, then, that the working of the Father and of the Son takes place as well in saints as in sinners, in rational beings and in dumb animals; nay, even in those things which are without life, and in all things universally which exist; but that the operation of the Holy Spirit does not take place at all in those things which are without life, or in those which, although living, are yet dumb; nay, is not found even in those who are endued indeed with reason, but are engaged in evil courses, and not at all converted to a better life. In those persons alone do I think that the operation of the Holy Spirit takes place, who are already turning to a better life, and walking along the way which leads to Jesus Christ, i.e., who are engaged in the performance of good actions, and who abide in God.

6. That the working of the Father and the Son operates both in saints and in sinners, is manifest from this, that all who are rational beings are partakers of the word, i.e., of reason, and by this means bear certain seeds, implanted within them, of wisdom and justice, which is Christ. Now, in Him who truly exists, and who said by Moses, "I AM WHO I AM,"[9] all things, whatever they are, participate; which participation in God the Father is shared both by just men and sinners, by rational and irrational beings, and by all things universally which exist.

[1] Gal. iii. 3.
[2] Isa. xlii. 5.
[3] Isa. vi. 3.
[4] Hab. iii. 2.
[5] Luke x. 22.
[6] 1 Cor. ii. 10.
[7] Cf. John xvi. 12, 13, and xiv. 26.
[8] John iii. 8.

[9] Ex. iii. 14.

The Apostle Paul also shows truly that all have a share in Christ, when he says, "Say not in thine heart, Who shall ascend into heaven? (i.e., to bring Christ down from above;) or who shall descend into the deep? (that is, to bring up Christ again from the dead.) But what saith the Scripture? The word is nigh thee, even in thy mouth, and in thy heart." [1] By which he means that Christ is in the heart of all, in respect of His being the word or reason, by participating in which they are rational beings. That declaration also in the Gospel, "If I had not come and spoken unto them, they had not had sin; but now they have no excuse for their sin," [2] renders it manifest and patent to all who have a rational knowledge of how long a time man is without sin, and from what period he is liable to it, how, by participating in the word or reason, men are said to have sinned, viz., from the time they are made capable of understanding and knowledge, when the reason implanted within has suggested to them the difference between good and evil; and after they have already begun to know what evil is, they are made liable to sin, if they commit it. And this is the meaning of the expression, that "men have no excuse for their sin," viz., that, from the time the divine word or reason has begun to show them internally the difference between good and evil, they ought to avoid and guard against that which is wicked: "For to him who knoweth to do good, and doeth it not, to him it is sin." [3] Moreover, that all men are not without communion with God, is taught in the Gospel thus, by the Saviour's words: "The kingdom of God cometh not with observation; neither shall they say, Lo here! or, lo there! but the kingdom of God is within you." [4] But here we must see whether this does not bear the same meaning with the expression in Genesis: "And He breathed into his face the breath of life, and man became a living soul." [5] For if this be understood as applying generally to all men, then all men have a share in God.

7. But if this is to be understood as spoken of the Spirit of God, since Adam also is found to have prophesied of some things, it may be taken not as of general application, but as confined to those who are saints. Finally, also, at the time of the flood, when all flesh had corrupted their way before God, it is recorded that God spoke thus, as of undeserving men and sinners: "My Spirit shall not abide with those men for ever, because they are flesh." [6] By which it is clearly shown that the Spirit of God is taken away from all who are unworthy. In the Psalms also it is written: "Thou wilt take away their spirit, and they will die, and return to their earth. Thou wilt send forth Thy Spirit, and they shall be created, and Thou wilt renew the face of the earth;" [7] which is manifestly intended of the Holy Spirit, who, after sinners and unworthy persons have been taken away and destroyed, creates for Himself a new people, and renews the face of the earth, when, laying aside, through the grace of the Spirit, the old man with his deeds, they begin to walk in newness of life. And therefore the expression is competently applied to the Holy Spirit, because He will take up His dwelling, not in all men, nor in those who are flesh, but in those whose land [8] has been renewed. Lastly, for this reason was the grace and revelation of the Holy Spirit bestowed by the imposition of the apostles' hands after baptism. Our Saviour also, after the resurrection, when old things had already passed away, and all things had become new, Himself a new man, and the first-born from the dead, His apostles also being renewed by faith in His resurrection, says, "Receive the Holy Spirit." [9] This is doubtless what the Lord the Saviour meant to convey in the Gospel, when He said that new wine cannot be put into old bottles, but commanded that the bottles should be made new, i.e., that men should walk in newness of life, that they might receive the new wine, i.e., the newness of grace of the Holy Spirit. In this manner, then, is the working of the power of God the Father and of the Son extended without distinction to every creature; but a share in the Holy Spirit we find possessed only by the saints. And therefore it is said, "No man can say that Jesus is Lord, but by the Holy Ghost." [10] And on one occasion, scarcely even the apostles themselves are deemed worthy to hear the words, "Ye shall receive the power of the Holy Ghost coming upon you." [11] For this reason, also, I think it follows that he who has committed a sin against the Son of man is deserving of forgiveness; because if he who is a participator of the word or reason of God cease to live agreeably to reason, he seems to have fallen into a state of ignorance or folly, and therefore to deserve forgiveness; whereas he who has been deemed worthy to have a portion of the Holy Spirit, and who has relapsed, is, by this very act and work, said to be guilty of blasphemy against the Holy Spirit. Let no one indeed suppose that we, from having said that the Holy Spirit is conferred upon the saints alone, but that the benefits or operations of the Father and of the Son extend

---

[1] Rom. x. 6–8.
[2] John xv. 22.
[3] Jas. iv. 17.
[4] Luke xvii. 20, 21.
[5] Gen. ii. 7.
[6] Gen. vi. 3.

[7] Ps. civ. 29, 30.
[8] Terra.
[9] John xx. 22.
[10] 1 Cor. xii. 3.
[11] Acts i. 8.

to good and bad, to just and unjust, by so doing give a preference to the Holy Spirit over the Father and the Son, or assert that His dignity is greater, which certainly would be a very illogical conclusion. For it is the peculiarity of His grace and operations that we have been describing. Moreover, nothing in the Trinity can be called greater or less, since the fountain of divinity alone contains all things by His word and reason, and by the Spirit of His mouth sanctifies all things which are worthy of sanctification, as it is written in the Psalm : " By the word of the LORD were the heavens strengthened, and all their power by the Spirit of His mouth." [1] There is also a special working of God the Father, besides that by which He bestowed upon all things the gift of natural life. There is also a special ministry of the Lord Jesus Christ to those upon whom he confers by nature the gift of reason, by means of which they are enabled to be rightly what they are. There is also another grace of the Holy Spirit, which is bestowed upon the deserving, through the ministry of Christ and the working of the Father, in proportion to the merits of those who are rendered capable of receiving it. This is most clearly pointed out by the Apostle Paul, when demonstrating that the power of the Trinity is one and the same, in the words, " There are diversities of gifts, but the same Spirit ; there are diversities of administrations, but the same Lord ; and there are diversities of operations, but it is the same God who worketh all in all. But the manifestation of the Spirit is given to every man to profit withal." [2] From which it most clearly follows that there is no difference in the Trinity, but that which is called the gift of the Spirit is made known through the Son, and operated by God the Father. " But all these worketh that one and the self-same Spirit, dividing to every one severally as He will." [3]

8. Having made these declarations regarding the Unity of the Father, and of the Son, and of the Holy Spirit, let us return to the order in which we began the discussion. God the Father bestows upon all, existence ; and participation in Christ, in respect of His being the word of reason, renders them rational beings. From which it follows that they are deserving either of praise or blame, because capable of virtue and vice. On this account, therefore, is the grace of the Holy Ghost present, that those beings which are not holy in their essence may be rendered holy by participating in it. Seeing, then, that firstly, they derive their existence from God the Father ; secondly, their rational nature from the Word ; thirdly, their holiness from the Holy Spirit, —

those who have been previously sanctified by the Holy Spirit are again made capable of receiving Christ, in respect that He is the righteousness of God ; and those who have earned advancement to this grade by the sanctification of the Holy Spirit, will nevertheless obtain the gift of wisdom according to the power and working of the Spirit of God. And this I consider is Paul's meaning, when he says that to " some is given the word of wisdom, to others the word of knowledge, according to the same Spirit." And while pointing out the individual distinction of gifts, he refers the whole of them to the source of all things in the words, "There are diversities of operations, but one God who worketh all in all." [4] Whence also the working of the Father, which confers existence upon all things, is found to be more glorious and magnificent, while each one, by participation in Christ, as being wisdom, and knowledge, and sanctification, makes progress, and advances to higher degrees of perfection ; and seeing it is by partaking of the Holy Spirit that any one is made purer and holier, he obtains, when he is made worthy, the grace of wisdom and knowledge, in order that, after all stains of pollution and ignorance are cleansed and taken away, he may make so great an advance in holiness and purity, that the nature which he received from God may become such as is worthy of Him who gave it to be pure and perfect, so that the being which exists may be as worthy as He who called it into existence. For, in this way, he who is such as his Creator wished him to be, will receive from God power always to exist, and to abide for ever. That this may be the case, and that those whom He has created may be unceasingly and inseparably present with HIM, WHO IS, it is the business of wisdom to instruct and train them, and to bring them to perfection by confirmation of His Holy Spirit and unceasing sanctification, by which alone are they capable of receiving God. In this way, then, by the renewal of the ceaseless working of Father, Son, and Holy Spirit in us, in its various stages of progress, shall we be able at some future time perhaps, although with difficulty, to behold the holy and the blessed life, in which (as it is only after many struggles that we are able to reach it) we ought so to continue, that no satiety of that blessedness should ever seize us ; but the more we perceive its blessedness, the more should be increased and intensified within us the longing for the same, while we ever more eagerly and freely receive and hold fast the Father, and the Son, and the Holy Spirit. But if satiety should ever take hold of any one of those who stand on the highest and perfect summit of attainment, I do not think that such an one would suddenly

[1] Ps. xxxiii. 6.
[2] 1 Cor. xii. 4-7.
[3] 1 Cor. xii. 11.

[4] 1 Cor. xii. 6.

be deposed from his position and fall away, but that he must decline gradually and little by little, so that it may sometimes happen that if a brief lapsus take place, and the individual quickly repent and return to himself, he may not utterly fall away, but may retrace his steps, and return to his former place, and again make good that which had been lost by his negligence.

CHAP. IV. — ON DEFECTION, OR FALLING AWAY.

1. To exhibit the nature of defection or falling away, on the part of those who conduct themselves carelessly, it will not appear out of place to employ a similitude by way of illustration. Suppose, then, the case of one who had become gradually acquainted with the art or science, say of geometry or medicine, until he had reached perfection, having trained himself for a lengthened time in its principles and practice, so as to attain a complete mastery over the art : to such an one it could never happen, that, when he lay down to sleep in the possession of his skill, he should awake in a state of ignorance. It is not our purpose to adduce or to notice here those accidents which are occasioned by any injury or weakness, for they do not apply to our present illustration. According to our point of view, then, so long as that geometer or physician continues to exercise himself in the study of his art and in the practice of its principles, the knowledge of his profession abides with him ; but if he withdraw from its practice, and lay aside his habits of industry, then, by his neglect, at first a few things will gradually escape him, then by and by more and more, until in course of time everything will be forgotten, and be completely effaced from the memory. It is possible, indeed, that when he has first begun to fall away, and to yield to the corrupting influence of a negligence which is small as yet, he may, if he be aroused and return speedily to his senses, repair those losses which up to that time are only recent, and recover that knowledge which hitherto had been only slightly obliterated from his mind. Let us apply this now to the case of those who have devoted themselves to the knowledge and wisdom of God, whose learning and diligence incomparably surpass all other training ; and let us contemplate, according to the form of the similitude employed, what is the acquisition of knowledge, or what is its disappearance, especially when we hear from the apostle what is said of those who are perfect, that they shall behold face to face the glory of the Lord in the revelation of His mysteries.

2. But in our desire to show the divine benefits bestowed upon us by Father, Son, and Holy Spirit, which Trinity is the fountain of all holiness, we have fallen, in what we have said, into a digression, having considered that the subject of the soul, which accidentally came before us, should be touched on, although cursorily, seeing we were discussing a cognate topic relating to our rational nature. We shall, however, with the permission of God through Jesus Christ and the Holy Spirit, more conveniently consider in the proper place the subject of all rational beings, which are distinguished into three genera and species.

CHAP. V. — ON RATIONAL NATURES.

1. After the dissertation, which we have briefly conducted to the best of our ability, regarding the Father, Son, and Holy Spirit, it follows that we offer a few remarks upon the subject of rational natures, and on their species and orders, or on the offices as well of holy as of malignant powers, and also on those which occupy an intermediate position between these good and evil powers, and as yet are placed in a state of struggle and trial. For we find in holy Scripture numerous names of certain orders and offices, not only of holy beings, but also of those of an opposite description, which we shall bring before us, in the first place ; and the meaning of which we shall endeavour, in the second place, to the best of our ability, to ascertain. There are certain holy angels of God whom Paul terms "ministering spirits, sent forth to minister for them who shall be heirs of salvation." [1] In the writings also of St. Paul himself we find him designating them, from some unknown source, as thrones, and dominions, and principalities, and powers ; and after this enumeration, as if knowing that there were still other rational offices [2] and orders besides those which he had named, he says of the Saviour : "Who is above all principality, and power, and might, and dominion, and every name that is named, not only in this world, but also in that which is to come." [3] From which he shows that there were certain beings besides those which he had mentioned, which may be named indeed in this world, but were not now enumerated by him, and perhaps were not known by any other individual ; and that there were others which may not be named in this world, but will be named in the world to come.

2. Then, in the next place, we must know that every being which is endowed with reason, and transgresses its statutes and limitations, is undoubtedly involved in sin by swerving from rectitude and justice. Every rational creature, therefore, is capable of earning praise and censure : of praise, if, in conformity to that reason which he possesses, he advance to better things ; of censure, if he fall away from the plan and

[1] Heb. i. 14.
[2] Officia.
[3] Eph. i. 21.

course of rectitude, for which reason he is justly liable to pains and penalties. And this also is to be held as applying to the devil himself, and those who are with him, and are called his angels. Now the titles of these beings have to be explained, that we may know what they are of whom we have to speak. The name, then, of Devil, and Satan, and Wicked One, who is also described as Enemy of God, is mentioned in many passages of Scripture. Moreover, certain angels of the devil are mentioned, and also a prince of this world, who, whether the devil himself or some one else, is not yet clearly manifest. There are also certain princes of this world spoken of as possessing a kind of wisdom which will come to nought; but whether these are those princes who are also the principalities with whom we have to wrestle, or other beings, seems to me a point on which it is not easy for any one to pronounce. After the principalities, certain powers also are named with whom we have to wrestle, and carry on a struggle even against the princes of this world and the rulers of this darkness. Certain spiritual powers of wickedness also, in heavenly places, are spoken of by Paul himself. What, moreover, are we to say of those wicked and unclean spirits mentioned in the Gospel? Then we have certain heavenly beings called by a similar name, but which are said to bend the knee, or to be about to bend the knee, at the name of Jesus; nay, even things on earth and things under the earth, which Paul enumerates in order. And certainly, in a place where we have been discussing the subject of rational natures, it is not proper to be silent regarding ourselves, who are human beings, and are called rational animals; nay, even this point is not to be idly passed over, that even of us human beings certain different orders are mentioned in the words, "The portion of the Lord is His people Jacob; Israel is the cord of His inheritance." [1] Other nations, moreover, are called a part of the angels; since "when the Most High divided the nations, and dispersed the sons of Adam, He fixed the boundaries of the nations according to the number of the angels of God." [2] And therefore, with other rational natures, we must also thoroughly examine the reason of the human soul.

3. After the enumeration, then, of so many and so important names of orders and offices, underlying which it is certain that there are personal existences, let us inquire whether God, the creator and founder of all things, created certain of them holy and happy, so that they could admit no element at all of an opposite kind, and certain others so that they were made capable

both of virtue and vice; or whether we are to suppose that He created some so as to be altogether incapable of virtue, and others again altogether incapable of wickedness, but with the power of abiding only in a state of happiness, and others again such as to be capable of either condition.[3] In order, now, that our first inquiry may begin with the names themselves, let us consider whether the holy angels, from the period of their first existence, have always been holy, and are holy still, and will be holy, and have never either admitted or had the power to admit any occasion of sin. Then in the next place, let us consider whether those who are called holy principalities began from the moment of their creation by God to exercise power over some who were made subject to them, and whether these latter were created of such a nature, and formed for the very purpose of being subject and subordinate. In like manner, also, whether those which are called powers were created of such a nature and for the express purpose of exercising power, or whether their arriving at that power and dignity is a reward and desert of their virtue. Moreover, also, whether those which are called thrones or seats gained that stability of happiness at the same time with their coming forth into being,[4] so as to have that possession from the will of the Creator alone; or whether those which are called dominions had their dominion conferred on them, not as a reward for their proficiency, but as the peculiar privilege of their creation,[5] so that it is something which is in a certain degree inseparable from them, and natural. Now, if we adopt the view that the holy angels, and the holy powers, and the blessed seats, and the glorious virtues, and the magnificent dominions, are to be regarded as possessing those powers and dignities and glories in virtue of their nature,[6] it will doubtless appear to follow that those beings which have been mentioned as holding offices of an opposite kind must be regarded in the same manner; so that those principalities with whom we have to struggle are to be viewed, not as having received that spirit of opposition and resistance to all good at a later period, or as falling away from good through the freedom of the will, but as having had it in themselves as the essence of their being from the beginning of their existence. In like manner also will it be the case with the powers and virtues, in none of which was wickedness subsequent or posterior to their first existence. Those also whom the apostle termed rulers and princes of the darkness of this world, are said, with respect to their

---

[1] Deut. xxxii. 9.
[2] Deut. xxxii. 8. The Septuagint here differs from the Masoretic text.

[3] [See note at end of chap. vi. S.]
[4] Simul cum substantiæ suæ prolatione — at the same time with the emanation of their substance.
[5] Conditionis prærogativa.
[6] Substantialiter.

rule and occupation of darkness, to fall not from perversity of intention, but from the necessity of their creation. Logical reasoning will compel us to take the same view with regard to wicked and malignant spirits and unclean demons. But if to entertain this view regarding malignant and opposing powers seem to be absurd, as it is certainly absurd that the cause of their wickedness should be removed from the purpose of their own will, and ascribed of necessity to their Creator, why should we not also be obliged to make a similar confession regarding the good and holy powers, that, viz., the good which is in them is not theirs by essential being, which we have manifestly shown to be the case with Christ and the Holy Spirit alone, as undoubtedly with the Father also? For it was proved that there was nothing compound in the nature of the Trinity, so that these qualities might seem to belong to it as accidental consequences. From which it follows, that in the case of every creature it is a result of his own works and movements, that those powers which appear either to hold sway over others or to exercise power or dominion, have been preferred to and placed over those whom they are said to govern or exercise power over, and not in consequence of a peculiar privilege inherent in their constitutions, but on account of merit.

4. But that we may not appear to build our assertions on subjects of such importance and difficulty on the ground of inference alone, or to require the assent of our hearers to what is only conjectural, let us see whether we can obtain any declarations from holy Scripture, by the authority of which these positions may be more credibly maintained. And, firstly, we shall adduce what holy Scripture contains regarding wicked powers; we shall next continue our investigation with regard to the others, as the Lord shall be pleased to enlighten us, that in matters of such difficulty we may ascertain what is nearest to the truth, or what ought to be our opinions agreeably to the standard of religion. Now we find in the prophet Ezekiel two prophecies written to the prince of Tyre, the former of which might appear to any one, before he heard the second also, to be spoken of some man who was prince of the Tyrians. In the meantime, therefore, we shall take nothing from that first prophecy; but as the second is manifestly of such a kind as cannot be at all understood of a man, but of some superior power which had fallen away from a higher position, and had been reduced to a lower and worse condition, we shall from it take an illustration, by which it may be demonstrated with the utmost clearness, that those opposing and malignant powers were not formed or created so by nature, but fell from a better to a worse position, and were converted into wicked beings; that those blessed powers also were not of such a nature as to be unable to admit what was opposed to them if they were so inclined and became negligent, and did not guard most carefully the blessedness of their condition. For if it is related that he who is called the prince of Tyre was amongst the saints, and was without stain, and was placed in the paradise of God, and adorned also with a crown of comeliness and beauty, is it to be supposed that such an one could be in any degree inferior to any of the saints? For he is described as having been adorned with a crown of comeliness and beauty, and as having walked stainless in the paradise of God: and how can any one suppose that such a being was not one of those holy and blessed powers which, as being placed in a state of happiness, we must believe to be endowed with no other honour than this? But let us see what we are taught by the words of the prophecy themselves. "The word of the LORD," says the prophet, "came to me, saying, Son of man, take up a lamentation over the prince of Tyre, and say to him, Thus saith the Lord GOD, Thou hast been the seal of a similitude, and a crown of comeliness among the delights of paradise; thou wert adorned with every good stone or gem, and wert clothed with sardonyx, and topaz, and emerald, and carbuncle, and sapphire, and jasper, set in gold and silver, and with agate, amethyst, and chrysolite, and beryl, and onyx: with gold also didst thou fill thy treasures, and thy storehouses within thee. From the day when thou wert created along with the cherubim, I placed thee in the holy mount of God. Thou wert in the midst of the fiery stones: thou wert stainless in thy days, from the day when thou wert created, until iniquities were found in thee: from the greatness of thy trade, thou didst fill thy storehouses with iniquity, and didst sin, and wert wounded from the mount of God. And a cherub drove thee forth from the midst of the burning stones; and thy heart was elated because of thy comeliness, thy discipline was corrupted along with thy beauty: on account of the multitude of thy sins, I cast thee forth to the earth before kings; I gave thee for a show and a mockery on account of the multitude of thy sins, and of thine iniquities: because of thy trade thou hast polluted thy holy places. And I shall bring forth fire from the midst of thee, and it shall devour thee, and I shall give thee for ashes and cinders on the earth in the sight of all who see thee: and all who know thee among the nations shall mourn over thee. Thou hast been made destruction, and thou shalt exist no longer for ever." [1] Seeing, then, that such are the words of the prophet, who is there that on hear-

---

[1] Ezek. xxviii. 11-19.

ing, "Thou wert a seal of a similitude, and a crown of comeliness among the delights of paradise," or that "From the day when thou wert created with the cherubim, I placed thee in the holy mount of God," can so enfeeble the meaning as to suppose that this language is used of some man or saint, not to say the prince of Tyre? Or what fiery stones can he imagine in the midst of which any man could live? Or who could be supposed to be stainless from the very day of his creation, and wickedness being afterwards discovered in him, it be said of him then that he was cast forth upon the earth? For the meaning of this is, that He who was not yet on the earth is said to be cast forth upon it: whose holy places also are said to be polluted. We have shown, then, that what we have quoted regarding the prince of Tyre from the prophet Ezekiel refers to an adverse power, and by it it is most clearly proved that that power was formerly holy and happy; from which state of happiness it fell from the time that iniquity was found in it, and was hurled to the earth, and was not such by nature and creation. We are of opinion, therefore, that these words are spoken of a certain angel who had received the office of governing the nation of the Tyrians, and to whom also their souls had been entrusted to be taken care of. But what Tyre, or what souls of Tyrians, we ought to understand, whether that Tyre which is situated within the boundaries of the province of Phœnicia, or some other of which this one which we know on earth is the model; and the souls of the Tyrians, whether they are those of the former or those which belong to that Tyre which is spiritually understood, does not seem to be a matter requiring examination in this place; lest perhaps we should appear to investigate subjects of so much mystery and importance in a cursory manner, whereas they demand a labour and work of their own.

5. Again, we are taught as follows by the prophet Isaiah regarding another opposing power. The prophet says, "How is Lucifer, who used to arise in the morning, fallen from heaven! He who assailed all nations is broken and beaten to the ground. Thou indeed saidst in thy heart, I shall ascend into heaven; above the stars of heaven shall I place my throne; I shall sit upon a lofty mountain, above the lofty mountains which are towards the north; I shall ascend above the clouds; I shall be like the Most High. Now shalt thou be brought down to the lower world, and to the foundations of the earth. They who see thee shall be amazed at thee, and shall say, This is the man who harassed the whole earth, who moved kings, who made the whole world a desert, who destroyed cities, and did not unloose those who were in chains. All the kings of the nations have slept in honour, every

one in his own house; but thou shalt be cast forth on the mountains, accursed with the many dead who have been pierced through with swords, and have descended to the lower world. As a garment clotted with blood, and stained, will not be clean; neither shalt thou be clean, because thou hast destroyed my land and slain my people: thou shalt not remain for ever, most wicked seed. Prepare thy sons for death on account of the sins of thy father, lest they rise again and inherit the earth, and fill the earth with wars. And I shall rise against them, saith the LORD of hosts, and I shall cause their name to perish, and their remains, and their seed."[1] Most evidently by these words is he shown to have fallen from heaven, who formerly was Lucifer, and who used to arise in the morning. For if, as some think, he was a nature of darkness, how is Lucifer said to have existed before? Or how could he arise in the morning, who had in himself nothing of the light? Nay, even the Saviour Himself teaches us, saying of the devil, "Behold, I see Satan fallen from heaven like lightning."[2] For at one time he was light. Moreover our Lord, who is the truth, compared the power of His own glorious advent to lightning, in the words, "For as the lightning shineth from the height of heaven even to its height again, so will the coming of the Son of man be."[3] And notwithstanding He compares him to lightning, and says that he fell from heaven, that He might show by this that he had been at one time in heaven, and had had a place among the saints, and had enjoyed a share in that light in which all the saints participate, by which they are made angels of light, and by which the apostles are termed by the Lord the light of the world. In this manner, then, did that being once exist as light before he went astray, and fell to this place, and had his glory turned into dust, which is peculiarly the mark of the wicked, as the prophet also says; whence, too, he was called the prince of this world, i.e., of an earthly habitation: for he exercised power over those who were obedient to his wickedness, since "the whole of this world" — for I term this place of earth, world — "lieth in the wicked one,"[4] and in this apostate. That he is an apostate, i.e., a fugitive, even the Lord in the book of Job says, "Thou wilt take with a hook the apostate dragon," i.e., a fugitive.[5] Now it is certain that by the dragon is understood the devil himself. If then they are called opposing powers, and are said to have been once without stain, while spotless purity exists in the essential being of none save the Father, Son, and Holy Spirit, but is an

---

[1] Isa. xiv. 12-22.
[2] Luke x. 18.
[3] Matt. xxiv. 27.
[4] 1 John v. 19.
[5] Job xl. 20 [LXX.].

accidental quality in every created thing; and since that which is accidental may also fall away, and since those opposite powers once were spotless, and were once among those which still remain unstained, it is evident from all this that no one is pure either by essence or nature, and that no one was by nature polluted. And the consequence of this is, that it lies within ourselves and in our own actions to possess either happiness or holiness; or by sloth and negligence to fall from happiness into wickedness and ruin, to such a degree that, through too great proficiency, so to speak, in wickedness (if a man be guilty of so great neglect), he may descend even to that state in which he will be changed into what is called an "opposing power."

CHAP. VI. — ON THE END OR CONSUMMATION.

1. An end or consummation would seem to be an indication of the perfection and completion of things. And this reminds us here, that if there be any one imbued with a desire of reading and understanding subjects of such difficulty and importance, he ought to bring to the effort a perfect and instructed understanding, lest perhaps, if he has had no experience in questions of this kind, they may appear to him as vain and superfluous; or if his mind be full of preconceptions and prejudices on other points, he may judge these to be heretical and opposed to the faith of the Church, yielding in so doing not so much to the convictions of reason as to the dogmatism of prejudice. These subjects, indeed, are treated by us with great solicitude and caution, in the manner rather of an investigation and discussion, than in that of fixed and certain decision. For we have pointed out in the preceding pages those questions which must be set forth in clear dogmatic propositions, as I think has been done to the best of my ability when speaking of the Trinity. But on the present occasion our exercise is to be conducted, as we best may, in the style of a disputation rather than of strict definition.

The end of the world, then, and the final consummation, will take place when every one shall be subjected to punishment for his sins; a time which God alone knows, when He will bestow on each one what he deserves. We think, indeed, that the goodness of God, through His Christ, may recall all His creatures to one end, even His enemies being conquered and subdued. For thus says holy Scripture, "The LORD said to My Lord, Sit Thou at My right hand, until I make Thine enemies Thy footstool."[1] And if the meaning of the prophet's language here be less clear, we may ascertain it from the Apostle Paul, who speaks more openly, thus: "For Christ must reign until He has put all enemies under His feet."[2] But if even that unreserved declaration of the apostle do not sufficiently inform us what is meant by "enemies being placed under His feet," listen to what he says in the following words, "For all things must be put under Him." What, then, is this "putting under" by which all things must be made subject to Christ? I am of opinion that it is this very subjection by which we also wish to be subject to Him, by which the apostles also were subject, and all the saints who have been followers of Christ. For the name "subjection," by which we are subject to Christ, indicates that the salvation which proceeds from Him belongs to His subjects, agreeably to the declaration of David, "Shall not my soul be subject unto God? From Him cometh my salvation."[3]

2. Seeing, then, that such is the end, when all enemies will be subdued to Christ, when death — the last enemy — shall be destroyed, and when the kingdom shall be delivered up by Christ (to whom all things are subject) to God the Father; let us, I say, from such an end as this, contemplate the beginnings of things. For the end is always like the beginning: and, therefore, as there is one end to all things, so ought we to understand that there was one beginning; and as there is one end to many things, so there spring from one beginning many differences and varieties, which again, through the goodness of God, and by subjection to Christ, and through the unity of the Holy Spirit, are recalled to one end, which is like unto the beginning: all those, viz., who, bending the knee at the name of Jesus, make known by so doing their subjection to Him: and these are they who are in heaven, on earth, and under the earth: by which three classes the whole universe of things is pointed out, those, viz., who from that one beginning were arranged, each according to the diversity of his conduct, among the different orders, in accordance with their desert; for there was no goodness in them by essential being, as in God and His Christ, and in the Holy Spirit. For in the Trinity alone, which is the author of all things, does goodness exist in virtue of essential being; while others possess it as an accidental and perishable quality, and only then enjoy blessedness, when they participate in holiness and wisdom, and in divinity itself. But if they neglect and despise such participation, then is each one, by fault of his own slothfulness, made, one more rapidly, another more slowly, one in a greater, another in a less degree, the cause of his own downfall. And since, as we have remarked, the lapse by which an individual falls away from his position is characterized by great

---

[1] Ps. cx. 1.

[2] 1 Cor. xv. 25.
[3] Ps. lxii. 1.

diversity, according to the movements of the mind and will, one man falling with greater ease, another with more difficulty, into a lower condition; in this is to be seen the just judgment of the providence of God, that it should happen to every one according to the diversity of his conduct, in proportion to the desert of his declension and defection. Certain of those, indeed, who remained in that beginning which we have described as resembling the end which is to come, obtained, in the ordering and arrangement of the world, the rank of angels; others that of influences, others of principalities, others of powers, that they may exercise power over those who need to have power upon their head. Others, again, received the rank of thrones, having the office of judging or ruling those who require this; others dominion, doubtless, over slaves; all of which are conferred by Divine Providence in just and impartial judgment according to their merits, and to the progress which they had made in the participation and imitation of God. But those who have been removed from their primal state of blessedness have not been removed irrecoverably, but have been placed under the rule of those holy and blessed orders which we have described; and by availing themselves of the aid of these, and being remoulded by salutary principles and discipline, they may recover themselves, and be restored to their condition of happiness. From all which I am of opinion, so far as I can see, that this order of the human race has been appointed in order that in the future world, or in ages to come, when there shall be the new heavens and new earth, spoken of by Isaiah, it may be restored to that unity promised by the Lord Jesus in His prayer to God the Father on behalf of His disciples: "I do not pray for these alone, but for all who shall believe on Me through their word: that they all may be one, as Thou, Father, art in Me, and I in Thee, that they also may be one in Us;"[1] and again, when He says: "That they may be one, even as We are one; I in them, and Thou in Me, that they may be made perfect in one."[2] And this is further confirmed by the language of the Apostle Paul: "Until we all come in the unity of the faith to a perfect man, to the measure of the stature of the fulness of Christ."[3] And in keeping with this is the declaration of the same apostle, when he exhorts us, who even in the present life are placed in the Church, in which is the form of that kingdom which is to come, to this same similitude of unity: "That ye all speak the same thing, and that there be no divisions among you; but that ye be perfectly joined together in the same mind and in the same judgment."[4]

3. It is to be borne in mind, however, that certain beings who fell away from that one beginning of which we have spoken, have sunk to such a depth of unworthiness and wickedness as to be deemed altogether undeserving of that training and instruction by which the human race, while in the flesh, are trained and instructed with the assistance of the heavenly powers; and continue, on the contrary, in a state of enmity and opposition to those who are receiving this instruction and teaching. And hence it is that the whole of this mortal life is full of struggles and trials, caused by the opposition and enmity of those who fell from a better condition without at all looking back, and who are called the devil and his angels, and the other orders of evil, which the apostle classed among the opposing powers. But whether any of these orders who act under the government of the devil, and obey his wicked commands, will in a future world be converted to righteousness because of their possessing the faculty of freedom of will, or whether persistent and inveterate wickedness may be changed by the power of habit into nature, is a result which you yourself, reader, may approve of, if neither in these present worlds which are seen and temporal, nor in those which are unseen and are eternal, that portion is to differ wholly from the final unity and fitness of things. But in the meantime, both in those temporal worlds which are seen, as well as in those eternal worlds which are invisible, all those beings are arranged, according to a regular plan, in the order and degree of their merits; so that some of them in the first, others in the second, some even in the last times, after having undergone heavier and severer punishments, endured for a lengthened period, and for many ages, so to speak, improved by this stern method of training, and restored at first by the instruction of the angels, and subsequently by the powers of a higher grade, and thus advancing through each stage to a better condition, reach even to that which is invisible and eternal, having travelled through, by a kind of training, every single office of the heavenly powers. From which, I think, this will appear to follow as an inference, that every rational nature may, in passing from one order to another, go through each to all, and advance from all to each, while made the subject of various degrees of proficiency and failure according to its own actions and endeavours, put forth in the enjoyment of its power of freedom of will.

---

[1] John xvii. 20, 21.
[2] John xvii. 22, 23.
[3] Eph. iv. 13.

[4] 1 Cor. i. 10.

4. But since Paul says that certain things are visible and temporal, and others besides these invisible and eternal, we proceed to inquire how those things which are seen are temporal — whether because there will be nothing at all after them in all those periods of the coming world, in which that dispersion and separation from the one beginning is undergoing a process of restoration to one and the same end and likeness; or because, while the form of those things which are seen passes away, their essential nature is subject to no corruption. And Paul seems to confirm the latter view, when he says, " For the fashion of this world passeth away." [1] David also appears to assert the same in the words, " The heavens shall perish, but Thou shalt endure ; and they all shall wax old as a garment, and Thou shalt change them like a vesture, and like a vestment they shall be changed." [2] For if the heavens are to be changed, assuredly that which is changed does not perish, and if the fashion of the world passes away, it is by no means an annihilation or destruction of their material substance that is shown to take place, but a kind of change of quality and transformation of appearance. Isaiah also, in declaring prophetically that there will be a new heaven and a new earth, undoubtedly suggests a similar view. For this renewal of heaven and earth, and this transmutation of the form of the present world, and this changing of the heavens, will undoubtedly be prepared for those who are walking along that way which we have pointed out above, and are tending to that goal of happiness to which, it is said, even enemies themselves are to be subjected, and in which God is said to be " all and in all." And if any one imagine that at the end material, i.e., bodily, nature will be entirely destroyed, he cannot in any respect meet my view, how beings so numerous and powerful are able to live and to exist without bodies, since it is an attribute of the divine nature alone — i.e., of the Father, Son, and Holy Spirit — to exist without any material substance, and without partaking in any degree of a bodily adjunct. Another, perhaps, may say that in the end every bodily substance will be so pure and refined as to be like the æther, and of a celestial purity and clearness. How things will be, however, is known with certainty to God alone, and to those who are His friends through Christ and the Holy Spirit.[3]

[1] 1 Cor. vii. 31.
[2] Ps. cii. 26.
[3] [The language used by Origen in this and the preceding chapter affords a remarkable illustration of that occasional extravagance in statements of facts and opinions, as well as of those strange imaginings and wild speculations as to the meaning of Holy Scripture, which brought upon him subsequently grave charges of error and heretical pravity. See Neander's *History of the Christian Religion and Church during the First Three Centuries* (Rose's translation), vol. ii. p. 217 et seqq., and Hagenbach's *History of Doctrines*, vol. i. p. 102 et seqq. See also *Prefatory Note to Origen's Works, supra*, p. 235. S.]

CHAP. VII. — ON INCORPOREAL AND CORPOREAL BEINGS.

1. The subjects considered in the previous chapter have been spoken of in general language, the nature of rational beings being discussed more by way of intelligent inference than strict dogmatic definition, with the exception of the place where we treated, to the best of our ability, of the persons of Father, Son, and Holy Spirit. We have now to ascertain what those matters are which it is proper to treat in the following pages according to our dogmatic belief, i.e., in agreement with the creed of the Church. All souls and all rational natures, whether holy or wicked, were formed or created, and all these, according to their proper nature, are incorporeal ; but although incorporeal, they were nevertheless created, because all things were made by God through Christ, as John teaches in a general way in his Gospel, saying, " In the beginning was the Word, and the Word was with God, and the Word was God. The same was in the beginning with God. All things were made by Him, and without Him was nothing made." [4] The Apostle Paul, moreover, describing created things by species and numbers and orders, speaks as follows, when showing that all things were made through Christ : " And in Him were all things created, that are in heaven, and that are in earth, visible and invisible, whether they be thrones, or dominions, or principalities, or powers : all things were created by Him, and in Him : and He is before all, and He is the head." [5] He therefore manifestly declares that in Christ and through Christ were all things made and created, whether things visible, which are corporeal, or things invisible, which I regard as none other than incorporeal and spiritual powers. But of those things which he had termed generally corporeal or incorporeal, he seems to me, in the words that follow, to enumerate the various kinds, viz., thrones, dominions, principalities, powers, influences.

These matters now have been previously mentioned by us, as we are desirous to come in an orderly manner to the investigation of the sun, and moon, and stars by way of logical inference, and to ascertain whether they also ought properly to be reckoned among the principalities on account of their being said to be created in Ἀρχάς, i.e., for the government of day and night ; or whether they are to be regarded as having only that government of day and night which they discharge by performing the office of illuminating them, and are not in reality chief of that order of principalities.

2. Now, when it is said that all things were

[4] John i. 1-3.
[5] Col. i. 16-18.

made by Him, and that in Him were all things created, both things in heaven and things on earth, there can be no doubt that also those things which are in the firmament, which is called heaven, and in which those luminaries are said to be placed, are included amongst the number of heavenly things. And secondly, seeing that the course of the discussion has manifestly discovered that all things were made or created, and that amongst created things there is nothing which may not admit of good and evil, and be capable of either, what are we to think of the following opinion which certain of our friends entertain regarding sun, moon, and stars, viz., that they are unchangeable, and incapable of becoming the opposite of what they are? Not a few have held that view even regarding the holy angels, and certain heretics also regarding souls, which they call spiritual natures.

In the first place, then, let us see what reason itself can discover respecting sun, moon, and stars, — whether the opinion, entertained by some, of their unchangeableness be correct, — and let the declarations of holy Scripture, as far as possible, be first adduced. For Job appears to assert that not only may the stars be subject to sin, but even that they are actually not clean from the contagion of it. The following are his words: "The stars also are not clean in Thy sight."[1] Nor is this to be understood of the splendour of their physical substance, as if one were to say, for example, of a garment, that it is not clean; for if such were the meaning, then the accusation of a want of cleanness in the splendour of their bodily substance would imply an injurious reflection upon their Creator. For if they are unable, through their own diligent efforts, either to acquire for themselves a body of greater brightness, or through their sloth to make the one they have less pure, how should they incur censure for being stars that are not clean, if they receive no praise because they are so?[2]

3. But to arrive at a clearer understanding on these matters, we ought first to inquire after this point, whether it is allowable to suppose that they are living and rational beings; then, in the next place, whether their souls came into existence at the same time with their bodies, or seem to be anterior to them; and also whether, after the end of the world, we are to understand that they are to be released from their bodies; and whether, as we cease to live, so they also will cease from illuminating the world. Although this inquiry may seem to be somewhat bold, yet, as we are incited by the desire of ascertaining the truth as far as possible, there seems no

absurdity in attempting an investigation of the subject agreeably to the grace of the Holy Spirit.

We think, then, that they may be designated as living beings, for this reason, that they are said to receive commandments from God, which is ordinarily the case only with rational beings. "I have given a commandment to all the stars,"[3] says the Lord. What, now, are these commandments? Those, namely, that each star, in its order and course, should bestow upon the world the amount of splendour which has been entrusted to it. For those which are called "planets" move in orbits of one kind, and those which are termed ἀπλανεῖς are different. Now it manifestly follows from this, that neither can the movement of that body take place without a soul, nor can living things be at any time without motion. And seeing that the stars move with such order and regularity, that their movements never appear to be at any time subject to derangement, would it not be the height of folly to say that so orderly an observance of method and plan could be carried out or accomplished by irrational beings? In the writings of Jeremiah, indeed, the moon is called the queen of heaven.[4] Yet if the stars are living and rational beings, there will undoubtedly appear among them both an advance and a falling back. For the language of Job, "the stars are not clean in His sight," seems to me to convey some such idea.

4. And now we have to ascertain whether those beings which in the course of the discussion we have discovered to possess life and reason, were endowed with a soul along with their bodies at the time mentioned in Scripture, when "God made two great lights, the greater light to rule the day, and the lesser light to rule the night, and the stars also,"[5] or whether their spirit was implanted in them, not at the creation of their bodies, but from without, after they had been already made. I, for my part, suspect that the spirit was implanted in them from without; but it will be worth while to prove this from Scripture: for it will seem an easy matter to make the assertion on conjectural grounds, while it is more difficult to establish it by the testimony of Scripture. Now it may be established conjecturally as follows. If the soul of a man, which is certainly inferior while it remains the soul of a man, was not formed along with his body, but is proved to have been implanted strictly from without, much more must this be the case with those living beings which are called heavenly. For, as regards man, how could the soul of him, viz., Jacob, who supplanted his brother in the womb, appear to be formed along with his body? Or how could his soul, or its

---

[1] Job xxv. 5.
[2] [See note, *supra*, p. 262. S.]

[3] Isa. xlv. 12.
[4] Jer. vii. 18.
[5] Gen. i. 16.

images, be formed along with his body, who, while lying in his mother's womb, was filled with the Holy Ghost? I refer to John leaping in his mother's womb, and exulting because the voice of the salutation of Mary had come to the ears of his mother Elisabeth. How could his soul and its images be formed along with his body, who, before he was created in the womb, is said to be known to God, and was sanctified by Him before his birth? Some, perhaps, may think that God fills individuals with His Holy Spirit, and bestows upon them sanctification, not on grounds of justice and according to their deserts, but undeservedly. And how shall we escape that declaration: "Is there unrighteousness with God? God forbid!"[1] or this: "Is there respect of persons with God?"[2] For such is the defence of those who maintain that souls come into existence with bodies. So far, then, as we can form an opinion from a comparison with the condition of man, I think it follows that we must hold the same to hold good with heavenly beings, which reason itself and scriptural authority show us to be the case with men.

5. But let us see whether we can find in holy Scripture any indications properly applicable to these heavenly existences. The following is the statement of the Apostle Paul: "The creature was made subject to vanity, not willingly, but by reason of Him who subjected the same in hope, because the creature itself also shall be delivered from the bondage of corruption into the glorious liberty of the children of God."[3] To what vanity, pray, was the creature made subject, or what creature is referred to, or how is it said "not willingly," or "in hope of what?" And in what way is the creature itself to be delivered from the bondage of corruption? Elsewhere, also, the same apostle says: "For the expectation of the creature waiteth for the manifestation of the sons of God."[4] And again in another passage, "And not only we, but the creation itself groaneth together, and is in pain until now."[5] And hence we have to inquire what are the groanings, and what are the pains. Let us see then, in the first place, what is the vanity to which the creature is subject. I apprehend that it is nothing else than the body; for although the body of the stars is ethereal, it is nevertheless material. Whence also Solomon appears to characterize the whole of corporeal nature as a kind of burden which enfeebles the vigour of the soul in the following language: "Vanity of vanities, saith the Preacher; all is vanity. I have looked, and seen all the works that are done under the sun; and, behold, all is vanity."[6] To this vanity, then, is the creature subject, that creature especially which, being assuredly the greatest in this world, holds also a distinguished principality of labour, i.e., the sun, and moon, and stars, are said to be subject to vanity, because they are clothed with bodies, and set apart to the office of giving light to the human race. "And this creature," he remarks, "was subjected to vanity not willingly." For it did not undertake a voluntary service to vanity, but because it was the will of Him who made it subject, and because of the promise of the Subjector to those who were reduced to this unwilling obedience, that when the ministry of their great work was performed, they were to be freed from this bondage of corruption and vanity when the time of the glorious redemption of God's children should have arrived. And the whole of creation, receiving this hope, and looking for the fulfilment of this promise now, in the meantime, as having an affection for those whom it serves, groans along with them, and patiently suffers with them, hoping for the fulfilment of the promises. See also whether the following words of Paul can apply to those who, although not willingly, yet in accordance with the will of Him who subjected them, and in hope of the promises, were made subject to vanity, when he says, "For I could wish to be dissolved," or "to return and be with Christ, which is far better."[7] For I think that the sun might say in like manner, "I would desire to be dissolved," or "to return and be with Christ, which is far better." Paul indeed adds, "Nevertheless, to abide in the flesh is more needful for you;" while the sun may say, "To abide in this bright and heavenly body is more necessary, on account of the manifestation of the sons of God." The same views are to be believed and expressed regarding the moon and stars.

Let us see now what is the freedom of the creature, or the termination of its bondage. When Christ shall have delivered up the kingdom to God even the Father, then also those living things, when they shall have first been made the kingdom of Christ, shall be delivered, along with the whole of that kingdom, to the rule of the Father, that when God shall be all in all, they also, since they are a part of all things, may have God in themselves, as He is in all things.

CHAP. VIII. — ON THE ANGELS.

1. A similar method must be followed in treating of the angels; nor are we to suppose that it is the result of accident that a particular office is assigned to a particular angel: as to

1 Rom. ix. 14.
2 Rom. ii. 11.
3 Cf. Rom. viii. 20, 21.
4 Rom. viii. 19.
5 Rom. viii. 22, cf. 23.
6 Eccles. i. 1, 14.
7 Phil. i. 23.

Raphael, e.g., the work of curing and healing; to Gabriel, the conduct of wars; to Michael, the duty of attending to the prayers and supplications of mortals. For we are not to imagine that they obtained these offices otherwise than by their own merits, and by the zeal and excellent qualities which they severally displayed before this world was formed; so that afterwards, in the order of archangels, this or that office was assigned to each one, while others deserved to be enrolled in the order of angels, and to act under this or that archangel, or that leader or head of an order. All of which things were disposed, as I have said, not indiscriminately and fortuitously, but by a most appropriate and just decision of God, who arranged them according to deserts, in accordance with His own approval and judgment: so that to one angel the Church of the Ephesians was to be entrusted; to another, that of the Smyrnæans; one angel was to be Peter's, another Paul's; and so on through every one of the little ones that are in the Church, for such and such angels as even daily behold the face of God must be assigned to each one of them; [1] and there must also be some angel that encampeth round about them that fear God. [2] All of which things, assuredly, it is to be believed, are not performed by accident or chance, or because they (the angels) were so created, lest on that view the Creator should be accused of partiality; but it is to be believed that they were conferred by God, the just and impartial Ruler of all things, agreeably to the merits and good qualities and mental vigour of each individual spirit.

2. And now let us say something regarding those who maintain the existence of a diversity of spiritual natures, that we may avoid falling into the silly and impious fables of such as pretend that there is a diversity of spiritual natures both among heavenly existences and human souls, and for that reason allege that they were called into being by different creators; for while it seems, and is really, absurd that to one and the same Creator should be ascribed the creation of different natures of rational beings, they are nevertheless ignorant of the cause of that diversity. For they say that it seems inconsistent for one and the same Creator, without any existing ground of merit, to confer upon some beings the power of dominion, and to subject others again to authority; to bestow a principality upon some, and to render others subordinate to rulers. Which opinions indeed, in my judgment, are completely rejected by following out the reasoning explained above, and by which

it was shown that the cause of the diversity and variety among these beings is due to their conduct, which has been marked either with greater earnestness or indifference, according to the goodness or badness of their nature, and not to any partiality on the part of the Disposer. But that this may more easily be shown to be the case with heavenly beings, let us borrow an illustration from what either has been done or is done among men, in order that from visible things we may, by way of consequence, behold also things invisible.

Paul and Peter are undoubtedly proved to have been men of a spiritual nature. When, therefore, Paul is found to have acted contrary to religion, in having persecuted the Church of God, and Peter to have committed so grave a sin as, when questioned by the maid-servant, to have asserted with an oath that he did not know who Christ was, how is it possible that these — who, according to those persons of whom we speak, were spiritual beings — should fall into sins of such a nature, especially as they are frequently in the habit of saying that a good tree cannot bring forth evil fruits? And if a good tree cannot produce evil fruit, and as, according to them, Peter and Paul were sprung from the root of a good tree, how should they be deemed to have brought forth fruits so wicked? And if they should return the answer which is generally invented, that it was not Paul who persecuted, but some other person, I know not whom, who was in Paul; and that it was not Peter who uttered the denial, but some other individual in him; how should Paul say, if he had not sinned, that "I am not worthy to be called an apostle, because I persecuted the Church of God?" [3] Or why did Peter weep most bitterly, if it were another than he who sinned? From which all their silly assertions will be proved to be baseless.

3. According to our view, there is no rational creature which is not capable both of good and evil. But it does not follow, that because we say there is no nature which may not admit evil, we therefore maintain that every nature has admitted evil, i.e., has become wicked. As we may say that the nature of every man admits of his being a sailor, but it does not follow from that, that every man will become so; or, again, it is possible for every one to learn grammar or medicine, but it is not therefore proved that every man is either a physician or a grammarian; so, if we say that there is no nature which may not admit evil, it is not necessarily indicated that it has done so. For, in our view, not even the devil himself was incapable of good; but although capable of admitting good, he did not therefore also desire it, or make any effort after virtue.

---

[1] Matt. xviii. 10.
[2] Ps. xxxiv. 7. Tum demun per singulos minimorum, qui sunt in ecclesiâ, qui vel qui adscribi singulis debeant angeli, qui etiam quotidie videant faciem Dei; sed et quis debeat esse angelus, qui circumdet in circuitu timentium Deum.

[3] 1 Cor. xv. 9.

For, as we are taught by those quotations which we adduced from the prophets, there was once a time when he was good, when he walked in the paradise of God between the cherubim. As he, then, possessed the power either of receiving good or evil, but fell away from a virtuous course, and turned to evil with all the powers of his mind, so also other creatures, as having a capacity for either condition, in the exercise of the freedom of their will, flee from evil, and cleave to good. There is no nature, then, which may not admit of good or evil, except the nature of God — the fountain of all good things — and of Christ; for it is wisdom, and wisdom assuredly cannot admit folly; and it is righteousness, and righteousness will never certainly admit of unrighteousness; and it is the Word, or Reason, which certainly cannot be made irrational; nay, it is also the light, and it is certain that the darkness does not receive the light. In like manner, also, the nature of the Holy Spirit, being holy, does not admit of pollution; for it is holy by nature, or essential being. If there is any other nature which is holy, it possesses this property of being made hŏly by the reception or inspiration of the Holy Spirit, not having it by nature, but as an accidental quality, for which reason it may be lost, in consequence of being accidental. So also a man may possess an accidental righteousness, from which it is possible for him to fall away. Even the wisdom which a man has is still accidental, although it be within our own power to become wise, if we devote ourselves to wisdom with the zeal and effort of our life; and if we always pursue the study of it, we may always be participators of wisdom: and that result will follow either in a greater or less degree, according to the desert of our life or the amount of our zeal. For the goodness of God, as is worthy of Him, incites and attracts all to that blissful end, where all pain, and sadness, and sorrow fall away and disappear.

4. I am of opinion, then, so far as appears to me, that the preceding discussion has sufficiently proved that it is neither from want of discrimination, nor from any accidental cause, either that the "principalities" hold their dominion, or the other orders of spirits have obtained their respective offices; but that they have received the steps of their rank on account of their merits, although it is not our privilege to know or inquire what those acts of theirs were, by which they earned a place in any particular order. It is sufficient only to know this much, in order to demonstrate the impartiality and righteousness of God, that, conformably with the declaration of the Apostle Paul, "there is no acceptance of persons with Him,"[1] who rather disposes every-

thing according to the deserts and moral progress of each individual. So, then, the angelic office does not exist except as a consequence of their desert; nor do "powers" exercise power except in virtue of their moral progress; nor do those which are called "seats," i.e., the powers of judging and ruling, administer their powers unless by merit; nor do "dominions" rule undeservedly, for that great and distinguished order of rational creatures among celestial existences is arranged in a glorious variety of offices. And the same view is to be entertained of those opposing influences which have given themselves up to such places and offices, that they derive the property by which they are made "principalities," or "powers," or rulers of the darkness of the world, or spirits of wickedness, or malignant spirits, or unclean demons, not from their essential nature, nor from their being so created, but have obtained these degrees in evil in proportion to their conduct, and the progress which they made in wickedness. And that is a second order of rational creatures, who have devoted themselves to wickedness in so headlong a course, that they are unwilling rather than unable to recall themselves; the thirst for evil being already a passion, and imparting to them pleasure. But the third order of rational creatures is that of those who are judged fit by God to replenish the human race, i.e., the souls of men, assumed in consequence of their moral progress into the order of angels; of whom we see some assumed into the number: those, viz., who have been made the sons of God, or the children of the resurrection, or who have abandoned the darkness, and have loved the light, and have been made children of the light; or those who, proving victorious in every struggle, and being made men of peace, have been the sons of peace, and the sons of God; or those who, mortifying their members on the earth, and, rising above not only their corporeal nature, but even the uncertain and fragile movements of the soul itself, have united themselves to the Lord, being made altogether spiritual, that they may be for ever one spirit with Him, discerning along with Him each individual thing, until they arrive at a condition of perfect spirituality, and discern all things by their perfect illumination in all holiness through the word and wisdom of God, and are themselves altogether undistinguishable by any one.

We think that those views are by no means to be admitted, which some are wont unnecessarily to advance and maintain, viz., that souls descend to such a pitch of abasement that they forget their rational nature and dignity, and sink into the condition of irrational animals, either large or small; and in support of these assertions they generally quote some pretended statements of Scripture, such as, that a beast, to which a

---

[1] Cf. Rom. ii. 11.

woman has unnaturally prostituted herself, shall be deemed equally guilty with the woman, and shall be ordered to be stoned ; or that a bull which strikes with its horn,[1] shall be put to death in the same way ; or even the speaking of Balaam's ass, when God opened its mouth, and the dumb beast of burden, answering with human voice, reproved the madness of the prophet. All of which assertions we not only do not receive, but, as being contrary to our belief, we refute and reject. After the refutation and rejection of such perverse opinions, we shall show, at the proper time and place, how those passages which they quote from the sacred Scriptures ought to be understood.

FRAGMENT FROM THE FIRST BOOK OF THE DE PRINCIPIIS.

Translated by Jerome in his Epistle to Avitus.

"It is an evidence of great negligence and sloth, that each one should fall down to such (a pitch of degradation), and be so emptied, as that, in coming to evil, he may be fastened to the gross body of irrational beasts of burden."

ANOTHER FRAGMENT FROM THE SAME.

Translated in the same Epistle to Avitus.

"At the end and consummation of the world, when souls and rational creatures shall have been sent forth as from bolts and barriers,[2] some of them walk slowly on account of their slothful habits, others fly with rapid flight on account of their diligence. And since all are possessed of free-will, and may of their own accord admit either of good or evil, the former will be in a worse condition than they are at present, while the latter will advance to a better state of things ; because different conduct and varying wills will admit of a different condition in either direction, i.e., angels may become men or demons, and again from the latter they may rise to be men or angels."

---

[1] [See Exod. xxi. 28, 29　S.]

[2] De quibusdam repagulis atque carceribus. There is an allusion here to the race-course and the mode of starting the chariots.

ORIGEN DE PRINCIPIIS.

BOOK II.

CHAP. I. — ON THE WORLD.

1. ALTHOUGH all the discussions in the preceding book have had reference to the world and its arrangements, it now seems to follow tnat we should specially re-discuss a few points respecting the world itself, i.e., its beginning and end, or those dispensations of Divine Providence which have taken place between the beginning and the end, or those events which are supposed to have occurred before the creation of the world, or are to take place after the end.

In this investigation, the first point which clearly appears is, that the world in all its diversified and varying conditions is composed not only of rational and diviner natures, and of a diversity of bodies, but of dumb animals, wild and tame beasts, of birds, and of all things which live in the waters ;[1] then, secondly, of places, i.e., of the heaven or heavens, and of the earth or water, as well as of the air, which is intermediate, and which they term æther, and of everything which proceeds from the earth or is born in it. Seeing, then,[2] there is so great a variety in the world, and so great a diversity among rational beings themselves, on account of which every other variety and diversity also is supposed to have come into existence, what other cause than this ought to be assigned for the existence of the world, especially if we have regard to that end by means of which it was shown in the preceding book that all things are to be restored to their original condition? And if this should seem to be logically stated, what other cause, as we have already said, are we to imagine for so great a diversity in the world, save the diversity and variety in the movements and declensions of those who fell from that primeval unity and harmony in which they were at first created by God, and who, being driven from that state of goodness, and drawn in various directions by the harassing influence of different motives and desires, have changed, according to their different tendencies, the single and undivided goodness of their nature into minds of various sorts?[3]

2. But God, by the ineffable skill of His wisdom, transforming and restoring all things, in whatever manner they are made, to some useful aim, and to the common advantage of all, recalls those very creatures which differed so much from each other in mental conformation to one agreement of labour and purpose ; so that, although they are under the influence of different motives, they nevertheless complete the fulness and perfection of one world, and the very variety of minds tends to one end of perfection. For it is one power which grasps and holds together all the diversity of the world, and leads the different movements towards one work, lest so immense an undertaking as that of the world should be dissolved by the dissensions of souls. And for this reason we think that God, the Father of all things, in order to ensure the salvation of all His creatures through the ineffable plan of His word and wisdom, so arranged each of these, that every spirit, whether soul or rational existence, however called, should not be compelled by force, against the liberty of his own will, to any other course than that to which the motives of his own mind led him (lest by so doing the power of exercising free-will should seem to be taken away, which certainly would produce a change in the nature of the being itself) ; and that the varying purposes of these would be suitably and usefully adapted to the harmony of one world, by some of them requiring help, and others being able to give it, and others again being the cause of struggle and contest to those who are making progress, amongst whom their diligence

---

[1] The words " in aquis " are omitted in Redepenning's edition.

[2] The original of this sentence is found at the close of the Emperor Justinian's Epistle to Menas, patriarch of Constantinople, and, literally translated, is as follows: " The world being so very varied, and containing so many different rational beings, what else ought we to say was the cause of its existence than the diversity of the falling away of those who decline from unity (τῆς ἑνάδος) in different ways?" — Ruæus. Lommatzsch adds a clause not contained in the note of the Benedictine editor: " And sometimes the soul selects the life that is in water" (ἔνυδρον).

[3] Lit. " into various qualities of mind."

would be deemed more worthy of approval, and the place of rank obtained after victory be held with greater certainty, which should be established by the difficulties of the contest.[1]

3. Although the whole world is arranged into offices of different kinds, its condition, nevertheless, is not to be supposed as one of internal discrepancies and discordances; but as our one body is provided with many members, and is held together by one soul, so I am of opinion that the whole world also ought to be regarded as some huge and immense animal, which is kept together by the power and reason of God as by one soul. This also, I think, is indicated in sacred Scripture by the declaration of the prophet, "Do not I fill heaven and earth? saith the Lord;"[2] and again, "The heaven is My throne, and the earth is My footstool;"[3] and by the Saviour's words, when He says that we are to swear "neither by heaven, for it is God's throne; nor by the earth, for it is His footstool."[4] To the same effect also are the words of Paul, in his address to the Athenians, when he says, "In Him we live, and move, and have our being."[5] For how do we live, and move, and have our being in God, except by His comprehending and holding together the whole world by His power? And how is heaven the throne of God, and the earth His footstool, as the Saviour Himself declares, save by His power filling all things both in heaven and earth, according to the Lord's own words? And that God, the Father of all things, fills and holds together the world with the fulness of His power, according to those passages which we have quoted, no one, I think, will have any difficulty in admitting. And now, since the course of the preceding discussion has shown that the different movements of rational beings, and their varying opinions, have brought about the diversity that is in the world, we must see whether it may not be appropriate that this world should have a termination like its beginning. For there is no doubt that its end must be sought amid much diversity and variety; which variety, being found to exist in the termination of the world, will again furnish ground and occasion for the diversities of the other world which is to succeed the present.

4. If now, in the course of our discussion, it has been ascertained that these things are so, it seems to follow that we next consider the nature of corporeal being, seeing the diversity in the world cannot exist without bodies. It is evident from the nature of things themselves, that bodily nature admits of diversity and variety of change, so that it is capable of undergoing all possible transformations, as, e.g., the conversion of wood into fire, of fire into smoke, of smoke into air, of oil into fire. Does not food itself, whether of man or of animals, exhibit the same ground of change? For whatever we take as food, is converted into the substance of our body. But how water is changed into earth or into air, and air again into fire, or fire into air, or air into water, although not difficult to explain, yet on the present occasion it is enough merely to mention them, as our object is to discuss the nature of bodily matter. By matter, therefore, we understand that which is placed under bodies, viz., that by which, through the bestowing and implanting of qualities, bodies exist; and we mention four qualities—heat, cold, dryness, humidity. These four qualities being implanted in the ὕλη, or matter (for matter is found to exist in its own nature without those qualities before mentioned), produce the different kinds of bodies. Although this matter is, as we have said above, according to its own proper nature without qualities, it is never found to exist without a quality. And I cannot understand how so many distinguished men have been of opinion that this matter, which is so great, and possesses such properties as to enable it to be sufficient for all the bodies in the world which God willed to exist, and to be the attendant and slave of the Creator for whatever forms and species He wished in all things, receiving into itself whatever qualities He desired to bestow upon it, was uncreated, i.e., not formed by God Himself, who is the Creator of all things, but that its nature and power were the result of chance. And I am astonished that they should find fault with those who deny either God's creative power or His providential administration of the world, and accuse them of impiety for thinking that so great a work as the world could exist without an architect or overseer; while they themselves incur a similar charge of impiety in saying that matter is uncreated, and co-eternal with the uncreated God. According to this view, then, if we suppose for the sake of argument that matter did not exist, as these maintain, saying that God could not create anything when nothing existed, without doubt He would have been idle, not having matter on which to operate, which matter they say was furnished Him not by His own arrangement, but by accident; and they think that this, which was discovered by chance, was able to suffice Him for an undertaking of so vast an extent, and for the manifestation of the power of His might, and by admitting the plan of all His wisdom, might be distinguished and formed into a world. Now this appears to me to be very absurd, and to be

---

[1] "Et diversi motus propositi earum (rationabilium subsistentiarum) ad unius mundi consonantiam competenter atque utiliter aptarentur, dum aliæ juvari indigent, aliæ juvare possunt, aliæ vero proficientibus certamina atque agones movent, in quibus eorum probabilior haberetur industria, et certior post victoriam reparati gradus statio teneretur, quæ per difficultates laborantium constituisset."

[2] Jer. xxiii. 24.
[3] Isa. lxvi. 1.
[4] Matt. v. 34.
[5] Acts xvii. 28.

the opinion of those men who are altogether ignorant of the power and intelligence of uncreated nature. But that we may see the nature of things a little more clearly, let it be granted that for a little time matter did not exist, and that God, when nothing formerly existed, caused those things to come into existence which He desired, why are we to suppose that God would create matter either better or greater, or of another kind, than that which He did produce from His own power and wisdom, in order that that might exist which formerly did not? Would He create a worse and inferior matter, or one the same as that which they call uncreated? Now I think it will very easily appear to any one, that neither a better nor inferior matter could have assumed the forms and species of the world, if it had not been such as that which actually did assume them. And does it not then seem impious to call that uncreated, which, if believed to be formed by God, would doubtless be found to be such as that which they call uncreated?

5. But that we may believe on the authority of holy Scripture that such is the case, hear how in the book of Maccabees, where the mother of seven martyrs exhorts her son to endure torture, this truth is confirmed; for she says, " I ask of thee, my son, to look at the heaven and the earth, and at all things which are in them, and beholding these, to know that God made all these things when they did not exist." [1] In the book of the Shepherd also, in the first commandment, he speaks as follows: " First of all believe that there is one God who created and arranged all things, and made all things to come into existence, and out of a state of nothingness." [2] Perhaps also the expression in the Psalms has reference to this: " He spake, and they were made; He commanded, and they were created." [3] For the words, " He spake, and they were made," appear to show that the substance of those things which exist is meant; while the others, " He commanded, and they were created," seem spoken of the qualities by which the substance itself has been moulded.

CHAP. II. — ON THE PERPETUITY OF BODILY NATURE.

1. On this topic some are wont to inquire whether, as the Father generates an uncreated Son, and brings forth a Holy Spirit, not as if He had no previous existence, but because the Father is the origin and source of the Son or Holy Spirit, and no anteriority or posteriority can be understood as existing in them; so also

a similar kind of union or relationship can be understood as subsisting between rational natures and bodily matter. And that this point may be more fully and thoroughly examined, the commencement of the discussion is generally directed to the inquiry whether this very bodily nature, which bears the lives and contains the movements of spiritual and rational minds, will be equally eternal with them, or will altogether perish and be destroyed. And that the question may be determined with greater precision, we have, in the first place, to inquire if it is possible for rational natures to remain altogether incorporeal after they have reached the summit of holiness and happiness (which seems to me a most difficult and almost impossible attainment), or whether they must always of necessity be united to bodies. If, then, any one could show a reason why it was possible for them to dispense wholly with bodies, it will appear to follow, that as a bodily nature, created out of nothing after intervals of time, was produced when it did not exist, so also it must cease to be when the purposes which it served had no longer an existence.

2. If, however, it is impossible for this point to be at all maintained, viz., that any other nature than the Father, Son, and Holy Spirit can live without a body, the necessity of logical reasoning compels us to understand that rational natures were indeed created at the beginning, but that material substance was separated from them only in thought and understanding, and appears to have been formed for them, or after them, and that they never have lived nor do live without it; for an incorporeal life will rightly be considered a prerogative of the Trinity alone. As we have remarked above, therefore, that material substance of this world, possessing a nature admitting of all possible transformations, is, when dragged down to beings of a lower order, moulded into the crasser and more solid condition of a body, so as to distinguish those visible and varying forms of the world; but when it becomes the servant of more perfect and more blessed beings, it shines in the splendour of celestial bodies, and adorns either the angels of God or the sons of the resurrection with the clothing of a spiritual body, out of all which will be filled up the diverse and varying state of the one world. But if any one should desire to discuss these matters more fully, it will be necessary, with all reverence and fear of God, to examine the sacred Scriptures with greater attention and diligence, to ascertain whether the secret and hidden sense within them may perhaps reveal anything regarding these matters; and something may be discovered in their abstruse and mysterious language, through the demonstration of the Holy Spirit to those who

---

[1] 2 Mac. vii. 28.
[2] *Hermæ Past.*, book ii. [See vol. ii. p. 20, of this series.　S.]
[3] Ps. cxlviii. 5.

are worthy, after many testimonies have been collected on this very point.

CHAP. III. — ON THE BEGINNING OF THE WORLD, AND ITS CAUSES.

1. The next subject of inquiry is, whether there was any other world before the one which now exists; and if so, whether it was such as the present, or somewhat different, or inferior; or whether there was no world at all, but something like that which we understand will be after the end of all things, when the kingdom shall be delivered up to God, even the Father; which nevertheless may have been the end of another world, — of that, namely, after which this world took its beginning; and whether the various lapses of intellectual natures provoked God to produce this diverse and varying condition of the world. This point also, I think, must be investigated in a similar way, viz., whether after this world there will be any (system of) preservation and amendment, severe indeed, and attended with much pain to those who were unwilling to obey the word of God, but a process through which, by means of instruction and rational training, those may arrive at a fuller understanding of the truth who have devoted themselves in the present life to these pursuits, and who, after having had their minds purified, have advanced onwards so as to become capable of attaining divine wisdom; and after this the end of all things will immediately follow, and there will be again, for the correction and improvement of those who stand in need of it, another world, either resembling that which now exists, or better than it, or greatly inferior; and how long that world, whatever it be that is to come after this, shall continue; and if there will be a time when no world shall anywhere exist, or if there has been a time when there was no world at all; or if there have been, or will be several; or if it shall ever come to pass that there will be one resembling another, like it in every respect, and indistinguishable from it.

2. That it may appear more clearly, then, whether bodily matter can exist during intervals of time, and whether, as it did not exist before it was made, so it may again be resolved into non-existence, let us see, first of all, whether it is possible for any one to live without a body. For if one person can live without a body, all things also may dispense with them; seeing our former treatise has shown that all things tend towards one end. Now, if all things may exist without bodies, there will undoubtedly be no bodily substance, seeing there will be no use for it. But how shall we understand the words of the apostle in those passages, in which, discussing the resurrection of the dead, he says, "This corruptible must put on incorruption, and this

mortal must put on immortality. When this corruptible shall have put on incorruption, and this mortal shall have put on immortality, then shall be brought to pass the saying which is written, Death is swallowed up in victory! Where, O death, is thy victory? O death, thy sting has been swallowed up: the sting of death is sin, and the strength of sin is the law." [1] Some such meaning, then, as this, seems to be suggested by the apostle. For can the expression which he employs, "this corruptible," and "this mortal," with the gesture, as it were, of one who touches or points out, apply to anything else than to bodily matter? This matter of the body, then, which is now corruptible shall put on incorruption when a perfect soul, and one furnished with the marks [2] of incorruption, shall have begun to inhabit it. And do not be surprised if we speak of a perfect soul as the clothing of the body (which, on account of the Word of God and His wisdom, is now named incorruption), when Jesus Christ Himself, who is the Lord and Creator of the soul, is said to be the clothing of the saints, according to the language of the apostle, "Put ye on the Lord Jesus Christ." [3] As Christ, then, is the clothing of the soul, so for a kind of reason sufficiently intelligible is the soul said to be the clothing of the body, seeing it is an ornament to it, covering and concealing its mortal nature. The expression, then, "This corruptible must put on incorruption," is as if the apostle had said, "This corruptible nature of the body must receive the clothing of incorruption — a soul possessing in itself incorruptibility," because it has been clothed with Christ, who is the Wisdom and Word of God. But when this body, which at some future period we shall possess in a more glorious state, shall have become a partaker of life, it will then, in addition to being immortal, become also incorruptible. For whatever is mortal is necessarily also corruptible; but whatever is corruptible cannot also be said to be mortal. We say of a stone or a piece of wood that it is corruptible, but we do not say that it follows that it is also mortal. But as the body partakes of life, then because life may be, and is, separated from it, we consequently name it mortal, and according to another sense also we speak of it as corruptible. The holy apostle therefore, with remarkable insight, referring to the general first cause of bodily matter, of which (matter), whatever be the qualities with which it is endowed (now indeed carnal, but by and by more refined and pure, which are termed spiritual), the soul makes constant use, says,

---

[1] 1 Cor. xv. 53–56; cf. Hos. xiii. 14 and Isa. xxv. 8.
[2] Dogmatibus. Schnitzer says that "dogmatibus" here yields no sense. He conjectures δείγμασι, and renders "proofs," "marks."
[3] Rom. xiii. 14.

"This corruptible must put on incorruption." And in the second place, looking to the special cause of the body, he says, "This mortal must put on immortality." Now, what else will incorruption and immortality be, save the wisdom, and the word, and the righteousness of God, which mould, and clothe, and adorn the soul? And hence it happens that it is said, "The corruptible will put on incorruption, and the mortal immortality." For although we may now make great proficiency, yet as we only know in part, and prophesy in part, and see through a glass, darkly, those very things which we seem to understand, this corruptible does not yet put on incorruption, nor is this mortal yet clothed with immortality; and as this training of ours in the body is protracted doubtless to a longer period, up to the time, viz., when those very bodies of ours with which we are enveloped may, on account of the word of God, and His wisdom and perfect righteousness, earn incorruptibility and immortality, therefore is it said, "This corruptible must put on incorruption, and this mortal must put on immortality."

3. But, nevertheless, those who think that rational creatures can at any time lead an existence out of the body, may here raise such questions as the following. If it is true that this corruptible shall put on incorruption, and this mortal put on immortality, and that death is swallowed up at the end; this shows that nothing else than a material nature is to be destroyed, on which death could operate, while the mental acumen of those who are in the body seems to be blunted by the nature of corporeal matter. If, however, they are out of the body, then they will altogether escape the annoyance arising from a disturbance of that kind. But as they will not be able immediately to escape all bodily clothing, they are just to be considered as inhabiting more refined and purer bodies, which possess the property of being no longer overcome by death, or of being wounded by its sting; so that at last, by the gradual disappearance of the material nature, death is both swallowed up, and even at the end exterminated, and all its sting completely blunted by the divine grace which the soul has been rendered capable of receiving, and has thus deserved to obtain incorruptibility and immortality. And then it will be deservedly said by all, "O death, where is thy victory? O death, where is thy sting? The sting of death is sin." If these conclusions, then, seem to hold good, it follows that we must believe our condition at some future time to be incorporeal; and if this is admitted, and all are said to be subjected to Christ, this (incorporeity) also must necessarily be bestowed on all to whom the subjection to Christ extends; since all who are subject to Christ will be in the end subject to God the Father, to whom Christ is said to deliver up the kingdom; and thus it appears that then also the need of bodies will cease.[1] And if it ceases, bodily matter returns to nothing, as formerly also it did not exist.

Now let us see what can be said in answer to those who make these assertions. For it will appear to be a necessary consequence that, if bodily nature be annihilated, it must be again restored and created; since it seems a possible thing that rational natures, from whom the faculty of free-will is never taken away, may be again subjected to movements of some kind, through the special act of the Lord Himself, lest perhaps, if they were always to occupy a condition that was unchangeable, they should be ignorant that it is by the grace of God and not by their own merit that they have been placed in that final state of happiness; and these movements will undoubtedly again be attended by variety and diversity of bodies, by which the world is always adorned; nor will it ever be composed (of anything) save of variety and diversity, — an effect which cannot be produced without a bodily matter.

4. And now I do not understand by what proofs they can maintain their position, who assert that worlds sometimes come into existence which are not dissimilar to each other, but in all respects equal. For if there is said to be a world similar in all respects (to the present), then it will come to pass that Adam and Eve will do the same things which they did before: there will be a second time the same deluge, and the same Moses will again lead a nation numbering nearly six hundred thousand out of Egypt; Judas will also a second time betray the Lord; Paul will a second time keep the garments of those who stoned Stephen; and everything which has been done in this life will be said to be repeated, — a state of things which I think cannot be established by any reasoning, if souls are actuated by freedom of will, and maintain either their advance or retrogression according to the power of their will. For souls are

---

[1] This passage is found in Jerome's *Epistle to Avitus;* and, literally translated, his rendering is as follows: " If these (views) are not contrary to the faith, we shall perhaps at some future time live without bodies. But if he who is perfectly subject to Christ is understood to be without a body, and all are to be subjected to Christ, we also shall be without bodies when we have been completely subjected to Him. If all have been subjected to God, all will lay aside their bodies, and the whole nature of bodily things will be dissolved into nothing; but if, in the second place, necessity shall demand, it will again come into existence on account of the fall of rational creatures. For God has abandoned souls to struggle and wrestling, that they may understand that they have obtained a full and perfect victory, not by their own bravery, but by the grace of God. And therefore I think that for a variety of causes are different worlds created, and the errors of those refuted who contend that worlds resemble each other." A fragment of the Greek original of the above is found in the Epistle of Justinian to the patriarch of Constantinople. " If the things subject to Christ shall at the end be subjected also to God, all will lay aside their bodies; and then, I think, there will be a dissolution (ἀνάλυσις) of the nature of bodies into non-existence (εἰς τὸ μὴ ὄν), to come a second time into existence, if rational (beings) should again gradually come down (ὑποκαταβῇ)."

not driven on in a cycle which returns after many ages to the same round, so as either to do or desire this or that ; but at whatever point the freedom of their own will aims, thither do they direct the course of their actions. For what these persons say is much the same as if one were to assert that if a medimnus of grain were to be poured out on the ground, the fall of the grain would be on the second occasion identically the same as on the first, so that every individual grain would lie for the second time close beside that grain where it had been thrown before, and so the medimnus would be scattered in the same order, and with the same marks as formerly ; which certainly is an impossible result with the countless grains of a medimnus, even if they were to be poured out without ceasing for many ages. So therefore it seems to me impossible for a world to be restored for the second time, with the same order and with the same amount of births, and deaths, and actions ; but that a diversity of worlds may exist with changes of no unimportant kind, so that the state of another world may be for some unmistakeable reasons better (than this), and for others worse, and for others again intermediate. But what may be the number or measure of this I confess myself ignorant, although, if any one can tell it, I would gladly learn.

5. But this world, which is itself called an age, is said to be the conclusion of many ages. Now the holy apostle teaches that in that age which preceded this, Christ did not suffer, nor even in the age which preceded that again ; and I know not that I am able to enumerate the number of anterior ages in which He did not suffer. I will show, however, from what statements of Paul I have arrived at this understanding. He says, "But now once in the consummation of ages, He was manifested to take away sin by the sacrifice of Himself."[1] For He says that He was once made a victim, and in the consummation of ages was manifested to take away sin. Now that after this age, which is said to be formed for the consummation of other ages, there will be other ages again to follow, we have clearly learned from Paul himself, who says, "That in the ages to come He might show the exceeding riches of His grace in His kindness towards us."[2] He has not said, "in the age to come," nor "in the two ages to come," whence I infer that by his language many ages are indicated. Now if there is something greater than ages, so that among created beings certain ages may be understood, but among other beings which exceed and surpass visible creatures, (ages still greater) (which perhaps will be the case at the restitution of all things, when the whole universe will come

to a perfect termination), perhaps that period in which the consummation of all things will take place is to be understood as something more than an age. But here the authority of holy Scripture moves me, which says, "For an age and more."[3] Now this word "more" undoubtedly means something greater than an age ; and see if that expression of the Saviour, "I will that where I am, these also may be with Me ; and as I and Thou are one, these also may be one in Us,"[4] may not seem to convey something more than an age and ages, perhaps even more than ages of ages, — that period, viz., when all things are now no longer in an age, but when God is in all.

6. Having discussed these points regarding the nature of the world to the best of our ability, it does not seem out of place to inquire what is the meaning of the term world, which in holy Scripture is shown frequently to have different significations. For what we call in Latin *mundus*, is termed in Greek κόσμος, and κόσμος signifies not only a world, but also an ornament. Finally, in Isaiah, where the language of reproof is directed to the chief daughters of Sion, and where he says, "Instead of an ornament of a golden head, thou wilt have baldness on account of thy works,"[5] he employs the same term to denote ornament as to denote the world, viz., κόσμος. For the plan of the world is said to be contained in the clothing of the high priest, as we find in the Wisdom of Solomon, where he says, "For in the long garment was the whole world."[6] That earth of ours, with its inhabitants, is also termed the world, as when Scripture says, "The whole world lieth in wickedness."[7] Clement indeed, a disciple of the apostles, makes mention of those whom the Greeks called Ἀντίχθονες, and other parts of the earth, to which no one of our people can approach, nor can any one of those who are there cross over to us, which he also termed worlds, saying, "The ocean is impassable to men ; and those are worlds which are on the other side of it, which are governed by these same arrangements of the ruling God."[8] That universe which is bounded by heaven and earth is also called a world, as Paul declares : "For the fashion of this world will pass away."[9] Our Lord and Saviour also points out a certain other world besides this visible one, which it would indeed be difficult to describe and make known. He says, "I am not of this world."[10] For, as if He were of a certain other world, He

---

[1] Heb. ix. 26.
[2] Eph. ii. 7.

[3] In sæculum et adhuc.
[4] Cf. John xvii. 24, 21, 22.
[5] Cf. Isa. iii. 24. Origen here quotes the Septuagint, which differs both from the Hebrew and the Vulgate: καὶ ἀντὶ τοῦ κόσμου τῆς κεφαλῆς τοῦ χρυσίου φαλάκρωμα ἕξεις διὰ τὰ ἔργά σου.
[6] Wisd. xviii. 24. Poderis, lit. "reaching to the feet."
[7] 1 John v. 19.
[8] Clemens Rom., Ep. i., *ad Cor.*, c. 20. [See vol. i. p. 10, of this series. S.]
[9] 1 Cor. vii. 31.
[10] John xvii. 16.

says, "I am not of this world." Now, of this world we have said beforehand, that the explanation was difficult; and for this reason, that there might not be afforded to any an occasion of entertaining the supposition that we maintain the existence of certain images which the Greeks call "ideas:" for it is certainly alien to our (writers) to speak of an incorporeal world existing in the imagination alone, or in the fleeting world of thoughts; and how they can assert either that the Saviour comes from thence, or that the saints will go thither, I do not see. There is no doubt, however, that something more illustrious and excellent than this present world is pointed out by the Saviour, at which He incites and encourages believers to aim. But whether that world to which He desires to allude be far separated and divided from this, either by situation, or nature, or glory; or whether it be superior in glory and quality, but confined within the limits of this world (which seems to me more probable), is nevertheless uncertain, and in my opinion an unsuitable subject for human thought. But from what Clement seems to indicate when he says, "The ocean is impassable to men, and those worlds which are behind it," speaking in the plural number of the worlds which are behind it, which he intimates are administered and governed by the same providence of the Most High God, he appears to throw out to us some germs of that view by which the whole universe of existing things, celestial and super-celestial, earthly and infernal, is generally called one perfect world, within which, or by which, other worlds, if any there are, must be supposed to be contained. For which reason he wished the globe of the sun or moon, and of the ôther bodies called planets, to be each termed worlds. Nay, even that pre-eminent globe itself which they call the non-wandering (ἀπλανῆ), they nevertheless desire to have properly called world. Finally, they summon the book of Baruch the prophet to bear witness to this assertion, because in it the seven worlds or heavens are more clearly pointed out. Nevertheless, above that sphere which they call non-wandering (ἀπλανῆ), they will have another sphere to exist, which they say, exactly as our heaven contains all things which are under it, comprehends by its immense size and indescribable extent the spaces of all the spheres together within its more magnificent circumference; so that all things are within it, as this earth of ours is under heaven. And this also is believed to be called in the holy Scriptures the good land, and the land of the living, having its own heaven, which is higher, and in which the names of the saints are said to be written, or to have been written, by the Saviour; by which heaven that earth is confined and shut in, which the Saviour

in the Gospel promises to the meek and merciful. For they would have this earth of ours, which formerly was named "Dry," to have derived its appellation from the name of that earth, as this heaven also was named firmament from the title of that heaven. But we have treated at greater length of such opinions in the place where we had to inquire into the meaning of the declaration, that in the beginning "God made the heavens and the earth." For another heaven and another earth are shown to exist besides that "firmament" which is said to have been made after the second day, or that "dry land" which was afterwards called "earth." Certainly, what some say of this world, that it is corruptible because it was made, and yet is not corrupted, because the will of God, who made it and holds it together lest corruption should rule over it, is stronger and more powerful than corruption, may more correctly be supposed of that world which we have called above a "non-wandering" sphere, since by the will of God it is not at all subject to corruption, for the reason that it has not admitted any causes of corruption, seeing it is the world of the saints and of the thoroughly purified, and not of the wicked, like that world of ours. We must see, moreover, lest perhaps it is with reference to this that the apostle says, "While we look not at the things which are seen, but at the things which are not seen; for the things which are seen are temporal, but the things which are unseen are eternal. For we know that if our earthly house of this tabernacle were dissolved, we have a building of God, an house not made with hands, eternal in the heavens." [1] And when he says elsewhere, "Because I shall see the heavens, the works of Thy fingers," [2] and when God said, regarding all things visible, by the mouth of His prophet, "My hand has formed all these things," [3] He declares that that eternal house in the heavens which He promises to His saints was not made with hands, pointing out, doubtless, the difference of creation in things which are seen and in those which are not seen. For the same thing is not to be understood by the expressions, "those things which are not seen," and "those things which are invisible." For those things which are invisible are not only not seen, but do not even possess the property of visibility, being what the Greeks call ἀσώματα, i.e., incorporeal; whereas those of which Paul says, "They are not seen," possess indeed the property of being seen, but, as he explains, are not yet beheld by those to whom they are promised.

7. Having sketched, then, so far as we could understand, these three opinions regarding the

---

[1] 2 Cor. iv. 18–v. 1.
[2] Ps. viii. 3.
[3] Isa. lxvi. 2.

end of all things, and the supreme blessedness, let each one of our readers determine for himself, with care and diligence, whether any one of them can be approved and adopted.[1] For it has been said that we must suppose either that an incorporeal existence is possible, after all things have become subject to Christ, and through Christ to God the Father, when God will be all and in all; or that when, notwithstanding all things have been made subject to Christ, and through Christ to God (with whom they formed also one spirit, in respect of spirits being rational natures), then the bodily substance itself also being united to most pure and excellent spirits, and being changed into an ethereal condition in proportion to the quality or merits of those who assume it (according to the apostle's words, "We also shall be changed"), will shine forth in splendour; or at least that when the fashion of those things which are seen passes away, and all corruption has been shaken off and cleansed away, and when the whole of the space occupied by this world, in which the spheres of the planets are said to be, has been left behind and beneath,[2] then is reached the fixed abode of the pious and the good situated above that sphere, which is called non-wandering (ἀπλανής), as in a good land, in a land of the living, which will be inherited by the meek and gentle; to which land belongs that heaven (which, with its more magnificent extent, surrounds and contains that land itself) which is called truly and chiefly heaven, in which heaven and earth, the end and perfection of all things, may be safely and most confidently placed, — where, viz., these, after their apprehension and their chastisement for the offences which they have undergone by way of purgation, may, after having fulfilled and discharged every obligation, deserve a habitation in that land; while those who have been obedient to the word of God, and have henceforth by their obedience shown themselves capable of wisdom, are said to deserve the kingdom of that heaven or heavens; and thus the prediction is more worthily fulfilled, "Blessed are the meek, for they shall inherit the earth;"[3] and, "Blessed are the poor in spirit, for they shall inherit the

kingdom of heaven;"[4] and the declaration in the Psalm, "He shall exalt thee, and thou shalt inherit the land."[5] For it is called a descent to this earth, but an exaltation to that which is on high. In this way, therefore, does a sort of road seem to be opened up by the departure of the saints from that earth to those heavens; so that they do not so much appear to abide in that land, as to inhabit it with an intention, viz., to pass on to the inheritance of the kingdom of heaven, when they have reached that degree of perfection also.

CHAP. IV. — THE GOD OF THE LAW AND THE PROPHETS, AND THE FATHER OF OUR LORD JESUS CHRIST, IS THE SAME GOD.

1. Having now briefly arranged these points in order as we best could, it follows that, agreeably to our intention from the first, we refute those who think that the Father of our Lord Jesus Christ is a different God from Him who gave the answers of the law to Moses, or commissioned the prophets, who is the God of our fathers, Abraham, Isaac, and Jacob. For in this article of faith, first of all, we must be firmly grounded. We have to consider, then, the expression of frequent recurrence in the Gospels, and subjoined to all the acts of our Lord and Saviour, "that it might be fulfilled which was spoken by this or that prophet," it being manifest that the prophets are the prophets of that God who made the world. From this therefore we draw the conclusion, that He who sent the prophets, Himself predicted what was to be foretold of Christ. And there is no doubt that the Father Himself, and not another different from Him, uttered these predictions. The practice, moreover, of the Saviour or His apostles, frequently quoting illustrations from the Old Testament, shows that they attribute authority to the ancients. The injunction also of the Saviour, when exhorting His disciples to the exercise of kindness, "Be ye perfect, even as your Father who is in heaven is perfect; for He commands His sun to rise upon the evil and the good, and sendeth rain on the just and on the unjust,"[6] most evidently suggests even to a person of feeble understanding, that He is proposing to the imitation of His disciples no other God than the maker of heaven and the bestower of the rain. Again, what else does the expression, which ought to be used by those who pray, "Our Father who art in heaven,"[7] appear to indicate, save that God is to be sought in the better parts of the world, i.e., of His creation? Further, do not those admirable principles which

---

[1] This passage is found in Jerome's *Epistle to Avitus*, and, literally translated, is as follows: "A threefold suspicion, therefore, is suggested to us regarding the end, of which the reader may examine which is the true and the better one. For we shall either live without a body, when, being subject to Christ, we shall be subject to God, and God shall be all in all; or, as things subject to Christ will be subject along with Christ Himself to God, and enclosed in one covenant, so all substance will be reduced to the best quality and dissolved into an ether, which is of a purer and simpler nature; or at least that sphere which we have called above ἀπλανῆ, and whatever is contained within its circumference (*circulo*), will be dissolved into nothing, but that one by which the anti-zone (ἀντιζώνη) itself is held together and surrounded will be called a good land: and, moreover, another sphere which surrounds this very earth itself with its revolution, and is called heaven, will be preserved for a habitation of the saints."

[2] Omnique hoc mundi statu, in quo planetarum dicuntur sphæræ, supergresso atque superato.

[3] Matt. v. 5.

[4] Matt. v. 3.

[5] Ps. xxxvii. 34.

[6] Matt. v. 48, 45.

[7] Matt. vi. 9.

He lays down respecting oaths, saying that we ought not to "swear either by heaven, because it is the throne of God; nor by the earth, because it is His footstool,"[1] harmonize most clearly with the words of the prophet, "Heaven is My throne, and the earth is My footstool?"[2] And also when casting out of the temple those who sold sheep, and oxen, and doves, and pouring out the tables of the money-changers, and saying, "Take these things hence, and do not make My Father's house a house of merchandise,"[3] He undoubtedly called Him His Father, to whose name Solomon had raised a magnificent temple. The words, moreover, "Have you not read what was spoken by God to Moses: I am the God of Abraham, and the God of Isaac, and the God of Jacob; He is not a God of the dead, but of the living,"[4] most clearly teach us, that He called the God of the patriarchs (because they were holy, and were alive) the God of the living, the same, viz., who had said in the prophets, "I am God, and besides Me there is no God."[5] For if the Saviour, knowing that He who is written in the law is the God of Abraham, and that it is the same who says, "I am God, and besides Me there is no God," acknowledges that very one to be His Father who is ignorant of the existence of any other God above Himself, as the heretics suppose, He absurdly declares Him to be His Father who does not know of a greater God. But if it is not from ignorance, but from deceit, that He says there is no other God than Himself, then it is a much greater absurdity to confess that His Father is guilty of falsehood. From all which this conclusion is arrived at, that He knows of no other Father than God, the Founder and Creator of all things.

2. It would be tedious to collect out of all the passages in the Gospels the proofs by which the God of the law and of the Gospels is shown to be one and the same. Let us touch briefly upon the Acts of the Apostles,[6] where Stephen and the other apostles address their prayers to that God who made heaven and earth, and who spoke by the mouth of His holy prophets, calling Him the "God of Abraham, of Isaac, and of Jacob;" the God who "brought forth His people out of the land of Egypt." Which expressions undoubtedly clearly direct our understandings to faith in the Creator, and implant an affection for Him in those who have learned piously and faithfully thus to think of Him; according to the words of the Saviour Himself, who, when He was asked which was the greatest commandment in the law, replied, "Thou shalt love the Lord thy God with all thy heart, and with all thy soul, and with all thy mind. And the second is like unto it, Thou shalt love thy neighbour as thyself.' And to these He added: "On these two commandments hang all the law and the prophets." How is it, then, that He commends to him whom He was instructing, and was leading to enter on the office of a disciple, this commandment above all others, by which undoubtedly love was to be kindled in him towards the God of that law, in asmuch as such had been declared by the law in these very words? But let it be granted, notwithstanding all these most evident proofs, that it is of some other unknown God that the Saviour says, "Thou shalt love the Lord thy God with all thy heart," etc., etc. How, in that case, if the law and the prophets are, as they say, from the Creator, i.e., from another God than He whom He calls good, shall that appear to be logically said which He subjoins, viz., that "on these two commandments hang the law and the prophets?" For how shall that which is strange and foreign to God depend upon Him? And when Paul says, "I thank my God, whom I serve in my spirit from my forefathers with pure conscience,"[8] he clearly shows that he came not to some new God, but to Christ. For what other forefathers of Paul can be intended, except those of whom he says, "Are they Hebrews? so am I; are they Israelites? so am I."[9] Nay, will not the very preface of his Epistle to the Romans clearly show the same thing to those who know how to understand the letters of Paul, viz., what God he preaches? For his words are: "Paul the servant of Jesus Christ, called to be an apostle, set apart to the Gospel of God, which He had promised afore by His prophets in the holy Scriptures concerning His Son, who was made of the seed of David according to the flesh, and who was declared to be the Son of God with power, according to the spirit of holiness, by the resurrection from the dead of Christ Jesus our Lord,"[10] etc. Moreover, also the following, "Thou shalt not muzzle the mouth of the ox that treadeth out the corn. Doth God take care for oxen? or saith he it altogether for our sakes? For our sakes, no doubt, this is written, that he that plougheth should plough in hope, and he that thresheth in hope of partaking of the fruits."[11] By which he manifestly shows that God, who gave the law on our account, i.e., on account of the apostles, says, "Thou shalt not muzzle the mouth of the ox that treadeth out the corn;" whose care was not for oxen, but for the apostles, who were preaching the Gospel of

---

[1] Matt. v. 34, 35.
[2] Isa. lxvi. 1.
[3] John ii. 16.
[4] Matt. xxii. 31, 32; cf. Ex. iii. 6.
[5] Isa. xlv. 6.
[6] Acts vii.

[7] Matt. xxii. 37, 39, 40.
[8] 2 Tim. i. 3.
[9] 2 Cor. xi. 22.
[10] Rom. i. 1-4.
[11] 1 Cor. ix. 9, 10; cf. Deut. xxv. 4.

Christ. In other passages also, Paul, embracing the promises of the law, says, "Honour thy father and thy mother, which is the first commandment with promise ; that it may be well with thee, and that thy days may be long upon the land, the good land, which the Lord thy God will give thee." [1] By which he undoubtedly makes known that the law, and the God of the law, and His promises, are pleasing to him.

3. But as those who uphold this heresy are sometimes accustomed to mislead the hearts of the simple by certain deceptive sophisms, I do not consider it improper to bring forward the assertions which they are in the habit of making, and to refute their deceit and falsehood. The following, then, are their declarations. It is written, that "no man hath seen God at any time." [2] But that God whom Moses preaches was both seen by Moses himself, and by his fathers before him ; whereas He who is announced by the Saviour has never been seen at all by any one. Let us therefore ask them and ourselves whether they maintain that He whom they acknowledge to be God, and allege to be a different God from the Creator, is visible or invisible. And if they shall say that He is visible, besides being proved to go against the declaration of Scripture, which says of the Saviour, " He is the image of the invisible God, the first-born of every creature," [3] they will fall also into the absurdity of asserting that God is corporeal. For nothing can be seen except by help of form, and size, and colour, which are special properties of bodies. And if God is declared to be a body, then He will also be found to be material, since every body is composed of matter. But if He be composed of matter, and matter is undoubtedly corruptible, then, according to them, God is liable to corruption ! We shall put to them a second question. Is matter made, or is it uncreated, i.e., not made ? And if they shall answer that it is not made, i.e., uncreated, we shall ask them if one portion of matter is God, and the other part the world ? But if they shall say of matter that it is made, it will undoubtedly follow that they confess Him whom they declare to be God to have been made ! — a result which certainly neither their reason nor ours can admit. But they will say, God is invisible. And what will you do? If you say that He is invisible by nature, then neither ought He to be visible to the Saviour. Whereas, on the contrary, God, the Father of Christ, is said to be seen, because " he who sees the Son," he says, "sees also the Father." [4] This certainly would press us very hard, were the

expression not understood by us more correctly of understanding, and not of seeing. For he who has understood the Son will understand the Father also. In this way, then, Moses too must be supposed to have seen God, not beholding Him with the bodily eye, but understanding Him with the vision of the heart and the perception of the mind, and that only in some degree. For it is manifest that He, viz., who gave answers to Moses, said, " You shall not see My face, but My hinder parts." [5] These words are, of course, to be understood in that mystical sense which is befitting divine words, those old wives' fables being rejected and despised which are invented by ignorant persons respecting the anterior and posterior parts of God. Let no one indeed suppose that we have indulged any feeling of impiety in saying that even to the Saviour the Father is not visible. Let him consider the distinction which we employ in dealing with heretics. For we have explained that it is one thing to see and to be seen, and another to know and to be known, or to understand and to be understood. [6] To see, then, and to be seen, is a property of bodies, which certainly will not be appropriately applied either to the Father, or to the Son, or to the Holy Spirit, in their mutual relations with one another. For the nature of the Trinity surpasses the measure of vision, granting to those who are in the body, i.e., to all other creatures, the property of vision in reference to one another. But to a nature that is incorporeal and for the most part intellectual, no other attribute is appropriate save that of knowing or being known, as the Saviour Himself declares when He says, " No man knoweth the Son, save the Father ; nor does any one know the Father, save the Son, and he to whom the Son will reveal Him." [7] It is clear, then, that He has not said, " No one has seen the Father, save the Son ; " but, " No one knoweth the Father, save the Son."

4. And now, if, on account of those expressions which occur in the Old Testament, as when God is said to be angry or to repent, or when any other human affection or passion is described, (our opponents) think that they are furnished with grounds for refuting us, who maintain that God is altogether impassible, and is to be regarded as wholly free from all affections of that kind, we have to show them that similar statements are found even in the parables of the Gospel ; as when it is said, that he who planted a vineyard, and let it out to husbandmen, who slew the servants that were sent to them, and at last put to death even the son,

[1] Eph. vi. 2, 3; cf. Ex. xx. 12.
[2] John i. 18.
[3] Col. i. 15.
[4] John xiv. 9.

[5] Ex. xxxiii. 20, cf. 23.
[6] Aliud sit videre et videri, et aliud nôsse et nosci, vel cognoscere atque cognosci.
[7] Matt. xi. 27.

is said in anger to have taken away the vineyard from them, and to have delivered over the wicked husbandmen to destruction, and to have handed over the vineyard to others, who would yield him the fruit in its season. And so also with regard to those citizens who, when the head of the household had set out to receive for himself a kingdom, sent messengers after him, saying, "We will not have this man to reign over us;"[1] for the head of the household having obtained the kingdom, returned, and in anger commanded them to be put to death before him, and burned their city with fire. But when we read either in the Old Testament or in the New of the anger of God, we do not take such expressions literally, but seek in them a spiritual meaning, that we may think of God as He deserves to be thought of. And on these points, when expounding the verse in the second Psalm, "Then shall He speak to them in His anger, and trouble them in His fury,"[2] we showed, to the best of our poor ability, how such an expression ought to be understood.

CHAP. V. — ON JUSTICE AND GOODNESS.

1. Now, since this consideration has weight with some, that the leaders of that heresy (of which we have been speaking) think they have established a kind of division, according to which they have declared that justice is one thing and goodness another, and have applied this division even to divine things, maintaining that the Father of our Lord Jesus Christ is indeed a good God, but not a just one, whereas the God of the law and the prophets is just, but not good; I think it necessary to return, with as much brevity as possible, an answer to these statements. These persons, then, consider goodness to be some such affection as would have benefits conferred on all, although the recipient of them be unworthy and undeserving of any kindness; but here, in my opinion, they have not rightly applied their definition, inasmuch as they think that no benefit is conferred on him who is visited with any suffering or calamity. Justice, on the other hand, they view as that quality which rewards every one according to his deserts. But here, again, they do not rightly interpret the meaning of their own definition. For they think that it is just to send evils upon the wicked and benefits upon the good; i.e., so that, according to their view, the just God does not appear to wish well to the bad, but to be animated by a kind of hatred against them. And they gather together instances of this, wherever they find a history in the Scriptures of the Old Testament, relating, e.g., the punishment of the deluge, or the fate of those who are described as perishing in it, or

the destruction of Sodom and Gomorrah by a shower of fire and brimstone, or the falling of all the people in the wilderness on account of their sins, so that none of those who had left Egypt were found to have entered the promised land, with the exception of Joshua and Caleb. Whereas from the New Testament they gather together words of compassion and piety, through which the disciples are trained by the Saviour, and by which it seems to be declared that no one is good save God the Father only; and by this means they have ventured to style the Father of the Saviour Jesus Christ a good God, but to say that the God of the world is a different one, whom they are pleased to term just, but not also good.

2. Now I think they must, in the first place, be required to show, if they can, agreeably to their own definition, that the Creator is just in punishing according to their deserts, either those who perished at the time of the deluge, or the inhabitants of Sodom, or those who had quitted Egypt, seeing we sometimes behold committed crimes more wicked and detestable than those for which the above-mentioned persons were destroyed, while we do not yet see every sinner paying the penalty of his misdeeds. Will they say that He who at one time was just has been made good? Or will they rather be of opinion that He is even now just, but is patiently enduring human offences, while that then He was not even just, inasmuch as He exterminated innocent and sucking children along with cruel and ungodly giants? Now, such are their opinions, because they know not how to understand anything beyond the letter; otherwise they would show how it is literal justice for sins to be visited upon the heads of children to the third and fourth generation, and on children's children after them. By us, however, such things are not understood literally; but, as Ezekiel taught[3] when relating the parable, we inquire what is the inner meaning contained in the parable itself. Moreover, they ought to explain this also, how He is just, and rewards every one according to his merits, who punishes earthly-minded persons and the devil, seeing they have done nothing worthy of punishment.[4] For they could not do any good if, according to them, they were of a wicked and ruined nature. For as they style Him a judge, He appears to be a judge not so much of actions as of natures; and if a bad nature cannot do good, neither can a good nature do evil. Then, in the next place, if He whom they call good is good to all, He is undoubtedly good also to those who are destined to perish. And why does He not save them? If He does not desire to do so, He will be no

---

[1] Luke xix. 14.
[2] Ps. ii. 5.

[3] Ezek. xviii. 3.
[4] [Cum nihil dignum pœna commiserint. S.]

longer good ; if He does desire it, and cannot effect it, He will not be omnipotent. Why do they not rather hear the Father of our Lord Jesus Christ in the Gospels, preparing fire for the devil and his angels? And how shall that proceeding, as penal as it is sad, appear to be, according to their view, the work of the good God? Even the Saviour Himself, the Son of the good God, protests in the Gospels, and declares that "if signs and wonders had been done in Tyre and Sidon, they would have repented [1] long ago, sitting in sackcloth and ashes." And when He had come near to those very cities, and had entered their territory, why, pray, does He avoid entering those cities, and exhibiting to them abundance of signs and wonders, if it were certain that they would have repented, after they had been performed, in sackcloth and ashes? But as He does not do this, He undoubtedly abandons to destruction those whom the language of the Gospel shows not to have been of a wicked or ruined nature, inasmuch as it declares they were capable of repentance. Again, in a certain parable of the Gospel, where the king enters in to see the guests reclining at the banquet, he beheld a certain individual not clothed with wedding raiment, and said to him, "Friend, how camest thou in hither, not having a wedding garment?" and then ordered his servants, "Bind him hand and foot, and cast him into outer darkness ; there will be weeping and gnashing of teeth." [2] Let them tell us who is that king who entered in to see the guests, and finding one amongst them with unclean garments, commanded him to be bound by his servants, and thrust out into outer darkness. Is he the same whom they call just? How then had he commanded good and bad alike to be invited, without directing their merits to be inquired into by his servants? By such procedure would be indicated, not the character of a just God who rewards according to men's deserts, as they assert, but of one who displays undiscriminating goodness towards all. Now, if this must necessarily be understood of the good God, i.e., either of Christ or of the Father of Christ, what other objection can they bring against the justice of God's judgment? Nay, what else is there so unjust charged by them against the God of the law as to order him who had been invited by His servants, whom He had sent to call good and bad alike, to be bound hand and foot, and to be thrown into outer darkness, because he had on unclean garments?

3. And now, what we have drawn from the authority of Scripture ought to be sufficient to refute the arguments of the heretics. It will not, however, appear improper if we discuss the matter with them shortly, on the grounds of reason itself. We ask them, then, if they know what is regarded among men as the ground of virtue and wickedness, and if it appears to follow that we can speak of virtues in God, or, as they think, in these two Gods. Let them give an answer also to the question, whether they consider goodness to be a virtue ; and as they will undoubtedly admit it to be so, what will they say of injustice? They will never certainly, in my opinion, be so foolish as to deny that justice is a virtue. Accordingly, if virtue is a blessing, and justice is a virtue, then without doubt justice is goodness. But if they say that justice is not a blessing, it must either be an evil or an indifferent thing. Now I think it folly to return any answer to those who say that justice is an evil, for I shall have the appearance of replying either to senseless words, or to men out of their minds. How can that appear an evil which is able to reward the good with blessings, as they themselves also admit? But if they say that it is a thing of indifference, it follows that since justice is so, sobriety also, and prudence, and all the other virtues, are things of indifference. And what answer shall we make to Paul, when he says, "If there be any virtue, and if there be any praise, think on these things, which ye have learned, and received, and heard, and seen in me?" [3] Let them learn, therefore, by searching the holy Scriptures, what are the individual virtues, and not deceive themselves by saying that that God who rewards every one according to his merits, does, through hatred of evil, recompense the wicked with evil, and not because those who have sinned need to be treated with severer remedies, and because He applies to them those measures which, with the prospect of improvement, seem nevertheless, for the present, to produce a feeling of pain. They do not read what is written respecting the hope of those who were destroyed in the deluge ; of which hope Peter himself thus speaks in his first Epistle : "That Christ, indeed, was put to death in the flesh, but quickened by the Spirit, by which He went and preached to the spirits who were kept in prison, who once were unbelievers, when they awaited the long-suffering of God in the days of Noah, when the ark was preparing, in which a few, i.e., eight souls, were saved by water. Whereunto also baptism by a like figure now saves you." [4] And with regard to Sodom and Gomorrah, let them tell us whether they believe the prophetic words to be those of the Creator God — of Him, viz., who is related to have rained upon them a shower of fire and brimstone. What does Ezekiel the prophet say

---

[1] Pœnitentiam egissent.
[2] Matt. xxii. 12, 13.

[3] Phil. iv. 8, 9.
[4] 1 Pet. iii. 18-21.

of them? "Sodom," he says, "shall be restored to her former condition."[1] But why, in afflicting those who are deserving of punishment, does He not afflict them for their good?—who also says to Chaldea, "Thou hast coals of fire, sit upon them; they will be a help to thee."[2] And of those also who fell in the desert, let them hear what is related in the seventy-eighth Psalm, which bears the superscription of Asaph; for he says, "When He slew them, then they sought Him."[3] He does not say that some sought Him after others had been slain, but he says that the destruction of those who were killed was of such a nature that, when put to death, they sought God. By all which it is established, that the God of the law and the Gospels is one and the same, a just and good God, and that He confers benefits justly, and punishes with kindness; since neither goodness without justice, nor justice without goodness, can display the (real) dignity of the divine nature.

We shall add the following remarks, to which we are driven by their subtleties. If justice is a different thing from goodness, then, since evil is the opposite of good, and injustice of justice, injustice will doubtless be something else than an evil; and as, in your opinion, the just man is not good, so neither will the unjust man be wicked; and again, as the good man is not just, so the wicked man also will not be unjust. But who does not see the absurdity, that to a good God one should be opposed that is evil; while to a just God, whom they allege to be inferior to the good, no one should be opposed! For there is none who can be called unjust, as there is a Satan who is called wicked. What, then, are we to do? Let us give up the position which we defend, for they will not be able to maintain that a bad man is not also unjust, and an unjust man wicked. And if these qualities be indissolubly inherent in these opposites, viz., injustice in wickedness, or wickedness in injustice, then unquestionably the good man will be inseparable from the just man, and the just from the good; so that, as we speak of one and the same wickedness in malice and injustice, we may also hold the virtue of goodness and justice to be one and the same.

4. They again recall us, however, to the words of Scripture, by bringing forward that celebrated question of theirs, affirming that it is written, "A bad tree cannot produce good fruits; for a tree is known by its fruit."[4] What, then, is their position? What sort of tree the law is, is shown by its fruits, i.e., by the language of its precepts.

For if the law be found to be good, then undoubtedly He who gave it is believed to be a good God. But if it be just rather than good, then God also will be considered a just legislator. The Apostle Paul makes use of no circumlocution, when he says, "The law is good; and the commandment is holy, and just, and good."[5] From which it is clear that Paul had not learned the language of those who separate justice from goodness, but had been instructed by that God, and illuminated by His Spirit, who is at the same time both holy, and good, and just; and speaking by whose Spirit he declared that the commandment of the law was holy, and just, and good. And that he might show more clearly that goodness was in the commandment to a greater degree than justice and holiness, repeating his words, he used, instead of these three epithets, that of goodness alone, saying, "Was then that which is good made death unto me? God forbid."[6] As he knew that goodness was the *genus* of the virtues, and that justice and holiness were *species* belonging to the *genus*, and having in the former verses named *genus* and *species* together, he fell back, when repeating his words, on the *genus* alone. But in those which follow he says, "Sin wrought death in me by that which is good,"[6] where he sums up generically what he had beforehand explained specifically. And in this way also is to be understood the declaration, "A good man, out of the good treasure of his heart, bringeth forth good things; and an evil man, out of the evil treasure, bringeth forth evil things."[7] For here also he assumed that there was a *genus* in good or evil, pointing out unquestionably that in a good man there were both justice, and temperance, and prudence, and piety, and everything that can be either called or understood to be good. In like manner also he said that a man was wicked who should without any doubt be unjust, and impure, and unholy, and everything which singly makes a bad man. For as no one considers a man to be wicked without these marks of wickedness (nor indeed can he be so), so also it is certain that without these virtues no one will be deemed to be good. There still remains to them, however, that saying of the Lord in the Gospel, which they think is given them in a special manner as a shield, viz., "There is none good but one, God the Father."[8] This word they declare is peculiar to the Father of Christ, who, however, is different from the God who is Creator of all things, to which Creator he gave no appellation of goodness. Let us see now if, in the Old Testament, the God of the prophets and the Creator and

---

[1] Ezek. xvi. 55, cf. 53.
[2] Isa. xlvii. 14, 15. The Septuagint here differs from the Hebrew: ἔχεις ἄνθρακας πυρός, κάθισαι ἐπ' αὐτούς, οὗτοι ἔσονταί σοι βοήθεια.
[3] Ps. lxxviii. 34.
[4] Matt. vii. 18, cf. xii. 33.

[5] Rom. vii. 12.
[6] Rom. vii. 13.
[7] Matt. xii. 35.
[8] Matt. xix. 17.

Legislator of the world is not called good. What are the expressions which occur in the Psalms? " How good is God to Israel, to the upright in heart!"[1] and, " Let Israel now say that He is good, that His mercy endureth for ever;"[2] the language in the Lamentations of Jeremiah, " The Lord is good to them that wait for Him, to the soul that seeketh Him."[3] As therefore God is frequently called good in the Old Testament, so also the Father of our Lord Jesus Christ is styled just in the Gospels. Finally, in the Gospel according to John, our Lord Himself, when praying to the Father, says, " O just Father, the world hath not known Thee."[4] And lest perhaps they should say that it was owing to His having assumed human flesh that He called the Creator of the world " Father," and styled Him " Just," they are excluded from such a refuge by the words that immediately follow, " The world hath not known Thee." But, according to them, the world is ignorant of the good God alone. For the world unquestionably recognises its Creator, the Lord Himself saying that the world loveth what is its own. Clearly, then, He whom they consider to be the good God, is called just in the Gospels. Any one may at leisure gather together a greater number of proofs, consisting of those passages, where in the New Testament the Father of our Lord Jesus Christ is called just, and in the Old also, where the Creator of heaven and earth is called good; so that the heretics, being convicted by numerous testimonies, may perhaps some time be put to the blush.

CHAP. VI. — ON THE INCARNATION OF CHRIST.

1. It is now time, after this cursory notice of these points, to resume our investigation of the incarnation of our Lord and Saviour, viz., how or why He became man. Having therefore, to the best of our feeble ability, considered His divine nature from the contemplation of His own works rather than from our own feelings, and having nevertheless beheld (with the eye) His visible creation while the invisible creation is seen by faith, because human frailty can neither see all things with the bodily eye nor comprehend them by reason, seeing we men are weaker and frailer than any other rational beings (for those which are in heaven, or are supposed to exist above the heaven, are superior), it remains that we seek a being intermediate between all created things and God, i.e., a Mediator, whom the Apostle Paul styles the " first-born of every creature."[5] Seeing, moreover, those declarations regarding His majesty which are contained in holy Scripture, that He is called the " image of the invisible God, and the first-born of every creature," and that " in Him were all things created, visible and invisible, whether they be thrones, or dominions, or principalities, or powers, all things were created by Him, and in Him: and He is before all things, and by Him all things consist,"[6] who is the head of all things, alone having as head God the Father; for it is written, " The head of Christ is God;"[7] seeing clearly also that it is written, " No one knoweth the Father, save the Son, nor doth any one know the Son, save the Father"[8] (for who can know what wisdom is, save He who called it into being? or, who can understand clearly what truth is, save the Father of truth? who can investigate with certainty the universal nature of His Word, and of God Himself, which nature proceeds from God, except God alone, with whom the Word was), we ought to regard it as certain that this Word, or Reason (if it is to be so termed), this Wisdom, this Truth, is known to no other than the Father only; and of Him it is written, that " I do not think that the world itself could contain the books which might be written,"[9] regarding, viz., the glory and majesty of the Son of God. For it is impossible to commit to writing (all) those particulars which belong to the glory of the Saviour. After the consideration of questions of such importance concerning the being of the Son of God, we are lost in the deepest amazement that such a nature, pre-eminent above all others, should have divested itself of its condition of majesty and become man, and tabernacled amongst men, as the grace that was poured upon His lips testifies, and as His heavenly Father bore Him witness, and as is confessed by the various signs and wonders and miracles[10] that were performed by Him; who also, before that appearance of His which He manifested in the body, sent the prophets as His forerunners, and the messengers of His advent; and after His ascension into heaven, made His holy apostles, men ignorant and unlearned, taken from the ranks of tax-gatherers or fishermen, but who were filled with the power of His divinity, to itinerate throughout the world, that they might gather together out of every race and every nation a multitude of devout believers in Himself.

2. But of all the marvellous and mighty acts related of Him, this altogether surpasses human admiration, and is beyond the power of mortal frailness to understand or feel, how that mighty power of divine majesty, that very Word of the Father, and that very wisdom of God, in which were created all things, visible and invisible, can

---

[1] Ps. lxxiii. 1.
[2] Ps. cxviii. 2.
[3] Lam. iii 25.
[4] John xvii. 25: Juste Pater.
[5] Col. i. 15.
[6] Col. i. 16, 17.
[7] 1 Cor. xi. 3.
[8] Matt. xi. 27.
[9] John xxi. 25.
[10] Virtutibus, probably for δυνάμεσιν.

be believed to have existed within the limits of that man who appeared in Judea; nay, that the Wisdom of God can have entered the womb of a woman, and have been born an infant, and have uttered wailings like the cries of little children! And that afterwards it should be related that He was greatly troubled in death, saying, as He Himself declared, "My soul is sorrowful, even unto death;"[1] and that at the last He was brought to that death which is accounted the most shameful among men, although He rose again on the third day. Since, then, we see in Him some things so human that they appear to differ in no respect from the common frailty of mortals, and some things so divine that they can appropriately belong to nothing else than to the primal and ineffable nature of Deity, the narrowness of human understanding can find no outlet; but, overcome with the amazement of a mighty admiration, knows not whither to withdraw, or what to take hold of, or whither to turn. If it think of a God, it sees a mortal; if it think of a man, it beholds Him returning from the grave, after overthrowing the empire of death, laden with its spoils. And therefore the spectacle is to be contemplated with all fear and reverence, that the truth of both natures may be clearly shown to exist in one and the same Being; so that nothing unworthy or unbecoming may be perceived in that divine and ineffable substance, nor yet those things which were done be supposed to be the illusions of imaginary appearances. To utter these things in human ears, and to explain them in words, far surpasses the powers either of our rank, or of our intellect and language. I think that it surpasses the power even of the holy apostles; nay, the explanation of that mystery may perhaps be beyond the grasp of the entire creation of celestial powers. Regarding Him, then, we shall state, in the fewest possible words, the contents of our creed rather than the assertions which human reason is wont to advance; and this from no spirit of rashness, but as called for by the nature of our arrangement, laying before you rather (what may be termed) our suspicions than any clear affirmations.

3. The Only-begotten of God, therefore, through whom, as the previous course of the discussion has shown, all things were made, visible and invisible, according to the view of Scripture, both made all things, and loves what He made. For since He is Himself the invisible image of the invisible God, He conveyed invisibly a share in Himself to all His rational creatures, so that each one obtained a part of Him exactly proportioned to the amount of affection with which he regarded Him. But since, agreeably to the faculty of free-will, variety and diversity characterized the individual souls, so that one was attached with a warmer love to the Author of its being, and another with a feebler and weaker regard, that soul (*anima*) regarding which Jesus said, "No one shall take my life (*animam*) from me,"[2] inhering, from the beginning of the creation, and afterwards, inseparably and indissolubly in Him, as being the Wisdom and Word of God, and the Truth and the true Light, and receiving Him wholly, and passing into His light and splendour, was made with Him in a pre-eminent degree[3] one spirit, according to the promise of the apostle to those who ought to imitate it, that "he who is joined in the Lord is one spirit."[4] This substance of a soul, then, being intermediate between God and the flesh — it being impossible for the nature of God to intermingle with a body without an intermediate instrument — the God-man is born, as we have said, that substance being the intermediary to whose nature it was not contrary to assume a body. But neither, on the other hand, was it opposed to the nature of that soul, as a rational existence, to receive God, into whom, as stated above, as into the Word, and the Wisdom, and the Truth, it had already wholly entered. And therefore deservedly is it also called, along with the flesh which it had assumed, the Son of God, and the Power of God, the Christ, and the Wisdom of God, either because it was wholly in the Son of God, or because it received the Son of God wholly into itself. And again, the Son of God, through whom all things were created, is named Jesus Christ and the Son of man. For the Son of God also is said to have died — in reference, viz., to that nature which could admit of death; and He is called the Son of man, who is announced as about to come in the glory of God the Father, with the holy angels. And for this reason, throughout the whole of Scripture, not only is the divine nature spoken of in human words, but the human nature is adorned by appellations of divine dignity. More truly indeed of this than of any other can the statement be affirmed, "They shall both be in one flesh, and are no longer two, but one flesh."[5] For the Word of God is to be considered as being more in one flesh with the soul than a man with his wife. But to whom is it more becoming to be also one spirit with God, than to this soul which has so joined itself to God by love as that it may justly be said to be one spirit with Him?

---

[1] Matt. xxvi. 38.

[2] John x. 18. "No other soul which descended into a human body has stamped on itself a pure and unstained resemblance of its former stamp, save that one of which the Saviour says, 'No one will take my soul from me, but I lay it down of myself.'" — Jerome, *Epistle to Avitus*, p. 763.

[3] Principaliter.

[4] 1 Cor. vi. 17.

[5] Gen. ii. 24; cf. Mark x. 8.

4. That the perfection of his love and the sincerity of his deserved affection [1] formed for it this inseparable union with God, so that the assumption of that soul was not accidental, or the result of a personal preference, but was conferred as the reward of its virtues, listen to the prophet addressing it thus : " Thou hast loved righteousness, and hated wickedness : therefore God, thy God, hath anointed thee with the oil of gladness above thy fellows." [2]　As a reward for its love, then, it is anointed with the oil of gladness ; i.e., the soul of Christ along with the Word of God is made Christ. Because to be anointed with the oil of gladness means nothing else than to be filled with the Holy Spirit. And when it is said " above thy fellows," it is meant that the grace of the Spirit was not given to it as to the prophets, but that the essential fulness of the Word of God Himself was in it, according to the saying of the apostle, " In whom dwelt all the fulness of the Godhead bodily." [3]　Finally, on this account he has not only said, " Thou hast loved righteousness ; " but he adds, " and Thou hast hated wickedness." For to have hated wickedness is what the Scripture says of Him, that " He did no sin, neither was any guile found in His mouth," [4] and that " He was tempted in all things like as we are, without sin." [5]　Nay, the Lord Himself also said, " Which of you will convince Me of sin ? " [6]　And again He says with reference to Himself, " Behold, the prince of this world cometh, and findeth nothing in Me." [7] All which (passages) show that in Him there was no sense of sin ; and that the prophet might show more clearly that no sense of sin had ever entered into Him, he says, " Before the boy could have knowledge to call upon father or mother, He turned away from wickedness." [8]

5. Now, if our having shown above that Christ possessed a rational soul should cause a difficulty to any one, seeing we have frequently proved throughout all our discussions that the nature of souls is capable both of good and evil, the difficulty will be explained in the following way. That the nature, indeed, of His soul was the same as that of all others cannot be doubted, otherwise it could not be called a soul were it not truly one. But since the power of choosing good and evil is within the reach of all, this soul which belonged to Christ elected to love righteousness, so that in proportion to the immensity of its love it clung to it unchangeably and in-

separably, so that firmness of purpose, and immensity of affection, and an inextinguishable warmth of love, destroyed all susceptibility (*sensum*) for alteration and change ; and that which formerly depended upon the will was changed by the power of long custom into nature ; and so we must believe that there existed in Christ a human and rational soul, without supposing that it had any feeling or possibility of sin.

6. To explain the matter more fully, it will not appear absurd to make use of an illustration, although on a subject of so much difficulty it is not easy to obtain suitable illustrations. However, if we may speak without offence, the metal iron is capable of cold and heat. If, then, a mass of iron be kept constantly in the fire, receiving the heat through all its pores and veins, and the fire being continuous and the iron never removed from it, it become wholly converted into the latter ; could we at all say of this, which is by nature a mass of iron, that when placed in the fire, and incessantly burning, it was at any time capable of admitting cold ? On the contrary, because it is more consistent with truth, do we not rather say, what we often see happening in furnaces, that it has become wholly fire, seeing nothing but fire is visible in it ? And if any one were to attempt to touch or handle it, he would experience the action not of iron, but of fire. In this way, then, that soul which, like an iron in the fire, has been perpetually placed in the Word, and perpetually in the Wisdom, and perpetually in God,[9] is God in all that it does, feels, and understands, and therefore can be called neither convertible nor mutable, inasmuch as, being incessantly heated, it possessed immutability from its union with the Word of God. To all the saints, finally, some warmth from the Word of God must be supposed to have passed ; and in this soul the divine fire itself must be believed to have rested, from which some warmth may have passed to others. Lastly, the expression, " God, thy God, anointed thee with the oil of gladness above thy fellows," [10] shows that that soul is anointed in one way with the oil of gladness, i.e., with the word of God and wisdom ; and his fellows, i.e., the holy prophets and apostles, in another. For they are said to have " run in the odour of his ointments ; " [11] and that soul was the vessel which contained that very ointment of whose fragrance all the worthy prophets and apostles were made partakers. As, then, the substance of an ointment is one thing and its odour another, so also Christ is one thing and His fellows another. And as the vessel itself, which contains the substance of the

---

[1] Meriti affectus.
[2] Ps. xlv. 7.
[3] Col. ii. 9.
[4] Isa. liii. 9.
[5] Heb. iv. 15.
[6] John viii. 46.
[7] John xiv. 30.
[8] This quotation is made up of two different parts of Isaiah: chap. viii. 4, " Before the child shall have knowledge to cry, My father and my mother ; " and chap. vii. 16, " Before the child shall know to refuse the evil, and choose the good."

[9] Semper in verbo, semper in sapientia, semper in Deo.
[10] Ps. xlv. 7.
[11] Illi enim in odore unguentorum ejus circumire dicuntur ; perhaps an allusion to Song of Sol. i. 3 or to Ps. xlv. 8.

ointment, can by no means admit any foul smell; whereas it is possible that those who enjoy its odour may, if they remove a little way from its fragrance, receive any foul odour which comes upon them : so, in the same way, was it impossible that Christ, being as it were the vessel itself, in which was the substance of the ointment, should receive an odour of an opposite kind, while they who are His "fellows" will be partakers and receivers of His odour, in proportion to their nearness to the vessel.

7. I think, indeed, that Jeremiah the prophet, also, understanding what was the nature of the wisdom of God in him, which was the same also which he had assumed for the salvation of the world, said, "The breath of our countenance is Christ the Lord, to whom we said, that under His shadow we shall live among the nations." [1] And inasmuch as the shadow of our body is inseparable from the body, and unavoidably performs and repeats its movements and gestures, I think that he, wishing to point out the work of Christ's soul, and the movements inseparably belonging to it, and which accomplished everything according to His movements and will, called this the shadow of Christ the Lord, under which shadow we were to live among the nations. For in the mystery of this assumption the nations live, who, imitating it through faith, come to salvation. David also, when saying, "Be mindful of my reproach, O Lord, with which they reproached me in exchange for Thy Christ," [2] seems to me to indicate the same. And what else does Paul mean when he says, "Your life is hid with Christ in God;" [3] and again in another passage, "Do you seek a proof of Christ, who speaketh in me?" [4] And now he says that Christ was hid in God. The meaning of which expression, unless it be shown to be something such as we have pointed out above as intended by the prophet in the words "shadow of Christ," exceeds, perhaps, the apprehension of the human mind. But we see also very many other statements in holy Scripture respecting the meaning of the word "shadow," as that well-known one in the Gospel according to Luke, where Gabriel says to Mary, "The Spirit of the Lord shall come upon thee, and the power of the Highest shall overshadow thee." [5] And the apostle says with reference to the law, that they who have circumcision in the flesh, "serve for the similitude and shadow of heavenly things." [6] And elsewhere, "Is not our life upon the earth a shadow?" [7] If, then, not only the law which is upon the earth is a shadow, but also all our

life which is upon the earth is the same, and we live among the nations under the shadow of Christ, we must see whether the truth of all these shadows may not come to be known in that revelation, when no longer through a glass, and darkly, but face to face, all the saints shall deserve to behold the glory of God, and the causes and truth of things. And the pledge of this truth being already received through the Holy Spirit, the apostle said, "Yea, though we have known Christ after the flesh, yet now henceforth know we Him no more." [8]

The above, meanwhile, are the thoughts which have occurred to us, when treating of subjects of such difficulty as the incarnation and deity of Christ. If there be any one, indeed, who can discover something better, and who can establish his assertions by clearer proofs from holy Scriptures, let his opinion be received in preference to mine.

CHAP. VII. — ON THE HOLY SPIRIT.

1. As, then, after those first discussions which, according to the requirements of the case, we held at the beginning regarding the Father, Son, and Holy Spirit, it seemed right that we should retrace our steps, and show that the same God was the creator and founder of the world, and the Father of our Lord Jesus Christ, i.e., that the God of the law and of the prophets and of the Gospel was one and the same; and that, in the next place, it ought to be shown, with respect to Christ, in what manner He who had formerly been demonstrated to be the Word and Wisdom of God became man; it remains that we now return with all possible brevity to the subject of the Holy Spirit.

It is time, then, that we say a few words to the best of our ability regarding the Holy Spirit, whom our Lord and Saviour in the Gospel according to John has named the Paraclete. For as it is the same God Himself, and the same Christ, so also is it the same Holy Spirit who was in the prophets and apostles, i.e., either in those who believed in God before the advent of Christ, or in those who by means of Christ have sought refuge in God. We have heard, indeed, that certain heretics have dared to say that there are two Gods and two Christs, but we have never known of the doctrine of two Holy Spirits being preached by any one. [9] For how could they maintain this out of Scripture, or what distinction could they lay down between Holy Spirit and Holy Spirit, if indeed any definition or description of Holy Spirit can be discovered? For

---

[1] Lam. iv. 20.
[2] Ps. lxxxix. 50, 51.
[3] Col. iii. 3.
[4] 2 Cor. xiii. 3.
[5] Luke i. 35.
[6] Heb. viii. 5.
[7] Job viii. 9.

[8] 2 Cor. v. 16.
[9] According to Pamphilus in his *Apology*, Origen, in a note on Tit. iii. 10, has made a statement the opposite of this. His words are : "But there are some also who say, that it was one Holy Spirit who was in the prophets, and another who was in the apostles of our Lord Jesus Christ." — RUÆUS.

although we should concede to Marcion or to Valentinus that it is possible to draw distinctions in the question of Deity, and to describe the nature of the good God as one, and that of the just God as another, what will he devise, or what will he discover, to enable him to introduce a distinction in the Holy Spirit? I consider, then, that they are able to discover nothing which may indicate a distinction of any kind whatever.

2. Now we are of opinion that every rational creature, without any distinction, receives a share of Him in the same way as of the Wisdom and of the Word of God. I observe, however, that the chief advent of the Holy Spirit is declared to men, after the ascension of Christ to heaven, rather than before His coming into the world. For, before that, it was upon the prophets alone, and upon a few individuals — if there happened to be any among the people deserving of it — that the gift of the Holy Spirit was conferred; but after the advent of the Saviour, it is written that the prediction of the prophet Joel was fulfilled, " In the last days it shall come to pass, and I will pour out my Spirit upon all flesh, and they shall prophesy," [1] which is similar to the well-known statement, " All nations shall serve Him." [2] By the grace, then, of the Holy Spirit, along with numerous other results, this most glorious consequence is clearly demonstrated, that with regard to those things which were written in the prophets or in the law of Moses, it was only a few persons at that time, viz., the prophets themselves, and scarcely another individual out of the whole nation, who were able to look beyond the mere corporeal meaning and discover something greater, i.e., something spiritual, in the law or in the prophets; but now there are countless multitudes of believers who, although unable to unfold methodically and clearly the results of their spiritual understanding,[3] are nevertheless most firmly persuaded that neither ought circumcision to be understood literally, nor the rest of the Sabbath, nor the pouring out of the blood of an animal, nor that answers were given by God to Moses on these points. And this method of apprehension is undoubtedly suggested to the minds of all by the power of the Holy Spirit.

3. And as there are many ways of apprehending Christ, who, although He is wisdom, does not act the part or possess the power of wisdom in all men, but only in those who give themselves to the study of wisdom in Him; and who, although called a physician, does not act as one towards all, but only towards those who under-

stand their feeble and sickly condition, and flee to His compassion that they may obtain health; so also I think is it with the Holy Spirit, in whom is contained every kind of gifts. For on some is bestowed by the Spirit the word of wisdom, on others the word of knowledge, on others faith; and so to each individual of those who are capable of receiving Him, is the Spirit Himself made to be that quality, or understood to be that which is needed by the individual who has deserved to participate.[4] These divisions and differences not being perceived by those who hear Him called Paraclete in the Gospel, and not duly considering in consequence of what work or act He is named the Paraclete, they have compared Him to some common spirits or other, and by this means have tried to disturb the Churches of Christ, and so excite dissensions of no small extent among brethren; whereas the Gospel shows Him to be of such power and majesty, that it says the apostles could not yet receive those things which the Saviour wished to teach them until the advent of the Holy Spirit, who, pouring Himself into their souls, might enlighten them regarding the nature and faith of the Trinity. But these persons, because of the ignorance of their understandings, are not only unable themselves logically to state the truth, but cannot even give their attention to what is advanced by us; and entertaining unworthy ideas of His divinity, have delivered themselves over to errors and deceits, being depraved by a spirit of error, rather than instructed by the teaching of the Holy Spirit, according to the declaration of the apostle, " Following the doctrine of devils, forbidding to marry, to the destruction and ruin of many, and to abstain from meats, that by an ostentatious exhibition of stricter observance they may seduce the souls of the innocent." [5]

4. We must therefore know that the Paraclete is the Holy Spirit, who teaches truths which cannot be uttered in words, and which are, so to speak, unutterable, and "which it is not lawful for a man to utter," [6] i.e., which cannot be indicated by human language. The phrase " it is not lawful " is, we think, used by the apostle instead of " it is not possible ; " as also is the case in the passage where he says, " All things are lawful for me, but all things are not expedient : all things are lawful for me; but all things edify not." [7] For those things which are in our power because we may have them, he says are lawful for us. But the Paraclete, who is called the Holy Spirit, is so called from His work of consolation, *para-*

---

[1] Joel ii. 28.
[2] Ps. lxxii. 11.
[3] Qui licet non omnes possint per ordinem atque ad liquidum spiritualis intelligentiæ explanare consequentiam.

[4] Ita per singulos, qui eum capere possunt, hoc efficitur, vel hoc intelligitur ipse Spiritus, quo indiget ille, qui eum participare meruerit. Schnitzer renders, " And so, in every one who is susceptible of them, the Spirit is exactly that which the receiver chiefly needs."
[5] 1 Tim. iv. 1-3.
[6] 2 Cor. xii. 4.
[7] 1 Cor. x. 23.

clesis being termed in Latin *consolatio*. For if any one has deserved to participate in the Holy Spirit by the knowledge of His ineffable mysteries, he undoubtedly obtains comfort and joy of heart. For since he comes by the teaching of the Spirit to the knowledge of the reasons of all things which happen — how or why they occur — his soul can in no respect be troubled, or admit any feeling of sorrow; nor is he alarmed by anything, since, clinging to the Word of God and His wisdom, he through the Holy Spirit calls Jesus Lord. And since we have made mention of the Paraclete, and have explained as we were able what sentiments ought to be entertained regarding Him; and since our Saviour also is called the Paraclete in the Epistle of John, when he says, "If any of us sin, we have a Paraclete with the Father, Jesus Christ the righteous, and He is the propitiation for our sins;"[1] let us consider whether this term Paraclete should happen to have one meaning when applied to the Saviour, and another when applied to the Holy Spirit. Now Paraclete, when spoken of the Saviour, seems to mean intercessor. For in Greek, Paraclete has both significations — that of intercessor and comforter. On account, then, of the phrase which follows, when he says, "And He is the propitiation for our sins," the name Paraclete seems to be understood in the case of our Saviour as meaning intercessor; for He is said to intercede with the Father because of our sins. In the case of the Holy Spirit, the Paraclete must be understood in the sense of comforter, inasmuch as He bestows consolation upon the souls to whom He openly reveals the apprehension of spiritual knowledge.

CHAP. VIII. — ON THE SOUL (ANIMA).

1. The order of our arrangement now requires us, after the discussion of the preceding subjects, to institute a general inquiry regarding the soul;[2] and, beginning with points of inferior importance, to ascend to those that are of greater. Now, that there are souls[3] in all living things, even in those which live in the waters, is, I suppose, doubted by no one. For the general opinion of all men maintains this; and confirmation from the authority of holy Scripture is added, when it is said that "God made great whales, and every living creature[4] that moveth which the waters brought forth after their kind."[5] It is confirmed also from the common intelligence of reason, by those who lay down in certain words a definition of soul. For soul is defined as follows: a substance $\phi a\nu\tau a\sigma\tau\iota\kappa\dot{\eta}$ and $\dot{o}\rho\mu\eta\tau\iota\kappa\dot{\eta}$,

which may be rendered into Latin, although not so appropriately, *sensibilis et mobilis*.[6] This certainly may be said appropriately of all living beings, even of those which abide in the waters; and of winged creatures too, this same definition of *anima* may be shown to hold good. Scripture also has added its authority to a second opinion, when it says, "Ye shall not eat the blood, because the life[7] of all flesh is its blood; and ye shall not eat the life with the flesh;"[8] in which it intimates most clearly that the blood of every animal is its life. And if any one now were to ask how it can be said with respect to bees, wasps, and ants, and those other things which are in the waters, oysters and cockles, and all others which are without blood, and are most clearly shown to be living things, that the "life of all flesh is the blood," we must answer, that in living things of that sort the force which is exerted in other animals by the power of red blood is exerted in them by that liquid which is within them, although it be of a different colour; for colour is a thing of no importance, provided the substance be endowed with life.[9] That beasts of burden or cattle of smaller size are endowed with souls,[10] there is, by general assent, no doubt whatever. The opinion of holy Scripture, however, is manifest, when God says, "Let the earth bring forth the living creature after its kind, four-footed beasts, and creeping things, and beasts of the earth after their kind."[11] And now with respect to man, although no one entertains any doubt, or needs to inquire, yet holy Scripture declares that "God breathed into his countenance the breath of life, and man became a living soul."[12] It remains that we inquire respecting the angelic order whether they also have souls, or are souls; and also respecting the other divine and celestial powers, as well as those of an opposite kind. We nowhere, indeed, find any authority in holy Scripture for asserting that either the angels, or any other divine spirits that are ministers of God, either possess souls or are called souls, and yet they are felt by very many persons to be endowed with life. But with regard to God, we find it written as follows: "And I will put My soul upon that soul which has eaten blood, and I will root him out from among his people;"[13] and also in another passage, "Your new moons, and sabbaths, and great days, I will not accept; your fasts, and holidays,

---

[1] 1 John ii. 1, 2.
[2] Anima.
[3] Animæ.
[4] Animam animantium.
[5] Gen. i. 21: $\pi\hat{a}\sigma a\nu \psi\upsilon\chi\dot{\eta}\nu \zeta\dot{\omega}\omega\nu$, Sept.

[6] Erasmus remarks, that $\phi a\nu\tau a\sigma\tau\iota\kappa\dot{\eta}$ may be rendered *imaginitiva*, which is the understanding: $\dot{o}\rho\mu\eta\tau\iota\kappa\dot{\eta}$, *impulsiva*, which refers to the affections (Schnitzer).
[7] Animam.
[8] Lev. xvii. 14: $\dot{\eta} \psi\upsilon\chi\dot{\eta} \pi\dot{a}\sigma\eta\varsigma \sigma a\rho\kappa\dot{o}\varsigma a\dot{\iota}\mu a a\dot{\upsilon}\tau o\hat{\upsilon} \dot{\epsilon}\sigma\tau\iota$, Sept.
[9] Vitalis.
[10] Animantia.
[11] Gen. i. 24, living creature, *animam*.
[12] Gen. ii. 7, *animam viventem*.
[13] Lev. xvii. 10. It is clear that in the text which Origen or his translator had before him he must have read $\psi\upsilon\chi\dot{\eta}$ instead of $\pi\rho\dot{o}\sigma\omega\pi o\nu$: otherwise the quotation would be inappropriate (Schnitzer).

and festal days, My soul hateth." [1]　And in the twenty-second Psalm, regarding Christ — for it is certain, as the Gospel bears witness, that this Psalm is spoken of Him — the following words occur : " O Lord, be not far from helping me ; look to my defence: O God, deliver my soul from the sword, and my beloved one from the hand of the dog ; " [2] although there are also many other testimonies respecting the soul of Christ when He tabernacled in the flesh.

2. But the nature of the incarnation will render unnecessary any inquiry into the soul of Christ.　For as He truly possessed flesh, so also He truly possessed a soul.　It is difficult indeed both to feel and to state how that which is called in Scripture the soul of God is to be understood ; for we acknowledge that nature to be simple, and without any intermixture or addition.　In whatever way, however, it is to be understood, it seems, meanwhile, to be named the soul of God ; whereas regarding Christ there is no doubt. And therefore there seems to me no absurdity in either understanding or asserting some such thing regarding the holy angels and the other heavenly powers, since that definition of soul appears applicable also to them.　For who can rationally deny that they are " sensible and moveable ? "　But if that definition appear to be correct, according to which a soul is said to be a substance rationally " sensible and moveable," the same definition would seem also to apply to angels.　For what else is in them than rational feeling and motion?　Now those beings who are comprehended under the same definition have undoubtedly the same substance. Paul indeed intimates that there is a kind of animal-man [3] who, he says, cannot receive the things of the Spirit of God, but declares that the doctrine of the Holy Spirit seems to him foolish, and that he cannot understand what is to be spiritually discerned.　In another passage he says it is sown an animal body, and arises a spiritual body, pointing out that in the resurrection of the just there will be nothing of an animal nature.　And therefore we inquire whether there happen to be any substance which, in respect of its being *anima*, is imperfect.　But whether it be imperfect because it falls away from perfection, or because it was so created by God, will form the subject of inquiry when each individual topic shall begin to be discussed in order.　For if the animal man receive not the things of the Spirit of God, and because he is animal, is unable to admit the understanding of a better, i.e., of a divine nature, it is for this reason perhaps that Paul, wishing to teach us more plainly what that is by means of which we are

able to comprehend those things which are of the Spirit, i.e., spiritual things, conjoins and associates with the Holy Spirit an understanding [4] rather than a soul. [5]　For this, I think, he indicates when he says, " I will pray with the spirit, I will pray with the understanding also ; I will sing with the spirit, I will sing with the understanding also." [6]　And he does not say that " I will pray with the soul," but with the spirit and the understanding.　Nor does he say, " I will sing with the soul," but with the spirit and the understanding.

3. But perhaps this question is asked, If it be the understanding which prays and sings with the spirit, and if it be the same which receives both perfection and salvation, how is it that Peter says, " Receiving the end of your faith, even the salvation of your souls ? " [7]　If the soul neither prays nor sings with the spirit, how shall it hope for salvation ? or when it attains to blessedness, shall it be no longer called a soul ? [8] Let us see if perhaps an answer may be given in this way, that as the Saviour came to save what was lost, that which formerly was said to be lost is not lost when it is saved ; so also, perhaps, this which is saved is called a soul, and when it has been placed in a state of salvation will receive a name from the Word that denotes its more perfect condition.　But it appears to some that this also may be added, that as the thing which was lost undoubtedly existed before it was lost, at which time it was something else than destroyed, so also will be the case when it is no longer in a ruined condition.　In like manner also, the soul which is said to have perished will appear to have been something at one time, when as yet it had not perished, and on that account would be termed soul, and being again freed from destruction, it may become a second time what it was before it perished, and be called a soul.　But from the very signification of the name soul which the Greek word conveys, it has appeared to a few curious inquirers that a meaning of no small importance may be suggested. For in sacred language God is called a fire, as when Scripture says, " Our God is a consuming fire." [9]　Respecting the substance of the angels also it speaks as follows : " Who maketh His

---

[1] Isa. i. 13, 14.
[2] Ps. xxii. 19, 20, unicam meam, μονογενῆ μου.
[3] Animalem.

[4] Mens.
[5] Anima.
[6] 1 Cor. xiv. 15.
[7] 1 Pet. i. 9.
[8] These words are found in Jerome's *Epistle to Avitus*, and, literally translated, are as follows: " Whence infinite caution is to be employed, lest perchance, after souls have obtained salvation and come to the blessed life, they should cease to be souls.　For as our Lord and Saviour came to seek and to save what might cease to be lost ; so the soul which was lost, and for whose salvation the Lord came, shall, when it has been saved, cease to be a soul. This point in like manner must be examined, whether, as that which has been lost was at one time not lost, and a time will come when it will be no longer lost ; so also at some time a soul may not have been a soul, and a time may be when it will by no means continue to be a soul."　A portion of the above is also found, in the original Greek, in the Emperor Justinian's Letter to Menas, Patriarch of Constantinople.
[9] Deut. iv. 24.

angels spirits, and His ministers a burning fire;"[1] and in another place, "The angel of the LORD appeared in a flame of fire in the bush."[2] We have, moreover, received a commandment to be "fervent in spirit;"[3] by which expression undoubtedly the Word of God is shown to be hot and fiery. The prophet Jeremiah also hears from Him, who gave him his answers, "Behold, I have given My words into thy mouth a fire."[4] As God, then, is a fire, and the angels a flame of fire, and all the saints are fervent in spirit, so, on the contrary, those who have fallen away from the love of God are undoubtedly said to have cooled in their affection for Him, and to have become cold. For the Lord also says, that, "because iniquity has abounded, the love of many will grow cold."[5] Nay, all things, whatever they are, which in holy Scripture are compared with the hostile power, the devil is said to be perpetually finding cold; and what is found to be colder than he? In the sea also the dragon is said to reign. For the prophet[6] intimates that the serpent and dragon, which certainly is referred to one of the wicked spirits, is also in the sea. And elsewhere the prophet says, "I will draw out my holy sword upon the dragon the flying serpent, upon the dragon the crooked serpent, and will slay him."[7] And again he says: "Even though they hide from my eyes, and descend into the depths of the sea, there will I command the serpent, and it shall bite them."[8] In the book of Job also, he is said to be the king of all things in the waters.[9] The prophet[10] threatens that evils will be kindled by the north wind upon all who inhabit the earth. Now the north wind is described in holy Scripture as cold, according to the statement in the book of Wisdom, "That cold north wind;"[11] which same thing also must undoubtedly be understood of the devil. If, then, those things which are holy are named fire, and light, and fervent, while those which are of an opposite nature are said to be cold; and if the love of many is said to wax cold; we have to inquire whether perhaps the name soul, which in Greek is termed ψυχή, be so termed from growing cold[12] out of a better and more divine condition, and be thence derived, because it seems to have cooled from that natural and divine warmth, and therefore has been placed in its present position, and called

by its present name. Finally, see if you can easily find a place in holy Scripture where the soul is properly mentioned in terms of praise: it frequently occurs, on the contrary, accompanied with expressions of censure, as in the passage, "An evil soul ruins him who possesses it;"[13] and, "The soul which sinneth, it shall die."[14] For after it has been said, "All souls are Mine; as the soul of the father, so also the soul of the son is Mine,"[15] it seemed to follow that He would say, "The soul that doeth righteousness, it shall be saved," and "The soul which sinneth, it shall die." But now we see that He has associated with the soul what is censurable, and has been silent as to that which was deserving of praise. We have therefore to see if, perchance, as we have said is declared by the name itself, it was called ψυχή, i.e., *anima*, because it has waxed cold from the fervour of just things,[16] and from participation in the divine fire, and yet has not lost the power of restoring itself to that condition of fervour in which it was at the beginning. Whence the prophet also appears to point out some such state of things by the words, "Return, O my soul, unto thy rest."[17] From all which this appears to be made out, that the understanding, falling away from its status and dignity, was made or named soul; and that, if repaired and corrected, it returns to the condition of the understanding.[18]

4. Now, if this be the case, it seems to me that this very decay and falling away of the understanding is not the same in all, but that this conversion into a soul is carried to a greater or less degree in different instances, and that certain understandings retain something even of their former vigour, and others again either nothing or a very small amount. Whence some are found from the very commencement of their lives to be of more active intellect, others again of a slower habit of mind, and some are born wholly obtuse, and altogether incapable of instruction. Our statement, however, that the

---

[1] Ps. civ. 4; cf. Heb. i. 7.
[2] Ex. iii. 2.
[3] Rom. xii. 11.
[4] Cf. Jer. i. 9. The word "fire" is found neither in the Hebrew nor in the Septuagint.
[5] Matt. xxiv. 12.
[6] Cf. Ezek. xxxii. 2 seqq.
[7] Isa. xxvii. 1.
[8] Amos ix. 3.
[9] Job xli. 34 [LXX.].
[10] Jer. i. 14.
[11] Ecclus. xliii. 20.
[12] ψυχή from ψύχεσθαι.

[13] Ecclus. vi. 4.
[14] Ezek. xviii. 4, cf. 20.
[15] Ezek. xviii. 4, 19.
[16] "By falling away and growing cold from a spiritual life, the soul has become what it now is, but is capable also of returning to what it was at the beginning, which I think is intimated by the prophet in the words, 'Return, O my soul, unto thy rest,' so as to be wholly this."—*Epistle of Justinian to Patriarch of Constantinople.*
[17] Ps. cxvi. 7.
[18] "The understanding (Νοῦς) somehow, then, has become a soul, and the soul, being restored, becomes an understanding. The understanding falling away, was made a soul, and the soul, again, when furnished with virtues, will become an understanding. For if we examine the case of Esau, we may find that he was condemned because of his ancient sins in a worse course of life. And respecting the heavenly bodies we must inquire, that not at the time when the world was created did the soul of the sun, or whatever else it ought to be called, begin to exist, but before that it entered that shining and burning body. We may hold similar opinions regarding the moon and stars, that, for the foregoing reasons, they were compelled, unwillingly, to subject themselves to vanity on account of the rewards of the future; and to do, not their own will, but the will of their Creator, by whom they were arranged among their different offices."—*Jerome's Epistle to Avitus.* From these, as well as other passages, it may be seen how widely Rufinus departed in his translation from the original.

understanding is converted into a soul, or whatever else seems to have such a meaning, the reader must carefully consider and settle for himself, as these views are not be regarded as advanced by us in a dogmatic manner, but simply as opinions, treated in the style of investigation and discussion. Let the reader take this also into consideration, that it is observed with regard to the soul of the Saviour, that of those things which are written in the Gospel, some are ascribed to it under the name of soul, and others under that of spirit. For when it wishes to indicate any suffering or perturbation affecting Him, it indicates it under the name of soul; as when it says, " Now is My soul troubled ; " [1] and, " My soul is sorrowful, even unto death ; " [2] and, " No man taketh My soul [3] from Me, but I lay it down of Myself." [4] Into the hands of His Father He commends not His soul, but His spirit ; and when He says that the flesh is weak, He does not say that the soul is willing, but the spirit : whence it appears that the soul is something intermediate between the weak flesh and the willing spirit.

5. But perhaps some one may meet us with one of those objections which we have ourselves warned you of in our statements, and say, " How then is there said to be also a soul of God?" To which we answer as follows : That as with respect to everything corporeal which is spoken of God, such as fingers, or hands, or arms, or eyes, or feet, or mouth, we say that these are not to be understood as human members, but that certain of His powers are indicated by these names of members of the body ; so also we are to suppose that it is something else which is pointed out by this title — soul of God. And if it is allowable for us to venture to say anything more on such a subject, the soul of God may perhaps be understood to mean the only-begotten Son of God. For as the soul, when implanted in the body, moves all things in it, and exerts its force over everything on which it operates ; so also the only-begotten Son of God, who is His Word and Wisdom, stretches and extends to every power of God, being implanted in it ; and perhaps to indicate this mystery is God either called or described in Scripture as a body. We must, indeed, take into consideration whether it is not perhaps on this account that the soul of God may be understood to mean His only-begotten Son, because He Himself came into this world of affliction, and descended into this valley of tears, and into this place of our humiliation ; as He says in the Psalm, " Because Thou hast humiliated us in the place of

affliction." [5] Finally, I am aware that certain critics, in explaining the words used in the Gospel by the Saviour, " My soul is sorrowful, even unto death," have interpreted them of the apostles, whom He termed His soul, as being better than the rest of His body. For as the multitude of believers is called His body, they say that the apostles, as being better than the rest of the body, ought to be understood to mean His soul.

We have brought forward as we best could these points regarding the rational soul, as topics of discussion for our readers, rather than as dogmatic and well-defined propositions. And with respect to the souls of animals and other dumb creatures, let that suffice which we have stated above in general terms.

CHAP. IX. — ON THE WORLD AND THE MOVEMENTS OF RATIONAL CREATURES, WHETHER GOOD OR BAD ; AND ON THE CAUSES OF THEM.

1. But let us now return to the order of our proposed discussion, and behold the commencement of creation, so far as the understanding can behold the beginning of the creation of God. In that commencement,[6] then, we are to suppose that God created so great a number of rational or intellectual creatures (or by whatever name they are to be called), which we have formerly termed understandings, as He foresaw would be sufficient. It is certain that He made them according to some definite number, predetermined by Himself : for it is not to be imagined, as some would have it, that creatures have not a limit, because where there is no limit there can neither be any comprehension nor any limitation. Now if this were the case, then certainly created things could neither be restrained nor administered by God. For, naturally, whatever is infinite will also be incomprehensible. Moreover, as Scripture says, " God has arranged all things in number and measure ; " [7] and therefore number will be correctly applied to rational creatures or understandings, that they may be so numerous as to admit of being arranged, governed, and controlled by God. But measure will be appropriately applied to a material body ; and this measure, we are to believe, was created by God such as He knew would be sufficient for the adorning of the world. These, then, are the

---

[1] John xii. 27.
[2] Matt. xxvi. 38.
[3] Animam.
[4] John x. 18.

[5] Ps. xliv. 19.
[6] The original of this passage is found in Justinian's Epistle to Menas, Patriarch of Constantinople, *apud finem*. " In that beginning which is cognisable by the understanding, God, by His own will, caused to exist as great a number of intelligent beings as was sufficient ; for we must say that the power of God is finite, and not, under pretence of praising Him, take away His limitation. For if the divine power be infinite, it must of necessity be unable to understand even itself, since that which is naturally illimitable is incapable of being comprehended. He made things therefore so great as to be able to apprehend and keep them under His power, and control them by His providence : so also He prepared matter of such a size ($\tau o\sigma a\nu\tau\eta\nu$ $\ddot{\nu}\lambda\eta\nu$) as He had the power to ornament."
[7] Wisdom xi. 20: " Thou hast ordered all things in measure, and number, and weight."

things which we are to believe were created by God in the beginning, i.e., before all things. And this, we think, is indicated even in that beginning which Moses has introduced in terms somewhat ambiguous, when he says, " In the beginning God made the heaven and the earth." [1] For it is certain that the firmament is not spoken of, nor the dry land, but that heaven and earth from which this present heaven and earth which we now see afterwards borrowed their names.

2. But since those rational natures, which we have said above were made in the beginning, were created when they did not previously exist, in consequence of this very fact of their non-existence and commencement of being, are they necessarily changeable and mutable ; since whatever power was in their substance was not in it by nature, but was the result of the goodness of their Maker. What they are, therefore, is neither their own nor endures for ever, but is bestowed by God. For it did not always exist ; and everything which is a gift may also be taken away, and disappear. And a reason for removal will consist in the movements of souls not being conducted according to right and propriety. For the Creator gave, as an indulgence to the understandings created by Him, the power of free and voluntary action, by which the good that was in them might become their own, being preserved by the exertion of their own will ; but slothfulness, and a dislike of labour in preserving what is good, and an aversion to and a neglect of better things, furnished the beginning of a departure from goodness. But to depart from good is nothing else than to be made bad. For it is certain that to want goodness is to be wicked. Whence it happens that, in proportion as one falls away from goodness, in the same proportion does he become involved in wickedness. In which condition, according to its actions, each understanding, neglecting goodness either to a greater or more limited extent, was dragged into the opposite of good, which undoubtedly is evil. From which it appears that the Creator of all things admitted certain seeds and causes of variety and diversity, that He might create variety and diversity in proportion to the diversity of understandings, i.e., of rational creatures, which diversity they must be supposed to have conceived from that cause which we have mentioned above. And what we mean by variety and diversity is what we now wish to explain.

3. Now we term world everything which is above the heavens, or in the heavens, or upon the earth, or in those places which are called the lower regions, or all places whatever that anywhere exist, together with their inhabitants. This whole, then, is called world. In which world

certain beings are said to be super-celestial, i.e., placed in happier abodes, and clothed with heavenly and resplendent bodies ; and among these many distinctions are shown to exist, the apostle, e.g., saying, " That one is the glory of the sun, another the glory of the moon, another the glory of the stars ; for one star differeth from another star in glory." [2]   Certain beings are called earthly, and among them, i.e., among men, there is no small difference ; for some of them are Barbarians, others Greeks ; and of the Barbarians some are savage and fierce, and others of a milder disposition. And certain of them live under laws that have been thoroughly approved ; others, again, under laws of a more common or severe kind ; [3] while some, again, possess customs of an inhuman and savage character, rather than laws. And certain of them, from the hour of their birth, are reduced to humiliation and subjection, and brought up as slaves, being placed under the dominion either of masters, or princes, or tyrants. Others, again, are brought up in a manner more consonant with freedom and reason : some with sound bodies, some with bodies diseased from their early years ; some defective in vision, others in hearing and speech ; some born in that condition, others deprived of the use of their senses immediately after birth, or at least undergoing such misfortune on reaching manhood. And why should I repeat and enumerate all the horrors of human misery, from which some have been free, and in which others have been involved, when each one can weigh and consider them for himself ? There are also certain invisible powers to which earthly things have been entrusted for administration ; and amongst them no small difference must be believed to exist, as is also found to be the case among men. The Apostle Paul indeed intimates that there are certain lower powers,[4] and that among them, in like manner, must undoubtedly be sought a ground of diversity. Regarding dumb animals, and birds, and those creatures which live in the waters, it seems superfluous to inquire ; since it is certain that these ought to be regarded not as of primary, but of subordinate rank.

4. Seeing, then, that all things which have been created are said to have been made through Christ, and in Christ, as the Apostle Paul most clearly indicates, when he says, " For in Him and by Him were all things created, whether things in heaven or things on earth, visible and invisible, whether they be thrones, or powers, or principalities, or dominions ; all things were created by Him, and in Him ; " [5] and as in his

---

[1] Gen. i. 1.

[2] 1 Cor. xv. 41.
[3] Vilioribus et asperioribus.
[4] Inferna.
[5] Col. i. 16.

Gospel John indicates the same thing, saying, "In the beginning was the Word, and the Word was with God, and the Word was God : the same was in the beginning with God : all things were made by Him ; and without Him was not anything made ; "[1] and as in the Psalm also it is written, " In wisdom hast Thou made them all ; "[2] — seeing, then, Christ is, as it were, the Word and Wisdom, and so also the Righteousness, it will undoubtedly follow that those things which were created in the Word and Wisdom are said to be created also in that righteousness which is Christ ; that in created things there may appear to be nothing unrighteous or accidental, but that all things may be shown to be in conformity with the law of equity and righteousness. How, then, so great a variety of things, and so great a diversity, can be understood to be altogether just and righteous, I am sure no human power or language can explain, unless as prostrate suppliants we pray to the Word, and Wisdom, and Righteousness Himself, who is the only-begotten Son of God, and who, pouring Himself by His graces into our senses, may deign to illuminate what is dark, to lay open what is concealed, and to reveal what is secret ; if, indeed, we should be found either to seek, or ask, or knock so worthily as to deserve to receive when we ask, or to find when we seek, or to have it opened to us when we knock. Not relying, then, on our own powers, but on the help of that Wisdom which made all things, and of that Righteousness which we believe to be in all His creatures, although we are in the meantime unable to declare it, yet, trusting in His mercy, we shall endeavour to examine and inquire how that great variety and diversity in the world may appear to be consistent with all righteousness and reason. I mean, of course, merely reason in general ; for it would be a mark of ignorance either to seek, or of folly to give, a special reason for each individual case.

5. Now, when we say that this world was established in the variety in which we have above explained that it was created by God, and when we say that this God is good, and righteous, and most just, there are numerous individuals, especially those who, coming from the school of Marcion, and Valentinus, and Basilides, have heard that there are souls of different natures, who object to us, that it cannot consist with the justice of God in creating the world to assign to some of His creatures an abode in the heavens, and not only to give such a better habitation, but also to grant them a higher and more honourable position ; to favour others with the grant of principalities ; to bestow powers upon some, dominions on others ; to confer upon some the most honourable seats in the celestial tribunals ; to enable some to shine with more resplendent glory, and to glitter with a starry splendour ; to give to some the glory of the sun, to others the glory of the moon, to others the glory of the stars ; to cause one star to differ from another star in glory. And, to speak once for all, and briefly, if the Creator God wants neither the will to undertake nor the power to complete a good and perfect work, what reason can there be that, in the creation of rational natures, i.e., of beings of whose existence He Himself is the cause, He should make some of higher rank, and others of second, or third, or of many lower and inferior degrees? In the next place, they object to us, with regard to terrestrial beings, that a happier lot by birth is the case with some rather than with others ; as one man, e.g., is begotten of Abraham, and born of the promise ; another, too, of Isaac and Rebekah, and who, while still in the womb, supplants his brother, and is said to be loved by God before he is born. Nay, this very circumstance, — especially that one man is born among the Hebrews, with whom he finds instruction in the divine law ; another among the Greeks, themselves also wise, and men of no small learning ; and then another amongst the Ethiopians, who are accustomed to feed on human flesh ; or amongst the Scythians, with whom parricide is an act sanctioned by law ; or amongst the people of Taurus, where strangers are offered in sacrifice, — is a ground of strong objection. Their argument accordingly is this : If there be this great diversity of circumstances, and this diverse and varying condition by birth, in which the faculty of free-will has no scope (for no one chooses for himself either where, or with whom, or in what condition he is born) ; if, then, this is not caused by the difference in the nature of souls, i.e., that a soul of an evil nature is destined for a wicked nation, and a good soul for a righteous nation, what other conclusion remains than that these things must be supposed to be regulated by accident and chance? And if that be admitted, then it will be no longer believed that the world was made by God, or administered by His providence ; and as a consequence, a judgment of God upon the deeds of each individual will appear a thing not to be looked for. In which matter, indeed, what is clearly the truth of things is the privilege of Him alone to know who searches all things, even the deep things of God.

6. We, however, although but men, not to nourish the insolence of the heretics by our silence, will return to their objections such answers as occur to us, so far as our abilities enable us. We have frequently shown, by those declarations which we were able to produce from the holy Scriptures, that God, the Creator of all

[1] John i. 1, 2.
[2] Ps. civ. 24.

things, is good, and just, and all-powerful. When He in the beginning created those beings which He desired to create, i.e., rational natures, He had no other reason for creating them than on account of Himself, i.e., His own goodness. As He Himself, then, was the cause of the existence of those things which were to be created, in whom there was neither any variation nor change, nor want of power, He created all whom He made equal and alike, because there was in Himself no reason for producing variety and diversity. But since those rational creatures themselves, as we have frequently shown, and will yet show in the proper place, were endowed with the power of free-will, this freedom of will incited each one either to progress by imitation of God, or reduced him to failure through negligence. And this, as we have already stated, is the cause of the diversity among rational creatures, deriving its origin not from the will or judgment of the Creator, but from the freedom of the individual will. Now God, who deemed it just to arrange His creatures according to their merit, brought down these different understandings into the harmony of one world, that He might adorn, as it were, one dwelling, in which there ought to be not only vessels of gold and silver, but also of wood and clay (and some indeed to honour, and others to dishonour), with those different vessels, or souls, or understandings. And these are the causes, in my opinion, why that world presents the aspect of diversity, while Divine Providence continues to regulate each individual according to the variety of his movements, or of his feelings and purpose. On which account the Creator will neither appear to be unjust in distributing (for the causes already mentioned) to every one according to his merits; nor will the happiness or unhappiness of each one's birth, or whatever be the condition that falls to his lot, be deemed accidental; nor will different creators, or souls of different natures, be believed to exist.

7. But even holy Scripture does not appear to me to be altogether silent on the nature of this secret, as when the Apostle Paul, in discussing the case of Jacob and Esau, says: "For the children being not yet born, neither having done any good or evil, that the purpose of God according to election might stand, not of works, but of Him who calleth, it was said, The elder shall serve the younger, as it is written, Jacob have I loved, but Esau have I hated." [1] And after that, he answers himself, and says, "What shall we say then? Is there unrighteousness with God?" And that he might furnish us with an opportunity of inquiring into these matters, and of ascertaining how these things do not happen without a reason, he answers himself, and

says, "God forbid." [2] For the same question, as it seems to me, which is raised concerning Jacob and Esau, may be raised regarding all celestial and terrestrial creatures, and even those of the lower world as well. And in like manner it seems to me, that as he there says, "The children being not yet born, neither having done any good or evil," so it might also be said of all other things, "When they were not yet" created, "neither had yet done any good or evil, that the decree of God according to election may stand," that (as certain think) some things on the one hand were created heavenly, some on the other earthly, and others, again, beneath the earth, "not of works" (as they think), "but of Him who calleth," what shall we say then, if these things are so? "Is there unrighteousness with God? God forbid." As, therefore, when the Scriptures are carefully examined regarding Jacob and Esau, it is not found to be unrighteousness with God that it should be said, before they were born, or had done anything in this life, "the elder shall serve the younger;" and as it is found not to be unrighteousness that even in the womb Jacob supplanted his brother, if we feel that he was worthily beloved by God, according to the deserts of his previous life, so as to deserve to be preferred before his brother; so also is it with regard to heavenly creatures, if we notice that diversity was not the original condition of the creature, but that, owing to causes that have previously existed, a different office is prepared by the Creator for each one in proportion to the degree of his merit, on this ground, indeed, that each one, in respect of having been created by God an understanding, or a rational spirit, has, according to the movements of his mind and the feelings of his soul, gained for himself a greater or less amount of merit, and has become either an object of love to God, or else one of dislike to Him; while, nevertheless, some of those who are possessed of greater merit are ordained to suffer with others for the adorning of the state of the world, and for the discharge of duty to creatures of a lower grade, in order that by this means they themselves may be participators in the endurance of the Creator, according to the words of the apostle: "For the creature was made subject to vanity, not willingly, but by reason of him who hath subjected the same in hope." [3] Keeping in view, then, the sentiment expressed by the apostle, when, speaking of the birth of Esau and Jacob, he says, "Is there unrighteousness with God? God forbid," I think it right that this same sentiment should be carefully applied to the case of all other

---

[1] Rom. ix. 11, 12.

[2] The text runs, "Respondet sibi ipse, et ait." on which Ruæus remarks that the sentence is incomplete, and that "absit" probably should be supplied. This conjecture has been adopted in the translation.

[3] Rom. viii. 20, 21.

creatures, because, as we formerly remarked, the righteousness of the Creator ought to appear in everything. And this, it appears to me, will be seen more clearly at last, if each one, whether of celestial or terrestrial or infernal beings, be said to have the causes of his diversity in himself, and antecedent to his bodily birth. For all things were created by the Word of God, and by His Wisdom, and were set in order by His Justice. And by the grace of His compassion He provides for all men, and encourages all to the use of whatever remedies may lead to their cure, and incites them to salvation.

8. As, then, there is no doubt that at the day of judgment the good will be separated from the bad, and the just from the unjust, and all by the sentence of God will be distributed according to their deserts throughout those places of which they are worthy, so I am of opinion some such state of things was formerly the case, as, God willing, we shall show in what follows. For God must be believed to do and order all things and at all times according to His judgment. For the words which the apostle uses when he says, " In a great house there are not only vessels of gold and silver, but also of wood and of earth, and some to honour and some to dishonour ; "[1] and those which he adds, saying, " If a man purge himself, he will be a vessel unto honour, sanctified and meet for the Master's use, unto every good work,"[2] undoubtedly point out this, that he who shall purge himself when he is in this life, will be prepared for every good work in that which is to come ; while he who does not purge himself will be, according to the amount of his impurity, a vessel unto dishonour, i.e., unworthy. It is therefore possible to understand that there have been also formerly rational vessels, whether purged or not, i.e., which either purged themselves or did not do so, and that consequently every vessel, according to the measure of its purity or impurity, received a place, or region, or condition by birth, or an office to discharge, in this world. All of which, down to the humblest, God providing for and distinguishing by the power of His wisdom, arranges all things by His controlling judgment, according to a most impartial retribution, so far as each one ought to be assisted or cared for in conformity with his deserts. In which certainly every principle of equity is shown, while the inequality of circumstances preserves the justice of a retribution according to merit. But the grounds of the merits in each individual case are only recognised truly and clearly by God Himself, along with His only-begotten Word, and His Wisdom, and the Holy Spirit.

CHAP. X. — ON THE RESURRECTION, AND THE JUDGMENT, THE FIRE OF HELL, AND PUNISHMENTS.

1. But since the discourse has reminded us of the subjects of a future judgment and of retribution, and of the punishments of sinners, according to the threatenings of holy Scripture and the contents of the Church's teaching — viz., that when the time of judgment comes, everlasting fire, and outer darkness, and a prison, and a furnace, and other punishments of like nature, have been prepared for sinners — let us see what our opinions on these points ought to be.[3] But that these subjects may be arrived at in proper order, it seems to me that we ought first to consider the nature of the resurrection, that we may know what that (body) is which shall come either to punishment, or to rest, or to happiness ; which question in other treatises which we have composed regarding the resurrection we have discussed at greater length, and have shown what our opinions were regarding it. But now, also, for the sake of logical order in our treatise, there will be no absurdity in re-stating a few points from such works, especially since some take offence at the creed of the Church, as if our belief in the resurrection were foolish, and altogether devoid of sense ; and these are principally heretics, who, I think, are to be answered in the following manner. If they also admit that there is a resurrection of the dead, let them answer us this, What is that which died? Was it not a body? It is of the body, then, that there will be a resurrection. Let them next tell us if they think that we are to make use of bodies or not. I think that when the Apostle Paul says, that " it is sown a natural body, it will arise a spiritual body,"[4] they cannot deny that it is a body which arises, or that in the resurrection we are to make use of bodies. What then? If it is certain that we are to make use of bodies, and if the bodies which have fallen are declared to rise again (for only that which before has fallen can be properly said to rise again), it can be a matter of doubt to no one that they rise again, in order that we may be clothed with them a second time at the resurrection. The one thing is closely connected with the other. For if bodies rise again, they undoubtedly rise to be coverings for us ; and if it is necessary for us to be invested with bodies, as it is certainly necessary, we ought to be invested with no other than our own. But if it is true that these rise again, and that they arise " spiritual " bodies, there can be no doubt that they are said to rise from the dead, after casting away corruption and laying aside mortality ;

---

[1] 2 Tim. ii. 20.
[2] 2 Tim. ii. 21.

[3] [Elucidation I.]
[4] 1 Cor. xv. 44: natural, animale (ψυχικόν).

otherwise it will appear vain and superfluous for any one to arise from the dead in order to die a second time. And this, finally, may be more distinctly comprehended thus, if one carefully consider what are the qualities of an animal body, which, when sown into the earth, recovers the qualities of a spiritual body. For it is out of the animal body that the very power and grace of the resurrection educe the spiritual body, when it transmutes it from a condition of indignity to one of glory.

2. Since the heretics, however, think themselves persons of great learning and wisdom, we shall ask them if every body has a form of some kind, i.e., is fashioned according to some shape. And if they shall say that a body is that which is fashioned according to no shape, they will show themselves to be the most ignorant and foolish of mankind. For no one will deny this, save him who is altogether without any learning. But if, as a matter of course, they say that every body is certainly fashioned according to some definite shape, we shall ask them if they can point out and describe to us the shape of a spiritual body; a thing which they can by no means do. We shall ask them, moreover, about the differences of those who rise again. How will they show that statement to be true, that there is "one flesh of birds, another of fishes; bodies celestial, and bodies terrestrial; that the glory of the celestial is one, and the glory of the terrestrial another; that one is the glory of the sun, another the glory of the moon, another the glory of the stars; that one star differeth from another star in glory; and that so is the resurrection of the dead?"[1] According to that gradation, then, which exists among heavenly bodies, let them show to us the differences in the glory of those who rise again; and if they have endeavoured by any means to devise a principle that may be in accordance with the differences in heavenly bodies, we shall ask them to assign the differences in the resurrection by a comparison of earthly bodies. Our understanding of the passage indeed is, that the apostle, wishing to describe the great difference among those who rise again in glory, i.e., of the saints, borrowed a comparison from the heavenly bodies, saying, "One is the glory of the sun, another the glory of the moon, another the glory of the stars." And wishing again to teach us the differences among those who shall come to the resurrection, without having purged themselves in this life, i.e., sinners, he borrowed an illustration from earthly things, saying, "There is one flesh of birds, another of fishes." For heavenly things are worthily compared to the saints, and earthly things to sinners. These statements are made

in reply to those who deny the resurrection of the dead, i.e., the resurrection of bodies.

3. We now turn our attention to some of our own (believers), who, either from feebleness of intellect or want of proper instruction, adopt a very low and abject view of the resurrection of the body. We ask these persons in what manner they understand that an animal body is to be changed by the grace of the resurrection, and to become a spiritual one; and how that which is sown in weakness will arise in power; how that which is planted in dishonour will arise in glory; and that which was sown in corruption, will be changed to a state of incorruption. Because if they believe the apostle, that a body which arises in glory, and power, and incorruptibility, has already become spiritual, it appears absurd and contrary to his meaning to say that it can again be entangled with the passions of flesh and blood, seeing the apostle manifestly declares that "flesh and blood shall not inherit the kingdom of God, nor shall corruption inherit incorruption." But how do they understand the declaration of the apostle, "We shall all be changed?" This transformation certainly is to be looked for, according to the order which we have taught above; and in it, undoubtedly, it becomes us to hope for something worthy of divine grace; and this we believe will take place in the order in which the apostle describes the sowing in the ground of a "bare grain of corn, or of any other fruit," to which "God gives a body as it pleases Him," as soon as the grain of corn is dead. For in the same way also our bodies are to be supposed to fall into the earth like a grain; and (that germ being implanted in them which contains the bodily substance) although the bodies die, and become corrupted, and are scattered abroad, yet by the word of God, that very germ which is always safe in the substance of the body, raises them from the earth, and restores and repairs them, as the power which is in the grain of wheat, after its corruption and death, repairs and restores the grain into a body having stalk and ear. And so also to those who shall deserve to obtain an inheritance in the kingdom of heaven, that germ of the body's restoration, which we have before mentioned, by God's command restores out of the earthly and animal body a spiritual one, capable of inhabiting the heavens; while to each one of those who may be of inferior merit, or of more abject condition, or even the lowest in the scale, and altogether thrust aside, there is yet given, in proportion to the dignity of his life and soul, a glory and dignity of body, — nevertheless in such a way, that even the body which rises again of those who are to be destined to everlasting fire or to severe punishments, is by the very change of the resurrection so incorruptible,

---

[1] 1 Cor. xv. 39-42.

that it cannot be corrupted and dissolved even by severe punishments. If, then, such be the qualities of that body which will arise from the dead, let us now see what is the meaning of the threatening of eternal fire.

4. We find in the prophet Isaiah, that the fire with which each one is punished is described as his own; for he says, "Walk in the light of your own fire, and in the flame which ye have kindled." [1] By these words it seems to be indicated that every sinner kindles for himself the flame of his own fire, and is not plunged into some fire which has been already kindled by another, or was in existence before himself. Of this fire the fuel and food are our sins, which are called by the Apostle Paul wood, and hay, and stubble." [2] And I think that, as abundance of food, and provisions of a contrary kind and amount, breed fevers in the body, and fevers, too, of different sorts and duration, according to the proportion in which the collected poison [3] supplies material and fuel for disease (the quality of this material, gathered together from different poisons, proving the causes either of a more acute or more lingering disease); so, when the soul has gathered together a multitude of evil works, and an abundance of sins against itself, at a suitable time all that assembly of evils boils up to punishment, and is set on fire to chastisements; when the mind itself, or conscience, receiving by divine power into the memory all those things of which it had stamped on itself certain signs and forms at the moment of sinning, will see a kind of history, as it were, of all the foul, and shameful, and unholy deeds which it has done, exposed before its eyes: then is the conscience itself harassed, and, pierced by its own goads, becomes an accuser and a witness against itself. And this, I think, was the opinion of the Apostle Paul himself, when he said, "Their thoughts mutually accusing or excusing them in the day when God will judge the secrets of men by Jesus Christ, according to my Gospel." [4] From which it is understood that around the substance of the soul certain tortures are produced by the hurtful affections of sins themselves.

5. And that the understanding of this matter may not appear very difficult, we may draw some considerations from the evil effects of those passions which are wont to befall some souls, as when a soul is consumed by the fire of love, or wasted away by zeal or envy, or when the passion of anger is kindled, or one is consumed by the greatness of his madness or his sorrow; on which occasions some, finding the excess of these evils unbearable, have deemed it more tolerable to submit to death than to endure perpetually torture of such a kind. You will ask indeed whether, in the case of those who have been entangled in the evils arising from those vices above enumerated, and who, while existing in this life, have been unable to procure any amelioration for themselves, and have in this condition departed from the world, it be sufficient in the way of punishment that they be tortured by the remaining in them of these hurtful affections, i.e., of the anger, or of the fury, or of the madness, or of the sorrow, whose fatal poison was in this life lessened by no healing medicine; or whether, these affections being changed, they will be subjected to the pains of a general punishment. Now I am of opinion that another species of punishment may be understood to exist; because, as we feel that when the limbs of the body are loosened and torn away from their mutual supports, there is produced pain of a most excruciating kind, so, when the soul shall be found to be beyond the order, and connection, and harmony in which it was created by God for the purposes of good and useful action and observation, and not to harmonize with itself in the connection of its rational movements, it must be deemed to bear the chastisement and torture of its own dissension, and to feel the punishments of its own disordered condition. And when this dissolution and rending asunder of soul shall have been tested by the application of fire, a solidification undoubtedly into a firmer structure will take place, and a restoration be effected.

6. There are also many other things which escape our notice, and are known to Him alone who is the physician of our souls. For if, on account of those bad effects which we bring upon ourselves by eating and drinking, we deem it necessary for the health of the body to make use of some unpleasant and painful drug, sometimes even, if the nature of the disease demand, requiring the severe process of the amputating knife; and if the virulence of the disease shall transcend even these remedies, the evil has at last to be burned out by fire; how much more is it to be understood that God our Physician, desiring to remove the defects of our souls, which they had contracted from their different sins and crimes, should employ penal measures of this sort, and should apply even, in addition, the punishment of fire to those who have lost their soundness of mind! Pictures of this method of procedure are found also in the holy Scriptures. In the book of Deuteronomy, the divine word threatens sinners with the punishments of fevers, and colds, and jaundice, [5] and with the pains of

---

[1] Isa. l. 11.
[2] 1 Cor. iii. 12.
[3] Intemperies.
[4] Rom. ii. 15, 16.

[5] Aurigine [aurugine]. Deut. xxviii.

feebleness of vision, and alienation of mind, and paralysis, and blindness, and weakness of the reins. If any one, then, at his leisure gather together out of the whole of Scripture all the enumerations of diseases which in the threatenings addressed to sinners are called by the names of bodily maladies, he will find that either the vices of souls, or their punishments, are figuratively indicated by them. To understand now, that in the same way in which physicians apply remedies to the sick, in order that by careful treatment they may recover their health, God so deals towards those who have lapsed and fallen into sin, is proved by this, that the cup of God's fury is ordered, through the agency of the prophet Jeremiah,[1] to be offered to all nations, that they may drink it, and be in a state of madness, and vomit it forth. In doing which, He threatens them, saying, That if any one refuse to drink, he shall not be cleansed.[2] By which certainly it is understood that the fury of God's vengeance is profitable for the purgation of souls. That the punishment, also, which is said to be applied by fire, is understood to be applied with the object of healing, is taught by Isaiah, who speaks thus of Israel: "The Lord will wash away the filth of the sons or daughters of Zion, and shall purge away the blood from the midst of them by the spirit of judgment, and the spirit of burning."[3] Of the Chaldeans he thus speaks: "Thou hast the coals of fire; sit upon them: they will be to thee a help."[4] And in other passages he says, "The Lord will sanctify in a burning fire;"[5] and in the prophecies of Malachi he says, "The Lord sitting will blow, and purify, and will pour forth the cleansed sons of Judah."[6]

7. But that fate also which is mentioned in the Gospels as overtaking unfaithful stewards, who, it is said, are to be divided, and a portion of them placed along with unbelievers, as if that portion which is not their own were to be sent elsewhere, undoubtedly indicates some kind of punishment on those whose spirit, as it seems to me, is shown to be separated from the soul. For if this Spirit is of divine nature, i.e., is understood to be a Holy Spirit, we shall understand this to be said of the gift of the Holy Spirit: that when, whether by baptism, or by the grace of the Spirit, the word of wisdom, or the word of knowledge, or of any other gift, has been bestowed upon a man, and not rightly administered, i.e., either buried in the earth or tied up in a napkin, the gift of the Spirit will certainly be withdrawn from his soul, and the other portion which remains, that is, the substance of the soul, will be assigned

its place with unbelievers, being divided and separated from that Spirit with whom, by joining itself to the Lord, it ought to have been one spirit. Now, if this is not to be understood of the Spirit of God, but of the nature of the soul itself, that will be called its better part which was made in the image and likeness of God; whereas the other part, that which afterwards, through its fall by the exercise of free-will, was assumed contrary to the nature of its original condition of purity,—this part, as being the friend and beloved of matter, is punished with the fate of unbelievers. There is also a third sense in which that separation may be understood, this viz., that as each believer, although the humblest in the Church, is said to be attended by an angel, who is declared by the Saviour always to behold the face of God the Father, and as this angel was certainly one with the object of his guardianship; so, if the latter is rendered unworthy by his want of obedience, the angel of God is said to be taken from him, and then that part of him — the part, viz., which belongs to his human nature — being rent away from the divine part, is assigned a place along with unbelievers, because it has not faithfully observed the admonitions of the angel allotted it by God.

8. But the outer darkness, in my judgment, is to be understood not so much of some dark atmosphere without any light, as of those persons who, being plunged in the darkness of profound ignorance, have been placed beyond the reach of any light of the understanding. We must see, also, lest this perhaps should be the meaning of the expression, that as the saints will receive those bodies in which they have lived in holiness and purity in the habitations of this life, bright and glorious after the resurrection, so the wicked also, who in this life have loved the darkness of error and the night of ignorance, may be clothed with dark and black bodies after the resurrection, that the very mist of ignorance which had in this life taken possession of their minds within them, may appear in the future as the external covering of the body. Similar is the view to be entertained regarding the prison. Let these remarks, which have been made as brief as possible, that the order of our discourse in the meantime might be preserved, suffice for the present occasion.

CHAP. XI. — ON COUNTER PROMISES.[7]

1. Let us now briefly see what views we are to form regarding promises.

It is certain that there is no living thing which can be altogether inactive and immoveable, but delights in motion of every kind, and in perpetual activity and volition; and this nature, I

[1] Cf. Jer. xxv. 15, 16.
[2] Cf. Jer. xxv. 28, 29.
[3] Isa. iv. 4.
[4] Isa. xlvii. 14, 15; vid. note, chap. v. § 3 [p. 280, supra. S.].
[5] Isa. x. 17, cf. lxvi. 16.
[6] Cf. Mal. iii. 3.
[7] Repromissionibus.

think it evident, is in all living things. Much more, then, must a rational animal, i.e., the nature of man, be in perpetual movement and activity. If, indeed, he is forgetful of himself, and ignorant of what becomes him, all his efforts are directed to serve the uses of the body, and in all his movements he is occupied with his own pleasures and bodily lusts; but if he be one who studies to care or provide for the general good, then, either by consulting for the benefit of the state or by obeying the magistrates, he exerts himself for that, whatever it is, which may seem certainly to promote the public advantage. And if now any one be of such a nature as to understand that there is something better than those things which seem to be corporeal, and so bestow his labour upon wisdom and science, then he will undoubtedly direct all his attention towards pursuits of that kind, that he may, by inquiring into the truth, ascertain the causes and reason of things. As therefore, in this life, one man deems it the highest good to enjoy bodily pleasures, another to consult for the benefit of the community, a third to devote attention to study and learning; so let us inquire whether in that life which is the true one (which is said to be hidden with Christ in God, i.e., in that eternal life), there will be for us some such order and condition of existence.

2. Certain persons, then, refusing the labour of thinking, and adopting a superficial view of the letter of the law, and yielding rather in some measure to the indulgence of their own desires and lusts, being disciples of the letter alone, are of opinion that the fulfilment of the promises of the future are to be looked for in bodily pleasure and luxury; and therefore they especially desire to have again, after the resurrection, such bodily structures[1] as may never be without the power of eating, and drinking, and performing all the functions of flesh and blood, not following the opinion of the Apostle Paul regarding the resurrection of a spiritual body. And consequently they say, that after the resurrection there will be marriages, and the begetting of children, imagining to themselves that the earthly city of Jerusalem is to be rebuilt, its foundations laid in precious stones, and its walls constructed of jasper, and its battlements of crystal; that it is to have a wall composed of many precious stones, as jasper, and sapphire, and chalcedony, and emerald, and sardonyx, and onyx, and chrysolite, and chrysoprase, and jacinth, and amethyst. Moreover, they think that the natives of other countries are to be given them as the ministers of their pleasures, whom they are to employ either as tillers of the field or builders of walls, and by whom their ruined and fallen city is again to be

raised up; and they think that they are to receive the wealth of the nations to live on, and that they will have control over their riches; that even the camels of Midian and Kedar will come, and bring to them gold, and incense, and precious stones. And these views they think to establish on the authority of the prophets by those promises which are written regarding Jerusalem; and by those passages also where it is said, that they who serve the Lord shall eat and drink, but that sinners shall hunger and thirst; that the righteous shall be joyful, but that sorrow shall possess the wicked. And from the New Testament also they quote the saying of the Saviour, in which He makes a promise to His disciples concerning the joy of wine, saying, "Henceforth I shall not drink of this cup, until I drink it with you new in My Father's kingdom."[2] They add, moreover, that declaration, in which the Saviour calls those blessed who now hunger and thirst,[3] promising them that they shall be satisfied; and many other scriptural illustrations are adduced by them, the meaning of which they do not perceive is to be taken figuratively. Then, again, agreeably to the form of things in this life, and according to the gradations of the dignities or ranks in this world, or the greatness of their powers, they think they are to be kings and princes, like those earthly monarchs who now exist; chiefly, as it appears, on account of that expression in the Gospel: "Have thou power over five cities."[4] And to speak shortly, according to the manner of things in this life in all similar matters, do they desire the fulfilment of all things looked for in the promises, viz., that what now is should exist again. Such are the views of those who, while believing in Christ, understand the divine Scriptures in a sort of Jewish sense, drawing from them nothing worthy of the divine promises.

3. Those, however, who receive the representations of Scripture according to the understanding of the apostles, entertain the hope that the saints will eat indeed, but that it will be the bread of life, which may nourish the soul with the food of truth and wisdom, and enlighten the mind, and cause it to drink from the cup of divine wisdom, according to the declaration of holy Scripture: "Wisdom has prepared her table, she has killed her beasts, she has mingled her wine in her cup, and she cries with a loud voice, Come to me, eat the bread which I have prepared for you, and drink the wine which I have mingled."[5] By this food of wisdom, the understanding, being nourished to an entire and perfect condition like that in which man was made at

---

[1] Carnes.

[2] Matt. xxvi. 29.
[3] Matt. v. 6.
[4] Cf. Luke xix. 19 and 17.
[5] Cf. Prov. ix. 1-5.

the beginning, is restored to the image and likeness of God ; so that, although an individual may depart from this life less perfectly instructed, but who has done works that are approved of,[1] he will be capable of receiving instruction in that Jerusalem, the city of the saints, i.e., he will be educated and moulded, and made a living stone, a stone elect and precious, because he has undergone with firmness and constancy the struggles of life and the trials of piety ; and will there come to a truer and clearer knowledge of that which here has been already predicted, viz., that " man shall not live by bread alone, but by every word which proceedeth from the mouth of God." [2]   And they also are to be understood to be the princes and rulers who both govern those of lower rank, and instruct them, and teach them, and train them to divine things.

4. But if these views should not appear to fill the minds of those who hope for such results with a becoming desire, let us go back a little, and, irrespective of the natural and innate longing of the mind for the thing itself, let us make inquiry so that we may be able at last to describe, as it were, the very forms of the bread of life, and the quality of that wine, and the peculiar nature of the principalities, all in conformity with the spiritual view of things.[3]   Now, as in those arts which are usually performed by means of manual labour, the reason why a thing is done, or why it is of a special quality, or for a special purpose, is an object of investigation to the mind,[4] while the actual work itself is unfolded to view by the agency of the hands ; so, in those works of God which were created by Him, it is to be observed that the reason and understanding of those things which we see done by Him remains undisclosed.   And as, when our eye beholds the products of an artist's labour, the mind, immediately on perceiving anything of unusual artistic excellence, burns to know of what nature it is, or how it was formed, or to what purposes it was fashioned ; so, in a much greater degree, and in one that is beyond all comparison, does the mind burn with an inexpressible desire to know the reason of those things which we see done by God.   This desire, this longing, we believe to be unquestionably implanted within us by God ; and as the eye naturally seeks the light and vision, and our body naturally desires food and drink, so our mind is possessed with a becoming and natural desire to become acquainted with the truth of God and the causes of things.   Now we have received this desire from God, not in order that it should never be

gratified or be *capable* of gratification ; otherwise the love of truth would appear to have been implanted by God into our minds to no purpose, if it were never to have an opportunity of satisfaction.   Whence also, even in this life, those who devote themselves with great labour to the pursuits of piety and religion, although obtaining only some small fragments from the numerous and immense treasures of divine knowledge, yet, by the very circumstance that their mind and soul is engaged in these pursuits, and that in the eagerness of their desire they outstrip themselves, do they derive much advantage ; and, because their minds are directed to the study and love of the investigation of truth, are they made fitter for receiving the instruction that is to come ; as if, when one would paint an image, he were first with a light pencil to trace out the outlines of the coming picture, and prepare marks for the reception of the features that are to be afterwards added, this preliminary sketch in outline is found to prepare the way for the laying on of the true colours of the painting ; so, in a measure, an outline and sketch may be traced on the tablets of our heart by the pencil of our Lord Jesus Christ.   And therefore perhaps is it said, " Unto every one that hath shall be given, and be added." [5]   By which it is established, that to those who possess in this life a kind of outline of truth and knowledge, shall be added the beauty of a perfect image in the future.

5. Some such desire, I apprehend, was indicated by him who said, "I am in a strait betwixt two, having a desire to depart, and to be with Christ, which is far better ; " [6] knowing that when he should have returned to Christ he would then know more clearly the reasons of all things which are done on earth, either respecting man, or the soul of man, or the mind ; or regarding any other subject, such as, for instance, what is the Spirit that operates, what also is the vital spirit, or what is the grace of the Holy Spirit that is given to believers.   Then also will he understand what Israel appears to be, or what is meant by the diversity of nations ; what the twelve tribes of Israel mean, and what the individual people of each tribe.   Then, too, will he understand the reason of the priests and Levites, and of the different priestly orders, the type of which was in Moses, and also what is the true meaning of the jubilees, and of the weeks of years with God. He will see also the reasons for the festival days, and holy days, and for all the sacrifices and purifications.   He will perceive also the reason of the purgation from leprosy, and what the different kinds of leprosy are, and the reason of the purgation of those who lose their seed.   He will

---

[1] Opera probabilia.
[2] Deut. viii. 3.
[3] The passage is somewhat obscure, but the rendering in the text seems to convey the meaning intended.
[4] Versatur in sensu.

[5] Luke xix. 26; cf. Matt. xxv. 29.
[6] Phil. i. 23.

come to know, moreover, what are the good influences,[1] and their greatness, and their qualities; and those too which are of a contrary kind, and what the affection of the former, and what the strife-causing emulation of the latter is towards men. He will behold also the nature of the soul, and the diversity of animals (whether of those which live in the water, or of birds, or of wild beasts), and why each of the genera is subdivided into so many species; and what intention of the Creator, or what purpose of His wisdom, is concealed in each individual thing. He will become acquainted, too, with the reason why certain properties are found associated with certain roots or herbs, and why, on the other hand, evil effects are averted by other herbs and roots. He will know, moreover, the nature of the apostate angels, and the reason why they have power to flatter in some things those who do not despise them with the whole power of faith, and why they exist for the purpose of deceiving and leading men astray. He will learn, too, the judgment of Divine Providence on each individual thing; and that, of those events which happen to men, none occur by accident or chance, but in accordance with a plan so carefully considered, and so stupendous, that it does not overlook even the number of the hairs of the heads, not merely of the saints, but perhaps of all human beings, and the plan of which providential government extends even to caring for the sale of two sparrows for a denarius, whether sparrows there be understood figuratively or literally. Now indeed this providential government is still a subject of investigation, but then it will be fully manifested. From all which we are to suppose, that meanwhile not a little time may pass by until the reason of those things only which are upon the earth be pointed out to the worthy and deserving after their departure from life, that by the knowledge of all these things, and by the grace of full knowledge, they may enjoy an unspeakable joy. Then, if that atmosphere which is between heaven and earth is not devoid of inhabitants, and those of a rational kind, as the apostle says, "Wherein in times past ye walked according to the course of this world, according to the prince of the power of the air, the spirit who now worketh in the children of disobedience."[2] And again he says, "We shall be caught up in the clouds to meet Christ in the air, and so shall we ever be with the Lord."[3]

6. We are therefore to suppose that the saints will remain there until they recognise the twofold mode of government in those things which are performed in the air. And when I say "two-fold mode," I mean this: When we were upon earth, we saw either animals or trees, and beheld the differences among them, and also the very great diversity among men; but although we saw these things, we did not understand the reason of them; and this only was suggested to us from the visible diversity, that we should examine and inquire upon what principle these things were either created or diversely arranged. And a zeal or desire for knowledge of this kind being conceived by us on earth, the full understanding and comprehension of it will be granted after death, if indeed the result should follow according to our expectations. When, therefore, we shall have fully comprehended its nature, we shall understand in a twofold manner what we saw on earth. Some such view, then, must we hold regarding this abode in the air. I think, therefore, that all the saints who depart from this life will remain in some place situated on the earth, which holy Scripture calls paradise, as in some place of instruction, and, so to speak, class-room or school of souls, in which they are to be instructed regarding all the things which they had seen on earth, and are to receive also some information respecting things that are to follow in the future, as even when in this life they had obtained in some degree indications of future events, although "through a glass darkly," all of which are revealed more clearly and distinctly to the saints in their proper time and place. If any one indeed be pure in heart, and holy in mind, and more practised in perception, he will, by making more rapid progress, quickly ascend to a place in the air, and reach the kingdom of heaven, through those mansions, so to speak, in the various places which the Greeks have termed spheres, i.e., globes, but which holy Scripture has called heavens; in each of which he will first see clearly what is done there, and in the second place, will discover the reason why things are so done: and thus he will in order pass through all gradations, following Him who hath passed into the heavens, Jesus the Son of God, who said, "I will that where I am, these may be also."[4] And of this diversity of places He speaks, when He says, "In My Father's house are many mansions." He Himself is everywhere, and passes swiftly through all things; nor are we any longer to understand Him as existing in those narrow limits in which He was once confined for our sakes, i.e., not in that circumscribed body which He occupied on earth, when dwelling among men, according to which He might be considered as enclosed in some one place.

7. When, then, the saints shall have reached the celestial abodes, they will clearly see the nature of the stars one by one, and will under-

---

[1] Virtutes.
[2] Eph. ii. 2. There is an evident omission of some words in the text, such as, "They will enter into it," etc.
[3] 1 Thess. iv. 17.

[4] John xvii. 24.

stand whether they are endued with life, or their condition, whatever it is. And they will comprehend also the other reasons for the works of God, which He Himself will reveal to them. For He will show to them, as to children, the causes of things and the power of His creation,[1] and will explain why that star was placed in that particular quarter of the sky, and why it was separated from another by so great an intervening space ; what, e.g., would have been the consequence if it had been nearer or more remote ; or if that star had been larger than this, how the totality of things would not have remained the same, but all would have been transformed into a different condition of being. And so, when they have finished all those matters which are connected with the stars, and with the heavenly revolutions, they will come to those which are not seen, or to those whose names only we have heard, and to things which are invisible, which the Apostle Paul has informed us are numerous, although what they are, or what difference may exist among them, we cannot even conjecture by our feeble intellect. And thus the rational nature, growing by each individual step, not as it grew in this life in flesh, and body, and soul, but enlarged in understanding and in power of perception, is raised as a mind already perfect to perfect knowledge, no longer at all impeded by those carnal senses, but increased in intellectual growth ; and ever gazing purely, and, so to speak face to face, on the causes of things, it attains perfection, firstly, viz., that by which it ascends to (the truth),[2] and secondly, that by which it abides in it, having problems and the understanding of things, and the causes of events, as the food on which it may feast. For as in this life our bodies grow physically to what they are through a sufficiency of food in early life supplying the means of increase, but after the due height has been attained we use food no longer to grow, but to live, and to be preserved in life by it ; so also I think that the mind, when it has attained perfection, eats and avails itself of suitable and appropriate food in such a degree, that nothing ought to be either deficient or superfluous. And in all things this food is to be understood as the contemplation and understanding of God, which is of a measure appropriate and suitable to this nature, which was made and created ; and this measure it is proper should be observed by every one of those who are beginning to see God, i.e., to understand Him through purity of heart.

---

[1] Virtutem suæ conditionis. Seine Schöpferkraft (Schnitzer).

[2] In id: To that state of the soul in which it gazes purely on the causes of things.

ORIGEN DE PRINCIPIIS.

BOOK III.

PREFACE OF RUFINUS.

READER, remember me in your prayers, that we too may deserve to be made emulators of the spirit. The two former books on *The Principles* I translated not only at your instance, but even under pressure from you during the days of Lent;[1] but as you, my devout brother Macarius, were not only living near me during that time, but had more leisure at your command than now, so I also worked the harder; whereas I have been longer in explaining these two latter books, seeing you came less frequently from a distant extremity of the city to urge on my labour. Now if you remember what I warned you of in my former preface, — that certain persons would be indignant, if they did not hear that we spoke some evil of Origen, — that, I imagine, you have forthwith experienced, has come to pass. But if those demons[2] who excite the tongues of men to slander were so infuriated by that work, in which he had not as yet fully unveiled their secret proceedings, what, think you, will be the case in this, in which he will expose all those dark and hidden ways, by which they creep into the hearts of men, and deceive weak and unstable souls? You will immediately see all things thrown into confusion, seditions stirred up, clamours raised throughout the whole city, and that individual summoned to receive sentence of condemnation who endeavoured to dispel the diabolical darkness of ignorance by means of the light of the Gospel lamp.[3] Let such things, however, be lightly esteemed by him who is desirous of being trained in divine learning, while retaining in its integrity the rule of the Catholic faith.[4] I think it necessary, however, to remind you that the principle observed in the former books has been observed also in these, viz., not to translate what appeared contrary to Origen's other opinions, and to our own belief, but to pass by such passages as being interpolated and forged by others. But if he has appeared to give expression to any novelties regarding rational creatures (on which subject the essence of our faith does not depend), for the sake of discussion and of adding to our knowledge, when perhaps it was necessary for us to answer in such an order some heretical opinions, I have not omitted to mention these either in the present or preceding books, unless when he wished to repeat in the following books what he had already stated in the previous ones, when I have thought it convenient, for the sake of brevity, to curtail some of these repetitions. Should any one, however, peruse these passages from a desire to enlarge his knowledge, and not to raise captious objections, he will do better to have them expounded by persons of skill. For it is an absurdity to have the fictions of poetry and the ridiculous plays of comedy[5] interpreted by grammarians, and to suppose that without a master and an interpreter any one is able to learn those things which are spoken either of God or of the heavenly virtues, and of the whole universe of things, in which some deplorable error either of pagan philosophers or of heretics is confuted; and the result of which is, that men would rather rashly and ignorantly condemn things that are difficult and obscure, than ascertain their meaning by diligence and study.

---

[1] Diebus quadragesimæ.
[2] Dæmones.
[3] Evangelicæ lucernæ lumine diabolicas ignorantiæ tenebras.
[4] Salvâ fidei Catholicæ regula. [This remonstrance of Rufinus deserves candid notice. He reduces the liberties he took with his author to two heads: (1) omitting what Origen himself contradicts, and (2) what was interpolated by those who thus vented their own heresies under a great name. "To our own belief," may mean what is contrary to the faith, as reduced to technical formula, at Nicæa; i.e., *Salva regula fidei*. Note examples in the parallel columns following.]
[5] Comœdiarum ridiculas fabulas.

TRANSLATED FROM LATIN OF RUFINUS.

CHAP. I. — ON THE FREEDOM OF THE WILL.[1]

1. Some such opinions, we believe, ought to be entertained regarding the divine promises, when we direct our understanding to the contemplation of that eternal and infinite world, and gaze on its ineffable joy and blessedness. But as the preaching of the Church includes a belief in a future and just judgment of God, which belief incites and persuades men to a good and virtuous life, and to an avoidance of sin by all possible means ; and as by this it is undoubtedly indicated that it is within our own power to devote ourselves either to a life that is worthy of praise, or to one that is worthy of censure, I therefore deem it necessary to say a few words regarding the freedom of the will, seeing that this topic has been treated by very many writers in no mean style. And that we may ascertain more easily what is the freedom of the will, let us inquire into the nature of will and of desire.[3]

2. Of all things which move, some have the cause of their motion within themselves, others receive it from without : and all those things only are moved from without which are without life, as stones, and pieces of wood, and whatever things are of such a nature as to be held together by the constitution of their matter alone, or of their bodily substance.[5] That view must indeed be dismissed which would regard the dissolution of bodies by corruption as motion, for it has no bearing upon our present purpose. Others, again, have the cause of motion in themselves, as animals, or trees, and all things which are held together by natural life or soul ; among which some think ought to be classed the veins of metals. Fire, also, is supposed to be the cause of its own motion, and perhaps also springs of water. And of those things which have the causes of their motion in themselves, some are said to be moved out of themselves, others by themselves. And they so distinguish them, because those things are moved out of themselves which are alive indeed, but have no soul ;[7] whereas those things which have a soul are moved by themselves, when a phantasy,[8] i.e., a desire or incitement, is presented to them, which excites them to move towards something. Finally, in certain things endowed with a soul, there is such a phantasy, i.e., a will or feeling,[9] as by a kind of natural instinct calls them forth, and arouses them to orderly and regular motion ; as we see to be the case with spiders, which are

TRANSLATION FROM THE GREEK.

CHAP. I. — ON THE FREEDOM OF THE WILL,[2] WITH AN EXPLANATION AND INTERPRETATION OF THOSE STATEMENTS OF SCRIPTURE WHICH APPEAR TO NULLIFY IT.

1. Since in the preaching of the Church there is included the doctrine respecting a just judgment of God, which, when believed to be true, incites those who hear it to live virtuously, and to shun sin by all means, inasmuch as they manifestly acknowledge that things worthy of praise and blame are within our own power, come and let us discuss by themselves a few points regarding the freedom of the will — a question of all others most necessary. And that we may understand what the freedom of the will is, it is necessary to unfold the conception of it,[4] that this being declared with precision, the subject may be placed before us.

2. Of things that move, some have the cause of their motion within themselves ; others, again, are moved only from without. Now only portable things are moved from without, such as pieces of wood, and stones, and all matter that is held together by their constitution alone.[6] And let that view be removed from consideration which calls the flux of bodies motion, since it is not needed for our present purpose. But animals and plants have the cause of their motion within themselves, and in general whatever is held together by nature and a soul, to which class of things they say that metals also belong. And besides these, fire too is self-moved, and perhaps also fountains of water. Now, of those things which have the cause of their movement within themselves, some, they say, are moved out of themselves, others from themselves : things without life, out of themselves ; animate things, from themselves. For animate things are moved from themselves, a phantasy[10] springing up in

---

[1] The whole of this chapter has been preserved in the original Greek, which is *literally* translated in corresponding portions on each page, so that the differences between Origen's own words and the amplifications and alterations of the paraphrase of Rufinus may be at once patent to the reader.   [2] περὶ τοῦ αὐτεξουσίου.   [3] Natura ipsius arbitrii voluntatisque.   [4] τὴν ἔννοιαν αὐτοῦ ἀναπτύξαι.
[5] Quæcunque hujusmodi sunt, quæ solo habitu materiæ suæ vel corporum constant.   [6] ὑπὸ ἕξεως μόνης.
[7] Non tamen animantia sunt.   [8] Phantasia.   [9] Voluntas vel sensus.   [10] φαντασίας.

FROM THE LATIN.

stirred up in a most orderly manner by a phantasy, i.e., a sort of wish and desire for weaving, to undertake the production of a web, some natural movement undoubtedly calling forth the effort to work of this kind. Nor is this very insect found to possess any other feeling than the natural desire of weaving; as in like manner bees also exhibit a desire to form honeycombs, and to collect, as they say, aerial honey.[2]

3. But since a rational animal not only has within itself these natural movements, but has moreover, to a greater extent than other animals, the power of reason, by which it can judge and determine regarding natural movements, and disapprove and reject some, while approving and adopting others, so by the judgment of this reason may the movements of men be governed and directed towards a commendable life. And from this it follows that, since the nature of this reason which is in man has within itself the power of distinguishing between good and evil, and while distinguishing possesses the faculty of selecting what it has approved, it may justly be deemed worthy of praise in choosing what is good, and deserving of censure in following that which is base or wicked. This indeed must by no means escape our notice, that in some dumb animals there is found a more regular movement [4] than in others, as in hunting-dogs or war-horses, so that they may appear to some to be moved by a kind of rational sense. But we must believe this to be the result not so much of reason as of some natural instinct,[6] largely bestowed for purposes of that kind. Now, as we had begun to remark, seeing that such is the nature of a rational animal, some things may happen to us human beings from without; and these, coming in contact with our sense of sight, or hearing, or any other of our senses, may incite and arouse us to good movements, or the contrary; and seeing they come to us from an external source, it is not within our own power to prevent their coming. But to determine and approve what use we ought to make of those things which thus happen, is the duty of no other than of that reason within us, i.e., of our own judgment; by the decision of which reason we use the incitement, which comes to us from without for that purpose, which reason approves, our natural movements being determined by its authority either to good actions or the reverse.

4. If any one now were to say that those things which happen to us from an external cause, and call forth our movements, are of such a nature that it is impossible to resist them, whether they incite us to good or evil, let the holder of this opinion turn his attention for a little upon himself, and carefully inspect the movements of his own

FROM THE GREEK.

them which incites to effort. And again, in certain animals phantasies are formed which call forth an effort, the nature of the phantasy[1] stirring up the effort in an orderly manner, as in the spider is formed the phantasy of weaving; and the attempt to weave follows, the nature of its phantasy inciting the insect in an orderly manner to this alone. And besides its phantasial nature, nothing else is believed to belong to the insect.[3] And in the bee there is formed the phantasy to produce wax.

3. The rational animal, however, has, in addition to its phantasial nature, also reason, which judges the phantasies, and disapproves of some and accepts others, in order that the animal may be led according to them. Therefore, since there are in the nature of reason aids towards the contemplation of virtue and vice, by following which, after beholding good and evil, we select the one and avoid the other, we are deserving of praise when we give ourselves to the practice of virtue, and censurable when we do the reverse. We must not, however, be ignorant that the greater part of the nature assigned to all things is a varying quantity [5] among animals, both in a greater and a less degree; so that the instinct in hunting-dogs and in war-horses approaches somehow, so to speak, to the faculty of reason. Now, to fall under some one of those external causes which stir up within us this phantasy or that, is confessedly not one of those things that are dependent upon ourselves; but to determine that we shall use the occurrence in this way or differently, is the prerogative of nothing else than of the reason within us, which, as occasion offers,[7] arouses us towards efforts inciting to what is virtuous and becoming, or turns us aside to what is the reverse.

4. But if any one maintain that this very external cause is of such a nature that it is impossible to resist it when it comes in such a way, let him turn his attention to his own feelings and movements, (and see) whether there

---

[1] φύσεως φανταστικῆς.   [2] Mella, ut aiunt, aeria congregandi. Rufinus seems to have read, in the original, ἀεροπλαστεῖν instead of κηροπλαστεῖν,—an evidence that he followed in general the worst readings (Redepenning).   [3] καὶ οὐδενὸς ἄλλου μετὰ τὴν φανταστικὴν αὐτοῦ φύσιν πεπιστευμένου τοῦ ζώου.   [4] Ordinatior quidem motus.   [5] ποσῶς.   [6] Incentivo quodam et naturali motu.   [7] παρὰ τὰς ἀφορμάς.

mind, unless he has discovered already, that when an enticement to any desire arises, nothing is accomplished until the assent of the soul is gained, and the authority of the mind has granted indulgence to the wicked suggestion ; so that a claim might seem to be made by two parties on certain probable grounds as to a judge residing within the tribunals of our heart, in order that, after the statement of reasons, the decree of execution may proceed from the judgment of reason.[2] For, to take an illustration : if, to a man who has determined to live continently and chastely, and to keep himself free from all pollution with women, a woman should happen to present herself, inciting and alluring him to act contrary to his purpose, that woman is not a complete and absolute cause or necessity of his transgressing,[4] since it is in his power, by remembering his resolution, to bridle the incitements to lust, and by the stern admonitions of virtue to restrain the pleasure of the allurement that solicits him ; so that, all feeling of indulgence being driven away, his determination may remain firm and enduring. Finally, if to any men of learning, strengthened by divine training, allurements of that kind present themselves, remembering forthwith what they are, and calling to mind what has long been the subject of their meditation and instruction, and fortifying themselves by the support of a holier doctrine, they reject and repel all incitement to pleasure, and drive away opposing lusts by the interposition of the reason implanted within them.

5. Seeing, then, that these positions are thus established by a sort of natural evidence, is it not superfluous to throw back the causes of our actions on those things which happen to us from without, and thus transfer the blame from ourselves, on whom it wholly lies? For this is to say that we are like pieces of wood, or stones, which have no motion in themselves, but receive the causes of their motion from without. Now such an assertion is neither true nor becoming, and is invented only that the freedom of the will may be denied ; unless, indeed, we are to suppose that the freedom of the will consists in this, that nothing which happens to us from without can incite us to good or evil. And if any one were to refer the causes of our faults to the natural disorder[8] of the body, such a theory is proved to be contrary to the reason of all teaching.[9] For, as we see in very many individuals, that after living unchastely and intemperately, and after being the captives of luxury and lust, if they should happen to be aroused by the word of teaching and instruction to enter upon a better course of life, there takes place so great a change, that from being luxurious and wicked men, they are converted into those who are sober, and most chaste and gentle ; so, again, we see in the case of those who are quiet and honest, that after associating with restless and shameless individuals, their good morals are corrupted by evil conversation, and they

is not an approval, and assent, and inclination of the controlling principle towards some object on account of some specious arguments.[1] For, to take an instance, a woman who has appeared before a man that has determined to be chaste, and to refrain from carnal intercourse, and who has incited him to act contrary to his purpose, is not a perfect[3] cause of annulling his determination. For, being altogether pleased with the luxury and allurement of the pleasure, and not wishing to resist it, or to keep his purpose, he commits an act of licentiousness. Another man, again (when the same things have happened to him who has received more instruction, and has disciplined himself[5]), encounters, indeed, allurements and enticements ; but his reason, as being strengthened to a higher point, and carefully trained, and confirmed in its views towards a virtuous course, or being near to confirmation,[6] repels the incitement, and extinguishes the desire.

5. Such being the case, to say that we are moved from without, and to put away the blame from ourselves, by declaring that we are like to pieces of wood and stones, which are dragged about by those causes that act upon them from without, is neither true nor in conformity with reason, but is the statement of him who wishes to destroy[7] the conception of free-will. For if we were to ask such an one what was free-will, he would say that it consisted in this, that when purposing to do some thing, no external cause came inciting to the reverse. But to blame, on the other hand, the mere constitution of the body,[10] is absurd ; for the disciplinary reason,[11] taking hold of those who are most intemperate and savage (if they will follow her exhortation), effects a transformation, so that the alteration and change for the better is most extensive, — the most licentious men frequently becoming better than those who formerly did not seem to be such by nature ; and

---

[1] διὰ τάσδε τὰς πιθανότητας.　[2] Ita ut etiam verisimilibus quibusdam causis intra cordis nostri tribunalia velut judici residenti ex utrâque parte adhiberi videatur assertio, ut causis prius expositis gerendi sententia de rationis judicio proferatur.　[3] αὐτοτελής.
[4] Causa ei perfecta et absoluta vel necessitas prævaricandi.　[5] ἠσκηκότι.　[6] ἐγγύς γε τοῦ βεβαιωθῆναι γεγενημένος.
[7] παραχαράττειν.　[8] Naturalem corporis intemperiem; ψιλὴν τὴν κατασκευήν.　[9] Contra rationem totius eruditionis. In the Greek, "contra rationem" is expressed by παρὰ τὸ ἐναργές ἐστι: and the words λόγου παιδευτικοῦ (rendered by Rufinus "totius eruditionis," and connected with "contra rationem") belong to the following clause.　[10] ψιλὴν τὴν κατασκευήν.　[11] λόγου παιδευτικοῦ.

become like those whose wickedness is complete.[1] And this is the case sometimes with men of mature age, so that such have lived more chastely in youth than when more advanced years have enabled them to indulge in a freer mode of life. The result of our reasoning, therefore, is to show that those things which happen to us from without are not in our own power; but that to make a good or bad use of those things which do so happen, by help of that reason which is within us, and which distinguishes and determines how these things ought to be used, *is* within our power.

6. And now, to confirm the deductions of reason by the authority of Scripture — viz., that it is our own doing whether we live rightly or not, and that we are not compelled, either by those causes which come to us from without, or, as some think, by the presence of fate — we adduce the testimony of the prophet Micah, in these words: "If it has been announced to thee, O man, what is good, or what the LORD requires of thee, except that thou shouldst do justice, and love mercy, and be ready to walk with the Lord thy God."[4] Moses also speaks as follows: "I have placed before thy face the way of life and the way of death: choose what is good, and walk in it."[5] Isaiah, moreover, makes this declaration: "If you are willing, and hear me, ye shall eat the good of the land. But if you be unwilling, and will not hear me, the sword shall consume you; for the mouth of the LORD has spoken this."[7] In the Psalm, too, it is written: "If My people had heard Me, if Israel had walked in My ways, I would have humbled her enemies to nothing;"[8] by which he shows that it was in the power of the people to hear, and to walk in the ways of God. The Saviour also saying, "I say unto you, Resist not evil;"[9] and, "Whoever shall be angry with his brother, shall be in danger of the judgment;"[10] and, "Whosoever shall look upon a woman to lust after her, hath already committed adultery with her in his heart;"[12] and in issuing certain other commands, — conveys no other meaning than this, that it is in our own power to observe what is commanded. And therefore we are rightly rendered liable to condemnation if we transgress those commandments which we are able to keep. And hence He Himself also declares: "Every one who hears my words, and doeth

the most savage men passing into such a state of mildness,[2] that those persons who never at any time were so savage as they were, appear savage in comparison, so great a degree of gentleness having been produced within them. And we see other men, most steady and respectable, driven from their state of respectability and steadiness by intercourse with evil customs, so as to fall into habits of licentiousness, often beginning their wickedness in middle age, and plunging into disorder after the period of youth has passed, which, so far as its nature is concerned, is unstable. Reason, therefore, demonstrates that external events do not depend on us, but that it is our own business to use them in this way or the opposite, having received reason as a judge and an investigator[3] of the manner in which we ought to meet those events that come from without.

6. Now, that it is our business to live virtuously, and that God asks this of us, as not being dependent on Him nor on any other, nor, as some think, upon fate, but as being our own doing, the prophet Micah will prove when he says: "If it has been announced to thee, O man, what is good, or what does the LORD require of thee, except to do justice and to love mercy?"[4] Moses also: "I have placed before thy face the way of life, and the way of death: choose what is good, and walk in it."[6] Isaiah too: "If you are willing, and hear me, ye shall eat the good of the land; but if ye be unwilling, and will not hear me, the sword will consume you: for the mouth of the LORD hath spoken it."[7] And in the Psalms: "If My people had heard Me, and Israel had walked in My ways, I would have humbled their enemies to nothing, and laid My hand upon those that afflicted them;"[11] showing that it was in the power of His people to hear and to walk in the ways of God. And the Saviour also, when He commands, "But I say unto you, Resist not evil;"[9] and, "Whosoever shall be angry with his brother, shall be in danger of the judgment;"[10] and, "Whosoever shall look upon a

---

[1] Quibus nihil ad turpitudinem deest.   [2] ἡμερότητος.   [3] ἐξεταστήν.   [4] Mic. vi. 8.   [5] Deut. xxx. 15.   [6] Cf. Deut. xxx. 15, 16, cf. 19.   [7] Isa. i. 19, 20.   [8] Ps. lxxxi. 13, 14.   [9] Matt. v. 39.   [10] Matt. v. 22.   [11] Ps. lxxxi. 13, 14.   [12] Matt. v. 28.

them, I will show to whom he is like : he is like a wise man who built his house upon a rock," etc.[1] So also the declaration : " Whoso heareth these things, and doeth them not, is like a foolish man, who built his house upon the sand," etc.[3] Even the words addressed to those who are on His right hand, " Come unto Me, all ye blessed of My Father," etc. ; " for I was an hungered, and ye gave Me to eat; I was thirsty, and ye gave Me drink,"[5] manifestly show that it depended upon themselves, that either these should be deserving of praise for doing what was commanded and receiving what was promised, or those deserving of censure who either heard or received the contrary, and to whom it was said, " Depart, ye cursed, into everlasting fire." Let us observe also, that the Apostle Paul addresses us as having power over our own will, and as possessing in ourselves the causes either of our salvation or of our ruin : " Dost thou despise the riches of His goodness, and of His patience, and of His long-suffering, not knowing that the goodness of God leadeth thee to repentance ? But, according to thy hardness and impenitent heart, thou art treasuring up for thyself wrath on the day of judgment and of the revelation of the just judgment of God, who will render to every one according to his work : to those who by patient continuance in well-doing seek for glory and immortality, eternal life ;[8] while to those who are contentious, and believe not the truth, but who believe iniquity, anger, indignation, tribulation, and distress, on every soul of man that worketh evil, on the Jew first, and (afterwards) on the Greek ; but glory, and honour, and peace to every one that doeth good, to the Jew first, and (afterwards) to the Greek."[11] You will find also innumerable other passages in holy Scripture, which manifestly show that we possess freedom of will. Otherwise there would be a contrariety in commandments being given us, by observing which we may be saved, or by transgressing which we may be condemned, if the power of keeping them were not implanted in us.

woman to lust after her, hath already committed adultery with her in his heart ;"[2] and by any other commandment which He gives, declares that it lies with ourselves to keep what is enjoined, and that we shall reasonably[4] be liable to condemnation if we transgress. And therefore He says in addition : " He that heareth My words and doeth them, shall be likened to a prudent man, who built his house upon a rock," etc., etc. ; " while he that heareth them, but doeth them not, is like a foolish man, who built his house upon the sand," etc.[6] And when He says to those on His right hand, " Come, ye blessed of My Father,' etc. ; " for I was an hungered, and ye gave Me to eat ; I was athirst, and ye gave Me to drink,"[7] it is exceedingly manifest that He gives the promises to these as being deserving of praise. But, on the contrary, to the others, as being censurable in comparison with them, He says, " Depart, ye cursed into everlasting fire ! "[9] And let us observe how Paul also converses[10] with us as having freedom of will, and as being ourselves the cause of ruin or salvation, when he says, " Dost thou despise the riches of His goodness and of His patience, and of His long-suffering ; not knowing that the goodness of God leadeth thee to repentance ? But, according to thy hardness and impenitent heart, thou art treasuring up for thyself wrath on the day of wrath and revelation of the righteous judgment of God ; who will render to every one according to his works : to those who, by patient continuance in well-doing, seek for glory and immortality, eternal life ; while to those who are contentious, and believe not the truth, but who believe iniquity, anger, wrath, tribulation, and distress, on every soul of man that worketh evil ; on the Jew first, and on the Greek ; but glory, and honour, and peace to every one that worketh good ; to the Jew first, and to the Greek."[11] There are, indeed, innumerable passages in the Scriptures which establish with exceeding clearness the existence of freedom of will.

7. But, seeing there are found in the sacred Scriptures

7. But, since certain declarations of

---

[1] Matt. vii. 24.   [2] Matt. v. 28.   [3] Matt. vii. 26.   [4] εὐλόγως.   [5] Matt. xxv. 34 sq.   [6] Cf. Matt. vii. 26.   [7] Matt. xxv. 34.
[8] The words in the text are: His qui secundum patientiam boni operis, gloria et incorruptio, qui quærunt vitam eternam.
[9] Matt. xxv. 41.   [10] διαλέγεται.   [11] Rom. ii. 4-10.

themselves certain expressions occurring in such a connection, that the opposite of this may appear capable of being understood from them, let us bring them forth before us, and, discussing them according to the rule of piety,[1] let us furnish an explanation of them, in order that from those few passages which we now expound, the solution of those others which resemble them, and by which any power over the will seems to be excluded, may become clear. Those expressions, accordingly, make an impression on very many, which are used by God in speaking of Pharaoh, as when He frequently says, " I will harden Pharaoh's heart."[2] For if he is hardened by God, and commits sin in consequence of being so hardened, the cause of his sin is not himself. And if so, it will appear that Pharaoh does not possess freedom of will ; and it will be maintained, as a consequence, that, agreeably to this illustration, neither do others who perish owe the cause of their destruction to the freedom of their own will. That expression, also, in Ezekiel, when he says, " I will take away their stony hearts, and will give them hearts of flesh, that they may walk in My precepts, and keep My ways,"[4] may impress some, inasmuch as it seems to be a gift of God, either to walk in His ways or to keep His precepts,[5] if He take away that stony heart which is an obstacle to the keeping of His commandments, and bestow and implant a better and more impressible heart, which is called now[6] a heart of flesh. Consider also the nature of the answer given in the Gospel by our Lord and Saviour to those who inquired of Him why He spoke to the multitude in parables. His words are : " That seeing they may not see ; and hearing they may hear, and not understand ; lest they should be converted, and their sins be forgiven them."[7] The words, moreover, used by the Apostle Paul, that " it is not of him that willeth, nor of him that runneth, but of God that showeth mercy ; "[8] in another passage also, ' that to will and to do are of God : "[9] and again, elsewhere, " Therefore hath He mercy upon whom He will, and whom He will He hardeneth. Thou wilt say then unto me, Why doth He yet find fault? For who shall resist His will? O man, who art thou that repliest against God? Shall the thing formed say to him who hath formed it, Why hast thou made me thus? Hath not the potter power over the clay, of the same lump to make one vessel unto honour, and another to dishonour? "[10] — these and similar declarations seem to have no small influence in preventing very many from believing that every one is to be considered as having freedom over his own will, and in making it appear to be a consequence of the will of God whether a man is either saved or lost.

the Old Testament and of the New lead to the opposite conclusion — namely, that it does not depend on ourselves to keep the commandments and to be saved, or to transgress them and to be lost — let us adduce them one by one, and see the explanations of them, in order that from those which we adduce, any one selecting in a similar way all the passages that seem to nullify free-will, may consider what is said about them by way of explanation. And now, the statements regarding Pharaoh have troubled many, respecting whom God declared several times, " I will harden Pharaoh's heart."[3] For if he is hardened by God, and commits sin in consequence of being hardened, he is not the cause of sin to himself ; and if so, then neither does Pharaoh possess free-will. And some one will say that, in a similar way, they who perish have not free-will, and will not perish of themselves. The declaration also in Ezekiel, " I will take away their stony hearts, and will put in them hearts of flesh, that they may walk in My precepts, and keep My commandments,"[4] might lead one to think that it was God who gave the power to walk in His commandments, and to keep His precepts, by His withdrawing the hindrance — the stony heart, and implanting a better — a heart of flesh. And let us look also at the passage in the Gospel — the answer which the Saviour returns to those who inquired why He spake to the multitude in parables. His words are : " That seeing they might not see ; and hearing they may hear, and not understand ; lest they should be converted, and their sins be forgiven them."[11] The passage also in Paul : " It is not of him that willeth, nor of him that runneth, but of God that showeth mercy."[8] The declarations, too, in other places, that " both to will and to do are of God ; "[12] " that God hath mercy upon whom He will have mercy, and whom He will He hardeneth. Thou wilt say then, Why doth He yet find fault? For who hath resisted His will? " " The per-

---

[1] Secundum pietatis regulam.   [2] Ex. iv. 21, etc.   [3] Ex. iv. 21, cf. vii. 3.   [4] Ezek. xi. 19, 20.   [5] Justificationes.
[6] The word " now " is added, as the term " flesh" is frequently used in the New Testament in a bad sense (Redepenning).
[7] Mark iv. 12.   [8] Rom. ix. 16.   [9] Phil. ii. 13.   [10] Rom. ix. 18 sq.   [11] Cf. Mark iv. 12 and Luke viii. 10.   [12] Cf. Phil. ii. 13.

suasion is of Him that calleth, an
not of us." [1] " Nay, O man, who ar
thou that repliest against God? Sha
the thing formed say to him that hat
formed it, Why hast thou made m
thus? Hath not the potter powe
over the clay, of the same lump t
make one vessel unto honour, an
another unto dishonour ? " [2]   Nov
these passages are sufficient of them
selves to trouble the multitude, as i
man were not possessed of free-will
but as if it were God who saves an
destroys whom He will.

8. Let us begin, then, with those words which were
spoken to Pharaoh, who is said to have been hardened
by God, in order that he might not let the people go ;
and, along with his case, the language of the apostle also
will be considered, where he says, "Therefore He hath
mercy on whom He will, and whom He will He hardeneth." [3] For it is on these passages chiefly that the heretics rely, asserting that salvation is not in our own power,
but that souls are of such a nature as must by all means be
either lost or saved ; and that in no way can a soul which
is of an evil nature become good, or one which is of a
virtuous nature be made bad. And hence they maintain
that Pharaoh, too, being of a ruined nature, was on that
account hardened by God, who hardens those that are
of an earthly nature, but has compassion on those who
are of a spiritual nature. Let us see, then, what is the
meaning of their assertion ; and let us, in the first place,
request them to tell us whether they maintain that the
soul of Pharaoh was of an earthly nature, such as they
term lost. They will undoubtedly answer that it was of
an earthly nature. If so, then to believe God, or to obey
Him, when his nature opposed his so doing, was an impossibility. And if this were his condition by nature,
what further need was there for his heart to be hardened,
and this not once, but several times, unless indeed because it was possible for him to yield to persuasion? Nor
could any one be said to be hardened by another, save
him who of himself was not obdurate. And if he were
not obdurate of himself, it follows that neither was he of
an earthly nature, but such an one as might give way when
overpowered [5] by signs and wonders. But he was necessary for God's purpose, in order that, for the saving of the
multitude, He might manifest in him His power by his
offering resistance to numerous miracles, and struggling
against the will of God, and his heart being by this means
said to be hardened. Such are our answers, in the first
place, to these persons ; and by these their assertion may
be overturned, according to which they think that Pharaoh
was destroyed in consequence of his evil nature.[7] And
with regard to the language of the Apostle Paul, we must
answer them in a similar way. For who are they whom
God hardens, according to your view? Those, namely,
whom you term of a ruined nature, and who, I am to

8. Let us begin, then, with what i
said about Pharaoh — that he wa
hardened by God, that he might no
send away the people ; along wit
which will be examined also the state
ment of the apostle, "Therefore hat
He mercy on whom He will hav
mercy, and whom He will He hard
eneth." [4] And certain of those wh
hold different opinions misuse thes
passages, themselves also almost de
stroying free-will by introducing ruine
natures incapable of salvation, an
others saved which it is impossibl
can be lost ; and Pharaoh, they say
as being of a ruined nature, is there
fore hardened by God, who has merc
upon the spiritual, but hardens th
earthly. Let us see now what the
mean. For we shall ask them if Pha
raoh was of an earthy nature ; an
when they answer, we shall say that h
who is of an earthy nature is alto
gether disobedient to God : but i
disobedient, what need is there of hi
heart being hardened, and that no
once, but frequently? Unless per
haps, since it was possible for him t
obey (in which case he would certainl
have obeyed, as not being earthy
when hard pressed by the signs an
wonders), God needs him to be dis
obedient to a greater degree,[6] in orde
that He may manifest His might
deeds for the salvation of the multi
tude, and therefore hardens his heart
This will be our answer to them i
the first place, in order to overtur
their supposition that Pharaoh was o
a ruined nature. And the same repl
must be given to them with respect t
the statement of the apostle. Fo
whom does God harden? Those wh

---

[1] Gal. v. 8.   [2] Rom. ix. 20, 21.   [3] Rom. ix. 18.   [4] Cf. Rom. ix. 18.   [5] Obstupefactus.   [6] χρῄζει δὲ αὐτοῦ ὁ Θεὸς . . . ἐπ
πλεῖον ἀπειθοῦντος.   [7] Naturaliter.

suppose, would have done something else had they not been hardened. If, indeed, they come to destruction in consequence of being hardened, they no longer perish naturally, but in virtue of what befalls them. Then, in the next place, upon whom does God show mercy? On those, namely, who are to be saved. And in what respect do those persons stand in need of a second compassion, who are to be saved once by their nature, and so come naturally to blessedness, except that it is shown even from their case, that, because it was possible for them to perish, they therefore obtain mercy, that so they may not perish, but come to salvation, and possess the kingdom of the good. And let this be our answer to those who devise and invent the fable [1] of good or bad natures, i.e., of earthly or spiritual souls, in consequence of which, as they say, each one is either saved or lost.

9. And now we must return an answer also to those who would have the God of the law to be just only, and not also good; and let us ask such in what manner they consider the heart of Pharaoh to have been hardened by God — by what acts or by what prospective arrangements.[2] For we must observe the conception of a God [3] who in our opinion is both just and good, but according to them only just. And let them show us how a God whom they also acknowledge to be just, can with justice cause the heart of a man to be hardened, that, in consequence of that very hardening, he may sin and be ruined. And how shall the justice of God be defended, if He Himself is the cause of the destruction of those whom, owing to their unbelief (through their being hardened), He has afterwards condemned by the authority of a judge? For why does He blame him, saying, "But since thou wilt not let My people go, lo, I will smite all the first-born in Egypt, even thy first-born," [5] and whatever else was spoken through Moses by God to Pharaoh? For it behoves every one who maintains the truth of what is recorded in Scripture, and who desires to show that the God of the law and the prophets is just, to render a reason for all these things, and to show how there is in them nothing at all derogatory to the justice of God, since, although they deny His goodness, they admit that He is a just judge, and creator of the world. Different, however, is the method of our reply to those who assert that the creator of this world is a malignant being, i.e., a devil.

perish, as if they would obey unless they were hardened, or manifestly those who would be saved because they are not of a ruined nature. And on whom has He mercy? Is it on those who are to be saved? And how is there need of a second mercy for those who have been prepared once for salvation, and who will by all means become blessed on account of their nature? Unless perhaps, since they are capable of incurring destruction, if they did not receive mercy, they will obtain mercy, in order that they may not incur that destruction of which they are capable, but may be in the condition of those who are saved. And this is our answer to such persons.

9. But to those who think they understand the term "hardened," we must address the inquiry, What do they mean by saying that God, by His working, hardens the heart, and with what purpose does He do this? For let them observe the conception [4] of a God who is in reality just and good; but if they will not allow this, let it be conceded to them for the present that He is just; and let them show how the good and just God, or the just God only, appears to be just, in hardening the heart of him who perishes because of his being hardened: and how the just God becomes the cause of destruction and disobedience, when men are chastened by Him on account of their hardness and disobedience. And why does He find fault with him, saying, "Thou wilt not let My people go;" [6] "Lo, I will smite all the first-born in Egypt, even thy first-born;" [7] and whatever else is recorded as spoken from God to Pharaoh through the intervention of Moses? For he who believes that the Scriptures are true, and that God is just, must necessarily endeavour, if he be honest,[8] to show how God, in using such expressions, may be distinctly [9] understood to be just. But if any one should stand, declaring with uncovered head that the Creator of the world was inclined to wickedness,[10] we should need other words to answer them.

---

[1] Commentitias fabulas introducunt.   [2] Quid faciente vel quid prospiciente.   [3] Prospectus et intuitus Dei. Such is the rendering of ἔννοια by Rufinus.   [4] ἔννοιαν.   [5] Ex. ix. 17, cf. xi. 5 and xii. 12.   [6] Cf. Ex. iv. 23 and ix. 17.   [7] Cf. Ex. xii. 12.   [8] εὐγνωμονῇ.   [9] τρανῶς.   [10] ἀπογραψάμενός τις γυμνῇ τῇ κεφαλῇ ἵστατο πρὸς τὸ πονηρὸν εἶναι τὸν δημιουργόν.

10. But since we acknowledge the God who spoke by Moses to be not only just, but also good, let us carefully inquire how it is in keeping with the character of a just and good Deity to have hardened the heart of Pharaoh. And let us see whether, following the example of the Apostle Paul, we are able to solve the difficulty by help of some parallel instances : if we can show, e.g., that by one and the same act God has pity upon one individual, but hardens another ; not purposing or desiring that he who is hardened should be so, but because, in the manifestation of His goodness and patience, the heart of those who treat His kindness and forbearance with contempt and insolence is hardened by the punishment of their crimes being delayed ; while those, on the other hand, who make His goodness and patience the occasion of their repentance and reformation, obtain compassion. To show more clearly, however, what we mean, let us take the illustration employed by the Apostle Paul in the Epistle to the Hebrews, where he says, " For the earth, which drinketh in the rain that cometh oft upon it, and bringeth forth herbs meet for them by whom it is dressed, will receive blessing from God ; but that which beareth thorns and briers is rejected, and is nigh unto cursing, whose end is to be burned." [3] Now from those words of Paul which we have quoted, it is clearly shown that by one and the same act on the part of God — that, viz., by which He sends rain upon the earth — one portion of the ground, when carefully cultivated, brings forth good fruits ; while another, neglected and uncared for, produces thorns and thistles. And if one, speaking as it were in the person of the rain,[4] were to say, " It is I, the rain, that have made the good fruits, and it is I that have caused the thorns and thistles to grow," however hard [6] the statement might appear, it would nevertheless be true ; for unless the rain had fallen, neither fruits, nor thorns, nor thistles would have sprung up, whereas by the coming of the rain the earth gave birth to both. Now, although it is due to the beneficial action of the rain that the earth has produced herbs of both kinds, it is not to the rain that the diversity of the herbs is properly to be ascribed ; but on those will justly rest the blame for the bad seed, who, although they might have turned up the ground by frequent ploughing, and have broken the clods by repeated harrowing, and have extirpated all useless and noxious weeds, and have cleared and prepared the fields for the coming showers by all the labour and toil which cultivation demands, have nevertheless neglected to do this, and who will accordingly reap briers and thorns, the most appropriate fruit of their sloth. And the consequence therefore is, that while the rain falls in kindness and impartiality [7] equally upon the whole earth, yet, by one and the same operation of the rain, that soil which is cultivated yields with a blessing useful fruits to the diligent and careful cultivators, while that which has become hardened through the neglect of the husbandman brings forth only thorns and thistles. Let us there-

10. But since they say that they regard Him as a just God, and we as one who is at the same time good and just, let us consider how the good and just God could harden the heart of Pharaoh. See, then, whether, by an illustration used by the apostle in the Epistle to the Hebrews, we are able to prove that by one operation [1] God has mercy upon one man while He hardens another, although not intending to harden ; but, (although) having a good purpose, hardening follows as a result of the inherent principle of wickedness in such persons,[2] and so He is said to harden him who is hardened. " The earth," he says, " which drinketh in the rain that cometh oft upon it, and bringeth forth herbs meet for them for whom it is dressed, receiveth blessing from God ; but that which beareth thorns and briers is rejected, and is nigh to cursing, whose end is to be burned." [3] As respects the rain, then, there is one operation ; and there being one operation as regards the rain, the ground which is cultivated produces fruit, while that which is neglected and is barren produces thorns. Now, it might seem profane [5] for Him who rains to say, " I produced the fruits, and the thorns that are in the earth ; " and yet, although profane, it is true. For, had rain not fallen, there would have been neither fruits nor thorns ; but, having fallen at the proper time and in moderation, both were produced. The ground, now, which drank in the rain which often fell upon it, and yet produced thorns and briers, is rejected and nigh to cursing. The blessing, then, of the rain descended even upon the inferior land ; but it, being neglected and uncultivated, yielded thorns and thistles. In the same way, therefore, the wonderful works also done by God are, as it were, the rain ; while the differing purposes are, as it were, the cultivated and neglected land, being (yet), like earth, of one nature.

---

[1] ἐνεργείᾳ.   [2] διὰ τὸ τῆς κακίας ὑποκείμενον τοῦ παρ᾽ ἑαυτοῖς κακοῦ.   [3] Heb. vi. 7, 8.   [4] Ex personâ imbrium. ,   [5] δύσφημον.
[6] Dure.   [7] Bonitas et æquitas imbrium.

fore view those signs and miracles which were done by God, as the showers furnished by Him from above ; and the purpose and desires of men, as the cultivated and uncultivated soil, which is of one and the same nature indeed, as is every soil compared with another, but not in one and the same state of cultivation. From which it follows that every one's will,[1] if untrained, and fierce, and barbarous, is either hardened by the miracles and wonders of God, growing more savage and thorny than ever, or it becomes more pliant, and yields itself up with the whole mind to obedience, if it be cleared from vice and subjected to training.

11. But, to establish the point more clearly, it will not be superfluous to employ another illustration, as if, e.g., one were to say that it is the sun which hardens and liquefies, although liquefying and hardening are things of an opposite nature. Now it is not incorrect to say that the sun, by one and the same power of its heat, melts wax indeed, but dries up and hardens mud :[3] not that its power operates one way upon mud, and in another way upon wax ; but that the qualities of mud and wax are different, although according to nature they are one thing,[4] both being from the earth. In this way, then, one and the same working upon the part of God, which was administered by Moses in signs and wonders, made manifest the hardness of Pharaoh, which he had conceived in the intensity of his wickedness,[5] but exhibited the obedience of those other Egyptians who were intermingled with the Israelites, and who are recorded to have quitted Egypt at the same time with the Hebrews. With respect to the statement that the heart of Pharaoh was subdued by degrees, so that on one occasion he said, " Go not far away ; ye shall go a three days' journey, but leave your wives, and your children, and your cattle,"[8] and as regards any other statements, according to which he appears to yield gradually to the signs and wonders, what else is shown, save that the power of the signs and miracles was making some impression on him, but not so much as it ought to have done ? For if the hardening were of such a nature as many take it to be, he would not indeed have given way even in a few instances. But I think there is no absurdity in explaining the tropical or figurative[9] nature of that language employed in speaking of " hardening," according to common usage. For those masters who are remarkable for kindness to their slaves, are frequently accustomed to say to the latter, when, through much patience and indulgence on their part, they have become insolent and worthless : " It is I that have made you what you are ; I have spoiled you ; it is my endurance that has made you good for nothing : I am to blame for your perverse and wicked habits, because I do not have you immediately punished for every delinquency according to your deserts." For we must first attend to the tropical or figurative meaning of the language, and so come to see the force of the expression, and not find fault with the word, whose inner meaning we do not ascertain.

11. And as if the sun, uttering a voice, were to say, " I liquefy and dry up," liquefaction and drying up being opposite things, he would not speak falsely as regards the point in question ;[2] wax being melted and mud being dried by the same heat ; so the same operation, which was performed through the instrumentality of Moses, proved the hardness of Pharaoh on the one hand, the result of his wickedness, and the yielding of the mixed Egyptian multitude who took their departure with the Hebrews. And the brief statement[6] that the heart of Pharaoh was softened, as it were, when he said, " But ye shall not go far : ye will go a three days' journey, and leave your wives,"[7] and anything else which he said, yielding little by little before the signs, proves that the wonders made some impression even upon him, but did not accomplish all (that they might). Yet even this would not have happened, if that which is supposed by the many — the hardening of Pharaoh's heart — had been produced by God Himself. And it is not absurd to soften down such expressions agreeably to common usage :[10] for good masters often say to their slaves, when spoiled by their kindness and forbearance, " I have made you bad, and I am to blame for offences of such enormity." For we must attend to the character and force of the phrase, and not argue sophistically,[11] disregarding the meaning of the expression. Paul accordingly, having examined these points clearly, says to the sinner : " Or despisest thou the riches of His goodness, and forbearance, and long-suffering ; not knowing that the goodness of God leadeth thee to repentance ?

---

[1] Propositum.   [2] παρὰ τὸ ὑποκείμενον.   [3] Limum.   [4] Cum utique secundum naturam unum sit conceperat.   [5] Malitiæ suæ intentione sermonis.   [6] καὶ τὸ κατὰ τὸ βραχὺ δὲ ἀναγεγράφθαι.   [7] Cf. Ex. viii. 28, 29.   [8] Cf. Ex. viii. 27-29.   [9] Tropum vel figuram sermonis.   [10] οὐκ ἄτοπον δὲ καὶ ἀπὸ συνηθείας τὰ τοιαῦτα παραμυθήσασθαι.   [11] συκοφαντεῖν.

Finally, the Apostle Paul, evidently treating of such, says to him who remained in his sins: "Despisest thou the riches of His goodness, and forbearance, and long-suffering; not knowing that the goodness of God leadeth thee to repentance? but, after thy hardness and impenitent heart, treasurest up unto thyself wrath on the day of wrath and revelation of the righteous judgment of God."[1] Such are the words of the apostle to him who is in his sins. Let us apply these very expressions to Pharaoh, and see if they also are not spoken of him with propriety, since, according to his hardness and impenitent heart, he treasured and stored up for himself wrath on the day of wrath, inasmuch as his hardness could never have been declared and manifested, unless signs and wonders of such number and magnificence had been performed.

12. But if the proofs which we have adduced do not appear full enough, and the similitude of the apostle seem wanting in applicability,[3] let us add the voice of prophetic authority, and see what the prophets declare regarding those who at first, indeed, leading a righteous life, have deserved to receive numerous proofs of the goodness of God, but afterwards, as being human beings, have fallen astray, with whom the prophet, making himself also one, says: "Why, O LORD, hast Thou made us to err from Thy way? and hardened our heart, that we should not fear Thy name? Return, for Thy servants' sake, for the tribes of Thine inheritance, that we also for a little may obtain some inheritance from Thy holy hill."[5] Jeremiah also employs similar language: "O LORD, Thou hast deceived us, and we were deceived; Thou hast held (us), and Thou hast prevailed."[7] The expression, then, "Why, O Lord, hast Thou hardened our heart, that we should not fear Thy name?" used by those who prayed for mercy, is to be taken in a figurative, moral acceptation,[8] as if one were to say, "Why hast Thou spared us so long, and didst not requite us when we sinned, but didst abandon us, that so our wickedness might increase, and our liberty of sinning be extended when punishment ceased?" In like manner, unless a horse continually feel the spur[9] of his rider, and have his mouth abraded by a bit,[10] he becomes hardened. And a boy also, unless constantly disciplined by chastisement, will grow up to be an insolent youth, and one ready to fall headlong into vice. God accordingly abandons and neglects those whom He has judged undeserving of chastisement: "For whom the Lord loveth He chasteneth, and scourgeth every son whom He receiveth."[11] From which we are to suppose that those are to be received into the rank and affection of sons, who have deserved to be scourged and chastened by the Lord, in order that they also, through endurance of trials and tribulations, may be able to say, "Who shall separate us from the love of God which is in Christ Jesus? shall tribulation, or anguish, or famine, or nakedness, or peril, or sword?"[12] For by all these is each one's resolu-

but, after thy hardness and impenitei heart, treasurest up unto thyself wrat against the day of wrath and revel tion of the righteous judgment c God."[1] Now, let what the apostl says to the sinner be addressed Pharaoh, and then the announcemen made to him will be understood t have been made with peculiar fitnes as to one who, according to his har ness and unrepentant heart, was trea uring up to himself wrath; seeing tha his hardness would not have bee proved nor made manifest unless mir cles had been performed, and miracle too, of such magnitude and impoi tance.

12. But since such narratives ar slow to secure assent,[2] and are cor sidered to be forced,[4] let us see fron the prophetical declarations also, wha those persons say, who, although the have experienced the great kindnes of God, have not lived virtuously, bu have afterwards sinned. "Why, (LORD, hast Thou made us to err fron Thy ways? Why hast Thou hardene our heart, so as not to fear Thy name Return for Thy servants' sake, for th tribes of Thine inheritance, that w may inherit a small portion of Th holy mountain."[6] And in Jeremiah "Thou hast deceived me, O LORI and I was deceived; Thou wei strong, and Thou didst prevail."[7] Fc the expression, "Why hast Thou hard ened our heart, so as not to fear Th name?" uttered by those who ar begging to receive mercy, is in it nature as follows: "Why hast Tho spared us so long, not visiting us be cause of our sins, but deserting u until our transgressions come to height?" Now He leaves the greate part of men unpunished, both in oi der that the habits of each one ma be examined, so far as it depend upon ourselves, and that the virtuou may be made manifest in consequenc of the test applied; while the other not escaping notice from God — fc He knows all things before they exi — but from the rational creation an themselves, may afterwards obtain th means of cure, seeing they would no have known the benefit had they no

---

[1] Rom. ii. 4, 5.　　[2] δυσπειθεῖς.　　[3] Et apostolicæ similitudinis parum munimenti habere adhuc videtur assertio.　　[4] βίαιοι.
[5] Isa. lxiii. 17, 18.　Here the Septuagint differs from the Masoretic text.　　[6] Isa. lxiii. 17, 18.　　[7] Jer. xx. 7.
[8] Morali utique tropo accipiendum　　[9] Ferratum calcem.　　[10] Frenis ferratis.　　[11] Heb. xii. 6.　　[12] Rom. viii. 35.

tion manifested and displayed, and the firmness of his perseverance made known, not so much to God, who knows all things before they happen, as to the rational and heavenly virtues,[2] who have obtained a part in the work of procuring human salvation, as being a sort of assistants and ministers to God. Those, on the other hand, who do not yet offer themselves to God with such constancy and affection, and are not ready to come into His service, and to prepare their souls for trial, are said to be abandoned by God, i.e., not to be instructed, inasmuch as they are not prepared for instruction, their training or care being undoubtedly postponed to a later time. These certainly do not know what they will obtain from God, unless they first entertain the desire of being benefited ; and this finally will be the case, if a man come first to a knowledge of himself, and feel what are his defects, and understand from whom he either ought or can seek the supply of his deficiencies. For he who does not know beforehand of his weakness or his sickness, cannot seek a physician ; or at least, after recovering his health, that man will not be grateful to his physician who did not first recognise the dangerous nature of his ailment. And so, unless a man has first ascertained the defects of his life, and the evil nature of his sins, and made this known by confession from his own lips, he cannot be cleansed or acquitted, lest he should be ignorant that what he possesses has been bestowed on him by favour, but should consider as his own property what flows from the divine liberality, which idea undoubtedly generates arrogance of mind and pride, and finally becomes the cause of the individual's ruin. And this, we must believe, was the case with the devil, who viewed as his own, and not as given him by God, the primacy[7] which he held at the time when he was unstained ;[8] and thus was fulfilled in him the declaration, that " every one who exalteth himself shall be abased."[9] From which it appears to me that the divine mysteries were concealed from the wise and prudent, according to the statement of Scripture, that " no flesh should glory before God,"[10] and revealed to children — to those, namely, who, after they have become infants and little children, i.e., have returned to the humility and simplicity of children, then make progress ; and on arriving at perfection, remember that they have obtained their state of happiness, not by their own merits, but by the grace and compassion of God.

13. It is therefore by the sentence of God that he is abandoned who deserves to be so, while over some sinners God exercises forbearance ; not, however, without a definite principle of action.[11] Nay, the very fact that He is long-suffering conduces to the advantage of those very persons, since the soul over which He exercises this providential care is immortal ; and, as being immortal and everlasting, it is not, although not immediately cared for, excluded from salvation, which is postponed to a more convenient time. For perhaps it is expedient for those who have been more deeply imbued with the poison of

condemned themselves. It is of advantage to each one, that he perceive his own peculiar nature[1] and the grace of God. For he who does not perceive his own weakness and the divine favour, although he receive a benefit, yet, not having made trial of himself, nor having condemned himself, will imagine that the benefit conferred upon him by the grace of Heaven is his own doing. And this imagination, producing also vanity,[3] will be the cause of a downfall : which, we conceive, was the case with the devil, who attributed to himself the priority which he possessed when in a state of sinlessness.[4] " For every one that exalteth himself shall be abased," and " every one that humbleth himself shall be exalted."[5] And observe, that for this reason divine things have been concealed from the wise and prudent, in order, as says the apostle, that " no flesh should glory in the presence of God ; "[6] and they have been revealed to babes, to those who after childhood have come to better things, and who remember that it is not so much from their own effort, as by the unspeakable goodness (of God), that they have reached the greatest possible extent of blessedness.

13. It is not without reason, then, that he who is abandoned, is abandoned to the divine judgment, and that God is long-suffering with certain sinners ; but because it will be for their advantage, with respect to the immortality of the soul and the unending world,[12] that they be not quickly brought[13] into a state of salvation, but be conducted to it more slowly, after having experienced many

[1] ἰδιότητος.   [2] Rationabilibus cœlestibusque virtutibus.   [3] φυσιωσιν.   [4] ἄμωμος.   [5] Cf. Luke xiv. 11.   [6] Cf. 1 Cor. i. 29.
[7] Primatus.   [8] Immaculatus.   [9] Luke xviii. 14.   [10] 1 Cor. i. 29.   [11] Non tamen sine certâ ratione.   [12] τὸν ἄπειρον αἰῶνα.
[13] συνεργηθῆναι.

wickedness to obtain this salvation at a later period. For as medical men sometimes, although they could quickly cover over the scars of wounds, keep back and delay the cure for the present, in the expectation of a better and more perfect recovery, knowing that it is more salutary to retard the treatment in the cases of swellings caused by wounds, and to allow the malignant humours to flow off for a while, rather than to hasten a superficial cure, by shutting up in the veins the poison of a morbid humour, which, excluded from its customary outlets, will undoubtedly creep into the inner parts of the limbs, and penetrate to the very vitals of the viscera, producing no longer mere disease in the body, but causing destruction to life ; so, in like manner, God also, who knows the secret things of the heart, and foreknows the future, in much forbearance allows certain events to happen, which, coming from without upon men, cause to come forth into the light the passions and vices which are concealed within, that by their means those may be cleansed and cured who, through great negligence and carelessness, have admitted within themselves the roots and seeds of sins, so that, when driven outwards and brought to the surface, they may in a certain degree be cast forth and dispersed.[1] And thus, although a man may appear to be afflicted with evils of a serious kind, suffering convulsions in all his limbs, he may nevertheless, at some future time, obtain relief and a cessation from his trouble ; and, after enduring his afflictions to satiety, may, after many sufferings, be restored again to his (proper) condition. For God deals with souls not merely with a view to the short space of our present life, included within sixty years[4] or more, but with reference to a perpetual and never-ending period, exercising His providential care over souls that are immortal, even as He Himself is eternal and immortal. For He made the rational nature, which He formed in His own image and likeness, incorruptible ; and therefore the soul, which is immortal, is not excluded by the shortness of the present life from the divine remedies and cures.

14. But let us take from the Gospels also the similitudes of those things which we have mentioned, in which is described a certain rock, having on it a little superficial earth, on which, when a seed falls, it is said quickly to spring up ; but when sprung up, it withers as the sun ascends in the heavens, and dies away, because it did not cast its root deeply into the ground.[7] Now this rock undoubtedly represents the human soul, hardened on account of its own negligence, and converted into stone because of its wickedness. For God gave no one a stony heart by a creative act ; but each individual's heart is said to become stony through his own wickedness and disobedience. As, therefore, if one were to blame a husbandman for not casting his seed more quickly upon rocky ground, because seed cast upon other rocky soil was seen to spring up speedily, the husbandman would certainly say in reply : "I sow this soil more slowly, for this reason,

evils. For as physicians, who are able to cure a man quickly, when they suspect that a hidden poison exists in the body, do the reverse of healing, making this more certain through their very desire to heal, deeming it better for a considerable time to retain the patient under inflammation and sickness, in order that he may recover his health more surely, than to appear to produce a rapid recovery, and afterwards to cause a relapse, and (thus) that hasty cure last only for a time ; in the same way, God also, who knows the secret things of the heart, and foresees future events, in His long-suffering, permits (certain events to occur), and by means of those things which happen from without extracts the secret evil, in order to cleanse him who through carelessness has received the seeds of sin, that having vomited them forth when they came to the surface, although he may have been deeply involved in evils, he may afterwards obtain healing after his wickedness, and be renewed.[2] For God governs souls not with reference, let me say, to the fifty[3] years of the present life, but with reference to an illimitable[5] age : for He made the thinking principle immortal in its nature, and kindred to Himself ; and the rational soul is not, as in this life, excluded from cure.

14. Come now, and let us use the following image[6] from the Gospel. There is a certain rock, with a little surface-soil, on which, if seeds fall, they quickly spring up ; but when sprung up, as not having root, they are burned and withered when the sun has arisen. Now this rock is a human soul, hardened on account of its negligence, and converted to stone because of its wickedness ; for no one receives from God a heart created of stone, but it becomes such in consequence of wickedness. If one then, were to find fault with the husbandman for not sowing his seed sooner upon the rocky soil, when he

---

[1] Digeri. The rendering "dispersed" seems to agree best with the meaning intended to be conveyed.   [2] ἀναστοιχειωθῆναι.
[3] πεντηκονταετίαν. Rufinus has "sexaginta annos."   [4] In the Greek the term is πεντηκονταετίαν.   [5] ἀπέραντον αἰῶνα.
[6] εἰκόνι.   [7] Cf. Matt. xiii. 5, 6.

that it may retain the seed which it has received; for it suits this ground to be sown somewhat slowly, lest perhaps the crop, having sprouted too rapidly, and coming forth from the mere surface of a shallow soil, should be unable to withstand the rays of the sun." Would not he who formerly found fault acquiesce in the reasons and superior knowledge of the husbandman, and approve as done on rational grounds what formerly appeared to him as founded on no reason? And in the same way, God, the thoroughly skilled husbandman of all His creation, undoubtedly conceals and delays to another time those[1] things which we think ought to have obtained health sooner, in order that not the outside of things, rather than the inside, may be cured. But if any one now were to object to us that certain seeds do even fall upon rocky ground, i.e., on a hard and stony heart, we should answer that even this does not happen without the arrangement of Divine Providence; inasmuch as, but for this, it would not be known what condemnation was incurred by rashness in hearing and indifference in investigation,[3] nor, certainly, what benefit was derived from being trained in an orderly manner. And hence it happens that the soul comes to know its defects, and to cast the blame upon itself, and, consistently with this, to reserve and submit itself to training, i.e., in order that it may see that its faults must first be removed, and that then it must come to receive the instruction of wisdom. As, therefore, souls are innumerable, so also are their manners, and purposes, and movements, and appetencies, and incitements different, the variety of which can by no means be grasped by the human mind; and therefore to God alone must be left the art, and the knowledge, and the power of an arrangement of this kind, as He alone can know both the remedies for each individual soul, and measure out the time of its cure. It is He alone then who, as we said, recognises the ways of individual men, and determines by what way He ought to lead Pharaoh, that through him His name might be named in all the earth, having previously chastised him by many blows, and finally drowning him in the sea. By this drowning, however, it is not to be supposed that God's providence as regards Pharaoh was terminated; for we must not imagine, because he was drowned, that therefore he had forthwith completely[5] perished: "for in the hand of God are both we and our words; all wisdom, also, and knowledge of workmanship,"[6] as Scripture declares. But these points we have discussed according to our ability, treating of that chapter[7] of Scripture in which it is said that God hardened the heart of Pharaoh, and agreeably to the statement, "He hath mercy on whom He will have mercy, and whom He will He hardeneth."[9]

15. Let us now look at those passages of Ezekiel where he says, "I will take away from them their stony heart, and I will put in them a heart of flesh, that they may walk in My statutes, and keep Mine ordinances.[10]

saw other rocky ground which had received seed flourishing, the husbandman would reply, "I shall sow this ground more slowly, casting in seeds that will be able to retain their hold, this slower method being better for the ground, and more secure than that which receives the seed in a more rapid manner, and more upon the surface." (The person finding fault) would yield his assent to the husbandman, as one who spoke with sound reason, and who acted with skill: so also the great Husbandman of all nature postpones that benefit which might be deemed premature,[2] that it may not prove superficial. But it is probable that here some one may object to us with reference to this: "Why do some of the seeds fall upon the earth that has superficial soil, the soul being, as it were, a rock?" Now we must say, in answer to this, that it was better for this soul, which desired better things precipitately,[4] and not by a way which led to them, to obtain its desire, in order that, condemning itself on this account, it may, after a long time, endure to receive the husbandry which is according to nature. For souls are, as one may say, innumerable; and their habits are innumerable, and their movements, and their purposes, and their assaults, and their efforts, of which there is only one admirable administrator, who knows both the seasons, and the fitting helps, and the avenues, and the ways, viz., the God and Father of all things, who knows how He conducts even Pharaoh by so great events, and by drowning in the sea, with which latter occurrence His superintendence of Pharaoh does not cease. For he was not annihilated when drowned: "For in the hand of God are both we and our words; all wisdom also, and knowledge of workmanship."[8] And such is a moderate defence with regard to the statements that "Pharaoh's heart was hardened," and that "God hath mercy upon whom He will have mercy, and whom He will He hardeneth."

15. Let us look also at the declaration in Ezekiel, which says, "I shall take away their stony hearts, and will put in them hearts of flesh, that they

---

[1] Hæc.　　[2] τάχιον.　　[3] Perscrutationis improbitas.　　[4] προπετέστερον, καὶ οὐχὶ ὁδῷ ἐπ' αὐτὰ ὁδευσάσῃ.　　[5] Substantialiter.
[6] Wisd. vii. 16.　　[7] Capitulum.　　[8] Cf. Wisd. vii. 16.　　[9] Rom. ix. 18.　　[10] Ezek. xi. 19, 20.

For if God, when He pleases, takes away a heart of stone and bestows a heart of flesh, that His ordinances may be observed and His commandments may be obeyed, it will then appear that it is not in our power to put away wickedness. For the taking away of a stony heart seems to be nothing else than the removal of the wickedness by which one is hardened, from whomsoever God pleases to remove it. Nor is the bestowal of a heart of flesh, that the precepts of God may be observed and His commandments obeyed, any other thing than a man becoming obedient, and no longer resisting the truth, but performing works of virtue. If, then, God promises to do this, and if, before He takes away the stony heart, we are unable to remove it from ourselves, it follows that it is not in our power, but in God's only, to cast away wickedness. And again, if it is not our doing to form within us a heart of flesh, but the work of God alone, it will not be in our power to live virtuously, but it will in everything appear to be a work of divine grace. Such are the assertions of those who wish to prove from the authority of Holy Scripture that nothing lies in our own power. Now to these we answer, that these passages are not to be so understood, but in the following manner. Take the case of one who was ignorant and untaught, and who, feeling the disgrace of his ignorance, should, driven either by an exhortation from some person, or incited by a desire to emulate other wise men, hand himself over to one by whom he is assured that he will be carefully trained and competently instructed. If he, then, who had formerly hardened himself in ignorance, yield himself, as we have said, with full purpose of mind to a master, and promise to obey him in all things, the master, on seeing clearly the resolute nature of his determination; will appropriately promise to take away all ignorance, and to implant knowledge within his mind ; not that he undertakes to do this if the disciple refuse or resist his efforts, but only on his offering and binding himself to obedience in all things. So also the Word of God promises to those who draw near to Him, that He will take away their stony heart, not indeed from those who do not listen to His word, but from those who receive the precepts of His teaching ; as in the Gospels we find the sick approaching the Saviour, asking to receive health, and thus at last be cured. And in order that the blind might be healed and regain their sight, their part consisted in making supplication to the Saviour, and in believing that their cure could be effected by Him ; while His part, on the other hand, lay in restoring to them the power of vision. And in this way also does the Word of God promise to bestow instruction by taking away the stony heart, i.e., by the removal of wickedness, that so men may be able to walk in the divine precepts, and observe the commandments of the law.

may walk in My statutes and keep My precepts."[1] For if God, when He wills, takes away the stony hearts, and implants hearts of flesh, so that His precepts are obeyed and His commandments are observed, it is not in our power to put away wickedness. For the taking away of the stony hearts is nothing else than the taking away of the wickedness, according to which one is hardened, from him from whom God wills to take it ; and the implanting of a heart of flesh, so that a man may walk in the precepts of God and keep His commandments, what else is it than to become somewhat yielding and unresistent to the truth, and to be capable of practising virtues? And if God promises to do this, and if, before He takes away the stony hearts, we do not lay them aside, it is manifest that it does not depend upon ourselves to put away wickedness ; and if it is not we who do anything towards the production within us of the heart of flesh, but if it is God's doing, it will not be our own act to live agreeably to virtue, but altogether (the result of) divine grace. Such will be the statements of him who, from the mere words (of Scripture), annihilates free-will.[2] But we shall answer, saying, that we ought to understand these passages thus : That as a man, e.g., who happened to be ignorant and uneducated, on perceiving his own defects, either in consequence of an exhortation from his teacher, or in some other way, should spontaneously give himself up to him whom he considers able to introduce[3] him to education and virtue ; and, on his yielding himself up, his instructor promises that he will take away his ignorance, and implant instruction, not as if it contributed nothing to his training, and to the avoiding of ignorance, that he brought himself to be healed, but because the instructor promised to improve him who desired improvement ; so, in the same way, the Word of God promises to take away wickedness, which it calls a stony heart, from those who come to it, not if they are unwilling, but (only) if they submit themselves to the Physician of the sick, as in the Gospels

[1] Ezek. xi. 19, 20.   [2] ἀπὸ τῶν ψιλῶν ῥητῶν τὸ ἐφ' ἡμῖν ἀναιρῶν.   [3] χειραγωγήσειν.

the sick are found coming to the Saviour, and asking to obtain healing, and so are cured. And, let me say, the recovery of sight by the blind is, so far as their request goes, the act of those who believe that they are capable of being healed; but as respects the restoration of sight, it is the work of our Saviour. Thus, then, does the Word of God promise to implant knowledge in those who come to it, by taking away the stony and hard heart, which is wickedness, in order that one may walk in the divine commandments, and keep the divine injunctions.

16. There is next brought before us that declaration uttered by the Saviour in the Gospel: "That seeing they may see, and not perceive; and hearing they may hear, and not understand; lest they should happen to be converted, and their sins be forgiven them." [1] On which our opponent will remark: "If those who shall hear more distinctly are by all means to be corrected and converted, and converted in such a manner as to be worthy of receiving the remission of sins, and if it be not in their own power to hear the word distinctly, but if it depend on the Instructor to teach more openly and distinctly, while he declares that he does not proclaim to them the word with clearness, lest they should perhaps hear and understand, and be converted, and be saved, it will follow, certainly, that their salvation is not dependent upon themselves. And if this be so, then we have no free-will either as regards salvation or destruction." Now were it not for the words that are added, "Lest perhaps they should be converted, and their sins be forgiven them," we might be more inclined to return the answer, that the Saviour was unwilling that those individuals whom He foresaw would not become good, should understand the mysteries of the kingdom of heaven, and that therefore He spoke to them in parables; but as that addition follows, "Lest perhaps they should be converted, and their sins be forgiven them," the explanation is rendered more difficult. And, in the first place, we have to notice what defence this passage furnishes against those heretics who are accustomed to hunt out of the Old Testament any expressions which seem, according to their view, to predicate severity and cruelty of God the Creator, as when He is described as being affected with the feeling of vengeance or punishment, or by any of those emotions, however named, from which they deny the existence of goodness in the Creator; for they do not judge of the Gospels with the same mind and feelings, and do not observe whether any such statements are found in them as they condemn and censure in the Old Testament. For manifestly, in the passage referred to, the Saviour is shown, as they themselves admit, not to speak distinctly, for this very reason, that men may not be converted, and

16. There was after this the passage from the Gospel, where the Saviour said, that for this reason did He speak to those without in parables, that "seeing they may not see, and hearing they may not understand; lest they should be converted, and their sins be forgiven them." [1] Now, our opponent will say, "If some persons are assuredly converted on hearing words of greater clearness, so that they become worthy of the remission of sins, and if it does not depend upon themselves to hear these words of greater clearness, but upon him who teaches, and he for this reason does not announce them to them more distinctly, lest they should see and understand, it is not within the power of such to be saved; and if so, we are not possessed of free-will as regards salvation and destruction." Effectual, indeed, would be the reply to such arguments, were it not for the addition, "Lest they should be converted, and their sins be forgiven them," — namely, that the Saviour did not wish those who were not to become good and virtuous to understand the more mystical (parts of His teaching), and for this reason spake to them in parables; but now, on account of the words, "Lest they should be converted, and their sins be forgiven them," the defence is more difficult. In the first place, then, we must notice the passage in its bearing on the heretics, who hunt out those portions from the Old Testament where is exhibited, as they themselves daringly assert, the cruelty [2] of the Creator of the world [3]

---

[1] Mark iv. 12.   [2] ὠμότης.   [3] δημιουργοῦ.

when converted, receive the remission of sins. Now, if the words be understood according to the letter merely, nothing less, certainly, will be contained in them than in those passages which they find fault with in the Old Testament. And if they are of opinion that any expressions occurring in such a connection in the New Testament stand in need of explanation, it will necessarily follow that those also occurring in the Old Testament, which are the subject of censure, may be freed from aspersion by an explanation of a similar kind, so that by such means the passages found in both Testaments may be shown to proceed from one and the same God. But let us return, as we best may, to the question proposed.

17. We said formerly, when discussing the case of Pharaoh, that sometimes it does not lead to good results for a man to be cured too quickly, especially if the disease, being shut up within the inner parts of the body, rage with greater fierceness. Whence God, who is acquainted with secret things, and knows all things before they happen, in His great goodness delays the cure of such, and postpones their recovery to a remoter period, and, so to speak, cures them by not curing them, lest a too favourable state of health [4] should render them incurable. It is therefore possible that, in the case of those to whom, as being " without," the words of our Lord and Saviour were addressed, He, seeing from His scrutiny of the hearts and reins that they were not yet able to receive teaching of a clearer type, veiled by the covering of language the meaning of the profounder mysteries, lest perhaps, being rapidly converted and healed, i.e., having quickly obtained the remission of their sins, they should again easily slide back into the same disease which they

in His purpose of avenging and punishing the wicked,[1] or by whatever other name they wish to designate such a quality, so speaking only that they may say that goodness does not exist in the Creator ; and who do not deal with the New Testament in a similar manner, nor in a spirit of candour,[2] but pass by places similar to those which they consider censurable in the Old Testament. For manifestly, and according to the Gospel, is the Saviour shown, as they assert, by His former words, not to speak distinctly for this reason, that men might not be converted, and, being converted, might become deserving of the remission of sins : which statement of itself is nothing inferior [3] to those passages from the Old Testament which are objected to. And if they seek to defend the Gospel, we must ask them whether they are not acting in a blameworthy manner in dealing differently with the same questions ; and, while not stumbling against the New Testament, but seeking to defend it, they nevertheless bring a charge against the Old regarding similar points, whereas they ought to offer a defence in the same way of the passages from the New. And therefore we shall force them, on account of the resemblances, to regard all as the writings of one God. Come, then, and let us, to the best of our ability, furnish an answer to the question submitted to us.

17. We asserted also, when investigating the subject of Pharaoh, that sometimes a rapid cure is not for the advantage of those who are healed, if, after being seized by troublesome diseases, they should easily get rid of those by which they had been entangled. For, despising the evil as one that is easy of cure, and not being on their guard a second time against falling into it, they will be involved in it (again). Wherefore, in the case of such persons, the everlasting God, the Knower of secrets, who knows all things before they exist, in conformity with His goodness, delays sending them more rapid assistance, and, so to speak, in helping them does not help, the latter course being to their advan-

---

[1] ἡ ἀμυντικὴ καὶ ἀνταποδοτικὴ τῶν χειρόνων προαίρεσις.   [2] εὐγνωμόνως.   [3] οὐδενὸς ἔλαττον.   [4] Prospera sanitas.

had found could be healed without any difficulty. For if this be the case, no one can doubt that the punishment is doubled, and the amount of wickedness increased; since not only are the sins which had appeared to be forgiven repeated, but the court [1] of virtue also is desecrated when trodden by deceitful and polluted beings,[2] filled within with hidden wickedness. And what remedy can there ever be for those who, after eating the impure and filthy food of wickedness, have tasted the pleasantness of virtue, and received its sweetness into their mouths, and yet have again betaken themselves to the deadly and poisonous provision of sin? And who doubts that it is better for delay and a temporary abandonment to occur, in order that if, at some future time, they should happen to be satiated with wickedness, and the filth with which they are now delighted should become loathsome, the word of God may at last be appropriately made clear to them, and that which is holy be not given to the dogs, nor pearls be cast before swine, which will trample them under foot, and turn, moreover, and rend and assault those who have proclaimed to them the word of God? These, then, are they who are said to be "without," undoubtedly by way of contrast with those who are said to be "within," and to hear the word of God with greater clearness. And yet those who are "without" do hear the word, although it is covered by parables, and overshadowed by proverbs. There are others, also, besides those who are without, who are called Tyrians, and who do not hear at all, respecting whom the Saviour knew that they would have repented long ago, sitting in sackcloth and ashes, if the miracles performed among others had been done amongst them, and yet these do not hear those things which are heard even by those who are "without:" and I believe, for this reason, that the rank of such in wickedness was far lower and worse than that of those who are said to be "without," i.e., who are not far from those who are within, and who have deserved to hear the word, although in parables; and because, perhaps, their cure was delayed to that time when it will be more tolerable for them on the day of judgment, than for those before whom those miracles which are recorded were performed, that so at last, being then relieved from the weight of their sins, they may enter with more ease and power of endurance upon the way of safety. And this is a point which I wish impressed upon those who peruse these pages, that with respect to topics of such difficulty and obscurity we use our utmost endeavour, not so much to ascertain clearly the solutions of the questions (for every one will do this as the Spirit gives him utterance), as to maintain the rule of faith in the most unmistakeable manner,[7] by striving to show that the providence of God, which equitably administers all things, governs also immortal souls on the justest principles, (conferring rewards) according to the merits and motives of each individual; the present economy of things [8] not being confined within the life of this world, but the pre-existing state of merit always furnishing the ground for

tage. It is probable, then, that those "without," of whom we are speaking, having been foreseen by the Saviour, according to our supposition, as not (likely) to prove steady in their conversion,[3] if they should hear more clearly the words that were spoken, were (so) treated by the Saviour as not to hear distinctly the deeper (things of His teaching),[4] lest, after a rapid conversion, and after being healed by obtaining remission of sins, they should despise the wounds of their wickedness, as being slight and easy of healing, and should again speedily relapse into them. And perhaps also, suffering punishment for their former transgressions against virtue, which they had committed when they had forsaken her, they had not yet filled up the (full) time; in order that, being abandoned by the divine superintendence, and being filled [5] to a greater degree by their own evils which they had sown, they may afterwards be called to a more stable repentance; so as not to be quickly entangled again in those evils in which they had formerly been involved when they treated with insolence the requirements of virtue, and devoted themselves to worse things. Those, then, who are said to be "without" (manifestly by comparison with those "within"), not being very far from those "within," while those "within" hear clearly, do themselves hear indistinctly, because they are addressed in parables; but nevertheless they do hear. Others, again, of those "without," who are called Tyrians, although it was foreknown that they would have repented long ago, sitting in sackcloth and ashes, had the Saviour come near their borders, do not hear even those words which are heard by those "without" (being, as is probable, very far inferior in merit to those "without"[6]), in order that at another season, after it has been more tolerable for them than for those who did not receive the word (among whom he mentioned also the Tyrians), they may, on hearing the word at a more appropriate time, obtain a more lasting repentance. But observe whether, besides our desire to investigate (the truth),

---

[1] Aula.　　[2] Mentes.　　[3] ἐωραμένους οὐ βεβαίους ἔσεσθαι ἐν τῇ ἐπιστροφῇ.　　[4] τῶν βαθυτέρων.　　[5] ἐπὶ πλεῖον ἐμφορηθέντας.
[6] ὡς εἰκὸς μᾶλλον πόρρω ὄντες τῆς ἀξίας τῶν ἔξω.　　[7] Evidentissimâ assertione pietatis regulam teneamus.　　[8] Dispensatio humana.

FROM THE LATIN.

the state that is to follow,[1] and thus by an eternal and immutable law of equity, and by the controlling influence of Divine Providence, the immortal soul is brought to the summit of perfection. If one, however, were to object to our statement, that the word of preaching was purposely put aside by certain men of wicked and worthless character, and (were to inquire) why the word was preached to those over whom the Tyrians, who were certainly despised, are preferred in comparison (by which proceeding, certainly, their wickedness was increased, and their condemnation rendered more severe, that they should hear the word who were not to believe it), they must be answered in the following manner: God, who is the Creator of the minds of all men, foreseeing complaints against His providence, especially on the part of those who say, "How could we believe when we neither beheld those things which others saw, nor heard those words which were preached to others? in so far is the blame removed from us, since they to whom the word was announced, and the signs manifested, made no delay whatever, but became believers, overpowered by the very force of the miracles;" wishing to destroy the grounds for complaints of this kind, and to show that it was no concealment of Divine Providence, but the determination of the human mind which was the cause of their ruin, bestowed the grace of His benefits even upon the unworthy and the unbelieving, that every mouth might indeed be shut, and that the mind of man might know that all the deficiency was on its own part, and none on that of God; and that it may, at the same time, be understood and recognised that he receives a heavier sentence of condemnation who has despised the divine benefits conferred upon him than he who has not deserved to obtain or hear them, and that it is a peculiarity of divine compassion, and a mark of the extreme justice of its administration, that it sometimes conceals from certain individuals the opportunity of either seeing or hearing the mysteries of divine power, lest, after beholding the power of the miracles, and recognising and hearing the mysteries of its wisdom, they should, on treating them with contempt and indifference, be punished with greater severity for their impiety.

18. Let us now look to the expression, "It is not of him that willeth, nor of him that runneth, but of God that showeth mercy."[4] For our opponents assert, that if it does not depend upon him that willeth, nor on him that runneth, but on God that showeth mercy, that a man be saved, our salvation is not in our own power. For our nature is such as to admit of our either being saved or not, or else our salvation rests solely on the will of Him who, if He wills it, shows mercy, and confers salvation. Now let us inquire, in the first place, of such persons, whether

FROM THE GREEK.

we do not rather strive to maintain an attitude of piety in everything regarding God and His Christ,[2] seeing we endeavour by every means to prove that, in matters so great and so peculiar regarding the varied providence of God, He takes an oversight of the immortal soul. If, indeed, one were to inquire regarding those things that are objected to, why those who saw wonders and who heard divine words are not benefited, while the Tyrians would have repented if such had been performed and spoken amongst them; and should ask, and say, Why did the Saviour proclaim such to these persons, to their own hurt, that their sin might be reckoned to them as heavier? we must say, in answer to such an one, that He who understands the dispositions[3] of all those who find fault with His providence— (alleging) that it is owing to it that they have not believed, because it did not permit them to see what it enabled others to behold, and did not arrange for them to hear those words by which others, on hearing them, were benefited — wishing to prove that their defence is not founded on reason, He grants those advantages which those who blame His administration asked; in order that, after obtaining them, they may notwithstanding be convicted of the greatest impiety in not having even then yielded themselves to be benefited, and may cease from such audacity; and having been made free in respect to this very point, may learn that God occasionally, in conferring benefits upon certain persons, delays and procrastinates, not conferring the favour of seeing and hearing those things which, when seen and heard, would render the sin of those who did not believe, after acts so great and peculiar, heavier and more serious.

18. Let us look next at the passage: "So, then, it is not of him that willeth, nor of him that runneth, but of God that showeth mercy."[4] For they who find fault say: If "it is not of him that willeth, nor of him that runneth, but of God that showeth mercy," salvation does not depend upon ourselves, but upon the arrangement[5] made by Him who has formed[6] us

---

[1] Futuri status causam præstat semper anterior meritorum status. ἀγωνιζόμεθα τηρεῖν περὶ Θεοῦ, etc.   [3] διαθέσεις.   [4] Rom. ix. 16.   [2] εἰ μὴ μᾶλλον ἡμεῖς πρὸς τῷ ἐξεταστικῷ καὶ τὸ εὐσεβὲς παντὴ   [5] κατασκευῆς.   [6] κατασκευάσαντος.

to desire blessings be a good or evil act; and whether to hasten after good as a final aim [2] be worthy of praise. If they were to answer that such a procedure was deserving of censure, they would evidently be mad; for all holy men both desire blessings and run after them, and certainly are not blameworthy. How, then, is it that he who is not saved, if he be of an evil nature, desires blessings, and runs after them, but does not find them? For they say that a bad tree does not bring forth good fruits, whereas it is a good fruit to desire blessings. And how is the fruit of a bad tree good? And if they assert that to desire blessings, and to run after them, is an act of indifference,[4] i.e., neither good nor bad, we shall reply, that if it be an indifferent act to desire blessings, and to run after them, then the opposite of that will also be an indifferent act, viz., to desire evils, and to run after them; whereas it is certain that it is not an indifferent act to desire evils, and to run after them, but one that is manifestly wicked. It is established, then, that to desire and follow after blessings is not an indifferent, but a virtuous proceeding.

Having now repelled these objections by the answer which we have given, let us hasten on to the discussion of the subject itself, in which it is said, " It is not of him that willeth, nor of him that runneth, but of God that showeth mercy." [8] In the book of Psalms — in the Songs of Degrees, which are ascribed to Solomon — the following statement occurs : " Except the LORD build the house, they labour in vain that build it ; except the LORD keep the city, the watchman waketh but in vain." [9] By which words he does not indeed indicate that we should cease from building or watching over the safe keeping of that city which is within us ; but what he points out is this, that whatever is built without God, and whatever is guarded without him, is built in vain, and guarded to no purpose. For in all things that are well built and well protected, the Lord is held to be the cause either of the building or of its protection. As if, e.g., we were to behold some magnificent structure and mass of splendid building reared with beauteous architectural skill, would we not justly and deservedly say that such was built not by human power, but by divine help and might? And yet from such a statement it will not be meant that the labour and industry of human effort were inactive, and effected nothing at all. Or again, if we were to see some city surrounded by a severe blockade of the enemy, in which threatening engines were brought against the walls, and the place hard pressed by a vallum, and weapons, and fire, and all the instruments of war, by which destruction is prepared, would we not rightly and deservedly say, if the enemy were repelled and put to flight, that the deliverance had been wrought for the liberated city by God? And yet we would not mean, by so speaking, that either the vigilance of the sentinels, or the alertness of the young men,[11] or the protection of the guards, had been wanting. And the apostle also must be understood in a similar manner, because the human will alone is not sufficient to obtain salvation ; nor is any mortal running able to win

such as we are, or on the purpose [1] of Him who showeth mercy when he pleases. Now we must ask these persons the following questions : Whether to desire what is good is virtuous or vicious ; and whether the desire to run in order to reach the goal in the pursuit of what is good be worthy of praise or censure? And if they shall say that it is worthy of censure, they will return an absurd answer ; [3] since the saints desire and run, and manifestly in so acting do nothing that is blameworthy. But if they shall say that it is virtuous to desire what is good, and to run after what is good, we shall ask them how a perishing nature desires better things ; [5] for it is like an evil tree producing good fruit, since it is a virtuous act to desire better things. They will give (perhaps) a third answer, that to desire and run after what is good is one of those things that are indifferent,[6] and neither beautiful [7] nor wicked. Now to this we must say, that if to desire and to run after what is good be a thing of indifference, then the opposite also is a thing of indifference, viz., to desire what is evil, and to run after it. But it is not a thing of indifference to desire what is evil, and to run after it. And therefore also, to desire what is good, and to run after it, is not a thing of indifference. Such, then, is the defence which I think we can offer to the statement, that " it is not of him that willeth, nor of him that runneth, but of God that showeth mercy." [8] Solomon says in the book of Psalms (for the Song of Degrees [10] is his, from which we shall quote the words) : " Unless the LORD build the house, they labour in vain that build it ; except the LORD keep the city, the watchman waketh in vain : " [9] not dissuading us from building, nor teaching us not to keep watch in order to guard the city in our soul, but showing that what is built without God, and does not receive a guard from Him, is built in vain and watched to no purpose, because God might reasonably be entitled the Lord of the building ; and the Governor of all things, the Ruler of the guard of the city. As, then, if we were to say that such a building is not the work of the builder, but of God,

---

[1] προαιρέσεως. [2] Ad finem boni. [3] παρὰ τὴν ἐνάργειαν. [4] Medium est velle bona. [5] τὰ κρείττονα. [6] τῶν μέσων ἐστί.
[7] ἀστεῖον. [8] Rom. ix. 16. [9] Ps. cxxvii. 1. [10] ᾠδὴ τῶν ἀναβαθμῶν. [11] Procinctum juvenum.

the heavenly (rewards), and to obtain the prize of our high calling [1] of God in Christ Jesus, unless this very good will of ours, and ready purpose, and whatever that diligence within us may be, be aided or furnished with divine help.   And therefore most logically [2] did the apostle say, that "it is not of him that willeth, nor of him that runneth, but of God that showeth mercy;" in the same manner as if we were to say of agriculture what is actually written : " I planted, Apollos watered ; but God gave the increase.   So then neither is he that planteth anything, neither he that watereth ; but God that giveth the increase." [4]   As, therefore, when a field has brought good and rich crops to perfect maturity, no one would piously and logically assert that the husbandman had made those fruits, but would acknowledge that they had been produced by God ; so also is our own perfection brought about, not indeed by our remaining inactive and idle,[5] (but by some activity on our part) : and yet the consummation of it will not be ascribed to us, but to God, who is the first and chief cause of the work.   So, when a ship has overcome the dangers of the sea, although the result be accomplished by great labour on the part of the sailors, and by the aid of all the art of navigation, and by the zeal and carefulness of the pilot, and by the favouring influence of the breezes, and the careful observation of the signs of the stars, no one in his sound senses would ascribe the safety of the vessel, when, after being tossed by the waves, and wearied by the billows, it has at last reached the harbour in safety, to anything else than to the mercy of God.   Not even the sailors or pilot venture to say, "I have saved the ship," but they refer all to the mercy of God ; not that they feel that they have contributed no skill or labour to save the ship, but because they know that while they contributed the labour, the safety of the vessel was ensured by God.   So also in the race of our life we ourselves must expend labour, and bring diligence and zeal to bear ; but it is from God that salvation is to be hoped for as the fruit of our labour.   Otherwise, if God demand none of our labour, His commandments will appear to be superfluous.   In vain, also, does Paul blame some for having fallen from the truth, and praise others for abiding in the faith ; and to no purpose does he deliver certain precepts and institutions to the Churches : in vain, also, do we ourselves either desire or run after what is good.   But it is certain that these things are not done in vain ; and it is certain that neither do the apostles give instructions in vain, nor the Lord enact laws without a reason.   It follows, therefore, that we declare it to be in vain, rather, for the heretics to speak evil of these good declarations.

and that it was not owing to the successful effort of the watcher, but of the God who is over all, that such a city suffered no injury from its enemies, we should not be wrong,[3] it being understood that something also had been done by human means, but the benefit being gratefully referred to God who brought it to pass ; so, seeing that the (mere) human desire is not sufficient to attain the end, and that the running of those who are, as it were, athletes, does not enable them to gain the prize of the high calling of God in Christ Jesus — for these things are accomplished with the assistance of God — it is well said that " it is not of him that willeth, nor of him that runneth, but of God that showeth mercy."   As if also it were said with regard to husbandry what also is actually recorded : " I planted, Apollos watered ; and God gave the increase. So then neither is he that planteth anything, neither he that watereth ; but God that giveth the increase." [4]   Now we could not piously assert that the production of full crops was the work of the husbandman, or of him that watered, but the work of God.   So also our own perfection is brought about, not as if we ourselves did nothing ;[6] for it is not completed [7] by us, but God produces the greater part of it.   And that this assertion may be more clearly believed, we shall take an illustration from the art of navigation.   For in comparison with the effect of the winds,[8] and the mildness of the air,[9] and the light of the stars, all co-operating in the preservation of the crew, what proportion [10] could the art of navigation be said to bear in the bringing of the ship into harbour? — since even the sailors themselves, from piety, do not venture to assert often that they had saved the ship, but refer all to God ; not as if they had done nothing, but because what had been done by Providence was infinitely [11] greater than what had been effected by their art.   And in the matter of our salvation, what is done by God is infinitely greater than what is done by ourselves ; and therefore, I think, is it

---

[1] Supernæ vocationis.   [2] Valde consequenter.   [3] οὐκ ἂν πταίοιμεν.   [4] 1 Cor. iii. 6, 7.   [5] "Nostra perfectio non quidem nobis cessantibus et otiosis efficitur."   There is an ellipsis of some such words as, "but by activity on our part."   [6] ἡ ἡμετέρα τελείωσις οὐχὶ μηδὲν ἡμῶν πραξάντων γίνεται.   [7] ἀπαρτίζεται.   [8] πνοήν.   [9] εὐκρασίαν.   [10] ἀριθμόν.   [11] εἰς ὑπερβολὴν πολλαπλάσιον.

said that "it is not of him that willeth, nor of him that runneth, but of God that showeth mercy." For if in the manner which they imagine we must explain the statement,[1] that "it is not of him that willeth, nor of him that runneth, but of God that showeth mercy," the commandments are superfluous; and it is in vain that Paul himself blames some for having fallen away, and approves of others as having remained upright, and enacts laws for the Churches: it is in vain also that we give ourselves up to desire better things, and in vain also (to attempt) to run. But it is not in vain that Paul gives such advice, censuring some and approving of others; nor in vain that we give ourselves up to the desire of better things, and to the chase after things that are pre-eminent. They have accordingly not well explained the meaning of the passage.[2]

19. After this there followed this point, that "to will and to do are of God."[3] Our opponents maintain that if to will be of God, and if to do be of Him, or if, whether we act or desire well or ill, it be of God, then in that case we are not possessed of free-will. Now to this we have to answer, that the words of the apostle do not say that to will evil is of God, or that to will good is of Him; nor that to do good or evil is of God; but his statement is a general one, that to will and to do are of God. For as we have from God this very quality, that we are men,[4] that we breathe, that we move; so also we have from God (the faculty) by which we will, as if we were to say that our power of motion is from God,[6] or that the performing of these duties by the individual members, and their movements, are from God. From which, certainly, I do not understand this, that because the hand moves, e.g., to punish unjustly, or to commit an act of theft, the act is of God, but only that the power of motion[8] is from God; while it is our duty to turn those movements, the power of executing which we have from God, either to purposes of good or evil. And so what the apostle says is, that we receive indeed the power of volition, but that we misuse the will either to good or evil desires. In a similar way, also, we must judge of results.

19. Besides these, there is the passage, "Both to will and to do are of God."[3] And some assert that, if to will be of God, and to do be of God, and if, whether we will evil or do evil, these (movements) come to us from God, then, if so, we are not possessed of free-will. But again, on the other hand, when we will better things, and do things that are more excellent,[5] seeing that willing and doing are from God, it is not we who have done the more excellent things, but we only appeared (to perform them), while it was God that bestowed them;[7] so that even in this respect we do not possess free-will. Now to this we have to answer, that the language of the apostle does not assert that to will evil is of God, or to will good is of Him (and similarly with respect to doing better and worse); but that to will in a general[9] way, and to run in a general way, (are from Him). For as we have from God (the property) of being living things and human beings, so also have we that of willing generally, and, so to speak, of motion in general. And as, possessing (the property) of life and of motion, and of moving, e.g., these members, the hands or the feet, we could not rightly say[10] that we had from God this

---

1 ἐκλαμβάνειν. 2 ἐξειλήφασι τὰ κατὰ τὸν τόπον. 3 Cf. Phil. ii. 13. 4 Hoc ipsum, quod homines sumus. 5 τὰ διαφέροντα.
6 Sicut dicamus, quod movemur, ex Deo est. 7 ἡμεῖς μὲν ἐδόξαμεν, ὁ δὲ Θεὸς ταῦτα ἐδωρήσατο. 8 Hoc ipsum, quod movetur.
9 τὸ καθόλου θέλειν. 10 εὐλόγως.

20. But with respect to the declaration of the apostle, "Therefore hath He mercy on whom He will have mercy, and whom He will He hardeneth. Thou wilt say then unto me, Why doth He yet find fault? For who hath resisted His will? Nay but, O man, who art thou that repliest against God? Shall the thing formed say to him that formed it, Why hast thou made me thus? Hath not the potter power over the clay, of the same lump to make one vessel unto honour, and another unto dishonour?"[4] Some one will perhaps say, that as the potter out of the same lump makes some vessels to honour, and others to dishonour, so God creates some men for perdition, and others for salvation; and that it is not therefore in our own power either to be saved or to perish; by which reasoning we appear not to be possessed of free-will. We must answer those who are of this opinion with the question, Whether it is possible for the apostle to contradict himself? And if this cannot be imagined of an apostle, how shall he appear, according to them, to be just in blaming those who committed fornication in Corinth, or those who sinned, and did not repent of their unchastity, and fornication, and uncleanness, which they had committed? How, also, does he greatly praise those who acted rightly, like the house of Onesiphorus, saying, "The Lord give mercy to the house of Onesiphorus; for he oft refreshed me, and was not ashamed of my chain: but, when he had come to Rome, he sought me out very diligently, and found me. The Lord grant unto him that he may find mercy of the Lord in that day."[5] Now it is not consistent with apostolic gravity to blame him who is worthy of blame, i.e., who has sinned, and greatly to praise him who is deserving of praise for his good works; and again, as if it were in no one's power to do any good or evil, to say that it was the Creator's doing that every one should act virtuously or wickedly, seeing He makes one vessel to honour, and another to dishonour. And how can he add that statement, "We must all stand before the judgment-seat of Christ, that every one of us may receive in his body, according to what he hath done, whether it be good or bad?"[6] For what reward of good will be conferred on him who could not commit evil, being formed by the Creator to that very end? or what punishment will deservedly be inflicted on him who was unable to do good in consequence of the creative act of

species of motion,[1] whereby we moved to strike, or destroy, or take away another's goods, but that we had received from Him simply the generic[2] power of motion, which we employed to better or worse purposes; so we have obtained from God (the power) of acting, in respect of our being living things, and (the power) to will from the Creator,[3] while we employ the power of will, as well as that of action, for the noblest objects, or the opposite.

20. Still the declaration of the apostle will appear to drag us to the conclusion that we are not possessed of freedom of will, in which, objecting against himself, he says, "Therefore hath He mercy on whom He will have mercy, and whom He will He hardeneth. Thou wilt say then unto me, Why doth He yet find fault? For who hath resisted His will? Nay but, O man, who art thou that repliest against God? Shall the thing formed say to him that formed it, Why hast thou made me thus? Hath not the potter power over the clay, of the same lump to make one vessel unto honour, and another unto dishonour?"[4] For it will be said: If the potter of the same lump make some vessels to honour and others to dishonour, and God thus form some men for salvation and others for ruin, then salvation or ruin does not depend upon ourselves, nor are we possessed of free-will. Now we must ask him who deals so with these passages, whether it is possible to conceive of the apostle as contradicting himself. I presume, however, that no one will venture to say so. If, then, the apostle does not utter contradictions, how can he, according to him who so understands him, reasonably find fault, censuring the individual at Corinth who had committed fornication, or those who had fallen away, and had not repented of the licentiousness and impurity of which they had been guilty? And how can he bless those whom he praises as having done well, as he does the house of Onesiphorus in these words: "The Lord give mercy to the house of Onesiphorus; for he oft refreshed me, and was not ashamed of my chain:

---

[1] τὸ εἰδικὸν τόδε.   [2] τὸ μὲν γενικὸν, τὸ κινεῖσθαι.   [3] δημιουργοῦ.   [4] Rom. ix. 18–21.   [5] 2 Tim. i. 16–18.   [6] 2 Cor. v. 10.

his Maker?[1] Then, again, how is not this opposed to that other declaration elsewhere, that "in a great house there are not only vessels of gold and silver, but also of wood and of earth, and some to honour, and some to dishonour. If a man therefore purge himself from these, he shall be a vessel unto honour, sanctified, and meet for the Master's use, prepared unto every good work."[4] He, accordingly, who purges himself, is made a vessel unto honour, while he who has disdained to cleanse himself from his impurity is made a vessel unto dishonour. From such declarations, in my opinion, the cause of our actions can in no degree be referred to the Creator. For God the Creator makes a certain vessel unto honour, and other vessels to dishonour; but that vessel which has cleansed itself from all impurity He makes a vessel unto honour, while that which has stained itself with the filth of vice He makes a vessel unto dishonour. The conclusion from which, accordingly, is this, that the cause of each one's actions is a pre-existing one; and then every one, according to his deserts, is made by God either a vessel unto honour or dishonour. Therefore every individual vessel has furnished to its Creator out of itself the causes and occasions of its being formed by Him to be either a vessel unto honour or one unto dishonour. And if the assertion appear correct, as it certainly is, and in harmony with all piety, that it is due to previous causes that every vessel be prepared by God either to honour or to dishonour, it does not appear absurd that, in discussing remoter causes in the same order, and in the same method, we should come to the same conclusion respecting the nature of souls, and (believe) that this was the reason why Jacob was beloved before he was born into this world, and Esau hated, while he still was contained in the womb of his mother.

but, when he was in Rome, he sought me out very diligently, and found me. The Lord grant to him that he may find mercy of the Lord in that day."[2] It is not consistent for the same apostle[3] to blame the sinner as worthy of censure, and to praise him who had done well as deserving of approval; and again, on the other hand, to say, as if nothing depended on ourselves, that the cause was in the Creator[5] why the one vessel was formed to honour, and the other to dishonour. And how is this statement correct:[6] "For we must all appear before the judgment-seat of Christ; that every one may receive the things done in his body, according to that he hath done, whether it be good or bad,"[7] since they who have done evil have advanced to this pitch of wickedness[8] because they were created vessels unto dishonour, while they that have lived virtuously have done good because they were created from the beginning for this purpose, and became vessels unto honour? And again, how does not the statement made elsewhere conflict with the view which these persons draw from the words which we have quoted (that it is the fault of the Creator that one vessel is in honour and another in dishonour), viz., "that in a great house there are not only vessels of gold and silver, but also of wood and of earth; and some to honour, and some to dishonour. If a man therefore purge himself, he shall be a vessel unto honour, sanctified, and meet for the Master's use, and prepared unto every good work;"[4] for if he who purges himself becomes a vessel unto honour, and he who allows himself to remain unpurged[9] becomes a vessel unto dishonour, then, so far as these words are concerned, the Creator is not at all to blame. For the Creator makes vessels of honour and vessels of dishonour, not from the beginning according to His foreknowledge,[10] since He does not condemn or justify beforehand[11] according to it; but (He makes) those into vessels of honour who purged themselves, and those into vessels of dishonour who allowed

---

[1] Ex ipsâ conditoris creatione.   [2] 2 Tim. i. 16-18.   [3] οὐ κατὰ τὸν αὐτὸν δὴ ἀπόστολόν ἐστι.   [4] 2 Tim. ii. 20, 21.
[5] παρὰ τὴν αἰτίαν τοῦ δημιουργοῦ.   [6] ὑγιές.   [7] 2 Cor. v. 10.   [8] ἐπὶ τοῦτο πράξεως.   [9] ἀπερικάθαρτον ἑαυτὸν περιιδών.
[10] πρόγνωσιν.   [11] πρ'...κρίνει ἢ προδικαιοῖ.

themselves to remain unpurged : so that it results from older causes [1] (which operated) in the formation of the vessels unto honour and dishonour, that one was created for the former condition, and another for the latter. But if we once admit that there were certain older causes (at work) in the forming of a vessel unto honour, and of one unto dishonour, what absurdity is there in going back to the subject of the soul, and (in supposing) that a more ancient cause for Jacob being loved and for Esau being hated existed with respect to Jacob before his assumption of a body, and with regard to Esau before he was conceived in the womb of Rebecca?

21. Nay, that very declaration, that from the same lump a vessel is formed both to honour and to dishonour, will not push us hard ; for we assert that the nature of all rational souls is the same, as one lump of clay is described as being under the treatment of the potter. Seeing, then, the nature of rational creatures is one, God, according to the previous grounds of merit,[3] created and formed out of it, as the potter out of the one lump, some persons to honour and others to dishonour. Now, as regards the language of the apostle, which he utters as if in a tone of censure, " Nay but, O man, who art thou that repliest against God?" he means, I think, to point out that such a censure does not refer to any believer who lives rightly and justly, and who has confidence in God, i.e., to such an one as Moses was, of whom Scripture says that " Moses spake, and God answered him by a voice ; "[5] and as God answered Moses, so also does every saint answer God. But he who is an unbeliever, and loses confidence in answering before God owing to the unworthiness of his life and conversation, and who, in relation to these matters, does not seek to learn and make progress, but to oppose and resist, and who, to speak more plainly, is such an one as to be able to say those words which the apostle indicates, when he says, " Why, then, does He yet find fault? for who will resist His will?" — to such an one may the censure of the apostle rightly be directed, " Nay but, O man, who art thou that repliest against God?" This censure accordingly applies not to believers and saints, but to unbelievers and wicked men.

Now, to those who introduce souls of different natures,[7] and who turn this declaration of the apostle to the support of their own opinion, we have to reply as follows : If even they are agreed as to what the apostle says, that out of the one lump are formed both those who are made to honour and those who are made to dishonour, whom they term of a nature that is to be saved and destroyed, there will then be no longer souls of different natures, but one nature for all. And if they admit that one and the same potter may undoubtedly denote one Creator, there will not

21. And at the same time, it is clearly shown that, as far as regards the underlying nature,[2] as there is one (piece) of clay which is under the hands of the potter, from which piece vessels are formed unto honour and dishonour ; so the one nature of every soul being in the hands of God, and, so to speak, there being (only) one lump of reasonable beings,[4] certain causes of more ancient date led to some being created vessels unto honour, and others vessels unto dishonour. But if the language of the apostle convey a censure when he says, " Nay but, O man, who art thou that repliest against God?" it teaches us that he who has confidence before God, and is faithful, and has lived virtuously, would not hear the words, " Who art thou that repliest against God ? " Such an one, e. g., as Moses was, " For Moses spake, and God answered him with a voice ; "[6] and as God answers Moses, so does a saint also answer God. But he who does not possess this confidence, manifestly, either because he has lost it, or because he investigates these matters not from a love of knowledge, but from a desire to find fault,[8] and who therefore says, " Why does He yet find fault? for who hath resisted His will?" would merit the language of censure, which says, " Nay but, O man, who art thou that repliest against God ? "

Now to those who introduce different natures, and who make use

---

[1] ἐκ πρεσβυτέρων αἰτιῶν.　[2] ὅσον ἐπὶ τῇ ὑποκειμένῃ φύσει.　[3] Secundum præcedentes meritorum causas.　[4] ἑνὸς φυράματος τῶν λογικῶν ὑποστασεων.　[5] Ex. xix. 19.　[6] Cf. Ex. xix. 19.　[7] Diversas animarum naturas.　[8] κατὰ φιλονεικίαν.

be different creators either of those who are saved, or of those who perish. Now, truly, let them choose whether they will have a good Creator to be intended who creates bad and ruined men, or one who is not good, who creates good men and those who are prepared to honour. For the necessity of returning an answer will extort from them one of these two alternatives. But according to our declaration, whereby we say that it is owing to preceding causes that God makes vessels either to honour or to dishonour, the approval of God's justice is in no respect limited. For it is possible that this vessel, which owing to previous causes was made in this world to honour, may, if it behave negligently, be converted in another world, according to the deserts of its conduct, into a vessel unto dishonour: as again, if any one, owing to preceding causes, was formed by his Creator in this life a vessel unto dishonour, and shall mend his ways and cleanse himself from all filth and vice, he may, in the new world, be made a vessel to honour, sanctified and useful, and prepared unto every good work. Finally, those who were formed by God in this world to be Israelites, and who have lived a life unworthy of the nobility of their race, and have fallen away from the grandeur of their descent, will, in the world to come, in a certain degree [3] be converted, on account of their unbelief, from vessels of honour into vessels of dishonour; while, on the other hand, many who in this life were reckoned among Egyptian or Idumean vessels, having adopted the faith and practice of Israelites, when they shall have done the works of Israelites, and shall have entered the Church of the Lord, will exist as vessels of honour in the revelation of the sons of God. From which it is more agreeable to the rule of piety to believe that every rational being, according to his purpose and manner of life, is converted, sometimes from bad to good, and falls away sometimes from good to bad: that some abide in good, and others advance to a better condition, and always ascend to higher things, until they reach the highest grade of all; while others, again, remain in evil, or, if the wickedness within them begin to spread itself further, they descend to a worse condition, and sink into the lowest depth of wickedness. Whence also we must suppose that it is possible there may be some who began at first indeed with small offences, but who have poured out wickedness to such a degree, and attained such proficiency in evil, that in the measure of their wickedness they are equal even to the opposing powers: and again, if, by means of many severe administrations of punishment, they are able at some future time to recover their senses, and gradually attempt to find healing for their wounds, they may, on ceasing from their wickedness, be restored to a state of goodness. Whence we are of opinion that, seeing the soul, as we have frequently said, is immortal and eternal, it is possible that, in the many and endless periods of duration in the immeasurable and different worlds, it may descend from the highest good to the lowest evil, or be restored from the lowest evil to the highest good.

of the declaration of the apostle (to support their view), the following must be our answer. If they maintain [1] that those who perish and those who are saved are formed of one lump, and that the Creator of those who are saved is the Creator also of them who are lost, and if He is good who creates not only spiritual but also earthy (natures) (for this follows from their view), it is nevertheless possible that he who, in consequence of certain former acts of righteousness, [2] had now been made a vessel of honour, but who had not (afterwards) acted in a similar manner, nor done things befitting a vessel of honour, was converted in another world into a vessel of dishonour; as, on the other hand, it is possible that he who, owing to causes more ancient than the present life, was here a vessel of dishonour, may after reformation become in the new creation "a vessel of honour, sanctified and meet for the Master's use, prepared unto every good work." And perhaps those who are now Israelites, not having lived worthily of their descent, will be deprived of their rank, being changed, as it were, from vessels of honour into those of dishonour; and many of the present Egyptians and Idumeans who came near to Israel, when they shall have borne fruit to a larger extent, shall enter into the Church of the Lord, being no longer accounted Egyptians and Idumeans, but becoming Israelites: so that, according to this view, it is owing to their (varying) purposes that some advance from a worse to a better condition, and others fall from better to worse; while others, again, are preserved in a virtuous course, or ascend from good to better; and others, on the contrary, remain in a course of evil, or from bad become worse, as their wickedness flows on.

---

[1] σώζουσι. [2] ἐκ προτέρων τινῶν κατορθωμάτων. [3] Quodammodo.

22. But since the words of the apostle, in what he says regarding vessels of honour or dishonour, that "if a man therefore purge himself, he will be a vessel unto honour, sanctified and meet for the Master's service, and prepared unto every good work," appear to place nothing in the power of God, but all in ourselves; while in those in which he declares that "the potter hath power over the clay, to make of the same lump one vessel to honour, another to dishonour," he seems to refer the whole to God, — it is not to be understood that those statements are contradictory, but that the two meanings are to be reduced to agreement, and one signification must be drawn from both, viz., that we are not to suppose either that those things which are in our own power can be done without the help of God, or that those which are in God's hand can be brought to completion without the intervention of our acts, and desires, and intention; because we have it not in our own power so to will or do anything, as not to know that this very faculty, by which we are able to will or to do, was bestowed on us by God, according to the distinction which we indicated above. Or again, when God forms vessels, some to honour and others to dishonour, we are to suppose that He does not regard either our wills, or our purposes, or our deserts, to be the causes of the honour or dishonour, as if they were a sort of matter from which He may form the vessel of each one of us either to honour or to dishonour; whereas the very movement of the soul itself, or the purpose of the understanding, may of itself suggest to him, who is not unaware of his heart and the thoughts of his mind, whether his vessel ought to be formed to honour or to dishonour. But let these points suffice, which we have discussed as we best could, regarding the questions connected with the freedom of the will.[6]

22. But since the apostle in one place does not pretend that the becoming of a vessel unto honour or dishonour depends upon God, but refers back the whole to ourselves, saying, "If, then, a man purge himself, he will be a vessel unto honour, sanctified, meet for the Master's use, and prepared unto every good work;" and elsewhere does not even pretend that it is dependent upon ourselves, but appears to attribute the whole to God, saying, "The potter hath power over the clay, of the same lump to make one vessel unto honour and another to dishonour;" and as his statements are not contradictory, we must reconcile them, and extract one complete statement from both. Neither does our own power,[1] apart from the knowledge[2] of God, compel us to make progress; nor does the knowledge of God (do so), unless we ourselves also contribute something to the good result; nor does our own power, apart from the knowledge of God, and the use of the power that worthily belongs to us,[3] make a man become (a vessel) unto honour or dishonour; nor does the will of God alone[4] form a man to honour or to dishonour, unless He hold our will to be a kind of matter that admits of variation,[5] and that inclines to a better or worse course of conduct. And these observations are sufficient to have been made by us on the subject of free-will.

---

[1] τὸ ἐφ' ἡμῖν.   [2] ἐπιστήμη: probably in the sense of πρόγνωσις.   [3] τῆς καταχρήσεως τοῦ κατ' ἀξίαν τοῦ ἐφ' ἡμῖν.   "Nec sine usu liberi nostri arbitrii, quod peculiare nobis et meriti nostri est" (Redepenning).   [4] οὔτε τοῦ ἐπὶ τῷ Θεῷ μόνον.   [5] ὕλην τινὰ διαφορᾶς.
[6] [Elucidation II.]

CHAP. II. — ON THE OPPOSING POWERS.

1. We have now to notice, agreeably to the statements of Scripture, how the opposing powers, or the devil himself, contends with the human race, inciting and instigating men to sin. And in the first place, in the book of Genesis,[1] the serpent is described as having seduced Eve; regarding whom, in the work entitled *The Ascension of Moses*[2] (a little treatise, of which the Apostle Jude makes mention in his Epistle), the archangel Michael, when disputing with the devil regarding the body of Moses, says that the serpent, being inspired by the devil, was the cause of Adam and Eve's transgression. This also is made a subject of inquiry by some, viz., who the angel was that, speaking from heaven to Abraham, said, "Now I know that thou fearest God, and on my account hast not spared thy beloved son, whom thou lovedst."[3] For he is manifestly described as an angel who said that he knew then that Abraham feared God, and had not spared his beloved son, as the Scripture declares, although he did not say that it was on account of God that Abraham had done this, but on his, that is, the speaker's account. We must also ascertain who

---

[1] Gen. iii.
[2] This apocryphal work, entitled in Hebrew פטירת משה, and in Greek Ἀνάληψις, or Ἀνάβασις Μωυσέως, is mentioned by several ancient writers; e.g., by Athanasius, in his *Synopsis Sacræ Scripturæ;* Nicephorus Constantinopolitanus in his *Stichometria*, appended to the *Chronicon* of Eusebius (where he says the Ἀνάληψις contained 1400 verses), in the Acts of the Council of Nice, etc., etc. (Ruæus).

[3] Gen. xxii. 12. The reading in the text is according to the Septuagint and Vulgate, with the exception of the words " quem dilexisti," which are an insertion.

that is of whom it is stated in the book of Exodus that he wished to slay Moses, because he was taking his departure for Egypt;[1] and afterwards, also, who he is that is called the destroying[2] angel, as well as he who in the book of Leviticus is called Apopompæus, i.e., Averter, regarding whom Scripture says, "One lot for the Lord, and one lot for Apopompæus, i.e., the Averter."[3] In the first book of Kings, also, an evil spirit is said to strangle[4] Saul; and in the third book, Micaiah the prophet says, "I saw the Lord of Israel sitting on His throne, and all the host of heaven standing by Him, on His right hand and on His left. And the Lord said, Who will deceive Achab king of Israel, that he may go up and fall at Ramoth-gilead? And one said on this manner, and another said on that manner. And there came forth a spirit, and stood before the Lord, and said, I will deceive him. And the Lord said to him, Wherewith? And he said, I will go forth, and I will be a lying spirit in the mouth of all his prophets. And He said, Thou shalt deceive him, and prevail also: go forth, and do so quickly. And now therefore the Lord hath put a lying spirit in the mouth of all thy prophets: the Lord hath spoken evil concerning thee."[5] Now by this last quotation it is clearly shown that a certain spirit, from his own (free) will and choice, elected to deceive (Achab), and to work a lie, in order that the Lord might mislead the king to his death, for he deserved to suffer. In the first book of Chronicles also it is said, "The devil, Satan, stood up against Israel, and provoked David to number the people."[6] In the Psalms, moreover, an evil angel is said to harass[7] certain persons. In the book of Ecclesiastes, too, Solomon says, "If the spirit of the ruler rise up against thee, leave not thy place; for soundness will restrain many transgressions."[8] In Zechariah[9] we read that the devil stood on the right hand of Joshua, and resisted him. Isaiah says that the sword of the Lord arises against the dragon, the crooked[10] serpent.[11] And what shall I say of Ezekiel, who in his second vision prophesies most unmistake-

ably to the prince of Tyre regarding an opposing power, and who says also that the dragon dwells in the rivers of Egypt?[12] Nay, with what else are the contents of the whole work which is written regarding Job occupied, save with the (doings) of the devil, who asks that power may be given him over all that Job possesses, and over his sons, and even over his person? And yet the devil is defeated through the patience of Job. In that book the Lord has by His answers imparted much information regarding the power of that dragon which opposes us. Such, meanwhile, are the statements made in the Old Testament, so far as we can at present recall them, on the subject of hostile powers being either named in Scripture, or being said to oppose the human race, and to be afterwards subjected to punishment.

Let us now look also to the New Testament, where Satan approaches the Saviour, and tempts Him: wherein also it is stated that evil spirits and unclean demons, which had taken possession of very many, were expelled by the Saviour from the bodies of the sufferers, who are said also to be made free by Him. Even Judas, too, when the devil had already put it in his heart to betray Christ, afterwards received Satan wholly into him; for it is written, that after the sop "Satan entered into him."[13] And the Apostle Paul teaches us that we ought not to give place to the devil; but "put on," he says, "the armour of God, that ye may be able to resist the wiles of the devil:"[14] pointing out that the saints have to "*wrestle* not against flesh and blood, but against principalities, against powers, against the rulers of the darkness of this world, against spiritual wickedness in high places."[15] Nay, he says that the Saviour even was crucified by the princes of this world, who shall come to nought,[16] whose wisdom also, he says, he does not speak. By all this, therefore, holy Scripture teaches us that there are certain invisible enemies that fight against us, and against whom it commands us to arm ourselves. Whence, also, the more simple among the believers in the Lord Christ are of opinion, that all the sins which men have committed are caused by the persistent efforts of these opposing powers exerted upon the minds of sinners, because in that invisible struggle these powers are found to be superior (to man). For if, for example, there were no devil, no single human being[17] would go astray.

2. We, however, who see the reason (of the thing) more clearly, do not hold this opinion, taking into account those (sins) which mani-

---

[1] Cf. Ex. iv. 24-26.
[2] Ex. xii. 23, exterminator. *Percussor*, Vulgate; ὀλοθρεύων, Sept.
[3] Lev. xvi. 8. Ἀποπομπαῖος is the reading of the Sept., "Caper emissarius" of the Vulgate, לַעֲזָאזֵל of the Masoretic text. Cf. Fürst and Gesenius s.v. Rufinus translates Apopompæus by "transmissor."
[4] 1 Sam. xviii. 10, effocare. Septuagint has ἔπεσε: Vulgate, "invasit;" the Masoretic text תִּצְלַח, fell on.
[5] 1 Kings xxii. 19-23.
[6] 1 Chron. xxi. 1.
[7] Atterere.
[8] Eccles. x. 4, "For yielding pacifieth great offences." The words in the text are, "Quoniam sanitas compescet multa peccata." The Vulgate has, "Curatio faciet cessare peccata maxima." The Septuagint reads, Ἴαμα καταπαύσει ἁμαρτίας μεγάλας: while the Masoretic text has מַרְפֵּא (curatio).
[9] Zech. iii. 1.
[10] Perversum.
[11] Isa xxvii. 1.
[12] Ezek. xxviii. 12 sq.
[13] Cf. John xiii. 27.
[14] Eph. vi. 13.
[15] Eph. vi. 12.
[16] Cf. 1 Cor. ii. 6.
[17] Nemo hominum omnino.

festly originate as a necessary consequence of our bodily constitution.[1] Must we indeed suppose that the devil is the cause of our feeling hunger or thirst? Nobody, I think, will venture to maintain that. If, then, he is not the cause of our feeling hunger and thirst, wherein lies the difference when each individual has attained the age of puberty, and that period has called forth the incentives of the natural heat? It will undoubtedly follow, that as the devil is not the cause of our feeling hunger and thirst, so neither is he the cause of that appetency which naturally arises at the time of maturity, viz., the desire of sexual intercourse. Now it is certain that this cause is not always so set in motion by the devil that we should be obliged to suppose that bodies would not possess a desire for intercourse of that kind if the devil did not exist. Let us consider, in the next place, if, as we have already shown, food is desired by human beings, not from a suggestion of the devil, but by a kind of natural instinct, whether, if there were no devil, it were possible for human experience to exhibit such restraint in partaking of food as never to exceed the proper limits ; i.e., that no one would either take otherwise than the case required, or more than reason would allow ; and so it would result that men, observing due measure and moderation in the matter of eating, would never go wrong. I do not think, indeed, that so great moderation could be observed by men (even if there were no instigation by the devil inciting thereto), as that no individual, in partaking of food, would go beyond due limits and restraint, until he had learned to do so from long usage and experience. What, then, is the state of the case? In the matter of eating and drinking it was possible for us to go wrong, even without any incitement from the devil, if we should happen to be either less temperate or less careful (than we ought) ; and are we to suppose, then, in our appetite for sexual intercourse, or in the restraint of our natural desires, our condition is not something similar?[2] I am of opinion, indeed, that the same course of reasoning must be understood to apply to other natural movements, as those of covetousness, or of anger, or of sorrow, or of all those generally which through the vice of intemperance exceed the natural bounds of moderation. There are therefore manifest reasons for holding the opinion, that as in good things the human will[3] is of itself weak to accomplish any good (for it is by divine help that it is brought to perfection in everything) ; so also, in things of an opposite nature we receive certain initial elements, and, as it were, seeds of sins, from those things which we use agreeably

to nature ;[4] but when we have indulged them beyond what is proper, and have not resisted the first movements to intemperance, then the hostile power, seizing the occasion of this first transgression, incites and presses us hard in every way, seeking to extend our sins over a wider field, and furnishing us human beings with occasions and beginnings of sins, which these hostile powers spread far and wide, and, if possible, beyond all limits. Thus, when men at first for a little desire money, covetousness begins to grow as the passion increases, and finally the fall into avarice takes place. And after this, when blindness of mind has succeeded passion, and the hostile powers, by their suggestions, hurry on the mind, money is now no longer desired, but stolen, and acquired by force, or even by shedding human blood. Finally, a confirmatory evidence of the fact that vices of such enormity proceed from demons, may be easily seen in this, that those individuals who are oppressed either by immoderate love, or incontrollable anger, or excessive sorrow, do not suffer less than those who are bodily vexed by devils. For it is recorded in certain histories, that some have fallen into madness from a state of love, others from a state of anger, not a few from a state of sorrow, and even from one of excessive joy ; which results, I think, from this, that those opposing powers, i.e., those demons, having gained a lodgment in their minds which has been already laid open to them by intemperance, have taken complete possession of their sensitive nature,[5] especially when no feeling of the glory of virtue has aroused them to resistance.

3. That there are certain sins, however, which do not proceed from the opposing powers, but take their beginnings from the natural movements of the body, is manifestly declared by the Apostle Paul in the passage : " The flesh lusteth against the Spirit, and the Spirit against the flesh : and these are contrary the one to the other ; so that ye cannot do the things that ye would." [6] If, then, the flesh lust against the Spirit, and the Spirit against the flesh, we have occasionally to wrestle against flesh and blood, i.e., as being men, and walking according to the flesh, and not capable of being tempted by greater than human temptations ; since it is said of us, " There hath no temptation taken you, but such as is common to man : but God is faithful, who will not suffer you to be tempted above that ye are able." [7] For as the presidents of the public games do not allow the competitors to enter the lists indiscriminately or fortuitously, but after a careful examination, pairing in a most impartial consid-

---

[1] Ex corporali necessitate descendunt.
[2] Quod non simile aliquid pateremur?
[3] Propositum.

[4] Quæ in usu naturaliter habentur.
[5] Sensum eorum penitus possederint.
[6] Gal. v. 17.
[7] 1 Cor. x. 13.

eration either of size or age, this individual with that — boys, e.g., with boys, men with men, who are nearly related to each other either in age or strength ; so also must we understand the procedure of divine providence, which arranges on most impartial principles all who descend into the struggles of this human life, according to the nature of each individual's power, which is known only to Him who alone beholds the hearts of men : so that one individual fights against one temptation of the flesh,[1] another against a second ; one is exposed to its influence for so long a period of time, another only for so long ; one is tempted by the flesh to this or that indulgence, another to one of a different kind ; one has to resist this or that hostile power, another has to combat two or three at the same time ; or at one time this hostile influence, at another that ; at some particular date having to resist one enemy, and at another a different one ; being, after the performance of certain acts, exposed to one set of enemies, after others to a second. And observe whether some such state of things be not indicated by the language of the apostle : "God is faithful, who will not suffer you to be tempted above what ye are able,"[2] i.e., each one is tempted in proportion to the amount of his strength or power of resistance.[3] Now, although we have said that it is by the just judgment of God that every one is tempted according to the amount of his strength, we are not therefore to suppose that he who is tempted ought by all means to prove victorious in the struggle ; in like manner as he who contends in the lists, although paired with his adversary on a just principle of arrangement, will nevertheless not necessarily prove conqueror. But unless the powers of the combatants are equal, the prize of the victor will not be justly won ; nor will blame justly attach to the vanquished, because He allows us indeed to be tempted, but not "beyond what we are able : " for it is in proportion to our strength that we are tempted ; and it is not written that, in temptation, He will make also a way to escape so as that we should bear it, but a way to escape so as that we should be able to bear it.[4] But it depends upon ourselves to use either with energy or feebleness this power which He has given us. For there is no doubt that under every temptation we have a power of endurance, if we employ properly the strength that is granted us. But it is not the same thing to possess the *power* of conquering and to be victorious, as the apostle himself has shown in very cautious language, saying, "God will make a way

to escape, that you may be *able* to bear it,"[5] not that you *will* bear it. For many do not sustain temptation, but are overcome by it. Now God enables us not to sustain (temptation), (otherwise there would appear to be no struggle), but to have the *power* of sustaining it.[6] But this power which is given us to enable us to conquer may be used, according to our faculty of free-will, either in a diligent manner, and then we prove victorious, or in a slothful manner, and then we are defeated. For if such a power were wholly given us as that we must by all means prove victorious, and never be defeated, what further reason for a struggle could remain to him who cannot be overcome? Or what merit is there in a victory, where the power of successful resistance[7] is taken away? But if the possibility of conquering be equally conferred on us all, and if it be in our own power how to use this possibility, i.e., either diligently or slothfully, then will the vanquished be justly censured, and the victor be deservedly lauded. Now from these points which we have discussed to the best of our power, it is, I think, clearly evident that there are certain transgressions which we by no means commit under the pressure of malignant powers ; while there are others, again, to which we are incited by instigation on their part to excessive and immoderate indulgence. Whence it follows that we have to inquire how those opposing powers produce these incitements within us.

4. With respect to the thoughts which proceed from our heart, or the recollection of things which we have done, or the contemplation of any things or causes whatever, we find that they sometimes proceed from ourselves, and sometimes are originated by the opposing powers ; not seldom also are they suggested by God, or by the holy angels. Now such a statement will perhaps appear incredible,[8] unless it be confirmed by the testimony of holy Scripture. That, then, thoughts arise within ourselves, David testifies in the Psalms, saying, "The thought of a man will make confession to Thee, and the rest of the thought shall observe to Thee a festival day."[9] That this, however, is also brought about by the opposing powers, is shown by Solomon in the book of Ecclesiastes in the following manner : "If the spirit of the ruler rise up against thee, leave not thy place ; for soundness restrains great offences."[10] The Apostle Paul also will bear testimony to the same point in the words : "Casting down imaginations, and every high thing that exalted itself against the knowl-

---

[1] Carnem talem.
[2] 1 Cor. x. 13.
[3] Pro virtutis suæ quantitate, vel possibilitate.
[4] Nec tamen scriptum est, quia faciet in tentatione etiam exitum sustinendi, sed exitum ut sustinere possimus.

[5] 1 Cor. x. 13.
[6] Ut sustinere possimus.
[7] Repugnandi vincendique.
[8] Fabulosum.
[9] Ps. lxxvi. 10. Such is the reading of the Vulgate and of the Septuagint. The authorized version follows the Masoretic text.
[10] Eccles. x. 4; cf. note 8, p. 329.

edge of Christ."[1]　That it is an effect due to God, nevertheless, is declared by David, when he says in the Psalms, "Blessed is the man whose help is in Thee, O Lord, Thy ascents (are) in his heart."[2]　And the apostle says that "God put it into the heart of Titus."[3]　That certain thoughts are suggested to men's hearts either by good or evil angels, is shown both by the angel that accompanied Tobias,[4] and by the language of the prophet, where he says, "And the angel who spoke in me answered."[5]　The book of the Shepherd[6] declares the same, saying that each individual is attended by two angels; that whenever good thoughts arise in our hearts, they are suggested by the good angel; but when of a contrary kind, they are the instigation of the evil angel.　The same is declared by Barnabas in his Epistle,[7] where he says there are two ways, one of light and one of darkness, over which he asserts that certain angels are placed, — the angels of God over the way of light, the angels of Satan over the way of darkness.　We are not, however, to imagine that any other result follows from what is suggested to our heart, whether good or bad, save a (mental) commotion only, and an incitement instigating us either to good or evil.　For it is quite within our reach, when a malignant power has begun to incite us to evil, to cast away from us the wicked suggestions, and to resist the vile inducements, and to do nothing that is at all deserving of blame.　And, on the other hand, it is possible, when a divine power calls us to better things, not to obey the call; our freedom of will being preserved to us in either case.　We said, indeed, in the foregoing pages, that certain recollections of good or evil actions were suggested to us either by the act of divine providence or by the opposing powers, as is shown in the book of Esther, when Artaxerxes had not remembered the services of that just man Mordecai, but, when wearied out with his nightly vigils, had it put into his mind by God to require that the annals of his great deeds should be read to him; whereon, being reminded of the benefits received from Mordecai, he ordered his enemy Haman to be hanged, but splendid honours to be conferred on him, and impunity from the threatened danger to be granted to the whole of

the holy nation.　On the other hand, however, we must suppose that it was through the hostile influence of the devil that the suggestion was introduced into the minds of the high priests and the scribes which they made to Pilate, when they came and said, "Sir, we remember that that deceiver said, while he was yet alive, After three days I will rise again."[8]　The design of Judas, also, respecting the betrayal of our Lord and Saviour, did not originate in the wickedness of his mind alone.　For Scripture testifies that the "devil had already put it into his heart to betray Him."[9]　And therefore Solomon rightly commanded, saying, "Keep thy heart with all diligence."[10]　And the Apostle Paul warns us: "Therefore we ought to give the more earnest heed to the things which we have heard, lest perhaps we should let them slip."[11]　And when he says, "Neither give place to the devil,"[12] he shows by that injunction that it is through certain acts, or a kind of mental slothfulness, that room is made for the devil, so that, if he once enter our heart, he will either gain possession of us, or at least will pollute the soul, if he has not obtained the entire mastery over it, by casting on us his fiery darts; and by these we are sometimes deeply wounded, and sometimes only set on fire.　Seldom indeed, and only in a few instances, are these fiery darts quenched, so as not to find a place where they may wound, i.e., when one is covered by the strong and mighty shield of faith.　The declaration, indeed, in the Epistle to the Ephesians, "We wrestle not against flesh and blood, but against principalities, against powers, against the rulers of the darkness of this world, against spiritual wickedness in high places,"[13] must be so understood as if "we" meant, "I Paul, and you Ephesians, and all who have not to wrestle against flesh and blood:" for such have to struggle against principalities and powers, against the rulers of the darkness of this world, not like the Corinthians, whose struggle was as yet against flesh and blood, and who had been overtaken by no temptation but such as is common to man.

5. We are not, however, to suppose that each individual has to contend against all these (adversaries).　For it is impossible for any man, although he were a saint, to carry on a contest against all of them at the same time.　If that indeed were by any means to be the case, as it is certainly impossible it should be so, human nature could not possibly bear it without undergoing entire destruction.[14]　But as, for example,

---

[1] 2 Cor. x. 5.
[2] Ps. lxxxiv. 5. The words in the text are: Beatus vir, cujus est susceptio apud te, Domine, adscensus in corde ejus. The Vulgate reads: Beatus vir, cujus est auxilium abs te: ascensiones in corde suo disposuit. The Septuagint the same. The Masoretic text has מְסִלּוֹת ("festival march or procession:" Furst). Probably the Septuagint and Vulgate had מַעֲלוֹת before them, the similarity between Samech and Ayin accounting for the error in transcription.
[3] 2 Cor. viii. 16.
[4] [See book of Tobit, chaps. v. vi. S.]
[5] Zech. i. 14. The Vulgate, Septuagint, and Masoretic text all have "in me," although the Authorized Version reads "with me."
[6] Shepherd of Hermas, Command. vi. 2. See vol. ii. p. 24.
[7] Epistle of Barnabas. See vol. i. pp. 148, 149.

[8] Matt. xxvii. 63.
[9] John xiii. 2.
[10] Prov. iv. 23.
[11] Heb. ii. 1.
[12] Eph. iv. 27.
[13] Eph. vi. 12.
[14] Sine maxima subversione sui.

if fifty soldiers were to say that they were about to engage with fifty others, they would not be understood to mean that one of them had to contend against the whole fifty, but each one would rightly say that "our battle was against fifty," all against all; so also this is to be understood as the apostle's meaning, that all the athletes and soldiers of Christ have to wrestle and struggle against all the adversaries enumerated,—the struggle having, indeed, to be maintained against all, but by single individuals either with individual powers, or at least in such manner as shall be determined by God, who is the just president of the struggle. For I am of opinion that there is a certain limit to the powers of human nature, although there may be a Paul, of whom it is said, "He is a chosen vessel unto Me;"[1] or a Peter, against whom the gates of hell do not prevail; or a Moses, the friend of God: yet not one of them could sustain, without destruction to himself,[2] the whole simultaneous assault of these opposing powers, unless indeed the might of Him alone were to work in him, who said, "Be of good cheer, I have overcome the world."[3] And therefore Paul exclaims with confidence, "I can do all things through Christ, who strengtheneth me;"[4] and again, "I laboured more abundantly than they all; yet not I, but the grace of God which was with me."[5] On account, then, of this power, which certainly is not of human origin, operating and speaking in him, Paul could say, "For I am persuaded that neither death, nor life, nor angels, nor principalities, nor powers, nor things present, nor things to come, nor height, nor depth, nor power, nor any other creature, shall be able to separate us from the love of God, which is in Christ Jesus our Lord."[6] For I do not think that human nature can alone of itself maintain a contest with angels, and with the powers of the height and of the abyss,[7] and with any other creature; but when it feels the presence of the Lord dwelling within it, confidence in the divine help will lead it to say, "The LORD is my light, and my salvation; whom shall I fear? The LORD is the protector of my life; of whom shall I be afraid? When the enemies draw near to me, to eat my flesh, my enemies who trouble me, they stumbled and fell. Though an host encamp against me, my heart shall not fear; though war should rise against me, in Him shall I be confident."[8] From which I infer that a man perhaps would never be able of himself to vanquish an opposing power, unless

he had the benefit of divine assistance. Hence, also, the angel is said to have wrestled with Jacob. Here, however, I understand the writer to mean, that it was not the same thing for the angel to have wrestled *with* Jacob, and to have wrestled *against* him; but the angel that wrestles with him is he who was present with him in order to secure his safety, who, after knowing also his moral progress, gave him in addition the name of Israel, i.e., he is *with* him in the struggle, and assists him in the contest; seeing there was undoubtedly another angel against whom he contended, and against whom he had to carry on a contest. Finally, Paul has not said that we wrestle *with* princes, or *with* powers, but *against* principalities and powers. And hence, although Jacob wrestled, it was unquestionably *against* some one of those powers which, Paul declares, resist and contend with the human race, and especially with the saints. And therefore at last the Scripture says of him that "he wrestled with the angel, and had power with God," so that the struggle is supported by help of the angel, but the prize of success conducts the conqueror to God.

6. Nor are we, indeed, to suppose that struggles of this kind are carried on by the exercise of bodily strength, and of the arts of the wrestling school;[9] but spirit contends with spirit, according to the declaration of Paul, that our struggle is against principalities, and powers, and the rulers of the darkness of this world. Nay, the following is to be understood as the nature of the struggles; when, e.g., losses and dangers befall us, or calumnies and false accusations are brought against us, it not being the object of the hostile powers that we should suffer these (trials) only, but that by means of them we should be driven either to excess of anger or sorrow, or to the last pitch of despair; or at least, which is a greater sin, should be forced, when fatigued and overcome by any annoyances, to make complaints against God, as one who does not administer human life justly and equitably; the consequence of which is, that our faith may be weakened, or our hopes disappointed, or we may be compelled to give up the truth of our opinions, or be led to entertain irreligious sentiments regarding God. For some such things are written regarding Job, after the devil had requested God that power should be given him over his goods. By which also we are taught, that it is not by any accidental attacks that we are assailed, whenever we are visited with any such loss of property, nor that it is owing to chance when one of us is taken prisoner, or when the dwellings in which those who are dear to us are crushed to death, fall in

---

[1] Acts ix. 15.
[2] Sine aliquâ pernicie sui.
[3] John xvi. 33.
[4] Phil iv. 13.
[5] 1 Cor. xv. 10.
[6] Rom. viii. 38, 39. The word "virtus," δύναμις, occurring in the text, is not found in the *text. recept.* Tischendorf reads Δυναμεις *in loco* (edit. 7). So also Codex Sinaiticus.
[7] Excelsa et profunda.
[8] Ps. xxvii. 1–3.

[9] Palæstricæ artis exercitiis.

ruins; for, with respect to all these occurrences, every believer ought to say, "Thou couldst have no power at all against Me, except it were given thee from above."[1] For observe that the house of Job did not fall upon his sons until the devil had first received power against them; nor would the horsemen have made an irruption in three bands,[2] to carry away his camels or his oxen, and other cattle, unless they had been instigated by that spirit to whom they had delivered themselves up as the servants of his will. Nor would that fire, as it seemed to be, or thunderbolt, as it has been considered, have fallen upon the sheep of the patriarch, until the devil had said to God, "Hast Thou not made a hedge about all that is without and within his house, and around all the rest of his property? But now put forth Thy hand, and touch all that he hath, (and see) if he do not renounce Thee to Thy face."[3]

7. The result of all the foregoing remarks is to show, that all the occurrences in the world which are considered to be of an intermediate kind, whether they be mournful or otherwise, are brought about, not indeed by God, and yet not without Him; while He not only does not prevent those wicked and opposing powers that are desirous to bring about these things (from accomplishing their purpose), but even permits them to do so, although only on certain occasions and to certain individuals, as is said with respect to Job himself, that for a certain time he was made to fall under the power of others, and to have his house plundered by unjust persons. And therefore holy Scripture teaches us to receive all that happens as sent by God, knowing that without Him no event occurs. For how can we doubt that such is the case, viz., that nothing comes to man without (the will of) God, when our Lord and Saviour declares, "Are not two sparrows sold for a farthing? and one of them shall not fall on the ground without your Father who is in heaven."[4] But the necessity of the case has drawn us away in a lengthened digression on the subject of the struggle waged by the hostile powers against men, and of those sadder events which happen to human life, i.e., its temptations — according to the declaration of Job, "Is not the whole life of man upon the earth a temptation?"[5] — in order that the manner of their occurrence, and the spirit in which we should regard them, might be clearly

shown. Let us notice next, how men fall away into the sin of false knowledge, or with what object the opposing powers are wont to stir up conflict with us regarding such things.

CHAP. III. — ON THREEFOLD WISDOM.

1. The holy apostle, wishing to teach us some great and hidden truth respecting science and wisdom, says, in the first Epistle to the Corinthians: "We speak wisdom among them that are perfect; yet not the wisdom of this world, nor of the princes of the world, that come to nought: but we speak the wisdom of God in a mystery, even the hidden wisdom, which God ordained before the world unto our glory: which none of the princes of the world knew: for had they known it, they would not have crucified the Lord of glory."[6] In this passage, wishing to describe the different kinds of wisdom, he points out that there is a wisdom of this world, and a wisdom of the princes of this world, and another wisdom of God. But when he uses the expression "wisdom of the princes of this world," I do not think that he means a wisdom common to all the princes of this world, but one rather that is peculiar to certain individuals among them. And again, when he says, "We speak the wisdom of God in a mystery, even the hidden wisdom, which God ordained before the world unto our glory,"[7] we must inquire whether his meaning be, that this is the same wisdom of God which was hidden from other times and generations, and was not made known to the sons of men, as it has now been revealed to His holy apostles and prophets, and which was also that wisdom of God before the advent of the Saviour, by means of which Solomon obtained his wisdom, and in reference to which the language of the Saviour Himself declared, that what He taught was greater than Solomon, in these words, "Behold, a greater than Solomon is here,"[8] — words which show, that those who were instructed by the Saviour were instructed in something higher than the knowledge of Solomon. For if one were to assert that the Saviour did indeed Himself possess greater knowledge, but did not communicate more to others than Solomon did, how will that agree with the statement which follows: "The queen of the south shall rise up in the judgment, and condemn the men of this generation, because she came from the ends of the earth to hear the wisdom of Solomon; and, behold, a greater than Solomon is here?" There is therefore a wisdom of this world, and also probably a wisdom belonging to each individual prince of this world. But with respect to

---

[1] John xix. 11.
[2] Tribus ordinibus.
[3] Cf. Job i. 10, 11. "Nisi in faciem benedixerit tibi." The Hebrew verb בָּרַךְ has the double signification of "blessing" and "cursing." Cf. Davidson's *Commentary on Job*, p. 7. Septuag. εὐλογήσει.
[4] Matt. x. 29.
[5] Cf. Job vii. 1. The Septuagint reads, πότερον οὐχὶ πειρατήριον, etc.; the Vulgate, "militia;" the Masoretic text has צָבָא. Cf. Davidson's *Commentary on Job, in loc.*

[6] 1 Cor. ii. 6-8.
[7] 1 Cor. ii. 7.
[8] Matt. xii. 42.

the wisdom of God alone, we perceive that this is indicated, that it operated to a less degree in ancient and former times, and was (afterwards) more fully revealed and manifested through Christ. We shall inquire, however, regarding the wisdom of God in the proper place.

2. But now, since we are treating of the manner in which the opposing powers stir up those contests, by means of which false knowledge is introduced into the minds of men, and human souls led astray, while they imagine that they have discovered wisdom, I think it necessary to name and distinguish the wisdom of this world, and of the princes of this world, that by so doing we may discover who are the fathers of this wisdom, nay, even of these kinds of wisdom.[1] I am of opinion, therefore, as I have stated above, that there is another wisdom of this world besides those (different kinds of) wisdom[2] which belong to the princes of this world, by which wisdom those things seem to be understood and comprehended which belong to this world. This wisdom, however, possesses in itself no fitness for forming any opinion either respecting divine things,[3] or the plan of the world's government, or any other subjects of importance, or regarding the training for a good or happy life ; but is such as deals wholly with the art of poetry, e.g., or that of grammar, or rhetoric, or geometry, or music, with which also, perhaps, medicine should be classed. In all these subjects we are to suppose that the wisdom of this world is included. The wisdom of the princes of this world, on the other hand, we understand to be such as the secret and occult philosophy, as they call it, of the Egyptians, and the astrology of the Chaldeans and Indians, who make profession of the knowledge of high things,[4] and also that manifold variety of opinion which prevails among the Greeks regarding divine things. Accordingly, in the holy Scriptures we find that there are princes over individual nations ; as in Daniel[5] we read that there was a prince of the kingdom of Persia, and another prince of the kingdom of Græcia, who are clearly shown, by the nature of the passage, to be not human beings, but certain powers. In the prophecies of Ezekiel,[6] also, the prince of Tyre is unmistakeably shown to be a kind of spiritual power. When these, then, and others of the same kind, possessing each his own wisdom, and building up his own opinions and sentiments, beheld our Lord and Saviour professing and declaring that He had for this purpose come into the world, that all the opinions of science, falsely

so called, might be destroyed, not knowing what was concealed within Him, they forthwith laid a snare for Him : for " the kings of the earth set themselves, and the rulers assembled together, against the LORD and His Christ."[7] But their snares being discovered, and the plans which they had attempted to carry out being made manifest when they crucified the Lord of glory, therefore the apostle says, " We speak wisdom among them that are perfect, but not the wisdom of this world, nor of the princes of this world, who are brought to nought, which none of the princes of this world knew : for had they known it, they would not have crucified the Lord of glory."[8]

3. We must, indeed, endeavour to ascertain whether that wisdom[9] of the princes of this world, with which they endeavour to imbue men, is introduced into their minds by the opposing powers, with the purpose of ensnaring and injuring them, or only for the purpose of deceiving them, i.e., not with the object of doing any hurt to man ; but, as these princes of this world esteem such opinions to be true, they desire to impart to others what they themselves believe to be the truth : and this is the view which I am inclined to adopt. For as, to take an illustration,, certain Greek authors, or the leaders of some heretical sect, after having imbibed an error in doctrine instead of the truth, and having come to the conclusion in their own minds that such *is* the truth, proceed, in the next place, to endeavour to persuade others of the correctness of their opinions ; so, in like manner, are we to suppose is the procedure of the princes of this world, in which to certain spiritual powers has been assigned the rule over certain nations, and who are termed on that account the princes of this world. There are besides, in addition to these princes, certain special energies[10] of this world, i.e., spiritual powers, which bring about certain effects, which they have themselves, in virtue of their freedom of will, chosen to produce, and to these belong those princes who practise the wisdom of this world : there being, for example, a peculiar energy and power, which is the inspirer of poetry ; another, of geometry ; and so a separate power, to remind us of each of the arts and professions of this kind. Lastly, many Greek writers have been of opinion that the art of poetry cannot exist without madness ;[11] whence also it is several times related in their histories, that those whom they call poets[12] were suddenly filled with a kind of spirit of madness. And what are we to say also of those whom they

---

[1] Sapientiarum harum.
[2] Sapientias illas.
[3] De divinitate.
[4] De scientiâ excelsi pollicentium.
[5] Cf. Dan. x.
[6] Cf. Ezek. xxvi.

[7] Ps. ii. 2.
[8] 1 Cor. ii. 6-8.
[9] Istæ sapientiæ.
[10] Energiæ.
[11] Insania.
[12] Vates.

call diviners,[1] from whom, by the working of those demons who have the mastery over them, answers are given in carefully constructed verses? Those persons, too, whom they term Magi or Malevolent,[2] frequently, by invoking demons over boys of tender years, have made them repeat poetical compositions which were the admiration and amazement of all. Now these effects we are to suppose are brought about in the following manner: As holy and immaculate souls, after devoting themselves to God with all affection and purity, and after preserving themselves free from all contagion of evil spirits,[3] and after being purified by lengthened abstinence, and imbued with holy and religious training, assume by this means a portion of divinity, and earn the grace of prophecy, and other divine gifts; so also are we to suppose that those who place themselves in the way of the opposing powers, i.e., who purposely admire and adopt their manner of life and habits,[4] receive their inspiration, and become partakers of their wisdom and doctrine. And the result of this is, that they are filled with the working of those spirits to whose service they have subjected themselves.

4. With respect to those, indeed, who teach differently regarding Christ from what the rule of Scripture allows, it is no idle task to ascertain whether it is from a treacherous purpose that these opposing powers, in their struggles to prevent a belief in Christ, have devised certain fabulous and impious doctrines; or whether, on hearing the word of Christ, and not being able to cast it forth from the secrecy of their conscience, nor yet to retain it pure and holy, they have, by means of vessels that were convenient to their use,[5] and, so to speak, through their prophets, introduced various errors contrary to the rule of Christian truth. Now we are to suppose rather that apostate and refugee powers,[6] which have departed from God out of the very wickedness of their mind and will,[7] or from envy of those for whom there is prepared (on their becoming acquainted with the truth) an ascent to the same rank, whence they themselves had fallen, did, in order to prevent any progress of that kind, invent these errors and delusions of false doctrine. It is then clearly established, by many proofs, that while the soul of man exists in this body, it may admit different energies, i.e., operations, from a diversity of good and evil spirits. Now, of wicked spirits there is a twofold mode of operation: i.e., when they either take complete and entire possession of the mind,[8] so

as to allow their captives [9] the power neither of understanding nor feeling; as, for instance, is the case with those commonly called possessed,[10] whom we see to be deprived of reason, and insane (such as those were who are related in the Gospel to have been cured by the Saviour); or when by their wicked suggestions they deprave a sentient and intelligent soul with thoughts of various kinds, persuading it to evil, of which Judas is an illustration, who was induced at the suggestion of the devil to commit the crime of treason, according to the declaration of Scripture, that "the devil had already put it into the heart of Judas Iscariot to betray him." [11]

But a man receives the energy, i.e., the working, of a good spirit, when he is stirred and incited to good, and is inspired to heavenly or divine things; as the holy angels and God Himself wrought in the prophets, arousing and exhorting them by their holy suggestions to a better course of life, yet so, indeed, that it remained within the will and judgment of the individual, either to be willing or unwilling to follow the call to divine and heavenly things. And from this manifest distinction, it is seen how the soul is moved by the presence of a better spirit, i.e., if it encounter no perturbation or alienation of mind whatever from the impending inspiration, nor lose the free control of its will; as, for instance, is the case with all, whether prophets or apostles, who ministered to the divine responses without any perturbation of mind.[12] Now, that by the suggestions of a good spirit the memory of man is aroused to the recollection of better things, we have already shown by previous instances, when we mentioned the cases of Mordecai and Artaxerxes.

5. This too, I think, should next be inquired into, viz., what are the reasons why a human soul is acted on at one time by good (spirits), and at another by bad: the grounds of which I suspect to be older than the bodily birth of the individual, as John (the Baptist) showed by his leaping and exulting in his mother's womb, when the voice of the salutation of Mary reached the ears of his mother Elisabeth; and as Jeremiah the prophet declares, who was known to God before he was formed in his mother's womb, and before he was born was sanctified by Him, and while yet a boy received the grace of prophecy.[13] And again, on the other hand, it is shown beyond a doubt, that some have been possessed by hostile spirits from the very beginning of their lives: i.e., some were born with an evil spirit; and others, according

---

[1] Divinos.
[2] Magi vel malefici.
[3] Dæmonum.
[4] Id est, industria vita, vel studio amico illis et accepto.
[5] Per vasa opportuna sibi.
[6] Apostatæ et refugæ virtutes.
[7] Propositi.
[8] Penitus ex integro.

[9] Eos quos obsederint.
[10] Energumenos.
[11] John xix. 2.
[12] [See Oehler's *Old Testament Theology*, § 207, "Psychological Definition of the Prophetic State in Ancient Times," pp. 468, 469. S.]
[13] Jer. i. 5, 6.

to credible histories, have practised divination [1] from childhood. Others have been under the influence of the demon called Python, i.e., the ventriloquial spirit, from the commencement of their existence. To all which instances, those who maintain that everything in the world is under the administration of Divine Providence (as is also our own belief), can, as it appears to me, give no other answer, so as to show that no shadow of injustice rests upon the divine government, than by holding that there were certain causes of prior existence, in consequence of which the souls, before their birth in the body, contracted a certain amount of guilt in their sensitive nature, or in their movements, on account of which they have been judged worthy by Divine Providence of being placed in this condition. For a soul is always in possession of free-will, as well when it is in the body as when it is without it; and freedom of will is always directed either to good or evil. Nor can any rational and sentient being, i.e., a mind or soul, exist without some movement either good or bad. And it is probable that these movements furnish grounds for merit even before they do anything in this world; so that on account of these merits or grounds they are, immediately on their birth, and even before it, so to speak, assorted by Divine Providence for the endurance either of good or evil.

Let such, then, be our views respecting those events which appear to befall men, either immediately after birth, or even before they enter upon the light. But as regards the suggestions which are made to the soul, i.e, to the faculty of human thought, by different spirits, and which arouse men to good actions or the contrary, even in such a case we must suppose that there sometimes existed certain causes anterior to bodily birth. For occasionally the mind, when watchful, and casting away from it what is evil, calls to itself the aid of the good; or if it be, on the contrary, negligent and slothful, it makes room through insufficient caution for these spirits, which, lying in wait secretly like robbers, contrive to rush into the minds of men when they see a lodgment made for them by sloth; as the Apostle Peter says, "that our adversary the devil goes about like a roaring lion, seeking whom he may devour." [2] On which account our heart must be kept with all carefulness both by day and night, and no place be given to the devil; but every effort must be used that the ministers of God — those spirits, viz., who were sent to minister to them who are called to be heirs of salvation [3] — may find a place within us, and be delighted to enter into the guest-chamber [4] of

our soul, and dwelling within us may guide us by their counsels; if, indeed, they shall find the habitation of our heart adorned by the practice of virtue and holiness. But let that be sufficient which we have said, as we best could, regarding those powers which are hostile to the human race.

CHAP. IV. — ON HUMAN TEMPTATIONS.

1. And now the subject of human temptations must not, in my opinion, be passed over in silence, which take their rise sometimes from flesh and blood, or from the wisdom of flesh and blood, which is said to be hostile to God. And whether the statement be true which certain allege, viz., that each individual has as it were two souls, we shall determine after we have explained the nature of those temptations, which are said to be more powerful than any of human origin, i.e., which we sustain from principalities and powers, and from the rulers of the darkness of this world, and from spiritual wickedness in high places, or to which we are subjected from wicked spirits and unclean demons. Now, in the investigation of this subject, we must, I think, inquire according to a logical method whether there be in us human beings, who are composed of soul and body and vital spirit, some other element, possessing an incitement of its own, and evoking a movement towards evil. For a question of this kind is wont to be discussed by some in this way: whether, viz., as two souls are said to co-exist within us, the one is more divine and heavenly and the other inferior; or whether, from the very fact that we inhere in bodily structures which according to their own proper nature are dead, and altogether devoid of life (seeing it is from us, i.e., from our souls, that the material body derives its life, it being contrary and hostile to the spirit), we are drawn on and enticed to the practice of those evils which are agreeable to the body; or whether, thirdly (which was the opinion of some of the Greek philosophers), although our soul is one in substance, it nevertheless consists of several elements, and one portion of it is called rational and another irrational, and that which is termed the irrational part is again separated into two affections — those of covetousness and passion. These three opinions, then, regarding the soul, which we have stated above, we have found to be entertained by some, but that one of them, which we have mentioned as being adopted by certain Grecian philosophers, viz., that the soul is tripartite, I do not observe to be greatly confirmed by the authority of holy Scripture; while with respect to the remaining two there is found a considerable number of passages in the holy Scriptures which seem capable of application to them.

---

[1] Divinasse.
[2] 1 Pet. v. 8.
[3] Heb. i. 14.
[4] Hospitium.

2. Now, of these opinions, let us first discuss that which is maintained by some, that there is in us a good and heavenly soul, and another earthly and inferior; and that the better soul is implanted within us from heaven, such as was that which, while Jacob was still in the womb, gave him the prize of victory in supplanting his brother Esau, and which in the case of Jeremiah was sanctified from his birth, and in that of John was filled by the Holy Spirit from the womb. Now, that which they term the inferior soul is produced, they allege, along with the body itself out of the seed of the body, whence they say it cannot live or subsist beyond the body, on which account also they say it is frequently termed flesh. For the expression, "The flesh lusteth against the Spirit," [1] they take to be applicable not to the flesh, but to this soul, which is properly the soul of the flesh. From these words, moreover, they endeavour notwithstanding to make good the declaration in Leviticus: "The life of all flesh is the blood thereof." [2] For, from the circumstance that it is the diffusion of the blood throughout the whole flesh which produces life in the flesh, they assert that this soul, which is said to be the life of all flesh, is contained in the blood. This statement, moreover, that the flesh struggles against the spirit, and the spirit against the flesh; and the further statement, that "the life of all flesh is the blood thereof," is, according to these writers, simply calling the wisdom of the flesh by another name, because it is a kind of material spirit, which is not subject to the law of God, nor can be so, because it has earthly wishes and bodily desires. And it is with respect to this that they think the apostle uttered the words: "I see another law in my members, warring against the law of my mind, and bringing me into captivity to the law of sin which is in my members." [3] And if one were to object to them that these words were spoken of the nature of the body, which indeed, agreeably to the peculiarity of its nature, is dead, but is said to have sensibility, or wisdom, [4] which is hostile to God, or which struggles against the spirit; or if one were to say that, in a certain degree, the flesh itself was possessed of a voice, which should cry out against the endurance of hunger, or thirst, or cold, or of any discomfort arising either from abundance or poverty, — they would endeavour to weaken and impair the force of such (arguments), by showing that there were many other mental perturbations [5] which derive their origin in no respect from the flesh, and yet against which the spirit struggles, such as ambition, avarice, emulation, envy, pride, and others like these;

and seeing that with these the human mind or spirit wages a kind of contest, they lay down as the cause of all these evils, nothing else than this corporal soul, as it were, of which we have spoken above, and which is generated from the seed by a process of traducianism. They are accustomed also to adduce, in support of their assertion, the declaration of the apostle, "Now the works of the flesh are manifest, which are these, fornication, uncleanness, lasciviousness, idolatry, poisonings, [6] hatred, contentions, emulations, wrath, quarrelling, dissensions, heresies, sects, envyings, drunkenness, revellings, and the like;" [7] asserting that all these do not derive their origin from the habits or pleasures of the flesh, so that all such movements are to be regarded as inherent in that substance which has not a soul, i.e., the flesh. The declaration, moreover, "For ye see your calling, brethren, how that not many wise men among you according to the flesh are called," [8] would seem to require to be understood as if there were one kind of wisdom, carnal and material, and another according to the spirit, the former of which cannot indeed be called wisdom, unless there be a soul of the flesh, which is wise in respect of what is called carnal wisdom. And in addition to these passages they adduce the following: "Since the flesh lusteth against the Spirit, and the Spirit against the flesh, so that we cannot do the things that we would." [9] What are these things now respecting which he says, "that we cannot do the things that we would?" It is certain, they reply, that the spirit cannot be intended; for the will of the spirit suffers no hindrance. But neither can the flesh be meant, because if it has not a soul of its own, neither can it assuredly possess a will. It remains, then, that the will of this soul be intended which is capable of having a will of its own, and which certainly is opposed to the will of the spirit. And if this be the case, it is established that the will of the soul is something intermediate between the flesh and the spirit, undoubtedly obeying and serving that one of the two which it has elected to obey. And if it yield itself up to the pleasures of the flesh, it renders men carnal; but when it unites itself with the spirit, it produces men of the Spirit, and who on that account are termed spiritual. And this seems to be the meaning of the apostle in the words, "But ye are not in the flesh, but in the Spirit." [10]

We have accordingly to ascertain what is this very will (intermediate) between flesh and spirit, besides that will which is said to belong to the flesh or the spirit. For it is held as certain, that

---

[1] Gal. v. 17.
[2] Lev. xvii. 14.
[3] Rom. vii. 23.
[4] Sensum vel sapientiam.
[5] Passiones animæ.

[6] Veneficia. Φαρμακεία. "Witchcraft" (Auth. Version).
[7] Gal. v. 19-21.
[8] 1 Cor. i. 26.
[9] Gal. v. 17.
[10] Rom. viii. 9.

everything which is said to be a work of the spirit is (a product of) the will of the spirit, and everything that is called a work of the flesh (proceeds from) the will of the flesh. What else then, besides these, is that will of the soul which receives a separate name,[1] and which will, the apostle being opposed to our executing, says: "Ye cannot do the things that ye would?" By this it would seem to be intended, that it ought to adhere to neither of these two, i.e., to neither flesh nor spirit. But some one will say, that as it is better for the soul to execute its own will than that of the flesh; so, on the other hand, it is better to do the will of the spirit than its own will. How, then, does the apostle say, "that ye cannot do the things that ye would?" Because in that contest which is waged between flesh and spirit, the spirit is by no means certain of victory, it being manifest that in very many individuals the flesh has the mastery.

3. But since the subject of discussion on which we have entered is one of great profundity, which it is necessary to consider in all its bearings,[2] let us see whether some such point as this may not be determined: that as it is better for the soul to follow the spirit when the latter has overcome the flesh, so also, if it seem to be a worse course for the former to follow the flesh in its struggles against the spirit, when the latter would recall the soul to its influence, it may nevertheless appear a more advantageous procedure for the soul to be under the mastery of the flesh than to remain under the power of its own will. For, since it is said to be neither hot nor cold, but to continue in a sort of tepid condition, it will find conversion a slow and somewhat difficult undertaking. If indeed it clung to the flesh, then, satiated at length, and filled with those very evils which it suffers from the vices of the flesh, and wearied as it were by the heavy burdens of luxury and lust, it may sometimes be converted with greater ease and rapidity from the filthiness of matter to a desire for heavenly things, and (to a taste for) spiritual graces. And the apostle must be supposed to have said, that "the Spirit contends against the flesh, and the flesh against the Spirit, so that we cannot do the things that we would" (those things, undoubtedly, which are designated as being beyond the will of the spirit, and the will of the flesh), meaning (as if we were to express it in other words) that it is

better for a man to be either in a state of virtue or in one of wickedness, than in neither of these; but that the soul, before its conversion to the spirit, and its union with it,[3] appears during its adherence to the body, and its meditation of carnal things, to be neither in a good condition nor in a manifestly bad one, but resembles, so to speak, an animal. It is better, however, for it, if possible, to be rendered spiritual through adherence to the spirit; but if that cannot be done, it is more expedient for it to follow even the wickedness of the flesh, than, placed under the influence of its own will, to retain the position of an irrational animal.

These points we have now discussed, in our desire to consider each individual opinion, at greater length than we intended, that those views might not be supposed to have escaped our notice which are generally brought forward by those who inquire whether there is within us any other soul than this heavenly and rational one, which is naturally opposed to the latter, and is called either the flesh, or the wisdom of the flesh, or the soul of the flesh.

4. Let us now see what answer is usually returned to these statements by those who maintain that there is in us one movement, and one life, proceeding from one and the same soul, both the salvation and the destruction of which are ascribed to itself as a result of its own actions. And, in the first place, let us notice of what nature those commotions[4] of the soul are which we suffer, when we feel ourselves inwardly drawn in different directions; when there arises a kind of contest of thoughts in our hearts, and certain probabilities are suggested us, agreeably to which we lean now to this side, now to that, and by which we are sometimes convicted of error, and sometimes approve of our acts.[5] It is nothing remarkable, however, to say of wicked spirits, that they have a varying and conflicting judgment, and one out of harmony with itself, since such is found to be the case in all men, whenever, in deliberating upon an uncertain event, council is taken, and men consider and consult what is to be chosen as the better and more useful course. It is not therefore surprising that, if two probabilities meet, and suggest opposite views, they should drag the mind in contrary directions. For example, if a man be led by reflection to believe and to fear God, it cannot then be said that the flesh contends against the Spirit; but, amidst the uncertainty of what may be true and advantageous, the mind is drawn in opposite directions. So, also, when it is supposed that the flesh provokes to the indulgence of lust, but

---

[1] The text here is very obscure, and has given some trouble to commentators. The words are: "Quæ ergo ista est præter hæc voluntas animæ quæ extrinsecus nominatur," etc. Redepenning understands "extrinsecus" as meaning "seorsim," "insuper," and refers to a note of Origen upon the Epistle to the Romans (tom. i. p. 466): "Et idcirco extrinsecus eam (animam, corporis et spiritus mentione factâ, Rom. i. 3, 4) apostolus non nominat, sed carnem tantum vel spiritum," etc. Schnitzer supposes that in the Greek the words were, Τῆς ἔξω καλουμένης, where ἔξω is to be taken in the sense of κάτω, so that the expression would mean "anima inferior."

[2] In quâ necesse est ex singulis quibusque partibus quæ possunt moveri discutere.

[3] Priusquam — unum efficiatur cum eo.

[4] Passiones.

[5] Quibus nunc quidem arguimur, nunc vero nosmet ipsos amplectimur.

better counsels oppose allurements of that kind, we are not to suppose that it is one life which is resisting another, but that it is the tendency of the nature of the body, which is eager to empty out and cleanse the places filled with seminal moisture ; as, in like manner, it is not to be supposed that it is any opposing power, or the life of another soul, which excites within us the appetite of thirst, and impels us to drink, or which causes us to feel hunger, and drives us to satisfy it. But as it is by the natural movements of the body that food and drink are either desired or rejected,[1] so also the natural seed, collected together in course of time in the various vessels, has an eager desire to be expelled and thrown away, and is so far from never being removed, save by the impulse of some exciting cause, that it is even sometimes spontaneously emitted. When, therefore, it is said that " the flesh struggles against the Spirit," these persons understand the expression to mean that habit or necessity, or the delights of the flesh, arouse a man, and withdraw him from divine and spiritual things. For, owing to the necessity of the body being drawn away, we are not allowed to have leisure for divine things, which are to be eternally advantageous. So again, the soul, devoting itself to divine and spiritual pursuits, and being united to the spirit, is said to fight against the flesh, by not permitting it to be relaxed by indulgence, and to become unsteady through the influence of those pleasures for which it feels a natural delight. In this way, also, they claim to understand the words, " The wisdom of the flesh is hostile to God,"[2] not that the flesh really has a soul, or a wisdom of its own. But as we are accustomed to say, by an abuse[3] of language, that the earth is thirsty, and wishes to drink in water, this use of the word " wishes " is not proper, but catachrestic, — as if we were to say again, that this house wants to be rebuilt,[4] and many other similar expressions ; so also is the wisdom of the flesh to be understood, or the expression, that " the flesh lusteth against the Spirit." They generally connect with these the expression, " The voice of thy brother's blood crieth unto Me from the ground."[5] For what cries unto the Lord is not properly the blood which was shed ; but the blood is said improperly to cry out, vengeance being demanded upon him who had shed it. The declaration also of the apostle, " I see another law in my members, warring against the law of my mind,"[6] they so understand as if he had said, That he who wishes to devote himself to the word of God is, on account

of his bodily necessities and habits, which like a sort of law are ingrained in the body, distracted, and divided, and impeded, lest, by devoting himself vigorously to the study of wisdom, he should be enabled to behold the divine mysteries.

5. With respect, however, to the following being ranked among the works of the flesh, viz., heresies, and envyings, and contentions, or other (vices), they so understand the passage, that the mind, being rendered grosser in feeling, from its yielding itself to the passions of the body, and being oppressed by the mass of its vices, and having no refined or spiritual feelings, is said to be made flesh, and derives its name from that in which it exhibits more vigour and force of will.[7] They also make this further inquiry, " Who will be found, or who will be said to be, the creator of this evil sense, called the sense of the flesh ? " Because they defend the opinion that there is no other creator of soul and flesh than God. And if we were to assert that the good God created anything in His own creation that was hostile to Himself, it would appear to be a manifest absurdity. If, then, it is written, that " carnal wisdom is enmity against God,"[8] and if this be declared to be a result of creation, God Himself will appear to have formed a nature hostile to Himself, which cannot be subject to Him nor to His law, as if it were (supposed to be) an animal of which such qualities are predicated. And if this view be admitted, in what respect will it appear to differ from that of those who maintain that souls of different natures are created, which, according to their natures,[9] are destined either to be lost or saved ? But this is an opinion of the heretics alone, who, not being able to maintain the justice of God on grounds of piety, compose impious inventions of this kind. And now we have brought forward to the best of our ability, in the person of each of the parties, what might be advanced by way of argument regarding the several views, and let the reader choose out of them for himself that which he thinks ought to be preferred.

CHAP. V. — THAT THE WORLD TOOK ITS BEGINNING IN TIME.

1. And now, since there is one of the articles of the Church [10] which is held principally in consequence of our belief in the truth of our sacred history, viz., that this world was created and took its beginning at a certain time, and, in conformity to the cycle of time [11] decreed to all things, is to be destroyed on account of its corruption, there seems no absurdity in re-discussing a few

---

[1] Evacuantur.
[2] Cf. Rom. viii. 2.
[3] Abusive = improperly used.
[4] Recomponi vult.
[5] Gen. iv. 10.
[6] Rom. vii. 23.

[7] Plus studii vel propositi.
[8] Rom. viii. 7.
[9] Naturaliter.
[10] De ecclesiasticis definitionibus unum.
[11] Consummationem sæculi.

points connected with this subject. And so far, indeed, as the credibility of Scripture is concerned, the declarations on such a matter seem easy of proof. Even the heretics, although widely opposed on many other things, yet on this appear to be at one, yielding to the authority of Scripture.

Concerning, then, the creation of the world, what portion of Scripture can give us more information regarding it, than the account which Moses has transmitted respecting its origin? And although it comprehends matters of profounder significance than the mere historical narrative appears to indicate, and contains very many things that are to be spiritually understood, and employs the letter, as a kind of veil, in treating of profound and mystical subjects; nevertheless the language of the narrator shows that all visible things were created at a certain time. But with regard to the consummation of the world, Jacob is the first who gives any information, in addressing his children in the words: "Gather yourselves together unto me, ye sons of Jacob, that I may tell you what shall be in the last days," or "after the last days." [1] If, then, there be "last days," or a period "succeeding the last days," the days which had a beginning must necessarily come to an end. David, too, declares: "The heavens shall perish, but Thou shalt endure; yea, all of them shall wax old as doth a garment: as a vesture shalt Thou change them, and they shall be changed: but Thou art the same, and Thy years shall have no end." [2] Our Lord and Saviour, indeed, in the words, "He who made them at the beginning, made them male and female," [3] Himself bears witness that the world was created; and again, when He says, "Heaven and earth shall pass away, but My word shall not pass away," [4] He points out that they are perishable, and must come to an end. The apostle, moreover, in declaring that "the creature was made subject to vanity, not willingly, but by reason of Him who hath subjected the same in hope, because the creature itself also shall be delivered from the bondage of corruption into the glorious liberty of the children of God," [5] manifestly announces the end of the world; as he does also when he again says, "The fashion of this world passeth away." [6] Now, by the expression which he employs, "that the creature was made subject to vanity," he shows that there was a beginning to this world: for if the creature were made subject to vanity on account of some hope, it was

certainly made subject from a cause; and seeing it was from a cause, it must necessarily have had a beginning: for, without some beginning, the creature could not be subject to vanity, nor could that (creature) hope to be freed from the bondage of corruption, which had not begun to serve. But any one who chooses to search at his leisure, will find numerous other passages in holy Scripture in which the world is both said to have a beginning and to hope for an end.

2. Now, if there be any one who would here oppose either the authority or credibility of our Scriptures, [7] we would ask of him whether he asserts that God can, or cannot, comprehend all things? To assert that He cannot, would manifestly be an act of impiety. If then he answer, as he must, that God comprehends all things, it follows from the very fact of their being capable of comprehension, that they are understood to have a beginning and an end, seeing that which is altogether without any beginning cannot be at all comprehended. For however far understanding may extend, so far is the faculty of comprehending illimitably withdrawn and removed when there is held to be no beginning.

3. But this is the objection which they generally raise: they say, "If the world had its beginning in time, what was God doing before the world began? For it is at once impious and absurd to say that the nature of God is inactive and immoveable, or to suppose that goodness at one time did not do good, and omnipotence at one time did not exercise its power." Such is the objection which they are accustomed to make to our statement that this world had its beginning at a certain time, and that, agreeably to our belief in Scripture, we can calculate the years of its past duration. To these propositions I consider that none of the heretics can easily return an answer that will be in conformity with the nature of their opinions. But we can give a logical answer in accordance with the standard of religion, [8] when we say that not then for the first time did God begin to work when He made this visible world; but as, after its destruction, there will be another world, so also we believe that others existed before the present came into being. And both of these positions will be confirmed by the authority of holy Scripture. For that there will be another world after this, is taught by Isaiah, who says, "There will be new heavens, and a new earth, which I shall make to abide in my sight, saith the LORD;" [9] and that before this world others also existed is shown by Ecclesiastes, in the words: "What is that which hath been? Even that which shall be. And what is that which has been created?

---

[1] Gen. xlix. 1. The Vulgate has, "In diebus novissimis;" the Sept. 'Επ' ἐσχάτων τῶν ἡμερῶν:" the Masoretic text, בְּאַחֲרִית.

[2] Ps. cii. 26, 27.
[3] Matt. xix. 4.
[4] Matt. xxiv. 35.
[5] Rom. viii. 20, 21.
[6] 1 Cor. vii. 31.

[7] Auctoritate Scripturæ nostræ, vel fidei.
[8] Regulam pietatis.
[9] Cf. Isa. lxvi. 22.

Even this which is to be created : and there is nothing altogether new under the sun. Who shall speak and declare, Lo, this is new? It hath already been in the ages which have been before us." [1] By these testimonies it is established both that there were ages [2] before our own, and that there will be others after it. It is not, however, to be supposed that several worlds existed at once, but that, after the end of this present world, others will take their beginning ; respecting which it is unnecessary to repeat each particular statement, seeing we have already done so in the preceding pages.

4. This point, indeed, is not to be idly passed by, that the holy Scriptures have called the creation of the world by a new and peculiar name, terming it καταβολή, which has been very improperly translated into Latin by "constitutio ;" for in Greek καταβολή signifies rather "dejicere," i.e., to cast downwards, — a word which has been, as we have already remarked, improperly translated into Latin by the phrase "constitutio mundi," as in the Gospel according to John, where the Saviour says, "And there will be tribulation in those days, such as was not since the beginning of the world ;" [3] in which passage καταβολή is rendered by beginning (constitutio), which is to be understood as above explained. The apostle also, in the Epistle to the Ephesians, has employed the same language, saying, "Who hath chosen us before the foundation of the world ;" [4] and this foundation he calls καταβολή, to be understood in the same sense as before. It seems worth while, then, to inquire what is meant by this new term ; and I am, indeed, of opinion [5]

that, as the end and consummation of the saints will be in those (ages) which are not seen, and are eternal, we must conclude (as frequently pointed out in the preceding pages), from a contemplation of that very end, that rational creatures had also a similar beginning. And if they had a beginning such as the end for which they hope, they existed undoubtedly from the very beginning in those (ages) which are not seen, and are eternal. [6] And if this is so, then there has been a descent from a higher to a lower condition, on the part not only of those souls who have deserved the change by the variety of their movements, but also on that of those who, in order to serve the whole world, were brought down from those higher and invisible spheres to these lower and visible ones, although against their will — "Because the creature was subjected to vanity, not willingly, but because of Him who subjected the same in hope ;" [7] so that both sun, and moon, and stars, and angels might discharge their duty to the world, and to those souls which, on account of their excessive mental defects, stood in need of bodies of a grosser and more solid nature ; and for the sake of those for whom this arrangement was necessary, this visible world was also called into being. From this it follows, that by the use of the word καταβολή, a descent from a higher to a lower condition, shared by all in common, would seem to be pointed out. The hope indeed of freedom is entertained by the whole of creation — of being liberated from the corruption of slavery — when the sons of God, who either fell away or were scattered abroad, [8] shall be gathered together into one, or when they shall have fulfilled their other duties in this world, which are known to God alone, the Disposer of all things. We are, indeed, to suppose that the world was created of such quality and capacity as to contain not only all those souls which it was determined should be trained in this world, but also all those powers which were prepared to attend, and serve, and assist them. For it is established by many declarations that all rational creatures are of one nature : on which ground alone could the justice of God in all His dealings with them be de-

---

[1] Cf. Eccles. i. 9, 10. The text is in conformity with the Septuag.: Τί τὸ γεγονός; Αὐτὸ τὸ γενησόμενον. Καὶ τί τὸ πεποιημένον; Αὐτὸ τὸ ποιηθησόμενον. Καὶ οὐκ ἔστι πᾶν πρόσφατον ὑπὸ τὸν ἥλιον. Ὅς λαλήσει καὶ ἐρεῖ. Ἰδὲ τοῦτο καινόν ἐστιν, ἤδη γέγονεν ἐν τοῖς αἰῶσι τοῖς γενομένοις ἀπὸ ἐμπροσθεν ἡμῶν.

[2] Sæcula.

[3] Matt. xxiv. 21.

[4] Eph. i. 4.

[5] The following is Jerome's version of this passage (Epistle to Avitus): "A divine habitation, and a true rest above (apud superos), I think is to be understood, where rational creatures dwell, and where, before their descent to a lower position, and removal from invisible to visible (worlds), and fall to earth, and need of gross bodies, they enjoyed a former blessedness. Whence God the Creator made for them bodies suitable to their humble position, and created this visible world, and sent into the world ministers for the salvation and correction of those who had fallen: of whom some were to obtain certain localities, and be subject to the necessities of the world; others were to discharge with care and attention the duties enjoined upon them at all times, and which were known to God, the Arranger (of all things). And of these, the sun, moon, and stars, which are called 'creature' by the apostle, received the more elevated places of the world. Which 'creature' was made subject to vanity, in that it was clothed with gross bodies, and was open to view; and yet was subject to vanity, not voluntarily, but because of the will of Him who subjected the same in hope." And again: "While others, whom we believe to be angels, at different places and times, which the Arranger alone knows, serve the government of the world." And a little further on: "Which order of things is regulated by the providential government of the whole world: some powers falling down from a loftier position, others gradually sinking to earth: some falling voluntarily, others being cast down against their will: some undertaking, of their own accord, the service of stretching out the hand to those who fall; others being compelled to persevere for so long a time in the duty which they have undertaken." And again: "Whence it follows that, on account of the various movements, various worlds also are created; and after this world which we now inhabit, there will be another greatly dissimilar. But no other being save God alone, the Creator of all things,

can arrange the deserts (of all), both to the time to come and to that which preceded. suitably to the differing lapses and advances (of individuals), and to the rewards of virtues or the punishment of vices, both in the present and in the future, and in all (times), and to conduct them all again to one end: for He knows the causes why He allows some to enjoy their own will, and to fall from a higher rank to the lowest condition; and why He begins to visit others, and bring them back gradually, as if by giving them His hand, to their pristine state, and placing them in a lofty position" (Ruæus).

[6] [According to Hagenbach (History of Doctrines, vol. i. p. 167), "Origen formally adopts the idea of original sin, by asserting that the human soul does not come into the world in a state of innocence, because it has already sinned in a former state. . . . And yet, subsequent times, especially after Jerome, have seen in Origen the precursor of Pelagius. Jerome calls the opinion that man can be without sin, Origenis ramusculus." S.]

[7] Cf. Rom. viii. 20, 21.

[8] Dispersi.

fended, seeing every one has the reason in himself, why he has been placed in this or that rank in life.

5. This arrangement of things, then, which God afterwards appointed (for He had, from the very origin of the world, clearly perceived the reasons and causes affecting those who, either owing to mental deficiencies, deserved to enter into bodies, or those who were carried away by their desire for visible things, and those also who, either willingly or unwillingly, were compelled, (by Him who subjected the same in hope), to perform certain services to such as had fallen into that condition), not being understood by some, who failed to perceive that it was owing to preceding causes, originating in free-will, that this variety of arrangement had been instituted by God, they have concluded that all things in this world are directed either by fortuitous movements or by a necessary fate, and that nothing is within the power of our own will. And, therefore, also they were unable to show that the providence of God was beyond the reach of censure.

6. But as we have said that all the souls who lived in this world stood in need of many ministers, or rulers, or assistants ; so, in the last times, when the end of the world is already imminent and near, and the whole human race is verging upon the last destruction, and when not only those who were governed by others have been reduced to weakness, but those also to whom had been committed the cares of government, it was no longer such help nor such defenders that were needed, but the help of the Author and Creator Himself was required to restore to the one the discipline of obedience, which had been corrupted and profaned, and to the other the discipline of rule. And hence the only-begotten Son of God, who was the Word and the Wisdom of the Father, when He was in the possession of that glory with the Father, which He had before the world was, divested Himself[1] of it, and, taking the form of a servant, was made obedient unto death, that He might teach obedience to those who could not otherwise than by obedience obtain salvation. He restored also the laws of rule and government[2] which had been corrupted, by subduing all enemies under His feet, that by this means (for it was necessary that He should reign until He had put all enemies under His feet, and destroyed the last enemy — death) He might teach rulers themselves moderation in their government. As He had come, then, to restore the discipline, not only of government, but of obedience, as we have said, accomplishing in Himself first what He desired to be accomplished by others, He

became obedient to the Father, not only to the death of the cross, but also, in the end of the world, embracing in Himself all whom He subjects to the Father, and who by Him come to salvation, He Himself, along with them, and in them, is said also to be subject to the Father ; all things subsisting in Him, and He Himself being the Head of all things, and in Him being the salvation and the fulness of those who obtain salvation. And this consequently is what the apostle says of Him : "And when all things shall be subjected to Him, then shall the Son also Himself be subject to Him that put all things under Him, that God may be all in all."

7. I know not, indeed, how the heretics, not understanding the meaning of the apostle in these words, consider the term[3] "subjection" degrading as applied to the Son ; for if the propriety of the title be called in question, it may easily be ascertained from making a contrary supposition. Because if it be not good to be in subjection, it follows that the opposite will be good, viz., not to be in subjection. Now the language of the apostle, according to their view, appears to indicate by these words, "And when all things shall be subdued unto Him, then shall the Son also Himself be subject unto Him that put all things under Him,"[4] that He, who is not now in subjection to the Father, will become subject to Him when the Father shall have first subdued all things unto Him. But I am astonished how it can be conceived to be the meaning, that He who, while all things are not yet subdued to Him, is not Himself in subjection, should — at a time when all things have been subdued to Him, and when He has become King of all men, and holds sway over all things — be supposed then to be made subject, seeing He was not formerly in subjection ; for such do not understand that the subjection of Christ to the Father indicates that our happiness has attained to perfection, and that the work undertaken by Him has been brought to a victorious termination, seeing He has not only purified the power of supreme government over the whole of creation, but presents to the Father the principles of the obedience and subjection of the human race in a corrected and improved condition.[5] If, then, that subjection be held to be good and salutary by which the Son is said to be subject to the Father, it is an extremely rational and logical inference to deduce that the subjection also of enemies, which is said to be made to the Son of God, should be understood as being also salutary and useful ; as if, when the

---

[1] Exinanivit semet ipsum.
[2] Regendi regnandique.

[3] [Elucidation II.]
[4] 1 Cor. xv. 28.
[5] Cum non solum regendi ac regnandi summam, quam in universam emendaverit creaturam, verum etiam obedientiæ et subjectione correcta reparataque humani generis Patri offerat instituta.

Son is said to be subject to the Father, the perfect restoration of the whole of creation is signified, so also, when enemies are said to be subjected to the Son of God, the salvation of the conquered and the restoration of the lost is in that understood to consist.

8. This subjection, however, will be accomplished in certain ways, and after certain training, and at certain times; for it is not to be imagined that the subjection is to be brought about by the pressure of necessity (lest the whole world should then appear to be subdued to God by force), but by word, reason, and doctrine; by a call to a better course of things, by the best systems of training, by the employment also of suitable and appropriate threatenings, which will justly impend over those who despise any care or attention to their salvation and usefulness. In a word, we men also, in training either our slaves or children, restrain them by threats and fear while they are, by reason of their tender age, incapable of using their reason; but when they have begun to understand what is good, and useful, and honourable, the fear of the lash being over, they acquiesce through the suasion of words and reason in all that is good. But how, consistently with the preservation of freedom of will in all rational creatures, each one ought to be regulated, i.e., who they are whom the word of God finds and trains, as if they were already prepared and capable of it; who they are whom it puts off to a later time; who these are from whom it is altogether concealed, and who are so situated as to be far from hearing it; who those, again, are who despise the word of God when made known and preached to them, and who are driven by a kind of correction and chastisement to salvation, and whose conversion is in a certain degree demanded and extorted; who those are to whom certain opportunities of salvation are afforded, so that sometimes, their faith being proved by an answer alone,[1] they have unquestionably obtained salvation;[2] — from what causes or on what occasions these results take place, or what the divine wisdom sees within them, or what movements of their will leads God so to arrange all these things, is known to Him alone, and to His only-begotten Son, through whom all things were created and restored, and to the Holy Spirit, through whom all things are sanctified, who proceedeth from the Father,[3] to whom be glory for ever and ever. Amen.

CHAP. VI. — ON THE END OF THE WORLD.

1. Now, respecting the end of the world and the consummation of all things, we have stated in the preceding pages, to the best of our ability, so far as the authority of holy Scripture enabled us, what we deem sufficient for purposes of instruction; and we shall here only add a few admonitory remarks, since the order of investigation has brought us back to the subject. The highest good, then, after the attainment of which the whole of rational nature is seeking, which is also called the end of all blessings,[4] is defined by many philosophers as follows : The highest good, they say, is to become as like to God as possible. But this definition I regard not so much as a discovery of theirs, as a view derived from holy Scripture. For this is pointed out by Moses, before all other philosophers, when he describes the first creation of man in these words : "And God said, Let Us make man in Our own image, and after Our likeness;"[5] and then he adds the words : "So God created man in His own image : in the image of God created He him; male and female created He them, and He blessed them."[6] Now the expression, "In the image[7] of God created He him," without any mention of the word "likeness,"[8] conveys no other meaning than this, that man received the dignity of God's image at his first creation; but that the perfection of his likeness has been reserved for the consummation, — namely, that he might acquire it for himself by the exercise of his own diligence in the imitation of God, the possibility of attaining to perfection being granted him at the beginning through the dignity of the divine image, and the perfect realization of the divine likeness being reached in the end by the fulfilment of the (necessary) works. Now, that such is the case, the Apostle John points out more clearly and unmistakeably, when he makes this declaration : "Little children, we do not yet know what we shall be; but if a revelation be made to us from the Saviour, ye will say, without any doubt, we shall be like Him."[9] By which expression he points out with the utmost certainty, that not only was the end of all things to be hoped for, which he says was still unknown to him, but also the likeness to God, which will be conferred in proportion to the completeness of our deserts. The Lord Himself, in the Gospel, not only declares that these same results are future, but that they are to be brought about by His own intercession, He Himself deigning to obtain them from the Father for His disciples, saying, "Father, I will that where I am, these also may be with

---

[1] By a profession of faith in baptism.

[2] Indubitatam ceperit salutem.

[3] It was not until the third Synod of Toledo, A.D. 589, that the "Filioque" clause was added to the Creed of Constantinople, — this difference forming, as is well known, one of the dogmatic grounds for the disunion between the Western and Eastern Churches down to the present day, the latter Church denying that the Spirit proceedeth from the Father *and the Son*. [See Elucidation III.]

[4] Finis omnium: "bonorum" understood.

[5] Gen. i. 26.

[6] Gen. i. 27, 28.

[7] Imago.

[8] Similitudo.

[9] Cf. 1 John iii. 2.

Me ; and as Thou and I are one, they also may
be one in Us." [1]   In which the divine likeness
itself already appears to advance, if we may so
express ourselves, and from being merely similar,
to become the same,[2] because undoubtedly in
the consummation or end God is " all and in all."
And with reference to this, it is made a question
by some [3] whether the nature of bodily matter,
although cleansed and purified, and rendered
altogether spiritual, does not seem either to offer
an obstruction towards attaining the dignity of
the (divine) likeness, or to the property of unity,[4]
because neither can a corporeal nature appear
capable of any resemblance to a divine nature,
which is certainly incorporeal ; nor can it be
truly and deservedly designated one with it, especially since we are taught by the truths of our
religion that that which alone is one, viz., the
Son with the Father, must be referred to a peculiarity of the (divine) nature.

2. Since, then, it is promised that in the end
God will be all and in all, we are not, as is fitting,
to suppose that animals, either sheep or other
cattle, come to that end, lest it should be implied
that God dwelt even in animals, whether sheep
or other cattle ; and so, too, with pieces of wood
or stones, lest it should be said that God is in
these also. So, again, nothing that is wicked
must be supposed to attain to that end, lest,
while God is said to be in all things, He may
also be said to be in a vessel of wickedness. For
if we now assert that God is everywhere and in
all things, on the ground that nothing can be
empty of God, we nevertheless do not say that

He is now " all things " in those in whom He is.
And hence we must look more carefully as to
what that is which denotes the perfection of
blessedness and the end of things, which is not
only said to be God in all things, but also " all
in all." Let us then inquire what all those things
are which God is to become in all.

3. I am of opinion that the expression, by
which God is said to be " all in all," means that
He is " all " in each individual person. Now
He will be " all " in each individual in this
way : when all which any rational understanding, cleansed from the dregs of every sort of
vice, and with every cloud of wickedness completely swept away, can either feel, or understand, or think, will be wholly God ; and when
it will no longer behold or retain anything else
than God, but when God will be the measure
and standard of all its movements ; and thus
God will be " all," for there will no longer be
any distinction of good and evil, seeing evil nowhere exists ; for God is all things, and to Him
no evil is near : nor will there be any longer a
desire to eat from the tree of the knowledge of
good and evil, on the part of him who is always
in the possession of good, and to whom God is
all. So then, when the end has been restored to
the beginning, and the termination of things
compared with their commencement, that condition of things will be re-established in which
rational nature was placed, when it had no need
to eat of the tree of the knowledge of good and
evil ; so that when all feeling of wickedness has
been removed, and the individual has been purified and cleansed, He who alone is the one good
God becomes to him " all," and that not in the
case of a few individuals, or of a considerable
number, but He Himself is " all in all." And
when death shall no longer anywhere exist, nor
the sting of death, nor any evil at all, then verily
God will be " all in all." But some are of
opinion that that perfection and blessedness of
rational creatures, or natures, can only remain in
that same condition of which we have spoken
above, i.e., that all things should possess God,
and God should be to them all things, if they
are in no degree prevented by their union with
a bodily nature. Otherwise they think that the
glory of the highest blessedness is impeded by
the intermixture of any material substance.[5] But

---

[1] Cf. John xvii. 24 : cf. 21.
[2] Ex simili unum fieri.
[3] Jerome, in his *Epistle to Avitus*, No. 94, has the passage
thus : " Since, as we have already frequently observed, the beginning
is generated again from the end, it is a question whether then also
there will be bodies, or whether existence will be maintained at some
time without them when they shall have been annihilated, and thus
the life of incorporeal beings must be believed to be incorporeal, as
we know is the case with God. And there is no doubt that if all the
bodies which are termed visible by the apostle, belong to that sensible
world, the life of incorporeal beings will be incorporeal." And a little
after : " That expression, also, used by the apostle, ' The whole creation will be freed from the bondage of corruption into the glorious liberty of the children of God ' (Rom. viii. 21), we so understand, that
we say it was the first creation of rational and incorporeal beings
which is not subject to corruption, because it was not clothed with
bodies ; for wherever bodies are, corruption immediately follows.
But afterwards it will be freed from the bondage of corruption, when
they shall have received the glory of the sons of God, and God shall
be all in all." And in the same place : " That we must believe the
end of all things to be incorporeal, the language of the Saviour Himself leads us to think, when He says, ' As I and Thou are one, so
may they also be one in Us ' (John xvii. 21). For we ought to know
what God is, and what the Saviour will be in the end, and how the
likeness of the Father and the Son has been promised to the saints ;
for as they are one in Him, so they also are one in them. For we
must adopt the view, either that the God of all things is clothed with
a body, and as we are enveloped with flesh, so He also with some
material covering, that the likeness of the life of God may be in the
end produced also in the saints ; or if this hypothesis is unbecoming,
especially in the judgment of those who desire, even in the smallest
degree, to feel the majesty of God, and to look upon the glory of His
uncreated and all-surpassing nature, we are forced to adopt the other
alternative, and despair either of attaining any likeness to God, if we
are to inhabit for ever the same bodies, or if the blessedness of the
same life with God is promised to us, we must live in the same state
as that in which God lives." All these points have been omitted by
Rufinus as erroneous, and statements of a different kind here and
there inserted instead (Ruæus).
[4] Ad unitatis proprietatem.

[5] " Here the honesty of Rufinus in his translation seems very
suspicious ; for Origen's well-known opinion regarding the sins and
lapses of blessed spirits he here attributes to others. Nay, even the
opinion which he introduces Origen as ascribing to others, he exhibits him as refuting a little further on, sec. 6, in these words : ' And
in this condition (of blessedness) we are to believe that, by the will
of the Creator, it will abide for ever without any change,' etc. I suspect, therefore, that all this is due to Rufinus himself, and that he has
inserted it, instead of what is found in the beginning of the chapter,
sec. 1, and which in Jerome's *Epistle to Avitus* stands as follows :
' Nor is there any doubt that, after certain intervals of time, matter
will again exist, and bodies be formed, and a diversity be established
in the world, on account of the varying wills of rational creatures,
who, after (enjoying) perfect blessedness down to the end of all

this subject we have discussed at greater length, as may be seen in the preceding pages.

4. And now, as we find the apostle making mention of a spiritual body, let us inquire, to the best of our ability, what idea we are to form of such a thing. So far, then, as our understanding can grasp it, we consider a spiritual body to be of such a nature as ought to be inhabited not only by all holy and perfect souls, but also by all those creatures which will be liberated from the slavery of corruption. Respecting the body also, the apostle has said, "We have a house not made with hands, eternal in the heavens,"[1] i.e., in the mansions of the blessed. And from this statement we may form a conjecture, how pure, how refined, and how glorious are the qualities of that body, if we compare it with those which, although they are celestial bodies, and of most brilliant splendour, were nevertheless made with hands, and are visible to our sight. But of that body it is said, that it is a house not made with hands, but eternal in the heavens. Since, then, those things "which are seen are temporal, but those things which are not seen are eternal,"[2] all those bodies which we see either on earth or in heaven, and which are capable of being seen, and have been made with hands, but are not eternal, are far excelled in glory by that which is not visible, nor made with hands, but is eternal. From which comparison it may be conceived how great are the comeliness, and splendour, and brilliancy of a spiritual body; and how true it is, that "eye hath not seen, nor ear heard, nor hath it entered into the heart of man to conceive, what God hath prepared for them that love Him."[3] We ought not, however, to doubt that the nature of this present body of ours may, by the will of God, who made it what it is, be raised to those qualities of refinement, and purity, and splendour (which characterize the body referred to), according as the condition of things requires, and the deserts of our rational nature shall demand. Finally, when the world required variety and diversity, matter yielded itself with all docility throughout the diverse appear-

ances and species of things to the Creator, as to its Lord and Maker, that He might educe from it the various forms of celestial and terrestrial beings. But when things have begun to hasten to that consummation that all may be one, as the Father is one with the Son, it may be understood as a rational inference, that where all are one, there will no longer be any diversity.

5. The last enemy, moreover, who is called death, is said on this account to be destroyed, that there may not be anything left of a mournful kind when death does not exist, nor anything that is adverse when there is no enemy. The destruction of the last enemy, indeed, is to be understood, not as if its substance, which was formed by God, is to perish, but because its mind and hostile will, which came not from God, but from itself, are to be destroyed. Its destruction, therefore, will not be its non-existence, but its ceasing to be an enemy, and (to be) death. For nothing is impossible to the Omnipotent, nor is anything incapable of restoration[4] to its Creator : for He made all things that they might exist, and those things which were made for existence cannot cease to be.[5] For this reason also will they admit of change and variety, so as to be placed, according to their merits, either in a better or worse position ; but no destruction of substance can befall those things which were created by God for the purpose of permanent existence.[6] For those things which agreeably to the common opinion are believed to perish, the nature either of our faith or of the truth will not permit us to suppose to be destroyed. Finally, our flesh is supposed by ignorant men and unbelievers to be destroyed after death, in such a degree that it retains no relic at all of its former substance. We, however, who believe in its resurrection, understand that a change only has been produced by death, but that its substance certainly remains ; and that by the will of its Creator, and at the time appointed, it will be restored to life ; and that a second time a change will take place in it, so that what at first was flesh (formed) out of earthly soil, and was afterwards dissolved by death, and again reduced to dust and ashes ("For dust thou art,"[7] it is said, "and to dust shalt thou return"), will be again raised from the earth, and shall after this, according to the merits of the indwelling soul, advance to the glory of a spiritual body.

6.' Into this condition, then, we are to suppose that all this bodily substance of ours will be

---

things, have gradually fallen away to a lower condition, and received into them so much wickedness, that they are converted into an opposite condition, by their unwillingness to retain their original state, and to preserve their blessedness uncorrupted. Nor is this point to be suppressed, that many rational creatures retain their first condition (*principium*) even to the second and third and fourth worlds, and allow no room for any change within them; while others, again, will lose so little of their pristine state, that they will appear to have lost almost nothing, and some are to be precipitated with great destruction into the lowest pit. And God, the disposer of all things, when creating His worlds, knows how to treat each individual agreeably to his merits, and He is acquainted with the occasions and causes by which the government (*gubernacula*) of the world is sustained and commenced; so that he who surpassed all others in wickedness, and brought himself completely down to the earth, is made in another world, which is afterwards to be formed, a devil, the beginning of the creation of the Lord (Job xl. 19), to be mocked by the angels who have lost the virtue of their original condition' (*exordii virtutem*)." — Ruæus.

[1] 2 Cor. v. 1.
[2] 2 Cor. iv. 18.
[3] 1 Cor. ii. 9; cf. Isa. lxiv. 4.

[4] Insanabile.
[5] ["Origen went so far, that, contrary to the general opinion, he allowed Satan the glimmer of a hope of future grace. . . . He is here speaking of the last enemy, death; but it is evident, from the context, that he identifies death with the devil," etc. (Hagenbach's *History of Doctrines*, vol. i. p. 145-147. See also, *supra*, book i. vi. 3. p. 261.) S.]
[6] Ut essent et permanerent.
[7] Gen. iii. 19.

brought, when all things shall be re-established in a state of unity, and when God shall be all in all. And this result must be understood as being brought about, not suddenly, but slowly and gradually, seeing that the process of amendment and correction will take place imperceptibly in the individual instances during the lapse of countless and unmeasured ages, some outstripping others, and tending by a swifter course towards perfection,[1] while others again follow close at hand, and some again a long way behind ; and thus, through the numerous and uncounted orders of progressive beings who are being reconciled to God from a state of enmity, the last enemy is finally reached, who is called death, so that he also may be destroyed, and no longer be an enemy. When, therefore, all rational souls shall have been restored to a condition of this kind, then the nature of this body of ours will undergo a change into the glory of a spiritual body. For as we see it not to be the case with rational natures, that some of them have lived in a condition of degradation owing to their sins, while others have been called to a state of happiness on account of their merits ; but as we see those same souls who had formerly been sinful, assisted, after their conversion and reconciliation to God, to a state of happiness ; so also are we to consider, with respect to the nature of the body, that the one which we now make use of in a state of meanness, and corruption, and weakness, is not a different body from that which we shall possess in incorruption, and in power, and in glory ; but that the same body, when it has cast away the infirmities in which it is now entangled, shall be transmuted into a condition of glory, being rendered spiritual, so that what was a vessel of dishonour may, when cleansed, become a vessel unto honour, and an abode of blessedness. And in this condition, also, we are to believe, that by the will of the Creator, it will abide for ever without any change, as is confirmed by the declaration of the apostle, when he says, "We have a house, not made with hands, eternal in the heavens." For the faith of the Church[2] does not admit the view of certain Grecian philosophers, that there is besides the body, composed of four elements, another fifth body, which is different in all its parts, and diverse from this our present body ; since neither out of sacred Scripture can any produce the slightest suspicion of evidence for such an opinion, nor can any rational inference from things allow the reception of it, especially when the holy apostle manifestly declares, that it is not new bodies which are given to those who rise from the dead, but that they receive those identical ones which they had possessed when living, transformed from an inferior into a better condition. For his words are : "It is sown an animal body, it will rise a spiritual body ; it is sown in corruption, it will arise in incorruption : it is sown in weakness, it will arise in power : it is sown in dishonour, it will arise in glory."[3] As, therefore, there is a kind of advance in man, so that from being first an animal being, and not understanding what belongs to the Spirit of God, he reaches by means of instruction the stage of being made a spiritual being, and of judging all things, while he himself is judged by no one ; so also, with respect to the state of the body, we are to hold that this very body which now, on account of its service to the soul, is styled an animal body, will, by means of a certain progress, when the soul, united to God, shall have been made one spirit with Him (the body even then ministering, as it were, to the spirit), attain to a spiritual condition and quality, especially since, as we have often pointed out, bodily nature was so formed by the Creator, as to pass easily into whatever condition he should wish, or the nature of the case demand.

7. The whole of this reasoning, then, amounts to this : that God created two general natures, — a visible, i.e., a corporeal nature ; and an invisible nature, which is incorporeal. Now these two natures admit of two different permutations. That invisible and rational nature changes in mind and purpose, because it is endowed with freedom of will,[4] and is on this account found sometimes to be engaged in the practice of good, and sometimes in that of the opposite. But this corporeal nature admits of a change in substance ; whence also God, the arranger of all things, has the service of this matter at His command in the moulding, or fabrication, or re-touching of whatever He wishes, so that corporeal nature may be transmuted, and transformed into any forms or species whatever, according as the deserts of things may demand ; which the prophet evidently has in view when he says, "It is God who makes and transforms all things."[5]

8. And now the point for investigation is, whether, when God shall be all in all, the whole of bodily nature will, in the consummation of all things, consist of one species, and the sole quality of body be that which shall shine in the indescribable glory which is to be regarded as the future possession of the spiritual body. For if we rightly understand the matter, this is the statement of Moses in the beginning of his book, when he says, "In the beginning God created the heavens and the earth."[6] For this is the

---

[1] Ad summa.
[2] [Elucidation IV.]
[3] 1 Cor. xv. 28.
[4] [Elucidation V.]
[5] Cf. Ps. cii. 25, 26.
[6] Gen. i. 1.

beginning of all creation : to this beginning the end and consummation of all things must be recalled, i.e., in order that that heaven and that earth may be the habitation and resting-place of the pious ; so that all the holy ones, and the meek, may first obtain an inheritance in that land, since this is the teaching of the law, and of the prophets, and of the Gospel. In which land I believe there exist the true and living forms of that worship which Moses handed down under the shadow of the law ; of which it is said, that "they serve unto the example and shadow of heavenly things " [1] — those, viz., who were in subjection in the law. To Moses himself also was the injunction given, " Look that thou make them after the form and pattern which were showed thee on the mount." [2]   From which it appears to me, that as on this earth the law was a sort of schoolmaster to those who by it were to be conducted to Christ, in order that, being instructed and trained by it, they might more easily, after the training of the law, receive the more perfect principles of Christ ; so also another earth, which receives into it all the saints, may first imbue and mould them by the institutions of the true and everlasting law, that they may more easily gain possession of those perfect institutions of heaven, to which nothing can be added ; in which there will be, of a truth, that Gospel which is called everlasting, and that Testament, ever new, which shall never grow old.

9. In this way, accordingly, we are to suppose that at the consummation and restoration of all things, those who make a gradual advance, and who ascend (in the scale of improvement), will arrive in due measure and order at that land, and at that training which is contained in it, where they may be prepared for those better institutions to which no addition can be made. For, after His agents and servants, the Lord Christ, who is King of all, will Himself assume the kingdom ; i.e., after instruction in the holy virtues, He will Himself instruct those who are capable of receiving Him in respect of His being wisdom, reigning in them until He has subjected them to the Father, who has subdued all things to Himself, i.e., that when they shall have been made capable of receiving God, God may be to them all in all.   Then accordingly, as a necessary consequence, bodily nature will obtain that highest condition [3] to which nothing more can be added.   Having discussed, up to this point, the quality of bodily nature, or of spiritual body, we leave it to the choice of the reader to determine what he shall consider best.   And here we may bring the third book to a conclusion.

---

[1] Heb. viii. 5.
[2] Ex. xxv. 40.

[3] Jerome (*Epistle to Avitus*, No. 94) says that Origen, "after a most lengthened discussion, in which he asserts that all bodily nature is to be changed into attenuated and spiritual bodies, and that all substance is to be converted into one body of perfect purity, and more brilliant than any splendour (*mundissimum et omni splendore purius*), and such as the human mind cannot now conceive," adds at the last, " And God will be ' all in all,' so that the whole of bodily nature may be reduced into that substance which is better than all others, into the divine, viz., than which none is better."   From which, since it seems to follow that God possesses a body, although of extreme tenuity (*licet tenuissimum*), Rufinus has either suppressed this view, or altered the meaning of Origen's words (Ruæus).

ORIGEN DE PRINCIPIIS.

BOOK IV.

TRANSLATED FROM THE LATIN OF RUFINUS.

CHAP. I. — THAT THE SCRIPTURES ARE DIVINELY INSPIRED.

1. But as it is not sufficient, in the discussion of matters of such importance, to entrust the decision to the human senses and to the human understanding, and to pronounce on things invisible as if they were seen by us,[1] we must, in order to establish the positions which we have laid down, adduce the testimony of Holy Scripture. And that this testimony may produce a sure and unhesitating belief, either with regard to what we have still to advance, or to what has been already stated, it seems necessary to show, in the first place, that the Scriptures themselves are divine, i.e., were inspired by the Spirit of God. We shall therefore with all possible brevity draw forth from the Holy Scriptures themselves, such evidence on this point as may produce upon us a suitable impression, (making our quotations) from Moses, the first legislator of the Hebrew nation, and from the words of Jesus Christ, the Author and Chief of the Christian religious system.[3] For although there have been numerous legislators among the Greeks and Barbarians, and also countless teachers and philosophers who professed to declare the truth, we do not remember any legislator who was able to produce in the minds of foreign nations an affection and a zeal (for him) such as led them either voluntarily to adopt his laws, or to defend them with all the efforts of their mind. No one, then, has been able to introduce and make known what seemed to himself the truth, among, I do not say many foreign nations, but even amongst the individuals of one single nation, in such a manner that a knowledge and belief of the same should extend to all. And yet there can be no doubt that it was the wish of the legislators that their laws should be observed by all men, if possible ; and of the teachers, that what appeared to themselves to be truth, should become known to all. But knowing that they could

TRANSLATION FROM THE GREEK.

CHAP. I. — ON THE INSPIRATION OF HOLY SCRIPTURE, AND HOW THE SAME IS TO BE READ AND UNDERSTOOD, AND WHAT IS THE REASON OF THE UNCERTAINTY IN IT ; AND OF THE IMPOSSIBILITY OR IRRATIONALITY OF CERTAIN THINGS IN IT, TAKEN ACCORDING TO THE LETTER.

(The translation from the Greek is designedly literal, that the difference between the original and the paraphrase of Rufinus may be more clearly seen.)

1. Since, in our investigation of matters of such importance, not satisfied with the common opinions, and with the clear evidence of visible things,[2] we take in addition, for the proof of our statements, testimonies from what are believed by us to be divine writings, viz., from that which is called the Old Testament, and that which is styled the New, and endeavour by reason to confirm our faith ; and as we have not yet spoken of the Scriptures as divine, come and let us, as if by way of an epitome, treat of a few points respecting them, laying down those reasons which lead us to regard them as divine writings. And before making use of the words of the writings themselves, and of the things which are exhibited in them, we must make the following statement regarding Moses and Jesus Christ, — the lawgiver of the Hebrews, and the Introducer of the saving doctrines according to Christianity. For, although there have been very many legislators among the Greeks and Barbarians, and teachers who announced opinions which professed to be the truth, we have heard of no legislator who was able to imbue other nations with a zeal for the

---

[1] Visibiliter de invisibilibus pronunciare.   [2] τῇ ἐναργείᾳ τῶν βλεπομένων.   [3] Principis Christianorum religionis et dogmatis.

by no means succeed in producing any such mighty power within them as would lead foreign nations to obey their laws, or have regard to their statements, they did not venture even to essay the attempt, lest the failure of the undertaking should stamp their conduct with the mark of imprudence. And yet there are throughout the whole world — throughout all Greece, and all foreign countries — countless individuals who have abandoned the laws of their country, and those whom they had believed to be gods, and have yielded themselves up to the obedience of the law of Moses, and to the discipleship and worship of Christ; and have done this, not without exciting against themselves the intense hatred of the worshippers of images, so as frequently to be exposed to cruel tortures from the latter, and sometimes even to be put to death. And yet they embrace, and with all affection preserve, the words and teaching of Christ.

2. And we may see, moreover, how that religion itself grew up in a short time, making progress by the punishment and death of its worshippers, by the plundering of their goods, and by the tortures of every kind which they endured; and this result is the more surprising, that even the teachers of it themselves neither were men of skill,[1] nor very numerous; and yet these words are preached throughout the whole world, so that Greeks and Barbarians, wise and foolish, adopt the doctrines of the Christian religion.[3] From which it is no doubtful inference, that it is not by human power or might that the words of Jesus Christ come to prevail with all faith and power over the understandings and souls of all men. For, that these results were both predicted by Him, and established by divine answers proceeding from Him, is clear from His own words: "Ye shall be brought before governors and kings for My sake, for a testimony against them and the Gentiles."[7] And again: "This Gospel of the kingdom shall be preached among all nations."[8] And again: "Many shall say to Me in that day, Lord, Lord, have we not eaten and drunk in Thy name, and in Thy name cast out devils? And I will say unto them, Depart from Me, ye workers of iniquity, I never knew you."[9] If these

reception of his words; and although those who professed to philosophize about truth brought forward a great apparatus of apparent logical demonstration, no one has been able to impress what was deemed by him the truth upon other nations, or even on any number of persons worth mentioning in a single nation. And yet not only would the legislators have liked to enforce those laws which appeared to be good, if possible, upon the whole human race, but the teachers also to have spread what they imagined to be truth everywhere throughout the world. But as they were unable to call men of other languages and from many nations to observe their laws, and accept their teaching, they did not at all attempt to do this, considering not unwisely the impossibility of such a result happening to them. Whereas all Greece, and the barbarous part of our world, contains innumerable zealots, who have deserted the laws of their fathers and the established gods, for the observance of the laws of Moses and the discipleship of the words of Jesus Christ; although those who clave to the law of Moses were hated by the worshippers of images, and those who accepted the words of Jesus Christ were exposed, in addition, to the danger of death.

2. And if we observe how powerful the word has become in a very few years, notwithstanding that against those who acknowledged Christianity conspiracies were formed, and some of them on its account put to death, and others of them lost their property, and that, notwithstanding the small number of its teachers,[2] it was preached everywhere throughout tne world, so that Greeks and Barbarians, wise and foolish, gave themselves up to the worship that is through Jesus,[4] we have no difficulty in saying that the result is beyond any human power,[5] Jesus having taught with all authority and persuasiveness that His word should not be overcome; so that we may rightly regard as oracular responses[6] those utterances of His, such as, "Ye shall be brought before governors and kings for My sake, for a testimony against them and the Gentiles;"[7] and, "Many shall say unto Me in that day, Lord, Lord, have we not eaten in Thy name, and drunk in Thy name, and in Thy name cast out devils? And I shall

---

[1] Satis idonei.　　[2] οὐδὲ τῶν διδασκάλων πλεοναζόντων.　　[3] Religionem Christianæ doctrinæ.　　[4] τῇ διὰ Ἰησοῦ θεοσεβείᾳ.
[5] μεῖζον ἢ κατὰ ἄνθρωπον τὸ πρᾶγμα εἶναι.　　[6] χρησμούς.　　[7] Matt. x. 18.　　[8] Cf. Matt. xxiv. 14.　　[9] Cf. Matt. vii. 22, 23.

sayings, indeed, had been so uttered by Him, and yet if these predictions had not been fulfilled, they might perhaps appear to be untrue,[2] and not to possess any authority. But now, when His declarations do pass into fulfilment, seeing they were predicted with such power and authority, it is most clearly shown to be true that He, when He was made man, delivered to men the precepts of salvation.[3]

3. What, then, are we to say of this, which the prophets had beforehand foretold of Him, that princes would not cease from Judah, nor leaders from between his thighs, until He should come for whom it has been reserved (viz., the kingdom), and until the expectation of the Gentiles should come? For it is most distinctly evident from the history itself, from what is clearly seen at the present day, that from the times of Christ onwards there were no kings amongst the Jews. Nay, even all those objects of Jewish pride,[8] of which they vaunted so much, and in which they exulted, whether regarding the beauty of the temple or the ornaments of the altar, and all those sacerdotal fillets and robes of the high priests, were all destroyed together. For the prophecy was fulfilled which had declared, " For the children of Israel shall abide many days without king and prince : there shall be no victim, nor altar, nor priesthood, nor answers." [10] These testimonies, accordingly, we employ against those who seem to assert that what is spoken in Genesis by Jacob refers to Judah ; and who say that there still remains a prince of the race of Judah — he, viz., who is the prince of their nation, whom they style Patriarch [11] — and that there cannot fail (a ruler) of his seed, who will remain until the advent of that Christ whom they picture to themselves. But if the prophet's words be true, when he says, " The children of Israel shall abide many days without king, without prince ; and there shall be no victim, nor altar, nor priesthood ; " [13] and if, certainly, since the overthrow of the temple, victims are neither offered, nor any altar found, nor any priesthood exists, it is most certain that, as it is written, princes have departed from Judah, and a leader from between his thighs, until the coming of Him for whom it has been reserved. It is established, then, that He is come for whom it has been reserved, and in whom is the expectation of the Gentiles. And this manifestly seems to be fulfilled in the multitude of those who have believed on God through Christ out of the different nations.

say unto them, Depart from Me, ye workers of iniquity, I never knew you." [1] Now it was perhaps (once) probable that, in uttering these words, He spoke them in vain, so that they were not true ; but when that which was delivered with so much authority *has* come to pass, it shows that God, having really become man, delivered to men the doctrines of salvation.[4]

3. And what need is there to mention also that it was predicted of Christ [5] that then would the rulers fail from Judah, and the leaders from his thighs,[6] when He came for whom it is reserved (the kingdom, namely) ; and that the expectation of the Gentiles should dwell in the land ? [7] For it is clearly manifest from the history, and from what is seen at the present day, that from the times of Jesus there were no longer any who were called kings of the Jews ; [9] all those Jewish institutions on which they prided themselves — I mean those arrangements relating to the temple and the altar, and the offering of the service, and the robes of the high priest — having been destroyed. For the prophecy was fulfilled which said, " The children of Israel shall sit many days, there being no king, nor ruler, nor sacrifice, nor altar, nor priesthood, nor responses." [10] And these predictions we employ to answer those who, in their perplexity as to the words spoken in Genesis by Jacob to Judah, assert that the Ethnarch,[12] being of the race of Judah, is the ruler of the people, and that there will not fail some of his seed, until the advent of that Christ whom they figure to their imagination. But if " the children of Israel are to sit many days without a king, or ruler, or altar, or priesthood, or responses ; " and if, since the temple was destroyed, there exists no longer sacrifice, nor altar, nor priesthood, it is manifest that the ruler *has* failed out of Judah, and the leader from between his thighs. And since the prediction declares that " the ruler shall not fail from Judah, and the leader from between his thighs, until what is reserved for Him shall come," it is manifest that He is come to whom (belongs) what is reserved — the expectation of the Gentiles. And this is clear from the multitude of the heathen who have believed on God through Jesus Christ.

[1] Cf. Matt. vii. 22, 23. [2] Fortasse minus vera esse viderentur. [3] Salutaria præcepta. [4] σωτήρια δόγματα. [5] προεφητεύθη ὁ Χριστός. [6] ἐκ τῶν μηρῶν. [7] ἐπιδημήσῃ. [8] Illæ omnes ambitiones Judaicæ. [9] οὐκ ἔτι βασιλεῖς Ἰουδαίαν ἐχρημάτισαν. [10] Cf. Hos. iii. 4. Quoted from the Septuagint. [11] On the Patriarch of the Jews, cf. Milman's *History of the Jews*, vol. ii. p. 399 sq., and vol. iii. p. 7 sq. [12] Termed by Rufinus " Patriarch." [13] Deut. xxxii.

4. In the song of Deuteronomy,[1] also, it is prophetically declared that, on account of the sins of the former people, there was to be an election of a foolish nation, — no other, certainly, than that which was brought about by Christ; for thus the words run: "They have moved Me to anger with their images, and I will stir them up to jealousy; I will arouse them to anger against a foolish nation."[3] We may therefore evidently see how the Hebrews, who are said to have excited God's anger by means of those (idols), which are no gods, and to have aroused His wrath by their images, were themselves also excited to jealousy by means of a foolish nation, which God hath chosen by the advent of Jesus Christ and His disciples. For the following is the language of the apostle: "For ye see your calling, brethren, how that not many wise men among you after the flesh, not many mighty, not many noble (are called): but God has chosen the foolish things of the world, and the things which are not, to destroy the things which formerly existed."[4] Carnal Israel, therefore, should not boast; for such is the term used by the apostle: "No flesh, I say, should glory in the presence of God."[5]

5. What are we to say, moreover, regarding those prophecies of Christ contained in the Psalms, especially the one with the superscription, "A song for the Beloved;"[7] in which it is stated that "His tongue is the pen of a ready writer; fairer than the children of men;" that "grace is poured into His lips?" Now, the indication that grace has been poured upon His lips is this, that, after a short period had elapsed — for He taught only during a year and some months[8] — the whole world, nevertheless, became filled with His doctrine, and with faith in His religion. There arose, then, "in His days righteous men, and abundance of peace,"[9] abiding even to the end, which end is entitled "the taking away of the moon;" and "His dominion shall extend from sea to sea, and from the river to the ends of the earth."[10] There was a sign also given to the house of David. For a virgin conceived, and bare Emmanuel, which, when interpreted, signifies, "God with us: know it, O nations, and be overcome."[11] For we are conquered and overcome, who are of the Gentiles, and remain as a kind of spoils of His victory, who have subjected our necks to His grace. Even the place of His birth was predicted in the prophecies of

4. And in the song in Deuteronomy,[*] also, it is prophetically made known that, on account of the sins of the former people,[2] there was to be an election of foolish nations, which has been brought to pass by no other than by Jesus. "For they," He says, "moved Me to jealousy with that which is not God, they have provoked Me to anger with their idols; and I will move them to jealousy with those which are not a people, and will provoke them to anger with a foolish nation."[3] Now it is possible to understand with all clearness how the Hebrews, who are said to have moved God to jealousy by that which is not God, and to have provoked Him to anger by their idols, were (themselves) aroused to jealousy by that which was not a people — the foolish nation, namely, which God chose by the advent of Jesus Christ and His disciples. We see, indeed, "our calling, that not many wise men after the flesh, not many mighty, not many noble (are called); but God hath chosen the foolish things of the world to confound the wise; and base things, and things that are despised, hath God chosen, and things that are not, to bring to nought the things which formerly existed;"[6] and let not the Israel according to the flesh, which is called by the apostle "flesh," boast in the presence of God.

5. And what are we to say regarding the prophecies of Christ in the Psalms, there being a certain ode with the superscription "For the Beloved,"[7] whose "tongue" is said to be the "pen of a ready writer, who is fairer than the sons of men," since "grace was poured on His lips?" For a proof that grace was poured on His lips is this, that although the period of His teaching was short — for He taught somewhere about a year and a few months — the world has been filled with his teaching, and with the worship of God (established) through Him. For there arose "in His days righteousness and abundance of peace,"[9] which abides until the consummation, which has been called the taking away of the moon; and He continues "ruling from sea to sea, and from the rivers to the ends of the earth."[10] And to the house of David has been given a sign: for the Virgin bore, and was pregnant,[12] and brought forth a son, and His name is Emmanuel, which is, "God with us;" and as the same prophet

---

[1] Deut. xxxii. [2] τοῦ προτέρου λαοῦ. [3] Deut. xxxii. 21. [4] 1 Cor. i. 26–28. Quæ erant prius. [5] 1 Cor. i. 29. [6] Cf. 1 Cor. i. 26–28. "The things which formerly existed, τὰ πρότερον ὄντα." [7] Ps. xlv. 1, 2. [8] [See note *infra*, Contra Celsum, B. II. cap xii. S.] [9] Cf. Ps. lxxii. 7. [10] Ps. lxxii. 8. [11] Cf. Isa. viii. 8, 9. Quoted from the Septuagint. [12] ἔτεκε καὶ ἐν γαστρὶ ἔσχε, καὶ ἔτεκεν υἱόν.

Micah, who said, "And thou, Bethlehem, land of Judah, art by no means small among the leaders of Judah: for out of thee shall come forth a Leader, who shall rule My people Israel." [1] The weeks of years, also, which the prophet Daniel had predicted, extending to the leadership of Christ,[3] have been fulfilled. Moreover, he is at hand, who in the book of Job[4] is said to be about to destroy the huge beast, who also gave power to his own disciples to tread on serpents and scorpions, and on all the power of the enemy, without being injured by him. But if any one will consider the journeys of Christ's apostles throughout the different places, in which as His messengers they preached the Gospel, he will find that both what they ventured to undertake is beyond the power of man, and what they were enabled to accomplish is from God alone. If we consider how men, on hearing that a new doctrine was introduced by these, were able to receive them; or rather, when desiring often to destroy them, they were prevented by a divine power which was in them, we shall find that in this nothing was effected by human strength, but that the whole was the result of the divine power and providence, — signs and wonders, manifest beyond all doubt, bearing testimony to their word and doctrine.

6. These points now being briefly established, viz., regarding the deity of Christ, and the fulfilment of all that was prophesied respecting Him, I think that this position also has been made good, viz., that the Scriptures themselves, which contained these predictions, were divinely inspired, — those, namely, which had either foretold His advent, or the power of His doctrine, or the bringing over of all nations (to His obedience). To which this remark must be added, that the divinity and inspiration both of the predictions of the prophets and of the law of Moses have been clearly revealed and confirmed, especially since the advent of Christ into the world. For before the fulfilment of those events which were predicted by them, they could not, although true and inspired by God, be shown to be so, because they were as yet unfulfilled. But the coming of Christ was a declaration that their statements were true and divinely inspired, although it was certainly doubtful before that whether there would be an accomplishment of those things which had been foretold.

says, the prediction has been fulfilled, "God (is) with us; know it, O nations, and be overcome; ye who are strong, be vanquished:"[2] for we of the heathen have been overcome and vanquished, we who have been taken by the grace of His teaching. The place also of His birth has been foretold in (the prophecies of) Micah: "For thou, Bethlehem," he says, "land of Judah, art by no means the least among the rulers of Judah; for out of thee shall come forth a Ruler, who shall rule My people Israel." [1] And according to Daniel, seventy weeks were fulfilled until (the coming of) Christ the Ruler.[5] And He came, who, according to Job,[6] has subdued the great fish,[7] and has given power to His true disciples to tread upon serpents and scorpions, and all the power of the enemy,[8] without sustaining any injury from them. And let one notice also the universal advent of the apostles sent by Jesus to announce the Gospel, and he will see both that the undertaking was beyond human power, and that the commandment came from God. And if we examine how men, on hearing new doctrines, and strange words, yielded themselves up to these teachers, being overcome, amid the very desire to plot against them, by a divine power that watched over these (teachers), we shall not be incredulous as to whether they also wrought miracles, God bearing witness to their words both by signs, and wonders, and divers miracles.

6. And while we thus briefly[9] demonstrate the deity of Christ, and (in so doing) make use of the prophetic declarations regarding Him, we demonstrate at the same time that the writings which prophesied of Him were divinely inspired; and that those documents which announced His coming and His doctrine were given forth with all power and authority, and that on this account they obtained the election from the Gentiles.[10] We must say, also, that the divinity of the prophetic declarations, and the spiritual nature of the law of Moses, shone forth after the advent of Christ. For before the advent of Christ it was not altogether possible to exhibit manifest proofs of the divine inspiration of the ancient Scripture; whereas His coming led those who might suspect the law and the prophets not to be divine, to the clear conviction that they were

---

[1] Cf. Mic. v. 2 with Matt. ii. 6.　　[2] Cf Isa. viii. 8, 9.　Quoted from the Septuagint.　　[3] Cf. Dan. ix. 25.　Ad ducem Christum; "To Messiah the Prince," Auth. Vers.　　[4] The allusion is perhaps to Job xli. 1.　　[5] Cf. Dan. ix. 25.　　[6] Cf. Job xl. and xli.　[7] τὸ μέγα κῆτος.　　[8] Cf. Luke x. 19.　　[9] ὡς ἐν ἐπιτομῇ.　　[10] διὰ τοῦτο τῆς ἀπὸ τῶν ἐθνῶν ἐκλογῆς κεκρατηκότα.

If any one, moreover, consider the words of the prophets with all the zeal and reverence which they deserve, it is certain that, in the perusal and careful examination thus given them, he will feel his mind and senses touched by a divine breath, and will acknowledge that the words which he reads were no human utterances, but the language of God; and from his own emotions he will feel that these books were the composition of no human skill, nor of any mortal eloquence, but, so to speak, of a style that is divine.[2] The splendour of Christ's advent, therefore, illuminating the law of Moses by the light of truth, has taken away that veil which had been placed over the letter (of the law), and has unsealed, for every one who believes upon Him, all the blessings which were concealed by the covering of the word.

7. It is, however, a matter attended with considerable labour, to point out, in every instance, how and when the predictions of the prophets were fulfilled, so as to appear to confirm those who are in doubt, seeing it is possible for every one who wishes to become more thoroughly acquainted with these things, to gather abundant proofs from the records of the truth themselves. But if the sense of the letter, which is beyond man, does not appear to present itself at once, on the first glance, to those who are less versed in divine discipline, it is not at all to be wondered at, because divine things are brought down somewhat slowly to (the comprehension of) men, and elude the view in proportion as one is either sceptical or unworthy. For although it is certain that all things which exist in this world, or take place in it, are ordered by the providence of God, and certain events indeed do appear with sufficient clearness to be under the disposal of His providential government, yet others again unfold themselves so mysteriously and incomprehensibly, that the plan of Divine Providence with regard to them is completely concealed; so that it is occasionally believed by some that particular occurrences do not belong to (the plan of) Providence, because the principle eludes their grasp, according to which the works of Divine Providence are administered with indescribable skill; which principle of administration, however, is not equally concealed from all. For even among men themselves, one individual devotes less consideration to it, another more; while by every man, He who is on earth, whoever is the inhabitant of heaven, is more acknowledged.[7] And the nature of bodies is clear to us in one way, that of trees in another, that of animals in a third; the nature of souls, again, is concealed in a different way; and the manner in which the diverse movements of ra-

composed by (the aid of) heavenly grace. And he who reads the words of the prophets with care and attention, feeling by the very perusal the traces of the divinity that is in them, will be led by his own emotions to believe that those words which have been deemed to be the words of God are not the compositions of men. The light, moreover, which was contained in the law of Moses, but which had been concealed by a veil, shone forth at the advent of Jesus, the veil being taken away, and those blessings, the shadow of which was contained in the letter, coming forth gradually to the knowledge (of men).

7. It would be tedious now to enumerate the most ancient prophecies respecting each future event, in order that the doubter, being impressed by their divinity, may lay aside all hesitation and distraction, and devote himself with his whole soul to the words of God. But if in every part of the Scriptures the superhuman element of thought[3] does not seem to present itself to the uninstructed, that is not at all wonderful; for, with respect to the works of that providence which embraces the whole world, some show with the utmost clearness that they are works of providence, while others are so concealed as to seem to furnish ground for unbelief with respect to that God who orders all things with unspeakable skill and power. For the artistic plan[4] of a providential Ruler is not so evident in those matters belonging to the earth, as in the case of the sun, and moon, and stars; and not so clear in what relates to human occurrences, as it is in the souls and bodies of animals, — the object and reason of the impulses, and phantasies and natures of animals, and the structure of their bodies, being carefully ascertained by those who attend to these things.[5] But as (the doctrine of) providence is not at all weakened[6] (on account of those things which are not understood) in the eyes of those who have once honestly accepted it, so neither is the divinity of Scripture, which extends to the whole of it, (lost) on account of the inability of our weakness to discover in every expression the hidden splendour of the doctrines

---

[1] ἰχνος ἐνθουσιασμοῦ.   [2] Divino, ut ita dixerim, cothurno.   [3] τὸ ὑπὲρ ἄνθρωπον τῶν νοημάτων.   [4] ὁ τεχνικὸς λόγος.
[5] Σφόδρα τοῦ πρὸς τί καὶ ἕνεκα τίνος εὑρισκομένου τοῖς τούτων ἐπιμελομένοις, περὶ τὰς ὁρμὰς, καὶ τὰς φαντασίας, καὶ φύσεις τῶν ζώων, καὶ τὰς κατασκευὰς τῶν σωμάτων.   [6] χρεοκοπεῖται.
[7] " Nam et inter ipsos homines ab alio minus, ab alio amplius consideratur: plus vero ab omni homine, qui in terris est, quis-quis ille est cœli habitator, agnoscitur." The translation of Rufinus, as Redepenning remarks, seems very confused. Probably also the text is corrupt. The Greek without doubt gives the genuine thought of Origen. By omitting the *ab* we approximate to the Greek, and get: " but he, whoever he be, who is inhabitant of heaven, is better known than any man who is on the earth;" or according to the punctuation in the old editions, " but he who is inhabitant of heaven is better known than any man on earth, whoever he be."

tional understandings are ordered by Providence, eludes the view of men in a greater degree, and even, in my opinion, in no small degree that of the angels also. But as the existence of divine providence is not refuted by those especially who are certain of its existence, but who do not comprehend its workings or arrangements by the powers of the human mind ; so neither will the divine inspiration of holy Scripture, which extends throughout its body, be believed to be non-existent, because the weakness of our understanding is unable to trace out the hidden and secret meaning in each individual word, the treasure of divine wisdom being hid in the vulgar and unpolished vessels of words,[3] as the apostle also points out when he says, " We have this treasure in earthen vessels," [4] that the virtue of the divine power may shine out the more brightly, no colouring of human eloquence being intermingled with the truth of the doctrines. For if our books induced men to believe because they were composed either by rhetorical arts or by the wisdom of philosophy, then undoubtedly our faith would be considered to be based on the art of words, and on human wisdom, and not upon the power of God ; whereas it is now known to all that the word of this preaching has been so accepted by numbers throughout almost the whole world, because they understood their belief to rest not on the persuasive words of human wisdom, but on the manifestation of the Spirit and of power. On which account, being led by a heavenly, nay, by a more than heavenly power, to faith and acceptance,[8] that we may worship the sole Creator of all things as our God, let us also do our utmost endeavour, by abandoning the language of the elements of Christ, which are but the first beginnings of wisdom, to go on to perfection, in order that that wisdom which is given to them who are perfect, may be given to us also. For such is the promise of him to whom was entrusted the preaching of this wisdom, in the words : " Howbeit we speak wisdom among them that are perfect ; yet not the wisdom of this world, nor of the princes of this world, who will be brought to nought ; " [10] by which he shows that this wisdom of ours has nothing in common, so far as regards the beauty of language, with the wisdom of this world. This wisdom, then, will be inscribed more clearly and perfectly on our hearts, if it be made known to us according to the revelation of the mystery which has been hid from eternity,[11] but now is manifest through the Scriptures of prophecy, and the advent of our Lord and Saviour Jesus Christ, to whom be glory for ever. Amen.

Many, not understanding the Scriptures in a spiritual sense, but incorrectly,[12] have fallen into heresies.

8. These particulars, then, being briefly stated regarding the inspiration of the sacred Scriptures by

veiled in common and unattractive phráseology.[1] For we have the treasure in earthen vessels, that the excellency of the power of God may shine forth, and that it may not be deemed to proceed from us (who are but) human beings. For if the hackneyed [2] methods of demonstration (common) among men, contained in the books (of the Bible), had been successful in producing conviction, then our faith would rightly have been supposed to rest on the wisdom of men, and not on the power of God ; but now it is manifest to every one who lifts up his eyes, that the word and preaching have not prevailed among the multitude "by persuasive words of wisdom, but by demonstration of the Spirit and of power." [5] Wherefore, since a celestial or even a super-celestial power compels us to worship the only Creator, let us leave the doctrine of the beginning of Christ, i.e., the elements,[6] and endeavour to go on to perfection, in order that the wisdon spoken to the perfect may be spoken to us also. For he who possesses it promises to speak wisdom among them that are perfect, but another wisdom than that of this world, and of the rulers of this world, which is brought to nought. And this wisdom will be distinctly stamped [7] upon us, and will produce a revelation of the mystery that was kept silent in the eternal ages,[9] but now has been manifested through the prophetic Scriptures, and the appearance of our Lord and Saviour Jesus Christ, to whom be glory for ever and ever. Amen.

8. Having spoken thus briefly [13] on the subject of the divine inspiration of the

---

[1] ἐν εὐτελεῖ καὶ εὐκαταφρονήτῳ λέξει.   [2] καθημαξευμέναι.   [3] In vilioribus et incomptis verborum vasculis.   [4] Cf. 2 Cor. iv. 7.
[5] 1 Cor. ii. 4.   [6] τῆς στοιχειώσεως.   [7] ἐντυπωθήσεται.   [8] Ad fidem credulitatemque.   [9] χρόνοις αἰωνίοις.   [10] 1 Cor. ii. 6.
[11] Temporibus eternis.   [12] Male.   [13] ὡς ἐν ἐπιδρομῇ.

the Holy Spirit, it seems necessary to explain this point also, viz., how certain persons, not reading them correctly, have given themselves over to erroneous opinions, inasmuch as the procedure to be followed, in order to attain an understanding of the holy writings, is unknown to many. The Jews, in fine, owing to the hardness of their heart, and from a desire to appear wise in their own eyes, have not believed in our Lord and Saviour, judging that those statements which were uttered respecting Him ought to be understood literally, i.e., that He ought in a sensible and visible manner to preach deliverance to the captives, and first build a city which they truly deem the city of God, and cut off at the same time the chariots of Ephraim,[5] and the horse from Jerusalem ; that He ought also to eat butter and honey,[6] in order to choose the good before He should come to know how to bring forth evil.[7] They think, also, that it has been predicted that the wolf — that four-footed animal — is, at the coming of Christ, to feed with the lambs, and the leopard to lie down with kids, and the calf and the bull to pasture with lions, and that they are to be led by a little child to the pasture ; that the ox and the bear are to lie down together in the green fields, and that their young ones are to be fed together ; that lions also will frequent stalls with the oxen, and feed on straw. And seeing that, according to history, there was no accomplishment of any of those things predicted of Him, in which they believed the signs of Christ's advent were especially to be observed, they refused to acknowledge the presence of our Lord Jesus Christ ; nay, contrary to all the principles of human and divine law,[9] i.e., contrary to the faith of prophecy, they crucified Him for assuming to Himself the name of Christ. Thereupon the heretics, reading that it is written in the law, " A fire has been kindled in Mine anger ; "[11] and that " I the Lord am a jealous (God), visiting the sins of the fathers upon the children unto the third and fourth generation ; "[12] and that " it repenteth Me that I anointed Saul to be king ; "[13] and, " I am the Lord, who make peace and create evil ; "[14] and again, " There is not evil in a city which the Lord hath not done ; "[15] and, " Evils came down from the Lord upon the gates of Jerusalem ; "[16] and, " An evil spirit from the Lord plagued Saul ; "[17] and reading many other passages similar to these, which are found in Scripture, they did not venture to assert that these were not the Scriptures of God, but they considered them to be the words of that creator God whom the Jews worshipped, and who, they judged, ought to be regarded as just only, and not also as good ; but that the Saviour had come to announce to us a more perfect God, who, they allege, is not the creator of the world, — there being different and discordant opinions

holy Scriptures, it is necessary to proceed to the (consideration of the) manner in which they are to be read and understood, seeing numerous errors have been committed in consequence of the method in which the holy documents[1] ought to be examined,[2] not having been discovered by the multitude. For both the hardened in heart, and the ignorant persons[3] belonging to the circumcision, have not believed on our Saviour, thinking that they are following the language of the prophecies respecting Him, and not perceiving in a manner palpable to their senses[4] that He had proclaimed liberty to the captives, nor that He had built up what they truly consider the city of God, nor cut off " the chariots of Ephraim, and the horse from Jerusalem," [5] nor eaten butter and honey, and, before knowing or preferring the evil, had selected the good.[6] And thinking, moreover, that it was prophesied that the wolf — the four-footed animal — was to feed with the lamb, and the leopard to lie down with the kid, and the calf and bull and lion to feed together, being led by a little child, and that the ox and bear were to pasture together, their young ones growing up together, and that the lion was to eat straw like the ox :[8] seeing none of these things visibly accomplished during the advent of Him who is believed by us to be Christ, they did not accept our Lord Jesus ; but, as having called Himself Christ improperly,[10] they crucified Him. And those belonging to heretical sects reading this (statement), " A fire has been kindled in Mine anger ; "[11] and this, " I am a jealous God, visiting the iniquities of the fathers upon the children unto the third and fourth generation ; "[12] and this, " I repent of having anointed Saul to be king ; "[13] and this, " I am a God that maketh peace, and createth evil ; "[14] and, among others, this, " There is not wickedness in the city which the Lord hath not done ; "[15] and again this, " Evils came down from the Lord upon the gates of Jerusalem ; "[16] and, " An evil spirit from the Lord plagued Saul ; "[17] and countless other passages like these — they have not ventured to disbelieve these as the Scriptures of God ; but believing them to be the (words) of the Demiurge, whom the Jews worship, they thought that as the Demiurge was an imperfect and unbenevo-

---

[1] τὰ ἅγια ἀναγνώσματα.　　[2] πῶς δεῖ ἐφοδεύειν.　　[3] οἱ ἰδιῶται τῶν ἐκ τῆς περιτομῆς.　　[4] αἰσθητῶς.　　[5] Cf. Zech. ix. 10.
[6] Cf. Isa. vii. 15.　　[7] Ut priusquam cognosceret proferre malum, eligeret bonum.　　[8] Cf. Isa. xi. 6, 7.　　[9] Contra jus fasque.
[10] παρὰ τὸ δέον.　　[11] Cf. Jer. xv. 14.　　[12] Cf. Ex. xx. 5.　　[13] Cf. 1 Sam. xv. 11.　　[14] Cf. Isa. xlv. 7.　　[15] Cf. Amos iii. 6.
[16] Cf. Mic. i. 12.　　[17] Cf. 1 Sam. xvi. 14, xviii. 10.

among them even on this very point, because, when they once depart from a belief in God the Creator, who is Lord of all, they have given themselves over to various inventions and fables, devising certain (fictions), and asserting that some things were visible, and made by one (God), and that certain other things were invisible, and were created by another, according to the vain and fanciful suggestions of their own minds. But not a few also of the more simple of those, who appear to be restrained within the faith of the Church, are of opinion that there is no greater God than the Creator, holding in this a correct and sound opinion ; and yet they entertain regarding Him such views as would not be entertained regarding the most unjust and cruel of men.

9. Now the reason of the erroneous apprehension of all these points on the part of those whom we have mentioned above, is no other than this, that holy Scripture is not understood by them according to its spiritual, but according to its literal meaning. And therefore we shall endeavour, so far as our moderate capacity will permit, to point out to those who believe the holy Scriptures to be no human compositions, but to be written by inspiration of the Holy Spirit, and to be transmitted and entrusted to us by the will of God the Father, through His only-begotten Son Jesus Christ, what appears to us, who observe things by a right way of understanding,[3] to be the standard and discipline delivered to the apostles by Jesus Christ, and which they handed down in succession to their posterity, the teachers of the holy Church. Now, that there are certain mystical economies[5] indicated in holy Scripture, is admitted by all, I think, even the simplest of believers. But what these are, or of what kind they are, he who is rightly minded, and not overcome with the vice of boasting, will scrupulously[6] acknowledge himself to be ignorant. For if any one, e.g., were to adduce the case of the daughters of Lot, who seem, contrary to the law of God,[7] to have had intercourse with their father, or that of the two wives of Abraham, or of the two sisters who were married to Jacob, or of the two handmaids who increased the number of his sons, what other answer could be returned than that these were certain mysteries,[8] and forms of spiritual things, but that we are ignorant of what nature they are ? Nay, even when we read of the construction of the tabernacle, we deem it certain that the written descriptions are the figures of certain hidden things ; but to adapt these to their appropriate standards, and to open up

lent God, the Saviour had come to announce a more perfect Deity, who, they say, is not the Demiurge, being of different opinions regarding Him ; and having once departed from the Demiurge, who is the only uncreated God, they have given themselves up to fictions, inventing to themselves hypotheses, according to which they imagine that there are some things which are visible, and certain other things which are not visible, all which are the fancies of their own minds. And yet, indeed, the more simple among those who profess to belong to the Church have supposed that there is no deity greater than the Demiurge, being right in so thinking, while they imagine regarding Him such things as would not be believed of the most savage and unjust of mankind.

9. Now the cause, in all the points previously enumerated, of the false opinions, and of the impious statements or ignorant assertions[1] about God, appears to be nothing else than the not understanding the Scripture according to its spiritual meaning, but the interpretation of it agreeably to the mere letter. And therefore, to those who believe that the sacred books are not the compositions of men, but that they were composed by inspiration[2] of the Holy Spirit, agreeably to the will of the Father of all things through Jesus Christ, and that they have come down to us, we must point out the ways (of interpreting them) which appear (correct) to us, who cling to the standard[4] of the heavenly Church of Jesus Christ according to the succession of the apostles. Now, that there are certain mystical economies made known by the holy Scriptures, all — even the most simple of those who adhere to the word — have believed ; but what these are, candid and modest individuals confess that they know not. If, then, one were to be perplexed about the intercourse of Lot with his daughters, and about the two wives of Abraham, and the two sisters married to Jacob, and the two handmaids who bore him children, they can return no other answer than this, that these are mysteries not understood by us. Nay, also, when the (description of the) fitting out of the tabernacle is read, believing that what is written is a type,[9] they seek

---

1 ἰδιωτικῶν.　　2 ἐπιπνοίας.
3 The text, as it stands, is probably corrupt: " Propter quod conabimur pro mediocritate sensus nostri his, qui credunt Scripturas sanctas non humana verba aliqua esse composita, sed Sancti Spiritus inspiratione conscripta, et voluntate Dei patris per unigenitum filium suum Jesum Christum nobis quoque esse tradita et commissa, quæ nobis videntur, recta via intelligentiæ observantibus, demonstrare illam regulam et disciplinam, quam ab Jesu Christo traditam sibi apostoli per successionem posteris quoque suis, sanctam ecclesiam docentibus, tradiderunt."
4 κανόνος.　　5 Dispensationes.　　6 Religiosius.　　7 Contra fas.　　8 Sacramenta quædam.　　9 τύπους εἶναι τὰ γεγραμμένα.

and discuss every individual point, I consider to be exceedingly difficult, not to say impossible. That that description, however, is, as I have said, full of mysteries, does not escape even the common understanding. But all the narrative portion, relating either to the marriages, or to the begetting of the children, or to battles of different kinds, or to any other histories whatever, what else can they be supposed to be, save the forms and figures of hidden and sacred things? As men, however, make little effort to exercise their intellect, or imagine that they possess knowledge before they really learn, the consequence is that they never begin to have knowledge ; or if there be no want of a desire, at least, nor of an instructor, and if divine knowledge be sought after, as it ought to be, in a religious and holy spirit, and in the hope that many points will be opened up by the revelation of God—since to human sense they are exceedingly difficult and obscure—then, perhaps, he who seeks in such a manner will find what it is lawful[1] to discover.

10. But lest this difficulty perhaps should be supposed to exist only in the language of the prophets, seeing the prophetic style is allowed by all to abound in figures and enigmas, what do we find when we come to the Gospels? Is there not hidden there also an inner, namely a divine sense, which is revealed by that grace alone which he had received who said, " But we have the mind of Christ, that we might know the things freely given to us by God. Which things also we speak, not in the words which man's wisdom teaches, but which the Spirit teacheth?"[2] And if one now were to read the revelations which were made to John, how amazed would he not be that there should be contained within them so great an amount of hidden, ineffable mysteries,[4] in which it is clearly understood, even by those who cannot comprehend *what* is concealed, that *something* certainly *is* concealed. And yet are not the Epistles of the Apostles, which seem to some to be plainer, filled with meanings so profound, that by means of them, as by some small receptacle,[5] the clearness of incalculable light[6] appears to be poured into those who are capable of understanding the meaning of divine wisdom? And therefore, because this is the case, and because there are many who go wrong in this life, I do not consider that it is easy to pronounce, without danger, that any one knows or understands those things, which, in order to be opened up, need the key of knowledge ; which key, the Saviour declared, lay with those who were skilled in the law. And here, although it is a digression, I think we should inquire of those who assert that before the advent of the Saviour there was no truth among those who were engaged in the study of the

to adapt what they can to each particular related about the tabernacle,—not being wrong so far as regards their belief that the tabernacle is a type of *something*, but erring sometimes in adapting the description of that of which the tabernacle is a type, to some special thing in a manner worthy of Scripture. And all the history that is considered to tell of marriages, or the begetting of children, or of wars, or any histories whatever that are in circulation among the multitude, they declare to be types ; but of what in each individual instance, partly owing to their habits not being thoroughly exercised—partly, too, owing to their precipitation—sometimes, even when an individual does happen to be well trained and clear-sighted, owing to the excessive difficulty of discovering things on the part of men,—the nature of each particular regarding these (types) is not clearly ascertained.

10. And what need is there to speak of the prophecies, which we all know to be filled with enigmas and dark sayings? And if we come to the Gospels, the exact understanding of these also, as being the mind of Christ, requires the grace that was given to him who said, " But we have the mind of Christ, that we might know the things freely given to us by God. Which things also we speak, not in the words which man's wisdom teacheth, but which the Spirit teacheth."[3] And who, on reading the revelations made to John, would not be amazed at the unspeakable mysteries therein concealed, and which are evident (even) to him who does not comprehend what is written? And to what person, skilful in investigating words, would the Epistles of the Apostles seem to be clear and easy of understanding, since even in them there are countless numbers of most profound ideas, which, (issuing forth) as by an aperture, admit of no rapid comprehension?[7] And therefore, since these things are so, and since innumerable individuals fall into mistakes, it is not safe in reading (the Scriptures) to declare that one easily understands what needs the key of knowledge, which the Saviour declares is with the lawyers. And let those answer who will not allow that the truth was with these before the advent of Christ, how the key of knowledge is said by our Lord Jesus Christ to be with those who, as they allege,

---

[1] Fas.　　[2] Cf. 1 Cor. ii. 16 and 12, 13.　　[3] 1 Cor. ii. 12, 13, and 16 ad fin.　　[4] Tantam occultationem ineffabilium sacramentorum.
[5] Per breve quoddam receptaculum.　　[6] Immensæ lucis claritas.
[7] Μυρίων ὅσων κἀκεῖ, ὡς δὶ ὀπῆς, μεγίστων καὶ πλείστων νοημάτων οὐ βραχεῖαν ἀφορμὴν παρεχόντων.

law, how it could be said by our Lord Jesus Christ that the keys of knowledge were with them, who had the books of the prophets and of the law in their hands. For thus did He speak: "Woe unto you, ye teachers of the law, who have taken away the key of knowledge: ye entered not in yourselves, and them who wished to enter in ye hindered." [3]

11. But, as we had begun to observe, the way which seems to us the correct one for the understanding of the Scriptures, and for the investigation of their meaning, we consider to be of the following kind: for we are instructed by Scripture itself in regard to the ideas which we ought to form of it. In the Proverbs of Solomon we find some such rule as the following laid down, respecting the consideration of holy Scripture: "And do thou," he says, "describe these things to thyself in a threefold manner, in counsel and knowledge, and that thou mayest answer the words of truth to those who have proposed them to thee." [6] Each one, then, ought to describe in his own mind, in a threefold manner, the understanding of the divine letters, — that is, in order that all the more simple individuals may be edified, so to speak, by the very body of Scripture; for such we term that common and historical sense: while, if some have commenced to make considerable progress, and are able to see something more (than that), *they* may be edified by the very soul of Scripture. Those, again, who are perfect, and who resemble those of whom the apostle says, "We speak wisdom among them that are perfect, but not the wisdom of this world, nor of the princes of this world, who will be brought to nought; but we speak the wisdom of God, hidden in a mystery, which God hath decreed before the ages unto our glory;" [7] — all such as these may be edified by the spiritual law itself (which has a shadow of good things to come), as if by the Spirit. For as man is said to consist of body, and soul, and spirit, so also does sacred Scripture, which has been granted by the divine bounty [8] for the salvation of man; which we see pointed out, moreover, in the little book of *The Shepherd*, which seems to be despised by some, where Hermas is commanded to write two little books, and afterwards to announce to the presbyters of the Church what he learned from the Spirit. For these are the words that are written: "And you will write," he says, "two books; and you will give the one to Clement, and the other to Grapte. [9] And let Grapte admonish the widows and orphans, and let Clement send through all the cities

had not the books which contain the secrets [1] of knowledge, and perfect mysteries. [2] For His words run thus: "Woe unto you, ye lawyers! for ye have taken away the key of knowledge: ye have not entered in yourselves, and them that were entering in ye hindered." [3]

11. The way, then, as it appears to us, in which we ought to deal with the Scriptures, and extract from them their meaning, is the following, which has been ascertained from the Scriptures themselves. By Solomon in the Proverbs we find some such rule as this enjoined respecting the divine doctrines of Scripture: [4] "And do thou portray them in a threefold manner, in counsel and knowledge, to answer words of truth to them who propose them to thee." [5] The individual ought, then, to portray the ideas of holy Scripture in a threefold manner upon his own soul; in order that the simple man may be edified by the "flesh," as it were, of the Scripture, for so we name the obvious sense; while he who has ascended a certain way (may be edified) by the "soul," as it were. The perfect man, again, and he who resembles those spoken of by the apostle, when he says, "We speak wisdom among them that are perfect, but not the wisdom of the world, nor of the rulers of this world, who come to nought; but we speak the wisdom of God in a mystery, the hidden wisdom, which God hath ordained before the ages, unto our glory," [7] (may receive edification) from the spiritual law, which has a shadow of good things to come. For as man consists of body, and soul, and spirit, so in the same way does Scripture, which has been arranged to be given by God for the salvation of men. And therefore we deduce this also from a book which is despised by some — *The Shepherd* — in respect of the command given to Hermas to write two books, and after so doing to announce to the presbyters of the Church what he had learned from the Spirit. The words are as follows: "You will write two books, and give one to Clement, and one to Grapte. And Grapte shall admonish

---

[1] ἀπόρρητα.   [2] παντελῆ μυστήρια.   [3] Luke xi. 52.

[4] The Septuagint: Καὶ σὺ δὲ ἀπόγραψαι αὐτὰ σεαυτῷ τρισσῶς, εἰς βουλὴν καὶ γνῶσιν ἐπὶ τὸ πλάτος τῆς καρδίας σου· διδάσκω οὖν σε ἀληθῆ λόγον, καὶ γνῶσιν ἀληθῆ ὑπακούειν, τοῦ ἀποκρίνεσθαι σε λόγους ἀληθείας τοῖς προβαλλομένοις σοι. The Vulgate reads: Ecce, descripsi eam tibi tripliciter, in cogitationibus et scientia, ut ostenderem tibi firmitatem et eloquia veritatis, respondere ex his illis, qui miserunt te.   [5] Cf. note 4, *ut supra*.

[6] Cf. Prov. xxii. 20, 21. The Masoretic text reads: הֲלֹא כָתַבְתִּי לְךָ שָׁלִישִׁים (*keri* שָׁלְשִׁים) בְּמוֹעֵצוֹת וָדָעַת: לְהוֹדִיעֲךָ קֹשְׁטְ אִמְרֵי אֱמֶת לְהָשִׁיב אֲמָרִים אֱמֶת לְשֹׁלְחֶיךָ.

[7] 1 Cor. ii. 6, 7.   [8] Largitione.

[9] [Hermas, vol. ii. pp. 3, 8, 12, this series. Origen seems to overrule this contempt of a minority; and, what is more strange, he appears to have accepted the fiction of the *Pauline* Hermas as authentic history. How naturally this became the impression in the East has been explained; and the *De Principiis*, it must not be forgotten, was not the product of the author's mature mind.]

which are abroad, while you will announce to the presbyters of the Church." Grapte, accordingly, who is commanded to admonish the orphans and widows, is the pure understanding of the letter itself; by which those youthful minds are admonished, who have not yet deserved to have God as their Father, and are on that account styled orphans. They, again, are the widows, who have withdrawn themselves from the unjust man, to whom they had been united contrary to law; but who have remained widows, because they have not yet advanced to the stage of being joined to a heavenly Bridegroom. Clement, moreover, is ordered to send into those cities which are abroad what is written to those individuals who already are withdrawing from the letter, — as if the meaning were to those souls who, being built up by this means, have begun to rise above the cares of the body and the desires of the flesh; while he himself, who had learned from the Holy Spirit, is commanded to announce, not by letter nor by book, but by the living voice, to the presbyters of the Church of Christ, i.e., to those who possess a mature faculty of wisdom, capable of receiving spiritual teaching.

12. This point, indeed, is not to be passed by without notice, viz., that there are certain passages of Scripture where this "body," as we termed it, i.e., this inferential historical sense,[4] is not always found, as we shall prove to be the case in the following pages, but where that which we termed "soul" or "spirit" can only be understood. And this, I think, is indicated in the Gospels, where there are said to be placed, according to the manner of purification among the Jews, six water-vessels, containing two or three firkins[5] a-piece; by which, as I have said, the language of the Gospel seems to indicate, with respect to those who are secretly called by the apostle "Jews," that they are purified by the word of Scripture, — receiving indeed sometimes two firkins, i.e., the understanding of the "soul" or "spirit," according to our statement as above; sometimes even three (firkins), when in the reading (of Scripture) the "bodily" sense, which is the "historical," may be preserved for the edification of the people. Now six water-vessels are appropriately spoken of, with regard to those persons who are purified by being placed in the world; for we read that in six days — which is the perfect number — this world and all things in it were finished. How great, then, is the utility of this first "historical" sense which we have mentioned, is attested by the multitude of all believers, who believe with adequate faith and simplicity, and does not need much argument, because it is openly manifest to all; whereas of that sense which we have called above the "soul," as it were, of Scripture, the Apostle Paul has given us numerous examples in the first Epistle to the Corinthians. For we find the expression, "Thou shalt not muzzle the

the widows and the orphans, and Clement will send to the cities abroad, while you will announce to the presbyters of the Church." Now Grapte, who admonishes the widows and the orphans, is the mere letter (of Scripture), which admonishes those who are yet children in soul, and not able to call God their Father, and who are on that account styled orphans, — admonishing, moreover, those who no longer have an unlawful bridegroom,[1] but who remain widows, because they have not yet become worthy of the (heavenly) Bridegroom; while Clement, who is already beyond the letter, is said to send what is written to the cities abroad, as if we were to call these the "souls," who are above (the influence of) bodily (affections) and degraded[2] ideas, — the disciple of the Spirit himself being enjoined to make known, no longer by letters, but by living words, to the presbyters of the whole Church of God, who have become grey[3] through wisdom.

12. But as there are certain passages of Scripture which do not at all contain the "corporeal" sense, as we shall show in the following (paragraphs), there are also places where we must seek only for the "soul," as it were, and "spirit" of Scripture. And perhaps on this account the water-vessels containing two or three firkins a-piece are said to lie for the purification of the Jews, as we read in the Gospel according to John: the expression darkly intimating, with respect to those who (are called) by the apostle "Jews" secretly, that they are purified by the word of Scripture, receiving sometimes two firkins, i.e., so to speak, the "psychical" and "spiritual" sense; and sometimes three firkins, since some have, in addition to those already mentioned, also the "corporeal" sense, which is capable of (producing) edification. And six water-vessels are reasonably (appropriate) to those who are purified in the world, which was made in six days — the perfect number. That the first "sense," then, is profitable in this respect, that it is capable of imparting edification, is testified by the multitudes of genuine and simple believers; while of that interpretation which is referred back to the "soul," there is an illustration in Paul's first Epistle to the Corinthians. The expression is, "Thou shalt not muzzle the mouth of the ox that treadeth out the corn;"[6] to which he adds, "Doth God

---

[1] παρανόμῳ νυμφίῳ.　　[2] τῶν κάτω νοημάτων.　　[3] πεπολιωμένοις.　　[4] Consequentia historialis intelligentiæ.　　[5] Metretes.
[6] Cf. 1 Cor. ix. 9 and Deut. xxv. 4.

mouth of the ox that treadeth out the corn."[1] And afterwards, when explaining what precept ought to be understood by this, he adds the words : "Doth God take care for oxen? or saith He it altogether for our sakes? For our sakes, no doubt, this is written ; that he who plougheth should plough in hope, and he that thresheth, in hope of partaking."[2] Very many other passages also of this nature, which are in this way explained of the law, contribute extensive information to the hearers.

13. Now a "spiritual" interpretation is of this nature : when one is able to point out what are the heavenly things of which these serve as the patterns and shadow, who are Jews "according to the flesh," and of what things future the law contains a shadow, and any other expressions of this kind that may be found in holy Scripture ; or when it is a subject of inquiry, what is that wisdom hidden in a mystery which "God ordained before the world for our glory, which none of the princes of this world knew ;"[3] or the meaning of the apostle's language, when, employing certain illustrations from Exodus or Numbers, he says : "These things happened to them in a figure,[5] and they are written on our account, on whom the ends of the ages have come."[6] Now, an opportunity is afforded us of understanding of what those things which happened to them were figures, when he adds : "And they drank of that spiritual Rock which followed them, and that Rock was Christ."[7] In another Epistle also, when referring to the tabernacle, he mentions the direction which was given to Moses : "Thou shalt make (all things) according to the pattern which was showed thee in the mount."[8] And writing to the Galatians, and upbraiding certain individuals who seem to themselves to read the law, and yet without understanding it, because of their ignorance of the fact that an allegorical meaning underlies what is written, he says to them in a certain tone of rebuke : "Tell me, ye who desire to be under the law, do ye not hear the law? For it is written that Abraham had two sons ; the one by a bond-maid, the other by a free woman. But he who was of the bond-woman was born according to the flesh ; but he of the free woman was by promise. Which things are an allegory : for these are the two covenants."[9] And here this point is to be attended to, viz., the caution with which the apostle employs the expression, "Ye who are under the law, do ye not hear the law?" Do ye not *hear*, i.e., do ye not understand and know? In the Epistle to the Colossians, again, briefly summing up and condensing the meaning of the whole law, he says : "Let no man therefore judge you in meat, or in drink, or in respect of holy days, or of the new moon, or of the Sabbath, which are a shadow of things to come."[11] Writing to the Hebrews

take care of oxen? or saith He it altogether for our sakes? For our sakes, no doubt, this was written : that he that plougheth should plough in hope, and that he who thresheth, in hope of partaking."[2] And there are numerous interpretations adapted to the multitude which are in circulation, and which edify those who are unable to understand profounder meanings, and which have somewhat the same character.

13. But the interpretation is "spiritual," when one is able to show of what heavenly things the Jews "according to the flesh" served as an example and a shadow, and of what future blessings the law contains a shadow. And, generally, we must investigate, according to the apostolic promise, "the wisdom in a mystery, the hidden wisdom which God ordained before the world for the glory" of the just, which "none of the princes of this world knew."[4] And the same apostle says somewhere, after referring to certain events mentioned as occurring in Exodus and Numbers, "that these things happened to them figuratively, but that they were written on our account, on whom the ends of the world are come."[6] And he gives an opportunity for ascertaining of what things these were patterns, when he says : "For they drank of the spiritual Rock that followed them, and that Rock was Christ."[7] And in another Epistle, when sketching the various matters relating to the tabernacle, he used the words : "Thou shalt make everything according to the pattern showed thee in the mount."[8] Moreover, in the Epistle to the Galatians, as if upbraiding those who think that they read the law, and yet do not understand it, judging that those do not understand it who do not reflect that allegories are contained under what is written, he says : "Tell me, ye that desire to be under the law, do ye not hear the law? For it is written, Abraham had two sons ; the one by the bond-maid, the other by the free woman. But he who was by the bond-maid was born according to the flesh ; but he of the free woman was by promise. Which things are an allegory :[10] for these are the two covenants," and so on. Now we must carefully observe each word employed by him. He says : "Ye who desire to be under the law," not "Ye that are under the law ;" and, "Do ye not

---

[1] Cf. 1 Cor. ix. 9 and Deut. xxv. 4. [2] Cf. 1 Cor. ix. 9, 10. [3] Cf. 1 Cor. ii. 7. [4] Cf. 1 Cor. ii. 6, 7, 8. [5] In figurâ. Greek (*text. recept.*) τύποι. Lachmann reads τυπικῶς. [6] 1 Cor. x. 11. [7] 1 Cor. x. 4. [8] Cf. Ex. xxv. 40 and Heb. viii. 5. [9] Gal. iv. 21-24. [10] ἀλληγορούμενα. [11] Col. ii. 16.

also, and treating of those who belong to the circumcision, he says : " Those who serve to the example and shadow of heavenly things." [1] Now perhaps, through these illustrations, no doubt will be entertained regarding the five books of Moses, by those who hold the writings of the apostle, as divinely inspired. And if they require, with respect to the rest of the history, that those events which are contained in it should be considered as having happened for an ensample to those of whom they are written, we have observed that this also has been stated in the Epistle to the Romans, where the apostle adduces an instance from the third book of Kings, saying, " I have left me seven thousand men who have not bowed the knee to Baal ; " [3] which expression Paul understood as figuratively spoken of those who are called Israelites according to the election, in order to show that the advent of Christ had not only now been of advantage to the Gentiles, but that very many even of the race of Israel had been called to salvation.

14. This being the state of the case, we shall sketch out, as if by way of illustration and pattern, what may occur to us with regard to the manner in which holy Scripture is to be understood on these several points, repeating in the first instance, and pointing out this fact, that the Holy Spirit, by the providence and will of God, through the power of His only-begotten Word, who was in the beginning God with God, enlightened the ministers of truth, the prophets and apostles, to understand the mysteries of those things or causes which take place among men, or with respect to men.[6] And by " men," I now mean souls that are placed in bodies, who, relating those mysteries that are known to them, and revealed through Christ, as if they were a kind of human transactions, or handing down certain legal observances and injunctions, described them figuratively ; [7] not that any one who pleased might view these expositions as deserving to be trampled under foot, but that he who should devote himself with all chastity, and sobriety, and watchfulness, to studies of this kind, might be able by this means to trace out the meaning of the Spirit of God, which is perhaps lying profoundly buried, and the context, which may be pointing again in another direction than the ordinary usage of speech would indicate.

hear the law ?" — " hearing " being understood to mean " comprehending " and " knowing." And in the Epistle to the Colossians, briefly abridging the meaning of the whole legislation, he says : " Let no man therefore judge you in meat, or in drink, or in respect of a festival, or of a new moon, or of Sabbaths, which are a shadow of things to come." [2] Moreover, in the Epistle to the Hebrews, discoursing of those who belong to the circumcision, he writes : " who serve for an ensample and shadow of heavenly things." [1] Now it is probable that, from these illustrations, those will entertain no doubt with respect to the five books of Moses, who have once given in their adhesion to the apostle, as divinely inspired ; [4] but do you wish to know, with regard to the rest of the history, if it also happened as a pattern ? We must note, then, the expression in the Epistle to the Romans, " I have left to myself seven thousand men, who have not bowed the knee to Baal," [3] quoted from the third book of Kings, which Paul has understood as equivalent (in meaning) to those who are Israelites according to election, because not only were the Gentiles benefited by the advent of Christ, but also certain of the race of God.[5]

14. This being the state of the case, we have to sketch what seem to us to be the marks of the (true) understanding of Scriptures. And, in the first place, this must be pointed out, that the object of the Spirit, which by the providence of God, through the Word who was in the beginning with God, illuminated the ministers of truth, the prophets and apostles, was especially (the communication) of ineffable mysteries regarding the affairs of men (now by men I mean those souls that make use of bodies), in order that he who is capable of instruction may by investigation, and by devoting himself to the study of the profundities of meaning contained in the words, become a participator of all the doctrines of his counsel. And among those matters which relate to souls (who cannot otherwise obtain perfection apart from the rich and wise truth of God), the (doctrines) belonging to God and His only-begotten Son are necessarily laid down as primary, viz., of what nature He is, and in what manner He is the Son of God, and what are the causes of His

---

[1] Heb. viii. 5.   [2] Col. ii. 16.   [3] Rom. xi. 4; cf. 1 Kings xix. 18.   [3 Kings according to the Septuagint and Vulgate enumeration. S.]
[4] ὡς θεῖον ἄνδρα.   [5] τινὰς ἀπὸ τοῦ θείου γένους, i.e., Israelites.   [6] Quæ inter homines, vel de hominibus geruntur.   [7] Figuraliter describebant.

And in this way he might become a sharer in the knowledge of the Spirit, and a partaker in the divine counsel, because the soul cannot come to the perfection of knowledge otherwise than by inspiration of the truth of the divine wisdom. Accordingly, it is of God, i.e. of the Father, and of the Son, and of the Holy Spirit, that these men, filled with the Divine Spirit, chiefly treat; then the mysteries relating to the Son of God — how the Word became flesh, and why He descended even to the assumption of the form of a servant — are the subject, as I have said, of explanation by those persons who are filled with the Divine Spirit. It next followed, necessarily, that they should instruct mortals by divine teaching, regarding rational creatures, both those of heaven and the happier ones of earth; and also (should explain) the differences among souls, and the origin of these differences; and then should tell what this world is, and why it was created; whence also sprung the great and terrible wickedness which extends over the earth. And whether that wickedness is found on this earth only, or in other places, is a point which it was necessary for us to learn from divine teaching. Since, then, it was the intention of the Holy Spirit to enlighten with respect to these and similar subjects, those holy souls who had devoted themselves to the service of the truth, this object was kept in view, in the second place, viz., for the sake of those who either could not or would not give themselves to this labour and toil by which they might deserve to be instructed in or to recognise things of such value and importance, to wrap up and conceal, as we said before, in ordinary language, under the covering of some history and narrative of visible things, hidden mysteries. There is therefore introduced the narrative of the visible creation, and the creation and formation of the first man; then the offspring which followed from him in succession, and some of the actions which were done by the good among his posterity, are related, and occasionally certain crimes also, which are stated to have been committed by them as being human; and afterwards certain unchaste or wicked deeds also are narrated as being the acts of the wicked. The description of battles, moreover, is given in a wonderful manner, and the alternations of victors and vanquished, by which certain ineffable mysteries are made known to those who know how to investigate statements of that kind. By an admirable discipline of wisdom, too, the law of truth, even of the prophets, is implanted in the Scriptures of the law, each of which is woven by a divine art of wisdom, as a kind of covering and veil of spiritual truths; and this is what we have called the "body" of Scripture, so that also, in this way, what we have called the covering of the letter, woven by the art of wisdom, might be capable of edifying and profiting many, when others would derive no benefit.

descending even to (the assumption of) human flesh, and of complete humanity; and what, also, is the operation of this (Son), and upon whom and when exercised. And it was necessary also that the subject of kindred beings, and other rational creatures, both those who are divine and those who have fallen from blessedness, together with the reasons of their fall, should be contained in the divine teaching; and also that of the diversities of souls, and of the origin of these diversities, and of the nature of the world, and the cause of its existence. We must learn also the origin of the great and terrible wickedness which overspreads the earth, and whether it is confined to this earth only, or prevails elsewhere. Now, while these and similar objects were present to the Spirit, who enlightened the souls of the holy ministers of the truth, there was a second object, for the sake of those who were unable to endure the fatigue of investigating matters so important, viz., to conceal the doctrine relating to the previously mentioned subjects, in expressions containing a narrative which conveyed an announcement regarding the things of the visible creation,[1] the creation of man, and the successive descendants of the first men until they became numerous; and other histories relating the acts of just men, and the sins occasionally committed by these same men as being human beings, and the wicked deeds, both of unchastity and vice, committed by sinful and ungodly men. And what is most remarkable, by the history of wars, and of the victors, and the vanquished, certain mysteries are indicated to those who are able to test these statements. And more wonderful still, the laws of truth are predicted by the written legislation; — all these being described in a connected series, with a power which is truly in keeping with the wisdom of God. For it was intended that the covering also of the spiritual truths — I mean the "bodily" part of Scripture — should not be without profit in many cases, but should be capable of improving the multitude, according to their capacity.

---

[1] περὶ τῶν αἰσθητῶν δημιουργημάτων.

FROM THE LATIN.

15. But as if, in all the instances of this covering (i.e., of this history), the logical connection and order of the law had been preserved, we would not certainly believe, when thus possessing the meaning of Scripture in a continuous series, that anything else was contained in it save what was indicated on the surface ; so for that reason divine wisdom took care that certain stumbling-blocks, or interruptions,[3] to the historical meaning should take place, by the introduction into the midst (of the narrative) of certain impossibilities and incongruities ; that in this way the very interruption of the narrative might, as by the interposition of a bolt, present an obstacle to the reader, whereby he might refuse to acknowledge the way which conducts to the ordinary meaning ; and being thus excluded and debarred from it, we might be recalled to the beginning of another way, in order that, by entering upon a narrow path, and passing to a loftier and more sublime road, he might lay open the immense breadth of divine wisdom.[5] This, however, must not be unnoted by us, that as the chief object of the Holy Spirit is to preserve the coherence of the spiritual meaning, either in those things which ought to be done or which have been already performed, if He anywhere finds that those events which, according to the history, took place, can be adapted to a spiritual meaning, He composed a texture of both kinds in one style of narration, always concealing the hidden meaning more deeply ; but where the historical narrative could not be made appropriate to the spiritual coherence of the occurrences, He inserted sometimes certain things which either did not take place or could not take place ; sometimes also what might happen, but what did not : and He does this at one time in a few words, which, taken in their "bodily" meaning, seem incapable of containing truth, and at another by the insertion of many. And this we find frequently to be the case in the legislative portions, where there are many things manifestly useful among the "bodily" precepts, but a very great number also in which no principle of utility is at all discernible, and sometimes even things which are judged to be impossibilities. Now all this, as we have remarked, was done by the Holy Spirit in order that, seeing those events which lie on the surface can be neither true nor useful, we may be led to the investigation of that truth which is more deeply concealed, and to the ascertaining of a meaning worthy of God in those Scriptures which we believe to be inspired by Him.

16. Nor was it only with regard to those Scriptures which were composed down to the advent of Christ that the Holy Spirit thus dealt ; but as being one and the same Spirit, and proceeding from one God, He dealt in the same way with the evangelists and apostles. For even those narratives which He in-

FROM THE GREEK.

15. But since, if the usefulness of the legislation, and the sequence and beauty of the history, were universally evident of itself,[2] we should not believe that any other thing could be understood in the Scriptures save what was obvious, the word of God has arranged that certain stumbling-blocks, as it were, and offences, and impossibilities, should be introduced into the midst of the law and the history, in order that we may not, through being drawn away in all directions by the merely attractive nature of the language,[4] either altogether fall away from the (true) doctrines, as learning nothing worthy of God, or, by not departing from the letter, come to the knowledge of nothing more divine. And this also we must know, that the principal aim being to announce the "spiritual" connection in those things that are done, and that ought to be done, where the Word found that things done according to the history could be adapted to these mystical senses, He made use of them, concealing from the multitude the deeper meaning ; but where, in the narrative of the development of super-sensual things,[6] there did not follow the performance of those certain events, which was already indicated by the mystical meaning, the Scripture interwove in the history (the account of) some event that did not take place, sometimes what could not have happened ; sometimes what could, but did not. And sometimes a few words are interpolated which are not true in their literal acceptation,[7] and sometimes a larger number. And a similar practice also is to be noticed with regard to the legislation, in which is often to be found what is useful in itself, and appropriate to the times of the legislation ; and sometimes also what does not appear to be of utility ; and at other times impossibilities are recorded for the sake of the more skilful and inquisitive, in order that they may give themselves to the toil of investigating what is written, and thus attain to a becoming conviction of the manner in which a meaning worthy of God must be sought out in such subjects.

16. It was not only, however, with the (Scriptures composed) before the advent (of Christ) that the Spirit thus dealt ; but as being the same Spirit, and (proceeding) from the one God, He did the same thing both with the evangelists and the apostles,

---

[1] γλαφυρόν.   [2] αὐτόθεν.   [3] Intercapedines.   [4] ὑπὸ τῆς λέξεως ἑλκόμενοι τὸ ἀγωγὸν ἄκρατον ἐχούσης.
[5] Ut ita celsioris cujusdam et eminentioris tramitis per angusti callis ingressum immensam divinæ scientiæ latitudinem pandat.
[6] ἐν τῇ διηγήσει τῆς περὶ τῶν νοητῶν ἀκολουθίας.   [7] κατὰ τὸ σῶμα.

spired them to write were not composed without the aid of that wisdom of His, the nature of which we have above explained. Whence also in· them were intermingled not a few things by which, the historical order of the narrative being interrupted and broken up, the attention of the reader might be recalled, by the impossibility of the case, to an examination of the inner meaning. But, that our meaning may be ascertained by the facts themselves, let us examine the passages of Scripture. Now who is there, pray, possessed of understanding, that will regard the statement as appropriate,[2] that the first day, and the second, and the third, in which also both evening and morning are mentioned, existed without sun, and moon, and stars — the first day even without a sky? And who is found so ignorant as to suppose that God, as if He had been a husbandman, planted trees in paradise, in Eden towards the east, and a tree of life in it, i.e., a visible and palpable tree of wood,[3] so that any one eating of it with bodily teeth should obtain life, and, eating again of another tree, should come to the knowledge of good and evil? No one, I think, can doubt that the statement that God walked in the afternoon in paradise, and that Adam lay hid under a tree, is related figuratively in Scripture, that some mystical meaning may be indicated by it. The departure of Cain from the presence of the Lord will manifestly cause a careful reader to inquire what is the presence of God, and how any one can go out from it. But not to extend the task which we have before us beyond its due limits, it is very easy for any one who pleases to gather out of holy Scripture what is recorded indeed as having been done, but what nevertheless cannot be believed as having reasonably and appropriately occurred according to the historical account. The same style of Scriptural narrative occurs abundantly in the Gospels, as when the devil is said to have placed Jesus on a lofty mountain, that he might show Him from thence all the kingdoms of the world, and the glory of them. How could it literally come to pass, either that Jesus should be led up by the devil into a high mountain, or that the latter should show him all the kingdoms of the world (as if they were lying beneath his bodily eyes, and adjacent to one mountain), i.e., the kingdoms of the Persians, and Scythians, and Indians? or how could he show in what manner the kings of these kingdoms are glorified by men? And many other instances similar to this will be found in the Gospels by any one who will read them with attention, and will observe that in those narratives which appear to be literally recorded, there are inserted and interwoven things which cannot be admitted historically, but which may be accepted in a spiritual signification.[6]

— as even these do not contain throughout a pure history of events, which are interwoven indeed according to the letter, but which did not actually occur.[1] Nor even do the law and the commandments wholly convey what is agreeable to reason. For who that has understanding will suppose that the first, and second, and third day, and the evening and the morning, existed without a sun, and moon, and stars? and that the first day was, as it were, also without a sky? And who is so foolish as to suppose that God, after the manner of a husbandman, planted a paradise in Eden, towards the east, and placed in it a tree of life, visible and palpable, so that one tasting of the fruit by the bodily teeth obtained life? and again, that one was a partaker of good and evil by masticating what was taken from the tree? And if God is said to walk in the paradise in the evening, and Adam to hide himself under a tree, I do not suppose that any one doubts that these things figuratively indicate certain mysteries, the history having taken place in appearance, and not literally.[4] Cain also, when going forth from the presence of God, certainly appears to thoughtful men as likely to lead the reader to inquire what is the presence of God, and what is the meaning of going out from Him. And what need is there to say more, since those who are not altogether blind can collect countless instances of a similar kind recorded as having occurred, but which did not literally[5] take place? Nay, the Gospels themselves are filled with the same kind of narratives; e.g., the devil leading Jesus up into a high mountain, in order to show him from thence the kingdoms of the whole world, and the glory of them. For who is there among those who do not read such accounts carelessly, that would not condemn those who think that with the eye of the body — which requires a lofty height in order that the parts lying (immediately) under and adjacent may be seen — the kingdoms of the Persians, and Scythians, and Indians, and Parthians, were beheld, and the manner in which their princes are glorified among men? And the attentive reader may notice in the Gospels innumerable other passages like these, so that he will be convinced that in the histories that are literally re-

---

[1] Οὐδὲ τούτων πάντῃ ἄκρατον τὴν ἱστορίαν τῶν προσυφασμένων κατὰ τὸ σωματικὸν ἐχόντων, μὴ γεγενημένων· οὐδὲ τὴν νομοθεσίαν καὶ τὰς ἐντολὰς πάντως τὸ εὔλογον ἐμφαίνοντα. One MS. reads γεγενημένην, referring to ἱστορίαν, on which one editor remarks, "Hic <t in sequentibus imploro fidem codicum!"
[2] Consequenter, alii "convenienter." [3] Lignum. [4] διὰ δοκούσης ἱστορίας καὶ οὐ σωματικῶς γεγενημένης. [5] κατὰ τὴν λέξιν.
[6] [See note, p. 262, *supra*. See also Dr. Lee, *The Inspiration of Holy Scripture*, pp. 523-527. S.]

17. In the passages containing the commandments also, similar things are found. For in the law Moses is commanded to destroy every male that is not circumcised on the eighth day, which is exceedingly incongruous,[2] since it would be necessary, if it were related that the law was executed according to the history, to command those parents to be punished who did not circumcise their children, and also those who were the nurses of little children. The declaration of Scripture now is, "The uncircumcised male, i.e., who shall not have been circumcised, shall be cut off from his people."[3] And if we are to inquire regarding the impossibilities of the law, we find an animal called the goat-stag,[4] which cannot possibly exist, but which, as being in the number of clean beasts, Moses commands to be eaten ; and a griffin,[5] which no one ever remembers or heard of as yielding to human power, but which the legislator forbids to be used for food. Respecting the celebrated[6] observance of the Sabbath also he thus speaks : "Ye shall sit, every one in your dwellings ; no one shall move from his place on the Sabbath-day."[8] Which precept it is impossible to observe literally ; for no man can sit a whole day so as not to move from the place where he sat down. With respect to each one of these points now, those who belong to the circumcision, and all who would have no more meaning to be found in sacred Scripture than what is indicated by the letter, consider that there should be no investigation regarding the goat-stag, and the griffin, and the vulture ; and they invent some empty and trifling tales about the Sabbath, drawn from some traditional sources or other, alleging that every one's place is computed to him within two thousand cubits."[10] Others, again, among whom is Dositheus the Samaritan, censure indeed expositions of this kind, but themselves lay down something more ridiculous, viz., that each one must remain until the evening in the posture, place, or position in which he found himself on the Sabbath-day ; i.e., if found sitting, he is to sit the whole day, or if reclining, he is to recline the whole day. Moreover, the injunction which runs, "Bear no burden on the Sabbath-day,"[12] seems to me an impossibility. For the Jewish doctors, in consequence of these (prescriptions), have betaken themselves, as the holy apostle says, to innumerable fables, saying that it is not accounted a burden if a man wear shoes without nails, but that it is a burden if shoes with nails be worn ; and that if it be carried on one shoulder, they consider it a burden ; but if on both, they declare it to be none.

corded, circumstances that did not occur are inserted.

17. And if we come to the legislation of Moses, many of the laws manifest the irrationality, and others the impossibility, of their literal[1] observance. The irrationality (in this), that the people are forbidden to eat vultures, although no one even in the direst famines was (ever) driven by want to have recourse to this bird ; and that children eight days old, which are uncircumcised, are ordered to be exterminated from among their people, it being necessary, if the law were to be carried out at all literally with regard to these, that their fathers, or those with whom they are brought up, should be commanded to be put to death. Now the Scripture says : "Every male that is uncircumcised, who shall not be circumcised on the eighth day, shall be cut off from among his people."[7] And if you wish to see impossibilities contained in the legislation, let us observe that the goat-stag is one of those animals that cannot exist, and yet Moses commands us to offer it as being a clean beast ; whereas a griffin, which is not recorded ever to have been subdued by man, the lawgiver forbids to be eaten. Nay, he who carefully considers (the famous injunction relating to) the Sabbath, "Ye shall sit each one in your dwellings : let no one go out from his place on the seventh day,"[9] will deem it impossible to be literally observed : for no living being is able to sit throughout a whole day, and remain without moving from a sitting position. And therefore those who belong to the circumcision, and all who desire that no meaning should be exhibited, save the literal one, do not investigate at all such subjects as those of the goat-stag and griffin and vulture, but indulge in foolish talk on certain points, multiplying words and adducing tasteless[11] traditions ; as, for example, with regard to the Sabbath, saying that two thousand cubits is each one's limit.[13] Others, again, among whom is Dositheus the Samaritan, condemning such an interpretation, think that in the position in which a man is found on the Sabbath-day, he is to remain until evening. Moreover, the not carrying of a burden on the Sabbath-day is an impossibility ; and therefore the Jewish teach-

---

[1] ὅσον ἐπὶ τῷ καθ' ἑαυτοὺς τηρεῖσθαι.   [2] Inconsequens.   [3] Cf. Gen. xvii. 14.
[4] Tragelaphus: "wild goat," Auth. Vers. Deut. xiv. 5; Heb. אַקֹּו, ἅπαξ λεγ.
[5] Gryphus: "ossifrage," Auth. Vers. Lev. xi. 13; Heb. פֶּרֶס.   [6] Opinatissimâ.   [7] Gen. xvii. 14.   [8] Cf. Ex. xvi. 29.
[9] Ex. xvi. 29.   [10] Ulnas.   [11] ψυχρὰς παραδόσεις.   [12] Jer. xvii. 21.   [13] τόπον ἑκάστῳ εἶναι δισχιλίους πήχεις.

FROM THE LATIN.

FROM THE GREEK.

ers have fallen into countless absurdities,[1] saying that a shoe of such a kind was a burden, but not one of another kind; and that a sandal which had nails was a burden, but not one that was without them; and in like manner what was borne on one shoulder (was a load), but not that which was carried on both.

18. And now, if we institute a similar examination with regard to the Gospels, how shall it appear otherwise than absurd to take the injunction literally, "Salute no man by the way?"[2] And yet there are simple individuals, who think that our Saviour gave this command to His apostles! How, also, can it appear possible for such an order as this to be observed, especially in those countries where there is a rigorous winter, attended by frost and ice, viz., that one should possess "neither two coats, nor shoes?"[2] And this, that when one is smitten on the right cheek, he is ordered to present the left also, since every one who strikes with the *right* hand smites the *left* cheek? This precept also in the Gospels must be accounted among impossibilities, viz., that if the right eye "offend" thee, it is to be plucked out; for even if we were to suppose that bodily eyes were spoken of, how shall it appear appropriate, that when both eyes have the property of sight, the responsibility of the "offence" should be transferred to one eye, and that the right one? Or who shall be considered free of a crime of the greatest enormity, that lays hands upon himself? But perhaps the Epistles of the Apostle Paul will appear to be beyond this. For what is his meaning, when he says, "Is any man called, being circumcised? Let him not become uncircumcised."[4] This expression indeed, in the first place, does not on careful consideration seem to be spoken with reference to the subject of which he was treating at the time, for this discourse consisted of injunctions relating to marriage and to chastity; and these words, therefore, will have the appearance of an unnecessary addition to such a subject. In the second place, however, what objection would there be, if, for the sake of avoiding that unseemliness which is caused by circumcision, a man were able to become uncircumcised?[6] And, in the third place, that is altogether impossible.

The object of all these statements on our part, is to show that it was the design of the Holy Spirit, who deigned to bestow upon us the sacred Scriptures, to show that we were not to be edified by the letter alone, or by everything in it, — a thing which we see to be frequently impossible and inconsistent; for in that way not only absurdities, but impossibilities, would be the result; but that we are to understand that certain occurrences were interwoven in this "visible" history, which, when considered and un-

18. And if we go to the Gospel and institute a similar examination, what would be more irrational than (to take literally the injunction), "Salute no man by the way,"[2] which simple persons think the Saviour enjoined on the apostles? The command, moreover, that the right cheek should be smitten, is most incredible, since every one who strikes, unless he happen to have some bodily defect,[3] smites the *left* cheek with his *right* hand. And it is impossible to take (literally, the statement) in the Gospel about the "offending" of the right eye. For, to grant the possibility of one being "offended" by the sense of sight, how, when there are two eyes that see, should the blame be laid upon the right eye? And who is there that, condemning himself for having looked upon a woman to lust after her, would rationally transfer the blame to the right eye alone, and throw *it* away? The apostle, moreover, lays down the law, saying, "Is any man called, being circumcised? Let him not become uncircumcised."[4] In the first place, any one will see that he does not utter these words in connection with the subject before him. For, when laying down precepts on marriage and purity, how will it not appear that he has introduced these words at random?[5] But, in the second place, who will say that a man does wrong who endeavours to become uncircumcised, if that be possible, on account of the disgrace that is considered by the multitude to attach to circumcision.

All these statements have been made by us, in order to show that the design of that divine power which gave us the sacred Scriptures is, that we should not receive what is presented by the letter alone (such things being sometimes not true in their literal acceptation, but absurd and impossible), but that certain things have been introduced into the actual history and into the legislation that are useful in their literal sense.[7]

---

1 Εἰς ἀπεραντολογίαν ἐληλύθασι.　　2 Luke x. 4.　　3 εἰ μὴ ἄρα πεπονθώς τι παρὰ φύσιν‾ τυγχάνοι.　　4 1 Cor. vii. 18.　　5 εἰκῇ.
6 Secundo vero, quid obesset, si obscœnitatis vitandæ causa ejus, quæ ex circumcisione est, posset aliquis revocare præputium?
7 καὶ τῇ κατὰ τὸ ῥητὸν χρησίμων νομοθεσίᾳ.

derstood in their inner meaning, give forth a law which is advantageous to men and worthy of God.

19. Let no one, however, entertain the suspicion that we do not believe any history in Scripture to be real, because we suspect certain events related in it not to have taken place; or that no precepts of the law are to be taken literally, because we consider certain of them, in which either the nature or possibility of the case so requires, incapable of being observed; or that we do not believe those predictions which were written of the Saviour to have been fulfilled in a manner palpable to the senses; or that His commandments are not to be literally obeyed. We have therefore to state in answer, since we are manifestly so of opinion, that the truth of the history may and ought to be preserved in the majority of instances. For who can deny that Abraham was buried in the double cave [3] at Hebron, as well as Isaac and Jacob, and each of their wives? Or who doubts that Shechem was given as a portion to Joseph? [4] or that Jerusalem is the metropolis of Judea, on which the temple of God was built by Solomon?—and countless other statements. For the passages which hold good in their historical acceptation are much more numerous than those which contain a purely spiritual meaning. Then, again, who would not maintain that the command to "honour thy father and thy mother, that it may be well with thee," [5] is sufficient of itself without any spiritual meaning, and necessary for those who observe it? especially when Paul also has confirmed the command by repeating it in the same words. And what need is there to speak of the prohibitions, "Thou shalt not commit adultery," "Thou shalt not steal," "Thou shalt not bear false witness," [7] and others of the same kind? And with respect to the precepts enjoined in the Gospels, no doubt can be entertained that very many of these are to be literally observed, as e.g., when our Lord says, "But I say unto you, Swear not at all;" [8] and when He says, "Whosoever looketh upon a woman to lust after her, hath committed adultery with her already in his heart;" [9] the admonitions also which are found in the writings of the Apostle Paul, "Warn them that are unruly, comfort the feeble-minded, support the weak, be patient towards all men," [12] and very many others. And yet I have no doubt that an attentive reader will, in numerous instances, hesitate whether this or that history can be considered to be literally true or not; or whether this or that precept ought to be observed according to the letter or no. And therefore great pains and labour are to be employed, until every reader reverentially understand that he is dealing with divine and not human words inserted in the sacred books.

19. But that no one may suppose that we assert respecting the whole that no history is real [1] because a certain one is not; and that no law is to be literally observed, because a certain one, (understood) according to the letter, is absurd or impossible; or that the statements regarding the Saviour are not true in a manner perceptible to the senses; [2] or that no commandment and precept of His ought to be obeyed;—we have to answer that, with regard to certain things, it is perfectly clear to us that the historical account is true; as that Abraham was buried in the double cave at Hebron, as also Isaac and Jacob, and the wives of each of them; and that Shechem was given as a portion to Joseph; [4] and that Jerusalem is the metropolis of Judea, in which the temple of God was built by Solomon; and innumerable other statements. For the passages that are true in their historical meaning are much more numerous than those which are interspersed with a purely spiritual signification. And again, who would not say that the command which enjoins to "honour thy father and thy mother, that it may be well with thee," [5] is useful, apart from all allegorical meaning, [6] and ought to be observed, the Apostle Paul also having employed these very same words? And what need is there to speak of the (prohibitions), "Thou shalt not commit adultery," "Thou shalt not kill," "Thou shalt not steal," "Thou shalt not bear false witness?" [7] And again, there are commandments contained in the Gospel which admit of no doubt whether they are to be observed according to the letter or not; e.g., that which says, "But I say unto you, Whoever is angry with his brother," [10] and so on. And again, "But I say unto you, Swear not at all." [11] And in the writings of the apostle the literal sense is to be retained: "Warn them that are unruly, comfort the feeble-minded, support the weak, be patient towards all men;" [12] although it is possible for those ambitious of a deeper meaning to retain the profundities of the wisdom of God, without setting aside the commandment in its literal meaning. [13] The careful (reader), however, will be in doubt [14] as to certain points, being unable to show without

[1] γέγονεν.   [2] κατὰ τὸ αἰσθητόν.   [3] Duplici spelunca.   [4] Cf. Gen. xlviii. 22 and Josh. xxiv. 32.   [5] Cf. Ex. xx. 12 and Eph. vi. 2, 3.   [6] χωρὶς πάσης ἀναγωγῆς.   [7] Cf. Ex. xx. 13–16.   [8] Cf. Matt. v. 34.   [9] Matt. v. 28.   [10] [Matt. v. 22.]   [11] Matt. v. 34.   [12] 1 Thess. v. 14.   [13] Εἰ καὶ παρὰ τοῖς φιλοτιμοτέροις δύναται σώζειν ἕκαστον αὐτῶν, μετὰ τοῦ μὴ ἀθετεῖσθαι τὴν κατὰ τὸ ῥητὸν ἐντολὴν, βάθη Θεοῦ σοφίας.   [14] περιελκυσθήσεται.

long investigation whether this history so deemed literally occurred or not, and whether the literal meaning of this law is to be observed or not. And therefore the exact reader must, in obedience to the Saviour's injunction to "search the Scriptures," [1] carefully ascertain in how far the literal meaning is true, and in how far impossible; and so far as he can, trace out, by means of similar statements, the meaning everywhere scattered through Scripture of that which cannot be understood in a literal signification.

20. The understanding, therefore, of holy Scripture which we consider ought to be deservedly and consistently maintained, is of the following kind. A certain nation is declared by holy Scripture to have been chosen by God upon the earth, which nation has received several names: for sometimes the whole of it is termed Israel, and sometimes Jacob; and it was divided by Jeroboam son of Nebat into two portions; and the ten tribes which were formed under him were called Israel, while the two remaining ones (with which were united the tribe of Levi, and that which was descended from the royal race of David) was named Judah. Now the whole of the country possessed by that nation, which it had received from God, was called Judea, in which was situated the metropolis, Jerusalem; and it is called metropolis, being as it were the mother of many cities, the names of which you will frequently find mentioned here and there in the other books of Scripture, but which are collected together into one catalogue in the book of Joshua the son of Nun.[4]

20. Since, therefore, as will be clear to those who read, the connection taken literally is impossible, while the sense preferred [2] is not impossible, but even the true one, it must be our object to grasp the whole meaning, which connects the account of what is literally impossible in an intelligible manner with what is not only not impossible, but also historically true, and which is allegorically understood, in respect of its not having literally occurred.[3] For, with respect to holy Scripture, our opinion is that the whole of it has a "spiritual," but not the whole a "bodily" meaning, because the bodily meaning is in many places proved to be impossible. And therefore great attention must be bestowed by the cautious reader on the divine books, as being divine writings; the manner of understanding which appears to us to be as follows:—The Scriptures relate that God chose a certain nation upon the earth, which they call by several names. For the whole of this nation is termed Israel, and also Jacob. And when it was divided in the times of Jeroboam the son of Nebat, the ten tribes related as being subject to him were called Israel; and the remaining two, along with the tribe of Levi, being ruled over by the descendants of David, were named Judah. And the whole of the territory which the people of this nation inhabited, being given them by God, receives the name of Judah, the metropolis of which is Jerusalem,—a metropolis, namely, of numerous cities, the names of which lie scattered about in many other passages (of Scripture), but are enumerated together in the book of Joshua the son of Nun.[5]

21. This, then, being the state of the case, the holy apostle desiring to elevate in some degree, and

21. Such, then, being the state of the case, the apostle, elevating our power of

---

[1] John v. 39.　　[2] ὁ προηγούμενος.
[3] Ὅλον τὸν νοῦν φιλοτιμητέον καταλαμβάνειν, συνείροντα τὸν περὶ τῶν κατὰ τὴν λέξιν ἀδυνάτων λόγον νοητῶς τοῖς οὐ μόνον οὐκ ἀδυνάτοις, ἀλλὰ καὶ ἀληθέσι κατὰ τὴν ἱστορίαν, συναλληγορουμένοις τοῖς ὅσον ἐπὶ τῇ λέξει, μὴ γεγενημένοις.
[4] In libro Jesu Naue.　　[5] ἐν Ἰησοῦ τῷ τοῦ Ναυῆ.

to raise our understanding above the earth, says in a certain place, "Behold Israel after the flesh;" [1] by which he certainly means that there is another Israel which is not according to the flesh, but according to the Spirit. And again in another passage, "For they are not all Israelites who are of Israel." [2]

discernment (above the letter), says somewhere, "Behold Israel after the flesh," [1] as if there were an Israel "according to the Spirit." And in another place he says, "For they who are the children of the flesh are not the children of God;" nor are "they all Israel who are of Israel;" [3] nor is "he a Jew who is one outwardly, nor is that 'circumcision' which is outward in the flesh: but he is a Jew who is one 'inwardly;' and circumcision is that of the heart, in the spirit, and not in the letter." [4] For if the judgment respecting the "Jew inwardly" be adopted, we must understand that, as there is a "bodily" race of Jews, so also is there a race of "Jews inwardly," the soul having acquired this nobility for certain mysterious reasons. Moreover, there are many prophecies which predict regarding Israel and Judah what is about to befall them. And do not such promises as are written concerning them, in respect of their being mean in expression, and manifesting no elevation (of thought), nor anything worthy of the promise of God, need a mystical interpretation? And if the "spiritual" promises are announced by visible signs, then they to whom the promises are made are not "corporeal." And not to linger over the point of the Jew who is a Jew "inwardly," nor over that of the Israelite according to the "inner man" — these statements being sufficient for those who are not devoid of understanding — we return to our subject, and say that Jacob is the father of the twelve patriarchs, and they of the rulers of the people; and these, again, of the other Israelites. Do not, then, the "corporeal" Israelites refer their descent to the rulers of the people, and the rulers of the people to the patriarchs, and the patriarchs to Jacob, and those still higher up; while are not the "spiritual" Israelites, of whom the "corporeal" Israelites were the type, sprung from the families, and the families from the tribes, and the tribes from some one individual whose descent is not of a "corporeal" but of a better kind, — he, too, being born of Isaac, and he of Abraham, — all going back to Adam, whom the apostle declares to be Christ? For every beginning of those families which have relation to God as to the Father of all, took its commencement lower down with Christ, who is next to the God and Father of all,[5] being thus the Father of every soul, as

---

[1] 1 Cor. x. 18.　　[2] Rom. ix. 6.　　[3] Rom. ix. 6, 8.　　[4] Rom. ii. 28, 29.

[5] Πᾶσα γὰρ ἀρχὴ πατριῶν τῶν ὡς πρὸς τὸν τῶν ὅλων Θεόν, κατωτέρω ἀπὸ τοῦ Χριστοῦ ἤρξατο τοῦ μετὰ τὸν τῶν ὅλων Θεὸν καὶ πατέρα.

Adam is the father of all men. And if Eve also is intended by the apostle to refer to the Church, it is not surprising that Cain, who was born of Eve, and all after him, whose descent goes back to Eve, should be types of the Church, inasmuch as in a pre-eminent sense they are all descended from the Church.

22. Being taught, then, by him that there is one Israel according to the flesh, and another according to the Spirit, when the Saviour says, " I am not sent but to the lost sheep of the house of Israel," [1] we do not understand these words as those do who savour of earthly things, i.e., the Ebionites, who derive the appellation of " poor " from their very name (for " Ebion " means " poor " in Hebrew [2]) ; but we understand that there exists a race of souls which is termed " Israel," as is indicated by the interpretation of the name itself : for Israel is interpreted to mean a " mind," or " man seeing God." The apostle, again, makes a similar revelation respecting Jerusalem, saying, " The Jerusalem which is above is free, which is the mother of us all." [4] And in another of his Epistles he says : " But ye are come unto mount Zion, and to the city of the living God, and to the heavenly Jerusalem, and to an innumerable company of angels, and to the Church of the first-born which is written in heaven." [5] If, then, there are certain souls in this world who are called Israel, and a city in heaven which is called Jerusalem, it follows that those cities which are said to belong to the nation of Israel have the heavenly Jerusalem as their metropolis ; and that, agreeably to this, we understand as referring to the whole of Judah (of which also we are of opinion that the prophets have spoken in certain mystical narratives), any predictions delivered either regarding Judea or Jerusalem, or invasions of any kind, which the sacred histories declare to have happened to Judea or Jerusalem. Whatever, then, is either narrated or predicted of Jerusalem, must, if we accept the words of Paul as those of Christ speaking in him, be understood as spoken in conformity with his opinion regarding that city which he calls the heavenly Jerusalem, and all those places or cities which are said to be cities of the holy land, of which Jerusalem is the metropolis. For we are to suppose that it is from these very cities that the Saviour, wishing to raise us to a higher grade of intelligence, promises to those who have well managed the money entrusted to them by Himself, that they are to have power over ten or five cities. If, then, the prophecies delivered concerning Judea, and Jerusalem, and Judah, and Israel, and Jacob, not being understood by us in a carnal sense, signify certain divine mysteries, it certainly follows that those prophecies also which were delivered either concerning Egypt or the Egyptians,

22. Now, if the statements made to us regarding Israel, and its tribes and its families, are calculated to impress us, when the Saviour says, " I was not sent but to the lost sheep of the house of Israel," [1] we do not understand the expression as the Ebionites do, who are poor in understanding (deriving their name from the poverty of their intellect — " Ebion " signifying " poor " in Hebrew), so as to suppose that the Saviour came specially to the " carnal " Israelites ; for " they who are the children of the flesh are not the children of God." [3] Again, the apostle teaches regarding Jerusalem as follows : " The Jerusalem which is above is free, which is the mother of us all." [4] And in another Epistle : " But ye are come unto mount Zion, and to the city of the living God, to the heavenly Jerusalem, and to an innumerable company of angels, to the general assembly and to the Church of the first-born which are written in heaven." [6] If, then, Israel is among the race of souls, [7] and if there is in heaven a city of Jerusalem, it follows that the cities of Israel have for their metropolis the heavenly Jerusalem, and it consequently is the metropolis of all Judea. Whatever, therefore, is predicted of Jerusalem, and spoken of it, if we listen to the words of Paul as those of God, and of one who utters wisdom, we must understand the Scriptures as speaking of the heavenly city, and of the whole territory included within the cities of the holy land. For perhaps it is to these cities that the Saviour refers us, when to those who have gained credit by having managed their " pounds " well, He assigns the presidency over five or ten cities. If, therefore, the prophecies relating to Judea, and Jerusalem, and Israel, and Judah, and Jacob, not being understood by us in a " carnal " sense, indicate some such mysteries (as already mentioned), it will follow also that the predictions concerning Egypt and the Egyptians, Babylon and the Babylonians, Tyre and the Tyrians, Sidon and the Si-

---

[1] Matt. xv. 24. [2] Ebion, Heb. אֶבְיוֹן, (from אָבָה, to desire), lit. " wishing," " desiring ; " secondarily, " poor."

[3] Rom. ix. 8. [See Dr. Burton's *Inquiry into the Heresies of the Apostolic Age* (Bampton Lectures), pp. 184, 185, 498, 499. S.]

[4] Gal. iv. 26.   [5] Cf. Heb. xii. 22, 23.   [6] Heb. xii. 22, 23.   [7] ἐν ψυχῶν γένει.

or Babylonia and the Babylonians, and Sidon and the Sidonians, are not to be understood as spoken of that Egypt which is situated on the earth, or of the earthly Babylon, Tyre, or Sidon. Nor can those predictions which the prophet Ezekiel delivered concerning Pharaoh king of Egypt, apply to any man who may seem to have reigned over Egypt, as the nature of the passage itself declares. In a similar manner also, what is spoken of the prince of Tyre cannot be understood of any man or king of Tyre. And how could we possibly accept, as spoken of a man, what is related in many passages of Scripture, and especially in Isaiah, regarding Nebuchadnezzar? For he is not a man who is said to have "fallen from heaven," or who was "Lucifer," or who "arose in the morning." But with respect to those predictions which are found in Ezekiel concerning Egypt, such as that it is to be destroyed in forty years, so that the foot of man should not be found within it, and that it should suffer such devastation, that throughout the whole land the blood of men should rise to the knees, I do not know that any one possessed of understanding could refer this to that earthly Egypt which adjoins Ethiopia. But let us see whether it may not be understood more fittingly in the following manner: viz., that as there is a heavenly Jerusalem and Judea, and a nation undoubtedly which inhabits it, and is named Israel; so also it is possible that there are certain localities near to these which may seem to be called either Egypt, or Babylon, or Tyre, or Sidon, and that the princes of these places, and the souls, if there be any, that inhabit them, are called Egyptians, Babylonians, Tyrians, and Sidonians. From whom also, according to the mode of life which they lead there, a sort of captivity would seem to result, in consequence of which they are said to have fallen from Judea into Babylonia or Egypt, from a higher and better condition, or to have been scattered into other countries.

23. For perhaps as those who, departing this world in virtue of that death which is common to all, are arranged, in conformity with their actions and deserts — according as they shall be deemed worthy — some in the place which is called "hell,"[1] others in the bosom of Abraham, and in different localities or mansions; so also from those places, as if dying there, if the expression can be used,[3] do they come down from the "upper world"[4] to this "hell." For that "hell" to which the souls of the dead are conducted from this world, is, I believe, on account of this distinction, called the "lower hell" by Scripture, as is said in the book of Psalms: "Thou hast delivered my soul from the lowest hell."[6] Every one, accordingly, of those who descend to the earth is, according to his deserts, or agreeably to the position which he occupied there, ordained to be born in this world, in a different country, or among a different

donians, or the other nations, are spoken not only of these "bodily" Egyptians, and Babylonians, and Tyrians, and Sidonians, but also of their "spiritual" (counterparts) For if there be "spiritual" Israelites, it follows that there are also "spiritual" Egyptians and Babylonians. For what is related in Ezekiel concerning Pharaoh king of Egypt does not at all apply to the case of a certain man who ruled or was said to rule over Egypt, as will be evident to those who give it careful consideration. Similarly what is said about the ruler of Tyre cannot be understood of a certain man who ruled over Tyre. And what is said in many places, and especially in Isaiah, of Nebuchadnezzar, cannot be explained of that individual. For the man Nebuchadnezzar neither fell from heaven, nor was he the morning star, nor did he arise upon the earth in the morning. Nor would any man of understanding interpret what is said in Ezekiel about Egypt — viz., that in forty years it should be laid desolate, so that the footstep of man should not be found thereon, and that the ravages of war should be so great that the blood should run throughout the whole of it, and rise to the knees — of that Egypt which is situated beside the Ethiopians whose bodies are blackened by the sun.

23. And perhaps as those here, dying according to the death common to all, are, in consequence of the deeds done here, so arranged as to obtain different places according to the proportion of their sins, if they should be deemed worthy of the place called Hades;[2] so those there dying, so to speak, descend into this Hades, being judged deserving of different abodes — better or worse — throughout all this space of earth, and (of being descended) from parents of different kinds,[5] so that an Israelite may sometimes fall among Scythians, and an Egyptian descend into Judea. And yet the Saviour came to gather together the lost sheep of the house of Israel; but many of the Israelites not having yielded to His teaching

---

[1] Infernus.   [2] τοῦ καλουμένου χωρίου ᾅδου.   [3] Velut illic, si dici potest, morientes.   [4] A superis.
[5] καὶ παρὰ τοισδε, ἢ τοῖσδε τοῖς πατράσι.   [6] Cf. Ps. xxx. 3 and Deut. xxxii. 22.

nation, or in a different mode of life, or surrounded by infirmities of a different kind, or to be descended from religious parents, or parents who are not religious; so that it may sometimes happen that an Israelite descends among the Scythians, and a poor Egyptian is brought down to Judea. And yet our Saviour came to gather together the lost sheep of the house of Israel; and as many of the Israelites did not accept His teaching, those who belonged to the Gentiles were called. From which it will appear to follow, that those prophecies which are delivered to the individual nations ought to be referred rather to the souls, and to their different heavenly mansions. Nay, the narratives of the events which are said to have happened either to the nation of Israel, or to Jerusalem, or to Judea, when assailed by this or that nation, cannot in many instances be understood as having actually [3] occurred, and are much more appropriate to those nations of souls who inhabit that heaven which is said to pass away, or who even now are supposed to be inhabitants of it.

If now any one demand of us clear and distinct declarations on these points out of holy Scripture, we must answer that it was the design of the Holy Spirit, in those portions which appear to relate the history of events, rather to cover and conceal the meaning: in those passages, e.g., where they are said to go down into Egypt, or to be carried captive to Babylonia, or when in these very countries some are said to be brought to excessive humiliation, and to be placed under bondage to their masters; while others, again, in these very countries of their captivity, were held in honour and esteem, so as to occupy positions of rank and power, and were appointed to the government of provinces;—all which things, as we have said, are kept hidden and covered in the narratives of holy Scripture, because "the kingdom of heaven is like a treasure hid in a field; which when a man findeth, he hideth it, and for joy thereof goeth away and selleth all that he hath, and buyeth that field." [1] By which similitude, consider whether it be not pointed out that the very soil and surface, so to speak, of Scripture — that is, the literal meaning — is the field, filled with plants and flowers of all kinds; while that deeper and profounder "spiritual" meaning are the very hidden treasures of wisdom and knowledge which the Holy Spirit by Isaiah calls the dark and invisible and hidden treasures, for the finding out of which the divine help is required: for God alone can burst the brazen gates by which they are enclosed and concealed, and break in pieces the iron bolts and levers by which access is prevented to all those things which are written and concealed in Genesis respecting the different kinds of souls, and of those seeds and generations which either have a close connection with Israel [5] or are widely separated from his descendants; as well as what is that descent

those from the Gentiles were called. . . . And these points, as we suppose, have been concealed in the histories. For "the kingdom of heaven is like a treasure hid in a field; the which when a man hath found, he hideth, and for joy thereof goeth and selleth all that he hath, and buyeth that field." [1] Let us notice, then, whether the apparent and superficial and obvious meaning of Scripture does not resemble a field filled with plants of every kind, while the things lying in it, and not visible to all, but buried, as it were, under the plants that are seen, are the hidden treasures of wisdom and knowledge; which the Spirit through Isaiah [2] calls dark and invisible and concealed, God alone being able to break the brazen gates that conceal them, and to burst the iron bars that are upon the gates, in order that all the statements in the book of Genesis may be discovered which refer to the various genuine kinds, and seeds, as it were, of souls, which stand nearly related to Israel, or at a distance from it; and the descent into Egypt of the seventy souls, that they may there become as the "stars of heaven in multitude." But since not all who are of them are the light of the world — "for not all who are of Israel are Israel" [4] — they become from seventy souls as the "sand that is beside the sea-shore innumerable."

---

[1] Matt. xiii. 44. [2] Cf. Isa. xlv. 3. [3] Corporaliter. [4] Rom. ix. 6. [5] Ad propinquitatem pertinent Israel.

FROM THE LATIN.

of seventy souls into Egypt, which seventy souls became in that land as the stars of heaven in multitude.
But as not all of them were the light of this world —
"for all who are of Israel are not Israel" [1] — they
grow from being seventy souls to be an important
people,[2] and as the "sand by the sea-shore innumerable."

---

[1] Rom. ix. 6.　　　　　　　[2] Ex ipsis Septuaginta animabus fiunt aliqui.

FROM THE LATIN.

24. This descent of the holy fathers into
Egypt will appear as granted to this world by
the providence of God for the illumination of
others, and for the instruction of the human
race, that so by this means the souls of others
might be assisted in the work of enlightenment.
For to them was first granted the privilege of
converse with God, because theirs is the only
race which is said to see God ; this being the
meaning, by interpretation, of the word " Israel." [1] And now it follows that, agreeably to
this view, ought the statement to be accepted
and explained that Egypt was scourged with ten
plagues, to allow the people of God to depart,
or the account of what was done with the people
in the wilderness, or of the building of the tabernacle by means of contributions from all the
people, or of the wearing of the priestly robes,
or of the vessels of the public service, because,
as it is written, they truly contain within them
the "shadow and form of heavenly things."
For Paul openly says of them, that "they serve
unto the example and shadow of heavenly
things." [2] There are, moreover, contained in
this same law the precepts and institutions, according to which men are to live in the holy
land. Threatenings also are held out as impending over those who shall transgress the law ;
different kinds of purifications are moreover prescribed for those who required purification, as
being persons who were liable to frequent pollution, that by means of these they may arrive
at last at that one purification after which no
further pollution is permitted. The very people
are numbered, though not all ; for the souls of
children are not yet old enough to be numbered
according to the divine command : nor are those
souls who cannot become the head of another,
but are themselves subordinated to others as to
a head, who are called "women," who certainly
are not included in that numbering which is enjoined by God ; but they alone are numbered
who are called "men," by which it might be
shown that the women could not be counted
separately,[3] but were included in those called
men. Those, however, especially belong to the
sacred number, who are prepared to go forth to
the battles of the Israelites, and are able to fight
against those public and private enemies [4] whom
the Father subjects to the Son, who sits on His
right hand that He may destroy all principality
and power, and by means of these bands of His
soldiery, who, being engaged in a warfare for
God, do not entangle themselves in secular business, He may overturn the Kingdom of His
adversary ; by whom the shields of faith are
borne, and the weapons of wisdom brandished ;
among whom also the helmet of hope and salvation gleams forth, and the breastplate of
brightness fortifies the breast that is filled with
God. Such soldiers appear to me to be indicated, and to be prepared for wars of this kind,
in those persons who in the sacred books are
ordered by God's command to be numbered.
But of these, by far the more perfect and distinguished are shown to be those of whom the
very hairs of the head are said to be numbered.
Such, indeed, as were punished for their sins,
whose bodies fell in the wilderness, appear to
possess a resemblance to those who had made
indeed no little progress, but who could not at
all, for various reasons, attain to the end of perfection ; because they are reported either to
have murmured, or to have worshipped idols, or
to have committed fornication, or to have done
some evil work which the mind ought not ever
to conceive. I do not consider the following
even to be without some mystical meaning,[5] viz.
that certain (of the Israelites), possessing many
flocks and animals, take possession by anticipation of a country adapted for pasture and the
feeding of cattle, which was the very first that
the right hand of the Hebrews had secured in

---

[1] Cf. Gen. xxxii. 28-30.
[2] Heb. viii. 5.

[3] Extrinsecus.
[4] Hostes inimicosque.
[5] Ne illud quidem sacramento aliquo vacuum puto.

war.[1] For, making a request of Moses to receive this region, they are divided off by the waters of the Jordan, and set apart from any possession in the holy land. And this Jordan, according to the form of heavenly things, may appear to water and irrigate thirsty souls, and the senses that are adjacent to it.[2] In connection with which, even this statement does not appear superfluous, that Moses indeed hears from God what is described in the book of Leviticus, while in Deuteronomy it is the people that are the auditors of Moses, and who learn from him what they could not hear from God. For as Deuteronomy is called, as it were, the second law, which to some will appear to convey this signification, that when the first law which was given through Moses had come to an end, so a second legislation seems to have been enacted, which was specially transmitted by Moses to his successor Joshua, who is certainly believed to embody a type[3] of our Saviour, by whose second law — that is, the precepts of the Gospel — all things are brought to perfection.

25. We have to see, however, whether this deeper meaning may not perhaps be indicated, viz., that as in Deuteronomy the legislation is made known with greater clearness and distinctness than in those books which were first written, so also by that advent of the Saviour which He accomplished in His state of humiliation, when He assumed the form of a servant, that more celebrated and renowned second advent in the glory of His Father may not be pointed out, and in it the types of Deuteronomy may be fulfilled, when in the kingdom of heaven all the saints shall live according to the laws of the everlasting Gospel; and as in His coming now He fulfilled that law which has a shadow of good things to come, so also by that (future) glorious advent will be fulfilled and brought to perfection the shadows of the present advent. For thus spake the prophet regarding it: "The breath of our countenance, Christ the Lord, to whom we said, that under Thy shadow we shall live among the nations;"[4] at the time, viz., when He will more worthily transfer all the saints from a temporal to an everlasting Gospel, according to the designation, employed by John in the Apocalypse, of "an everlasting Gospel."[5]

26. But let it be sufficient for us in all these matters to adapt our understanding to the rule of religion, and so to think of the words of the Holy Spirit as not to deem the language the ornate composition of feeble human eloquence, but to hold, according to the scriptural statement, that "all the glory of the King is within,"[6] and that the treasure of divine meaning is enclosed within the frail vessel of the common letter. And if any curious reader were still to ask an explanation of individual points, let him come and hear, along with ourselves, how the Apostle Paul, seeking to penetrate by help of the Holy Spirit, who searches even the "deep things" of God, into the depths of divine wisdom and knowledge, and yet, unable to reach the end, so to speak, and to come to a thorough knowledge, exclaims in despair and amazement, "Oh the depth of the riches of the knowledge and wisdom of God!"[7] Now, that it was from despair of attaining a perfect understanding that he uttered this exclamation, listen to his own words: "How unsearchable are God's judgments! and His ways, how past finding out!"[7] For he did not say that God's judgments were difficult to discover, but that they were altogether inscrutable; nor that it was (simply) difficult to trace out His ways, but that they were altogether past finding out. For however far a man may advance in his investigations, and how great soever the progress that he may make by unremitting study, assisted even by the grace of God, and with his mind enlightened, he will not be able to attain to the end of those things which are the object of his inquiries. Nor can any created mind deem it possible in any way to attain a full comprehension (of things); but after having discovered certain of the objects of its research, it sees again others which have still to be sought out. And even if it should succeed in mastering these, it will see again many others succeeding them which must form the subject of investigation. And on this account, therefore, Solomon, the wisest of men, beholding by his wisdom the nature of things, says, "I said, I will become wise; and wisdom herself was made far from me, far further than it was; and a profound depth, who shall find?"[8] Isaiah also, knowing that the beginnings of things could not be discovered by a mortal nature, and not even by those natures which, although more divine than human, were nevertheless themselves created or formed; knowing then, that by none of these could either the beginning or the end be discovered, says, "Tell the former things which have been, and we know that ye are gods; or announce what are the last things, and then we shall see that ye are gods."[9] For my Hebrew teacher also used thus to teach, that as the beginning or end of all things could be

---

[1] Quem primum omnium Israelitici belli dextra defenderat.
[2] Rigare et inundare animas sitientes, et sensus adjacentes sibi.
[3] Formam.
[4] Lam. iv. 20.
[5] Cf. Rev. xiv. 6.

[6] Omnis gloria regis intrinsecus est. Heb., Sept., and Vulgate all read, "daughter of the king." Probably the omission of "filiæ" in the text may be due to an error of the copyists. [Cf. Ps. xlv. 13.]
[7] Rom. xi. 33.
[8] [Eccles. vii. 23, 24.] The Septuagint reads: Εἶπα, Σοφισθήσομαι· καὶ αὕτη ἐμακρύνθη ἀπ' ἐμοῦ, μακρὰν ὑπὲρ ὃ ἦν, καὶ βαθὺ βάθος, τίς εὑρήσει αὐτό; the Vulgate translates this literally.
[9] Cf. Isa. xli. 22, 23.

comprehended by no one, save only our Lord Jesus Christ and the Holy Spirit, so under the form of a vision Isaiah spake of two seraphim alone, who with two wings cover the countenance of God, and with two His feet, and with two do fly, calling to each other alternately, and saying, "Holy, holy, holy is the LORD God of Sabaoth; the whole earth is full of Thy glory."[1] That the seraphim alone have both their wings over the face of God, and over His feet, we venture to declare as meaning that neither the hosts of holy angels, nor the "holy seats," nor the "dominions," nor the "principalities," nor the "powers," can fully understand the beginning of all things, and the limits of the universe. But we are to understand that those "saints" whom the Spirit has enrolled, and the "virtues," approach very closely to those very beginnings, and attain to a height which the others cannot reach; and yet whatever it be that these "virtues" have learned through revelation from the Son of God and from the Holy Spirit — and they will certainly be able to learn very much, and those of higher rank much more than those of a lower — nevertheless it is impossible for them to comprehend all things, according to the statement, "The most part of the works of God are hid."[2] And therefore also it is to be desired that every one, according to his strength, should ever stretch out to those things that are before, "forgetting the things that are behind," both to better works and to a clearer apprehension and understanding, through Jesus Christ our Saviour, to whom be glory for ever!

27. Let every one, then, who cares for truth, be little concerned about words and language, seeing that in every nation there prevails a different usage of speech; but let him rather direct his attention to the meaning conveyed by the words, than to the nature of the words that convey the meaning, especially in matters of such importance and difficulty: as, e.g., when it is an object of investigation whether there is any "substance" in which neither colour, nor form, nor touch, nor magnitude is to be understood as existing visible to the mind alone, which any one names as he pleases; for the Greeks call such ἀσώματον, i.e., "incorporeal," while holy Scripture declares it to be "invisible," for Paul calls Christ the "image of the invisible God," and says again, that by Christ were created all things "visible and invisible." And by this it is declared that there are, among created things, certain "substances" that are, according to their peculiar nature, invisible. But although these are not themselves "corporeal," they nevertheless make use of bodies, while they are themselves better than any bodily substances. But that "substance" of the Trinity which is th[e] beginning and cause of all things, "from whic[h] are all things, and through which are all thing[s] and in which are all things," cannot be believe[d] to be either a body or in a body, but is altogethe[r] incorporeal. And now let it suffice to hav[e] spoken briefly on these points (although in [a] digression, caused by the nature of the subject) in order to show that there are certain thing[s] the meaning of which cannot be unfolded at a[ll] by any words of human language, but which ar[e] made known more through simple apprehensio[n] than by any properties of words. And unde[r] this rule must be brought also the understandin[g] of the sacred Scripture, in order that its state ments may be judged not according to the worth lessness of the letter, but according to the divinit[y] of the Holy Spirit, by whose inspiration the[y] were caused to be written.

SUMMARY (OF DOCTRINE) REGARDING THE FATHER THE SON, AND THE HOLY SPIRIT, AND THE OTHE[R] TOPICS DISCUSSED IN THE PRECEDING PAGES.

28. It is now time, after the rapid considera tion which to the best of our ability we hav[e] given to the topics discussed, to recapitulate, b[y] way of summing up what we have said in di[f] ferent places, the individual points, and first o[f] all to restate our conclusions regarding th[e] Father, and the Son, and the Holy Spirit.

Seeing God the Father is invisible and in separable from the Son, the Son is not generate[d] from Him by "prolation," as some suppose For if the Son be a "prolation" of the Fathe[r] (the term "prolation" being used to signify suc[h] a generation as that of animals or men usuall[y] is), then, of necessity, both He who "prolated" and He who *was* "prolated" are corporeal. Fo[r] we do not say, as the heretics suppose, that som[e] part of the substance of God was converted int[o] the Son, or that the Son was procreated by th[e] Father out of things non-existent,[3] i.e., beyon[d] His own substance, so that there once was [a] time when He did not exist; but, putting awa[y] all corporeal conceptions, we say that the Wor[d] and Wisdom was begotten out of the invisibl[e] and incorporeal without any corporeal feeling, a[s] if it were an act of the will proceeding fro[m] the understanding. Nor, seeing He is called th[e] Son of (His) love, will it appear absurd if in thi[s] way He be called the Son of (His) will. Na[y] John also indicates that "God is Light,"[4] an[d] Paul also declares that the Son is the splendou[r] of everlasting light.[5] As light, accordingly, coul[d] never exist without splendour, so neither can th[e]

---

[1] Isa. vi. 3.
[2] Cf. Ecclus. xvi. 21.

[3] Ex nullis substantibus.
[4] 1 John i. 5.
[5] Cf. Heb. i. 3.

Son be understood to exist without the Father; for He is called the "express image of His person,"[1] and the Word and Wisdom. How, then, can it be asserted that there once was a time when He was not the Son? For that is nothing else than to say that there was once a time when He was not the Truth, nor the Wisdom, nor the Life, although in all these He is judged to be the perfect essence of God the Father; for these things cannot be severed from Him, or even be separated from His essence. And although these qualities are said to be many in understanding,[2] yet in their nature and essence they are one, and in them is the fulness of divinity. Now this expression which we employ — "that there never was a time when He did not exist" — is to be understood with an allowance. For these very words "when" or "never" have a meaning that relates to time, whereas the statements made regarding Father, Son, and Holy Spirit are to be understood as transcending all time, all ages, and all eternity. For it is the Trinity alone which exceeds the comprehension not only of temporal but even of eternal intelligence; while other things which are not included in it[3] are to be measured by times and ages. This Son of God, then, in respect of the Word being God, which was in the beginning with God, no one will logically suppose to be contained in any place; nor yet in respect of His being "Wisdom," or "Truth," or the "Life," or "Righteousness," or "Sanctification," or "Redemption:" for all these properties do not require space to be able to act or to operate, but each one of them is to be understood as meaning those individuals who participate in His virtue and working.

29. Now, if any one were to say that, through those who are partakers of the "Word" of God, or of His "Wisdom," or His "Truth," or His "Life," the Word and Wisdom itself appeared to be contained in a place, we should have to say to him in answer, that there is no doubt that Christ, in respect of being the "Word" or "Wisdom," or all other things, was in Paul, and that he therefore said, "Do you seek a proof of Christ speaking in me?"[4] and again, "I live, yet not I, but Christ liveth in me."[5] Seeing, then, He was in Paul, who will doubt that He was in a similar manner in Peter and in John, and in each one of the saints; and not only in those who are upon the earth, but in those also who are in heaven? For it is absurd to say that Christ was in Peter and in Paul, but not in Michael the archangel, nor in Gabriel. And from this it is distinctly shown that the divinity of the Son of God was not shut up in some place; otherwise it would have been in it only, and not in another. But since, in conformity with the majesty of its incorporeal nature, it is confined to no place; so, again, it cannot be understood to be wanting in any. But this is understood to be the sole difference, that although He is in different individuals as we have said — as Peter, or Paul, or Michael, or Gabriel — He is not in a similar way in all beings whatever. For He is more fully and clearly, and, so to speak, more openly in archangels than in other holy men.[6] And this is evident from the statement, that when all who are saints have arrived at the summit of perfection, they are said to be made like, or equal to, the angels, agreeably to the declaration in the Gospels.[7] Whence it is clear that Christ is in each individual in as great a degree as the amount of his deserts allows.[8]

30. Having, then, briefly restated these points regarding the nature of the Trinity, it follows that we notice shortly this statement also, that "by the Son" are said to be created "all things that are in heaven, and that are in earth, visible and invisible, whether they be thrones, or dominions, or principalities, or powers: all things were created by Him, and for Him; and He is before all, and all things consist by Him, who is the Head."[9] In conformity with which John also in his Gospel says: "All things were created by Him; and without Him was not anything made."[10] And David, intimating that the mystery of the entire Trinity was (concerned) in the creation of all things, says: "By the Word of the LORD were the heavens made; and all the host of them by the Spirit of His mouth."[11]

After these points we shall appropriately remind (the reader) of the bodily advent and incarnation of the only-begotten Son of God, with respect to whom we are not to suppose that all the majesty of His divinity is confined within the limits of His slender body, so that all the "word" of God, and His "wisdom," and "essential truth," and "life," was either rent asunder from the Father, or restrained and confined within the narrowness of His bodily person, and is not to be considered to have operated anywhere besides; but the cautious acknowledgment of a religious man ought to be between the two, so that it ought neither to be believed that anything of divinity was wanting in Christ, nor that any separation at all was made from the essence of the Father, which is everywhere. For some such meaning seems to be indicated

---

[1] Cf. Heb. i. 3.
[2] Quæ quidem quamvis intellectu multa esse dicantur.
[3] Quæ sunt extra Trinitatem.
[4] Cf. 2 Cor. xiii. 3.
[5] Gal. ii. 20.

[6] Quam in aliis sanctis viris. "Aliis" is found in the MSS., but is wanting in many editions.
[7] Cf. Matt. xxii. 30 and Luke xx. 36.
[8] Unde constat in singulis quibusque tantum effici Christum, quantum ratio indulserit meritorum.
[9] Cf. Col. i. 16-18.
[10] John i. 3.
[11] Ps. xxxiii. 6.

by John the Baptist, when he said to the multitude in the bodily absence of Jesus, "There standeth one among you whom ye know not: He it is who cometh after me, the latchet of whose shoes I am not worthy to unloose."[1] For it certainly could not be said of Him, who was absent, so far as His bodily presence is concerned, that He was standing in the midst of those among whom the Son of God was not bodily present.

31. Let no one, however, suppose that by this we affirm that some portion of the divinity of the Son of God was in Christ, and that the remaining portion was elsewhere or everywhere, which may be the opinion of those who are ignorant of the nature of an incorporeal and invisible essence. For it is impossible to speak of the parts of an incorporeal being, or to make any division of them; but He is in all things, and through all things, and above all things, in the manner in which we have spoken above, i.e., in the manner in which He is understood to be either "wisdom," or the "word," or the "life," or the "truth," by which method of understanding all confinement of a local kind is undoubtedly excluded. The Son of God, then, desiring for the salvation of the human race to appear unto men, and to sojourn among them, assumed not only a human body, as some suppose, but also a soul resembling our souls indeed in nature, but in will and power[2] resembling Himself, and such as might unfailingly accomplish all the desires and arrangements of the "word" and "wisdom." Now, that He had a soul,[3] is most clearly shown by the Saviour in the Gospels, when He said, "No man taketh my life from me, but I lay it down of myself. I have power to lay down my life, and I have power to take it again."[4] And again, "My soul is sorrowful even unto death."[5] And again, "Now is my soul troubled."[6] For the "Word" of God is not to be understood to be a "sorrowful and troubled" soul, because with the authority of divinity He says, "I have power to lay down my life." Nor yet do we assert that the Son of God was in that soul as he was in the soul of Paul or Peter and the other saints, in whom Christ is believed to speak as He does in Paul. But regarding all these we are to hold, as Scripture declares, "No one is clean from filthiness, not even if his life lasted but a single day."[7] But this soul which was in Jesus, before it knew the evil, selected the good; and because He loved righteousness, and hated iniquity, therefore God

"anointed Him with the oil of gladness above His fellows."[8] He is anointed, then, with the oil of gladness when He is united to the "word" of God in a stainless union, and by this means alone of all souls was incapable of sin, because it was capable of (receiving) well and fully the Son of God; and therefore also it is one with Him, and is named by His titles, and is called Jesus Christ, by whom all things are said to be made. Of which soul, seeing it had received into itself the whole wisdom of God, and the truth, and the life, I think that the apostle also said this: "Our life is hidden with Christ in God; but when Christ, who is our life, shall appear, then shall we also appear with him in glory."[9] For what other Christ can be here understood, who is said to be hidden in God, and who is afterwards to appear, except Him who is related to have been anointed with the oil of gladness, i.e., to have been filled with God essentially,[10] in whom he is now said to be hidden? For on this account is Christ proposed as an example to all believers, because as He always, even before he knew evil at all, selected the good, and loved righteousness, and hated iniquity, and therefore God anointed Him with the oil of gladness; so also ought each one, after a lapse or sin, to cleanse himself from his stains, making Him his example, and, taking Him as the guide of his journey, enter upon the steep way of virtue, that so perchance by this means, as far as possible we may, by imitating Him, be made partakers of the divine nature, according to the words of Scripture: "He that saith that he believeth in Christ, ought so to walk, as He also walked."[11]

This "word," then, and this "wisdom," by the imitation of which we are said to be either wise or rational (beings), becomes "all things to all men, that it may gain all;" and because it is made weak, it is therefore said of it, "Though He was crucified through weakness, yet He liveth by the power of God."[12] Finally, to the Corinthians who were weak, Paul declares that he "knew nothing, save Jesus Christ, and Him crucified."[13]

32. Some, indeed, would have the following language of the apostle applied to the soul itself, as soon as it had assumed flesh from Mary,[14] viz., "Who, being in the form of God, thought it not robbery to be equal with God, but divested Himself (of His glory),[15] taking upon Himself the form of a servant;"[16] since He undoubtedly re-

1 Cf. John i. 26, 27.
2 Proposito vero et virtute similem sibi.
3 Animam.
4 John x. 18.
5 Matt. xxvi. 38.
6 John xii. 27.
7 Cf. Job xv. 14.

8 Ps. xlv. 7.
9 Cf. Col. iii. 3, 4.
10 Substantialiter.
11 Cf. 1 John ii. 6.
12 2 Cor. xiii. 4.
13 1 Cor. ii. 2.
14 De Maria corpus assumsit.
15 Semet ipsum exinanivit.
16 Phil. ii. 6, 7.

stored it to the form of God by means of better examples and training, and recalled it to that fulness of which He had divested Himself.

As now by participation in the Son of God one is adopted as a son,[1] and by participating in that wisdom which is in God is rendered wise, so also by participation in the Holy Spirit is a man rendered holy and spiritual. For it is one and the same thing to have a share in the Holy Spirit, which is (the Spirit) of the Father and the Son, since the nature of the Trinity is one and incorporeal. And what we have said regarding the participation of the soul is to be understood of angels and heavenly powers in a similar way as of souls, because every rational creature needs a participation in the Trinity.

Respecting also the plan of this visible world — seeing one of the most important questions usually raised is as to the manner of its existence — we have spoken to the best of our ability in the preceding pages, for the sake of those who are accustomed to seek the grounds of their belief in our religion, and also for those who stir against us heretical questions, and who are accustomed to bandy about[2] the word " matter," which they have not yet been able to understand ; of which subject I now deem it necessary briefly to remind (the reader).

33. And, in the first place, it is to be noted that we have nowhere found in the canonical Scriptures,[3] up to the present time, the word " matter " used for that substance which is said to underlie bodies. For in the expression of Isaiah, " And he shall devour ὕλη," i.e., matter, " like hay," [4] when speaking of those who were appointed to undergo their punishments, the word " matter " was used instead of " sins." And if this word " matter " should happen to occur in any other passage, it will never be found, in my opinion, to have the signification of which we are now in quest, unless perhaps in the book which is called the Wisdom of Solomon, a work which is certainly not esteemed authoritative by all.[5] In that book, however, we find written as follows : " For thy almighty hand, that made the world out of shapeless matter, wanted not means to send among them a multitude of bears and fierce lions." [6] Very many, indeed, are of opinion that the matter of which things are made is itself signified in the language used by Moses in the beginning of Genesis : " In the beginning God made heaven and earth ; and the earth was invisible, and not arranged : "[7] for by

the words " invisible and not arranged " Moses would seem to mean nothing else than shapeless matter. But if this be truly matter, it is clear then that the original elements of bodies[8] are not incapable of change. For those who posited " atoms " — either those particles which are incapable of subdivision, or those which are subdivided into equal parts — or any one element, as the principles of bodily things, could not posit the word " matter " in the proper sense of the term among the first principles of things. For if they will have it that matter underlies every body — a substance convertible or changeable, or divisible in all its parts — they will not, as is proper, assert that it exists without qualities. And with them we agree, for we altogether deny that matter ought to be spoken of as " unbegotten " or " uncreated," agreeably to our former statements, when we pointed out that from water, and earth, and air or heat, different kinds of fruits were produced by different kinds of trees ; or when we showed that fire, and air, and water, and earth were alternately converted into each other, and that one element was resolved into another by a kind of mutual consanguinity ; and also when we proved that from the food either of men or animals the substance of the flesh was derived, or that the moisture of the natural seed was converted into solid flesh and bones ; — all which go to prove that the substance of the body is changeable, and may pass from one quality into all others.

34. Nevertheless we must not forget that a substance never exists without a quality, and that it is by an act of the understanding alone that this (substance) which underlies bodies, and which is capable of quality, is discovered to be matter. Some indeed, in their desire to investigate these subjects more profoundly, have ventured to assert that bodily nature[9] is nothing else than qualities. For if hardness and softness, heat and cold, moisture and aridity, be qualities ; and if, when these or other (qualities) of this sort be cut away, nothing else is understood to remain, then all things will appear to be " qualities." And therefore also those persons who make these assertions have endeavoured to maintain, that since all who say that matter was uncreated will admit that qualities were created by God, it may be in this way shown that even according to them matter was not uncreated ; since qualities constitute everything, and these are declared by all without contradiction to have been made by God. Those, again, who would make out that qualities are superimposed from without upon a certain underlying matter, make use of illustrations of this kind : e.g., Paul un-

[1] In filium adoptatur.
[2] Ventilare.
[3] In Scripturis canonicis.
[4] Isa. x. 17, καὶ φάγεται ὡσεὶ χόρτον τὴν ὕλην, Sept. The Vulgate follows the Masoretic text.
[5] [Elucidation VI].
[6] Wisd. xi. 17.
[7] Gen. i. 2, " invisibilis et incomposita; " " inanis et vacua," Vulg.

[8] Initia corporum.
[9] Naturam corpoream.

doubtedly is either silent, or speaks, or watches, or sleeps, or maintains a certain attitude of body; for he is either in a sitting, or standing, or recumbent position. For these are "accidents" belonging to men, without which they are almost never found. And yet our conception of man does not lay down any of these things as a definition of him; but we so understand and regard him by their means, that we do not at all take into account the reason of his (particular) condition either in watching, or in sleeping, or in speaking, or in keeping silence, or in any other action that must necessarily happen to men.[1] If any one, then, can regard Paul as being without all these things which are capable of happening, he will in the same way also be able to understand this underlying (substance) without qualities. When, then, our mind puts away all qualities from its conception, and gazes, so to speak, upon the underlying element alone, and keeps its attention closely upon it, without any reference to the softness or hardness, or heat or cold, or humidity or aridity of the substance, then by means of this somewhat simulated process of thought[2] it will appear to behold matter clear from qualities of every kind.

35. But some one will perhaps inquire whether we can obtain out of Scripture any grounds for such an understanding of the subject. Now I think some such view is indicated in the Psalms, when the prophet says, "Mine eyes have seen thine imperfection:"[3] by which the mind of the prophet, examining with keener glance the first principles of things, and separating in thought and imagination only between matter and its qualities, perceived the imperfection of God, which certainly is understood to be perfected by the addition of qualities. Enoch also, in his book, speaks as follows: "I have walked on even to imperfection;"[4] which expression I consider may be understood in a similar manner, viz., that the mind of the prophet proceeded in its scrutiny and investigation of all visible things, until it arrived at that first beginning in which it beheld imperfect matter (existing) without "qualities." For it is written in the same book of Enoch, "I beheld the whole of matter;"[5] which is so understood as if he had said: "I

---

[1] Nec tamen sensus noster manifeste de eo aliquid horum definit, sed ita eum per hæc intelligimus, vel consideramus, ut non omnino rationem status ejus comprehendamus, vel in eo, quod vigilat, vel in eo, quod dormit, aut in quo loquitur, vel tacet, et si qua alia sunt, quæ accidere necesse est hominibus.

[2] Tunc simulatâ quodammodo cogitatione.

[3] Ps. cxxxix. 16, τὸ ἀκατέργαστόν μου εἰδοσαν οἱ ὀφθαλμοί σου, Sept.; "Imperfectum meum viderunt oculi tui," Vulg. (same as in the text.) גָּלְמִי רָאוּ עֵינֶיךָ — "Thine eyes did see my substance, yet being imperfect," Auth. Vers. Cf. Gesenius and Fürst, s.v., גֹּלֶם.

[4] Ambulavi usque ad imperfectum: cf. Book of Enoch, chap. xvii.

[5] Universas materias perspexi; cf. Book of Enoch, chap. xvii. [On this apocryphal book, see the learned remarks of Dr. Pusey in his reply to Canon Farrar, *What is of Faith as to Everlasting Punishment;* pp. 52-59. London, 1881.]

have clearly seen all the divisions of matter which are broken up from one into each individual species either of men, or animals, or of the sky, or of the sun, or of all other things in this world." After these points, now, we proved to the best of our power in the preceding pages that all things which exist were made by God, and that there was nothing which was not made, save the nature of the Father, and the Son, and the Holy Spirit; and that God, who is by nature good, desiring to have those upon whom He might confer benefits, and who might rejoice in receiving His benefits, created creatures worthy (of this), i.e., who were capable of receiving Him in a worthy manner, who, He says, are also begotten by Him as his sons. He made all things, moreover, by number and measure. For there is nothing before God without either limit or measure. For by His power He comprehends all things, and He Himself is comprehended by the strength of no created thing, because that nature is known to itself alone. For the Father alone knoweth the Son, and the Son alone knoweth the Father, and the Holy Spirit alone searcheth even the deep things of God. All created things, therefore, i.e., either the number of rational beings or the measure of bodily matter, are distinguished by Him as being within a certain number or measurement; since, as it was necessary for an intellectual nature to employ bodies, and this nature is shown to be changeable and convertible by the very condition of its being created (for what did not exist, but began to exist, is said by this very circumstance to be of mutable nature), it can have neither goodness nor wickedness as an essential, but only as an accidental attribute of its being. Seeing, then, as we have said, that rational nature was mutable and changeable, so that it made use of a different bodily covering of this or that sort of quality, according to its merits, it was necessary, as God foreknew there would be diversities in souls or spiritual powers, that He should create also a bodily nature the qualities of which might be changed at the will of the Creator into all that was required. And this bodily nature must last as long as those things which require it is a covering: for there will be always rational natures which need a bodily covering; and there will therefore always be a bodily nature whose coverings must necessarily be used by rational creatures, unless some one be able to demonstrate by arguments that a rational nature can live without a body. But how difficult — nay, how almost impossible — this is for our understanding, we have shown in the preceding pages, in our discussion of the individual topics.

36. It will not, I consider, be opposed to the nature of our undertaking, if we restate with all possible brevity our opinions on the immortality

of rational natures. Every one who participates in anything, is unquestionably of one essence and nature with him who is partaker of the same thing. For example, as all eyes participate in the light, so accordingly all eyes which partake of the light are of one nature; but although every eye partakes of the light, yet, inasmuch as one sees more clearly, and another more obscurely, every eye does not equally share in the light. And again, all hearing receives voice or sound, and therefore all hearing is of one nature; but each one hears more rapidly or more slowly, according as the quality of his hearing is clear and sound. Let us pass now from these sensuous illustrations to the consideration of intellectual things. Every mind which partakes of intellectual light ought undoubtedly to be of one nature with every mind which partakes in a similar manner of intellectual light. If the heavenly virtues, then, partake of intellectual light, i.e., of divine nature, because they participate in wisdom and holiness, and if human souls have partaken of the same light and wisdom, and thus are mutually of one nature and of one essence, — then, since the heavenly virtues are incorruptible and immortal, the essence of the human soul will also be immortal and incorruptible. And not only so, but because the nature of Father, and Son, and Holy Spirit, of whose intellectual light alone all created things have a share, is incorruptible and eternal, it is altogether consistent and necessary that every substance which partakes of that eternal nature should last for ever, and be incorruptible and eternal, so that the eternity of divine goodness may be understood also in this respect, that they who obtain its benefits are also eternal. But as, in the instances referred to, a diversity in the participation of the light was observed, when the glance of the beholder was described as being duller or more acute, so also a diversity is to be noted in the participation of Father, Son, and Holy Spirit, varying with the degree of zeal or capacity of mind. If such were not the case,[1] we have to consider whether it would not seem to be an act of impiety to say that the mind which is capable of (receiving) God should admit of a destruction of its essence;[2] as if the very fact that it is able to feel and understand God could not suffice for its perpetual existence, especially since, if even through neglect the mind fall away from a pure and complete reception of God, it nevertheless contains within it certain seeds of restoration and renewal to a better understanding, seeing the "inner," which is also called the "rational" man, is renewed after "the image and likeness of God, who cre-

ated him." And therefore the prophet says, "All the ends of the earth shall remember, and turn unto the Lord; and all the kindreds of the nations shall worship before Thee."[3]

37. If any one, indeed, venture to ascribe essential corruption to Him who was made after the image and likeness of God, then, in my opinion, this impious charge extends even to the Son of God Himself, for He is called in Scripture the image of God.[4] Or he who holds this opinion would certainly impugn the authority of Scripture, which says that man was made in the image of God; and in him are manifestly to be discovered traces of the divine image, not by any appearance of the bodily frame, which is corruptible, but by mental wisdom, by justice, moderation, virtue, wisdom, discipline; in fine, by the whole band of virtues, which are innate in the essence of God, and which may enter into man by diligence and imitation of God; as the Lord also intimates in the Gospel, when He says, "Be ye therefore merciful, as your Father also is merciful;"[5] and, "Be ye perfect, even as your Father also is perfect."[6] From which it is clearly shown that all these virtues are perpetually in God, and that they can never approach to or depart from Him, whereas by men they are acquired only slowly, and one by one. And hence also by these means they seem to have a kind of relationship with God; and since God knows all things, and none of things intellectual in themselves can elude His notice[7] (for God the Father alone, and His only-begotten Son, and the Holy Spirit, not only possess a knowledge of those things which they have created, but also of themselves), a rational understanding also, advancing from small things to great, and from things visible to things invisible, may attain to a more perfect knowledge. For it is placed in the body, and advances from sensible things themselves, which are corporeal, to things that are intellectual. But lest our statement that things intellectual are not cognisable by the senses should appear unbecoming, we shall employ the instance of Solomon, who says, "You will find also a divine sense;"[8] by which he shows that those things which are intellectual are to be sought out not by means of a bodily sense, but by a certain other which he calls "divine." And with this sense must we look on each of those rational beings which we have enumerated above; and with this sense are to be understood those words which we speak, and those statements to be weighed which we com-

---

[1] Alioquin.
[2] Substantialem interitum.

[3] Ps. xxii. 27.
[4] Cf. Col. i. 15 and 2 Cor. iv. 4.
[5] Luke vi. 36.
[6] Matt. v. 48.
[7] Nihil eum rerum intellectualium ex se lateat.
[8] Cf. Prov. ii. 5, ἐπίγνωσιν Θεοῦ εὑρήσεις (Sept.), Scientiam Dei invenies (Vulg.). דַּעַת אֱלֹהִים תִּמְצָא.

mit to writing. For the divine nature knows even those thoughts which we revolve within us in silence. And on those matters of which we have spoken, or on the others which follow from them, according to the rule above laid down, are our opinions to be formed.

ELUCIDATIONS.

I.

(Teaching of the Church, p. 240.)

It is noteworthy how frequently our author employs this expression in this immediate connection. Concerning the punishment of the wicked he asserts a " clearly defined teaching." He shows what the Church's teaching " has laid down" touching demons and angels. Touching the origin of the world, he again asserts the Church's teaching, and then concedes, that, over and above what he maintains, there is "no clear statement regarding it,"—i.e., the creation and its antecedents. Elsewhere he speaks of "the faith of the Church," and all this as something accepted by all Christians recognised as orthodox or Catholics.

Not to recur to the subject of the creeds [1] known at this period in the East and West, this frequent recognition of a system of theology, or something like it, starts some interesting inquiries. We have space to state only some of them :—

1. Was Origen here speaking of the catechetical school of Alexandria, and assuming its teaching to be that of the whole Church?

2. If so, was not this recognition of the Alexandrian leadership the precursor of that terrible shock which was given to Christendom by the rise of Arianism out of such a stronghold of orthodoxy?

3. Does not the power of Athanasius to stand "against the world" assure us that he was strong in the position that "the teaching of the Church," in Alexandria and elsewhere, was against Arius, whom he was able to defeat by *prescription* as well as by Scripture?

4. Is it not clear that all this was asserted, held, and defined without help from the West, and that the West merely responded *Amen* to what Alexandria had taught from the beginning?

5. Is not the evidence overwhelming, that nothing but passive testimony was thus far heard of in connection with the see of Rome?

6. If the "teaching of the Church," then, was so far independent of that see that Christendom neither waited for its voice, nor recognised it as of any exceptional importance in the definition of the faith and the elimination of heresy, is it not evident that the entire fabric of the Middle-Age polity in the West has its origin in times and manners widely differing from the Apostolic Age and that of the Ante-Nicene Fathers?

II.

(Subjection, p. 343.)

The *subordination* of the Son, as held by all Nicene Christians, is defended by Bull [2] at great length and with profound learning. It is my purpose elsewhere to quote his splendid tribute to the substantial orthodoxy of Origen. Professor Shedd, in his work on *Christian Doctrine*,[3] pronounces the Nicene Creed " *the received* creed-statement among all Trinitarian Churches." I assume that this note will be of interest to all theological minds. For an unsatisfactory and meagre account of primitive creeds, see Bunsen, *Hippol.*, iii. pp. 125–132.

---

[1] On which consult Dupin, and, for another view, Bunsen's *Hippolytus.* See also p. 383, *infra.*
[2] Vol. v. p. 134, and *passim* to 745; also vi. 368.
[3] Vol. ii. p. 438.

III.

(Proceedeth from the Father, p. 344.)

The double procession is no part of the Creed of Christendom; nor did it become fixed in the West, till, by the influence of Charlemagne, the important but not immaculate Council of Frankfort (A.D. 794) completed the work of Toledo, and committed the whole West to its support. The Anglican Church recites the *Filioque* liturgically, but explains its adhesion to this *formula* in a manner satisfactory to the Easterns. It has no rightful place in the Creed, however; and its retention in the Nicene Symbol is a just offence, not only to the Greeks, but against the great canon, *Quod semper,* etc.

Compare Pearson on the *Creed,*[1] and these candid words : " Although the addition of words to the formal Creed *be not justifiable,*" etc. Consult the valuable work of Theophanes Procopowicz, Bishop of Novgorod, which contains a history of the literature of the subject down to his times.[2] It is a matter debated anew in our own age, in view of advances to the Greeks made by Dr. Döllinger and the Old Catholics. Let me refer to a volume almost equally learned and ill-digested,[3] written by a clever author who was perverted to Romanism, and returned, after many years, to the Church of England. It bears the marks of many unreal impressions received during his " Babylonish captivity." I refer to a work of E. S. Foulkes.

IV.

(The faith of the Church, p. 347.)

Before the Nicene Council local creeds were in use, all agreeing substantially; all scriptural, but some more full than others. Of these the ancient Symbol of Jerusalem was chief, and this forms the base of the Nicene Creed. It is here noteworthy that Origen speaks of " the faith " as something settled and known : clearly, he did not intentionally transgress it. Bull says,[4] " Græci Scriptores Ante-Nicæni τὸν κανόνα τῆς πίστεως passim in scriptis suis commemorant." See the Jerusalem Creed, on the same page ; and note, the Church of Jerusalem is called by the Second Œcumenical Council (A.D. 381), " the mother of all the Churches." So ignorant were the Fathers of that date of any other " mother Church," that they address this very statement to the clergy of Rome.[5] Compare Eusebius, book iv. cap. viii.

V.

(Endowed with freedom of will, p. 347.)

Elsewhere in this treatise our author defines the will as " able to resist external causes." The profound work of Edwards needs no words of mine.[6] As an example of logic the most acute, it is the glory of early American literature. I read it eagerly during my college course, while under the guidance of my instructor in philosophy, the amiable and profound Dr. Tappan (afterwards president of the University of Michigan), who taught us to admire it, but not to regard it as infallible. See his vigorous review of Edwards,[7] in which he argues as a disciple of Coleridge and of Plato.

On allied subjects, let me refer to Wiggers's *Augustinismus,* etc., translated by Professor Emerson of Andover ;[8] also to Bledsoe's *Theodicy,*[9] heretofore cited. I venture to say, that, among the thinkers of America, and as Christian philosophers, both Bledsoe and Tappan are less known and honoured than they deserve to be.

---

[1] pp. 521-526.   [2] *Tractatus de Processione Spiritus Sancti,* Gothæ, A.D. 1772.   [3] *Christendom's Divisions,* London, 1865.
[4] Vol. vi. p. 132, 133.   [5] Theodoret, book v. cap. ix.   [6] Ed. Converse, New York, 1829.
[7] *A Review of Edwards's Inquiry,* by Henry Philip Tappan, New York, 1839.   [8] New York, 1840.
[9] New York, 1854. See vol. ii. p. 522, this series.

VI.

(Not esteemed authoritative by all, p. 379.)

Not by Jerome, nor Rufinus, nor Chrysostom. Gregory the Great, Bishop of Rome, is also shown by Lardner (*Credib.*, v. 127) to have quoted "the wisdom of Solomon" only as the sayings of a wise man; not at all as Scripture. The Easterns are equally represented by John Damascene (A.D. 730), who says of this book that it is one of those "excellent and useful" books which are not reckoned with the hagiographa. But Methodius is an exception; for he quotes this book *twice* (says Lardner) as if it were Scripture, and certainly cites it not infrequently. Yet his testimony does not amount, perhaps, to more than an acceptance of the same as only *deutero-canonical;* i.e., as one of the books read in the Church for instruction, but not appealed to as establishing any doctrine otherwise unknown to the Church. We may examine this subject when we come to Methodius, in vol. vi. of this series.

NOTE.

THIS is a convenient place for the following tables, compiled from Eusebius as far as his history goes; i.e. A.D. 305. See also Dr. Robinson's *Researches*.

I. THE SEE OF JERUSALEM.

1. James, the Lord's brother.	14. Joseph.	27. Antoninus.
2. Simeon.	15. Judah.	28. Valens.
3. Justus.	16. Marcus.	29. Dolichianus.
4. Zacchæus.	17. Cassian.	30. Narcissus.
5. Tobias.	18. Publius.	31. Dius.
6. Benjamin.	19. Maximus.	32. Germanio.
7. John.	20. Julian.	33. Gordius.
8. Matthew.	21. Caius.	34. Narcissus II.
9. Philip.	22. Symmachus.	35. Alexander.
10. Seneca.	23. Caius II.	36. Mazabanes.
11. Justus.	24. Julian II.	37. Hymenæus.
12. Levi.	25. Capito.	38. Zabdas.
13. Ephres.	26. Maximus II.	39. Hermon, A.D. 300.

II. THE SEE OF ALEXANDRIA.

1. Annianus.	7. Marcus.	13. Dionysius.
2. Avilius.	8. Celadion.	14. Maximus.
3. Cerdon.	9. Aggripinus.	15. Theonas.
4. Primus.	10. Julianus.	16. Peter.
5. Justus.	11. Demetrius.	17. Achillas.
6. Eumenes.	12. Heraclas.	18. Alexander,[1] A.D. 326.

[1] Alexander, dying just after the Nicene Council, was succeeded by the great Athanasius.

A LETTER TO ORIGEN FROM AFRICANUS ABOUT THE HISTORY OF SUSANNA.

GREETING, my lord and son, most worthy Origen, from Africanus.[1] In your sacred discussion with Agnomon you referred to that prophecy of Daniel which is related of his youth. This at that time, as was meet, I accepted as genuine. Now, however, I cannot understand how it escaped you that this part of the book is spurious. For, in sooth, this section, although apart from this it is elegantly written, is plainly a more modern forgery. There are many proofs of this. When Susanna is condemned to die, the prophet is seized by the Spirit, and cries out that the sentence is unjust. Now, in the first place, it is always in some other way that Daniel prophesies — by visions, and dreams, and an angel appearing to him, never by prophetic inspiration. Then, after crying out in this extraordinary fashion, he detects them in a way no less incredible, which not even Philistion the play-writer would have resorted to. For, not satisfied with rebuking them through the Spirit, he placed them apart, and asked them severally where they saw her committing adultery. And when the one said, "Under a holm-tree" (*prinos*), he answered that the angel would saw him asunder (*prisein*); and in a similar fashion menaced the other who said, "Under a mastich-tree" (*schinos*), with being rent asunder (*schisthenai*). Now, in Greek, it happens that "holm-tree" and "saw asunder," and "rend" and "mastich-tree"

sound alike; but in Hebrew they are quite distinct. But all the books of the Old Testament have been translated from Hebrew into Greek.

2. Moreover, how is it that they who were captives among the Chaldæans, lost and won at play,[2] thrown out unburied on the streets, as was prophesied of the former captivity, their sons torn from them to be eunuchs, and their daughters to be concubines, as had been prophesied; how is it that such could pass sentence of death, and that on the wife of their king Joakim, whom the king of the Babylonians had made partner of his throne? Then if it was not this Joakim, but some other from the common people, whence had a captive such a mansion and spacious garden? But a more fatal objection is, that this section, along with the other two at the end of it, is not contained in the Daniel received among the Jews. And add that, among all the many prophets who had been before, there is no one who has quoted from another word for word. For they had no need to go a-begging for words, since their own were true; but this one, in rebuking one of those men, quotes the words of the Lord: "The innocent and righteous shalt thou not slay." From all this I infer that this section is a later addition. Moreover, the style is different. I have struck the blow; do you give the echo; answer, and instruct me. Salute all my masters. The learned all salute thee. With all my heart I pray for your and your circle's health.

[1] [See Routh's *Reliquiæ*, vol. ii. p. 115; also Euseb., i. 7, and Socrates, ii. 35. He ranks with the great pupils of the Alexandrian school, with which, however, he seems to have had only a slight personal relation. Concerning this Epistle to Origen, and the answer of the latter, consult Routh's very full annotations (*ut supra*, pp. 312-328). Concerning Gregory Thaumaturgus, the greatest of Origen's pupils, we shall know more when we come to vol. vi. of this series. He died *circa* 270].

[2] Nolte would change ἠστραγαλωμένοι (or ἀστραγαλώμενοι, as Wetsten. has it), which is a ἅπαξ εἰρημένον, into στραγγαλωμένοι or ἐστραγγαλωμένοι, "strangled." He compares Tob. ii. 3.

A LETTER FROM ORIGEN TO AFRICANUS.

ORIGEN to Africanus, a beloved brother in God the Father, through Jesus Christ, His holy Child, greeting. Your letter, from which I learn what you think of the Susanna in the Book of Daniel, which is used in the Churches, although apparently somewhat short, presents in its few words many problems, each of which demands no common treatment, but such as oversteps the character of a letter, and reaches the limits of a discourse.[1] And I, when I consider, as best I can, the measure of my intellect, that I may know myself, am aware that I am wanting in the accuracy necessary to reply to your letter; and that the more, that the few days I have spent in Nicomedia have been far from sufficient to send you an answer to all your demands and queries even after the fashion of the present epistle. Wherefore pardon my little ability, and the little time I had, and read this letter with all indulgence, supplying anything I may omit.

2. You begin by saying, that when, in my discussion with our friend Bassus, I used the Scripture which contains the prophecy of Daniel when yet a young man in the affair of Susanna, I did this as if it had escaped me that this part of the book was spurious. You say that you praise this passage as elegantly written, but find fault with it as a more modern composition, and a forgery; and you add that the forger has had recourse to something which not even Philistion the play-writer would have used in his puns between *prinos* and *prisein*, *schinos* and *schisis*, which words as they sound in Greek can be used in this way, but not in Hebrew. In answer to this, I have to tell you what it behoves us to do in the cases not only of the History of Susanna, which is found in every Church of Christ in that Greek copy which the Greeks use, but is not in the Hebrew, or of the two other passages you mention at the end of the book containing the history of Bel and the Dragon, which likewise are not in the Hebrew copy of Daniel; but of thousands of other passages also which I found in many places when with my little strength I was collating the Hebrew copies with ours. For in Daniel itself I found the word "bound" followed in our versions by very many verses which are not in the Hebrew at all, beginning (according to one of the copies which circulate in the Churches) thus: "Ananias, and Azarias, and Misael prayed and sang unto God," down to "O, all ye that worship the Lord, bless ye the God of gods. Praise Him, and say that His mercy endureth for ever and ever. And it came to pass, when the king heard them singing, and saw them that they were alive." Or, as in another copy, from "And they walked in the midst of the fire, praising God and blessing the Lord," down to "O, all ye that worship the Lord, bless ye the God of gods. Praise Him, and say that His mercy endureth to all generations."[2] But in the Hebrew copies the words, "And these three men, Sedrach, Misach, and Abednego fell down bound into the midst of the fire," are immediately followed by the verse, "Nabouchodonosor the king was astonished, and rose up in haste, and spake, and said unto his counsellors." For so Aquila, following the Hebrew reading, gives it, who has obtained the credit among the Jews of having interpreted the Scriptures with no ordinary care, and whose version is most commonly used by those who do not know Hebrew, as the one which has been most successful. Of the copies in my possession whose readings I gave, one follows the Seventy, and the other Theodotion; and just as the History of Susanna which you call a forgery is found in both, together with the passages at the end of Daniel, so they give also these passages, amounting to, make a rough guess, to more than two hundred verses.

3. And in many other of the sacred books I found sometimes more in our copies than in the Hebrew, sometimes less. I shall adduce a few examples, since it is impossible to give them all. Of the Book of Esther neither the prayer of Mardochaios nor that of Esther, both fitted to

1 [See Dr. Pusey's *Lectures on Daniel the Prophet*, lect. vi. p. 326, 327; also *The Uncanonical and Apocryphal Scriptures*, by Rev. R. W. Churton, B.D. (1884), pp. 389-404. S.]

2 "The Song of the Three Holy Children" (in the Apocrypha).

edify the reader, is found in the Hebrew. Neither are the letters; [1] nor the one written to Amman about the rooting up of the Jewish nation, nor that of Mardochaios in the name of Artaxerxes delivering the nation from death. Then in Job, the words from "It is written, that he shall rise again with those whom the Lord raises," to the end, are not in the Hebrew, and so not in Aquila's edition; while they are found in the Septuagint and in Theodotion's version, agreeing with each other at least in sense. And many other places I found in Job where our copies have more than the Hebrew ones, sometimes a little more, and sometimes a great deal more: a little more, as when to the words, "Rising up in the morning, he offered burnt-offerings for them according to their number," they add, "one heifer for the sin of their soul;" and to the words, "The angels of God came to present themselves before God, and the devil came with them," "from going to and fro in the earth, and from walking up and down in it." Again, after "The LORD gave, the LORD has taken away," the Hebrew has not, "It was so, as seemed good to the Lord." Then our copies are very much fuller than the Hebrew, when Job's wife speaks to him, from "How long wilt thou hold out? And he said, Lo, I wait yet a little while, looking for the hope of my salvation," down to "that I may cease from my troubles, and my sorrows which compass me." For they have only these words of the woman, "But say a word against God, and die."

4. Again, through the whole of Job there are many passages in the Hebrew which are wanting in our copies, generally four or five verses, but sometimes, however, even fourteen, and nineteen, and sixteen. But why should I enumerate all the instances I collected with so much labour, to prove that the difference between our copies and those of the Jews did not escape me? In Jeremiah I noticed many instances, and indeed in that book I found much transposition and variation in the readings of the prophecies. Again, in Genesis, the words, "God saw that it was good," when the firmament was made, are not found in the Hebrew, and there is no small dispute among them about this; and other instances are to be found in Genesis, which I marked, for the sake of distinction, with the sign the Greeks call an obelisk, as on the other hand I marked with an asterisk those passages in our copies which are not found in the Hebrew. What needs there to speak of Exodus, where there is such diversity in what is said about the tabernacle and its court, and the ark, and the garments of the high priest and the priests, that

sometimes the meaning even does not seem to be akin? And, forsooth, when we notice such things, we are forthwith to reject as spurious the copies in use in our Churches, and enjoin the brotherhood to put away the sacred books current among them, and to coax the Jews, and persuade them to give us copies which shall be untampered with, and free from forgery! Are we to suppose that that Providence which in the sacred Scriptures has ministered to the edification of all the Churches of Christ, had no thought for those bought with a price, for whom Christ died; [2] whom, although His Son, God who is love spared not, but gave Him up for us all, that with Him He might freely give us all things? [3]

5. In all these cases consider whether it would not be well to remember the words, "Thou shalt not remove the ancient landmarks which thy fathers have set." [4] Nor do I say this because I shun the labour of investigating the Jewish Scriptures, and comparing them with ours, and noticing their various readings. This, if it be not arrogant to say it, I have already to a great extent done to the best of my ability, labouring hard to get at the meaning in all the editions and various readings; [5] while I paid particular attention to the interpretation of the Seventy, lest I might to be found to accredit any forgery to the Churches which are under heaven, and give an occasion to those who seek such a starting-point for gratifying their desire to slander the common brethren, and to bring some accusation against those who shine forth in our community. And I make it my endeavour not to be ignorant of their various readings, lest in my controversies with the Jews I should quote to them what is not found in their copies, and that I may make some use of what is found there, even although it should not be in our Scriptures. For if we are so prepared for them in our discussions, they will not, as is their manner, scornfully laugh at Gentile believers for their ignorance of the true reading as they have them. So far as to the History of Susanna not being found in the Hebrew.

6. Let us now look at the things you find fault with in the story itself. And here let us begin with what would probably make any one averse to receiving the history: I mean the play of

---

[1] This should probably be corrected, with Pat. Jun., into, "Nor are the letters, *neither*," etc.

[2] 1 Cor. vi. 20; Rom. xiv. 15.
[3] Rom. viii. 32.
[4] Prov. xxii. 28.
[5] Origen's most important contribution to biblical literature was his elaborate attempt to rectify the text of the Septuagint by collating it with the Hebrew original and other Greek versions. On this he spent twenty-eight years, during which he travelled through the East collecting materials. The form in which he first issued the result of his labours was that of the *Tetrapla*, which presented in four columns the texts of the LXX., Aquila, Symmachus, and Theodotion. He next issued the *Hexapla*, in which the Hebrew text was given, first in Hebrew and then in Greek letters. Of some books he gave two additional Greek versions, whence the title *Octapla;* and there was even a seventh Greek version added for some books. Unhappily this great work, which extended to nearly fifty volumes, was never transcribed, and so perished (Kitto, *Cycl.*).

words between *prinos* and *prisis*, *schinos* and *schisis*. You say that you can see how this can be in Greek, but that in Hebrew the words are altogether distinct. On this point, however, I am still in doubt; because, when I was considering this passage (for I myself saw this difficulty), I consulted not a few Jews about it, asking them the Hebrew words for *prinos* and *prisein*, and how they would translate *schinos* the tree, and how *schisis*. And they said that they did not know these Greek words *prinos* and *schinos*, and asked me to show them the trees, that they might see what they called them. And I at once (for the truth's dear sake) put before them pieces of the different trees. One of them then said, that he could not with any certainty give the Hebrew name of anything not mentioned in Scripture, since, if one was at a loss, he was prone to use the Syriac word instead of the Hebrew one; and he went on to say, that some words the very wisest could not translate. "If, then," said he, "you can adduce a passage in any Scripture where the *schinos* is mentioned, or the *prinos*, you will find there the words you seek, together with the words which have the same sound; but if it is nowhere mentioned, we also do not know it." This, then, being what the Hebrews said to whom I had recourse, and who were acquainted with the history, I am cautious of affirming whether or not there is any correspondence to this play of words in the Hebrew. Your reason for affirming that there is not, you yourself probably know.

7. Moreover, I remember hearing from a learned Hebrew, said among themselves to be the son of a wise man, and to have been specially trained to succeed his father, with whom I had intercourse on many subjects, the names of these elders, just as if he did not reject the History of Susanna, as they occur in Jeremias as follows: "The LORD make thee like Zedekias and Achiab, whom the king of Babylon roasted in the fire, for the iniquity they did in Israel."[1] How, then, could the one be sawn asunder by an angel, and the other rent in pieces? The answer is, that these things were prophesied not of this world, but of the judgment of God, after the departure from this world. For as the lord of that wicked servant who says, "My lord delayeth his coming," and so gives himself up to drunkenness, eating and drinking with drunkards, and smiting his fellow-servants, shall at his coming "cut him asunder, and appoint him his portion with the unbelievers,"[2] even so the angels appointed to punish will accomplish these things (just as they will cut asunder the wicked steward of that passage) on these men, who were called indeed elders, but who administered their stew-

ardship wickedly. One will saw asunder him who was waxen old in wicked days, who had pronounced false judgment, condemning the innocent, and letting the guilty go free;[3] and another will rend in pieces him of the seed of Chanaan, and not of Judah, whom beauty had deceived, and whose heart lust had perverted.[4]

8. And I knew another Hebrew, who told about these elders such traditions as the following: that they pretended to the Jews in captivity, who were hoping by the coming of Christ to be freed from the yoke of their enemies, that they could explain clearly the things concerning Christ, . . . and that they so deceived the wives of their countrymen.[5] Wherefore it is that the prophet Daniel calls the one "waxen old in wicked days," and says to the other, "Thus have ye dealt with the children of Israel; but the daughters of Juda would not abide your wickedness."

9. But probably to this you will say, Why then is the "History" not in their Daniel, if, as you say, their wise men hand down by tradition such stories? The answer is, that they hid from the knowledge of the people as many of the passages which contained any scandal against the elders, rulers, and judges, as they could, some of which have been preserved in uncanonical writings (Apocrypha). As an example, take the story told about Esaias, and guaranteed by the Epistle to the Hebrews, which is found in none of their public books. For the author of the Epistle to the Hebrews, in speaking of the prophets, and what they suffered, says, "They were stoned, they were sawn asunder, they were slain with the sword."[6] To whom, I ask, does the "sawn asunder" refer (for by an old idiom, not peculiar to Hebrew, but found also in Greek, this is said in the plural, although it refers to but one person)? Now we know very well that tradition says that Esaias the prophet was sawn asunder; and this is found in some apocryphal work, which probably the Jews have purposely tampered with, introducing some phrases manifestly incorrect, that discredit might be thrown on the whole.

However, some one hard pressed by this argument may have recourse to the opinion of those who reject this Epistle as not being Paul's; against whom I must at some other time use other arguments to prove that it is Paul's.[7] At present I shall adduce from the Gospel what Jesus Christ testifies concerning the prophets, together with a story which He refers to, but

---

[1] Jer. xxix. 22, 23.
[2] Luke xii. 45, 46.

[3] Susanna 52, 53.
[4] Susanna 56.
[5] Et utrumque sigillatim in quamcunque mulierem incidebat, et cui vitium afferre cupiebat, ei secreto affirmasse sibi a Deo datum e suo semine progignere Christum. Hinc spe gignendi Christum decepta mulier, sui copiam decipienti faciebat, et sic civium uxores stuprabant seniores Achiab et Sedekias.
[6] Heb. xi. 37.
[7] [See note *supra*, p. 239. S.]

which is not found in the Old Testament, since in it also there is a scandal against unjust judges in Israel. The words of our Saviour run thus: "Woe unto you, scribes and Pharisees, hypocrites! because ye build the tombs of the prophets, and garnish the sepulchres of the righteous, and say, If we had been in the days of our fathers, we would not have been partakers with them in the blood of the prophets. Wherefore be ye witnesses unto yourselves, that ye are the children of them which killed the prophets. Fill ye up then the measure of your fathers. Ye serpents, ye generation of vipers, how can ye escape the damnation of Gehenna? Wherefore, behold, I send unto you prophets, and wise men, and scribes; and some of them ye shall kill and crucify; and some of them shall ye scourge in your synagogues, and persecute them from city to city: that upon you may come all the righteous blood shed upon the earth, from the blood of righteous Abel unto the blood of Zacharias, son of Barachias, whom ye slew between the temple and the altar. Verily I say unto you, All these things shall come upon this generation." And what follows is of the same tenor: "O Jerusalem, Jerusalem, thou that killest the prophets, and stonest them which are sent unto thee, how often would I have gathered thy children together, even as a hen gathereth her chickens under her wings, and ye would not! Behold, your house is left unto you desolate." [1]

Let us see now if in these cases we are not forced to the conclusion, that while the Saviour gives a true account of them, none of the Scriptures which could prove what He tells are to be found. For they who build the tombs of the prophets and garnish the sepulchres of the righteous, condemning the crimes their fathers committed against the righteous and the prophets, say, "If we had been in the days of our fathers, we would not have been partakers with them in the blood of the prophets." [2] In the blood of what prophets, can any one tell me? For where do we find anything like this written of Esaias, or Jeremias, or any of the twelve, or Daniel? Then about Zacharias the son of Barachias, who was slain between the temple and the altar, we learn from Jesus only, not knowing it otherwise from any Scripture. Wherefore I think no other supposition is possible, than that they who had the reputation of wisdom, and the rulers and elders, took away from the people every passage which might bring them into discredit among the people. We need not wonder, then, if this history of the evil device of the licentious elders against Susanna is true, but was concealed and removed from the Scriptures by men themselves

not very far removed from the counsel of these elders.

In the Acts of the Apostles also, Stephen, in his other testimony, says, "Which of the prophets have not your fathers persecuted? And they have slain them which showed before of the coming of the Just One; of whom ye have been now the betrayers and murderers." [3] That Stephen speaks the truth, every one will admit who receives the Acts of the Apostles; but it is impossible to show from the extant books of the Old Testament how with any justice he throws the blame of having persecuted and slain the prophets on the fathers of those who believed not in Christ. And Paul, in the first Epistle to the Thessalonians, testifies this concerning the Jews: "For ye, brethren, became followers of the Churches of God which in Judea are in Christ Jesus: for ye also have suffered like things of your own countrymen, even as they have of the Jews; who both killed the Lord Jesus and their own prophets, and have persecuted us; and they please not God, and are contrary to all men." [4] What I have said is, I think, sufficient to prove that it would be nothing wonderful if this history were true, and the licentious and cruel attack was actually made on Susanna by those who were at that time elders, and written down by the wisdom of the Spirit, but removed by these rulers of Sodom,[5] as the Spirit would call them.

10. Your next objection is, that in this writing Daniel is said to have been seized by the Spirit, and to have cried out that the sentence was unjust; while in that writing of his which is universally received he is represented as prophesying in quite another manner, by visions and dreams, and an angel appearing to him, but never by prophetic inspiration. You seem to me to pay too little heed to the words, "At sundry times, and in divers manners, God spake in time past unto the fathers by the prophets." [6] This is true not only in the general, but also of individuals. For if you notice, you will find that the same saints have been favoured with divine dreams and angelic appearances and (direct) inspirations. For the present it will suffice to instance what is testified concerning Jacob. Of dreams from God he speaks thus: "And it came to pass, at the time that the cattle conceived, that I saw them before my eyes in a dream, and, behold, the rams and he-goats which leaped upon the sheep and the goats, white-spotted, and speckled, and grisled. And the angel of God spake unto me in a dream, saying, Jacob. And I said, What is it? And he said, Lift up thine eyes and see, the goats and rams leaping

---

[1] Matt. xxiii. 29–38.
[2] Matt. xxiii. 30.

[3] Acts vii. 52.
[4] 1 Thess. ii. 14, 15.
[5] Isa. i. 10.
[6] Heb. i. 1.

on the goats and sheep, white-spotted, and speckled, and grisled : for I have seen all that Laban doeth unto thee. I am God, who appeared unto thee in the place of God, where thou anointedst to Me there a pillar, and vowedst a vow there to Me : now arise, get thee out from this land, and return unto the land of thy kindred." [1]

And as to an appearance (which is better than a dream), he speaks as follows about himself : "And Jacob was left alone ; and there wrestled a man with him until the breaking of the day. And he saw that he prevailed not against him, and he touched the breadth of his thigh ; and the breadth of Jacob's thigh grew stiff while he was wrestling with him. And he said to him, Let me go, for the day breaketh. And he said, I will not let thee go, except thou bless me. And he said unto him, What is thy name? And he said, Jacob. And he said to him, Thy name shall be called no more Jacob, but Israel shall be thy name : for thou hast prevailed with God, and art powerful with men. And Jacob asked him, and said, Tell me thy name. And he said, Wherefore is it that thou dost ask after my name? And he blessed him there. And Jacob called the name of the place Vision of God : for I have seen God face to face, and my life is preserved. And the sun rose, when the vision of God passed by." [2] And that he also prophesied by inspiration, is evident from this passage : " And Jacob called unto his sons, and said, Gather yourselves together, that I may tell you what shall befall you in the last days. Gather yourselves together, and hear, ye sons of Jacob ; and hearken unto Israel your father. Reuben, my first-born, my might, and the beginning of my children, hard to be born, hard and stubborn. Thou wert wanton, boil not over like water ; because thou wentest up to thy father's bed ; then defiledst thou the couch to which thou wentest up." [3] And so with the rest : it was by inspiration that the prophetic blessings were pronounced. We need not wonder, then, that Daniel sometimes prophesied by inspiration, as when he rebuked the elders sometimes, as you say, by dreams and visions, and at other times by an angel appearing unto him.

11. Your other objections are stated, as it appears to me, somewhat irreverently, and without the becoming spirit of piety. I cannot do better than quote your very words : "Then, after crying out in this extraordinary fashion, he detects them in a way no less incredible, which not even Philistion the play-writer would have resorted to. For, not satisfied with rebuking them through the Spirit, he placed them apart,

and asked them severally where they saw her committing adultery ; and when the one said, 'Under a holm-tree' (*prinos*), he answered that the angel would saw him asunder (*prisein*) ; and in a similar fashion threatened the other, who said, 'Under a mastich-tree' (*schinos*), with being rent asunder."

You might as reasonably compare to Philistion the play-writer, a story somewhat like this one, which is found in the third book of Kings, which you yourself will admit to be well written. Here is what we read in Kings : —

"Then there appeared two women that were harlots before the king, and stood before him. And the one woman said, To me, my lord, I and this woman dwell in one house ; and we were delivered in the house. And it came to pass, the third day after that I was delivered, that this woman was delivered also : and we were together ; there is no one in our house except us two. And this woman's child died in the night ; because she overlaid it. And she arose at midnight, and took my son from my arms. And thine handmaid slept. And she laid it in her bosom, and laid her dead child in my bosom. And I arose in the morning to give my child suck, and he was dead ; but when I had considered it in the morning, behold, it was not my son which I did bear. And the other woman said, Nay ; the dead is thy son, but the living is my son. And the other said, No ; the living is my son, but the dead is thy son. Thus they spake before the king. Then said the king, Thou sayest, This is my son that liveth, and thy son is the dead : and thou sayest, Nay ; but thy son is the dead, and my son is the living. And the king said, Bring me a sword. And they brought a sword before the king. And the king said, Divide the living child in two, and give half to the one, and half to the other. Then spake the woman whose the living child was unto the king (for her bowels yearned after her son), and she said, To me, my lord, give her the living child, and in no wise slay it. But the other said, Let it be neither mine nor thine, but divide it. Then the king answered and said, Give the child to her which said, Give her the living child, and in no wise slay it : for she is the mother of it. And all Israel heard of the judgment which the king had judged ; and they feared the face of the king : for they saw that the wisdom of God was in him to do judgment." [4]

For if we were at liberty to speak in this scoffing way of the Scriptures in use in the Churches, we should rather compare this story of the two harlots to the play of Philistion than that of the chaste Susanna. And just as the people would

---

[1] Gen. xxxi. 10–13.
[2] Gen. xxxii. 24–31.
[3] Gen. xlix. 1–4.

[4] 1 Kings iii. 16–28.

not have been persuaded if Solomon had merely said, "Give this one the living child, for she is the mother of it;" so Daniel's attack on the elders would not have been sufficient had there not been added the condemnation from their own mouth, when both said that they had seen her lying with the young man under a tree, but did not agree as to what kind of tree it was. And since you have asserted, as if you knew for certain, that Daniel in this matter judged by inspiration (which may or may not have been the case), I would have you notice that there seem to me to be some analogies in the story of Daniel to the judgment of Solomon, concerning whom the Scripture testifies that the people saw that the wisdom of God was in him to do judgment.[1] This might be said also of Daniel, for it was because wisdom was in him to do judgment that the elders were judged in the manner described.

12. I had nearly forgotten an additional remark I have to make about the *prino-prisein* and *schino-schisein* difficulty; that is, that in our Scriptures there are many etymological fancies, so to call them, which in the Hebrew are perfectly suitable, but not in the Greek. It need not surprise us, then, if the translators of the History of Susanna contrived it so that they found out some Greek words, derived from the same root, which either corresponded exactly to the Hebrew form (though this I hardly think possible), or presented some analogy to it. Here is an instance of this in our Scripture. When the woman was made by God from the rib of the man, Adam says, "She shall be called woman, because she was taken out of her husband." Now the Jews say that the woman was called "*Essa*," and that "taken" is a translation of this word, as is evident from "*chos isouoth essa*," which means, "I have taken the cup of salvation;"[2] and that "*is*" means "man," as we see from "*Hesre aïs*," which is, "Blessed is the man."[3] According to the Jews, then, "*is*" is "man," and "*essa*" "woman," because she was taken out of her husband (*is*). It need not then surprise us if some interpreters of the Hebrew "Susanna," which had been concealed among them at a very remote date, and had been preserved only by the more learned and honest, should have either given the Hebrew word for word, or hit upon some analogy to the Hebrew forms, that the Greeks might be able to follow them. For in many other passages we can find traces of this kind of contrivance on the part of the translators, which I noticed when I was collating the various editions.

13. You raise another objection, which I give

in your own words: "Moreover, how is it that they, who were captives among the Chaldeans, lost and won at play, thrown out unburied on the streets, as was prophesied of the former captivity, their sons torn from them to be eunuchs, and their daughters to be concubines, as had been prophesied; how is it that such could pass sentence of death, and that on the wife of their king Joakim, whom the king of the Babylonians had made partner of his throne? Then, if it was not this Joakim, but some other from the common people, whence had a captive such a mansion and spacious garden?"

Where you get your "lost and won at play, and thrown out unburied on the streets," I know not, unless it is from Tobias; and Tobias (as also Judith), we ought to notice, the Jews do not use. They are not even found in the Hebrew Apocrypha, as I learned from the Jews themselves. However, since the Churches use Tobias, you must know that even in the captivity some of the captives were rich and well to do. Tobias himself says, "Because I remembered God with all my heart; and the Most High gave me grace and beauty in the eyes of Nemessarus, and I was his purveyor; and I went into Media, and left in trust with Gabael, the brother of Gabrias, at Ragi, a city of Media, ten talents of silver."[4] And he adds, as if he were a rich man, "In the days of Nemessarus I gave many alms to my brethren. I gave my bread to the hungry, and my clothes to the naked: and if I saw any of my nation dead, and cast outside the walls of Nineve, I buried him; and if king Senachereim had slain any when he came fleeing from Judea, I buried them privily (for in his wrath he killed many)." Think whether this great catalogue of Tobias's good deeds does not betoken great wealth and much property, especially when he adds, "Understanding that I was sought for to be put to death, I withdrew myself for fear, and all my goods were forcibly taken away."[5]

And another captive, Dachiacharus, the son of Ananiel, the brother of Tobias, was set over all the exchequer of the kingdom of king Acherdon; and we read, "Now Achiacharus was cupbearer, and keeper of the signet, and steward and overseer of the accounts."[6]

Mardochaios, too, frequented the court of the king, and had such boldness before him, that he was inscribed among the benefactors of Artaxerxes.

Again we read in Esdras, that Neemias, a cupbearer and eunuch of the king, of Hebrew race, made a request about the rebuilding of the temple, and obtained it; so that it was granted to

---

[1] 1 Kings iii. 28.
[2] Ps. cxvi. 13.
[3] Ps. i. 1.

[4] Tob. i. 12–14.
[5] Tob. i. 19.
[6] Tob. i. 22.

him, with many more, to return and build the temple again. Why then should we wonder that one Joakim had garden, and house, and property, whether these were very expensive or only moderate, for this is not clearly told us in the writing?

14. But you say, "How could they who were in captivity pass sentence of death?" asserting, I know not on what grounds, that Susanna was the wife of a king, because of the name Joakim. The answer is, that it is no uncommon thing, when great nations become subject, that the king should allow the captives to use their own laws and courts of justice. Now, for instance, that the Romans rule, and the Jews pay the half-shekel to them, how great power by the concession of Cæsar the ethnarch has; so that we, who have had experience of it, know that he differs in little from a true king! Private trials are held according to the law, and some are condemned to death. And though there is not full licence for this, still it is not done without the knowledge of the ruler, as we learned and were convinced of when we spent much time in the country of that people. And yet the Romans only take account of two tribes, while at that time besides Judah there were the ten tribes of Israel. Probably the Assyrians contented themselves with holding them in subjection, and conceded to them their own judicial processes.

15. I find in your letter yet another objection in these words: "And add, that among all the many prophets who had been before, there is no one who has quoted from another word for word. For they had no need to go a-begging for words, since their own were true. But this one, in rebuking one of these men, quotes the words of the Lord, 'The innocent and righteous shalt thou not slay.'" I cannot understand how, with all your exercise in investigating and meditating on the Scriptures, you have not noticed that the prophets continually quote each other almost word for word. For who of all believers does not know the words in Esaias? "And in the last days the mountain of the LORD shall be manifest, and the house of the LORD on the top of the mountains, and it shall be exalted above the hills; and all nations shall come unto it. And many people shall go and say, Come ye, and let us go up to the mountain of the LORD, unto the house of the God of Jacob; and He will teach us His way, and we will walk in it: for out of Zion shall go forth a law, and a word of the LORD from Jerusalem. And He shall judge among the nations, and shall rebuke many people; and they shall beat their swords into ploughshares, and their spears into pruning-hooks: nation shall not lift up sword against nation, neither shall they learn war any more."[1]

But in Micah we find a parallel passage, which is almost word for word: "And in the last days the mountain of the LORD shall be manifest, established on the top of the mountains, and it shall be exalted above the hills; and people shall hasten unto it. And many nations shall come, and say, Come, let us go up to the mountain of the LORD, to the house of the God of Jacob; and they will teach us His way, and we will walk in His paths: for a law shall go forth from Zion, and a word of the LORD from Jerusalem. And He shall judge among many people, and rebuke strong nations; and they shall beat their swords into ploughshares, and their spears into pruning-hooks: nation shall not lift up a sword against nation, neither shall they learn war any more."[2]

Again, in First Chronicles, the psalm which is put in the hands of Asaph and his brethren to praise the Lord, beginning, "Give thanks unto the LORD, call upon His name,"[3] is in the beginning almost identical with Ps. cv., down to "and do my prophets no harm;" and after that it is the same as Ps. xcvi., from the beginning of that psalm, which is something like this, "Praise the Lord all the earth," down to "For He cometh to judge the earth." (It would have taken up too much time to quote more fully; so I have given these short references, which are sufficient for the matter before us.) And you will find the law about not bearing a burden on the Sabbath-day in Jeremias, as well as in Moses.[4] And the rules about the passover, and the rules for the priests, are not only in Moses, but also at the end of Ezekiel.[5] I would have quoted these, and many more, had I not found that from the shortness of my stay in Nicomedia my time for writing you was already too much restricted.

Your last objection is, that the style is different. This I cannot see.

This, then, is my defence. I might, especially after all these accusations, speak in praise of this history of Susanna, dwelling on it word by word, and expounding the exquisite nature of the thoughts. Such an encomium, perhaps, some of the learned and able students of divine things may at some other time compose. This, however, is my answer to your strokes, as you call them. Would that I could instruct you! But I do not now arrogate that to myself. My lord and dear brother Ambrosius, who has written this at my dictation, and has, in looking over it, corrected as he pleased, salutes you. His faithful spouse, Marcella, and her children, also salute you. Also Anicetus. Do you salute our dear father Apollinarius, and all our friends.

---

[1] Isa. ii. 2–4.

[2] Mic. iv. 1–3.
[3] 1 Chron. xvi. 8.
[4] Ex. xxxv. 2; Num. xv. 32; Jer. xvii. 21–24.
[5] In Levit. *passim;* Ezek. xliii. xliv. xlv. xlvi.

A LETTER FROM ORIGEN TO GREGORY.[1]

1. GREETING in God, my most excellent sir, and venerable son Gregory, from Origen. A natural readiness of comprehension, as you well know, may, if practice be added, contribute somewhat to the contingent end, if I may so call it, of that which any one wishes to practise. Thus, your natural good parts might make of you a finished Roman lawyer or a Greek philosopher, so to speak, of one of the schools in high reputation. But I am anxious that you should devote all the strength of your natural good parts to Christianity for your end ; and in order to this, I wish to ask you to extract from the philosophy of the Greeks what may serve as a course of study or a preparation for Christianity, and from geometry and astronomy what will serve to explain the sacred Scriptures, in order that all that the sons of the philosophers are wont to say about geometry and music, grammar, rhetoric, and astronomy, as fellow-helpers to philosophy, we may say about philosophy itself, in relation to Christianity.

2. Perhaps something of this kind is shadowed forth in what is written in Exodus from the mouth of God, that the children of Israel were commanded to ask from their neighbours, and those who dwelt with them, vessels of silver and gold, and raiment, in order that, by spoiling the Egyptians, they might have material for the preparation of the things which pertained to the service of God. For from the things which the children of Israel took from the Egyptians the vessels in the holy of holies were made, — the ark with its lid, and the cherubim, and the mercy-seat, and the golden coffer, where was the manna, the angels' bread. These things were probably made from the best of the Egyptian gold. An inferior kind would be used for the solid golden candlestick near the inner veil, and its branches, and the golden table on which were the pieces of shewbread, and the golden censer between them. And if there was a third and fourth quality of gold, from it would be made the holy vessels ; and the other things would be made of Egyptian silver. For when the children of Israel dwelt in Egypt, they gained this from their dwelling there, that they had no lack of such precious material for the utensils of the service of God. And of the Egyptian raiment were probably made all those things which, as the Scripture mentions, needed sewed and embroidered work, sewed with the wisdom of God, the one to the other, that the veils might be made, and the inner and the cuter courts. And why should I go on, in this untimely digression, to set forth how useful to the children of Israel were the things brought from Egypt, which the Egyptians had not put to a proper use, but which the Hebrews, guided by the wisdom of God, used for God's service? Now the sacred Scripture is wont to represent as an evil the going down from the land of the children of Israel into Egypt, indicating that certain persons get harm from sojourning among the Egyptians, that is to say, from meddling with the knowledge of this world, after they have subscribed to the law of God, and the Israelitish service of Him. Ader[2] at least, the Idumæan, so long as he was in the land of Israel, and had not tasted the bread of the Egyptians, made no idols. It was when he fled from the wise Solomon, and went down into Egypt, as it were flying from the wisdom of God, and was made a kinsman of Pharaoh by marrying his wife's sister, and begetting a child, who was brought up with the children of Pharaoh, that he did this. Wherefore, although he did return to the land of Israel, he returned only to divide the people of God, and to make them say to the golden calf, " These be thy gcds, O Israel, which brought thee up from the land of Egypt."[3] And I may tell you from my experience, that not many take from Egypt only the useful, and go away and use it for the service of God ; while Ader the Idumæan has many brethren. These are they who, from their Greek studies, produce heretical notions, and set them up, like the golden calf, in Bethel, which signifies " God's house." In these words also

---

[1] This Gregory, styled the Wonder-worker, (Thaumaturgus) was afterwards bishop of Neo-Cæsarea.

[2] Origen evidently confounds Hadad the Edomite, of 1 Kings xi. 14, with Jeroboam.

[3] [1 Kings xii. 28. S.]

there seems to me an indication that they have set up their own imaginations in the Scriptures, where the word of God dwells, which is called in a figure Bethel. The other figure, the word says, was set up in Dan. Now the borders of Dan are the most extreme, and nearest the borders of the Gentiles, as is clear from what is written in Joshua, the son of Nun. Now some of the devices of these brethren of Ader, as we call them, are also very near the borders of the Gentiles.

3. Do you then, my son, diligently apply yourself to the reading of the sacred Scriptures. Apply yourself, I say. For we who read the things of God need much application, lest we should say or think anything too rashly about them. And applying yourself thus to the study of the things of God, with faithful prejudgments such as are well pleasing to God, knock at its locked door, and it will be opened to you by the porter, of whom Jesus says, "To him the porter opens." [1] And applying yourself thus to the divine study, seek aright, and with unwavering trust in God, the meaning of the holy Scriptures, which so many have missed. Be not satisfied with knocking and seeking; for prayer is of all things indispensable to the knowledge of the things of God. For to this the Saviour exhorted, and said not only, "Knock, and it shall be opened to you; and seek, and ye shall find," [2] but also, "Ask, and it shall be given unto you." [3] My fatherly love to you has made me thus bold; but whether my boldness be good, God will know, and His Christ, and all partakers of the Spirit of God and the Spirit of Christ. May you also be a partaker, and be ever increasing your inheritance, that you may say not only, "We are become partakers of Christ," [4] but also partakers of God.

[1] John x. 3.
[2] Matt. vii. 7.
[3] Luke xi. 9.
[4] Heb. iii. 14.

ELUCIDATION.

THIS golden letter, doubtless genuine, was attended with very great consequences, of which we shall gather more hereafter. It is worthy of the solemn consideration of young students to whom this page may come. Gregory was unbaptized when Origen (*circa* A.D. 230) thus addressed his conscience.

On the letters here inserted, let me refer the student to Routh, *Reliqu.*, ii. pp. 312–327; also same vol., pp. 222–228; also iii. 254–256.

For the facts concerning this letter to Gregory, see Cave, i. p. 400.

ORIGEN AGAINST CELSUS.

BOOK I.

PREFACE.

1. WHEN false witnesses testified against our Lord and Saviour Jesus Christ, He remained silent; and when unfounded charges were brought against Him, He returned no answer, believing that His whole life and conduct among the Jews were a better refutation than any answer to the false testimony, or than any formal defence against the accusations. And I know not, my pious Ambrosius,[1] why you wished me to write a reply to the false charges brought by Celsus against the Christians, and to his accusations directed against the faith of the Churches in his treatise; as if the facts themselves did not furnish a manifest refutation, and the doctrine a better answer than any writing, seeing it both disposes of the false statements, and does not leave to the accusations any credibility or validity. Now, with respect to our Lord's silence when false witness was borne against Him, it is sufficient at present to quote the words of Matthew, for the testimony of Mark is to the same effect. And the words of Matthew are as follow: "And the high priest and the council sought false witness against Jesus to put Him to death, but found none, although many false witnesses came forward. At last two false witnesses came and said, This fellow said, I am able to destroy the temple of God, and after three days to build it up. And the high priest arose, and said to Him, Answerest thou nothing to what these witness against thee? But Jesus held His peace."[2] And that He returned no answer when falsely accused, the following is the statement: "And Jesus stood before the governor; and he asked Him, saying, Art Thou the King of the Jews? And Jesus said to him, Thou sayest. And when He was accused of the chief priests and elders,

He answered nothing. Then said Pilate unto Him, Hearest thou not how many things they witness against Thee? And He answered him to never a word, insomuch that the governor marvelled greatly."[3]

2. It was, indeed, matter of surprise to men even of ordinary intelligence, that one who was accused and assailed by false testimony, but who was able to defend Himself, and to show that He was guilty of none of the charges (alleged), and who might have enumerated the praiseworthy deeds of His own life, and His miracles wrought by divine power, so as to give the judge an opportunity of delivering a more honourable judgment regarding Him, should not have done this, but should have disdained such a procedure, and in the nobleness of His nature have contemned His accusers.[4] That the judge would, without any hesitation, have set Him at liberty if He had offered a defence, is clear from what is related of him when he said, "Which of the two do ye wish that I should release unto you, Barabbas or Jesus, who is called Christ?"[5] and from what the Scripture adds, "For he knew that for envy they had delivered Him."[6] Jesus, however, is at all times assailed by false witnesses, and, while wickedness remains in the world, is ever exposed to accusation. And yet even now He continues silent before these things, and makes no audible answer, but places His defence in the lives of His genuine disciples, which are a pre-eminent testimony, and one that rises superior to all false witness, and refutes and overthrows all unfounded accusations and charges.

3. I venture, then, to say that this "apology" which you require me to compose will somewhat weaken that defence (of Christianity) which rests on facts, and that power of Jesus which is manifest to those who are not altogether devoid of perception. Notwithstanding, that we may

---

[1] This individual is mentioned by Eusebius (*Eccles. Hist.*, vi. c. 18) as having been converted from the heresy of Valentinus to the faith of the Church by the efforts of Origen. [Lardner (*Credib.*, vii. 210-212) is inclined to "place" Celsus in the year 176. Here and elsewhere this learned authority is diffuse on the subject, and merits careful attention.]
[2] Cf. Matt. xxvi. 59-63.

[3] Cf. Matt. xxvii. 11-14.
[4] Μεγαλοφυῶς ὑπερεωρακέναι τοὺς κατηγόρους.
[5] Cf. Matt. xxvii. 17.
[6] Cf. Matt. xxvii. 18.

not have the appearance of being reluctant to undertake the task which you have enjoined, we have endeavoured, to the best of our ability, to suggest, by way of answer to each of the statements advanced by Celsus, what seemed to us adapted to refute them, although his arguments have no power to shake the faith of any (true) believer. And forbid, indeed, that any one should be found who, after having been a partaker in such a love of God as was (displayed) in Christ Jesus, could be shaken in his purpose by the arguments of Celsus, or of any such as he. For Paul, when enumerating the innumerable causes which generally separate men from the love of Christ and from the love of God in Christ Jesus (to all of which, the love that was in himself rose superior), did not set down argument among the grounds of separation. For observe that he says, firstly : "Who shall separate us from the love of Christ? Shall tribulation, or distress, or persecution, or famine, or nakedness, or peril, or sword? (as it is written, For Thy sake we are killed all the day long; we are accounted as sheep for the slaughter.) Nay, in all these things we are more than conquerors through Him that loved us." [1] And secondly, when laying down another series of causes which naturally tend to separate those who are not firmly grounded in their religion, he says : "For I am persuaded that neither death, nor life, nor angels, nor principalities, nor powers, nor things present, nor things to come, nor height, nor depth, nor any other creature, shall be able to separate us from the love of God, which is in Christ Jesus our Lord." [2]

4. Now, truly, it is proper that *we* should feel elated because afflictions, or those other causes enumerated by Paul, do not separate us (from Christ) ; but not that Paul and the other apostles, and any other resembling them, (should entertain that feeling), because they were far exalted above such things when they said, "In all these things we are *more* than conquerors through Him that loved us," [3] which is a stronger statement than that they are simply "conquerors." But if it be proper for apostles to entertain a feeling of elation in not being separated from the love of God that is in Christ Jesus our Lord, that feeling will be entertained by them, because neither death, nor life, nor angels, nor principalities, nor any of the things that follow, can separate them from the love of God which is in Christ Jesus our Lord. And therefore I do not congratulate that believer in Christ whose faith can be shaken by Celsus — who no longer shares the common life of men, but has long since departed — or by any apparent plausibility of argument. [4] For I do not know in what rank to place him who has need of arguments written in books in answer to the charges of Celsus against the Christians, in order to prevent him from being shaken in his faith, and confirm him in it. But nevertheless, since in the multitude of those who are considered believers some such persons might be found as would have their faith shaken and overthrown by the writings of Celsus, but who might be preserved by a reply to them of such a nature as to refute his statements and to exhibit the truth, we have deemed it right to yield to your injunction, and to furnish an answer to the treatise which you sent us, but which I do not think that any one, although only a short way advanced in philosophy, will allow to be a "True Discourse," as Celsus has entitled it.

5. Paul, indeed, observing that there are in Greek philosophy certain things not to be lightly esteemed, which are plausible in the eyes of the many, but which represent falsehood as truth, says with regard to such : "Beware lest any man spoil you through philosophy and vain deceit, after the tradition of men, after the rudiments of the world, and not after Christ." [5] And seeing that there was a kind of greatness manifest in the words of the world's wisdom, he said that the words of the philosophers were "according to the rudiments of the world." No man of sense, however, would say that those of Celsus were "according to the rudiments of the world." Now those words, which contained some element of deceitfulness, the apostle named "vain deceit," probably by way of distinction from a deceit that was not "vain;" and the prophet Jeremiah observing this, ventured to say to God, "O LORD, Thou hast deceived me, and I was deceived; Thou art stronger than I, and hast prevailed." [6] But in the language of Celsus there seems to me to be no deceitfulness at all, not even that which is "vain;" such deceitfulness, viz., as is found in the language of those who have founded philosophical sects, and who have been endowed with no ordinary talent for such pursuits. And as no one would say that any ordinary error in geometrical demonstrations was intended to deceive, or would describe it for the sake of exercise in such matters; [7] so those opinions which are to be styled "vain deceit," and the "tradition of men," and "according to the rudiments of the world," must have some resemblance to the views of those who have been the founders of philosophical sects, (if such titles are to be appropriately applied to them).

---

[1] 1 Rom. viii. 35-37.
[2] Rom. viii. 38, 39.
[3] Rom. viii. 37, ὑπερνικῶμεν.
[4] ἤ τινος πιθανότητος λόγου.
[5] Col. ii. 8.
[6] Cf. Jer. xx. 7.
[7] Καὶ ὥσπερ οὐ τὸ τυχὸν τῶν ψευδομένων ἐν γεωμετρικοῖς θεωρήμασι ψευδογραφούμενόν τις ἄν λέγοι, ἤ καὶ ἀναγράφοι γυμνασίου ἔνεκεν τοῦ ἀπὸ τοιούτων. Cf. note of Ruæus *in loc.*

6. After proceeding with this work as far as the place where Celsus introduces the Jew disputing with Jesus, I resolved to prefix this preface to the beginning (of the treatise), in order that the reader of our reply to Celsus might fall in with it first, and see that this book has been composed not for those who are thorough believers, but for such as are either wholly unacquainted with the Christian faith, or for those who, as the apostle terms them, are "weak in the faith;" regarding whom he says, "Him that is weak in the faith receive ye."[1] And this preface must be my apology for beginning my answer to Celsus on one plan, and carrying it on on another. For my first intention was to indicate his principal objections, and then briefly the answers that were returned to them, and subsequently to make a systematic treatise of the whole discourse.[2] But afterwards, circumstances themselves suggested to me that I should be economical of my time, and that, satisfied with what I had already stated at the commencement, I should in the following part grapple closely, to the best of my ability, with the charges of Celsus. I have therefore to ask indulgence for those portions which follow the preface towards the beginning of the book. And if you are not impressed by the powerful arguments which succeed, then, asking similar indulgence also with respect to them, I refer you, if you still desire an argumentative solution of the objections of Celsus, to those men who are wiser than myself, and who are able by words and treatises to overthrow the charges which he brings against us. But better is the man who, although meeting with the work of Celsus, needs no answer to it at all, but who despises all its contents, since they are contemned, and with good reason, by every believer in Christ, through the Spirit that is in him.

CHAP. I.

The first point which Celsus brings forward, in his desire to throw discredit upon Christianity, is, that the Christians entered into secret associations with each other contrary to law, saying, that "of associations some are public, and that these are in accordance with the laws; others, again, secret, and maintained in violation of the laws." And his wish is to bring into disrepute what are termed the "love-feasts"[3] of the Christians, as if they had their origin in the common danger, and were more binding than any oaths. Since, then, he babbles about the public law, alleging that the associations of the Christians are in violation of it, we have to reply, that if a man were placed among Scythians, whose laws were unholy,[4] and having no opportunity of escape, were compelled to live among them, such an one would with good reason, for the sake of the law of truth, which the Scythians would regard as wickedness,[5] enter into associations contrary to their laws, with those likeminded with himself; so, if truth is to decide, the laws of the heathens which relate to images, and an atheistical polytheism, are "Scythian" laws, or more impious even than these, if there be any such. It is not irrational, then, to form associations in opposition to existing laws, if done for the sake of the truth. For as those persons would do well who should enter into a secret association in order to put to death a tyrant who had seized upon the liberties of a state, so Christians also, when tyrannized over by him who is called the devil, and by falsehood, form leagues contrary to the laws of the devil, against his power, and for the safety of those others whom they may succeed in persuading to revolt from a government which is, as it were, "Scythian," and despotic.

CHAP. II.

Celsus next proceeds to say, that the system of doctrine, viz., Judaism, upon which Christianity depends, was barbarous in its origin. And with an appearance of fairness, he does not reproach Christianity[6] because of its origin among barbarians, but gives the latter credit for their ability in discovering (such) doctrines. To this, however, he adds the statement, that the Greeks are more skilful than any others in judging, establishing, and reducing to practice the discoveries of barbarous nations. Now this is our answer to his allegations, and our defence of the truths contained in Christianity, that if any one were to come from the study of Grecian opinions and usages to the Gospel, he would not only decide that its doctrines were true, but would by practice establish their truth, and supply whatever seemed wanting, from a Grecian point of view, to their demonstration, and thus confirm the truth of Christianity. We have to say, moreover, that the Gospel has a demonstration of its own, more divine than any established by Grecian dialectics. And this diviner method is called by the apostle the "manifestation of the Spirit and of power:" of "the Spirit," on account of the prophecies, which are sufficient to produce faith in any one who reads them, especially in those things which relate to Christ; and of "power," because of the signs and wonders which we must believe to have been performed, both on many other grounds, and on this, that traces of them are still preserved among those

---

[1] Rom. xiv. 1.
[2] σωματοποιῆσαι.
[3] τὴν καλουμένην ἀγάπην.

[4] ἀθέσμους.
[5] παρανομίαν.
[6] τῷ λόγῳ.

who regulate their lives by the precepts of the Gospel.

CHAP. III.

After this, Celsus proceeding to speak of the Christians teaching and practising their favourite doctrines in secret, and saying that they do this to some purpose, seeing they escape the penalty of death which is imminent, he compares their dangers with those which were encountered by such men as Socrates for the sake of philosophy; and here he might have mentioned Pythagoras as well, and other philosophers. But our answer to this is, that in the case of Socrates the Athenians immediately afterwards repented; and no feeling of bitterness remained in their minds regarding him, as also happened in the history of Pythagoras. The followers of the latter, indeed, for a considerable time established their schools in that part of Italy called Magna Græcia; but in the case of the Christians, the Roman Senate, and the princes of the time, and the soldiery, and the people, and the relatives of those who had become converts to the faith, made war upon their doctrine, and would have prevented (its progress), overcoming it by a confederacy of so powerful a nature, had it not, by the help of God, escaped the danger, and risen above it, so as (finally) to defeat the whole world in its conspiracy against it.

CHAP. IV.

Let us notice also how he thinks to cast discredit upon our system of morals,[1] alleging that it is only common to us with other philosophers, and no venerable or new branch of instruction. In reply to which we have to say, that unless all men had naturally impressed upon their minds sound ideas of morality, the doctrine of the punishment of sinners would have been excluded by those who bring upon themselves the righteous judgments of God. It is not therefore matter of surprise that the same God should have sown in the hearts of all men those truths which He taught by the prophets and the Saviour, in order that at the divine judgment every man may be without excuse, having the "requirements[2] of the law written upon his heart," — a truth obscurely alluded to by the Bible[3] in what the Greeks regard as a myth, where it represents God as having with His own finger written down the commandments, and given them to Moses, and which the wickedness of the worshippers of the calf made him break in pieces, as if the flood of wickedness, so to speak, had swept them away. But Moses having again hewn tables of stone, God wrote the commandments a second time,

and gave them to him; the prophetic word preparing the soul, as it were, after the first transgression, for the writing of God a second time.

CHAP. V.

Treating of the regulations respecting idolatry as being peculiar to Christianity, Celsus establishes their correctness, saying that the Christians do not consider those to be gods that are made with hands, on the ground that it is not in conformity with right reason (to suppose) that images, fashioned by the most worthless and depraved of workmen, and in many instances also provided by wicked men, can be (regarded as) gods. In what follows, however, wishing to show that this is a common opinion, and one not first discovered by Christianity, he quotes a saying of Heraclitus to this effect: "That those who draw near to lifeless images, as if they were gods, act in a similar manner to those who would enter into conversation with houses." Respecting this, then, we have to say, that ideas were implanted in the minds of men like the principles of morality, from which not only Heraclitus, but any other Greek or barbarian, might by reflection have deduced the same conclusion; for he states that the Persians also were of the same opinion, quoting Herodotus as his authority. We also can add to these Zeno of Citium, who in his *Polity* says: "And there will be no need to build temples, for nothing ought to be regarded as sacred, or of much value, or holy, which is the work of builders and of mean men." It is evident, then, with respect to this opinion (as well as others), that there has been engraven upon the hearts of men by the finger of God a sense of the duty that is required.

CHAP. VI.

After this, through the influence of some motive which is unknown to me, Celsus asserts that it is by the names of certain demons, and by the use of incantations, that the Christians appear to be possessed of (miraculous) power; hinting, I suppose, at the practices of those who expel evil spirits by incantations. And here he manifestly appears to malign the Gospel. For it is not by incantations that Christians seem to prevail (over evil spirits), but by the name of Jesus, accompanied by the announcement of the narratives which relate to Him; for the repetition of these has frequently been the means of driving demons out of men, especially when those who repeated them did so in a sound and genuinely believing spirit. Such power, indeed, does the name of Jesus possess over evil spirits, that there have been instances where it was effectual, when it was pronounced even by bad men, which Jesus Himself taught

---

[1] τὸν ἠθικὸν τόπον.
[2] τὸ βούλημα τοῦ νόμου.
[3] ὁ λόγος.

(would be the case), when He said: "Many shall say to Me in that day, In Thy name we have cast out devils, and done many wonderful works."[1] Whether Celsus omitted this from intentional malignity, or from ignorance, I do not know. And he next proceeds to bring a charge against the Saviour Himself, alleging that it was by means of sorcery that He was able to accomplish the wonders which He performed; and that foreseeing that others would attain the same knowledge, and do the same things, making a boast of doing them by help of the power of God, He excludes such from His kingdom. And his accusation is, that if they are justly excluded, while He Himself is guilty of the same practices, He is a wicked man; but if He is not guilty of wickedness in doing such things, neither are they who do the same as He. But even if it be impossible to show by what power Jesus wrought these miracles, it is clear that Christians employ no spells or incantations, but the simple name of Jesus, and certain other words in which they repose faith, according to the holy Scriptures.

CHAP. VII.

Moreover, since he frequently calls the Christian doctrine a secret system (of belief), we must confute him on this point also, since almost the entire world is better acquainted with what Christians preach than with the favourite opinions of philosophers. For who is ignorant of the statement that Jesus was born of a virgin, and that He was crucified, and that His resurrection is an article of faith among many, and that a general judgment is announced to come, in which the wicked are to be punished according to their deserts, and the righteous to be duly rewarded? And yet the mystery of the resurrection, not being understood,[2] is made a subject of ridicule among unbelievers. In these circumstances, to speak of the Christian doctrine as a *secret* system, is altogether absurd. But that there should be certain doctrines, not made known to the multitude, which are (revealed) after the exoteric ones have been taught, is not a peculiarity of Christianity alone, but also of philosophic systems, in which certain truths are exoteric and others esoteric. Some of the hearers of Pythagoras were content with his *ipse dixit;* while others were taught in secret those doctrines which were not deemed fit to be communicated to profane and insufficiently prepared ears. Moreover, all the mysteries that are celebrated everywhere throughout Greece and barbarous countries, although held in secret, have

no discredit thrown upon them, so that it is in vain that he endeavours to calumniate the secret doctrines of Christianity, seeing he does not correctly understand its nature.

CHAP. VIII.

It is with a certain eloquence,[3] indeed, that he appears to advocate the cause of those who bear witness to the truth of Christianity by their death, in the following words: "And I do not maintain that if a man, who has adopted a system of good doctrine, is to incur danger from men on that account, he should either apostatize, or feign apostasy, or openly deny his opinions." And he condemns those who, while holding the Christian views, either pretend that they do not, or deny them, saying that "he who holds a certain opinion ought not to feign recantation, or publicly disown it." And here Celsus must be convicted of self-contradiction. For from other treatises of his it is ascertained that he was an Epicurean; but here, because he thought that he could assail Christianity with better effect by not professing the opinions of Epicurus, he pretends that there is a something better in man than the earthly part of his nature, which is akin to God, and says that "they in whom this element, viz., the soul, is in a healthy condition, are ever seeking after their kindred nature, meaning God, and are ever desiring to hear something about Him, and to call it to remembrance." Observe now the insincerity of his character! Having said a little before, that "the man who had embraced a system of good doctrine ought not, even if exposed to danger on that account from men, to disavow it, or pretend that he had done so, nor yet openly disown it," he now involves himself in all manner of contradictions. For he knew that if he acknowledged himself an Epicurean, he would not obtain any credit when accusing those who, in any degree, introduce the doctrine of Providence, and who place a God over the world. And we have heard that there were two individuals of the name of Celsus, both of whom were Epicureans; the earlier of the two having lived in the time of Nero, but this one in that of Adrian, and later.

CHAP. IX.

He next proceeds to recommend, that in adopting opinions we should follow reason and a rational guide,[4] since he who assents to opinions without following this course is very liable to be deceived. And he compares inconsiderate believers to Metragyrtæ, and soothsayers, and Mithræ, and Sabbadians, and to anything else

---

[1] Cf. Matt. vii. 22.
[2] The words, as they stand in the text of Lommatzsch, are, ἀλλὰ καὶ μὴν νοηθὲν τὸ περὶ τῆς ἀναστάσεως μυστήριον. Ruæus would read μή instead of μήν. This emendation has been adopted in the translation.

[3] δεινότητος.
[4] λόγῳ καὶ λογικῷ ὁδηγῷ.

that one may fall in with, and to the phantoms of Hecate, or any other demon or demons. For as amongst such persons are frequently to be found wicked men, who, taking advantage of the ignorance of those who are easily deceived, lead them away whither they will, so also, he says, is the case among Christians. And he asserts that certain persons who do not wish either to give or receive a reason for their belief, keep repeating, "Do not examine, but believe !" and, "Your faith will save you !" And he alleges that such also say, "The wisdom of this life is bad, but that foolishness is a good thing !" To which we have to answer, that if it were possible for all to leave the business of life, and devote themselves to philosophy, no other method ought to be adopted by any one, but this alone. For in the Christian system also it will be found that there is, not to speak at all arrogantly, at least as much of investigation into articles of belief, and of explanation of dark sayings, occurring in the prophetical writings, and of the parables in the Gospels, and of countless other things, which either were narrated or enacted with a symbolical signification,[1] (as is the case with other systems). But since the course alluded to is impossible, partly on account of the necessities of life, partly on account of the weakness of men, as only a very few individuals devote themselves earnestly to study,[2] what better method could be devised with a view of assisting the multitude, than that which was delivered by Jesus to the heathen? And let us inquire, with respect to the great multitude of believers, who have washed away the mire of wickedness in which they formerly wallowed, whether it were better for them to believe without a reason, and (so) to have become reformed and improved in their habits, through the belief that men are chastised for sins, and honoured for good works ; or not to have allowed themselves to be converted on the strength of mere faith, but (to have waited) until they could give themselves to a thorough examination of the (necessary) reasons. For it is manifest that, (on such a plan), all men, with very few exceptions, would not obtain this (amelioration of conduct) which they have obtained through a simple faith, but would continue to remain in the practice of a wicked life. Now, whatever other evidence can be furnished of the fact, that it was not without divine intervention that the philanthropic scheme of Christianity was introduced among men, this also must be added. For a pious man will not believe that even a physician of the body, who restores the sick to better health, could take up his abode in any city or country without divine

permission, since no good happens to men without the help of God. And if he who has cured the *bodies* of many, or restored them to better health, does not effect his cures without the help of God, how much more He who has healed the *souls* of many, and has turned them (to virtue), and improved their nature, and attached them to God who is over all things, and taught them to refer every action to His good pleasure, and to shun all that is displeasing to Him, even to the least of their words or deeds, or even of the thoughts of their hearts?

CHAP. X.

In the next place, since our opponents keep repeating those statements about faith, we must say that, considering it as a useful thing for the multitude, we admit that we teach those men to believe without reasons, who are unable to abandon all other employments, and give themselves to an examination of arguments ; and our opponents, although they do not acknowledge it, yet practically do the same. For who is there that, on betaking himself to the study of philosophy, and throwing himself into the ranks of some sect, either by chance,[3] or because he is provided with a teacher of that school, adopts such a course for any other reason, except that he *believes* his particular sect to be superior to any other? For, not waiting to hear the arguments of all the other philosophers, and of all the different sects, and the reasons for condemning one system and for supporting another, he in this way elects to become a Stoic, e.g., or a Platonist, or a Peripatetic, or an Epicurean, or a follower of some other school, and is thus borne, although they will not admit it, by a kind of irrational impulse to the practice, say of Stoicism, to the disregard of the others ; despising either Platonism, as being marked by greater humility than the others ; or Peripateticism, as more human, and as admitting with more fairness[4] than other systems the blessings of human life. And some also, alarmed at first sight[5] about the doctrine of providence, from seeing what happens in the world to the vicious and to the virtuous, have rashly concluded that there is no divine providence at all, and have adopted the views of Epicurus and Celsus.

CHAP. XI.

Since, then, as reason teaches, we must repose faith in some one of those who have been the introducers of sects among the Greeks or Barbarians, why should we not rather believe in God who is over all things, and in Him who teaches

---

[1] συμβολικῶς γεγενημένων, ἢ νενομοθετημένων.
[2] σφόδρα ὀλίγων ἐπὶ τὸν λόγον ᾀττόντων.

[3] ἀποκληρωτικῶς.
[4] μᾶλλον εὐγνωμόνως.
[5] ἀπὸ πρώτης προσβολῆς.

that worship is due to God alone, and that other things are to be passed by, either as non-existent, or as existing indeed, and worthy of honour, but not of worship and reverence? And respecting these things, he who not only believes, but who contemplates things with the eye of reason, will state the demonstrations that occur to him, and which are the result of careful investigation. And why should it not be more reasonable, seeing all human things are dependent upon faith, to believe God rather than them? For who enters on a voyage, or contracts a marriage, or becomes the father of children, or casts seed into the ground, without believing that better things will result from so doing, although the contrary might and sometimes does happen? And yet the belief that better things, even agreeably to their wishes, will follow, makes all men venture upon uncertain enterprises, which may turn out differently from what they expect. And if the hope and belief of a better future be the support of life in every uncertain enterprise, why shall not this faith rather be rationally accepted by him who believes on better grounds than he who sails the sea, or tills the ground, or marries a wife, or engages in any other human pursuit, in the existence of a God who was the Creator of all these things, and in Him who with surpassing wisdom and divine greatness of mind dared to make known this doctrine to men in every part of the world, at the cost of great danger, and of a death considered infamous, which He underwent for the sake of the human race; having also taught those who were persuaded to embrace His doctrine at the first, to proceed, under the peril of every danger, and of ever impending death, to all quarters of the world to ensure the salvation of men?

CHAP. XII.

In the next place, when Celsus says in express words, "If they would answer me, not as if I were asking for information, for I am acquainted with all their opinions, but because I take an equal interest in them all, it would be well. And if they will not, but will keep reiterating, as they generally do, 'Do not investigate,' etc., they must, he continues, explain to me at least of what nature these things are of which they speak, and whence they are derived," etc. Now, with regard to his statement that he "is acquainted with all our doctrines," we have to say that this is a boastful and daring assertion; for if he had read the prophets in particular, which are full of acknowledged difficulties, and of declarations that are obscure to the multitude, and if he had perused the parables of the Gospels, and the other writings of the law and of the Jewish history, and the utterances of the apostles, and had read them candidly, with a desire to enter into

their meaning, he would not have expressed himself with such boldness, nor said that he "was acquainted with all their doctrines." Even we ourselves, who have devoted much study to these writings, would not say that "we were acquainted with everything," for we have a regard for truth. Not one of us will assert, "I know all the doctrines of Epicurus," or will be confident that he knows all those of Plato, in the knowledge of the fact that so many differences of opinion exist among the expositors of these systems. For who is so daring as to say that he knows all the opinions of the Stoics or of the Peripatetics? Unless, indeed, it should be the case that he has heard this boast, "I know them all," from some ignorant and senseless individuals, who do not perceive their own ignorance, and should thus imagine, from having had such persons as his teachers, that he was acquainted with them all. Such an one appears to me to act very much as a person would do who had visited Egypt (where the Egyptian *savans*, learned in their country's literature, are greatly given to philosophizing about those things which are regarded among them as divine, but where the vulgar, hearing certain myths, the reasons of which they do not understand, are greatly elated because of their fancied knowledge), and who should imagine that he is acquainted with the whole circle of Egyptian knowledge, after having been a disciple of the ignorant alone, and without having associated with any of the priests, or having learned the mysteries of the Egyptians from any other source. And what I have said regarding the learned and ignorant among the Egyptians, I might have said also of the Persians; among whom there are mysteries, conducted on rational principles by the learned among them, but understood in a symbolical sense by the more superficial of the multitude.[1] And the same remark applies to the Syrians, and Indians, and to all those who have a literature and a mythology.

CHAP. XIII.

But since Celsus has declared it to be a saying of many Christians, that "the wisdom of this life is a bad thing, but that foolishness is good," we have to answer that he slanders the Gospel, not giving the words as they actually occur in the writings of Paul, where they run as follow: "If any one among you seemeth to be wise in this world, let him become a fool, that he may become wise. For the wisdom of this world is foolishness with God."[2] The apostle, therefore, does not say simply that "wisdom is fool-

---

[1] Παρ' οἷς εἰσι τελεταί, πρεσβευόμεναι μὲν λογικῶς ὑπὸ τῶν παρ' αὐτοῖς λογίων, συμβολικῶς δὲ γινόμεναι ὑπὸ τῶν παρ' αὐτοῖς πολλῶν καὶ ἐπιπολαιοτέρων. For γινόμεναι Ruæus prefers γινωσκόμεναι, which is adopted in the translation.
[2] 1 Cor. iii. 18, 19.

ishness with God," but "the wisdom of *this world*." And again, not, "If any one among you seemeth to be wise, let him become a fool universally;" but, "let him become a fool *in this world*, that he may become wise." We term, then, "the wisdom of this world," every false system of philosophy, which, according to the Scriptures, is brought to nought; and we call foolishness good, not without restriction, but when a man becomes foolish as to *this world*. As if we were to say that the Platonist, who believes in the immortality of the soul, and in the doctrine of its metempsychosis,[1] incurs the charge of folly with the Stoics, who discard this opinion; and with the Peripatetics, who babble about the subtleties of Plato; and with the Epicureans, who call it superstition to introduce a providence, and to place a God over all things. Moreover, that it is in agreement with the spirit of Christianity, of much more importance to give our assent to doctrines upon grounds of reason and wisdom than on that of faith merely, and that it was only in certain circumstances that the latter course was desired by Christianity, in order not to leave men altogether without help, is shown by that genuine disciple of Jesus, Paul, when he says: "For after that, in the wisdom of God, the world by wisdom knew not God, it pleased God by the foolishness of preaching to save them that believe."[2] Now by these words it is clearly shown that it is by the wisdom of God that God ought to be known. But as this result did not follow, it pleased God a second time to save them that believe, not by "folly" *universally*, but by such foolishness as depended on preaching. For the preaching of Jesus Christ as crucified is the "foolishness" of preaching, as Paul also perceived, when he said, "But we preach Christ crucified, to the Jews a stumbling-block, and to the Greeks foolishness; but to them who are called, both Jews and Greeks, Christ the power of God, and wisdom of God."[3]

CHAP. XIV.

Celsus, being of opinion that there is to be found among many nations a general relationship of doctrine, enumerates all the nations which gave rise to such and such opinions; but for some reason, unknown to me, he casts a slight upon the Jews, not including them amongst the others, as having either laboured along with them, and arrived at the same conclusions, or as having entertained similar opinions on many subjects. It is proper, therefore,

to ask him why he gives credence to the histories of Barbarians and Greeks respecting the antiquity of those nations of whom he speaks, but stamps the histories of this nation alone as false. For if the respective writers related the events which are found in these works in the spirit of truth, why should we distrust the prophets of the Jews alone? And if Moses and the prophets have recorded many things in their history from a desire to favour their own system, why should we not say the same of the historians of other countries? Or, when the Egyptians or their histories speak evil of the Jews, are they to be believed on that point; but the Jews, when saying the same things of the Egyptians, and declaring that they had suffered great injustice at their hands, and that on this account they had been punished by God, are to be charged with falsehood? And this applies not to the Egyptians alone, but to others; for we shall find that there was a connection between the Assyrians and the Jews, and that this is recorded in the ancient histories of the Assyrians. And so also the Jewish historians (I avoid using the word "prophets," that I may not appear to prejudge the case) have related that the Assyrians were enemies of the Jews. Observe at once, then, the arbitrary procedure of this individual, who believes the histories of these nations on the ground of their being learned, and condemns others as being wholly ignorant. For listen to the statement of Celsus: "There is," he says, "an authoritative account from the very beginning, respecting which there is a constant agreement among all the most learned nations, and cities, and men." And yet he will not call the Jews a learned nation in the same way in which he does the Egyptians, and Assyrians, and Indians, and Persians, and Odrysians, and Samothracians, and Eleusinians.

CHAP. XV.

How much more impartial than Celsus is Numenius the Pythagorean, who has given many proofs of being a very eloquent man, and who has carefully tested many opinions, and collected together from many sources what had the appearance of truth; for, in the first book of his treatise *On the Good*, speaking of those nations who have adopted the opinion that God is incorporeal, he enumerates the Jews also among those who hold this view; not showing any reluctance to use even the language of their prophets in his treatise, and to give it a metaphorical signification. It is said, moreover, that Hermippus has recorded in his first book, *On Lawgivers*, that it was from the Jewish people that Pythagoras derived the philosophy which he introduced among the Greeks. And there is extant a work by the historian Hecataeus, treat-

---

[1] μετενσωματώσεως.
[2] Ἔτι δὲ ὅτι καὶ κατὰ τὸ τῷ λόγῳ ἀρέσκον, πολλῷ διαφέρει μετὰ λόγου καὶ σοφίας συγκατατίθεσθαι τοῖς δόγμασιν, ἤπερ μετὰ ψιλῆς τῆς πίστεως· καὶ ὅτι κατὰ περίστασιν καὶ τοῦτ' ἐβουλήθη ὁ Λόγος, ἵνα μὴ πάντη ἀνωφελεῖς ἐάσῃ τοὺς ἀνθρώπους, δηλοῖ ὁ τοῦ Ἰησοῦ γνήσιος μαθητής, etc.
[3] 1 Cor. i. 23, 24.

ing of the Jews, in which so high a character is bestowed upon that nation for its learning, that Herennius Philo, in his treatise on the Jews, has doubts in the first place, whether it is really the composition of the historian; and says, in the second place, that if really his, it is probable that he was carried away by the plausible nature of the Jewish history, and so yielded his assent to their system.

CHAP. XVI.

I must express my surprise that Celsus should class the Odrysians, and Samothracians, and Eleusinians, and Hyperboreans among the most ancient and learned nations, and should not deem the Jews worthy of a place among such, either for their learning or their antiquity, although there are many treatises in circulation among the Egyptians, and Phœnicians, and Greeks, which testify to their existence as an ancient people, but which I have considered it unnecessary to quote. For any one who chooses may read what Flavius Josephus has recorded in his two books, *On the Antiquity* [1] *of the Jews*, where he brings together a great collection of writers, who bear witness to the antiquity of the Jewish people; and there exists the *Discourse to the Greeks* of Tatian the younger,[2] in which with very great learning he enumerates those historians who have treated of the antiquity of the Jewish nation and of Moses. It seems, then, to be not from a love of truth, but from a spirit of hatred, that Celsus makes these statements, his object being to asperse the origin of Christianity, which is connected with Judaism. Nay, he styles the Galactophagi of Homer, and the Druids of the Gauls, and the Getæ, most learned and ancient tribes, on account of the resemblance between their traditions and those of the Jews, although I know not whether any of their histories survive; but the Hebrews alone, as far as in him lies, he deprives of the honour both of antiquity and learning. And again, when making a list of ancient and learned men who have conferred benefits upon their contemporaries (by their deeds), and upon posterity by their writings, he excluded Moses from the number; while of Linus, to whom Celsus assigns a foremost place in his list, there exists neither laws nor discourses which produced a change for the better among any tribes; whereas a whole nation, dispersed throughout the entire world, obey the laws of Moses. Consider, then, whether it is not from open malevolence that he has expelled Moses from his catalogue of learned men, while asserting that Linus, and Musæus, and Orpheus, and Pherecydes, and the Persian Zo-

roaster, and Pythagoras, discussed these topics, and that their opinions were deposited in books, and have thus been preserved down to the present time. And it is intentionally also that he has omitted to take notice of the myth, embellished chiefly by Orpheus, in which the gods are described as affected by human weaknesses and passions.

CHAP. XVII.

In what follows, Celsus, assailing the Mosaic history, finds fault with those who give it a tropical and allegorical signification. And here one might say to this great man, who inscribed upon his own work the title of a *True Discourse*, "Why, good sir, do you make it a boast to have it recorded that the gods should engage in such adventures as are described by your learned poets and philosophers, and be guilty of abominable intrigues, and of engaging in wars against their own fathers, and of cutting off their secret parts, and should dare to commit and to suffer such enormities; while Moses, who gives no such accounts respecting God, nor even regarding the holy angels, and who relates deeds of far less atrocity regarding men (for in his writings no one ever ventured to commit such crimes as Kronos did against Uranus, or Zeus against his father, or that of the father of men and gods, who had intercourse with his own daughter), should be considered as having deceived those who were placed under his laws, and to have led them into error?" And here Celsus seems to me to act somewhat as Thrasymachus the Platonic philosopher did, when he would not allow Socrates to answer regarding justice, as he wished, but said, "Take care not to say that utility is justice, or duty, or anything of that kind." For in like manner Celsus assails (as he thinks) the Mosaic histories, and finds fault with those who understand them allegorically, at the same time bestowing also some praise upon those who do so, to the effect that they are more impartial (than those who do not); and thus, as it were, he prevents by his cavils those who are able to show the true state of the case from offering such a defence as they would wish to offer.[3]

CHAP. XVIII.

And challenging a comparison of book with book, I would say, "Come now, good sir, take down the poems of Linus, and of Musæus, and of Orpheus, and the writings of Pherecydes, and carefully compare these with the laws of Moses — histories with histories, and ethical discourses with laws and commandments — and see

---

[1] [ἀρχαιότητος. See Josephus's *Works*, for the treatise in two books, usually designated, as written, *Against Apion.* S.]
[2] [See vol. ii. pp. 80, 81. S.]

[3] Οἱονεὶ κωλύεται, κατηγορήσας ὡς βούλεται, ἀπολογεῖσθαι τοὺς δυναμένους ὡς πέφυκεν ἔχειν τὰ πράγματα. We have taken κωλύεται as middle. Some propose κωλύει. And we have read βούλονται, a lection which is given by a second hand in one MS.

which of the two are the better fitted to change the character of the hearer on the very spot, and which to harden[1] him in his wickedness ; and observe that your series of writers display little concern for those readers who are to peruse them at once unaided,[2] but have composed their philosophy (as you term it) for those who are able to comprehend its metaphorical and allegorical signification ; whereas Moses, like a distinguished orator who meditates some figure of Rhetoric, and who carefully introduces in every part language of twofold meaning, has done this in his five books : neither affording, in the portion which relates to morals, any handle to his Jewish subjects for committing evil ; nor yet giving to the few individuals who were endowed with greater wisdom, and who were capable of investigating his meaning, a treatise devoid of material for speculation. But of your learned poets the very writings would seem no longer to be preserved, although they would have been carefully treasured up if the readers had perceived any benefit (likely to be derived from them) ; whereas the works of Moses have stirred up many, who were even aliens to the manners of the Jews, to the belief that, as these writings testify, the first who enacted these laws and delivered them to Moses, was the God who was the Creator of the world. For it became the Creator of the universe, after laying down laws for its government, to confer upon His words a power which might subdue all men in every part of the earth.[3] And this I maintain, having as yet entered into no investigation regarding Jesus, but still demonstrating that Moses, who is far inferior to the Lord, is, as the *Discourse* will show, greatly superior to your wise poets and philosophers."

CHAP. XIX.

After these statements, Celsus, from a secret desire to cast discredit upon the Mosaic account of the creation, which teaches that the world is not yet ten thousand years old, but very much under that, while concealing his wish, intimates his agreement with those who hold that the world is uncreated. For, maintaining that there have been, from all eternity, many conflagrations and many deluges, and that the flood which lately took place in the time of Deucalion is comparatively modern, he clearly demonstrates to those who are able to understand him, that, in his opinion, the world was uncreated. But let this assailant of the Christian faith tell us by what arguments he was compelled to accept the statement that there have been many conflagra-

tions and many cataclysms, and that the flood which occurred in the time of Deucalion, and the conflagration in that of Phaëthon, were more recent than any others. And if he should put forward the dialogues of Plato (as evidence) on these subjects, we shall say to him that it is allowable for us also to believe that there resided in the pure and pious soul of Moses, who ascended above all created things, and united himself to the Creator of the universe, and who made known divine things with far greater clearness than Plato, or those other wise men (who lived) among the Greeks and Romans, a spirit which was divine. And if he demands of us our reasons for such a belief, let him first give grounds for his own unsupported assertions, and then we shall show that this view of ours is the correct one.

CHAP. XX.

And yet, against his will, Celsus is entangled into testifying that the world is comparatively modern, and not yet ten thousand years old, when he says that the Greeks consider those things as ancient, because, owing to the deluges and conflagrations, they have not beheld or received any memorials of older events. But let Celsus have, as his authorities for the myth regarding the conflagrations and inundations, those persons who, in his opinion, are the most learned of the Egyptians, traces of whose wisdom are to be found in the worship of irrational animals, and in arguments which prove that such a worship of God is in conformity with reason, and of a secret and mysterious character. The Egyptians, then, when they boastfully give their own account of the divinity of animals, are to be considered wise ; but if any Jew, who has signified his adherence to the law and the lawgiver, refer everything to the Creator of the universe, and the only God, he is, in the opinion of Celsus and those like him, deemed inferior to him who degrades the Divinity not only to the level of rational and mortal animals, but even to that of irrational also ! — a view which goes far beyond the mythical doctrine of transmigration, according to which the soul falls down from the summit of heaven, and enters into the body of brute beasts, both tame and savage ! And if the Egyptians related fables of this kind, they are believed to convey a philosophical meaning by their enigmas and mysteries ; but if Moses compose and leave behind him histories and laws for an entire nation, they are to be considered as empty fables, the language of which admits of no allegorical meaning !

CHAP. XXI.

The following is the view of Celsus and the Epicureans : " Moses having," he says, "learned the doctrine which is to be found existing among

---

[1] Ἐπιτρίψαι. Other readings are ἐπιστρέψαι and ἀποστρέψαι, which convey the opposite meaning.
[2] αὐτόθεν.
[3] [See Dr. Waterland's charge to the clergy, on " The Wisdom of the Ancients borrowed from Divine Revelation," *Works*, vol. v. pp. 10, 24. S.]

wise nations and eloquent men, obtained the reputation of divinity." Now, in answer to this we have to say, that it may be allowed him that Moses did indeed hear a somewhat ancient doctrine, and transmitted the same to the Hebrews; that if the doctrine which he heard was false, and neither pious nor venerable, and if notwithstanding, he received it and handed it down to those under his authority, he is liable to censure; but if, as you assert, he gave his adherence to opinions that were wise and true, and educated his people by means of them, what, pray, has he done deserving of condemnation? Would, indeed, that not only Epicurus, but Aristotle, whose sentiments regarding providence are not so impious (as those of the former), and the Stoics, who assert that God is a body, had heard such a doctrine! Then the world would not have been filled with opinions which either disallow or enfeeble the action of providence, or introduce a corrupt corporeal principle, according to which the god of the Stoics is a body, with respect to whom they are not afraid to say that he is capable of change, and may be altered and transformed in all his parts, and, generally, that he is capable of corruption, if there be any one to corrupt him, but that he has the good fortune to escape corruption, because there is none to corrupt. Whereas the doctrine of the Jews and Christians, which preserves the immutability and unalterableness of the divine nature, is stigmatized as impious, because it does not partake of the profanity of those whose notions of God are marked by impiety, but because it says in the supplication addressed to the Divinity, "Thou art the same," [1] it being, moreover, an article of faith that God has said, "I change not." [2]

CHAP. XXII.

After this, Celsus, without condemning circumcision as practised by the Jews, asserts that this usage was derived from the Egyptians; thus believing the Egyptians rather than Moses, who says that Abraham was the first among men who practised the rite. And it is not Moses alone who mentions the name of Abraham, assigning to him great intimacy with God; but many also of those who give themselves to the practice of the conjuration of evil spirits, employ in their spells the expression "God of Abraham," pointing out by the very name the friendship (that existed) between that just man and God. And yet, while making use of the phrase "God of Abraham," they do not know who Abraham is! And the same remark applies to Isaac, and Jacob, and Israel; which names, although confessedly Hebrew, are frequently introduced by

those Egyptians who profess to produce some wonderful result by means of their knowledge. The rite of circumcision, however, which began with Abraham, and was discontinued by Jesus, who desired that His disciples should not practise it, is not before us for explanation; for the present occasion does not lead us to speak of such things, but to make an effort to refute the charges brought against the doctrine of the Jews by Celsus, who thinks that he will be able the more easily to establish the falsity of Christianity, if, by assailing its origin in Judaism, he can show that the latter also is untrue.

CHAP. XXIII.

After this, Celsus next asserts that "Those herdsmen and shepherds who followed Moses as their leader, had their minds deluded by vulgar deceits, and so supposed that there was one God." Let him show, then, how, after this irrational departure, as he regards it, of the herdsmen and shepherds from the worship of many gods, he himself is able to establish the multiplicity of deities that are found amongst the Greeks, or among those other nations that are called Barbarian. Let him establish, therefore, the existence of Mnemosyne, the mother of the Muses by Zeus; or of Themis, the parent of the Hours; or let him prove that the ever naked Graces can have a real, substantial existence. But he will not be able to show, from any actions of theirs, that these fictitious representations [3] of the Greeks, which have the appearance of being invested with bodies, are (really) gods. And why should the fables of the Greeks regarding the gods be true, any more than those of the Egyptians for example, who in their language know nothing of a Mnemosyne, mother of the nine Muses; nor of a Themis, parent of the Hours; nor of a Euphrosyne, one of the Graces; nor of any other of these names? How much more manifest (and how much better than all these inventions!) is it that, convinced by what we see, in the admirable order of the world, we should worship the Maker of it as the one Author of one effect, and which, as being wholly in harmony with itself, cannot on that account have been the work of many makers; and that we should believe that the whole heaven is not held together by the movements of many souls, for one is enough, which bears the whole of the non-wandering [4] sphere from east to west, and embraces within it all things which the world requires, and which are not self-existing! For all are parts of the world, while God is no part of the whole. But God cannot be imperfect, as a part is imperfect. And

---

perhaps profounder consideration will show, that as God is not a part, so neither is He properly the whole, since the whole is composed of parts ; and reason will not allow us to believe that the God who is over all is composed of parts, each one of which cannot do what all the other parts can.

CHAP. XXIV.

After this he continues : " These herdsmen and shepherds concluded that there was but one God, named either the Highest, or Adonai, or the Heavenly, or Sabaoth, or called by some other of those names which they delight to give this world ; and they knew nothing beyond that." And in a subsequent part of his work he says, that " It makes no difference whether the God who is over all things be called by the name of Zeus, which is current among the Greeks, or by that, e.g., which is in use among the Indians or Egyptians." Now, in answer to this, we have to remark that this involves a deep and mysterious subject — that, viz., respecting the nature of names : it being a question whether, as Aristotle thinks, names were bestowed by arrangement, or, as the Stoics hold, by nature ; the first words being imitations of things, agreeably to which the names were formed, and in conformity with which they introduce certain principles of etymology ; or whether, as Epicurus teaches (differing in this from the Stoics), names were given by nature, — the first men having uttered certain words varying with the circumstances in which they found themselves. If, then, we shall be able to establish, in reference to the preceding statement, the nature of powerful names, some of which are used by the learned amongst the Egyptians, or by the Magi among the Persians, and by the Indian philosophers called Brahmans, or by the Samanæans, and others in different countries ; and shall be able to make out that the so-called magic is not, as the followers of Epicurus and Aristotle suppose, an altogether uncertain thing, but is, as those skilled in it prove, a consistent system, having words which are known to exceedingly few ; then we say that the name Sabaoth, and Adonai, and the other names treated with so much reverence among the Hebrews, are not applicable to any ordinary created things, but belong to a secret theology which refers to the Framer of all things. These names, accordingly, when pronounced with that attendant train of circumstances which is appropriate to their nature, are possessed of great power ; and other names, again, current in the Egyptian tongue, are efficacious against certain demons who can only do certain things ; and other names in the Persian language have corresponding power over other spirits ; and so on in every individual nation, for different purposes.

And thus it will be found that, of the various demons upon the earth, to whom different localities have been assigned, each one bears a name appropriate to the several dialects of place and country. He, therefore, who has a nobler idea, however small, of these matters, will be careful not to apply differing names to different things ; lest he should resemble those who mistakenly apply the name of God to lifeless matter, or who drag down the title of "the Good " from the First Cause, or from virtue and excellence, and apply it to blind Plutus, and to a healthy and well-proportioned mixture of flesh and blood and bones, or to what is considered to be noble birth.[1]

CHAP. XXV.

And perhaps there is a danger as great as that which degrades the name of "God," or of "the Good," to improper objects, in changing the name of God according to a secret system, and applying those which belong to inferior beings to greater, and *vice versa*. And I do not dwell on this, that when the name of Zeus is uttered, there is heard at the same time that of the son of Kronos and Rhea, and the husband of Hera, and brother of Poseidon, and father of Athene, and Artemis, who was guilty of incest with his own daughter Persephone ; or that Apollo immediately suggests the son of Leto and Zeus, and the brother of Artemis, and half-brother of Hermes ; and so with all the other names invented by these wise men of Celsus, who are the parents of these opinions, and the ancient theologians of the Greeks. For what are the grounds for deciding that he should on the one hand be properly called Zeus, and yet on the other should not have Kronos for his father and Rhea for his mother ? And the same argument applies to all the others that are called gods. But this charge does not at all apply to those who, for some mysterious reason, refer the word Sabaoth, or Adonai, or any of the other names to the (true) God. And when one is able to philosophize about the mystery of names, he will find much to say respecting the titles of the angels of God, of whom one is called Michael, and another Gabriel, and another Raphael, appropriately to the duties which they discharge in the world, according to the will of the God of all things. And a similar philosophy of names applies also to our Jesus, whose name has already been seen, in an unmistakeable manner, to have expelled myriads of evil spirits from the souls and bodies (of men), so great was the power which it exerted upon those from whom the spirits were driven out. And while still upon the subject of names, we have to mention that those who are skilled in

---

[1] Ἐπὶ τὸν τυφλὸν πλοῦτον, καὶ ἐπὶ τὴν σαρκῶν καὶ αἱμάτων καὶ ὀστέων συμμετρίαν ἐν ὑγιείᾳ καὶ εὐεξίᾳ, ἢ τὴν νομιζομένην εὐγένειαν.

the use of incantations, relate that the utterance of the same incantation in its proper language can accomplish what the spell professes to do; but when translated into any other tongue, it is observed to become inefficacious and feeble. And thus it is not the things signified, but the qualities and peculiarities of words, which possess a certain power for this or that purpose. And so on such grounds as these we defend the conduct of the Christians, when they struggle even to death to avoid calling God by the name of Zeus, or to give Him a name from any other language. For they either use the common name — God — indefinitely, or with some such addition as that of the "Maker of all things," "the Creator of heaven and earth" — He who sent down to the human race those good men, to whose names that of God being added, certain mighty works are wrought among men. And much more besides might be said on the subject of names, against those who think that we ought to be indifferent as to our use of them. And if the remark of Plato in the *Philebus* should surprise us, when he says, "My fear, O Protagoras, about the names of the gods is no small one," seeing Philebus in his discussion with Socrates had called pleasure a "god," how shall we not rather approve the piety of the Christians, who apply none of the names used in the mythologies to the Creator of the world? And now enough on this subject for the present.

CHAP. XXVI.

But let us see the manner in which this Celsus, who professes to know everything, brings a false accusation against the Jews, when he alleges that "they worship angels, and are addicted to sorcery, in which Moses was their instructor." Now, in what part of the writings of Moses he found the lawgiver laying down the worship of angels, let him tell, who professes to know all about Christianity and Judaism; and let him show also how sorcery can exist among those who have accepted the Mosaic law, and read the injunction, "Neither seek after wizards, to be defiled by them."[1] Moreover, he promises to show afterwards "how it was through ignorance that the Jews were deceived and led into error." Now, if he had discovered that the ignorance of the Jews regarding Christ was the effect of their not having heard the prophecies about Him, he would show with truth how the Jews fell into error. But without any wish whatever that this should appear, he views as Jewish errors what are no errors at all. And Celsus having promised to make us acquainted, in a subsequent part of his work, with the doctrines of Judaism, proceeds in the first place to speak

of our Saviour as having been the leader of our generation, in so far as we are Christians,[2] and says that "a few years ago he began to teach this doctrine, being regarded by Christians as the Son of God." Now, with respect to this point — His prior existence a few years ago — we have to remark as follows. Could it have come to pass without divine assistance, that Jesus, desiring during these years to spread abroad His words and teaching, should have been so successful, that everywhere throughout the world, not a few persons, Greeks as well as Barbarians, learned as well as ignorant, adopted His doctrine, so that they struggled even to death in its defence, rather than deny it, which no one is ever related to have done for any other system? I indeed, from no wish to flatter[3] Christianity, but from a desire thoroughly to examine the facts, would say that even those who are engaged in the healing of numbers of sick persons, do not attain their object — the cure of the body — without divine help; and if one were to succeed in delivering souls from a flood of wickedness, and excesses, and acts of injustice, and from a contempt of God, and were to show, as evidence of such a result, one hundred persons improved in their natures (let us suppose the number to be so large), no one would reasonably say that it was without divine assistance that he had implanted in those hundred individuals a doctrine capable of removing so many evils. And if any one, on a candid consideration of these things, shall admit that no improvement ever takes place among men without divine help, how much more confidently shall he make the same assertion regarding Jesus, when he compares the former lives of many converts to His doctrine with their after conduct, and reflects in what acts of licentiousness and injustice and covetousness they formerly indulged, until, as Celsus, and they who think with him, allege, "they were deceived," and accepted a doctrine which, as these individuals assert, is destructive of the life of men; but who, from the time that they adopted it, have become in some way meeker, and more religious, and more consistent, so that certain among them, from a desire of exceeding chastity, and a wish to worship God with greater purity, abstain even from the permitted indulgences of (lawful) love.

CHAP. XXVII.

Any one who examines the subject will see that Jesus attempted and successfully accomplished works beyond the reach of human power. For although, from the very beginning, all things opposed the spread of His doctrine in the world,

---

[1] Lev. xix. 31.

— both the princes of the times, and their chief captains and generals, and all, to speak generally, who were possessed of the smallest influence, and in addition to these, the rulers of the different cities, and the soldiers, and the people, — yet it proved victorious, as being the Word of God, the nature of which is such that it cannot be hindered; and becoming more powerful than all such adversaries, it made itself master of the whole of Greece, and a considerable portion of Barbarian lands, and converted countless numbers of souls to His religion. And although, among the multitude of converts to Christianity, the simple and ignorant necessarily outnumbered the more intelligent, as the former class always does the latter, yet Celsus, unwilling to take note of this, thinks that this philanthropic doctrine, which reaches to every soul under the sun, is vulgar,[1] and on account of its vulgarity and its want of reasoning power, obtained a hold only over the ignorant. And yet he himself admits that it was not the simple alone who were led by the doctrine of Jesus to adopt His religion; for he acknowledges that there were amongst them some persons of moderate intelligence, and gentle disposition, and possessed of understanding, and capable of comprehending allegories.

CHAP. XXVIII.

And since, in imitation of a rhetorician training a pupil, he introduces a Jew, who enters into a personal discussion with Jesus, and speaks in a very childish manner, altogether unworthy of the grey hairs of a philosopher, let me endeavour, to the best of my ability, to examine his statements, and show that he does not maintain, throughout the discussion, the consistency due to the character of a Jew. For he represents him disputing with Jesus, and confuting Him, as he thinks, on many points; and in the first place, he accuses Him of having "invented his birth from a virgin," and upbraids Him with being "born in a certain Jewish village, of a poor woman of the country, who gained her subsistence by spinning, and who was turned out of doors by her husband, a carpenter by trade, because she was convicted of adultery; that after being driven away by her husband, and wandering about for a time, she disgracefully gave birth to Jesus, an illegitimate child, who having hired himself out as a servant in Egypt on account of his poverty, and having there acquired some miraculous powers, on which the Egyptians greatly pride themselves, returned to his own country, highly elated on account of them, and by means of these proclaimed himself a God." Now, as I cannot allow anything said by unbe-

lievers to remain unexamined, but must investigate everything from the beginning, I give it as my opinion that all these things worthily harmonize with the predictions that Jesus is the Son of God.

CHAP. XXIX.

For birth is an aid towards an individual's becoming famous, and distinguished, and talked about; viz., when a man's parents happen to be in a position of rank and influence, and are possessed of wealth, and are able to spend it upon the education of their son, and when the country of one's birth is great and illustrious; but when a man having all these things against him is able, notwithstanding these hindrances, to make himself known, and to produce an impression on those who hear of him, and to become distinguished and visible to the whole world which speaks of him as it did not do before, how can we help admiring such a nature as being both noble in itself, and devoting itself to great deeds and possessing a courage which is not by any means to be despised? And if one were to examine more fully the history of such an individual, why should he not seek to know in what manner, after being reared up in frugality and poverty, and without receiving any complete education, and without having studied systems and opinions by means of which he might have acquired confidence to associate with multitudes and play the demagogue, and attract to himself many hearers, he nevertheless devoted himself to the teaching of new opinions, introducing among men a doctrine which not only subverted the customs of the Jews, while preserving due respect for their prophets, but which especially overturned the established observances of the Greeks regarding the Divinity? And how could such a person — one who had been so brought up, and who, as his calumniators admit, had learned nothing great from men — have been able to teach, in a manner not at all to be despised, such doctrines as he did regarding the divine judgment, and the punishments that are to overtake wickedness, and the rewards that are to be conferred upon virtue; so that not only rustic and ignorant individuals were won by his words, but also not a few of those who were distinguished by their wisdom, and who were able to discern the hidden meaning in those more common doctrines, as they were considered, which were in circulation, and which secret meaning enwrapped, so to speak, some more recondite signification still? The Seriphian, in Plato, who reproaches Themistocles after he had become celebrated for his military skill, saying that his reputation was due not to his own merits, but to his good fortune in having been born in the most illustrious country in Greece, received

[1] ἰδιωτικήν.

from the good-natured Athenian, who saw that his native country did contribute to his renown, the following reply : " Neither would I, had I been a Seriphian, have been so distinguished as I am, nor would you have been a Themistocles, even if you had had the good fortune to be an Athenian !"   And now, our Jesus, who is reproached with being born in a village, and that not a Greek one, nor belonging to any nation widely esteemed, and being despised as the son of a poor labouring woman, and as having on account of his poverty left his native country and hired himself out in Egypt, and being, to use the instance already quoted, not only a Seriphian, as it were, a native of a very small and undistinguished island, but even, so to speak, the meanest of the Seriphians, has yet been able to shake [1] the whole inhabited world not only to a degree far above what Themistocles the Athenian ever did, but beyond what even Pythagoras, or Plato, or any other wise man in any part of the world whatever, or any prince or general, ever succeeded in doing.[2]

CHAP. XXX.

Now, would not any one who investigated with ordinary care the nature of these facts, be struck with amazement at this man's victory? — with his complete success in surmounting by his reputation all causes that tended to bring him into disrepute, and with his superiority over all other illustrious individuals in the world?   And yet it is a rare thing for distinguished men to succeed in acquiring a reputation for several things at once.   For one man is admired on account of his wisdom, another for his military skill, and some of the Barbarians for their marvellous powers of incantation, and some for one quality, and others for another ; but not many have been admired and acquired a reputation for many things at the same time ; whereas this man, in addition to his other merits, is an object of admiration both for his wisdom, and for his miracles, and for his power of government.   For he persuaded some to withdraw themselves from their laws, and to secede to him, not as a tyrant would do, nor as a robber, who arms [3] his followers against men ; nor as a rich man, who bestows help upon those who come to him ; nor as one of those who confessedly are deserving of censure ; but as a teacher of the doctrine regarding the God of all things, and of the worship which belongs to Him, and of all moral precepts which are able to secure the favour of the

Supreme God to him who orders his life in conformity therewith.   Now, to Themistocles, or to any other man of distinction, nothing happened to prove a hindrance to their reputation ; whereas to this man, besides what we have already enumerated, and which are enough to cover with dishonour the soul of a man even of the most noble nature, there was that apparently infamous death of crucifixion, which was enough to efface his previously acquired glory, and to lead those who, as they who disavow his doctrine assert, were formerly deluded by him to abandon their delusion, and to pass condemnation upon their deceiver.

CHAP. XXXI.

And besides this, one may well wonder how it happened that the disciples — if, as the calumniators of Jesus say, they did not see Him after His resurrection from the dead, and were not persuaded of His divinity — were not afraid to endure the same sufferings with their Master, and to expose themselves to danger, and to leave their native country to teach, according to the desire of Jesus, the doctrine delivered to them by Him.   For I think that no one who candidly examines the facts would say that these men devoted themselves to a life of danger for the sake of the doctrine of Jesus, without a profound belief which He had wrought in their minds of its truth, not only teaching them to conform to His precepts, but others also, and to conform, moreover, when manifest destruction to life impended over him who ventured to introduce these new opinions into all places and before all audiences, and who could retain as his friend no human being who adhered to the former opinions and usages.   For did not the disciples of Jesus see, when they ventured to prove not only to the Jews from their prophetic Scriptures that this is He who was spoken of by the prophets, but also to the other heathen nations, that He who was crucified yesterday or the day before underwent this death voluntarily on behalf of the human race, — that this was analogous to the case of those who have died for their country in order to remove pestilence, or barrenness, or tempests?   For it is probable that there is in the nature of things, for certain mysterious reasons which are difficult to be understood by the multitude, such a virtue that one just man, dying a voluntary death for the common good, might be the means of removing wicked spirits, which are the cause of plagues, or barrenness, or tempests, or similar calamities.   Let those, therefore, who would disbelieve the statement that Jesus died on the cross on behalf of men, say whether they also refuse to accept the many accounts current both among Greeks and Barbarians, of persons who have laid down their

---

[1] σεῖσαι.

[2] [This striking chapter is cited, as a specimen of Christian eloquence, in the important work of Guillon, *Cours d' Eloquence Sacrée*, Bruxelles, 1828].

[3] Gelenius reads ὁπλίζων (instead of ἀλείφων), which has been adopted in the translation.

lives for the public advantage, in order to remove those evils which had fallen upon cities and countries? Or will they say that such events actually happened, but that no credit is to be attached to that account which makes this so-called man to have died to ensure the destruction of a mighty evil spirit, the ruler of evil spirits, who had held in subjection the souls of all men upon earth? And the disciples of Jesus, seeing this and much more (which, it is probable, they learned from Jesus in private), and being filled, moreover, with a divine power (since it was no mere poetical virgin that endowed them with strength and courage, but the true wisdom and understanding of God), exerted all their efforts "to become distinguished among all men," not only among the Argives, but among all the Greeks and Barbarians alike, and "so bear away for themselves a glorious renown." [1]

CHAP. XXXII.

But let us now return to where the Jew is introduced, speaking of the mother of Jesus, and saying that "when she was pregnant she was turned out of doors by the carpenter to whom she had been betrothed, as having been guilty of adultery, and that she bore a child to a certain soldier named Panthera;" and let us see whether those who have blindly concocted these fables about the adultery of the Virgin with Panthera, and her rejection by the carpenter, did not invent these stories to overturn His miraculous conception by the Holy Ghost: for they could have falsified the history in a different manner, on account of its extremely miraculous character, and not have admitted, as it were against their will, that Jesus was born of no ordinary human marriage. It was to be expected, indeed, that those who would not believe the miraculous birth of Jesus would invent some falsehood. And their not doing this in a credible manner, but (their) preserving the fact that it was not by Joseph that the Virgin conceived Jesus, rendered the falsehood very palpable to those who can understand and detect such inventions. Is it at all agreeable to reason, that he who dared to do so much for the human race, in order that, as far as in him lay, all the Greeks and Barbarians, who were looking for divine condemnation, might depart from evil, and regulate their entire conduct in a manner pleasing to the Creator of the world, should not have had a miraculous birth, but one the vilest and most disgraceful of all? And I will ask of them as Greeks, and particularly of Celsus, who either holds or not the sentiments of Plato, and at any rate quotes them, whether He who sends souls down into the bodies of men, degraded Him

who was to dare such mighty acts, and to teach so many men, and to reform so many from the mass of wickedness in the world, to a birth more disgraceful than any other, and did not rather introduce Him into the world through a lawful marriage? Or is it not more in conformity with reason, that every soul, for certain mysterious reasons (I speak now according to the opinion of Pythagoras, and Plato, and Empedocles, whom Celsus frequently names), is introduced into a body, and introduced according to its deserts and former actions? It is probable, therefore, that this soul also, which conferred more benefit by its residence in the flesh than that of many men (to avoid prejudice, I do not say "all"), stood in need of a body not only superior to others, but invested with all excellent qualities.

CHAP. XXXIII.

Now if a particular soul, for certain mysterious reasons, is not deserving of being placed in the body of a wholly irrational being, nor yet in that of one purely rational, but is clothed with a monstrous body, so that reason cannot discharge its functions in one so fashioned, which has the head disproportioned to the other parts, and altogether too short; and another receives such a body that the soul is a little more rational than the other; and another still more so, the nature of the body counteracting to a greater or less degree the reception of the reasoning principle; why should there not be also some soul which receives an altogether miraculous body, possessing some qualities common to those of other men, so that it may be able to pass through life with them, but possessing also some quality of superiority, so that the soul may be able to remain untainted by sin? And if there be any truth in the doctrine of the physiognomists, whether Zopyrus, or Loxus, or Polemon, or any other who wrote on such a subject, and who profess to know in some wonderful way that all bodies are adapted to the habits of the souls, must there have been for that soul which was to dwell with miraculous power among men, and work mighty deeds, a body produced, as Celsus thinks, by an act of adultery between Panthera and the Virgin?! Why, from such unhallowed intercourse there must rather have been brought forth some fool to do injury to mankind, — a teacher of licentiousness and wickedness, and other evils; and not of temperance, and righteousness, and the other virtues!

CHAP. XXXIV.

But it was, as the prophets also predicted, from a virgin that there was to be born, according to the promised sign, one who was to give His name to the fact, showing that at His birth

---

[1] Cf. Homer's *Iliad*, v. 2, 3.

God was to be with man. Now it seems to me appropriate to the character of a Jew to have quoted the prophecy of Isaiah, which says that Immanuel was to be born of a virgin. This, however, Celsus, who professes to know everything, has not done, either from ignorance or from an unwillingness (if he had read it and voluntarily passed it by in silence) to furnish an argument which might defeat his purpose. And the prediction runs thus : " And the LORD spake again unto Ahaz, saying, Ask thee a sign of the LORD thy God ; ask it either in the depth or in the height above. But Ahaz said, I will not ask, neither will I tempt the LORD. And he said, Hear ye now, O house of David ; is it a small thing for you to weary men, but will ye weary my God also? Therefore the Lord Himself shall give you a sign. Behold, a virgin shall conceive, and bear a son, and shall call His name Immanuel, which is, being interpreted, God with us." [1] And that it was from intentional malice that Celsus did not quote this prophecy, is clear to me from this, that although he makes numerous quotations from the Gospel according to Matthew, as of the star that appeared at the birth of Christ, and other miraculous occurrences, he has made no mention at all of this. Now, if a Jew should split words, and say that the words are not, " Lo, a virgin," but, " Lo, a young woman," [2] we reply that the word " Olmah " — which the Septuagint have rendered by " a virgin," and others by " a young woman " — occurs, as they say, in Deuteronomy, as applied to a " virgin," in the following connection : " If a damsel that is a virgin be betrothed unto an husband, and a man find her in the city, and lie with her ; then ye shall bring them both out unto the gate of that city, and ye shall stone them with stones that they die ; the damsel,[3] because she cried not, being in the city ; and the man, because he humbled his neighbour's wife." [4] And again : " But if a man find a betrothed damsel in a field, and the man force her, and lie with her : then the man only that lay with her shall die : but unto the damsel [5] ye shall do nothing ; there is in her no sin worthy of death."

CHAP. XXXV.

But that we may not seem, because of a Hebrew word, to endeavour to persuade those who are unable to determine whether they ought to believe it or not, that the prophet spoke of this man being born of a virgin, because at his birth these words, " God with us," were uttered, let us make good our point from the words

themselves. The Lord is related to have spoken to Ahaz thus : " Ask a sign for thyself from the LORD thy God, either in the depth or height above ; " [6] and afterwards the sign is given, " Behold, a virgin shall conceive, and bear a son." [7] What kind of sign, then, would that have been — a young woman who was not a virgin giving birth to a child? And which of the two is the more appropriate as the mother of Immanuel (i.e., " God with us "), — whether a woman who has had intercourse with a man, and who has conceived after the manner of women, or one who is still a pure and holy virgin? Surely it is appropriate only to the latter to produce a being at whose birth it is said, " God with us." And should he be so captious as to say that it is to Ahaz that the command is addressed, " Ask for thyself a sign from the LORD thy God," we shall ask in return, who in the times of Ahaz bore a son at whose birth the expression is made use of, " Immanuel," i.e., " God with us ? " And if no one can be found, then manifestly what was said to Ahaz was said to the house of David, because it is written that the Saviour was born of the house of David according to the flesh ; and this sign is said to be " in the depth or in the height," since " He that descended is the same also that ascended up far above all heavens, that He might fill all things." [8] And these arguments I employ as against a Jew who believes in prophecy. Let Celsus now tell me, or any of those who think with him, with what meaning the prophet utters either these statements about the future, or the others which are contained in the prophecies? Is it with any foresight of the future or not? If with a foresight of the future, then the prophets were divinely inspired ; if with no foresight of the future, let him explain the meaning of one who speaks thus boldly regarding the future, and who is an object of admiration among the Jews because of his prophetic powers.

CHAP. XXXVI.

And now, since we have touched upon the subject of the prophets, what we are about to advance will be useful not only to the Jews, who believe that they spake by divine inspiration, but also to the more candid among the Greeks. To these we say that we must necessarily admit that the Jews had prophets, if they were to be kept together under that system of law which had been given them, and were to believe in the Creator of the world, as they had learned, and to be without pretexts, so far as the law was concerned, for apostatizing to the polytheism of the heathen. And we establish this necessity in

---

[1] Cf. Isa. vii. 10-14 with Matt. i. 23.
[2] νεᾶνις.
[3] νεᾶνιν.
[4] Cf. Deut. xxii. 23, 24.
[5] τῇ νεάνιδι.

[6] Cf. Isa. vii. 11.
[7] Isa. vii. 14.
[8] Cf. Eph. iv. 10.

the following manner. "For the nations," as it is written in the law of the Jews itself, "shall hearken unto observers of times, and diviners;"[1] but to that people it is said: "But as for thee, the LORD thy God hath not suffered thee so to do."[1] And to this is subjoined the promise: "A prophet shall the LORD thy God raise up unto thee from among thy brethren."[2] Since, therefore, the heathen employ modes of divination either by oracles or by omens, or by birds, or by ventriloquists, or by those who profess the art of sacrifice, or by Chaldean genealogists — all which practices were forbidden to the Jews — this people, if they had no means of attaining a knowledge of futurity, being led by the passion common to humanity of ascertaining the future, would have despised their own prophets, as not having in them any particle of divinity; and would not have accepted any prophet after Moses, nor committed their words to writing, but would have spontaneously betaken themselves to the divining usages of the heathen, or attempted to establish some such practices amongst themselves. There is therefore no absurdity in their prophets having uttered predictions even about events of no importance, to soothe those who desire such things, as when Samuel prophesies regarding three she-asses which were lost,[3] or when mention is made in the third book of Kings respecting the sickness of a king's son.[4] And why should not those who desired to obtain auguries from idols be severely rebuked by the administrators of the law among the Jews? — as Elijah is found rebuking Ahaziah, and saying, "Is it because there is not a God in Israel that ye go to inquire of Baalzebub, god of Ekron?"[5]

CHAP. XXXVII.

I think, then, that it has been pretty well established not only that our Saviour was to be born of a virgin, but also that there were prophets among the Jews who uttered not merely general predictions about the future, — as, e.g., regarding Christ and the kingdoms of the world, and the events that were to happen to Israel, and those nations which were to believe on the Saviour, and many other things concerning Him, — but also prophecies respecting particular events; as, for instance, how the asses of Kish, which were lost, were to be discovered, and regarding the sickness which had fallen upon the son of the king of Israel, and any other recorded circumstance of a similar kind. But as a further answer to the Greeks, who do not believe in the

birth of Jesus from a virgin, we have to say that the Creator has shown, by the generation of several kinds of animals, that what He has done in the instance of one animal, He could do, if it pleased Him, in that of others, and also of man himself. For it is ascertained that there is a certain female animal which has no intercourse with the male (as writers on animals say is the case with vultures), and that this animal, without sexual intercourse, preserves the succession of race. What incredibility, therefore, is there in supposing that, if God wished to send a divine teacher to the human race, He caused Him to be born in some manner different from the common![6] Nay, according to the Greeks themselves, all men were not born of a man and woman. For if the world has been created, as many even of the Greeks are pleased to admit, then the first men must have been produced not from sexual intercourse, but from the earth, in which spermatic elements existed; which, however, I consider more incredible than that Jesus was born like other men, so far as regards the half of his birth. And there is no absurdity in employing Grecian histories to answer Greeks, with the view of showing that we are not the only persons who have recourse to miraculous narratives of this kind. For some have thought fit, not in regard to ancient and heroic narratives, but in regard to events of very recent occurrence, to relate as a possible thing that Plato was the son of Amphictione, Ariston being prevented from having marital intercourse with his wife until she had given birth to him with whom she was pregnant by Apollo. And yet these are veritable fables, which have led to the invention of such stories concerning a man whom they regarded as possessing greater wisdom and power than the multitude, and as having received the beginning of his corporeal substance from better and diviner elements than others, because they thought that this was appropriate to persons who were too great to be human beings. And since Celsus has introduced the Jew disputing with Jesus, and tearing in pieces, as he imagines, the fiction of His birth from a virgin, comparing the Greek fables about Danaë, and Melanippe, and Auge, and Antiope, our answer is, that such language becomes a buffoon, and not one who is writing in a serious tone.

CHAP. XXXVIII.

But, moreover, taking the history, contained in the Gospel according to Matthew, of our Lord's descent into Egypt, he refuses to believe the miraculous circumstances attending it, viz., either that the angel gave the divine intimation,

---

[1] Cf. Deut. xviii. 14.
[2] Cf. Deut. xviii. 15.
[3] Cf. 1 Sam. ix. 10.
[4] Cf. 1 Kings xiv. 12. [See note 3, *supra*, p. 362. S.]
[5] Cf. 2 Kings i. 3.

[6] Πεποίηκεν ἀντὶ σπερματικοῦ λόγου, τοῦ ἐκ μίξεως τῶν ἀρρένων ταῖς γυναιξί, ἀλλῳ τρόπῳ γενέσθαι τὸν λόγον τοῦ τεχθησομένου.

or that our Lord's quitting Judea and residing in Egypt was an event of any significance ; but he invents something altogether different, admitting somehow the miraculous works done by Jesus, by means of which He induced the multitude to follow Him as the Christ. And yet he desires to throw discredit on them, as being done by help of magic and not by divine power ; for he asserts "that he (Jesus), having been brought up as an illegitimate child, and having served for hire in Egypt, and then coming to the knowledge of certain miraculous powers, returned from thence to his own country, and by means of those powers proclaimed himself a god." Now I do not understand how a magician should exert himself to teach a doctrine which persuades us always to act as if God were to judge every man for his deeds ; and should have trained his disciples, whom he was to employ as the ministers of his doctrine, in the same belief. For did the latter make an impression upon their hearers, after they had been so taught to work miracles ; or was it without the aid of these ? The assertion, therefore, that they did no miracles at all, but that, after yielding their belief to arguments which were not at all convincing, like the wisdom of Grecian dialectics,[1] they gave themselves up to the task of teaching the new doctrine to those persons among whom they happened to take up their abode, is altogether absurd. For in what did they place their confidence when they taught the doctrine and disseminated the new opinions ? But if they indeed wrought miracles, then how can it be believed that magicians exposed themselves to such hazards to introduce a doctrine which forbade the practice of magic ?

CHAP. XXXIX.

I do not think it necessary to grapple with an argument advanced not in a serious but in a scoffing spirit, such as the following : "If the mother of Jesus was beautiful, then the god whose nature is not to love a corruptible body, had intercourse with her because she was beautiful ; " or, "It was improbable that the god would entertain a passion for her, because she was neither rich nor of royal rank, seeing no one, even of her neighbours, knew her." And it is in the same scoffing spirit that he adds : "When hated by her husband, and turned out of doors, she was not saved by divine power, nor was her story believed. Such things, he says, have no connection with the kingdom of heaven." In what respect does such language differ from that of those who pour abuse on others on the public streets, and whose words are unworthy of any serious attention ?

CHAP. XL.

After these assertions, he takes from the Gospel of Matthew, and perhaps also from the other Gospels, the account of the dove alighting upon our Saviour at His baptism by John, and desires to throw discredit upon the statement, alleging that the narrative is a fiction. Having completely disposed, as he imagined, of the story of our Lord's birth from a virgin, he does not proceed to deal in an orderly manner with the accounts that follow it ; since passion and hatred observe no order, but angry and vindictive men slander those whom they hate, as the feeling comes upon them, being prevented by their passion from arranging their accusations on a careful and orderly plan. For if he had observed a proper arrangement, he would have taken up the Gospel, and, with the view of assailing it, would have objected to the first narrative, then passed on to the second, and so on to the others. But now, after the birth from a virgin, this Celsus, who professes to be acquainted with all our history, attacks the account of the appearance of the Holy Spirit in the form of a dove at the baptism. He then, after that, tries to throw discredit upon the prediction that our Lord was to come into the world. In the next place, he runs away to what immediately follows the narrative of the birth of Jesus — the account of the star, and of the wise men who came from the east to worship the child. And you yourself may find, if you take the trouble, many confused statements made by Celsus throughout his whole book ; so that even in this account he may, by those who know how to observe and require an orderly method of arrangement, be convicted of great rashness and boasting, in having inscribed upon his work the title of *A True Discourse*, — a thing which is never done by a learned philosopher. For Plato says, that it is not an indication of an intelligent man to make strong assertions respecting those matters which are somewhat uncertain ; and the celebrated Chrysippus even, who frequently states the reasons by which he is decided, refers us to those whom we shall find to be abler speakers than himself. This man, however, who is wiser than those already named, and than all the other Greeks, agreeably to his assertion of being acquainted with everything, inscribed upon his book the words, *A True Discourse !*

CHAP. XLI.

But, that we may not have the appearance of intentionally passing by his charges through inability to refute them, we have resolved to answer

---

[1] This difficult passage is rendered in the Latin translation: " but that, after they had believed (in Christ), they with no adequate supply of arguments, such as is furnished by the Greek dialectics, gave themselves up," etc.

each one of them separately according to our ability, attending not to the connection and sequence of the nature of the things themselves, but to the arrangement of the subjects as they occur in this book. Let us therefore notice what he has to say by way of impugning the bodily appearance of the Holy Spirit to our Saviour in the form of a dove. And it is a Jew who addresses the following language to Him whom we acknowledge to be our Lord Jesus : " When you were bathing," says the Jew, " beside John, you say that what had the appearance of a bird from the air alighted upon you." And then this same Jew of his, continuing his interrogations, asks, " What credible witness beheld this appearance ? or who heard a voice from heaven declaring you to be the Son of God ? What proof is there of it, save your own assertion, and the statement of another of those individuals who have been punished along with you ? "

CHAP. XLII.

Before we begin our reply, we have to remark that the endeavour to show, with regard to almost any history, however true, that it actually occurred, and to produce an intelligent conception regarding it, is one of the most difficult undertakings that can be attempted, and is in some instances an impossibility. For suppose that some one were to assert that there never had been any Trojan war, chiefly on account of the impossible narrative interwoven therewith, about a certain Achilles being the son of a sea-goddess Thetis and of a man Peleus, or Sarpedon being the son of Zeus, or Ascalaphus and Ialmenus the sons of Ares, or Æneas that of Aphrodite, how should we prove that such was the case, especially under the weight of the fiction attached, I know not how, to the universally prevalent opinion that there was really a war in Ilium between Greeks and Trojans ? And suppose, also, that some one disbelieved the story of Œdipus and Jocasta, and of their two sons Eteocles and Polynices, because the sphinx, a kind of half-virgin, was introduced into the narrative, how should we demonstrate the reality of such a thing ? And in like manner also with the history of the Epigoni, although there is no such marvellous event interwoven with it, or with the return of the Heracleidæ, or countless other historical events. But he who deals candidly with histories, and would wish to keep himself also from being imposed upon by them, will exercise his judgment as to what statements he will give his assent to, and what he will accept figuratively, seeking to discover the meaning of the authors of such inventions, and from what statements he will withhold his belief, as having been written for the gratification of certain individuals. And we have said this by way of anti-cipation respecting the whole history related in the Gospels concerning Jesus, not as inviting men of acuteness to a simple and unreasoning faith, but wishing to show that there is need of candour in those who are to read, and of much investigation, and, so to speak, of insight into the meaning of the writers, that the object with which each event has been recorded may be discovered.

CHAP. XLIII.

We shall therefore say, in the first place, that if he who disbelieves the appearance of the Holy Spirit in the form of a dove had been described as an Epicurean, or a follower of Democritus, or a Peripatetic, the statement would have been in keeping with the character of such an objector. But now even this Celsus, wisest of all men, did not perceive that it is to a Jew, who believes more incredible things contained in the writings of the prophets than the narrative of the appearance of the dove, that he attributes such an objection ! For one might say to the Jew, when expressing his disbelief of the appearance, and thinking to assail it as a fiction, " How are you able to prove, sir, that the Lord spake to Adam, or to Eve, or to Cain, or to Noah, or to Abraham, or to Isaac, or to Jacob, those words which He is recorded to have spoken to these men ? " And, to compare history with history, I would say to the Jew, " Even your own Ezekiel writes, saying, ' The heavens were opened, and I saw a vision of God.' [1] After relating which, he adds, ' This was the appearance of the likeness of the glory of the Lord ; and He said to me,' " [2] etc. Now, if what is related of Jesus be false, since we cannot, as you suppose, clearly prove it to be true, it being seen or heard by Himself alone, and, as you appear to have observed, also by one of those who were punished, why should we not rather say that Ezekiel also was dealing in the marvellous when he said, " The heavens were opened," etc.? Nay, even Isaiah asserts, " I saw the Lord of hosts sitting on a throne, high and lifted up ; and the seraphim stood round about it : the one had six wings, and the other had six wings." [3] How can we tell whether he really saw them or not ? Now, O Jew, you have believed these visions to be true, and to have been not only shown to the prophet by a diviner Spirit, but also to have been both spoken and recorded by the same. And who is the more worthy of belief, when declaring that the heavens were opened before him, and that he heard a voice, or beheld the Lord of Sabaoth sitting upon a throne high and lifted up, — whether Isaiah and Ezekiel or Jesus ? Of the former, indeed, no work has been found equal

---

[1] Cf. Ezek. i. 1.
[2] Cf. Ezek. i. 28 and ii. 1.
[3] Cf. Isa. vi. 1, 2.

to those of the latter ; whereas the good deeds of Jesus have not been confined solely to the period of His tabernacling in the flesh, but up to the present time His power still produces conversion and amelioration of life in those who believe in God through Him. And a manifest proof that these things are done by His power, is the fact that, although, as He Himself said, and as is admitted, there are not labourers enough to gather in the harvest of souls, there really is nevertheless such a great harvest of those who are gathered together and conveyed into the everywhere existing threshing-floors and Churches of God.

CHAP. XLIV.

And with these arguments I answer the Jew, not disbelieving, I who am a Christian, Ezekiel and Isaiah, but being very desirous to show, on the footing of our common belief, that this man is far more worthy of credit than they are when He says that He beheld such a sight, and, as is probable, related to His disciples the vision which He saw, and told them of the voice which He heard. But another party might object, that not all those who have narrated the appearance of the dove and the voice from heaven heard the accounts of these things from Jesus, but that that Spirit which taught Moses the history of events before his own time, beginning with the creation, and descending down to Abraham his father, taught also the writers of the Gospel the miraculous occurrence which took place at the time of Jesus' baptism. And he who is adorned with the spiritual gift,[1] called the " word of wisdom," will explain also the reason of the heavens opening, and the dove appearing, and why the Holy Spirit appeared to Jesus in the form of no other living thing than that of a dove. But our present subject does not require us to explain this, our purpose being to show that Celsus displayed no sound judgment in representing a Jew as disbelieving, on such grounds, a fact which has greater probability in its favour than many events in which he firmly reposes confidence.

CHAP. XLV.

And I remember on one occasion, at a disputation held with certain Jews who were reputed learned men, having employed the following argument in the presence of many judges : " Tell me, sirs," I said, " since there are two individuals who have visited the human race, regarding whom are related marvellous works surpassing human power — Moses, viz., your own legislator, who wrote about himself, and Jesus our teacher, who has left no writings regarding Himself, but to whom testimony is borne by the disciples in the Gos-

pels — what are the grounds for deciding that Moses is to be believed as speaking the truth, although the Egyptians slander him as a sorcerer, and as appearing to have wrought his mighty works by jugglery, while Jesus is not to be believed because you are His accusers? And yet there are nations which bear testimony in favour of both : the Jews to Moses ; and the Christians, who do not deny the prophetic mission of Moses, but proving from that very source the truth of the statement regarding Jesus, accept as true the miraculous circumstances related of Him by His disciples. Now, if ye ask us for the reasons of our faith in Jesus, give yours first for believing in Moses, who lived before Him, and then we shall give you ours for accepting the latter. But if you draw back, and shirk a demonstration, then we, following your own example, decline for the present to offer any demonstration likewise. Nevertheless, admit that ye have no proof to offer for Moses, and then listen to our defence of Jesus derived from the law and the prophets. And now observe what is almost incredible ! It is shown from the declarations concerning Jesus, contained in the law and the prophets, that both Moses and the prophets were truly prophets of God."

CHAP. XLVI.

For the law and the prophets are full of marvels similar to those recorded of Jesus at His baptism, viz., regarding the dove and the voice from heaven. And I think the wonders wrought by Jesus are a proof of the Holy Spirit's having then appeared in the form of a dove, although Celsus, from a desire to cast discredit upon them, alleges that He performed only what He had learned among the Egyptians. And I shall refer not only to His miracles, but, as is proper, to those also of the apostles of Jesus. For they could not without the help of miracles and wonders have prevailed on those who heard their new doctrines and new teachings to abandon their national usages, and to accept their instructions at the danger to themselves even of death. And there are still preserved among Christians traces of that Holy Spirit which appeared in the form of a dove. They expel evil spirits, and perform many cures, and foresee certain events, according to the will of the Logos. And although Celsus, or the Jew whom he has introduced, may treat with mockery what I am going to say, I shall say it nevertheless, — that many have been converted to Christianity as if against their will, some sort of spirit having suddenly transformed their minds from a hatred of the doctrine to a readiness to die in its defence, and having appeared to them either in a waking vision or a dream of the night. Many such instances have we known, which, if we were to commit to writ-

---

[1] χαρίσματι.

ing, although they were seen and witnessed by ourselves, we should afford great occasion for ridicule to unbelievers, who would imagine that we, like those whom they suppose to have invented such things, had ourselves also done the same. But God is witness of our conscientious desire, not by false statements, but by testimonies of different kinds, to establish the divinity of the doctrine of Jesus. And as it is a Jew who is perplexed about the account of the Holy Spirit having descended upon Jesus in the form of a dove, we would say to him, "Sir, who is it that says in Isaiah, 'And now the Lord hath sent me and His Spirit?'"[1] In which sentence, as the meaning is doubtful — viz., whether the Father and the Holy Spirit sent Jesus, or the Father sent both Christ and the Holy Spirit — the latter is correct. For, because the Saviour was sent, afterwards the Holy Spirit was sent also, that the prediction of the prophet might be fulfilled; and as it was necessary that the fulfilment of the prophecy should be known to posterity, the disciples of Jesus for that reason committed the result to writing.

CHAP. XLVII.

I would like to say to Celsus, who represents the Jew as accepting somehow John as a Baptist, who baptized Jesus, that the existence of John the Baptist, baptizing for the remission of sins, is related by one who lived no great length of time after John and Jesus. For in the 18th book of his *Antiquities*[2] *of the Jews*, Josephus bears witness to John as having been a Baptist, and as promising purification to those who underwent the rite. Now this writer, although not believing in Jesus as the Christ, in seeking after the cause of the fall of Jerusalem and the destruction of the temple, whereas he ought to have said that the conspiracy against Jesus was the cause of these calamities befalling the people, since they put to death Christ, who was a prophet, says nevertheless — being, although against his will, not far from the truth — that these disasters happened to the Jews as a punishment for the death of James the Just, who was a brother of Jesus (called Christ), — the Jews having put him to death, although he was a man most distinguished for his justice.[3] Paul, a genuine disciple of Jesus, says that he regarded this James as a brother of the Lord, not so much on account of their relationship by blood, or of their being brought up together, as because of his virtue and doctrine.[4] If, then, he says that it was on account of James that the desolation of Jerusalem was made to overtake the Jews, how should it not be more in accordance with reason to say that it happened on account (of the death) of Jesus Christ, of whose divinity so many Churches are witnesses, composed of those who have been converted from a flood of sins, and who have joined themselves to the Creator, and who refer all their actions to His good pleasure.

CHAP. XLVIII.

Although the Jew, then, may offer no defence for himself in the instances of Ezekiel and Isaiah, when we compare the opening of the heavens to Jesus, and the voice that was heard by Him, to the similar cases which we find recorded in Ezekiel and Isaiah, or any other of the prophets, we nevertheless, so far as we can, shall support our position, maintaining that, as it is a matter of belief that in a *dream* impressions have been brought before the minds of many, some relating to divine things, and others to future events of this life, and this either with clearness or in an enigmatic manner, — a fact which is manifest to all who accept the doctrine of providence; so how is it absurd to say that the mind which could receive impressions in a *dream* should be impressed also in a waking vision, for the benefit either of him on whom the impressions are made, or of those who are to hear the account of them from him? And as in a dream we fancy that we hear, and that the organs of hearing are actually impressed, and that we see with our eyes — although neither the bodily organs of sight nor hearing are affected, but it is the mind alone which has these sensations — so there is no absurdity in believing that similar things occurred to the prophets, when it is recorded that they witnessed occurrences of a rather wonderful kind, as when they either heard the words of the Lord or beheld the heavens opened. For I do not suppose that the visible heaven was actually opened, and its physical structure divided, in order that Ezekiel might be able to record such an occurrence. Should not, therefore, the same be believed of the Saviour by every intelligent hearer of the Gospels? — although such an occurrence may be a stumbling-block to the simple, who in their simplicity would set the whole world in movement, and split in sunder the compact and mighty body of the whole heavens. But he who examines such matters more profoundly will say, that there being, as the Scripture calls it, a kind of general divine perception which the blessed man alone knows how to discover, according to the saying of Solomon, "Thou shalt find the knowledge of God;"[5] and as there are various forms of this perceptive power, such as a faculty of vision

---

[1] Cf. Isa. xlviii. 16.
[2] [ἀρχαιολογίας. S.] Cf. Joseph., *Antiq.*, book xviii. c. v. sec. 2.
[3] [*Ibid.*, b. xx. c. ix. § 1. S.]
[4] Cf. Gal. i. 19.

[5] Cf. Prov. ii. 5.

which can naturally see things that are better than bodies, among which are ranked the cherubim and seraphim; and a faculty of hearing which can perceive voices which have not their being in the air; and a sense of taste which can make use of living bread that has come down from heaven, and that giveth life unto the world; and so also a sense of smelling, which scents such things as leads Paul to say that he is a sweet savour of Christ unto God;[1] and a sense of touch, by which John says that he "handled with his hands of the Word of life;"[2]—the blessed prophets having discovered this divine perception, and seeing and hearing in this divine manner, and tasting likewise, and smelling, so to speak, with no sensible organs of perception, and laying hold on the Logos by faith, so that a healing effluence from it comes upon them, saw in this manner what they record as having seen, and heard what they say they heard, and were affected in a similar manner to what they describe when eating the roll of a book that was given them.[3] And so also Isaac smelled the savour of his son's divine garments,[4] and added to the spiritual blessing these words: "See, the savour of my son is as the savour of a full field which the LORD blessed."[5] And similarly to this, and more as a matter to be understood by the mind than to be perceived by the senses, Jesus touched the leper,[6] to cleanse him, as I think, in a twofold sense,—freeing him not only, as the multitude heard, from the visible leprosy by visible contact, but also from that other leprosy, by His truly divine touch. It is in this way, accordingly, that John testifies when he says, "I beheld the Spirit descending from heaven like a dove, and it abode upon Him. And I knew Him not; but He that sent me to baptize with water, the same said to me, Upon whom you will see the Spirit descending, and abiding on Him, the same is He that baptizeth with the Holy Ghost. And I saw, and bear witness, that this is the Son of God."[7] Now it was to Jesus that the heavens were opened; and on that occasion no one except John is recorded to have seen them opened. But with respect to this opening of the heavens, the Saviour, foretelling to His disciples that it would happen, and that they would see it, says, "Verily, verily, I say unto you, Ye shall see the heavens opened, and the angels of God ascending and descending upon the Son of man."[8] And so Paul was carried away into the third heaven, having previously seen it opened, since he was a disciple of

Jesus. It does not, however, belong to our present object to explain why Paul says, "Whether in the body, I know not; or whether out of the body, I know not: God knoweth."[9] But I shall add to my argument even those very points which Celsus imagines, viz., that Jesus Himself related the account of the opening of the heavens, and the descent of the Holy Spirit upon Him at the Jordan in the form of a dove, although the Scripture does not assert that He saw it. For this great man did not perceive that it was not in keeping with Him who commanded His disciples on the occasion of the vision on the mount, "Tell what ye have seen to no man, until the Son of man be risen from the dead,"[10] to have related to His disciples what was seen and heard by John at the Jordan. For it may be observed as a trait of the character of Jesus, that He on all occasions avoided unnecessary talk about Himself; and on that account said, "If I speak of Myself, My witness is not true."[11] And since He avoided unnecessary talk about Himself, and preferred to show by acts rather than words that He was the Christ, the Jews for that reason said to Him, "If Thou art the Christ, tell us plainly."[12] And as it is a Jew who, in the work of Celsus, uses the language to Jesus regarding the appearance of the Holy Spirit in the form of a dove, "This is your own testimony, unsupported save by one of those who were sharers of your punishment, whom you adduce," it is necessary for us to show him that such a statement is not appropriately placed in the mouth of a Jew. For the Jews do not connect John with Jesus, nor the punishment of John with that of Christ. And by this instance, this man who boasts of universal knowledge is convicted of not knowing what words he ought to ascribe to a Jew engaged in a disputation with Iesus.

CHAP. XLIX.

After this he wilfully sets aside, I know not why, the strongest evidence in confirmation of the claims of Jesus, viz., that His coming was predicted by the Jewish prophets—Moses, and those who succeeded as well as preceded that legislator—from inability, as I think, to meet the argument that neither the Jews nor any other heretical sect refuse to believe that Christ was the subject of prophecy. But perhaps he was unacquainted with the prophecies relating to Christ. For no one who was acquainted with the statements of the Christians, that many prophets foretold the advent of the Saviour, would have ascribed to a Jew sentiments which

---

[1] Cf. 2 Cor. ii. 15.
[2] Cf. 1 John i. 1.
[3] Cf. Ezek. iii. 2, 3.
[4] Ὠσφράνθη τῆς ὀσμῆς τῶν τοῦ υἱοῦ θειοτέρων ἱματίων.
[5] Cf. Gen. xxvii. 27.
[6] Cf. Matt. viii. 3.
[7] Cf. John i. 32–34.
[8] Cf. John i. 51.

[9] Cf. 2 Cor. xii. 2.
[10] Cf. Matt. xvii. 9.
[11] John v. 31.
[12] John x. 24.

it would have better befitted a Samaritan or a Sadducee to utter; nor would the Jew in the dialogue have expressed himself in language like the following : " But my prophet once declared in Jerusalem, that the Son of God will come as the Judge of the righteous and the Punisher of the wicked." Now it is not one of the prophets merely who predicted the advent of Christ. But although the Samaritans and Sadducees, who receive the books of Moses alone, would say that there were contained in them predictions regarding Christ, yet certainly not in Jerusalem, which is not even mentioned in the times of Moses, was the prophecy uttered. It were indeed to be desired, that all the accusers of Christianity were equally ignorant with Celsus, not only of the facts, but of the bare letter of Scripture, and would so direct their assaults against it, that their arguments might not have the least available influence in shaking, I do not say the faith, but the little faith of unstable and temporary believers. A Jew, however, would not admit that any prophet used the expression, " The 'Son of God' will come ; " for the term which they employ is, " The 'Christ of God' will come." And many a time indeed do they directly interrogate us about the " Son of God," saying that no such being exists, or was made the subject of prophecy. We do not of course assert that the " Son of God " is not the subject of prophecy ; but we assert that he most inappropriately attributes to the Jewish disputant, who would not allow that He was, such language as, " My prophet once declared in Jerusalem that the 'Son of God' will come."

CHAP. L.

In the next place, as if the only event predicted were this, that He was to be "the Judge of the righteous and the Punisher of the wicked," and as if neither the place of His birth, nor the sufferings which He was to endure at the hands of the Jews, nor His resurrection, nor the wonderful works which He was to perform, had been made the subject of prophecy, he continues : " Why should it be you alone, rather than innumerable others, who existed after the prophecies were published, to whom these predictions are applicable ? " And desiring, I know not how, to suggest to others the possibility of the notion that they themselves were the persons referred to by the prophets, he says that " some, carried away by enthusiasm, and others having gathered a multitude of followers, give out that the Son of God is come down from heaven." Now we have not ascertained that such occurrences are admitted to have taken place among the Jews. We have to remark then, in the first place, that many of the prophets have uttered predictions

in all kinds of ways [1] regarding Christ ; some by means of dark sayings, others in allegories or in some other manner, and some also in express words. And as in what follows he says, in the character of the Jew addressing the converts from his own nation, and repeating emphatically and malevolently, that " the prophecies referred to the events of his life may also suit other events as well," we shall state a few of them out of a greater number ; and with respect to these, any one who chooses may say what he thinks fitted to ensure a refutation of them, and which may turn away intelligent believers from the faith.

CHAP. LI.

Now the Scripture speaks, respecting the place of the Saviour's birth — that the Ruler was to come forth from Bethlehem — in the following manner : "And thou Bethlehem, house of Ephrata, art not the least among the thousands of Judah : for out of thee shall He come forth unto Me who is to be Ruler in Israel ; and His goings forth have been of old, from everlasting." [2] Now this prophecy could not suit any one of those who, as Celsus' Jew says, were fanatics and mob-leaders, and who gave out that they had come from heaven, unless it were clearly shown that He had been born in Bethlehem, or, as another might say, had come forth from Bethlehem to be the leader of the people. With respect to the birth of Jesus in Bethlehem, if any one desires, after the prophecy of Micah and after the history recorded in the Gospels by the disciples of Jesus, to have additional evidence from other sources, let him know that, in conformity with the narrative in the Gospel regarding His birth, there is shown at Bethlehem the cave [3] where He was born, and the manger in the cave where He was wrapped in swaddling-clothes. And this sight is greatly talked of in surrounding places, even among the enemies of the faith, it being said that in this cave was born that Jesus who is worshipped and reverenced by the Christians. [4] Moreover, I am of opinion that, before the advent of Christ, the chief priests and scribes of the people, on account of the distinctness and clearness of this prophecy, taught that in Bethlehem the Christ was to be born. And this opinion had prevailed also extensively among the Jews ; for which reason it is related that Herod, on inquiring at the chief priests and scribes of the people, heard from them that the Christ was to be born in Bethlehem of Judea,

---

[1] παντοδαπῶς προεῖπον.
[2] Cf. Mic. v. 2 and Matt. ii. 6.
[3] [See Dr. Spencer's *The East: Sketches of Travel in Egypt and the Holy Land*, pp. 362-365, London, Murray, 1850, an interesting work by my esteemed collaborator.]
[4] [Concerning this, besides Dr. Robinson (ii. 159), consult Dean Stanley, *Sinai and Palestine*, p. 433. But compare Van Lennep, *Bible Lands*, p. 804; Roberts' *Holy Land*, capp. 85, 87, vol. ii., London.]

"whence David was." It is stated also in the Gospel according to John, that the Jews declared that the Christ was to be born in Bethlehem, "whence David was."[1] But after our Lord's coming, those who busied themselves with overthrowing the belief that the place of His birth had been the subject of prophecy from the beginning, withheld such teaching from the people ; acting in a similar manner to those individuals who won over those soldiers of the guard stationed around the tomb who had seen Him arise from the dead, and who instructed these eye-witnesses to report as follows : " Say that His disciples, while we slept, came and stole Him away. And if this come to the governor's ears, we shall persuade him, and secure you."[2]

CHAP. LII.

Strife and prejudice are powerful instruments in leading men to disregard even those things which are abundantly clear ; so that they who have somehow become familiar with certain opinions, which have deeply imbued their minds, and stamped them with a certain character, will not give them up. For a man will abandon his habits in respect to other things, although it may be difficult for him to tear himself from them, more easily than he will surrender his opinions. Nay, even the former are not easily put aside by those who have become accustomed to them ; and so neither houses, nor cities, nor villages, nor intimate acquaintances, are willingly forsaken when we are prejudiced in their favour. This, therefore, was a reason why many of the Jews at that time disregarded the clear testimony of the prophecies, and miracles which Jesus wrought, and of the sufferings which He is related to have endured. And that human nature is thus affected, will be manifest to those who observe that those who have once been prejudiced in favour of the most contemptible and paltry traditions of their ancestors and fellow-citizens, with difficulty lay them aside. For example, no one could easily persuade an Egyptian to despise what he had learned from his fathers, so as no longer to consider this or that irrational animal as a god, or not to guard against eating, even under the penalty of death, of the flesh of such an animal. Now, if in carrying our examination of this subject to a considerable length, we have enumerated the points respecting Bethlehem, and the prophecy regarding it, we consider that we were obliged to do this, by way of defence against those who would assert that if the prophecies current among the Jews regarding Jesus were so clear as we represent them, why did they not at His coming give in

their adhesion to His doctrine, and betake themselves to the better life pointed out by Him? Let no one, however, bring such a reproach against believers, since he may see that reasons of no light weight are assigned by those who have learned to state them, for their faith in Jesus.

CHAP. LIII.

And if we should ask for a second prophecy, which may appear to us to have a clear reference to Jesus, we would quote that which was written by Moses very many years before the advent of Christ, when he makes Jacob, on his departure from this life, to have uttered predictions regarding each of his sons, and to have said of Judah along with the others : " The ruler will not fail from Judah, and the governor from his loins, until that which is reserved for him come."[3] Now, any one meeting with this prophecy, which is in reality much older than Moses, so that one who was not a believer might suspect that it was not written by him, would be surprised that Moses should be able to predict that the princes of the Jews, seeing there are among them twelve tribes, should be born of the tribe of Judah, and should be the rulers of the people ; for which reason also the whole nation are called Jews, deriving their name from the ruling tribe. And, in the second place, one who candidly considers the prophecy, would be surprised how, after declaring that the rulers and governors of the people were to proceed from the tribe of Judah, he should determine also the limit of their rule, saying that " the ruler should not fail from Judah, nor the governor from his loins, until there should come that which was reserved for him, and that He is the expectation of the Gentiles."[4] For He came for whom these things were reserved, viz., the Christ of God, the ruler of the promises of God. And manifestly He is the only one among those who preceded, and, I might make bold to say, among those also who followed Him, who was the expectation of the Gentiles ; for converts from among all the Gentile nations have believed on God through Him, and that in conformity with the prediction of Isaiah, that in His name the Gentiles had hoped : " In Thy name shall the Gentiles hope."[5] And this man said also to those who are in prison, as every man is a captive to the chains of his sins, " Come forth ; " and to the ignorant, " Come into the light : " these things also having been thus foretold : " I have given Thee for a covenant of the people, to establish the earth, to

---

[1] Cf. John vii. 42.
[2] Cf. Matt. xxviii. 13, 14.

[3] Cf. Gen. xlix. 10, ἕως ἂν ἔλθῃ τὰ ἀποκείμενα αὐτῷ. This is one of the passages of the Septuagint which Justin Martyr charges the Jews with corrupting ; the true reading, according to him, being ἕως ἂν ἔλθῃ ᾧ ἀπόκειται. Cf. Justin Martyr, Dialogue with Trypho, vol. i. p. 259.
[4] Cf. Gen. xlix. 10.
[5] Isa. xlii. 4. (Sept.)

cause to inherit the desolate heritage ; saying to the prisoners, Go forth ; and to them that are in darkness, Show yourselves." [1] And we may see at the appearing of this man, by means of those who everywhere throughout the world have reposed a simple faith in Him, the fulfilment of this prediction : " They shall feed in the ways, and their pastures shall be in all the beaten tracks." [2]

CHAP. LIV.

And since Celsus, although professing to know all about the Gospel, reproaches the Saviour because of His sufferings, saying that He received no assistance from the Father, or was unable to aid Himself ; we have to state that His sufferings were the subject of prophecy, along with the cause of them ; because it was for the benefit of mankind that He should die on their account,[3] and should suffer stripes because of His condemnation. It was predicted, moreover, that some from among the Gentiles would come to the knowledge of Him (among whom the prophets are not included) ; and it had been declared that He would be seen in a form which is deemed dishonourable among men. The words of prophecy run thus : " Lo, my Servant shall have understanding, and shall be exalted and glorified, and raised exceedingly high. In like manner, many shall be astonished at Thee ; so Thy form shall be in no reputation among men, and Thy glory among the sons of men. Lo, many nations shall marvel because of Him ; and kings shall close their mouths : because they, to whom no message about Him was sent, shall see Him ; and they who have not heard of Him, shall have knowledge of Him." [4] " Lord, who hath believed our report? and to whom was the arm of the LORD revealed? We have reported, as a child before Him, as a root in a thirsty ground. He has no form nor glory ; and we beheld Him, and He had not any form nor beauty : but His appearance was without honour, and deficient more than that of all men. He was a man under suffering, and who knew how to bear sickness : because His countenance was averted, He was treated with disrespect, and was made of no account. This man bears our sins, and suffers pain on our behalf ; and we regarded Him as in trouble, and in suffering, and as ill-treated. But He was wounded for our sins, and bruised for our iniquities. The chastisement of our peace was upon Him ; by His stripes we were healed. We all, like sheep, wandered from the way. A man wandered in his way, and the Lord delivered Him on account of our sins ; and He, because of His evil treatment, opens not His mouth. As a sheep was He led to slaughter ; and as a lamb before her shearer is dumb, so He opens not His mouth. In His humiliation His judgment was taken away. And who shall describe His generation? because His life is taken away from the earth ; because of the iniquities of My people was He led unto death." [5]

CHAP. LV.

Now I remember that, on one occasion, at a disputation held with certain Jews, who were reckoned wise men, I quoted these prophecies ; to which my Jewish opponent replied, that these predictions bore reference to the whole people, regarded as *one individual*, and as being in a state of dispersion and suffering, in order that many proselytes might be gained, on account of the dispersion of the Jews among numerous heathen nations. And in this way he explained the words, " Thy form shall be of no reputation among men ; " and then, " They to whom no message was sent respecting him shall see ; " and the expression, " A man under suffering." Many arguments were employed on that occasion during the discussion to prove that these predictions regarding one particular person were not rightly applied by them to the whole nation. And I asked to what character the expression would be appropriate, " This man bears our sins, and suffers pain on our behalf ; " and this, " But He was wounded for our sins, and bruised for our iniquities ; " and to whom the expression properly belonged, " By His stripes were we healed." For it is manifest that it is they who had been sinners, and had been healed by the Saviour's sufferings (whether belonging to the Jewish nation or converts from the Gentiles), who use such language in the writings of the prophet who foresaw these events, and who, under the influence of the Holy Spirit, appiled these words to a person. But we seemed to press them hardest with the expression, " Because of the iniquities of My people was He led away unto death." For if the people, according to them, are the subject of the prophecy, how is the man said to be led away to death because of the iniquities of the people of God, unless he be a different person from that people of God? And who is this person save Jesus Christ, by whose stripes they who believe on Him are healed, when " He had spoiled the principalities and powers (that were over us), and had made a show of them openly on His cross?" [6] At another time we may explain the several parts of the prophecy, leaving none of them unexamined. But these matters have been treated at greater length, necessarily as I think, on account of the

---

[1] Cf. Isa. xlix. 8, 9.
[2] Isa. xlix. 9.
[3] ὑπέρ αὐτῶν.
[4] Cf. Isa. lii. 13-15 in the Septuagint version (Roman text).

[5] Cf. Isa. liii. 1-8 in the Septuagint version (Roman text).
[6] [Col. ii. 15, S.]

language of the Jew, as quoted in the work of Celsus.

CHAP. LVI.

Now it escaped the notice of Celsus, and of the Jew whom he has introduced, and of all who are not believers in Jesus, that the prophecies speak of two advents of Christ: the former characterized by human suffering and humility, in order that Christ, being with men, might make known the way that leads to God, and might leave no man in this life a ground of excuse, in saying that he knew not of the judgment to come; and the latter, distinguished only by glory and divinity, having no element of human infirmity intermingled with its divine greatness. To quote the prophecies at length would be tedious; and I deem it sufficient for the present to quote a part of the forty-fifth Psalm, which has this inscription, in addition to others, "A Psalm for the Beloved," where God is evidently addressed in these words: "Grace is poured into Thy lips: therefore God will bless Thee for ever and ever. Gird Thy sword on Thy thigh, O mighty One, with Thy beauty and Thy majesty. And stretch forth, and ride prosperously, and reign, because of Thy truth, and meekness, and righteousness; and Thy right hand shall lead Thee marvellously. Thine arrows are pointed, O mighty One; the people will fall under Thee in the heart of the enemies of the King." [1] But attend carefully to what follows, where He is called God: "For Thy throne, O God, is for ever and ever: a sceptre of righteousness is the sceptre of Thy kingdom. Thou hast loved righteousness, and hated iniquity: therefore God, even Thy God, hath anointed Thee with the oil of gladness above Thy fellows." [2] And observe that the prophet, speaking familiarly to God, whose "throne is for ever and ever," and "a sceptre of righteousness the sceptre of His kingdom," says that this God has been anointed by a God who was His God, and anointed, because more than His fellows He had loved righteousness and hated iniquity. And I remember that I pressed the Jew, who was deemed a learned man, very hard with this passage; and he, being perplexed about it, gave such an answer as was in keeping with his Judaistic views, saying that the words, "Thy throne, O God, is for ever and ever: a sceptre of righteousness is the sceptre of Thy kingdom," are spoken of the God of all things; and these, "Thou hast loved righteousness and hated iniquity, therefore Thy God hath anointed Thee," etc., refer to the Messiah.[3]

CHAP. LVII.

The Jew, moreover, in the treatise, addresses the Saviour thus: "If you say that every man, born according to the decree of Divine Providence, is a son of God, in what respect should you differ from another?" In reply to whom we say, that every man who, as Paul expresses it, is no longer under fear, as a schoolmaster, but who chooses good for its own sake, is "a son of God;" but this man is distinguished far and wide above every man who is called, on account of his virtues, a son of God, seeing He is, as it were, a kind of source and beginning of all such. The words of Paul are as follow: "For ye have not received the spirit of bondage again to fear; but ye have received the Spirit of adoption, whereby we cry, Abba, Father." [4] But, according to the Jew of Celsus, "countless individuals will convict Jesus of falsehood, alleging that those predictions which were spoken of him were intended of them." We are not aware, indeed, whether Celsus knew of any who, after coming into this world, and having desired to act as Jesus did, declared themselves to be also the "sons of God," or the "power" of God. But since it is in the spirit of truth that we examine each passage, we shall mention that there was a certain Theudas among the Jews before the birth of Christ, who gave himself out as some great one, after whose death his deluded followers were completely dispersed. And after him, in the days of the census, when Jesus appears to have been born, one Judas, a Galilean, gathered around him many of the Jewish people, saying he was a wise man, and a teacher of certain new doctrines. And when he also had paid the penalty of his rebellion, his doctrine was overturned, having taken hold of very few persons indeed, and these of the very humblest condition. And after the times of Jesus, Dositheus the Samaritan also wished to persuade the Samaritans that he was the Christ predicted by Moses; and he appears to have gained over some to his views. But it is not absurd, in quoting the extremely wise observation of that Gamaliel named in the book of Acts, to show how those persons above mentioned were strangers to the promise, being neither "sons of God" nor "powers" of God, whereas Christ Jesus was truly the Son of God. Now Gamaliel, in the passage referred to, said: "If this counsel or this work be of men, it will come to nought" (as also did the designs of those men already mentioned after their death); "but if it be of God, ye cannot overthrow this doctrine, lest haply ye be found even to fight against God." [5] There was also Simon the Samaritan

---

[1] Ps. xlv. 2–5.
[2] Ps. xlv. 6, 7.
[3] πρὸς τὸν Χριστόν.

[4] Rom. viii. 15.
[5] Cf. Acts v. 38, 39.

magician, who wished to draw away certain by his magical arts. And on that occasion he was successful; but now-a-days it is impossible to find, I suppose, thirty of his followers in the entire world, and probably I have even overstated the number. There are exceedingly few in Palestine; while in the rest of the world, through which he desired to spread the glory of his name, you find it nowhere mentioned. And where it is found, it is found quoted from the Acts of the Apostles; so that it is to Christians that he owes this mention of himself, the unmistakeable result having proved that Simon was in no respect divine.

CHAP. LVIII.

After these matters this Jew of Celsus, instead of the Magi mentioned in the Gospel, says that "Chaldeans are spoken of by Jesus as having been induced to come to him at his birth, and to worship him while yet an infant as a God, and to have made this known to Herod the tetrarch; and that the latter sent and slew all the infants that had been born about the same time, thinking that in this way he would ensure his death among the others; and that he was led to do this through fear that, if Jesus lived to a sufficient age, he would obtain the throne." See now in this instance the blunder of one who cannot distinguish between Magi and Chaldeans, nor perceive that what they profess is different, and so has falsified the Gospel narrative. I know not, moreover, why he has passed by in silence the cause which led the Magi to come, and why he has not stated, according to the scriptural account, that it was a star seen by them in the east. Let us see now what answer we have to make to these statements. The star that was seen in the east we consider to have been a new star, unlike any of the other well-known planetary bodies, either those in the firmament above or those among the lower orbs, but partaking of the nature of those celestial bodies which appear at times, such as comets, or those meteors which resemble beams of wood, or beards, or wine jars, or any of those other names by which the Greeks are accustomed to describe their varying appearances. And we establish our position in the following manner.

CHAP. LIX.

It has been observed that, on the occurrence of great events, and of mighty changes in terrestrial things, such stars are wont to appear, indicating either the removal of dynasties or the breaking out of wars, or the happening of such circumstances as may cause commotions upon the earth. But we have read in the *Treatise on Comets* by Chaeremon the Stoic, that on some occasions also, when *good* was to happen, comets made their appearance; and he gives an account of such instances. If, then, at the commencement of new dynasties, or on the occasion of other important events, there arises a comet so called, or any similar celestial body, why should it be matter of wonder that at the birth of Him who was to introduce a new doctrine to the human race, and to make known His teaching not only to Jews, but also to Greeks, and to many of the barbarous nations besides, a star should have arisen? Now I would say, that with respect to comets there is no prophecy in circulation to the effect that such and such a comet was to arise in connection with a particular kingdom or a particular time; but with respect to the appearance of a star at the birth of Jesus there is a prophecy of Balaam recorded by Moses to this effect: "There shall arise a star out of Jacob, and a man shall rise up out of Israel." [1] And now, if it shall be deemed necessary to examine the narrative about the Magi, and the appearance of the star at the birth of Jesus, the following is what we have to say, partly in answer to the Greeks, and partly to the Jews.

CHAP. LX.

To the Greeks, then, I have to say that the Magi, being on familiar terms with evil spirits, and invoking them for such purposes as their knowledge and wishes extend to, bring about such results only as do not appear to exceed the superhuman power and strength of the evil spirits, and of the spells which invoke them, to accomplish; but should some greater manifestation of divinity be made, then the powers of the evil spirits are overthrown, being unable to resist the light of divinity. It is probable, therefore, that since at the birth of Jesus "a multitude of the heavenly host," as Luke records, and as I believe, "praised God, saying, Glory to God in the highest, and on earth peace, good-will towards men," the evil spirits on that account became feeble, and lost their strength, the falsity of their sorcery being manifested, and their power being broken; this overthrow being brought about not only by the angels having visited the terrestrial regions on account of the birth of Jesus, but also by the power of Jesus Himself, and His innate divinity. The Magi, accordingly, wishing to produce the customary results, which formerly they used to perform by means of certain spells and sorceries, sought to know the reason of their failure, conjecturing the cause to be a great one; and beholding a divine sign in the heaven, they desired to learn its signification. I am therefore of opinion that, possessing as they did the prophecies of Balaam, which Moses also records, inasmuch as Balaam was celebrated for

---

[1] Cf. Num. xxiv. 17 (Septuag.).

such predictions, and finding among them the prophecy about the star, and the words, "I shall show him to him, but not now; I deem him happy, although he will not be near,"[1] they conjectured that the man whose appearance had been foretold along with that of the star, had actually come into the world; and having pre-determined that he was superior in power to all demons, and to all common appearances and powers, they resolved to offer him homage. They came, accordingly, to Judea, persuaded that some king had been born; but not know-ing over what kingdom he was to reign, and being ignorant also of the place of his birth, bringing gifts, which they offered to him as one whose nature partook, if I may so speak, both of God and of a mortal man, — gold, viz., as to a king; myrrh, as to one who was mortal; and incense, as to a God; and they brought these offerings after they had learned the place of His birth. But since He was a God, the Saviour of the human race, raised far above all those angels which minister to men, an angel rewarded the piety of the Magi for their worship of Him, by making known to them that they were not to go back to Herod, but to return to their own homes by another way.

CHAP. LXI.

That Herod conspired against the Child (al-though the Jew of Celsus does not believe that this really happened), is not to be wondered at. For wickedness is in a certain sense blind, and would desire to defeat fate, as if it were stronger than it. And this being Herod's condition, he both believed that a king of the Jews had been born, and yet cherished a purpose contradictory of such a belief; not seeing that the Child is assuredly either a king and will come to the throne, or that he is not to be a king, and that his death, therefore, will be to no purpose. He desired accordingly to kill Him, his mind being agitated by contending passions on account of his wickedness, and being instigated by the blind and wicked devil who from the very beginning plotted against the Saviour, imagining that He was and would become some mighty one. An angel, however, perceiving the course of events, intimated to Joseph, although Celsus may not believe it, that he was to withdraw with the Child and His mother into Egypt, while Herod slew all the infants that were in Bethlehem and the surrounding borders, in the hope that he would thus destroy Him also who had been born King of the Jews. For he saw not the sleepless guardian power that is around those who deserve to be protected and preserved for the salvation of men, of whom Jesus is the first,

superior to all others in honour and excellence, who was to be a King indeed, but not in the sense that Herod supposed, but in that in which it became God to bestow a kingdom, — for the benefit, viz., of those who were to be under His sway, who was to confer no ordinary and unim-portant blessings, so to speak, upon His subjects, but who was to train them and to subject them to laws that were truly from God. And Jesus, knowing this well, and denying that He was a king in the sense that the multitude expected, but declaring the superiority of His kingdom, says: "If My kingdom were of this world, then would My servants fight, that I should not be delivered to the Jews: but now is My kingdom not of this world."[2] Now, if Celsus had seen this, he would not have said: "But if, then, this was done in order that you might not reign in his stead when you had grown to man's estate; why, after you did reach that estate, do you not become a king, instead of you, the Son of God, wandering about in so mean a condition, hiding yourself through fear, and leading a miserable life up and down?" Now, it is not dishonour-able to avoid exposing one's self to dangers, but to guard carefully against them, when this is done, not through fear of death, but from a desire to benefit others by remaining in life, until the proper time come for one who has assumed human nature to die a death that will be useful to mankind. And this is plain to him who reflects that Jesus died for the sake of men, — a point of which we have. spoken to the best of our ability in the preceding pages.

CHAP. LXII.

And after such statements, showing his igno-rance even of the number of the apostles, he proceeds thus: "Jesus having gathered around him ten or eleven persons of notorious charac-ter, the very wickedest of tax-gatherers and sail-ors, fled in company with them from place to place, and obtained his living in a shameful and importunate manner." Let us to the best of our power see what truth there is in such a state-ment. It is manifest to us all who possess the Gospel narratives, which Celsus does not appear even to have read, that Jesus selected twelve apostles, and that of these Matthew alone was a tax-gatherer; that when he calls them indiscrim-inately sailors, he probably means James and John, because they left their ship and their father Zebedee, and followed Jesus; for Peter and his brother Andrew, who employed a net to gain their necessary subsistence, must be classed not as sailors, but as the Scripture describes them, as fishermen. The Lebes[3] also, who was a follower

---

of Jesus, may have been a tax-gatherer; but he was not of the number of the apostles, except according to a statement in one of the copies of Mark's Gospel.[1] And we have not ascertained the employments of the remaining disciples, by which they earned their livelihood before becoming disciples of Jesus. I assert, therefore, in answer to such statements as the above, that it is clear to all who are able to institute an intelligent and candid examination into the history of the apostles of Jesus, that it was by help of a divine power that these men taught Christianity, and succeeded in leading others to embrace the word of God. For it was not any power of speaking, or any orderly arrangement of their message, according to the arts of Grecian dialectics or rhetoric, which was in them the effective cause of converting their hearers. Nay, I am of opinion that if Jesus had selected some individuals who were wise according to the apprehension of the multitude, and who were fitted both to think and speak so as to please them, and had used such as the ministers of His doctrine, He would most justly have been suspected of employing artifices, like those philosophers who are the leaders of certain sects, and consequently the promise respecting the divinity of His doctrine would not have manifested itself; for had the doctrine and the preaching consisted in the persuasive utterance and arrangement of words, then faith also, like that of the philosophers of the world in their opinions, would have been through the wisdom of men, and not through the power of God. Now, who is there, on seeing fishermen and tax-gatherers, who had not acquired even the merest elements of learning (as the Gospel relates of them, and in respect to which Celsus believes that they speak the truth, inasmuch as it is their own ignorance which they record), discoursing boldly not only among the Jews of faith in Jesus, but also preaching Him with success among other nations, would not inquire whence they derived this power of persuasion, as theirs was certainly not the common method followed by the multitude? And who would not say that the promise, "Follow Me, and I will make you fishers of men,"[2] had been accomplished by Jesus in the history of His apostles by a sort of divine power? And to this also, Paul, referring in terms of commendation, as we have stated a little above, says: "And my speech and my preaching was not with enticing words of man's wisdom, but in demonstration of the Spirit and of power; that your faith should not stand in the wisdom of men, but in the power of God."[3] For, according to the predictions in the prophets, foretelling the preach-

ing of the Gospel, "the Lord gave the word in great power to them who preached it, even the King of the powers of the Beloved,"[4] in order that the prophecy might be fulfilled which said, "His words shall run very swiftly."[5] And we see that "the voice of the apostles of Jesus has gone forth into all the earth, and their words to the end of the world."[6] On this account are they who hear the word powerfully proclaimed filled with power, which they manifest both by their dispositions and their lives, and by struggling even to death on behalf of the truth; while some are altogether empty, although they profess to believe in God through Jesus, inasmuch as, not possessing any divine power, they have the appearance only of being converted to the word of God. And although I have previously mentioned a Gospel declaration uttered by the Saviour, I shall nevertheless quote it again, as appropriate to the present occasion, as it confirms both the divine manifestation of our Saviour's foreknowledge regarding the preaching of His Gospel, and the power of His word, which without the aid of teachers gains the mastery over those who yield their assent to persuasion accompanied with divine power; and the words of Jesus referred to are, "The harvest is plenteous, but the labourers are few; pray ye therefore the Lord of the harvest, that He will send forth labourers into His harvest."[7]

CHAP. LXIII.

And since Celsus has termed the apostles of Jesus men of infamous notoriety, saying that they were tax-gatherers and sailors of the vilest character, we have to remark, with respect to this charge, that he seems, in order to bring an accusation against Christianity, to believe the Gospel accounts only where he pleases, and to express his disbelief of them, in order that he may not be forced to admit the manifestations of Divinity related in these same books; whereas one who sees the spirit of truth by which the writers are influenced, ought, from their narration of things of inferior importance, to believe also the account of divine things. Now in the general Epistle of Barnabas, from which perhaps Celsus took the statement that the apostles were notoriously wicked men, it is recorded that "Jesus selected His own apostles, as persons who were more guilty of sin than all other evil-doers."[8] And in the Gospel according to Luke, Peter says to Jesus, "Depart from me, O Lord, for I am a sinful man."[9] Moreover, Paul, who himself also at a later time became an apostle

---

[1] Cf. Mark iii. 18 with Matt. x. 3.
[2] Matt. iv. 19.
[3] Cf. 1 Cor. ii. 4, 5.

[4] Cf. Ps. lxviii. 11 (Septuag.).
[5] Ps. cxlvii. 15.
[6] Ps. xix. 4.
[7] Matt. ix. 37, 38.
[8] *Epistle of Barnabas*, chap. v. vol. i p. 139.
[9] Luke v. 8.

of Jesus, says in his Epistle to Timothy, " This is a faithful saying, that Jesus Christ came into the world to save sinners, of whom I am the chief." [1] And I do not know how Celsus should have forgotten or not have thought of saying something about Paul, the founder, after Jesus, of the Churches that are in Christ. He saw, probably, that anything he might say about that apostle would require to be explained, in consistency with the fact that, after being a persecutor of the Church of God, and a bitter opponent of believers, who went so far even as to deliver over the disciples of Jesus to death, so great a change afterwards passed over him, that he preached the Gospel of Jesus from Jerusalem round about to Illyricum, and was ambitious to carry the glad tidings where he needed not to build upon another man's foundation, but to places where the Gospel of God in Christ had not been proclaimed at all. What absurdity, therefore, is there, if Jesus, desiring to manifest to the human race the power which He possesses to heal souls, should have selected notorious and wicked men, and should have raised them to such a degree of moral excellence, that they became a pattern of the purest virtue to all who were converted by their instrumentality to the Gospel of Christ?

CHAP. LXIV.

But if we were to reproach those who have been converted with their former lives, then we would have occasion to accuse Phædo also, even after he became a philosopher ; since, as the history relates, he was drawn away by Socrates from a house of bad fame [2] to the pursuits of philosophy. Nay, even the licentious life of Polemo, the successor of Xenocrates, will be a subject of reproach to philosophy ; whereas even in these instances we ought to regard it as a ground of praise, that reasoning was enabled, by the persuasive power of these men, to convert from the practice of such vices those who had been formerly entangled by them. Now among the Greeks there was only one Phædo, I know not if there were a second, and one Polemo, who betook themselves to philosophy, after a licentious and most wicked life ; while with Jesus there were not only at the time we speak of, the twelve disciples, but many more at all times, who, becoming a band of temperate men, speak in the following terms of their former lives : " For we ourselves also were sometimes foolish, disobedient, deceived, serving divers lusts and pleasures, living in malice and envy, hateful, and hating one another. But after that the kindness and love of God our Saviour towards man

appeared, by the washing of regeneration, and renewing of the Holy Ghost, which He shed upon us richly," [3] we became such as we are. For " God sent forth His Word and healed them, and delivered them from their destructions," [4] as the prophet taught in the book of Psalms. And in addition to what has been already said, I would add the following : that Chrysippus, in his treatise on the *Cure of the Passions*, in his endeavours to restrain the passions of the human soul, not pretending to determine what opinions are the true ones, says that according to the principles of the different sects are those to be cured who have been brought under the dominion of the passions, and continues : " And if pleasure be an end, then by it must the passions be healed ; and if there be three kinds of chief blessings, still, according to this doctrine, it is in the same way that those are to be freed from their passions who are under their dominion ; " whereas the assailants of Christianity do not see in how many persons the passions have been brought under restraint, and the flood of wickedness checked, and savage manners softened, by means of the Gospel. So that it well became those who are ever boasting of their zeal for the public good, to make a public acknowledgement of their thanks to that doctrine which by a new method led men to abandon many vices, and to bear their testimony at least to it, that even though not the truth, it has at all events been productive of benefit to the human race.

CHAP. LXV.

And since Jesus, in teaching His disciples not to be guilty of rashness, gave them the precept, " If they persecute you in this city, flee ye into another ; and if they persecute you in the other, flee again into a third," [5] to which teaching He added the example of a consistent life, acting so as not to expose Himself to danger rashly, or unseasonably, or without good grounds ; from this Celsus takes occasion to bring a malicious and slanderous accusation, — the Jew whom he brings forward saying to Jesus, " In company with your disciples you go and hide yourself in different places." Now similar to what has thus been made the ground of a slanderous charge against Jesus and His disciples, do we say was the conduct recorded of Aristotle. This philosopher, seeing that a court was about to be summoned to try him, on the ground of his being guilty of impiety on account of certain of his philosophical tenets which the Athenians regarded as impious, withdrew from Athens, and fixed his school in Chalcis, defending his course of procedure to his friends by saying, " Let us

---

[1] Cf. 1 Tim. i. 15.
[2] ἀπὸ οἰκήματος. Such is the reading in the text of Lommatzsch. Hœschel and Spencer read ἀπὸ οἰκήματος ἐτείου, and Ruæus proposes ἑταιρίου.

[3] Cf. Tit. iii. 3-6.
[4] Cf. Ps. cvii. 20.
[5] Cf. Matt. x. 23.

depart from Athens, that we may not give the Athenians a handle for incurring guilt a second time, as formerly in the case of Socrates, and so prevent them from committing a second act of impiety against philosophy." He further says, "that Jesus went about with His disciples, and obtained His livelihood in a disgraceful and importunate manner." Let him show wherein lay the disgraceful and importunate element in their manner of subsistence. For it is related in the Gospels, that there were certain women who had been healed of their diseases, among whom also was Susanna, who from their own possessions afforded the disciples the means of support. And who is there among philosophers, that, when devoting himself to the service of his acquaintances, is not in the habit of receiving from them what is needful for his wants? Or is it only in them that such acts are proper and becoming; but when the disciples of Jesus do the same, they are accused by Celsus of obtaining their livelihood by disgraceful importunity?

CHAP. LXVI.

And in addition to the above, this Jew of Celsus afterwards addresses Jesus: "What need, moreover, was there that you, while still an infant, should be conveyed into Egygt? Was it to escape being murdered? But then it was not likely that a God should be afraid of death; and yet an angel came down from heaven, commanding you and your friends to flee, lest ye should be captured and put to death! And was not the great God, who had already sent two angels on your account, able to keep you, His only Son, there in safety?" From these words Celsus seems to think that there was no element of divinity in the human body and soul of Jesus, but that His body was not even such as is described in the fables of Homer; and with a taunt also at the blood of Jesus which was shed upon the cross, he adds that it was not

"Ichor, such as flows in the veins of the blessed gods." [1]

We now, believing Jesus Himself, when He says respecting His divinity, "I am the way, and the truth, and the life," [2] and employs other terms of similar import; and when He says respecting His being clothed with a human body, "And now ye seek to kill Me, a man that hath told you the truth," [3] conclude that He was a kind of compound being. And so it became Him who was making provision for His sojourning in the world as a human being, not to expose Himself unseasonably to the danger of death. And in like manner it was necessary that He should be taken away by His parents, acting under the instruc-

tions of an angel from heaven, who communicated to them the divine will, saying on the first occasion, "Joseph, thou son of David, fear not to take unto thee Mary thy wife; for that which is conceived in her is of the Holy Ghost;" [4] and on the second, "Arise, and take the young Child, and His mother, and flee into Egypt; and be thou there until I bring thee word: for Herod will seek the young Child to destroy Him." [5] Now, what is recorded in these words appears to me to be not at all marvellous. For in either passage of Scripture it is stated that it was in a dream that the angel spoke these words; and that in a dream certain persons may have certain things pointed out to them to do, is an event of frequent occurrence to many individuals, — the impression on the mind being produced either by an angel or by some other thing. Where, then, is the absurdity in believing that He who had once become incarnate, should be led also by human guidance to keep out of the way of dangers? Not indeed from any impossibility that it should be otherwise, but from the moral fitness that ways and means should be made use of to ensure the safety of Jesus. And it was certainly better that the Child Jesus should escape the snare of Herod, and should reside with His parents in Egypt until the death of the conspirator, than that Divine Providence should hinder the free-will of Herod in his wish to put the Child to death, or that the fabled poetic helmet of Hades should have been employed, or anything of a similar kind done with respect to Jesus, or that they who came to destroy Him should have been smitten with blindness like the people of Sodom. For the sending of help to Him in a very miraculous and unnecessarily public manner, would not have been of any service to Him who wished to show that as a man, to whom witness was borne by God, He possessed within that form which was seen by the eyes of men some higher element of divinity, — that which was properly the Son of God — God the Word — the power of God, and the wisdom of God — He who is called the Christ. But this is not a suitable occasion for discussing the composite nature of the incarnate Jesus; the investigation into such a subject being for believers, so to speak, a sort of private question.

CHAP. LXVII.

After the above, this Jew of Celsus, as if he were a Greek who loved learning, and were well instructed in Greek literature, continues: "The old mythological fables, which attributed a divine origin to Perseus, and Amphion, and Æacus, and Minos, were not believed by us. Nevertheless,

---

[1] Cf. *Iliad*, v. 340.
[2] John xiv. 6.
[3] Cf. John viii. 40.

[4] Cf. Matt. i. 20.
[5] Cf. Matt. ii. 13.

that they might not appear unworthy of credit, they represented the deeds of these personages as great and wonderful, and truly beyond the power of man ; but what hast thou done that is noble or wonderful either in deed or in word? Thou hast made no manifestation to us, although they challenged you in the temple to exhibit some unmistakeable sign that you were the Son of God." In reply to which we have to say: Let the Greeks show to us, among those who have been enumerated, any one whose deeds have been marked by a utility and splendour extending to after generations, and which have been so great as to produce a belief in the fables which represented them as of divine descent. But these Greeks can show us nothing regarding those men of whom they speak, which is even inferior by a great degree to what Jesus did ; unless they take us back to their fables and histories, wishing us to believe them without any reasonable grounds, and to discredit the Gospel accounts even after the clearest evidence. For we assert that the whole habitable world contains evidence of the works of Jesus, in the existence of those Churches of God which have been founded through Him by those who have been converted from the practice of innumerable sins.[1] And the name of Jesus can still remove distractions from the minds of men, and expel demons, and also take away diseases ; and produce a marvellous meekness of spirit and complete change of character, and a humanity, and goodness, and gentleness in those individuals who do not feign themselves to be Christians for the sake of subsistence or the supply of any mortal wants, but who have honestly accepted the doctrine concerning God and Christ, and the judgment to come.

CHAP. LXVIII.

But after this, Celsus, having a suspicion that the great works performed by Jesus, of which we have named a few out of a great number, would be brought forward to view, affects to grant that those statements may be true which are made regarding His cures, or His resurrection, or the feeding of a multitude with a few loaves, from which many fragments remained over, or those other stories which Celsus thinks the disciples have recorded as of a marvellous nature ; and he adds : "Well, let us believe that these were actually wrought by you." But then he immediately compares them to the tricks of jugglers, who profess to do more wonderful things, and to the feats performed by those who have been taught by Egyptians, who in the

middle of the market-place, in return for a few obols, will impart the knowledge of their most venerated arts, and will expel demons from men, and dispel diseases, and invoke the souls of heroes, and exhibit expensive banquets, and tables, and dishes, and dainties having no real existence, and who will put in motion, as if alive, what are not really living animals, but which have only the appearance of life. And he asks, "Since, then, these persons can perform such feats, shall we of necessity conclude that they are 'sons of God,' or must we admit that they are the proceedings of wicked men under the influence of an evil spirit?" You see that by these expressions he allows, as it were, the existence of magic. I do not know, however, if he is the same who wrote several books against it. But, as it helped his purpose, he compares the (miracles) related of Jesus to the results produced by magic. There would indeed be a resemblance between them, if Jesus, like the dealers in magical arts, had performed His works only for show ; but now there is not a single juggler who, by means of his proceedings, invites his spectators to reform their manners, or trains those to the fear of God who are amazed at what they see, nor who tries to persuade them so to live as men who are to be justified[2] by God. And jugglers do none of these things, because they have neither the power nor the will, nor any desire to busy themselves about the reformation of men, inasmuch as their own lives are full of the grossest and most notorious sins. But how should not He who, by the miracles which He did, induced those who beheld the excellent results to undertake the reformation of their characters, manifest Himself not only to His genuine disciples, but also to others, as a pattern of most virtuous life, in order that His disciples might devote themselves to the work of instructing men in the will of God, and that the others, after being more fully instructed by His word and character than by His miracles, as to how they were to direct their lives, might in all their conduct have a constant reference to the good pleasure of the universal God? And if such were the life of Jesus, how could any one with reason compare Him with the sect of impostors, and not, on the contrary, believe, according to the promise, that He was God, who appeared in human form to do good to our race?

CHAP. LXIX.

After this, Celsus, confusing together the Christian doctrine and the opinions of some heretical sect, and bringing them forward as charges that were applicable to all who believe in the divine word, says : "Such a body as yours could not

---

[1] [Note the words, "The whole habitable world," and comp. cap. iii., *supra*, "the defeat of the whole world." In cap. vii. is another important testimony. "Countless numbers" is the phrase in cap. xxvii. See cap. xxix. also, *ad finem.* Such evidence cannot be explained away.]

[2] ὡς δικαιωθησομένους.

have belonged to God." Now, in answer to this, we have to say that Jesus, on entering into the world, assumed, as one born of a woman, a human body, and one which was capable of suffering a natural death. For which reason, in addition to others, we say that He was also a great wrestler;[1] having, on account of His human body, been tempted in all respects like other men, but no longer as men, with sin as a consequence, but being altogether without sin. For it is distinctly clear to us that "He did no sin, neither was guile found in His mouth; and as one who knew no sin,"[2] God delivered Him up as pure for all who had sinned. Then Celsus says: "The body of god would not have been so generated as you, O Jesus, were." He saw, besides, that if, as it is written, it had been born, His body somehow might be even more divine than that of the multitude, and in a certain sense a body of god. But he disbelieves the accounts of His conception by the Holy Ghost, and believes that He was begotten by one Panthera, who corrupted the Virgin, "because a god's body would not have been so generated as you were." But we have spoken of these matters at greater length in the preceding pages.

CHAP. LXX.

He asserts, moreover, that "the body of a god is not nourished with such food (as was that of Jesus)," since he is able to prove from the Gospel narratives both that He partook of food, and food of a particular kind. Well, be it so. Let him assert that He ate the passover with His disciples, when He not only used the words, "With desire have I desired to eat this passover with you," but also actually partook of the same. And let him say also, that He experienced the sensation of thirst beside the well of Jacob, and drank of the water of the well. In what respect do these facts militate against what we have said respecting the nature of His body? Moreover, it appears indubitable that after His resurrection He ate a piece of fish; for, according to our view, He assumed a (true) body, as one born of a woman. "But," objects Celsus, "the body of a god does not make use of such a voice as that of Jesus, nor employ such a method of persuasion as he." These are, indeed, trifling and altogether contemptible objections. For our

reply to him will be, that he who is believed among the Greeks to be a god, viz., the Pythian and Didymean Apollo, makes use of such a voice for his Pythian priestess at Delphi, and for his prophetess at Miletus; and yet neither the Pythian nor Didymean is charged by the Greeks with not being a god, nor any other Grecian deity whose worship is established in one place. And it was far better, surely, that a god should employ a voice which, on account of its being uttered with power, should produce an indescribable sort of persuasion in the minds of the hearers.

CHAP. LXXI.

Continuing to pour abuse upon Jesus as one who, on account of his impiety and wicked opinions, was, so to speak, hated by God, he asserts that "these tenets of his were those of a wicked and God-hated sorcerer." And yet, if the name and the thing be properly examined, it will be found an impossibility that man should be hated by God, seeing God loves all existing things, and "hateth nothing of what He has made," for He created nothing in a spirit of hatred. And if certain expressions in the prophets convey such an impression, they are to be interpreted in accordance with the general principle by which Scripture employs such language with regard to God as if He were subject to human affections. But what reply need be made to him who, while professing to bring foreward credible statements, thinks himself bound to make use of calumnies and slanders against Jesus, as if He were a wicked sorcerer? Such is not the procedure of one who seeks to make good his case, but of one who is in an ignorant and unphilosophic state of mind, inasmuch as the proper course is to state the case, and candidly to investigate it; and, according to the best of his ability, to bring forward what occurs to him with regard to it. But as the Jew of Celsus has, with the above remarks, brought to a close his charges against Jesus, so we also shall here bring to a termination the contents of our first book in reply to him. And if God bestow the gift of that truth which destroys all falsehood, agreeably to the words of the prayer, "Cut them off in thy truth,"[3] we shall begin, in what follows, the consideration of the second appearance of the Jew, in which he is represented by Celsus as addressing those who have become converts to Jesus.

---

[1] μέγαν ἀγωνιστήν.
[2] [1 Pet. ii. 22; 2 Cor. v. 21. S.]

[3] Ps. liv. 5.

ORIGEN AGAINST CELSUS.

BOOK II.

CHAP. I.

THE first book of our answer to the treatise of Celsus, entitled *A True Discourse*, which concluded with the representation of the Jew addressing Jesus, having now extended to a sufficient length, we intend the present part as a reply to the charges brought by him against those who have been converted from Judaism to Christianity.[1] And we call attention, in the first place, to this special question, viz., why Celsus, when he had once resolved upon the introduction of individuals upon the stage of his book, did not represent the Jew as addressing the converts from heathenism rather than those from Judaism, seeing that his discourse, if directed to us, would have appeared more likely to produce an impression.[2] But probably this claimant to universal knowledge does not know what is appropriate in the matter of such representations; and therefore let us proceed to consider what he has to say to the converts from Judaism. He asserts that "they have forsaken the law of their fathers, in consequence of their minds being led captive by Jesus; that they have been most ridiculously deceived, and that they have become deserters to another name and to another mode of life." Here he has not observed that the Jewish converts have not deserted the law of their fathers, inasmuch as they live according to its prescriptions, receiving their very name from the poverty of the law, according to the literal acceptation of the word; for Ebion signifies "poor" among the Jews,[3] and those Jews who have received Jesus as Christ are called by the name of Ebionites. Nay, Peter himself seems to have observed for a considerable time the Jewish observances enjoined by the law of Moses, not having yet learned from Jesus to ascend from the law that is regulated according to the letter, to that which is interpreted according to the spirit,—a fact which we learn from the Acts of the Apostles. For on the day after the angel of God appeared to Cornelius, suggesting to him "to send to Joppa, to Simon surnamed Peter," Peter "went up into the upper room to pray about the sixth hour. And he became very hungry, and would have eaten: but while they made ready he fell into a trance, and saw heaven opened, and a certain vessel descending unto him, as it had been a great sheet knit at the four corners, and let down to the earth; wherein were all manner of four-footed beasts, and creeping things of the earth, and fowls of the air. And there came a voice to him, Rise, Peter; kill, and eat. But Peter said, Not so, Lord; for I have never eaten anything that is common or unclean. And the voice spake unto him again the second time, What God hath cleansed, that call thou not common."[4] Now observe how, by this instance, Peter is represented as still observing the Jewish customs respecting clean and unclean animals. And from the narrative that follows, it is manifest that he, as being yet a Jew, and living according to their traditions, and despising those who were beyond the pale of Judaism, stood in need of a vision to lead him to communicate to Cornelius (who was not an Israelite according to the flesh), and to those who were with him, the word of faith. Moreover, in the Epistle to the Galatians, Paul states that Peter, still from fear of the Jews, ceased upon the arrival of James to eat with the Gentiles, and "separated himself from them, fearing them that were of the circumcision;"[5] and the rest of the Jews, and Barnabas also, followed the same course. And certainly it was quite consistent that those should not abstain from the observance of Jewish usages who were sent to minister to the circumcision, when they who "seemed to be pillars" gave the right hand of fellowship to Paul and Barnabas, in order that, while devoting themselves to the circumcision, the latter might preach to the Gentiles. And

[1] [Comp. Justin, *Dial. with Trypho (passim)*, vol. i., this series.]
[2] πιθανώτατος.
[3] אֶבְיוֹן.
[4] Cf. Acts x. 9-15.
[5] Cf. Gal. ii. 12.

why do I mention that they who preached to the circumcision withdrew and separated themselves from the heathen, when even Paul himself " became as a Jew to the Jews, that he might gain the Jews?" Wherefore also in the Acts of the Apostles it is related that he even brought an offering to the altar, that he might satisfy the Jews that he was no apostate from their law.[1] Now, if Celsus had been acquainted with all these circumstances, he would not have represented the Jew holding such language as this to the converts from Judaism : " What induced you, my fellow-citizens, to abandon the law of your fathers, and to allow your minds to be led captive by him with whom we have just conversed, and thus be most ridiculously deluded, so as to become deserters from us to another name, and to the practices of another life?"

CHAP. II.

Now, since we are upon the subject of Peter, and of the teachers of Christianity to the circumcision, I do not deem it out of place to quote a certain declaration of Jesus taken from the Gospel according to John, and to give the explanation of the same. For it is there related that Jesus said : " I have yet many things to say unto you, but ye cannot bear them now. Howbeit when He, the Spirit of truth, is come, He will guide you into all the truth : for He shall not speak of Himself ; but whatsoever He shall hear, that shall He speak."[2] And when we inquire what were the " many things " referred to in the passage which Jesus had to say to His disciples, but which they were not then able to bear, I have to observe that, probably because the apostles were Jews, and had been trained up according to the letter of the Mosaic law, He was unable to tell them what was the true law, and how the Jewish worship consisted in the pattern and shadow of certain heavenly things, and how future blessings were foreshadowed by the injunctions regarding meats and drinks, and festivals, and new moons, and sabbaths. These were many of the subjects which He had to explain to them ; but as He saw that it was a work of exceeding difficulty to root out of the mind opinions that have been almost born with a man, and amid which he has been brought up till he reached the period of maturity, and which have produced in those who have adopted them the belief that they are divine, and that it is an act of impiety to overthrow them ; and to demonstrate by the superiority of Christian doctrine, that is, by the truth, in a manner to convince the hearers, that such opinions were but " loss and dung," He postponed such a task to a future

season — to that, namely, which followed His passion and resurrection. For the bringing of aid unseasonably to those who were not yet capable of receiving it, might have overturned the idea which they had already formed of Jesus, as the Christ, and the Son of the living God. And see if there is not some well-grounded reason for such a statement as this, " I have many things to say unto you, but ye cannot bear them now ; " seeing there are many points in the law which require to be explained and cleared up in a spiritual sense, and these the disciples were in a manner unable to bear, having been born and brought up amongst Jews. I am of opinion, moreover, that since these rites were typical, and the truth was that which was to be taught them by the Holy Spirit, these words were added, " When He is come who is the Spirit of truth, He will lead you into all the truth ; " as if He had said, into all the truth about those things which, being to you but types, ye believed to constitute a true worship which ye rendered unto God. And so, according to the promise of Jesus, the Spirit of truth came to Peter, saying to him, with regard to the four-footed beasts, and creeping things of the earth, and fowls of the air : "Arise, Peter ; kill, and eat." And the Spirit came to him while he was still in a state of superstitious ignorance ; for he said, in answer to the divine command, " Not so Lord ; for I have never yet eaten anything common or unclean." He instructed him, however, in the true and spiritual meaning of meats, by saying, " What God hath cleansed, that call not thou common." And so, after that vision, the Spirit of truth, which conducted Peter into all the truth, told him the many things which he was unable to bear when Jesus was still with him in the flesh. But I shall have another opportunity of explaining those matters, which are connected with the literal acceptation of the Mosaic law.

CHAP. III.

Our present object, however, is to expose the ignorance of Celsus, who makes this Jew of his address his fellow-citizen and the Israelitish converts in the following manner : " What induced you to abandon the law of your fathers?" etc. Now, how should they have abandoned the law of their fathers, who are in the habit of rebuking those who do not listen to its commands, saying, " Tell me, ye who read the law, do ye not hear the law? For it is written, that Abraham had two sons ; " and so on, down to the place, " which things are an allegory,"[3] etc.? And how have they abandoned the law of their fathers, who are ever speaking of the usages of their fathers in such words as these : " Or does

---

[1] Cf. Acts xxi. 26.
[2] John xvi. 12, 13.
[3] Gal. iv. 21, 22, 24.

not the law say these things also? For it is written in the law of Moses, Thou shalt not muzzle the mouth of the ox that treadeth out the corn. Doth God care for oxen? or saith He it altogether for our sakes? for for our sakes it was written," and so on?[1] Now, how confused is the reasoning of the Jew in regard to these matters (although he had it in his power to speak with greater effect) when he says: "Certain among you have abandoned the usages of our fathers under a pretence of explanations and allegories; and some of you, although, as ye pretend, interpreting them in a spiritual manner, nevertheless do observe the customs of our fathers; and some of you, without any such interpretation, are willing to accept Jesus as the subject of prophecy, and to keep the law of Moses according to the customs of the fathers, as having in the words the whole mind of the Spirit." Now how was Celsus able to see these things so clearly in this place, when in the subsequent parts of his work he makes mention of certain godless heresies altogether alien from the doctrine of Jesus, and even of others which leave the Creator out of account altogether, and does not appear to know that there are Israelites who are converts to Christianity, and who have not abandoned the law of their fathers? It was not his object to investigate everything here in the spirit of truth, and to accept whatever he might find to be useful; but he composed these statements in the spirit of an enemy, and with a desire to overthrow everything as soon as he heard it.

CHAP. IV.

The Jew, then, continues his address to converts from his own nation thus: "Yesterday and the day before, when we visited with punishment the man who deluded you, ye became apostates from the law of your fathers;" showing by such statements (as we have just demonstrated) anything but an exact knowledge of the truth. But what he advances afterwards seems to have some force, when he says: "How is it that you take the beginning of your system from our worship, and when you have made some progress you treat it with disrespect, although you have no other foundation to show for your doctrines than our law?" Now, certainly the introduction to Christianity is through the Mosaic worship and the prophetic writings; and after the introduction, it is in the interpretation and explanation of these that progress takes place, while those who are introduced prosecute their investigations into "the mystery according to revelation, which was kept secret since the world began, but now is made manifest in the Scriptures of the prophets,"[2] and by the appearance of our Lord Jesus

Christ. But they who advance in the knowledge of Christianity do not, as ye allege, treat the things written in the law with disrespect. On the contrary, they bestow upon them greater honour, showing what a depth of wise and mysterious reasons is contained in these writings, which are not fully comprehended by the Jews, who treat them superficially, and as if they were in some degree even fabulous.[3] And what absurdity should there be in our system — that is, the Gospel — having the law for its foundation, when even the Lord Jesus Himself said to those who would not believe upon Him: "If ye had believed Moses, ye would have believed Me, for he wrote of Me. But if ye do not believe his writings, how shall ye believe My words?"[4] Nay, even one of the evangelists — Mark — says: "The beginning of the Gospel of Jesus Christ, as it is written in the prophet Isaiah, Behold, I send My messenger before Thy face, who shall prepare Thy way before Thee,"[5] which shows that the beginning of the Gospel is connected with the Jewish writings. What force, then, is there in the objection of the Jew of Celsus, that "if any one predicted to us that the Son of God was to visit mankind, he was one of our prophets, and the prophet of our God?" Or how is it a charge against Christianity, that John, who baptized Jesus, was a Jew? For although He was a Jew, it does not follow that every believer, whether a convert from heathenism or from Judaism, must yield a literal obedience to the law of Moses.

CHAP. V.

After these matters, although Celsus becomes tautological in his statements about Jesus, repeating for the second time that "he was punished by the Jews for his crimes," we shall not again take up the defence, being satisfied with what we have already said. But, in the next place, as this Jew of his disparages the doctrine regarding the resurrection of the dead, and the divine judgment, and of the rewards to be bestowed upon the just, and of the fire which is to devour the wicked, as being stale[6] opinions, and thinks that he will overthrow Christianity by asserting that there is nothing new in its teaching upon these points, we have to say to him, that our Lord, seeing the conduct of the Jews not to be at all in keeping with the teaching of the prophets, inculcated by a parable that the kingdom of God would be taken from them, and given to the converts from heathenism. For which reason, now, we may also see of a truth that all the doctrines of the Jews of the present

---

[1] 1 Cor. ix. 8–10.
[2] Rom. xvi. 25, 26.
[3] τῶν ἐπιπολαιότερον καὶ μυθικώτερον αὐτοῖς ἐντυγχανόντων.
[4] John v. 46, 47.
[5] Mark i. 1, 2.
[6] ἑωλα.

day are mere trifles and fables,[1] since they have not the light that proceeds from the knowledge of the Scriptures; whereas those of the Christians are the truth, having power to raise and elevate the soul and understanding of man, and to persuade him to seek a citizenship, not like the earthly[2] Jews here below, but in heaven. And this result shows itself among those who are able to see the grandeur of the ideas contained in the law and the prophets, and who are able to commend them to others.

CHAP. VI.

But let it be granted that Jesus observed all the Jewish usages, including even their sacrificial observances, what does that avail to prevent our recognising Him as the Son of God? Jesus, then, is the Son of God, who gave the law and the prophets; and we, who belong to the Church, do not transgress the law, but have escaped the mythologizings[3] of the Jews, and have our minds chastened and educated by the mystical contemplation of the law and the prophets. For the prophets themselves, as not resting the sense of these words in the plain history which they relate, nor in the legal enactments taken according to the word and letter, express themselves somewhere, when about to relate histories, in words like this, "I will open my mouth in parables, I will utter hard sayings of old;"[4] and in another place, when offering up a prayer regarding the law as being obscure, and needing divine help for its comprehension, they offer up this prayer, "Open Thou mine eyes, that I may behold wondrous things out of Thy law."[5]

CHAP. VII.

Moreover, let them show where there is to be found even the appearance of language dictated by arrogance,[6] and proceeding from Jesus. For how could an arrogant man thus express himself, "Learn of Me, for I am meek and lowly of heart, and you shall find rest for your souls?"[7] or how can He be styled arrogant, who after supper laid aside His garments in the presence of His disciples, and, after girding Himself with a towel, and pouring water into a basin, proceeded to wash the feet of each disciple, and rebuked him who was unwilling to allow them to be washed, with the words, "Except I wash thee, thou hast no part with Me?"[8] Or how could He be called such who said, "I was amongst you, not as he that sitteth at meat, but as he that serveth?"[9] And let any one show what were the falsehoods which He uttered, and let him point out what are great and what are small falsehoods, that he may prove Jesus to have been guilty of the former. And there is yet another way in which we may confute him. For as one falsehood is not less or more false than another, so one truth is not less or more true than another. And what charges of impiety he has to bring against Jesus, let the Jew of Celsus especially bring forward. Was it impious to abstain from corporeal circumcision, and from a literal Sabbath, and literal festivals, and literal new moons, and from clean and unclean meats, and to turn the mind to the good and true and spiritual law of God, while at the same time he who was an ambassador for Christ knew how to become to the Jews as a Jew, that he might gain the Jews, and to those who are under the law, as under the law, that he might gain those who are under the law?

CHAP. VIII.

He says, further, that "many other persons would appear such as Jesus was, to those who were willing to be deceived." Let this Jew of Celsus then show us, not many persons, nor even a few, but a single individual, such as Jesus was, introducing among the human race, with the power that was manifested in Him, a system of doctrine and opinions beneficial to human life, and which converts men from the practice of wickedness. He says, moreover, that this charge is brought against the Jews by the Christian converts, that they have not believed in Jesus as in God. Now on this point we have, in the preceding pages, offered a preliminary defence, showing at the same time in what respects we understand Him to be God, and in what we take Him to be man. "How should we," he continues, "who have made known to all men that there is to come from God one who is to punish the wicked, treat him with disregard when he came?" And to this, as an exceedingly silly argument, it does not seem to me reasonable to offer any answer. It is as if some one were to say, "How could we, who teach temperance, commit any act of licentiousness? or we, who are ambassadors for righteousness, be guilty of any wickedness?" For as these inconsistencies are found among men, so, to say that they believed the prophets when speaking of the future advent of Christ, and yet refused their belief to Him when He came, agreeably to prophetic statement, was quite in keeping with human nature. And since we must add another reason, we shall remark that this very result was foretold by the prophets. Isaiah distinctly declares: "Hearing ye shall hear, and shall not understand; and seeing ye

---

[1] μύθους καὶ λήρους.
[2] τοῖς κάτω Ἰουδαίοις.
[3] μυθολογίας.
[4] Ps. lxxviii. 2.
[5] Ps. cxix. 18.
[6] ἀλαζονεία.
[7] Matt. xi. 29.
[8] John xiii. 8.

[9] Luke xxii. 27.

shall see, and shall not perceive : for the heart
of this people has become fat," [1] etc.   And let
them explain why it was predicted to the Jews,
that although they both heard and saw, they
would not understand what was said, nor perceive what was seen as they ought.   For it is
indeed manifest, that when they beheld Jesus
they did not see who He was; and when they
heard Him, they did not understand from His
words the divinity that was in Him, and which
transferred God's providential care, hitherto exercised over the Jews, to His converts from the
heathen.   Therefore we may see, that after the
advent of Jesus the Jews were altogether abandoned, and possess now none of what were considered their ancient glories, so that there is no
indication of any Divinity abiding amongst them.
For they have no longer prophets nor miracles,
traces of which to a considerable extent are still
found among Christians, and some of them more
remarkable than any that existed among the
Jews ; and these we ourselves have witnessed, if
our testimony may be received.[2]   But the Jew of
Celsus exclaims : " Why did we treat him, whom
we announced beforehand, with dishonour?   Was
it that we might be chastised more than others?"
To which we have to answer, that on account of
their unbelief, and the other insults which they
heaped upon Jesus, the Jews will not only suffer
more than others in that judgment which is believed to impend over the world, but have even
already endured such sufferings.   For what nation is an exile from their own metropolis, and
from the place sacred to the worship of their
fathers, save the Jews alone?   And these calamities they have suffered, because they were a most
wicked nation, which, although guilty of many
other sins, yet has been punished so severely for
none, as for those that were committed against
our Jesus.

CHAP. IX.

The Jew continues his discourse thus : " How
should we deem him to be a God, who not only
in other respects, as was currently reported, performed none of his promises, but who also, after
we had convicted him, and condemned him as
deserving of punishment, was found attempting
to conceal himself, and endeavouring to escape
in a most disgraceful manner, and who was betrayed by those whom he called disciples?   And
yet," he continues, " he who was a God could
neither flee nor be led away a prisoner ; and
least of all could he be deserted and delivered
up by those who had been his associates, and

had shared all things in common, and had had
him for their teacher, who was deemed to be a
Saviour, and a son of the greatest God, and an
angel."   To which we reply, that even we do
not suppose the body of Jesus, which was then
an object of sight and perception, to have been
God.   And why do I say His body?   Nay, not
even His soul, of which it is related, " My soul
is exceeding sorrowful, even unto death." [3]   But
as, according to the Jewish manner of speaking,
" I am the Lord, the God of all flesh," and,
" Before Me there was no God formed, neither
shall there be after Me," God is believed to be
He who employs the soul and body of the
prophet as an instrument ; and as, according to
the Greeks, he who says,

" I know both the number of the sand, and the measures
    of the sea,
And I understand a dumb man, and hear him who
    does not speak," [4]

is considered to be a god when speaking, and
making himself heard through the Pythian
priestess ; so, according to our view, it was the
Logos God, and Son of the God of all things,
who spake in Jesus these words, " I am the way,
and the truth, and the life ; " and these, " I am
the door ; " and these, " I am the living bread
that came down from heaven ; " and other expressions similar to these.   We therefore charge
the Jews with not acknowledging Him to be
God, to whom testimony was borne in many passages by the prophets, to the effect that He was
a mighty power, and a God next to [5] the God
and Father of all things.   For we assert that it
was to Him the Father gave the command, when
in the Mosaic account of the creation He uttered
the words, " Let there be light," and " Let there
be a firmament," and gave the injunctions with
regard to those other creative acts which were
performed ; and that to Him also were addressed
the words, " Let Us make man in Our own image
and likeness ; " and that the Logos, when commanded, obeyed all the Father's will.   And we
make these statements not from our own conjectures, but because we believe the prophecies cir-
culated among the Jews, in which it is said of
God, and of the works of creation, in express
words, as follows : " He spake, and they were

---

[1] Isa. vi. 9.
[2] [" The Fathers, while they refer to extraordinary divine agency
going on in their own day, also with one consent represent miracles
as having ceased since the apostolic era," — MOZLEY's Bampton Lectures, *On Miracles*, p. 165.   See also, Newman's *Essay on the Miracles of the Early Ages*, quoted by Mozley.   S.]

[3] Matt. xxvi. 38.
[4] Herodot., i. cap. 47.
[5] καὶ Θεὸν κατὰ τὸν τῶν ὅλων Θεὸν καὶ πατέρα.   " Ex mente
Origenis, inquit Boherellus, vertendum ' Secundo post universi Deum
atque parentem loco;" non cum interprete Gelenio, ' Ipsius rerum
universarum Dei atque Parentis testimonio.'   Nam si hic esset sensus,
frustra post ὑπὸ τῶν προφητῶν, adderetur κατὰ τὸν Θεόν.   Præte-
rea, hæc epitheta, τὸν τῶν ὅλων Θεὸν καὶ πατέρα, manifestam continent antithesin ad ista, μεγάλην ὄντα δύναμιν καὶ Θεόν, ut Pater
supra Filium evehatur, quemadmodum evehitur, ab Origene infra
libro octavo, num. 15.   Τοῦ, κατά, inferiorem ordinem denotantis ex-
empla afferre supersedeo, cum obvia sint." — RUÆUS.   [See also
Liddon's Bampton Lectures on *The Divinity of our Lord and
Saviour Jesus Christ*, p. 414, where he says, " Origen maintains
Christ's true divinity against the contemptuous criticisms of Celsus"
(book ii. 9, 16, seq.; vii. 53, etc.).   S.]

made ; He commanded, and they were created." [1] Now if God gave the command, and the creatures were formed, who, according to the view of the spirit of prophecy, could He be that was able to carry out such commands of the Father, save Him who, so to speak, is the living Logos and the Truth? And that the Gospels do not consider him who in Jesus said these words, " I am the way, and the truth, and the life," to have been of so circumscribed a nature, [2] as to have an existence nowhere out of the soul and body of Jesus, is evident both from many considerations, and from a few instances of the following kind which we shall quote. John the Baptist, when predicting that the Son of God was to appear immediately, not in that body and soul, but as manifesting Himself everywhere, says regarding Him : "There stands in the midst of you One whom ye know not, who cometh after me." [3] For if he had thought that the Son of God was only there, where was the visible body of Jesus, how could he have said, " There stands in the midst of you One whom ye know not ? " And Jesus Himself, in raising the minds of His disciples to higher thoughts of the Son of God, says : "Where two or three are gathered together in My name, there am I in the midst of you." [4] And of the same nature is His promise to His disciples : " Lo, I am with you alway, even to the end of the world." [5] And we quote these passages, making no distinction between the Son of God and Jesus. For the soul and body of Jesus formed, after the οἰκονομία, one being with the Logos of God. Now if, according to Paul's teaching, " he that is joined unto the Lord is one spirit," [6] every one who understands what being joined to the Lord is, and who has been actually joined to Him, is one spirit with the Lord ; how should not that being be one in a far greater and more divine degree, which was once united with the Logos of God? [7] He, indeed, manifested Himself among the Jews as the power of God, by the miracles which He performed, which Celsus suspected were accomplished by sorcery, but which by the Jews of that time were attributed, I know not why, to Beelzebub, in the words : " He casteth out devils through Beelzebub, the prince of the devils." [8] But these our Saviour convicted of uttering the greatest absurdities, from the fact that the kingdom of evil was not yet come to an end. And this will be evident to all intelligent readers of the Gospel narrative, which it is not now the time to explain.

CHAP. X.

But what promise did Jesus make which He did not perform? Let Celsus produce any instance of such, and make good his charge. But he will be unable to do so, especially since it is from mistakes, arising either from misapprehension of the Gospel narratives, or from Jewish stories, that he thinks to derive the charges which he brings against Jesus or against ourselves. Moreover, again, when the Jew says, "We both found him guilty, and condemned him as deserving of death," let them show how they who sought to concoct false witness against Him proved Him to be guilty. Was not the great charge against Jesus, which His accusers brought forward, this, that He said, " I am able to destroy the temple of God, and after three days to raise it up again?" [9] But in so saying, He spake of the temple of His body ; while they thought, not being able to understand the meaning of the speaker, that His reference was to the temple of stone, which was treated by the Jews with greater respect than He was who ought to have been honoured as the true Temple of God — the Word, and the Wisdom, and the Truth. And who can say that "Jesus attempted to make His escape by disgracefully concealing Himself?" Let any one point to an act deserving to be called disgraceful. And when he adds, " he was taken prisoner," I would say that, if to be taken prisoner implies an act done against one's will, then Jesus was not taken prisoner ; for at the fitting time He did not prevent Himself falling into the hands of men, as the Lamb of God, that He might take away the sin of the world. For, knowing all things that were to come upon Him, He went forth, and said to them, " Whom seek ye ? " and they answered, "Jesus of Nazareth ; " and He said unto them, "I am He." And Judas also, who betrayed Him, was standing with them. When, therefore, He had said to them, " I am He," they went backwards and fell to the ground. Again He asked them, " Whom seek ye ? " and they said again, " Jesus of Nazareth." Jesus said to them, " I told you I am He ; if then ye seek Me, let these go away." [10] Nay, even to Him who wished to help Him, and who smote the high priest's servant, and cut off his ear, He said : " Put up thy sword into its sheath : for all they who draw the sword shall perish by the sword. Thinkest thou that I cannot even now pray to My Father, and He will presently give Me more than twelve legions of angels? But how then should the Scriptures be fulfilled, that

---

[1] Ps. cxlviii. 5.
[2] περιγεγραμμένον τινά.
[3] John i. 26.
[4] Matt. xviii. 20.
[5] Matt. xxviii. 20.
[6] 1-Cor. vi. 17.
[7] εἰ γὰρ κατὰ τὴν Παύλου διδασκαλίαν, λέγοντος · "ὁ κολλώμενος τῷ κυρίῳ, ἕν πνεῦμά ἐστι." πᾶς ὁ νοήσας τί τὸ κολλᾶσθαι τῷ κυρίῳ, καὶ κολληθεὶς αὐτῷ, ἕν ἐστι πνεῦμα πρὸς τὸν κύριον· πῶς οὐ πολλῷ μᾶλλον θειοτέρως καὶ μειζόνως ἕν ἐστι τό ποτε σύνθετον πρὸς τὸν λόγον τοῦ Θεοῦ;
[8] Matt. xii. 24.

[9] Matt. xxvi. 61.
[10] John xviii. 4 sqq.

thus it must be?"[1] And if any one imagines these statements to be inventions of the writers of the Gospels, why should not those statements rather be regarded as inventions which proceeded from a spirit of hatred and hostility against Jesus and the Christians? and these the truth, which proceed from those who manifest the sincerity of their feelings towards Jesus, by enduring everything, whatever it may be, for the sake of His words? For the reception by the disciples of such power of endurance and resolution continued even to death, with a disposition of mind that would not invent regarding their Teacher what was not true, is a very evident proof to all candid judges that they were fully persuaded of the truth of what they wrote, seeing they submitted to trials so numerous and so severe, for the sake of Him whom they believed to be the Son of God.

CHAP. XI.

In the next place, that He was betrayed by those whom He called His disciples, is a circumstance which the Jew of Celsus learned from the Gospels; calling the one Judas, however, "many disciples," that he might seem to add force to the accusation. Nor did he trouble himself to take note of all that is related concerning Judas; how this Judas, having come to entertain opposite and conflicting opinions regarding his Master, neither opposed Him with his whole soul, nor yet with his whole soul preserved the respect due by a pupil to his teacher. For he that betrayed Him gave to the multitude that came to apprehend Jesus, a sign, saying, "Whomsoever I shall kiss, it is he; seize ye him," — retaining still some element of respect for his Master: for unless he had done so, he would have betrayed Him, even publicly, without any pretence of affection. This circumstance, therefore, will satisfy all with regard to the purpose of Judas, that along with his covetous disposition, and his wicked design to betray his Master, he had still a feeling of a mixed character in his mind, produced in him by the words of Jesus, which had the appearance (so to speak) of some remnant of good. For it is related that, "when Judas, who betrayed Him, knew that He was condemned, he repented, and brought back the thirty pieces of silver to the high priest and elders, saying, I have sinned, in that I have betrayed the innocent blood. But they said, What is that to us? see thou to that;"[2] — and that, having thrown the money down in the temple, he departed, and went and hanged himself. But if this covetous Judas, who also stole the money placed in the bag for the relief of the poor, repented, and brought back the thirty pieces of silver to the chief priests and elders, it is clear that the instructions of Jesus had been able to produce some feeling of repentance in his mind, and were not altogether despised and loathed by this traitor. Nay, the declaration, "I have sinned, in that I have betrayed the innocent blood," was a public acknowledgment of his crime. Observe, also, how exceedingly passionate[3] was the sorrow for his sins that proceeded from that repentance, and which would not suffer him any longer to live; and how, after he had cast the money down in the temple, he withdrew, and went away and hanged himself: for he passed sentence upon himself, showing what a power the teaching of Jesus had over this sinner Judas, this thief and traitor, who could not always treat with contempt what he had learned from Jesus. Will Celsus and his friends now say that those proofs which show that the apostasy of Judas was not a complete apostasy, even after his attempts against his Master, are inventions, and that this alone is true, viz., that one of His disciples betrayed Him; and will they add to the Scriptural account that he betrayed Him also with his whole heart? To act in this spirit of hostility with the same writings, both as to what we are to believe and what we are not to believe, is absurd.[4] And if we must make a statement regarding Judas which may overwhelm our opponents with shame, we would say that, in the book of Psalms, the whole of the 108th contains a prophecy about Judas, the beginning of which is this: "O God, hold not Thy peace before my praise; for the mouth of the sinner, and the mouth of the crafty man, are opened against me."[5] And it is predicted in this psalm, both that Judas separated himself from the number of the apostles on account of his sins, and that another was selected in his place; and this is shown by the words: "And his bishopric let another take."[6] But suppose now that He had been betrayed by some one of His disciples, who was possessed by a worse spirit than Judas, and who had completely poured out, as it were, all the words which he had heard from Jesus, what would this contribute to an accusation against Jesus or the Christian religion? And how will this demonstrate its doctrine to be false? We have replied in the preceding chapter to the statements which follow this, showing that Jesus was not taken prisoner when attempting to flee, but that He gave Himself up voluntarily for the sake of us all. Whence it follows, that even if He were bound, He was bound agreeably to His own will; thus teaching us the lesson that we should undertake similar things for the sake of religion in no spirit of unwillingness.

---

[1] Matt. xxvi. 52-54.
[2] Matt. xxvii. 3-5.

[3] διάπυρος καὶ σφόδρα.
[4] ἀπίθανον.
[5] Ps. cix. 1, 2. [cviii. 1, 2, Sept. S.]
[6] Ps. cix. 8. [cviii. 8, Sept. S.]

CHAP. XII.

And the following appear to me to be childish assertions, viz., that "no good general and leader of great multitudes was ever betrayed; nor even a wicked captain of robbers and commander of very wicked men, who seemed to be of any use to his associates; but Jesus, having been betrayed by his subordinates, neither governed like a good general, nor, after deceiving his disciples, produced in the minds of the victims of his deceit that feeling of good-will which, so to speak, would be manifested towards a brigand chief." Now one might find many accounts of generals who were betrayed by their own soldiers, and of robber chiefs who were captured through the instrumentality of those who did not keep their bargains with them. But grant that no general or robber chief was ever betrayed, what does that contribute to the establishment of the fact as a charge against Jesus, that one of His disciples became His betrayer? And since Celsus makes an ostentatious exhibition of philosophy, I would ask of him, If, then, it was a charge against Plato, that Aristotle, after being his pupil for twenty years, went away and assailed his doctrine of the immortality of the soul, and styled the ideas of Plato the merest trifling?[1] And if I were still in doubt, I would continue thus: Was Plato no longer mighty in dialectics, nor able to defend his views, after Aristotle had taken his departure; and, on that account, are the opinions of Plato false? Or may it not be, that while Plato is true, as the pupils of his philosophy would maintain, Aristotle was guilty of wickedness and ingratitude towards his teacher? Nay, Chrysippus also, in many places of his writings, appears to assail Cleanthes, introducing novel opinions opposed to his views, although the latter had been his teacher when he was a young man, and began the study of philosophy. Aristotle, indeed, is said to have been Plato's pupil for twenty years, and no inconsiderable period was spent by Chrysippus in the school of Cleanthes; while Judas did not remain so much as three years with Jesus.[2] But from the narratives of the lives of philosophers we might take many instances similar to those on which Celsus founds a charge against Jesus on account of Judas. Even the Pythagoreans erected cenotaphs[3] to those who, after betaking themselves to philosophy, fell back again into their ignorant mode of life; and yet neither was Pythagoras nor his followers, on that account, weak in argument and demonstration.

CHAP. XIII.

This Jew of Celsus continues, after the above, in the following fashion: "Although he could state many things regarding the events of the life of Jesus which are true, and not like those which are recorded by the disciples, he willingly omits them." What, then, are those true statements, unlike the accounts in the Gospels, which the Jew of Celsus passes by without mention? Or is he only employing what appears to be a figure of speech,[4] in pretending to have something to say, while in reality he had nothing to produce beyond the Gospel narrative which could impress the hearer with a feeling of its truth, and furnish a clear ground of accusation against Jesus and His doctrine? And he charges the disciples with having invented the statement that Jesus foreknew and foretold all that happened to Him; but the truth of this statement we shall establish, although Celsus may not like it, by means of many other predictions uttered by the Saviour, in which He foretold what would befall the Christians in after generations. And who is there who would not be astonished at this prediction: "Ye shall be brought before governors and kings for My sake, for a testimony against them and the Gentiles;"[5] and at any others which He may have delivered respecting the future persecution of His disciples? For what system of opinions ever existed among men on account of which others are punished, so that any one of the accusers of Jesus could say that, foreseeing the impiety or falsity of his opinions to be the ground of an accusation against them, he thought that this would redound to his credit, that he had so predicted regarding it long before? Now if any deserve to be brought, on account of their opinions, before governors and kings, what others are they, save the Epicureans, who altogether deny the existence of providence? And also the Peripatetics, who say that prayers are of no avail, and sacrifices offered as to the Divinity? But some one will say that the Samaritans suffer persecution because of their religion. In answer to whom we shall state that the Sicarians,[6] on account of the practice of circumcision, as mutilating themselves contrary to the established laws and the customs permitted to the Jews alone, are put to death. And you never hear a judge inquiring whether a Sicarian who strives to live according to this established religion of his will be released from punishment if he apostatizes, but will be led away to death if he con-

[1] τερετίσματα.
[2] [See *De Princip.*, iv. i. 5, where Origen gives the length of our Lord's ministry as "only a year and a few months." S.]
[3] Cf. Clem. Alex., *Strom.*, v. c. ix. [See vol. ii. pp. 457, 458. S.]

[4] δοκούσῃ δεινότητι ῥητορικῇ.
[5] Matt. x. 18.
[6] Modestinus, lib. vi. *Regularum, ad legem Corneliam d Sicariis:* "Circumcidere filios suos Judæis tantum rescripto div Pii permittitur: in non ejusdem religionis qui hoc fecerit, castranti pœna irrogatur."

tinues firm ; for the evidence of the circumcision is sufficient to ensure the death of him who has undergone it. But Christians alone, according to the prediction of their Saviour, " Ye shall be brought before governors and kings for My sake," are urged up to their last breath by their judges to deny Christianity, and to sacrifice according to the public customs ; and after the oath of abjuration, to return to their homes, and to live in safety. And observe whether it is not with great authority that this declaration is uttered : " Whosoever therefore shall confess Me before men, him will I confess also before My Father who is in heaven. And whosoever shall deny Me before men," [1] etc. And go back with me in thought to Jesus when He uttered these words, and see His predictions not yet accomplished. Perhaps you will say, in a spirit of incredulity, that he is talking folly, and speaking to no purpose, for his words will have no fulfilment ; or, being in doubt about assenting to his words, you will say, that if these predictions be fulfilled, and the doctrine of Jesus be established, so that governors and kings think of destroying those who acknowledge Jesus, then we shall believe that he utters these prophecies as one who has received great power from God to implant this doctrine among the human race, and as believing that it will prevail. And who will not be filled with wonder, when he goes back in thought to Him who then taught and said, " This Gospel shall be preached throughout the whole world, for a testimony against them and the Gentiles," [2] and beholds, agreeably to His words, the Gospel of Jesus Christ preached in the whole world under heaven to Greeks and Barbarians, wise and foolish alike ? For the word, spoken with power, has gained the mastery over men of all sorts of nature, and it is impossible to see any race of men which has escaped accepting the teaching of Jesus. But let this Jew of Celsus, who does not believe that He foreknew all that happened to Him, consider how, while Jerusalem was still standing, and the whole Jewish worship celebrated in it, Jesus foretold what would befall it from the hand of the Romans. For they will not maintain that the acquaintances and pupils of Jesus Himself handed down His teaching contained in the Gospels without committing it to writing, and left His disciples without the memoirs of Jesus contained in their works. [3] Now in these

it is recorded, that " when ye shall see Jerusalem compassed about with armies, then shall ye know that the desolation thereof is nigh." [4] But at that time there were no armies around Jerusalem, encompassing and enclosing and besieging it ; for the siege began in the reign of Nero, and lasted till the government of Vespasian, whose son Titus destroyed Jerusalem, on account, as Josephus says, of James the Just, the brother of Jesus who was called Christ, but in reality, as the truth makes clear, on account of Jesus Christ the Son of God.

CHAP. XIV.

Celsus, however, accepting or granting that Jesus foreknew what would befall Him, might think to make light of the admission, as he did in the case of the miracles, when he alleged that they were wrought by means of sorcery ; for he might say that many persons by means of divination, either by auspices, or auguries, or sacrifices, or nativities, have come to the knowledge of what was to happen. But this concession he would not make, as being too great a one ; and although he somehow granted that Jesus worked miracles, he thought to weaken the force of this by the charge of sorcery. Now Phlegon, in the thirteenth or fourteenth book, I think, of his Chronicles, not only ascribed to Jesus a knowledge of future events (although falling into confusion about some things which refer to Peter, as if they referred to Jesus), but also testified that the result corresponded to His predictions. So that he also, by these very admissions regarding foreknowledge, as if against his will, expressed his opinion that the doctrines taught by the fathers of our system were not devoid of divine power.

CHAP. XV.

Celsus continues : " The disciples of Jesus, having no undoubted fact on which to rely, devised the fiction that he foreknew everything before it happened ; " not observing, or not wishing to observe, the love of truth which actuated the writers, who acknowledged that Jesus had told His disciples beforehand, " All ye shall be offended because of Me this night," — a statement which was fulfilled by their all being offended ; and that He predicted to Peter, " Before the cock crow, thou shalt deny Me thrice," which was followed by Peter's threefold denial. Now if they had not been lovers of truth, but, as Celsus supposes, inventors of fictions, they would not have represented Peter as denying, nor His disciples as being offended. For although these events actually happened, who could have proved that they turned out in that manner ? And yet, according to all probability,

---

[1] Matt. x. 18.
[2] Matt. xxiv. 14.
[3] [" Celsus quotes the writings of the disciples of Jesus concerning His life, as possessing unquestioned authority; and that these were the four canonical Gospels is proved both by the absence of all evidence to the contrary, and by the special facts which he brings forward. And not only this, but both Celsus and Porphyry appear to have been acquainted with the Pauline Epistles " (Westcott's *History of the Canon of the New Testament*, pp. 464, 465, 137, 138, 401, 402). See also *infra*, cap. lxxiv. S.]

[4] [Luke xxi. 20. S.]

these were matters which ought to have been passed over in silence by men who wished to teach the readers of the Gospels to despise death for the sake of confessing Christianity. But now, seeing that the word, by its power, will gain the mastery over men, they related those facts which they have done, and which, I know not how, were neither to do any harm to their readers, nor to afford any pretext for denial.

CHAP. XVI.

Exceedingly weak is his assertion, that "the disciples of Jesus wrote such accounts regarding him, by way of extenuating the charges that told against him : as if," he says, "any one were to say that a certain person was a just man, and yet were to show that he was guilty of injustice ; or that he was pious, and yet had committed murder ; or that he was immortal, and yet was dead ; subjoining to all these statements the remark that he had foretold all these things." Now his illustrations are at once seen to be inappropriate ; for there is no absurdity in Him who had resolved that He would become a living pattern to men, as to the manner in which they were to regulate their lives, showing also how they ought to die for the sake of their religion, apart altogether from the fact that His death on behalf of men was a benefit to the whole world, as we proved in the preceding book. He imagines, moreover, that the whole of the confession of the Saviour's sufferings confirms his objection instead of weakening it. For he is not acquainted either with the philosophical remarks of Paul,[1] or the statements of the prophets, on this subject. And it escaped him that certain heretics have declared that Jesus underwent His sufferings in appearance, not in reality. For had he known, he would not have said : "For ye do not even allege this, that he seemed to wicked men to suffer this punishment, though not undergoing it in reality ; but, on the contrary, ye acknowledge that he openly suffered." But we do not view His sufferings as having been merely in appearance, in order that His resurrection also may not be a false, but a real event. For he who really died, actually arose, if he did arise ; whereas he who appeared only to have died, did not in reality arise. But since the resurrection of Jesus Christ is a subject of mockery to unbelievers, we shall quote the words of Plato,[2] that Erus the son of Armenius rose from the funeral pile twelve days after he had been laid upon it, and gave an account of what he had seen in Hades ; and as we are replying to unbelievers, it will not be altogether useless to refer in this place to what Heraclides[3]

relates respecting the woman who was deprived of life. And many persons are recorded to have risen from their tombs, not only on the day of their burial, but also on the day following. What wonder is it, then, if in the case of One who performed many marvellous things, both beyond the power of man and with such fulness of evidence, that he who could not deny their performance, endeavoured to calumniate them by comparing them to acts of sorcery, should have manifested also in His death some greater display of divine power, so that His soul, if it pleased, might leave its body, and having performed certain offices out of it, might return again at pleasure ? And such a declaration is Jesus said to have made in the Gospel of John, when He said : "No man taketh My life from Me, but I lay it down of Myself. I have power to lay it down, and I have power to take it again."[4] And perhaps it was on this account that He hastened His departure from the body, that He might preserve it, and that His legs might not be broken, as were those of the robbers who were crucified with Him. "For the soldiers brake the legs of the first, and of the other who was crucified with Him ; but when they came to Jesus, and saw that He was dead, they brake not His legs."[5] We have accordingly answered the question, "How is it credible that Jesus could have predicted these things?" And with respect to this, "How could the dead man be immortal?" let him who wishes to understand know, that it is not the dead man who is immortal, but He who rose from the dead. So far, indeed, was the dead man from being immortal, that even the Jesus before His decease — the compound being, who was to suffer death — was not immortal.[6] For no one is immortal who is destined to die ; but he is immortal when he shall no longer be subject to death. But "Christ, being raised from the dead, dieth no more : death hath no more dominion over Him ;"[7] although those may be unwilling to admit this who cannot understand how such things should be said.

CHAP. XVII.

Extremely foolish also is his remark, "What god, or spirit, or prudent man would not, on foreseeing that such events were to befall him, avoid them if he could ; whereas he threw himself headlong into those things which he knew beforehand were to happen?" And yet Socrates knew that he would die after drinking the hemlock, and it was in his power, if he had allowed himself to be persuaded by Crito, by escaping

---

[1] ὅσα περὶ τούτου καὶ παρὰ τῷ Παύλῳ πεφιλοσόφηται.
[2] Cf. Plato, de Rep., x. p. 614.
[3] Cf. Plin., Nat. Hist., vii. c. 52.

[4] John x. 18.
[5] John xix. 32, 33.
[6] Οὐ μόνον οὖν οὐχ ὁ νεκρὸς ἀθάνατος, ἀλλ' οὐδ' ὁ πρὸ τοῦ νεκροῦ Ἰησοῦς ὁ σύνθετος ἀθάνατος ἦν, ὅς γε ἔμελλε τεθνήξεσθαι.
[7] Rom. vi. 9.

from prison, to avoid these calamities; but nevertheless he decided, as it appeared to him consistent with right reason, that it was better for him to die as became a philosopher, than to retain his life in a manner unbecoming one. Leonidas also, the Lacedæmonian general, knowing that he was on the point of dying with his followers at Thermopylæ, did not make any effort to preserve his life by disgraceful means, but said to his companions, "Let us go to breakfast, as we shall sup in Hades." And those who are interested in collecting stories of this kind, will find numbers of them. Now, where is the wonder if Jesus, knowing all things that were to happen, did not avoid them, but encountered what He foreknew; when Paul, His own disciple, having heard what would befall him when he went up to Jerusalem, proceeded to face the danger, reproaching those who were weeping around him, and endeavouring to prevent him from going up to Jerusalem? Many also of our contemporaries, knowing well that if they made a confession of Christianity they would be put to death, but that if they denied it they would be liberated, and their property restored, despised life, and voluntarily selected death for the sake of their religion.

CHAP. XVIII.

After this the Jew makes another silly remark, saying, "How is it that, if Jesus pointed out beforehand both the traitor and the perjurer, they did not fear him as a God, and cease, the one from his intended treason, and the other from his perjury?" Here the learned Celsus did not see the contradiction in his statement: for if Jesus foreknew events as a God, then it was impossible for His foreknowledge to prove untrue; and therefore it was impossible for him who was known to Him as going to betray Him not to execute his purpose, nor for him who was rebuked as going to deny Him not to have been guilty of that crime. For if it had been possible for the one to abstain from the act of betrayal, and the other from that of denial, as having been warned of the consequences of these actions beforehand, then His words were no longer true, who predicted that the one would betray Him and the other deny Him. For if He had foreknowledge of the traitor, He knew the wickedness in which the treason originated, and this wickedness was by no means taken away by the foreknowledge. And, again, if He had ascertained that one would deny Him, He made that prediction from seeing the weakness out of which that act of denial would arise, and yet this weakness was not to be taken away thus at once [1] by the foreknowledge. But whence he derived the

statement, "that these persons betrayed and denied him without manifesting any concern about him," I know not; for it was proved, with respect to the traitor, that it is false to say that he betrayed his master without an exhibition of anxiety regarding Him. And this was shown to be equally true of him who denied Him; for he went out, after the denial, and wept bitterly.

CHAP. XIX.

Superficial also is his objection, that "it is always the case when a man against whom a plot is formed, and who comes to the knowledge of it, makes known to the conspirators that he is acquainted with their design, that the latter are turned from their purpose, and keep upon their guard." For many have continued to plot even against those who were acquainted with their plans. And then, as if bringing his argument to a conclusion, he says: "Not because these things were predicted did they come to pass, for that is impossible; but since they have come to pass, their being predicted is shown to be a falsehood: for it is altogether impossible that those who heard beforehand of the discovery of their designs, should carry out their plans of betrayal and denial!" But if his premises are overthrown, then his conclusion also falls to the ground, viz., "that we are not to believe, because these things were predicted, that they have come to pass." Now we maintain that they not only came to pass as being possible, but also that, because they came to pass, the fact of their being predicted is shown to be true; for the truth regarding future events is judged of by results. It is false, therefore, as asserted by him, that the prediction of these events is proved to be untrue; and it is to no purpose that he says, "It is altogether impossible for those who heard beforehand that their designs were discovered, to carry out their plans of betrayal and denial."

CHAP. XX.

Let us see how he continues after this: "These events," he says, "he predicted as being a God, and the prediction must by all means come to pass. God, therefore, who above all others ought to do good to men, and especially to those of his own household, led on his own disciples and prophets, with whom he was in the habit of eating and drinking, to such a degree of wickedness, that they became impious and unholy men. Now, of a truth, he who shared a man's table would not be guilty of conspiring against him; but after banqueting with God, he became a conspirator. And, what is still more absurd, God himself plotted against the members of his own table, by converting them into traitors and villains!" Now, since you wish me

---

[1] οὕτως ἀθρόως.

to answer even those charges of Celsus which seem to me frivolous,[1] the following is our reply to such statements. Celsus imagines that an event, predicted through foreknowledge, comes to pass because it was predicted; but we do not grant this, maintaining that he who foretold it was not the cause of its happening, because he foretold it would happen; but the future event itself, which would have taken place though not predicted, afforded the occasion to him, who was endowed with foreknowledge, of foretelling its occurrence. Now, certainly this result is present to the foreknowledge of him who predicts an event, when it is possible that it may or may not happen, viz., that one or other of these things will take place. For we do not assert that he who foreknows an event, by secretly taking away the possibility of its happening or not, makes any such declaration as this: "This shall infallibly happen, and it is impossible that it can be otherwise." And this remark applies to all the foreknowledge of events dependent upon ourselves, whether contained in the sacred Scriptures or in the histories of the Greeks. Now, what is called by logicians an "idle argument,"[2] which is a sophism, will be no sophism as far as Celsus can help, but according to sound reasoning it is a sophism. And that this may be seen, I shall take from the Scriptures the predictions regarding Judas, or the foreknowledge of our Saviour regarding him as the traitor; and from the Greek histories the oracle that was given to Laius, conceding for the present its truth, since it does not affect the argument. Now, in Ps. cviii., Judas is spoken of by the mouth of the Saviour, in words beginning thus: "Hold not Thy peace, O God of my praise; for the mouth of the wicked and the mouth of the deceitful are opened against me." Now, if you carefully observe the contents of the psalm, you will find that, as it was foreknown that he would betray the Saviour, so also was he considered to be himself the cause of the betrayal, and deserving, on account of his wickedness, of the imprecations contained in the prophecy. For let him suffer these things, "because," says the psalmist, "he remembered not to show mercy, but persecuted the poor and needy man." Wherefore it was possible for him to show mercy, and not to persecute him whom he did persecute. But although he might have done these things, he did not do them, but carried out the act of treason, so as to merit the curses pronounced against him in the prophecy.

And in answer to the Greeks we shall quote the following oracular response to Laius, as recorded by the tragic poet, either in the exact words of the oracle or in equivalent terms. Future events are thus made known to him by the oracle: "Do not try to beget children against the will of the gods. For if you beget a son, your son shall murder you; and all your household shall wade in blood."[3] Now from this it is clear that it was within the power of Laius not to try to beget children, for the oracle would not have commanded an impossibility; and it was also in his power to do the opposite, so that neither of these courses was compulsory. And the consequence of his not guarding against the begetting of children was, that he suffered from so doing the calamities described in the tragedies relating to Œdipus and Jocasta and their sons. Now that which is called the "idle argument," being a quibble, is such as might be applied, say in the case of a sick man, with the view of sophistically preventing him from employing a physician to promote his recovery; and it is something like this: "If it is decreed that you should recover from your disease, you will recover whether you call in a physician or not; but if it is decreed that you should not recover, you will not recover whether you call in a physician or no. But it is certainly decreed either that you should recover, or that you should not recover; and therefore it is in vain that you call in a physician." Now with this argument the following may be wittily compared: "If it is decreed that you should beget children, you will beget them, whether you have intercourse with a woman or not. But if it is decreed that you should not beget children, you will not do so, whether you have intercourse with a woman or no. Now, certainly, it is decreed either that you should beget children or not; therefore it is in vain that you have intercourse with a woman." For, as in the latter instance, intercourse with a woman is not employed in vain, seeing it is an utter impossibility for him who does not use it to beget children; so, in the former, if recovery from disease is to be accomplished by means of the healing art, of necessity the physician is summoned, and it is therefore false to say that "in vain do you call in a physician." We have brought forward all these illustrations on account of the assertion of this learned Celsus, that "being a God He predicted these things, and the predictions must *by all means* come to pass." Now, if by "*by all means*" he means "*necessarily*," we cannot admit this. For it was quite possible, also, that they might *not* come to pass. But if he uses "*by all means*" in the sense of "*simple futurity*,"[4] which nothing hinders from being true (although it was possible that they might not happen), he does not at all touch my

---

1 εὐτελέσι.
2 ἀργὸς λόγος.

3 Euripid., *Phœnissæ*, 18–20.
4 ἀντὶ τοῦ ἔσται.

argument; nor did it follow, from Jesus having predicted the acts of the traitor or the perjurer, that it was the same thing with His being the cause of such impious and unholy proceedings. For He who was amongst us, and knew what was in man, seeing his evil disposition, and foreseeing what he would attempt from his spirit of covetousness, and from his want of stable ideas of duty towards his Master, along with many other declarations, gave utterance to this also: "He that dippeth his hand with Me in the dish, the same shall betray Me."[1]

CHAP. XXI.

Observe also the superficiality and manifest falsity of such a statement of Celsus, when he asserts "that he who was partaker of a man's table would not conspire against him; and if he would not conspire against a man, much less would he plot against a God after banqueting with him." For who does not know that many persons, after partaking of the salt on the table,[2] have entered into a conspiracy against their entertainers? The whole of Greek and Barbarian history is full of such instances. And the Iambic poet of Paros,[3] when upbraiding Lycambes with having violated covenants confirmed by the salt of the table, says to him: —

"But thou hast broken a mighty oath — that, viz., by the salt of the table."

And they who are interested in historical learning, and who give themselves wholly to it, to the neglect of other branches of knowledge more necessary for the conduct of life,[4] can quote numerous instances, showing that they who shared in the hospitality of others entered into conspiracies against them.

CHAP. XXII.

He adds to this, as if he had brought together an argument with conclusive demonstrations and consequences, the following: "And, which is still more absurd, God himself conspired against those who sat at his table, by converting them into traitors and impious men." But how Jesus could either conspire or convert His disciples into traitors or impious men, it would be impossible for him to prove, save by means of such a deduction as any one could refute with the greatest ease.

CHAP. XXIII.

He continues in this strain: "If he had determined upon these things, and underwent chastisement in obedience to his Father, it is manifest that, being a God, and submitting voluntarily,

those things that were done agreeably to his own decision were neither painful nor distressing." But he did not observe that here he was at once contradicting himself. For if he granted that He was chastised because He had determined upon these things, and had submitted Himself to His Father, it is clear that He actually suffered punishment, and it was impossible that what was inflicted on Him by His chastisers should not be painful, because pain is an involuntary thing. But if, because He was willing to suffer, His inflictions were neither painful nor distressing, how did He grant that "He was chastised?" He did not perceive that when Jesus had once, by His birth, assumed a body, He assumed one which was capable both of suffering pains, and those distresses incidental to humanity, if we are to understand by distresses what no one voluntarily chooses. Since, therefore, He voluntarily assumed a body, not wholly of a different nature from that of human flesh, so along with His body He assumed also its sufferings and distresses, which it was not in His power to avoid enduring, it being in the power of those who inflicted them to send upon Him things distressing and painful. And in the preceding pages we have already shown, that He would not have come into the hands of men had He not so willed. But He did come, because He was willing to come, and because it was manifest beforehand that His dying upon behalf of men would be of advantage to the whole human race.

CHAP. XXIV.

After this, wishing to prove that the occurrences which befell Him were painful and distressing, and that it was impossible for Him, had He wished, to render them otherwise, he proceeds: "Why does he mourn, and lament, and pray to escape the fear of death, expressing himself in terms like these: 'O Father, if it be possible, let this cup pass from Me?'"[4] Now in these words observe the malignity of Celsus, how not accepting the love of truth which actuates the writers of the Gospels (who might have passed over in silence those points which, as Celsus thinks, are censurable, but who did not omit them for many reasons, which any one, in expounding the Gospel, can give in their proper place), he brings an accusation against the Gospel statement, grossly exaggerating the facts, and quoting what is not written in the Gospels, seeing it is nowhere found that Jesus lamented. And he changes the words in the expression, "Father, if it be possible, let this cup pass from Me," and does not give what follows immediately after, which manifests at once the ready obedience of Jesus to His Father, and His greatness of mind,

---

[1] Matt. xxvi. 23.
[2] ἁλῶν καὶ τραπέζης.
[3] Archilochus.
[4] Guietus would expunge these words as "inept."

[5] Matt. xxvi. 39.

and which runs thus: "Nevertheless, not as I will, but as Thou wilt." [1] Nay, even the cheerful obedience of Jesus to the will of His Father in those things which He was condemned to suffer, exhibited in the declaration, "If this cup cannot pass from Me except I drink it, Thy will be done," he pretends not to have observed, acting here like those wicked individuals who listen to the Holy Scriptures in a malignant spirit, and "who talk wickedness with lofty head." For they appear to have heard the declaration, "I kill," [2] and they often make it to us a subject of reproach; but the words, "I will make alive," they do not remember, — the whole sentence showing that those who live amid public wickedness, and who work wickedly, are put to death by God, and that a better life is infused into them instead, even one which God will give to those who have died to sin. And so also these men have heard the words, "I will smite;" but they do not see these, "and I will heal," which are like the words of a physician, who cuts bodies asunder, and inflicts severe wounds, in order to extract from them substances that are injurious and prejudicial to health, and who does not terminate his work with pains and lacerations, but by his treatment restores the body to that state of soundness which he has in view. Moreover, they have not heard the whole of the announcement, "For He maketh sore, and again bindeth up;" but only this part, "He maketh sore." So in like manner acts this Jew of Celsus, who quotes the words, "O Father, would that this cup might pass from Me;" but who does not add what follows, and which exhibits the firmness of Jesus, and His preparedness for suffering. But these matters, which afford great room for explanation from the wisdom of God, and which may reasonably be pondered over [3] by those whom Paul calls "perfect" when he said, "We speak wisdom among them who are perfect," [4] we pass by for the present, and shall speak for a little of those matters which are useful for our present purpose.

CHAP. XXV.

We have mentioned in the preceding pages that there are some of the declarations of Jesus which refer to that Being in Him which was the "first-born of every creature," such as, "I am the way, and the truth, and the life," and such like; and others, again, which belong to that in Him which is understood to be man, such as, "But now ye seek to kill Me, a man that hath told you the truth which I have heard of the Father." [5] And here, accordingly, he describe the element of weakness belonging to huma flesh, and that of readiness of spirit which existe in His humanity: the element of weakness i the expression, "Father, if it be possible, le this cup pass from Me;" the readiness of th spirit in this, "Nevertheless, not as I will, but a Thou wilt." And since it is proper to observ the order of our quotations, observe that, in th first place, there is mentioned only the singl instance, as one would say, indicating the weak ness of the flesh; and afterwards those othe instances, greater in number, manifesting th willingness of the spirit. For the expression "Father, if it be possible, let this cup pass from Me," is only one: whereas more numerous ar those others, viz., "Not as I will, but as Tho wilt;" and, "O My Father, if this cup cann pass from Me except I drink it, Thy will b done." It is to be noted also, that the word are not, "let this cup depart from Me;" bu that the whole expression is marked by a ton of piety and reverence, "Father, if it be possi ble, let this cup pass from Me." I know, indeed that there is another explanation of this passag to the following effect: — The Saviour, foresee ing the sufferings which the Jewish people an the city of Jerusalem were to undergo in requita of the wicked deeds which the Jews had dare to perpetrate upon Him, from no other motiv than that of the purest philanthropy toward them, and from a desire that they might escap the impending calamities, gave utterance to the prayer, "Father, if it be possible, let this cu pass from Me." It is as if He had said, "Be cause of My drinking this cup of punishmen the whole nation will be forsaken by Thee, pray, if it be possible, that this cup may pas from Me, in order that Thy portion, which wa guilty of such crimes against Me, may not b altogether deserted by Thee." But if, as Celsu would allege, "nothing at that time was done t Jesus which was either painful or distressing, how could men afterwards quote the example o Jesus as enduring sufferings for the sake of reli gion, if He did *not* suffer what are human suffer ings, but only had the *appearance* of so doing?

CHAP. XXVI.

This Jew of Celsus still accuses the disciple of Jesus of having invented these statements saying to them: "Even although guilty of false hood, ye have not been able to give a colour of credibility to your inventions." In answer t which we have to say, that there was an eas method of concealing these occurrences, — that viz., of not recording them at all. For if th Gospels had not contained the accounts of thes

---

[1] Matt. xxvi. 39.
[2] Deut. xxxii. 39.
[3] καὶ ταῦτα δὲ, πολλὴν ἔχοντα διήγησιν ἀπὸ σοφίας Θεοῦ οἷς ὁ Παῦλος ὠνόμασε τελείοις εὐλόγως παραδοθησομένην.
[4] 1 Cor. ii. 6.

[5] John viii. 40.

things, who could have reproached us with Jesus having spoken such words during His stay upon the earth? Celsus, indeed, did not see that it was an inconsistency for the same persons both to be deceived regarding Jesus, believing Him to be God, and the subject of prophecy, and to invent fictions about Him, knowing manifestly that these statements were false. Of a truth, therefore, they were not guilty of inventing untruths, but such were their real impressions, and they recorded them truly; or else they were guilty of falsifying the histories, and did not entertain these views, and were not deceived when they acknowledged Him to be God.

CHAP. XXVII.

After this he says, that certain of the Christian believers, like persons who in a fit of drunkenness lay violent hands upon themselves, have corrupted the Gospel from its original integrity, to a threefold, and fourfold, and many-fold degree, and have remodelled it, so that they might be able to answer objections. Now I know of no others who have altered the Gospel, save the followers of Marcion, and those of Valentinus, and, I think, also those of Lucian. But such an allegation is no charge against the Christian system, but against those who dared so to trifle with the Gospels. And as it is no ground of accusation against philosophy, that there exist Sophists, or Epicureans, or Peripatetics, or any others, whoever they may be, who hold false opinions; so neither is it against genuine Christianity that there are some who corrupt the Gospel histories, and who introduce heresies opposed to the meaning of the doctrine of Jesus.

CHAP. XXVIII.

And since this Jew of Celsus makes it a subject of reproach that Christians should make use of the prophets, who predicted the events of Christ's life, we have to say, in addition to what we have already advanced upon this head, that it became him to spare individuals, as he says, and to expound the prophecies themselves, and after admitting the probability of the Christian interpretation of them, to show how the use which they make of them may be overturned.[1] For in this way he would not appear hastily to assume so important a position on small grounds, and particularly when he asserts that the " prophecies agree with ten thousand other things more credibly than with Jesus." And he ought to have carefully met this powerful argument of the Christians, as being the strongest which they adduce,

and to have demonstrated with regard to each particular prophecy, that it can apply to other events with greater probability than to Jesus. He did not, however, perceive that this was a plausible argument to be advanced against the Christians only by one who was an opponent of the prophetic writings; but Celsus has here put in the mouth of a Jew an objection which a Jew would not have made. For a Jew will not admit that the prophecies may be applied to countless other things with greater probability than to Jesus; but he will endeavour, after giving what appears to him the meaning of each, to oppose the Christian interpretation, not indeed by any means adducing convincing reasons, but only attempting to do so.

CHAP. XXIX.

In the preceding pages we have already spoken of this point, viz., the prediction that there were to be two advents of Christ to the human race, so that it is not necessary for us to reply to the objection, supposed to be urged by a Jew, that " the prophets declare the coming one to be a mighty potentate, Lord of all nations and armies." But it is in the spirit of a Jew, I think, and in keeping with their bitter animosity, and baseless and even improbable calumnies against Jesus, that he adds : " Nor did the prophets predict such a pestilence." [2] For neither Jews, nor Celsus, nor any other, can bring any argument to prove that a pestilence converts men from the practice of evil to a life which is according to nature, and distinguished by temperance and other virtues.

CHAP. XXX.

This objection also is cast in our teeth by Celsus : " From such signs and misinterpretations, and from proofs so mean, no one could prove him to be God, and the Son of God." Now it was his duty to enumerate the alleged misinterpretations, and to prove them to be such, and to show by reasoning the meanness of the evidence, in order that the Christian, if any of his objections should seem to be plausible, might l e able to answer and confute his arguments. What he said, however, regarding Jesus, did indeed come to pass, because He was a mighty potentate, although Celsus refuses to see that it so happened, notwithstanding that the clearest evidence proves it true of Jesus. " For as the sun," he says, " which enlightens all other objects, first makes himself visible, so ought the Son of God to have done." We would say in reply, that so He did; for righteousness has arisen in His days, and there is abundance of peace, which took its commencement at His

---

[1] The original here is probably corrupt: Ὅτι ἐχρῆν αὐτὸν (ὥς φησι) φειδόμενον ἀνθρώπων αὐτὰς ἐκθέσθαι τὰς προφητείας, καὶ συναγορεύσαντα ταῖς πιθανότησιν αὐτῶν, τὴν φαινομένην αὐτῶν ἀνατροπὴν τῆς χρήσεως τῶν προφητικῶν ἐκθέσθαι. For φειδόμενον Boherellus would read κηδόμενον, and τὴν φαινομένην αὐτῷ ἀνατροπήν.

[2] ὄλεθρον.

birth, God preparing the nations for His teaching, that they might be under one prince, the king of the Romans, and that it might not, owing to the want of union among the nations, caused by the existence of many kingdoms, be more difficult for the apostles of Jesus to accomplish the task enjoined upon them by their Master, when He said, " Go and teach all nations." Moreover it is certain that Jesus was born in the reign of Augustus, who, so to speak, fused together into one monarchy the many populations of the earth. Now the existence of many kingdoms would have been a hindrance to the spread of the doctrine of Jesus throughout the entire world ; not only for the reasons mentioned, but also on account of the necessity of men everywhere engaging in war, and fighting on behalf of their native country, which was the case before the times of Augustus, and in periods still more remote, when necessity arose, as when the Peloponnesians and Athenians warred against each other, and other nations in like manner. How, then, was it possible for the Gospel doctrine of peace, which does not permit men to take vengeance even upon enemies, to prevail throughout the world, unless at the advent of Jesus[1] a milder spirit had been everywhere introduced into the conduct of things?

CHAP. XXXI.

He next charges the Christians witn being " guilty of sophistical reasoning, in saying that the Son of God is the Logos Himself." And he thinks that he strengthens the accusation, because " when we declare the Logos to be the Son of God, we do not present to view a pure and holy Logos, but a most degraded man, who was punished by scourging and crucifixion." Now, on this head we have briefly replied to the charges of Celsus in the preceding pages, where Christ was shown to be the first-born of all creation, who assumed a body and a human soul ; and that God gave commandment respecting the creation of such mighty things in the world, and they were created ; and that He who received the command was God the Logos. And seeing it is a Jew who makes these statements in the work of Celsus, it will not be out of place to quote the declaration, " He sent His word, and healed them, and delivered them from their destruction," [2] — a passage of which we spoke a little ago. Now, although I have conferred with many Jews who professed to be learned men, I never heard any one expressing his approval of the statement that the Logos is the Son of God, as Celsus declares they do, in putting into the

mouth of the Jew such a declaration as this : " If your Logos is the Son of God, we also give our assent to the same."

CHAP. XXXII.

We have already shown that Jesus can be regarded neither as an arrogant man, nor a sorcerer ; and therefore it is unnecessary to repeat our former arguments, lest, in replying to the tautologies of Celsus, we ourselves should be guilty of needless repetition. And now, in finding fault with our Lord's genealogy, there are certain points which occasion some difficulty even to Christians, and which, owing to the discrepancy between the genealogies, are advanced by some as arguments against their correctness, but which Celsus has not even mentioned. For Celsus, who is truly a braggart, and who professes to be acquainted with all matters relating to Christianity, does not know how to raise doubts in a skilful manner against the credibility of Scripture. But he asserts that the " framers of the genealogies, from a feeling of pride, made Jesus to be descended from the first man, and from the kings of the Jews." And he thinks that he makes a notable charge when he adds, that " the carpenter s wife could not have been ignorant of the fact, had she been of such illustrious descent." But what has this to do with the question? Granted that she was not ignorant of her descent, how does that affect the result? Suppose that she *were* ignorant, how could her ignorance prove that she was not descended from the first man, or could not derive her origin from the Jewish kings? Does Celsus imagine that the poor must always be descended from ancestors who are poor, or that kings are always born of kings? But it appears folly to waste time upon such an argument as this, seeing it is well known that, even in our own days, some who are poorer than Mary are descended from ancestors of wealth and distinction, and that rulers of nations and kings have sprung from persons of no reputation.

CHAP. XXXIII.

" But," continues Celsus, " what great deeds did Jesus perform as being a God? Did he put his enemies to shame, or bring to a ridiculous conclusion what was designed against him?" Now to this question, although we are able to show the striking and miraculous character of the events which befell Him, yet from what other source can we furnish an answer than from the Gospel narratives, which state that " there was an earthquake, and that the rocks were split asunder, and the tombs opened, and the veil of the temple rent in twain from top to bottom, and that darkness prevailed in the day-time, the

---

[1] [In fulfilment of the great plan foreshadowed in Daniel, and promised by Haggai (ii. 7), where I adhere to the Anglican version and the Vulgate.]
[2] Ps. cvii. 20.

sun failing to give light?"[1] But if Celsus believe the Gospel accounts when he thinks that he can find in them matter of charge against the Christians, and refuse to believe them when they establish the divinity of Jesus, our answer to him is: "Sir,[2] either disbelieve all the Gospel narratives, and then no longer imagine that you can found charges upon them; or, in yielding your belief to their statements, look in admiration on the Logos of God, who became incarnate, and who desired to confer benefits upon the whole human race. And this feature evinces the nobility of the work of Jesus, that, down to the present time, those whom God wills are healed by His name.[3] And with regard to the eclipse in the time of Tiberius Cæsar, in whose reign Jesus appears to have been crucified, and the great earthquakes which then took place, Phlegon too, I think, has written in the thirteenth or fourteenth book of his Chronicles."[4]

CHAP. XXXIV.

This Jew of Celsus, ridiculing Jesus, as he imagines, is described as being acquainted with the Bacchæ of Euripides, in which Dionysus says:—

"The divinity himself will liberate me whenever I wish."[5]

Now the Jews are not much acquainted with Greek literature; but suppose that there was a Jew so well versed in it (as to make such a quotation on his part appropriate), how (does it follow) that Jesus *could* not liberate Himself, because He did not do so? For let him believe from our own Scriptures that Peter obtained his freedom after having been bound in prison, an angel having loosed his chains; and that Paul, having been bound in the stocks along with Silas in Philippi of Macedonia, was liberated by divine power, when the gates of the prison were opened. But it is probable that Celsus treats these accounts with ridicule, or that he never read them; for he would probably say in reply, that there are certain sorcerers who are able by incantations to unloose chains and to open doors, so that he would liken the events related in our histories to the doings of sorcerers. "But," he continues, "no calamity happened even to him who condemned him, as there did to Pentheus, viz., madness or discerption."[6] And yet he does not know that it was not so much Pilate that condemned Him (who knew that "for envy the Jews had delivered Him"), as the Jewish nation, which *has* been condemned by God, and rent in

pieces, and dispersed over the whole earth, in a degree far beyond what happened to Pentheus. Moreover, why did he intentionally omit what is related of Pilate's wife, who beheld a vision, and who was so moved by it as to send a message to her husband, saying: "Have thou nothing to do with that just man; for I have suffered many things this day in a dream because of Him?"[7] And again, passing by in silence the proofs of the divinity of Jesus, Celsus endeavours to cast reproach upon Him from the narratives in the Gospel, referring to those who mocked Jesus, and put on Him the purple robe, and the crown of thorns, and placed the reed in His hand. From what source now, Celsus, did you derive these statements, save from the Gospel narratives? And did you, accordingly, see that they were fit matters for reproach, while they who recorded them did not think that you, and such as you, would turn them into ridicule; but that others would receive from them an example how to despise those who ridiculed and mocked Him on account of His religion, who appropriately laid down His life for its sake? Admire rather their love of truth, and that of the Being who bore these things voluntarily for the sake of men, and who endured them with all constancy and long-suffering. For it is not recorded that He uttered any lamentation, or that after His condemnation He either did or uttered anything unbecoming.

CHAP. XXXV.

But in answer to this objection, "If not before, yet why now, at least, does he not give some manifestation of his divinity, and free himself from this reproach, and take vengeance upon those who insult both him and his Father?" We have to reply, that it would be the same thing as if we were to say to those among the Greeks who accept the doctrine of providence, and who believe in portents, Why does God not punish those who insult the Divinity, and subvert the doctrine of providence? For as the Greeks would answer such objections, so would we, in the same, or a more effective manner. There was not only a portent from heaven—the eclipse of the sun—but also the other miracles, which show that the crucified One possessed something that was divine, and greater than was possessed by the majority of men.

CHAP. XXXVI.

Celsus next says: "What is the nature of the ichor in the body of the crucified Jesus? Is it 'such as flows in the bodies of the immortal gods?'"[8] He puts this question in a spirit of mockery; but we shall show from the serious

[1] Cf. Matt. xxvii. 51, 52; cf. Luke xxiii. 44, 45.
[2] ὦ οὗτος.
[3] [Testimony not to be scorned.]
[4] On Phlegon, cf. note in Migne, pp. 823, 854. [See also vol. iii. Elucidation V. p. 58.]
[5] Eurip., *Bacchæ*, 498 (ed. Dindorf).
[6] Cf. Euseb., *Hist. Eccles.*, bk. ii. c. vii.

[7] Matt. xxvii. 19.
[8] Cf. *Iliad*, v. 340.

narratives of the Gospels, although Celsus may not like it, that it was no mythic and Homeric ichor which flowed from the body of Jesus, but that, after His death, "one of the soldiers with a spear pierced His side, and there came thereout blood and water. And he that saw it bare record, and his record is true, and he knoweth that he saith the truth."[1] Now, in other dead bodies the blood congeals, and pure water does not flow forth ; but the miraculous feature in the case of the dead body of Jesus was, that around the dead body blood and water flowed forth from the side. But if this Celsus, who, in order to find matter of accusation against Jesus and the Christians, extracts from the Gospel even passages which are incorrectly interpreted, but passes over in silence the evidences of the divinity of Jesus, would listen to divine portents, let him read the Gospel, and see that even the centurion, and they who with him kept watch over Jesus, on seeing the earthquake, and the events that occurred, were greatly afraid, saying, "This man was the Son of God."[2]

CHAP. XXXVII.

After this, he who extracts from the Gospel narrative those statements on which he thinks he can found an accusation, makes the vinegar and the gall a subject of reproach to Jesus, saying that "he rushed with open mouth[3] to drink of them, and could not endure his thirst as any ordinary man frequently endures it." Now this matter admits of an explanation of a peculiar and figurative kind ; but on the present occasion, the statement that the prophets predicted this very incident may be accepted as the more common answer to the objection. For in the sixty-ninth Psalm there is written, with reference to Christ : " And they gave me gall for my meat, and in my thirst they gave me vinegar to drink."[4] Now, let the Jews say who it is that the prophetic writing represents as uttering these words ; and let them adduce from history one who received gall for his food, and to whom vinegar was given as drink. Would they venture to assert that the Christ whom they expect still to come might be placed in such circumstances? Then we would say, What prevents the prediction from having been already accomplished? For this very prediction was uttered many ages before, and is sufficient, along with the other prophetic utterances, to lead him who fairly examines the whole matter to the conclusion that Jesus is He who was prophesied of as Christ, and as the Son of God.

CHAP. XXXVIII.

The Jew next remarks : "You, O sincere believers,[5] find fault with us, because we do not recognise this individual as God, nor agree with you that he endured these (sufferings) for the benefit of mankind, in order that we also might despise punishment." Now, in answer to this, we say that we blame the Jews, who have been brought up under the training of the law and the prophets (which foretell the coming of Christ), because they neither refute the arguments which we lay before them to prove that He is the Messiah,[6] adducing such refutation as a defence of their unbelief; nor yet, while not offering any refutation, do they believe in Him who was the subject of prophecy, and who clearly manifested through His disciples, even after the period of His appearance in the flesh, that He underwent these things for the benefit of mankind ; having, as the object of His first advent, not to condemn men and their actions[7] before He had instructed them, and pointed out to them their duty,[8] nor to chastise the wicked and save the good, but to disseminate His doctrine in an extraordinary[9] manner, and with the evidence of divine power, among the whole human race, as the prophets also have represented these things. And we blame them, moreover, because they did not believe in Him who gave evidence of the power that was in Him, but asserted that He cast out demons from the souls of men through Beelzebub the prince of the demons ; and we blame them because they slander the philanthropic character of Him, who overlooked not only no city, but not even a single village in Judea, that He might everywhere announce the kingdom of God, accusing Him of leading the wandering life of a vagabond, and passing an anxious existence in a disgraceful body. But there is no disgrace in enduring such labours for the benefit of all those who may be able to understand Him.

CHAP. XXXIX.

And how can the following assertion of this Jew of Celsus appear anything else than a manifest falsehood, viz., that Jesus, "having gained over no one during his life, not even his own disciples, underwent these punishments and sufferings?" For from what other source sprang the envy which was aroused against Him by the Jewish high priests, and elders, and scribes, save from the fact that multitudes obeyed and followed Him, and were led into the deserts not

---

[1] Cf. John xix. 34, 35.
[2] Cf. Matt. xxvii. 54.
[3] χανδόν.
[4] Ps. lxix. 21.

[5] ὦ πιστότατοι.
[6] τὸν Χριστόν.
[7] τὰ ἀνθρώπων.
[8] μαρτύρασθαι περὶ τῶν πρακτέων.
[9] παραδόξως.

only by the persuasive [1] language of Him whose words were always appropriate to His hearers, but who also by His miracles made an impression on those who were not moved to belief by His words? And is it not a manifest falsehood to say that " he did not gain over even his own disciples," who exhibited, indeed, at that time some symptoms of human weakness arising from cowardly fear — for they had not yet been disciplined to the exhibition of full courage — but who by no means abandoned the judgments which they had formed regarding Him as the Christ? For Peter, after his denial, perceiving to what a depth of wickedness he had fallen, " went out and wept bitterly ; " while the others, although stricken with dismay on account of what had happened to Jesus (for they still continued to admire Him), had, by His glorious appearance,[2] their belief more firmly established than before that He was the Son of God.

CHAP. XL.

It is, moreover, in a very unphilosophical spirit that Celsus imagines our Lord's pre-eminence among men to consist, not in the preaching of salvation and in a pure morality, but in acting contrary to the character of that personality which He had taken upon Him, and in not dying, although He had assumed mortality ; or, if dying, yet at least not such a death as might serve as a pattern to those who were to learn by that very act how to die for the sake of religion, and to comport themselves boldly through its help, before those who hold erroneous views on the subject of religion and irreligion, and who regard religious men as altogether irreligious, but imagine those to be most religious who err regarding God, and who apply to everything rather than to God the ineradicable [3] idea of Him (which is implanted in the human mind), and especially when they eagerly rush to destroy those who have yielded themselves up with their whole soul (even unto death), to the clear evidence of one God who is over all things.

CHAP. XLI.

In the person of the Jew, Celsus continues to find fault with Jesus, alleging that " he did not show himself to be pure from all evil." Let Celsus state from what " evil " our Lord did not show Himself to be pure. If he means that He was not pure from what is properly termed " evil," let him clearly prove the existence of any wicked work in Him. But if he deems poverty and the cross to be evils, and conspiracy on the part of wicked men, then it is clear that

he would say that evil had happened also to Socrates, who was unable to show himself pure from evils. And how great also the other band of poor men is among the Greeks, who have given themselves to philosophical pursuits, and have voluntarily accepted a life of poverty, is known to many among the Greeks from what is recorded of Democritus, who allowed his property to become pasture for sheep ; and of Crates, who obtained his freedom by bestowing upon the Thebans the price received for the sale of his possessions. Nay, even Diogenes himself, from excessive poverty, came to live in a tub ; and yet, in the opinion of no one possessed of moderate understanding, was Diogenes on that account considered to be in an evil (sinful) condition.

CHAP. XLII.

But further, since Celsus will have it that " Jesus was not irreproachable," let him instance any one of those who adhere to His doctrine, who has recorded anything that could truly furnish ground of reproach against Jesus ; or if it be not from these that he derives his matter of accusation against Him, let him say from what quarter he has learned that which has induced him to say that He is not free from reproach. Jesus, however, performed all that He promised to do, and by which He conferred benefits upon his adherents. And we, continually seeing fulfilled all that was predicted by Him before it happened, viz., that this Gospel of His should be preached throughout the whole world, and that His disciples should go among all nations and announce His doctrine ; and, moreover, that they should be brought before governors and kings on no other account than because of His teaching ; we are lost in wonder at Him, and have our faith in Him daily confirmed. And I know not by what greater or more convincing proofs Celsus would have Him confirm His predictions ; unless, indeed, as seems to be the case, not understanding that the Logos had become the man Jesus, he would have Him to be subject to no human weakness, nor to become an illustrious pattern to men of the manner in which they ought to bear the calamities of life, although these appear to Celsus to be most lamentable and disgraceful occurrences, seeing that he regards labour [4] to be the greatest of evils, and pleasure the perfect good, — a view accepted by none of those philosophers who admit the doctrine of providence, and who allow that courage, and fortitude, and magnanimity are virtues. Jesus, therefore, by His sufferings cast no discredit upon the faith of which He was the object ; but rather confirmed the same among those who would approve of manly courage, and among those who were

---

[1] τῆς τῶν λόγων αὐτοῦ ἀκολουθίας.
[2] ἐπιφανείας.
[3] τὴν περὶ αὐτοῦ ἀδιάστροφον ἔννοιαν.

[4] πόνον.

taught by Him that what was truly and properly the happy life was not here below, but was to be found in that which was called, according to His own words, the "coming world;" whereas in what is called the "present world" life is a calamity, or at least the first and greatest struggle of the soul.[1]

CHAP. XLIII.

Celsus next addresses to us the following remark: "You will not, I suppose, say of him, that, after failing to gain over those who were in this world, he went to Hades to gain over those who were there." But whether he like it or not, we assert that not only while Jesus was in the body did He win over not a few persons merely, but so great a number, that a conspiracy was formed against Him on account of the multitude of His followers; but also, that when He became a soul, without the covering of the body, He dwelt among those souls which were without bodily covering, converting such of them as were willing to Himself, or those whom He saw, for reasons known to Him alone, to be better adapted to such a course.[2]

CHAP. XLIV.

Celsus in the next place says, with indescribable silliness: "If, after inventing defences which are absurd, and by which ye were ridiculously deluded, ye imagine that you really make a good defence, what prevents you from regarding those other individuals who have been condemned, and have died a miserable death, as greater and more divine messengers of heaven (than Jesus)?" Now, that manifestly and clearly there is no similarity between Jesus, who suffered what is described, and those who have died a wretched death on account of their sorcery, or whatever else be the charge against them, is patent to every one. For no one can point to any acts of a sorcerer which turned away souls from the practice of the many sins which prevail among men, and from the flood of wickedness (in the world).[3] But since this Jew of Celsus compares Him to robbers, and says that "any similarly shameless fellow might be able to say regarding even a robber and murderer whom punishment had overtaken, that such an one was not a robber, but a god, because he predicted to his fellow-robbers that he would suffer such punishment as he actually did suffer," it might, in the first place, be answered, that it is not because He predicted that He would suffer such things that we entertain those opinions regarding Jesus which lead us to have confidence in Him, as one who has come down to us from God. And,

in the second place, we assert that this very comparison[4] has been somehow foretold in the Gospels; since God was numbered with the transgressors by wicked men, who desired rather a "murderer" (one who for sedition and murder had been cast into prison) to be released unto them, and Jesus to be crucified, and who crucified Him between two robbers. Jesus, indeed, is ever crucified with robbers among His genuine disciples and witnesses to the truth, and suffers the same condemnation which they do among men. And we say, that if those persons have any resemblance to robbers, who on account of their piety towards God suffer all kinds of injury and death, that they may keep it pure and unstained, according to the teaching of Jesus, then it is clear also that Jesus, the author of such teaching, is with good reason compared by Celsus to the captain of a band of robbers. But neither was He who died for the common good of mankind, nor they who suffered because of their religion, and alone of all men were persecuted because of what appeared to them the right way of honouring God, put to death in accordance with justice, nor was Jesus persecuted without the charge of impiety being incurred by His persecutors.

CHAP. XLV.

But observe the superficial nature of his argument respecting the former disciples of Jesus, in which he says: "In the next place, those who were his associates while alive, and who listened to his voice, and enjoyed his instructions as their teacher, on seeing him subjected to punishment and death, neither died with him, nor for him, nor were even induced to regard punishment with contempt, but denied even that they were his disciples, whereas now ye die along with him." And here he believes the sin which was committed by the disciples while they were yet beginners and imperfect, and which is recorded in the Gospels, to have been actually committed, in order that he may have matter of accusation against the Gospel; but their upright conduct after their transgression, when they behaved with courage before the Jews, and suffered countless cruelties at their hands, and at last suffered death for the doctrine of Jesus, he passes by in silence. For he would neither hear the words of Jesus, when He predicted to Peter, "When thou shalt be old, thou shalt stretch forth thy hands,"[5] etc., to which the Scripture adds, "This spake He, signifying by what death he should glorify God;" nor how James the brother of John — an apostle, the brother of an apostle — was slain with the sword by Herod for the doctrine of Christ;

---

[1] ἀγῶνα τὸν πρῶτον καὶ μέγιστον τῆς ψυχῆς.
[2] [See Dean Plumptre's The Spirits in Prison: Studies on the Life after Death, p. 85. S.]
[3] τῆς κατὰ τὴν κακίαν χύσεως.

[4] καὶ ταῦτα.
[5] John xxi. 18, 19.

nor even the many instances of boldness displayed by Peter and the other apostles because of the Gospel, and " how they went forth from the presence of the Sanhedrim after being scourged, rejoicing that they were counted worthy to suffer shame for His name," [1] and so surpassing many of the instances related by the Greeks of the fortitude and courage of their philosophers. From the very beginning, then, this was inculcated as a precept of Jesus among His hearers, which taught men to despise the life which is eagerly sought after by the multitude, but to be earnest in living the life which resembles that of God.

CHAP. XLVI.

But how can this Jew of Celsus escape the charge of falsehood, when he says that Jesus, " when on earth, gained over to himself only ten sailors and tax-gatherers of the most worthless character, and not even the whole of these?" Now it is certain that the Jews themselves would admit that He drew over not ten persons merely, nor a hundred, nor a thousand, but on one occasion five thousand at once, and on another four thousand; and that He attracted them to such a degree that they followed Him even into the deserts, which alone could contain the assembled multitude of those who believed in God through Jesus, and where He not only addressed to them discourses, but also manifested to them His works. And now, through his tautology, he compels us also to be tautological, since we are careful to guard against being supposed to pass over any of the charges advanced by him; and therefore, in reference to the matter before us, following the order of his treatise as we have it, he says: " Is it not the height of absurdity to maintain, that if, while he himself was alive, he won over not a single person to his views, after his death any who wish are able to gain over such a multitude of individuals?" Whereas he ought to have said, in consistency with truth, that if, after His death, not simply those who will, but they who have the will and the power, can gain over so many proselytes, how much more consonant to reason is it, that while He was alive He should, through the greater power of His words and deeds, have won over to Himself manifold greater numbers of adherents?

CHAP. XLVII.

He represents, moreover, a statement of his own as if it were an answer to one of his questions, in which he asks : " By what train of argument were you led to regard him as the Son of God?" For he makes us answer that " we were won over to him, because [2] we know that his punishment was undergone to bring about the destruction of the father of evil." Now we were won over to His doctrine by innumerable other considerations, of which we have stated only the smallest part in the preceding pages; but, if God permit, we shall continue to enumerate them, not only while dealing with the so-called *True Discourse* of Celsus, but also on many other occasions. And, as if we said that we consider Him to be the Son of God because He suffered punishment, he asks : " What then? have not many others, too, been punished, and that not less disgracefully?" And here Celsus acts like the most contemptible enemies of the Gospel, and like those who imagine that it follows as a consequence from our history of the crucified Jesus, that we should worship those who have undergone crucifixion!

CHAP. XLVIII.

Celsus, moreover, unable to resist the miracles which Jesus is recorded to have performed, has already on several occasions spoken of them slanderously as works of sorcery; and we also on several occasions have, to the best of our ability, replied to his statements. And now he represents us as saying that " we deemed Jesus to be the Son of God, because he healed the lame and the blind." And he adds : " Moreover, as you assert, he raised the dead." That He healed the lame and the blind, and that therefore we hold Him to be the Christ and the Son of God, is manifest to us from what is contained in the prophecies : " Then the eyes of the blind shall be opened, and the ears of the deaf shall hear; then shall the lame man leap as an hart." [3] And that He also raised the dead, and that it is no fiction of those who composed the Gospels, is shown by this, that if it had been a fiction, *many* individuals would have been represented as having risen from the dead, and these, too, such as had been many years in their graves. But as it is no fiction, they are very easily counted of whom this is related to have happened; viz., the daughter of the ruler of the synagogue (of whom I know not why He said, " She is not dead, but sleepeth," stating regarding her something which does not apply to all who die) ; and the only son of the widow, on whom He took compassion and raised him up, making the bearers of the corpse to stand still ; and the third instance, that of Lazarus, who had been four days in the grave. Now, regarding these cases we would say to all persons of candid mind, and especially to the Jew, that as

[1] Acts v. 41.

[2] The reading in the text is εἰ καὶ ἴσμεν; for which both Bohereau and De la Rue propose ἐπεὶ ἴσμεν, which has been adopted in the translation: cf. ἐπεὶ ἐκολάσθη, *infra*.

[3] Cf. Isa. xxxv. 5, 6.

there were many lepers in the days of Elisha the prophet, and none of them was healed save Naaman the Syrian, and many widows in the days of Elijah the prophet, to none of whom was Elijah sent save to Sarepta in Sidonia (for the widow there had been deemed worthy by a divine decree of the miracle which was wrought by the prophet in the matter of the bread) ; so also there were many dead in the days of Jesus, but those only rose from the grave whom the Logos knew to be fitted for a resurrection, in order that the works done by the Lord might not be merely symbols of certain things, but that by the very acts themselves He might gain over many to the marvellous doctrine of the Gospel. I would say, moreover, that, agreeably to the promise of Jesus, His disciples performed even greater works than these miracles of Jesus, which were perceptible only to the senses.[1] For the eyes of those who are blind in soul are ever opened ; and the ears of those who were deaf to virtuous words, listen readily to the doctrine of God, and of the blessed life with Him ; and many, too, who were lame in the feet of the "inner man," as Scripture calls it, having now been healed by the word, do not simply leap, but leap as the hart, which is an animal hostile to serpents, and stronger than all the poison of vipers. And these lame who have been healed, receive from Jesus power to trample, with those feet in which they were formerly lame, upon the serpents and scorpions of wickedness, and generally upon all the power of the enemy ; and though they tread upon it, they sustain no injury, for they also have become stronger than the poison of all evil and of demons.

CHAP. XLIX.

Jesus, accordingly, in turning away the minds of His disciples, not merely from giving heed to sorcerers in general, and those who profess in any other manner to work miracles — for His disciples did not need to be so warned — but from such as gave themselves out as the Christ of God, and who tried by certain apparent[2] miracles to gain over to them the disciples of Jesus, said in a certain passage : "Then, if any man shall say unto you, Lo, here is Christ, or there ; believe it not. For there shall arise false Christs, and false prophets, and shall show great signs and wonders ; insomuch that, if it were possible, they shall deceive the very elect. Behold, I have told you before. Wherefore, if they shall say unto you, Behold, he is in the desert, go not forth ; behold, he is in the secret chambers, believe it not. For as the lightning cometh out of the east, and shineth even to the west, so also shall the coming of the Son of man be."[3] And

in another passage : "Many will say unto Me in that day, Lord, Lord, have we not eaten and drunk in Thy name, and by Thy name have cast out demons, and done many wonderful works? And then will I say unto them, Depart from Me, because ye are workers of iniquity."[4] But Celsus, wishing to assimilate the miracles of Jesus to the works of human sorcery, says in express terms as follows : "O light and truth ! he distinctly declares, with his own voice, as ye yourselves have recorded, that there will come to you even others, employing miracles of a similar kind, who are wicked men, and sorcerers ; and he calls him who makes use of such devices, one Satan. So that Jesus himself does not deny that these works at least are not at all divine, but are the acts of wicked men ; and being compelled by the force of truth, he at the same time not only laid open the doings of others, but convicted himself of the same acts. Is it not, then, a miserable inference, to conclude from the same works that the one is God and the other sorcerers? Why ought the others, because of these acts, to be accounted wicked rather than this man, seeing they have him as their witness against himself? For he has himself acknowledged that these are not the works of a divine nature, but the inventions of certain deceivers, and of thoroughly wicked men." Observe, now, whether Celsus is not clearly convicted of slandering the Gospel by such statements, since what Jesus says regarding those who are to work signs and wonders is different from what this Jew of Celsus alleges it to be. For if Jesus had simply told His disciples to be on their guard against those who professed to work miracles, without declaring what they would give themselves out to be, then perhaps there would have been some ground for his suspicion. But since those against whom Jesus would have us to be on our guard give themselves out as the Christ — which is not a claim put forth by sorcerers — and since He says that even some who lead wicked lives will perform miracles in the name of Jesus, and expel demons out of men, sorcery in the case of these individuals, or any suspicion of such, is rather, if we may so speak, altogether banished, and the divinity of Christ established, as well as the divine mission[5] of His disciples ; seeing that it is possible that one who makes use of His name, and who is wrought upon by some power, in some way unknown, to make the pretence that he is the Christ, should seem to perform miracles like those of Jesus, while others through His name should do works resembling those of His genuine disciples.

Paul, moreover, in the second Epistle to the Thessalonians, shows in what manner there will

---

[1] ὧν Ἰησοῦς αἰσθητῶν.
[2] φαντασιῶν.
[3] Matt. xxiv. 23-27.

[4] Cf. Matt. vii. 22, 23, with Luke xiii. 26, 27.
[5] θειότης, lit. divinity.

one day be revealed "the man of sin, the son of perdition, who opposeth and exalteth himself above all that is called God, or that is worshipped ; so that he sitteth in the temple of God, showing himself that he is God." [1] And again he says to the Thessalonians : "And now ye know what withholdeth that he might be revealed in his time. For the mystery of iniquity doth already work : only he who now letteth will let, until he be taken out of the way : and then shall that Wicked be revealed, whom the Lord will consume with the spirit of His mouth, and shall destroy with the brightness of His coming : even him, whose cunning is after the working of Satan, with all power, and signs, and lying wonders, and with all deceivableness of unrighteousness in them that perish." [2] And in assigning the reason why the man of sin is permitted to continue in existence, he says : " Because they received not the love of the truth, that they might be saved. And for this cause God shall send them strong delusion, that they should believe a lie ; that they all might be damned who believed not the truth, but had pleasure in unrighteousness." [3] Let any one now say whether any of the statements in the Gospel, or in the writings of the apostle, could give occasion for the suspicion that there is therein contained any prediction of sorcery. Any one, moreover, who likes may find the prophecy in Daniel respecting antichrist.[4] But Celsus falsifies the words of Jesus, since He did not say that others would come working similar miracles to Himself, but who are wicked men and sorcerers, although Celsus asserts that He uttered such words. For as the power of the Egyptian magicians was not similar to the divinely-bestowed grace of Moses, but the issue clearly proved that the acts of the former were the effect of magic, while those of Moses were wrought by divine power ; so the proceedings of the antichrists, and of those who feign that they can work miracles as being the disciples of Christ, are said to be lying signs and wonders, prevailing with all deceivableness of unrighteousness among them that perish ; whereas the works of Christ and His disciples had for their fruit, not deceit, but the salvation of human souls. And who would rationally maintain that an improved moral life, which daily lessened the number of a man's offences, could proceed from a system of deceit?

CHAP. LI.

Celsus, indeed, evinced a slight knowledge of Scripture when he made Jesus say, that it is "a certain Satan who contrives such devices ; " although he begs the question [5] when he asserts that " Jesus did not deny that these works have in them nothing of divinity, but proceed from wicked men," for he makes things which differ in kind to be the same. Now, as a wolf is not of the same species as a dog, although it may appear to have some resemblance in the figure of its body and in its voice, nor a common wood-pigeon [6] the same as a dove,[7] so there is no resemblance between what is done by the power of God and what is the effect of sorcery. And we might further say, in answer to the calumnies of Celsus, Are those to be regarded as miracles which are wrought through sorcery by wicked demons, but those not which are performed by a nature that is holy and divine ? and does human life endure the worse, but never receive the better ? Now it appears to me that we must lay it down as a general principle, that as, wherever anything that is evil would make itself to be of the same nature with the good, there must by all means be something that is good opposed to the evil ; so also, in opposition to those things which are brought about by sorcery, there must also of necessity be some things in human life which are the result of divine power. And it follows from the same, that we must either annihilate both, and assert that neither exists, or, assuming the one, and particularly the evil, admit also the reality of the good. Now, if one were to lay it down that works are wrought by means of sorcery, but would not grant that there are also works which are the product of divine power, he would seem to me to resemble him who should admit the existence of sophisms and plausible arguments, which have the appearance of establishing the truth, although really undermining it, while denying that truth had anywhere a home among men, or a dialectic which differed from sophistry. But if we once admit that it is consistent with the existence of magic and sorcery (which derive their power from evil demons, who are spell-bound by elaborate incantations, and become subject to sorcerers) that some works must be found among men which proceed from a power that is divine, why shall we not test those who profess to perform them by their lives and morals, and the consequences of their miracles, viz., whether they tend to the injury of men or to the reformation of conduct? What minister of evil demons, e.g., can do such things ? and by means of what incantations and magic arts? And who, on the other hand, is it that, having his soul and his spirit, and I imagine also his body, in a pure and holy state, receives a divine spirit, and performs such works in order to benefit men, and to lead them to believe on

---

[1] 2 Thess. ii. 3, 4.
[2] 2 Thess. ii. 6-10.
[3] 2 Thess. ii. 10-12.
[4] Cf. Dan. vii. 26.

[5] συναρπάζει τὸν λόγον.
[6] φάσσα.
[7] περιστερά.

the true God? But if we must once investigate (without being carried away by the miracles themselves) who it is that performs them by help of a good, and who by help of an evil power, so that we may neither slander all without discrimination, nor yet admire and accept all as divine, will it not be manifest, from what occurred in the times of Moses and Jesus, when entire nations were established in consequence of their miracles, that these men wrought by means of divine power what they are recorded to have performed? For wickedness and sorcery would not have led a whole nation to rise not only above idols and images erected by men, but also above all created things, and to ascend to the uncreated origin of the God of the universe.

CHAP. LII.

But since it is a Jew who makes these assertions in the treatise of Celsus, we would say to him : Pray, friend, why do you believe the works which are recorded in your writings as having been performed by God through the instrumentality of Moses to be really divine, and endeavour to refute those who slanderously assert that they were wrought by sorcery, like those of the Egyptian magicians ; while, in imitation of your Egyptian opponents, you charge those which were done by Jesus, and which, you admit, were actually performed, with not being divine? For if the final result, and the founding of an entire nation by the miracles of Moses, manifestly demonstrate that it was God who brought these things to pass in the time of Moses the Hebrew lawgiver, why should not such rather be shown to be the case with Jesus, who accomplished far greater works than those of Moses? For the former took those of his own nation, the descendants of Abraham, who had observed the rite of circumcision transmitted by tradition, and who were careful observers of the Abrahamic usages, and led them out of Egypt, enacting for them those laws which you believe to be divine ; whereas the latter ventured upon a greater undertaking, and superinduced upon the pre-existing constitution, and upon ancestral customs and modes of life agreeable to the existing laws, a constitution in conformity with the Gospel. And as it was necessary, in order that Moses should find credit not only among the elders, but the common people, that there should be performed those miracles which he is recorded to have performed, why should not Jesus also, in order that He may be believed on by those of the people who had learned to ask for signs and wonders, need [1] to work such miracles as, on account of their greater grandeur and divinity (in comparison with those of Moses), were able to convert

men from Jewish fables, and from the human traditions which prevailed among them, and make them admit that He who taught and did such things was greater than the prophets? For how was not He greater than the prophets, who was proclaimed by them to be the Christ, and the Saviour of the human race?

CHAP. LIII.

All the arguments, indeed, which this Jew of Celsus advances against those who believe on Jesus, may, by parity of reasoning, be urged as ground of accusation against Moses : so that there is no difference in asserting that the sorcery practised by Jesus and that by Moses were similar to each other,[2] — both of them, so far as the language of this Jew of Celsus is concerned, being liable to the same charge ; as, e.g., when this Jew says of Christ, " But, O light and truth ! Jesus with his own voice expressly declares, as you yourselves have recorded, that there will appear among you others also, who will perform miracles like mine, but who are wicked men and sorcerers," some one, either Greek or Egyptian, or any other party who disbelieved the Jew, might say respecting Moses, " But, O light and truth ! Moses with his own voice expressly declares, as ye also have recorded, that there will appear among you others also, who will perform miracles like mine, but who are wicked men and sorcerers. For it is written in your law, ' If there arise among you a prophet, or a dreamer of dreams, and giveth thee a sign or a wonder, and the sign or wonder come to pass whereof he spake unto thee, saying, Let us go after other gods which thou hast not known, and let us serve them ; thou shalt not hearken to the words of that prophet, or dreamer of dreams,' "[3] etc. Again, perverting the words of Jesus, he says, " And he terms him who devises such things, one Satan ; " while one, applying this to Moses, might say, " And he terms him who devises such things, a prophet who dreams dreams." And as this Jew asserts regarding Jesus, that " even he himself does not deny that these works have in them nothing of divinity, but are the acts of wicked men ; " so any one who disbelieves the writings of Moses might say, quoting what has been already said, the same thing, viz., that, " even Moses does not deny that these works have in them nothing of divinity, but are the acts of wicked men." And he will do the same thing also with respect to this : " Being compelled by the force of truth, Moses at the same time both exposed the doings of others, and convicted himself of the same." And when the Jew says, " Is it not a wretched inference from the same acts, to con-

---

[1] [δεήσεται. S.]

[2] ὥστε μηδὲν διαφέρειν παραπλήσιον εἶναι λέγειν γοητείαν την Ἰησοῦ τῇ Μωϋσέως.

[3] Deut. xiii. 1-3.

clude that the one is a God, and the others sorcerers?" one might object to him, on the ground of those words of Moses already quoted, "Is it not then a wretched inference from the same acts, to conclude that the one is a prophet and servant of God, and the others sorcerers?" But when, in addition to those comparisons which I have already mentioned, Celsus, dwelling upon the subject, adduces this also: "Why from these works should the others be accounted wicked, rather than this man, seeing they have him as a witness against himself?"—we, too, shall adduce the following, in addition to what has been already said: "Why, from those passages in which Moses forbids us to believe those who exhibit signs and wonders, ought we to consider such persons as wicked, rather than Moses, because he calumniates some of them in respect of their signs and wonders?" And urging more to the same effect, that he may appear to strengthen his attempt, he says: "He himself acknowledged that these were not the works of a divine nature, but were the inventions of certain deceivers, and of very wicked men." Who, then, is "himself?" You, O Jew, say that it is Jesus; but he who accuses you as liable to the same charges, will transfer this "himself" to the person of Moses.

CHAP. LIV.

After this, forsooth, the Jew of Celsus, to keep up the character assigned to the Jew from the beginning, in his address to those of his countrymen who had become believers, says: "By what, then, were you induced (to become his followers)? Was it because he foretold that after his death he would rise again?" Now this question, like the others, can be retorted upon Moses. For we might say to the Jew: "By what, then, were *you* induced (to become the follower of Moses)? Was it because he put on record the following statement about his own death: 'And Moses, the servant of the LORD, died there, in the land of Moab, according to the word of the LORD; and they buried him in Moab, near the house of Phogor: and no one knoweth his sepulchre until this day?'"[1] For as the Jew casts discredit upon the statement, that "Jesus foretold that after His death He would rise again," another person might make a similar assertion about Moses, and would say in reply, that Moses also put on record (for the book of Deuteronomy is his composition) the statement, that "no one knoweth his sepulchre until this day," in order to magnify and enhance the importance of his place of burial, as being unknown to mankind.

CHAP. LV.

The Jew continues his address to those of his countrymen who are converts, as follows: "Come now, let us grant to you that the prediction was actually uttered. Yet how many others are there who practise such juggling tricks, in order to deceive their simple hearers, and who make gain by their deception?—as was the case, they say, with Zamolxis[2] in Scythia, the slave of Pythagoras; and with Pythagoras himself in Italy; and with Rhampsinitus[3] in Egypt (the latter of whom, they say, played at dice with Demeter in Hades, and returned to the upper world with a golden napkin which he had received from her as a gift); and also with Orpheus[4] among the Odrysians, and Protesilaus in Thessaly, and Hercules[4] at Cape Tænarus, and Theseus. But the question is, whether any one who was really dead ever rose with a veritable body.[5] Or do you imagine the statements of others not only to be myths, but to have the appearance of such, while you have discovered a becoming and credible termination to your drama in the voice from the cross, when he breathed his last, and in the earthquake and the darkness? That while alive he was of no assistance to himself, but that when dead he rose again, and showed the marks of his punishment, and how his hands were pierced with nails: who beheld this? A half-frantic[6] woman, as you state, and some other one, perhaps, of those who were engaged in the same system of delusion, who had either dreamed so, owing to a peculiar state of mind,[7] or under the influence of a wandering imagination had formed to himself an appearance according to his own wishes,[8] which has been the case with numberless individuals; or, which is most probable, one who desired to impress others with this portent, and by such a falsehood to furnish an occasion to impostors like himself."

Now, since it is a Jew who makes these statements, we shall conduct the defence of our Jesus as if we were replying to a Jew, still continuing the comparison derived from the accounts regarding Moses, and saying to him: "How many others are there who practise similar juggling tricks to those of Moses, in order to deceive their silly hearers, and who make gain by their deception?" Now this objection would be more appropriate in the mouth of one who did not believe in Moses (as we might quote the instances of Zamolxis and Pythagoras, who were

---

[1] Cf. Deut. xxxiv. 5, 6.

[2] Cf. Herodot., iv. 95.
[3] Cf. Herodot., ii. 122.
[4] Cf. Diodor., iv., *Bibl. Hist.*
[5] αὐτῷ σώματι. [See Mozley's Bampton Lectures *On Miracles*, 3d ed., p. 297: "That a man should rise from the dead, was treated by them (the heathen) as an absolutely incredible fact." S.]
[6] γυνὴ πάροιστρος.
[7] κατά τινα διάθεσιν ὀνειρώξας.
[8] ἢ κατὰ τὴν αὑτοῦ βούλησιν δόξῃ πεπλανημένῃ φαντασιωθείς.

engaged in such juggling tricks) than in that of a Jew, who is not very learned in the histories of the Greeks. An Egyptian, moreover, who did not believe the miracles of Moses, might credibly adduce the instance of Rhampsinitus, saying that it was far more credible that he had descended to Hades, and had played at dice with Demeter, and that after stealing from her a golden napkin he exhibited it as a sign of his having been in Hades, and of his having returned thence, than that Moses should have recorded that he entered into the darkness, where God was, and that he alone, above all others, drew near to God. For the following is his statement: "Moses alone shall come near the LORD; but the rest shall not come nigh."[1] We, then, who are the disciples of Jesus, say to the Jew who urges these objections: "While assailing our belief in Jesus, defend yourself, and answer the Egyptian and the Greek objectors: what will you say to those charges which you brought against our Jesus, but which also might be brought against Moses first? And if you should make a vigorous effort to defend Moses, as indeed his history does admit of a clear and powerful defence, you will unconsciously, in your support of Moses, be an unwilling assistant in establishing the greater divinity of Jesus."

CHAP. LVI.

But since the Jew says that these histories of the alleged descent of heroes to Hades, and of their return thence, are juggling impositions,[2] maintaining that these heroes disappeared for a certain time, and secretly withdrew themselves from the sight of all men, and gave themselves out afterwards as having returned from Hades, —for such is the meaning which his words seem to convey respecting the Odrysian Orpheus, and the Thessalian Protesilaus, and the Tænarian Hercules, and Theseus also, — let us endeavour to show that the account of Jesus being raised from the dead cannot possibly be compared to these. For each one of the heroes respectively mentioned might, had he wished, have secretly withdrawn himself from the sight of men, and returned again, if so determined, to those whom he had left; but seeing that Jesus was crucified before all the Jews, and His body slain in the presence of His nation, how can they bring themselves to say that He practised a similar deception[3] with those heroes who are related to have gone down to Hades, and to have returned thence? But we say that the following consideration might be adduced, perhaps, as a defence of the public crucifixion of Jesus, especially

in connection with the existence of those stories of heroes who are supposed to have been compelled[4] to descend to Hades: that if we were to suppose Jesus to have died an obscure death, so that the fact of His decease was not patent to the whole nation of the Jews, and afterwards to have actually risen from the dead, there would, in such a case, have been ground for the same suspicion entertained regarding the heroes being also entertained regarding Himself. Probably, then, in addition to other causes for the crucifixion of Jesus, this also may have contributed to His dying a conspicuous death upon the cross, that no one might have it in his power to say that He voluntarily withdrew from the sight of men, and seemed only to die, without really doing so; but, appearing again, made a juggler's trick[5] of the resurrection from the dead. But a clear and unmistakeable proof of the fact I hold to be the undertaking of His disciples, who devoted themselves to the teaching of a doctrine which was attended with danger to human life, — a doctrine which they would not have taught with such courage had they invented the resurrection of Jesus from the dead; and who also, at the same time, not only prepared others to despise death, but were themselves the first to manifest their disregard for its terrors.

CHAP. LVII.

But observe whether this Jew of Celsus does not talk very blindly, in saying that it is impossible for any one to rise from the dead with a veritable body, his language being: "But this is the question, whether any one who was really dead ever rose again with a veritable body?" Now a Jew would not have uttered these words, who believed what is recorded in the third and fourth books of Kings regarding little children, of whom the one was raised up by Elijah,[6] and the other by Elisha.[7] And on this account, too, I think it was that Jesus appeared to no other nation than the Jews, who had become accustomed to miraculous occurrences; so that, by comparing what they themselves believed with the works which were done by Him, and what was related of Him, they might confess that He, in regard to whom greater things were done, and by whom mightier marvels were performed, was greater than all those who preceded Him.

CHAP. LVIII.

Further, after these Greek stories which the Jew adduced respecting those who were guilty

---

[1] Cf. Ex. xxiv. 2.
[2] τερατείας.
[3] πῶς οἴονται τὸ παραπλήσιον πλάσασθαι λέγειν αὐτὸν τοῖς ἱστορουμένοις, etc.

[4] καταβεβηκέναι βίᾳ. Bohereau proposes the omission of βίᾳ.
[5] ἐτερατεύσατο.
[6] Cf. 1 Kings xvii. 21, 22. [3 Kings, Sept. and Vulg. S.]
[7] Cf. 2 Kings iv. 34, 35. [4 Kings, Sept. and Vulg. S.]

of juggling practices,[1] and who pretended to have risen from the dead, he says to those Jews who are converts to Christianity : "Do you imagine the statements of others not only to be myths, but to have the appearance of such, while you have discovered a becoming and credible termination to your drama in the voice from the cross, when he breathed his last?" We reply to the Jew : "What you adduce as myths, we regard also as such ; but the statements of the Scriptures which are common to us both, in which not you only, but we also, take pride, we do not at all regard as myths. And therefore we accord our belief to those who have therein related that some rose from the dead, as not being guilty of imposition ; and to Him especially there mentioned as having risen, who both predicted the event Himself, and was the subject of prediction by others. And His resurrection is more miraculous than that of the others in this respect, that they were raised by the prophets Elijah and Elisha, while He was raised by none of the prophets, but by His Father in heaven. And therefore His resurrection also produced greater results than theirs. For what great good has accrued to the world from the resurrection of the children through the instrumentality of Elijah and Elisha, such as has resulted from the preaching of the resurrection of Jesus, accepted as an article of belief, and as effected through the agency of divine power?"

CHAP. LIX.

He imagines also that both the earthquake and the darkness were an invention ;[2] but regarding these, we have in the preceding pages made our defence, according to our ability, adducing the testimony of Phlegon, who relates that these events took place at the time when our Saviour suffered.[3] And he goes on to say, that "Jesus, while alive, was of no assistance to himself, but that he arose after death, and exhibited the marks of his punishment, and showed how his hands had been pierced by nails." We ask him what he means by the expression, "was of no assistance to himself?" For if he means it to refer to want of virtue, we reply that He *was* of very great assistance. For He neither uttered nor committed anything that was improper, but was truly "led as a sheep to the slaughter, and was dumb as a lamb before the shearer ;"[4] and the Gospel testifies that He opened not His mouth. But if Celsus applies the expression to things indifferent and corporeal,[5] (meaning that in such Jesus could render

no help to Himself,) we say that we have proved from the Gospels that He went voluntarily to encounter His sufferings. Speaking next of the statements in the Gospels, that after His resurrection He showed the marks of His punishment, and how His hands had been pierced, he asks, "Who beheld this?" And discrediting the narrative of Mary Magdalene, who is related to have seen Him, he replies, "A half-frantic woman, as ye state." And because she is not the only one who is recorded to have seen the Saviour after His resurrection, but others also are mentioned, this Jew of Celsus calumniates these statements also in adding, "And some one else of those engaged in the same system of deception ! "

CHAP. LX.

In the next place, as if this were possible, viz., that the image of a man who was dead could appear to another as if he were still living, he adopts this opinion as an Epicurean, and says, " That some one having so dreamed owing to a peculiar state of mind, or having, under the influence of a perverted imagination, formed such an appearance as he himself desired, reported that such had been seen ; and this," he continues, "has been the case with numberless individuals." But even if this statement of his seems to have a considerable degree of force, it is nevertheless only fitted to confirm a necessary doctrine, that the soul of the dead exists in a separate state (from the body) ; and he who adopts such an opinion does not believe without good reason in the immortality, or at least continued existence, of the soul, as even Plato says in his treatise on the Soul that shadowy phantoms of persons already dead have appeared to some around their sepulchres. Now the phantoms which exist about the soul of the dead are produced by some substance, and this substance is in the soul, which exists apart in a body said to be of splendid appearance.[6] But Celsus, unwilling to admit any such view, will have it that some dreamed a waking dream,[7] and, under the influence of a perverted imagination, formed to themselves such an image as they desired. Now it is not irrational to believe that a dream may take place while one is asleep ; but to suppose a waking vision in the case of those who are not altogether out of their senses, and under the influence of delirium or hypochondria, is incredible. And Celsus, seeing this, called the woman "half-mad," — a statement which is not made by the history recording the fact, but from which he took occasion to charge the occurrences with being untrue.

---

[1] τερατευομένοις.
[2] τερατείαν.
[3] [See cap. xxxiii., note, p. 445, *supra*.]
[4] Isa. liii. 7.
[5] εἰ δὲ τὸ "ἐπήρκεσεν" ἀπὸ τῶν μέσων καὶ σωματικῶν λαμβάνει.

[6] τὰ μὲν οὖν γινόμενα περὶ ψυχῆς τεθνηκότων φαντάσματα ἀπό τινος ὑποκειμένου γίνεται, τοῦ κατὰ τὴν ὑφεστηκυῖαν ἐν τῷ καλουμένῳ αὐγοειδεῖ σώματι ψυχήν. Cf. note in Benedictine ed.
[7] ὕπαρ.

CHAP. LXI.

Jesus accordingly, as Celsus imagines, exhibited after His death only the appearance of wounds received on the cross, and was not in reality so wounded as He is described to have been ; whereas, according to the teaching of the Gospel — some portions of which Celsus arbitrarily accepts, in order to find ground of accusation, and other parts of which he rejects — Jesus called to Him one of His disciples who was sceptical, and who deemed the miracle an impossibility. That individual had, indeed, expressed his belief in the statement of the woman who said that she had seen Him, because he did not think it impossible that the soul of a dead man could be seen ; but he did not yet consider the report to be true that He had been raised in a body, which was the antitype of the former.[1] And therefore he did not merely say, " Unless I see, I will not believe ; " but he added, " Unless I put my hand into the print of the nails, and lay my hands upon His side, I will not believe." These words were spoken by Thomas, who deemed it possible that the body of the soul[2] might be seen by the eye of sense, resembling in all respects its former appearance,

> " Both in size, and in beauty of eyes,
> And in voice ; "

and frequently, too,

" Having, also, such garments around the person[3] (as when alive)."

Jesus accordingly, having called Thomas, said, " Reach hither thy finger, and behold My hands ; and reach hither thy hand, and thrust it into My side : and be not faithless, but believing." [4]

CHAP. LXII.

Now it followed from all the predictions which were uttered regarding Him — amongst which was this prediction of the resurrection — and from all that was done by Him, and from all the events which befell Him, that this event should be marvellous above all others. For it had been said beforehand by the prophet in the person of Jesus : " My flesh shall rest in hope, and Thou wilt not leave my soul in Hades, and wilt not suffer Thine Holy One to see corruption." [5] And truly, after His resurrection, He existed in a body intermediate, as it were, between the grossness of that which He had before His sufferings, and the appearance of a soul uncovered by such a body. And hence it was, that when His disciples were together, and Thomas with them, there "came Jesus, the doors being shut, and stood in

the midst, and said, Peace be unto you. Then saith He to Thomas, Reach hither thy finger," [6] etc. And in the Gospel of Luke also, while Simon and Cleopas were conversing with each other respecting all that had happened to them, Jesus " drew near, and went with them. And their eyes were holden, that they should not know Him. And He said unto them, What manner of communications are these that ye have one to another, as ye walk?" And when their eyes were opened, and they knew Him, then the Scripture says, in express words, " And He vanished out of their sight." [7] And although Celsus may wish to place what is told of Jesus, and of those who saw Him after His resurrection, on the same level with imaginary appearances of a different kind, and those who have invented such, yet to those who institute a candid and intelligent examination, the events will appear only the more miraculous.

CHAP. LXIII.

After these points, Celsus proceeds to bring against the Gospel narrative a charge which is not to be lightly passed over, saying that " if Jesus desired to show that his power was really divine, he ought to have appeared to those who had ill-treated him, and to him who had condemned him, and to all men universally." For it appears to us also to be true, according to the Gospel account, that He was not seen after His resurrection in the same manner as He used formerly to show Himself — publicly, and to all men. But it is recorded in the Acts, that "being seen during forty days," He expounded to His disciples " the things pertaining to the kingdom of God." [8] And in the Gospels [9] it is not stated that He was always with them ; but that on one occasion He appeared in their midst, after eight days, when the doors were shut, and on another in some similar fashion. And Paul also, in the concluding portions of the first Epistle to the Corinthians, in reference to His not having publicly appeared as He did in the period before He suffered, writes as follows : " For I delivered unto you first of all that which I also received, how that Christ died for our sins according to the Scriptures ; and that He was seen of Cephas, then of the twelve : after that He was seen of above five hundred brethren at once, of whom the greater part remain unto the present time, but some are fallen asleep. After that He was seen of James, then of all the apostles. And last of all He was seen of me also, as of one born out of due time." [10] I am of opinion now

---

1 ἐν σώματι ἀντιτύπῳ ἐγηγέρθαι.
2 ψυχῆς σῶμα.
3 Cf. Homer, *Iliad*, xxiii. 66, 67.
4 Cf. John xx. 27.
5 Ps. xvi. 9, 10.

6 John xx. 26, 27.
7 Luke xxiv. 15, 31.
8 Acts i. 3.
9 Cf. John xx. 26.
10 1 Cor. xv. 3-8.

that the statements in this passage contain some great and wonderful mysteries, which are beyond the grasp not merely of the great multitude of ordinary believers, but even of those who are far advanced (in Christian knowledge), and that in them the reason would be explained why He did not show Himself, after His resurrection from the dead, in the same manner as before that event. And in a treatise of this nature, composed in answer to a work directed against the Christians and their faith, observe whether we are able to adduce a few rational arguments out of a greater number, and thus make an impression upon the hearers of this apology.

CHAP. LXIV.

Although Jesus was only a single individual, He was nevertheless more things than one, according to the different standpoint from which He might be regarded;[1] nor was He seen in the same way by all who beheld Him. Now, that He was more things than one, according to the varying point of view, is clear from this statement, "I am the way, and the truth, and the life;" and from this, "I am the bread;" and this, "I am the door," and innumerable others. And that when seen He did not appear in like fashion to all those who saw Him, but according to their several ability to receive Him, will be clear to those who notice why, at the time when He was about to be transfigured on the high mountain, He did not admit all His apostles (to this sight), but only Peter, and James, and John, because they alone were capable of beholding His glory on that occasion, and of observing the glorified appearance of Moses and Elijah, and of listening to their conversation, and to the voice from the heavenly cloud. I am of opinion, too, that before He ascended the mountain where His disciples came to Him alone, and where He taught them the beatitudes, when He was somewhere in the lower part of the mountain, and when, as it became late, He healed those who were brought to Him, freeing them from all sickness and disease, He did not appear the same person to the sick, and to those who needed His healing aid, as to those who were able by reason of their strength to go up the mountain along with Him. Nay, even when He interpreted privately to His own disciples the parables which were delivered to the multitudes without, from whom the explanation was withheld, as they who heard them explained were endowed with higher organs of hearing than they who heard them without explanation, so was it altogether the same with the eyes of their soul, and, I think, also with those of their body.[2]

And the following statement shows that He had not always the same appearance, viz., that Judas, when about to betray Him, said to the multitudes who were setting out with him, as not being acquainted with Him, "Whomsoever I shall kiss, the same is He."[3] And I think that the Saviour Himself indicates the same thing by the words: "I was daily with you, teaching in the temple, and ye laid no hold on Me."[4] Entertaining, then, such exalted views regarding Jesus, not only with respect to the Deity within, and which was hidden from the view of the multitude, but with respect to the transfiguration of His body, which took place when and to whom He would, we say, that before Jesus had "put off the governments and powers,"[5] and while as yet He was not dead unto sin, all men were capable of seeing Him; but that, when He had "put off the governments and powers," and had no longer anything which was capable of being seen by the multitude, all who had formerly seen Him were not now able to behold Him. And therefore, sparing them, He did not show Himself to all after His resurrection from the dead.

CHAP. LXV.

And why do I say "to all?" For even with His own apostles and disciples He was not perpetually present, nor did He constantly show Himself to them, because they were not able without intermission[6] to receive His divinity. For His deity was more resplendent after He had finished the economy[7] (of salvation): and this Peter, surnamed Cephas, the first-fruits as it were of the apostles, was enabled to behold, and along with him the twelve (Matthias having been substituted in room of Judas); and after them He appeared to the five hundred brethren at once, and then to James, and subsequently to all the others besides the twelve apostles, perhaps to the seventy also, and lastly to Paul, as to one born out of due time, and who knew well how to say, "Unto me, who am less than the least of all saints, is this grace given;" and probably the expression "least of all" has the same meaning with "one born out of due time." For as no one could reasonably blame Jesus for not having admitted all His apostles to the high mountain, but only the three already mentioned, on the occasion of His transfiguration, when He was about to manifest the splendour which appeared in His garments, and the glory of Moses and Elias talking with Him, so none could reasonably object to the statements of the apostles, who introduce the appearance of Jesus after His resurrection as having been made not to all, but

---

[1] πλείονα τῇ ἐπινοίᾳ ἦν.
[2] οὕτω καὶ ταῖς ὄψεσι πάντως μὲν τῆς ψυχῆς, ἐγὼ δ᾽ ἡγοῦμαι, ὅτι καὶ τοῦ σώματος.

[3] Matt. xxvi. 48.
[4] Matt. xxvi. 55.
[5] τὸν μὴ ἀπεκδυσάμενον, etc. Cf. Alford, *in loco* (Col. ii. 15).
[6] διηνεκῶς.
[7] τὴν οἰκονομίαν τελέσαντος.

to those only whom He knew to have received eyes capable of seeing His resurrection. I think, moreover, that the following statement regarding Him has an apologetic value [1] in reference to our subject, viz. : "For to this end Christ died, and rose again, that He might be Lord both of the dead and living." [2] For observe, it is conveyed in these words, that Jesus died that He might be Lord of the dead ; and that He rose again to be Lord not only of the dead, but also of the living. And the apostle understands, undoubtedly, by the dead over whom Christ is to be Lord, those who are so called in the first Epistle to the Corinthians, "For the trumpet shall sound, and the dead shall be raised incorruptible ; " [3] and by the living, those who are to be changed, and who are different from the dead who are to be raised. And respecting the living the words are these, "And we shall be changed ; " an expression which follows immediately after the statement, "The dead shall be raised first." [4] Moreover, in the first Epistle to the Thessalonians, describing the same change in different words, he says, that they who sleep are not the same as those who are alive ; his language being, "I would not have you to be ignorant, brethren, concerning them who are asleep, that ye sorrow not, even as others which have no hope. For if we believe that Jesus died, and rose again, even so them also that sleep in Jesus will God bring with Him. For this we say unto you by the word of the Lord, that we who are alive and remain unto the coming of the Lord, shall not prevent them that are asleep." [5] The explanation which appeared to us to be appropriate to this passage, we gave in the exegetical remarks which we have made on the first Epistle to the Thessalonians.

CHAP. LXVI.

And be not surprised if all the multitudes who have believed on Jesus do not behold His resurrection, when Paul, writing to the Corinthians, can say to them, as being incapable of receiving greater matters, "For I determined not to know anything among you, save Jesus Christ, and Him crucified ; " [6] which is the same as saying, "Hitherto ye were not able, neither yet now are ye able, for ye are still carnal." [7] The Scripture, therefore, doing everything by appointment of God, has recorded of Jesus, that before His sufferings He appeared to all indifferently, but not always ; while after His sufferings He no longer appeared to all in the same way, but with a certain discrimination which measured out to each

his due. And as it is related that "God appeared to Abraham," or to one of the saints, and this "appearance" was not a thing of constant occurrence, but took place at intervals, and not to all, so understand that the Son of God appeared in the one case on the same principle that God appeared to the latter. [8]

CHAP. LXVII.

To the best of our ability, therefore, as in a treatise of this nature, we have answered the objection, that "if Jesus had really wished to manifest his divine power, he ought to have shown himself to those who ill-treated him, and to the judge who condemned him, and to all without reservation." There was, however, no obligation on Him to appear either to the judge who condemned Him, or to those who ill-treated Him. For Jesus spared both the one and the other, that they might not be smitten with blindness, as the men of Sodom were when they conspired against the beauty of the angels entertained by Lot. And here is the account of the matter : "But the men put forth their hand, and pulled Lot into the house to them, and shut to the door. And they smote the men who were at the door of the house with blindness, both small and great ; so that they wearied themselves to find the door." [9] Jesus, accordingly, wished to show that His power was divine to each one who was capable of seeing it, and according to the measure of His capability. And I do not suppose that He guarded against being seen on any other ground than from a regard to the fitness of those who were incapable of seeing Him. And it is in vain for Celsus to add, "For he had no longer occasion to fear any man after his death, being, as you say, a God ; nor was he sent into the world at all for the purpose of being hid." Yet He was sent into the world not only to become known, but also to be hid. For all that He was, was not known even to those to whom He was known, but a certain part of Him remained concealed even from them ; and to some He was not known at all. And He opened the gates of light to those who were the sons of darkness and of night, and had devoted themselves to becoming the sons of light and of the day. For our Saviour Lord, like a good physician, came rather to us who were full of sins, than to those who were righteous.

CHAP. LXVIII.

But let us observe how this Jew of Celsus asserts that, "if this at least would have helped to manifest his divinity, he ought accordingly

---

[1] χρήσιμον δ' οἶμαι πρὸς ἀπολογίαν τῶν προκειμένων.
[2] Cf. Rom. xiv. 9.
[3] 1 Cor. xv. 52.
[4] Cf. 1 Cor. xv. 52 with 1 Thess. iv. 16.
[5] Cf. 1 Thess. iv. 13-15.
[6] 1 Cor. ii. 2.
[7] Cf. 1 Cor. iii. 2, 3.

[8] οὕτω μοι νόει καὶ τὸν υἱὸν τοῦ Θεοῦ ὦφθαι τῇ παραπλησίᾳ εἰς τὸ περὶ ἐκείνων, εἰς τὸ ὦφθαι αὐτοῖς τὸν Θεόν, κρίσει.
[9] Cf. Gen. xix. 10, 11. [Also Jude 7, "strange (or *other*) flesh."]

to have at once disappeared from the cross." Now this seems to me to be like the argument of those who oppose the doctrine of providence, and who arrange things differently from what they are, and allege that the world would be better if it were as they arrange it. Now, in those instances in which their arrangement is a possible one, they are proved to make the world, so far as depends upon them, worse by their arrangement than it actually is; while in those cases in which they do not portray things worse than they really are, they are shown to desire impossibilities; so that in either case they are deserving of ridicule. And here, accordingly, that there was no impossibility in His coming, as a being of diviner nature, in order to disappear when He chose, is clear from the very nature of the case; and is certain, moreover, from what is recorded of Him, in the judgment of those who do not adopt certain portions merely of the narrative that they may have ground for accusing Christianity, and who consider other portions to be fiction. For it is related in St. Luke's Gospel, that Jesus after His resurrection took bread, and blessed it, and breaking it, distributed it to Simon and Cleopas; and when they had received the bread, "their eyes were opened, and they knew Him, and He vanished out of their sight."[1]

CHAP. LXIX.

But we wish to show that His instantaneous bodily disappearance from the cross was not better fitted to serve the purposes of the whole economy of salvation (than His remaining upon it was). For the mere letter and narrative of the events which happened to Jesus do not present the whole view of the truth. For each one of them can be shown, to those who have an intelligent apprehension of Scripture, to be a symbol of something else. Accordingly, as His crucifixion contains a truth, represented in the words, "I am crucified with Christ," and intimated also in these, "God forbid that I should glory, save in the cross of our Lord Jesus Christ, by whom the world is crucified to me, and I unto the world;"[2] and as His death was necessary, because of the statement, "For in that He died, He died unto sin once,"[3] and this, "Being made conformable to His death,'[4] and this, "For if we be dead with Him, we shall also live with Him:"[5] so also His burial has an application to those who have been made conformable to His death, who have been both crucified with Him, and have died with Him; as is declared by Paul, "For we were buried with Him by bap-

tism, and have also risen with Him."[6] These matters, however, which relate to His burial, and His sepulchre, and him who buried Him, we shall expound at greater length on a more suitable occasion, when it will be our professed purpose to treat of such things. But, for the present, it is sufficient to notice the clean linen in which the pure body of Jesus was to be enwrapped, and the new tomb which Joseph had hewn out of the rock, where "no one was yet lying,"[7] or, as John expresses it, "wherein was never man yet laid."[8] And observe whether the harmony of the three evangelists here is not fitted to make an impression: for they have thought it right to describe the tomb as one that was "quarried or hewn out of the rock;" so that he who examines the words of the narrative may see something worthy of consideration, both in them and in the *newness* of the tomb, — a point mentioned by Matthew and John,[9] — and in the statement of Luke and John,[10] that no one had ever been interred therein before. For it became Him, who was unlike other dead men (but who even in death manifested signs of life in the water and the blood), and who was, so to speak, a *new* dead man, to be laid in a new and clean tomb, in order that, as His birth was purer than any other (in consequence of His being born, not in the way of ordinary generation, but of a virgin), His burial also might have the purity symbolically indicated in His body being deposited in a sepulchre which was new, not built of stones gathered from various quarters, and having no natural unity, but quarried and hewed out of *one* rock, united together in all its parts. Regarding the explanation, however, of these points, and the method of ascending from the narratives themselves to the things which they symbolized, one might treat more profoundly, and in a manner more adapted to their divine character, on a more suitable occasion, in a work expressly devoted to such subjects. The literal narrative, however, one might thus explain, viz., that it was appropriate for Him who had resolved to endure suspension upon the cross, to maintain all the accompaniments of the character He had assumed, in order that He who as a man had been put to death, and who as a man had died, might also as a man be buried. But even if it had been related in the Gospels, according to the view of Celsus, that Jesus had immediately disappeared from the cross, he and other unbelievers would have found fault with the narrative, and would have brought against it some such objection as this: "Why, pray, did he disappear after he had been put upon the cross, and not

[1] Cf. Luke xxiv. 30, 31.
[2] Cf. Gal. vi. 14.
[3] Rom. vi. 10.
[4] Phil. iii. 10.
[5] 2 Tim. ii. 11.

[6] Cf. Rom. vi. 4.
[7] Luke xxiii. 53, οὐκ ἦν οὔπω οὐδεὶς κείμενος.
[8] John xix. 41, ἐν ᾧ οὐδέπω οὐδεὶς ἐτέθη.
[9] Cf. Matt. xxvii. 60 with John xix. 41.
[10] Cf. Luke xxiii. 53 with John xix. 41.

disappear before he suffered?" If, then, after learning from the Gospels that He did not at once disappear from the cross, they imagine that they can find fault with the narrative, because it did not invent, as they consider it ought to have done, any such instantaneous disappearance, but gave a true account of the matter, is it not reasonable that they should accord their faith also to His resurrection, and should believe that He, according to His pleasure, on one occasion, when the doors were shut, stood in the midst of His disciples, and on another, after distributing bread to two of His acquaintances, immediately disappeared from view, after He had spoken to them certain words?

CHAP. LXX.

But how is it that this Jew of Celsus could say that Jesus concealed Himself? For his words regarding Him are these: "And who that is sent as a messenger ever conceals himself when he ought to make known his message?" Now, He did not conceal Himself, who said to those who sought to apprehend Him, "I was daily teaching openly in the temple, and ye laid no hold upon Me." But having once already answered this charge of Celsus, now again repeated, we shall content ourselves with what we have formerly said. We have answered, also, in the preceding pages, this objection, that "while he was in the body, and no one believed upon him, he preached to all without intermission; but when he might have produced a powerful belief in himself after rising from the dead, he showed himself secretly only to one woman, and to his own boon companions."[1] Now it is not true that He showed Himself only to one woman; for it is stated in the Gospel according to Matthew, that "in the end of the Sabbath, as it began to dawn towards the first day of the week, came Mary Magdalene, and the other Mary, to see the sepulchre. And, behold, there had been a great earthquake: for the angel of the Lord had descended from heaven, and come and rolled back the stone."[2] And, shortly after, Matthew adds: "And, behold, Jesus met *them*" — clearly meaning the afore-mentioned Marys — "saying, All hail. And they came and held Him by the feet, and worshipped Him."[3] And we answered, too, the charge, that "while undergoing his punishment he was seen by all, but after his resurrection only by one," when we offered our defence of the fact that "He was not seen by all." And now we might say that His merely human attributes were visible to all men, but those which were divine in their nature — I speak of the attributes not as related, but as distinct[4] — were not capable of being received by all. But observe here the manifest contradiction into which Celsus falls. For having said, a little before, that Jesus had appeared secretly to one woman and His own boon companions, he immediately subjoins: "While undergoing his punishment he was seen by all men, but after his resurrection by one, whereas the opposite ought to have happened." And let us hear what he means by "ought to have happened." The being seen by all men while undergoing His punishment, but after His resurrection only by one individual, are opposites.[5] Now, so far as his language conveys a meaning, he would have that to take place which is both impossible and absurd, viz., that while undergoing His punishment He should be seen only by one individual, but after His resurrection by all men! or else how will you explain his words, "The opposite ought to have happened?"

CHAP. LXXI.

Jesus taught us who it was that sent Him, in the words, "None knoweth the Father but the Son;"[6] and in these, "No man hath seen God at any time; the only-begotten Son, who is in the bosom of the Father, He hath declared Him."[7] He, treating of Deity, stated to His true disciples the doctrine regarding God; and we, discovering traces of such teaching in the Scripture narratives, take occasion from such to aid our theological conceptions,[8] hearing it declared in one passage, that "God is light, and in Him there is no darkness at all;"[9] and in another, "God is a Spirit, and they that worship Him must worship Him in spirit and in truth."[10] But the purposes for which the Father sent Him are innumerable; and these any one may ascertain who chooses, partly from the prophets who prophesied of Him, and partly from the narratives of the evangelists. And not a few things also will he learn from the apostles, and especially from Paul. Moreover, those who are pious He leadeth to the light, and those who sin He will punish, — a circumstance which Celsus not observing, has represented Him "as one who will lead the pious to the light, and who will have mercy on others, whether they sin or repent."[11]

---

[1] τοῖς ἑαυτοῦ θιασώταις.
[2] Matt. xxviii. 1, 2.
[3] Matt. xxviii. 9.

[4] λέγω δὲ οὐ περὶ τῶν σχέσιν πρὸς ἕτερα ἐχόντων, ἀλλὰ περὶ τῶν κατὰ διαφοράν.
[5] ἐναντίον τὸν μὲν κολαζόμενον πᾶσιν ἑωρᾶσθαι, ἀναστάντα δὲ ἑνί. The Benedictine editor reads τὸν μὲν κολαζόμενον, and Bohereau proposes ἐναντίον τῷ κολαζομένῳ μὲν, etc.
[6] Cf. Luke x. 22.
[7] John i. 18.
[8] ὧν ἴχνη ἐν τοῖς γεγραμμένοις εὑρίσκοντες ἀφορμὰς ἔχομεν θεολογεῖν.
[9] 1 John i. 5.
[10] John iv. 24.
[11] The text is, τοὺς δὲ ἁμαρτάνοντας ἢ μεταγνόντας ἐλεήσων. Bohereau would read μὴ μεταγνόντας, or would render the passage as if the reading were ἢ ἁμαρτάνοντας, ἢ μεταγνόντας. This suggestion has been adopted in the translation.

CHAP. LXXII.

After the above statements, he continues : " If he wished to remain hid, why was there heard a voice from heaven proclaiming him to be the Son of God ? And if he did not seek to remain concealed, why was he punished ? or why did he die ?" Now, by such questions he thinks to convict the histories of discrepancy, not observing that Jesus neither desired all things regarding Himself to be known to all whom He happened to meet, nor yet all things to be unknown. Accordingly, the voice from heaven which proclaimed Him to be the Son of God, in the words, " This is my beloved Son, in whom I am well pleased," [1] is not stated to have been audible to the multitudes, as this Jew of Celsus supposed. The voice from the cloud on the high mountain, moreover, was heard only by those who had gone up with Him. For the divine voice is of such a nature, as to be heard only by those whom the speaker wishes to hear it. And I maintain, that the voice of God which is referred to, is neither air which has been struck, nor any concussion of the air, nor anything else which is mentioned in treatises on the voice ; [2] and therefore it is heard by a better and more divine organ of hearing than that of sense. And when the speaker will not have his voice to be heard by all, he that has the finer ear hears the voice of God, while he who has the ears of his soul deadened does not perceive that it is God who speaks. These things I have mentioned because of his asking, " Why was there heard a voice from heaven proclaiming him to be the Son of God ?" while with respect to the query, " Why was he punished, if he wished to remain hid ?" what has been stated at greater length in the preceding pages on the subject of His suffering may suffice.

CHAP. LXXIII.

The Jew proceeds, after this, to state as a consequence what does not follow from the premises ; for it does *not* follow from " His having wished, by the punishments which He underwent, to teach us also to despise death," that after His resurrection He should openly summon all men to the light, and instruct them in the object of His coming. For He had formerly summoned all men to the light in the words, " Come unto Me, all ye that labour and are heavy laden, and I will give you rest." [3] And the object of His coming had been explained at great length in His discourses on the beatitudes, and in the announcements which followed them, and in the parables, and in His conversations with the scribes and Pharisees. And the instruction afforded us by the Gospel of John, shows that the eloquence of Jesus consisted not in words, but in deeds ; while it is manifest from the Gospel narratives that His speech was " with power," on which account also they marvelled at Him.

CHAP. LXXIV.

In addition to all this, the Jew further says : " All these statements are taken from your own books, in addition to which we need no other witness ; for ye fall upon your own swords." [4] Now we have proved that many foolish assertions, opposed to the narratives of our Gospels, occur in the statements of the Jew, either with respect to Jesus or ourselves. And I do not think that he has shown that " we fall upon our own swords ; " but he only so imagines. And when the Jew adds, in a general way, this to his former remarks : " O most high and heavenly one ! what God, on appearing to men, is received with incredulity ? " we must say to him, that according to the accounts in the law of Moses, God is related to have visited the Hebrews in a most public manner, not only in the signs and wonders performed in Egypt, and also in the passage of the Red Sea, and in the pillar of fire and cloud of light, but also when the Decalogue was announced to the whole people, and yet was received with incredulity by those who saw these things : for had they believed what they saw and heard, they would not have fashioned the calf, nor changed their own glory into the likeness of a grass-eating calf ; nor would they have said to one another with reference to the calf, " These be thy gods, O Israel, who brought thee up out of the land of Egypt." [5] And observe whether it is not entirely in keeping with the character of the same people, who formerly refused to believe such wonders and such appearances of divinity, throughout the whole period of wandering in the wilderness, as they are recorded in the law of the Jews to have done, to refuse to be convinced also, on occasion of the glorious advent of Jesus, by the mighty words which were spoken by Him with authority, and the marvels which He performed in the presence of all the people.

CHAP. LXXV.

I think what has been stated is enough to convince any one that the unbelief of the Jews with regard to Jesus was in keeping with what is related of this people from the beginning. For I would say in reply to this Jew of Celsus, when he asks, " What God that appeared among men is received with incredulity, and that, too, when

---

[1] Matt. iii. 17.
[2] οὐδέπω δὲ λέγω, ὅτι οὐ πάντως ἐστὶν ἀὴρ πεπληγμένος· ἡ πληγὴ ἀέρος, ἤ ὅ τι ποτὲ λέγεται ἐν τοῖς περὶ φωνῆς.
[3] Cf. Matt. xi. 28.

[4] αὐτοὶ γὰρ ἑαυτοῖς περιπίπτετε. [See note *supra*, cap. xiii. p. 437. S.]
[5] Cf. Ex. xxxii. 4.

appearing to those who expect him? or why, pray, is he not recognized by those who have been long looking for him?" what answer, friends, would you have us return to your [1] questions? Which class of miracles, in your judgment, do you regard as the greater? Those which were wrought in Egypt and the wilderness, or those which we declare that Jesus performed among you? For if the former are in your opinion greater than the latter, does it not appear from this very fact to be in conformity with the character of those who disbelieved the greater to despise the less? And this is the opinion entertained with respect to our accounts of the miracles of Jesus. But if those related of Jesus are considered to be as great as those recorded of Moses, what strange thing has come to pass among a nation which has manifested incredulity with regard to the commencement of both dispensations?[2] For the·beginning of the legislation was in the time of Moses, in whose work are recorded the sins of the unbelievers and wicked among you, while the commencement of our legislation and second covenant is admitted to have been in the time of Jesus. And by your unbelief of Jesus ye show that ye are the sons of those who in the desert discredited the divine appearances; and thus what was spoken by our Saviour will be applicable also to you who believed not on Him: "Therefore ye bear witness that ye allow the deeds of your fathers."[3] And there is fulfilled among you also the prophecy which said: "Your life shall hang in doubt before your eyes, and you will have no assurance of your life."[4] For ye did not believe in the life which came to visit the human race.

CHAP. LXXVI.

Celsus, in adopting the character of a Jew, could not discover any objections to be urged against the Gospel which might not be retorted on him as liable to be brought also against the law and the prophets. For he censures Jesus in such words as the following: "He makes use of threats, and reviles men on light grounds, when he says, 'Woe unto you,' and 'I tell you beforehand.' For by such expressions he manifestly acknowledges his inability to persuade; and this would not be the case with a God, or even a prudent man." Observe, now, whether these charges do not manifestly recoil upon the Jew. For in the writings of the law and the prophets God makes use of threats and revilings, when He employs language of not less severity than that

found in the Gospel, such as the following expressions of Isaiah: "Woe unto them that join house to house, and lay field to field;"[5] and, "Woe unto them that rise up early in the morning that they may follow strong drink;"[6] and, "Woe unto them that draw their sins after them as with a long rope;"[7] and, "Woe unto them that call evil good, and good evil;"[8] and, "Woe unto those of you who are mighty to drink wine;"[9] and innumerable other passages of the same kind. And does not the following resemble the threats of which he speaks: "Ah sinful nation, a people laden with iniquity, a seed of evildoers, children that are corrupters?"[10] and so on, to which he subjoins such threats as are equal in severity to those which, he says, Jesus made use of. For is it not a threatening, and a great one, which declares, "Your country is desolate, your cities are burned with fire: your land, strangers devour it in your presence, and it is desolate, as overthrown by strangers?"[11] And are there not revilings in Ezekiel directed against the people, when the Lord says to the prophet, "Thou dwellest in the midst of scorpions?"[12] Were you serious, then, Celsus, in representing the Jew as saying of Jesus, that "he makes use of threats and revilings on slight grounds, when he employs the expressions, 'Woe unto you,' and 'I tell you beforehand?'" Do you not see that the charges which this Jew of yours brings against Jesus might be brought by him against God? For the God who speaks in the prophetic writings is manifestly liable to the same accusations, as Celsus regards them, of inability to persuade. I might, moreover, say to this Jew, who thinks that he makes a good charge against Jesus by such statements, that if he undertakes, in support of the scriptural account, to defend the numerous curses recorded in the books of Leviticus and Deuteronomy, we should make as good, or better, a defence of the revilings and threatenings which are regarded as having been spoken by Jesus. And as respects the law of Moses itself, we are in a position to make a better defence of it than the Jew is, because we have been taught by Jesus to have a more intelligent apprehension of the writings of the law. Nay, if the Jew perceive the meaning of the prophetic Scriptures, he will be able to show that it is for no light reason that God employs threatenings and revilings, when He says, "Woe unto you," and "I tell you beforehand." And how should God employ such expressions for the conversion of men, which Celsus thinks that even

---

[1] The text reads ἡμῶν, for which Bohereau and the Benedictine editor propose either ὑμᾶς or ἡμᾶς, the former of which is preferred by Lommatzsch.

[2] κατ' ἀμφοτέρας τὰς ἀρχὰς τῶν πραγμάτων ἀπιστοῦντι;

[3] Cf. Luke xi. 48.

[4] Cf. Deut. xxviii. 66.

[5] Isa. v. 8.
[6] Isa. v. 11.
[7] Isa. v. 18.
[8] Isa. v. 20.
[9] Isa. v. 22.
[10] Cf. Isa. i. 4.
[11] Isa. i. 7.
[12] Ezek. ii. 6.

a prudent man would not have recourse to? But Christians, who know only one God — the same who spoke in the prophets and in the Lord (Jesus) — can prove the reasonableness of those threatenings and revilings, as Celsus considers and entitles them. And here a few remarks shall be addressed to this Celsus, who professes both to be a philosopher, and to be acquainted with all our system. How is it, friend, when Hermes, in Homer, says to Odysseus,

"Why, now, wretched man, do you come wandering alone over the mountain-tops?"[1]

that you are satisfied with the answer, which explains that the Homeric Hermes addresses such language to Odysseus to remind him of his duty,[2] because it is characteristic of the Sirens to flatter and to say pleasing things, around whom

"Is a huge heap of bones,"[3]

and who say,

"Come hither, much lauded Odysseus, great glory of the Greeks;"[4]

whereas, if our prophets and Jesus Himself, in order to turn their hearers from evil, make use of such expressions as "Woe unto you," and what you regard as revilings, there is no condescension in such language to the circumstances of the hearers, nor any application of such words to them as healing[5] medicine? Unless, indeed, you would have God, or one who partakes of the divine nature, when conversing with men, to have regard to His own nature alone, and to what is worthy of Himself, but to have no regard to what is fitting to be brought before men who are under the dispensation and leading of His word, and with each one of whom He is to converse agreeably to his individual character. And is it not a ridiculous assertion regarding Jesus, to say that He was unable to persuade men, when you compare the state of matters not only among the Jews, who have many such instances recorded in the prophecies, but also among the Greeks, among whom all of those who have attained great reputation for their wisdom have been unable to persuade those who conspired against them, or to induce their judges or accusers to cease from evil, and to endeavour to attain to virtue by the way of philosophy?

CHAP. LXXVII.

After this the Jew remarks, manifestly in accordance with the Jewish belief: "We certainly hope that there will be a bodily resurrection, and that we shall enjoy an eternal life; and the example and archetype of this will be He who is

sent to us, and who will show that nothing is impossible with God." We do not know, indeed, whether the Jew would say of the expected Christ, that He exhibits in Himself an example of the resurrection; but let it be supposed that he both thinks and says so. We shall give this answer, then, to him who has told us that he drew his information from our own writings: "Did you read those writings, friend, in which you think you discover matter of accusation against us, and not find there the resurrection of Jesus, and the declaration that He was the first-born from the dead? Or because you will not allow such things to have been recorded, were they not actually recorded?" But as the Jew still admits the resurrection of the body, I do not consider the present a suitable time to discuss the subject with one who both believes and says that there is a bodily resurrection, whether he has an articulate[6] understanding of such a topic, and is able to plead well on its behalf,[7] or not, but has only given his assent to it as being of a legendary character.[8] Let the above, then, be our reply to this Jew of Celsus. And when he adds, "Where, then, is he, that we may see him and believe upon him?" we answer: Where is He now who spoke in the prophecies, and who wrought miracles, that we may see and believe that He is part of God? Are *you* to be allowed to meet the objection, that God does not perpetually show Himself to the Hebrew nation, while *we* are not to be permitted the same defence with regard to Jesus, who has both once risen Himself, and led His disciples to believe in His resurrection, and so thoroughly persuaded them of its truth, that they show to all men by their sufferings how they are able to laugh at all the troubles of life, beholding the life eternal and the resurrection clearly demonstrated to them both in word and deed?

CHAP. LXXVIII.

The Jew continues: "Did Jesus come into the world for this purpose, that we should not believe him?" To which we immediately answer, that He did not come with the object of producing incredulity among the Jews; but knowing beforehand that such would be the result, He foretold it, and made use of their unbelief for the calling of the Gentiles. For through their sin salvation came to the Gentiles, respecting whom the Christ who speaks in the prophecies says, "A people whom I did not know became subject to Me: they were obedient to the hearing of My ear;"[9] and, "I was found of them who sought Me not; I became manifest to those

---

[1] Cf. *Odyss.*, x. 281.
[2] ὑπὲρ ἐπιστροφῆς.
[3] Cf. *Odyss.*, xii. 45.
[4] *Ibid.*, xii. 184.
[5] παιώνιον φάρμακον.

[6] εἴτε διαρθροῦντα τὸ τοιοῦτον παρ᾽ ἑαυτῷ.
[7] καὶ δυνάμενον πρεσβεῦσαι περὶ τοῦ λόγου καλῶς.
[8] ἀλλὰ μυθικώτερον συγκατατιθέμενον
[9] Cf. 2 Sam. xxii. 44, 45.

who inquired not after Me." [1] It is certain, moreover, that the Jews were punished even in this present life, after treating Jesus in the manner in which they did. And let the Jews assert what they will when we charge them with guilt, and say, "Is not the providence and goodness of God most wonderfully displayed in your punishment, and in your being deprived of Jerusalem, and of the sanctuary, and of your splendid worship?" For whatever they may say in reply with respect to the providence of God, we shall be able more effectually to answer it by remarking, that the providence of God was wonderfully manifested in using the transgression of that people for the purpose of calling into the kingdom of God, through Jesus Christ, those from among the Gentiles who were strangers to the covenant and aliens to the promises. And these things were foretold by the prophets, who said that, on account of the transgressions of the Hebrew nation, God would make choice, not of a nation, but of individuals chosen from all lands; [2] and, having selected the foolish things of the world, would cause an ignorant nation to become acquainted with the divine teaching, the kingdom of God being taken from the one and given to the other. And out of a larger number it is sufficient on the present occasion to adduce the prediction from the song in Deuteronomy regarding the calling of the Gentiles, which is as follows, being spoken in the person of the Lord: "They have moved Me to jealousy with those who are not gods; they have provoked Me to anger with their idols: and I will move them to jealousy with those who are not a people; I will provoke them to anger with a foolish nation." [3]

CHAP. LXXIX.

The conclusion of all these arguments regarding Jesus is thus stated by the Jew: "He was therefore a man, and of such a nature, as the truth itself proves, and reason demonstrates him to be." I do not know, however, whether a man who had the courage to spread throughout the entire world his doctrine of religious worship and teaching, [4] could accomplish what he wished

without the divine assistance, and could rise superior to all who withstood the progress of his doctrine — kings and rulers, and the Roman senate, and governors in all places, and the common people. And how could the nature of a man possessed of no inherent excellence convert so vast a multitude? For it would not be wonderful if it were only the wise who were so converted; but it is the most irrational of men and those devoted to their passions, and who by reason of their irrationality, change with the greater difficulty so as to adopt a more temperate course of life. And yet it is because Christ was the power of God and the wisdom of the Father that He accomplished, and still accomplishes, such results, although neither the Jews nor Greeks who disbelieve His word will so admit. And therefore we shall not cease to believe in God, according to the precepts of Jesus Christ, and to seek to convert those who are blind on the subject of religion, although it is they who are truly blind themselves that charge us with blindness: and they, whether Jews or Greeks, who lead astray those that follow them, accuse us of seducing men — a good seduction, truly! — that they may become temperate instead of dissolute, or at least may make advances to temperance; may become just instead of unjust, or at least may tend to become so; prudent instead of foolish, or be on the way to become such; and instead of cowardice, meanness, and timidity, may exhibit the virtues of fortitude and courage, especially displayed in the struggles undergone for the sake of their religion towards God, the Creator of all things. Jesus Christ therefore came announced beforehand, not by one prophet, but by all; and it was a proof of the ignorance of Celsus, to represent a Jew as saying that one prophet only had predicted the advent of Christ. But as this Jew of Celsus, after being thus introduced, asserting that these things were indeed in conformity with his own law, has somewhere here ended his discourse, with a mention of other matters not worthy of remembrance, I too shall here terminate this second book of my answer to his treatise. But if God permit, and the power of Christ abide in my soul, I shall endeavour in the third book to deal with the subsequent statements of Celsus.

---

[1] Cf. Isa. lxv. 1.
[2] οὐχὶ ἔθνος, ἀλλὰ λογάδας πανταχόθεν.
[3] Cf. Deut. xxxii. 21.
[4] τὴν κατ' αὐτὸν θεοσέβειαν καὶ διδασκαλίαν.

ORIGEN AGAINST CELSUS.

BOOK III.

CHAP. I.

IN the first book of our answer to the work of Celsus, who had boastfully entitled the treatise which he had composed against us *A True Discourse*, we have gone through, as you enjoined, my faithful Ambrosius, to the best of our ability, his preface, and the parts immediately following it, testing each one of his assertions as we went along, until we finished with the tirade[1] of this Jew of his, feigned to have been delivered against Jesus. And in the second book we met, as we best could, all the charges contained in the invective[1] of the said Jew, which were levelled at us who are believers in God through Christ; and now we enter upon this third division of our discourse, in which our object is to refute the allegations which he makes in his own person.

He gives it as his opinion, that "the controversy between Jews and Christians is a most foolish one," and asserts that "the discussions which we have with each other regarding Christ differ in no respect from what is called in the proverb, 'a fight about the shadow of an ass;'"[2] and thinks that "there is nothing of importance[3] in the investigations of the Jews and Christians: for both believe that it was predicted by the Divine Spirit that one was to come as a Saviour to the human race, but do not yet agree on the point whether the person predicted has actually come or not." For we Christians, indeed, have believed in Jesus, as He who came according to the predictions of the prophets. But the majority of the Jews are so far from believing in Him, that those of them who lived at the time of His coming conspired against Him; and those of the present day, approving of what the Jews of former times dared to do against Him, speak evil of Him, asserting that it was by means of sorcery[4] that he passed himself off for Him who

was predicted by the prophets as the One who was to come, and who was called, agreeably to the traditions of the Jews,[5] the Christ.

CHAP. II.

But let Celsus, and those who assent to his charges, tell us whether it is at all like "an ass's shadow," that the Jewish prophets should have predicted the birth-place of Him who was to be the ruler of those who had lived righteous lives, and who are called the "heritage" of God;[6] and that Emmanuel should be conceived by a virgin; and that such signs and wonders should be performed by Him who was the subject of prophecy; and that His word should have such speedy course, that the voice of His apostles should go forth into all the earth; and that He should undergo certain sufferings after His condemnation by the Jews; and that He should rise again from the dead. For was it by chance[7] that the prophets made these announcements, with no persuasion of the truth in their minds,[8] moving them not only to speak, but to deem their announcements worthy of being committed to writing? And did so great a nation as that of the Jews, who had long ago received a country of their own wherein to dwell, recognise certain men as prophets, and reject others as utterers of false predictions, without any conviction of the soundness of the distinction?[8] And was there no motive which induced them to class with the books of Moses, which were held as sacred, the words of those persons who were afterwards deemed to be prophets? And can those who charge the Jews and Christians with folly, show us how the Jewish nation could have continued to subsist, had there existed among them no promise of the knowledge of future events? and how, while each of the surrounding nations believed, agreeably to their ancient institutions, that they

---

[1] δημηγορίας: cf. book i. c. 71.
[2] κατὰ τὴν παροιμίαν καλουμένης ὄνου σκιᾶς μάχης. On this proverb, see Zenobius, *Centuria Sexta*, adag. 28, and the note of Schottius. Cf. also Suidas, s.v. ὄνου σκιά. — DE LA RUE.
[3] σεμνόν.
[4] διά τινος γοητείας.

[5] κατὰ τὰ Ἰουδαίων πάτρια.
[6] τῶν χρηματιζόντων μερίδος Θεοῦ.
[7] ἆρα γὰρ ὡς ἔτυχε.
[8] σὺν οὐδεμιᾷ πιθανότητι.

received oracles and predictions from those whom they accounted gods, this people alone, who were taught to view with contempt all those who were considered gods by the heathen, as not being gods, but demons, according to the declaration of the prophets, " For all the gods of the nations are demons," [1] had among them no one who professed to be a prophet, and who could restrain such as, from a desire to know the future, were ready to desert [2] to the demons [1] of other nations? Judge, then, whether it were not a necessity, that as the whole nation had been taught to despise the deities of other lands, they should have had an abundance of prophets, who made known events which were of far greater importance in themselves,[3] and which surpassed the oracles of all other countries.

CHAP. III.

In the next place, miracles were performed in all countries, or at least in many of them, as Celsus himself admits, instancing the case of Æsculapius, who conferred benefits on many, and who foretold future events to entire cities, which were dedicated to him, such as Tricca, and Epidaurus, and Cos, and Pergamus ; and along with Æsculapius he mentions Aristeas of Proconnesus, and a certain Clazomenian, and Cleomedes of Astypalæa. But among the Jews alone, who say they are dedicated to the God of all things, there was wrought no miracle or sign which might help to confirm their faith in the Creator of all things, and strengthen their hope of another and better life ! But how can they imagine such a state of things? For they would immediately have gone over to the worship of those demons which gave oracles and performed cures, and deserted the God who was believed, as far as words went,[4] to assist them, but who never manifested to them His visible presence. But if this result has not taken place, and if, on the contrary, they have suffered countless calamities rather than renounce Judaism and their law, and have been cruelly treated, at one time in Assyria, at another in Persia, and at another under Antiochus, is it not in keeping with the probabilities of the case [5] for those to suppose who do not yield their belief to their miraculous histories and prophecies, that the events in question could not be inventions, but that a certain divine Spirit being in the holy souls of the prophets, as of men who underwent

any labour for the cause of virtue, *did* move them to prophesy some things relating to their contemporaries, and others to their posterity but chiefly regarding a certain personage who was to come as a Saviour to the human race?

CHAP. IV.

And if the above be the state of the case how do Jews and Christians search after " the shadow of an ass," in seeking to ascertain from those prophecies which they believe in common whether He who was foretold has come, or has not yet arrived, and is still an object of expectation? But even suppose [6] it be granted to Celsus that it was not Jesus who was announced by the prophets, then, even on such a hypothesis, the investigation of the sense of the prophetic writings is no search after " the shadow of an ass," if He who was spoken of can be clearly pointed out, and it can be shown both what sort of person He was predicted to be, and what He was to do, and, if possible, when He was to arrive. But in the preceding pages we have already spoken on the point of Jesus being the individual who was foretold to be the Christ, quoting a few prophecies out of a larger number. Neither Jews nor Christians, then, are wrong in assuming that the prophets spoke under divine influence ; [7] but they are in error who form erroneous opinions respecting Him who was expected to be the prophets to come, and whose person and character were made known in their " true discourses."[8]

CHAP. V.

Immediately after these points, Celsus, imagining that the Jews are Egyptians by descent, and had abandoned Egypt, after revolting against the Egyptian state, and despising the customs of that people in matters of worship, says that " they suffered from the adherents of Jesus, who believed in Him as the Christ, the same treatment which they had inflicted upon the Egyptians ; and that the cause which led to the new state of things [8] in either instance was rebellion against the state." Now let us observe what Celsus has here done. The ancient Egyptians, after inflicting many cruelties upon the Hebrew race, who had settled in Egypt owing to a famine which had broken out in Judea, suffered, in consequence of their injustice to strangers and suppliants, that punishment which divine Providence had decreed was to fall on the whole nation for having combined against an entire people, who had been their guests, and who had done them no harm ; and after being smitten by plagues from God, they allowed them, with difficulty,

---

[1] Ps. xcvi. 5, δαιμόνια, "idols," Auth. Vers. We have in this passage, and in many others, the identification of the δαίμονες or gods of the heathen with the δαίμονες or δαιμόνια, "evil spirits," or angels, supposed to be mentioned in Gen. vi. 2.

[2] The reading in the text is αὐτομολεῖν, on which Bohereau, with whom the Benedictine editor agrees, remarks that we must either read αὐτομολήσοντας, or understand some such word as ἑτοίμους before αὐτομολεῖν.

[3] τὸ μεῖζον αὐτόθεν.

[4] μέχρι λόγου.

[5] πῶς οὐχὶ ἐξ εἰκότων κατασκευάζεται.

[6] καθ' ὑπόθεσιν.

[7] θεόθεν.

[8] Τῆς καινοτομίας.

and after a brief period, to go wherever they liked, as being unjustly detained in slavery. Because, then, they were a selfish people, who honoured those who were in any degree related to them far more than they did strangers of better lives, there is not an accusation which they have omitted to bring against Moses and the Hebrews, — not altogether denying, indeed, the miracles and wonders done by him, but alleging that they were wrought by sorcery, and not by divine power. Moses, however, not as a magician, but as a devout man, and one devoted to the God of all things, and a partaker in the divine Spirit, both enacted laws for the Hebrews, according to the suggestions of the Divinity, and recorded events as they happened with perfect fidelity.

CHAP. VI.

Celsus, therefore, not investigating in a spirit of impartiality the facts, which are related by the Egyptians in one way, and by the Hebrews in another, but being bewitched, as it were,[1] in favour of the former, accepted as true the statements of those who had oppressed the strangers, and declared that the Hebrews, who had been unjustly treated, had departed from Egypt after revolting against the Egyptians, — not observing how impossible it was for so great a multitude of rebellious Egyptians to become a nation, which, dating its origin from the said revolt, should change its language at the time of its rebellion, so that those who up to that time made use of the Egyptian tongue, should completely adopt, all at once, the language of the Hebrews ! Let it be granted, however, according to his supposition, that on abandoning Egypt they did conceive a hatred also of their mother tongue,[2] how did it happen that after so doing they did not rather adopt the Syrian or Phœnician language, instead of preferring the Hebrew, which is different from both ? But reason seems to me to demonstrate that the statement is false, which makes those who were Egyptians by race to have revolted against Egyptians, and to have left the country, and to have proceeded to Palestine, and occupied the land now called Judea. For Hebrew was the language of their fathers before their descent into Egypt ; and the Hebrew letters, employed by Moses in writing those five books which are deemed sacred by the Jews, were different from those of the Egyptians.

CHAP. VII.

In like manner, as the statement is false " that the Hebrews, being (originally) Egyptians, dated the commencement (of their political existence) from the time of their rebellion," so also is this,

" that in the days of Jesus others who were Jews rebelled against the Jewish state, and became His followers ; " for neither Celsus nor they who think with him are able to point out any act on the part of Christians which savours of rebellion. And yet, if a revolt had led to the formation of the Christian commonwealth, so that it derived its existence in this way from that of the Jews, who were permitted to take up arms in defence of the members of their families, and to slay their enemies, the Christian Lawgiver would not have altogether forbidden the putting of men to death ; and yet He nowhere teaches that it is right for His own disciples to offer violence to any one, however wicked. For He did not deem it in keeping with such laws as His, which were derived from a divine source, to allow the killing of any individual whatever. Nor would the Christians, had they owed their origin to a rebellion, have adopted laws of so exceedingly mild a character as not to allow them, when it was their fate to be slain as sheep, on any occasion to resist their persecutors. And truly, if we look a little deeper into things, we may say regarding the exodus from Egypt, that it is a miracle if a whole nation *at once* adopted the language called Hebrew, as if it had been a gift from heaven, when one of their own prophets said, " As they went forth from Egypt, they heard a language which they did not understand." [3]

CHAP. VIII.

In the following way, also, we may conclude that they who came out of Egypt with Moses were not Egyptians ; for if they had been Egyptians, their *names* also would be Egyptian, because in every language the designations (of persons and things) are kindred to the language.[4] But if it is certain, from the names being Hebrew, that the people were not Egyptians, — and the Scriptures are full of Hebrew names, and these bestowed, too, upon their children while they were in Egypt, — it is clear that the Egyptian account is false, which asserts that they were Egyptians, and went forth from Egypt with Moses. Now it is absolutely certain[5] that, being descended, as the Mosaic history records, from Hebrew ancestors, they employed a language from which they also took the names which they conferred upon their children. But with regard to the Christians, because they were taught not to avenge themselves upon their enemies (and have thus observed laws of a mild and philanthropic character) ; and because they would not, although able, have made war even if they had received authority to do so, — they have obtained this reward from God, that He

---

[1] Προκαταληφθεὶς ὡς ὑπὸ φίλτρων τῶν Αἰγυπτίων.
[2] Τὴν σύντροφον φωνήν.

[3] Cf. Ps. lxxxi. 5.
[4] Συγγενεῖς εἰσιν αἱ προσηγορίαι.
[5] Σαφῶς ἐναργές.

has always warred in their behalf, and on certain occasions has restrained those who rose up against them and desired to destroy them. For in order to remind others, that by seeing a *few* engaged in a struggle for their religion, they also might be better fitted to despise death, some, on special occasions, and these individuals who can be easily numbered, have endured death for the sake of Christianity, — God not permitting the whole nation to be exterminated, but desiring that it should continue, and that the whole world should be filled with this salutary and religious doctrine.[1] And again, on the other hand, that those who were of weaker minds might recover their courage and rise superior to the thought of death, God interposed His providence on behalf of believers, dispersing by an act of His will alone all the conspiracies formed against them ; so that neither kings, nor rulers, nor the populace, might be able to rage against them beyond a certain point. Such, then, is our answer to the assertions of Celsus, "that a revolt was the original commencement of the ancient Jewish state, and subsequently of Christianity."

CHAP. IX.

But since he is manifestly guilty of falsehood in the statements which follow, let us examine his assertion when he says, "If all men wished to become Christians, the latter would not desire such a result." Now that the above statement is false is clear from this, that Christians do not neglect, as far as in them lies, to take measures to disseminate their doctrine throughout the whole world. Some of them, accordingly, have made it their business to itinerate not only through cities, but even villages and country houses,[2] that they might make converts to God. And no one would maintain that they did this for the sake of gain, when sometimes they would not accept even necessary sustenance ; or if at any time they were pressed by a necessity of this sort, were contented with the mere supply of their wants, although many were willing to share (their abundance) with them, and to bestow help upon them far above their need. At the present day, indeed, when, owing to the multitude of Christian believers, not only rich men, but persons of rank, and delicate and high-born ladies, receive the teachers of Christianity, some perhaps will dare to say that it is for the sake of a little glory[3] that certain individuals assume the office of Christian instructors. It is impossible, however, rationally to entertain such a suspicion

with respect to Christianity in its beginnings, whe[re] the danger incurred, especially by its teachers was great ; while at the present day the dis[?] credit attaching to it among the rest of mankin[d] is greater than any supposed honour enjoye[d] among those who hold the same belief, espe[?] cially when such honour is not shared by all. I[t] is false, then, from the very nature of the case to say that "if all men wished to become Chris[?] tians, the latter would not desire such a result."

CHAP. X.

But observe what he alleges as a proof of hi[s] statement : "Christians at first were few in num[?] ber, and held the same opinions ; but when the[y] grew to be a great multitude, they were divide[d] and separated, each wishing to have his ow[n] individual party :[4] for this was their object from the beginning." That Christians at first wer[e] few in number, in comparison with the multi[?] tudes who subsequently became Christian, is un[?] doubted ; and yet, all things considered, the[y] were not so very few.[5] For what stirred up th[e] envy of the Jews against Jesus, and arouse[d] them to conspire against Him, was the grea[t] number of those who followed Him into th[e] wilderness, — five thousand men on one occa[?] sion, and four thousand on another, having at tended Him thither, without including the wome[n] and children. For such was the charm[6] of Je sus' words, that not only were *men* willing t[o] follow Him to the wilderness, but *women* also forgetting[7] the weakness of their sex and a re gard for outward propriety[8] in thus followin[g] their Teacher into desert places. Children, too who are altogether unaffected by such emotions, either following their parents, or perhaps at tracted also by His divinity, in order that i[t] might be implanted within them, became Hi[s] followers along with their parents. But let i[t] be granted that Christians were few in numbe[r] at the beginning, how does that help to prov[e] that Christians would be unwilling to make al[l] men believe the doctrine of the Gospel ?

CHAP. XI.

He says, in addition, that "all the Christian[s] were of one mind," not observing, even in thi[s] particular, that from the beginning there wer[e] differences of opinion among believers regardin[g] the meaning[10] of the books held to be divine At all events, while the apostles were still preach ing, and while eye-witnesses of (the works of

---

[1] [Gibbon, in the sixteenth chapter of his *Decline and Fall of the Roman Empire*, quotes the first part of this sentence as proving that "the learned Origen declares, in the most express terms, that the number of martyrs was very inconsiderable." But see Guizot's note on the passage. S.]

[2] Ἐπαύλεις.

[3] Δοξάριον.

[4] στάσεις ἰδίας.

[5] καί τοι οὐ πάντη ἦσαν ὀλίγοι.

[6] ἴυγξ.

[7] The reading in Spencer's and the Benedictine edition is ὑπο τεμνομένας, for which Lommatzsch reads ὑπομεμνημένας.

[8] καὶ τὸ δοκοῦν.

[9] ἀπαθέστατα.

[10] Ἐκδοχήν.

esus were still teaching His doctrine, there was no small discussion among the converts from Judaism regarding Gentile believers, on the point whether they ought to observe Jewish customs, or should reject the burden of clean and unclean meats, as not being obligatory on those who had abandoned their ancestral Gentile customs, and had become believers in Jesus. Nay, even in the Epistles of Paul, who was contemporary with those who had seen Jesus, certain particulars are found mentioned as having been the subject of dispute, — viz., respecting the resurrection,[1] and whether it were already past, and the day of the Lord, whether it were nigh at hand[2] or not. Nay, the very exhortation to "avoid profane and vain babblings, and oppositions of science falsely so called : which some professing, have erred concerning the faith,"[3] is enough to show that from the very beginning, when, as Celsus imagines, believers were few in number, there were certain doctrines interpreted in different ways.[4]

CHAP. XII.

In the next place, since he reproaches us with the existence of heresies in Christianity as being a ground of accusation against it, saying that 'when Christians had greatly increased in numbers, they were divided and split up into factions, each individual desiring to have his own party ;" and further, that " being thus separated through their numbers, they confute one another, still having, so to speak, one *name* in common, if indeed they still retain it. And this is the only thing which they are yet ashamed to abandon, while other matters are determined in different ways by the various sects." In reply to which, we say that heresies of different kinds have never originated from any matter in which the principle involved was not important and beneficial to human life. For since the science of medicine is useful and necessary to the human race, and many are the points of dispute in it respecting the manner of curing bodies, there are found, for this reason, numerous heresies confessedly prevailing in the science of medicine among the Greeks, and also, I suppose, among those barbarous nations who profess to employ medicine. And, again, since philosophy makes a profession of the truth, and promises a knowledge of existing things with a view to the regulation of life, and endeavours to teach what is advantageous to our race, and since the investigation of these matters is attended with great differences of opinion,[5] innumerable heresies have conse-

quently sprung up in philosophy, some of which are more celebrated than others. Even Judaism itself afforded a pretext for the origination of heresies, in the different acceptation accorded to the writings of Moses and those of the prophets. So, then, seeing Christianity appeared an object of veneration to men, not to the more servile class alone, as Celsus supposes, but to many among the Greeks who were devoted to literary pursuits,[6] there necessarily originated heresies, — not at all, however, as the result of faction and strife, but through the earnest desire of many literary men to become acquainted with the doctrines of Christianity. The consequence of which was, that, taking in different acceptations those discourses which were believed by all to be divine, there arose heresies, which received their names from those individuals who admired, indeed, the origin of Christianity, but who were led, in some way or other, by certain plausible reasons, to discordant views. And yet no one would act rationally in avoiding medicine because of its heresies ; nor would he who aimed at that which is seemly[7] entertain a hatred of philosophy, and adduce its many heresies as a pretext for his antipathy. And so neither are the sacred books of Moses and the prophets to be condemned on account of the heresies in Judaism.

CHAP. XIII.

Now, if these arguments hold good, why should we not defend, in the same way, the existence of heresies in Christianity? And respecting these, Paul appears to me to speak in a very striking manner when he says, " For there must be heresies among you, that they who are approved may be made manifest among you."[8] For as that man is "approved" in medicine who, on account of his experience in various (medical) heresies, and his honest examination of the majority of them, has selected the preferable system, — and as the great proficient in philosophy is he who, after acquainting himself experimentally with the various views, has given in his adhesion to the best, — so I would say that the wisest Christian was he who had carefully studied the heresies both of Judaism and Christianity. Whereas he who finds fault with Christianity because of its heresies would find fault also with the teaching of Socrates, from whose school have issued many others of discordant views. Nay, the opinions of Plato might be chargeable with error, on account of Aristotle's having separated from his school, and founded a new one, — on which subject we have remarked in the preceding book. But it appears to me

---

[1] Cf. 1 Cor. xv. 12 sqq.
[2] Cf. 2 Thess. ii. 2.
[3] Cf. 1 Tim. vi. 20.
[4] Τινὲς παρεκδοχαί. [He admits the fact, but does not justify such oppositions.]
[5] πολλὴν ἔχει διολκήν.

[6] φιλολόγον.
[7] τὸ πρέπον.
[8] 1 Cor. xi. 19.

that Celsus has become acquainted with certain heresies which do not possess even the *name* of Jesus in common with us. Perhaps he had heard of the sects called Ophites and Cainites, or some others of a similar nature, which had departed in all points from the teaching of Jesus. And yet surely this furnishes no ground for a charge against the *Christian* doctrine.

CHAP. XIV.

After this he continues : " Their union is the more wonderful, the more it can be shown to be based on no substantial reason. And yet rebellion is a substantial reason, as well as the advantages which accrue from it, and the fear of external enemies. Such are the causes which give stability to their faith." To this we answer, that our union does thus rest upon a reason, or rather not upon a reason, but upon the divine working,[1] so that its commencement was God's teaching men, in the prophetical writings, to expect the advent of Christ, who was to be the Saviour of mankind. For in so far as this point is not really refuted (although it may *seem* to be by unbelievers), in the same proportion is the doctrine commended as the doctrine of God, and Jesus shown to be the Son of God both before and after His incarnation. I maintain, moreover, that even after His incarnation, He is always found by those who possess the acutest spiritual vision to be most God-like, and to have really come down to us from God, and to have derived His origin or subsequent development not from human wisdom, but from the manifestation[2] of God within Him, who by His manifold wisdom and miracles established Judaism first, and Christianity afterwards ; and the assertion that rebellion, and the advantages attending it, were the originating causes of a doctrine which has converted and improved so many men was effectually refuted.

CHAP. XV.

But again, that it is not the fear of external enemies which strengthens our union, is plain from the fact that this cause, by God's will, has already, for a considerable time, ceased to exist. And it is probable that the secure existence, so far as regards the world, enjoyed by believers at present, will come to an end, since those who calumniate Christianity in every way are again attributing the present frequency of rebellion to the multitude of believers, and to their not being persecuted by the authorities as in old times. For we have learned from the Gospel neither to relax our efforts in days of peace, and to give ourselves up to repose, nor, when the world makes war upon us, to become cowards, and

apostatize from the love of the God of all thing which is in Jesus Christ. And we clearly mani fest the illustrious nature of our origin, and do not (as Celsus imagines) conceal it, when we impress upon the minds of our first converts contempt for idols, and images of all kinds, and besides this, raise their thoughts from the wor ship of created things instead of God, and elevate them to the universal Creator ; clearly showing Him to be the subject of prophecy, both from the predictions regarding Him — of which there are many — and from those traditions which have been carefully investigated by such as are able intelligently to understand the Gospels, and the declarations of the apostles.

CHAP. XVI.

" But what the legends are of every kind which we gather together, or the terrors which we in vent," as Celsus without proof asserts, he who likes may show. I know not, indeed, what he means by " inventing terrors," unless it be ou doctrine of God as Judge, and of the condem nation of men for their deeds, with the various proofs derived partly from Scripture, partly from probable reason. And yet — for truth is pre cious — Celsus says, at the close, " Forbid tha either I, or these, or any other individual should ever reject the doctrine respecting the future punishment of the wicked and the reward of the good ! " What terrors, then, if you except the doctrine of punishment, do we invent and im pose upon mankind? And if he should reply that " we weave together erroneous opinions drawn from ancient sources, and trumpet them aloud, and sound them before men, as the priest of Cybele clash their cymbals in the ears of those who are being initiated in their mysteries ; "[3] we shall ask him in reply, " Erroneous opinions from what ancient sources?" For, whether he refers to Grecian accounts, which taught the existence of courts of justice under the earth, or Jewish which, among other things, predicted the life that follows the present one ; he will be unable to show that we who, striving to believe on grounds of reason, regulate our lives in con formity with such doctrines, have failed correctly to ascertain the truth.[4]

CHAP. XVII.

He wishes, indeed, to compare the articles of our faith to those of the Egyptians ; " among whom, as you approach their sacred edifices, are to be seen splendid enclosures, and groves, and

---

[1] θείας ἐνεργείας.
[2] ἐπιφανείας.

[3] τὰ τοῦ παλαιοῦ λόγου παρακούσματα συμπλάττοντες, τούτοι προκαταυλοῦμεν καὶ προκατηχοῦμεν τοὺς ἀνθρώπους, ὡς οἱ του κορυβαντιζομένους περιβομβοῦντες.
[4] οὐκ ἂν ἔχοι παραστῆσαι, ὅτι ἡμεῖς μὲν ἐν παρακούσμασι γενόμενοι τῆς ἀληθείας, ὅσοι γε πειρώμεθα μετὰ λόγου πιστεύειν πρὸς τὰ τοιαῦτα ζῶμεν δόγματα.

large and beautiful gateways,[1] and wonderful temples, and magnificent tents around them, and ceremonies of worship full of superstition and mystery ; but when you have entered, and passed within, the object of worship is seen to be a cat, or an ape, or a crocodile, or a goat, or a dog !" Now, what is the resemblance[2] between us and the splendours of Egyptian worship which are seen by those who draw near their temples? And where is the resemblance to those irrational animals which are worshipped within, after you pass through the splendid gateways? Are our prophecies, and the God of all things, and the injunctions against images,[3] objects of reverence in the view of Celsus also, and Jesus Christ crucified, the analogue to the worship of the irrational animal? But if he should assert this — and I do not think that he will maintain anything else — we shall reply that we have spoken in the preceding pages at greater length in defence of those charges affecting Jesus, showing that what appeared to have happened to Him in the capacity of His human nature, was fraught with benefit to all men, and with salvation to the whole world.

CHAP. XVIII.

In the next place, referring to the statements of the Egyptians, who talk loftily about irrational animals, and who assert that they are a sort of symbols of God, or anything else which their prophets, so termed, are accustomed to call them, Celsus says that "an impression is produced in the minds of those who have learned these things ; that they have not been initiated in vain ; "[4] while with regard to the truths which are taught in our writings to those who have made progress in the study of Christianity (through that which is called by Paul the gift consisting in the "word of wisdom" through the Spirit, and in the "word of knowledge" according to the Spirit), Celsus does not seem even to have formed an idea,[5] judging not only from what he has already said, but from what he subsequently adds in his attack upon the Christian system, when he asserts that Christians "repel every wise man from the doctrine of their faith, and invite only the ignorant and the vulgar ; " on which assertions we shall remark in due time, when we come to the proper place.

CHAP. XIX.

He says, indeed, that "we ridicule the Egyptians, although they present many by no means contemptible mysteries[6] for our consideration, when they teach us that such rites are acts of worship offered to eternal ideas, and not, as the multitude think, to ephemeral animals ; and that we are silly, because we introduce nothing nobler than the goats and dogs of the Egyptian worship in our narratives about Jesus." Now to this we reply, "Good sir,[7] (suppose that) you are right in eulogizing the fact that the Egyptians present to view many by no means contemptible mysteries, and obscure explanations about the animals (worshipped) among them, you nevertheless do not act consistently in accusing us as if you believed that *we* had nothing to state which was worthy of consideration, but that all *our* doctrines were contemptible and of no account, seeing we unfold[8] the narratives concerning Jesus according to the 'wisdom of the word' to those who are 'perfect' in Christianity. Regarding whom, as being competent to understand the wisdom that is in Christianity, Paul says : 'We speak wisdom among them that are perfect ; yet not the wisdom of this world, nor of the princes of this world, who come to nought, but we speak the wisdom of God in a mystery, even the hidden wisdom, which God ordained before the world unto our glory ; which none of the princes of this world knew.' "[9]

CHAP. XX.

And we say to those who hold similar opinions to those of Celsus : "Paul then, we are to suppose, had before his mind the idea of no pre-eminent wisdom when he professed to speak wisdom among them that are perfect?" Now, as he spoke with his customary boldness when in making such a profession he said that *he* was possessed of no wisdom, we shall say in reply : first of all examine the Epistles of him who utters these words, and look carefully at the meaning of each expression in them — say, in those to the Ephesians, and Colossians, and Thessalonians, and Philippians, and Romans, — and show two things, both that you understand Paul's words, and that you can demonstrate any of them to be silly or foolish. For if any one give himself to their attentive perusal, I am well assured either that he will be amazed at the understanding of the man who can clothe great ideas in common language ; or if he be not amazed, he will only exhibit himself in a ridiculous light, whether he simply state the meaning of the writer as if he had comprehended it, or try to controvert and confute what he only imagined that he understood !

---

[1] προπυλαίων μεγέθη τε καὶ κάλλη.
[2] τὸ ἀνάλογον.
[3] [Clearly coincident with Clement and other early Fathers on this head.]
[4] φαντασίαν ἐξαποστέλλειν τοῖς ταῦτα μεμαθηκόσιν, ὅτι μὴ μάτην μεμύηνται.
[5] πεφαντάσθαι.

[6] αἰνίγματα.
[7] ὦ γενναίε.
[8] διεξοδεύωμεν.
[9] 1 Cor. ii. 6-8.

CHAP. XXI.

And I have not yet spoken of the observance[1] of all that is written in the Gospels, each one of which contains much doctrine difficult to be understood, not merely by the multitude, but even by certain of the more intelligent, including a very profound explanation of the parables which Jesus delivered to "those without," while reserving the exhibition of their full meaning[2] for those who had passed beyond the stage of exoteric teaching, and who came to Him privately in the house. And when he comes to understand it, he will admire the reason why some are said to be "without," and others "in the house." And again, who would not be filled with astonishment that is able to comprehend the movements[3] of Jesus; ascending at one time a mountain for the purpose of delivering certain discourses, or of performing certain miracles, or for His own transfiguration, and descending again to heal the sick and those who were unable to follow Him whither His disciples went? But it is not the appropriate time to describe at present the truly venerable and divine contents of the Gospels, or the mind of Christ — that is, the wisdom and the word — contained in the writings of Paul. But what we have said is sufficient by way of answer to the unphilosophic sneers[4] of Celsus, in comparing the inner mysteries of the Church of God to the cats, and apes, and crocodiles, and goats, and dogs of Egypt.

CHAP. XXII.

But this low jester[5] Celsus, omitting no species of mockery and ridicule which can be employed against us, mentions in his treatise the Dioscuri, and Hercules, and Æsculapius, and Dionysus, who are believed by the Greeks to have become gods after being men, and says that "we cannot bear to call such beings gods, because they were at first men,[6] and yet they manifested many noble qualities, which were displayed for the benefit of mankind, while we assert that Jesus was seen after His death by His own followers;" and he brings against us an additional charge, as if we said that "He was seen indeed, but was only a shadow!" Now to this we reply, that it was very artful of Celsus not here clearly to indicate that he did not regard these beings as gods, for he was afraid of the opinion of those who might peruse his treatise, and who might suppose him to be an atheist; whereas, if he had paid respect to what appeared to him to be the truth, he would not have *feigned* to regard

them as gods.[7] Now to either of the allegations we are ready with an answer. Let us, accordingly, to those who do *not* regard them as gods reply as follows: These beings, then, are not gods at all; but agreeably to the view of those who think that the soul of man perishes immediately (after death), the souls of these men also perished; or according to the opinion of those who say that the soul continues to subsist or is immortal, these men continue to exist or are immortal, and they are not gods but heroes, — or not even heroes, but simply souls. If, then, on the one hand, you suppose them *not* to exist, we shall have to prove the doctrine of the soul's immortality, which is to us a doctrine of preeminent importance ;[8] if, on the other hand, they *do* exist, we have *still* to prove[9] the doctrine of immortality, not only by what the Greeks have so well said regarding it, but also in a manner agreeable to the teaching of Holy Scripture. And we shall demonstrate that it is impossible for those who were polytheists during their lives to obtain a better country and position after their departure from this world, by quoting the histories that are related of them, in which is recorded the great dissoluteness of Hercules, and his effeminate bondage with Omphale, together with the statements regarding Æsculapius, that their Zeus struck him dead by a thunderbolt. And of the Dioscuri, it will be said that they die often —

"At one time live on alternate days, and at another
 Die, and obtain honour equally with the gods."[10]

How, then, can they reasonably imagine that one of these is to be regarded as a god or a hero?

CHAP. XXIII.

But we, in proving the facts related of our Jesus from the prophetic Scriptures, and comparing afterwards His history with them, demonstrate that no dissoluteness on His part is recorded. For even they who conspired against Him, and who sought false witnesses to aid them, did not find even any plausible grounds for advancing a false charge against Him, so as to accuse Him of licentiousness; but His death was indeed the result of a conspiracy, and bore no resemblance to the death of Æsculapius by lightning. And what is there that is venerable in the madman Dionysus, and his female garments, that *he* should be worshipped as a god? And if they who would defend such beings betake themselves to allegorical interpretations, we

---

[1] τηρήσεως.
[2] σαφήνειαν.
[3] μεταβάσεις.
[4] ἀφιλόσοφον χλεύην.
[5] βωμολόχος.
[6] The reading in the text is καὶ πρῶτοι, for which Bohereau proposes τὸ πρῶτον, which we have adopted in the translation.

[7] We have followed in the translation the emendation of Guietus, who proposes εἰ δὲ τὴν φαινομένην αὐτῷ ἀλήθειαν ἐπρέσβευσεν, οὐκ ἄν, κ.τ.λ., instead of the textual reading, εἰ τε τῆς φαινομένης αὐτῷ ἀληθείας ἐπρέσβευσεν, οὐκ ἄν, κ.τ.λ.
[8] τὸν προηγούμενον ἡμῖν περὶ ψυχῆς κατασκευαστέον λόγον.
[9] Bohereau conjectures, with great probability, that instead of ἀποδεκτέον, we ought to read ἀποδεικτέον.
[10] Cf. Hom., *Odyss.*, xi. 303 and 304.

must examine each individual instance, and ascertain whether it is well founded,[1] and also in each particular case, whether those beings can have a real existence, and are deserving of respect and worship who were torn by the Titans, and cast down from their heavenly throne. Whereas our Jesus, who appeared to the members of His own troop[2] — for I will take the word that Celsus employs — did *really* appear, and Celsus makes a false accusation against the Gospel in saying that what appeared was a shadow. And let the statements of their histories and that of Jesus be carefully compared together. Will Celsus have the former to be true, but the latter, although recorded by eye-witnesses who showed by their acts that they clearly understood the nature of what they had seen, and who manifested their state of mind by what they cheerfully underwent for the sake of His Gospel, to be inventions? Now, who is there that, desiring to act always in conformity with right reason, would yield his assent at random[3] to what is related of the one, but would rush to the history of Jesus, and without examination refuse to believe what is recorded of Him?[4]

CHAP. XXIV.

And again, when it is said of Æsculapius that a great multitude both of Greeks and Barbarians acknowledge that they have frequently seen, and still see, no mere phantom, but Æsculapius himself, healing and doing good, and foretelling the future; Celsus requires us to believe this, and finds no fault with the believers in Jesus, when we express our belief in such stories, but when we give our assent to the disciples, and eye-witnesses of the miracles of Jesus, who clearly manifest the honesty of their convictions (because we see their guilelessness, as far as it is possible to see the conscience revealed in writing), we are called by him a set of "silly" individuals, although he cannot demonstrate that an incalculable[5] number, as he asserts, of Greeks and Barbarians acknowledge the existence of Æsculapius; while we, if we deem this a matter of importance, can clearly show a countless multitude of Greeks and Barbarians who acknowledge the existence of Jesus. And some give evidence of their having received through this faith a marvellous power by the cures which they perform, invoking no other name over those who need their help than that of the God of all things, and of Jesus, along with a mention of His history. For by these means we too have seen many persons freed from grievous calamities, and

from distractions of mind,[6] and madness, and countless other ills, which could be cured neither by men nor devils.

CHAP. XXV.

Now, in order to grant that there did exist a healing spirit named Æsculapius, who used to cure the bodies of men, I would say to those who are astonished at such an occurrence, or at the prophetic knowledge of Apollo, that since the cure of bodies is a thing indifferent,[7] and a matter within the reach not merely of the good,[8] but also of the bad; and as the foreknowledge of the future is also a thing indifferent — for the possessor of foreknowledge does not necessarily manifest the possession of virtue — you must show that they who practise healing or who foretell the future are in no respect wicked, but exhibit a perfect pattern of virtue, and are not far from being regarded as gods. But they will *not* be able to show that they are virtuous who practise the art of healing, or who are gifted with foreknowledge, seeing many who are not fit to live are related to have been healed; and these, too, persons whom, as leading improper lives, no wise physician would wish to heal. And in the responses of the Pythian oracle also you may find some injunctions which are not in accordance with reason, two of which we will adduce on the present occasion; viz., when it gave commandment that Cleomedes[9] — the boxer, I suppose — should be honoured with divine honours, seeing some great importance or other attaching to his pugilistic skill, but did not confer either upon Pythagoras or upon Socrates the honours which it awarded to pugilism; and also when it called Archilochus "the servant of the Muses" — a man who employed his poetic powers upon topics of the most wicked and licentious nature, and whose public character was dissolute and impure — and entitled him "pious,"[10] in respect of his being the servant of the Muses, who are deemed to be goddesses! Now I am inclined to think that no one would assert that he was a "pious" man who was not adorned with all moderation and virtue, or that a decorous[11] man would utter such expressions as are contained in the unseemly[12] iambics of Archilochus. And if nothing that is divine in itself is shown to belong either to the healing skill of Æsculapius or the prophetic power of Apollo, how could any one, even were I to grant that the facts are as alleged, reasonably worship them as pure divinities? — and especially when the prophetic spirit of Apollo, pure from any body of earth, secretly

---

[1] εἰ τὸ ὑγιὲς ἔχουσιν.
[2] θιασώταις.
[3] ἀποκληρωτικῶς.
[4] εἰς δὲ τὰ περὶ τούτου ἀνεξετάστως ὁρμῶν ἀπιστῆσαι τοῖς περὶ αὐτοῦ;
[5] ἀμύθητον.

[6] ἐκστάσεων.
[7] μέσον.
[8] ἀστείους.
[9] Cf. Smith's *Dict. of Biograph.*, s.v.
[10] εὐσεβῆ.
[11] κόσμιος.
[12] οἱ μὴ σεμνοί.

enters through the private parts the person of her who is called the priestess, as she is seated at the mouth of the Pythian cave ! [1] Whereas regarding Jesus and His power we have no such notion; for the body which was born of the Virgin was composed of human material, and capable of receiving human wounds and death.

CHAP. XXVI.

Let us see what Celsus says next, when he adduces from history marvellous occurrences, which in themselves seem to be incredible, but which are not discredited by him, so far at least as appears from his words. And, in the first place, regarding Aristeas of Proconnesus, of whom he speaks as follows : "Then, with respect to Aristeas of Proconnesus, who disappeared from among men in a manner so indicative of divine intervention,[2] and who showed himself again in so unmistakeable a fashion, and on many subsequent occasions visited many parts of the world, and announced marvellous events, and whom Apollo enjoined the inhabitants of Metapontium to regard as a god, no one considers him to be a god." This account he appears to have taken from Pindar and Herodotus. It will be sufficient, however, at present to quote the statement of the latter writer from the fourth book of his histories, which is to the following effect : "Of what country Aristeas, who made these verses, was, has already been mentioned, and I shall now relate the account I heard of him in Proconnesus and Cyzicus. They say that Aristeas, who was inferior to none of the citizens by birth, entering into a fuller's shop in Proconnesus, died suddenly, and that the fuller, having closed his workshop, went to acquaint the relatives of the deceased. When the report had spread through the city that Aristeas was dead, a certain Cyzicenian, arriving from Artace, fell into a dispute with those who made the report, affirming that he had met and conversed with him on his way to Cyzicus, and he vehemently disputed the truth of the report; but the relations of the deceased went to the fuller's shop, taking with them what was necessary for the purpose of carrying the body away; but when the house was opened, Aristeas was not to be seen, either dead or alive. They say that afterwards, in the seventh year, he appeared in Proconnesus, composed those verses which by the Greeks are now called Arimaspian, and having composed them, disappeared a second time. Such is the story current in these cities. But these things I know happened to the Metapontines in Italy 340 years after the second dis-

appearance of Aristeas, as I discovered by computation in Proconnesus and Metapontium. The Metapontines say that Aristeas himself, having appeared in their country, exhorted them to erect an altar to Apollo, and to place near it a statue bearing the name of Aristeas the Proconnesian ; for he said that Apollo had visited their country only of all the Italians, and that he himself, who was now Aristeas, accompanied him ; and that when he accompanied the god he was a crow ; and after saying this he vanished. And the Metapontines say they sent to Delphi to inquire of the god what the apparition of the man meant ; but the Pythian bade them obey the apparition, and if they obeyed it would conduce to their benefit. They accordingly, having received this answer, fulfilled the injunctions. And now, a statue bearing the name of Aristeas is placed near the image of Apollo, and around it laurels are planted : the image is placed in the public square. Thus much concerning Aristeas."[3]

CHAP. XXVII.

Now, in answer to this account of Aristeas, we have to say, that if Celsus had adduced it as history, without signifying his own assent to its truth, it is in a different way that we should have met his argument. But since he asserts that he "disappeared through the intervention of the divinity," and "showed himself again in an unmistakeable manner," and "visited many parts of the world," and "made marvellous announcements ;" and, moreover, that there was "an oracle of Apollo, enjoining the Metapontines to treat Aristeas as a god," he gives the accounts relating to him as upon his own authority, and with his full assent. And (this being the case), we ask, How is it possible that, while supposing the marvels related by the disciples of Jesus regarding their Master to be wholly fictitious, and finding fault with those who believe them, you, O Celsus, do not regard these stories of yours to be either products of jugglery[4] or inventions? And how,[5] while charging others with an irrational belief in the marvels recorded of Jesus, can you show yourself justified in giving credence to such statements as the above, without producing some proof or evidence of the alleged occurrences having taken place? Or do Herodotus and Pindar appear to you to speak the truth, while they who have made it their concern to *die* for the doctrine of Jesus, and who have left to their successors writings so remarkable on the truths which they believed, entered for the sake of "fictions" (as you consider them), and "myths," and "juggleries," upon a

---

[1] ὅτε διὰ τοῦ Πυθίου στομίου περικαθεζομένη τῇ καλουμένῃ προφήτιδι πνεῦμα διὰ τῶν γυναικείων ὑπεισέρχεται τὸ μαντικὸν, ὁ Ἀπόλλων, τὸ καθαρὸν ἀπὸ γηΐνου σώματος. Boherellus conjectures τὸ μαντικὸν τοῦ Ἀπόλλωνος τὸ καθαρόν.
[2] οὕτω δαιμονίως.

[3] Herod., book iv. chaps. 14 and 15 (Cary's transl.).
[4] τερατείαν.
[5] Guietus conjectures, καὶ πῶς, ὦ λῷστε.

struggle which entails a life of danger and a death of violence? Place yourself, then, as a neutral party, between what is related of Aristeas and what is recorded of Jesus, and see whether, from the result, and from the benefits which have accrued from the reformation of morals, and to the worship of the God who is over all things, it is not allowable to conclude that we must believe the events recorded of Jesus not to have happened without the divine intervention, but that this was not the case with the story of Aristeas the Proconnesian.

CHAP. XXVIII.

For with what purpose in view did Providence accomplish the marvels related of Aristeas? And to confer what benefit upon the human race did such remarkable events, as you regard them, take place? You cannot answer. But we, when we relate the events of the history of Jesus, have no ordinary defence to offer for their occurrence;—this, viz., that God desired to commend the doctrine of Jesus as a doctrine which was to save mankind, and which was based, indeed, upon the apostles as foundations of the rising [1] edifice of Christianity, but which increased in magnitude also in the succeeding ages, in which not a few cures are wrought in the name of Jesus, and certain other manifestations of no small moment have taken place. Now what sort of person is Apollo, who enjoined the Metapontines to treat Aristeas as a god? And with what object does he do this? And what advantage was he procuring to the Metapontines from this divine worship, if they were to regard him as a god, who a little ago was a mortal? And yet the recommendations of Apollo (viewed by us as a demon who has obtained the honour of libation and sacrificial odours [2]) regarding this Aristeas appear to you to be worthy of consideration; while those of the God of all things, and of His holy angels, made known beforehand through the prophets — not *after* the birth of Jesus, but *before* He appeared among men — do not stir you up to admiration, not merely of the prophets who received the Divine Spirit, but of Him also who was the object of their predictions, whose entrance into life was so clearly predicted many years beforehand by numerous prophets, that the whole Jewish people who were hanging in expectation of the coming of Him who was looked for, did, after the advent of Jesus, fall into a keen dispute with each other; and that a great multitude of them acknowledged Christ, and believed Him to be the object of prophecy, while others did not believe in Him, but, despising the meekness of those who,

on account of the teaching of Jesus, were unwilling to cause even the most trifling sedition, dared to inflict on Jesus those cruelties which His disciples have so truthfully and candidly recorded, without secretly omitting from their marvellous history of Him what seems to the multitude to bring disgrace upon the doctrine of Christianity. But both Jesus Himself and His disciples desired that His followers should believe not merely in His Godhead and miracles, as if He had not also been a partaker of human nature, and had assumed the human flesh which "lusteth against the Spirit;" [3] but they saw also that the power which had descended into human nature, and into the midst of human miseries, and which had assumed a human soul and body, contributed through faith, along with its divine elements, to the salvation of believers, [4] when they see that from Him there began the union of the divine with the human nature, in order that the human, by communion with the divine, might rise to be divine, not in Jesus alone, but in all those who not only believe, but [5] enter upon the life which Jesus taught, and which elevates to friendship with God and communion with Him every one who lives according to the precepts of Jesus.

CHAP. XXIX.

According to Celsus, then, Apollo wished the Metapontines to treat Aristeas as a god. But as the Metapontines considered the evidence in favour of Aristeas being a man — and probably not a virtuous one — to be stronger than the declaration of the oracle to the effect that he was a god or worthy of divine honours, they for that reason would not obey Apollo, and consequently no one regarded Aristeas as a god. But with respect to Jesus we would say that, as it was of advantage to the human race to accept him as the Son of God — God come in a human soul and body — and as this did not seem to be advantageous to the gluttonous appetites [6] of the demons which love bodies, and to those who deem them to be gods on that account, the demons that are on earth (which are supposed to be gods by those who are not instructed in the nature of demons), and also their worshippers, were desirous to prevent the spread of the doctrine of Jesus; for they saw that the libations and odours in which they greedily delighted were being swept away by the prevalence of the instructions of Jesus. But the God who sent Jesus dissipated all the conspiracies of the demons, and

---

[1] τῆς καταβαλλομένης οἰκοδομῆς.

[2] τοῦ καθ᾽ ἡμᾶς δαίμονος, λαχόντος γέρας λοιβῆς τε κνίσσης τε.

[3] ὡς οὐ κοινωνήσαντος τῇ ἀνθρωπίνῃ φύσει, οὐδ᾽ ἀναλαβόντος τὴν ἐν ἀνθρώποις σάρκα ἐπιθυμοῦσαν κατὰ τοῦ πνεύματος.

[4] Ἀλλὰ γὰρ καὶ τὴν καταβᾶσαν εἰς ἀνθρωπίνην φύσιν καὶ εἰς ἀνθρωπίνας περιστάσεις δύναμιν, καὶ ἀναλαβοῦσαν ψυχὴν καὶ σῶμα ἀνθρώπινον, ἑώρων ἐκ τοῦ πιστεύεσθαι μετὰ τῶν θειοτέρων συμβαλλομένην εἰς σωτηρίαν τοῖς πιστεύουσιν.

[5] μετὰ τοῦ πιστεύειν. Others read, μετὰ το πιστεύειν.

[6] λιχνεία.

made the Gospel of Jesus to prevail throughout the whole world for the conversion and reformation of men, and caused Churches to be everywhere established in opposition to those of superstitious and licentious and wicked men; for such is the character of the multitudes who constitute the citizens [1] in the assemblies of the various cities. Whereas the Churches of God which are instructed by Christ, when carefully contrasted with the assemblies of the districts in which they are situated, are as beacons [2] in the world; for who would not admit that even the inferior members of the Church, and those who in comparison with the better are less worthy, are nevertheless more excellent than many of those who belong to the assemblies in the different districts?

CHAP. XXX.

For the Church [3] of God, e.g., which is at Athens, is a meek and stable body, as being one which desires to please God, who is over all things; whereas the assembly [4] of the Athenians is given to sedition, and is not at all to be compared to the Church of God in that city. And you may say the same thing of the Church of God at Corinth, and of the assembly of the Corinthian people; and also of the Church of God at Alexandria, and of the assembly of the people of Alexandria. And if he who hears this be a candid man, and one who investigates things with a desire to ascertain the truth, he will be filled with admiration of Him who not only conceived the design, but also was able to secure in all places the establishment of Churches of God alongside [5] of the assemblies of the people in each city. In like manner, also, in comparing the council [6] of the Church of God with the council in any city, you would find that certain councillors [7] of the Church are worthy to rule in the city of God, if there be any such city in the whole world; [8] whereas the councillors in all other places exhibit in their characters no quality worthy of the conventional [9] superiority which they appear to enjoy over their fellow-citizens. And so, too, you must compare *the ruler* of the *Church* in each city with the ruler of the *people* of the city, in order to observe that even amongst those councillors and rulers of the Church of God who come very far short of their duty, and who lead more indolent lives than others who

are more energetic, it is nevertheless possible to discover a general superiority in what relates to the progress of virtue over the characters of the councillors and rulers in the various cities. [10]

CHAP. XXXI.

Now if these things be so, why should it not be consistent with reason to hold with regard to Jesus, who was able to effect results so great, that there dwelt in *Him* no ordinary divinity? while this was not the case either with the Proconnesian Aristeas (although Apollo would have him regarded as a god), or with the other individuals enumerated by Celsus when he says, "No one regards Abaris the Hyperborean as a god, who was possessed of such power as to be borne along like an arrow from a bow." [11] For with what object did the deity who bestowed upon this Hyperborean Abaris the power of being carried along like an arrow, confer upon him such a gift? Was it that the human race might be benefited thereby, [12] or did he himself obtain any advantage from the possession of such a power?—always supposing it to be conceded that these statements are not wholly inventions, but that the thing actually happened through the co-operation of some demon. But if it be recorded that my Jesus was received up into glory, [13] I perceive the divine arrangement [14] in such an act, viz., because God, who brought this to pass, commends in this way the Teacher to those who witnessed it, in order that as men who are contending not for human doctrine, but for divine teaching, they may devote themselves as far as possible to the God who is over all, and may do all things in order to please Him, as those who are to receive in the divine judgment the reward of the good or evil which they have wrought in this life.

CHAP. XXXII.

But as Celsus next mentions the case of the Clazomenian, subjoining to the story about him this remark, "Do they not report that his soul frequently quitted his body, and flitted about in an incorporeal form? and yet men did not regard him as a god," we have to answer that probably certain wicked demons contrived that such statements should be committed to writing (for I do not believe that they contrived that such a thing should actually *take place*), in order that the predictions regarding Jesus, and the discourses ut-

---

[1] τοιαῦτα γὰρ τὰ πανταχοῦ πολιτευόμενα ἐν ταῖς ἐκκλησίαις τῶν πόλεων πλήθη.
[2] φωστῆρες. [Phil. ii. 15. Very noteworthy are the details of this and the following chapter, and their defiant comparisons.]
[3] ἐκκλησία.
[4] ἐκκλησία.
[5] παροικούσας.
[6] βουλήν.
[7] βουλευταί.
[8] εὔροις ἄν τινες μὲν τῆς ἐκκλησίας βουλευταὶ ἄξιοί εἰσιν, εἰ τίς ἐστιν ἐν τῷ πάντι πόγις τοῦ Θεοῦ, ἐν ἐκείνῃ πολιτεύεσθαι. Boherellus conjectures εὔροις ἄν ὅτι τινὲς μὲν, κ.τ.λ.
[9] τῆς ἐκ κατατάξεως ὑπεροχῆς.

[10] ὅτι καὶ ἐπὶ τῶν σφόδρα ἀποτυγχανομένων βουλευτῶν καὶ ἀρχόντων ἐκκλησίας Θεοῦ, καὶ ῥαθυμότερον παρὰ τοὺς εὐτονωτέρως βιοῦντας, οὐδὲν ἧττόν ἐστιν εὑρεῖν ὡς εἰπεῖν ὑπεροχήν, τὴν ἐν τῇ ἐπὶ τὰς ἀρετὰς προκοπῇ, παρὰ τὰ ἔθη τῶν ἐν ταῖς πόλεσι βουλευτῶν καὶ ἀρχόντων. Boherellus conjectures ῥαθυμοτέρων.
[11] ὥστε οἰστῷ βέλει συμφέρεσθαι. Spencer and Bohereau would delete βέλει as a gloss.
[12] Guietus would insert ἢ before ἵνα τι ὠφεληθῇ. This emendation is adopted in the translation.
[13] Cf. 1 Tim. iii. 16.
[14] τὴν οἰκονομίαν.

ered by Him, might either be evil spoken of, as inventions like these, or might excite no surprise, as not being more remarkable than other occurrences. But my Jesus said regarding His own soul (which was separated from the body, not by virtue of any human necessity, but by the miraculous power which was given Him also for this purpose): "No one taketh my life from Me, but I lay it down of Myself. I have power to lay it down, and I have power to take it again." [1] For as He had power to lay it down, He laid it down when He said, "Father, why hast Thou forsaken Me? And when He had cried with a loud voice, He gave up the ghost," [2] anticipating the public executioners of the crucified, who break the legs of the victims, and who do so in order that their punishment may not be further prolonged. And He "took His life," when He manifested Himself to His disciples, having in their presence foretold to the unbelieving Jews, "Destroy this temple, and in three days I will raise it up again," [3] and "He spake this of the temple of His body;" the prophets, moreover, having predicted such a result in many other passages of their writings, and in this, "My flesh also shall rest in hope: for Thou wilt not leave my soul in hell, neither wilt Thou suffer Thine Holy One to see corruption." [4]

CHAP. XXXIII.

Celsus, however, shows that he has read a good many Grecian histories, when he quotes further what is told of Cleomedes of Astypalæa, "who," he relates, "entered into an ark, and although shut up within it, was not found therein, but through some arrangement of the divinity, flew out, when certain persons had cut open the ark in order to apprehend him." Now this story, if an invention, as it appears to be, cannot be compared with what is related of Jesus, since in the lives of such men there is found no indication of their possessing the divinity which is ascribed to them; whereas the divinity of Jesus is established both by the existence of the Churches of the saved,[5] and by the prophecies uttered concerning Him, and by the cures wrought in His name, and by the wisdom and knowledge which are in Him, and the deeper truths which are discovered by those who know how to ascend from a simple faith, and to investigate the meaning which lies in the divine Scriptures, agreeably to the injunctions of Jesus, who said, "Search the Scriptures," [6] and to the wish of Paul, who taught that "we ought to know how to answer every man;" [7] nay, also of him who

said, "Be ready always to give an answer to every man that asketh of you a reason of the faith [8] that is in you." [9] If he wishes to have it conceded, however, that it is not a fiction, let him show with what object this supernatural power made him, through some arrangement of the divinity, flee from the ark. For if he will adduce any reason worthy of consideration, and point out any purpose worthy of God in conferring such a power on Cleomedes, we will decide on the answer which we ought to give; but if he fail to say anything convincing on the point, clearly because no reason *can* be discovered, then we shall either speak slightingly of the story to those who have not accepted it, and charge it with being false, or we shall say that some demoniac power, casting a glamour over the eyes, produced, in the case of the Astypalæan, a result like that which is produced by the performers of juggling tricks,[10] while Celsus thinks that with respect to him he has spoken like an oracle, when he said that "by some divine arrangement he flew away from the ark."

CHAP. XXXIV.

I am, however, of opinion that these individuals are the only instances with which Celsus was acquainted. And yet, that he might appear voluntarily to pass by other similar cases, he says, "And one might name many others of the same kind." Let it be granted, then, that many such persons have existed who conferred no benefit upon the human race: what would each one of their acts be found to amount to in comparison with the work of Jesus, and the miracles related of Him, of which we have already spoken at considerable length? He next imagines that, "in worshipping him who," as *he* says, "was taken prisoner and put to death, we are acting like the Getæ who worship Zamolxis, and the Cilicians who worship Mopsus, and the Acarnanians who pay divine honours to Amphilochus, and like the Thebans who do the same to Amphiaraus, and the Lebadians to Trophonius." Now in these instances we shall prove that he has compared us to the foregoing without good grounds. For these different tribes erected temples and statues to those individuals above enumerated, whereas we have refrained from offering to the Divinity honour by any such means (seeing they are adapted rather to demons, which are somehow fixed in a certain place which they prefer to any other, or which take up their dwell-

---

[1] Cf. John x. 18.
[2] Cf. Matt. xxvii. 46–50.
[3] Cf. John ii. 19.
[4] Ps. xvi. 9, 10.
[5] τῶν ὠφελουμένων.
[6] John v. 39.
[7] Cf. Col. iv. 6.

[8] πίστεως.
[9] 1 Pet. iii. 15.
[10] ἤτοι διαβαλοῦμεν τοῖς αὐτὴν μὴ παραδεξαμένοις, καὶ ἐγκαλέσομεν τῇ ἱστορίᾳ ὡς οὐκ ἀληθεῖ, ἢ δαιμόνιόν τι φήσομεν παραπλήσιον τοῖς ἐπιδεικνυμένοις γόησιν ἀπάτῃ ὀφθαλμῶν πεποιηκέναι καὶ περὶ τὸν Ἀστυπαλαιέα. Spencer in his edition includes μὴ in brackets, and renders, "Aut eos incusabimus, qui istam virtutem admiserint."

ing, as it were, after being removed (from one place to another) by certain rites and incantations), and are lost in reverential wonder at Jesus, who has recalled our minds from all sensible things, as being not only corruptible, but destined to corruption, and elevated them to honour the God who is over all with prayers and a righteous life, which we offer to Him as being intermediate between the nature of the uncreated and that of all created things,[1] and who bestows upon us the benefits which come from the Father, and who as High Priest conveys our prayers to the supreme God.

CHAP. XXXV.

But I should like, in answer to him who for some unknown reason advances such statements as the above, to make in a conversational way[2] some such remarks as the following, which seem not inappropriate to him. Are then those persons whom you have mentioned nonentities, and is there no power in Lebadea connected with Trophonius, nor in Thebes with the temple of Amphiaraus, nor in Acarnania with Amphilochus, nor in Cilicia with Mopsus? Or is there in such persons some being, either a demon, or a hero, or even a god, working works which are beyond the reach of man? For if he answer that there is nothing either demoniacal or divine about these individuals more than others, then let him at once make known his own opinion, as being that of an Epicurean, and of one who does not hold the same views with the Greeks, and who neither recognises demons nor worships gods as do the Greeks; and let it be shown that it was to no purpose that he adduced the instances previously enumerated (as if he believed them to be true), together with those which he adds in the following pages. But if he will assert that the persons spoken of are either demons, or heroes, or even gods, let him notice that he will establish by what he has admitted a result which he does not desire, viz., that Jesus also was some such being; for which reason, too, he was able to demonstrate to not a few that He had come down from God to visit the human race. And if he once admit this, see whether he will not be forced to confess that He is mightier than those individuals with whom he classed Him, seeing none of the latter forbids the offering of honour to the others; while He, having confidence in Himself, because He is more powerful than all those others, forbids them to be received as divine[3] because they are wicked demons, who

have taken possession of places on earth, through inability to rise to the purer and diviner region, whither the grossnesses of earth and its countless evils cannot reach.

CHAP. XXXVI.

But as he next introduces the case of the favourite of Adrian (I refer to the accounts regarding the youth Antinous, and the honours paid him by the inhabitants of the city of Antinous in Egypt), and imagines that the honour paid to him falls little short of that which we render to Jesus, let us show in what a spirit of hostility this statement is made. For what is there in common between a life lived among the favourites of Adrian, by one who did not abstain even from unnatural lusts, and that of the venerable Jesus, against whom even they who brought countless other charges, and who told so many falsehoods, were not able to allege that He manifested, even in the slightest degree, any tendency to what was licentious?[4] Nay, further, if one were to investigate, in a spirit of truth and impartiality, the stories relating to Antinous, he would find that it was due to the magical arts and rites of the Egyptians that there was even the *appearance* of his performing anything (marvellous) in the city which bears his name, and that too only after his decease,—an effect which is said to have been produced in other temples by the Egyptians, and those who are skilled in the arts which they practise. For they set up in certain places demons claiming prophetic or healing power, and which frequently torture those who seem to have committed any mistake about ordinary kinds of food, or about touching the dead body of a man, that they may have the appearance of alarming the uneducated multitude. Of this nature is the being that is considered to be a god in Antinoopolis in Egypt, whose (reputed) virtues are the lying inventions of some who live by the gain derived therefrom;[5] while others, deceived by the demon placed there, and others again convicted by a weak conscience, actually think that they are paying a divine penalty inflicted by Antinous. Of such a nature also are the mysteries which they perform, and the seeming predictions which they utter. Far different from such are those of Jesus. For it was no company of sorcerers, paying court to a king or ruler at his bidding, who seemed to have made him a god; but the Architect of the universe Himself, in keeping with the marvellously persuasive power of His words,[6] commended Him as worthy of honour, not only to those men who were well disposed, but to demons also, and other unseen powers,

---

[1] ἃς προσάγομεν αὐτῷ, ὡς διὰ μεταξὺ ὄντος τῆς τοῦ ἀγενήτου καὶ τῆς τῶν γενητῶν πάντων φύσεως. "Hoeschel (itemque Spencérus ad marg.) suspicabatur legendum: ὡς δὴ μεταξὺ ὄντος. Male. Nihil mutari necesse est. Agitur quippe de precibus, quas offerimus Deo ' per eum qui veluti medius est inter increatam naturam et creatam.' "—RUÆUS.

[2] ἀδολεσχῆσαι.

[3] τὰς τούτων ἀποδοχάς.

[4] ὡς κᾶν τὸ τυχὸν ἀκολασίας κᾶν ἐπ' ὀλίγον γευσαμένον;

[5] οὗ ἀρετὰς οἱ μέν τινες κυβευτικώτερον ζῶντες καταψεύδονται.

[6] ἀκολούθως τῇ ἐν τῷ λέγειν τερατίως πιστικῇ δυνάμει.

which even at the present time show that they either fear the name of Jesus as that of a being of superior power, or reverentially accept Him as their legal ruler.[1] For if the commendation had not been given Him by God, the demons would not have withdrawn from those whom they had assailed, in obedience to the mere mention of His name.

CHAP. XXXVII.

The Egyptians, then, having been taught to worship Antinous, will, if you compare him with Apollo or Zeus, endure such a comparison, Antinous being magnified in their estimation through being classed with these deities; for Celsus is clearly convicted of falsehood when he says, "that they will not endure his being compared with Apollo or Zeus." Whereas Christians (who have learned that their eternal life consists in knowing the only true God, who is over all, and Jesus Christ, whom He has sent; and who have learned also that all the gods of the heathen are greedy demons, which flit around sacrifices and blood, and other sacrificial accompaniments,[2] in order to deceive those who have not taken refuge with the God who is over all, but that the divine and holy angels of God are of a different nature and will[3] from all the demons on earth, and that they are known to those exceedingly few persons who have carefully and intelligently investigated these matters) will not endure a comparison to be made between them and Apollo or Zeus, or any being worshipped with odour and blood and sacrifices; some of them, so acting from their extreme simplicity, not being able to give a reason for their conduct, but sincerely observing the precepts which they have received; others, again, for reasons not to be lightly regarded, nay, even of a profound description, and (as a Greek would say) drawn from the inner nature of things;[4] and amongst the latter of these God is a frequent subject of conversation, and those who are honoured by God, through His only-begotten Word, with participation in His divinity, and therefore also in His name. They speak much, too, both regarding the angels of God and those who are opposed to the truth, but have been deceived; and who, in consequence of being deceived, call them gods or angels of God, or good demons, or heroes who have become such by the transference into them of a good human soul.[5] And such Christians will also show, that as in philosophy there are many who appear to be in possession of the truth, who have yet either de-

ceived themselves by plausible arguments, or by rashly assenting to what was brought forward and discovered by others; so also, among those souls which exist apart from bodies, both angels and demons, there are some which have been induced by plausible reasons to declare themselves gods. And because it was impossible that the reasons of such things could be discovered by men with perfect exactness, it was deemed safe that no mortal should entrust himself to any being as to God, with the exception of Jesus Christ, who is, as it were, the Ruler over all things, and who both beheld these weighty secrets, and made them known to a few.

CHAP. XXXVIII.

The belief, then, in Antinous,[6] or any other such person, whether among the Egyptians or the Greeks, is, so to speak, unfortunate; while the belief in Jesus would seem to be either a fortunate one, or the result of thorough investigation, having the appearance of the former to the multitude, and of the latter to exceedingly few.[7] And when I speak of a certain belief being, as the multitude would call it, unfortunate, I in such a case refer the cause to God, who knows the reasons of the various fates allotted to each one who enters human life. The Greeks, moreover, will admit that even amongst those who are considered to be most largely endowed with wisdom, good fortune has had much to do, as in the choice of teachers of one kind rather than another, and in meeting with a better class of instructors (there being teachers who taught the most opposite doctrines), and in being brought up in better circumstances; for the bringing up of many has been amid surroundings of such a kind, that they were prevented from ever receiving any idea of better things, but constantly passed their life, from their earliest youth, either as the favourites of licentious men or of tyrants, or in some other wretched condition which forbade the soul to look upwards. And the causes of these varied fortunes, according to all probability, are to be found in the reasons of providence, though it is not easy for men to ascertain these; but I have said what I have done by way of digression from the main body of my subject, on account of the proverb, that "such is the power of faith, because it seizes that which first presents itself."[8] For it was necessary, owing to the different methods of education, to speak of the differences of belief among men, some of whom are more, others less fortunate in their belief; and

---

[1] ὡς κατὰ νόμους αὐτῶν ἄρχοντος.
[2] ἀποφοράς.
[3] προαιρέσεως.
[4] ἐσωτερικῶν καὶ ἐποπτικῶν.
[5] ἢ ἥρωας ἐκ μεταβολῆς συστάντας ἀγαθῆς ἀνθρωπίνης ψυχῆς.

[6] [See vol. ii. p. 185, and the stinging reference of Justin, vol. i. p. 172, this series.]
[7] περὶ δὲ τοῦ Ἰησοῦ ἤτοι δόξασα ἂν εἶναι εὐτυχῆς, ἢ καὶ βεβασανισμένως ἐξητασμένη, δοκοῦσα μὲν εὐτυχῆς παρὰ τοῖς πολλοῖς, βεβασανισμένως δὲ ἐξητασμένη παρὰ πάνυ ὀλιγωτάτοις.
[8] τοσοῦτον ποιεῖ πίστις, ὁποία δὴ προκατασχοῦσα.

from this to proceed to show that what is termed good or bad fortune would appear to contribute, even in the case of the most talented, to their appearing to be more fully endowed with reason, and to give their assent on grounds of reason to the majority of human opinions. But enough on these points.

CHAP. XXXIX.

We must notice the remarks which Celsus next makes, when he says to us, that "faith, having taken possession of our minds, makes us yield the assent which we give to the doctrine of Jesus;" for of a truth it is faith which does produce such an assent. Observe, however, whether that faith does not of itself exhibit what is worthy of praise, seeing we entrust ourselves to the God who is over all, acknowledging our gratitude to Him who has led us to such a faith, and declaring that He could not have attempted or accomplished such a result without the divine assistance. And we have confidence also in the intentions of the writers of the Gospels, observing their piety and conscientiousness, manifested in their writings, which contain nothing that is spurious, or deceptive,[1] or false, or cunning; for it is evident to us that souls unacquainted with those artifices which are taught by the cunning sophistry of the Greeks (which is characterized by great plausibility and acuteness), and by the kind of rhetoric in vogue in the courts of justice, would not have been able thus to invent occurrences which are fitted of themselves to conduct to faith, and to a life in keeping with faith. And I am of opinion that it was on this account that Jesus wished to employ such persons as teachers of His doctrines, viz., that there might be no ground for any suspicion of plausible sophistry, but that it might clearly appear to all who were capable of understanding, that the guileless purpose of the writers being, so to speak, marked with great simplicity, was deemed worthy of being accompanied by a diviner power, which accomplished far more than it seemed possible could be accomplished by a periphrasis of words, and a weaving of sentences, accompanied by all the distinctions of Grecian art.

CHAP. XL.

But observe whether the principles of our faith, harmonizing with the general ideas implanted in our minds at birth, do not produce a change upon those who listen candidly to its statements; for although a perverted view of things, with the aid of much instruction to the same effect, has been able to implant in the minds of the multitude the belief that images are gods, and that things made of gold, and silver, and ivory, and stone are deserving of wor-

ship, yet common sense[2] forbids the supposition that God is at all a piece of corruptible matter, or is honoured when made to assume by men a form embodied in dead matter, fashioned according to some image or symbol of His appearance. And therefore we say at once of images that they are not gods, and of such creations (of art) that they are not to be compared with the Creator, but are small in contrast with the God who is over all, and who created, and upholds, and governs the universe. And the rational soul recognising, as it were, its relationship (to the divine), at once rejects what it for a time supposed to be gods, and resumes its natural love[3] for its Creator; and because of its affection towards Him, receives Him also who first presented these truths to all nations through the disciples whom He had appointed, and whom He sent forth, furnished with divine power and authority, to proclaim the doctrine regarding God and His kingdom.

CHAP. XLI.

But since he has charged us, I know not how often already, "with regarding this Jesus, who was but a mortal body, as a God, and with supposing that we act piously in so doing," it is superfluous to say any more in answer to this, as a great deal has been said in the preceding pages. And yet let those who make this charge understand that He whom we regard and believe to have been from the beginning God, and the Son of God, is the very Logos, and the very Wisdom, and the very Truth; and with respect to His mortal body, and the human soul which it contained, we assert that not by their communion merely with Him, but by their unity and intermixture,[4] they received the highest powers, and after participating in His divinity, were changed into God. And if any one should feel a difficulty at our saying this regarding His body, let him attend to what is said by the Greeks regarding matter, which, properly speaking, being without qualities, receives such as the Creator desires to invest it with, and which frequently divests itself of those which it formerly possessed, and assumes others of a different and higher kind. And if these opinions be correct, what is there wonderful in this, that the mortal quality of the body of Jesus, if the providence of God has so willed it, should have been changed into one that was ethereal and divine?[5]

[1] κυβευτικόν.

[2] ἡ κοινὴ ἔννοια.
[3] φίλτρον φυσικόν.
[4] ἀλλὰ καὶ ἑνώσει καὶ ἀνακράσει.
[5] [" By means of Origen the idea of a proper reasonable soul in Christ received a new dogmatical importance. This point, which up to this time had been altogether untouched with controversy with the Patripassians, was now for the first time expressly brought forward in a synod held against Beryllus of Bostra, A.D. 244, and the doctrine of a reasonable human soul in Christ settled as a doctrine of the Church." — NEANDER'S History (ut supra), vol. ii. p. 309, with the references there. See also Waterland's Works, vol. i. pp. 330, 331. S.]

CHAP. XLII.

Celsus, then, does not speak as a good reasoner,[1] when he compares the mortal flesh of Jesus to gold, and silver, and stone, asserting that the former is more liable to corruption than the latter. For, to speak correctly, that which is incorruptible is not more free from corruption than another thing which is incorruptible, nor that which is corruptible more liable to corruption than another corruptible thing. But, admitting that there are degrees of corruptibility, we can say in answer, that if it is possible for the matter which underlies all qualities to exchange some of them, how should it be impossible for the flesh of Jesus also to exchange qualities, and to become such as it was proper for a body to be which had its abode in the ether and the regions above it, and possessing no longer the infirmities belonging to the flesh, and those properties which Celsus terms "impurities," and in so terming them, speaks unlike a philosopher? For that which is properly impure, is so because of its wickedness. Now the nature of body is not impure; for in so far as it is bodily nature, it does not possess vice, which is the generative principle of impurity. But, as he had a suspicion of the answer which we would return, he says with respect to the change of the body of Jesus, "Well, after he has laid aside these qualities, he will be a God:" (and if so), why not rather Æsculapius, and Dionysus, and Hercules? To which we reply, "What great deed has Æsculapius, or Dionysus, or Hercules wrought?" And what individuals will they be able to point out as having been improved in character, and made better by their words and lives, so that they may make good their claim to be gods? For let us peruse the many narratives regarding them, and see whether they were free from licentiousness, or injustice, or folly, or cowardice. And if nothing of that kind be found in them, the argument of Celsus might have force, which places the forenamed individuals upon an equality with Jesus. But if it is certain that, although some things are reported of them as reputable, they are recorded, nevertheless, to have done innumerable things which are contrary to right reason, how could you any longer say, with any show of reason, that these men, on putting aside their mortal body, became gods rather than Jesus?

CHAP. XLIII.

He next says of us, that "we ridicule those who worship Jupiter, because his tomb is pointed out in the island of Crete; and yet we worship him who rose from the tomb,[2] although ignorant of the grounds[3] on which the Cretans observe

such a custom." Observe now that he thus undertakes the defence of the Cretans, and of Jupiter, and of his tomb, alluding obscurely to the allegorical notions, in conformity with which the myth regarding Jupiter is said to have been invented; while he assails us who acknowledge that our Jesus has been buried, indeed, but who maintain that He has also been *raised* from the tomb, — a statement which the Cretans have not yet made regarding Jupiter. But since he appears to admit that the tomb of Jupiter is in Crete, when he says that "we are ignorant of the grounds on which the Cretans observe such a custom," we reply that Callimachus the Cyrenian, who had read innumerable poetic compositions, and nearly the whole of Greek history, was not acquainted with any allegorical meaning which was contained in the stories about Jupiter and his tomb; and accordingly he accuses the Cretans in his hymn addressed to Jupiter, in the words:[4] —

"The Cretans are always liars: for thy tomb, O king,
The Cretans have reared; and yet thou didst not die,
For thou ever livest."

Now he who said, "Thou didst not die, for thou ever livest," in denying that Jupiter's tomb was in Crete, records nevertheless that in Jupiter there was the beginning of death.[5] But birth upon earth is the beginning of death. And his words run: —

"And Rhea bore thee among the Parrhasians;" —

whereas he ought to have seen, after denying that the birth of Jupiter took place in Crete because of his tomb, that it was quite congruous with his birth in Arcadia that he who was born should also die. And the following is the manner in which Callimachus speaks of these things: "O Jupiter, some say that thou wert born on the mountains of Ida, others in Arcadia. Which of them, O father, have lied? The Cretans are always liars," etc. Now it is Celsus who made us discuss these topics, by the unfair manner in which he deals with Jesus, in giving his assent to what is related about His death and burial, but regarding as an invention His resurrection from the dead, although this was not only foretold by innumerable prophets, but many proofs also were given of His having appeared after death.

CHAP. XLIV.

After these points Celsus quotes some objections against the doctrine of Jesus, made by a very few individuals who are considered Christians, not of the more intelligent, as he supposes, but of the more ignorant class, and asserts that "the following are the rules laid down by them. Let no one come to us who has been instructed,

---

[1] διαλεκτικός.
[2] τὸν ἀπὸ τοῦ τάφου.
[3] οὐκ εἰδότες πῶς καὶ καθό.

[4] Cf. Callimach., *Hymn*, i. Cf. also Tit. i. 12.
[5] τὴν ἀρχὴν τοῦ θανάτου γεγονέναι περὶ τὸν Δία.

or who is wise or prudent (for such qualifications are deemed evil by us); but if there be any ignorant, or unintelligent, or uninstructed, or foolish persons, let them come with confidence. By which words, acknowledging that such individuals are worthy of their God, they manifestly show that they desire and are able to gain over only the silly, and the mean, and the stupid, with women and children." [1] In reply to which, we say that, as if, while Jesus teaches continence, and says, "Whosoever looketh upon a woman to lust after her, hath already committed adultery with her in his heart," one were to behold a few of those who are deemed to be Christians living licentiously, he would most justly blame them for living contrary to the teaching of Jesus, but would act most unreasonably if he were to charge the Gospel with their censurable conduct; so, if he found nevertheless that the doctrine of the Christians invites men to wisdom, the blame then must remain with those who rest in their own ignorance, and who utter, not what Celsus relates (for although some of them are simple and ignorant, they do not speak so shamelessly as he alleges), but other things of much less serious import, which, however, serve to turn aside men from the practice of wisdom.

CHAP. XLV.

But that the object of Christianity [2] is that we should become wise, can be proved not only from the ancient Jewish writings, which we also use, but especially from those which were composed after the time of Jesus, and which are believed among the Churches to be divine. Now, in the fiftieth Psalm, David is described as saying in his prayer to God these words: "The unseen and secret things of Thy wisdom Thou hast manifested to me." [3] Solomon, too, because he asked for wisdom, received it; and if any one were to peruse the Psalms, he would find the book filled with many maxims of wisdom; and the evidences of his wisdom may be seen in his treatises, which contain a great amount of wisdom expressed in few words, and in which you will find many laudations of wisdom, and encouragements towards obtaining it. So wise, moreover, was Solomon, that "the queen of Sheba, having heard his name, and the name of the LORD, came to try him with difficult questions, and spake to him all things, whatsoever were in her heart; and Solomon answered her all her questions. There was no question omitted

by the king which he did not answer her. And the queen of Sheba saw all the wisdom of Solomon, and the possessions which he had, [4] and there was no more spirit in her. [5] And she said to the king, The report is true which I heard in mine own land regarding thee and thy wisdom; and I believed not them who told me, until I had come, and mine eyes have seen it. And, lo, they did not tell me the half. Thou hast added wisdom and possessions above all the report which I heard." [6] It is recorded also of him, that "God gave Solomon wisdom and understanding exceeding much, and largeness of heart, even as the sand that is on the sea-shore. And the wisdom that was in Solomon greatly excelled the wisdom of all the ancients, and of all the wise men of Egypt; and he was wiser than all men, even than Gethan the Ezrahite, and Emad, and Chalcadi, and Aradab, the sons of Madi. And he was famous among all the nations round about. And Solomon spake three thousand proverbs, and his songs were five thousand. And he spake of trees, from the cedar that is in Lebanon even to the hyssop which springeth out of the wall; and also of fishes and of beasts. And all nations came to hear the wisdom of Solomon, and from all the kings of the earth who had heard of the fame of his wisdom." [7]

And to such a degree does the Gospel desire that there should be wise men among believers, that for the sake of exercising the understanding of its hearers, it has spoken certain truths in enigmas, others in what are called "dark" sayings, others in parables, and others in problems. [8] And one of the prophets — Hosea — says at the end of his prophecies: "Who is wise, and he will understand these things? or prudent, and he shall know them?" [9] Daniel, moreover, and his fellow-captives, made such progress in the learning which the wise men around the king in Babylon cultivated, that they were shown to excel all of them in a tenfold degree. And in the book of Ezekiel it is said to the ruler of Tyre, who greatly prided himself on his wisdom, "Art thou wiser than Daniel? Every secret was not revealed to thee." [10]

CHAP. XLVI.

And if you come to the books written after the time of Jesus, you will find that those multitudes of believers who hear the parables, as it were, "without," and worthy only of exoteric doctrines, while the disciples learn in private the explanation of the parables. For, privately, to

---

[1] [The sarcastic raillery of Celsus in regard to the ignorance and low social scale of the early converts to Christianity is in keeping with his whole tone and manner. On the special value of the evidence of early Christian writers, such as Justin Martyr, Clement, Origen, etc., to the truth and power, among men of all classes, of the Gospel of our Lord, see Rawlinson's Bampton Lectures, The Historical Evidences of the Truth of the Scripture Records, Lect. viii. pp. 207, 420, et seqq. (Amer. ed. 1860). S.]

[2] ὁ λόγος.

[3] τὰ ἄδηλα καὶ τὰ κρύφια τῆς σοφίας σου ἐδήλωσάς μοι.

[4] τὰ κατ᾽ αὐτόν.

[5] καὶ ἐξ αὐτῆς ἐγένετο.

[6] Cf. 1 Kings x. 1–9.

[7] Cf. 1 Kings iv. 29–34. The text reads, περὶ πάντων τῶν βασιλέων τῆς γῆς, for which παρά has been substituted.

[8] καὶ ἄλλα διὰ προβλημάτων.

[9] Hos. xiv. 9.

[10] Cf. Ezek. xxviii. 3.

His own disciples did Jesus open up all things, esteeming above the multitudes those who desired to know His wisdom. And He promises to those who believe upon Him to send them wise men and scribes, saying, "Behold, I will send unto you wise men and scribes, and some of them they shall kill and crucify."[1] And Paul also, in the catalogue of "charismata" bestowed by God, placed first "the word of wisdom," and second, as being inferior to it, "the word of knowledge," but third, and lower down, "faith."[2] And because he regarded "the word" as higher than miraculous powers, he for that reason places "workings of miracles" and "gifts of healings" in a lower place than the gifts of the word. And in the Acts of the Apostles Stephen bears witness to the great learning of Moses, which he had obtained wholly from ancient writings not accessible to the multitude. For he says: "And Moses was learned in all the wisdom of the Egyptians."[3] And therefore, with respect to his miracles, it was suspected that he wrought them perhaps, not in virtue of his professing to come from God, but by means of his Egyptian knowledge, in which he was well versed. For the king, entertaining such a suspicion, summoned the Egyptian magicians, and wise men, and enchanters, who were found to be of no avail as against the wisdom of Moses, which proved superior to all the wisdom of the Egyptians.

CHAP. XLVII.

But it is probable that what is written by Paul in the first Epistle to the Corinthians,[4] as being addressed to Greeks who prided themselves greatly on their Grecian wisdom, has moved some to believe that it was not the object of the Gospel to win wise men. Now, let him who is of this opinion understand that the Gospel, as censuring wicked men, says of them that they are wise not in things which relate to the understanding, and which are unseen and eternal; but that in busying themselves about things of sense alone, and regarding these as all-important, they are wise men of the world: for as there are in existence a multitude of opinions, some of them espousing the cause of matter and bodies,[5] and asserting that everything is corporeal which has a substantial existence,[6] and that besides these nothing else exists, whether it be called invisible or incorporeal, it says also that these constitute the wisdom of the world, which perishes and fades away, and belongs only to this age, while those opinions which raise the soul from things here to the blessedness which is with God, and to His kingdom, and which teach men to

despise all sensible and visible things as existing only for a season, and to hasten on to things invisible, and to have regard to those things which are not seen, — these, it says, constitute the wisdom of God. But Paul, as a lover of truth, says of certain wise men among the Greeks, when their statements are true, that "although they knew God, they glorified Him not as God, neither were thankful."[7] And he bears witness that they knew God, and says, too, that this did not happen to them without divine permission, in these words: "For God showed it unto them;"[8] dimly alluding, I think, to those who ascend from things of sense to those of the understanding, when he adds, "For the invisible things of God from the creation of the world are clearly seen, being understood by the things that are made, even His eternal power and Godhead; so that they are without excuse: because that, when they knew God, they glorified Him not as God, neither were thankful."[9]

CHAP. XLVIII.

And perhaps also from the words, "For ye see your calling, brethren, how that not many wise men after the flesh, not many mighty, not many noble, are called: but God hath chosen the foolish things of the world to confound the wise; and the base things, and the things which are despised, hath God chosen, and things which are not, to bring to nought things that are, that no flesh may glory in His presence;"[10] some have been led to suppose that no one who is instructed, or wise, or prudent, embraces the Gospel. Now, in answer to such an one, we would say that it has not been stated that "no wise man according to the flesh," but that "not many wise men according to the flesh," are called. It is manifest, further, that amongst the characteristic qualifications of those who are termed "bishops," Paul, in describing what kind of man the bishop ought to be, lays down as a qualification that he should also be a teacher, saying that he ought to be able to convince the gainsayers, that by the wisdom which is in him he may stop the mouths of foolish talkers and deceivers.[11] And as he selects for the episcopate a man who has been once married[12] rather than he who has twice entered the married state,[13] and a man of blameless life rather than one who is liable to censure, and a sober man rather than one who is not such, and a prudent man rather

---

[1] Cf. Matt. xxiii. 34.
[2] Cf. 1 Cor. xii. 8.
[3] Acts vii. 22.
[4] Cf. 1 Cor. i. 18, etc.
[5] τὰ μὲν συναγορεύοντα ὑγῇ καὶ σώμασι.
[6] τὰ προηγουμένως ὑφεστηκότα.

[7] Cf. Rom. i. 21.
[8] Rom. i. 19.
[9] Cf. Rom. i. 20–22.
[10] Cf. 1 Cor. i. 26–28.
[11] Cf. Tit. i. 9, 10.
[12] Μονόγαμον. Cf. *Can. Apost.*, c. xvii.: "ὁ δυσὶ γάμοις συμπλακεὶς μετὰ τὸ βάπτισμα, ἢ παλλακὴν κτησάμενος, οὐ δύναται εἶναι ἐπίσκοπος, ἢ πρεσβύτερος, ἢ διάκονος, ἢ ὅλως τοῦ καταλόγου τοῦ ἱερατικοῦ." Cf. note in Benedictine ed.
[13] [Origen agrees with Tertullian, *passim*, on this subject. Hippolytus makes Callistus, Bishop of Rome, the first to depart from this principle, — accepting "digamists and trigamists."]

than one who is not prudent, and a man whose behaviour is decorous rather than he who is open to the charge even of the slightest indecorum, so he desires that he who is to be chosen by preference for the office of a bishop should be apt to teach, and able to convince the gainsayers. How then can Celsus justly charge us with saying, "Let no one come to us who is 'instructed,' or 'wise,' or 'prudent?'" Nay, let him who wills come to us "instructed," and "wise," and "prudent;" and none the less, if any one be ignorant and unintelligent, and uninstructed and foolish, let him also come: for it is these whom the Gospel promises to cure, when they come, by rendering them all worthy of God.

CHAP. XLIX.

This statement also is untrue, that it is "only foolish and low individuals, and persons devoid of perception, and slaves, and women, and children, of whom the teachers of the divine word wish to make converts." Such indeed does the Gospel invite, in order to make them better; but it invites also others who are very different from these, since Christ is the Saviour of all men, and especially of them that believe, whether they be intelligent or simple; and "He is the propitiation with the Father for our sins; and not for ours only, but also for the sins of the whole world."[1] After this it is superfluous for us to wish to offer a reply to such statements of Celsus as the following: "For why is it an evil to have been educated, and to have studied the best opinions, and to have both the reality and appearance of wisdom? What hindrance does this offer to the knowledge of God? Why should it not rather be an assistance, and a means by which one might be better able to arrive at the truth?" Truly it is no evil to have been educated, for education is the way to virtue; but to rank those amongst the number of the educated who hold erroneous opinions is what even the wise men among the Greeks would not do. On the other hand, who would not admit that to have studied the best opinions is a blessing? But what shall we call the best, save those which are true, and which incite men to virtue? Moreover, it is an excellent thing for a man to *be* wise, but not to *seem* so, as Celsus says. And it is no hindrance to the knowledge of God, but an assistance, to have been educated, and to have studied the best opinions, and to be wise. And it becomes us rather than Celsus to say this, especially if it be shown that he is an Epicurean.

CHAP. L.

But let us see what those statements of his are which follow next in these words: "Nay, we see, indeed, that even those individuals, who in the market-places perform the most disgraceful tricks, and who gather crowds around them, would never approach an assembly of wise men, nor dare to exhibit their arts among them; but wherever they see young men, and a mob of slaves, and a gathering of unintelligent persons, thither they thrust themselves in, and show themselves off." Observe, now, how he slanders us in these words, comparing us to those who in the market-places perform the most disreputable tricks, and gather crowds around them! What disreputable tricks, pray, do we perform? Or what is there in *our* conduct that resembles theirs, seeing that by means of readings, and explanations of the things read, we lead men to the worship of the God of the universe, and to the cognate virtues, and turn them away from contemning Deity, and from all things contrary to right reason? Philosophers verily would wish to collect together such hearers of their discourses as exhort men to virtue, — a practice which certain of the Cynics especially have followed, who converse publicly with those whom they happen to meet. Will they maintain, then, that these who do not gather together persons who are considered to have been educated, but who invite and assemble hearers from the public street, resemble those who in the market-places perform the most disreputable tricks, and gather crowds around them? Neither Celsus, however, nor any one who holds the same opinions, will blame those who, agreeably to what they regard as a feeling of philanthropy, address their arguments to the ignorant populace.

CHAP. LI.

And if they are not to be blamed for so doing, let us see whether Christians do not exhort multitudes to the practice of virtue in a greater and better degree than they. For the philosophers who converse in public do not pick and choose their hearers, but he who likes stands and listens. The Christians, however, having previously, so far as possible, tested the souls of those who wish to become their hearers, and having previously instructed[2] them in private, when they appear (before entering the community) to have sufficiently evinced their desire towards a virtuous life, introduce them then, and not before, privately forming one class of those who are beginners, and are receiving admission, but who have not yet obtained the mark of complete purification; and another of those who have manifested to the best of their ability their intention to desire no other things than are approved by Christians; and among these there are certain persons appointed to make inquiries regard-

---

[1] Cf. 1 John ii. 2.

[2] προεπᾴσαντες.

ing the lives and behaviour of those who join them, in order that they may prevent those who commit acts of infamy from coming into their public assembly, while those of a different character they receive with their whole heart, in order that they may daily make them better. And this is their method of procedure, both with those who are sinners, and especially with those who lead dissolute lives, whom they exclude from their community, although, according to Celsus, they resemble those who in the market-places perform the most shameful tricks. Now the venerable school of the Pythagoreans used to erect a cenotaph to those who had apostatized from their system of philosophy, treating them as dead; but the Christians lament as dead those who have been vanquished by licentiousness or any other sin, because they are lost and dead to God, and as being risen from the dead (if they manifest a becoming change) they receive them afterwards, at some future time, after a greater interval than in the case of those who were admitted at first, but not placing in any office or post of rank in the Church of God those who, after professing the Gospel, lapsed and fell.

CHAP. LII.

Observe now with regard to the following statement of Celsus, "We see also those persons who in the market-places perform most disreputable tricks, and collect crowds around them," whether a manifest falsehood has not been uttered, and things compared which have no resemblance. He says that these individuals, to whom he compares us, who "perform the most disreputable tricks in the market-places and collect crowds, would never approach an assembly of wise men, nor dare to show off their tricks before them; but wherever they see young men, and a mob of slaves, and a gathering of foolish people, thither do they thrust themselves in and make a display." Now, in speaking thus he does nothing else than simply load us with abuse, like the women upon the public streets, whose object is to slander one another; for we do everything in our power to secure that our meetings should be composed of wise men, and those things among us which are especially excellent and divine we then venture to bring forward publicly in our discussions when we have an abundance of intelligent hearers, while we conceal and pass by in silence the truths of deeper import when we see that our audience is composed of simpler minds, which need such instruction as is figuratively termed "milk."

CHAP. LIII.

For the word is used by our Paul in writing to the Corinthians, who were Greeks, and not yet purified in their morals: "I have fed you with milk, not with meat; for hitherto ye were not able to bear it, neither yet now are ye able, for ye are yet carnal: for whereas there is among you envying and strife, are ye not carnal, and walk as men?"[1] Now the same writer,[2] knowing that there was a certain kind of nourishment better adapted for the soul, and that the food of those young[3] persons who were admitted was compared to milk, continues: "And ye are become such as have need of milk, and not of strong meat. For every one that useth milk is unskilful in the word of righteousness; for he is a babe. But strong meat belongeth to them that are of full age, even those who by reason of use have their senses exercised to discern both good and evil."[4] Would then those who believe these words to be well spoken, suppose that the noble doctrines of our faith would never be mentioned in an assembly of wise men, but that wherever (our instructors) see young men, and a mob of slaves, and a collection of foolish individuals, they bring publicly forward divine and venerable truths, and before such persons make a display of themselves in treating of them? But it is clear to him who examines the whole spirit of our writings, that Celsus is animated with a hatred against the human race resembling that of the ignorant populace, and gives utterance to these falsehoods without examination.

CHAP. LIV.

We acknowledge, however, although Celsus will not have it so, that we *do* desire to instruct all men in the word of God, so as to give to young men the exhortations which are appropriate to them, and to show to slaves how they may recover freedom of thought,[5] and be ennobled by the word. And those amongst us who are the ambassadors of Christianity sufficiently declare that they are debtors[6] to Greeks and Barbarians, to wise men and fools, (for they do not deny their obligation to cure the souls even of foolish persons,) in order that as far as possible they may lay aside their ignorance, and endeavour to obtain greater prudence, by listening also to the words of Solomon: "Oh, ye fools, be of an understanding heart,"[7] and "Who is the most simple among you, let him turn unto me;"[8] and wisdom exhorts those who are devoid of understanding in the words, "Come, eat of my bread, and drink of the wine which I have mixed for you. Forsake folly that ye may

---

1　[1 Cor. iii. 2, 3. S.]
2　[See note *supra*, p. 239. S.]
3　νηπίων.
4　Heb. v. 12–14.
5　ἐλεύθερον ἀναλαβόντες φρόνημα.
6　Cf. Rom. i. 14.
7　Cf. Prov. viii. 5.
8　Cf. Prov. ix. 4.

live, and correct understanding in knowledge." [1]
This too would I say (seeing it bears on the
point),[2] in answer to the statement of Celsus :
Do not philosophers invite young men to their
lectures ? and do they not encourage young men
to exchange a wicked life for a better? and do
they not desire slaves to learn philosophy? Must
we find fault, then, with philosophers who have
exhorted slaves to the practice of virtue? with
Pythagoras for having so done with Zamolxis,
Zeno with Perseus, and with those who recently
encouraged Epictetus to the study of philosophy? Is it indeed permissible for you, O Greeks,
to call youths and slaves and foolish persons to
the study of philosophy, but if *we* do so, we do
not act from philanthropic motives in wishing
to heal every rational nature with the medicine
of reason, and to bring them into fellowship
with God, the Creator of all things? These remarks, then, may suffice in answer to what are
slanders rather than accusations [3] on the part of
Celsus.

CHAP. LV.

But as Celsus delights to heap up calumnies
against us, and, in addition to those which he
has already uttered, has added others, let us examine these also, and see whether it be the Christians or Celsus who have reason to be ashamed
of what is said. He asserts, "We see, indeed,
in private houses workers in wool and leather,
and fullers, and persons of the most uninstructed
and rustic character, not venturing to utter a
word in the presence of their elders and wiser
masters ;[4] but when they get hold of the children
privately, and certain women as ignorant as themselves, they pour forth wonderful statements, to
the effect that they ought not to give heed to
their father and to their teachers, but should
obey them ; that the former are foolish and stupid, and neither know nor can perform anything
that is really good, being preoccupied with empty
trifles ; that *they* alone know how men ought to
live, and that, if the children obey them, they
will both be happy themselves, and will make
their home happy also. And while thus speaking, if they see one of the instructors of youth
approaching, or one of the more intelligent class,
or even the father himself, the more timid among
them become afraid, while the more forward incite the children to throw off the yoke, whisper-
ing that in the presence of father and teachers
they neither will nor can explain to them any
good thing, seeing they turn away with aversion

from the silliness and stupidity of such persons
as being altogether corrupt, and far advanced in
wickedness, and such as would inflict punishment
upon them ; but that if they wish (to avail themselves of their aid,) they must leave their father
and their instructors, and go with the women
and their playfellows to the women's apartments,
or to the leather shop, or to the fuller's shop,
that they may attain to perfection ; — and by
words like these they gain them over."

CHAP. LVI.

Observe now how by such statements he depreciates those amongst us who are teachers of
the word, and who strive in every way to raise
the soul to the Creator of all things, and who
show that we ought to despise things "sensible,"
and "temporal," and "visible," and to do our
utmost to reach communion with God, and the
contemplation of things that are "intelligent,"
and "invisible," and a blessed life with God,
and the friends of God ; comparing them to
"workers in wool in private houses, and to
leather-cutters, and to fullers, and to the most
rustic of mankind, who carefully incite young
boys to wickedness, and women to forsake their
fathers and teachers, and follow them." Now
let Celsus point out from what wise parent, or
from what teachers, we keep away children and
women, and let him ascertain by comparison
among those children and women who are adherents of our doctrine, whether any of the
opinions which they formerly heard are better
than ours, and in what manner we draw away
children and women from noble and venerable
studies, and incite them to worse things. But
he will not be able to make good any such
charge against us, seeing that, on the contrary, we
turn away women from a dissolute life, and from
being at variance with those with whom they
live, from all mad desires after theatres and
dancing, and from superstition ; while we train
to habits of self-restraint boys just reaching the
age of puberty, and feeling a desire for sexual
pleasures, pointing out to them not only the disgrace which attends those sins, but also the state
to which the soul of the wicked is reduced
through practices of that kind, and the judgments which it will suffer, and the punishments
which will be inflicted.

CHAP. LVII.

But who are the teachers whom we call triflers
and fools, whose defence is undertaken by Celsus, as of those who teach better things? (I
know not,) unless he deem those to be good
instructors of women, and no triflers, who invite
them to superstition and to unchaste spectacles,
and those, moreover, to be teachers not devoid

---

[1] Cf. Prov. ix. 5, 6.
[2] διὰ τὰ ἐγκείμενα.
[3] λοιδορίας μᾶλλον ἢ κατηγορίας.
[4] The allusion is to the practice of wealthy Greeks and Romans
having among their slaves artificers of various kinds, for whose service there was constant demand in the houses and villas of the rich,
and who therefore had their residence in or near the dwelling of their
master. Many of these artificers seem, from the language of Celsus,
to have been converts to Christianity.

of sense who lead and drag the young men to all those disorderly acts which we know are often committed by them. We indeed call away these also, as far as we can, from the dogmas of philosophy to our worship of God, by showing forth its excellence aud purity. But as Celsus, by his statements, has declared that we do not do so, but that we call only the foolish, I would say to him, "If you had charged us with withdrawing from the study of philosophy those who were already preoccupied with it, you would not have spoken the truth, and yet your charge would have had an appearance of probability; but when you now say that we draw away our adherents from good teachers, show who are those other teachers save the teachers of philosophy, or those who have been appointed to give instruction in some useful branch of study." [1]

He will be unable, however, to show any such; while we promise, openly and not in secret, that *they* will be happy who live according to the word of God, and who look to Him in all things, and who do everything, whatever it is, as if in the presence of God. Are these the instructions of workers in wool, and of leather-cutters, and fullers, and uneducated rustics? But such an assertion he cannot make good.

CHAP. LVIII.

But those who, in the opinion of Celsus, resemble the workers in wool in private houses, and the leather-cutters, and fullers, and uneducated rustics, will, he alleges, in the presence of father or teachers be unwilling to speak, or unable to explain to the boys anything that is good. In answer to which, we would say, What kind of father, my good sir, and what kind of teacher, do you mean? If you mean one who approves of virtue, and turns away from vice, and welcomes what is better, then know, that with the greatest boldness will we declare our opinions to the children, because we will be in good repute with such a judge. But if, in the presence of a father who has a hatred of virtue and goodness, we keep silence, and also before those who teach what is contrary to sound doctrine, do not blame us for so doing, since you will blame us without good reason. You, at all events, in a case where fathers deemed the mysteries of philosophy an idle and unprofitable occupation for their sons, and for young men in general, would not, in teaching philosophy, make known its secrets before worthless parents; but, desiring to keep apart those sons of wicked parents who had been turned towards the study of philosophy, you would observe the proper seasons, in order that

the doctrines of philosophy might reach the minds of the young men. And we say the same regarding our teachers. For if we turn (our hearers) away from those instructors who teach obscene comedies and licentious iambics, and many other things which neither improve the speaker nor benefit the hearers (because the latter do not know how to listen to poetry in a philosophic frame of mind, nor the former how to say to each of the young men what tends to his profit), we are not, in following such a course, ashamed to confess what we do. But if you will show me teachers who train young men for philosophy, and who exercise them in it, I will not from such turn away young men, but will try to raise them, as those who have been previously exercised in the whole circle of learning and in philosophical subjects, to the venerable and lofty height of eloquence which lies hid from the multitude of Christians, where are discussed topics of the greatest importance, and where it is demonstrated and shown that they have been treated philosophically both by the prophets of God and the apostles of Jesus.

CHAP. LIX.

Immediately after this, Celsus, perceiving that he has slandered us with too great bitterness, as if by way of defence expresses himself as follows: "That I bring no heavier charge than what the truth compels me, any one may see from the following remarks. Those who invite to participation in other mysteries, make proclamation as follows: 'Every one who has clean hands, and a prudent tongue;' [2] others again thus: 'He who is pure from all pollution, and whose soul is conscious of no evil, and who has lived well and justly.' Such is the proclamation made by those who promise purification from sins. [3] But let us hear what kind of persons these Christians invite. Every one, they say, who is a sinner, who is devoid of understanding, who is a child, and, to speak generally, whoever is unfortunate, him will the kingdom of God receive. Do you not call him a sinner, then, who is unjust, and a thief, and a housebreaker, and a poisoner, and a committer of sacrilege, and a robber of the dead? What others would a man invite if he were issuing a proclamation for an assembly of robbers?" Now, in answer to such statements, we say that it is not the same thing to invite those who are *sick in soul* to be *cured*, and those who are *in health* to the *knowledge* and *study* of divine things. We, however, keeping both these things in view, at first invite all men to be healed, and exhort those

---

[1] Παράστησον τοὺς διδασκάλους ἄλλους παρὰ τοὺς φιλοσοφίας διδασκάλους, ἢ τοὺς κατά τι τῶν χρησίμων πεποιημένους.

[2] φωνὴν συνετός.
[3] [Much is to be gathered from this and the following chapters, of the evangelical character of primitive preaching and discipline.]

who are sinners to come to the consideration of the doctrines which teach men not to sin, and those who are devoid of understanding to those which beget wisdom, and those who are children to rise in their thoughts to manhood, and those who are simply [1] unfortunate to good fortune,[2] or — which is the more appropriate term to use — to blessedness.[3] And when those who have been turned towards virtue have made progress, and have shown that they have been purified by the word, and have led as far as they can a better life, then and not before do we invite them to participation in our mysteries. "For we speak wisdom among them that are perfect."[4]

CHAP. LX.

And as we teach, moreover, that "wisdom will not enter into the soul of a base man, nor dwell in a body that is involved in sin,"[5] we say, Whoever has clean hands, and therefore lifts up holy hands to God, and by reason of being occupied with elevated and heavenly things, can say, "The lifting up of my hands is as the evening sacrifice,"[6] let him come to us; and whoever has a wise tongue through meditating on the law of the Lord day and night, and by "reason of habit has his senses exercised to discern between good and evil," let him have no reluctance in coming to the strong and rational sustenance which is adapted to those who are athletes in piety and every virtue. And since the grace of God is with all those who love with a pure affection the teacher of the doctrines of immortality, whoever is pure not only from all defilement, but from what are regarded as lesser transgressions, let him be boldly initiated in the mysteries of Jesus, which properly are made known only to the holy and the pure. The initiated of Celsus accordingly says, "Let him whose soul is conscious of no evil come." But he who acts as initiator, according to the precepts of Jesus, will say to those who have been purified in heart, "He whose soul has, for a long time, been conscious of no evil, and especially since he yielded himself to the healing of the word, let such an one hear the doctrines which were spoken in private by Jesus to His genuine disciples." Therefore in the comparison which he institutes between the procedure of the initiators into the Grecian mysteries, and the teachers of the doctrine of Jesus, he does not know the difference between inviting the wicked to be healed, and initiating those already purified into the sacred mysteries !

CHAP. LXI.

Not to *participation in mysteries*, then, and to *fellowship in the wisdom hidden in a mystery*, which God ordained before the world to the glory of His saints,[7] do we invite the *wicked* man, and the *thief*, and the *housebreaker*, and the *poisoner*, and the *committer of sacrilege*, and the *plunderer of the dead*, and all those others whom Celsus may enumerate in his exaggerating style, but such as these we invite to be *healed*. For there are in the divinity of the word some helps towards the cure of those who are sick, respecting which the word says, "They that be whole need not a physician, but they that are sick;"[8] others, again, which to the pure in soul and body exhibit "the revelation of the mystery, which was kept secret since the world began, but now is made manifest by the Scriptures of the prophets,"[9] and "by the appearing of our Lord Jesus Christ,"[10] which "appearing" is manifested to each one of those who are perfect, and which enlightens the reason[11] in the true[12] knowledge of things. But as he exaggerates the charges against us, adding, after his list of those vile individuals whom he has mentioned, this remark, "What other persons would a robber summon to himself by proclamation?" we answer such a question by saying that a robber summons around him individuals of such a character, in order to make use of their villany against the men whom they desire to slay and plunder. A Christian, on the other hand, even though he invite those whom the robber invites, invites them to a very different vocation, viz., to bind up these wounds by His word, and to apply to the soul, festering amid evils, the drugs obtained from the word, and which are analogous to the wine and oil, and plasters, and other healing appliances which belong to the art of medicine.

CHAP. LXII.

In the next place, throwing a slur[13] upon the exhortations spoken and written to those who have led wicked lives, and which invite them to repentance and reformation of heart, he asserts that we say "that it was to sinners that God has been sent." Now this statement of his is much the same as if he were to find fault with certain persons for saying that on account of the sick who were living in a city, a physician had been sent them by a very benevolent monarch.[14] God the Word was sent, indeed, as a physician

---

[1] ἁπλῶς.
[2] εὐδαιμονίαν.
[3] μακαριότητα.
[4] Cf. 1 Cor. ii. 6.
[5] Wisd. Solom. i. 4.
[6] Cf. Ps. cxli. 2.
[7] Cf. 1 Cor. ii. 7.
[8] Matt. ix. 12.
[9] Rom. xvi. 25, 26.
[10] Cf. 2 Tim. i. 10.
[11] τὸ ἡγεμονικόν.
[12] ἀψευδῆ.
[13] συκοφαντῶν.
[14] [The reproaches of the scoffer are very instructive as to the *real* nature of the primitive dealing with sinners and with sin.]

to sinners, but as a teacher of divine mysteries to those who are already pure and who sin no more. But Celsus, unable to see this distinction, — for he had no desire to be animated with a love of truth, — remarks, "Why was he not sent to those who were without sin? What evil is it not to have committed sin?" To which we reply, that if by those "who were without sin" he means those who sin no more, then our Saviour Jesus was sent even to such, but not as a physician. While if by those "who were without sin" he means such as have never at any time sinned, — for he made no distinction in his statement, — we reply that it is impossible for a man thus to be without sin. And this we say, excepting, of course, the man understood to be in Christ Jesus,[1] who "did no sin." It is with a malicious intent, indeed, that Celsus says of us that we assert that "God will receive the unrighteousness man if he humble himself on account of his wickedness, but that He will not receive the righteous man, although he look up to Him, (adorned) with virtue from the beginning." Now we assert that it is impossible for a man to look up to God (adorned) with virtue from the beginning. For wickedness must necessarily first exist in men. As Paul also says, "When the commandment came, sin revived, and I died."[2] Moreover, we do not teach regarding the unrighteous man, that it is sufficient for him to humble himself on account of his wickedness in order to his being accepted by God, but that God will accept him if, after passing condemnation upon himself for his past conduct, he walk humbly on account of it, and in a becoming manner for the time to come.

CHAP. LXIII.

After this, not understanding how it has been said that "every one who exalted himself shall be abased;"[3] nor (although taught even by Plato) that "the good and virtuous man walketh humbly and orderly;" and ignorant, moreover, that we give the injunction, "Humble yourselves, therefore, under the mighty hand of God, that He may exalt you in due time;"[4] he says that "those persons who preside properly over a trial make those individuals who bewail before them their evil deeds to cease from their piteous wailings, lest their decisions should be determined rather by compassion than by a regard to truth; whereas God does not decide in accordance with truth, but in accordance with flattery."[5] Now, what words of flattery and piteous wailing are contained in the Holy Scriptures

when the sinner says in his prayers to God, " I have acknowledged my sin, and mine iniquity have I not hid. I said, I will confess my transgression to the Lord," etc., etc.? For is he able to show that a procedure of this kind is not adapted to the conversion of sinners, who humble themselves in their prayers under the hand of God? And, becoming confused by his efforts to accuse us, he contradicts himself; appearing at one time to know a man "without sin," and "a righteous man, who can look up to God (adorned) with virtue from the beginning;" and at another time accepting our statement that there is no man altogether righteous, or without sin;[6] for, as if he admitted its truth, he remarks, "This is indeed apparently true, that somehow the human race is naturally inclined to sin." In the next place, as if all men were not invited by the word, he says, "All men, then, without distinction, ought to be invited, since all indeed are sinners." And yet, in the preceding pages, we have pointed out the words of Jesus : "Come unto Me, *all* ye that labour and are heavy laden, and I will give you rest."[7] *All* men, therefore, labouring and being heavy laden on account of the nature of sin, are invited to the rest spoken of in the word of God, "for God sent His word, and healed them, and delivered them from their destructions."[8]

CHAP. LXIV.

But since he says, in addition to this, "What is this preference of sinners over others?" and makes other remarks of a similar nature, we have to reply that absolutely a sinner is not preferred before one who is not a sinner; but that sometimes a sinner, who has become conscious of his own sin, and for that reason comes to repentance, being humbled on account of his sins, is preferred before one who is accounted a lesser sinner, but who does not consider himself one, but exalts himself on the ground of certain good qualities which he thinks he possesses, and is greatly elated on their account. And this is manifest to those who are willing to peruse the Gospels in a spirit of fairness, by the parable of the publican, who said, "Be merciful to me a sinner,"[9] and of the Pharisee who boasted with a certain wicked self-conceit in the words, " I thank Thee that I am not as other men are, extortioners, unjust, adulterers, or even as this publican."[10] For Jesus subjoins to his narrative of them both the words : "This man went down

---

[1] ὑπεξαιρομένου τοῦ κατὰ τὸν Ἰησοῦν νοουμένου ἀνθρώπου
[2] Rom. vii. 9.
[3] Cf. Matt. xxiii. 12.
[4] 1 Pet. v. 6.
[5] πρὸς κολακείαν.

[6] In the text it is put interrogatively: τίς ἄνθρωπος τελέως δίκαιος; ἢ τίς ἀναμάρτητος; The allusion seems to be to Job xv. 14 (Sept.): τίς γὰρ ὢν βροτὸς, ὅτι ἔσται ἄμεμπτος; ἢ ὡς ἐσόμενος δίκαιος γεννητὸς γυναικός;
[7] Matt. xi. 28.
[8] Ps. cvii. 20.
[9] Luke xviii. 13.
[10] Luke xviii. 11.

to his house justified rather than the other : for every one that exalteth himself shall be abased ; and he that humbleth himself shall be exalted." [1] We utter no blasphemy, then, against God, neither are we guilty of falsehood, when we teach that every man, whoever he may be, is conscious of human infirmity in comparison with the greatness of God, and that we must ever ask from Him, who alone is able to supply our deficiencies, what is wanting to our (mortal) nature.

CHAP. LXV.

He imagines, however, that we utter these exhortations for the conversion of sinners, because we are able to gain over no one who is really good and righteous, and therefore open our gates to the most unholy and abandoned of men. But if any one will fairly observe our assemblies, we can present a greater number of those who have been converted from not a very wicked life, than of those who have committed the most abominable sins. For naturally those who are conscious to themselves of better things, desire that those promises may be true which are declared by God regarding the reward of the righteous, and thus assent more readily to the statements (of Scripture) than those do who have led very wicked lives, and who are prevented by their very consciousness (of evil) from admitting that they will be punished by the Judge of all with such punishment as befits those who have sinned so greatly, and as would not be inflicted by the Judge of all contrary to right reason.[2] Sometimes, also, when very abandoned men are willing to accept the doctrine of (future) punishment, on account of the hope which is based upon repentance, they are prevented from so doing by their habit of sinning, being constantly dipped,[3] and, as it were, dyed[4] in wickedness, and possessing no longer the power to turn from it easily to a proper life, and one regulated according to right reason. And although Celsus observes this, he nevertheless, I know not why, expresses himself in the following terms : " And yet, indeed, it is manifest to every one that no one by chastisement, much less by merciful treatment, could effect a complete change in those who are sinners both by nature and custom, for to change nature is an exceedingly difficult thing. But they who are without sin are partakers of a better life."

CHAP. LXVI.

Now here Celsus appears to me to have committed a great error, in refusing to those who are sinners by nature, and also by habit, the possibility of a complete transformation, alleging that they cannot be cured even by punishment. For it clearly appears that all men are inclined to sin by nature,[5] and some not only by nature but by practice, while not all men are incapable of an entire transformation. For there are found in every philosophical sect, and in the word of God, persons who are related to have undergone so great a change that they may be proposed as a model of excellence of life. Among the names of the heroic age some mention Hercules and Ulysses, among those of later times, Socrates, and of those who have lived very recently, Musonius.[6] Not only against us, then, did Celsus utter the calumny, when he said that " it was manifest to every one that those who were given to sin by nature and habit could not by any means — even by punishments — be completely changed for the better," but also against the noblest names in philosophy, who have not denied that the recovery of virtue was a possible thing for men. But although he did not express his meaning with exactness, we shall nevertheless, though giving his words a more favourable construction, convict him of unsound reasoning. For his words were : " Those who are inclined to sin by nature and habit, no one could completely reform even by chastisement ; " and his words, as we understood them, we refuted to the best of our ability.[7]

CHAP. LXVII.

It is probable, however, that he meant to convey some such meaning as this, that those who were both by nature and habit given to the commission of those sins which are committed by the most abandoned of men, could not be completely transformed even by punishment. And yet this is shown to be false from the history of certain philosophers. For who is there that would not rank among the most abandoned of men the individual who somehow submitted to yield himself to his master, when he placed him in a brothel,[8] that he might allow himself to be polluted by any one who liked? And yet such a circumstance is related of Phædo ! And who will not agree that he who burst, accompanied with a flute-player and a party of revellers, his profligate associates, into the school of the venerable Xenocrates, to insult a man who was the admiration of his friends, was not one of the greatest miscreants [9] among mankind? Yet, notwithstanding this, reason was powerful enough

---

[1] Luke xviii. 14.
[2] καὶ οὐ παρὰ τὸν ὀρθὸν λόγον προσάγοιτο ὑπὸ τοῦ ἐπὶ πᾶσι δικαστοῦ. [See infra, book iv. cap. lxxix, and Elucidations there named.]
[3] [ἐπιμόνως βεβαμμένοι. S.]
[4] [ὡσπερεὶ δευσοποιηθέντες ἀπὸ τῆς κακίας. S.]

[5] [Let us note this in passing, as balancing some other expressions which could not have been used after the Pelagian controversy.]
[6] He is said to have been either a Babylonian or Tyrrhenian, and to have lived in the rein of Nero. Cf. Philostratus, iv. 12. — RUÆUS.
[7] καὶ τὸ ἐξακουόμενον ἀπὸ τῆς λέξεως, ὡς δυνατὸν ἡμῖν, ἀνετρέψαμεν.
[8] ἐπὶ τέγους. [" Ut quidam scripserunt," says Hoffmann.]
[9] μιαρώτατον ἀνθρώπων.

to effect their conversion, and to enable them to make such progress in philosophy, that the one was deemed worthy by Plato to recount the discourse of Socrates on immortality, and to record his firmness in prison, when he evinced his contempt of the hemlock, and with all fearlessness and tranquillity of mind treated of subjects so numerous and important, that it is difficult even for those to follow them who are giving their utmost attention, and who are disturbed by no distraction ; while Polemon, on the other hand, who from a profligate became a man of most temperate life, was successor in the school of Xenocrates, so celebrated for his venerable character. Celsus then does not speak the truth when he says " that sinners by nature and habit cannot be completely reformed even by chastisement."

CHAP. LXVIII.

That philosophical discourses, however, distinguished by orderly arrangement and elegant expression,[1] should produce such results in the case of those individuals just enumerated, and upon others[2] who have led wicked lives, is not at all to be wondered at. But when we consider that those discourses, which Celsus terms " vulgar,"[3] are filled with power, as if they were spells, and see that they at once convert multitudes from a life of licentiousness to one of extreme regularity,[4] and from a life of wickedness to a better, and from a state of cowardice or unmanliness to one of such high-toned courage as to lead men to despise even death through the piety which shows itself within them, why should we not justly admire the power which they contain? For the words of those who at the first assumed the office of (Christian) ambassadors, and who gave their labours to rear up the Churches of God, — nay, their preaching also, — were accompanied with a persuasive power, though not like that found among those who profess the philosophy of Plato, or of any other merely human philosopher, which possesses no other qualities than those of human nature. But the demonstration which followed the words of the apostles of Jesus was given from God, and was accredited[5] by the Spirit and by power. And therefore *their* word ran swiftly and speedily, or rather the word of *God* through their instrumentality, transformed numbers of persons who had been sinners both by nature and habit, whom no one could have reformed by punishment, but who were changed by the word, which moulded and transformed them according to its pleasure.

CHAP. LXIX.

Celsus continues in his usual manner, asserting that " to change a nature entirely is exceedingly difficult." We, however, who know of only one nature in every rational soul, and who maintain that none has been created evil by the Author of all things, but that many have *become* wicked through education, and perverse example, and surrounding influences,[6] so that wickedness has been naturalized[7] in some individuals, are persuaded that for the word of God to change a nature in which evil has been naturalized is not only not impossible, but is even a work of no very great difficulty, if a man only believe that he must entrust himself to the God of all things, and do everything with a view to please Him with whom it cannot be[8] that

" Both good and bad are in the same honour,
Or that the idle man and he who laboured much
　　Perish alike."[9]

But even if it be exceedingly difficult to effect a change in some persons, the cause must be held to lie in their own will, which is reluctant to accept the belief that the God over all things is a just Judge of all the deeds done during life. For deliberate choice and practice[10] avail much towards the accomplishment of things which appear to be very difficult, and, to speak hyperbolically, almost impossible. Has the nature of man, when desiring to walk along a rope extended in the air through the middle of the theatre, and to carry at the same time numerous and heavy weights, been able by practice and attention to accomplish such a feat ; but when desiring to live in conformity with the practice of virtue, does it find it impossible to do so, although formerly it may have been exceedingly wicked ? See whether he who holds such views does not bring a charge against the nature of the Creator of the rational animal[11] rather than against the creature, if He has formed the nature of man with powers for the attainment of things of such difficulty, and of no utility whatever, but has rendered it incapable of securing its own blessedness. But these remarks may suffice as an answer to the assertion that "entirely to change a nature is exceedingly difficult." He alleges, in the next place, that " they who are without sin are partakers of a better life ; " not making it clear what he means by " those who are without sin," whether those who are so from the beginning (of their lives), or those who become so by a transformation. Of those who were so from the beginning of their lives, there cannot possibly be any ; while those who are so after a

---

1 Ἀλλὰ τὴν μὲν τάξιν καὶ σύνθεσιν καὶ φράσιν τῶν ἀπὸ φιλοσοφίας λόγων.
2 The reading in the text is ἄλλως, for which ἄλλους has been conjectured by Ruæus and Boherellus, and which has been adopted in the translation.
3 ἰδιωτικούς.
4 εὐσταθέστατον.
5 πιστικὴ ἀπὸ πνεύματος.

6 παρὰ τὰς ἀνατροφὰς, καὶ τὰς διαστροφὰς, καὶ τὰς περιηχήσεις.
7 φυσιωθῆναι.
8 [παρ' ᾧ οὐκ ἔστιν. S.]
9 Cf. *Iliad*, ix. 319, 320.
10 προαίρεσις καὶ ἄσκησις.
11 τοῦ λογικοῦ ζώου.

transformation (of heart) are found to be few in number, being those who have become so after giving in their allegiance to the saving word. And they were not such when they gave in their allegiance. For, apart from the aid of the word, and that too the word of perfection, it is impossible for a man to become free from sin.

CHAP. LXX.

In the next place, he objects to the statement, as if it were maintained by us, that "God will be able to do all things," not seeing even here how these words are meant, and what "the *all things*" are which are included in it, and how it is said that God "will be able." But on these matters it is not necessary to speak; for although he might with a show of reason have opposed this proposition, he has not done so. Perhaps he did not understand the arguments which might be plausibly used against it, or if he did, he saw the answers that might be returned. Now in our judgment God can do everything which it is possible for Him to do without ceasing to be God, and good, and wise. But Celsus asserts — not comprehending the meaning of the expression "God can do all things " — "that He will not desire to do anything wicked," admitting that He has the *power*, but not the *will*, to commit evil. We, on the contrary, maintain that as that which by nature possesses the property of sweetening other things through its own inherent sweetness cannot produce bitterness contrary to its own peculiar nature,[1] nor that whose nature it is to produce light through its being light can cause darkness; so neither is God able to commit wickedness, for the power of doing evil is contrary to His deity and its omnipotence. Whereas if any one among existing things is able to commit wickedness from being inclined to wickedness by nature, it does so from not having in its nature the ability not to do evil.

CHAP. LXXI.

He next assumes what is not granted by the more rational class of believers, but what perhaps is considered to be true by some who are devoid of intelligence, — viz., that "God, like those who are overcome with pity, being Himself overcome, alleviates the sufferings of the wicked through pity for their wailings, and casts off the good, who do nothing of that kind, which is the height of injustice." Now, in our judgment, God lightens the suffering of no wicked man who has not betaken himself to a virtuous life, and casts off no one who is already good, nor yet alleviates the suffering of any one who mourns, simply because he utters lamentation, or

takes pity upon him, to use the word pity in its more common acceptation.[2] But those who have passed severe condemnation upon themselves because of their sins, and who, as on that account, lament and bewail themselves as lost, so far as their previous conduct is concerned, and who have manifested a satisfactory change, are received by God on account of their repentance, as those who have undergone a transformation from a life of great wickedness. For virtue, taking up her abode in the souls of these persons, and expelling the wickedness which had previous possession of them, produces an oblivion of the past. And even although virtue do not effect an entrance, yet if a considerable progress take place in the soul, even that is sufficient, in the proportion that it is progressive, to drive out and destroy the flood of wickedness, so that it almost ceases to remain in the soul.

CHAP. LXXII.

In the next place, speaking as in the person of a teacher of our doctrine, he expresses himself as follows : " Wise men reject what we say, being led into error, and ensnared by their wisdom." In reply to which we say that, since wisdom is the knowledge of divine and human things and of their causes, or, as it is defined by the word of God, " the breath of the power of God, and a pure influence flowing from the glory of the Almighty ; and the brightness of the everlasting light, and the unspotted mirror of the power of God, and the image of His goodness," [3] no one who was really wise would reject what is said by a Christian acquainted with the principles of Christianity, or would be led into error, or ensnared by it. For true wisdom does not mislead, but ignorance does, while of existing things knowledge alone is permanent, and the truth which is derived from wisdom. But if, contrary to the definition of wisdom, you call any one whatever who dogmatizes with sophistical opinions wise, we answer that in conformity with what *you* call wisdom, such an one rejects the words of God, being misled and ensnared by plausible sophisms. And since, according to our doctrine, wisdom is not the knowledge of evil, but the knowledge of evil, so to speak, is in those who hold false opinions and who are deceived by them, I would therefore in such persons term it ignorance rather than wisdom.

CHAP. LXXIII.

After this he again slanders the ambassador of Christianity, and gives out regarding him that he relates "ridiculous things," although he does not show or clearly point out what are the things

---

[1] ὥσπερ οὐ δύναται τὸ πεφυκὸς γλυκαίνειν τῷ γλυκυ τυγχάνειν πικράζειν, παρὰ τὴν αὐτοῦ μόνην αἰτίαν.

[2] ἵνα κοινότερον τῷ ἐλέει χρήσωμαι.
[3] Cf. Wisd. of Solom. vii. 25, 26.

which he calls "ridiculous." And in his slanders he says that "no wise man believes the Gospel, being driven away by the multitudes who adhere to it." And in this he acts like one who should say that owing to the multitude of those ignorant persons who are brought into subjection to the laws, no wise man would yield obedience to Solon, for example, or to Lycurgus, or Zaleucus, or any other legislator, and especially if by wise man he means one who is wise (by living) in conformity with virtue. For, as with regard to these ignorant persons, the legislators, according to their ideas of utility, caused them to be surrounded with appropriate guidance and laws, so God, legislating through Jesus Christ for men in all parts of the world, brings to Himself even those who are not wise in the way in which it is possible for such persons to be brought to a better life. And God, well knowing this, as we have already shown in the preceding pages, says in the books of Moses: "They have moved Me to jealousy with that which is not God; they have provoked Me to anger with their idols: and I will move them to jealousy with those which are not a people; I will provoke them to anger with a foolish nation."[1] And Paul also, knowing this, said, "But God hath chosen the foolish things of the world to confound the wise,"[2] calling, in a general way, wise all who appear to have made advances in knowledge, but have fallen into an atheistic polytheism, since "professing themselves to be wise they became fools, and changed the glory of the incorruptible God into an image made like to corruptible man, and to birds, and four-footed beasts, and creeping things."[3]

CHAP. LXXIV.

He accuses the Christian teacher, moreover, of "seeking after the unintelligent." In answer, we ask, Whom do you mean by the "unintelligent?" For, to speak accurately, every wicked man is "unintelligent." If then by "unintelligent" you mean the wicked, do you, in drawing men to philosophy, seek to gain the wicked or the virtuous?[4] But it is impossible to gain the virtuous, because they have already given themselves to philosophy. The wicked, then, (you try to gain;) but if they are wicked, are they "unintelligent?" And many such you seek to win over to philosophy, and you therefore seek the "unintelligent." But if I seek after those who are thus termed "unintelligent," I act like a benevolent physician, who should seek after the sick in order to help and cure them. If, however, by "unintelligent" you mean persons who

are not clever,[5] but the inferior class of men intellectually,[6] I shall answer that I endeavour to improve such also to the best of my ability, although I would not desire to build up the Christian community out of such materials. For I seek in preference those who are more clever and acute, because they are able to comprehend the meaning of the hard sayings, and of those passages in the law, and prophecies, and Gospels, which are expressed with obscurity, and which you have despised as not containing anything worthy of notice, because you have not ascertained the meaning which they contain, nor tried to enter into the aim of the writers.

CHAP. LXXV.

But as he afterwards says that "the teacher of Christianity acts like a person who promises to restore patients to bodily health, but who prevents them from consulting skilled physicians, by whom his ignorance would be exposed," we shall inquire in reply, "What are the physicians to whom you refer, from whom we turn away ignorant individuals? For you do not suppose that we exhort those to embrace the Gospel who are devoted to philosophy, so that you would regard the latter as the physicians from whom we keep away such as we invite to come to the word of God." He indeed will make no answer, because he cannot name the physicians; or else he will be obliged to betake himself to those of them who are ignorant, and who of their own accord servilely yield themselves to the worship of many gods, and to whatever other opinions are entertained by ignorant individuals. In either case, then, he will be shown to have employed to no purpose in his argument the illustration of "one who keeps others away from skilled physicians." But if, in order to preserve from the philosophy of Epicurus, and from such as are considered physicians after his system, those who are deceived by them, why should we not be acting most reasonably in keeping such away from a dangerous disease caused by the physicians of Celsus, — that, viz., which leads to the annihilation of providence, and the introduction of pleasure as a good? But let it be conceded that we do keep away those whom we encourage to become our disciples from other philosopher-physicians, — from the Peripatetics, for example, who deny the existence of providence and the relation of Deity to man, — why shall we not piously train[7] and heal those who have been thus encouraged, persuading them to devote themselves to the God of all things, and

---

[1] Cf. Deut. xxxii. 21.
[2] Cf. 1 Cor. i. 27.
[3] Rom. i. 22, 23.
[4] ἀστείους.

[5] τοὺς μὴ ἐντρεχεῖς.
[6] The reading in the text is τερατωδεστέρους, of which Ruæus remarks, "Hic nullum habet locum." Καταδεεστέρους has been conjectured instead, and has been adopted in the translation.
[7] For εὐσεβεῖς in the text, Boherellus conjectures εὐσεβῶς.

free those who yield obedience to us from the great wounds inflicted by the words of such as are deemed to be philosophers? Nay, let it also be admitted that we turn away from physicians of the sect of the Stoics, who introduce a corruptible god, and assert that his essence consists of a body, which is capable of being changed and altered in all its parts,[1] and who also maintain that all things will one day perish, and that God alone will be left; why shall we not even thus emancipate our subjects from evils, and bring them by pious arguments to devote themselves to the Creator, and to admire the Father of the Christian system, who has so arranged that instruction of the most benevolent kind, and fitted for the conversion of souls,[2] should be distributed throughout the whole human race? Nay, if we should cure those who have fallen into the folly of believing in the transmigration of souls through the teaching of physicians, who will have it that the rational nature descends sometimes into all kinds of irrational animals, and sometimes into that state of being which is incapable of using the imagination,[3] why should we not improve the souls of our subjects by means of a doctrine which does not teach that a state of insensibility or irrationalism is produced in the wicked instead of punishment, but which shows that the labours and chastisements inflicted upon the wicked by God are a kind of medicines leading to conversion? For those who are intelligent Christians,[4] keeping this in view, deal with the simple-minded, as parents do with very young[5] children. We do not betake ourselves then to young persons and silly rustics, saying to them, "Flee from physicians." Nor do we say, "See that none of you lay hold of knowledge;" nor do we assert that "knowledge is an evil;" nor are we mad enough to say that "knowledge causes men to lose their soundness of mind." We would not even say that any one ever perished through wisdom; and although we give instruction, we never say, "Give heed to me," but "Give heed to the God of all things, and to Jesus, the giver of instruction concerning Him." And none of us is so great a braggart[6] as to say what Celsus put in the mouth of one of our teachers to his acquaintances, "I alone will save you." Observe here the lies which he utters against us! Moreover, we do *not* assert that

"true physicians destroy those whom they promise to cure."

CHAP. LXXVI.

And he produces a second illustration to our disadvantage, saying that "our teacher acts like a drunken man, who, entering a company of drunkards, should accuse those who are sober of being drunk." But let him show, say from the writings of Paul, that the apostle of Jesus gave way to drunkenness, and that his words were not those of soberness; or from the writings of John, that his thoughts do not breathe a spirit of temperance and freedom from the intoxication of evil. No one, then, who is of sound mind, and teaches the doctrines of Christianity, gets drunk with wine; but Celsus utters these calumnies against us in a spirit very unlike that of a philosopher. Moreover, let Celsus say who those "sober" persons are whom the ambassadors of Christianity accuse. For in our judgment all are intoxicated who address themselves to inanimate objects as to God. And why do I say "intoxicated?" "Insane" would be the more appropriate word for those who hasten to temples and worship images or animals as divinities. And they too are not less insane who think that images, fashioned by men of worthless and sometimes most wicked character, confer any honour upon genuine divinities.[7]

CHAP. LXXVII.

He next likens our teacher to one suffering from ophthalmia, and his disciples to those suffering from the same disease, and says that "such an one amongst a company of those who are afflicted with ophthalmia, accuses those who are sharp-sighted of being blind." Who, then, would we ask, O Greeks, are they who in our judgment do not see, save those who are unable to look up from the exceeding greatness of the world and its contents, and from the beauty of created things, and to see that they ought to worship, and admire, and reverence Him alone who made these things, and that it is not befitting to treat with reverence anything contrived by man, and applied to the honour of God, whether it be without a reference to the Creator, or with one?[8] For, to compare with that illimitable excellence, which surpasses all created being, things which ought not to be brought into comparison with it, is the act of those whose understanding is darkened. We do not then say that those who are

---

[1] θεὸν φθαρτὸν εἰσαγόντων, καὶ τὴν οὐσίαν αὐτοῦ λεγόντων σῶμα τρεπτὸν διόλου καὶ ἀλλοιωτὸν καὶ μεταβλητόν.

[2] The words in the text are, φιλανθρωπότατα ἐπιστρεπτικὸν, καὶ ψυχῶν μαθήματα οἰκονομήσαντα, for which we have adopted in the translation the emendation of Boherellus, φιλανθρωπότατα καὶ ψυχῶν ἐπιστρεπτικὰ μαθήματα.

[3] ἀλλὰ κἂν τοὺς πεπονθότας τὴν περὶ τῆς μετενσωματώσεως ἄνοιαν ἀπὸ ἰατρῶν, τῶν καταβιβαζόντων τὴν λογικὴν φύσιν ὅτε μὲν ἐπὶ τὴν ἄλογον πᾶσαν, ὁτὲ δὲ καὶ ἐπὶ τὴν ἀφάνταστον.

[4] Instead of οἱ φρονίμως Χριστιανοὶ ζῶντες, as in the text, Ruæus and Boherellus conjecture οἱ φρονίμως Χριστιανίζοντες, etc.

[5] τοὺς κομιδῇ νηπίους.

[6] ἀλαζών.

[7] [See vol. iii. Elucidation I. p. 76, this series; and as against the *insanity* of the Deutero-Nicene Council (A.D. 787) note this prophetic protest. Condemned at Frankfort (A.D. 794) by Anglicans and Gallicans. See Sir W. Palmer, *Treatise on the Church*, part iv. 10, sect. 4. The Council of Frankfort is the pivot of history as to the division between East and West, the rise of Gallicanism, and of the Anglican Reformation.]

[8] εἴτε χωρὶς τοῦ δημιουργοῦ θεοῦ εἴτε καὶ μετ' ἐκείνου.

sharp-sighted are suffering from ophthalmia or blindness; but we assert that those who, in ignorance of God, give themselves to temples and images, and so-called sacred seasons,[1] are blinded in their minds, and especially when, in addition to their impiety, they live also in licentiousness, not even inquiring after any honourable work whatever, but doing everything that is of a disgraceful character.

CHAP. LXXVIII.

After having brought against us charges of so serious a kind, he wishes to make it appear that, although he has others to adduce, he passes them by in silence. His words are as follows: "These charges I have to bring against them, and others of a similar nature, not to enumerate them one by one, and I affirm that they are in error, and that they act insolently towards God, in order to lead on wicked men by empty hopes, and to persuade them to despise better things, saying that if they refrain from them it will be better for them." In answer to which, it might be said that from the power which shows itself in those who are converted to Christianity, it is not at all the "wicked" who are won over to the Gospel, as the more simple class of persons, and, as many would term them, the "unpolished."[2] For such individuals, through fear of the punishments that are threatened, which arouses and exhorts them to refrain from those actions which are followed by punishments, strive to yield themselves up to the Christian religion, being influenced by the power of the word to such a degree, that through fear of what are called in the word "everlasting punishments," they despise all the tortures which are devised against them among men, — even death itself, with countless other evils, — which no wise man would say is the act of persons of wicked mind. How can temperance and sobermindedness, or benevolence and liberality, be practised by a man of wicked mind? Nay, even the fear of God cannot be felt by such an one, with respect to which, because it is useful to the many, the Gospel encourages those who are not yet able to choose that which ought to be chosen for its own sake, to select it as the greatest blessing, and one above all promise; for this principle cannot be implanted in him who prefers to live in wickedness.

CHAP. LXXIX.

But if in these matters any one were to imagine that it is superstition rather than wickedness which appears in the multitude of those who believe the word, and should charge our doctrine

with making men superstitious, we shall answer him by saying that, as a certain legislator[3] replied to the question of one who asked him whether he had enacted for his citizens the best laws, that he had not given them absolutely the best, but the best which they were capable of receiving; so it might be said by the Father of the Christian doctrine, I have given the best laws and instruction for the improvement of morals of which the many were capable, not threatening sinners with imaginary labours and chastisements, but with such as are real, and necessary to be applied for the correction of those who offer resistance, although they do not at all understand the object of him who inflicts the punishment, nor the effect of the labours. For the doctrine of punishment is both attended with utility, and is agreeable to truth, and is stated in obscure terms with advantage.[4] Moreover, as for the most part it is not the wicked whom the ambassadors of Christianity gain over, neither do we insult God. For we speak regarding Him both what is true, and what appears to be clear to the multitude, but not so clear to them as it is to those few who investigate the truths of the Gospel in a philosophical manner.

CHAP. LXXX.

Seeing, however, that Celsus alleges that "Christians are won over by us through vain hopes," we thus reply to him when he finds fault with our doctrine of the blessed life, and of communion with God: "As for you, good sir, they also are won over by vain hopes who have accepted the doctrine of Pythagoras and Plato regarding the soul, that it is its nature to ascend to the vault[5] of heaven, and in the super-celestial space to behold the sights which are seen by the blessed spectators above. According to you, O Celsus, they also who have accepted the doctrine of the duration of the soul (after death), and who lead a life through which they become heroes, and make their abodes with the gods, are won over by vain hopes. Probably also they who are persuaded that the soul comes (into the body) from without, and that it will be withdrawn from the power of death,[6] would be said by Celsus to be won over by empty hopes. Let him then come forth to the contest, no longer concealing the sect to which he belongs, but

---

[1] ἱερομηνίας.

[2] The reading in the text is κομψοί, which is so opposed to the sense of the passage, that the conjecture of Guietus, ἀκομψοί, has been adopted in the translation.

[3] [i.e., Solon. S.]

[4] [See Gieseler's *Church History*, vol. i. p. 212 (also 213), with references there. But see Elucidation IV. p. 77, vol. iii., this series, and Elucidation at close of this book. See also Robertson's *History of the Church*, vol. i. p. 156. S.]

[5] ἀψῖδα.

[6] Τάχα δὲ καὶ οἱ πεισθέντες περὶ τοῦ θύραθεν νοῦ, ὡς θανάτου καινοῦ διεξαγωγὴν ἔξοντος, etc. Locus certe obscurus, cui lucem afferre conatur Boherellus, legendo divisim ὡς θανάτου καὶ νοῦ διεξαγωγὴν ἔξοντος, ut sensus sit "morti etiam mentem subductum iri." Nam si θύραθεν ἧκει νοῦς, consequens est ut θανάτου καὶ νοῦς διεξαγωγὴν ἔχῃ. Cf. Aristot., lib. ii. c. 3, *de generatione animæ lium.*—SPENCER.

confessing himself to be an Epicurean, and let him meet the arguments, which are not lightly advanced among Greeks and Barbarians, regarding the immortality of the soul, or its duration (after death), or the immortality of the thinking principle;[1] and let him prove that these are words which deceive with empty hopes those who give their assent to them; but that the adherents of his philosophical system are pure from empty hopes, and that they indeed lead to hopes of good, or — what is more in keeping with his opinions — give birth to no hope at all, on account of the immediate and complete destruction of the soul (after death). Unless, perhaps, Celsus and the Epicureans will deny that it is a vain hope which they entertain regarding *their* end, — pleasure, — which, according to them, is the supreme good, and which consists in the permanent health of the body, and the hope regarding it which is entertained by Epicurus.[2]

CHAP. LXXXI.

And do not suppose that it is not in keeping with the Christian religion for me to have accepted, against Celsus, the opinions of those philosophers who have treated of the immortality or after-duration of the soul; for, holding certain views in common with them, we shall more conveniently establish our position, that the future life of blessedness shall be for those only who have accepted the religion which is according to Jesus, and that devotion towards the Creator of all things which is pure and sincere, and unmingled with any created thing whatever. And let him who likes show what " better things " we

persuade men to despise, and let him compare the blessed end with God in Christ, — that is the word, and the wisdom, and all virtue, — which, according to our view, shall be bestowed by the gift of God, on those who have lived a pure and blameless life, and who have felt a single and undivided love for the God of all things, with that end which is to follow according to the teaching of each philosophic sect whether it be Greek or Barbarian, or according to the professions of religious mysteries;[3] and let him prove that the end which is predicted by any of the others is superior to that which we promise, and consequently that that is true, and ours not befitting the gift of God, nor those who have lived a good life; or let him prove that these words were not spoken by the divine Spirit who filled the souls of the holy prophets. And let him who likes show that those words which are acknowledged among all men to be human are superior to those which are proved to be divine, and uttered by inspiration.[4] And what are the "better" things from which we teach those who receive them that it would be better to abstain? For if it be not arrogant so to speak, it is self-evident that nothing can be denied which is better than to entrust oneself to the God of all, and yield oneself up to the doctrine which raises us above all created things, and brings us, through the animate and living word — which is also living wisdom and the Son of God — to God who is over all. However, as the third book of our answers to the treatise of Celsus has extended to a sufficient length, we shall here bring our present remarks to a close, and in what is to follow shall meet what Celsus has subsequently written.

---

[1] ἢ τῆς τοῦ νοῦ ἀθανασίας.

[2] Εἰ μὴ ἄρα Κέλσος καὶ οἱ Ἐπικούρειοι οὐ φήσουσι κούφην εἶναι ἐλπίδα τὴν περὶ τοῦ τέλους αὐτῶν τῆς ἡδονῆς, ἥτις κατ᾽ αὐτούς ἐστι τὸ ἀγαθὸν, τὸ τῆς σαρκὸς εὐσταθὲς κατάστημα, καὶ τὸ περὶ ταύτης πιστὸν Ἐπικούρῳ ἐλπισμα.

[3] τῷ καθ᾽ ἑκάστην φιλοσόφων αἵρεσιν ἐν Ἕλλησιν ἢ βαρβάροις, ἢ μυστηριώδη ἐπαγγελίαν, τέλει.

[4] [Note the testimony to divine inspiration.]

ORIGEN AGAINST CELSUS.

BOOK IV.

CHAP. I.

HAVING, in the three preceding books, fully stated what occurred to us by way of answer to the treatise of Celsus, we now, reverend Ambrosius, with prayer to God through Christ, offer this fourth book as a reply to what follows. And we pray that words may be given us, as it is written in the book of Jeremiah that the Lord said to the prophet: "Behold, I have put My words in thy mouth as fire. See, I have set thee this day over the nations, and over the kingdoms, to root out and to pull down, and to destroy, and to throw down, and to build and to plant." [1] For we need words now which will root out of every wounded soul the reproaches uttered against the truth by this treatise of Celsus, or which proceed from opinions like his. And we need also thoughts which will pull down all edifices based on false opinions, and especially the edifice raised by Celsus in his work, which resembles the building of those who said, "Come, let us build us a city, and a tower whose top shall reach to heaven." [2] Yea, we even require a wisdom which will throw down all high things that rise against the knowledge of God,[3] and especially that height of arrogance which Celsus displays against us. And in the next place, as we must not stop with rooting out and pulling down the hindrances which have just been mentioned, but must, in room of what has been rooted out, plant the plants of "God's husbandry; " [4] and in place of what has been pulled down, rear up the building of God, and the temple of His glory, — we must for that reason pray also to the Lord, who bestowed the gifts named in the book of Jeremiah, that He may grant even to us words adapted both for building up the (temple) of Christ, and for planting the spiritual law, and the prophetic words referring to the same.[5] And above all is it necessary to show, as against the assertions of Celsus which follow those he has already made, that the prophecies regarding Christ are true predictions. For, arraying himself at the same time against both parties — against the Jews on the one hand, who deny that the advent of Christ has taken place, but who expect it as future, and against Christians on the other, who acknowledge that Jesus is the Christ spoken of in prophecy — he makes the following statement : —

CHAP. II.

" But that certain Christians and (all) Jews should maintain, the former that there *has* already descended, the latter that there *will* descend, upon the earth a certain God, or Son of a God, who will make the inhabitants of the earth righteous,[6] is a most shameless assertion, and one the refutation of which does not need many words." Now here he appears to pronounce correctly regarding not "certain" of the Jews, but *all* of them, that they imagine that there is a certain (God) who will descend upon the earth ; and with regard to Christians, that *certain of them* say that He has already come down.   For he means those who prove from the Jewish Scriptures that the advent of Christ has already taken place, and he seems to know that there are certain heretical sects which deny that Christ Jesus was predicted by the prophets.   In the preceding pages, however, we have already discussed, to the best of our ability, the question of Christ having been the subject of prophecy, and therefore, to avoid tautology, we do not repeat much that might be advanced upon this head. Observe, now, that if he had wished with a kind of apparent force[7] to subvert faith in the prophetic writings, either with regard to the future or past advent of Christ, he ought to have set forth the prophecies which we Christians and Jews quote in our discussions with each other.   For in this way he would have

---

[1] Cf. Jer. i. 9, 10.
[2] Cf. Gen. xi. 4.
[3] Cf. 2 Cor. x. 5.
[4] Cf. 1 Cor. iii. 9.
[5] τοὺς ἀνάλογον αὐτῷ προφητικοὺς λόγους.

[6] δικαιωτής.
[7] ἀκολουθίας.

appeared to turn aside those who are carried away by the plausible character [1] of the prophetic statements, as he regards it, from assenting to their truth, and from believing, on account of these prophecies, that Jesus is the Christ; whereas now, being unable to answer the prophecies relating to Christ, or else not knowing at all what are the prophecies relating to Him, he brings forward no prophetic declaration, although there are countless numbers which refer to Christ; but he thinks that he prefers an accusation against the prophetic Scriptures, while he does not even state what he himself would call their "plausible character!" He is not, however, aware that it is not at all the Jews who say that Christ will descend as a God, or the Son of a God, as we have shown in the foregoing pages. And when he asserts that "he is said by us to have already come, but by the Jews that his advent as Messiah [2] is still future," he appears by the very charge to censure our statement as one that is most shameless, and which needs no lengthened refutation.

CHAP. III.

And he continues: "What is the meaning of such a descent upon the part of God?" not observing that, according to our teaching, the meaning of the descent is pre-eminently to convert what are called in the Gospel the lost "sheep of the house of Israel;" and secondly, to take away from them, on account of their disobedience, what is called the "kingdom of God," and to give to other husbandmen than the ancient Jews, viz., to the Christians, who will render to God the fruits of His kingdom in due season (each action being a "fruit of the kingdom").[3] We shall therefore, out of a greater number, select a few remarks by way of answer to the question of Celsus, when he says, "What is the meaning of such a descent upon the part of God?" And Celsus here returns to himself an answer which would have been given neither by Jews nor by us, when he asks, "Was it in order to learn what goes on amongst men?" For not one of us asserts that it was in order to learn what goes on amongst men that Christ entered into this life. Immediately after, however, as if some would reply that it *was* "in order to learn what goes on among men," he makes this objection to his own statement: "Does he not know all things?" Then, as if we were to answer that He *does* know all things, he raises a new question, saying, "Then he does know, but does not make (men) better, nor is it possible for him by means of his divine power to make

(men) better." Now all this on his part is silly talk; [4] for God, by means of His word, which is continually passing from generation to generation into holy souls, and constituting them friends of God and prophets, *does* improve those who listen to His words; and by the coming of Christ He improves, through the doctrine of Christianity, not those who are unwilling, but those who have chosen the better life, and that which is pleasing to God. I do not know, moreover, what kind of improvement Celsus wished to take place when he raised the objection, asking, "Is it then not possible for him, by means of his divine power, to make (men) better, unless he send some one for that special purpose?"[5] Would he then have the improvement to take place by God's filling the minds of men with new ideas, removing at once the (inherent) wickedness, and implanting virtue (in its stead)?[6] Another person now would inquire whether this was not inconsistent or impossible in the very nature of things; we, however, would say, "Grant it to be so, and let it be possible." Where, then, is our free will?[7] and what credit is there in assenting to the truth? or how is the rejection of what is false praiseworthy? But even if it were once granted that such a course was not only possible, but could be accomplished with propriety (by God), why would not one rather inquire (asking a question like that of Celsus) why it was not possible for God, by means of His divine power, to create men who needed no improvement, but who were of themselves virtuous and perfect, evil being altogether non-existent? These questions may perplex ignorant and foolish individuals, but not him who sees into the nature of things; for if you take away the spontaneity of virtue, you destroy its essence. But it would need an entire treatise to discuss these matters; and on this subject the Greeks have expressed themselves at great length in their works on providence. They truly would not say what Celsus has expressed in words, that "God knows (all things) indeed, but does not make (men) better, nor is able to do so by His divine power." We ourselves have spoken in many parts of our writings on these points to the best of our ability, and the Holy Scriptures have established the same to those who are able to understand them.

CHAP. IV.

The argument which Celsus employs against us and the Jews will be turned against himself

---

[1] πιθανότητος.

[2] Δικαιωτής, not Δικαστής.

[3] τοὺς καρποὺς τῆς τοῦ Θεοῦ βασιλείας ἀποδώσουσι τῷ Θεῷ, ἐν τοῖς ἑκάστης πράξεως οὔσης καρποῦ τῆς βασιλείας καιροῖς.

[4] εὐήθως.

[5] The word φύσει which is found in the text seems out of place, and has been omitted in the translation, agreeably to the emendation of Boherellus.

[6] Ἆρα γὰρ ἤθελε φαντασιουμένοις τοῖς ἀνθρώποις ὑπὸ Θεοῦ, ἀπειληφότος μὲν ἀθρόως τὴν κακίαν, ἐμφύοντος δὲ τὴν ἀρετήν, τὴν ἐπανόρθωσιν γενέσθαι;

[7] ποῦ οὖν τὸ ἐφ' ἡμῖν;

hus: My good sir, does the God who is over all things know what takes place among men, or does He not know? Now if you admit the existence of a God and of providence, as your treatise indicates, He must of necessity know. And if He does know, why does He not make (men) better? Is it obligatory, then, on *us* to defend God's procedure in not making men better, although He knows their state, but not equally binding on *you*, who do not distinctly show by your treatise that you are an Epicurean, but pretend to recognise a providence, to explain why God, although knowing all that takes place among men, does not make them better, nor by divine power liberate all men from evil? We are not ashamed, however, to say that God is constantly sending (instructors) in order to make men better; for there are to be found amongst men reasons [1] given by God which exhort them to enter on a better life. But there are many diversities amongst those who serve God, and they are few in number who are perfect and pure ambassadors of the truth, and who produce a complete reformation, as did Moses and the prophets. But above all these, great was the reformation effected by Jesus, who desired to heal not only those who lived in one corner of the world, but as far as in Him lay, men in every country, for He came as the Saviour of *all* men.

CHAP. V.

The illustrious [2] Celsus, taking occasion I know not from what, next raises an additional objection against us, as if we asserted that "God Himself will come down to men." He imagines also that it follows from this, that "He has left His own abode;" for he does not know the power of God, and that "the Spirit of the Lord filleth the world, and that which upholdeth all things hath knowledge of the voice." [3] Nor is he able to understand the words, "Do I not fill heaven and earth? saith the LORD." [4] Nor does he see that, according to the doctrine of Christianity, we all "in Him live, and move, and have our being," [5] as Paul also taught in his address to the Athenians; and therefore, although the God of the universe should through His own power descend with Jesus into the life of men, and although the Word which was in the beginning with God, which is also God Himself, should come to us, He does not give His place or vacate His own seat, so that one place should be empty of Him, and another which did not formerly contain Him be filled. But the power and divinity of God comes through him whom God chooses, and resides in him in whom it finds a place, not changing its situation, nor leaving its own place empty and filling another: for, in speaking of His quitting one place and occupying another, we do not mean such expressions to be taken *topically;* but we say that the soul of the bad man, and of him who is overwhelmed in wickedness, is abandoned by God, while we mean that the soul of him who wishes to live virtuously, or of him who is making progress (in a virtuous life), or who is already living conformably thereto, is filled with or becomes a partaker of the Divine Spirit. It is not necessary, then, for the descent of Christ, or for the coming of God to men, that He should abandon a greater seat, and that things on earth should be changed, as Celsus imagines when he says, "If you were to change a single one, even the least, of things on earth, all things would be overturned and disappear." And if we must speak of a change in any one by the appearing of the power of God, and by the entrance of the word among men, we shall not be reluctant to speak of changing from a wicked to a virtuous, from a dissolute to a temperate, and from a superstitious to a religious life, the person who has allowed the word of God to find entrance into his soul.

CHAP. VI.

But if you will have us to meet the most ridiculous among the charges of Celsus, listen to him when he says: "Now God, being unknown amongst men, and deeming himself on that account to have less than his due,[6] would desire to make himself known, and to make trial both of those who believe upon him and of those who do not, like those of mankind who have recently come into the possession of riches, and who make a display of their wealth; and thus they testify to an excessive but very mortal ambition on the part of God." [7] We answer, then, that God, not being known by wicked men, would desire to make Himself known, not because He thinks that He meets with less than His due, but because the knowledge of Him will free the possessor from unhappiness. Nay, not even with the desire to try those who do or who do not believe upon Him, does He, by His unspeakable and divine power, Himself take up His abode in certain individuals, or send His Christ; but He does this in order to liberate from all their wretchedness those who do believe upon Him, and who accept His divinity, and that those who do *not* believe may no longer have this as a ground of excuse, viz., that their unbelief is the consequence of their not having

---

[1] οἱ γὰρ ἐπὶ τὰ βέλτιστα προκαλούμενοι λόγοι, Θεοῦ αὐτοὺς δεδωκότος, εἰσὶν ἐν ἀνθρώποις.

[2] γενναιότατος.

[3] Wisd. Solom. i. 7, καὶ τὸ συνέχον τὰ πάντα γνῶσιν ἔχει φωνῆς.

[4] Cf. Jer. xxiii. 24.

[5] Cf. Acts xvii. 28.

[6] καὶ παρὰ τοῦτ' ἔλαττον ἔχειν δοκῶν.

[7] καθάπερ οἱ νεόπλουτοι τῶν ἀνθρώπων ἐπιδεικτιῶντες, πολλήν τινα καὶ πάνυ θνητὴν φιλοτιμίαν τοῦ Θεοῦ καταμαρτυροῦσι.

heard the word of instruction. What argument, then, proves that it follows from our views that God, according to our representations, is "like those of mankind who have recently come into the possession of riches, and who make a display of their wealth?" For God makes no display towards us, from a desire that we should understand and consider His pre-eminence; but desiring that the blessedness which results from His being known by us should be implanted in our souls, He brings it to pass through Christ, and His ever-indwelling word, that we come to an intimate fellowship [1] with Him. No mortal ambition, then, does the Christian doctrine testify as existing on the part of God.

CHAP. VII.

I do not know how it is, that after the foolish remarks which he has made upon the subject which we have just been discussing, he should add the following, that "God does not desire to make himself known for his own sake, but because he wishes to bestow upon us the knowledge of himself for the sake of our salvation, in order that those who accept it may become virtuous and be saved, while those who do not accept may be shown to be wicked and be punished." And yet, after making such a statement, he raises a new objection, saying: "After so long a period of time,[2] then, did God now bethink himself of making men live righteous lives,[3] but neglect to do so before?" To which we answer, that there never was a time when God did not wish to make men live righteous lives; but He continually evinced His care for the improvement of the rational animal,[4] by affording him occasions for the exercise of virtue. For in every generation the wisdom of God, passing into those souls which it ascertains to be holy, converts them into friends and prophets of God. And there may be found in the sacred book (the names of) those who in each generation were holy, and were recipients of the Divine Spirit, and who strove to convert their contemporaries so far as in their power.

CHAP. VIII.

And it is not matter of surprise that in certain generations there have existed prophets who, in the reception of divine influence,[5] surpassed, by means of their stronger and more powerful (religious) life, other prophets who were their contemporaries, and others also who lived before and after them. And so it is not at all wonderful that there should also have been a time when

something of surpassing excellence[6] took up it abode among the human race, and which wa distinguished above all that preceded or eve that followed. But there is an element of pro found mystery in the account of these things and one which is incapable of being received b the popular understanding. And in order tha these difficulties should be made to disappear and that the objections raised against the adven of Christ should be answered — viz., that, "afte so long a period of time, then, did God now be think himself of making men live righteous lives but neglect to do so before?" — it is necessar to touch upon the narrative of the divisions (o the nations), and to make it evident why it was that "when the Most High divided the nations when He separated the sons of Adam, He se the bounds of the nations according to the num ber of the angels of God, and the portion of th LORD was His people Jacob, Israel the cord o His inheritance;" [7] and it will be necessary t state the reason why the birth of each man too place within each particular boundary, unde him who obtained the boundary by lot, an how it rightly happened that "the portion of th LORD was His people Jacob, and Israel the cor of His inheritance," and why formerly the por tion of the LORD was His people Jacob, an Israel the cord of His inheritance. But wit respect to those who come after, it is said to th Saviour by the Father, "Ask of Me, and I wi give Thee the heathen for Thine inheritance and the uttermost parts of the earth for Th possession." [8] For there are certain connecte and related reasons, bearing upon the differen treatment of human souls, which are difficult t state and to investigate.[9]

CHAP. IX.

There came, then, although Celsus may no wish to admit it, after the numerous prophet who were the reformers of that well-known Israel the Christ, the Reformer of the whole world, wh did not need to employ against men whips, an chains, and tortures, as was the case unde the former economy. For when the sower wen forth to sow, the doctrine sufficed to sow th word everywhere. But if there is a time comin which will necessarily circumscribe the duratio of the world, by reason of its having had a be ginning, and if there is to be an end to the world and after the end a just judgment of all things, i will be incumbent on him who treats the decla rations of the Gospels philosophically, to estab lish these doctrines by arguments of all kinds

---

[1] οἰκείωσιν.
[2] μετὰ τοσοῦτον αἰῶνα.
[3] δικαιῶσαι.
[4] τὸ λογικὸν ζῷον.
[5] ἐν τῇ παραδοχῇ τῆς θειότητος.

[6] ἐξαίρετόν τι χρῆμα.
[7] Deut. xxxii. 8, 9 (according to the LXX.).
[8] Cf. Ps. ii. 8.
[9] Εἰσὶ γάρ τινες εἱρμοὶ καὶ ἀκολουθίαι ἄφατοι καὶ ἀνεκδιήγητοι περὶ τῆς κατὰ τὰς ἀνθρωπίνας ψυχὰς διαφόρου οἰκονομίας.

not only derived directly from the sacred Scriptures, but also by inferences deducible from them; while the more numerous and simpler class of believers, and those who are unable to comprehend the many varied aspects of the divine wisdom, must entrust themselves to God, and to the Saviour of our race, and be contented with His " ipse dixit," [1] instead of this or any other demonstration whatever.

CHAP. X.

In the next place, Celsus, as is his custom, having neither proved nor established anything, proceeds to say, as if we talked of God in a manner that was neither holy nor pious, that " it is perfectly manifest that they babble about God in a way that is neither holy nor reverential;" and he imagines that we do these things to excite the astonishment of the ignorant, and that we do not speak the truth regarding the necessity of punishments for those who have sinned. And accordingly he likens us to those who " in the Bacchic mysteries introduce phantoms and objects of terror." With respect to the mysteries of Bacchus, whether there is any trustworthy [2] account of them, or none that is such, let the Greeks tell, and let Celsus and his boon-companions [3] listen. But we defend our own procedure, when we say that our object is to reform the human race, either by the threats of punishments which we are persuaded are necessary for the whole world, [4] and which perhaps are not without use [5] to those who are to endure them; or by the promises made to those who have lived virtuous lives, and in which are contained the statements regarding the blessed termination which is to be found in the kingdom of God, reserved for those who are worthy of becoming His subjects.

CHAP. XI.

After this, being desirous to show that it is nothing either wonderful or new which we state regarding floods or conflagrations, but that, from misunderstanding the accounts of these things which are current among Greeks or barbarous nations, we have accorded our belief to our own Scriptures when treating of them, he writes as follows : " The belief has spread among them, from a misunderstanding of the accounts of these occurrences, that after lengthened cycles of time, and the returns and conjunctions of planets, conflagrations and floods are wont to happen, and because after the last flood, which took place in the time of Deucalion, the lapse of time, agreeably

to the vicissitude of all things, requires a conflagration; and this made them give utterance to the erroneous opinion that God will descend, bringing fire like a torturer." Now in answer to this we say, that I do not understand how Celsus, who has read a great deal, and who shows that he has perused many histories, had not his attention arrested [6] by the antiquity of Moses, who is related by certain Greek historians to have lived about the time of Inachus the son of Phoroneus, and is acknowledged by the Egyptians to be a man of great antiquity, as well as by those who have studied the history of the Phœnicians. And any one who likes may peruse the two books of Flavius Josephus on the antiquities of the Jews, in order that he may see in what way Moses was more ancient than those who asserted that floods and conflagrations take place in the world after long intervals of time; which statement Celsus alleges the Jews and Christians to have misunderstood, and, not comprehending what was said about a conflagration, to have declared that " God will descend, bringing fire like a torturer." [7]

CHAP. XII.

Whether, then, there are cycles of time, and floods, or conflagrations which occur periodically or not, and whether the Scripture is aware of this, not only in many passages, but especially where Solomon [8] says, " What is the thing which hath been? Even that which shall be. And what is the thing which hath been done? Even that which shall be done," [9] etc., etc., belongs not to the present occasion to discuss. For it is sufficient only to observe, that Moses and certain of the prophets, being men of very great antiquity, did not receive from others the statements relating to the (future) conflagration of the world; but, on the contrary (if we must attend to the matter of time [10]), others rather misunderstanding them, and not inquiring accurately into their statements, invented the fiction of the same events recurring at certain intervals, and differing neither in their essential nor accidental qualities. [11] But we do not refer either the deluge or the conflagration to cycles and planetary periods; but the cause of them we declare to be the extensive prevalence of wickedness, [12] and its (consequent) removal by a deluge or a conflagration. And if the voices of the prophets say that God " comes down," who has said, " Do I not fill heaven and earth? saith the LORD," [13] the term

---

1 αὐτὸς ἔφα.
2 [The word " reliable " is used here. I cannot let it stand, and have supplied an English word instead].
3 συνθιασῶται.
4 τῷ παντί.
5 οὐκ ἀχρήστους. On Origen's views respecting rewards and punishments, cf. Huet's *Origeniana*, book ii. question xi.

6 οὐκ ἐπέστη.
7 δίκην βασανιστοῦ πῦρ φέρων.
8 [Note this testimony to the authorship of *Koheleth*, and that it is Scripture.]
9 Cf. Eccles. i. 9.
10 εἰ χρὴ ἐπιστήσαντα τοῖς χρόνοις εἰπεῖν.
11 ἀνέπλασαν κατὰ περιόδους ταυτότητας, καὶ ἀπαραλλάκτους τοῖς ἰδίοις ποιοῖς καὶ τοῖς συμβεβηκόσιν αὐτοῖς.
12 κακίαν ἐπὶ πλεῖον χεομένην.
13 Cf. Jer. xxiii. 24.

is used in a figurative sense. For God "comes down" from His own height and greatness when He arranges the affairs of men, and especially those of the wicked. And as custom leads men to say that teachers "condescend" [1] to children, and wise men to those youths who have just betaken themselves to philosophy, not by "descending" in a *bodily* manner; so, if God is said anywhere in the holy Scriptures to "come down," it is understood as spoken in conformity with the usage which so employs the word, and in like manner also with the expression "go up." [2]

CHAP. XIII.

But as it is in mockery that Celsus says we speak of "God coming down like a torturer bearing fire," and thus compels us unseasonably to investigate words of deeper meaning, we shall make a few remarks, sufficient to enable our hearers to form an idea [3] of the defence which disposes of the ridicule of Celsus against us, and then we shall turn to what follows. The divine word says that our God is "a consuming fire," [4] and that "He draws rivers of fire before Him;" [5] nay, that He even entereth in as "a refiner's fire, and as a fuller's herb," [6] to purify His own people. But when He is said to be a "consuming fire," we inquire what are the things which are appropriate to be consumed by God. And we assert that they are wickedness, and the works which result from it, and which, being figuratively called "wood, hay, stubble," [7] God consumes as a fire. The wicked man, accordingly, is said to build up on the previously-laid foundation of reason, "wood, and hay, and stubble." If, then, any one can show that these words were differently understood by the writer, and can prove that the wicked man *literally* [8] builds up "wood, or hay, or stubble," it is evident that the fire must be understood to be material, and an object of sense. But if, on the contrary, the works of the wicked man are spoken of *figuratively* under the names of "wood, or hay, or stubble," why does it not at once occur (to inquire) in what sense the word "fire" is to be taken, so that "wood" of such a kind should be consumed? for (the Scripture) says: "The fire will try each man's work of what sort it is. If any man's work abide which he hath built thereupon, he shall receive a reward. If any man's work be burned, he shall suffer loss." [9] But what work can be spoken of in these words as being "burned," save all that results from wickedness? There-

fore our God is a "consuming fire" in the sense in which we have taken the word; and thus He enters in as a "refiner's fire," to refine the rational nature, which has been filled with the lead of wickedness, and to free it from the other impure materials, which adulterate the natural gold or silver, so to speak, of the soul. [10] And, in like manner, "rivers of fire" are said to be before God, who will thoroughly cleanse away the evil which is intermingled throughout the whole soul. [11] But these remarks are sufficient in answer to the assertion, "that thus they were made to give expression to the erroneous opinion that God will come down bearing fire like a torturer."

CHAP. XIV.

But let us look at what Celsus next with great ostentation announces in the following fashion "And again," he says, "let us resume the subject from the beginning, with a larger array of proofs. And I make no new statement, but say what has been long settled. God is good, and beautiful, and blessed, and that in the best and most beautiful degree. [12] But if he come down among men, he must undergo a change, and a change from good to evil, from virtue to vice, from happiness to misery, and from best to worst. Who, then, would make choice of such a change? It is the nature of a mortal, indeed to undergo change and remoulding, but of an immortal to remain the same and unaltered God, then, could not admit of such a change." Now it appears to me that the fitting answer has been returned to these objections, when I have related what is called in Scripture the "condescension" [13] of God to human affairs; for which purpose He did not need to undergo a transformation, as Celsus thinks we assert, nor a change from good to evil, nor from virtue to vice, nor from happiness to misery, nor from best to worst. For, continuing unchangeable in His essence, He condescends to human affairs by the economy of His providence. [14] We show, accordingly, that the holy Scriptures represent God as unchangeable, both by such words as "Thou art the same," [15] and "I change not;" [16] whereas the gods of Epicurus, being composed of atoms, and, so far as their structure is concerned, capable of dissolution, endeavour to throw off the atoms which contain the elements of destruction. Nay, even the god of the Stoics, as being corporeal, at one time has his whole essence composed of the guiding principle [17] when the conflagration (of the

1 συγκαταβαίνειν.
2 [On this figure (*anthropopathy*) see vol. ii. p. 363, this series.]
3 γεῦσαι.
4 Cf. Deut. iv. 24, ix. 3.
5 Cf. Dan. vii. 10.
6 Cf. Mal. iii. 2.
7 Cf. 1 Cor. iii. 12.
8 σωματικῶς.
9 Cf. 1 Cor. iii. 13–15.

10 τὴν τοῦ χρυσοῦ (ἵν' οὕτως ὀνομάσω), φύσιν τῆς ψυχῆς, ἢ τὴν ἀργύρου, δολωσάντων.
11 [See note *supra*, cap. x. S.]
12 Ὁ Θεὸς ἀγαθός ἐστι, καὶ καλὸς, καὶ εὐδαίμων, καὶ ἐν τῷ καλλίστῳ καὶ ἀρίστῳ.
13 κατάβασιν.
14 τῇ προνοίᾳ καὶ τῇ οἰκονομίᾳ.
15 Ps. cii. 27.
16 Mal. iii. 6.
17 ἡγεμονικόν.

world) takes place; and at another, when a re-arrangement of things occurs, he again becomes partly material.[1] For even the Stoics were un-able distinctly to comprehend the natural idea of God, as of a being altogether incorruptible and simple, and uncompounded and indivisible.

CHAP. XV.

And with respect to His having descended among men, He was "previously in the form of God;"[2] and through benevolence, divested Him-self (of His glory), that He might be capable of being received by men. But He did not, I imagine, undergo any change from "good to evil," for "He did no *sin;*"[3] nor from "virtue to vice," for "He knew no *sin.*"[4] Nor did He pass from "happiness to misery," but He hum-bled Himself, and nevertheless was blessed, even when His humiliation was undergone in order to benefit our race. Nor was there any change in Him from "best to worst," for how can good-ness and benevolence be of "the worst?" Is it befitting to say of the physician, who looks on dreadful sights and handles unsightly objects in order to cure the sufferers, that he passes from "good to evil," or from "virtue to vice," or from "happiness to misery?" And yet the physician, in looking on dreadful sights and handling un-sightly objects, does not wholly escape the possi-bility of being involved in the same fate. But He who heals the wounds of our souls, through the word of God that is in Him, is Himself in-capable of admitting any wickedness. But if the immortal God — the Word[5] — by assuming a mortal body and a human soul, appears to Celsus to undergo a change and transformation, let him learn that the Word, still remaining essentially the Word, suffers none of those things which are suffered by the body or the soul; but, condescending occasionally to (the weakness of) him who is unable to look upon the splendours and brilliancy of Deity, He becomes as it were flesh, speaking with a literal voice, until he who has received Him in such a form is able, through being elevated in some slight degree by the teaching of the Word, to gaze upon what is, so to speak, His real and pre-eminent appearance.[6]

CHAP. XVI.

For there are different appearances, as it were, of the Word, according as He shows Himself to each one of those who come to His doctrine;

and this in a manner corresponding to the con-dition of him who is just becoming a disciple, or of him who has made a little progress, or of him who has advanced further, or of him who has already *nearly* attained to virtue, or who has even *already* attained it. And hence it is not the case, as Celsus and those like him would have it, that our God was transformed, and as-cending the lofty mountain, showed that His real appearance was something different, and far more excellent than what those who remained below, and were unable to follow Him on high, beheld. For those below did not possess eyes capable of seeing the transformation of the Word into His glorious and more divine condition. But with difficulty were they able to receive Him as He was; so that it might be said of Him by those who were unable to behold His more excellent nature: "We saw Him, and He had no form nor comeliness; but His form was mean,[7] and inferior to that of the sons of men."[8] And let these remarks be an answer to the suppositions of Celsus, who does not understand the changes or transformations of Jesus, as related in the histories, nor His mortal and immortal nature.[9]

CHAP. XVII.

But will not those narratives, especially when they are understood in their proper sense, appear far more worthy of respect than the story that Dionysus was deceived by the Titans, and ex-pelled from the throne of Jupiter, and torn in pieces by them, and his remains being after-wards put together again, he returned as it were once more to life, and ascended to heaven? Or are the Greeks at liberty to refer such stories to the doctrine of the soul, and to interpret them figuratively, while the door of a consistent ex-planation, and one everywhere in accord and harmony with the writings of the Divine Spirit, who had His abode in pure souls, is closed against *us?* Celsus, then, is altogether ignorant of the purpose of our writings, and it is there-fore upon his own acceptation of them that he casts discredit, and not upon their real meaning; whereas, if he had reflected on what is appro-priate[10] to a soul which is to enjoy an everlasting life, and on the opinion which we are to form of its essence and principles, he would not so have ridiculed the entrance of the immortal into a mortal body, which took place not according to the metempsychosis of Plato, but agreeably to another and higher view of things. And he would have observed one "descent," distin-guished by its great benevolence, undertaken to convert (as the Scripture mystically terms them)

---

[1] The reading in the text is, ἐπὶ μέρους γίνεται αὐτῆς, which is thus corrected by Guietus: ἐπιμερὴς γίνεται αὐτός.
[2] Cf. Phil. ii. 6, 7.
[3] Cf. 1 Pet. ii. 22.
[4] Cf. 2 Cor. v. 21.
[5] [Gieseler cites this chapter (and cap. xix. *infra*) to show that Origen taught that the Logos did not assume a human body. Could words be stronger to the contrary? "He becomes, *as it were,* flesh," is used below to guard against transmutation.]
[6] προηγουμένην.

[7] ἄτιμον.
[8] ἐκλεῖπον.
[9] [The transfiguration did not conflict with his *mortal* nature, nor the incarnation with his *immortality*.]
[10] τί ἀκολουθεῖ.

the "lost sheep of the house of Israel," which had strayed down from the mountains, and to which the Shepherd is said in certain parables to have gone down, leaving on the mountains those "which had not strayed."

CHAP. XVIII.

But Celsus, lingering over matters which he does not understand, leads us to be guilty of tautology, as we do not wish even in appearance to leave any one of his objections unexamined. He proceeds, accordingly, as follows: "God either really changes himself, as these assert, into a mortal body, and the impossibility of that has been already declared; or else he does *not* undergo a change, but only causes the beholders to imagine so, and thus deceives them, and is guilty of falsehood. Now deceit and falsehood are nothing but evils, and would only be employed as a medicine, either in the case of sick and lunatic friends, with a view to their cure, or in that of enemies when one is taking measures to escape danger. But no sick man or lunatic is a friend of God, nor does God fear any one to such a degree as to shun danger by leading him into error." Now the answer to these statements might have respect partly to the nature of the Divine Word, who is God, and partly to the soul of Jesus. As respects the nature of the Word, in the same way as the quality of the food changes in the nurse into milk with reference to the nature of the child, or is arranged by the physician with a view to the good of his health in the case of a sick man, or (is specially) prepared for a stronger man, because he possesses greater vigour, so does God appropriately change, in the case of each individual, the power of the Word to which belongs the natural property of nourishing the human soul. And to one is given, as the Scripture terms it, "the sincere milk of the word;" and to another, who is weaker, as it were, "herbs;" and to another who is full-grown, "strong meat." And the Word does not, I imagine, prove false to His own nature, in contributing nourishment to each one, according as he is capable of receiving Him.[1] Nor does He mislead or prove false. But if one were to take the change as referring to the soul of Jesus after it had entered the body, we would inquire in what sense the term "change" is used. For if it be meant to apply to its essence, such a supposition is inadmissible, not only in relation to the soul of Jesus, but also to the rational soul of any other being. And if it be alleged that it suffers anything from the body when united with it, or from the place to which it has come, then what inconvenience[2]

can happen to the Word who, in great benevolence, brought down a Saviour to the human race? — seeing none of those who formerly professed to effect a cure could accomplish so much as that soul showed *it* could do, by what it performed, even by voluntarily descending to the level of human destinies for the benefit of our race. And the Divine Word, well knowing this, speaks to that effect in many passages of Scripture, although it is sufficient at present to quote one testimony of Paul to the following effect: "Let this mind be in you which was also in Christ Jesus; who, being in the form of God, thought it not robbery to be equal with God, but made Himself of no reputation, and took upon Him the form of a servant, and was made in the likeness of men; and being found in fashion as a man, He humbled Himself, and became obedient unto death, even the death of the cross. Wherefore God also hath highly exalted Him, and given Him a name which is above every name."[3]

CHAP. XIX.

Others, then, may concede to Celsus that God does not undergo a change, but leads the spectators to imagine that He does; whereas we who are persuaded that the advent of Jesus among men was no mere appearance, but a real manifestation, are not affected by this charge of Celsus. We nevertheless will attempt a reply, because you assert, Celsus, do you not, that it is sometimes allowable to employ deceit and falsehood by way, as it were, of medicine?[4] Where, then, is the absurdity, if such a saving result were to be accomplished, that some such events should have taken place? For certain words, when savouring of falsehood, produce upon such characters a corrective effect (like the similar declarations of physicians to their patients), rather than when spoken in the spirit of truth. This, however, must be our defence against other opponents. For there is no absurdity in Him who healed sick friends, healing the dear human race by means of such remedies as He would not employ preferentially, but only according to circumstances.[5] The human race, moreover, when in a state of mental alienation, had to be cured by methods which the Word saw would aid in bringing back those so afflicted to a sound state of mind. But Celsus says also, that "one acts thus towards enemies when taking measures to escape danger. But God does not fear any one, so as to escape danger by leading into error those who conspire against him." Now it is altogether unnecessary and absurd to answer a charge which is advanced by no one

---

[1] [Such are the *accommodations* reflected upon by Gieseler. See Book III. cap. lxxix., *supra*.]
[2] τί ἄτοπον.

[3] Phil. ii. 5–9.
[4] ὅμως δ᾽ ἀπολογησόμεθα, ὅτι οὐ φῄς, ὦ Κέλσε, ὡς ἐν φαρμάκου μοίρᾳ ποτὲ δίδοται χρῆσθαι τῷ πλανᾷν καὶ τῷ ψεύδεσθαι;
[5] προηγουμένως, ἀλλ᾽ ἐκ περιστάσεως.

against our Saviour. And we have already replied, when answering other charges, to the statement that "no one who is either in a state of sickness or mental alienation is a friend of God." For the answer is, that such arrangements have been made, not for the sake of those who, being already friends, afterwards fell sick or became afflicted with mental disease, but in order that those who were still enemies through sickness of the soul, and alienation of the natural reason, might become the friends of God. For it is distinctly stated that Jesus endured all things on behalf of sinners, that He might free them from sin, and convert them to righteousness.

CHAP. XX.

In the next place, as he represents the Jews accounting in a way peculiar to themselves for their belief that the advent of Christ among them is still in the future, and the Christians as maintaining in *their* way that the coming of the Son of God into the life of men has already taken place, let us, as far as we can, briefly consider these points. According to Celsus, the Jews say that "(human) life, being filled with all wickedness, needed one sent from God, that the wicked might be punished, and all things purified in a manner analogous to the first deluge which happened." And as the Christians are said to make statements additional to this, it is evident that he alleges that they admit these. Now, where is the absurdity in the coming of one who is, on account of the prevailing flood of wickedness, to purify the world, and to treat every one according to his deserts? For it is not in keeping with the character of God that the diffusion of wickedness should not cease, and all things be renewed. The Greeks, moreover, know of the earth's being purified at certain times by a deluge or a fire, as Plato, too, says somewhere to this effect: "And when the gods overwhelm the earth, purifying it with water, some of them on the mountains,"[1] etc., etc. Must it be said, then, that if the Greeks make such assertions, they are to be deemed worthy of respect and consideration, but that if we too maintain certain of these views, which are quoted with approval by the Greeks, they cease to be honourable? And yet they who care to attend to the connection and truth of all our records, will endeavour to establish not only the antiquity of the writers, but the venerable nature of their writings, and the consistency of their several parts.

CHAP. XXI.

But I do not understand how he can imagine the overturning of the tower (of Babel) to have happened with a similar object to that of the deluge, which effected a purification of the earth, according to the accounts both of Jews and Christians. For, in order that the narrative contained in Genesis respecting the tower may be held to convey no secret meaning, but, as Celsus supposes, may be taken as true to the letter,[2] the event does not on such a view appear to have taken place for the purpose of purifying the earth; unless, indeed, he imagines that the so-called confusion of tongues is such a purificatory process. But on this point, he who has the opportunity will treat more seasonably when his object is to show not only what is the meaning of the narrative in its historical connection, but what metaphorical meaning may be deduced from it.[3] Seeing that he imagines, however, that Moses, who wrote the account of the tower, and the confusion of tongues, has perverted the story of the sons of Aloeus,[4] and referred it to the tower, we must remark that I do not think any one prior to the time of Homer[5] has mentioned the sons of Aloeus, while I am persuaded that what is related about the tower has been recorded by Moses as being much older not only than Homer, but even than the invention of letters among the Greeks. Who, then, are the perverters of each other's narratives? Whether do they who relate the story of the Aloadæ pervert the history of the time, or he who wrote the account of the tower and the confusion of tongues the story of the Aloadæ? Now to impartial hearers Moses appears to be more ancient than Homer. The destruction by fire, moreover, of Sodom and Gomorrah on account of their sins, related by Moses in Genesis, is compared by Celsus to the story of Phaëthon, — all these statements of his resulting from one blunder, viz., his not attending to the (greater) antiquity of Moses.[6] For they who relate the story of Phaëthon seem to be younger even than Homer, who, again, is much younger than Moses. We do not deny, then, that the purificatory fire and the destruction of the world took place in order that evil might be swept away, and all things be renewed; for we assert that we have learned these things from the sacred books of the prophets. But since, as we have said in the preceding pages, the prophets, in uttering many predictions regarding future events, show that they have spoken the truth concerning many things that are past, and thus give evidence of the indwelling of the Divine Spirit, it is manifest that, with respect to things still future, we should repose faith in them, or rather in the Divine Spirit that is in them.

---

[1] Cf. Plato in the *Timæus*, and book iii., *de Legibus*.

[2] σαφής.
[3] Ἐπὰν τὸ προκείμενον ᾖ παραστῆσαι καὶ τὰ τῆς κατὰ τὸν τόπον ἱστορίας τινὰ ἔχοι λόγον, καὶ τὰ τῆς περὶ αὐτοῦ ἀναγωγῆς.
[4] Otus and Ephialtes. Cf. Smith's *Dict. of Myth. and Biog.*, s.v.
[5] Cf. Hom., *Odyss.*, xi. 305.
[6] [Demonstrated by Justin, vol. i. pp. 277, 278, this series.]

CHAP. XXII.

But, according to Celsus, " the Christians, making certain additional statements to those of the Jews, assert that the Son of God has been already sent on account of the sins of the Jews ; and that the Jews having chastised Jesus, and given him gall to drink, have brought upon themselves the divine wrath." And any one who likes may convict this statement of falsehood, if it be not the case that the whole Jewish nation was overthrown within one single generation after Jesus had undergone these sufferings at their hands. For forty and two years, I think, after the date of the crucifixion of Jesus, did the destruction of Jerusalem take place. Now it has never been recorded, since the Jewish nation began to exist, that they have been expelled for so long a period from their venerable temple-worship [1] and service, and enslaved by more powerful nations; for if at any time they appeared to be abandoned because of their sins, they were notwithstanding visited (by God),[2] and returned to their own country, and recovered their possessions, and performed unhindered the observances of their law. One fact, then, which proves that Jesus was something divine and sacred,[3] is this, that Jews should have suffered on His account now for a lengthened time calamities of such severity. And we say with confidence that they will never be restored to their former condition.[4] For they committed a crime of the most unhallowed kind, in conspiring against the Saviour of the human race in that city where they offered up to God a worship containing the symbols of mighty mysteries. It accordingly behoved that city where Jesus underwent these sufferings to perish utterly, and the Jewish nation to be overthrown, and the invitation to happiness offered them by God to pass to others, — the Christians, I mean, to whom has come the doctrine of a pure and holy worship, and who have obtained new laws, in harmony with the established constitution in all countries ; [5] seeing those which were formerly imposed, as on a single nation which was ruled by princes of its own race and of similar manners,[6] could not now be observed in all their entirety.

CHAP. XXIII.

In the next place, ridiculing after his usual style the race of Jews and Christians, he compares them all " to a flight of bats or to a swarm of ants issuing out of their nest, or to frogs holding council in a marsh, or to worms crawl-

ing together in the corner of a dunghill, and quarrelling with one another as to which of them were the greater sinners, and asserting that God shows and announces to us all things beforehand ; and that, abandoning the whole world, and the regions of heaven,[7] and this great earth, he becomes a citizen [8] among us alone, and to us alone makes his intimations, and does not cease sending and inquiring, in what way we may be associated with him for ever." And in his fictitious representation, he compares us to " worms which assert that there is a God, and that immediately after him, we who are made by him are altogether like unto God, and that all things have been made subject to us, — earth, and water, and air, and stars, — and that all things exist for our sake, and are ordained to be subject to us." And, according to his representation, the worms — that is, we ourselves — say that " now, since certain amongst us commit sin, God will come or will send his Son to consume the wicked with fire, that the rest of us may have eternal life with him." And to all this he subjoins the remark, that " such wranglings would be more endurable amongst worms and frogs than betwixt Jews and Christians."

CHAP. XXIV.

In reply to these, we ask of those who accept such aspersions as are scattered against us, Do you regard all men as a collection of bats, or as frogs, or as worms, in consequence of the pre-eminence of God? or do you not include the rest of mankind in this proposed comparison, but on account of their possession of reason, and of the established laws, treat *them* as men, while you hold cheap [9] *Christians* and *Jews*, because their opinions are distasteful to you, and compare them to the animals above mentioned? And whatever answer you may return to our question, we shall reply by endeavouring to show that such assertions are most unbecoming, whether spoken of all men in general, or of us in particular. For, let it be supposed that you say justly that all men, as compared with God, are (rightly) likened to these worthless [10] animals, since their littleness is not at all to be compared with the superiority of God, what then do you mean by littleness? Answer me, good sirs. If you refer to littleness of body, know that superiority and inferiority, if truth is to be judge, are not determined by a bodily standard.[11] For, on such a view, vultures [12] and elephants would be superior to us men ; for they are larger, and stronger, and longer-lived than

---

1 ἁγιστείας.
2 ἐπεσκοπήθησαν.
3 Θεῖόν τι καὶ ἱερὸν χρῆμα γεγονέναι τὸν Ἰησοῦν.
4 οὐδ᾽ ἀποκατασταθήσονται. [A very bold and confident assertion this must have seemed sixteen hundred years ago.]
5 καὶ ἁρμόζοντας τῇ πανταχοῦ καθεστώσῃ πολιτείᾳ.
6 ὑπὸ οἰκείων καὶ ὁμοήθων.
7 τὴν οὐράνιον φοράν.
8 ἐμπολιτεύεται.
9 ἐξευτελίζοντες.
10 εὐτελέσι.
11 οὐκ ἐν σώματι κρίνεται.
12 γύπες: γρύπες?

we. But no sensible person would maintain that these irrational creatures are superior to rational beings, merely on account of their bodies : for the possession of reason raises a rational being to a vast superiority over all irrational creatures. Even the race of virtuous and blessed beings would admit this, whether they are, as ye say, good demons, or, as we are accustomed to call them, the angels of God, or any other natures whatever superior to that of man, since the rational faculty within them has been made perfect, and endowed with all virtuous qualities.[1]

<h3 style="text-align:center">CHAP. XXV.</h3>

But if you depreciate the littleness of man, not on account of his body, but of his soul, regarding it as inferior to that of other rational beings, and especially of those who are virtuous ; and inferior, because evil dwells in it, — why should those among Christians who are wicked, and those among the Jews who lead sinful lives, be termed a collection of bats, or ants, or worms, or frogs, rather than those individuals among other nations who are guilty of wickedness? — seeing, in this respect, any individual whatever, especially if carried away by the tide of evil, is, in comparison with the rest of mankind, a bat, and worm, and frog, and ant. And although a man may be an orator like Demosthenes, yet, if stained with wickedness like his,[2] and guilty of deeds proceeding, like his, from a wicked nature ; or an Antiphon, who was also considered to be indeed an orator, yet who annihilated the doctrine of providence in his writings, which were entitled *Concerning Truth*, like that discourse of Celsus, — such individuals are notwithstanding worms, rolling in a corner of the dung-heap of stupidity and ignorance. Indeed, whatever be the nature of the rational faculty, it could not reasonably be compared to a worm, because it possesses capabilities of virtue.[3] For these adumbrations[4] towards virtue do not allow of those who possess the power of acquiring it, and who are incapable of wholly losing its seeds, to be likened to a worm. It appears, therefore, that neither can men in general be deemed worms in comparison with God. For reason, having its beginning in the reason of God, cannot allow of the rational animal being considered wholly alien from Deity. Nor can those among Christians and Jews who are wicked, and who, in truth, are neither Christians nor Jews, be compared, more than other wicked men, to worms rolling in a corner of a

dunghill. And if the nature of reason will not permit of such comparisons, it is manifest that we must not calumniate human nature, which has been formed for virtue, even if it should sin through ignorance, nor liken it to animals of the kind described.

<h3 style="text-align:center">CHAP. XXVI.</h3>

But if it is on account of those opinions of the Christians and Jews which displease Celsus (and which he does not at all appear to understand) that they are to be regarded as worms and ants, and the rest of mankind as different, let us examine the acknowledged opinions of Christians and Jews,[5] and compare them with those of the rest of mankind, and see whether it will not appear to those who have once admitted that certain men are worms and ants, that *they* are the worms and ants and frogs who have fallen away from sound views of God, and, under a vain appearance of piety,[6] worship either irrational animals, or images, or other objects, the works of men's hands ;[7] whereas, from the beauty of such, they ought to admire the Maker of them, and worship Him : while those are indeed men, and more honourable than men (if there be anything that is so), who, in obedience to their reason, are able to ascend from stocks and stones,[8] nay, even from what is reckoned the most precious of all matter — silver and gold ; and who ascend up also from the beautiful things in the world to the Maker of all, and entrust themselves to Him who alone is able to satisfy[9] all existing things, and to overlook the thoughts of all, and to hear the prayers of all ; who send up their prayers to Him, and do all things as in the presence of Him who beholds everything, and who are careful, as in the presence of the Hearer of all things, to say nothing which might not with propriety be reported to God. Will not such piety as this — which can be overcome neither by labours, nor by the dangers of death, nor by logical plausibilities[10] — be of no avail in preventing those who have obtained it from being any longer compared to worms, even if they had been so represented before their assumption of a piety so remarkable? Will they who subdue that fierce longing for sexual pleasures which has reduced the souls of many to a weak and feeble condition, and who subdue it because they are persuaded that they cannot otherwise have communion with God, unless they ascend to Him through the exercise of temperance, appear to you to be the brothers of worms, and relatives of ants, and to

<hr>

1 καὶ κατὰ πᾶσαν ἀρετὴν πεποίωται.
2 The allusion may possibly be to his flight from the field of Chæronea, or to his avarice, or to the alleged impurity of his life, which is referred to by Plutarch in his *Lives of the Ten Orators.* — SPENCER.
3 ἀφορμὰς ἔχον πρὸς ἀρετήν.
4 ὑποτυπώσεις.

5 τὰ αὐτόθεν πᾶσι προφαινόμενα δόγματα Χριστιανῶν καὶ Ἰουδαίων.
6 φαντασίᾳ δ᾽ εὐσεβείας.
7 ἢ καὶ τὰ δημιουργήματα.
8 λίθων καὶ ξύλων.
9 διαρκεῖν.
10 ὑπὸ λογικῶν πιθανοτήτων.

bear a likeness to frogs? What! is the brilliant quality of justice, which keeps inviolate the rights common to our neighbour, and our kindred, and which observes fairness, and benevolence, and goodness, of no avail in saving him who practises it from being termed a bird of the night? And are not they who wallow in dissoluteness, as do the majority of mankind, and they who associate promiscuously with common harlots, and who teach that such practices are not wholly contrary to propriety, worms who roll in mire?— especially when they are compared with those who have been taught not to take the "members of Christ," and the body inhabited by the Word, and make them the "members of a harlot;" and who have already learned that the body of the rational being, as consecrated to the God of all things, is the temple of the God whom they worship, becoming such from the pure conceptions which they entertain of the Creator, and who also, being careful not to corrupt the temple of God by unlawful pleasure, practise temperance as constituting piety towards God!

CHAP. XXVII.

And I have not yet spoken of the other evils which prevail amongst men, from which even those who have the appearance of philosophers are not speedily freed, for in philosophy there are many pretenders. Nor do I say anything on the point that many such evils are found to exist among those who are neither Jews nor Christians. Of a truth, such evil practices do not at all prevail among *Christians*, if you properly examine what constitutes a Christian. Or, if any persons of that kind should be discovered, they are at least not to be found among those who frequent the assemblies, and come to the public prayers, without their being excluded from them, unless it should happen, and that rarely, that some one individual of such a character escapes notice in the crowd. We, then, are not worms who assemble together; who take our stand against the Jews on those Scriptures which they believe to be divine, and who show that He who was spoken of in prophecy *has* come, and that *they* have been abandoned on account of the greatness of their sins, and that *we* who have accepted the Word have the highest hopes in God, both because of our faith in Him, and of His ability to receive us into His communion pure from all evil and wickedness of life. If a man, then, should call himself a Jew or a Christian, he would not say without qualification that God had made the whole world, and the vault of heaven[1] for us in particular. But if a man is, as Jesus taught, pure in heart, and meek, and peaceful, and cheerfully submits to dangers for

the sake of his religion, such an one might reasonably have confidence in God, and with a full apprehension of the word contained in the prophecies, might say this also: "All these things has God shown beforehand, and announced to us who believe."

CHAP. XXVIII.

But since he has represented those whom he regards as worms, viz., the Christians, as saying that "God, having abandoned the heavenly regions, and despising this great earth, takes up His abode amongst us alone, and to us alone makes His announcements, and ceases not His messages and inquiries as to how we may become His associates for ever," we have to answer that he attributes to us words which we never uttered, seeing we both read and know that God loves all existing things, and loathes[2] nothing which He has made, for He would not have created anything in hatred. We have, moreover, read the declaration: "And Thou sparest all things, because they are Thine, O lover of souls. For Thine incorruptible Spirit is in all. And therefore those also who have fallen away for a little time Thou rebukest, and admonishest, reminding them of their sins."[3] How can we assert that "God, leaving the regions of heaven, and the whole world, and despising this great earth, takes up His abode amongst us only," when we have found that all thoughtful persons must say in their prayers, that "the earth is full of the mercy of the LORD,"[4] and that "the mercy of the Lord is upon all flesh;"[5] and that God, being good, "maketh His sun to arise upon the evil and the good, and sendeth His rain upon the just and the unjust;"[6] and that He encourages us to a similar course of action, in order that we may become His sons, and teaches us to extend the benefits which we enjoy, so far as in our power, to all men? For He Himself is said to be the Saviour of all men, especially of them that believe;[7] and His Christ to be the "propitiation for our sins, and not for ours only, but also for the sins of the whole world."[8] And this, then, is our answer to the allegations of Celsus. Certain other statements, in keeping with the character of the Jews, might be made by some of that nation, but certainly not by the Christians, who have been taught that "God commendeth His love towards us, in that, while we were yet sinners, Christ died for us;"[9] and although "scarcely for a righteous man will one die, yet peradventure for a good man some

---

1 τὴν οὐράνιον φοράν.
2 βδελύσσεται.
3 Cf. Wisd. of Solom. xi. 26, xii. 1, 2.
4 Ps. xxxiii. 5.
5 Ecclus. xviii. 13.
6 Cf. Matt. v. 45.
7 Cf. 1 Tim. iv. 10.
8 Cf. 1 John ii. 2.
9 Cf. Rom. v. 8.

would even dare to die." [1] But now is Jesus declared to have come for the sake of sinners in all parts of the world (that they may forsake their sin, and entrust themselves to God), being called also, agreeably to an ancient custom of these Scriptures, the "Christ of God."

CHAP. XXIX.

But Celsus perhaps has misunderstood certain of those whom he has termed "worms," when they affirm that "God exists, and that *we* are next to Him." And he acts like those who would find fault with an entire sect of philosophers, on account of certain words uttered by some rash youth who, after a three days' attendance upon the lectures of a philosopher, should exalt himself above other people as inferior to himself, and devoid of philosophy. For we know that there are many creatures more honourable [2] than man ; and we have read that "God standeth in the congregation of gods," [3] but of gods who are not worshipped by the nations, "for all the gods of the nations are idols." [4] We have read also, that "God, standing in the congregation of the gods, judgeth among the gods." [5] We know, moreover, that "though there be that are called gods, whether in heaven or in earth (as there be gods many and lords many), but to us there is one God, the Father, of whom are all things, and we in Him ; and one Lord Jesus Christ, by whom are all things, and we by Him." [6] And we know that in this way the angels are superior to men ; so that men, when made perfect, become like the angels. "For in the resurrection they neither marry nor are given in marriage, but the righteous are as the angels in heaven," [7] and also become "equal to the angels." [8] We know, too, that in the arrangement of the universe there are certain beings termed "thrones," and others "dominions," and others "powers," and others "principalities ; " and we see that we men, who are far inferior to these, may entertain the hope that by a virtuous life, and by acting in all things agreeably to reason, we may rise to a likeness with all these. And, lastly, because "it doth not yet appear what we shall be ; but we know that when He shall appear, we shall be like God, and shall see Him as He is." [9] And if any one were to maintain what is asserted by some (either by those who possess intelligence or who do not, but have misconceived sound reason), that "God exists, and *we* are next to Him," I would interpret the word "we," by using in its stead, "We who act according to reason," or rather, "We *virtuous*, who act according to reason." [10] For, in our opinion, the same virtue belongs to *all* the blessed, so that the virtue of man and of God is identical. [11] And therefore we are taught to become "perfect," as our Father in heaven is perfect. [12] No good and virtuous man, then, is a "worm rolling in filth," nor is a pious man an "ant," nor a righteous man a "frog ; " nor could one whose soul is enlightened with the bright light of truth be reasonably likened to a "bird of the night."

CHAP. XXX.

It appears to me that Celsus has also misunderstood this statement, "Let Us make man in Our image and likeness ; " [13] and has therefore represented the "worms" as saying that, being created by God, we altogether resemble Him. If, however, he had known the difference between man being created "in the image of God" and "after His likeness," and that God is recorded to have said, "Let Us make man after Our image and likeness," but that He made man "after the image" of God, but not then also "after His likeness," [14] he would not have represented us as saying that "we are altogether like Him." Moreover, we do not assert that the stars are subject to us ; since the resurrection which is called the "resurrection of the just," and which is understood by wise men, is compared to the sun, and moon, and stars, by him who said, "There is one glory of the sun, and another glory of the moon, and another glory of the stars ; for one star differeth from another star in glory. So also is the resurrection of the dead." [15] Daniel also prophesied long ago regarding these things. [16] Celsus says further, that we assert that "all things have been arranged so as to be subject to us," having perhaps heard some of the intelligent among us speaking to that effect, and perhaps also not understanding the saying, that "he who is the greatest amongst us is the servant of all." [17] And if the Greeks say, "Then sun and moon are the slaves of mortal men," [18] they express approval of the statement, and give an explanation of its meaning ; but since such a statement is either not made at all by us, or is expressed in a different way,

---

[1] Cf. Rom. v. 7.
[2] τιμιώτερα.
[3] Cf. Ps. lxxxii. 1.
[4] δαιμόνια. Cf. Ps. xcvi. 5.
[5] Cf. Ps. lxxxii. 1.
[6] 1 Cor. viii. 5, 6.
[7] Cf. Matt. xxii. 30.
[8] Cf. Luke xx. 36.
[9] Cf. 1 John iii. 2.

[10] καὶ τοῦτό γ' ἂν ἑρμηνεύοιμι, τὸ "ἡμεῖς" λέγων ἀντὶ τοῦ οἱ λογικοὶ, καὶ ἔτι μᾶλλον, οἱ σπουδαῖοι λογικοί.
[11] ὥστε καὶ ἡ αὐτὴ ἀρετὴ ἀνθρώπου καὶ Θεοῦ. Cf. Cicero, *de Leg.*, i.: "Jam vero virtus eadem in homine ac deo est, neque ullo alio in genio praeterea. Est autem virtus nihil aliud, quam in se perfecta, et ad summum perducta natura. Est igitur homini cum Deo similitudo." Cf. also Clemens Alex., *Strom.*, vii. c. 14: Οὐ γὰρ, καθάπερ οἱ Στωικοὶ, ἀθέως, πάνυ τὴν αὐτὴν ἀρετὴν ἀνθρώπου λέγομεν καὶ Θεοῦ. [See vol. ii. p. 549. S.] Cf. Theodoret, *Serm.*, xi.—SPENCER.
[12] Cf. Matt. v. 48.
[13] Cf. Gen. i. 26.
[14] Cf. Gen. i. 27.
[15] Cf. 1 Cor. xv. 41, 42.
[16] Cf. Dan. xii. 3.
[17] Cf. Matt. xx. 27.
[18] Cf. Eurip., *Phoeniss.*, 546, 547.

Celsus here too falsely accuses us. Moreover, we who, according to Celsus, are "worms," are represented by him as saying that, "seeing some among us are guilty of sin, God will come to us, or will send His own Son, that He may consume the wicked, and that we other frogs may enjoy eternal life with Him." Observe how this venerable philosopher, like a low buffoon,[1] turns into ridicule and mockery, and a subject of laughter, the announcement of a divine judgment, and of the punishment of the wicked, and of the reward of the righteous; and subjoins to all this the remark, that "such statements would be more endurable if made by worms and frogs than by Christians and Jews who quarrel with one another!" We shall not, however, imitate his example, nor say similar things regarding those philosophers who profess to know the nature of all things, and who discuss with each other the manner in which all things were created, and how the heaven and earth originated, and all things in them; and how the souls (of men), being either unbegotten, and not created by God, are yet governed by Him, and pass from one body to another;[2] or being formed at the same time with the body, exist for ever or pass away. For instead of treating with respect and accepting the intention of those who have devoted themselves to the investigation of the truth, one might mockingly and revilingly say that such men were "worms," who did not measure themselves by their corner of their dung-heap in human life, and who accordingly gave forth their opinions on matters of such importance as if they understood them, and who strenuously assert that they have obtained a view of those things which cannot be seen without a higher inspiration and a diviner power. "For no man knoweth the things of a man, save the spirit of man which is in him: even so the things of God knoweth no man, but the Spirit of God."[3] We are not, however, mad, nor do we compare such human wisdom (I use the word "wisdom" in the common acceptation), which busies itself not about the affairs of the multitude, but in the investigation of truth, to the wrigglings of worms or any other such creatures; but in the spirit of truth, we testify of certain Greek philosophers that they knew God, seeing "He manifested Himself to them,"[4] although "they glorified Him not as God, neither were thankful, but became vain in their imaginations; and professing themselves to be wise, they became foolish, and changed the glory of the incorruptible God into an image made like to corruptible man, and to birds, and four-footed beasts, and creeping things."[5]

CHAP. XXXI.

After this, wishing to prove that there is no difference between Jews and Christians, and those animals previously enumerated by him, he asserts that the Jews were "fugitives from Egypt, who never performed anything worthy of note, and never were held in any reputation or account."[6] Now, on the point of their not being fugitives, nor Egyptians, but Hebrews who settled in Egypt, we have spoken in the preceding pages. But if he thinks his statement, that "they were never held in any reputation or account," to be proved, because no remarkable event in their history is found recorded by the Greeks, we would answer, that if one will examine their polity from its first beginning, and the arrangement of their laws, he will find that they were men who represented upon earth the shadow of a heavenly life, and that amongst them God is recognised as nothing else, save He who is over all things, and that amongst them no maker of images was permitted to enjoy the rights of citizenship.[7] For neither painter nor image-maker existed in their state, the law expelling all such from it; that there might be no pretext for the construction of images, — an art which attracts the attention of foolish men, and which drags down the eyes of the soul from God to earth.[8] There was, accordingly, amongst them a law to the following effect: "Do not transgress the law, and make to yourselves a graven image, any likeness of male or female; either a likeness of any one of the creatures that are upon the earth, or a likeness of any winged fowl that flieth under the heaven, or a likeness of any creeping thing that creepeth upon the earth, or a likeness of any of the fishes which are in the waters under the earth."[9] The law, indeed, wished them to have regard to the truth of each individual thing, and not to form representations of things contrary to reality, feigning the appearance merely of what was really male or really female, or the nature of animals, or of birds, or of creeping things, or of fishes. Venerable, too, and grand was this prohibition of theirs: "Lift not up thine eyes unto heaven, lest, when thou seest the sun, and the moon, and the stars, and all the host of heaven, thou shouldst be led astray to worship them, and serve them."[10] And what a *régime*[11] was that under which the whole nation was placed, and which rendered it impossible for any effeminate person to appear in public;[12] and worthy of admiration, too, was the arrangement by which harlots were removed out of the state,

---

[1] βωμολόχος.
[2] καὶ ἀμείβουσι σώματα.
[3] Cf. 1 Cor. ii. 11.
[4] Cf. Rom. i. 19.
[5] Rom. i. 21-23.

[6] οὔτ' ἐν λόγῳ οὔτ' ἐν ἀριθμῷ αὐτοὺς ποτε γεγενημένους.
[7] ἐπολιτεύετο.
[8] [See note on Book III. cap. lxxvi. *supra*, and to vol. iii. p. 76, this series.]
[9] Cf. Deut. iv. 16-18.
[10] Cf. Deut. iv. 19.
[11] πολιτεία.
[12] οὐδὲ φαίνεσθαι θηλυδρίαν οἷόν τ' ἦν.

those incentives to the passions of the youth! Their courts of justice also were composed of men of the strictest integrity, who, after having for a lengthened period set the example of an unstained life, were entrusted with the duty of presiding over the tribunals, and who, on account of the superhuman purity of their character,[1] were said to be gods, in conformity with an ancient Jewish usage of speech. Here was the spectacle of a whole nation devoted to philosophy; and in order that there might be leisure to listen to their sacred laws, the days termed "Sabbath," and the other festivals which existed among them, were instituted. And why need I speak of the orders of their priests and sacrifices, which contain innumerable indications (of deeper truths) to those who wish to ascertain the signification of things?

CHAP. XXXII.

But since nothing belonging to human nature is permanent, this polity also must gradually be corrupted and changed. And Providence, having remodelled their venerable system where it needed to be changed, so as to adapt it to men of all countries, gave to believers of all nations, in place of the Jews, the venerable religion of Jesus, who, being adorned not only with understanding, but also with a share of divinity,[2] and having overthrown the doctrine regarding earthly demons, who delight in frankincense, and blood, and in the exhalations of sacrificial odours, and who, like the fabled Titans or Giants, drag down men from thoughts of God; and having Himself disregarded their plots, directed chiefly against the better class of men, enacted laws which ensure happiness to those who live according to them, and who do not flatter the demons by means of sacrifices, but altogether despise them, through help of the word of God, which aids those who look upwards to Him. And as it was the will of God that the doctrine of Jesus should prevail amongst men, the demons could effect nothing, although straining every nerve[3] to accomplish the destruction of Christians; for they stirred up both princes, and senates, and rulers in every place, — nay, even nations themselves, who did not perceive the irrational and wicked procedure of the demons, — against the word, and those who believed in it; yet, notwithstanding, the word of God, which is more powerful than all other things, even when meeting with opposition, deriving from the opposition, as it were, a means of increase, advanced onwards, and won many souls, such being the will of God. And we have offered these remarks by way of a necessary digression. For we wished to answer

the assertion of Celsus concerning the Jews, that they were "fugitives from Egypt, and that these men, beloved by God, never accomplished anything worthy of note." And further, in answer to the statement that "they were never held in any reputation or account," we say, that living apart as a "chosen nation and a royal priesthood," and shunning intercourse with the many nations around them, in order that their morals might escape corruption, they enjoyed the protection of the divine power, neither coveting like the most of mankind the acquisition of other kingdoms, nor yet being abandoned so as to become, on account of their smallness, an easy object of attack to others, and thus be altogether destroyed; and this lasted so long as they were worthy of the divine protection. But when it became necessary for them, as a nation wholly given to sin, to be brought back by their sufferings to their God, they were abandoned (by Him), sometimes for a longer, sometimes for a shorter period, until in the time of the Romans, having committed the greatest of sins in putting Jesus to death, they were completely deserted.

CHAP. XXXIII.

Immediately after this, Celsus, assailing the contents of the first book of Moses, which is entitled "Genesis," asserts that "the Jews accordingly endeavoured to derive their origin from the first race of jugglers and deceivers,[4] appealing to the testimony of dark and ambiguous words, whose meaning was veiled in obscurity, and which they misinterpreted[5] to the unlearned and ignorant, and that, too, when such a point had never been called in question during the long preceding period." Now Celsus appears to me in these words to have expressed very obscurely the meaning which he intended to convey. It is probable, indeed, that his obscurity on this subject is intentional, inasmuch as he saw the strength of the argument which establishes the descent of the Jews from their ancestors; while again, on the other hand, he wished not to appear ignorant that the question regarding the Jews and their descent was one that could not be lightly disposed of. It is certain, however, that the Jews trace their genealogy back to the three fathers, Abraham, Isaac, and Jacob. And the names of these individuals possess such efficacy, when united with the name of God, that not only do those belonging to the nation employ in their prayers to God, and in the exorcising of demons, the words, "God of Abraham,[6] and God of Isaac, and God of Jacob,"

---

[1] οἵ τινες διὰ τὸ καθαρὸν ἦθος, καὶ τὸ ὑπὲρ ἄνθρωπον.
[2] θείᾳ μοίρᾳ.
[3] καίτοιγε πάντα κάλων κινήσαντες.

[4] ἀπὸ πρώτης σπορᾶς γοήτων καὶ πλάνων ἀνθρώπων.
[5] παρεξηγούμενοι.
[6] [This *formula* he regards as an adumbration of the Triad (see our vol. ii. p. 101): thus, "the God of Abraham" = Fatherhood; "of Isaac" = Sonship; "of Jacob" = Wisdom, and the Founder of the New Israel.]

but so also do almost all those who occupy themselves with incantations and magical rites. For there is found in treatises on magic in many countries such an invocation of God, and assumption of the divine name, as implies a familiar use of it by these men in their dealings with demons. These facts, then — adduced by Jews and Christians to prove the sacred character of Abraham, and Isaac, and Jacob, the fathers of the Jewish race — appear to me not to have been altogether unknown to Celsus, but not to have been distinctly set forth by him, because he was unable to answer the argument which might be founded on them.

CHAP. XXXIV.

For we inquire of all those who employ such invocations of God, saying : Tell us, friends, who was Abraham, and what sort of person was Isaac, and what power did Jacob possess, that the appellation " God," when joined with their name, could effect such wonders? And from whom have you learned, or can you learn, the facts relating to these individuals? And who has occupied himself with writing a history about them, either directly magnifying these men by ascribing to them mysterious powers, or hinting obscurely at their possession of certain great and marvellous qualities, patent to those who are qualified to see them?[1] And when, in answer to our inquiry, no one can show from what history — whether Greek or Barbarian — or, if not a history, yet at least from what mystical narrative,[2] the accounts of these men are derived, we shall bring forward the book entitled " Genesis," which contains the acts of these men, and the divine oracles addressed to them, and will say, Does not the use by you of the names of these three ancestors of the race, establishing in the clearest manner that effects not to be lightly regarded are produced by the invocation of them, evidence the divinity of the men?[3] And yet we know them from no other source than the sacred books of the Jews ! Moreover, the phrases, " the God of Israel," and " the God of the Hebrews," and " the God who drowned in the Red Sea the king of Egypt and the Egyptians," are *formulæ*[4] frequently employed against demons and certain wicked powers. And we learn the history of the names and their interpretation from those Hebrews, who in their national literature and national

tongue dwell with pride upon these things, and explain their meaning. How, then, should the Jews attempt to derive their origin from the first race of those whom Celsus supposed to be jugglers and deceivers, and shamelessly endeavour to trace themselves and their beginning back to these? — whose names, being Hebrew, are an evidence to the Hebrews, who have their sacred books written in the Hebrew language and letters, that their nation is akin to these men. For up to the present time, the Jewish names belonging to the Hebrew language were either taken from their writings, or generally from words the meaning of which was made known by the Hebrew language.

CHAP. XXXV.

And let any one who peruses the treatise of Celsus observe whether it does not convey some such insinuation as the above, when he says : " And they attempted to derive their origin from the first race of jugglers and deceivers, appealing to the testimony of dark and ambiguous words, whose meaning was veiled in obscurity." For these names are indeed obscure, and not within the comprehension and knowledge of many, though not in our opinion of doubtful meaning, even although assumed by those who are aliens to our religion ; but as, according to Celsus, they do not[5] convey any ambiguity, I am at a loss to know why he has rejected them. And yet, if he had wished honestly to overturn the genealogy which he deemed the Jews to have so shamelessly arrogated, in boasting of Abraham and his descendants (as their progenitors), he ought to have quoted *all* the passages bearing on the subject ; and, in the first place, to have advocated his cause with such arguments as he thought likely to be convincing, and in the next to have bravely[6] refuted, by means of what appeared to him to be the true meaning, and by arguments in its favour, the errors existing on the subject. But neither Celsus nor any one else will be able, by their discussions regarding the nature of names employed for miraculous purposes, to lay down the correct doctrine regarding them, and to demonstrate that those men were to be lightly esteemed whose names merely, not among their countrymen alone, but also amongst foreigners, could accomplish (such results). He ought to have shown, moreover, how we, in misinterpreting[7] the passages in which these names are found, deceive our hearers, as he imagines, while he himself, who boasts that he is not ignorant or unintelligent, gives the true interpretation of them. And he hazarded

---

[1] εἴτε καὶ αὐτόθεν σεμνύνουσαν ἐν ἀπορρήτοις τοὺς ἄνδρας, εἴτε καὶ δι' ὑπονοιῶν αἰνισσομένην τινὰ μεγάλα καὶ θαυμάσια τοῖς θεωρῆσαι αὐτὰ δυναμένοις;

[2] μυστικῆς ἀναγραφῆς.

[3] ἐροῦμέν τε· ὅτι μήποτε τὸ καὶ ὑφ' ὑμῶν παραλαμβάνεσθαι τὰ ὀνόματα τῶν τριῶν τούτων γεναρχῶν τοῦ ἔθνους, τῇ ἐναργείᾳ καταλαμβανόντων, οὐκ εὐκαταφρόνητα ἀνύεσθαι ἐκ τῆς κατεπικλήσεως αὐτῶν, παρίστησι τὸ θεῖον τῶν ἀνδρῶν; Guietus would expunge the words τῇ ἐναργείᾳ καταλαμβανόντων.

[4] [See p. 511, *supra*, on the *formula* of benediction and exorcism, and compare Num. vi. 24.]

[5] κατὰ δὲ Κέλσον, οὐ παριστάντα. *Libri editi ad oram* ὡς παριστάντα.

[6] γενναίως.

[7] παρεξηγούμενοι.

the assertion,[1] in speaking of those names, from which the Jews deduce their genealogies, that "never, during the long antecedent period, has there been any dispute about these names, but that at the present time the Jews dispute about them with certain others," whom he does not mention. Now, let him who chooses show who these are that dispute with the Jews, and who adduce even probable arguments to show that Jews and Christians do not decide correctly on the points relating to these names, but that there are others who have discussed these questions with the greatest learning and accuracy. But we are well assured that none can establish anything of the sort, it being manifest that these names are derived from the Hebrew language, which is found only among the Jews.

CHAP. XXXVI.

Celsus in the next place, producing from history other than that of the divine record, those passages which bear upon the claims to great antiquity put forth by many nations, as the Athenians, and Egyptians, and Arcadians, and Phrygians, who assert that certain individuals have existed among them who sprang from the earth, and who each adduce proofs of these assertions, says: "The Jews, then, leading a grovelling life[2] in some corner of Palestine, and being a wholly uneducated people, who had not heard that these matters had been committed to verse long ago by Hesiod and innumerable other inspired men, wove together some most incredible and insipid stories,[3] viz., that a certain man was formed by the hands of God, and had breathed into him the breath of life, and that a woman was taken from his side, and that God issued certain commands, and that a serpent opposed these, and gained a victory over the commandments of God; thus relating certain old wives' fables, and most impiously representing God as weak at the very beginning (of things), and unable to convince even a single human being whom He Himself had formed." By these instances, indeed, this deeply read and learned Celsus, who accuses Jews and Christians of ignorance and want of instruction, clearly evinces the accuracy of his knowledge of the chronology of the respective historians, whether Greek or Barbarian, since he imagines that Hesiod and the "innumerable" others, whom he styles "inspired" men, are older than Moses and his writings — that very Moses who is shown to be much older than the time of the Trojan war! It is not the Jews, then, who have composed incredible and insipid stories regarding the birth of man from the earth, but these

"inspired" men of Celsus, Hesiod and his other "innumerable" companions, who, having neither learned nor heard of the far older and most venerable accounts existing in Palestine, have written such histories as their Theogonies, attributing, so far as in their power, "generation" to their deities, and innumerable other absurdities. And these are the writers whom Plato expels from his "State" as being corrupters of the youth,[4] — Homer, viz., and those who have composed poems of a similar description! Now it is evident that Plato did not regard as "inspired" those men who had left behind them such works. But perhaps it was from a desire to cast reproach upon us, that this Epicurean Celsus, who is better able to judge than Plato (if it be the same Celsus who composed two other books against the Christians), called those individuals "inspired" whom he did not in reality regard as such.

CHAP. XXXVII.

He charges us, moreover, with introducing "a man formed by the *hands* of God," although the book of Genesis has made no mention of the "hands" of God, either when relating the creation or the "fashioning"[5] of the man; while it is Job and David who have used the expression, "Thy hands have made me and fashioned me;"[6] with reference to which it would need a lengthened discourse to point out the sense in which these words were understood by those who used them, both as regards the difference between "making" and "fashioning," and also the "hands" of God. For those who do not understand these and similar expressions in the sacred Scriptures, imagine that we attribute to the God who is over all things a form[7] such as that of man; and according to their conceptions, it follows that we consider the body of God to be furnished with wings, since the Scriptures, literally understood, attribute such appendages to God. The subject before us, however, does not require us to interpret these expressions; for, in our explanatory remarks upon the book of Genesis, these matters have been made, to the best of our ability, a special subject of investigation. Observe next the malignity[8] of Celsus in what follows. For the Scripture, speaking of the "fashioning"[9] of the man, says, "And breathed into his face the breath of life, and the man became a living soul."[10] Whereon Celsus, wishing maliciously to ridicule the "inbreathing into his face of the breath of life," and not understanding

---

[1] παρέρριψε.
[2] συγκύψαντες.
[3] ἀμουσότατα.

[4] Cf. Plato, *de Repub.*, book ii. etc.
[5] ἐπὶ τῆς πλάσεως.
[6] Cf. Job x. 8 and Ps. cxix. 73.
[7] σχῆμα.
[8] κακοήθειαν.
[9] πλάσεως.
[10] Gen. ii. 7; Heb. בְּאַפָּיו, LXX. πρόσωπον.

the sense in which the expression was employed, states that "they composed a story that a man was fashioned by the hands of God, and was inflated by breath blown into him," [1] in order that, taking the word "inflated" to be used in a similar way to the inflation of skins, he might ridicule the statement, "He breathed into his face the breath of life," — terms which are used figuratively, and require to be explained in order to show that God communicated to man of His incorruptible Spirit; as it is said, "For Thine incorruptible Spirit is in all things." [2]

CHAP. XXXVIII.

In the next place, as it is his object to slander our Scriptures, he ridicules the following statement: "And God caused a deep sleep to fall upon Adam, and he slept: and He took one of his ribs, and closed up the flesh instead thereof. And the rib, which He had taken from the man, made He a woman," [3] and so on; without quoting the words, which would give the hearer the impression that they are spoken with a figurative meaning. He would not even have it appear that the words were used allegorically, although he says afterwards, that "the more modest among Jews and Christians are ashamed of these things, and endeavour to give them somehow an allegorical signification." Now we might say to him, Are the statements of your "inspired" Hesiod, which he makes regarding the woman in the form of a myth, to be explained allegorically, in the sense that she was given by Jove to men as an evil thing, and as a retribution for the theft of "the fire;" [4] while that regarding the woman who was taken from the side of the man (after he had been buried in deep slumber), and was formed by God, appears to you to be related without any rational meaning and secret signification? [5] But is it not uncandid, not to ridicule the former as myths, but to admire them as philosophical ideas in a mythical dress, and to treat with contempt [6] the latter, as offending the understanding, and to declare that they are of no account? For if, because of the mere phraseology, we are to find fault with what is intended to have a secret meaning, see whether the following lines of Hesiod, a man, as you say, "inspired," are not better fitted to excite laughter : —

"'Son of Iapetus!' with wrathful heart
Spake the cloud-gatherer: 'Oh, unmatched in art!
Exultest thou in this the flame retrieved,
And dost thou triumph in the god deceived?
But thou, with the posterity of man,
Shalt rue the fraud whence mightier ills began;

[1] εμφυσώμενον.
[2] Wisd. of Solom. xii. 1.
[3] Cf. Gen. ii. 21, 22.
[4] αντι του πυρός.
[5] χωρις παντος λόγου καί τινος επικρύψεως.
[6] μοχθίζειν.

I will send evil for thy stealthy fire,
While all embrace it, and their bane desire.'
The sire, who rules the earth, and sways the pole,
Had said, and laughter fill'd his secret soul.
He bade the artist-god his hest obey,
And mould with tempering waters ductile clay:
Infuse, as breathing life and form began,
The supple vigour, and the voice of man:
Her aspect fair as goddesses above,
A virgin's likeness, with the brows of love.
He bade Minerva teach the skill that dyes
The web with colours, as the shuttle flies;
He called the magic of Love's Queen to shed
A nameless grace around her courteous head;
Instil the wish that longs with restless aim,
And cares of dress that feed upon the frame:
Bade Hermes last implant the craft refined
Of artful manners, and a shameless mind.
He said; their king th' inferior powers obeyed:
The fictile likeness of a bashful maid
Rose from the temper'd earth, by Jove's behest,
Under the forming god; the zone and vest
Were clasp'd and folded by Minerva's hand:
The heaven-born graces, and persuasion bland
Deck'd her round limbs with chains of gold: the hours
Of loose locks twined her temples with spring flowers.
The whole attire Minerva's curious care
Form'd to her shape, and fitted to her air.
But in her breast the herald from above,
Full of the counsels of deep thundering Jove,
Wrought artful manners, wrought perfidious lies,
And speech that thrills the blood, and lulls the wise.
Her did th' interpreter of gods proclaim,
And named the woman with Pandora's name;
Since all the gods conferr'd their gifts, to charm,
For man's inventive race, this beauteous harm." [7]

Moreover, what is said also about the casket is fitted of itself to excite laughter; for example : —

"Whilome on earth the sons of men abode
From ills apart, and labour's irksome load,
And sore diseases, bringing age to man;
Now the sad life of mortals is a span.
The woman's hands a mighty casket bear;
She lifts the lid; she scatters griefs in air:
Alone, beneath the vessel's rims detained,
Hope still within th' unbroken cell remained,
Nor fled abroad; so will'd cloud-gatherer Jove:
The woman's hand had dropp'd the lid above." [8]

Now, to him who would give to these lines a grave allegorical meaning (whether any such meaning be contained in them or not), we would say: Are the Greeks alone at liberty to convey a philosophic meaning in a secret covering? or perhaps also the Egyptians, and those of the Barbarians who pride themselves upon their mysteries and the truth (which is concealed within them); while the Jews alone, with their lawgiver and historians, appear to you the most unintelligent of men? And is this the only nation which has not received a share of divine power, and which yet was so grandly instructed how to rise upwards to the uncreated nature of God, and to gaze on Him alone, and to expect from Him alone (the fulfilment of) their hopes?

[7] Hesiod, *Works and Days*, i. 73-114 (Elton's translation [in substance. S.]).
[8] Hesiod, *Works and Days*, i. 125-134 (Elton's translation [in substance. S.]).

CHAP. XXXIX.

But as Celsus makes a jest also of the serpent, as counteracting the injunctions given by God to the man, taking the narrative to be an old wife's fable,[1] and has purposely neither mentioned the paradise[2] of God, nor stated that God is said to have planted it in Eden towards the east, and that there afterwards sprang up from the earth every tree that was beautiful to the sight, and good for food, and the tree of life in the midst of the paradise, and the tree of the knowledge of good and evil, and the other statements which follow, which might of themselves lead a candid reader to see that all these things had not inappropriately an allegorical meaning, let us contrast with this the words of Socrates regarding Eros in the Symposium of Plato, and which are put in the mouth of Socrates as being more appropriate than what was said regarding him by all the others at the Symposium. The words of Plato are as follow : "When Aphrodite was born, the gods held a banquet, and there was present, along with the others, Porus the son of Metis. And after they had dined, Penia[3] came to beg for something (seeing there was an entertainment), and she stood at the gate. Porus meantime, having become intoxicated with the nectar (for there was then no wine), went into the garden of Zeus, and, being heavy with liquor, lay down to sleep. Penia accordingly formed a secret plot, with a view of freeing herself from her condition of poverty,[4] to get a child by Porus, and accordingly lay down beside him, and became pregnant with Eros. And on this account Eros has become the follower and attendant of Aphrodite, having been begotten on her birthday feast,[5] and being at the same time by nature a lover of the beautiful, because Aphrodite too is beautiful. Seeing, then, that Eros is the son of Porus and Penia, the following is his condition.[6] In the first place, he is always poor, and far from being delicate and beautiful, as most persons imagine ; but is withered, and sunburnt,[7] and unshod, and without a home, sleeping always upon the ground, and without a covering ; lying in the open air beside gates, and on public roads ; possessing the nature of his mother, and dwelling continually with indigence.[8] But, on the other hand, in conformity with the character of his father, he is given to plotting against the beautiful and the good, being courageous, and hasty, and vehement ;[9] a keen[10] hunter, perpet-

ually devising contrivances ; both much given to forethought, and also fertile in resources ;[11] acting like a philosopher throughout the whole of his life ; a terrible[12] sorcerer, and dealer in drugs, and a sophist as well ; neither immortal by nature nor yet mortal, but on the same day, at one time he flourishes and lives when he has plenty, and again at another time dies, and once more is recalled to life through possessing the nature of his father. But the supplies furnished to him are always gradually disappearing, so that he is never at any time in want, nor yet rich ; and, on the other hand, he occupies an intermediate position between wisdom and ignorance."[13] Now, if those who read these words were to imitate the malignity of Celsus — which be it far from Christians to do ! — they would ridicule the myth, and would turn this great Plato into a subject of jest ; but if, on investigating in a philosophic spirit what is conveyed in the dress of a myth, they should be able to discover the meaning of Plato, (they will admire)[14] the manner in which he was able to conceal, on account of the multitude, in the form of this myth, the great ideas which presented themselves to him, and to speak in a befitting manner to those who know how to ascertain from the myths the true meaning of him who wove them together. Now I have brought forward this myth occurring in the writings of Plato, because of the mention in it of the garden of Zeus, which appears to bear some resemblance to the paradise of God, and of the comparison between Penia and the serpent, and the plot against Porus by Penia, which may be compared with the plot of the serpent against the man. It is not very clear, indeed, whether Plato fell in with these stories by chance, or whether, as some think, meeting during his visit to Egypt with certain individuals who philosophized on the Jewish mysteries, and learning some things from them, he may have preserved a few of their ideas, and thrown others aside, being careful not to offend the Greeks by a complete adoption of all the points of the philosophy of the Jews, who were in bad repute with the multitude, on account of the foreign character of their laws and their peculiar polity. The present, however, is not the proper time for explaining either the myth of Plato, or the story of the serpent and the paradise of God, and all that is related to have taken place in it, as in our exposition of the book of Genesis we have especially occupied ourselves as we best could with these matters.

---

1 "μῦθόν τινα" παραπλήσιον τοῖς παραδιδομένοις ταῖς γραυσίν.
2 παράδεισος.
3 Penia, poverty ; Porus, abundance.
4 διὰ τὴν αὑτῆς ἀπορίαν.
5 ἐν τοῖς ἐκείνης γενεθλίοις.
6 ἐν τοιαύτῃ τύχῃ καθέστηκε.
7 σκληρὸς καὶ αὐχμηρός.
8 ἐνδείᾳ.
9 σύντονος.
10 δεινός.

11 καὶ φρονήσεως ἐπιθυμητὴς καὶ πόριμος.
12 δεινὸς γόης.
13 [Plato, *Symposion*, xxiii. p. 203. S.]
14 Boherellus, quem Ruæus sequitur, in notis; "Ante voces: τίνα τρόπον, videtur deesse: θαυμάσονται, aut quid simile."— LOMMATZSCH.

CHAP. XL.

But as he asserts that "the Mosaic narrative most impiously represents God as in a state of weakness from the very commencement (of things), and as unable to gain over (to obedience) even one single man whom He Himself had formed," we say in answer that the objection [1] is much the same as if one were to find fault with the existence of evil, which God has not been able to prevent even in the case of a single individual, so that *one* man might be found from the very beginning of things who was born into the world untainted by sin. For as those whose business it is to defend the doctrine of providence do so by means of arguments which are not to be despised,[2] so also the subjects of Adam and his son will be philosophically dealt with by those who are aware that in the Hebrew language Adam signifies man; and that in those parts of the narrative which appear to refer to Adam as an individual, Moses is discoursing upon the nature of man in general.[3] For "in Adam" (as the Scripture [4] says) "all die," and were condemned in the likeness of Adam's transgression, the word of God asserting this not so much of *one particular individual* as of the *whole human race*. For in the connected series of statements which appears to apply as to one particular individual, the curse pronounced upon Adam is regarded as common to all (the members of the race), and what was spoken with reference to the woman is spoken of *every* woman without exception.[5] And the expulsion of the man and woman from paradise, and their being clothed with tunics of skins (which God, because of the transgression of men, made for those who had sinned), contain a certain secret and mystical doctrine (far transcending that of Plato) of the soul's losing its wings,[6] and being borne downwards to earth, until it can lay hold of some stable resting-place.

CHAP. XLI.

After this he continues as follows: "They speak, in the next place, of a deluge, and of a monstrous [7] ark, having within it all things, and of a dove and a crow [8] as messengers, falsifying and recklessly altering [9] the story of Deucalion; not expecting, I suppose, that these things would come to light, but imagining that they were inventing stories merely for young children." Now in these remarks observe the hostility — so un-

becoming a philosopher — displayed by this man towards this very ancient Jewish narrative. For, not being able to say anything against the history of the deluge, and not perceiving what he might have urged against the ark and its dimensions, — viz., that, according to the general opinion, which accepted the statements that it was three hundred cubits in length, and fifty in breadth, and thirty in height, it was impossible to maintain that it contained (all) the animals that were upon the earth, fourteen specimens of every clean and four of every unclean beast, — he merely termed it "monstrous, containing all things within it." Now wherein was its "monstrous" character, seeing it is related to have been a hundred years in building, and to have had the three hundred cubits of its length and the fifty of its breadth contracted, until the thirty cubits of its height terminated in a top one cubit long and one cubit broad? Why should we not rather admire a structure which resembled an extensive city, if its measurements be taken to mean what they are capable of meaning,[10] so that it was nine myriads of cubits long in the base, and two thousand five hundred in breadth? [11] And why should we not admire the design evinced in having it so compactly built, and rendered capable of sustaining a tempest which caused a deluge? For it was not daubed with pitch, or any material of that kind, but was securely coated with bitumen. And is it not a subject of admiration, that by the providential arrangement of God, the elements of all the races were brought into it, that the earth might receive again the seeds of all living things, while God made use of a most righteous man to be the progenitor of those who were to be born after the deluge?

CHAP. XLII.

In order to show that he had read the book of Genesis, Celsus rejects the story of the dove, although unable to adduce any reason which might prove it to be a fiction. In the next place, as his habit is, in order to put the narrative in a more ridiculous light, he converts the "raven" into a "crow," and imagines that Moses so wrote, having recklessly altered the accounts related of the Grecian Deucalion; unless perhaps he regards the narrative as not having proceeded from Moses, but from *several* individuals, as appears from his employing the *plural* number in the expressions, "falsifying and recklessly altering the story of Deucalion," [12] as well as from the words, "For *they* did not expect, I suppose, that these things would come to light." But

---

1 τὸ λεγόμενον.

2 εὐκαταφρονήτων.

3 φυσιολογεῖ Μωϋσῆς τὰ περὶ τῆς τοῦ ἀνθρώπου φύσεως.

4 Cf. 1 Cor. xv. 22 with Rom. v. 14.

5 οὐκ ἔστι καθ᾽ ἧς οὐ λέγεται.

6 πτερορρυούσης. This is a correction for πτεροφυούσης, the textual reading in the Benedictine and Spencer's edd.

7 ἀλλόκοτον.

8 κορώνη.

9 παραχαράττοντες καὶ ῥᾳδιουργοῦντες.

10 τῷ δυνάμει λέγεσθαι τὰ μέτρα.

11 [This question, which is little short of astounding, illustrates the marvellous reach and play of Origen's fancy at times. See note *supra*, p. 262. S.]

12 παραχαράττοντες καὶ ῥᾳδιουργοῦντες.

how should they, who gave their Scriptures to the *whole* nation, not expect that they would come to light, and who predicted, moreover, that this religion should be proclaimed to *all* nations? Jesus declared, "The kingdom of God shall be taken from you, and given to a nation bringing forth the fruits thereof;"[1] and in uttering these words to the Jews, what other meaning did He intend to convey than this, viz., that He Himself should, through his divine power, bring forth into light the whole of the Jewish Scriptures, which contain the mysteries of the kingdom of God? If, then, they peruse the Theogonies of the Greeks, and the stories about the twelve gods, they impart to them an air of dignity, by investing them with an allegorical signification; but when they wish to throw contempt upon our biblical narratives, they assert that they are fables, clumsily invented for infant children!

CHAP. XLIII.

"Altogether absurd, and out of season,"[2] he continues, "is the (account of the) begetting of children," where, although he has mentioned no names, it is evident that he is referring to the history of Abraham and Sarah. Cavilling also at the "conspiracies of the brothers," he alludes either to the story of Cain plotting against Abel,[3] or, in addition, to that of Esau against Jacob;[4] and (speaking) of "a father's sorrow," he probably refers to that of Isaac on account of the absence of Jacob, and perhaps also to that of Jacob because of Joseph having been sold into Egypt. And when relating the "crafty procedure of mothers," I suppose he means the conduct of Rebecca, who contrived that the blessing of Isaac should descend, not upon Esau, but upon Jacob. Now if we assert that in all these cases God interposed in a very marked degree,[5] what absurdity do we commit, seeing we are persuaded that He never withdraws His providence[6] from those who devote themselves to Him in an honourable and vigorous[7] life? He ridicules, moreover, the acquisition of property made by Jacob while living with Laban, not understanding to what these words refer: "And those which had no spots were Laban's, and those which were spotted were Jacob's;"[8] and he says that "God presented his sons with asses, and sheep, and camels,"[9] and did not see that "all these things happened unto them for ensamples, and were written for our sake, upon whom the

ends of the world are come."[10] The varying customs (prevailing among the different nations) becoming famous,[11] are regulated by the word of God, being given as a possession to him who is figuratively termed Jacob. For those who become converts to Christ from among the heathen, are indicated by the history of Laban and Jacob.

CHAP. XLIV.

And erring widely from the meaning of Scripture, he says that "God gave wells[12] also to the righteous." Now he did not observe that the righteous do not construct cisterns,[13] but dig wells, seeking to discover the inherent ground and source of potable blessings,[14] inasmuch as they receive in a figurative sense the commandment which enjoins, "Drink waters from your own vessels, and from your own wells of fresh water. Let not your water be poured out beyond your own fountain, but let it pass into your own streets. Let it belong to you alone, and let no alien partake with thee."[15] Scripture frequently makes use of the histories of real events, in order to present to view more important truths, which are but obscurely intimated; and of this kind are the narratives relating to the "wells," and to the "marriages," and to the various acts of "sexual intercourse" recorded of righteous persons, respecting which, however, it will be more seasonable to offer an explanation in the exegetical writings referring to those very passages. But that wells were constructed by righteous men in the land of the Philistines, as related in the book of Genesis,[16] is manifest from the wonderful wells which are shown at Ascalon, and which are deserving of mention on account of their structure, so foreign and peculiar compared with that of other wells. Moreover, that both young women[17] and female servants are to be understood metaphorically, is not *our* doctrine merely, but one which we have received from the beginning from wise men, among whom a certain one said, when exhorting his hearers to investigate the figurative meaning: "Tell me, ye that read the law, do ye not hear the law? For it is written that Abraham had two sons; the one by a bond maid, the other by a free woman. But he who was of the bond woman was born after the flesh; but he of the free woman was by promise. Which things are an allegory: for

---

[1] Cf. Matt. xxi. 43.
[2] ἔξωρον.
[3] Cf. Gen. iv. 8.
[4] Cf. Gen. xxvii. 41.
[5] ἄγχιστα δὲ τούτοις πᾶσι συμπολιτευόμενον.
[6] θειότητα.
[7] ἐρρωμένως.
[8] Cf. Gen. xxx. 42 (LXX.). "The feebler were Laban's, and the stronger Jacob's" (Auth. Vers.).
[9] Cf. Gen. xxx. 43.

[10] Cf. 1 Cor. x. 11.
[11] παρ' οἷς τὰ ποικίλα ἤθη ἐπίσημα γενόμενα, τῷ λογῷ τοῦ Θεοῦ πολιτεύεται, δοθέντα κτῆσις τῷ τροπικῶς καλουμένῳ Ἰακώβ: ἐπίσημα is the term employed to denote the "spotted" cattle of Laban, and is here used by Origen in its figurative sense of "distinguished," thus playing on the double meaning of the word.
[12] φρέατα.
[13] λάκκους.
[14] τὴν ἐνυπάρχουσαν γῆν καὶ ἀρχὴν τῶν ποτίμων ἀγαθῶν. Boherellus proposes: τὴν ἐνυπάρχουσαν πηγὴν καὶ ἀρχὴν τῶν ποτίμων ὑδάτων.
[15] Cf. Prov. v. 15–17.
[16] Cf. Gen. xxvi. 15.
[17] νύμφας.

these are the two covenants; the one from the Mount Sinai, which gendereth to bondage, which is Agar."[1] And a little after, "But Jerusalem which is above is free, which is the mother of us all." And any one who will take up the Epistle to the Galatians may learn how the passages relating to the "marriages," and the intercourse with "the maid-servants," have been allegorized; the Scripture desiring us to imitate not the literal acts of those who did these things, but (as the apostles of Jesus are accustomed to call them) the spiritual.

CHAP. XLV.

And whereas Celsus ought to have recognised the love of truth displayed by the writers of sacred Scripture, who have not concealed even what is to their discredit,[2] and thus been led to accept the other and more marvellous accounts as true, he has done the reverse, and has characterized the story of Lot and his daughters (without examining either its literal or its figurative meaning) as "worse than the crimes of Thyestes." The figurative signification of that passage of history it is not necessary at present to explain, nor what is meant by Sodom, and by the words of the angels to him who was escaping thence, when they said : "Look not behind thee, neither stay thou in all the surrounding district; escape to the mountain, lest thou be consumed;"[3] nor what is intended by Lot and his wife, who became a pillar of salt because she turned back; nor by his daughters intoxicating their father, that they might become mothers by him. But let us in a few words soften down the repulsive features of the history. The nature of actions — good, bad, and indifferent — has been investigated by the Greeks; and the more successful of such investigators[4] lay down the principle that intention alone gives to actions the character of good or bad, and that all things which are done without a purpose are, strictly speaking, indifferent; that when the intention is directed to a becoming end, it is praiseworthy; when the reverse, it is censurable. They have said, accordingly, in the section relating to "things indifferent," that, strictly speaking, for a man to have sexual intercourse with his daughters is a thing indifferent, although such a thing ought not to take place in established communities. And for the sake of hypothesis, in order to show that such an act belongs to the class of things indifferent, they have assumed the case of a wise man being left with an only daughter, the entire human race besides having perished; and they put the question whether the father can fitly have

intercourse with his daughter, in order, agreeably to the supposition, to prevent the extermination of mankind. Is this to be accounted sound reasoning among the Greeks, and to be commended by the influential[5] sect of the Stoics; but when young maidens, who had heard of the burning of the world, though without comprehending (its full meaning), saw fire devastating their city and country, and supposing that the only means left of rekindling the flame[6] of human life lay in their father and themselves, should, on such a supposition, conceive the desire that the world should continue, shall their conduct be deemed worse than that of the wise man who, according to the hypothesis of the Stoics, acts becomingly in having intercourse with his daughter in the case already supposed, of all men having been destroyed? I am not unaware, however, that some have taken offence at the desire[7] of Lot's daughters, and have regarded their conduct as very wicked; and have said that two accursed nations — Moab and Ammon — have sprung from that unhallowed intercourse. And yet truly sacred Scripture is nowhere found distinctly approving of their conduct as good, nor yet passing sentence upon it as blameworthy. Nevertheless, whatever be the real state of the case, it admits not only of a figurative meaning, but also of being defended on its own merits.[8]

CHAP. XLVI.

Celsus, moreover, sneers at the "hatred" of Esau (to which, I suppose, he refers) against Jacob, although he was a man who, according to the Scriptures, is acknowledged to have been wicked; and not clearly stating the story of Simeon and Levi, who sallied out (on the Shechemites) on account of the insult offered to their sister, who had been violated by the son of the Shechemite king, he inveighs against their conduct. And passing on, he speaks of "brothers selling (one another)," alluding to the sons of Jacob; and of "a brother sold," Joseph to wit; and of "a father deceived," viz., Jacob, because he entertained no suspicion of his sons when they showed him Joseph's coat of many colours, but believed their statement, and mourned for his son, who was a slave in Egypt, as if he were dead. And observe in what a spirit of hatred and falsehood Celsus collects together the statements of the sacred history; so that wherever it appeared to him to contain a ground of accusation he produces the passage, but wherever there is any exhibition of virtue worthy of mention —

---

[1] Cf. Gal. iv. 21–24.
[2] τὰ ἀπεμφαίνοντα.
[3] Gen. xix. 17.
[4] οἱ ἐπιτυγχάνοντές γε αὐτῶν,

[5] οὐκ εὐκαταφρόνητος αὐτοῖς.
[6] ζώπυρον.
[7] βουλήματι.
[8] ἔχει δέ τινα καὶ καθ' αὐτὸ ἀπολογίαν. [Our Edinburgh translator gives a misleading rendering here. Origen throughout this part of his argument is reasoning *ad hominem*, and has shown that Greek philosophy sustains this idea.]

as when Joseph would not gratify the lust of his mistress, refusing alike her allurements and her threats — he does not even mention the circumstance ! He should see, indeed, that the conduct of Joseph was far superior to what is related of Bellerophon,[1] since the former chose rather to be shut up in prison than do violence to his virtue. For although he might have offered a just defence against his accuser, he magnanimously remained silent, entrusting his cause to God.

CHAP. XLVII.

Celsus next, for form's sake,[2] and with great want of precision, speaks of "the dreams of the chief butler and chief baker, and of Pharaoh, and of the explanation of them, in consequence of which Joseph was taken out of prison in order to be entrusted by Pharaoh with the second place in Egypt." What absurdity, then, did the history contain, looked at even in itself, that it should be adduced as matter of accusation by this Celsus, who gave the title of *True Discourse* to a treatise not containing doctrines, but full of charges against Jews and Christians? He adds : " He who had been sold behaved kindly to his brethren (who had sold him), when they were suffering from hunger, and had been sent with their asses to purchase (provisions) ; " although he has not related these occurrences (in his treatise). But he *does* mention the circumstance of Joseph making himself known to his brethren, although I know not with what view, or what absurdity he can point out in such an occurrence ; since it is impossible for Momus himself, we might say, to find any reasonable fault with events which, apart from their figurative meaning, present so much that is attractive. He relates, further, that "Joseph, who had been sold as a slave, was restored to liberty, and went up with a solemn procession to his father's funeral," and thinks that the narrative furnishes matter of accusation against us, as he makes the following remark : " By whom (Joseph, namely) the illustrious and divine nation of the Jews, after growing up in Egypt to be a multitude of people, was commanded to sojourn somewhere beyond the limits of the kingdom, and to pasture their flocks in districts of no repute." Now the words, " that they were commanded to pasture their flocks in districts of no repute," are an addition, proceeding from his own feelings of hatred ; for he has not shown that Goshen, the district of Egypt, is a place of no repute. The exodus of the people from Egypt he calls a flight, not at all remembering what is written in the book of Exodus regarding the departure of the Hebrews from the land of Egypt. We have enumerated these instances to show that what, literally considered, might appear to furnish ground of accusation, Celsus has not succeeded in proving to be either objectionable or foolish, having utterly failed to establish the evil character, as he regards it, of our Scriptures.

CHAP. XLVIII.

In the next place, as if he had devoted himself solely to the manifestation of his hatred and dislike of the Jewish and Christian doctrine, he says : "The more modest of Jewish and Christian writers give all these things an allegorical meaning ; " and, " Because they are ashamed of these things, they take refuge in allegory." Now one might say to him, that if we must admit fables and fictions, whether written with a concealed meaning or with any other object, to be shameful narratives when taken in their literal acceptation,[3] of what histories can this be said more truly than of the Grecian? In these histories, gods who are sons castrate the gods who are their fathers, and gods who are parents devour their own children, and a goddess-mother gives to the " father of gods and men " a stone to swallow instead of his own son, and a father has intercourse with his daughter, and a wife binds her own husband, having as her allies in the work the brother of the fettered god and his own daughter ! But why should I enumerate these absurd stories of the Greeks regarding their gods, which are most shameful in themselves, even though invested with an allegorical meaning? (Take the instance) where Chrysippus of Soli, who is considered to be an ornament of the Stoic sect, on account of his numerous and learned treatises, explains a picture at Samos, in which Juno was represented as committing unspeakable abominations with Jupiter. This reverend philosopher says in his treatises, that matter receives the spermatic words[4] of the god, and retains them within herself, in order to ornament the universe. For in the picture at Samos Juno represents matter, and Jupiter god. Now it is on account of these, and of countless other similar fables, that we would not even in word call the God of all things Jupiter, or the sun Apollo, or the moon Diana. But we offer to the Creator a worship which is pure, and speak with religious respect of His noble works of creation, not contaminating even in word the things of God ; approving of the language of Plato in the *Philebus*, who would not admit that pleasure was a goddess, " so great is my reverence, Protarchus," he says, " for the very names of the gods." We verily entertain such reverence for the name of God, and for His noble works of creation, that we would not, even under

---

[1] Cf. Homer, *Iliad*, vi. 160.
[2] ὁσίας ἕνεκεν.
[3] κατὰ τὴν πρώτην ἐκδοχήν.
[4] τοὺς σπερματικοὺς λόγους.

pretext of an allegorical meaning, admit any fable which might do injury to the young.

CHAP. XLIX.

If Celsus had read the Scriptures in an impartial spirit, he would not have said that "our writings are incapable of admitting an allegorical meaning." For from the prophetic Scriptures, in which historical events are recorded (not from the historical), it is possible to be convinced that the historical portions also were written with an allegorical purpose, and were most skilfully adapted not only to the multitude of the simpler believers, but also to the few who are able or willing to investigate matters in an intelligent spirit. If, indeed, those writers at the present day who are deemed by Celsus the "more modest of the Jews and Christians" were the (first) allegorical interpreters of our Scriptures, he would have the appearance, perhaps, of making a plausible allegation. But since the very fathers and authors of the doctrines themselves give them an allegorical signification, what other inference can be drawn than that they were composed so as to be allegorically understood in their chief signification?[1] And we shall adduce a few instances out of very many to show that Celsus brings an empty charge against the Scriptures, when he says "that they are incapable of admitting an allegorical meaning." Paul, the apostle of Jesus, says: "It is written in the law, Thou shalt not muzzle the mouth of the ox that treadeth out the corn. Doth God take care for oxen? or saith He it altogether for our sakes? For our sakes, no doubt, this is written, that he that plougheth should plough in hope, and he that thresheth in hope of partaking."[2] And in another passage the same Paul says: "For it is written, For this cause shall a man leave his father and mother, and shall be joined to his wife, and they two shall be one flesh. This is a great mystery; but I speak concerning Christ and the Church."[3] And again, in another place: "We know that all our fathers were under the cloud, and all passed through the sea; and were all baptized unto Moses in the cloud, and in the sea."[4] Then, explaining the history relating to the manna, and that referring to the miraculous issue of the water from the rock, he continues as follows: "And they did all eat the same spiritual meat, and did all drink the same spiritual drink. For they drank of that spiritual Rock that followed them, and that Rock was Christ."[5] Asaph, moreover, who, in showing the histories in Exo-

dus and Numbers to be full of difficulties and parables,[6] begins in the following manner, as recorded in the book of Psalms, where he is about to make mention of these things: "Give ear, O my people, to my law: incline your ears to the words of my mouth. I will open my mouth in parables; I will utter dark sayings of old, which we have heard and known, and our fathers have told us."[7]

CHAP. L.

Moreover, if the law of Moses had contained nothing which was to be understood as having a secret meaning, the prophet would not have said in his prayer to God, "Open Thou mine eyes, and I will behold wondrous things out of Thy law;"[8] whereas he knew that there was a veil of ignorance lying upon the heart of those who read but do not understand the figurative meaning, which veil is taken away by the gift of God, when He hears him who has done all that he can,[9] and who by reason of habit has his senses exercised to distinguish between good and evil, and who continually utters the prayer, "Open Thou mine eyes, and I will behold wondrous things out of Thy law." And who is there that, on reading of the dragon that lives in the Egyptian river,[10] and of the fishes which lurk in his scales, or of the excrement of Pharaoh which fills the mountains of Egypt,[11] is not led at once to inquire who he is that fills the Egyptian mountains with his stinking excrement, and what the Egyptian mountains are; and what the rivers in Egypt are, of which the aforesaid Pharaoh boastfully says, "The rivers are mine, and I have made them;"[10] and who the dragon is, and the fishes in its scales, — and this so as to harmonize with the interpretation to be given of the rivers? But why establish at greater length what needs no demonstration? For to these things applies the saying: "Who is wise, and he shall understand these things? or who is prudent, and he shall know them?"[12] Now I have gone at some length into the subject, because I wished to show the unsoundness of the assertion of Celsus, that "the more modest among the Jews and Christians endeavour somehow to give these stories an allegorical signification, although some of them do not admit of this, but on the contrary are exceedingly silly inventions." Much rather are the stories of the Greeks not only very silly, but very impious inventions. For our narratives keep expressly in view the multitude of simpler believers, which was not done by those who invented the Grecian fables. And therefore not

---

[1] κατὰ τὸν προηγούμενον νοῦν.
[2] Cf. 1 Cor. ix. 9, 10, and Deut. xxv. 4.
[3] Cf. Eph. v. 31, 32. Cf Gen. ii. 24.
[4] Cf. 1 Cor. x. 1, 2.
[5] Cf. 1 Cor. x. 3, 4.

[6] προβλήματα καὶ παραβολαί.
[7] Cf. Ps. lxxviii. 1-3.
[8] Cf Ps. cxix. 18.
[9] ἐπὰν ἐπακούσῃ τοῦ παρ' ἑαυτοῦ πάντα ποιήσαντος.
[10] Cf. Ezek. xxix. 3.
[11] Cf. Ezek. xxxii. 5, 6.
[12] Cf. Hos xiv. 9.

without propriety does Plato expel from his state all fables and poems of such a nature as those of which we have been speaking.

CHAP. LI.

Celsus appears to me to have heard that there are treatises in existence which contain allegorical explanations of the law of Moses. These, however, he could not have read; for if he had, he would not have said: "The allegorical explanations, however, which have been devised, are much more shameful and absurd than the fables themselves, inasmuch as they endeavour to unite with marvellous and altogether insensate folly things which cannot at all be made to harmonize." He seems to refer in these words to the works of Philo, or to those of still older writers, such as Aristobulus. But I conjecture that Celsus has not read their books, since it appears to me that in many passages they have so successfully hit the meaning (of the sacred writers), that even Grecian philosophers would have been captivated by their explanations; for in their writings we find not only a polished style, but exquisite thoughts and doctrines, and a rational use of what Celsus imagines to be fables in the sacred writings. I know, moreover, that Numenius the Pythagorean — a surpassingly excellent expounder of Plato, and who held a foremost place as a teacher of the doctrines of Pythagoras — in many of his works quotes from the writings of Moses and the prophets, and applies to the passages in question a not improbable allegorical meaning, as in his work called *Epops*, and in those which treat of "Numbers" and of "Place." And in the third book of his dissertation on *The Good*, he quotes also a narrative regarding Jesus — without, however, mentioning His name — and gives it an allegorical signification, whether successfully or the reverse I may state on another occasion. He relates also the account respecting Moses, and Jannes, and Jambres.[1] But we are not elated on account of this instance, though we express our approval of Numenius, rather than of Celsus and other Greeks, because he was willing to investigate our histories from a desire to acquire knowledge, and was (duly) affected by them as narratives which were to be allegorically understood, and which did not belong to the category of foolish compositions.

CHAP. LII.

After this, selecting from all the treatises which contain allegorical explanations and interpretations, expressed in a language and style not to be despised, the least important,[2] such as might contribute, indeed, to strengthen the faith of the multitude of simple believers, but were not adapted to impress those of more intelligent mind, he continues: "Of such a nature do I know the work to be, entitled *Controversy between one Papiscus and Jason*, which is fitted to excite pity and hatred instead of laughter. It is not my purpose, however, to confute the statements contained in such works; for their fallacy is manifest to all, especially if any one will have the patience to read the books themselves. Rather do I wish to show that Nature teaches this, that God made nothing that is mortal, but that His works, whatever they are, are immortal, and theirs mortal. And the soul[3] is the work of God, while the nature of the body is different. And in this respect there is no difference between the body of a bat, or of a worm, or of a frog, and that of a man; for the matter[4] is the same, and their corruptible part is alike." Nevertheless I could wish that every one who heard Celsus declaiming and asserting that the treatise entitled *Controversy between Jason and Papiscus regarding Christ* was fitted to excite not laughter, but hatred, could take the work into his hands, and patiently listen to its contents; that, finding in it nothing to excite hatred, he might condemn Celsus out of the book itself. For if it be impartially perused, it will be found that there is nothing to excite even laughter in a work in which a Christian is described as conversing with a Jew on the subject of the Jewish Scriptures, and proving that the predictions regarding Christ fitly apply to Jesus; although the other disputant maintains the discussion in no ignoble style, and in a manner not unbecoming the character of a Jew.

CHAP. LIII.

I do not know, indeed, how he could conjoin things that do not admit of union, and which cannot exist together at the same time in human nature, in saying, as he did, that "the above treatise deserved to be treated both with pity and hatred." For every one will admit that he who is the object of pity is not at the same moment an object of hatred, and that he who is the object of hatred is not at the same time a subject of pity. Celsus, moreover, says that it was not his purpose to refute such statements, because he thinks that their absurdity is evident to all, and that, even before offering any logical refutation, they will appear to be bad, and to merit both pity and hatred. But we invite him who peruses this reply of ours to the charges of Celsus to have patience, and to listen to our sacred writings themselves, and, as far as possible, to form an opinion from their *contents* of the purpose of the writers, and of their con-

---

[1] Cf. 2 Tim. iii. 8. [Note this testimony concerning Numenius.]
[2] τὸ εὐτελέστερον.
[3] ψυχή.
[4] ὕλη.

sciences and disposition of mind ; for he will discover that they are men who strenuously contend for what they uphold, and that some of them show that the history which they narrate is one which they have both seen and experienced,[1] which was miraculous, and worthy of being recorded for the advantage of their future hearers. Will any one indeed venture to say that it is not the source and fountain of all blessing[2] (to men) to believe in the God of all things, and to perform all our actions with the view of pleasing Him in everything whatever, and not to entertain even a thought unpleasing to Him, seeing that not only our words and deeds, but our very thoughts, will be the subject of future judgment? And what other arguments would more effectually lead human nature to adopt a virtuous life, than the belief or opinion that the supreme God beholds all things, not only what is said and done, but even what is thought by us? And let any one who likes compare any other system which at the same time converts and ameliorates, not merely one or two individuals, but, as far as in it lies, countless numbers, that by the comparison of both methods he may form a correct idea of the arguments which dispose to a virtuous life.

CHAP. LIV.

But as in the words which I quoted from Celsus, which are a paraphrase from the *Timæus*, certain expressions occur, such as, " God made nothing mortal, but immortal things alone, while mortal things are the works of others, and the soul is a work of God, but the nature of the body is different, and there is no difference between the body of a man and that of a bat, or of a worm, or of a frog ; for the matter is the same, and their corruptible part alike," — let us discuss these points for a little ; and let us show that Celsus either does not disclose his Epicurean opinions, or, as might be said by one person, has exchanged them for better, or, as another might say, has nothing in common save the name, with Celsus, the Epicurean. For he ought, in giving expression to such opinions, and in proposing to contradict not only us, but the by no means obscure sect of philosophers who are the adherents of Zeno of Citium, to have proved that the bodies of animals are not the work of God, and that the great skill displayed in their construction did not proceed from the highest intelligence. And he ought also, with regard to the countless diversities of plants, which are regulated by an inherent, incomprehensible nature,[3] and which have been created

for the by no means despicable[4] use of man in general, and of the animals which minister to man, whatever other reasons may be adduced for their existence,[5] not only to have stated his opinion, but also to have shown us that it was no perfect intelligence which impressed these qualities upon the matter of plants. And when he had once represented (various) divinities as the creators of all the bodies, the soul alone being the work of God, why did not he, who separated these great acts of creation, and apportioned them among a plurality of creators, next demonstrate by some convincing reason the existence of these diversities among divinities, some of which construct the bodies of men, and others — those, say, of beasts of burden, and others — those of wild animals? And he who saw that some divinities were the creators of dragons, and of asps, and of basilisks, and others of each plant and herb according to its species, ought to have explained the causes of these diversities. For probably, had he given himself carefully to the investigation of each particular point, he would either have observed that it was one God who was the creator of all, and who made each thing with a certain object and for a certain reason ; or if he had failed to observe this, he would have discovered the answer which he ought to return to those who assert that corruptibility is a thing indifferent in its nature ; and that there was no absurdity in a world which consists of diverse materials, being formed by one architect, who constructed the different kinds of things so as to secure the good of the whole. Or, finally, he ought to have expressed no opinion at all on so important a doctrine, since he did not intend to prove what he professed to demonstrate ; unless, indeed, he who censures others for professing a simple faith, would have us to believe his mere assertions, although he gave out that he would not merely assert, but would prove his assertions.

CHAP. LV.

But I maintain that, if he had had the patience (to use his own expression) to listen to the writings of Moses and the prophets, he would have had his attention arrested by the circumstance that the expression " God made " is applied to heaven and earth, and to what is called the firmament, and also to the lights and stars ; and after these, to the great fishes, and to every living thing among creeping animals which the waters brought forth after their kinds, and to every fowl of heaven after its kind ; and after these, to the wild beasts of the earth after their kind, and the beasts after their kind, and to

---

[1] The reading in the text of Spencer and of the Benedictine ed. is καταλειφθεῖσαν, for which Lommatzsch has adopted the conjecture of Boherellus, καταληφθεῖσαν.
[2] ὠφελείας.
[3] ὑπ' ἐνυπαρχούσης ἀφαντάστου φύσεως διοικουμένων.

[4] πρὸς χρείαν οὐκ εὐκαταφρόνητον.
[5] ὅπως ποτὲ ἄλλως ὄντων.

every creeping thing upon the earth after its kind ; and last of all to man. The expression "made," however, is not applied to other things ; but it is deemed sufficient to say regarding light, "And it was light ;" and regarding the one gathering together of all the waters that are under the whole heaven, "It was so." And in like manner also, with regard to what grew upon the earth, where it is said, "The earth brought forth grass, and herb yielding seed after its kind and after its likeness, and the fruit-tree yielding fruit, whose seed is in itself, after its kind, upon the earth." He would have inquired, moreover, whether the recorded commands of God respecting the coming into existence of each part of the world were addressed to one thing or to several ;[1] and he would not lightly have charged with being unintelligible, and as having no secret meaning, the accounts related in these books, either by Moses, or, as *we* would say, by the Divine Spirit speaking in Moses, from whom also he derived the power of prophesying ; since he "knew both the present, and the future, and the past," in a higher degree than those priests who are alleged by the poets to have possessed a knowledge of these things.

CHAP. LVI.

Moreover, since Celsus asserts that "the soul is the work of God, but that the nature of body is different ; and that in this respect there is no difference between the body of a bat, or of a worm, or of a frog, and that of a man, for the matter is the same, and their corruptible part alike," — we have to say in answer to this argument of his, that if, since the same matter underlies the body of a bat, or of a worm, or of a frog, or of a man, these bodies will differ in no respect from one another, it is evident then that these bodies also will differ in no respect from the sun, or the moon, or the stars, or the sky, or any other thing which is called by the Greeks a god, cognisable by the senses.[2] For the same matter, underlying *all* bodies, is, properly speaking, without qualities and without form, and derives its qualities from some (other) source, I know not whence, since Celsus will have it that nothing corruptible can be the work of God. Now the corruptible part of everything whatever, being produced from the same underlying matter, must necessarily be the same, by Celsus' own showing ; unless, indeed, finding himself here hard pressed, he should desert Plato, who makes the soul arise from a certain bowl,[3] and take refuge with Aristotle and the Peripatetics, who maintain that the ether is *immaterial*,[4] and con-

sists of a fifth nature, separate from the other four elements,[5] against which view both the Platonists and the Stoics have nobly protested. And we too, who are despised by Celsus, will contravene it, seeing we are required to explain and maintain the following statement of the prophet : "The heavens shall perish, but Thou remainest : and they all shall wax old as a garment ; and as a vesture shalt Thou fold them up, and they shall be changed : but Thou art the same."[6] These remarks, however, are sufficient in reply to Celsus, when he asserts that "the soul is the work of God, but that the nature of body is different ;" for from his argument it follows that there is no difference between the body of a bat, or of a worm, or of a frog, and that of a heavenly[7] being.

CHAP. LVII.

See, then, whether we ought to yield to one who, holding such opinions, calumniates the Christians, and thus abandon a doctrine which explains the difference existing among bodies as due to the different qualities, internal and external, which are implanted in them. For we, too, know that there are "bodies celestial, and bodies terrestrial ;" and that "the glory of the celestial is one, and the glory of the terrestrial another ;" and that even the glory of the celestial bodies is not alike : for "one is the glory of the sun, and another the glory of the stars ;" and among the stars themselves, "one star differeth from another star in glory."[8] And therefore, as those who expect the resurrection of the dead, we assert that the qualities which are in bodies undergo change : since some bodies, which are sown in corruption, are raised in incorruption ; and others, sown in dishonour, are raised in glory ; and others, again, sown in weakness, are raised in power ; and those which are sown natural bodies, are raised as spiritual.[9] That the matter which underlies bodies is capable of receiving those qualities which the Creator pleases to bestow, is a point which all of us who accept the doctrine of providence firmly hold ; so that, if God so willed, one quality is at the present time implanted in this portion of matter, and afterwards another of a different and better kind. But since there are, from the beginning of the world, laws[10] established for the purpose of regulating the changes of bodies, and which will continue while the world lasts, I do not know whether, when a new and different

---

[1] τίνι ἢ τίσιν.
[2] αἰσθητοῦ θεοῦ.
[3] Cf. Plato in *Timæo*.
[4] ἄϋλον.

[5] πέμπτης παρὰ τὰ τέσσαρα στοιχεῖα εἶναι φύσεως.
[6] Cf. Ps. cii. 26, 27.
[7] αἰθερίου.
[8] Cf. 1 Cor. xv. 41, etc.
[9] Cf. 1 Cor. xv. 44.
[10] ὀδοί.

order of things has succeeded [1] after the destruction of the world, and what our Scriptures call the end [2] (of the ages), it is not wonderful that at the present time a snake should be formed out of a dead man, growing, as the multitude affirm, out of the marrow of the back,[3] and that a bee should spring from an ox, and a wasp from a horse, and a beetle from an ass, and, generally, worms from the most of bodies. Celsus, indeed, thinks that this can be shown to be the consequence of none of these bodies being the work of God, and that qualities (I know not whence it was so arranged that one should spring out of another) are not the work of a divine intelligence, producing the changes which occur in the qualities of matter.

CHAP. LVIII.

But we have something more to say to Celsus, when he declares that "the soul is the work of God, and that the nature of body is different," and puts forward such an opinion not only without proof, but even without clearly defining his meaning; for he did not make it evident whether he meant that every soul is the work of God, or only the rational soul. This, then, is what we have to say: If every soul is the work of God, it is manifest that those of the meanest irrational animals are God's work, so that the nature of all bodies is different from that of the soul. He appears, however, in what follows, where he says that "irrational animals are more beloved by God than we, and have a purer knowledge of divinity," to maintain that not only is the soul of man, but in a much greater degree that of irrational animals, the work of God; for this follows from their being said to be more beloved by God than we. Now if the rational soul alone be the work of God, then, in the first place, he did not clearly indicate that such was his opinion; and in the second place, this deduction follows from his indefinite language regarding the soul — viz., whether not every one, but only the rational, is the work of God — that neither is the nature of all bodies different (from the soul). But if the nature of all bodies be not different, although the body of each animal correspond to its soul, it is evident that the body of that animal whose soul was the work of God, would differ from the body of that animal in which dwells a soul which was not the work of God. And so the assertion will be false, that there is no difference between the body of a bat, or of a worm, or of a frog, and that of a man.

CHAP. LIX.

For it would, indeed, be absurd that certain stones and buildings should be regarded as more sacred or more profane than others, according as they were constructed for the honour of God, or for the reception of dishonourable and accursed persons;[4] while bodies should not differ from bodies, according as they are inhabited by rational or irrational beings, and according as these rational beings are the most virtuous or most worthless of mankind. Such a principle of distinction, indeed, has led some to deify the bodies of distinguished men,[5] as having received a virtuous soul, and to reject and treat with dishonour those of very wicked individuals. I do not maintain that such a principle has been always soundly exercised, but that it had its origin in a correct idea. Would a wise man, indeed, after the death of Anytus and Socrates, think of burying the bodies of both with like honours? And would he raise the same mound or tomb to the memory of both? These instances we have adduced because of the language of Celsus, that "none of these is the work of God" (where the words "of these" refer to the body of a man, or to the snakes which come out of the body; and to that of an ox, or of the bees which come from the body of an ox; and to that of a horse, or of an ass, and to the wasps which come from a horse, and the beetles which proceed from an ass); for which reason we have been obliged to return to the consideration of his statement, that "the soul is the work of God, but that the nature of body is different."

CHAP. LX.

He next proceeds to say, that "a common nature pervades all the previously mentioned bodies, and one which goes and returns the same amid recurring changes."[6] In answer to this, it is evident from what has been already said, that not only does a common nature pervade those bodies which have been previously enumerated, but the heavenly bodies as well. And if this is the case, it is clear also that, according to Celsus (although I do not know whether it is according to truth), it is one nature which goes and returns the same through all bodies amid recurring changes. It is evident also that this is the case in the opinion of those who hold that the world is to perish; while those also who hold the opposite view will endeavour to show, without the assumption of a fifth substance,[7] that in their judgment too it is one nature "which goes and returns the same through all bodies amid

---

[1] καινῆς διαδεξαμένης ὁδοῦ καὶ ἀλλοίας, etc. For διαδεξαμένης, Boherellus would read διαδεξομένης. Cf. Origen, de Princip., iii. c. 5; ii. c. 3. [See also Neander's Church History, vol. i. p.328, and his remarks on "the general ἀποκατάστασις" of Origen. S.]

[2] συντέλεια.

[3] Cf. Pliny, x. c. 66: "Anguem ex medullâ hominis spinæ gigni accepimus a multis." Cf. also Ovid, Metamorphos., xv. fab. iv.

[4] σωμάτων.

[5] τῶν διαφερόντων.

[6] καὶ μία εἰς ἀμοιβὴν παλίντροπον ἰοῦσα καὶ ἐπανιοῦσα.

[7] σῶμα.

recurring changes." And thus, even that which is perishable remains in order to undergo a change;[1] for the matter which underlies (all things), while its properties perish, still abides, according to the opinion of those who hold it to be uncreated. If, however, it can be shown by any arguments not to be uncreated, but to have been created for certain purposes, it is clear that it will not have the same nature of permanency which it would possess on the hypothesis of being uncreated. But it is not our object at present, in answering the charges of Celsus, to discuss these questions of natural philosophy.

CHAP. LXI.

He maintains, moreover, that "no product of matter is immortal." Now, in answer to this it may be said, that if no product of matter is immortal, then either the whole world is immortal, and thus not a product of matter, or it is *not* immortal. If, accordingly, the world is immortal (which is agreeable to the view of those who say that the soul alone is the work of God, and was produced from a certain bowl), let Celsus show that the world was not produced from a matter devoid of qualities, remembering his own assertion that "no product of matter is immortal." If, however, the world is not immortal (seeing it is a product of matter), but mortal, does it also perish, or does it not? For if it perish, it will perish as being a work of God; and then, in the event of the *world* perishing, what will become of the *soul*, which is also a work of God? Let Celsus answer this! But if, perverting the notion of immortality, he will assert that, although *perishable*, it is immortal, because it does not *really* perish; that it is *capable* of dying, but does not *actually* die, — it is evident that, according to him, there will exist something which is at the same time mortal and immortal, by being capable of both conditions; and that which does not die will be mortal, and that which is not immortal by nature will be termed in a peculiar sense immortal, because it does not die! According to what distinction, then, in the meaning of words, will he maintain that no product of matter is immortal? And thus you see that the ideas contained in his writings, when closely examined and tested, are proved *not* to be sound and incontrovertible.[2] And after making these assertions he adds: "On this point these remarks are sufficient; and if any one is capable of hearing and examining further, he will come to know (the truth)." Let us, then, who in his opinion are unintelligent individuals, see what will result from our being able to listen to him for a little, and so continue our investigation.

CHAP. LXII.

After these matters, then, he thinks that he can make us acquainted in a few words with the questions regarding the nature of evil, which have been variously discussed in many important treatises, and which have received very opposite explanations. His words are: "There neither were formerly, nor are there now, nor will there be again, more or fewer evils in the world (than have always been). For the nature of all things is one and the same, and the generation of evils is always the same." He seems to have paraphrased these words from the discussions in the *Theætetus*, where Plato makes Socrates say: "It is neither possible for evils to disappear from among men, nor for them to become established among the gods," and so on. But he appears to me not to have understood Plato correctly, although professing to include all truth[3] in this one treatise, and giving to his own book against us the title of *A True Discourse*. For the language in the *Timæus*, where it is said, "When the gods purify the earth with water," shows that the earth, when purified with water, contains less evil than it did before its purification. And this assertion, that there at one time were fewer evils in the world, is one which we make, in harmony with the opinion of Plato, because of the language in the *Theætetus*, where he says that "evils cannot disappear from among men."[4]

CHAP. LXIII.

I do not understand how Celsus, while admitting the existence of Providence, at least so far as appears from the language of this book, can say that there never existed (at any time) either more or fewer evils, but, as it were, a fixed number; thus annihilating the beautiful doctrine regarding the indefinite[5] nature of evil, and asserting that evil, even in its own nature,[6] is infinite. Now it appears to follow from the position, that there never have been, nor are now, nor ever will be, more or fewer evils in the world; that as, according to the view of those who hold the indestructibility of the world, the equipoise of the elements is maintained by a Providence (which does not permit one to gain the preponderance over the others, in order to prevent the destruction of the world), so a kind of Providence presides, as it were, over evils (the number of which is fixed),[7] to prevent their being either increased or diminished! In other ways, too, are the arguments of Celsus concerning evil confuted, by those philosophers who have investigated the subjects of good and evil,

---

[1] οὕτω δὲ καὶ τὸ ἀπολλύμενον εἰς μεταβολὴν διαμένει.
[2] διελέγχεται οὐκ ἐπιδεχόμενα τὸ γενναῖον καὶ ἀναντίρρητον.
[3] ὁ τὴν ἀλήθειαν ἐκπεριλαμβάνων.
[4] [Cf. Plato, *Theætetus*, xxv. p. 176. S.]
[5] ἀόριστον.
[6] καὶ τῷ ἰδίῳ λόγῳ.
[7] τοσοῖσδε τυγχάνουσιν.

and who have proved also from history that in former times it was without the city, and with their faces concealed by masks, that loose women hired themselves to those who wanted them; that subsequently, becoming more impudent, they laid aside their masks, though not being permitted by the laws to enter the cities, they (still) remained without them, until, as the dissoluteness of manners daily increased, they dared even to enter the cities. Such accounts are given by Chrysippus in the introduction to his work on *Good and Evil*. From this also it may be seen that evils both increase and decrease, viz., that those individuals who were called "Ambiguous"[1] used formerly to present themselves openly to view, suffering and committing all shameful things, while subserving the passions of those who frequented their society; but recently they have been expelled by the authorities.[2] And of countless evils which, owing to the spread of wickedness, have made their appearance in human life, we may say that formerly they did *not* exist. For the most ancient histories, which bring innumerable other accusations against sinful men, know nothing of the perpetrators of abominable[3] crimes.

CHAP. LXIV.

And now, after these arguments, and others of a similar kind, how can Celsus escape appearing in a ridiculous light, when he imagines that there never has been in the past, nor will be in the future, a greater or less number of evils? For although the nature of all things is one and the same, it does not at all follow that the production of evils is a constant quantity.[4] For although the nature of a certain individual is one and the same, yet his mind, and his reason, and his actions, are not always alike:[5] there being a time when he had not yet attained to reason; and another, when, with the possession of reason, he had become stained with wickedness, and when this increased to a greater or less degree; and again, a time when he devoted himself to virtue, and made greater or less progress therein, attaining sometimes the very summit of perfection, through longer or shorter periods of contemplation.[6] In like manner, we may make the same assertion in a higher degree of the nature of the universe,[7] that although it is one and the same in kind, yet neither do exactly the same things, nor yet things that are similar, occur in it; for we neither have invariably productive nor unproductive seasons, nor yet periods of continuous rain or of drought. And so in the same way, with regard to virtuous souls, there are neither appointed periods of fertility nor of barrenness; and the same is the case with the greater or less spread of evil. And those who desire to investigate all things to the best of their ability, must keep in view this estimate of evils, that their amount is not always the same, owing to the working of a Providence which either preserves earthly things, or purges them by means of floods and conflagrations; and effects this, perhaps, not merely with reference to things on earth, but also to the whole universe of things[8] which stands in need of purification, when the wickedness that is in it has become great.

CHAP. LXV.

After this Celsus continues: "It is not easy, indeed, for one who is not a philosopher to ascertain the origin of evils, though it is sufficient for the multitude to say that they do not proceed from God, but cleave to matter, and have their abode among mortal things; while the course[9] of mortal things being the same from beginning to end, the same things must always, agreeably to the appointed cycles,[10] recur in the past, present, and future." Celsus here observes that it is not easy for one who is not a philosopher to ascertain the origin of evils, as if it were an easy matter for a philosopher to gain this knowledge, while for one who is not a philosopher it was difficult, though still possible, for such an one, although with great labour, to attain it. Now, to this we say, that the origin of evils is a subject which is not easy even for a philosopher to master, and that perhaps it is impossible even for such to attain a clear understanding of it, unless it be revealed to them by divine inspiration, both what evils are, and how they originated, and how they shall be made to disappear. But although ignorance of God *is* an evil, and one of the greatest of these is not to know how God is to be served and worshipped, yet, as even Celsus would admit, there are undoubtedly some philosophers who have been ignorant of this, as is evident from the views of the different philosophical sects; whereas, according to our judgment, no one is capable of ascertaining the origin of evils who does not know that it is wicked to suppose that piety is preserved uninjured amid the laws that are established in different states, in conformity with the generally prevailing ideas of government.[11] No one, moreover, who has not heard what is related of him who is called "devil," and of his "angels," and what he was before he became a devil, and *how* he became

---

[1] Ἀμφίβολοι.
[2] Ἀγορανόμοι.
[3] ἀρρητοποιοὺς οὐκ ἴσασι.
[4] οὐ πάντως καὶ ἡ τῶν κακῶν γένεσις ἀεὶ ἡ αὐτή.
[5] οὐκ ἀεὶ τὰ αὐτά ἐστι περὶ τὸ ἡγεμονικὸν αὐτοῦ, καὶ τὸν λόγον αὐτοῦ, καὶ τὰς πράξεις.
[6] θεωρίαις.
[7] τῶν ὅλων.

[8] τὰ ἐν ὅλῳ τῷ κόσμῳ.
[9] περίοδος.
[10] κατὰ τὰς τεταγμένας ἀνακυκλήσεις.
[11] μὴ ἐγνωκὼς κακὸν εἶναι τὸ νομίζειν εὐσέβειαν σώζεσθαι ἐν τοῖς καθεστηκόσι κατὰ τὰς κοινότερον νοουμένας πολιτείας νόμοις.

such, and what was the cause of the simultaneous apostasy of those who are termed his angels, will be able to ascertain the origin of evils. But he who would attain to this knowledge must learn more accurately the nature of demons, and know that they are not the work of God so far as respects their demoniacal nature, but only in so far as they are possessed of reason; and also what their origin was, so that they became beings of such a nature, that while converted into demons, the powers of their mind[1] remain. And if there be any topic of human investigation which is difficult for our nature to grasp, certainly the origin of evils may be considered to be such.

CHAP. LXVI.

Celsus in the next place, as if he were able to tell certain secrets regarding the origin of evils, but chose rather to keep silence, and say only what was suitable to the multitude, continues as follows: " It is sufficient to say to the multitude regarding the origin of evils, that they do not proceed from God, but cleave to matter, and dwell among mortal things." It is true, certainly, that evils do not proceed from God; for according to Jeremiah, one of our prophets, it is certain that " out of the mouth of the Most High proceedeth not evil and good."[2] But to maintain that matter, dwelling among mortal things, is the cause of evils, is in our opinion not true. For it is the mind of each individual which is the cause of the evil which arises in him, and this is evil (in the abstract);[3] while the actions which proceed from it are wicked, and there is, to speak with accuracy, nothing else in our view that is evil. I am aware, however, that this topic requires very elaborate treatment, which (by the grace of God enlightening the mind) may be successfully attempted by him who is deemed by God worthy to attain the necessary knowledge on this subject.

CHAP. LXVII.

I do not understand how Celsus should deem it of advantage, in writing a treatise against us, to adopt an opinion which requires at least much plausible reasoning to make it appear, as far as he can do so, that " the course of mortal things is the same from beginning to end, and that the same things must always, according to the appointed cycles, recur in the past, present, and future." Now, if this be true, our free-will is annihilated.[4] For if, in the revolution of mortal things, the same events must perpetually occur in the past, present, and future, according to the

appointed cycles, it is clear that, of necessity, Socrates will always be a philosopher, and be condemned for introducing strange gods and for corrupting the youth. And Anytus and Melitus must always be his accusers, and the council of the Areopagus must ever condemn him to death by hemlock. And in the same way, according to the appointed cycles, Phalaris must always play the tyrant, and Alexander of Pheræ commit the same acts of cruelty, and those condemned to the bull of Phalaris continually pour forth their wailings from it. But if these things be granted, I do not see how our free-will can be preserved, or how praise or blame can be administered with propriety. We may say further to Celsus, in answer to such a view, that " if the course of mortal things be always the same from beginning to end, and if, according to the appointed cycles, the same events must always occur in the past, present, and future," then, according to the appointed cycles, Moses must again come forth from Egypt with the Jewish people, and Jesus again come to dwell in human life, and perform the same actions which (according to this view) he has done not once, but countless times, as the periods have revolved. Nay, Christians too will be the same in the appointed cycles; and Celsus will again write this treatise of his, which he has done innumerable times before.

CHAP. LXVIII.

Celsus, however, says that it is only " the course of *mortal* things which, according to the appointed cycles, must always be the same in the past, present, and future; " whereas the majority of the Stoics maintain that this is the case not only with the course of mortal, but also with that of immortal things, and of those whom they regard as gods. For after the conflagration of the world,[5] which has taken place countless times in the past, and will happen countless times in the future, there has been, and will be, the same arrangement of all things from the beginning to the end. The Stoics, indeed, in endeavouring to parry, I don't know how, the objections raised to their views, allege that as cycle after cycle returns, all men will be altogether unchanged[6] from those who lived in former cycles; so that Socrates will not live again, but one altogether like to Socrates, who will marry a wife exactly like Xanthippe, and will be accused by men exactly like Anytus and Melitus. I do not understand, however, how the world is to be always the same, and one individual not different from another, and yet the things in it not the same, though exactly alike. But the main argument in answer to the statements of Celsus

---

[1] τὸ ἡγεμονικόν.
[2] Cf. Lam. iii. 38. [In the Authorized Version and in the Vulgate the passage is interrogative. S.]
[3] ἥτις ἐστὶ τὸ κακόν.
[4] τὸ ἐφ' ἡμῖν ἀνῄρηται.

[5] τοῦ παντός.
[6] ἀπαραλλάκτους.

and of the Stoics will be more appropriately investigated elsewhere, since on the present occasion it is not consistent with the purpose we have in view to expatiate on these points.

CHAP. LXIX.

He continues to say that "neither have visible things [1] been given to man (by God), but each individual thing comes into existence and perishes for the sake of the safety of the whole, passing agreeably to the change, which I have already mentioned, from one thing to another." It is unnecessary, however, to linger over the refutation of these statements, which have been already refuted to the best of my ability. And the following, too, has been answered, viz., that "there will neither be more nor less good and evil among mortals." This point also has been referred to, viz., that "God does not need to amend His work afresh." [2] But it is not as a man who has imperfectly designed some piece of workmanship, and executed it unskilfully, that God administers correction to the world, in purifying it by a flood or by a conflagration, but in order to prevent the tide of evil from rising to a greater height; and, moreover, I am of opinion that it is at periods which are precisely determined beforehand that He sweeps wickedness away, so as to contribute to the good of the whole world. [3] If, however, he should assert that, after the disappearance of evil, it again comes into existence, such questions will have to be examined in a special treatise. [4] It is, then, always in order to repair what has become faulty [5] that God desires to amend His work afresh. For although, in the creation of the world, all things had been arranged by Him in the most beautiful and stable manner, He nevertheless needed to exercise some healing power upon those who were labouring under the disease of wickedness, and upon a whole world, which was polluted as it were thereby. But nothing has been neglected by God, or will be neglected by Him; for He does at each particular juncture what it becomes Him to do in a perverted and changed world. And as a husbandman performs different acts of husbandry upon the soil and its productions, according to the varying seasons of the year, so God administers entire ages of time, as if they were, so to speak, so many individual years, performing during each one of them what is requisite with a reasonable regard to the care of the world; and this, as it is truly understood by God alone, so also is it accomplished by Him.

CHAP. LXX.

Celsus has made a statement regarding evils of the following nature, viz., that "although a thing may seem to you to be evil, it is by no means certain that it is so; for you do not know what is of advantage to yourself, or to another, or to the whole world." Now this assertion is made with a certain degree of caution; [6] and it hints that the nature of evil is not wholly wicked, because that which may be considered so in individual cases, may contain something which is of advantage to the whole community. However, lest any one should mistake my words, and find a pretence of wrongdoing, as if his wickedness were profitable to the world, or at least *might* be so, we have to say, that although God, who preserves the free-will of each individual, may make use of the evil of the wicked for the administration of the world, so disposing them as to conduce to the benefit of the whole; yet, notwithstanding, such an individual is deserving of censure, and as such has been appointed for a use, which is a subject of loathing to each separate individual, although of advantage to the whole community. [7] It is as if one were to say that in the case of a city, a man who had committed certain crimes, and on account of these had been condemned to serve in public works that were useful to the community, did something that was of advantage to the entire city, while he himself was engaged in an abominable task, [8] in which no one possessed of moderate understanding would wish to be engaged. Paul also, the apostle of Jesus, teaches us that even the very wicked will contribute to the good of the whole, while in themselves they will be amongst the vile, but that the most virtuous men, too, will be of the greatest advantage to the world, and will therefore on that account occupy the noblest position. His words are: "But in a great house there are not only vessels of gold and silver, but also of wood and of earth; and some to honour, and some to dishonour. If a man therefore purge himself, he shall be a vessel unto honour, sanctified and meet for the Master's use, prepared unto every good work." [9] These remarks I have thought it necessary to make in reply to the assertion, that "although a thing may seem to you to be evil, it is by no means certain that it is so, for you do not know what is of advantage either to yourself or to another," in order that no one may take occasion from what has been said on the subject to commit sin, on the pretext that he will thus be useful to the world.

---

[1] τὰ ὁρώμενα.
[2] οὔτε τῷ Θεῷ καινοτέρας δεῖ διορθώσεως.
[3] ὅτι καὶ πάντη τεταγμένως αὐτὴν ἀφανίζων συμφερόντως τῷ παντί.
[4] [See note *supra*, p. 524. S.]
[5] τὰ σφάλματα ἀναλαμβάνειν.
[6] ἔχει τὶ εὐλαβές.
[7] καὶ ὡς ψεκτὸς κατατέτακται εἰς χρείαν ἀπευκταίαν μὲν ἑκάστῳ, χρήσιμον δὲ τῷ παντί.
[8] ἐν ἀπευκταίῳ πράγματι.
[9] Cf. 2 Tim. ii. 20, 21.

CHAP. LXXI.

But as, in what follows, Celsus, not understanding that the language of Scripture regarding God is adapted to an anthropopathic point of view,[1] ridicules those passages which speak of words of anger addressed to the ungodly, and of threatenings directed against sinners, we have to say that, as we ourselves, when talking with very young children, do not aim at exerting our own power of eloquence,[2] but, adapting ourselves to the weakness of our charge, both say and do those things which may appear to us useful for the correction and improvement of the children as children, so the word of God appears to have dealt with the history, making the capacity of the hearers, and the benefit which they were to receive, the standard of the appropriateness of its announcements (regarding Him). And, generally, with regard to such a style of speaking about God, we find in the book of Deuteronomy the following: "The LORD thy God bare with your manners, as a man would bear with the manners of his son."[3] It is, as it were, assuming the manners of a man in order to secure the advantage of men that the Scripture makes use of such expressions; for it would not have been suitable to the condition of the multitude, that what God had to say to them should be spoken by Him in a manner more befitting the majesty of His own person. And yet he who is anxious to attain a true understanding of holy Scripture, will discover the spiritual truths which are spoken by it to those who are called "spiritual," by comparing the meaning of what is addressed to those of weaker mind with what is announced to such as are of acuter understanding, both meanings being frequently found in the same passage by him who is capable of comprehending it.

CHAP. LXXII.

We speak, indeed, of the "wrath" of God. We do not, however, assert that it indicates any "passion" on His part, but that it is something which is asumed in order to discipline by stern means those sinners who have committed many and grievous sins. For that which is called God's "wrath," and "anger," is a means of discipline; and that such a view is agreeable to Scripture, is evident from what is said in the sixth Psalm, "O LORD, rebuke me not in Thine anger, neither chasten me in Thy hot displeasure;"[4] and also in Jeremiah, "O LORD, correct me, but with judgment: not in Thine anger, lest

Thou bring me to nothing."[5] Any one, moreover, who reads in the second book of Kings of the "wrath" of God, inducing David to number the people, and finds from the first book of Chronicles that it was the devil who suggested this measure, will, on comparing together the two statements, easily see for what purpose the "wrath" is mentioned, of which "wrath," as the Apostle Paul declares, all men are children: "We were by nature children of wrath, even as others."[6] Moreover, that "wrath" is no passion on the part of God, but that each one brings it upon himself by his sins, will be clear from the further statement of Paul: "Or despisest thou the riches of His goodness, and forbearance, and long-suffering, not knowing that the goodness of God leadeth thee to repentance? But after thy hardness and impenitent heart, treasurest up unto thyself wrath against the day of wrath, and revelation of the righteous judgment of God." How, then, can any one treasure up for himself "wrath" against a "day of wrath," if "wrath" be understood in the sense of "passion?" or how can the "passion of wrath" be a help to discipline? Besides, the Scripture, which tells us not to be angry at all, and which says in the thirty-seventh Psalm, "Cease from anger, and forsake wrath,"[7] and which commands us by the mouth of Paul to "put off all these, anger, wrath, malice, blasphemy, filthy communication,"[8] would not involve God in the same passion from which it would have us to be altogether free. It is manifest, further, that the language used regarding the wrath of God is to be understood *figuratively* from what is related of His "sleep," from which, as if awaking Him, the prophet says: "Awake, why sleepest Thou, Lord?"[9] and again: "Then the Lord awaked as one out of sleep, and like a mighty man that shouteth by reason of wine."[10] If, then, "sleep" must mean something else, and not what the first acceptation of the word conveys, why should not "wrath" also be understood in a similar way? The "threatenings," again, are intimations of the (punishments) which are to befall the wicked: for it is as if one were to call the words of a physician "threats," when he tells his patients, "I will have to use the knife, and apply cauteries, if you do not obey my prescriptions, and regulate your diet and mode of life in such a way as I direct you." It is no human passions, then, which we ascribe to God, nor impious opinions which we entertain of Him; nor do we err when we present the various narratives concerning Him, drawn from the Scriptures them-

---

[1] [See note, p. 502, *supra*.]
[2] οὐ τοῦ ἑαυτῶν ἐν τῷ λέγειν στοχαζόμεθα δυνατοῦ.
[3] Cf. Deut. i. 31. Origen appears to have read, not ἐτροφόρησεν, the common reading (Heb. אשׂ)), but ἐτροποφόρησεν, the reading of the Codex Alex.
[4] Cf. Ps. vi. 1.

[5] Cf. Jer. x. 24.
[6] Cf. Eph. ii. 3.
[7] Cf. Ps. xxxvii. 8.
[8] Cf. Col. iii. 8.
[9] Ps. xliv. 23.
[10] Cf. Ps. lxxviii. 65.

selves, after careful comparison one with another. For those who are wise ambassadors of the "word" have no other object in view than to free as far as they can their hearers from weak opinions, and to endue them with intelligence.

CHAP. LXXIII.

And as a sequel to his non-understanding of the statements regarding the "wrath" of God, he continues : "Is it not ridiculous to suppose that, whereas a *man*, who became angry with the Jews, slew them all from the youth upwards, and burned their city (so powerless were they to resist him), the mighty *God*, as they say, being angry, and indignant, and uttering threats, should, (instead of punishing them,) send His own *Son*, who endured the sufferings which He did?" If the Jews, then, after the treatment which they dared to inflict upon Jesus, perished with all their youth, and had their city consumed by fire, they suffered this punishment in consequence of no other wrath than that which they treasured up for themselves ; for the judgment of God against them, which was determined by the divine appointment, is termed "wrath" agreeably to a traditional usage of the Hebrews. And what the Son of the mighty God suffered, He suffered voluntarily for the salvation of men, as has been stated to the best of my ability in the preceding pages. He then continues : "But that I may speak not of the Jews alone (for that is not my object), but of the whole of nature, as I promised, I will bring out more clearly what has been already stated." Now what modest man, on reading these words, and knowing the weakness of humanity, would not be indignant at the offensive nature of the promise to give an account of the "whole of nature," and at an arrogance like that which prompted him to inscribe upon his book the title which he ventured to give it (of a True Discourse) ? But let us see what he has to say regarding the "whole of nature," and what he is to place "in a clearer light."

CHAP. LXXIV.

He next, in many words, blames us for asserting that God made all things for the sake of man. Because from the history of animals, and from the sagacity manifested by them, he would show that all things came into existence not more for the sake of man than of the irrational animals. And here he seems to me to speak in a similar manner to those who, through dislike of their enemies, accuse them of the same things for which their own friends are commended. For as, in the instance referred to, hatred blinds these persons from seeing that they are accusing their very dearest friends by the means through which they think they are slandering their ene-

mies ; so in the same way, Celsus also, becoming confused in his argument, does not see that he is bringing a charge against the philosophers of the Porch, who, not amiss, place man in the foremost rank, and rational nature in general before irrational animals, and who maintain that Providence created all things mainly on account of rational nature. Rational beings, then, as being the principal ones, occupy the place, as it were of children in the womb, while irrational and soulless beings hold that of the envelope which is created along with the child.[1] I think, too that as in cities the superintendents of the good and market discharge their duties for the sake of no other than human beings, while dogs and other irrational animals have the benefit of the superabundance ; so Providence provides *in a special manner* for rational creatures ; while this also follows, that irrational creatures likewise enjoy the benefit of what is done for the sake of man. And as he is in error who alleges that the superintendents of the markets[2] make provision in no greater degree for men than for dogs, because dogs also get their share of the goods ; so in a far greater degree are Celsus and they who think with him guilty of impiety towards the God who makes provision for rational beings, in asserting that His arrangements are made in no greater degree for the sustenance of human beings than for that of plants, and trees, and herbs, and thorns.

CHAP. LXXV.

For, in the first place, he is of opinion that "thunders, and lightnings, and rains are not the works of God,"—thus showing more clearly at last his Epicurean leanings ; and in the second place, that "even if one were to grant that these were the works of God, they are brought into existence not more for the support of us who are human beings, than for that of plants, and trees, and herbs, and thorns,"—maintaining, like a true Epicurean, that these things are the product of chance, and not the work of Providence. For if these things are of no more use to us than to plants, and trees, and herbs, and thorns, it is evident either that they do not proceed from Providence at all, or from a providence which does not provide for us in a greater degree than for trees, and herbs, and thorns. Now, either of these suppositions is impious in itself, and it would be foolish to refute such statements by answering any one who brought against us the charge of impiety ; for it is manifest to every one, from what has been said, who is the person guilty of impiety. In the next place, he adds : "Although you may say that these things, viz., plants, and trees, and

---

[1] καὶ λόγον μὲν ἔχει τὰ λογικά, ἅπερ ἐστὶ προηγούμενα, παίδων γεννωμένων· τὰ δ' ἄλογα καὶ τὰ ἄψυχα χωρίου συγκτιζομένου τᾷ παιδίῳ.
[2] ἀγορανόμοι.

herbs, and thorns, grow for the use of men, why will you maintain that they grow for the use of men rather than for that of the most savage of irrational animals?" Let Celsus then say distinctly that the great diversity among the products of the earth is not the work of Providence, but that a certain fortuitous concurrence of atoms[1] gave birth to qualities so diverse, and that it was owing to chance that so many kinds of plants, and trees, and herbs resemble one another, and that no disposing reason gave existence to them,[2] and that they do *not* derive their origin from an understanding that is beyond all admiration. We Christians, however, who are devoted to the worship of the only God, who created these things, feel grateful for them to Him who made them, because not only for us, but also (on our account) for the animals which are subject to us, He has prepared such a home,[3] seeing " He causeth the grass to grow for the cattle, and herb for the service of man, that He may bring forth food out of the earth, and wine that maketh glad the heart of man, and oil to make his face to shine, and bread which strengtheneth man's heart."[4] But that He should have provided food even for the most savage animals is not matter of surprise, for these very animals are said by some who have philosophized (upon the subject) to have been created for the purpose of affording exercise to the rational creature. And one of our own wise men says somewhere: ' Do not say, What is this? or Wherefore is that? for all things have been made for their uses. And do not say, What is this? or Wherefore is that? for everything shall be sought out in its season."[5]

CHAP. LXXVI.

After this, Celsus, desirous of maintaining that Providence created the products of the earth, not more on our account than on that of the most savage animals, thus proceeds: " We indeed by labour and suffering earn a scanty and toilsome subsistence,[6] while all things are produced for them without their sowing and ploughing." He does not observe that God, wishing to exercise the human understanding in all countries (that it might not remain idle and unacquainted with the arts), created man a being full of wants,[7] in order that by virtue of his very needy condition he might be compelled to be the inventor of arts, some of which minister to his subsistence, and others to his protection. For it was better that those who would not have

sought out divine things, nor engaged in the study of philosophy, should be placed in a condition of want, in order that they might employ their understanding in the invention of the arts, than that they should altogether neglect the cultivation of their minds, because their condition was one of abundance. The want of the necessaries of human life led to the invention on the one hand of the art of husbandry, on the other to that of the cultivation of the vine; again, to the art of gardening, and the arts of carpentry and smithwork, by means of which were formed the tools required for the arts which minister to the support of life. The want of covering, again, introduced the art of weaving, which followed that of wool-carding and spinning; and again, that of house-building: and thus the intelligence of men ascended even to the art of architecture. The want of necessaries caused the products also of other places to be conveyed, by means of the arts of sailing and pilotage,[8] to those who were without them; so that even on that account one might admire the Providence which made the rational being subject to want in a far higher degree than the irrational animals, and yet all with a view to his advantage. For the irrational animals have their food provided for them, because there is not in them even an impulse [9] towards the invention of the arts. They have, besides, a natural covering; for they are provided either with hair, or wings, or scales, or shells. Let the above, then, be our answer to the assertions of Celsus, when he says that " we indeed by labour and suffering earn a scanty and toilsome subsistence, while all things are produced for them without their sowing and ploughing."

CHAP. LXXVII.

In the next place, forgetting that his object is to accuse both Jews and Christians, he quotes against himself an iambic verse of Euripides, which is opposed to his view, and, joining issue with the words, charges them with being an erroneous statement. His words are as follow: " But if you will quote the saying of Euripides, that

'The Sun and Night are to mortals slaves,'[10]

why should they be so in a greater degree to us than to ants and flies? For the night is created for them in order that they may rest, and the day that they may see and resume their work." Now it is undoubted, that not only have certain of the Jews and Christians declared that the sun and the heavenly bodies [11] are our servants; but he also has said this, who, according to some, is

---

[1] συντυχία τις ἀτόμων.
[2] οὐδεὶς λόγος τεχνικὸς ὑπέστησεν αὐτά.
[3] ἑστίαν.
[4] Cf. Ps. civ. 14, 15.
[5] Cf. Ecclus. xxxix. 21, and 16, 17.
[6] μόλις καὶ ἐπιπόνως.
[7] ἐπιδεῆ.

[8] διὰ ναυτικῆς καὶ κυβερνητικῆς.
[9] ἀφορμήν.
[10] Cf. Eurip., *Phœniss.*, 546.
[11] τὰ ἐν οὐρανῷ.

the philosopher of the stage,[1] and who was a hearer of the lectures on the philosophy of nature delivered by Anaxagoras. But this man asserts that all things in the world are subject to all rational beings, — one rational nature being taken to represent all, on the principle of a part standing for the whole;[2] which, again, clearly appears from the verse: —

"The Sun and Night are to mortals slaves."

Perhaps the tragic poet meant the day when he said the sun, inasmuch as it is the cause of the day, — teaching that those things which most need the day and night are the things which are under the moon, and other things in a less degree than those which are upon the earth. Day and night, then, are subject to mortals, being created for the sake of rational beings. And if ants and flies, which labour by day and rest by night, have, besides, the benefit of those things which were created for the sake of men, we must not say that day and night were brought into being for the sake of ants and flies, nor must we suppose that they were created for the sake of nothing, but, agreeably to the design of Providence, were formed for the sake of man.

CHAP. LXXVIII.

He next proceeds further to object against himself[3] what is said on behalf of man, viz., that the irrational animals were created on his account, saying: "If one were to call us the lords of the animal creation because we hunt the other animals and live upon their flesh, we would say, Why were not *we* rather created on *their* account, since they hunt and devour us? Nay, *we* require nets and weapons, and the assistance of many persons, along with dogs, when engaged in the chase; while they are immediately and spontaneously provided by nature with weapons which easily bring us under their power." And here we may observe, that the gift of understanding has been bestowed upon us as a mighty aid, far superior to any weapon which wild beasts may seem to possess. We, indeed, who are far weaker in bodily strength than the beasts, and shorter in stature than some of them, yet by means of our understanding obtain the mastery, and capture the huge elephants. We subdue by our gentle treatment those animals whose nature it is to be tamed, while with those whose nature is different, or which do not appear likely to be of use to us when tamed, we take such precautionary measures, that when we desire it, we keep such wild beasts shut up; and when we

need the flesh of their bodies for food, we slaughter them, as we do those beasts which are not of a savage nature. The Creator, then, has constituted all things the servants of the rational being and of his natural understanding. For some purposes we require dogs, say as guardians of our sheep-folds, or of our cattle-yards, or goat-pastures, or of our dwellings; and for other purposes we need oxen, as for agriculture; and for others, again, we make use of those which bear the yoke, or beasts of burden. And so it may be said that the race of lions, and bears, and leopards, and wild boars, and such like, have been given to us in order to call into exercise the elements of the manly character that exist within us.

CHAP. LXXIX.

In the next place, in answer to the human race who perceive their own superiority, which far exceeds that of the irrational animals, he says, "With respect to your assertion, that God gave you the power to capture wild beasts, and to make your own use of them, we would say that, in all probability, before cities were built, and arts invented, and societies such as now exist were formed, and weapons and nets employed, men were generally caught and devoured by wild beasts, while wild beasts were very seldom captured by men." Now, in reference to this, observe that although men catch wild beasts, and wild beasts make prey of men, there is a great difference between the case of such as by means of their understanding obtain the mastery over those whose superiority consists in their savage and cruel nature, and that of those who do not make use of their understanding to secure their safety from injury by wild beasts. But when Celsus says, "before cities were built, and arts invented, and societies such as now exist were formed," he appears to have forgotten what he had before said, that "the world was uncreated and incorruptible, and that it was only the things on earth which underwent deluges and conflagrations, and that all these things did not happen at the same time." Now let it be granted that these admissions on his part are entirely in harmony with our views, though not at all with his, and his statements made above; yet what does it all avail to prove that in the beginning men were mostly captured and devoured by wild beasts, while wild beasts were never caught by men? For, since the world was created in conformity with the will of Providence, and God presided over the universe of things, it was necessary that the elements[4] of the human race should at the commencement of its existence be placed under some protection of the higher powers, so that there might be formed from the beginning

[1] ὁ κατά τινας Σκηνικὸς φιλόσοφος. Euripides himself is the person alluded to. He is called by Athenæus and Clemens Alexandrinus (*Strom.*, v. vol. ii. p. 461), ὁ ἐπὶ τῆς σκηνῆς φιλόσοφος. — De la Rue.
[2] συνεκδοχικῶς.
[3] ἑαυτῷ ἀνθυποφέρει.

[4] ζώπυρα.

union of the divine nature with that of men. And the poet of Ascra, perceiving this, sings : —

" For common then were banquets, and common were seats,
Alike to immortal gods and mortal men." [1]

CHAP. LXXX.

Those holy Scriptures, moreover, which bear the name of Moses, introduce the first men as hearing divine voices and oracles, and beholding sometimes the angels of God coming to visit them.[2] For it was probable that in the beginning of the world's existence human nature would be assisted to a greater degree (than afterwards), until progress had been made towards the attainment of understanding and the other virtues, and the invention of the arts, and they should thus be able to maintain life of themselves, and no longer stand in need of superintendents, and of those to guide them who do so with a miraculous manifestation of the means which subserve the will of God. Now it follows from this, that it is false that " in the beginning men were captured and devoured by wild beasts, while wild beasts were very seldom caught by men." And from this, too, it is evident that the following statement of Celsus is untrue, that " in this way God rather subjected men to wild beasts." For God did not subject men to wild beasts, but gave wild beasts to be a prey to the understanding of man, and to the arts, which are directed against them, and which are the product of the understanding. For it was not without the help of God [3] that men desired for themselves the means of protection against wild beasts, and of securing the mastery over them.

CHAP. LXXXI.

Our noble opponent, however, not observing how many philosophers there are who admit the existence of Providence, and who hold that Providence created all things for the sake of rational beings, overturns as far as he can those doctrines which are of use in showing the harmony that prevails in these matters between Christianity and philosophy ; nor does he see how great is the injury done to religion from accepting the statement that before God there is no difference between a man and an ant or a bee, but proceeds to add, that " if men appear to be superior to irrational animals on this account, that they have built cities, and make use of a political constitution, and forms of government, and sovereignties,[4] this is to say nothing to the purpose, for ants and bees do the same. Bees, indeed, have a sovereign, who has followers

and attendants ; and there occur among them wars and victories, and slaughterings of the vanquished,[5] and cities and suburbs, and a succession of labours, and judgments passed upon the idle and the wicked ; for the drones are driven away and punished." Now here he did not observe the difference that exists between what is done after reason and consideration, and what is the result of an irrational nature, and is purely mechanical. For the origin of these things is not explained by the existence of any rational principle in those who make them, because they do not possess any such principle ; but the most ancient Being, who is also the Son of God, and the King of all things that exist, has created an irrational nature, which, as being irrational, acts as a help to those who are deemed worthy of reason. Cities, accordingly, were established among men, with many arts and well-arranged laws ; while constitutions, and governments, and sovereignties among men are either such as are properly so termed, and which exemplify certain virtuous tendencies and workings, or they are those which are improperly so called, and which were devised, so far as could be done, in imitation of the former : for it was by contemplating these that the most successful legislators established the best constitutions, and governments, and sovereignties. None of these things, however, can be found among irrational animals, although Celsus may transfer rational names, and arrangements which belong to rational beings, as cities and constitutions, and rulers and sovereignties, even to ants and bees ; in respect to which matters, however, ants and bees merit no approval, because they do not act from reflection. But we ought to admire the divine nature, which extended even to irrational animals the capacity, as it were, of imitating rational beings, perhaps with a view of putting rational beings to shame ; so that by looking upon ants, for instance, they might become more industrious and more thrifty in the management of their goods ; while, by considering the bees, they might place themselves in subjection to their Ruler, and take their respective parts in those constitutional duties which are of use in ensuring the safety of cities.

CHAP. LXXXII.

Perhaps also the so-called wars among the bees convey instruction as to the manner in which wars, if ever there arise a necessity for them, should be waged in a just and orderly way among men. But the bees have no cities or suburbs ; while their hives and hexagonal cells, and succession of labours, are for the sake of men, who require honey for many purposes,

---

[1] Cf. Hesiod, *Fragmenta Incerta*, ed. Goettling, p. 231.
[2] [Cf. Wordsworth, *Excursion :* " He sat and talked," etc., book iv., *circa med.*]
[3] οὐ γὰρ ἀθεεί.
[4] ἡγεμονίαις.

[5] τῶν ἡττημένων αἱρέσεις. " Nota αἱρέσεις hoc loco sumi pro internecionibus, cædibus. Haud scio an alibi reperiatur pari significatu. Forte etiam scribendum καθαιρέσεις." — RUÆUS.

both for cure of disordered bodies, and as a pure article of food. Nor ought we to compare the proceedings taken by the bees against the drones with the judgments and punishments inflicted on the idle and wicked in cities. But, as I formerly said, we ought on the one hand in these things to admire the divine nature, and on the other to express our admiration of man, who is capable of considering and admiring all things (as co-operating with Providence), and who executes not merely the works which are determined by the providence of God, but also those which are the consequences of his own foresight.

CHAP. LXXXIII.

After Celsus has finished speaking of the bees, in order to depreciate (as far as he can) the cities, and constitutions, and governments, and sovereignties not only of us Christians, but of all mankind, as well as the wars which men undertake on behalf of their native countries, he proceeds, by way of digression, to pass a eulogy upon the ants, in order that, while praising them, he may compare the measures which men take to secure their subsistence with those adopted by these insects,[1] and so evince his contempt for the forethought which makes provision for winter, as being nothing higher than the irrational providence of the ants, as he regards it. it. Now might not some of the more simple-minded, and such as know not how to look into the nature of all things, be turned away (so far, at least, as Celsus could accomplish it) from helping those who are weighed down with the burdens (of life), and from sharing their toils, when he says of the ants, that "they help one another with their loads, when they see one of their number toiling under them?" For he who needs to be disciplined by the word, but who does not at all understand[2] its voice, will say: "Since, then, there is no difference between us and the ants, even when we help those who are weary with bearing their heavy burdens, why should we continue to do so to no purpose?" And would not the ants, as being irrational creature, be greatly puffed up, and think highly of themselves, because their works were compared to those of men? while men, on the other hand, who by means of their reason are enabled to hear how their philanthropy[3] towards others is contemned, would be injured, so far as could be effected by Celsus and his arguments: for he does not perceive that, while he wishes to turn away from Christianity those who read his treatise, he turns away also the sympathy of those who are not Christians from those who bear the

heaviest burdens (of life). Whereas, had he been a philosopher, who was capable of perceiving the good which men may do each other, he ought, in addition to not removing along with Christianity the blessings which are found amongst men, to have lent his aid to co-operate (if he had it in his power) with those principles of excellence which are common to Christianity and the rest of mankind. Moreover, even if the ants set apart in a place by themselves those grains which sprout forth, that they may not swell into bud, but may continue throughout the year as their food, this is not to be deemed as evidence of the existence of *reason* among ants, but as the work of the universal mother, Nature, which adorned even irrational animals, so that even the most insignificant is not omitted, but bears traces of the reason implanted in it by nature. Unless, indeed, by these assertions Celsus means obscurely to intimate (for in many instances he would like to adopt Platonic ideas) that all souls are of the same species, and that there is no difference between that of a man and those of ants and bees, which is the act of one who would bring down the soul from the vault of heaven, and cause it to enter not only a human body, but that of an animal. Christians, however, will not yield their assent to such opinions : for they have been instructed before now that the human soul was created in the image of God ; and they see that it is impossible for a nature fashioned in the divine image to have its (original) features altogether obliterated, and to assume others, formed after I know not what likeness of irrational animals.

CHAP. LXXXIV.

And since he asserts that, "when ants die, the survivors set apart a special place (for their interment), and that their ancestral sepulchres such a place is," we have to answer, that the greater the laudations which he heaps upon irrational animals, so much the more does he magnify (although against his will) the work of that reason which arranged all things in order, and points out the skill[4] which exists among men, and which is capable of adorning by its reason even the gifts which are bestowed by nature on the irrational creation. But why do I say "irrational," since Celsus is of opinion that these animals, which, agreeably to the common ideas of all men, are termed irrational, are not really so? Nor does *he* regard the ants as devoid of reason, who professed to speak of "universal nature," and who boasted of his truthfulness in the inscription of his book. For, speaking of the ants conversing with one another, he uses the following language : "And when they meet one another

---

[1] παραβάλῃ τῷ λόγῳ πρὸς τοὺς μύρμηκας. "Verba: τῷ λόγῳ πρὸς τοὺς μύρμηκας additititia videntur et recidenda."—Ruæus.
[2] ἐπαίων.
[3] τὸ κοινωνικόν.
[4] ἐντρέχειαν.

they enter into conversation, for which reason they never mistake their way ; consequently they possess a full endowment of reason, and some common ideas on certain general subjects, and a voice by which they express themselves regarding accidental things." [1] Now conversation between one man and another is carried on by means of a voice, which gives expression to the meaning intended, and which also gives utterances concerning what are called "accidental things ;" but to say that this was the case with ants would be a most ridiculous assertion.

CHAP. LXXXV.

He is not ashamed, moreover, to say, in addition to these statements (that the unseemly character [2] of his opinions may be manifest to those who will live after him) : " Come now, if one were to look down from heaven upon earth, in what respect would *our* actions appear to differ from those of ants and bees? " Now does he who, according to his own supposition, looks from heaven upon the proceedings of men and ants, look upon their bodies alone, and not rather have regard to the controlling reason which is called into action by reflection ; [3] while, on the other hand, the guiding principle of the latter is irrational, and set in motion irrationally by impulse and fancy, in conjunction with a certain natural apparatus ? [4] But it is absurd to suppose that he who looks from heaven upon earthly things would desire to look from such a distance upon the *bodies* of men and ants, and would not rather consider the nature of the guiding principles, and the source of impulses, whether that be rational or irrational. And if he once look upon the source of all impulses, it is manifest that he would behold also the difference which exists, and the superiority of man, not only over ants, but even over elephants. For he who looks from heaven will see among irrational creatures, however large their bodies, no other principle [5] than, so to speak, irrationality ; [6] while amongst rational beings he will discover reason, the common possession of men, and of divine and heavenly beings, and perhaps of the Supreme God Himself, on account of which man is said to have been created in the image of God, for the image of the Supreme God is his reason. [7]

CHAP. LXXXVI.

Immediately after this, as if doing his utmost to reduce the human race to a still lower position, and to bring them to the level of the irrational animals, and desiring to omit not a single circumstance related of the latter which manifests their greatness, he declares that " in certain individuals among the irrational creation there exists the power of sorcery ; " so that even in this particular men cannot specially pride themselves, nor wish to arrogate a superiority over irrational creatures. And the following are his words : " If, however, men entertain lofty notions because of their possessing the power of sorcery, yet even in that respect are serpents and eagles their superiors in wisdom ; for they are acquainted with many prophylactics against persons and diseases, and also with the virtues of certain stones which help to preserve their young. If men, however, fall in with these, they think that they have gained a wonderful possession." Now, in the first place, I know not why he should designate as sorcery the knowledge of natural prophylactics displayed by animals, — whether that knowledge be the result of experience, or of some natural power of apprehension ; [8] for the term "sorcery" has by usage been assigned to something else. Perhaps, indeed, he wishes quietly, as an Epicurean, to censure the entire use of such arts, as resting only on the professions of sorcerers. However, let it be granted him that men *do* pride themselves greatly upon the knowledge of such arts, whether they are sorcerers or not : how can serpents be in this respect wiser than men, when they make use of the well-known fennel [9] to sharpen their power of vision and to produce rapidity of movement, having obtained this natural power not from the exercise of reflection, but from the constitution of their body, [10] while men do not, like serpents, arrive at such knowledge merely by nature, but partly by experiment, partly by reason, and sometimes by reflection and knowledge ? So, if eagles, too, in order to preserve their young in the nest, carry thither the eagle-stone [11] when they have discovered it, how does it appear that they are wise, and more intelligent than men, who find out by the exercise of their reflective powers and of their understanding what has been bestowed by nature upon eagles as a gift?

CHAP. LXXXVII.

Let it be granted, however, that there are other prophylactics against poisons known to animals : what does that avail to prove that it is not nature, but reason, which leads to the discovery of such things among them? For if reason were the discoverer, this one thing (or, if you will, one or two more things) would not be (exclusive [12] of all others) the sole discovery

---

[1] οὐκοῦν καὶ λόγου συμπλήρωσίς ἐστι παρ' αὐτοῖς, καὶ κοιναὶ
ἔννοιαι καθολικῶν τινων, καὶ φωνή, καὶ τυγχάνοντα σημαινόμενα.
[2] ἀσχημοσύνην.
[3] οὐ κατανοεῖ δὲ τὸ λογικὸν ἡγεμονικὸν καὶ λογισμῷ κινούμενον;
[4] μετά τινος φυσικῆς ὑποκατασκευῆς;
[5] ἀρχήν.
[6] τὴν ἀλογίαν.
[7] λόγος.

[8] φυσικήν τινα κατάληψιν.
[9] τῷ μαράθρῳ.
[10] ἀλλ' ἐκ κατασκευῆς.
[11] [The ἀετίτης. See Pliny, *N. H.*, x. 4.]
[12] ἀποτεταγμένως.

made by serpents, and some other thing the sole discovery of the eagle, and so on with the rest of the animals; but as many discoveries would have been made amongst them as among men. But now it is manifest from the determinate inclination of the nature of each animal towards certain kinds of help, that they possess neither wisdom nor reason, but a natural constitutional tendency implanted by the Logos [1] towards such things in order to ensure the preservation of the animal. And, indeed, if I wished to join issue with Celsus in these matters, I might quote the words of Solomon from the book of Proverbs, which run thus: "There be four things which are little upon the earth, but these are wiser than the wise: The ants are a people not strong, yet they prepare their meat in the summer; the conies [2] are but a feeble folk, yet make they their houses in the rocks; the locusts have no king, yet go they forth in order at one command; and the spotted lizard,[3] though leaning upon its hands, and being easily captured, dwelleth in kings' fortresses." [4] I do not quote these words, however, as taking them in their literal signification, but, agreeably to the title of the book (for it is inscribed "Proverbs"), I investigate them as containing a secret meaning. For it is the custom of these writers (of Scripture) to distribute into many classes those writings which express one sense when taken literally,[5] but which convey a different signification as their hidden meaning; and one of these kinds of writing is "Proverbs." And for this reason, in our Gospels too, is our Saviour described as saying: "These things have I spoken to you in proverbs, but the time cometh when I shall no more speak unto you in proverbs." [6] It is not, then, the *visible* ants which are "wiser even than the wise," but they who are indicated as such under the "proverbial" style of expression. And such must be our conclusion regarding the rest of the animal creation, although Celsus regards the books of the Jews and Christians as exceedingly simple and commonplace,[7] and imagines that those who give them an allegorical interpretation do violence to the meaning of the writers. By what we have said, then, let it appear that Celsus calumniates us in vain, and let his assertions that serpents and eagles are wiser than men also receive their refutation.

CHAP. LXXXVIII.

And wishing to show at greater length that even the thoughts of God entertained by the

human race are not superior to those of all other mortal creatures, but that certain of the irrational animals are capable of thinking about Him regarding whom opinions so discordant have existed among the most acute of mankind — Greeks and Barbarians — he continues: "If, because man has been able to grasp the idea of God, he is deemed superior to the other animals, let those who hold this opinion know that this capacity will be claimed by many of the other animals; and with good reason: for what would any one maintain to be more divine than the power of foreknowing and predicting future events? Men accordingly acquire the art from the other animals, and especially from birds. And those who listen to the indications furnished by them, become possessed of the gift of prophecy. If, then, birds, and the other prophetic animals, which are enabled by the gift of God to foreknow events, instruct us by means of signs, so much the nearer do they seem to be to the society of God, and to be endowed with greater wisdom, and to be more beloved by Him. The more intelligent of men, moreover, say that the animals hold meetings which are more sacred than our assemblies, and that they know what is said at these meetings, and show that in reality they possess this knowledge, when, having previously stated that the birds have declared their intention of departing to some particular place, and of doing this thing or the other, the truth of their assertions is established by the departure of the birds to the place in question, and by their doing what was foretold. And no race of animals appears to be more observant of oaths than the elephants are, or to show greater devotion to divine things; and this, I presume, solely because they have some knowledge of God." See here now how he at once lays hold of, and brings forward as acknowledged facts, questions which are the subject of dispute among those philosophers, not only among the Greeks, but also among the Barbarians, who have either discovered or learned from certain demons some things about birds of augury and other animals, by which certain prophetic intimations are said to be made to men. For, in the first place, it has been disputed whether there *is* an art of augury, and, in general, a method of divination by animals, or not. And, in the second place, they who admit that there is an art of divination by birds, are not agreed about the manner of the divination; since some maintain that it is from certain demons or gods of divination [8] that the animals receive their impulses to action — the birds to flights and sounds of different kinds, and the other animals to movements of one sort

---

[1] ὑπὸ τοῦ Λόγου γεγενημένη.
[2] χοιρογρύλλιοι. Heb. שְׁפַנִּים.
[3] ἀσκαλαβώτης.
[4] Cf. Prov. xxx. 24-28.
[5] αὐτόθεν.
[6] John xvi. 25.
[7] ἰδιωτικά.

[8] θεῶν μαντικῶν.

or another. Others, again, believe that their souls are more divine in their nature, and fitted to operations of that kind, which is a most incredible supposition.

CHAP. LXXXIX.

Celsus, however, seeing he wished to prove by the foregoing statements that the irrational animals are more divine and intelligent than human beings, ought to have established at greater length the actual existence of such an art of divination, and in the next place have energetically undertaken its defence, and effectually refuted the arguments of those who would annihilate such arts of divination, and have overturned in a convincing manner also the arguments of those who say that it is from demons or from gods that animals receive the movements which lead them to divination, and to have proved in the next place that the soul of irrational animals is more divine than that of man. For, had he done so, and manifested a philosophical spirit in dealing with such things, we should to the best of our power have met his confident assertions, refuting in the first place the allegation that irrational animals are wiser than men, and showing the falsity of the statement that they have ideas of God more sacred than ours, and that they hold among themselves certain sacred assemblies. But now, on the contrary, *he* who accuses us because we believe in the Supreme God, requires us to believe that the souls of birds entertain ideas of God more divine and distinct than those of men. Yet if this is true, the birds have clearer ideas of God than Celsus himself; and it is not matter of surprise that it should be so with him, who so greatly depreciates human beings. Nay, so far as Celsus can make it appear, the birds possess grander and more divine ideas than, I do not say we Christians do, or than the Jews, who use the same Scriptures with ourselves, but even than are possessed by the theologians among the Greeks, for they were only human beings. According to Celsus, indeed, the tribe of birds that practise divination, forsooth, understand the nature of the Divine Being better than Pherecydes, and Pythagoras, and Socrates, and Plato! We ought then to go to the birds as our teachers, in order that as, according to the view of Celsus, they instruct us by their power of divination in the knowledge of future events, so also they may free men from doubts regarding the Divine Being, by imparting to them the clear ideas which they have obtained respecting Him! It follows, accordingly, that Celsus, who regards birds as superior to men, ought to employ them as his instructors, and not one of the Greek philosophers.

CHAP. XC.

But we have a few remarks to make, out of a larger number, in answer to these statements of Celsus, that we may show the ingratitude towards his Maker which is involved in his holding these false opinions.[1] For Celsus, although a man, and "being in honour,"[2] does not possess understanding, and therefore he did not compare himself with the birds and the other irrational animals, which he regards as capable of divining; but yielding to them the foremost place, he lowered himself, and as far as he could the whole human race with him (as entertaining lower and inferior views of God than the irrational animals), beneath the Egyptians, who worship irrational animals as divinities. Let the principal point of investigation, however, be this: whether there actually is or not an art of divination, by means of birds and other living things believed to have such power. For the arguments which tend to establish either view are not to be despised. On the one hand, it is pressed upon us not to admit such an art, lest the rational being should abandon the divine oracles, and betake himself to birds; and on the other, there is the energetic testimony of many, that numerous individuals have been saved from the greatest dangers by putting their trust in divination by birds. For the present, however, let it be granted that an art of divination does exist, in order that I may in this way show to those who are prejudiced on the subject, that if this be admitted, the superiority of man over irrational animals, even over those that are endowed with power of divination, is great, and beyond all reach of comparison with the latter. We have then to say, that if there was in them any divine nature capable of foretelling future events, and so rich (in that knowledge) as out of its superabundance to make them known to any man who wished to know them, it is manifest that they would know what concerned themselves far sooner (than what concerned others); and had they possessed this knowledge, they would have been upon their guard against flying to any particular place where men had planted snares and nets to catch them, or where archers took aim and shot at them in their flight. And especially, were eagles aware beforehand of the designs formed against their young, either by serpents crawling up to their nests and destroying them, or by men who take them for their amusement, or for any other useful purpose or service, they would not have placed their young in a spot where they were to be attacked; and, in general, not one of these animals would have been captured by men, because they were more divine and intelligent than they.

[1] τὴν ἀχάριστον ψευδοδοξίαν.
[2] Ps. xlix. 12.

CHAP. XCI.

But besides, if birds of augury converse with one another,[1] as Celsus maintains they do, the prophetic birds having a divine nature, and the other rational animals also ideas of the divinity and foreknowledge of future events; and if they had communicated this knowledge to others, the sparrow mentioned in Homer would not have built her nest in the spot where a serpent was to devour her and her young ones, nor would the serpent in the writings of the same poet have failed to take precautions against being captured by the eagle. For this wonderful poet says, in his poem regarding the former: —

" A mighty dragon shot, of dire portent;
From Jove himself the dreadful sign was sent.
Straight to the tree his sanguine spires he rolled,
And curled around in many a winding fold.
The topmost branch a mother-bird possessed;
Eight callow infants filled the mossy nest;
Herself the ninth: the serpent, as he hung,
Stretched his black jaws, and crashed the dying young;
While hovering near, with miserable moan,
The drooping mother wailed her children gone.
The mother last, as round the nest she flew,
Seized by the beating wing, the monster slew:
Nor long survived: to marble turned, he stands
A lasting prodigy on Aulis' sands.
Such was the will of Jove; and hence we dare
Trust in his omen, and support the war."[2]

And regarding the second — the bird — the poet says: —

" Jove's bird on sounding pinions beat the skies;
A bleeding serpent of enormous size,
His talons twined; alive, and curling round,
He stung the bird, whose throat received the wound.
Mad with the smart, he drops the fatal prey,
In airy circles wings his painful way,
Floats on the winds, and rends the heaven with cries;
Amidst the host, the fallen serpent lies.
They, pale with terror, mark its spires unrolled,
And Jove's portent with beating hearts behold."[3]

Did the eagle, then, possess the power of divination, and the serpent (since this animal also is made use of by the augurs) not? But as this distinction can be easily refuted, cannot the assertion that both were capable of divination be refuted also? For if the serpent had possessed this knowledge, would not he have been on his guard against suffering what he did from the eagle? And innumerable other instances of a similar character may be found, to show that animals do not possess a prophetic soul, but that, according to the poet and the majority of mankind, it is the " Olympian himself who sent him to the light." And it is with a symbolical meaning[4] that Apollo employs the hawk[5] as his

messenger, for the hawk[6] is called the " swift messenger of Apollo."[7]

CHAP. XCII.

In my opinion, however, it is certain wicked demons, and, so to speak, of the race of Titans or Giants, who have been guilty of impiety towards the true God, and towards the angels in heaven, and who have fallen from it, and who haunt the denser parts of bodies, and frequent unclean places upon earth, and who, possessing some power of distinguishing future events, because they are without bodies of earthly material, engage in an employment of this kind, and desiring to lead the human race away from the true God, secretly enter the bodies of the more rapacious and savage and wicked of animals, and stir them up to do whatever they choose, and at whatever time they choose: either turning the fancies of these animals to make flights and movements of various kinds, in order that men may be caught by the divining power that is in the irrational animals, and neglect to seek after the God who contains all things; or to search after the pure worship of God, but allow their reasoning powers to grovel on the earth, and amongst birds and serpents, and even foxes and wolves. For it has been observed by those who are skilled in such matters, that the clearest prognostications are obtained from animals of this kind; because the demons cannot act so effectively in the milder sort of animals as they can in these, in consequence of the similarity between them in point of wickedness; and yet it is not wickedness, but something like wickedness,[8] which exist in these animals.

CHAP. XCIII.

For which reason, whatever else there may be in the writings of Moses which excites my wonder, I would say that the following is worthy of admiration, viz., that Moses, having observed the varying natures of animals, and having either learned from God what was peculiar to them, and to the demons which are kindred to each of the animals, or having himself ascertained these things by his own wisdom, has, in arranging the different kinds of animals, pronounced all those which are supposed by the Egyptians and the rest of mankind to possess the power of divination to be unclean, and, as a general rule, all that are not of that class to be clean. And amongst the unclean animals mentioned by Moses are the wolf, and fox, and serpent, and eagle, and hawk, and such like. And, generally speaking, you will find that not only in the law, but also in the

---

[1] εἴπερ οἰωνοὶ οἰωνοῖς μάχονται. For μάχονται Ruæus conjectures διαλέγονται, which is adopted by Lommatzsch.
[2] Homer, *Iliad*, ii. 308 sq. (Pope's translation).
[3] Homer, *Iliad*, xii. 200 sq. (Pope's translation).
[4] κατὰ δέ τι σημεῖον.
[5] ἱέραξ.

[6] κίρκος, " the hen-harrier," " Falco," or " Circus pygargus." Cf. Liddell and Scott, s.v.
[7] Cf. Homer, *Odyss.*, xv. 526.
[8] καὶ οὐ κακίαν μὲν, οἱονεὶ δὲ κακίαν οὖσαν.

prophets, these animals are employed as examples of all that is most wicked ; and that a wolf or a fox is never mentioned for a good purpose. Each species of demon, consequently, would seem to possess a certain affinity with a certain species of animal. And as among men there are some who are stronger than others, and this not at all owing to their moral character, so, in the same way, some demons will be more powerful in things indifferent than others ; [1] and one class of them employs one kind of animal for the purpose of deluding men, in accordance with the will of him who is called in our Scriptures the "prince of this world," while others predict future events by means of another kind of animal. Observe, moreover, to what a pitch of wickedness the demons proceed, so that they even assume the bodies of weasels in order to reveal the future ! And now, consider with yourself whether it is better to accept the belief that it is the Supreme God and His Son who stir up the birds and the other living creatures to divination, or that those who stir up these creatures, and not human beings (although they are present before them), are wicked, and, as they are called by our Scriptures, unclean demons.

CHAP. XCIV.

But if the soul of birds is to be esteemed divine because future events are predicted by them, why should we not rather maintain, that when omens [2] are accepted by men, the souls of those are divine through which the omens are heard ? Accordingly, among such would be ranked the female slave mentioned in Homer, who ground the corn, when she said regarding the suitors : —

"For the very last time, now, will they sup here." [3]

This slave, then, was divine, while the great Ulysses, the friend of Homer's Pallas Athene, was *not* divine, but understanding the words spoken by this "divine" grinder of corn as an omen, rejoiced, as the poet says : —

"The divine Ulysses rejoiced at the omen." [4]

Observe, now, as the birds are possessed of a divine soul, and are capable of perceiving God, or, as Celsus says, the gods, it is clear that when we men also sneeze, we do so in consequence of a kind of divinity that is within us, and which imparts a prophetic power to our soul. For this belief is testified by many witnesses, and therefore the poet also says : —

"And while he prayed, he sneezed." [5]

And Penelope, too, said : —

'Perceiv'st thou not that at every word my son did sneeze ? " [6]

[1] ἐν μέσοις.
[2] κληδόνες.
[3] Cf. Homer, *Odyss.*, iv. 685; cf. also xx. 116, 119.
[4] Cf. Homer, *Odyss.*, xx. 120.
[5] Cf. Homer, *Odyss.*, xvii. 541.
[6] Cf. Homer, *Odyss.*, xvii. 545.

CHAP. XCV.

The true God, however, neither employs irrational animals, nor any individuals whom chance may offer,[7] to convey a knowledge of the future ; but, on the contrary, the most pure and holy of human souls, whom He inspires and endows with prophetic power. And therefore, whatever else in the Mosaic writings may excite our wonder, the following must be considered as fitted to do so : "Ye shall not practise augury, nor observe the flight of birds ; " [8] and in another place : "For the nations whom the LORD thy God will destroy from before thy face, shall listen to omens and divinations ; but as for thee, the LORD thy God has not suffered thee to do so." [9] And he adds : "A prophet shall the LORD your God raise up unto you from among your brethren." [10] On one occasion, moreover, God, wishing by means of an augur to turn away (His people) from the practice of divination, caused the spirit that was in the augur to speak as follows : "For there is no enchantment in Jacob, nor is there divination in Israel. In due time will it be declared to Jacob and Israel what the Lord will do." [11] And now, we who knew these and similar sayings wish to observe this precept with the mystical meaning, viz., "Keep thy heart with all diligence," [12] that nothing of a demoniacal nature may enter into our minds, or any spirit of our adversaries turn our imagination whither it chooses. But we pray that the light of the knowledge of the glory of God may shine in our hearts, and that the Spirit of God may dwell in our imaginations, and lead them to contemplate the things of God ; for "as many as are led by the Spirit of God, they are the sons of God." [13]

CHAP. XCVI.

We ought to take note, however, that the power of foreknowing the future is by no means a proof of divinity ; for in itself it is a thing indifferent, and is found occurring amongst both good and bad. Physicians, at any rate, by means of their professional skill foreknow certain things, although their character may happen to be bad. And in the same way also pilots, although perhaps wicked men, are able to foretell the signs [14] (of good or bad weather), and the approach of violent tempests of wind, and atmospheric changes,[15] because they gather this knowledge from experience and observation, although I do not suppose that on that account any one would

[7] οὔτε τοῖς τυχοῦσι τῶν ἀνθρώπων.
[8] Cf. Lev. xix. 26. The Septuagint here differs from the Masoretic text.
[9] Cf. Deut. xviii. 14, cf. 12.
[10] Cf. Deut. xviii. 15.
[11] Cf. Num. xxiii. 23.
[12] Prov. iv. 23.
[13] Cf. Rom. viii. 14.
[14] ἐπισημασίας.
[15] τροπάς.

term them " gods " if their characters happened to be bad. The assertion, then, of Celsus is false, when he says : "What could be called more divine than the power of foreknowing and fore-telling the future?" And so also is this, that "many of the animals claim to have ideas of God ; " for none of the irrational animals possess any idea of God. And wholly false, too, is his assertion, that " the irrational animals are nearer the society of God (than men)," when even men who are still in a state of wickedness, how-ever great their progress in knowledge, are far removed from that society. It is, then, those alone who are truly wise and sincerely religious who are nearer to God's society ; such persons as were our prophets, and Moses, to the latter of whom, on account of his exceeding purity, the Scripture said : " Moses alone shall come near the Lord, but the rest shall not come nigh." [1]

<h3 align="center">CHAP. XCVII.</h3>

How impious, indeed, is the assertion of this man, who charges us with impiety, that " not only are the irrational animals wiser than the human race, but that they are more beloved by God (than they) ! " And who would not be re-pelled (by horror) from paying any attention to a man who declared that a serpent, and a fox, and a wolf, and an eagle, and a hawk, were more beloved by God than the human race? For it follows from his maintaining such a position, that if these animals be more beloved by God than human beings, it is manifest that they are dearer to God than Socrates, and Plato, and Pythagoras, and Pherecydes, and those theolo-gians whose praises he had sung a little before. And one might address him with the prayer : " If these animals be dearer to God than men, may you be beloved of God along with them, and be made like to those whom you consider as dearer to Him than human beings ! " And let no one suppose that such a prayer is meant as an imprecation ; for who would not pray to resemble in all respects those whom he believes to be dearer to God than others, in order that he, like them, may enjoy the divine love? And as Celsus is desirous to show that the assemblies of the irrational animals are more sacred than ours, he ascribes the statement to that effect not to any ordinary individuals, but to persons of intelligence. Yet it is the virtuous alone who are truly wise, for no wicked man is so. He speaks, accordingly, in the following style : " Intelligent men say that these animals hold assemblies which are more sacred than ours, and that they know what is spoken at them, and actually prove that they are not without such knowledge, when they mention beforehand that the birds have

announced their intention of departing to a par ticular place, or of doing this thing or that, an then show that they *have* departed to the plac in question, and have done the particular thin, which was foretold." Now, truly, no person o intelligence ever related such things ; nor di any wise man ever say that the assemblies of th irrational animals were more sacred than thos of men. But if, for the purpose of examinin (the soundness of) his statements, we look t their consequences, it is evident that, in hi opinion, the assemblies of the irrational animal are more sacred than those of the venerabl Pherecydes, and Pythagoras, and Socrates, an Plato, and of philosophers in general ; whicl assertion is not only incongruous [2] in itself, bu full of absurdity. In order that we may believe however, that certain individuals *do* learn fron the indistinct sound of birds that they are abou to take their departure, and do this thing or that and announce these things beforehand, we woul say that this information is imparted to men b demons by means of signs, with the view o having men deceived by demons, and havin, their understanding dragged down from Goc and heaven to earth, and to places lower still.

<h3 align="center">CHAP. XCVIII.</h3>

I do not know, moreover, how Celsus coul hear of the elephants' (fidelity to) oaths, an of their great devotedness to our God, and o the knowledge which they possess of Him. Fo I know many wonderful things which are relatec of the nature of this animal, and of its gentl disposition. But I am not aware that any on has spoken of its observance of oaths ; unles indeed to its gentle disposition, and its observ ance of compacts, so to speak, when once con cluded between it and man, he give the nam of keeping its oath, which statement also ir itself is false. For although rarely, yet some times it has been recorded that, after their appar ent tameness, they have broken out against mer in the most savage manner, and have committec murder, and have been on that account con demned to death, because no longer of any use And seeing that after this, in order to establish (as he thinks he does) that the stork is mor pious than any human being, he adduces the accounts which are narrated regarding that crea ture's display of filial affection [3] in bringing fooc to its parents for their support, we have to say in reply, that this is done by the storks, not from a regard to what is proper, nor from reflection, bu from a natural instinct ; the nature which formec them being desirous to show an instance among the irrational animals which might put men to

---

[1] Cf. Ex. xxiv. 2.

[2] ἀπεμφαῖνον.
[3] ἀντιπελαργοῦντος.

shame, in the matter of exhibiting their gratitude to their parents. And if Celsus had known how great the difference is between acting in this way from reason, and from an irrational natural impulse, he would not have said that storks are more pious than human beings. But further, Celsus, is still contending for the piety of the irrational creation, quotes the instance of the Arabian bird the phœnix, which after many years repairs to Egypt, and bears thither its parent, when dead and buried in a ball of myrrh, and deposits its body in the Temple of the Sun. Now this story is indeed recorded, and, if it be true,[1] it is possible that it may occur in consequence of some provision of nature; divine providence freely displaying to human beings, by the differences which exist among living things, the variety of constitution which prevails in the world, and which extends even to birds, and in harmony with which He has brought into existence one creature, the only one of its kind, in order that by it men may be led to admire, not the creature, but Him who created it.

CHAP. XCIX.

In addition to all that he has already said, Celsus subjoins the following: "All things, accordingly, were not made for man, any more than they were made for lions, or eagles, or dolphins, but that this world, as being God's work, might be perfect and entire in all respects. For this reason all things have been adjusted, not with reference to each other, but with regard to their bearing upon the whole.[2] And God takes care of the whole, and (His) providence will never forsake it; and it does not become worse; nor does God after a time bring it back to himself; nor is He angry on account of men any more than on account of apes or flies; nor does He threaten these beings, each one of which has received its appointed lot in its proper place."

---

[1] [See. vol. i. pp. viii., 12, this series. Observe, Origen, *in Egypt*, doubts the story.]

[2] ἀλλ' εἰ μὴ πᾶν ἐργον. "Gelenius does not recognise these words, and Guietus regards them as superfluous." They are omitted in the translation.

Let us then briefly reply to these statements. I think, indeed, that I have shown in the preceding pages that all things were created for man, and every rational being, and that it was chiefly for the sake of the rational creature that the creation took place. Celsus, indeed, may say that this was done not more for man than for lions, or the other creatures which he mentions; but we maintain that the Creator did not form these things for lions, or eagles, or dolphins, but all for the sake of the rational creature, and "in order that this world, as being God's work, might be perfect and complete in all things." For to this sentiment we must yield our assent as being well said. And God takes care, not, as Celsus supposes, merely of the *whole*, but beyond the whole, in a special degree of every rational being. Nor will Providence ever abandon the whole; for although it should become more wicked, owing to the sin of the rational being, which is a portion of the whole, He makes arrangements to purify it, and after a time to bring back the whole to Himself. Moreover, He is not angry with apes or flies; but on human beings, as those who have transgressed the laws of nature, He sends judgments and chastisements, and threatens them by the mouth of the prophets, and by the Saviour who came to visit the whole human race, that those who hear the threatenings may be converted by them, while those who neglect these calls to conversion may deservedly suffer those punishments which it becomes God, in conformity with that will of His which acts for the advantage of the whole, to inflict upon those who need such painful discipline and correction. But as our fourth book has now attained sufficient dimensions, we shall here terminate our discourse. And may God grant, through His Son, who is God the Word, and Wisdom, and Truth, and Righteousness, and everything else which the sacred Scriptures when speaking of God call Him, that we may make a good beginning of the fifth book, to the benefit of our readers, and may bring it to a successful conclusion, with the aid of His word abiding in our soul.

ELUCIDATION.

(Stated in obscure terms, with advantage, p. 495.)

Turn back to the *Second Apology* of Justin (cap. ix.), "Eternal punishment not a mere threat;"[1] also to Clement (*Stromata*, iv. cap. xxiv.), "the reason and end of divine punishments."[2] Now compare Gieseler[3] (vol. i. p. 212) for what he so sweepingly asserts. And on the doctrine of Origen, let me quote a very learned and *on such points* a most capable judge, the late erudite and pious *half-Gallican* Dr. Pusey. He says:—

"Celsus and Origen are both witnesses that Christians believed in the eternity of punishment. Celsus, to weaken the force of the argument from the sufferings which the martyrs underwent sooner than abjure Christianity, tells Origen that heathen priests taught the same doctrine of eternal punishment as the Christians, and that the only question was, *which was right.*[4]

"Origen answers, 'I should say that the truth lies with those who are able to induce their hearers to *live as men convinced of the truth* of what they have heard. Jews and Christians have been thus affected by the doctrines which they hold about the world to come, the rewards of the righteous, and the punishments of the wicked. Who have been moved in this way, in regard to eternal punishments, by the teaching of heathen priests and mystagogues?'

"Origen's answer acknowledges that the doctrine of eternal punishment had been taught to Christians, that One [Christ] had taught it, and that it had produced the effects He had [in view] in teaching it; viz., to set Christians to strive with all their might to *conquer the sin* which produced it."[5]

On this most painful subject my natural feelings are much with Canon Farrar; but, after lifelong application to the subject, I must think Dr. Pusey holds with his Master, Christ. I feel willing to leave it all with Him who died for sinners, and the cross shuts my mouth. "Herein is love;" and I cannot dictate to such love, from my limited mind, and capacity, and knowledge of His universe. Here let "*every thought* be brought into captivity to the obedience of Christ." Let us sacrifice "imaginations and every high thing that exalteth itself," and leave our Master alike supreme in our affections and over our intellectual powers. He merits such subjection. Let us preach His words, and leave Him to explain them when He shall "condemn every tongue that shall rise against Him in judgment."

Let me also refer to Bledsoe's most solemn and searching reply to John Foster; also to his answer to Lord Kames's effort to help the Lord out of a supposed difficulty.[6] I am sorry that Tillotson exposed himself to a witty retort by the same author, in these words: "If the Almighty really undertook to deceive the world for its own good, it is a pity He did not take the precaution to prevent the archbishop from *detecting the cheat*, . . . not suffering his secret to get into the possession of one who has so indiscreetly published it." The awful importance of the subject, and the recently awakened interest in its discussion, have led me to enlarge this annotation.

---

[1] Our vol. i. p. 191.

[2] Our vol. ii. p. 437.

[3] Ed. Philadelphia, 1836.

[4] See this treatise, Book VIII. cap. xlviii., *infra*.

[5] *What is of Faith as to Everlasting Punishment?* in reply to Dr. Farrar's *Challenge*, 1879. By the Rev. E. B. Pusey, D.D., Oxford, 1881.

[6] *Theodicy*, pp. 295-311 (answer to Foster), p. 81 (to Lord Kames), p. 310 (to Tillotson). I must confess that Bledsoe is *paulo iniquior* when he gives no reference to Tillotson's language. If the retort is based on the sermon (xxxv. vol. iii. p. 350, ed. folio, 1720) on the "Eternity of Torment," however, I do not think it just. The latitudinarian primate restricts himself therein to a very guarded statement of that reserved right by which any governor commutes or remits punishment, though he cannot modify a promise of reward. I wish modern apologists for the divine sovereignty had not gone farther.

ORIGEN AGAINST CELSUS.

BOOK V.

CHAP. I.

It is not, my reverend Ambrosius, because we seek after many words — a thing which is forbidden, and in the indulgence of which it is impossible to avoid sin[1] — that we now begin the fifth book of our reply to the treatise of Celsus, but with the endeavour, so far as may be within our power, to leave none of his statements without examination, and especially those in which it might appear to some that he had skilfully assailed us and the Jews. If it were possible, indeed, for me to enter along with my words into the conscience of every one without exception who peruses this work, and to extract each dart which wounds him who is not completely protected with the "whole armour" of God, and apply a rational medicine to cure the wound inflicted by Celsus, which prevents those who listen to his words from remaining "sound in the faith," I would do so. But since it is the work of God alone, in conformity with His own Spirit, and along with that of Christ, to take up His abode invisibly in those persons whom He judges worthy of being visited ; so, on the other hand, is *our* object to try, by means of arguments and treatises, to confirm men in their faith, and to earn the name of "workmen needing not to be ashamed, rightly dividing the word of truth."[2] And there is one thing above all which it appears to us we ought to do, if we would discharge faithfully the task enjoined upon us by you, and that is to overturn to the best of our ability the confident assertions of Celsus. Let us then quote such assertions of his as follow those which we have already refuted (the reader must decide whether we have done so successfully or not), and let us reply to them. And may God grant that we approach not our subject with our understanding and reason empty and devoid of divine inspiration, that the faith of those whom we wish to aid may not depend upon human wisdom, but that, receiving the "mind" of Christ from His Father, who alone can bestow it, and being strengthened by participating in the word of God, we may pull down "every high thing that exalteth itself against the knowledge of God,"[3] and the imagination of Celsus, who exalts himself against us, and against Jesus, and also against Moses and the prophets, in order that He who "gave the word to those who published it with great power"[4] may supply us also, and bestow upon us "great power," so that faith in the word and power of God may be implanted in the minds of all who will peruse our work.

CHAP. II.

We have now, then, to refute that statement of his which runs as follows : " O Jews and Christians, no God or son of a God either came or will come down (to earth). But if you mean that certain angels did so, then what do you call them ? Are they gods, or some other race of beings ? Some other race of beings (doubtless), and in all probability demons." Now as Celsus here is guilty of repeating himself (for in the preceding pages such assertions have been frequently advanced by him), it is unnecessary to discuss the matter at greater length, seeing what we have already said upon this point may suffice. We shall mention, however, a few considerations out of a greater number, such as we deem in harmony with our former arguments, but which have not altogether the same bearing as they, and by which we shall show that in asserting generally that no God, or son of God, ever descended (among men), he overturns not only the opinions entertained by the majority of mankind regarding the manifestation of Deity, but also what was formerly admitted by himself. For if the general statement, that " no God or son

---

[1] Cf. Prov. x. 19.
[2] Cf. 2 Tim. ii. 15.
[3] Cf. 2 Cor. x. 5.
[4] Cf. Ps. lxviii. 11.

of God has come down or will come down," be truly maintained by Celsus, it is manifest that we have here overthrown the belief in the existence of gods upon the earth who had descended from heaven either to predict the future to mankind or to heal them by means of divine responses; and neither the Pythian Apollo, nor Æsculapius, nor any other among those supposed to have done so, would be a god descended from heaven. He might, indeed, either be a god who had obtained as his lot (the obligation) to dwell on earth for ever, and be thus a fugitive, as it were, from the abode of the gods, or he might be one who had no power to share in the society of the gods in heaven;[1] or else Apollo, and Æsculapius, and those others who are believed to perform acts on earth, would not be gods, but only certain demons, much inferior to those wise men among mankind, who on account of their virtue ascend to the vault[2] of heaven.

CHAP. III.

But observe how, in his desire to subvert our opinions, he who never acknowledged himself throughout his whole treatise to be an Epicurean, is convicted of being a deserter to that sect. And now is the time for you, (reader), who peruse the works of Celsus, and give your assent to what has been advanced, either to overturn the belief in a God who visits the human race, and exercises a providence over each individual man, or to grant this, and prove the falsity of the assertions of Celsus. If you, then, wholly annihilate providence, you will falsify those assertions of his in which he grants the existence of "God and a providence," in order that you may maintain the truth of your own position; but if, on the other hand, you still admit the existence of providence, because you do not assent to the dictum of Celsus, that "neither has a God nor the son of a God come down nor is to come down[3] to mankind," why not rather carefully ascertain from the statements made regarding Jesus, and the prophecies uttered concerning Him, who it is that we are to consider as having come down to the human race as God, and the Son of God? — whether that Jesus who said and ministered so much, or those who, under pretence of oracles and divinations, do not reform the morals of their worshippers, but who have besides apostatized from the pure and holy worship and honour due to the Maker of all things, and who tear away the souls of those who give heed to them from the one only visible and true God, under a pretence of paying honour to a multitude of deities?

CHAP. IV.

But since he says, in the next place, as if the Jews or Christians had answered regarding those who come down to visit the human race, that they were angels: "But if ye say that they are angels, what do you call them?" he continues, "Are they gods, or some other race of beings?" and then again introduces us as if answering, "Some other race of beings, and probably demons," — let us proceed to notice these remarks. For we indeed acknowledge that angels are "ministering spirits," and we say that "they are sent forth to minister for them who shall be heirs of salvation;"[4] and that they ascend, bearing the supplications of men, to the purest of the heavenly places in the universe, or even to supercelestial regions purer still;[5] and that they come down from these, conveying to each one, according to his deserts, something enjoined by God to be conferred by them upon those who are to be the recipients of His benefits. Having thus learned to call these beings "angels" from their employments, we find that because they are divine they are sometimes termed "god" in the sacred Scriptures,[6] but not so that we are commanded to honour and worship in place of God those who minister to us, and bear to us His blessings. For every prayer, and supplication, and intercession, and thanksgiving, is to be sent up to the Supreme God through the High Priest, who is above all the angels, the living Word and God. And to the Word Himself shall we also pray and make intercessions, and offer thanksgivings and supplications to Him, if we have the capacity of distinguishing between the proper use and abuse of prayer.[7]

CHAP. V.

For to invoke angels without having obtained a knowledge of their nature greater than is possessed by men, would be contrary to reason. But, conformably to our hypothesis, let this knowledge of them, which is something wonderful and mysterious, be obtained. Then this knowledge, making known to us their nature, and the offices to which they are severally appointed, will not permit us to pray with confidence to any other than to the Supreme God, who is sufficient for all things, and that through our Saviour the Son of God, who is the Word, and Wisdom, and Truth, and everything else which the writings of God's prophets and the apostles of Jesus entitle Him. And it is enough to secure that the holy angels of God be pro-

---

[1] τοῖς ἐκεῖ θεοῖς.
[2] ἀψίδα.
[3] κατέρχεσθαι.

[4] Cf. Heb. i. 14.
[5] ἐν τοῖς καθαρωτάτοις τοῦ κόσμου χωρίοις ἐπουρανίοις, ἢ καὶ τοῖς τούτων καθαρωτέροις ὑπερουρανίοις.
[6] Cf. Ps. lxxxvi. 8, xcvi. 4, cxxxvi. 2.
[7] ἐὰν δυνώμεθα κατακούειν τῆς περὶ προσευχῆς κυριολεξίας καὶ καταχρήσεως.

pitious to us,[1] and that they do all things on our behalf, that our disposition of mind towards God should imitate as far as it is within the power of human nature the example of these holy angels, who again follow the example of their God ; and that the conceptions which we entertain of His Son, the Word, so far as attainable by us, should not be opposed to the clearer conceptions of Him which the holy angels possess, but should daily approach these in clearness and distinctness.   But because Celsus has not read our holy Scriptures, he gives himself an answer as if it came from us, saying that we "assert that the angels who come down from heaven to confer benefits on mankind are a different race from the gods," and adds that " in all probability they would be called demons by us : " not observing that the name " demons " is not a term of indifferent meaning like that of " men," among whom some are good and some bad, nor yet a term of excellence like that of " the gods," which is applied not to wicked demons, or to statues, or to animals, but (by those who know divine things) to what is truly divine and blessed ; whereas the term " demons " is always applied to those wicked powers, freed from the encumbrance of a grosser body, who lead men astray, and fill them with distractions, and drag them down from God and supercelestial thoughts to things here below.

CHAP. VI.

He next proceeds to make the following statement about the Jews : — " The first point relating to the Jews which is fitted to excite wonder, is that they should worship the heaven and the angels who dwell therein, and yet pass by and neglect its most venerable and powerful parts, as the sun, the moon, and the other heavenly bodies, both fixed stars and planets, as if it were possible that ' the whole ' could be God, and yet its parts not divine ; or (as if it were reasonable) to treat with the greatest respect those who are said to appear to such as are in darkness somewhere, blinded by some crooked sorcery, or dreaming dreams through the influence of shadowy spectres,[2] while those who prophesy so clearly and strikingly to all men, by means of whom rain,, and heat, and clouds, and thunder (to which they offer worship), and lightnings, and fruits, and all kinds of productiveness, are brought about, — by means of whom God is revealed to them, — the most prominent heralds among those beings that are above, — those that are truly heavenly angels, — are to be regarded as of no account ! " In

making these statements, Celsus appears to have fallen into confusion, and to have penned them from false ideas of things which he did not understand ; for it is patent to all who investigate the practices of the Jews, and compare them with those of the Christians, that the Jews who follow the law, which, speaking in the person of God, says, " Thou shalt have no other gods before Me : thou shalt not make unto thee an image, nor a likeness of anything that is in heaven above, or that is in the earth beneath, or that is in the waters under the earth ; thou shalt not bow down to them, nor serve them," [3] worship nothing else than the Supreme God, who made the heavens, and all things besides.   Now it is evident that those who live according to the law, and worship the *Maker* of heaven, will not worship the heaven at the same time with God.   Moreover, no one who obeys the law of Moses will bow down to the angels who are in heaven ; and, in like manner, as they do not bow down to sun, moon, and stars, the host of heaven, they refrain from doing obeisance to heaven and its angels, obeying the law which. declares : " Lest thou lift up thine eyes to heaven, and when thou seest the sun, and the moon, and the stars, even all the host of heaven, shouldst be driven to worship them, and serve them, which the LORD thy God hath divided unto all nations." [4]

CHAP. VII.

Having, moreover, assumed that the Jews consider the heaven to be God, he adds that this is absurd ; finding fault with those who bow down to the heaven, but not also to the sun, and moon, and stars, saying that the Jews do this, as if it were possible that " the whole " should be God, and its several parts not divine.   And he seems to call the heaven " a whole," and sun, moon, and stars its several parts.   Now, certainly neither Jews nor Christians call the " heaven " God.   Let it be granted, however, that, as he alleges, the heaven *is* called God by the Jews, and suppose that sun, moon, and stars *are* parts of " heaven," — which is by no means true, for neither are the animals and plants upon the earth any portion of it, — how is it true, even according to the opinions of the Greeks, that if God be a whole, His parts also are divine ?   Certainly they say that the Cosmos taken as the whole [5] is God, the Stoics calling it the First God, the followers of Plato the Second, and some of them the Third.   According to these philosophers, then, seeing the whole Cosmos is God, its parts also are divine ; so that not only are human be-

---

[1] [Comp. Col. iii. 18 and cap. viii., *infra.*]

[2] ἢ τοὺς μὲν ἐν σκότῳ που ἐκ γοητείας οὐκ ὀρθῆς τυφλώττουσιν, ἢ δι᾽ ἀμυδρῶν φασμάτων ὀνειρώττουσιν ἐγχρίμπτειν λεγομένους, εὖ μάλα θρησκεύειν.

[3] Cf. Ex. xx. 3, 4, 5.

[4] Cf. Deut. iv. 19.

[5] τὸ ὅλον ὁ κόσμος.

ings divine, but the whole of the irrational creation, as being "*portions*" of the Cosmos; and
besides these, the plants also are divine. And if
the rivers, and mountains, and seas are portions
of the Cosmos, then, since the whole Cosmos is
God, are the rivers and seas also gods? But
even this the Greeks will not assert. Those,
however, who preside over rivers and seas
(either demons or gods, as they call them),
they would term gods. Now from this it follows
that the general statement of Celsus, even according to the Greeks, who hold the doctrine of
Providence, is false, that if any "whole" be a
god, its parts necessarily are divine. But it fol
lows from the doctrine of Celsus, that if the
Cosmos be God, all that is in it is divine, being
parts of the Cosmos. Now, according to this
view, animals, as flies, and gnats, and worms,
and every species of serpent, as well as of birds
and fishes, will be divine,—an assertion which
would not be made even by those who maintain
that the Cosmos is God. But the Jews, who live
according to the law of Moses, although they
may not know how to receive the secret meaning of the law, which is conveyed in obscure
language, will not maintain that either the heaven
or the angels are God.

CHAP. VIII.

As we allege, however, that he has fallen into
confusion in consequence of false notions which
he has imbibed, come and let us point them out
to the best of our ability, and show that although
Celsus considers it to be a Jewish custom to bow
down to the heaven and the angels in it, such a
practice is not at all Jewish, but is in violation
of Judaism, as it also is to do obeisance to sun,
moon, and stars, as well as images. You will
find at least in the book of Jeremiah the words
of God censuring by the mouth of the prophet
the Jewish people for doing obeisance to such
objects, and for sacrificing to the queen of heav-
en, and to all the host of heaven.[1] The writings
of the Christians, moreover, show, in censuring
the sins committed among the Jews, that when
God abandoned that people on account of certain sins, these sins (of idol-worship) also were
committed by them. For it is related in the
Acts of the Apostles regarding the Jews, that
"God turned, and gave them up to worship the
host of heaven; as it is written in the book of
the prophets, O ye house of Israel, have ye
offered to Me slain beasts and sacrifices by the
space of forty years in the wilderness? Yea, ye
took up the tabernacle of Moloch, and the star
of your god Remphan, figures which you made
to worship them."[2] And in the writings of Paul,

who was carefully trained in Jewish customs, and
converted afterwards to Christianity by a miraculous appearance of Jesus, the following words
may be read in the Epistle to the Colossians:
"Let no man beguile you of your reward in a
voluntary humility and worshipping of angels,
intruding into those things which he hath not
seen, vainly puffed up by his fleshly mind; and
not holding the Head, from which all the body
by joint and bands having nourishment ministered, and knit together, increaseth with the
increase of God."[3] But Celsus, having neither
read these verses, nor having learned their contents from any other source, has represented, I
know not how, the Jews as not transgressing
their law in bowing down to the heavens, and to
the angels therein.

CHAP. IX.

And still continuing a little confused, and not
taking care to see what was relevant to the
matter, he expressed his opinion that the Jews
were induced by the incantations employed in
jugglery and sorcery (in consequence of which
certain phantoms appear, in obedience to the
spells employed by the magicians) to bow down
to the angels in heaven, not observing that this
was contrary to their law, which said to them
who practised such observances: "Regard not
them which have familiar spirits,[4] neither seek
after wizards,[5] to be defiled by them: I am the
LORD your God."[6] He ought, therefore, either
not to have at all attributed this practice to the
Jews, seeing he has observed that they keep
their law, and has called them "those who live
according to their law;" or if he did attribute it,
he ought to have shown that the Jews did this
in violation of their code. But again, as they
transgress their law who offer worship to those
who are said to appear to them who are involved
in darkness and blinded by sorcery, and who
dream dreams, owing to obscure phantoms presenting themselves; so also do they transgress the
law who offer sacrifice to sun, moon, and stars.[7]
And there is thus great inconsistency in the same
individual saying that the Jews are careful to
keep their law by not bowing down to sun, and
moon, and stars, while they are not so careful to
keep it in the matter of heaven and the angels.

CHAP. X.

And if it be necessary for us to offer a defence
of our refusal to recognise as gods, equally with
angels, and sun, and moon, and stars, those who
are called by the Greeks "manifest and visible"

[1] Cf. Jer. vii. 17, 18.
[2] Cf. Acts vii. 42, 43.
[3] Cf. Col. ii. 18, 19.
[4] ἐγγαστριμύθοις.
[5] ἐπαοιδοῖς.
[6] Cf. Lev. xix. 31.
[7] The emendations of Ruæus have been adopted in the translation, the text being probably corrupt. Cf. Ruæus, *in loc.*

divinities, we shall answer that the law of Moses knows that these latter have been apportioned by God among all the nations under the heaven, but not amongst those who were selected by God as His chosen people above all the nations of the earth. For it is written in the book of Deuteronomy : "And lest thou lift up thine eyes unto heaven, and when thou seest the sun, and the moon, and the stars, even all the host of heaven, shouldst be driven to worship them, and serve them, which the LORD thy God hath divided unto all nations unto the whole heaven. But the LORD hath taken us, and brought us forth out of the iron furnace, even out of Egypt, to be unto Him a people of inheritance, as ye are this day." [1] The Hebrew people, then, being called by God a "chosen generation, and a royal priesthood, and a holy nation, and a purchased people," [2] regarding whom it was foretold to Abraham by the voice of the Lord addressed to him, "Look now towards heaven, and tell the stars, if thou be able to number them : and He said unto him, So shall thy seed be ; " [3] and having thus a hope that they would become as the stars of heaven, were not likely to bow down to those objects which they were to resemble as a result of their understanding and observing the law of God. For it was said to them : "The LORD our God hath multiplied us ; and, behold, ye are this day as the stars of heaven for multitude." [4] In the book of Daniel, also, the following prophecies are found relating to those who are to share in the resurrection : "And at that time thy people shall be delivered, every one that has been written in the book. And many of them that sleep in the dust [5] of the earth shall awake, some to everlasting life, and some to shame and everlasting contempt. And they that be wise shall shine as the brightness of the firmament, and (those) of the many righteous [6] as the stars for ever and ever," [7] etc. And hence Paul, too, when speaking of the resurrection, says : "And there are also celestial bodies, and bodies terrestrial : but the glory of the celestial is one, and the glory of the terrestrial is another. There is one glory of the sun, and another glory of the moon, and another glory of the stars ; for one star differeth from another star in glory. So also is the resurrection of the dead." [8] It was not therefore consonant to reason that those who had been taught sublimely [9] to ascend above all created things, and to hope for the enjoyment of the most glorious rewards

with God on account of their virtuous lives, and who had heard the words, "Ye are the light of the world," [10] and, "Let your light so shine before men, that they, seeing your good works, may glorify your Father who is in heaven," [11] and who possessed through practice this brilliant and unfading wisdom, or who had secured even the "very reflection of everlasting light," [12] should be so impressed with the (mere) *visible* light of sun, and moon, and stars, that, on account of that sensible light of theirs, they should deem themselves (although possessed of so great a rational light of knowledge, and of the true light, and the light of the world, and the light of men) to be somehow inferior to them, and to bow down to them ; seeing they ought to be worshipped, if they are to receive worship at all, not for the sake of the sensible light which is admired by the multitude, but because of the rational and true light, if indeed the stars in heaven are rational and virtuous beings, and have been illuminated with the light of knowledge by that wisdom which is the "reflection of everlasting light." For that sensible light of theirs is the work of the Creator of all things, while that rational light is derived perhaps from the principle of free-will within them. [13]

CHAP. XI.

But even this rational light itself ought not to be worshipped by him who beholds and understands the true light, by sharing in which these also are enlightened ; nor by him who beholds God, the Father of the true light, — of whom it has been said, "God is light, and in Him there is no darkness at all." [14] Those, indeed, who worship sun, moon, and stars because their light is visible and celestial, would not bow down to a spark of fire or a lamp upon earth, because they see the incomparable superiority of those objects which are deemed worthy of homage to the light of sparks and lamps. So those who understand that God is light, and who have apprehended that the Son of God is "the true light which lighteth every man that cometh into the world," and who comprehend also how He says, "I am the light of the world," would not rationally offer worship to that which is, as it were, a spark in sun, moon, and stars, in comparison with God, who is light of the true light. Nor is it with a view to depreciate these great works of God's creative power, or to call them, after the fashion of Anaxagoras, "fiery masses," [15] that we thus speak of sun, and moon, and stars ; but because we perceive the inexpressible superiority of the

---

[1] Cf. Deut. iv. 19, 20.
[2] Cf. 1 Pet. ii. 9.
[3] Cf. Gen. xv. 5.
[4] Cf. Deut. i. 10.
[5] χώματι.
[6] ἀπὸ τῶν δικαίων τῶν πολλῶν.
[7] Cf. Dan. xii. 1, 2, 3.
[8] Cf. 1 Cor. xv. 40–42.
[9] μεγαλοφυῶς.

[10] Matt. v. 14.
[11] Cf. Matt. v. 16.
[12] Cf. Origen, *de Principiis*, i. c. vii.
[13] ἐκ τοῦ ἐν αὐτοῖς αὐτεξουσίου ἐληλυθός.
[14] Cf. 1 John i. 5.
[15] μύδρον διάπυρον.

divinity of God, and that of His only-begotten Son, which surpasses all other things. And being persuaded that the sun himself, and moon, and stars pray to the Supreme God through His only-begotten Son, we judge it improper to pray to those beings who themselves offer up prayers (to God), seeing even they themselves would prefer that we should send up our requests to the God to whom they pray, rather than send them downwards to themselves, or apportion our power of prayer [1] between God and them.[2] And here I may employ this illustration, as bearing upon this point : Our Lord and Saviour, hearing Himself on one occasion addressed as "Good Master,"[3] referring him who used it to His own Father, said, "Why callest thou Me good? There is none good but one, that is, God the Father."[4] And since it was in accordance with sound reason that this should be said by the Son of His Father's love, as being the image of the goodness of God, why should not the sun say with greater reason to those that bow down to him, Why do you worship me? "for thou wilt worship the LORD thy God, and Him only shalt thou serve ;"[5] for it is He whom I and all who are with me serve and worship. And although one may not be so exalted (as the sun), nevertheless let such an one pray to the Word of God (who is able to heal him), and still more to His Father, who also to the righteous of former times " sent His word, and healed them, and delivered them from their destructions."[6]

CHAP. XII.

God accordingly, in His kindness, condescends to mankind, not in any local sense, but through His providence ;[7] while the Son of God, not only (when on earth), but at *all* times, is with His own disciples, fulfilling the promise, " Lo, I am with you always, even to the end of the world."[8] And if a branch cannot bear fruit except it abide in the vine, it is evident that the disciples also of the Word, who are the rational branches of the Word's true vine, cannot produce the fruits of virtue unless they abide in the true vine, the Christ of God, who is with us locally here below upon the earth, and who is with those who cleave to Him in all parts of the world, and is also in all places with those who do not know Him. Another is made manifest by that John who wrote the Gospel, when, speaking in the person of John the Baptist, he said, " There standeth one among you whom ye know

not ; He it is who cometh after me."[9] And it is absurd, when He who fills heaven and earth, and who said, " Do I not fill heaven and earth? saith the LORD," [10] is with us, and near us (for I believe Him when He says, " I am a God nigh at hand, and not afar off, saith the LORD " [11]), to seek to pray to sun or moon, or one of the stars, whose influence does not reach the whole of the world.[12] But, to use the very words of Celsus, let it be granted that "the sun, moon, and stars *do* foretell rain, and heat, and clouds, and thunders," why, then, if they really do foretell such great things, ought we not rather to do homage to God, whose servant they are in uttering these predictions, and show reverence to *Him* rather than His *prophets ?* Let them predict, then, the approach of lightnings, and fruits, and all manner of productions, and let all such things be under their administration ; yet we shall not on that account worship those who themselves offer worship, as we do not worship even Moses, and those prophets who came from God after him, and who predicted better things than rain, and heat, and clouds, and thunders, and lightnings, and fruits, and all sorts of productions visible to the senses. Nay, even if sun, and moon, and stars were able to prophesy better things than rain, not even then shall we worship *them*, but the *Father* of the prophecies which are in them, and the *Word* of God, their minister. But grant that they are His heralds, and truly messengers of heaven, why, even then ought we not to worship the *God* whom they only proclaim and announce, rather than those who are the *heralds* and *messengers ?*

CHAP. XIII.

Celsus, moreover, assumes that sun, and moon, and stars are regarded by us as of no account. Now, with regard to these, we acknowledge that they too are " waiting for the manifestation of the sons of God," being for the present subjected to the "vanity" of their material bodies, "by reason of Him who has subjected the same in hope." [13] But if Celsus had read the innumerable other passages where we speak of sun, moon, and stars, and especially these, — " Praise Him, all ye stars, and thou, O light," and, " Praise Him, ye heaven of heavens," [14] — he would not have said of us that we regard such mighty beings, which "greatly praise" the Lord God, as of no account. Nor did Celsus know the passage : " For the earnest expectation of the creature waiteth for the manifestation of the sons of God. For the creature was made subject to

---

[1] τὴν εὐκτικὴν δύναμιν.
[2] [See note in Migne's edition of Origen's *Works*, vol. i. p. 1195; also note *supra*, p. 262. S.].
[3] Cf. Matt. xix. 17; cf. Mark x. 18.
[4] Ibid.
[5] Cf. Deut. vi. 13.
[6] Cf. Ps. cvii. 20.
[7] προνοητικῶς.
[8] Matt. xxviii. 20.

[9] Cf. John i. 26, 27.
[10] Cf. Jer. xxiii. 24.
[11] Cf. Jer. xxiii. 23.
[12] ζητεῖν εὔχεσθαι τῷ μὴ φθάνοντι ἐπὶ τὰ σύμπαντα.
[13] Cf. Rom. viii. 19-21.
[14] Cf. Ps. cxlviii. 3, 4.

vanity, not willingly, but by reason of Him who hath subjected the same in hope; because the creature itself also shall be delivered from the bondage of corruption into the glorious liberty of the children of God."[1] · And with these words let us terminate our defence against the charge of not worshipping sun, moon, and stars. And let us now bring forward those statements of his which follow, that we may, God willing, address to him in reply such arguments as shall be suggested by the light of truth.

CHAP. XIV.

The following, then, are his words: "It is folly on their part to suppose that when God, as if He were a cook,[2] introduces the fire (which is to consume the world), all the rest of the human race will be burnt up, while they alone will remain, not only such of them as are then alive, but also those who are long since dead, which latter will arise from the earth clothed with the self-same flesh (as during life); for such a hope is simply one which might be cherished by worms. For what sort of human soul is that which would still long for a body that had been subject to corruption? Whence, also, this opinion of yours is not shared by some of the Christians, and they pronounce it to be exceedingly vile, and loathsome, and impossible; for what kind of body is that which, after being completely corrupted, can return to its original nature, and to that self-same first condition out of which it fell into dissolution? Being unable to return any answer, they betake themselves to a most absurd refuge, viz., that all things are possible to God. And yet God *cannot* do things that are disgraceful, nor does He wish to do things that are contrary to His nature; nor, if (in accordance with the wickedness of your own heart) you desired anything that was evil, would God accomplish it; nor must you believe at once that it will be done. For God does not rule the world in order to satisfy inordinate desires, or to allow disorder and confusion, but to govern a nature that is upright and just.[3] For the *soul*, indeed, He might be able to provide an everlasting life; while dead *bodies*, on the contrary, are, as Heraclitus observes, more worthless than dung. God, however, neither can nor will declare, contrary to all reason, that the flesh, which is full of those things which it is not even honourable to mention, is to exist for ever. For He is the reason of all things that exist, and therefore can do nothing either contrary to reason or contrary to Himself."

CHAP. XV.

Observe, now, here at the very beginning, how, in ridiculing the doctrine of a conflagration of the world, held by certain of the Greeks who have treated the subject in a philosophic spirit not to be depreciated, he would make us, "representing God, as it were, as a cook, hold the belief in a general conflagration;" not perceiving that, as certain Greeks were of opinion (perhaps having received their information from the ancient nation of the Hebrews), it is a purificatory fire which is brought upon the world, and probably also on each one of those who stand in need of chastisement by the fire and healing at the same time, seeing it *burns* indeed, but does not *consume*, those who are without a material body,[4] which needs to be consumed by that fire, and which burns and consumes those who by their actions, words, and thoughts have built up wood, or hay, or stubble, in that which is figuratively termed a "building."[5] And the holy Scriptures say that the Lord will, like a refiner's fire and fullers' soap,[6] visit each one of those who require purification, because of the intermingling in them of a flood of wicked matter proceeding from their evil nature; who need fire, I mean, to refine, as it were, (the dross of) those who are intermingled with copper, and tin, and lead. And he who likes may learn this from the prophet Ezekiel.[7] But that we say that God brings fire upon the world, not like a cook, but like a God, who is the benefactor of them who stand in need of the discipline of fire,[8] will be testified by the prophet Isaiah, in whose writings it is related that a sinful nation was thus addressed: "Because thou hast coals of fire, sit upon them: they shall be to thee a help."[9] Now the Scripture is appropriately adapted to the multitudes of those who are to peruse it, because it speaks obscurely of things that are sad and gloomy,[10] in order to terrify those who cannot by any other means be saved from the flood of their sins, although even then the attentive reader will clearly discover the end that is to be accomplished by these sad and painful punishments upon those who endure them. It is sufficient, however, for the present to quote the words of Isaiah: "For My name's sake will I show Mine anger, and My glory I will bring upon thee, that I may not destroy thee."[11] We have thus been under the necessity of referring in obscure terms to questions not fitted to the capacity of simple believers,[12] who require a

---

[1] Cf. Rom. viii. 19-21.
[2] ὥσπερ μάγειρος.
[3] οὐ γὰρ τῆς πλημμελοῦς ὀρέξεως, οὐδὲ τῆς πεπλανημένης ἀκοσμίας, ἀλλὰ τῆς ὀρθῆς καὶ δικαίας φύσεως Θεός ἐστιν ἀρχηγέτης.

[4] ὕλην.
[5] Cf. 1 Cor. iii. 12.
[6] Cf. Mal. iii. 2.
[7] Cf. Ezek. xxii. 18, 20.
[8] πόνου καὶ πυρός.
[9] Cf. Isa. xlvii. 14, 15.
[10] τὰ σκυθρωπά.
[11] Cf. Isa. xlviii. 9 (Septuagint).
[12] [See Robertson's *History of the Church*, vol. i. p. 156, 157. S.]

simpler instruction in words, that we might not appear to leave unrefuted the accusation of Celsus, that "God introduces the fire (which is to destroy the world), as if He were a cook."

CHAP. XVI.

From what has been said, it will be manifest to intelligent hearers how we have to answer the following: "All the rest of the race will be completely burnt up, and they alone will remain." It is not to be wondered at, indeed, if such thoughts have been entertained by those amongst us who are called in Scripture the "foolish things" of the world, and "base things," and "things which are despised," and "things which are not," because "by the foolishness of preaching it pleased God to save them that believe on Him, after that, in the wisdom of God, the world by wisdom knew not God,"[1] — because such individuals are unable to see distinctly the sense of each particular passage,[2] or unwilling to devote the necessary leisure to the investigation of Scripture, notwithstanding the injunction of Jesus, "Search the Scriptures."[3] The following, moreover, are his ideas regarding the fire which is to be brought upon the world by God, and the punishments which are to befall sinners. And perhaps, as it is appropriate to children that some things should be addressed to them in a manner befitting their infantile condition, to convert them, as being of very tender age, to a better course of life; so, to those whom the word terms "the foolish things of the world," and "the base," and "the despised," the just and obvious meaning of the passages relating to punishments is suitable, inasmuch as they cannot receive any other mode of conversion than that which is by fear and the presentation of punishment, and thus be saved from the many evils (which would befall them).[4] The Scripture accordingly declares that only those who are unscathed by the fire and the punishments are to remain, — those, viz., whose opinions, and morals, and mind have been purified to the highest degree; while, on the other hand, those of a different nature — those, viz., who, according to their deserts, require the administration of punishment by fire — will be involved in these sufferings with a view to an end which it is suitable for God to bring upon those who have been created in His image, but who have lived in opposition to the will of that nature which is according to His image. And this is our answer to the statement, "All the rest of the race will be completely burnt up, but they alone are to remain."

CHAP. XVII.

Then, in the next place, having either himself misunderstood the sacred Scriptures, or those (interpreters) by whom they were not understood, he proceeds to assert that "it is said by us that there will remain at the time of the visitation which is to come upon the world by the fire of purification, not only those who are then alive, but also those who are long ago dead;" not observing that it is with a secret kind of wisdom that it was said by the apostle of Jesus: "We shall not all sleep, but we shall all be changed, in a moment, in the twinkling of an eye, at the last trump; for the trumpet shall sound, and the dead shall be raised incorruptible, and we shall be changed."[5] Now he ought to have noticed what was the meaning of him who uttered these words, as being one who was by no means dead, who made a distinction between himself and those like him and the dead, and who said afterwards, "The dead shall be raised incorruptible," and "we shall be changed." And as a proof that such was the apostle's meaning in writing those words which I have quoted from the first Epistle to the Corinthians, I will quote also from the first to the Thessalonians, in which Paul, as one who is alive and awake, and different from those who are asleep, speaks as follows: "For this we say unto you by the word of the Lord, that we who are alive and remain unto the coming of the Lord, shall not prevent them who are asleep; for the Lord Himself shall descend from heaven with a shout, with the voice of the archangel, and with the trump of God."[6] Then, again, after this, knowing that there were others dead in Christ besides himself and such as he, he subjoins the words, "The dead in Christ shall rise first; then we who are alive and remain shall be caught up together with them in the clouds, to meet the Lord in the air."[7]

CHAP. XVIII.

But since he has ridiculed at great length the doctrine of the resurrection of the flesh, which has been preached in the Churches, and which is more clearly understood by the more intelligent believer; and as it is unnecessary again to quote his words, which have been already adduced, let us, with regard to the problem[8] (as in an apologetic work directed against an alien from the faith, and for the sake of those who are still "children, tossed to and fro, and carried about with every wind of doctrine, by the sleight of men, and cunning craftiness, whereby they lie

---

[1] Cf. 1 Cor. i. 21.
[2] τὰ κατὰ τοὺς τόπους.
[3] Cf. John v. 39.
[4] καὶ τῶν πολλῶν κακῶν ἀποχήν.

[5] Cf. 1 Cor. xv. 51, 52.
[6] Cf. 1 Thess. iv. 15, 16.
[7] Cf. 1 Thess. iv. 16, 17.
[8] περὶ τοῦ προβλήματος τούτου.

in wait to deceive " [1]), state and establish to the best of our ability a few points expressly intended for our readers.   Neither we, then, nor the holy Scriptures, assert that with the same bodies, without a change to a higher condition, " shall those who were long dead arise from the earth and live again ; " for in so speaking, Celsus makes a false charge against us.   For we may listen to many passages of Scripture treating of the resurrection in a manner worthy of God, although it may suffice for the present to quote the language of Paul from the first Epistle to the Corinthians, where he says : " But some man will say, How are the dead raised up? and with what body do they come?   Thou fool, that which thou sowest is not quickened, except it die.   And that which thou sowest, thou sowest not that body that shall be, but bare grain, it may chance of wheat, or of some other grain ; but God giveth it a body as it hath pleased Him, and to every seed his own body." [2]   Now, observe how in these words he says that there is sown, " not that body that shall be ; " but that of the body which is sown and cast naked into the earth (God giving to each seed its own body), there takes place as it were a resurrection : from the seed that was cast into the ground there arising a stalk, e.g., among such plants as the following, viz., the mustard plant, or of a larger tree, as in the olive,[3] or one of the fruit-trees.

CHAP. XIX.

God, then, gives to each thing its own body as He pleases : as in the case of plants that are sown, so also in the case of those beings who are, as it were, sown in dying, and who in due time receive, out of what has been " sown," the body assigned by God to each one according to his deserts.   And we may hear, moreover, the Scripture teaching us at great length the difference between that which is, as it were, " sown," and that which is, as it were, " raised " from it, in these words : " It is sown in corruption, it is raised in incorruption ; it is sown in dishonour, it is raised in glory ; it is sown in weakness, it is raised in power ; it is sown a natural body, it is raised a spiritual body." [4]   And let him who has the capacity understand the meaning of the words : " As is the earthy, such are they also that are earthy ; and as is the heavenly, such are they also that are heavenly.   And as we have borne the image of the earthy, we shall also bear the image of the heavenly." [5]   And although the apostle wished to conceal the secret meaning of the passage, which was not adapted to the simpler class of believers, and to the under-

standing of the common people, who are led by their faith to enter on a better course of life, he was nevertheless obliged afterwards to say (in order that we might not misapprehend his meaning), after " Let us bear the image of the heavenly," these words also : " Now this I say, brethren, that flesh and blood cannot inherit the kingdom of God ; neither doth corruption inherit incorruption." [6]   Then, knowing that there was a secret and mystical meaning in the passage, as was becoming in one who was leaving, in his Epistles, to those who were to come after him words full of significance, he subjoins the following, " Behold, I show you a mystery ; " [7] which is his usual style in introducing matters of a profounder and more mystical nature, and such as are fittingly concealed from the multitude, as is written in the book of Tobit : " It is good to keep close the secret of a king, but honourable to reveal the works of God," [8] — in a way consistent with truth and God's glory, and so as to be to the advantage of the multitude.   Our hope, then, is *not* " the hope of worms, nor does our soul long for a body that has seen corruption ; " for although it may require a body, for the sake of moving from place to place,[9] yet it understands — as having meditated on the wisdom (that is from above), agreeably to the declaration, " The mouth of the righteous will speak wisdom " [10] — the difference between the " earthly house," in which is the tabernacle of the building that is to be dissolved, and that in which the righteous do groan, being burdened, — not wishing to " put off " the tabernacle, but to be " clothed therewith," that by being clothed upon, mortality might be swallowed up of life.   For, in virtue of the whole nature of the body being corruptible, the corruptible tabernacle must put on incorruption ; and its other part, being mortal, and becoming liable to the death which follows sin, must put on immortality, in order that, when the corruptible shall have put on incorruption, and the mortal immortality, then shall come to pass what was predicted of old by the prophets, — the annihilation of the " victory " of death (because it had conquered and subjected us to his sway), and of its " sting," with which it stings the imperfectly defended soul, and inflicts upon it the wounds which result from sin.

CHAP. XX.

But since our views regarding the resurrection have, as far as time would permit, been stated in part on the present occasion (for we have systematically examined the subject in greater

[1] Cf. Eph. iv. 14.
[2] Cf. 1 Cor. xv. 35–38.
[3] ἐν ἐλαίας πυρῆνι.
[4] Cf. 1 Cor. xv. 42–44.
[5] Cf. 1 Cor. xv. 48, 49.

[6] Cf. 1 Cor. xv. 50.
[7] Cf. 1 Cor. xv. 51.
[8] Cf. Tobit xii. 7.
[9] διὰ τὰς τοπικὰς μεταβάσεις.
[10] Cf. Ps. xxxvii. 30.

detail in other parts of our writings) ; and as now we must by means of sound reasoning refute the fallacies of Celsus, who neither understands the meaning of our Scripture, nor has the capacity of judging that the meaning of our wise men is not to be determined by those individuals who make no profession of anything more than of a (simple) faith in the Christian system, let us show that men, not to be lightly esteemed on account of their reasoning powers and dialectic subtleties, have given expression to very absurd[1] opinions. And if we must sneer[2] at them as contemptible old wives' fables, it is at them rather than at our narrative that we must sneer. The disciples of the Porch assert, that after a period of years there will be a conflagration of the world, and after that an arrangement of things in which everything will be unchanged, as compared with the former arrangement of the world. Those of them, however, who evinced their respect for this doctrine have said that there will be a change, although exceedingly slight, at the end of the cycle, from what prevailed during the preceding.[3] And these men maintain, that in the succeeding cycle the same things will occur, and Socrates will be again the son of Sophroniscus, and a native of Athens ; and Phænarete, being married to Sophroniscus, will again become his mother. And although they do not mention the word "resurrection," they show in reality that Socrates, who derived his origin from seed, will spring from that of Sophroniscus, and will be fashioned in the womb of Phænarete ; and being brought up at Athens, will practise the study of philosophy, as if his former philosophy had arisen again, and were to be in no respect different from what it was before. Anytus and Melitus, too, will arise again as accusers of Socrates, and the Council of Areopagus will condemn him to death ! But what is more ridiculous still, is that Socrates will clothe himself with garments not at all different from those which he wore during the former cycle, and will live in the same unchanged state of poverty, and in the same unchanged city of Athens ! And Phalaris will again play the tyrant, and his brazen bull will pour forth its bellowings from the voices of victims within, unchanged from those who were condemned in the former cycle ! And Alexander of Pheræ, too, will again act the tyrant with a cruelty unaltered from the former time, and will condemn to death the same "unchanged" individuals as before. But what need is there to go into detail upon the doctrine held by the Stoic philosophers on such things, and which escapes the ridicule of Celsus, and is perhaps even venerated by him, since he regards Zeno as a wiser man than Jesus?

CHAP. XXI.

The disciples of Pythagoras, too, and of Plato, although they appear to hold the incorruptibility of the world, yet fall into similar errors. For as the planets, after certain definite cycles, assume the same positions, and hold the same relations to one another, all things on earth will, they assert, be like what they were at the time when the same state of planetary relations existed in the world. From this view it necessarily follows, that when, after the lapse of a lengthened cycle, the planets come to occupy towards each other the same relations which they occupied in the time of Socrates, Socrates will again be born of the same parents, and suffer the same treatment, being accused by Anytus and Melitus, and condemned by the Council of Areopagus ! The learned among the Egyptians, moreover, hold similar views, and yet they are treated with respect, and do not incur the ridicule of Celsus and such as he ; while we, who maintain that all things are administered by God in proportion to the relation of the free-will of each individual, and are ever being brought into a better condition, so far as they admit of being so,[4] and who know that the nature of our free-will admits of the occurrence of contingent events[5] (for it is incapable of receiving the wholly unchangeable character of God), yet do not appear to say anything worthy of a testing examination.

CHAP. XXII.

Let no one, however, suspect that, in speaking as we do, we belong to those who are indeed called Christians, but who set aside the doctrine of the resurrection as it is taught in Scripture. For these persons cannot, so far as their principles apply, at all establish that the stalk or tree which springs up comes from the grain of wheat, or anything else (which was cast into the ground) ; whereas we, who believe that that which is "sown" is not "quickened" unless it die, and that there is sown not that body that shall be (for God gives it a body as it pleases Him, raising it in incorruption after it is sown in corruption ; and after it is sown in dishonour, raising it in glory ; and after it is sown in weakness, raising it in power ; and after it is sown a natural body, raising it a spiritual), — we preserve both the doctrine[6] of the Church of Christ and the grandeur of the divine promise, proving also the possibility of its accomplishment not by mere assertion, but by arguments ; knowing that

---

[1] σφόδρ' ἀπεμφαίνοντα.
[2] μυχθίζειν.
[3] [Comp. book iv. capp. lxv.-lxix. pp. 526-528, *supra*.]

[4] κατὰ τὸ ἐνδεχόμενον.
[5] καὶ τὴν τοῦ ἐφ' ἡμῖν φύσιν γιγνώσκοντες ἐνδεχομένου ἃ ἐνδέχεται.
[6] βούλημα.

although heaven and earth, and the things that are in them, may pass away, yet His words regarding each individual thing, being, as parts of a whole, or species of a genus, the utterances of Him who was God the Word, who was in the beginning with God, shall by no means pass away. For we desire to listen to Him who said : "Heaven and earth shall pass away, but My words shall not pass away." [1]

CHAP. XXIII.

We, therefore, do not maintain that the body which has undergone corruption resumes its original nature, any more than the grain of wheat which has decayed returns to its former condition. But we do maintain, that as above the grain of wheat there arises a stalk, so a certain power [2] is implanted in the body, which is not destroyed, and from which the body is raised up in incorruption. The philosophers of the Porch, however, in consequence of the opinions which they hold regarding the unchangeableness of things after a certain cycle, assert that the body, after undergoing complete corruption, will return to its original condition, and will again assume that first nature from which it passed into a state of dissolution, establishing these points, as they think, by irresistible arguments. [3] We, however, do not betake ourselves to a most absurd refuge, saying that with God *all* things are possible ; for we know how to understand this word " all " as not referring either to things that are " non-existent " or that are inconceivable. But we maintain, at the same time, that God cannot do what is disgraceful, since then He would be capable of ceasing to be God ; for if He do anything that is disgraceful, He is not God. Since, however, he lays it down as a principle, that "God does not desire what is contrary to nature," we have to make a distinction, and say that if any one asserts that wickedness is contrary to nature, while we maintain that " God does not desire what is contrary to nature," — either what springs from wickedness or from an irrational principle, — yet, if such things happen according to the word and will of God, we must at once necessarily hold that they are not contrary to nature. Therefore things which are done by God, although they may be, or may *appear* to some to be incredible, are not contrary to nature. And if we must press the force of words, [4] we would say that, in comparison with what is generally understood as " nature," there *are* certain things which are *beyond* its power, which God could at any time do ; as, e.g., in raising man above the level of human nature, and

causing him to pass into a better and more divine condition, and preserving him in the same, so long as he who is the object of His care shows by his actions that he desires (the continuance of His help).

CHAP. XXIV.

Moreover, as we have already said that for God to desire anything unbecoming Himself would be destructive of His existence as Deity, we will add that if man, agreeably to the wickedness of his nature, should desire anything that is abominable, [5] God cannot grant it. And now it is from no spirit of contention that we answer the assertions of Celsus ; but it is in the spirit of truth that we investigate them, as assenting to his view that " He is the God, not of inordinate desires, nor of error and disorder, but of a nature just and upright," because He is the source of all that is good. And that He is able to provide an eternal life for the soul we acknowledge ; and that He possesses not only the " power," but the " will." In view, therefore, of these considerations, we are not at all distressed by the assertion of Heraclitus, adopted by Celsus, that " dead bodies are to be cast out as more worthless than dung ; " and yet, with reference even to this, one might say that dung, indeed, ought to be cast out, while the dead bodies of men, on account of the soul by which they were inhabited, especially if it had been virtuous, ought not to be cast out. For, in harmony with those laws which are based upon the principles of equity, bodies are deemed worthy of sepulture, with the honours accorded on such occasions, that no insult, so far as can be helped, may be offered to the soul which dwelt within, by casting forth the body (after the soul has departed) like that of the animals. Let it not then be held, contrary to reason, that it is the will of God to declare that the grain of wheat is not immortal, but the stalk which springs from it, while the body which is sown in corruption is not, but that which is raised by Him in incorruption. But according to Celsus, God Himself is the reason of all things, while according to our view it is His Son, of whom we say in philosophic language, " In the beginning was the Word, and the Word was with God, and the Word was God ; " [6] while in our judgment also, God cannot do anything which is contrary to reason, or contrary to Himself. [7]

CHAP. XXV.

Let us next notice the statements of Celsus, which follow the preceding, and which are as follow : " As the Jews, then, became a peculiar

---

[1] Cf. Matt. xxiv. 35; cf. Mark xiii. 31.
[2] λόγος.
[3] διαλεκτικαῖς ἀνάγκαις.
[4] εἰ δὲ χρὴ βεβιασμένως ὀνομάσαι.

[5] βδελυρόν.
[6] Cf. John i. 1.
[7] [See note *infra*, bk. vi. cap. xlvii. S.]

people, and enacted laws in keeping with the customs of their country,[1] and maintain them up to the present time, and observe a mode of worship which, whatever be its nature, is yet derived from their fathers, they act in these respects like other men, because each nation retains its ancestral customs, whatever they are, if they happen to be established among them. And such an arrangement appears to be advantageous, not only because it has occurred to the mind of other nations to decide some things differently, but also because it is a duty to protect what has been established for the public advantage ; and also because, in all probability, the various quarters of the earth were from the beginning allotted to different superintending spirits,[2] and were thus distributed among certain governing powers,[3] and in this manner the administration of the world is carried on. And whatever is done among each nation in this way would be rightly done, wherever it was agreeable to the wishes (of the superintending powers), while it would be an act of impiety to get rid of[4] the institutions established from the beginning in the various places." By these words Celsus shows that the Jews, who were formerly Egyptians, subsequently became a " peculiar people," and enacted laws which they carefully preserve. And not to repeat his statements, which have been already before us, he says that it is advantageous to the Jews to observe their ancestral worship, as other nations carefully attend to theirs. And he further states a deeper reason why it is of advantage to the Jews to cultivate their ancestral customs, in hinting dimly that those to whom was allotted the office of superintending the country which was being legislated for, enacted the laws of each land in co-operation with its legislators. He appears, then, to indicate that both the country of the Jews, and the nation which inhabits it, are superintended by one or more beings, who, whether they were one or more, co-operated with Moses, and enacted the laws of the Jews.

CHAP. XXVI.

"We must," he says, " observe the laws, not only because it has occurred to the mind of others to decide some things differently, but because it is a duty to protect what has been enacted for the public advantage, and also because, in all probability, the various quarters of the earth were from the beginning allotted to different superintending spirits, and were distributed among certain governing powers, and in this manner the administration of the world is

carried on." Thus Celsus, as if he had forgotten what he had said against the Jews, now includes them in the general eulogy which he passes upon all who observe their ancestral customs, remarking : "And whatever is done among each nation in this way, would be rightly done whenever agreeable to the wishes (of the superintendents)." And observe here, whether he does not openly, so far as he can, express a wish that the Jew should live in the observance of his own laws, and not depart from them, because he would commit an act of impiety if he apostatized ; for his words are : " It would be an act of impiety to get rid of the institutions established from the beginning in the various places." Now I should like to ask him, and those who entertain his views, who it was that distributed the various quarters of the earth from the beginning among the different superintending spirits ; and especially, who gave the country of the Jews, and the Jewish people themselves, to the one or more superintendents to whom it was allotted ? Was it, as Celsus would say, Jupiter who assigned the Jewish people and their country to a certain spirit or spirits ? And was it *his* wish, to whom they were thus assigned, to enact among them the laws which prevail, or was it *against* his will that it was done ? You will observe that, whatever be his answer, he is in a strait. But if the various quarters of the earth were *not* allotted by some one being to the various superintending spirits, then each one at random, and without the superintendence of a higher power, divided the earth according to chance ; and yet such a view is absurd, and destructive in no small degree of the providence of the God who presides over all things.

CHAP. XXVII.

Any one, indeed, who chooses, may relate how the various quarters of the earth, being distributed among certain governing powers, are administered by those who superintend them ; but let him tell us also how what is done among each nation is done rightly when agreeable to the wishes of the superintendents. Let him, for example, tell us whether the laws of the Scythians, which permit the murder of parents, are right laws ; or those of the Persians, which do not forbid the marriages of sons with their mothers, or of daughters with their own fathers. But what need is there for me to make selections from those who have been engaged in the business of enacting laws among the different nations, and to inquire how the laws are rightly enacted among each, according as they please the superintending powers ? Let Celsus, however, tell us how it would be an act of impiety to get rid of those ancestral laws which permit the marriages of mothers and daughters ; or

---

[1] καὶ κατὰ τὸ ἐπιχώριον νόμους θέμενοι.
[2] τὰ μέρη τῆς γῆς ἐξ ἀρχῆς ἄλλα ἄλλοις ἐπόπταις νενεμημένα.
[3] καὶ κατά τινας ἐπικρατείας διειλημμένα.
[4] παραλύειν.

which pronounce a man happy who puts an end to his life by hanging, or declare that they undergo entire purification who deliver themselves over to the fire, and who terminate their existence by fire ; and how it is an act of impiety to do away with those laws which, for example, prevail in the Tauric Chersonese, regarding the offering up of strangers in sacrifice to Diana, or among certain of the Libyan tribes regarding the sacrifice of children to Saturn. Moreover, this inference follows from the dictum of Celsus, that it is an act of impiety on the part of the Jews to do away with those ancestral laws which forbid the worship of any other deity than the Creator of all things. And it will follow, according to his view, that piety is not divine by its own nature, but by a certain (external) arrangement and appointment. For it is an act of piety among certain tribes to worship a crocodile, and to eat what is an object of adoration among other tribes ; while, again, with others it is a pious act to worship a calf, and among others, again, to regard the goat as a god. And, in this way, the same individual will be regarded as acting piously according to one set of laws, and impiously according to another ; and this is the most absurd result that can be conceived !

CHAP. XXVIII.

It is probable, however, that to such remarks as the above, the answer returned would be, that he was pious who kept the laws of his *own* country, and not at all chargeable with impiety for the non-observance of those of *other* lands ; and that, again, he who was deemed guilty of impiety among certain nations was not really so, when he worshipped his own gods, agreeably to his country's laws, although he made war against, and even feasted on,[1] those who were regarded as divinities among those nations which possessed laws of an opposite kind. Now, observe here whether these statements do not exhibit the greatest confusion of mind regarding the nature of what is just, and holy, and religious ; since there is no accurate definition laid down of these things, nor are they described as having a peculiar character of their own, and stamping as religious those who act according to their injunctions. If, then, religion, and piety, and righteousness belong to those things which are so only by comparison, so that the same act may be both pious and impious, according to different relations and different laws, see whether it will not follow that temperance[2] also is a thing of comparison, and courage as well, and prudence, and the other virtues, than which nothing could be more absurd ! What we have said, however, is sufficient

for the more general and simple class of answers to the allegations of Celsus. But as we think it likely that some of those who are accustomed to deeper investigation will fall in with this treatise, let us venture to lay down some considerations of a profounder kind, conveying a mystical and secret view respecting the original distribution of the various quarters of the earth among different superintending spirits ; and let us prove to the best of our ability, that our doctrine is free from the absurd consequences enumerated above.

CHAP. XXIX.

It appears to me, indeed, that Celsus has misunderstood some of the deeper reasons relating to the arrangement of terrestrial affairs, some of which are touched upon[3] even in Grecian history, when certain of those who are considered to be gods are introduced as having contended with each other about the possession of Attica ; while in the writings of the Greek poets also, some who are called gods are represented as acknowledging that certain places here are preferred by them[4] before others. The history of barbarian nations, moreover, and especially that of Egypt, contains some such allusions to the division of the so-called Egyptian nomes, when it states that Athena, who obtained Saïs by lot, is the same who also has possession of Attica. And the learned among the Egyptians can enumerate innumerable instances of this kind, although I do not know whether they include the Jews and their country in this division. And now, so far as testimonies outside the word of God bearing on this point are concerned, enough have been adduced for the present. We say, moreover, that our prophet of God and His genuine servant Moses, in his song in the book of Deuteronomy, makes a statement regarding the portioning out of the earth in the following terms : "When the Most High divided the nations, when He dispersed the sons of Adam, He set the bounds of the people according to the number of the angels of God ; and the LORD's portion was His people Jacob, and Israel the cord of His inheritance."[5] And regarding the distribution of the nations, the same Moses, in his work entitled Genesis, thus expresses himself in the style of a historical narrative : "And the whole earth was of one language and of one speech ; and it came to pass, as they journeyed from the east, that they found a plain in the land of Shinar, and they dwelt there."[6] A little further on he continues : "And the LORD came down to see the city and the tower, which the children of men had built. And the LORD said,

---

[1] καταθοινᾶται.
[2] σωφροσύνη.

[3] ἐφάπτεται.
[4] οἰκειοτέρους.
[5] Cf. Deut. xxxii. 8, 9 (LXX.).
[6] Cf. Gen. xi. 1, 2.

Behold, the people is one, and they have all one language ; and this they have begun to do : and now nothing will be restrained from them which they have imagined to do. Go to, let Us go down, and there confound their language, that they may not understand one another's speech. And the LORD scattered them abroad from thence upon the face of all the earth : and they left off to build the city and the tower. Therefore is the name of it called Confusion ;[1] because the LORD did there confound the language of all the earth : and from thence did the LORD scatter them abroad upon the face of all the earth."[2] In the treatise of Solomon, moreover, on "Wisdom," and on the events at the time of the confusion of languages, when the division of the earth took place, we find the following regarding Wisdom : "Moreover, the nations in their wicked conspiracy being confounded, she found out the righteous, and preserved him blameless unto God, and kept him strong in his tender compassion towards his son."[3] But on these subjects much, and that of a mystical kind, might be said ; in keeping with which is the following : "It is good to keep close the secret of a king,"[4] — in order that the doctrine of the entrance of souls into bodies (not, however, that of the transmigration from one body into another) may not be thrown before the common understanding, nor what is holy given to the dogs, nor pearls be cast before swine. For such a procedure would be impious, being equivalent to a betrayal of the mysterious declarations of God's wisdom, of which it has been well said : "Into a malicious soul wisdom shall not enter, nor dwell in a body subject to sin."[5] It is sufficient, however, to represent in the style of a historic narrative what is intended to convey a secret meaning in the garb of history, that those who have the capacity may work out for themselves all that relates to the subject. (The narrative, then, may be understood as follows.)

CHAP. XXX.

All the people upon the earth are to be regarded as having used one divine language, and so long as they lived harmoniously together were preserved in the use of this divine language, and they remained without moving from the east so long as they were imbued with the sentiments of the "light," and of the "reflection" of the eternal light.[6] But when they departed from the east, and began to entertain sentiments alien to those of the east,[7] they found a place in the land of Shinar (which, when interpreted, means "gnashing of teeth," by way of indicating symbolically that they had lost the means of their support), and in it they took up their abode. Then, desiring to gather together material things,[8] and to join to heaven what had no natural affinity for it, that by means of material things they might conspire against such as were immaterial, they said, "Come, let us made bricks, and burn them with fire." Accordingly, when they had hardened and compacted these materials of clay and matter, and had shown their desire to make brick into stone, and clay into bitumen, and by these means to build a city and a tower, the head of which was, at least in their conception, to reach up to the heavens, after the manner of the "high things which exalt themselves against the knowledge of God," each one was handed over (in proportion to the greater or less departure from the east which had taken place among them, and in proportion to the extent in which bricks had been converted into stones, and clay into bitumen, and building carried on out of these materials) to angels of character more or less severe, and of a nature more or less stern, until they had paid the penalty of their daring deeds ; and they were conducted by those angels, who imprinted on each his native language, to the different parts of the earth according to their deserts : some, for example, to a region of burning heat, others to a country which chastises its inhabitants by its cold ; others, again, to a land exceedingly difficult of cultivation, others to one less so in degree ; while a fifth were brought into a land filled with wild beasts, and a sixth to a country comparatively free of these.

CHAP. XXXI.

Now, in the next place, if any one has the capacity, let him understand that in what assumes the form of history, and which contains some things that are literally true, while yet it conveys a deeper meaning, those who preserved their original language continued, by reason of their not having migrated from the east, in possession of the east, and of their eastern language. And let him notice, that these alone became the portion of the Lord, and His people who were called Jacob, and Israel the cord of His inheritance ; and these alone were governed by a ruler who did not receive those who were placed under him for the purpose of punishment, as was the case with the others. Let him also, who has the capacity to perceive as far as mortals may, observe that in the body politic[9] of those who were assigned to the Lord as His pre-eminent portion, sins were committed, first of all, such as

---

[1] σύγχυσις.
[2] Cf. Gen. xi. 5-9.
[3] Cf. Wisd. of Sol. x. 5.
[4] Cf. Tobit xii. 7.
[5] Cf. Wisd. of Sol. i. 4.
[6] ἐς ὅσον εἰσὶ τὰ τοῦ φωτὸς καὶ τοῦ ἀπὸ φωτὸς αἰδίου ἀπαυγάσματος φρονοῦντες.
[7] ἀλλότρια ἀνατολῶν φρονοῦντες.

[8] τὰ τῆς ὕλης.
[9] πολιτείᾳ.

might be forgiven, and of such a nature as not to make the sinner worthy of entire desertion, while subsequently they became more numerous, though still of a nature to be pardoned. And while remarking that this state of matters continued for a considerable time, and that a remedy was always applied, and that after certain intervals these persons returned to their duty, let him notice that they were given over, in proportion to their transgressions, to those to whom had been assigned the other quarters of the earth; and that, after being at first slightly punished, and having made atonement,[1] they returned, as if they had undergone discipline,[2] to their proper habitations. Let him notice also that afterwards they were delivered over to rulers of a severer character — to Assyrians and Babylonians, as the Scriptures would call them. In the next place, notwithstanding that means of healing were being applied, let him observe that they were still multiplying their transgressions, and that they were on that account dispersed into other regions by the rulers of the nations that oppressed them. And their own ruler intentionally overlooked their oppression at the hands of the rulers of the other nations, in order that he also with good reason, as avenging himself, having obtained power to tear away from the other nations as many as he can, may do so, and enact for them laws, and point out a manner of life agreeably to which they ought to live, that so he may conduct them to the end to which those of the former people were conducted who did not commit sin.

CHAP. XXXII.

And by this means let those who have the capacity of comprehending truths so profound, learn that he to whom were allotted those who had not formerly sinned is far more powerful than the others, since he has been able to make a selection of individuals from the portion of the whole,[3] and to separate them from those who received them for the purpose of punishment, and to bring them under the influence of laws, and of a mode of life which helps to produce an oblivion of their former transgressions. But, as we have previously observed, these remarks are to be understood as being made by us with a concealed meaning, by way of pointing out the mistakes of those who asserted that "the various quarters of the earth were from the beginning distributed among different superintending spirits, and being allotted among certain governing powers, were administered in this way;" from which statement Celsus took occasion to make the remarks referred to. But since those who wandered away from the east were delivered over, on account of their sins, to "a reprobate mind," and to "vile affections," and to "uncleanness through the lusts of their own hearts,"[4] in order that, being sated with sin, they might hate it, we shall refuse our assent to the assertion of Celsus, that "because of the superintending spirits distributed among the different parts of the earth, what is done among each nation is rightly done;" for our desire is to do what is *not* agreeable to these spirits.[5] For we see that it is a religious act to do away with the customs originally established in the various places by means of laws of a better and more divine character, which were enacted by Jesus, as one possessed of the greatest power, who has rescued us "from the present evil world," and "from the princes of the world that come to nought;" and that it is a mark of irreligion not to throw ourselves at the feet of Him who has manifested Himself to be holier and more powerful than all other rulers, and to whom God said, as the prophets many generations before predicted: "Ask of Me, and I shall give Thee the heathen for Thine inheritance, and the uttermost parts of the earth for Thy possession."[6] For He, too, has become the "expectation" of us who from among the heathen have believed upon Him, and upon His Father, who is God over all things.

CHAP. XXXIII.

The remarks which we have made not only answer the statements of Celsus regarding the superintending spirits, but anticipate in some measure what he afterwards brings forward, when he says: "Let the second party come forward; and I shall ask them whence they come, and whom they regard as the originator of their ancestral customs. They will reply, No one, because they spring from the same source as the Jews themselves, and derive their instruction and superintendence[7] from no other quarter, and notwithstanding they have revolted from the Jews." Each one of us, then, is come "in the last days," when one Jesus has visited us, to the "visible mountain of the Lord," the Word that is above every word, and to the "house of God," which is "the Church of the living God, the pillar and ground of the truth."[8] And we notice how it is built upon "the tops of the mountains," i.e., the predictions of all the prophets, which are its foundations. And this house is exalted above the hills, i.e., those individuals among men who make a profession of superior attainments in wisdom and truth; and all the nations come to it, and the "many nations" go

---

[1] καὶ τίσαντας δίκην.
[2] ὡσπερεὶ παιδευθέντας.
[3] ἀπὸ τῆς πάντων μερίδος.

[4] Cf. Rom. i. 24, 26, 28.
[5] ἀλλὰ καὶ βουλόμεθα, οὐχ ὅπη ᾗ ἐκείνοις φίλον, ποιεῖν τὰ ἐκείνων.
[6] Ps. ii. 8.
[7] χοροστάτην.
[8] Cf. 1 Tim. iii. 15.

forth, and say to one another, turning to the religion which in the last days has shone forth through Jesus Christ: "Come ye, and let us go up to the mountain of the LORD, to the house of the God of Jacob; and He will teach us of His ways, and we will walk in them."[1] For the law came forth from the dwellers in Sion, and settled among us as a spiritual law. Moreover, the word of the Lord came forth from that very Jerusalem, that it might be disseminated through all places, and might judge in the midst of the heathen, selecting those whom it sees to be submissive, and rejecting[2] the disobedient, who are many in number. And to those who inquire of us whence we come, or who is our founder,[3] we reply that we are come, agreeably to the counsels of Jesus, to "cut down our hostile and insolent 'wordy'[4] swords into ploughshares, and to convert into pruning-hooks the spears formerly employed in war."[5] For we no longer take up "sword against nation," nor do we "learn war any more," having become children of peace, for the sake of Jesus, who is our leader, instead of those whom our fathers followed, among whom we were "strangers to the covenant," and having received a law, for which we give thanks to Him that rescued us from the error (of our ways), saying, "Our fathers honoured lying idols, and there is not among them one that causeth it to rain."[6] Our Superintendent, then, and Teacher, having come forth from the Jews, regulates the whole world by the word of His teaching. And having made these remarks by way of anticipation, we have refuted as well as we could the untrue statements of Celsus, by subjoining the appropriate answer.

CHAP. XXXIV.

But, that we may not pass without notice what Celsus has said between these and the preceding paragraphs, let us quote his words: "We might adduce Herodotus as a witness on this point, for he expresses himself as follows: 'For the people of the cities Marea and Apis, who inhabit those parts of Egypt that are adjacent to Libya, and who look upon themselves as Libyans, and not as Egyptians, finding their sacrificial worship oppressive, and wishing not to be excluded from the use of cows' flesh, sent to the oracle of Jupiter Ammon, saying that there was no relationship between them and the Egyptians, that they dwelt outside the Delta, that there was no community of sentiment between them and the Egyptians, and that they wished to be allowed to partake of all kinds of food. But the god would not allow them to do as they desired, saying that that country was a part of Egypt, which was watered by the inundation of the Nile, and that those were Egyptians who dwell to the south of the city of Elephantine, and drink of the river Nile.'[7] Such is the narrative of Herodotus. But," continues Celsus, "Ammon in divine things would not make a worse ambassador than the angels of the Jews,[8] so that there is nothing wrong in each nation observing its established method of worship. Of a truth, we shall find very great differences prevailing among the nations, and yet each seems to deem its own by far the best. Those inhabitants of Ethiopia who dwell in Meroe worship Jupiter and Bacchus alone; the Arabians, Urania and Bacchus only; all the Egyptians, Osiris and Isis; the Saïtes, Minerva; while the Naucratites have recently classed Serapis among their deities, and the rest according to their respective laws. And some abstain from the flesh of sheep, and others from that of crocodiles; others, again, from that of cows, while they regard swine's flesh with loathing. The Scythians, indeed, regard it as a noble act to banquet upon human beings. Among the Indians, too, there are some who deem themselves discharging a holy duty in eating their fathers, and this is mentioned in a certain passage by Herodotus. For the sake of credibility, I shall again quote his very words, for he writes as follows: 'For if any one were to make this proposal to all men, viz., to bid him select out of all existing laws the best, each would choose, after examination, those of his own country. Men each consider their own laws much the best, and therefore it is not likely than any other than a madman would make these things a subject of ridicule. But that such are the conclusions of all men regarding the laws, may be determined by many other evidences, and especially by the following illustration. Darius, during his reign, having summoned before him those Greeks who happened to be present at the time, inquired of them for how much they would be willing to eat their deceased fathers? their answer was, that for no consideration would they do such a thing. After this, Darius summoned those Indians who are called Callatians, who are in the habit of eating their parents, and asked of them in the presence of these Greeks, who learned what passed through an interpreter, for what amount of money they would undertake to burn their deceased fathers with fire? on which they raised a loud shout, and bade the king say no more.'[9] Such is the

---

[1] Cf. Isa. ii. 3.
[2] ἐλέγχῃ.
[3] ἀρχηγέτην.
[4] συγκόψαι τὰς πολεμικὰς ἡμῶν λογικὰς μαχαίρας καὶ ὑβριστικὰς εἰς ἄροτρα, καὶ τὰς κατὰ τὸ πρότερον ἡμῶν μάχιμον ξιβύνας εἰς δρέπανα μετασκευάζομεν.
[5] Cf. Isa. ii. 4.
[6] Cf. Jer. xvi. 19 and xiv. 22: ὡς ψευδῆ ἐκτήσαντο οἱ πατέρες ἡμῶν εἴδωλα, καὶ οὐκ ἔστιν ἐν αὐτοῖς ὑετίζων.

[7] Cf. Herodot., ii. 18.
[8] ὁ δὲ Ἄμμων οὐδέν τι κακίων διαπρεσβεῦσαι τὰ δαιμόνια, ἢ οἱ Ἰουδαίων ἄγγελοι.
[9] εὐφημεῖν μιν ἐκέλευον.

way, then, in which these matters are regarded. And Pindar appears to me to be right in saying that 'law' is the king of all things." [1]

CHAP. XXXV.

The argument of Celsus appears to point by these illustrations to this conclusion : that it is ' an obligation incumbent on all men to live according to their country's customs, in which case they will escape censure ; whereas the Christians, who have abandoned their native usages, and who are not one nation like the Jews, are to be blamed for giving their adherence to the teaching of Jesus." Let him then tell us whether it is a becoming thing for philosophers, and those who have been taught not to yield to superstition, to abandon their country's customs, so as to eat of those articles of food which are prohibited in their respective cities? or whether this proceeding of theirs is opposed to what is becoming? For if, on account of their philosophy, and the instructions which they have received against superstition, they should eat, in disregard of their native laws, what was interdicted by their fathers, why should the Christians (since the Gospel requires *them* not to busy themselves about statues and images, or even about any of the created works of God, but to ascend on high, and present the soul to the Creator), when acting in a similar manner to the philosophers, be censured for so doing? But if, for the sake of defending the thesis which he has proposed to himself, Celsus, or those who think with him, should say, that even one who had studied philosophy would keep his country's laws, then philosophers in Egypt, for example, would act most ridiculously in avoiding the eating of onions, in order to observe their country's laws, or certain parts of the body, as the head and shoulders, in order not to transgress the traditions of their fathers. And I do not speak of those Egyptians who shudder with fear at the discharge of wind from the body, because if any one of these were to become a philosopher, and still observe the laws of his country, he would be a ridiculous philosopher, acting very unphilosophically. [2] In the same way, then, he who has been led by the Gospel to worship the God of all things, and, from regard to his country's laws, lingers here below among images and statues of men, and does not desire to ascend to the Creator, will resemble those who have indeed learned philosophy, but who are afraid of things which ought to inspire no terrors, and who regard it as an act of impiety to eat of those things which have been enumerated.

CHAP. XXXVI.

But what sort of being is this Ammon of Herodotus, whose words Celsus has quoted, as if by way of demonstrating how each one ought to keep his country's laws? For this Ammon would not allow the people of the cities of Marea and Apis, who inhabit the districts adjacent to Libya, to treat as a matter of indifference the use of cows' flesh, which is a thing not only indifferent in its own nature, but which does not prevent a man from being noble and virtuous. If Ammon, then, forbade the use of cows' flesh, because of the advantage which results from the use of the animal in the cultivation of the ground, and in addition to this, because it is by the female that the breed is increased, the account would possess more plausibility. But now he simply requires that those who drink of the Nile should observe the laws of the Egyptians regarding kine. And hereupon Celsus, taking occasion to pass a jest upon the employment of the angels among the Jews as the ambassadors of God, says that " Ammon did not make a worse ambassador of divine things than did the angels of the Jews," into the meaning of whose words and manifestations he instituted no investigation ; otherwise he would have seen, that it is not for oxen that God is concerned, even where He may appear to legislate for them, or for irrational animals, but that what is written for the sake of men, under the appearance of relating to irrational animals, contains certain truths of nature. [3] Celsus, moreover, says that no wrong is committed by any one who wishes to observe the religious worship sanctioned by the laws of his country ; and it follows, according to his view, that the Scythians commit no wrong, when, in conformity with their country's laws, they eat human beings. And those Indians who eat their own fathers are considered, according to Celsus, to do a religious, or at least not a wicked act. He adduces, indeed, a statement of Herodotus which favours the principle that each one ought, from a sense of what is becoming, to obey his country's laws ; and he appears to approve of the custom of those Indians called Callatians, who in the time of Darius devoured their parents, since, on Darius inquiring for how great a sum of money they would be willing to lay aside this usage, they raised a loud shout, and bade the king say no more.

CHAP. XXXVII.

As there are, then, generally two laws presented to us, the one being the law of nature, of which God would be the legislator, and the

---

[1] Cf. Herodot., iii. 38.
[2] γέλοιος ἂν εἴη φιλόσοφος ἀφιλόσοφα πράττων.

[3] φυσιολογίαν.

other being the written law of cities, it is a proper thing, when the written law is not opposed to that of God, for the citizens not to abandon it under pretext of foreign customs; but when the law of nature, that is, the law of God, commands what is opposed to the written law, observe whether reason will not tell us to bid a long farewell to the written code, and to the desire of its legislators, and to give ourselves up to the legislator God, and to choose a life agreeable to His word, although in doing so it may be necessary to encounter dangers, and countless labours, and even death and dishonour. For when there are some laws in harmony with the will of God, which are opposed to others which are in force in cities, and when it is impracticable to please God (and those who administer laws of the kind referred to), it would be absurd to contemn those acts by means of which we may please the Creator of all things, and to select those by which we shall become displeasing to God, though we may satisfy unholy laws, and those who love them. But since it is reasonable in other matters to prefer the law of nature, which is the law of God, before the written law, which has been enacted by men in a spirit of opposition to the law of God, why should we not do this still more in the case of those laws which relate to God? Neither shall we, like the Ethiopians who inhabit the parts about Meroe, worship, as is their pleasure, Jupiter and Bacchus only; nor shall we at all reverence Ethiopian gods in the Ethiopian manner; nor, like the Arabians, shall we regard Urania and Bacchus alone as divinities; nor in any degree at all deities in which the difference of sex has been a ground of distinction (as among the Arabians, who worship Urania as a female, and Bacchus as a male deity); nor shall we, like all the Egyptians, regard Osiris and Isis as gods; nor shall we enumerate Athena among these, as the Saites are pleased to do. And if to the ancient inhabitants of Naucratis it seemed good to worship other divinities, while their modern descendants have begun quite recently to pay reverence to Serapis, who never was a god at all, we shall not on that account assert that a new being who was not formerly a god, nor at all known to men, is a deity. For the Son of God, "the First-born of all creation," although He seemed recently to have become incarnate, is not by any means on that account recent. For the holy Scriptures know Him to be the most ancient of all the works of creation;[1] for it was to Him that God said regarding the creation of man, "Let Us make man in Our image, after Our likeness."[2]

CHAP. XXXVIII.

I wish, however, to show how Celsus asserts without any good reason, that each one reveres his domestic and native institutions. For he declares that "those Ethiopians who inhabit Meroe know only of two gods, Jupiter and Bacchus, and worship these alone; and that the Arabians also know only of two, viz., Bacchus, who is also an Ethiopian deity, and Urania, whose worship is confined to them." According to his account, neither do the Ethiopians worship Urania, nor the Arabians Jupiter. If, then, an Ethiopian were from any accident to fall into the hands of the Arabians, and were to be judged guilty of impiety because he did not worship Urania, and for this reason should incur the danger of death, would it be proper for the Ethiopian to die, or to act contrary to his country's laws, and do obeisance to Urania? Now, if it would be proper for him to act contrary to the laws of his country, he will do what is not right, so far as the language of Celsus is any standard; while, if he should be led away to death, let him show the reasonableness of selecting such a fate. I know not whether, if the Ethiopian doctrine taught men to philosophize on the immortality of the soul, and the honour which is paid to religion, they would reverence those as deities who are deemed to be such by the laws of the country.[3] A similar illustration may be employed in the case of the Arabians, if from any accident they happened to visit the Ethiopians about Meroe. For, having been taught to worship Urania and Bacchus alone, they will not worship Jupiter along with the Ethiopians; and if, adjudged guilty of impiety, they should be led away to death, let Celsus tell us what it would be reasonable on their part to do. And with regard to the fables which relate to Osiris and Isis, it is superfluous and out of place at present to enumerate them. For although an allegorical meaning may be given to the fables, they will nevertheless teach us to offer divine worship to cold water, and to the earth, which is subject to men, and all the animal creation. For in this way, I presume, they refer Osiris to water, and Isis to earth; while with regard to Serapis the accounts are numerous and conflicting, to the effect that very recently he appeared in public, agreeably to certain juggling tricks performed at the desire of Ptolemy, who wished to show to the people of Alexandria as it were a visible god. And we have read in the writings of Numenius the Pythagorean regarding his formation, that he partakes of the essence of all the animals and plants that are under the control of nature, that he may appear

---

[1] πρεσβύτατον πάντων τῶν δημιουργημάτων.
[2] Cf. Gen. i. 26.

[3] This sentence is regarded by Guietus as an interpolation, which should be struck out of the text.

to have been fashioned into a god, not by the makers of images alone, with the aid of profane mysteries, and juggling tricks employed to invoke demons, but also by magicians and sorcerers, and those demons who are bewitched by their incantations.[1]

CHAP. XXXIX.

We must therefore inquire what may be fittingly eaten or not by the rational and gentle[2] animal, which acts always in conformity with reason; and not worship at random, sheep, or goats, or kine; to abstain from which is an act of moderation,[3] for much advantage is derived by men from these animals. Whereas, is it not the most foolish of all things to spare crocodiles, and to treat *them* as sacred to some fabulous divinity or other? For it is a mark of exceeding stupidity to spare those animals which do not spare us, and to bestow care on those which make a prey of human beings. But Celsus approves of those who, in keeping with the laws of their country, worship and tend crocodiles, and not a word does he say against them, while the Christians appear deserving of censure, who have been taught to loath evil, and to turn away from wicked works, and to reverence and honour virtue as being generated by God, and as being His Son. For we must not, on account of their feminine name and nature, regard wisdom and righteousness as females;[4] for these things are in our view the Son of God, as His genuine disciple has shown, when he said of Him, " Who of God is made to us wisdom, and righteousness, and sanctification, and redemption."[5] And although we may call Him a " second " God, let men know that by the term " second God " we mean nothing else than a virtue capable of including all other virtues, and a reason capable of containing all reason whatsoever which exists in all things, which have arisen naturally, directly, and for the general advantage, and which " reason," we say, dwelt in the soul of Jesus, and was united to Him in a degree far above all other souls, seeing He alone was enabled completely to receive the highest share in the absolute reason, and the absolute wisdom, and the absolute righteousness.

CHAP. XL.

But since, after Celsus had spoken to the above effect of the different kinds of laws, he adds the following remark, " Pindar appears to me to be correct in saying that law is king of all

things," let us proceed to discuss this assertion. What law do you mean to say, good sir, is " king of all things?" If you mean those which exist in the various cities, then such an assertion is not true. For all men are not governed by the same law. You ought to have said that " laws are kings of all men," for in every nation some law is king of all. But if you mean that which is law in the proper sense, then it is this which is by nature " king of all things;" although there are some individuals who, having like robbers abandoned the law, deny its validity, and live lives of violence and injustice. We Christians, then, who have come to the knowledge of the law which is by nature " king of all things," and which is the same with the law of God, endeavour to regulate our lives by its prescriptions, having bidden a long farewell to those of an unholy kind.

CHAP. XLI.

Let us notice the charges which are next advanced by Celsus, in which there is exceedingly little that has reference to the Christians, as most of them refer to the Jews. His words are: " If, then, in these respects the Jews were carefully to preserve their own law, they are not to be blamed for so doing, but those persons rather who have forsaken their own usages, and adopted those of the Jews. And if they pride themselves on it, as being possessed of superior wisdom, and keep aloof from intercourse with others, as not being equally pure with themselves, they have already heard that their doctrine concerning heaven is not peculiar to them, but, to pass by all others, is one which has long ago been received by the Persians, as Herodotus somewhere mentions. ' For they have a custom,' he says, ' of going up to the tops of the mountains, and of offering sacrifices to Jupiter, giving the name of Jupiter to the whole circle of the heavens.'[6] And I think," continues Celsus, " that it makes no difference whether you call the highest being Zeus, or Zen, or Adonai, or Sabaoth, or Ammoun like the Egyptians, or Pappæus like the Scythians. Nor would they be deemed at all holier than others in this respect, that they observe the rite of circumcision, for this was done by the Egyptians and Colchians before them; nor because they abstain from swine's flesh, for the Egyptians practised abstinence not only from it, but from the flesh of goats, and sheep, and oxen, and fishes as well; while Pythagoras and his disciples do not eat beans, nor anything that contains life. It is not probable, however, that they enjoy God's favour, or are loved by Him differently from others, or that angels were sent from heaven to them alone, as if they had had allotted

---

[1] ἵνα δόξη μετὰ τῶν ἀτελέστων τελετῶν, καὶ τῶν καλουσῶν δαίμονας μαγγανειῶν, οὐχ ὑπὸ ἀγαλματοποιῶν μόνων κατασκευάζεσθαι θεὸς, ἀλλὰ καὶ ὑπὸ μάγων, καὶ φαρμακῶν, καὶ τῶν ἐπωδαῖς αὐτῶν κηλουμένων δαιμόνων.

[2] ἡμέρῳ.

[3] μέτριον.

[4] οὐ γὰρ παρὰ τὸ θηλυκὸν ὄνομα, καὶ τῇ οὐσίᾳ θήλειαν νομισ-τέον εἶναι τὴν σοφίαν, καὶ τὴν δικαιοσύνην.

[5] Cf. 1 Cor. i. 30.

[6] Cf. Herodot., i. 131.

to them 'some region of the blessed,'[1] for we see both themselves and the country of which they were deemed worthy. Let this band,[2] then, take its departure, after paying the penalty of its vaunting, not having a knowledge of the great God, but being led away and deceived by the artifices of Moses, having become his pupil to no good end."

CHAP. XLII.

It is evident that, by the preceding remarks, Celsus charges the Jews with falsely giving themselves out as the chosen portion of the Supreme God above all other nations. And he accuses them of boasting, because they gave out that they knew the great God, although they did not really know Him, but were led away by the artifices of Moses, and were deceived by him, and became his disciples to no good end. Now we have in the preceding pages already spoken in part of the venerable and distinguished polity of the Jews, when it existed amongst them as a symbol of the city of God, and of His temple, and of the sacrificial worship offered in it and at the altar of sacrifice. But if any one were to turn his attention to the meaning of the legislator, and to the constitution which he established, and were to examine the various points relating to him, and compare them with the present method of worship among other nations, there are none which he would admire to a greater degree; because, so far as can be accomplished among mortals, everything that was not of advantage to the human race was withheld from them, and only those things which are useful bestowed.[3] And for this reason they had neither gymnastic contests, nor scenic representations, nor horse-races; nor were there among them women who sold their beauty to any one who wished to have sexual intercourse without offspring, and to cast contempt upon the nature of human generation. And what an advantage was it to be taught from their tender years to ascend above all visible nature, and to hold the belief that God was not fixed anywhere within its limits, but to look for Him on high, and beyond the sphere of all bodily substance![4] And how great was the advantage which they enjoyed in being instructed almost from their birth, and as soon as they could speak,[5] in the immortality of the soul, and in the existence of courts of justice under the earth, and in the rewards provided for those who have lived righteous lives! These truths, indeed, were proclaimed in the veil of fable to children, and to those whose views of things were childish; while to those who were

already occupied in investigating the truth, and desirous of making progress therein, these fables, so to speak, were transfigured into the truths which were concealed within them. And I consider that it was in a manner worthy of their name as the "portion of God" that they despised all kinds of divination, as that which bewitches men to no purpose, and which proceeds rather from wicked demons than from anything of a better nature; and sought the knowledge of future events in the souls of those who, owing to their high degree of purity, received the spirit of the Supreme God.

CHAP. XLIII.

But what need is there to point out how agreeable to sound reason, and unattended with injury either to master or slave, was the law that one of the same faith[6] should not be allowed to continue in slavery more than six years?[7] The Jews, then, cannot be said to preserve their own law in the same points with the other nations. For it would be censurable in them, and would involve a charge of insensibility to the superiority of their law, if they were to believe that they had been legislated for in the same way as the other nations among the heathen. And although Celsus will not admit it, the Jews nevertheless *are* possessed of a wisdom superior not only to that of the multitude, but also of those who have the appearance of philosophers; because those who engage in philosophical pursuits, after the utterance of the most venerable philosophical sentiments, fall away into the worship of idols and demons, whereas the very lowest Jew directs his look to the Supreme God alone; and they do well, indeed, so far as this point is concerned, to pride themselves thereon, and to keep aloof from the society of others as accursed and impious. And would that they had not sinned, and transgressed the law, and slain the prophets in former times, and in these latter days conspired against Jesus, that we might be in possession of a pattern of a heavenly city which even Plato would have sought to describe; although I doubt whether he could have accomplished as much as was done by Moses and those who followed him, who nourished a "chosen generation," and "a holy nation," dedicated to God, with words free from all superstition.

CHAP. XLIV.

But as Celsus would compare the venerable customs of the Jews with the laws of certain nations, let us proceed to look at them. He is of opinion, accordingly, that there is no differ-

---

[1] οἷον δή τινα μακάρων χώραν λαχοῦσιν.
[2] χορός.
[3] [Note this eulogy on the law, even though it "made nothing perfect."]
[4] ὑπὲρ τὰ σώματα.
[5] συμπληρώσει τοῦ λόγου.

[6] τὸν ἀπὸ τῶν αὐτῶν ὁρώμενον δογμάτων.
[7] Cf. Ex. xxi. 2 and Jer. xxxiv. 14. [An important comment on Mosaic servitude.]

ence between the doctrine regarding "heaven" and that regarding "God;" and he says that "the Persians, like the Jews, offer sacrifices to Jupiter upon the tops of the mountains," — not observing that, as the Jews were acquainted with one God, so they had only one holy house of prayer, and one altar of whole burnt-offerings, and one censer for incense, and one high priest of God. The Jews, then, had nothing in common with the Persians, who ascend the summits of their mountains, which are many in number, and offer up sacrifices which have nothing in common with those which are regulated by the Mosaic code, — in conformity to which the Jewish priests "served unto the example and shadow of heavenly things," explaining enigmatically the object of the law regarding the sacrifices, and the things of which these sacrifices were the symbols. The Persians therefore may call the "whole circle of heaven" Jupiter; but we maintain that "the heaven" is neither Jupiter nor God, as we indeed know that certain beings of a class inferior to God have ascended above the heavens and all visible nature: and in this sense we understand the words, "Praise God, ye heaven of heavens, and ye waters that be above the heavens: let them praise the name of the LORD." [1]

CHAP. XLV.

As Celsus, however, is of opinion that it matters nothing whether the highest being be called Jupiter, or Zen, or Adonai, or Sabaoth, or Ammoun (as the Egyptians term him), or Pappæus (as the Scythians entitle him), let us discuss the point for a little, reminding the reader at the same time of what has been said above upon this question, when the language of Celsus led us to consider the subject. And now we maintain that the nature of names is not, as Aristotle supposes, an enactment of those who impose them.[2] For the languages which are prevalent among men do not derive their origin from men, as is evident to those who are able to ascertain the nature of the charms which are appropriated by the inventors of the languages differently, according to the various tongues, and to the varying pronunciations of the names, on which we have spoken briefly in the preceding pages, remarking that when those names which in a certain language were possessed of a natural power were translated into another, they were no longer able to accomplish what they did before when uttered in their native tongues. And the same peculiarity is found to apply to men; for if we were to translate the name of one who was called from his birth by a certain appellation in the Greek language into the Egyp-

tian or Roman, or any other tongue, we could not make him do or suffer the same things which he would have done or suffered under the appellation first bestowed upon him. Nay, even if we translated into the Greek language the name of an individual who had been originally invoked in the Roman tongue, we could not produce the result which the incantation professed itself capable of accomplishing had it preserved the name first conferred upon him. And if these statements are true when spoken of the names of *men*, what are we to think of those which are transferred, for any cause whatever, to the *Deity?* For example, something is transferred [3] from the name Abraham when translated into Greek, and something is signified by that of Isaac, and also by that of Jacob; and accordingly, if any one, either in an invocation or in swearing an oath, were to use the expression, "the God of Abraham," and "the God of Isaac," and "the God of Jacob," he would produce certain effects, either owing to the nature of these names or to their powers, since even demons are vanquished and become submissive to him who pronounces these names; whereas if we say, "the god of the chosen father of the echo, and the god of laughter, and the god of him who strikes with the heel," [4] the mention of the name is attended with no result, as is the case with other names possessed of no power. And in the same way, if we translate the word "Israel" into Greek or any other language, we shall produce no result; but if we retain it as it is, and join it to those expressions to which such as are skilled in these matters think it ought to be united, there would then follow some result from the pronunciation of the word which would accord with the professions of those who employ such invocations. And we may say the same also of the pronunciation of "Sabaoth," a word which is frequently employed in incantations; for if we translate the term into "Lord of hosts," or "Lord of armies," or "Almighty" (different acceptation of it having been proposed by the interpreters), we shall accomplish nothing; whereas if we retain the original pronunciation, we shall, as those who are skilled in such matters maintain, produce some effect. And the same observation holds good of Adonai. If, then, neither "Sabaoth" nor "Adonai," when rendered into what appears to be their meaning in the Greek tongue, can accomplish anything, how much less would be the result among those who regard it as a matter of indifference whether the highest being be called Jupiter, or Zen, or Adonai, or Sabaoth!

---

[1] Cf. Ps. cxlviii. 4, 5.
[2] ὅτι ἡ τῶν ὀνομάτων φύσις οὐ θεμένων εἰσὶ νόμοι.

[3] μεταλαμβάνεται γάρ τι, φερ' εἰπεῖν. In the editions of Hœschel and Spencer, τι is wanting.
[4] ὁ θεὸς πατρὸς ἐκλεκτοῦ τῆς ἠχοῦς, καὶ ὁ θεὸς τοῦ γέλωτος, καὶ ὁ θεὸς τοῦ πτερνιστοῦ. Cf. note in Benedictine ed.

CHAP. XLVI.

It was for these and similar mysterious reasons, with which Moses and the prophets were acquainted, that they forbade the name of other gods to be pronounced by him who bethought himself of praying to the one Supreme God alone, or to be remembered by a heart which had been taught to be pure from all foolish thoughts and words. And for these reasons we should prefer to endure all manner of suffering rather than acknowledge Jupiter to be God. For we do not consider Jupiter and Sabaoth to be the same, nor Jupiter to be at all divine, but that some demon, unfriendly to men and to the true God, rejoices under this title.[1] And although the Egyptians were to hold Ammon before us under threat of death, we would rather die than address him as God, it being a name used in all probability in certain Egyptian incantations in which this demon is invoked. And although the Scythians may call Pappæus the supreme God, yet we will not yield our assent to this; granting, indeed, that there *is* a Supreme Deity, although we do not give the name Pappæus to Him as His proper title, but regard it as one which is agreeable to the demon to whom was allotted the desert of Scythia, with its people and its language. He, however, who gives God His title in the Scythian tongue, or in the Egyptian or in any language in which he has been brought up, will not be guilty of sin.[2]

CHAP. XLVII.

Now the reason why circumcision is practised among the Jews is not the same as that which explains its existence among the Egyptians and Colchians, and therefore it is not to be considered the same circumcision. And as he who sacrifices does not sacrifice to the same god, although he appears to perform the rite of sacrifice in a similar manner, and he who offers up prayer does not pray to the same divinity, although he asks the same things in his supplication; so, in the same way, if one performs the rite of circumcision, it by no means follows that it is not a different act from the circumcision performed upon another. For the purpose, and the law, and the wish of him who performs the rite, place the act in a different category. But that the whole subject may be still better understood, we have to remark that the term for "righteousness"[3] is the same among all the Greeks; but righteousness is shown to be one thing according to the view of Epicurus; and another according to the Stoics, who deny the

threefold division of the soul; and a different thing again according to the followers of Plato, who hold that righteousness is the proper business of the parts of the soul.[4] And so also the "courage"[5] of Epicurus is one thing, who would undergo some labours in order to escape from a greater number; and a different thing that of the philosopher of the Porch, who would choose all virtue for its own sake; and a different thing still that of Plato, who maintains that virtue itself is the act of the irascible part of the soul, and who assigns to it a place about the breast.[6] And so circumcision will be a different thing according to the varying opinions of those who undergo it. But on such a subject it is unnecessary to speak on this occasion in a treatise like the present; for whoever desires to see what led us to the subject, can read what we have said upon it in the Epistle of Paul to the Romans.

CHAP. XLVIII.

Although the Jews, then, pride themselves on çircumcision, they will separate it not only from that of the Colchians and Egyptians, but also from that of the Arabian Ishmaelites; and yet the latter was derived from their ancestor Abraham, the father of Ishmael, who underwent the rite of circumcision along with his father. The Jews say that the circumcision performed on the eighth day is the principal circumcision, and that which is performed according to circumstances is different; and probably it was performed on account of the hostility of some angel towards the Jewish nation, who had the power to injure such of them as were not circumcised, but was powerless against those who had undergone the rite. This may be said to appear from what is written in the book of Exodus, where the angel before the circumcision of Eliezer[7] was able to work against[8] Moses, but could do nothing after his son was circumcised. And when Zipporah had learned this, she took a pebble and circumcised her child, and is recorded, according to the reading of the common copies, to have said, "The blood of my child's circumcision is stayed," but according to the Hebrew text, "A bloody husband art thou to me."[9] For she had known the story about a certain angel having power before the shedding of the blood, but who became powerless through the blood of circumcision. For which reason the words were addressed to Moses, "A bloody husband art thou to me." But these things, which appear

---

[1] δαίμονα δέ τινα χαίρειν οὕτως ὀνομαζόμενον.
[2] [Note the bearing of this chapter on the famous controversy concerning the Chinese renderings of God's name.]
[3] δικαιοσύνη.
[4] ἰδιοπραγίαν τῶν μερῶν τῆς ψυχῆς.
[5] ἀνδρεία.
[6] τοῦ θυμικοῦ μέρους τῆς ψυχῆς φάσκοντος αὐτὸ εἶναι ἀρετὴν καὶ ἀποτάσσοντος αὐτῇ τόπον τὸν περὶ τὸν θώρακα.
[7] Cf. Ex. iv. 24, 25. Eliezer was one of the two sons of Moses. Cf. Ex. xviii. 4.
[8] ἐνεργεῖν κατὰ Μωϋσέως.
[9] Cf. Ex. iv. 25, 26.

rather of a curious nature, and not level to the comprehension of the multitude, I have ventured to treat at such length ; and now I shall only add, as becomes a Christian, one thing more, and shall then pass on to what follows. For this angel might have had power, I think, over those of the people who were not circumcised, and generally over all who worshipped only the Creator ; and this power lasted so long as Jesus had not assumed a human body. But when He had done this, and had undergone the rite of circumcision in His own person, all the power of the angel over those who practise the same worship, but are not circumcised,[1] was abolished ; for Jesus reduced it to nought by (the power of) His unspeakable divinity. And therefore His disciples are forbidden to circumcise themselves, and are reminded (by the apostle) : " If ye be circumcised, Christ shall profit you nothing."[2]

CHAP. XLIX.

But neither do the Jews pride themselves upon abstaining from swine's flesh, as if it were some great thing ; but upon their having ascertained the nature of clean and unclean animals, and the cause of the distinction, and of swine being classed among the unclean. And these distinctions were signs of certain things until the advent of Jesus ; after whose coming it was said to His disciple, who did not yet comprehend the doctrine concerning these matters, but who said, " Nothing that is common or unclean hath entered into my mouth,"[3] " What God hath cleansed, call not thou common." It therefore in no way affects either the Jews or us that the Egyptian priests abstain not only from the flesh of swine, but also from that of goats, and sheep, and oxen, and fish. But since it is not that " which entereth into the mouth that defiles a man," and since " meat does not commend us to God," we do not set great store on refraining from eating, nor yet are we induced to eat from a gluttonous appetite. And therefore, so far as we are concerned, the followers of Pythagoras, who abstain from all things that contain life, may do as they please ; only observe the different reason for abstaining from things that have life on the part of the Pythagoreans and our ascetics. For the former abstain on account of the fable about the transmigration of souls, as the poet says : —

" And some one, lifting up his beloved son,
    Will slay him after prayer ; O how foolish he ! "[4]

We, however, when we do abstain, do so because " we keep under our body, and bring it into subjection,"[5] and desire " to mortify our members that are upon the earth, fornication, uncleanness, inordinate affection, evil concupiscence ; "[6] and we use every effort to " mortify the deeds of the flesh."[7]

CHAP. L.

Celsus, still expressing his opinion regarding the Jews, says : " It is not probable that they are in great favour with God, or are regarded by Him with more affection than others, or that angels are sent by Him to them alone, as if to them had been allotted some region of the blessed. For we may see both the people themselves, and the country of which they were deemed worthy." We shall refute this, by remarking that it is evident that this nation *was* in great favour with God, from the fact that the God who presides over all things was called the God of the Hebrews, even by those who were aliens to our faith. And because they were in favour with God, they were not abandoned by Him ;[8] but although few in number, they continued to enjoy the protection of the divine power, so that in the reign of Alexander of Macedon they sustained no injury from him, although they refused, on account of certain covenants and oaths, to take up arms against Darius. They say that on that occasion the Jewish high priest, clothed in his sacred robe, received obeisance from Alexander, who declared that he had beheld an individual arrayed in this fashion, who announced to him in his sleep that he was to be the subjugator of the whole of Asia.[9] Accordingly, we Christians maintain that " it was the fortune of that people in a remarkable degree to enjoy God's favour, and to be loved by Him in a way different from others ; " but that this economy of things and this divine favour were transferred to us, after Jesus had conveyed the power which had been manifested among the Jews to those who had become converts to Him from among the heathen. And for this reason, although the Romans desired to perpetrate many atrocities against the Christians, in order to ensure their extermination, they were unsuccessful ; for there was a divine hand which fought on their behalf, and whose desire it was that the word of God should spread from one corner of the land of Judea throughout the whole human race.

---

[1] κατὰ τῶν ἐν τῇ θεοσεβείᾳ ταύτῃ περιτεμνομένων δύναμις. Boherellus inserts μή before περιτεμνομένων, which has been adopted in the text.
[2] Gal. v. 2.
[3] Cf. Acts x. 14.

[4] καί τις φίλον υἱὸν ἀείρας,
    σφάξει ἐπευχόμενος μέγα νήπιος.
—A verse of Empedocles, quoted by Plutarch, *de Superstitione*, c. xii. Spencer. Cf. note *in loc.* in Benedictine edition.

[5] Cf. 1 Cor. ix. 27.
[6] Cf. Col. iii. 5.
[7] Cf. Rom. viii. 13.
[8] καὶ ὡς εὐδοκιμοῦντές γε ὅσον οὐκ ἐγκατελείποντο. The negative particle (οὐκ) is wanting in the editions of Hœschel and Spencer, but is found in the Royal, Basil, and Vatican MSS. Guietus would delete ὅσον (which emendation has been adopted in the translation), while Boherellus would read ὅσοι instead. — RUÆUS.
[9] [Josephus, *Antiquities*, b. xi. cap. viii.]

CHAP. LI.

But seeing that we have answered to the best of our ability the charges brought by Celsus against the Jews and their doctrine, let us proceed to consider what follows, and to prove that it is no empty boast on our part when we make a profession of knowing the great God, and that we have not been led away by any juggling tricks[1] of Moses (as Celsus imagines), or even of our own Saviour Jesus; but that for a good end we listen to the God who speaks in Moses, and have accepted Jesus, whom he testifies to be God, as the Son of God, in hope of receiving the best rewards if we regulate our lives according to His word. And we shall willingly pass over what we have already stated by way of anticipation on the points, "whence we came, and who is our leader, and what law proceeded from Him." And if Celsus would maintain that there is no difference between us and the Egyptians, who worship the goat, or the ram, or the crocodile, or the ox, or the river-horse, or the dog-faced baboon,[2] or the cat, he can ascertain if it be so, and so may any other who thinks alike on the subject. We, however, have to the best of our ability defended ourselves at great length in the preceding pages on the subject of the honour which we render to our Jesus, pointing out that we have found the better part;[3] and that in showing that the truth which is contained in the teaching of Jesus Christ is pure and unmixed with error, we are not commending ourselves, but our Teacher, to whom testimony was borne through many witnesses by the Supreme God and the prophetic writings among the Jews, and by the very clearness of the case itself, for it is demonstrated that He could not have accomplished such mighty works without the divine help.

CHAP. LII.

But the statement of Celsus which we wish to examine at present is the following: "Let us then pass over the refutations which might be adduced against the claims of their teacher, and let him be regarded as really an angel. But is he the first and only one who came (to men), or were there others before him? If they should say that he is the only one, they would be convicted of telling lies against themselves. For they assert that on many occasions others came, and sixty or seventy of them together, and that these became wicked, and were cast under the earth and punished with chains, and that from this source originate the warm springs, which are their tears; and, moreover, that there came an angel to the tomb of this said being—according

to some, indeed, one, but according to others, two—who answered the women that he had arisen. For the Son of God could not himself, as it seems, open the tomb, but needed the help of another to roll away the stone. And again, on account of the pregnancy of Mary, there came an angel to the carpenter, and once more another angel, in order that they might take up the young Child and flee away (into Egypt). But what need is there to particularize everything, or to count up the number of angels said to have been sent to Moses, and others amongst them? If, then, others were sent, it is manifest that he also came from the same God. But he may be supposed to have the appearance of announcing something of greater importance (than those who preceded him), as if the Jews had been committing sin, or corrupting their religion, or doing deeds of impiety; for these things are obscurely hinted at."

CHAP. LIII.

The preceding remarks might suffice as an answer to the charges of Celsus, so far as regards those points in which our Saviour Jesus Christ is made the subject of special investigation. But that we may avoid the appearance of intentionally passing over any portion of his work, as if we were unable to meet him, let us, even at the risk of being tautological (since we are challenged to this by Celsus), endeavour as far as we can with all due brevity to continue our discourse, since perhaps something either more precise or more novel may occur to us upon the several topics. He says, indeed, that "he has omitted the refutations which have been adduced against the claims which Christians advance on behalf of their teacher," although he has *not* omitted anything which he was able to bring forward, as is manifest from his previous language, but makes this statement only as an empty rhetorical device. That we are not refuted, however, on the subject of our great Saviour, although the accuser may *appear* to refute us, will be manifest to those who peruse in a spirit of truth-loving investigation all that is predicted and recorded of Him. And, in the next place, since he considers that he makes a concession in saying of the Saviour, "Let him appear to be really an angel," we reply that we do not accept of such a concession from Celsus; but we look to the work of Him who came to visit the whole human race in His word and teaching, as each one of His adherents was capable of receiving Him. And this was the work of one who, as the prophecy regarding Him said, was not simply an angel, but the "Angel of the great counsel:"[4] for He announced to men the great

---

[1] γοητεία.
[2] τὸν κυνοκέφαλον.
[3] ὅτι κρεῖττον εὕρομεν.

[4] Cf. Isa. ix. 6 [according to Sept. See vol. i. pp. 223, 236, this series.]

counsel of the God and Father of all things regarding them, (saying) of those who yield themselves up to a life of pure religion, that they ascend by means of their great deeds to God; but of those who do not adhere to Him, that they place themselves at a distance from God, and journey on to destruction through their unbelief of Him. He then continues: "If even the angel came to men, is he the first and only one who came, or did others come on former occasions?" And he thinks he can meet either of these dilemmas at great length, although there is not a single real Christian who asserts that Christ was the only being that visited the human race. For, as Celsus says, "If they should say the only one," there are others who appeared to different individuals.

CHAP. LIV.

In the next place, he proceeds to answer himself as he thinks fit in the following terms: "And so he is not the only one who is recorded to have visited the human race, as even those who, under pretext of teaching in the name of Jesus, have apostatized from the Creator as an inferior being, and have given in their adherence to one who is a superior God and father of him who visited (the world), assert that before him certain beings came from the Creator to visit the human race." Now, as it is in the spirit of truth that we investigate all that relates to the subject, we shall remark that it is asserted by Apelles, the celebrated disciple of Marcion, who became the founder of a certain sect, and who treated the writings of the Jews as fabulous, that Jesus is the only one that came to visit the human race. Even against him, then, who maintained that Jesus was the only one that came from God to men, it would be in vain for Celsus to quote the statements regarding the descent of other angels, seeing Apelles discredits, as we have already mentioned, the miraculous narratives of the Jewish Scriptures; and much more will he decline to admit what Celsus has adduced, from not understanding the contents of the book of Enoch. No one, then, convicts us of falsehood, or of making contradictory assertions, as if we maintained both that our Saviour was the only being that ever came to men, and yet that many others came on different occasions. And in a most confused manner, moreover, does he adduce, when examining the subject of the visits of angels to men, what he has derived, without seeing its meaning, from the contents of the book of Enoch; for he does not appear to have read the passages in question, nor to have been aware that the books which bear the name Enoch [1] do not at all circulate in the Churches as divine, although it is from this source that he might be supposed to have obtained the statement, that "sixty or seventy angels descended at the same time, who fell into a state of wickedness."

CHAP. LV.

But, that we may grant to him in a spirit of candour what he has not discovered in the contents of the book of Genesis, that "the sons of God, seeing the daughters of men, that they were fair, took to them wives of all whom they chose," [2] we shall nevertheless even on this point persuade those who are capable of understanding the meaning of the prophet, that even before us there was one who referred this narrative to the doctrine regarding souls, which became possessed with a desire for the corporeal life of men, and this in metaphorical language, he said, was termed "daughters of men." But whatever may be the meaning of the "sons of God desiring to possess the daughters of men," it will not at all contribute to prove that Jesus was not the only one who visited mankind as an angel, and who manifestly became the Saviour and benefactor of all those who depart from the flood of wickedness. Then, mixing up and confusing whatever he had at any time heard, or had anywhere found written — whether held to be of divine origin among Christians or not — he adds: "The sixty or seventy who descended together were cast under the earth, and were punished with chains." And he quotes (as from the book of Enoch, but without naming it) the following: "And hence it is that the tears of these angels are warm springs," — a thing neither mentioned nor heard of in the Churches of God! For no one was ever so foolish as to materialize into human tears those which were shed by the angels who had come down from heaven. And if it were right to pass a jest upon what is advanced against us in a serious spirit by Celsus, we might observe that no one would ever have said that hot springs, the greater part of which are fresh water, were the tears of the angels, since tears are saltish in their nature, unless indeed the angels, in the opinion of Celsus, shed tears which are fresh.

CHAP. LVI.

Proceeding immediately after to mix up and compare with one another things that are dissimilar, and incapable of being united, he subjoins to his statement regarding the sixty or seventy angels who came down from heaven, and who, according to him, shed fountains of warm water for tears, the following: "It is related also that there came to the tomb of Jesus himself, according to some, two angels, accord-

---

[1] [See p. 380, *supra*.]

[2] [Gen. vi. 2. S.]

ing to others, one;" having failed to notice, I think, that Matthew and Mark speak of one, and Luke and John of two, which statements are not contradictory. For they who mention "one," say that it was he who rolled away the stone from the sepulchre; while they who mention "two," refer to those who appeared in shining raiment to the women that repaired to the sepulchre, or who were seen within sitting in white garments. Each of these occurrences might now be demonstrated to have actually taken place, and to be indicative of a figurative meaning existing in these "phenomena," (and intelligible) to those who were prepared to behold the resurrection of the Word. Such a task, however, does not belong to our present purpose, but rather to an exposition of the Gospel.[1]

CHAP. LVII.

Now, that miraculous appearances have sometimes been witnessed by human beings, is related by the Greeks; and not only by those of them who might be suspected of composing fabulous narratives, but also by those who have given every evidence of being genuine philosophers, and of having related with perfect truth what had happened to them. Accounts of this kind we have read in the writings of Chrysippus of Soli, and also some things of the same kind relating to Pythagoras; as well as in some of the more recent writers who lived a very short time ago, as in the treatise of Plutarch of Chæronea "on the Soul," and in the second book of the work of Numenius the Pythagorean on the "Incorruptibility of the Soul." Now, when such accounts are related by the Greeks, and especially by the philosophers among them, they are not to be received with mockery and ridicule, nor to be regarded as fictions and fables; but when those who are devoted to the God of all things, and who endure all kinds of injury, even to death itself, rather than allow a falsehood to escape their lips regarding God, announce the appearances of angels which they have themselves witnessed, they are to be deemed unworthy of belief, and their words are not to be regarded as true! Now it is opposed to sound reason to judge in this way whether individuals are speaking truth or falsehood. For those who act honestly, only after a long and careful examination into the details of a subject, slowly and cautiously express their opinion of the veracity or falsehood of this or that person with regard to the marvels which they may relate; since it is the case that neither do all men

show themselves worthy of belief, nor do all make it distinctly evident that they are relating to men only fictions and fables. Moreover, regarding the resurrection of Jesus from the dead, we have this remark to make, that it is not at all wonderful if, on such an occasion, either one or two angels should have appeared to announce that Jesus had risen from the dead, and to provide for the safety of those who believed in such an event to the advantage of their souls. Nor does it appear to me at all unreasonable, that those who believe in the resurrection of Jesus, and who manifest, as a fruit of their faith not to be lightly esteemed, their possession of a virtuous[2] life, and their withdrawal from the flood of evils, should not be unattended by angels who lend their help in accomplishing their conversion to God.

CHAP. LVIII.

But Celsus challenges the account also that an angel rolled away the stone from the sepulchre where the body of Jesus lay, acting like a lad at school, who should bring a charge against any one by help of a string of commonplaces. And, as if he had discovered some clever objection to the narrative, he remarks: "The Son of God, then, it appears, could not open his tomb, but required the aid of another to roll away the stone." Now, not to overdo the discussion of this matter, or to have the appearance of unreasonably introducing philosophical remarks, by explaining the figurative meaning at present, I shall simply say of the narrative alone, that it does appear in itself a more respectful proceeding, that the servant and inferior should have rolled away the stone, than that such an act should have been performed by Him whose resurrection was to be for the advantage of mankind. I do not speak of the desire of those who conspired against the Word, and who wished to put Him to death, and to show to all men that He *was* dead and non-existent,[3] that His tomb should not be opened, in order that no one might behold the Word alive after their conspiracy; but the "Angel of God" who came into the world for the salvation of men, with the help of another angel, proved more powerful than the conspirators, and rolled away the weighty stone, that those who deemed the Word to be dead might be convinced that He is not with the "departed," but is alive, and precedes those who are willing to follow Him, that He may manifest to them those truths which come after those which He formerly showed them at the time of their first entrance (into the school of Christianity), when they were as yet incapable of receiving deeper instruction. In the next

---

[1] [See Dr. Lee on *The Inspiration of Holy Scripture*, p. 383, where it is pointed out that the primitive Church was fully aware of the difficulties urged against the historic accuracy of the Four Gospels. Dr. Lee also notes that the culminating sarcasm of Gibbon's famous fifteenth chapter "has not even the poor merit of originality." S.]

[2] τὸν ἐρρωμένον βίον.
[3] καὶ τὸ μηδὲν τυγχάνοντα.

place, I do not understand what advantage he thinks will accrue to his purpose when he ridicules the account of "the angel's visit to Joseph regarding the pregnancy of Mary;" and again, that of the angel to warn the parents "to take up the new-born Child, whose life was in danger, and to flee with it into Egypt." Concerning these matters, however, we have in the preceding pages answered his statements. But what does Celsus mean by saying, that "according to the Scriptures, angels are recorded to have been sent to Moses, and others as well?" For it appears to me to contribute nothing to his purpose, and especially because none of them made any effort to accomplish, as far as in his power, the conversion of the human race from their sins. Let it be granted, however, that other angels were sent from God, but that he came to announce something of greater importance (than any others who preceded him); and when the Jews had fallen into sin, and corrupted their religion, and had done unholy deeds, transferred the kingdom of God to other husbandmen, who in all the Churches take special care of themselves,[1] and use every endeavour by means of a holy life, and by a doctrine conformable thereto, to win over to the God of all things those who would rush away from the teaching of Jesus.[2]

CHAP. LIX.

Celsus then continues: "The Jews accordingly, and these (clearly meaning the Christians), have the same God;" and as if advancing a proposition which would not be conceded, he proceeds to make the following assertion: "It is certain, indeed, that the members of the great Church[3] admit this, and adopt as true the accounts regarding the creation of the world which are current among the Jews, viz., concerning the six days and the seventh;" on which day, as the Scripture says, God "ceased"[4] from His works, retiring into the contemplation of Himself, but on which, as Celsus says (who does not abide by the letter of the history, and who does not understand its meaning), God "rested,"[5] — a term which is not found in the record. With respect, however, to the creation of the world, and the "rest[6] which is reserved after it for the people of God," the subject is extensive, and mystical, and profound, and difficult of explanation. In the next place, as it appears to me,

from a desire to fill up his book, and to give it an appearance of importance, he recklessly adds certain statements, such as the following, relating to the first man, of whom he says: "We give the same account as do the Jews, and deduce the same genealogy from him as they do." However, as regards "the conspiracies of brothers against one another," we know of none such, save that Cain conspired against Abel, and Esau against Jacob; but not Abel against Cain, nor Jacob against Esau: for if this had been the case, Celsus would have been correct in saying that we give the same accounts as do the Jews of "the conspiracies of brothers against one another." Let it be granted, however, that we speak of the same descent into Egypt as they, and of their return[7] thence, which was not a "flight,"[8] as Celsus considers it to have been, what does that avail towards founding an accusation against us or against the Jews? Here, indeed, he thought to cast ridicule upon us, when, in speaking of the Hebrew people, he termed their exodus a "flight;" but when it was his business to investigate the account of the punishments inflicted by God upon Egypt, that topic he purposely passed by in silence.

CHAP. LX.

If, however, it be necessary to express ourselves with precision in our answer to Celsus, who thinks that we hold the same opinions on the matters in question as do the Jews, we would say that we both agree that the books (of Scripture) were written by the Spirit of God, but that we do *not* agree about the meaning of their contents; for we do not regulate our lives like the Jews, because we are of opinion that the literal acceptation of the laws is not that which conveys the meaning of the legislation. And we maintain, that "when Moses is read, the veil is upon their heart,"[9] because the meaning of the law of Moses has been concealed from those who have not welcomed[10] the way which is by Jesus Christ. But we know that if one turn to the Lord (for "the Lord is that Spirit"), the veil being taken away, "he beholds, as in a mirror with unveiled face, the glory of the Lord" in those thoughts which are concealed in their literal expression, and to his own glory becomes a participator of the divine glory; the term "face" being used figuratively for the "understanding," as one would call it without a figure, in which is the face of the "inner man," filled with light and glory, flowing from the true comprehension of the contents of the law.

---

[1] ἑαυτῶν. Guietus would read αὐτῶν, to agree with τῶν ἐκκλησιῶν.
[2] Instead of τὰς ἀπὸ τῆς διδασκαλίας τοῦ Ἰησοῦ ἀφορμάς, Boherellus conjectures τοὺς ... ἀφορμῶντας, which has been adopted in the translation.
[3] τῶν ἀπὸ μεγάλης ἐκκλησίας.
[4] κατέπαυσεν.
[5] ἀναπαυσάμενος.
[6] σαββατισμοῦ.

[7] τὴν ἐκεῖθεν ἐπάνοδον.
[8] φυγήν.
[9] 2 Cor. iii. 15.
[10] ἀσπασαμένοις.

CHAP. LXI.

After the above remarks he proceeds as follows: "Let no one suppose that I am ignorant that some of them will concede that their God is the same as that of the Jews, while others will maintain that he is a different one, to whom the latter is in opposition, and that it was from the former that the Son came." Now, if he imagine that the existence of numerous heresies among the Christians is a ground of accusation against Christianity, why, in a similar way, should it not be a ground of accusation against philosophy, that the various sects of philosophers differ from each other, not on small and indifferent points, but upon those of the highest importance? Nay, medicine also ought to be a subject of attack, on account of its many conflicting schools. Let it be admitted, then, that there are amongst us some who deny that our God is the same as that of the Jews: nevertheless, on that account those are not to be blamed who prove from the same Scriptures that one and the same Deity is the God of the Jews and of the Gentiles alike, as Paul, too, distinctly says, who was a convert from Judaism to Christianity, "I thank my God, whom I serve from my forefathers with a pure conscience."[1] And let it be admitted also, that there is a third class who call certain persons "carnal," and others "spiritual," — I think he here means the followers of Valentinus, — yet what does this avail against us, who belong to the Church, and who make it an accusation against such as hold that certain natures are saved, and that others perish in consequence of their natural constitution?[2] And let it be admitted further, that there are some who give themselves out as Gnostics, in the same way as those Epicureans who call themselves philosophers: yet neither will they who annihilate the doctrine of providence be deemed true philosophers, nor those true Christians who introduce monstrous inventions, which are disapproved of by those who are the disciples of Jesus. Let it be admitted, moreover, that there are some who accept Jesus, and who boast on that account of being Christians, and yet would regulate their lives, like the Jewish multitude, in accordance with the Jewish law, — and these are the twofold sect of Ebionites, who either acknowledge with us that Jesus was born of a virgin, or deny this, and maintain that He was begotten like other human beings, — what does that avail by way of charge against such as belong to the Church, and whom Celsus has styled "those of the multitude?"[3] He adds, also, that certain of the Christians are believers in the Sibyl,[4] having

---

[1] 2 Tim. i. 3.
[2] ἐκ κατασκευῆς.
[3] ἀπὸ τοῦ πλήθους.
[4] Σιβυλλιστάς.

probably misunderstood some who blamed such as believed in the existence of a prophetic Sibyl, and termed those who held this belief Sibyllists.

CHAP. LXII.

He next pours down upon us a heap of names, saying that he knows of the existence of certain Simonians who worship Helene, or Helenus, as their teacher, and are called Helenians. But it has escaped the notice of Celsus that the Simonians do not at all acknowledge Jesus to be the Son of God, but term Simon the "power" of God, regarding whom they relate certain marvellous stories, saying that he imagined that if he could become possessed of similar powers to those with which he believed Jesus to be endowed, he too would become as powerful among men as Jesus was amongst the multitude. But neither Celsus nor Simon could comprehend how Jesus, like a good husbandman of the word of God, was able to sow the greater part of Greece, and of barbarian lands, with His doctrine, and to fill these countries with words which transform the soul from all that is evil, and bring it back to the Creator of all things. Celsus knows, moreover, certain Marcellians, so called from Marcellina, and Harpocratians from Salome, and others who derive their name from Mariamne, and others again from Martha. We, however, who from a love of learning examine to the utmost of our ability not only the contents of Scripture, and the differences to which they give rise, but have also, from love to the truth, investigated as far as we could the opinions of philosophers, have never at any time met with these sects. He makes mention also of the Marcionites, whose leader was Marcion.

CHAP. LXIII.

In the next place, that he may have the appearance of knowing still more than he has yet mentioned, he says, agreeably to his usual custom, that "there are others who have wickedly invented some being as their teacher and demon, and who wallow about in a great darkness, more unholy and accursed than that of the companions of the Egyptian Antinous." And he seems to me, indeed, in touching on these matters, to say with a certain degree of truth, that there are certain others who have wickedly invented another demon, and who have found him to be their lord, as they wallow about in the great darkness of their ignorance. With respect, however, to Antinous, who is compared with our Jesus, we shall not repeat what we have already said in the preceding pages. "Moreover," he continues, "these persons utter against one another dreadful blasphemies, saying all manner of things shameful to be spoken; nor will they yield in the slightest point for the sake of harmony, hating each other with a perfect hatred." Now, in answer to this, we have already said that in philosophy and medicine sects are to be found warring against sects. We, however, who are followers of the word of Jesus, and have exercised ourselves in thinking, and saying, and doing what is in harmony with His words, "when reviled, bless; being persecuted, we suffer it; being defamed, we entreat;"[1] and we would *not* utter "all manner of things shameful to be spoken" against those who have adopted different opinions from ours, but, if possible, use every exertion to raise them to a better condition through adherence to the Creator alone, and lead them to perform every act as those who will (one day) be judged. And if those who hold different opinions will not be convinced, we observe the injunction laid down for the treatment of such: "A man that is a heretic, after the first and second admonition, reject, knowing that he that is such is subverted, and sinneth, being condemned of himself."[2] Moreover, we who know the maxim, "Blessed are the peacemakers," and this also, "Blessed are the meek," would not regard with hatred the corrupters of Christianity, nor term those who had fallen into error Circes and flattering deceivers.[3]

CHAP. LXIV.

Celsus appears to me to have misunderstood the statement of the apostle, which declares that "in the latter times some shall depart from the faith, giving heed to seducing spirits and doctrines of devils; speaking lies in hypocrisy, having their conscience seared with a hot iron; forbidding to marry, and commanding to abstain from meats, which God hath created to be received with thanksgiving of them who believe;"[4] and to have misunderstood also those who employed these declarations of the apostle against such as had corrupted the doctrines of Christianity. And it is owing to this cause that Celsus has said that "certain among the Christians are called 'cauterized in the ears;'"[5] and also that some are termed "enigmas,"[6] — a term which we have never met. The expression "stumbling-block"[7] is, indeed, of frequent occurrence in these writings, — an appellation which we are accustomed to apply to those who turn away simple persons, and those who are easily deceived, from sound doctrine. But neither we, nor, I imagine, any other, whether Christian or

heretic, know of any who are styled Sirens, who betray and deceive,[8] and stop their ears, and change into swine those whom they delude. And yet this man, who affects to know everything, uses such language as the following: "You may hear," he says, "all those who differ so widely, and who assail each other in their disputes with the most shameless language, uttering the words, 'The world is crucified to me, and I unto the world.'" And this is the only phrase which, it appears, Celsus could remember out of Paul's writings; and yet why should we not also employ innumerable other quotations from the Scriptures, such as, "For though we do walk in the flesh, we do not war after the flesh; (for the weapons of our warfare are not carnal, but mighty through God to the pulling down of strongholds,) casting down imaginations, and every high thing that exalteth itself against the knowledge of God?"[9]

CHAP. LXV.

But since he asserts that "you may hear all those who differ so widely saying, 'The world is crucified to me, and I unto the world,'" we shall show the falsity of such a statement. For there are certain heretical sects which do not receive the Epistles of the Apostle Paul, as the two sects of Ebionites, and those who are termed Encratites.[10] Those, then, who do not regard the apostle as a holy and wise man, will not adopt his language, and say, "The world is crucified to me, and I unto the world." And consequently in this point, too, Celsus is guilty of falsehood. He continues, moreover, to linger over the accusations which he brings against the diversity of sects which exist, but does not appear to me to be accurate in the language which he employs, nor to have carefully observed or understood how it is that those Christians who have made progress in their studies say that they are possessed of greater knowledge than the Jews; and also, whether they acknowledge the same Scriptures, but interpret them differently, or whether they do not recognise these books as divine. For we find both of these views prevailing among the sects. He then continues: "Although they have no foundation for the doctrine, let us examine the system itself; and, in the first place, let us mention the corruptions which they have made through ignorance and misunderstanding, when in the discussion of elementary principles they express their opinions in the most absurd manner on things which they do not understand, such as the following." And then, to certain expressions which are continu-

---

[1] 1 Cor. iv. 12, 13.
[2] Tit. iii. 10, 11.
[3] Κίρκας καὶ κύκηθρα αἰμύλα.
[4] Cf. 1 Tim. iv. 1–3.
[5] ἀκοῆς καυστήρια. Cf. note in Benedictine ed.
[6] αἰνίγματα. Cf. note in Benedictine ed.
[7] σκανδάλου.

[8] ἐξορχουμένας καὶ σοφιστρίας.
[9] Cf. 2 Cor. x. 3–5.
[10] [Irenæus, vol. i. p. 353.]

ally in the mouths of the believers in Christianity, he opposes certain others from the writings of the philosophers, with the object of making it appear that the noble sentiments which Celsus supposes to be used by Christians have been expressed in better and clearer language by the philosophers, in order that he might drag away to the study of philosophy those who are caught by opinions which at once evidence their noble and religious character. We shall, however, here terminate the fifth book, and begin the sixth with what follows.

ORIGEN AGAINST CELSUS.

BOOK VI.

CHAP. I.

In beginning this our sixth book, we desire, my reverend Ambrosius, to answer in it those accusations which Celsus brings against the *Christians*, not, as might be supposed, those objections which he has adduced from *writers on philosophy*. For he has quoted a considerable number of passages, chiefly from Plato, and has placed alongside of these such declarations of holy Scripture as are fitted to impress even the intelligent mind; subjoining the assertion, that " these things are stated much better among the Greeks (than in the Scriptures), and in a manner which is free from all exaggerations [1] and promises on the part of God, or the Son of God." Now we maintain, that if it is the object of the ambassadors of the truth to confer benefits upon the greatest possible number, and, so far as they can, to win over to its side, through their love to men, every one without exception — intelligent as well as simple — not Greeks only, but also Barbarians (and great, indeed, is the humanity which should succeed in converting the rustic and the ignorant[2]), it is manifest that they must adopt a style of address fitted to do good to all, and to gain over to them men of every sort. Those, on the other hand, who turn away[3] from the ignorant as being mere slaves,[4] and unable to understand the flowing periods of a polished and logical discourse, and to devote their attention solely to such as have been brought up amongst literary pursuits,[5] confine their views of the public good within very strait and narrow limits.

CHAP. II.

I have made these remarks in reply to the charges which Celsus and others bring against the simplicity of the language of Scripture, which appears to be thrown into the shade by the splendour of polished discourse. For our prophets, and Jesus Himself, and His apostles, were careful to adopt[6] a style of address which should not merely convey the truth, but which should be fitted to gain over the multitude, until each one, attracted and led onwards, should ascend as far as he could towards the comprehension of those mysteries which are contained in these apparently simple words. For, if I may venture to say so, few have been benefited (if they have indeed been benefited at all) by the beautiful and polished style of Plato, and those who have written like him;[7] while, on the contrary, many have received advantage from those who wrote and taught in a simple and practical manner, and with a view to the wants of the multitude. It is easy, indeed, to observe that Plato is found only in the hands of those who profess to be literary men;[8] while Epictetus is admired by persons of ordinary capacity, who have a desire to be benefited, and who perceive the improvement which may be derived from his writings. Now we make these remarks, not to disparage Plato (for the great world of men has found even him useful), but to point out the aim of those who said: "And my speech and my preaching was not with enticing words of man's wisdom, but in demonstration of the Spirit and of power, that our faith should not stand in the wisdom of men, but in the power of God."[9] For the word of God declares that the preaching (although in itself true and most worthy of belief) is not sufficient to reach the human heart, unless a certain power be imparted to the speaker from God, and a grace appear upon his words; and it is only by the divine agency that this takes place in those who speak effectually. The prophet says in the sixty-seventh Psalm, that "the Lord will give a

---

[1] ἀνατάσεως.
[2] πολὺ δὲ τὸ ἥμερον ἐὰν . . . οἶος τέ τις γένηται ἐπιστρέφειν.
[3] πολλὰ χαίρειν φράσαντες.
[4] ἀνδραπόδοις.
[5] καὶ μὴ οἷοί τε κατακούειν τῆς ἐν φράσει λόγων καὶ τάξει ἀπαγγελλομένων ἀκολουθίας, μόνων ἐφρόντισαν τῶν ἀνατραφέντων ἐν λόγοις καὶ μαθήμασιν.

[6] ἐνεῖδον.
[7] [See Dr. Burton's Bampton Lectures *On the Heresies of the Apostolic Age*, pp. 198, 529. S.]
[8] φιλολόγων.
[9] 1 Cor. ii. 4, 5.

word with great power to them who preach." [1]
If, then, it should be granted with respect to
certain points, that the same doctrines are found
among the Greeks as in our own Scriptures, yet
they do not possess the same power of attracting
and disposing the souls of men to follow them.
And therefore the disciples of Jesus, men ignorant so far as regards Grecian philosophy, yet
traversed many countries of the world, impress-
ing, agreeably to the desire of the Logos, each
one of their hearers according to his deserts, so
that they received a moral amelioration in proportion to the inclination of their will to accept
of that which is good.

CHAP. III.

Let the ancient sages, then, make known their
sayings to those who are capable of understanding them. Suppose that Plato, for example, the
son of Ariston, in one of his Epistles, is discoursing about the "chief good," and that he says,
"The chief good can by no means be described
in words, but is produced by long habit, and
bursts forth suddenly as a light in the soul, as
from a fire which had leapt forth." We, then,
on hearing these words, admit that they are well
said, for it is God who revealed to men these as
well as all other noble expressions. And for this
reason it is that we maintain that those who have
entertained correct ideas regarding God, but who
have not offered to Him a worship in harmony
with the truth, are liable to the punishments which
fall on sinners. For respecting such Paul says in
express words : "The wrath of God is revealed
from heaven against all ungodliness and unrighteousness of men, who hold the truth in unrighteousness ; because that which may be known of
God is manifest in them ; for God hath showed
it unto them. For the invisible things of Him
from the creation of the world are clearly seen,
being understood by the things that are made,
even His eternal power and Godhead ; so that
they are without excuse : because that, when
they knew God, they glorified Him not as God,
neither were thankful ; but became vain in their
imaginations, and their foolish heart was darkened. Professing themselves to be wise, they
became fools, and changed the glory of the incorruptible God into an image made like to corruptible man, and to birds, and four-footed beasts,
and creeping things." [2] The truth, then, is verily
held (in unrighteousness), as our Scriptures testify, by those who are of opinion that "the chief
good cannot be described in words," but who assert that, "after long custom and familiar usage,[3]

a light becomes suddenly kindled in the soul, as
if by a fire springing forth, and that it now supports itself alone."

CHAP. IV.

Notwithstanding, those who have written in
this manner regarding the "chief good" will go
down to the Piræus and offer prayer to Artemis,
as if she were God, and will look (with approval)
upon the solemn assembly held by ignorant men ;
and after giving utterance to philosophical remarks of such profundity regarding the soul, and
describing its passage (to a happier world) after
a virtuous life, they pass from those great topics
which God has revealed to them, and adopt
mean and trifling thoughts, and offer a cock
to Æsculapius ! [4] And although they had been
enabled to form representations both of the "invisible things" of God and of the "archetypal
forms" of things from the creation of the world,
and from (the contemplation of) sensible things,
from which they ascend to those objects which
are comprehended by the understanding alone,
— and although they had no mean glimpses of
His "eternal power and Godhead," [5] they nevertheless became "foolish in their imaginations,"
and their "foolish heart" was involved in darkness and ignorance as to the (true) worship of
God. Moreover, we may see those who greatly
pride themselves upon their wisdom and theology
worshipping the image of a corruptible man, in
honour, they say, of Him, and sometimes even
descending, with the Egyptians, to the worship
of birds, and four-footed beasts, and creeping
things ! And although some may appear to have
risen above such practices, nevertheless they will
be found to have changed the truth of God into
a lie, and to worship and serve the "creature
more than the Creator." [6] As the wise and
learned among the Greeks, then, commit errors
in the service which they render to God, God
"chose the foolish things of the world to confound the wise ; and base things of the world,
and things that are weak, and things which are
despised, and things which are nought, to bring
to nought things that are ; " and this, truly,
"that no flesh should glory in the presence of
God." [7] Our wise men, however, — Moses, the
most ancient of them all, and the prophets who
followed him, — knowing that the chief good
could by no means be described in words, were
the first who wrote that, as God manifests Himself to the deserving, and to those who are qualified to behold Him,[8] He appeared to Abraham

---

[1] Such is the reading of the Septuagint version. The Masoretic
text has: "The Lord gave a word; of them who published it there
was a great host." [Cf. Ps. lxviii. 11. S.]

[2] Cf. Rom. i. 18-23.

[3] ἐκ πολλῆς συνουσίας γινομένης περὶ τὸ πρᾶγμα αὐτὸ, καὶ τοῦ
συζῆν.

[4] Cf. Plato, *Phædo* [lxvi. p. 118. S.]

[5] καὶ τὰ ἀόρατα τοῦ Θεοῦ, καὶ τὰς ἰδέας φαντασθέντες ἀπὸ τῆς
κτίσεως τοῦ κόσμου, καὶ τῶν αἰσθητῶν, ἀφ᾽ ὧν ἀναβαίνουσιν ἐπὶ τὰ
νοούμενα᾽ τήν τε ἀίδιον αὐτοῦ δύναμιν καὶ θειότητα οὐκ ἀγεννῶς
ἰδόντες, etc.

[6] Rom. i. 25.

[7] Cf. 1 Cor. i. 27, 28, 29.

[8] ἐπιτηδείοις.

or to Isaac, or to Jacob. But who He was that appeared, and of what form, and in what manner, and like to which of mortal beings,[1] they have left to be investigated by those who are able to show that they resemble those persons to whom God showed Himself: for He was seen not by their bodily eyes, but by the pure heart. For, according to the declaration of our Jesus, "Blessed are the pure in heart, for they shall see God."[2]

CHAP. V.

But that a light is suddenly kindled in the soul, as by a fire leaping forth, is a fact known long ago to our Scriptures; as when the prophet said, "Light ye for yourselves the light of knowledge."[3] John also, who lived after him, said, "That which was in the Logos was life, and the life was the light of men;"[4] which "true light lighteneth every man that cometh into the world" (i.e., the true world, which is perceived by the understanding[5]), and maketh him a light of the world: "For this light shone in our hearts, to give the light of the glorious Gospel of God in the face of Christ Jesus."[6] And therefore that very ancient prophet, who prophesied many generations before the reign of Cyrus (for he was older than he by more than fourteen generations), expressed himself in these words: "The LORD is my light and my salvation: whom shall I fear?"[7] and, "Thy law is a lamp unto my feet, and a light unto my path;"[8] and again, "The light of Thy countenance, O LORD, was manifested towards us;"[9] and, "In Thy light we shall see light."[10] And the Logos, exhorting us to come to this light, says, in the prophecies of Isaiah: "Enlighten thyself, enlighten thyself, O Jerusalem; for thy light is come, and the glory of the LORD is risen upon thee."[11] The same prophet also, when predicting the advent of Jesus, who was to turn away men from the worship of idols, and of images, and of demons, says, "To those that sat in the land and shadow of death, upon them hath the light arisen;"[12] and again, "The people that sat in darkness saw a great light."[12] Observe now the difference between the fine phrases of Plato respecting the "chief good," and the declarations of our prophets regarding

the "light" of the blessed; and notice that the truth as it is contained in Plato concerning this subject did not at all help his readers to attain to a pure worship of God, nor even himself, who could philosophize so grandly about the "chief good," whereas the simple language of the holy Scriptures has led to their honest readers being filled with a divine spirit;[13] and this light is nourished within them by the oil, which in a certain parable is said to have preserved the light of the torches of the five wise virgins.[14]

CHAP. VI.

Seeing, however, that Celsus quotes from an epistle of Plato another statement to the following effect, viz.: "If it appeared to me that these matters could be adequately explained to the multitude in writing and in oral address, what nobler pursuit in life could have been followed by me, than to commit to writing what was to prove of such advantage to human beings, and to lead the nature of all men onwards to the light?" — let us then consider this point briefly, viz., whether or not Plato were acquainted with any doctrines more profound than are contained in his writings, or more divine than those which he has left behind him, leaving it to each one to investigate the subject according to his ability, while we demonstrate that our prophets did know of greater things than any in the Scriptures, but which they did not commit to writing. Ezekiel, e.g., received a roll,[15] written within and without, in which were contained "lamentations," and "songs," and "denunciations;"[16] but at the command of the Logos he swallowed the book, in order that its contents might not be written, and so made known to unworthy persons. John also is recorded to have seen and done a similar thing.[17] Nay, Paul even heard "unspeakable words, which it is not lawful for a man to utter."[18] And it is related of Jesus, who was greater than all these, that He conversed with His disciples in private, and especially in their sacred retreats, concerning the Gospel of God; but the words which He uttered have not been preserved, because it appeared to the evangelists that they could not be adequately conveyed to the multitude in writing or in speech. And if it were not tiresome to repeat the truth regarding these illustrious individuals, I would say that they saw better than Plato (by means of the intelligence which they received by the grace of God), what things were to be committed to *writing*, and how this was to be done, and what was by no

---

[1] καὶ τίνι τῶν ἐν ἡμῖν. Boherellus understands ὅμοιος, which has been adopted in the translation.
[2] Cf. Matt. v. 8.
[3] Hos. x. 12. φωτίσατε ἑαυτοῖς φῶς γνώσεως (LXX.). The Masoretic text is, נִ֤ירוּ לָכֶם֙ נִ֔יר וְעֵ֖ת, where for וְעֵת (*and time*) the Septuagint translator apparently read דַּעַת (*knowledge*), ד and ו being interchanged for their similarity.
[4] Cf. John i. 3, 4.
[5] τὸν ἀληθινὸν καὶ νοητόν.
[6] Cf. 2 Cor. iv. 6.
[7] Ps. xxvii. 1 (attributed to David).
[8] Ps. cxix. 105.
[9] Ps. iv. 6 (Heb. "Lift up upon us," etc.).
[10] Ps. xxxvi. 9.
[11] Cf. Isa. lx. 1.
[12] Cf. Isa. ix. 2.

[13] ἐνθουσιᾷν.
[14] Cf. Matt. xxv. 4.
[15] κεφαλίδα βιβλίου.
[16] οὐαί: cf. Ezek. ii. 9, 10.
[17] Cf. Rev. x. 9.
[18] 2 Cor. xii. 4.

means to be written to the multitude, and what was to be expressed in *words*, and what was not to be so conveyed. And once more, John, in teaching us the difference between what ought to be committed to writing and what not, declares that he heard seven thunders instructing him on certain matters, and forbidding him to commit their words to writing.[1]

CHAP. VII.

There might also be found in the writings of Moses and of the prophets, who are older not only than Plato, but even than Homer and the invention of letters among the Greeks, passages worthy of the grace of God bestowed upon them, and filled with great thoughts, to which they gave utterance, but not because they understood Plato imperfectly, as Celsus imagines. For how was it possible that they should have heard one who was not yet born? And if any one should apply the words of Celsus to the apostles of Jesus, who were younger than Plato, say whether it is not on the very face of it an incredible assertion, that Paul the tentmaker, and Peter the fisherman, and John who left his father's nets, should, through misunderstanding the language of Plato in his Epistles, have expressed themselves as they have done regarding God? But as Celsus now, after having often required of us immediate assent (to his views), as if he were babbling forth something new in addition to what he has already advanced, only repeats himself,[2] what we have said in reply may suffice. Seeing, however, he produces another quotation from Plato, in which he asserts that the employment of the method of question and answer sheds light on the thoughts of those who philosophize like him, let us show from the holy Scriptures that the word of God also encourages us to the practice of dialectics : Solomon, e.g., declaring in one passage, that "instruction unquestioned goes astray ; "[3] and Jesus the son of Sirach, who has left us the treatise called "Wisdom," declaring in another, that "the knowledge of the unwise is as words that will not stand investigation."[4] Our methods of discussion, however, are rather of a gentle kind ; for we have learned that he who presides over the preaching of the word ought to be able to confute gainsayers. But if some continue indolent, and do not train themselves so as to attend to the reading of the word, and "to search the Scriptures," and, agreeably to the command of Jesus, to investigate the

meaning of the sacred writings, and to ask of God concerning them, and to keep "knocking" at what may be closed within them, the Scripture is not on that account to be regarded as devoid of wisdom.

CHAP. VIII.

In the next place, after other Platonic declarations, which demonstrate that "the good" can be known by few, he adds : "Since the multitude, being puffed up with a contempt for others, which is far from right, and being filled with vain and lofty hopes, assert that, because they have come to the knowledge of some venerable doctrines, certain things are true." "Yet although Plato predicted these things, he nevertheless does not talk marvels,[5] nor shut the mouth of those who wish to ask him for information on the subject of his promises ; nor does he command them to come at once and believe that a God of a particular kind exists, and that he has a son of a particular nature, who descended (to earth) and conversed with me." Now, in answer to this we have to say, that with regard to Plato, it is Aristander, I think, who has related that he was not the son of Ariston, but of a phantom, which approached Amphictione in the guise of Apollo. And there are several other of the followers of Plato who, in their lives of their master, have made the same statement. What are we to say, moreover, about Pythagoras, who relates the greatest possible amount of wonders, and who, in a general assembly of the Greeks, showed his ivory thigh, and asserted that he recognised the shield which he wore when he was Euphorbus, and who is said to have appeared on one day in two different cities ! He, moreover, who will declare that what is related of Plato and Socrates belongs to the marvellous, will quote the story of the swan which was recommended to Socrates while he was asleep, and of the master saying when he met the young man, "This, then, was the swan ! "[6] Nay, the third eye which Plato saw that he himself possessed, he will refer to the category of prodigies.[7] But occasion for slanderous accusations will never be wanting to those who are ill-disposed, and who wish to speak evil of what has happened to such as are raised above the multitude. Such persons will deride as a fiction even the demon of Socrates. We do not, then, relate marvels when we narrate the history of Jesus, nor have His genuine disciples recorded any such stories of Him ; whereas this Celsus, who professes universal knowledge, and who quotes many of the sayings of Plato, is,

---

1 Cf. Rev. x. 4.
2 πολλάκις δὲ ἤδη ὁ Κέλσος θρυλλήσας ὡς ἀξιούμενον εὐθέως πιστεύειν, ὡς καινόν τι παρὰ τὰ πρότερον εἰρημένα. Guietus thus amends the passage : πολλάκις δὲ ἤδη ὁ Κέλσος ἀξιούμενος εὐθέως πιστεύειν, ὡς καινόν τι παρὰ τὰ πρότερον εἰρημένα θρυλλήσας, etc. Boherellus would change ἀξιούμενον into ἀξιούμεν.
3 παιδεία ἀνεξέλεγκτος πλανᾶται: cf. Prov. x. 17 (Sept.).
4 γνῶσις ἀσυνέτου ἀδιεξέταστοι λόγοι: cf. Ecclus. xxi. 18.

5 οὐ τερατεύεται.
6 The night before Ariston brought Plato to Socrates as his pupil, the latter dreamed that a swan from the altar of Cupid alighted on his bosom. Cf. Pausanias in *Atticis*, p. 58.
7 " Alicubi forsan occurrit : me vero uspiam legisse non memini. Credo Platonem per tertium oculum suam πολυμάθειαν et scientiam, quâ ceteris anteibat, denotare voluisse." — SPENCER.

I think, intentionally silent on the discourse concerning the Son of God which is related in Plato's Epistle to Hermeas and Coriscus. Plato's words are as follows : " And calling to witness the God of all things — the ruler both of things present and things to come, father and lord both of the ruler and cause — whom, if we are philosophers indeed, we shall all clearly know, so far as it is possible for happy human beings to attain such knowledge." [1]

CHAP. IX.

Celsus quotes another saying of Plato to the following effect : " It has occurred to me to speak once more upon these subjects at greater length, as perhaps I might express myself about them more clearly than I have already done : for there is a certain ' real ' cause, which proves a hindrance in the way of him who has ventured, even to a slight extent, to write on such topics ; and as this has been frequently mentioned by me on former occasions, it appears to me that it ought to be stated now. In each of existing things, which are necessarily employed in the acquisition of knowledge, there are three elements ; knowledge itself is the fourth ; and that ought to be laid down as the fifth which is both capable of being known and is true. Of these, one is ' name ; ' the second is ' word ; ' the third, ' image ; ' the fourth, ' knowledge.' " [2] Now, according to this division, John is introduced before Jesus as the voice of one crying in the wilderness, so as to correspond with the "name" of Plato ; and the second after John, who is pointed out by him, is Jesus, with whom agrees the statement, " The Word became flesh;" and that corresponds to the " word " of Plato. Plato terms the third " image ; " but we, who apply the expression " image " to something different, would say with greater precision, that the mark of the wounds which is made in the soul by the word is the Christ which is in each one of us and this mark is impressed by Christ the Word.[3] And whether Christ, the wisdom which is in those of us who are perfect, correspond to the " fourth " element — knowledge — will become known to him who has the capacity to ascertain it.

CHAP. X.

He next continues : " You see how Plato, although maintaining that (the chief good) cannot be described in words, yet, to avoid the appearance of retreating to an irrefutable position, subjoins a reason in explanation of this difficulty, as even ' nothing ' [4] might perhaps be explained in words." But as Celsus adduces this to prove that we ought not to yield a simple assent, but to furnish a reason for our belief, we shall quote also the words of Paul, where he says, in censuring the hasty [5] believer, "unless ye have believed inconsiderately." [6] Now, through his practice of repeating himself, Celsus, so far as he can, forces us to be guilty of tautology, reiterating, after the boastful language which has been quoted, that " Plato is not guilty of boasting and falsehood, giving out that he has made some new discovery, or that he has come down from heaven to announce it, but acknowledges whence these statements are derived." Now, if one wished to reply to Celsus, one might say in answer to such assertions, that even Plato *is* guilty of boasting, when in the *Timæus* [7] he puts the following language in the mouth of Zeus : " Gods of gods, whose creator and father I am," and so on. And if any one will defend such language on account of the meaning which is conveyed under the name of Zeus, thus speaking in the dialogue of Plato, why should not he who investigates the meaning of the words of the Son of God, or those of the Creator [8] in the prophets, express a profounder meaning than any conveyed by the words of Zeus in the *Timæus ?* For the characteristic of divinity is the announcement of future events, predicted not by human power, but shown by the result to be due to a divine spirit in him who made the announcement. Accordingly, we do not say to each of our hearers, " Believe, first of all, that He whom I introduce to thee is the Son of God ; " but we put the Gospel before each one, as his character and disposition may fit him to receive it, inasmuch as we have learned to know " how we ought to answer every man." [9] And there are some who are capable of receiving nothing more than an exhortation to believe, and to these we address that alone ; while we approach others, again, as far as possible, in the way of demonstration, by means of question and answer. Nor do we at all say, as Celsus scoffingly alleges, " Believe that he whom I introduce to thee is the Son of God, although he was shamefully bound, and disgracefully punished, and very recently [10] was most contumeliously treated before the eyes of all men ; " neither do we add, " Believe it even the more (on that account)." For it is our endeavour to state, on each individual point, arguments more numerous even than we have brought forward in the preceding pages.

---

[1] Plato, *Epist.*, vi.
[2] ὧν ἓν μὲν ὄνομα· δεύτερον δὲ λόγος· τὸ δὲ τρίτον εἴδωλον· τὸ τέταρτον δὲ ἐπιστήμη.
[3] τρανότερον φήσομεν ἐν τῇ ψυχῇ γινόμενον μετὰ τὸν λόγον τῶν τραυμάτων τύπον, τοῦτον εἶναι τὸν ἐν ἑκάστῳ Χριστὸν, ἀτ᾽ὸ Χριστοῦ Λόγου.
[4] τὸ μηδέν.
[5] εἰκῇ πιστεύοντι.
[6] 1 Cor. xv. 2.
[7] [p. 41. S.]
[8] τοῦ δημιουργοῦ.
[9] Cf. Col. iv. 6.
[10] χθὲς καὶ πρώην.

CHAP. XI.

After this Celsus continues : " If these (meaning the Christians) bring forward this person, and others, again, a different individual (as the Christ), while the common and ready cry[1] of all parties is, ' Believe, if thou wilt be saved, or else begone,' what shall those do who are in earnest about their salvation? Shall they cast the dice, in order to divine whither they may betake themselves, and whom they shall join?" Now we shall answer this objection in the following manner, as the clearness of the case impels us to do. If it had been recorded that several individuals had appeared in human life as sons of God in the manner in which Jesus did, and if each of them had drawn a party of adherents to his side, so that, on account of the similarity of the profession (in the case of each individual) that he was the Son of God, he to whom his followers bore testimony to that effect was an object of dispute, there would have been ground for his saying, " If these bring forward this person, and others a different individual, while the common and ready cry of all parties is, ' Believe, if thou wilt be saved, or else begone,' " and so on ; whereas it has been proclaimed to the entire world that Jesus Christ is the only Son of God who visited the human race : for those who, like Celsus, have supposed that (the acts of Jesus) were a series of prodigies,[2] and who for that reason wished to perform acts of the same kind,[3] that they, too, might gain a similar mastery over the minds of men, were convicted of being utter nonentities.[4] Such were Simon, the Magus of Samaria, and Dositheus, who was a native of the same place ; since the former gave out that he was the power of God that is called great,[5] and the latter that he was the Son of God. Now Simonians are found nowhere throughout the world ; and yet, in order to gain over to himself many followers, Simon freed his disciples from the danger of death, which the Christians were taught to prefer, by teaching them to regard idolatry as a matter of indifference. But even at the beginning of their existence the followers of Simon were not exposed to persecution. For that wicked demon who was conspiring against the doctrine of Jesus, was well aware that none of his own maxims would be weakened by the teaching of Simon. The Dositheans, again, even in former times, did not rise to any eminence, and now they are completely extinguished, so that it is said their whole number does not

amount to thirty. Judas of Galilee also, as Luke relates in the Acts of the Apostles,[6] wished to call himself some great personage, as did Theudas before him ; but as their doctrine was not of God, they were destroyed, and all who obeyed them were immediately dispersed. We do not, then, " cast the dice in order to divine whither we shall betake ourselves, and whom we shall join," as if there were many claimants able to draw us after them by the profession of their having come down from God to visit the human race. On these points, however, we have said enough.

CHAP. XII.

Accordingly, let us pass on to another charge made by Celsus, who is not even acquainted with the words (of our sacred books), but who, from misunderstanding them, has said that " we declare the wisdom that is among men to be foolishness with God ; " Paul having said that " the wisdom of the *world* is foolishness with God."[7] Celsus says that " the reason of this has been stated long ago." And the reason he imagines to be, " our desire to win over by means of this saying the ignorant and foolish alone." But, as he himself has intimated, he has said the same thing before ; and we, to the best of our ability, replied to it. Notwithstanding this, however, he wished to show that this statement was an invention[8] of ours, and borrowed from the Grecian sages, who declare that human wisdom is of one kind, and divine of another. And he quotes the words of Heraclitus, where he says in one passage, that " man's method of action is not regulated by fixed principles, but that of God is ; "[9] and in another, that " a foolish man listens to a demon, as a boy does to a man." He quotes, moreover, the following from the *Apology of Socrates*, of which Plato was the author : " For I, O men of Athens, have obtained this name by no other means than by my wisdom. And of what sort is this wisdom ? Such, probably, as is human ; for in that respect I venture to think that I am in reality wise."[10] Such are the passages adduced by Celsus. But I shall subjoin also the following from Plato's letter to Hermeas, and Erastus, and Coriscus : " To Erastus and Coriscus I say, although I am an old man, that, in addition to this noble knowledge of ' forms ' (which they possess), they need a wisdom, with regard to the class of wicked and unjust persons, which may serve as a protective and repelling force against them. For they are inexperienced, in consequence of having passed a large portion of their lives with us, who are

---

[1] κοινὸν δὲ πάντων ἢ καὶ πρόχειρον. For ἢ, Boherellus reads ᾗ.
[2] οἱ γὰρ ὁμοίως Κελσῷ ὑπολαβόντες τετερατεῦσθαι. The word ὁμοίως formerly stood, in the text of Spencer and Ruæus, before τετερατεῦσθαι, but is properly expunged, as arising from the preceding ὁμοίως. Boherellus remarks : " Forte aliud quid exciderit, verbi gratiâ, τὰ τοῦ Ἰησοῦ."
[3] τερατεύσασθαι.
[4] τὸ οὐδέν.
[5] Cf. Acts viii. 10 [and vol. i. p. 187, this series].
[6] Cf. Acts v. 36, 37.
[7] Cf. 1 Cor. iii. 19.
[8] πεπλασμένον ἡμῖν.
[9] ἦθος γὰρ ἀνθρώπειον μὲν οὐκ ἔχει γνώμας, θεῖον δὲ ἔχει.
[10] Cf. Plato's *Apolog.*, v.

moderate [1] individuals, and not wicked. I have accordingly said that they need these things, in order that they may not be compelled to neglect the true wisdom, and to apply themselves in a greater degree than is proper to that which is necessary and human."

CHAP. XIII.

According to the foregoing, then, the one kind of wisdom is human, and the other divine. Now the "human" wisdom is that which is termed by us the wisdom of the "world," which is "foolishness with God;" whereas the "divine"—being different from the "human," because it is "divine"—comes, through the grace of God who bestows it, to those who have evinced their capacity for receiving it, and especially to those who, from knowing the difference between either kind of wisdom, say, in their prayers to God, "Even if one among the sons of men be perfect, while the wisdom is wanting that comes from Thee, he shall be accounted as nothing." [2] We maintain, indeed, that "human" wisdom is an exercise for the soul, but that "divine" wisdom is the "end," being also termed the "strong" meat of the soul by him who has said that "strong meat belongeth to them that are perfect, [3] even those who by reason of use have their senses exercised to discern both good and evil." [4] This opinion, moreover, is truly an ancient one, its antiquity not being referred back, as Celsus thinks, merely to Heraclitus and Plato. For before these individuals lived, the prophets distinguished between the two kinds of wisdom. It is sufficient for the present to quote from the words of David what he says regarding the man who is wise, according to divine wisdom, that "he will not see corruption when he beholds wise men dying." [5] Divine wisdom, accordingly, being different from faith, is the "first" of the so-called "charismata" of God; and the "second" after it — in the estimation of those who know how to distinguish such things accurately — is what is called "knowledge;" [6] and the "third"—seeing that even the more simple class of men who adhere to the service of God, so far as they can, must be saved — is faith. And therefore Paul says: "To one is given by the Spirit the word of wisdom; to another the word of knowledge by the same Spirit; to another faith by the same Spirit." [7] And therefore it is no ordinary individuals whom you will find to have participated in the "divine" wisdom, but the more excellent and distinguished among those who have given in their adherence to Christianity; for it is not "to the most ignorant, or servile, or most uninstructed of mankind," that one would discourse upon the topics relating to the divine wisdom.

CHAP. XIV.

In designating others by the epithets of "uninstructed, and servile, and ignorant," Celsus, I suppose, means those who are not acquainted with his laws, nor trained in the branches of Greek learning; while we, on the other hand, deem those to be "uninstructed" who are not ashamed to address (supplications) to inanimate objects, and to call upon those for health that have no strength, and to ask the dead for life, and to entreat the helpless for assistance. [8] And although some may say that these objects are not gods, but only imitations and symbols of real divinities, nevertheless these very individuals, in imagining that the hands of low mechanics [9] can frame imitations of divinity, are "uninstructed, and servile, and ignorant;" for we assert that the lowest [10] among us have been set free from this ignorance and want of knowledge, while the most intelligent can understand and grasp the divine hope. We do *not* maintain, however, that it is impossible for one who has not been trained in earthly wisdom to receive the "divine," but we *do* acknowledge that all human wisdom is "folly" in comparison with the "divine." In the next place, instead of endeavouring to adduce reasons, as he ought, for his assertions, he terms us "sorcerers," [11] and asserts that "we flee away with headlong speed [12] from the more polished [13] class of persons, because they are not suitable subjects for our impositions, while we seek to decoy [14] those who are more rustic." Now he did not observe that from the very beginning our wise men were trained in the external branches of learning: Moses, e.g., in all the wisdom of the Egyptians; Daniel, and Ananias, and Azariah, and Mishael, in all Assyrian learning, so that they were found to surpass in tenfold degree all the wise men of that country. At the present time, moreover, the Churches have, in proportion to the multitudes (of ordinary believers), a few "wise" men, who have come over to them from that wisdom which is said by us to be "according to the flesh;" [15] and they have also some who have advanced from it to that wisdom which is "divine."

---

1 μετρίων ὄντων.
2 Cf. Wisd. of Sol. ix. 6.
3 τέλειοι.
4 Heb. v. 14.
5 Ps. xlix. 9, 10 (LXX.).
6 γνῶσις.
7 1 Cor. xii. 8, 9. [See Gieseler's *Church History*, on "The Alexandrian Theology," vol. i. p. 212. S.]

8 τοὺς μὴ αἰσχυνομένους ἐν τῷ τοῖς ἀψύχοις προσλαλεῖν, καὶ περὶ μὲν ὑγείας τὸ ἀσθενὲς ἐπικαλουμένους, περὶ δὲ ζωῆς τὸ νεκρὸν ἀξιοῦντας, περὶ δὲ ἐπικουρίας τὸ ἀπορώτατον ἱκετεύοντας.
9 βαναύσων.
10 τοὺς ἐσχάτους.
11 γόητας.
12 προτροπάδην.
13 τοὺς χαριεστέρους.
14 παλεύομεν. [See note *supra*, p. 482. S.]
15 Cf. 1 Cor. i. 26.

CHAP. XV.

Celsus, in the next place, as one who has heard the subject of humility greatly talked about;[1] but who has not been at the pains to understand it,[2] would wish to speak evil of that humility which is practised among us, and imagines that it is borrowed from some words of Plato imperfectly understood, where he expresses himself in the *Laws* as follows : " Now God, according to the ancient account, having in Himself both the beginning and end and middle of all existing things, proceeds according to nature, and marches straight on.[3]   He is constantly followed by justice, which is the avenger of all breaches of the divine law : he who is about to become happy follows her closely in humility, and becomingly adorned."[4]   He did not observe, however, that in writers much older than Plato the following words occur in a prayer : " Lord, my heart is not haughty, nor mine eyes lofty, neither do I walk in great matters, nor in things too wonderful for me ; if I had not been humble,"[5] etc.   Now these words show that he who is of humble mind does not by any means humble himself in an unseemly or inauspicious manner, falling down upon his knees, or casting himself headlong on the ground, putting on the dress of the miserable, or sprinkling himself with dust.   But he who is of humble mind in the sense of the prophet, while "walking in great and wonderful things," which are above his capacity—viz., those doctrines that are truly great, and those thoughts that are wonderful—" humbles himself under the mighty hand of God." If there are some, however, who through their stupidity[6] have not clearly understood the doctrine of humiliation, and act as they do, it is not our doctrine which is to be blamed ; but we must extend our forgiveness to the stupidity[6] of those who aim at higher things, and owing to their fatuity of mind[7] fail to attain them.   He who is " humble and becomingly adorned," is so in a greater degree than Plato's " humble and becomingly adorned " individual : for he is becomingly adorned, on the one hand, because " he walks in things great and wonderful," which are beyond his capacity ; and humble, on the other hand, because, while being in the midst of such, he yet voluntarily humbles himself, not under any one at random, but under " the mighty hand of God," through Jesus Christ, the teacher of such instruction, "who did not deem equality with God a thing to be eagerly clung to, but made Himself of no reputation, and took on

Him the form of a servant, and being found in fashion as a man, humbled Himself, and became obedient unto death, even the death of the cross."[8]   And so great is this doctrine of humiliation, that it has no ordinary individual as its teacher ; but our great Saviour Himself says : " Learn of Me, for I am meek and lowly of heart, and ye shall find rest for your souls."[9]

CHAP. XVI.

In the next place, with regard to the declaration of Jesus against rich men, when He said, " It is easier for a camel to go through the eye of a needle, than for a rich man to enter into the kingdom of God," [10] Celsus alleges that this saying manifestly proceeded from Plato, and that Jesus perverted the words of the philosopher, which were, that " it was impossible to be distinguished for goodness, and at the same time for riches." [11]   Now who is there that is capable of giving even moderate attention to affairs — not merely among the believers on Jesus, but among the rest of mankind — that would not laugh at Celsus, on hearing that Jesus, who was born and brought up among the Jews, and was supposed to be the son of Joseph the carpenter, and who had not studied literature — not merely that of the Greeks, but not even that of the Hebrews — as the truth-loving Scriptures testify regarding Him,[12] had read Plato, and being pleased with the opinion he expressed regarding rich men, to the effect that " it was impossible to be distinguished for goodness and riches at the same time," had perverted this, and changed it into, " It is easier for a camel to go through the eye of a needle, than for a rich man to enter into the kingdom of God ! "   Now, if Celsus had not perused the Gospels in a spirit of hatred and dislike, but had been imbued with a love of truth, he would have turned his attention to the point why a camel — that one of animals which, as regards its physical structure, is crooked — was chosen as an object of comparison with a rich man, and what signification the " narrow eye of a needle " had for him who saw that "strait and narrow was the way that leadeth unto life ; [13] and to this point also, that this animal, according to the law, is described as " unclean," having one element of acceptability, viz., that it ruminates, but one of condemnation, viz., that it does not divide the hoof.   He would have inquired, moreover, how often the camel was adduced as an object of comparison in the sacred Scriptures, and in reference to what objects, that he might thus ascertain the mean-

---

1 ὡς περιηχηθεὶς τὰ περὶ ταπεινοφροσύνης.
2 μὴ ἐπιμελῶς αὐτὴν νοήσας.
3 εὐθεία περαίνει κατὰ φύσιν παραπορευόμενος.
4 Plato, *de Legibus*, iv. p. 716.
5 Ps. cxxxi. 1, 2 (LXX.).   The clause, " If I had not been humble," seems to belong to the following verse.
6 τῇ ἰδιωτείᾳ.
7 διὰ τὸν ἰδιωτισμόν.

8 Cf. Phil ii. 6, 8.
9 Cf. Matt. xi. 20.
10 Cf. Matt. xix. 24.
11 Cf. Plato, *de Legibus*, v. p. 743.
12 Cf. Matt. xiii. 54, Mark vi. 2, and John vii. 15.
13 Cf. Matt. vii. 14

ing of the Logos concerning the rich men. Nor would he have left without examination the fact that "the poor" are termed "blessed" by Jesus, while "the rich" are designated as "miserable;" and whether these words refer to the rich and poor who are visible to the senses, or whether there is any kind of poverty known to the Logos which is to be deemed "altogether blessed," and any rich man who is to be wholly condemned. For even a common individual would not thus indiscriminately have praised the poor, many of whom lead most wicked lives. But on this point we have said enough.

CHAP. XVII.

Since Celsus, moreover, from a desire to depreciate the accounts which our Scriptures give of the kingdom of God, has quoted none of them, as if they were unworthy of being recorded by him (or perhaps because he was unacquainted with them), while, on the other hand, he quotes the sayings of Plato, both from his *Epistles* and the *Phædrus*, as if these were divinely inspired, but our Scriptures were not, let us set forth a few points, for the sake of comparison with these plausible declarations of Plato, which did not, however, dispose the philosopher to worship in a manner worthy of him the Maker of all things. For he ought not to have adulterated or polluted this worship with what we call "idolatry," but what the many would describe by the term "superstition." Now, according to a Hebrew figure of speech, it is said of God in the eighteenth Psalm, that "He made darkness His secret place," [1] to signify that those notions which should be worthily entertained of God are invisible and unknowable, because God conceals Himself in darkness, as it were, from those who cannot endure the splendours of His knowledge, or are incapable of looking at them, partly owing to the pollution of their understanding, which is clothed with the body of mortal lowliness, and partly owing to its feebler power of comprehending God. And in order that it may appear that the knowledge of God has rarely been vouchsafed to men, and has been found in very few individuals, Moses is related to have entered into the darkness where God was.[2] And again, with regard to Moses it is said: "Moses alone shall come near the LORD, but the rest shall not come nigh." [3] And again, that the prophet may show the depth of the doctrines which relate to God, and which is unattainable by those who do not possess the "Spirit which searcheth all things, even the deep things of God," he added: "The abyss like a garment is His covering." [4] Nay,

our Lord and Saviour, the Logos of God, manifesting that the greatness of the knowledge of the Father is appropriately comprehended and known pre-eminently by Him alone, and in the second place by those whose minds are enlightened by the Logos Himself and God, declares: "No man knoweth the Son, but the Father; neither knoweth any man the Father but the Son, and he to whomsoever the Son will reveal Him." [5] For no one can worthily know the "uncreated" [6] and first-born of all created nature like the Father who begat Him, nor any one the Father like the living Logos, and His Wisdom and Truth.[7] By sharing in Him who takes away from the Father what is called "darkness," which He "made His secret place," and "the abyss," which is called His "covering," and in this way unveiling the Father, every one knows the Father who [8] is capable of knowing Him.

CHAP. XVIII.

I thought it right to quote these few instances from a much larger number of passages, in which our sacred writers express their ideas regarding God, in order to show that, to those who have eyes to behold the venerable character of Scripture, the sacred writings of the prophets contain things more worthy of reverence than those sayings of Plato which Celsus admires. Now the declaration of Plato, quoted by Celsus, runs as follows: "All things are around the King of all, and all things exist for his sake, and he is the cause of all good things. With things of the second rank he is second, and with those of the third rank he is third. The human soul, accordingly, is eager to learn what these things are, looking to such things as are kindred to itself, none of which is perfect. But as regards the King and those things which I mentioned, there is nothing which resembles them." [9] I might have mentioned, moreover, what is said of those beings which are called seraphim by the Hebrews, and described in Isaiah,[10] who cover the face and feet of God, and of those called cherubim, whom Ezekiel [11] has described, and the postures of these, and of the manner in which God is said to be borne upon the cherubim. But since they are mentioned in a very mysterious manner, on account of the unworthy and the indecent, who are unable to enter into

---

[1] Cf. Ps. xviii. 11.
[2] Cf. Ex. xx. 21.
[3] Cf. Ex. xxiv. 2.
[4] Cf. Ps. civ. 6.

[5] Cf. Matt. xi. 27.
[6] ἀγένητον. Locus diligenter notandus, ubi Filius e creaturarum numero diserte eximitur, dum ἀγένητος dicitur. At non dissimulandum in unico Cod. Anglicano secundo legi: τὸν γεννητόν: cf. *Origenianorum*, lib. ii. quæstio 2, num. 23. — RUÆUS.
[7] [Bishop Bull, in the *Defensio Fidei Nicenæ*, book ii. cap. ix. 9, says, " In these words, which are clearer than any light, Origen proves the absolutely divine and uncreated nature of the Son." S.]
[8] ὅ τι ποτ᾽ ἂν χωρῇ γιγνώσκειν. Boherellus proposes ὅστις ποτ᾽ ἂν χωρῇ, etc.
[9] Cf. Plato, *Epist.*, ii., ad Dionys.
[10] Cf. Isa. vi. 2.
[11] Cf. Ezek. i. and x.

the great thoughts and venerable nature of theology, I have not deemed it becoming to discourse of them in this treatise.

CHAP. XIX.

Celsus in the next place alleges, that "certain Christians, having misunderstood the words of Plato, loudly boast of a 'super-celestial' God, thus ascending beyond the heaven of the Jews." By these words, indeed, he does not make it clear whether they also ascend beyond the *God* of the Jews, or only beyond the heaven by which they swear. It is not our purpose at present, however, to speak of those who acknowledge another god than the one worshipped by the Jews, but to defend ourselves, and to show that it was impossible for the prophets of the Jews, whose writings are reckoned among ours, to have borrowed anything from Plato, because they were older than he. They did not then borrow from him the declaration, that "all things are around the King of all, and that all exist on account of him;" for we have learned that nobler thoughts than these have been uttered by the prophets, by Jesus Himself and His disciples, who have clearly indicated the meaning of the spirit that was in them, which was none other than the spirit of Christ. Nor was the philosopher the first to present to view the "super-celestial" place; for David long ago brought to view the profundity and multitude of the thoughts concerning God entertained by those who have ascended above visible things, when he said in the book of Psalms: "Praise God, ye heaven of heavens; and ye waters that be above the heavens, let them praise the name of the Lord."[1] I do not, indeed, deny that Plato learned from certain Hebrews the words quoted from the *Phædrus*, or even, as some have recorded, that he quoted them from a perusal of our prophetic writings, when he said: "No poet here below has ever sung of the super-celestial place, or ever will sing in a becoming manner," and so on. And in the same passage is the following: "For the essence, which is both colourless and formless, and which cannot be touched, which really exists, is the pilot of the soul, and is beheld by the understanding alone; and around it the genus of true knowledge holds this place."[2] Our Paul, moreover, educated by these words, and longing after things "supra-mundane" and "super-celestial," and doing his utmost for their sake to attain them, says in the second Epistle to the Corinthians: "For our light affliction, which is but for a moment, worketh for us a far more exceeding and eternal weight of glory; while we look not at the things which are seen, but at the

things which are not seen: for the things which are seen are temporal; but the things which are unseen are eternal."[3]

CHAP. XX.

Now, to those who are capable of understanding him, the apostle manifestly presents to view "things which are the objects of perception," calling them "things seen;" while he terms "unseen," things which are the object of the understanding, and cognisable by it alone. He knows, also, that things "seen" and visible are "temporal," but that things cognisable by the mind, and "not seen," are "eternal;" and desiring to remain in the contemplation of these, and being assisted by his earnest longing for them, he deemed all affliction as "light" and as "nothing," and during the season of afflictions and troubles was not at all bowed down by them, but by his contemplation of (divine) things deemed every calamity a light thing, seeing we also have "a great High Priest," who by the greatness of His power and understanding "has passed through the heavens, even Jesus the Son of God," who has promised to all that have truly learned divine things, and have lived lives in harmony with them, to go before them to the things that are supra-mundane; for His words are: "That where I go, ye may be also."[4] And therefore we hope, after the troubles and struggles which we suffer here, to reach the highest heavens,[5] and receiving, agreeably to the teaching of Jesus, the fountains of water that spring up unto eternal life, and being filled with the rivers of knowledge,[6] shall be united with those waters that are said to be above the heavens, and which praise His name. And as many of us[7] as praise Him shall not be carried about by the revolution of the heaven, but shall be ever engaged in the contemplation of the invisible things of God, which are no longer understood by us through the things which He hath made from the creation of the world, but seeing, as it was expressed by the true disciple of Jesus in these words, "then face to face;"[8] and in these, "When that which is perfect is come, then that which is in part will be done away."[9]

CHAP. XXI.

The Scriptures which are current in the Churches[10] of God do not speak of "seven"

---

[1] Ps. cxlviii. 4.
[2] Cf. Plato in *Phædro*, p. 247.

[3] Cf. 2 Cor. iv. 17, 18.
[4] Cf. John xiv. 3.
[5] πρὸς ἄκροις τοῖς οὐρανοῖς.
[6] ποταμοὺς τῶν θεωρημάτων.
[7] For ὅσον γε Boherellus proposes ὅσοι γε, which is adopted in the translation.
[8] Cf. 1 Cor. xiii. 12.
[9] Cf. 1 Cor. xiii. 10.
[10] [Bishop Pearson, in his *Exposition of the Creed*, Art. IX., notes that "Origen for the most part speaks of the Church in the plural number, αἱ ἐκκλησίαι." S.]

heavens, or of any definite number at all,[1] but they do appear to teach the existence of "heavens," whether that means the "spheres" of those bodies which the Greeks call "planets," or something more mysterious. Celsus, too, agreeably to the opinion of Plato,[2] asserts that souls can make their way to and from the earth through the planets; while Moses, our most ancient prophet, says that a divine vision was presented to the view of our prophet Jacob,[3] — a ladder stretching to heaven, and the angels of God ascending and descending upon it, and the Lord supported[4] upon its top, — obscurely pointing, by this matter of the ladder, either to the same truths which Plato had in view, or to something greater than these. On this subject Philo has composed a treatise which deserves the thoughtful and intelligent investigation of all lovers of truth.

CHAP. XXII.

After this, Celsus, desiring to exhibit his learning in his treatise against us, quotes also certain Persian mysteries, where he says: "These things are obscurely hinted at in the accounts of the Persians, and especially in the mysteries of Mithras, which are celebrated amongst them. For in the latter there is a representation of the two heavenly revolutions, — of the movement, viz., of the fixed[5] stars, and of that which takes place among the planets, and of the passage of the soul through these. The representation is of the following nature: There is a ladder with lofty gates,[6] and on the top of it an eighth gate. The first gate consists of lead, the second of tin, the third of copper, the fourth of iron, the fifth of a mixture of metals,[7] the sixth of silver, and the seventh of gold. The first gate they assign to Saturn, indicating by the 'lead' the slowness of this star; the second to Venus, comparing her to the splendour and softness of tin; the third to Jupiter, being firm[8] and solid; the fourth to Mercury, for both Mercury and iron are fit to endure all things, and are money-making and laborious;[9] the fifth to Mars, because, being composed of a mixture of metals, it is varied and unequal; the sixth, of silver, to the Moon; the seventh, of gold, to the Sun, — thus imitating the different colours of the two latter." He next proceeds to examine the reason of the stars being arranged in this order, which is symbolized by the names of the rest of matter.[10]

Musical reasons, moreover, are added or quoted by the Persian theology; and to these, again, he strives to add a second explanation, connected also with musical considerations. But it seems to me, that to quote the language of Celsus upon these matters would be absurd, and similar to what he himself has done, when, in his accusations against Christians and Jews, he quoted, most inappropriately, not only the words of Plato; but, dissatisfied even with these,[11] he adduced in addition the mysteries of the Persian Mithras, and the explanation of them. Now, whatever be the case with regard to these, — whether the Persians and those who conduct the mysteries of Mithras give false or true accounts regarding them, — why did he select these for quotation, rather than some of the other mysteries, with the explanation of them? For the mysteries of Mithras do not appear to be more famous among the Greeks than those of Eleusis, or than those in Ægina, where individuals are initiated in the rites of Hecate. But if he must introduce barbarian mysteries with their explanation, why not rather those of the Egyptians, which are highly regarded by many,[12] or those of the Cappadocians regarding the Comanian Diana, or those of the Thracians, or even those of the Romans themselves, who initiate the noblest members of their senate?[13] But if he deemed it inappropriate to institute a comparison with any of these, because they furnished no aid in the way of accusing Jews or Christians, why did it not also appear to him inappropriate to adduce the instance of the mysteries of Mithras?

CHAP. XXIII.

If one wished to obtain means for a profounder contemplation of the entrance of souls into divine things, not from the statements of that very insignificant sect from which he quoted, but from books — partly those of the Jews, which are read in their synagogues, and adopted by Christians, and partly from those of Christians alone — let him peruse, at the end of Ezekiel's prophecies, the visions beheld by the prophet, in which gates of different kinds are enumerated,[14] which obscurely refer to the different modes in which divine souls enter into a better world;[15] and let him peruse also, from the Apocalypse of John, what is related of the city of God, the heavenly Jerusalem, and of its foundations and gates.[16] And if he is capable of finding out also the road, which is indicated by symbols, of those who will march on to divine things, let him read

---

[1] [But see 2 Cor. xii. 2, and also Irenæus, vol. i. p. 405.]
[2] Cf. Plato in *Timæo*, p. 42.
[3] Cf. Gen. xxviii. 12, 13.
[4] ἐπεστηριγμένον.
[5] τῆς τε ἀπλανοῦς.
[6] κλίμαξ ἰψίπυλος. Boherellus conjectures ἑπτάπυλος.
[7] κεραστοῦ νομίσματος.
[8] τὴν χαλκοβάτην καὶ στερράν.
[9] τλήμονα γὰρ ἔργων ἀπάντων, καὶ χρηματιστὴν, καὶ πολύκμητον εἶναι, τόν τε σίδηρον καὶ τὸν Ἑρμῆν.
[10] τῆς λοιπῆς ὕλης. For ὕλης, another reading is πύλης.

[11] For ὡς ἐκείνοις ἀρκεῖσθαι, Spencer introduced into his text, οὐδ' ἐκείνοις ἀρκεῖσθαι, which has been adopted in the translation.
[12] ἐν οἷς πολλοὶ σεμνύνονται.
[13] ἀπὸ τῆς συγκλήτου βουλῆς.
[14] Cf. Ezek. xlviii.
[15] ἐπὶ τὰ κρείττονα.
[16] Cf. Rev. xxi.

the book of Moses entitled Numbers, and let him seek the help of one who is capable of initiating him into the meaning of the narratives concerning the encampments of the children of Israel; viz., of what sort those were which were arranged towards the east, as was the case with the first; and what those towards the south-west and south; and what towards the sea; and what the last were, which were stationed towards the north. For he will see that there is in the respective places a meaning [1] not to be lightly treated, nor, as Celsus imagines, such as calls only for silly and servile listeners: but he will distinguish in the encampments certain things relating to the numbers that are enumerated, and which are specially adapted to each tribe, of which the present does not appear to us to be the proper time to speak. Let Celsus know, moreover, as well as those who read his book, that in no part of the genuine and divinely accredited Scriptures are "seven" heavens mentioned; neither do our prophets, nor the apostles of Jesus, nor the Son of God Himself, repeat anything which they borrowed from the Persians or the Cabiri.

CHAP. XXIV.

After the instance borrowed from the Mithraic mysteries, Celsus declares that he who would investigate the Christian mysteries, along with the aforesaid Persian, will, on comparing the two together, and on unveiling the rites of the Christians, see in this way the difference between them. Now, wherever he was able to give the names of the various sects, he was nothing loth to quote those with which he thought himself acquainted; but when he ought most of all to have done this, if they were really known to him, and to have informed us which was the sect that makes use of the diagram he has drawn, he has not done so. It seems to me, however, that it is from some statements of a very insignificant sect called Ophites,[2] which he has misunderstood, that, in my opinion, he has partly borrowed what he says about the diagram.[3] Now, as we have always been animated by a love of learning,[4] we have fallen in with this diagram, and we have found in it the representations of men who, as Paul says, "creep into houses, and lead captive silly women laden with sins, led away with divers lusts; ever learning, and never able to come to the knowledge of the truth."[5] The diagram was, however, so destitute of all credibility, that neither these easily deceived women, nor the most rustic class of men, nor those who were ready to be led away by any

plausible pretender whatever, ever gave their assent to the diagram. Nor, indeed, have we ever met any individual, although we have visited many parts of the earth, and have sought out all those who anywhere made profession of knowledge, that placed any faith in this diagram.

CHAP. XXV.

In this diagram were described ten circles, distinct from each other, but united by one circle, which was said to be the soul of all things, and was called "Leviathan."[6] This Leviathan, the Jewish Scriptures say, whatever they mean by the expression, was created by God for a plaything;[7] for we find in the Psalms: "In wisdom hast Thou made all things: the earth is full of Thy creatures; so is this great and wide sea. There go the ships; small animals with great; there is this dragon, which Thou hast formed to play therein."[8] Instead of the word "dragon," the term "leviathan" is in the Hebrew. This impious diagram, then, said of this leviathan, which is so clearly depreciated by the Psalmist, that it was the soul which had travelled through all things! We observed, also, in the diagram, the being named "Behemoth," placed as it were under the lowest circle. The inventor of this accursed diagram had inscribed this leviathan at its circumference and centre, thus placing its name in two separate places. Moreover, Celsus says that the diagram was "divided by a thick black line, and this line he asserted was called Gehenna, which is Tartarus." Now as we found that Gehenna was mentioned in the Gospel as a place of punishment, we searched to see whether it is mentioned anywhere in the ancient Scriptures, and especially because the Jews too use the word. And we ascertained that where the valley of the son of Ennom was named in Scripture in the Hebrew, instead of "valley," with fundamentally the same meaning, it was termed both the valley of Ennom and also Geenna. And continuing our researches, we find that what was termed "Geenna," or "the valley of Ennom," was included in the lot of the tribe of Benjamin, in which Jerusalem also was situated. And seeking to ascertain what might be the inference from the heavenly Jerusalem belonging to the lot of Benjamin and the valley of Ennom, we find a certain confirmation of what is said regarding the place of punishment, intended for the purification of such souls as are to be purified by torments, agreeably to the saying: "The Lord cometh like a refiner's fire, and like fullers' soap: and He shall sit as a refiner and purifier of silver and of gold."[9]

---

1 θεωρήματα.
2 [Vol. i. p. 354, this series.]
3 "Utinam exstaret! Multum enim lucis procul dubio antiquissimorum Patrum libris, priscæ ecclesiæ temporibus, et quibusdam sacræ Scripturæ locis, accederet."—SPENCER.
4 κατὰ τὸ φιλομαθὲς ἡμῶν.
5 Cf. 2 Tim. iii. 6, 7.

6 Cf. note in Spencer's edition.
7 παίγνιον.
8 Cf. Ps. civ. 24-26.
9 Cf. Mal. iii. 2, 3.

CHAP. XXVI.

It is in the precincts of Jerusalem, then, that punishments will be inflicted upon those who undergo the process of purification,[1] who have received into the substance of their soul the elements of wickedness, which in a certain place[2] is figuratively termed " lead," and on that account iniquity is represented in Zechariah as sitting upon a " talent of lead."[3] But the remarks which might be made on this topic are neither to be made to all, nor to be uttered on the present occasion; for it is not unattended with danger to commit to writing the explanation of such subjects, seeing the multitude need no further instruction than that which relates to the punishment of sinners; while to ascend beyond this is not expedient, for the sake of those who are with difficulty restrained, even by fear of eternal punishment, from plunging into any degree of wickedness, and into the flood of evils which result from sin.[4] The doctrine of Geenna, then, is unknown both to the diagram and to Celsus: for had it been otherwise, the framers of the former would not have boasted of their pictures of animals and diagrams, as if the truth were represented by these; nor would Celsus, in his treatise against the Christians, have introduced among the charges directed against them statements which they never uttered, instead of what was spoken by some who perhaps are no longer in existence, but have altogether disappeared, or been reduced to a very few individuals, and these easily counted. And as it does not beseem those who profess the doctrines of Plato to offer a defence of Epicurus and his impious opinions, so neither is it for us to defend the diagram, or to refute the accusations brought against it by Celsus. We may therefore allow his charges on these points to pass as superfluous and useless,[5] for we would censure more severely than Celsus any who should be carried away by such opinions.

CHAP. XXVII.

After the matter of the diagram, he brings forward certain monstrous statements, in the form of question and answer,[6] regarding what is called by ecclesiastical writers the " seal," statements which did not arise from imperfect information; such as that " he who impresses the seal is called father, and he who is sealed is called young man and son; " and who answers, " I have been anointed with white ointment from the tree of life," — things which we never heard

to have occurred even among the heretics. In the next place, he determines even the number mentioned by those who deliver over the seal, as that " of *seven* angels, who attach themselves to both sides of the soul of the dying body; the one party being named angels of light, the others ' archontics; ' "[7] and he asserts that the " ruler of those named ' archontics ' is termed the ' accursed ' god." Then, laying hold of the expression, he assails, not without reason; those who venture to use such language; and on that account we entertain a similar feeling of indignation with those who censure such individuals, if indeed there exist any who call the God of the Jews — who sends rain and thunder, and who is the Creator of this world, and the God of Moses, and of the cosmogony which he records — an " accursed " divinity. Celsus, however, appears to have had in view, in employing these expressions, not a *rational*[8] object, but one of a most irrational kind, arising out of his hatred towards us, which is so unlike a philosopher. For his aim was, that those who are unacquainted with our customs should, on perusing his treatise, at once assail us as if we called the noble Creator of this world an " accursed divinity." He appears to me, indeed, to have acted like those Jews who, when Christianity began to be first preached, scattered abroad false reports of the Gospel, such as that " Christians offered up an infant in sacrifice, and partook of its flesh; " and again, " that the professors of Christianity, wishing to do the ' works of darkness,' used to extinguish the lights (in their meetings), and each one to have sexual intercourse with any woman whom he chanced to meet." These calumnies have long exercised, although unreasonably, an influence over the minds of very many, leading those who are aliens to the Gospel to believe that Christians are men of such a character; and even at the present day they mislead some, and prevent them from entering even into the simple intercourse of conversation with those who are Christians.

CHAP. XXVIII.

With some such object as this in view does Celsus seem to have been actuated, when he alleged that Christians term the Creator an " accursed divinity; " in order that he who believes these charges of his against us, should, if possible, arise and exterminate the Christians as the most impious of mankind. Confusing, moreover, things that are distinct,[9] he states also the reason why the God of the Mosaic cosmogony is termed " accursed," asserting that " such is his character, and worthy of execration in the

---

[1] χωνευομένων.
[2] ποῦ.
[3] Cf. Zech. v. 7.
[4] [See Dean Plumptre's *The Spirits in Prison*, on " The Universalism of Origen," p. 137, et seqq. S.]
[5] μάτην ἐκκείμενα.
[6] ἀλλόκοτα καὶ ἀμοιβαίας φωνάς.

[7] ἀρχοντικῶν.
[8] οὐκ εὐγνώμον ἀλλά . . . πάνυ ἀγνωμονέστατον.
[9] φύρων δὲ τὰ πράγματα.

opinion of those who so regard him, inasmuch
as he pronounced a curse upon the serpent, who
introduced the first human beings to the knowledge of good and evil." Now he ought to have
known that those who have espoused the cause
of the serpent, because he gave good advice to
the first human beings, and who go far beyond
the Titans and Giants of fable, and are on this
account called Ophites, are so far from being
Christians, that they bring accusations against
Jesus to as great a degree as Celsus himself; and
they do not admit any one into their assembly [1]
until he has uttered maledictions against Jesus.
See, then, how irrational is the procedure of
Celsus, who, in his discourse against the Christians, represents as such those who will not even
listen to the *name* of Jesus, or omit even that
He was a wise man, or a person of virtuous [2]
character! What, then, could evince greater
folly or madness, not only on the part of those
who wish to derive their name from the serpent
as the author of good,[3] but also on the part of
Celsus, who thinks that the accusations with
which the Ophites [4] are charged, are chargeable
also against the Christians! Long ago, indeed,
that Greek philosopher who preferred a state of
poverty,[5] and who exhibited the pattern of a
happy life, showing that he was not excluded
from happiness although he was possessed of
nothing,[6] termed himself a Cynic; while these
impious wretches, as not being human beings,
whose enemy the serpent is, but as being serpents, pride themselves upon being called Ophites
from the serpent, which is an animal most hostile to and greatly dreaded by man, and boast
of one Euphrates [7] as the introducer of these
unhallowed opinions.

CHAP. XXIX.

In the next place, as if it were the Christians
whom he was calumniating, he continues his accusations against those who termed the God of
Moses and of his law an "accursed" divinity;
and imagining that it is the Christians who so
speak, he expresses himself thus: "What could
be more foolish or insane than such senseless [8]
wisdom? For what blunder has the Jewish lawgiver committed? and why do you accept, by
means, as you say,[9] of a certain allegorical and
typical method of interpretation, the cosmogony
which he gives, and the law of the Jews, while it
is with unwillingness, O most impious man, that

you give praise to the Creator of the world, who
promised to give them all things; who promised
to multiply their race to the ends of the earth,
and to raise them up from the dead with the
same flesh and blood, and who gave inspiration [10]
to their prophets; and, again, you slander Him!
When you feel the force of such considerations,
indeed, you acknowledge that you worship the
same God; but when your teacher Jesus and
the Jewish Moses give contradictory decisions,[11]
you seek another God, instead of Him, and the
Father!" Now, by such statements, this illustrious philosopher Celsus distinctly slanders the
Christians, asserting that, when the Jews press
them hard, they acknowledge the same God as
they do; but that when Jesus legislates differently from Moses, they seek another god instead
of Him. Now, whether we are conversing with
the Jews, or are alone with ourselves, we know
of only one and the same God, whom the Jews
also worshipped of old time, and still profess to
worship as God, and we are guilty of no impiety
towards Him. We do *not* assert, however, that
God will raise men from the dead with the same
flesh and blood, as has been shown in the preceding pages; for we do not maintain that the
natural [12] body, which is sown in corruption, and
in dishonour, and in weakness, will rise again
such as it was sown. On such subjects, however, we have spoken at adequate length in the
foregoing pages.

CHAP. XXX.

He next returns to the subject of the Seven
ruling Demons,[13] whose names are not found
among Christians, but who, I think, are accepted
by the Ophites. We found, indeed, that in the
diagram, which on their account we procured a
sight of, the same order was laid down as that
which Celsus has given. Celsus says that "the
goat was shaped like a lion," not mentioning the
name given him by those who are truly the most
impious of individuals; whereas *we* discovered
that He who is honoured in holy Scripture as
the angel of the Creator is called by this accursed diagram Michael the Lion-like. Again,
Celsus says that the "second in order is a bull;"
whereas the diagram which we possessed made
him to be Suriel, the bull-like. Further, Celsus
termed the third "an amphibious sort of animal,
and one that hissed frightfully;" while the diagram described the third as Raphael, the serpent-like. Moreover, Celsus asserted that the
"fourth had the form of an eagle;" the diagram representing him as Gabriel, the eagle-like.
Again, the "fifth," according to Celsus, "had

---

[1] συνέδριον.
[2] μέτριος τὰ ἤθη.
[3] ἀρχηγοῦ τῶν καλῶν.
[4] Ὀφιανοι: cf. Irenæus, vol. i. pp. 354-358.
[5] τὴν εὐτέλειαν ἀγαπήσας.
[6] ἀπὸ τῆς παντελοῦς ἀκτημοσύνης.
[7] "Euphraten hujus hæresis auctorem solus Origenes tradit."—
Spencer; cf. note in Spencer's edition.
[8] ἀναισθήτου.
[9] Boherellus proposes φῆς for the textual reading φησί.

[10] καὶ τοῖς προφήταις ἐμπνέοντα.
[11] ὅταν δὲ τὰ ἐναντία ὁ σὸς διδάσκαλος Ἰησοῦς, καὶ ὁ Ἰουδαίων
Μωϋσῆς, νομοθετῇ.
[12] ψυχικόν.
[13] Cf. Spencer's note, as quoted in Benedictine edition.

the countenance of a bear;" and this, according to the diagram, was Thauthabaoth,[1] the bear-like. Celsus continues his account, that the "sixth was described as having the face of a dog;" and him the diagram called Erataoth. The "seventh," he adds, "had the countenance of an ass, and was named Thaphabaoth or Onoel;" whereas we discovered that in the diagram he is called Onoel, or Thartharaoth, being somewhat asinine in appearance. We have thought it proper to be exact in stating these matters, that we might not appear to be ignorant of those things which Celsus professed to know, but that we Christians, knowing them better than he, may demonstrate that these are not the words of Christians, but of those who are altogether alienated from salvation, and who neither acknowledge Jesus as Saviour, nor God, nor Teacher, nor Son of God.

CHAP. XXXI.

Moreover, if any one would wish to become acquainted with the artifices of those sorcerers, through which they desire to lead men away by their teaching (as if they possessed the knowledge of certain secret rites), but are not at all successful in so doing, let him listen to the instruction which they receive after passing through what is termed the "fence of wickedness,"[2] — gates which are subjected to the world of ruling spirits.[3] (The following, then, is the manner in which they proceed) : "I salute the one-formed[4] king, the bond of blindness, complete[5] oblivion, the first power, preserved by the spirit of providence and by wisdom, from whom I am sent forth pure, being already part of the light of the son and of the father : grace be with me ; yea, O father, let it be with me." They say also that the beginnings of the Ogdoad[6] are derived from this. In the next place, they are taught to say as follows, while passing through what they call Ialdabaoth : "Thou, O first and seventh, who art born to command with confidence, thou, O Ialdabaoth, who art the rational ruler of a pure mind, and a perfect work to son and father, bearing the symbol of life in the character of a type, and opening to the world the gate which thou didst close against thy kingdom, I pass again in freedom through thy realm. Let grace be with me ; yea, O father, let it be with me." They say, moreover, that the star Phænon[7] is in sym-

pathy[8] with the lion-like ruler. They next imagine that he who has passed through Ialdabaoth and arrived at Iao ought thus to speak : "Thou, O second Iao, who shinest by night,[9] who art the ruler of the secret mysteries of son and father, first prince of death, and portion of the innocent, bearing now mine own beard as symbol, I am ready to pass through thy realm, having strengthened him who is born of thee by the living word. Grace be with me ; father, let it be with me." They next come to Sabaoth, to whom they think the following should be addressed : " O governor of the fifth realm, powerful Sabaoth, defender of the law of thy creatures, who are liberated by thy grace through the help of a more powerful Pentad,[10] admit me, seeing the faultless symbol of their art, preserved by the stamp of an image, a body liberated by a Pentad. Let grace be with me, O father, let grace be with me." And after Sabaoth they come to Astaphæus, to whom they believe the following prayer should be offered : "O Astaphæus, ruler of the third gate, overseer of the first principle of water, look upon me as one of thine initiated,[11] admit me who am purified with the spirit of a virgin, thou who seest the essence of the world. Let grace be with me, O father, let grace be with me." After him comes Aloæus, who is to be thus addressed : " O Aloæus, governor of the second gate, let me pass, seeing I bring to thee the symbol of thy mother, a grace which is hidden by the powers of the realms.[12] Let grace be with me, O father, let it be with me." And last of all they name Horæus, and think that the following prayer ought to be offered to him : "Thou who didst fearlessly overleap the rampart of fire, O Horæus, who didst obtain the government of the first gate, let me pass, seeing thou beholdest the symbol of thine own power, sculptured[13] on the figure of the tree of life, and formed after this image, in the likeness of innocence. Let grace be with me, O father, let grace be with me."

CHAP. XXXII.

The supposed great learning of Celsus, which is composed, however, rather of curious trifles and silly talk than anything else, has made us touch upon these topics, from a wish to show to every one who peruses his treatise and our reply, that we have no lack of information on those subjects, from which he takes occasion to calumniate the Christians, who neither are acquainted with, nor concern themselves about, such mat-

---

[1] "Nescio, an hæresium Scriptores hujus Thauthabaoth, Erataoth, Thaphabaoth, Onoeles, et Thartharaoth, usquam meminerint. Hujus generis vocabula innumera invenies apud Epiphan., *Hær.*, 31, quæ est Valentinianorum, pp. 165-171." — SPENCER.

[2] φραγμὸν κακίας.

[3] πύλας ἀρχόντων αἰῶνι δεδεμένας.

[4] μονότροπον.

[5] λήθην ἀπερίσκεπτον.

[6] Ὀγδοάδος. Cf. Tertullian, *de Præscript. adv. Hæreticos,* cap. xxxiii. (vol. iii. p. 259), and other references in Benedictine ed.

[7] Φαίνων. "Ea, quæ Saturni stella dicitur, Φαίνων que a Græcis dicitur." — CICERO, *de Nat. Deorum,* book ii. c. 20.

[8] συμπαθεῖν.

[9] νυκτοφαῆς.

[10] πεντάδι δυνατωτέρᾳ.

[11] μύστην.

[12] χάριν κρυπτομένην δυνάμεσιν ἐξουσιῶν.

[13] For καταλυθέν Boherellus conjectures καταγλυφθέν, which has been adopted in the translation.

ters. For we, too, desired both to learn and set forth these things, in order that sorcerers might not, under pretext of knowing more than we, delude those who are easily carried away by the glitter[1] of names. And I could have given many more illustrations to show that we are acquainted with the opinions of these deluders,[2] and that we disown them, as being alien to ours, and impious, and not in harmony with the doctrines of true Christians, of which we are ready to make confession even to the death. It must be noticed, too, that those who have drawn up this array of fictions, have, from neither understanding magic, nor discriminating the meaning of holy Scripture, thrown everything into confusion; seeing that they have borrowed from magic the names of Ialdabaoth, and Astaphæus, and Horæus, and from the Hebrew Scriptures him who is termed in Hebrew Iao or Jah, and Sabaoth, and Adonæus, and Eloæus. Now the names taken from the Scriptures are names of one and the same God; which, not being understood by the enemies of God, as even themselves acknowledge, led to their imagining that Iao was a different God, and Sabaoth another, and Adonæus, whom the Scriptures term Adonai, a third besides, and that Eloæus, whom the prophets name in Hebrew Eloi, was also different.

CHAP. XXXIII.

Celsus next relates other fables, to the effect that "certain persons return to the shapes of the archontics,[3] so that some are called lions, others bulls, others dragons, or eagles, or bears, or dogs." We found also in the diagram which we possessed, and which Celsus called the "square pattern," the statements[4] made by these unhappy beings concerning the gates of Paradise. The flaming sword was depicted as the diameter of a flaming circle, and as if mounting guard over the tree of knowledge and of life. Celsus, however, either would not or could not repeat the harangues which, according to the fables of these impious individuals, are represented as spoken at each of the gates by those who pass through them; but this we have done in order to show to Celsus and those who read his treatise, that we know the depth of these unhallowed mysteries,[5] and that they are far removed from the worship which Christians offer up to God.

CHAP. XXXIV.

After finishing the foregoing, and those analogous matters which we ourselves have added,

Celsus continues as follows: "They continue to heap together one thing after another, — discourses of prophets, and circles upon circles, and effluents[6] from an earthly church, and from circumcision; and a power flowing from one Prunicos, a virgin and a living soul; and a heaven slain in order to live, and an earth slaughtered by the sword, and many put to death that they may live, and death ceasing in the world, when the sin of the world is dead; and, again, a narrow way, and gates that open spontaneously. And in all their writings (is mention made) of the tree of life, and a resurrection of the flesh by means[7] of the 'tree,' because, I imagine, their teacher was nailed to a cross, and was a carpenter by craft; so that if he had chanced to have been cast from a precipice, or thrust into a pit, or suffocated by hanging, or had been a leather-cutter, or stone-cutter, or worker in iron, there would have been (invented) a precipice of life beyond the heavens, or a pit of resurrection, or a cord of immortality, or a blessed stone, or an iron of love, or a sacred leather! Now what old woman would not be ashamed to utter such things in a whisper, even when making stories to lull an infant to sleep?" In using such language as this, Celsus appears to me to confuse together matters which he has imperfectly heard. For it seems likely that, even supposing that he had heard a few words traceable to some existing heresy, he did not clearly understand the meaning intended to be conveyed; but heaping the words together, he wished to show before those who knew nothing either of our opinions or of those of the heretics, that he was acquainted with all the doctrines of the Christians. And this is evident also from the foregoing words.

CHAP. XXXV.

It is our practice, indeed, to make use of the words of the prophets, who demonstrate that Jesus is the Christ predicted by them, and who show from the prophetic writings the events in the Gospels regarding Jesus have been fulfilled. But when Celsus speaks of "circles upon circles," (he perhaps borrowed the expression) from the aforementioned heresy, which includes in one circle (which they call the soul of all things, and Leviathan) the seven circles of archontic demons, or perhaps it arises from misunderstanding the preacher, when he says: "The wind goeth in a circle of circles, and returneth again upon its circles."[8] The expression, too, "effluents of an earthly church and of circumcision," was probably taken from the fact that the church on earth was called by some an efflu-

---

[1] φαντασίας.
[2] ἀπατεώνων.
[3] εἰς τὰς ἀρχοντικὰς μορφάς.
[4] Guietus thinks that some word has been omitted here, as ξίφος, which seems very probable.
[5] τὸ τῆς ἀτελέστου τελετῆς πέρας.

[6] ἀπορροίας.
[7] ἀπὸ ξύλου.
[8] Eccles. i. 6 (literally rendered). [Modern science demonstrates this physical truth.]

ent from a heavenly church and a better world; and that the circumcision described in the law was a symbol of the circumcision performed there, in a certain place set apart for purification. The adherents of Valentinus, moreover, in keeping with their system of error,[1] give the name of Prunicos to a certain kind of wisdom, of which they would have the woman afflicted with the twelve years' issue of blood to be the symbol; so that Celsus, who confuses together all sorts of opinions — Greek, Barbarian, and Heretical — having heard of her, asserted that it was a power flowing forth from one Prunicos, a virgin. The "living soul," again, is perhaps mysteriously referred by some of the followers of Valentinus to the being whom they term the psychic[2] creator of the world; or perhaps, in contradistinction to a "dead" soul, the "living" soul is termed by some, not inelegantly,[3] the soul of "him who is saved." I know nothing, however, of a "heaven which is said to be slain," or of an "earth slaughtered by the sword," or of many persons slain in order that they might live; for it is not unlikely that these were coined by Celsus out of his own brain.

eousness," which is an equivalent expression to "the gates of virtue," and these are ready to be opened to him who follows after virtuous pursuits. The subject of the "tree of life" will be more appropriately explained when we interpret the statements in the book of Genesis regarding the paradise planted by God. Celsus, moreover, has often mocked at the subject of a resurrection, — a doctrine which he did not comprehend; and on the present occasion, not satisfied with what he has formerly said, he adds, "And there is said to be a resurrection of the flesh by means of the tree;" not understanding, I think, the symbolical expression, that "through the tree came death, and through the tree comes life,"[9] because death was in Adam, and life in Christ. He next scoffs at the "tree," assailing it on two grounds, and saying, "For this reason is the tree introduced, either because our teacher was nailed to a cross, or because he was a carpenter by trade;" not observing that the tree of life is mentioned in the Mosaic writings, and being blind also to this, that in none of the Gospels current in the Churches[10] is Jesus Himself ever described as being a carpenter.[11]

CHAP. XXXVI.

We would say, moreover, that death ceases in the world when the sin of the world dies, referring the saying to the mystical words of the apostle, which run as follows: "When He shall have put all enemies under His feet, then the last enemy that shall be destroyed is death."[4] And also: "When this corruptible shall have put on incorruption, then shall be brought to pass the saying that is written, Death is swallowed up in victory."[5] The "strait descent,"[6] again, may perhaps be referred by those who hold the doctrine of transmigration of souls to that view of things. And it is not incredible that the gates which are said to open spontaneously are referred obscurely by some to the words, "Open to me the gates of righteousness, that I may go into them, and praise the Lord; this gate of the Lord, into it the righteous shall enter;"[7] and again, to what is said in the ninth psalm, "Thou that liftest me up from the gates of death, that I may show forth all Thy praise in the gates of the daughter of Zion."[8] The Scripture further gives the name of "gates of death" to those sins which lead to destruction, as it terms, on the contrary, good actions the "gates of Zion." So also "the gates of right-

CHAP. XXXVII.

Celsus, moreover, thinks that we have invented this "tree of life" to give an allegorical meaning to the cross; and in consequence of his error upon this point, he adds: "If he had happened to be cast down a precipice, or shoved into a pit, or suffocated by hanging, there would have been invented a precipice of life far beyond the heavens, or a pit of resurrection, or a cord of immortality." And again: "If the 'tree of life' were an invention, because he — Jesus — (is reported) to have been a carpenter, it would follow that if he had been a leather-cutter, something would have been said about holy leather; or had he been a stone-cutter, about a blessed stone; or if a worker in iron, about an iron of love." Now, who does not see at once[12] the paltry nature of his charge, in thus calumniating men whom he professed to convert on the ground of their being deceived? And after these remarks, he goes on to speak in a way quite in harmony with the tone of those who have invented the fictions of lion-like, and ass-headed, and serpent-like ruling angels,[13] and other similar absurdities, but which does not affect those who belong to the Church. Of a truth, even a drunken old woman would be ashamed to chaunt or whisper

---

[1] κατὰ τὴν πεπλανημένην ἑαυτῶν σοφίαν.
[2] ψυχικὸν δημιουργόν.
[3] οὐκ ἀγεννῶς.
[4] Cf. 1 Cor. xv. 25, 26.
[5] Cf. 1 Cor. xv. 54; cf. Hos. xiii. 14.
[6] κάθοδον στενήν.
[7] Cf. Ps. cxviii. 19, 20.
[8] Cf. Ps. ix. 13, 14.

[9] Cf. 1 Cor. xv. 22.
[10] [See note supra, p. 582. S.]
[11] Cf., however, Mark vi. 3. [Some MSS., though not of much value, have the reading here (Mark vi. 3), "Is not this the carpenter's son, the son of Mary?" Origen seems to have so read the evangelist. See Alford, in loc. S.]
[12] αὐτόθεν.
[13] ἄρχοντας.

to an infant, in order to lull him to sleep, any such fables as those have done who invented the beings with asses' heads, and the harangues, so to speak, which are delivered at each of the gates. But Celsus is not acquainted with the doctrines of the members of the Church, which very few have been able to comprehend, even of those who have devoted all their lives, in conformity with the command of Jesus, to the searching of the Scriptures, and have laboured to investigate the meaning of the sacred books, to a greater degree than Greek philosophers in their efforts to attain a so-called wisdom.

CHAP. XXXVIII.

Our noble (friend), moreover, not satisfied with the objections which he has drawn from the diagram, desires, in order to strengthen his accusations against us, who have nothing in common with it, to introduce certain other charges, which he adduces from the same (heretics), but yet as if they were from a different source. His words are : "And that is not the least of their marvels, for there are between the upper circles — those that are above the heavens — certain inscriptions of which they give the interpretation, and among others two words especially, 'a greater and a less,' which they refer to Father and Son." [1] Now, in the diagram referred to, we found the greater and the lesser circle, upon the diameter of which was inscribed "Father and Son ; " and between the greater circle (in which the lesser was contained) and another [2] composed of two circles, — the outer one of which was yellow, and the inner blue, — a barrier inscribed in the shape of a hatchet. And above it, a short circle, close to the greater of the two former, having the inscription "Love ; " and lower down, one touching the same circle, with the word "Life." And on the second circle, which was intertwined with and included two other circles, another figure, like a rhomboid, (entitled) "The foresight of wisdom." And within their point of common section was "The nature of wisdom." And above their point of common section was a circle, on which was inscribed "Knowledge ; " and lower down another, on which was the inscription, "Understanding." We have introduced these matters into our reply to Celsus, to show to our readers that we know better than he, and not by mere report, those things, even although we also disapprove of them. Moreover, if those who pride themselves upon such matters profess also a kind of magic and sorcery, — which, in their opinion, is the summit of wisdom, — we,

on the other hand, make no affirmation about it, seeing we never have discovered anything of the kind. Let Celsus, however, who has been already often convicted of false witness and irrational accusations, see whether he is not guilty of falsehood in these also, or whether he has not extracted and introduced into his treatise, statements taken from the writings of those who are foreigners and strangers to our Christian faith.

CHAP. XXXIX.

In the next place, speaking of those who employ the arts of magic and sorcery, and who invoke the barbarous names of demons, he remarks that such persons act like those who, in reference to the same things,[3] perform marvels before those who are ignorant that the names of demons among the Greeks are different from what they are among the Scythians. He then quotes a passage from Herodotus, stating that " Apollo is called Gongosyrus by the Scythians ; Poseidon, Thagimasada ; Aphrodite, Argimpasan ; Hestia, Tabiti." [4] Now, he who has the capacity can inquire whether in these matters Celsus and Herodotus are not both wrong ; for the Scythians do not understand the same thing as the Greeks, in what relates to those beings which are deemed to be gods. For how is it credible [5] that Apollo should be called Gongosyrus by the Scythians ? I do not suppose that Gongosyrus, when transferred into the Greek language, yields the same etymology as Apollo ; or that Apollo, in the dialect of the Scythians, has the signification of Gongosyrus. Nor has any such assertion hitherto been made regarding the other names,[6] for the Greeks took occasion from different circumstances and etymologies to give to those who are by them deemed gods the names which they bear ; and the Scythians, again, from another set of circumstances ; and the same also was the case with the Persians, or Indians, or Ethiopians, or Libyans, or with those who delight to bestow names (from fancy), and who do not abide by the just and pure idea of the Creator of all things. Enough, however, has been said by us in the preceding pages, where we wished to demonstrate that Sabaoth and Zeus were not the same deity, and where also we made some remarks, derived from the holy Scriptures, regarding the different dialects. We willingly, then, pass by these points, on which Celsus would make us repeat ourselves. In the next place, again, mixing up together matters which belong to magic and sorcery, and referring them perhaps to no one, — because of the non-existence

---

[1] ἄλλα τε, καὶ δύο ἄττα, μεῖζον τε καὶ μικρότερον υἱοῦ καὶ πατρός.

[2] For ἄλλους, the textual reading, Gelenius, with the approval of Boherellus, proposes καὶ ἄλλου συγκειμένου, which has been followed in the translation.

[3] ἐπὶ τοῖς αὐτοῖς ὑποκειμένοις.

[4] Cf. Herodot., iv. 59.

[5] ποῖα γὰρ πιθανότης.

[6] For the textual reading, οὔπω δὲ οὐδὲ περὶ τῶν λοιπῶν ταὐτόν τι ἐρεῖ, Boherellus conjectures εἴρηται, which has been adopted in the translation.

of any who practise magic under pretence of a worship of this character, — and yet, perhaps, having in view some who *do* employ such practices in the presence of the simple (that they may have the appearance of acting by divine power), he adds : "What need to number up all those who have taught methods of purification, or expiatory hymns, or spells for averting evil, or (the making of) images, or resemblances of demons, or the various sorts of antidotes against poison (to be found) [1] in clothes, or in numbers, or stones, or plants, or roots, or generally in all kinds of things?" In respect to these matters, reason does not require us to offer any defence, since we are not liable in the slightest degree to suspicions of such a nature.

CHAP. XL.

After these things, Celsus appears to me to act like those who, in their intense hatred of the Christians, maintain, in the presence of those who are utterly ignorant of the Christian faith, that they have actually ascertained that Christians devour the flesh of infants, and give themselves without restraint to sexual intercourse with their women. Now, as these statements have been condemned as falsehoods invented against the Christians, and this admission made by the multitude and those altogether aliens to our faith ; so would the following statements of Celsus be found to be calumnies invented against the Christians, where he says that " he has seen in the hands of certain presbyters belonging to our faith [2] barbarous books, containing the names and marvellous doings of demons ; " asserting further, that " these presbyters of our faith professed to do no good, but all that was calculated to injure human beings." Would, indeed, that all that is said by Celsus against the Christians was of such a nature as to be refuted by the multitude, who have ascertained by experience that such things are untrue, seeing that most of them have lived as neighbours with the Christians, and have not even heard of the existence of any such alleged practices !

CHAP. XLI.

In the next place, as if he had forgotten that it was his object to write against the Christians, he says that, " having become acquainted with one Dionysius, an Egyptian musician, the latter told him, with respect to magic arts, that it was only over the uneducated and men of corrupt morals that they had any power, while on philosophers they were unable to produce any effect, because they were careful to observe a healthy manner of life." If, now, it had been our purpose to treat of magic, we could have added a few remarks in addition to what we have already said on this topic ; but since it is only the more important matters which we have to notice in answer to Celsus, we shall say of magic, that any one who chooses to inquire whether philosophers were ever led captive by it or not, can read what has been written by Moiragenes regarding the memoirs of the magician and philosopher Apollonius of Tyana, in which this individual, who is not a Christian, but a philosopher, asserts that some philosophers of no mean note were won over by the magic power possessed by Apollonius, and resorted to him as a sorcerer ; and among these, I think, he especially mentioned Euphrates and a certain Epicurean. Now *we*, on the other hand, affirm, and have learned by experience, that they who worship the God of all things in conformity with the Christianity which comes by Jesus, and who live according to His Gospel, using night and day, continuously and becomingly, the prescribed prayers, are not carried away either by magic or demons. For verily " the angel of the LORD encamps round about them that fear Him, and delivereth them " [3] from all evil ; and the angels of the little ones in the Church, who are appointed to watch over them, are said always to behold the face of their Father who is in heaven,[4] whatever be the meaning of " face " or of " behold."

CHAP. XLII.

After these matters, Celsus brings the following charges against us from another quarter : " Certain most impious errors," he says, " are committed by them, due to their extreme ignorance, in which they have wandered away from the meaning of the divine enigmas, creating an adversary to God, the devil, and naming him in the Hebrew tongue, Satan. Now, of a truth, such statements are altogether of mortal invention,[5] and not even proper to be repeated, viz., that the mighty God, in His desire to confer good upon men, has yet one counterworking Him, and is helpless. The Son of God, it follows, is vanquished by the devil ; and being punished by him, teaches us also to despise the punishments which he inflicts, telling us beforehand that Satan, after appearing to men as He Himself had done, will exhibit great and marvellous works, claiming for himself the glory of God, but that those who wish to keep him at a distance ought to pay no attention to these works of Satan, but to place their faith in Him alone. Such statements are manifestly the words of a

---

[1] For αἰσθητῶν, Lommatzsch adopts the conjecture of Boherellus, approved by Ruæus, ἐσθῆτων.
[2] δόξης.

[3] Cf. Ps. xxxiv. 7.
[4] Cf. Matt. xviii. 10.
[5] θνητά. Instead of this reading, Guietus conjectures πτηκτά, which is approved of by Ruæus.

deluder, planning and manœuvring against those who are opposed to his views, and who rank themselves against them." In the next place, desiring to point out the "enigmas," our mistakes regarding which lead to the introduction of our views concerning Satan, he continues : " The ancients allude obscurely to a certain war among the gods, Heraclitus speaking thus of it : ' If one must say that there is a general war and discord, and that all things are done and administered in strife.' Pherecydes, again, who is much older than Heraclitus, relates a myth of one army drawn up in hostile array against another, and names Kronos as the leader of the one, and Ophioneus of the other, and recounts their challenges and struggles, and mentions that agreements were entered into between them, to the end that whichever party should fall into the Ocean ¹ should be held as vanquished, while those who had expelled and conquered them should have possession of heaven. The mysteries relating to the Titans and Giants also had some such (symbolical) meaning, as well as the Egyptian mysteries of Typhon, and Horus, and Osiris." After having made such statements, and not having got over the difficulty ² as to the way in which these accounts contain a higher view of things, while our accounts are erroneous copies of them, he continues his abuse of us, remarking that " these are not like the stories which are related of a devil, or demon, or, as he remarks with more truth, of a man who is an impostor, who wishes to establish an opposite doctrine." And in the same way he understands Homer, as if he referred obscurely to matters similar to those mentioned by Heraclitus, and Pherecydes, and the originators of the mysteries about the Titans and Giants, in those words which Hephæstus addresses to Hera, as follows : —

"Once in your cause I felt his matchless might,
Hurled headlong downward from the ethereal height." ³

And in those of Zeus to Hera : —

"Hast thou forgot, when, bound and fix'd on high,
From the vast concave of the spangled sky,
I hung thee trembling in a golden chain,
And all the raging gods opposed in vain?
Headlong I hurled them from the Olympian hall,
Stunn'd in the whirl, and breathless with the fall." ⁴

Interpreting, moreover, the words of Homer, he adds : "The words of Zeus addressed to Hera are the words of God addressed to matter ; and the words addressed to matter obscurely signify that the matter which at the beginning was in a state of discord (with God), was taken by Him, and bound together and arranged under laws,

which may be analogically compared to chains ; ⁵ and that by way of chastising the demons who create disorder in it, he hurls them down headlong to this lower world." These words of Homer, he alleges, were so understood by Pherecydes, when he said that beneath that region is the region of Tartarus, which is guarded by the Harpies and Tempest, daughters of Boreas, and to which Zeus banishes any one of the gods who becomes disorderly. With the same ideas also are closely connected the *peplos* of Athena, which is beheld by all in the procession of the *Panathenæa*. For it is manifest from this, he continues, that a motherless and unsullied demon ⁶ has the mastery over the daring of the Giants. While accepting, moreover, the fictions of the Greeks, he continues to heap against us such accusations as the following, viz., that " the Son of God is punished by the devil, and teaches us that we also, when punished by him, ought to endure it. Now these statements are altogether ridiculous. For it is the devil, I think, who ought rather to be punished, and those human beings who are calumniated by him ought not to be threatened with chastisement."

CHAP. XLIII.

Mark now, whether he who charges us with having committed errors of the most impious kind, and with having wandered away from the (true meaning) of the divine enigmas, is not himself clearly in error, from not observing that in the writings of Moses, which are much older not merely than Heraclitus and Pherecydes, but even than Homer, mention is made of this wicked one, and of his having fallen from heaven. For the serpent ⁷ — from whom the Ophioneus spoken of by Pherecydes is derived — having become the cause of man's expulsion from the divine Paradise, obscurely shadows forth something similar, having deceived the woman ⁸ by a promise of divinity and of greater blessings ; and her example is said to have been followed also by the man. And, further, who else could the destroying angel mentioned in the Exodus of Moses ⁹ be, than he who was the author of destruction to them that obeyed him, and did not withstand his wicked deeds, nor struggle against them? Moreover (the goat), which in the book of Leviticus ¹⁰ is sent away (into the wilderness), and which in the Hebrew language is named Azazel, was none other than this ; and it was necessary to send it away into the desert, and to treat it as an expiatory sacrifice, because

---

¹ Ὠγηνόν, i.e., in Oceanum, Hesych.; Ὠγήν, ὠκεανός, Suid.
² καὶ μὴ παραμυθησάμενος.
³ Cf. *Iliad*, i. 590 (Pope's translation).
⁴ Cf. *Iliad*, xv. 18-24 (Pope's translation).

⁵ ἀναλογίαις τισὶ συνέδησε καὶ ἐκόσμησεν ὁ Θεός.
⁶ ἀμήτωρ τις καὶ ἄχραντος δαίμων.
⁷ Cf. Gen. iii.
⁸ τὸ θηλύτερον γένος.
⁹ Cf. Ex. xii. 23.
¹⁰ Cf. Lev. xvi. 8.

on it the lot fell. For all who belong to the "worse" part, on account of their wickedness, being opposed to those who are God's heritage, are deserted by God.[1] Nay, with respect to the sons of Belial in the book of Judges,[2] whose sons are they said to be, save his, on account of their wickedness? And besides all these instances, in the book of Job, which is older even than Moses himself,[3] the devil is distinctly described as presenting himself before God,[4] and asking for power against Job, that he might involve him in trials[5] of the most painful kind ; the first of which consisted in the loss of all his goods and of his children, and the second in afflicting the whole body of Job with the so-called disease of elephantiasis.[6] I pass by what might be quoted from the Gospels regarding the devil who tempted the Saviour, that I may not appear to quote in reply to Celsus from more recent writings on this question. In the last (chapter)[7] also of Job, in which the Lord utters to Job amid tempest and clouds what is recorded in the book which bears his name, there are not a few things referring to the serpent. I have not yet mentioned the passages in Ezekiel,[8] where he speaks, as it were, of Pharaoh, or Nebuchadnezzar, or the prince of Tyre ; or those in Isaiah,[9] where lament is made for the king of Babylon, from which not a little might be learned concerning evil, as to the nature of its origin and generation, and as to how it derived its existence from some who had lost their wings,[10] and who had followed him who was the first to lose his own.

CHAP. XLIV.

For it is impossible that the good which is the result of accident, or of communication, should be like that good which comes by nature ; and yet the former will never be lost by him who, so to speak, partakes of the "living" bread with a view to his own preservation. But if it should fail any one, it must be through his own fault, in being slothful to partake of this "living bread" and "genuine drink," by means of which the wings, nourished and watered, are fitted for their purpose, even according to the saying of Solomon, the wisest of men, concerning the truly rich man, that "he made to himself wings like an eagle, and returns to the house of his patron."[11] For it became God, who

knows how to turn to proper account even those who in their wickedness have apostatized from Him, to place wickedness of this sort in some part of the universe, and to appoint a training-school of virtue, wherein those must exercise themselves who would desire to recover in a "lawful manner"[12] the possession (which they had lost) ; in order that being tested, like gold in the fire, by the wickedness of these, and having exerted themselves to the utmost to prevent anything base injuring their rational nature, they may appear deserving of an ascent to divine things, and may be elevated by the Word to the blessedness which is above all things, and so to speak, to the very summit of goodness. Now he who in the Hebrew language is named Satan, and by some Satanas — as being more in conformity with the genius of the Greek language — signifies, when translated into Greek, "adversary." But every one who prefers vice and a vicious life, is (because acting in a manner contrary to virtue) Satanas, that is, an "adversary" to the Son of God, who is righteousness, and truth, and wisdom.[13] With more propriety, however, is *he* called "adversary," who was the first among those that were living a peaceful and happy life to lose his wings, and to fall from blessedness ; he who, according to Ezekiel, walked faultlessly in all his ways, "until iniquity was found in him,"[14] and who being the "seal of resemblance" and the "crown of beauty" in the paradise of God, being filled as it were with good things, fell into destruction, in accordance with the word which said to him in a mystic sense : "Thou hast fallen into destruction, and shalt not abide for ever."[15] We have ventured somewhat rashly to make these few remarks, although in so doing we have added nothing of importance to this treatise. If any one, however, who has leisure for the examination of the sacred writings, should collect together from all sources and form into one body of doctrine what is recorded concerning the origin of evil, and the manner of its dissolution, he would see that the views of Moses and the prophets regarding Satan had not been even dreamed of either by Celsus or any one of those whose soul had been dragged down, and torn away from God, and from right views of Him, and from His word, by this wicked demon.

CHAP. XLV.

But since Celsus rejects the statements concerning Antichrist, as it is termed, having neither read what is said of him in the book of Daniel[16]

---

1 ἐναντίοι ὄντες τοῖς ἀπὸ τοῦ κλήρου τοῦ Θεοῦ, ἔρημοί εἰσι Θεοῦ.
2 [Judg. xix. 22. S.]
3 [See the elaborate article on the book of Job, by Canon Cook, in Dr. Smith's *Dictionary of the Bible*, vol. i. pp. 1087-1100. S.].
4 Cf. Job i., ii.
5 περιστάσεσι.
6 ἀγρίῳ ἐλέφαντι.
7 Cf. Job xl. 20.
8 Cf. Ezek. xxxii. 1-28.
9 Isa. xiv. 4 sqq.
10 πτερορρυησάντων. Cf. *supra*, bk. iv. cap. xl. p. 516.
11 Cf. Prov. xxiii. 5. [See Neander's *History of the Church*, vol. ii. p. 299, with Rose's note. S.]

12 Cf. 2 Tim. ii. 5.
13 Cf. 1 Cor. i. 30.
14 Cf. Ezek. xxviii. 15.
15 Cf. Ezek. xxviii. 19.
16 Cf. Dan. viii. 23.

nor in the writings of Paul,[1] nor what the Saviour in the Gospels[2] has predicted about his coming, we must make a few remarks upon this subject also; because, "as faces do not resemble faces,"[3] so also neither do men's "hearts" resemble one another. It is certain, then, that there will be diversities amongst the hearts of men, — those which are inclined to virtue not being all modelled and shaped towards it in the same or like degree; while others, through neglect of virtue, rush to the opposite extreme. And amongst the latter are some in whom evil is deeply engrained, and others in whom it is less deeply rooted. Where is the absurdity, then, in holding that there exist among men, so to speak, two extremes,[4] — the one of virtue, and the other of its opposite; so that the perfection of virtue dwells in the man who realizes the ideal given in Jesus, from whom there flowed to the human race so great a conversion, and healing, and amelioration, while the opposite extreme is in the man who embodies the notion of him that is named Antichrist? For God, comprehending all things by means of His foreknowledge, and foreseeing what consequences would result from both of these, wished to make these known to mankind by His prophets, that those who understand their words might be familiarized with the good, and be on their guard against its opposite. It was proper, moreover, that the one of these extremes, and the best of the two, should be styled the Son of God, on account of His pre-eminence; and the other, who is diametrically opposite, be termed the son of the wicked demon, and of Satan, and of the devil. And, in the next place, since evil is specially characterized by its diffusion, and attains its greatest height when it simulates the appearance of the good, for that reason are signs, and marvels, and lying miracles found to accompany evil, through the co-operation of its father the devil. For, far surpassing the help which these demons give to jugglers (who deceive men for the basest of purposes), is the aid which the devil himself affords in order to deceive the human race. Paul, indeed, speaks of him who is called Antichrist, describing, though with a certain reserve,[5] both the manner, and time, and cause of his coming to the human race. And notice whether his language on this subject is not most becoming, and undeserving of being treated with even the slightest degree of ridicule.

CHAP. XLVI.

It is thus that the apostle expresses himself: "We beseech you, brethren, by the coming of our Lord Jesus Christ, and by our gathering together unto Him, that ye be not soon shaken in mind, or be troubled, neither by word, nor by spirit, nor by letter as from us, as that the day of the Lord is at hand. Let no man deceive you by any means: for *that day shall not come*, except there come a falling away first, and that man of sin be revealed, the son of perdition; who opposeth and exalteth himself above all that is called God, or that is worshipped; so that he sitteth in the temple of God, showing himself that he is God. Remember ye not, that, when I was yet with you, I told you these things? And now ye know what withholdeth, that he might be revealed in his time. For the mystery of iniquity doth already work: only he who now letteth *will let*, until he be taken out of the way. And then shall that Wicked be revealed, whom the Lord shall consume with the spirit of His mouth, and shall destroy with the brightness of His coming: *even him*, whose coming is after the working of Satan, with all power, and signs, and lying wonders, and with all deceivableness of unrighteousness in them that perish; because they received not the love of the truth, that they might be saved. And for this cause God shall send them strong delusion, that they should believe a lie; that they all might be damned who believed not the truth, but had pleasure in unrighteousness."[6] To explain each particular here referred to does not belong to our present purpose. The prophecy also regarding Antichrist is stated in the book of Daniel, and is fitted to make an intelligent and candid reader admire the words as truly divine and prophetic; for in them are mentioned the things relating to the coming kingdom, beginning with the times of Daniel, and continuing to the destruction of the world. And any one who chooses may read it. Observe, however, whether the prophecy regarding Antichrist be not as follows: "And at the latter time of their kingdom, when their sins are coming to the full, there shall arise a king, bold in countenance, and understanding riddles. And his power shall be great, and he shall destroy wonderfully, and prosper, and practise; and shall destroy mighty men, and the holy people. And the yoke of his chain shall prosper: there is craft in his hand, and he shall magnify himself in his heart, and by craft shall destroy many; and he shall stand up for the destruction of many, and shall crush them as eggs in his hand."[7] What is stated by Paul in the words quoted from him, where he says, "so that he sitteth in the temple of God, showing himself that he is God,"[8] is in Daniel referred to in the following fashion: "And on the temple shall be

---

[1] Cf. 2 Thess. ii. 3, 4.
[2] Cf. Matt. xxiv. 4, 5.
[3] Cf. Prov. xxvii. 19.
[4] ἀκρότητας.
[5] μετά τινος ἐπικρύψεως. Cf. 2 Thess. ii. 9.

[6] 2 Thess. ii. 1-12.
[7] Cf. Dan. viii. 23-25 (LXX.).
[8] Cf. 2 Thess. ii. 4.

he abomination of desolations, and at the end
of the time an end shall be put to the desola-
ion."[1] So many, out of a greater number of
passages, have I thought it right to adduce, that
he hearer may understand in some slight degree
he meaning of holy Scripture, when it gives us
information concerning the devil and Antichrist;
and being satisfied with what we have quoted for
his purpose, let us look at another of the charges
of Celsus, and reply to it as we best may.

CHAP. XLVII.

Celsus, after what has been said, goes on as
follows: "I can tell how the very thing occurred,
viz., that they should call him 'Son of God.'
Men of ancient times termed this world, as being
born of God, both his child and his son.[2] Both
the one and other 'Son of God,' then, greatly
resembled each other." He is therefore of opinion that we employed the expression "Son of
God," having perverted[3] what is said of the
world, as being born of God, and being His
" Son," and " a God." For he was unable so to
consider the times of Moses and the prophets,
as to see that the Jewish prophets predicted generally that there was a " Son of God " long before
the Greeks and those men of ancient time of
whom Celsus speaks. Nay, he would not even
quote the passage in the letters of Plato, to which
we referred in the preceding pages, concerning
Him who so beautifully arranged this world, as
being the Son of God; lest he too should be
compelled by Plato, whom he often mentions
with respect, to admit that the architect of this
world *is* the Son of God, and that His Father is
the first God and Sovereign Ruler over all things.[4]
Nor is it at all wonderful if we maintain that the
soul of Jesus is made one with so great a Son
of God through the highest union with Him, being no longer in a state of separation from Him.
For the sacred language of holy Scripture knows
of other things also, which, although " dual " in
their own nature, are considered to be, and really
are, " one " in respect to one another. It is
said of husband and wife, " They are no longer
twain, but one flesh; "[5] and of the perfect man,
and of him who is joined to the true Lord,
Word, and Wisdom, and Truth, that " he who is
joined to the Lord is one spirit."[6] And if he
who " is joined to the Lord is one spirit," who
has been joined to the Lord, the Very Word,
and Wisdom, and Truth, and Righteousness, in
a more intimate union, or even in a manner at all

approaching to it than the soul of Jesus? And
if this be so, then the soul of Jesus and God the
Word — the first-born of every creature — are
no longer two, (but one).

CHAP. XLVIII.

In the next place, when the philosophers of
the Porch, who assert that the virtue of God and
man is the same, maintain that the God who is
over all things is not happier than *their* wise man,
but that the happiness of both is equal, Celsus
neither ridicules nor scoffs at their opinion. If,
however, holy Scripture says that the perfect
man is joined to and made one with the Very
Word by means of virtue, so that we infer that
the soul of Jesus is not separated from the first-
born of all creation, he laughs at Jesus being
called " Son of God," not observing what is said
of Him with a secret and mystical signification
in the holy Scriptures. But that we may win
over to the reception of our views those who are
willing to accept the inferences which flow from
our doctrines, and to be benefited thereby, we
say that the holy Scriptures declare the body of
Christ, animated by the Son of God, to be the
whole Church of God, and the members of this
body — considered as a whole — to consist of
those who are believers; since, as a soul vivifies
and moves the body, which of itself has not the
natural power of motion like a living being, so
the Word, arousing and moving the whole body,
the Church, to befitting action, awakens, moreover, each individual member belonging to the
Church, so that they do nothing apart from the
Word. Since all this, then, follows by a train of
reasoning not to be depreciated, where is the
difficulty in maintaining that, as the *soul* of Jesus
is joined in a perfect and inconceivable manner
with the very Word, so the person of Jesus, generally speaking,[7] is not separated from the only-
begotten and first-born of all creation, and is not
a different being from Him? But enough here
on this subject.

CHAP. XLIX.

Let us notice now what follows, where, expressing in a single word his opinion regarding
the Mosaic cosmogony, without offering, however,
a single argument in its support, he finds fault
with it, saying: " Moreover, their cosmogony is
extremely silly."[8] Now, if he had produced
some credible proofs of its silly character, we
should have endeavoured to answer them; but it
does not appear to me reasonable that I should
be called upon to demonstrate, in answer to his
mere *assertion*, that it is *not* " silly." If any one,
however, wishes to see the reasons which led us
to accept the Mosaic account, and the arguments

---

[1] Cf. Dan. ix. 27 (LXX.).
[2] παῖδά τε αὐτοῦ καὶ ἤθεον.
[3] παραποιήσαντας.
[4] [See Dr. Burton's learned discussion as to the Logos of Plato,
and the connection of Plato's doctrines with the Gospel of the Son of
God: *Bampton Lectures*, pp. 211–223, 537–547. See also Fisher's
Beginnings of Christianity, p. 147 (1877). S.]
[5] Cf. Gen. ii. 24.
[6] Cf. 1 Cor. vi. 17.

[7] ἀπαξαπλῶς.
[8] μάλα εὐηθική.

by which it may be defended, he may read what we have written upon Genesis, from the beginning of the book up to the passage, "And this is the book of the generation of men," [1] where we have tried to show from the holy Scriptures themselves what the "heaven" was which was created in the beginning; and what the "earth," and the "invisible part of the earth," and that which was "without form;" [2] and what the "deep" was, and the "darkness" that was upon it; and what the "water" was, and the "Spirit of God" which was "borne over it;" and what the "light" which was created, and what the "firmament," as distinct from the "heaven" which was created in the beginning; and so on with the other subjects that follow. Celsus has also expressed his opinion that the narrative of the creation of man is "exceedingly silly," without stating any proofs, or endeavouring to answer our arguments; for he had no evidence, in my judgment, which was fitted to overthrow the statement that "man has been made in the image of God." [3] He does not even understand the meaning of the "Paradise" that was planted by God, and of the life which man first led in it; and of that which resulted from accident, [4] when man was cast forth on account of his sin, and was settled opposite the Paradise of delight. Now, as he asserts that these are silly statements, let him turn his attention not merely to each one of them (in general), but to this in particular, "He placed the cherubim, and the flaming sword, which turned every way, to keep the way of the tree of life," [5] and say whether Moses wrote these words with no serious object in view, but in the spirit of the writers of the old Comedy, who have sportively related that "Prœtus slew Bellerophon," and that "Pegasus came from Arcadia." Now their object was to create laughter in composing such stories; whereas it is incredible that he who left behind him laws [6] for a whole nation, regarding which he wished to persuade his subjects that they were given by God, should have written words so little to the purpose, [7] and have said without any meaning, "He placed the cherubim, and the flaming sword, which turned every way, to keep the way of the tree of life," or made any other statement regarding the creation of man, which is the subject of philosophic investigation by the Hebrew sages.

CHAP. L.

In the next place, Celsus, after heaping together, simply as mere assertions, the varying opinions of some of the ancients regarding the world, and the origin of man, alleges that "Moses and the prophets, who have left to us our books, not knowing at all what the nature of the world is, and of man, have woven together a web of sheer nonsense." [8] If he had shown, now, how it appeared to him that the holy Scriptures contained "sheer nonsense," we should have tried to demolish the arguments which appeared to him to establish their nonsensical character; but on the present occasion, following his own example, we also sportively give it as our opinion that Celsus, knowing nothing at all about the nature of the meaning and language of the prophets, [9] composed a work which contained "sheer nonsense," and boastfully gave it the title of a "true discourse." And since he makes the statements about the "days of creation" ground of accusation, — as if he understood them clearly and correctly, some of which elapsed before the creation of light and heaven, and sun, and moon, and stars, and some of them after the creation of these, — we shall only make this observation, that Moses must then have forgotten that he had said a little before, "that in six days the creation of the world had been finished," and that in consequence of this act of forgetfulness he subjoins to these words the following: "This is the book of the creation of man, in the day when God made the heaven and the earth!" But it is not in the least credible, that after what he had said respecting the six days, Moses should immediately add, without a special meaning, the words, "in the day that God made the heavens and the earth;" and if any one thinks that these words may be referred to the statement, "In the beginning God made the heaven and the earth," let him observe that before the words, "Let there be light, and there was light," and these, "God called the light day," it has been stated that "in the beginning God made the heaven and the earth."

CHAP. LI.

On the present occasion, however, it is not our object to enter into an explanation of the subject of intelligent and sensible beings, [10] nor of the manner in which the different kinds [11] of days were allotted to both sorts, nor to investigate the details which belong to the subject, for we should need whole treatises for the exposition of the Mosaic cosmogony; and that work we had already performed, to the best of our ability, a considerable time before the commencement of this answer to Celsus, when we discussed with such measure of capacity as we then possessed

---

1 Cf. Gen. v. 1.
2 ἀκατασκεύαστον.
3 Cf. Gen. i. 26.
4 τὴν ἐκ περιστάσεως γενομένην.
5 Gen. iii. 24.
6 γραφάς.
7 ἀπρόσλογα.

8 συνθεῖναι λῆρον βαθύν.
9 ὅτι τίς ποτέ ἐστιν ἡ φύσις τοῦ νοῦ, καὶ τοῦ ἐν τοῖς προφήταις λόγου.
10 περὶ νοητῶν καὶ αἰσθητῶν.
11 αἱ φύσεις τῶν ἡμερῶν.

the question of the Mosaic cosmogony of the six days. We must keep in mind, however, that the Word promises to the righteous through the mouth of Isaiah, that days will come [1] when not the sun, but the LORD Himself, will be to them an everlasting light, and God will be their glory.[2] And it is from misunderstanding, I think, some pestilent heresy which gave an erroneous interpretation to the words, "Let there be light," as if they were the expression of a *wish*[3] merely on the part of the Creator, that Celsus made the remark : "The Creator did not borrow light from above, like those persons who kindle their lamps at those of their neighbours." Misunderstanding, moreover, another impious heresy, he has said : "If, indeed, there did exist an accursed god opposed to the great God, who did this contrary to his approval, why did he lend him the light?" So far are we from offering a defence of such puerilities, that we desire, on the contrary, distinctly to arraign the statements of these heretics as erroneous, and to undertake to refute, not those of their opinions with which we are *unacquainted*, as Celsus does, but those of which we have attained an accurate knowledge, derived in part from the statements of their own adherents, and partly from a careful perusal of their writings.

CHAP. LII.

Celsus proceeds as follows : "With regard to the origin of the world and its destruction, whether it is to be regarded as uncreated and indestructible, or as created indeed, but not destructible, or the reverse, I at present say nothing." For this reason we too say nothing on these points, as the work in hand does not require it. Nor do we allege that the Spirit of the universal God mingled itself in things here below as in things alien to itself,[4] as might appear from the expression, "The Spirit of God moved upon the water ; " nor do we assert that certain wicked devices directed against His Spirit, as if by a different creator from the great God, and which were tolerated by the Supreme Divinity, needed to be completely frustrated. And, accordingly, I have nothing further to say to those [5] who utter such absurdities ; nor to Celsus, who does not refute them with ability. For he ought either *not* to have mentioned such matters at all, or else, in keeping with that character for philanthropy which he assumes, have carefully set them forth, and then endeavoured to rebut these impious assertions. Nor have we ever heard that the great God, after giving his spirit to the creator, demands it back again. Proceeding next

foolishly to assail these impious assertions, he asks : "What god gives anything with the intention of demanding it back? For it is the mark of a needy person to demand back (what he has given), whereas God stands in need of nothing." To this he adds, as if saying something clever against certain parties : "Why, when he lent (his spirit), was he ignorant that he was lending it to an evil being?" He asks, further : "Why does he pass without notice [6] a wicked creator who was counter-working his purposes?"

CHAP. LIII.

In the next place, mixing up together various heresies, and not observing that some statements are the utterances of one heretical sect, and others of a different one, he brings forward the objections which we raised against Marcion.[7] And, probably, having heard them from some paltry and ignorant individuals,[8] he assails the very arguments which combat them, but not in a way that shows much intelligence. Quoting then our arguments against Marcion, and not observing that it is *against* Marcion that he is speaking, he asks : "Why does he send secretly, and destroy the works which he has created? Why does he secretly employ force, and persuasion, and deceit? Why does he allure those who, as ye assert, have been condemned or accused by him, and carry them away like a slave-dealer? Why does he teach them to steal away from their Lord? Why to flee from their father? Why does he claim them for himself against the father's will? Why does he profess to be the father of strange children?" To these questions he subjoins the following remark, as if by way of expressing his surprise : [9] "Venerable, indeed, is the god who desires to be the father of those sinners who are condemned by another (god), and of the needy,[10] and, as themselves say, of the very offscourings [11] (of men), and who is unable to capture and punish his messenger, who escaped from him!" After this, as if addressing us who acknowledge that this world is not the work of a different and strange god, he continues in the following strain : "If these are his works, how is it that God created evil? And how is it that he cannot persuade and admonish (men)? And how is it that he repents on account of the ingratitude and wickedness of men? He finds fault, moreover, with his own handwork,[12] and hates, and threatens, and destroys his own off-

---

[1] ἐν καταστάσει ἔσεσθαι ἡμέρας.
[2] Cf. Isa. lx. 19.
[3] εὐκτικῶς.
[4] ὡς ἐν ἀλλοτρίοις τοῖς τῇδε.
[5] μακρὰν χαιρέτωσαν.

[6] περιορᾷ.
[7] Cf. bk. v. cap. liv.
[8] The textual reading is, ἀπό τινων εὐτελῶς καὶ ἰδιωτικῶς, for which Ruæus reads, ἀπό τινων εὐτελῶν καὶ ἰδιωτικῶν, which emendation has been adopted in the translation.
[9] οἱονεὶ θαυμαστικῶς.
[10] ἀκλήρων.
[11] σκυβάλων.
[12] τέχνην.

spring? Whither can he transport them out of this world, which he himself has made?" Now it does not appear to me that by these remarks he makes clear what "evil" is; and although there have been among the Greeks many sects who differ as to the nature of good and evil, he hastily concludes, as if it were a consequence of our maintaining that this world also is a work of the universal God, that in *our* judgment *God* is the author of evil. Let it be, however, regarding evil as it may — whether created by God or not — it nevertheless follows only as a *result* when you compare the principal design.[1] And I am greatly surprised if the inference regarding God's authorship of evil, which he thinks follows from our maintaining that this world also is the work of the universal God, does not follow too from his *own* statements. For one might say to Celsus: "If these are His works, how is it that God created evil? and how is it that He cannot persuade and admonish men?" It is indeed the greatest error in reasoning to accuse those who are of different opinions of holding unsound doctrines, when the accuser himself is much more liable to the same charge with regard to his own.

CHAP. LIV.

Let us see, then, briefly what holy Scripture has to say regarding good and evil, and what answer we are to return to the questions, "How is it that God created evil?" and, "How is He incapable of persuading and admonishing men?" Now, according to holy Scripture, properly speaking, virtues and virtuous actions are good, as, properly speaking, the reverse of these are evil. We shall be satisfied with quoting on the present occasion some verses from the 34th Psalm, to the following effect: "They that seek the LORD shall not want any good thing. Come, ye children, hearken unto me; I will teach you the fear of the LORD. What man is he that desireth life, and loveth many days, that he may see good? Keep thy tongue from evil, and thy lips from speaking guile. Depart from evil, and do good."[2] Now, the injunctions to "depart from evil, and to do good," do not refer either to *corporeal* evils or *corporeal* blessings, as they are termed by some, nor to external things at all, but to blessings and evils of a *spiritual* kind; since he who departs from such evils, and performs such virtuous actions, will, as one who desires the true life, come to the enjoyment of it; and as one loving to see "good days," in which the word of righteousness will be the Sun, he will see them, God taking him away from this "present evil world,"[3] and from those evil days

concerning which Paul said: "Redeeming the time, because the days are evil."[4]

CHAP. LV.

Passages, indeed, might be found where corporeal and external (benefits) are improperly[5] called "good," — those things, viz., which contribute to the natural life, while those which do the reverse are termed "evil." It is in this sense that Job says to his wife: "If we have received good at the hand of the Lord, shall we not also receive evil!"[6] Since, then, there is found in the sacred Scriptures, in a certain passage, this statement put into the mouth of God, "I make peace, and create evil;"[7] and again another, where it is said of Him that "evil came down from the LORD to the gate of Jerusalem, the noise of chariots and horsemen,"[8] — passages which have disturbed many readers of Scripture, who are unable to see what Scripture means by "good" and "evil," — it is probable that Celsus, being perplexed thereby, gave utterance to the question, "How is it that God created evil?" or, perhaps, having heard some one discussing the matters relating to it in an ignorant manner, he made this statement which we have noticed. We, on the other hand, maintain that "evil," or "wickedness," and the actions which proceed from it, were *not* created by God. For if God created that which is *really* evil, how was it possible that the proclamation regarding (the last) judgment should be confidently announced,[9] which informs us that the wicked are to be punished for their evil deeds in proportion to the amount of their wickedness, while those who have lived a virtuous life, or performed virtuous actions, will be in the enjoyment of blessedness, and will receive rewards from God? I am well aware that those who would daringly assert that these evils were created by God will quote certain expressions of Scripture (in their support), because we are not able to show one consistent series[10] of passages; for although Scripture (generally) blames the wicked and approves of the righteous, it nevertheless contains some statements which, although comparatively[11] few in number, seem to disturb the minds of ignorant readers of holy Scripture. I have not, however, deemed it appropriate to my present treatise to quote on the present occasion those discordant statements, which are many in number,[12] and

---

[4] Cf. Eph. v. 16.
[5] καταχρηστικώτερον.
[6] Cf. Job ii. 10.
[7] Cf. Isa. xlv. 7.
[8] Cf. Mic. i. 12, 13. The rendering of the Heb. in the first clause of the thirteenth verse is different from that of the LXX.
[9] παρρησίαν ἔχειν.
[10] ὗφος.
[11] ὀλίγα must be taken *comparatively*, on account of the πολλάς that follows afterwards.
[12] πολλάς. See note 11.

---

[1] ἐκ παρακολουθήσεως γεγένηται τῆς πρὸς τὰ προηγούμενα.
[2] Cf. Ps. xxxiv. 10–14.
[3] Cf. Gal. i. 4.

heir explanations, which would require a long array of proofs. Evils, then, if those be meant which are *properly* so called, were *not* created by God ; but some, although *few* in comparison with the order of the *whole* world, *have* resulted from His principal works, as there follow from the chief works of the carpenter such things as spiral shavings and sawdust,[1] or as architects might appear to be the cause of the rubbish[2] which lies around their buildings in the form of the filth which drops from the stones and the plaster.

CHAP. LVI.

If we speak, however, of what are called " corporeal " and " external " evils, — which are improperly so termed, — then it may be granted that there *are* occasions when some of these have been called into existence by God, in order that by their means the conversion of certain individuals might be effected. And what absurdity would follow from such a course ? For as, if we should hear those sufferings[3] improperly termed " evils " which are inflicted by fathers, and instructors, and pedagogues upon those who are under their care, or upon patients who are operated upon or cauterized by the surgeons in order to effect a cure, we were to say that a father was ill-treating his son, or pedagogues and instructors their pupils, or physicians their patients, no blame would be laid upon the operators or chastisers ; so, in the same way, if God is said to bring upon men such evils for the conversion and cure of those who need this discipline, there would be no absurdity in the view, nor would " evils come down from the LORD upon the gates of Jerusalem," [4] — which evils consist of the punishments inflicted upon the Israelites by their enemies with a view to their conversion ; nor would one visit " with a rod the transgressions of those who forsake the law of the Lord, and their iniquities with stripes ; " [5] nor could it be said, " Thou hast coals of fire to set upon them ; they shall be to thee a help." [6] In the same way also we explain the expressions, " I, who make peace, and create evil ; " [7] for He calls into existence " corporeal " or " external " evils, while purifying and training those who would not be disciplined by the word and sound doctrine. This, then, is our answer to the question, " How is it that God created evil ? "

CHAP. LVII.

With respect to the question, " How is he incapable of persuading and admonishing men ? "

it has been already stated that, if such an objection were really a ground of charge, then the objection of Celsus might be brought against those who accept the doctrine of providence. Any one might answer the charge that God is incapable of admonishing men ; for He conveys His admonitions throughout the whole of Scripture, and by means of those persons who, through God's gracious appointment, are the instructors of His hearers. Unless, indeed, some peculiar meaning be understood to attach to the word " admonish," as if it signified both to penetrate into the mind of the person admonished, and to make him hear the words of his [8] instructor, which is contrary to the usual meaning of the word. To the objection, " How is he incapable of persuading ? " — which also might be brought against all who believe in providence, — we have to make the following remarks. Since the expression " to be persuaded " belongs to those words which are termed, so to speak, " reciprocal " [9] (compare the phrase " to shave a man," when he makes an effort to submit himself to the barber [10]), there is for this reason needed not merely the effort of him who persuades, but also the submission, so to speak, which is to be yielded to the persuader, or the acceptance of what is said by him. And therefore it must not be said that it is because God is *incapable* of persuading men that they are not persuaded, but because they will not accept the faithful words of God. And if one were to apply this expression to men who are the " artificers of persuasion," [11] he would not be wrong ; for it is possible for a man who has thoroughly learned the principles of rhetoric, and who employs them properly, to do his utmost to persuade, and yet appear to fail, because he cannot overcome the will of him who ought to yield to his persuasive arts. Moreover, that persuasion does not come from God, although persuasive words may be uttered by him, is distinctly taught by Paul, when he says : " This persuasion cometh not of him that calleth you." [12] Such also is the view indicated by these words : " If ye be willing and obedient, ye shall eat the good of the land ; but if ye refuse and rebel, a sword shall devour you." [13] For that one may (really) desire what is addressed to him by one who admonishes, and may become deserving of those promises of God which he hears, it is necessary to secure the will of the hearer, and his inclination to what is addressed to him. And therefore it appears to me, that in the book of Deuteronomy the following words

---

[1] τὰ ἑλικοειδῆ ξέσματα καὶ πρίσματα.
[2] τὰ παρακείμενα.
[3] πόνους.
[4] Cf. Mic. i. 12.
[5] Cf. Ps. lxxxix. 32.
[6] Cf. Isa. xlvii. 14, 15 (**LXX.**).
[7] Cf. Isa. xlv. 7.

[8] τὸ καὶ ἐπιτυγχάνειν ἐν τῷ νουθετουμένῳ καὶ ἀκούειν τὸν τοῦ διδάσκοντος λόγον.
[9] ὡσπερεὶ τῶν καλουμένων ἀντιπεπονθότων ἐστίν.
[10] ἀνάλογον τῷ κείρεσθαι ἄνθρωπον, ἐνεργοῦντα τὸ παρέχειν ἑαυτὸν τῷ κείροντι.
[11] πειθοῦς δημιουργῶν.
[12] Cf. Gal. v. 8.
[13] Cf. Isa. i. 19, 20.

are uttered with peculiar emphasis : "And now, O Israel, what doth the LORD thy God require of thee, but to fear the LORD thy God, and to walk in all His ways, and to love Him, and to keep His commandments?"[1]

CHAP. LVIII.

There is next to be answered the following query : "And how is it that he repents when men become ungrateful and wicked ; and finds fault with his own handwork, and hates, and threatens, and destroys his own offspring?" Now Celsus here calumniates and falsifies what is written in the book of Genesis to the following effect : "And the LORD God, seeing that the wickedness of men upon the earth was increasing, and that every one in his heart carefully meditated to do evil continually, was grieved[2] He had made man upon the earth. And God meditated in His heart, and said, I will destroy man, whom I have made, from the face of the earth, both man and beast, and creeping thing, and fowl of the air, because I am grieved[3] that I made them ; "[4] quoting words which are not written in Scripture, as if they conveyed the meaning of what was actually written. For there is no mention in these words of the repentance of God, nor of His blaming and hating His own handwork. And if there is the appearance of God threatening the catastrophe of the deluge, and thus destroying His own children in it, we have to answer that, as the soul of man is immortal, the supposed threatening has for its object the conversion of the hearers, while the destruction of men by the flood is a purification of the earth, as certain among the Greek philosophers of no mean repute have indicated by the expression : "When the gods purify the earth."[5] And with respect to the transference to God of those anthropopathic phrases, some remarks have been already made by us in the preceding pages.

CHAP. LIX.

Celsus, in the next place, suspecting, or perhaps seeing clearly enough, the answer which might be returned by those who defend the destruction of men by the deluge, continues : "But if he does not destroy his own offspring, whither does he convey them out of this world[6] which he himself created?" To this we reply, that God by no means removes out of the whole world, consisting of heaven and earth, those who suffered death by the deluge, but removes them from a life in the flesh, and, having set them free from their bodies, liberates them at the same time from an existence upon earth, which in many parts of Scripture it is usual to call the "world." In the Gospel according to John especially, we may frequently find the regions of earth[7] termed "world," as in the passage, "He was the true Light, which lighteneth every man that cometh into the 'world;'"[8] as also in this, "In the world ye shall have tribulation; but be of good cheer, I have overcome the world."[9] If, then, we understand by "removing out of the world" a transference from "regions on earth," there is nothing absurd in the expression. If, on the contrary, the system of things which consists of heaven and earth be termed "world," then those who perished in the deluge are by no means removed out of the so-called "world." And yet, indeed, if we have regard to the words, "Looking not at the things which are seen, but at the things which are not seen;"[10] and also to these, "For the invisible things of Him from the creation of the world are clearly seen, being understood by the things that are made,"[11] — we might say that he who dwells amid the "invisible" things, and what are called generally "things not seen," is gone out of the world, the Word having removed him hence, and transported him to the heavenly regions, in order to behold all beautiful things.

CHAP. LX.

But after this investigation of his assertions, as if his object were to swell his book by many words, he repeats, in different language, the same charges which we have examined a little ago, saying : "By far the most silly thing is the distribution of the creation of the world over certain days, *before days existed :* for, as the heaven was not yet created, nor the foundation of the earth yet laid,[12] nor the sun yet revolving,[13] how could there be *days?*" Now, what difference is there between these words and the following : "Moreover, taking and looking at these things from the beginning, would it not be absurd in the first and greatest God to issue the command, Let this (first thing) come into existence, and this second thing, and this (third) ; and after accomplishing so much on the first day, to do so much more again on the second, and third, and fourth, and fifth, and sixth?" We answered to the best of our ability this objection to God's "commanding this first, second, and third thing

---

[1] Cf. Deut. x. 12, 13.
[2] ἐνεθυμήθη, in all probability a corruption for ἐθυμώθη, which Hoeschel places in the text, and Spencer in the margin of his ed.: Heb. ‎וַיִּנָּחֶם.
[3] ἐνεθυμήθην. Cf. remark in note 2.
[4] Cf. Gen. vi. 5-7.
[5] Cf. Plato in *Timæo.*
[6] κόσμος.

[7] τὸν περίγειον τόπον.
[8] Cf. John i. 9.
[9] Cf. John xvi. 33.
[10] Cf. 2 Cor. iv. 18.
[11] Cf. Rom. i. 20.
[12] ἐρηρεισμένης.
[13] τῇδε φερομένου.

be created," when we quoted the words, "He said, and it was done; He commanded, and all things stood fast;"[1] remarking that the immediate[2] Creator, and, as it were, very Maker[3] of the world was the Word, the Son of God; while the Father of the Word, by commanding His own Son — the Word — to create the world, is *primarily* Creator. And with regard to the creation of the light upon the first day, and of the firmament upon the second, and of the gathering together of the waters that are under the heaven into their several reservoirs[4] on the third (the earth thus causing to sprout forth those fruits) which are under the control of nature alone[5]), and of the (great) lights and stars upon the fourth, and of aquatic[6] animals upon the fifth, and of land animals and man upon the sixth, we have treated to the best of our ability in our notes upon Genesis, as well as in the foregoing pages, when we found fault with those who, taking the words in their *apparent* signification, said that the time of six days was occupied in the creation of the world, and quoted the words: "These are the generations of the heavens and of the earth when they were created, in the day that the LORD God made the earth and the heavens."[7]

CHAP. LXI.

Again, not understanding the meaning of the words, "And God ended[8] on the sixth day His works which He had made, and ceased[9] on the seventh day from all His works which He had made: and God blessed the seventh day, and hallowed it, because on it He had ceased[9] from all His works which He had begun to make;"[10] and imagining the expression, "He *ceased* on the seventh day," to be the same as this, "He *rested*[11] on the seventh day," he makes the remark: "After this, indeed, he is weary, like a very bad workman, who stands in need of rest to refresh himself!" For he knows nothing of the day of the Sabbath and rest of God, which follows the completion of the world's creation, and which lasts during the duration of the world, and in which all those will keep festival with God who have done all *their* works in *their* six days, and who, because they have omitted none of their duties,[12] will ascend to the contemplation (of celestial things), and to the assembly of righteous and blessed beings. In the next place, as if either the Scriptures made such a statement, or

as if we ourselves so spoke of God as having rested from fatigue, he continues: "It is not in keeping with the fitness of things[13] that the first God should feel fatigue, or work with His hands,[14] or give forth commands." Celsus says, that "it is not in keeping with the fitness of things that the first God should feel fatigue. Now we would say that neither does God the Word feel fatigue, nor any of those beings who belong to a better and diviner order of things, because the sensation of fatigue is peculiar to those who are in the body. You can examine whether this is true of those who possess a body of any kind, or of those who have an *earthly* body, or one a little better than this. But "neither is it consistent with the fitness of things that the first God should work with His own hands." If you understand the words "work with His own hands" *literally*, then neither are they applicable to the *second* God, nor to any other being partaking of divinity. But suppose that they are spoken in an improper and figurative sense, so that we may translate the following expressions, "And the firmament showeth forth His handywork,"[15] and "the heavens are the work of Thy hands,"[16] and any other similar phrases, in a figurative manner, so far as respects the "hands" and "limbs" of Deity, where is the absurdity in the words, "God thus working with His own hands?" And as there is no absurdity in God thus working, so neither is there in His issuing "commands;" so that what is done at His bidding should be beautiful and praiseworthy, because it was God who commanded it to be performed.

CHAP. LXII.

Celsus, again, having perhaps misunderstood the words, "For the mouth of the LORD hath spoken it,"[17] or perhaps because some ignorant individuals had rashly ventured upon the explanation of such things, and not understanding, moreover, on what principles parts called after the names of the bodily members are assigned to the attributes[18] of God, asserts: "He has neither mouth nor voice." Truly, indeed, God can have no voice, if the voice is a concussion of the air, or a stroke on the air, or a species of air, or any other definition which may be given to the voice by those who are skilled in such matters; but what is called the "voice of God" is said to be *seen* as "God's voice" by the people in the passage; "And all the people saw the voice of God;"[19] the word "saw" being taken, agreeably to the custom of Scripture, in a spiritual

---

[1] Cf. Ps. xxxiii. 9.
[2] τὸν προσεχῶς δημιουργόν.
[3] αὐτουργόν.
[4] συναγωγάς.
[5] τὰ ὑπὸ μόνης φύσεως διοικούμενα.
[6] τὰ νηκτά.
[7] Cf. Gen. ii. 4.
[8] [συνετέλεσεν, *complevit.* S.]
[9] κατέπαυσεν.
[10] Cf. Gen. ii. 2, 3.
[11] ἀνεπαύσατο.
[12] τῶν ἐπιβαλλόντων.

[13] οὐ θέμις.
[14] χειρουργεῖν.
[15] Cf. Ps. xix. 1.
[16] Cf. Ps. cii. 25.
[17] Cf. Isa. i. 20.
[18] ἐπὶ τῶν δυνάμεων.
[19] Cf. Ex. xx- 18 (LXX.). The Masoretic text is different.

sense. Moreover, he alleges that "God possesses nothing else of which *we* have any knowledge ; " but of what things *we* have knowledge he gives no indication. If he means "limbs," we agree with him, understanding the things "of which we have knowledge" to be those called corporeal, and pretty generally so termed. But if we are to understand the words "of which *we* have knowledge" in a universal sense, then there are many things of which we have knowledge, (and which may be attributed to God) ; for He possesses virtue, and blessedness, and divinity. If we, however, put a higher meaning upon the words, "of which *we* have knowledge," since all that we know is less than God, there is no absurdity in our also admitting that God possesses none of those things "of which *we* have knowledge." For the attributes which belong to God are far superior to all things with which not merely the nature of man is acquainted, but even that of those who have risen far above it. And if he had read the writings of the prophets, David on the one hand saying, "But Thou art the same,"[1] and Malachi on the other, "I am (the LORD), and change not,"[2] he would have observed that none of us assert that there is any change in God, either in act or thought. For abiding the same, He administers mutable things according to their nature, and His word elects to undertake their administration.

CHAP. LXIII.

Celsus, not observing the difference between "after the image of God" and "God's image," next asserts that the "first-born of every creature" is the image of God, — the very word and truth, and also the very wisdom, being the image of His goodness, while man has been created *after* the image of God ; moreover, that every man whose head is Christ is the image and glory of God ; — and further, not observing to which of the characteristics of humanity the expression "after the image of God" belongs, and that it consists in a nature which never had nor longer has "the old man with his deeds," being called "after the image of Him who created it," from its not possessing these qualities, — he maintains : "Neither did He make man His image ; for God is not such an one, nor like any other species of (visible) being." Is it possible to suppose that the element which is "after the image of God" should exist in the inferior part — I mean the body — of a compound being like man, because Celsus has explained that to be made after the image of God ? For if that which is "after the image of God" be in the body only, the better part, the soul, has been deprived of that which is "after His image," and this

(distinction) exists in the corruptible body, — an assertion which is made by none of us. But if that which is "after the image of God" be in *both together*, then God must necessarily be a compound being, and consist, as it were, of soul and body, in order that the element which is "after God's image," the better part, may be in the soul ; while the inferior part, and that which "is according to the body," may be in the body, — an assertion, again, which is made by none of us. It remains, therefore, that that which is "after the image of God" must be understood to be in our "inner man," which is also renewed, and whose nature it is to be "after the image of Him who created it," when a man becomes "perfect," as "our Father in heaven is perfect," and hears the command, "Be ye holy, for I the LORD your God am holy,"[3] and learning the precept, "Be ye followers of God,"[4] receives into his virtuous soul the traits of God's image. The body, moreover, of him who possesses such a soul is a temple of God ; and in the soul God dwells, because it has been made after His image.[5]

CHAP. LXIV.

Celsus, again, brings together a number of statements, which he gives as admissions on our part, but which no intelligent Christian would allow. For not one of us asserts that "God partakes of form or colour." Nor does He even partake of "motion," because He stands firm, and His nature is permanent, and He invites the righteous man also to do the same, saying : "But as for thee, stand thou here by Me."[6] And if certain expressions indicate a kind of motion, as it were, on His part, such as this, "They heard the voice of the LORD God *walking* in the garden in the cool of the day,"[7] we must understand them in this way, that it is by sinners that God is understood as moving, or as we understand the "sleep" of God, which is taken in a figurative sense, or His "anger," or any other similar attribute. But "God does not partake even of substance."[8] For He is partaken of (by others) rather than that Himself partakes of them, and He is partaken of by those who have the Spirit of God. Our Saviour, also, does not partake of righteousness ; but being Himself "righteousness," He is partaken of by the righteous. A discussion about "substance" would be protracted and difficult, and especially if it were a question whether that which is permanent and immaterial be "sub-

---

[1] Cf. Ps. cii. 27.
[2] Cf. Mal. iii. 6.

[3] Lev. xi. 44.
[4] Cf. Eph. v. 1 (μιμηταί).
[5] The words as they stand in the text are probably corrupt: we have adopted in the translation the emendation of Guietus: ἔτι καὶ ναός ἐστι τοῦ Θεοῦ τὸ σῶμα τοῦ τοιαύτην ἔχοντος ψυχὴν, καὶ ἐν τῇ ψυχῇ διὰ τὸ κατ᾽ εἰκόνα, τὸν Θεόν.
[6] Deut. v. 31.
[7] Cf. Gen. iii. 8.
[8] οὐσία.

stance " properly so called, so that it would be found that God is *beyond* " substance," communicating of His " substance," by means of office and power,[1] to those to whom He communicates Himself by His Word, as He does to the Word Himself ; or even if He *is* " substance," yet He is said be in His nature " invisible," in these words respecting our Saviour, who is said to be " the image of the *invisible* God," [2] while from the term " invisible " it is indicated that He is " immaterial." It is also a question for investigation, whether the " only-begotten " and " first-born of every creature " is to be called " substance of substances," and " idea of ideas," and the " principle of all things," while above all there is His Father and God.[3]

CHAP. LXV.

Celsus proceeds to say of God that " of Him are all things," abandoning (in so speaking), I know not how, all his principles ; [4] while our Paul declares, that " of Him, and through Him, and to Him are all things," [5] showing that He is the beginning of the substance of all things by the words " of Him," and the bond of their subsistence by 'the expression "through Him," and their final end by the terms " to Him." Of a truth, God is of nothing. But when Celsus adds, that " He is not to be reached by word," [6] I make a distinction, and say that if he means the word that is in *us* — whether the word conceived in the mind, or the word that is uttered [7] — I, too, admit that God is not to be reached by word. If, however, we attend to the passage, " In the beginning was the Word, and the Word was with God, and the Word was God," [8] we are of opinion that God is to be reached by *this* Word, and is comprehended not by Him only, but by any one whatever to whom He may reveal the Father ; and thus we shall prove the falsity of the assertion of Celsus, when he says, " Neither is God to be reached by word." The statement, moreover, that " He cannot be expressed by name," requires to be taken with a distinction. If he means, indeed, that there is no word or sign [9] that can represent the attributes of God, the statement is true, since there are many qualities which cannot be indicated by words. Who, for

example, could describe in words the difference betwixt the quality of sweetness in a palm and that in a fig? And who could distinguish and set forth in words the peculiar qualities of each individual thing? It is no wonder, then, if in this way God cannot be described by name. But if you take the phrase to mean that it is possible to represent by words something of God's attributes, in order to lead the hearer by the hand,[10] as it were, and so enable him to comprehend something of God, so far as attainable by human nature, then there is no absurdity in saying that " He *can* be described by name." And we make a similar distinction with regard to the expression, " for He has undergone no suffering that can be conveyed by words." It *is* true that the Deity is beyond all suffering. And so much on this point.

CHAP. LXVI.

Let us look also at his next statement, in which he introduces, as it were, a certain person, who, after hearing what has been said. expresses himself in the following manner, " How, then, shall I know God? and how shall I learn the way that leads to Him? And how will you show Him to me? Because now, indeed, you throw darkness before my eyes, and I see nothing distinctly." He then answers, as it were, the individual who is thus perplexed, and thinks that he assigns the reason why darkness has been poured upon the eyes of him who uttered the foregoing words, when he asserts that " those whom one would lead forth out of darkness into the brightness of light, being unable to withstand its splendours, have their power of vision affected [11] and injured, and so imagine that they are smitten with blindness." In answer to this, we would say that all those indeed sit in darkness, and are rooted in it, who fix their gaze upon the evil handiwork of painters, and moulders and sculptors, and who will not look upwards, and ascend in thought from all visible and sensible things, to the Creator of all things, who is light ; while, on the other hand, every one is in light who has followed the radiance of the Word, who has shown in consequence of what ignorance, and impiety, and want of knowledge of divine things these objects were worshipped instead of God, and who has conducted the soul of him who desires to be saved towards the uncreated God, who is over all. For " the people that sat in darkness — the Gentiles — saw a great light, and to them who sat in the region and shadow of death light is sprung up," [12] — the God Jesus. No Christian, then, would give Celsus, or any accuser of the divine Word, the answer, " How shall I know God?" for each one of

---

[1] πρεσβείᾳ καὶ δυνάμει.
[2] Cf. Col. i. 15.
[3] [" It is a remarkable fact, that it was Origen who discerned the heresy outside the Church on its first rise, and actually gave the alarm, sixty years before Arius's day. See Athanasius, *De Decret. Nic.*, § 27; also the περὶ ἀρχῶν (if Rufinus may be trusted), for Origen's denouncement of the still more characteristic Arianism of the ἦν ὅτε οὐκ ἦν and the ἐξ οὐκ ὄντων." — Newman's *The Arians of the Fourth Century*, p. 97. See also Hagenbach's *History of Doctrines*, vol. i. pp. 130-133. S.]
[4] For αὐτοῦ Boherellus conjectures αὑτοῦ, and translates, "*Propria ipse principia*, quæ sunt Epicuri, *subruens*."
[5] Rom. xi. 36.
[6] οὐδὲ λόγῳ ἐφικτός.
[7] εἴτε ἐνδιαθέτῳ εἴτε καὶ προφορικῷ.
[8] John i. 1.
[9] οὐδὲν τῶν ἐν λέξεσι καὶ σημαινομένοις.

[10] χειραγωγῆσαι.
[11] κολάζεσθαι.
[12] Cf. Matt. iv. 16 and Isa. ix. 2.

them knows God according to his capacity. And no one asks, "How shall I learn the way which leads to Him?" because he has heard Him who says, "I am the way, and the truth, and the life,"[1] and has tasted, in the course of the journey, the happiness which results from it. And not a single Christian would say to Celsus, "How will you show me God?"

CHAP. LXVII.

The remark, indeed, was true which Celsus made, that any one, on hearing his words, would answer, seeing that his words *are* words of darkness, "You pour darkness before my eyes." Celsus verily, and those like him, do desire to pour darkness before our eyes: we, however, by means of the light of the Word, disperse the darkness of their impious opinions. The Christian, indeed, could retort on Celsus, who says nothing that is distinct or true, "I see nothing that is distinct among all *your* statements." It is not, therefore, "out of darkness" into "the brightness of light" that Celsus leads us forth: he wishes, on the contrary, to transport us from light into darkness, making the darkness light and the light darkness, and exposing himself to the woe well described by the prophet Isaiah in the following manner: "Woe unto them that put darkness for light, and light for darkness."[2] But we, the eyes of whose soul have been opened by the Word, and who see the difference between light and darkness, prefer by all means to take our stand "in the light," and will have nothing to do with darkness at all. The true light, moreover, being endued with life, knows to whom his full splendours are to be manifested, and to whom his light; for he does not display his brilliancy on account of the still existing weakness in the eyes of the recipient. And if we must speak at all of "sight being affected and injured," what other eyes shall we say are in this condition, than his who is involved in ignorance of God, and who is prevented by his passions from seeing the truth? Christians, however, by no means consider that they are blinded by the words of Celsus, or any other who is opposed to the worship of God. But let those who perceive that they are blinded by following multitudes who are in error, and tribes of those who keep festivals to demons, draw near to the Word, who can bestow the gift of sight,[3] in order that, like those poor and blind who had thrown themselves down by the wayside, and who were healed by Jesus because they said to Him, "Son of David, have mercy upon me," they too may receive mercy and recover their eyesight,[3] fresh and beautiful, as the Word of God can create it.

CHAP. LXVIII.

Accordingly, if Celsus were to ask us how we think we know God, and how we shall be saved by Him, we would answer that the Word of God, which entered into those who seek Him, or who accept Him when He appears, is able to make known and to reveal the Father, who was not seen (by any one) before the appearance of the Word. And who else is able to save and conduct the soul of man to the God of all things, save God the Word, who, "being in the beginning with God," became flesh for the sake of those who had cleaved to the flesh, and had become as flesh, that He might be received by those who could not behold Him, inasmuch as He was the Word, and was with God, and was God? And discoursing in human form,[4] and announcing Himself as flesh, He calls to Himself those who are flesh, that He may in the first place cause them to be transformed according to the Word that was made flesh, and afterwards may lead them upwards to behold Him as He was before He became flesh; so that they, receiving the benefit, and ascending from their great introduction to Him, which was according to the flesh, say, "Even if we have known Christ after the flesh, yet henceforth know we Him no more."[5] Therefore He became flesh, and having become flesh, "He tabernacled among us,"[6] not dwelling without us; and after tabernacling and dwelling *within* us, He did not continue in the form in which He first presented Himself, but caused us to ascend to the lofty mountain of His word, and showed us His own glorious form, and the splendour of His garments; and not His own form alone, but that also of the spiritual law, which is Moses, seen in glory along with Jesus. He showed to us, moreover, all prophecy, which did not perish even after His incarnation, but was received up into heaven, and whose symbol was Elijah. And he who beheld these things could say, "We beheld His glory, the glory as of the only-begotten of the Father, full of grace and truth."[6] Celsus, then, has exhibited considerable ignorance in the imaginary answer to his question which he puts into our mouth, "How we think we can know God? and how we know we shall be saved by Him?" for our answer is what we have just stated.

CHAP. LXIX.

Celsus, however, asserts that the answer which we give is based upon a probable conjecture,[7] admitting that he describes our answer in the following terms: "Since God is great and diffi-

---

[1] John xiv. 6.
[2] Cf. Isa. v. 20.
[3] ὀφθαλμούς.

[4] σωματικῶς.
[5] [2 Cor. v. 16. S.]
[6] Cf. John i. 14.
[7] εἰκότι στοχασμῷ.

cult to see,[1] He put His own Spirit into a body that resembled ours, and sent it down to us, that we might be enabled to hear Him and become acquainted with Him." But the God and Father of all things is not the only being that is great in our judgment; for He has imparted (a share) of Himself and His greatness to His Only-begotten and First-born of every creature, in order that He, being the image of the invisible God, might preserve, even in His greatness, the image of the Father. For it was not possible that there could exist a well-proportioned,[2] so to speak, and beautiful image of the invisible God, which did not at the same time preserve the image of His greatness. God, moreover, is in our judgment invisible, because He is not a body, while He *can* be seen by those who see with the heart, that is, the understanding; not indeed with any kind of heart, but with one which is pure. For it is inconsistent with the fitness of things that a polluted heart should look upon God; for that must be itself pure which would worthily behold that which is pure. Let it be granted, indeed, that God is "difficult to see," yet He is not the only being who is so; for His Only-begotten also is "difficult to see." For God the Word is "difficult to see," and so also is His[3] wisdom, by which God created all things. For who is capable of seeing the wisdom which is displayed in each individual part of the whole system of things, and by which God created every individual thing? It was not, then, because God was "difficult to see" that He sent God His Son to be an object "easy to be seen."[4] And because Celsus does not understand this, he has represented us as saying, "Because God was 'difficult to see,' He put His own Spirit in a body resembling ours, and sent it down to us, that we might be enabled to hear Him and become acquainted with Him." Now, as we have stated, the Son also is "difficult to see," because He is God the Word, through whom all things were made, and who "tabernacled amongst us."

CHAP. LXX.

If Celsus, indeed, had understood our teaching regarding the Spirit of God, and had known that "as many as are led by the Spirit of God, these are the sons of God,"[5] he would not have returned to himself the answer which he represents as coming from us, that "God put His own Spirit into a body, and sent it down to us;" for God is perpetually bestowing of His own Spirit to those who are capable of receiving it, although

it is not by way of division and separation that He dwells in (the hearts of) the deserving. Nor is the Spirit, in our opinion, a "body," any more than fire is a "body," which God is said to be in the passage, "Our God is a consuming fire."[6] For all these are figurative expressions, employed to denote the nature of "intelligent beings" by means of familiar and corporeal terms. In the same way, too, if sins are called "wood, and straw, and stubble," we shall not maintain that sins are corporeal; and if blessings are termed "gold, and silver, and precious stones,"[7] we shall not maintain that blessings are "corporeal;" so also, if God be said to be a fire that consumes wood, and straw, and stubble, and all substance[8] of sin, we shall not understand Him to be a "body," so neither do we understand Him to be a body if He should be called "fire." In this way, if God be called "spirit,"[9] we do not mean that He is a "body." For it is the custom of Scripture to give to "intelligent beings" the names of "spirits" and "spiritual things," by way of distinction from those which are the objects of "sense;" as when Paul says, "But our sufficiency is of God; who hath also made us able ministers of the New Testament; not of the letter, but of the spirit; for the letter killeth, but the spirit giveth life,"[10] where by the "letter" he means that "exposition of Scripture which is apparent to the senses,"[11] while by the "spirit" that which is the object of the "understanding." It is the same, too, with the expression, "God is a Spirit." And because the prescriptions of the law were obeyed both by Samaritans and Jews in a corporeal and literal[12] manner, our Saviour said to the Samaritan woman, "The hour is coming, when neither in Jerusalem, nor in this mountain, shall ye worship the Father. God is a Spirit; and they that worship Him must worship Him in spirit and in truth."[13] And by these words He taught men that God must be worshipped not in the flesh, and with fleshly sacrifices, but in the spirit. And He will be understood to be a Spirit in proportion as the worship rendered to Him is rendered in spirit, and with understanding. It is not, however, with images[14] that we are to worship the Father, but "in truth," which "came by Jesus Christ," after the giving of the law by Moses. For when we turn to the Lord (and the Lord is a Spirit[15]), He takes away the veil which lies upon the heart when Moses is read.

---

6 Cf. Heb. xii. 29.
7 Cf. 1 Cor. iii. 12.
8 πᾶσαν οὐσίαν.
9 πνεῦμα. There is an allusion to the two meanings of πνεῦμα, "wind" and "spirit."
10 2 Cor. iii. 5, 6.
11 τὴν αἰσθητὴν ἐκδοχήν.
12 τυπικῶς here evidently must have the above meaning.
13 Cf. John iv. 21, 24.
14 ἐν τύποις.
15 Cf. 2 Cor. iii. 17.

---

1 δυσθεώρητος.
2 σύμμετρον.
3 For οὑτωσί we have adopted the conjecture of Guietus, τούτου.
4 ὡς εὐθεώρητον.
5 Rom. viii. 14.

CHAP. LXXI.

Celsus accordingly, as not understanding the doctrine relating to the Spirit of God ("for the natural man receiveth not the things of the Spirit of God, for they are foolishness unto him; neither can he know them, because they are spiritually discerned"[1]), weaves together (such a web) as pleases himself,[2] imagining that we, in calling God a Spirit, differ in no respect in this particular from the Stoics among the Greeks, who maintain that "God is a Spirit, diffused through all things, and containing all things within Himself." Now the superintendence and providence of God does extend through all things, but not in the way that spirit does, according to the Stoics. Providence indeed contains all things that are its objects, and comprehends them all, but not as a containing body includes its contents, because they also are "body,"[3] but as a *divine* power does it comprehend what it contains. According to the philosophers of the Porch, indeed, who assert that principles are "corporeal," and who on that account make all things perishable, and who venture even to make the God of all things capable of perishing, the very Word of God, who descends even to the lowest of mankind, would be — did it not appear to them to be too gross an incongruity[4] — nothing else than a "corporeal" spirit; whereas, in our opinion, — who endeavour to demonstrate that the rational soul is superior to all "corporeal" nature, and that it is an invisible substance, and incorporeal, — God the Word, by whom all things were made, who came, in order that all things might be made by the Word, not to men only, but to what are deemed the very lowest of things, under the dominion of nature alone, would be no body. The Stoics, then, may consign all things to destruction by fire; we, however, know of no incorporeal substance that is destructible by fire, nor (do we believe) that the soul of man, or the substance of "angels," or of "thrones," or dominions," or "principalities," or "powers," can be dissolved by fire.

CHAP. LXXII.

It is therefore in vain that Celsus asserts, as one who knows not the nature of the Spirit of God, that "as the Son of God, who existed in a human body, is a Spirit, this very Son of God would not be immortal." He next becomes confused in his statements, as if there were some of us who did not admit that God is a Spirit, but maintain that only with regard to His Son,

and he thinks that he can answer us by saying that there "is no kind of spirit which lasts for ever." This is much the same as if, when we term God a "consuming fire," he were to say that there "is no kind of fire which lasts for ever;" not observing the sense in which we say that our God is a fire, and what the things are which He consumes, viz., sins, and wickedness. For it becomes a God of goodness, after each individual has shown, by his efforts, what kind of combatant he has been, to consume vice by the fire of His chastisements. He proceeds, in the next place, to assume what we do not maintain, that "God must necessarily have given up the ghost;" from which also it follows that Jesus could not have risen again with His body. For God would not have received back the spirit which He had surrendered after it had been stained by contact with the body. It is foolish, however, for us to answer statements as ours which were never made by us.

CHAP. LXXIII.

He proceeds to repeat himself, and after saying a great deal which he had said before, and ridiculing the birth of God from a virgin, — to which we have already replied as we best could, — he adds the following: "If God had wished to send down His Spirit from Himself, what need was there to breathe it into the womb of a woman? For as one who knew already how to form men, He could also have fashioned a body for this person, without casting His own Spirit into so much pollution;[5] and in this way He would not have been received with incredulity, if He had derived His existence immediately from above." He had made these remarks, because he knows not the pure and virgin birth, unaccompanied by any corruption, of that body which was to minister to the salvation of men. For, quoting the sayings of the Stoics,[6] and affecting not to know the doctrine about "things indifferent," he thinks that the divine nature was cast amid pollution, and was stained either by being in the body of a woman, until a body was formed around it, or by assuming a body. And in this he acts like those who imagine that the sun's rays are polluted by dung and by foul-smelling bodies, and do not remain pure amid such things. If, however, according to the view of Celsus, the body of Jesus had been fashioned without generation, those who beheld the body would at once have believed that it had not been formed by generation; and yet an object, when seen, does not at the same time indicate the nature of that from which it has derived its origin. For example,

---

[1] Cf. 1 Cor. ii. 14.
[2] ἑαυτῷ συνάπτει.
[3] οὐχ ὡς σῶμα δὲ περιέχον περιέχει, ὅτι καὶ σῶμά ἐστι τὸ περιεχόμενον.
[4] πάνυ ἀπεμφαῖνον.

[5] εἰς τοσοῦτον μίασμα.
[6] Cf. book iv. capp. xiv. and lxviii.

suppose that there were some honey (placed before one) which had not been manufactured by bees, no one could tell from the taste or sight that it was not their workmanship, because the honey which comes from bees does not make known its origin by the senses,[1] but experience alone can tell that it does not proceed from them. In the same way, too, experience teaches that wine comes from the vine, for taste does not enable us to distinguish (the wine) which comes from the vine. In the same manner, therefore, the visible[2] body does not make known the manner of its existence. And you will be induced to accept this view,[3] by (regarding) the heavenly bodies, whose existence and splendour we perceive as we gaze at them ; and yet, I presume, their appearance does not suggest to us whether they are created or uncreated ; and accordingly different opinions have existed on these points. And yet those who say that they are created are not agreed as to the manner of their creation, for their appearance does not suggest it, although the force of reason[4] may have discovered that they are created, and how their creation was effected.

CHAP. LXXIV.

After this he returns to the subject of Marcion's opinions (having already spoken frequently of them), and states some of them correctly, while others he has misunderstood ; these, however, it is not necessary for us to answer or refute. Again, after this he brings forward the various arguments that may be urged on Marcion's behalf, and also against him, enumerating what the opinions are which exonerate him from the charges, and what expose him to them ; and when he desires to support the statement which declares that Jesus has been the subject of prophecy, — in order to found a charge against Marcion and his followers, — he distinctly asks, " How could he, who was punished in such a manner, be shown to be God's Son, unless these things had been predicted of him ? " He next proceeds to jest, and, as his custom is, to pour ridicule upon the subject, introducing " two sons of God, one the son of the Creator,[5] and the other the son of Marcion's God ; and he portrays their single combats, saying that the Theomachies of the Fathers are like the battles between quails ;[6] or that the Fathers, becoming useless through age, and falling into their dotage,[7] do not meddle at all with one another, but leave their sons to fight it out." The remark which he made

formerly we will turn against himself : " What old woman would not be ashamed to lull a child to sleep with such stories as he has inserted in the work which he entitles *A True Discourse ?* For when he ought seriously[8] to apply himself to argument, he leaves serious argument aside, and betakes himself to jesting and buffoonery, imagining that he is writing mimes or scoffing verses ; not observing that such a method of procedure defeats his purpose, which is to make us abandon Christianity and give in our adherence to his opinions, which, perhaps, had they been stated with some degree of gravity,[9] would have appeared more likely to convince, whereas, since he continues to ridicule, and scoff, and play the buffoon, we answer that it is because he has no argument of weight[10] (for such he neither had, nor could understand) that he has betaken himself to such drivelling." [11]

CHAP. LXXV.

To the preceding remarks he adds the following : " Since a divine Spirit inhabited the body (of Jesus), it must certainly have been different from that of other beings, in respect of grandeur, or beauty, or strength, or voice, or impressiveness,[12] or persuasiveness. For it is impossible that He, to whom was imparted some divine quality beyond other beings, should not differ from others ; whereas this person did not differ in any respect from another, but was, as they report, little, and ill-favoured, and ignoble." [13] Now it is evident by these words, that when Celsus wishes to bring a charge against Jesus, he adduces the sacred writings, as one who believed them to be writings apparently fitted to afford a handle for a charge against Him ; but wherever, in the same writings, statements would appear to be made opposed to those charges which are adduced, he pretends not even to know them ! There are, indeed, admitted to be recorded some statements respecting the body of Jesus having been " ill-favoured ; " not, however, " ignoble," as has been stated, nor is there any certain evidence that he was " little." The language of Isaiah runs as follows, who prophesied regarding Him that He would come and visit the multitude, not in comeliness of form, nor in any surpassing beauty : " Lord, who hath believed our report, and to whom was the arm of the Lord revealed ? He made announcement before Him, as a child, as a root in a thirsty ground. He has no form nor glory, and we beheld Him, and He had no form nor beauty ; but His form was without

---

1 τῇ αἰσθήσει τὴν ἀρχήν.
2 τὸ αἰσθητὸν σῶμα.
3 προσαχθήσῃ δὲ τῷ λεγομένῳ.
4 κἂν βιασάμενος ὁ λόγος εὕρῃ.
5 τοῦ δημιουργοῦ.
6 ὀρτύγων.
7 ληροῦντας.

8 πραγματικῶς.
9 ἐσεμνολόγει.
10 σεμνῶν λόγων.
11 τοσαύτην φλυαρίαν.
12 κατάπληξιν.
13 ἀγενές.

honour, and inferior to that of the sons of men."[1] These passages, then, Celsus listened to, because he thought they were of use to him in bringing a charge against Jesus; but he paid no attention to the words of the 45th Psalm, and why it is then said, "Gird Thy sword upon Thy thigh, O most mighty, with Thy comeliness and beauty; and continue, and prosper, and reign."[2]

CHAP. LXXVI.

Let it be supposed, however, that he had not read the prophecy, or that he *had* read it, but had been drawn away by those who misinterpreted it as not being spoken of Jesus Christ. What has he to say of the Gospel, in the narratives of which Jesus ascended up into a high mountain, and was transfigured before the disciples, and was seen in glory, when both Moses and Elias, "being seen in glory, spake of the decease which He was about to accomplish at Jerusalem?"[3] or when the prophet says, "We beheld Him, and He had no form nor beauty," etc.? and Celsus accepts this prophecy as referring to Jesus, being blinded in so accepting it, and not seeing that it is a great proof that the Jesus who appeared to be "without form" was the Son of God, that His very appearance should have been made the subject of prophecy many years before His birth. But if another prophet speak of His comeliness and beauty, he will no longer accept the prophecy as referring to Christ! And if it were to be clearly ascertained from the Gospels that "He had no form nor beauty, but that His appearance was without honour, and inferior to that of the sons of men," it might be said that it was not with reference to the prophetic writings, but to the Gospels, that Celsus made his remarks. But now, as neither the Gospels nor the apostolic writings indicate that "He had no form nor beauty," it is evident that we must accept the declaration of the prophets as true of Christ, and this will prevent the charge against Jesus from being advanced.[4]

CHAP. LXXVII.

But again, how did he who said, "Since a divine Spirit inhabited the body (of Jesus), it must certainly have been different from that of other beings in respect of grandeur, or voice, or strength, or impressiveness, or persuasiveness," not observe the changing relation of His body according to the capacity of the spectators (ånd therefore its corresponding utility), inasmuch as it appeared to each one of such a nature as it was requisite for him to behold it? Moreover,

it is not a subject of wonder that the matter, which is by nature susceptible of being altered and changed, and of being transformed into anything which the Creator chooses, and is capable of receiving all the qualities which the Artificer desires, should at one time possess a quality, agreeably to which it is said, "He had no form nor beauty," and at another, one so glorious, and majestic, and marvellous, that the spectators of such surpassing loveliness — three disciples who had ascended (the mount) with Jesus — should fall upon their faces. He will say, however, that these are inventions, ana in no respect different from myths, as are also the other marvels related of Jesus; which objection we have answered at greater length in what has gone before. But there is also something mystical in this doctrine, which announces that the varying appearances of Jesus are to be referred to the nature of the divine Word, who does not show Himself in the same manner to the multitude as He does to those who are capable of following Him to the high mountain which we have mentioned; for to those who still remain below, and are not yet prepared to ascend, the Word "has neither form nor beauty," because to such persons His form is "without honour," and inferior to the words given forth by men, which are figuratively termed "sons of men." For we might say that the words of philosophers — who are "sons of men" — appear far more beautiful than the Word of God, who is proclaimed to the multitude, and who also exhibits (what is called) the "foolishness of preaching," and on account of this apparent "foolishness of preaching" those who look at this alone say, "We saw Him, but He had no form nor beauty." To those, indeed, who have received power to follow Him, in order that they may attend Him even when He ascends to the "lofty mount," He *has* a diviner appearance, which they behold, if there happens to be (among them) a Peter, who has received within himself the edifice of the Church based upon the Word, and who has gained such a habit (of goodness) that none of the gates of Hades will prevail against him, having been exalted by the Word from the gates of death, that he may "publish the praises of God in the gates of the daughter of Sion," and any others who have derived their birth from impressive preaching,[5] and who are not at all inferior to "sons of thunder." But how can Celsus and the enemies of the divine Word, and those who have not examined the doctrines of Christianity in the spirit of truth, know the meaning of the different appearances of Jesus? And I refer also to the different stages of His life, and to any actions performed by Him be-

---

[1] Cf. Isa. liii. 1–3 (LXX.). [See Bishop Pearson's *Exposition of the Creed*, Art. II., note. S.].
[2] Cf. Ps. xlv. 3, 4 (LXX.).
[3] [Luke ix. 31. S.]
[4] προβαίνειν.

[5] καὶ εἴ τινές εἰσιν ἐκ λόγων τὴν γένεσιν λαχόντες μεγαλοφώνων.

fore His sufferings, and after His resurrection from the dead.

CHAP. LXXVIII.

Celsus next makes certain observations of the following nature : "Again, if God, like Jupiter in the comedy, should, on awaking from a lengthened slumber, desire to rescue the human race from evil, why did He send this Spirit of which you speak into one corner (of the earth) ? He ought to have breathed it alike into many bodies, and have sent them out into all the world. Now the comic poet, to cause laughter in the theatre, wrote that Jupiter, after awakening, despatched Mercury to the Athenians and Lacedæmonians ; but do not you think that you have made the Son of God more ridiculous in sending Him to the Jews?" Observe in such language as this the irreverent character of Celsus, who, unlike a philosopher, takes the writer of a comedy, whose business is to cause laughter, and compares our God, the Creator of all things, to the being who, as represented in the play, on awaking, despatches Mercury (on an errand) ! We stated, indeed, in what precedes, that it was not as if awakening from a lengthened slumber that God sent Jesus to the human race, who has now, for good reasons, fulfilled the economy of His incarnation, but who has always conferred benefits upon the human race. For no noble deed has ever been performed amongst men, where the divine Word did not visit the souls of those who were capable, although for a little time, of admitting such operations of the divine Word. Moreover, the advent of Jesus apparently to one corner (of the earth) was founded on good reasons, since it was necessary that He who was the subject of prophecy should make His appearance among those who had become acquainted with the doctrine of one God, and who perused the writings of His prophets, and who had come to know the announcement of Christ, and that He should come to them at a time when the Word was about to be diffused from one corner over the whole world.

CHAP. LXXIX.

And therefore there was no need that there should everywhere exist many bodies, and many spirits like Jesus, in order that the whole world of men might be enlightened by the Word of God. For the one Word was enough, having arisen as the "Sun of righteousness," to send forth from Judea His coming rays into the soul of all who were willing to receive Him. But if any one desires to see many bodies filled with a divine Spirit, similar to the one Christ, ministering to the salvation of men everywhere, let him take note of those who teach the Gospel of Jesus in all lands in soundness of doctrine and

uprightness of life, and who are themselves termed "christs" by the holy Scriptures, in the passage, "Touch not Mine anointed,[1] and do not My prophets any harm."[2] For as we have heard that Antichrist cometh, and yet have learned that there are many antichrists in the world, in the same way, knowing that Christ has come, we see that, owing to Him, there are many christs in the world, who, like Him, have loved righteousness and hated iniquity, and therefore God, the God of Christ, anointed them also with the "oil of gladness." But inasmuch as He loved righteousness and hated iniquity above those who were His partners,[3] He also obtained the first-fruits of His anointing, and, if we must so term it, the entire unction of the oil of gladness ; while they who were His partners shared also in His unction, in proportion to their individual capacity. Therefore, since Christ is the Head of the Church, so that Christ and the Church form one body, the ointment descended from the head to the beard of Aaron, — the symbols of the perfect man, — and this ointment in its descent reached to the very skirt of his garment. This is my answer to the irreverent language of Celsus when he says, "He ought to have breathed (His Spirit) alike into many bodies, and have sent it forth into all the world." The comic poet, indeed, to cause laughter, has represented Jupiter asleep and awaking from slumber, and despatching Mercury to the Greeks ; but the Word, knowing that the nature of God is unaffected by sleep, may teach us that God administers in due season, and as right reason demands, the affairs of the world. It is not, however, a matter of surprise that, owing to the greatness and incomprehensibility[4] of the divine judgments, ignorant persons should make mistakes, and Celsus among them. There is therefore nothing ridiculous in the Son of God having been sent to the Jews, amongst whom the prophets had appeared, in order that, making a commencement among them in a bodily shape, He might arise with might and power upon a world of souls, which no longer desired to remain deserted by God.

CHAP. LXXX.

After this, it seemed proper to Celsus to term the Chaldeans a most divinely-inspired nation from the very earliest times,[5] from whom the delusive system of astrology[6] has spread abroad among men. Nay, he ranks the Magi also in the same category, from whom the art of magic derived its name and has been transmitted to

---

[1] τῶν χριστῶν μου.
[2] Cf. 1 Chron. xvi. 22 and Ps. cv. 15.
[3] τοὺς μετόχους αὐτοῦ.
[4] δυσδιηγήτους τὰς κρίσεις.
[5] ἐξ ἀρχῆς.
[6] γενεθλιαλογία.

other nations, to the corruption and destruction of those who employ it. In the preceding part of this work, (we mentioned) that, in·the opinion even of Celsus, the Egyptians also were guilty of error, because they had indeed solemn enclosures around what they considered their temples, while within them there was nothing save apes, or crocodiles, or goats, or asps, or some other animal ; but on the present occasion it pleases him to speak of the Egyptian people too as most divinely inspired, and that, too, from the earliest times, — perhaps because they made war upon the Jews from an early date. The Persians, moreover, who marry their own mothers,[1] and have intercourse with their own daughters, are, in the opinion of Celsus, an inspired race ; nay, even the Indians are so, some of whom, in the preceding, he mentioned as eaters of human flesh. To the Jews, however, especially those of ancient times, who employ none of these practices, he did not merely refuse the name of inspired, but declared that they would immediately perish. And this prediction he uttered respecting them, as being doubtless endued with prophetic power, not observing that the whole history of the Jews, and their ancient and venerable polity, were administered by God ; and that it is by their fall that salvation has come to the Gentiles, and that " their fall is the riches of the world, and the diminishing of them the riches of the Gentiles,"[2] until the fulness of the Gentiles come, that after that the whole of Israel, whom Celsus does not know, may be saved.

CHAP. LXXXI.

I do not understand, however, how he should say of God, that although " knowing all things, He was not aware of this, that He was sending His Son amongst wicked men, who were both to be guilty of sin, and to inflict punishment upon Him." Certainly he appears, in the present instance, to have forgotten that all the sufferings which Jesus was to undergo were foreseen by the Spirit of God, and foretold by His prophets ; from which it does not follow that " God did not know that He was sending His Son amongst wicked and sinful men, who were also to inflict punishment upon Him." He immediately adds, however, that " our defence on this point is that all these things were predicted." But as our sixth book has now attained sufficient dimensions, we shall stop here, and begin, God willing, the argument of the seventh, in which we shall consider the reasons which he thinks furnish an answer to our statement, that everything regarding Jesus was foretold by the prophets ; and as these are numerous, and require to be answered at length, we wished neither to cut the subject short, in consequence of the size of the present book, nor, in order to avoid doing so, to swell this sixth book beyond its proper proportions.

---

[1] [On the manners of heathen nations, note this. See 1 Cor. v. 1.]

[2] Cf. Rom. xi. 11, 12.

ORIGEN AGAINST CELSUS.

BOOK VII.

CHAP. I.

In the six former books we have endeavoured, reverend brother Ambrosius, according to our ability to meet the charges brought by Celsus against the Christians, and have as far as possible passed over nothing without first subjecting it to a full and close examination. And now, while we enter upon the seventh book, we call upon God through Jesus Christ, whom Celsus accuses, that He who is the truth of God would shed light into our hearts and scatter the darkness of error, in accordance with that saying of the prophet which we now offer as our prayer, "Destroy them by Thy truth."[1] For it is evidently the words and reasonings opposed to the truth that God destroys by His truth; so that when these are destroyed, all who are delivered from deception may go on with the prophet to say, "I will freely sacrifice unto Thee,"[2] and may offer to the Most High a reasonable and smokeless sacrifice.

CHAP. II.

Celsus now sets himself to combat the views of those who say that the Jewish prophets foretold events which happened in the life of Christ Jesus. At the outset let us refer to a notion he has, that those who assume the existence of another God besides the God of the Jews have no ground on which to answer his objections; while we who recognise the same God rely for our defence on the prophecies which were delivered concerning Jesus Christ. His words are: "Let us see how they can raise a defence. To those who admit another God, no defence is possible; and they who recognise the same God will always fall back upon the same reason, 'This and that must have happened.' And why? 'Because it had been predicted long before.'" To this we answer, that the arguments recently raised by Celsus against Jesus and Christians were so utterly feeble, that they might easily be

overthrown even by those who are impious enough to bring in another God. Indeed, were it not dangerous to give to the weak any excuse for embracing false notions, we could furnish the answer ourselves, and show Celsus how unfounded is his opinion, that those who admit another God are not in a position to meet his arguments. However, let us for the present confine ourselves to a defence of the prophets, in continuation of what we have said on the subject before.

CHAP. III.

Celsus goes on to say of us: "They set no value on the oracles of the Pythian priestess, of the priests of Dodona, of Clarus, of Branchidæ, of Jupiter Ammon, and of a multitude of others; although under their guidance we may say that colonies were sent forth, and the whole world peopled. But those sayings which were uttered or not uttered in Judea, after the manner of that country, as indeed they are still delivered among the people of Phœnicia and Palestine — these they look upon as marvellous sayings, and unchangeably true." In regard to the oracles here enumerated, we reply that it would be possible for us to gather from the writings of Aristotle and the Peripatetic school not a few things to overthrow the authority of the Pythian and the other oracles. From Epicurus also, and his followers, we could quote passages to show that even among the Greeks themselves there were some who utterly discredited the oracles which were recognised and admired throughout the whole of Greece. But let it be granted that the responses delivered by the Pythian and other oracles were not the utterances of false men who pretended to a divine inspiration; and let us see if, after all, we cannot convince any sincere inquirers that there is no necessity to attribute these oracular responses to any divinities, but that, on the other hand, they may be traced to wicked demons — to spirits which are at enmity with the human race, and which in this way wish to hinder the soul from rising upwards, from following the path of virtue, and from returning to God in sincere piety. It is said of the Pythian priestess, whose oracle seems to have been the most celebrated, that when she sat down at the mouth of the Castalian cave, the prophetic spirit of Apollo entered her private parts; and when she was filled with it, she gave utterance to responses which are regarded with awe as divine truths. Judge by this whether that spirit does not show its profane and impure nature, by choosing to enter the soul of the prophetess not through the more becoming medium of the bodily pores which are both open and invisible, but by means of what no modest man would ever see or speak of. And this occurs not once or twice, which would be more permissible, but as often as she was believed to receive inspiration from Apollo. Moreover, it is not the part of a divine spirit to drive the prophetess into such a state of ecstasy and madness that she loses control of herself. For he who is under the influence of the Divine Spirit ought to be the first to receive the beneficial effects; and these ought not to be first enjoyed by the persons who consult the oracle about the concerns of natural or civil life, or for purposes of temporal gain or interest; and, moreover, that should be the time of clearest perception, when a person is in close intercourse with the Deity.

CHAP. IV.

Accordingly, we can show from an examination of the sacred Scriptures, that the Jewish prophets, who were enlightened as far as was necessary for their prophetic work by the Spirit of God, were the first to enjoy the benefit of the inspiration; and by the contact — if I may so say — of the Holy Spirit they became clearer in mind, and their souls were filled with a brighter light. And the body no longer served as a hindrance to a virtuous life; for to that which we call "the lust of the flesh" it was deadened. For we are persuaded that the Divine Spirit "mortifies the deeds of the body," and destroys that enmity against God which the carnal passions serve to excite. If, then, the Pythian priestess is beside herself when she prophesies, what spirit must that be which fills her mind and clouds her judgment with darkness, unless it be of the same order with those demons which many Christians cast out of persons possessed with them? And this, we may observe, they do without the use of any curious arts of magic, or incantations, but merely by prayer and simple adjurations which the plainest person can use. Because for the most part it is unlettered persons who perform this work; thus making manifest the grace which is in the word of Christ, and the despicable weakness of demons, which, in order to be overcome and driven out of the bodies and souls of men, do not require the power and wisdom of those who are mighty in argument, and most learned in matters of faith.[1]

CHAP. V.

Moreover, if it is believed not only among Christians and Jews, but also by many others among the Greeks and Barbarians, that the human soul lives and subsists after its separation from the body; and if reason supports the idea that pure souls which are not weighed down with sin as with a weight of lead ascend on high to the region of purer and more ethereal bodies, leaving here below their grosser bodies along with their impurities; whereas souls that are polluted and dragged down to the earth by their sins, so that they are unable even to breathe upwards, wander hither and thither, at some times about sepulchres, where they appear as the apparitions of shadowy spirits, at others among other objects on the ground; — if this is so, what are we to think of those spirits that are attached for entire ages, as I may say, to particular dwellings and places, whether by a sort of magical force or by their own natural wickedness? Are we not compelled by reason to set down as evil such spirits as employ the power of prophesying — a power in itself neither good nor bad — for the purpose of deceiving men, and thus turn them away from God, and from the purity of His service? It is moreover evident that this is their character, when we add that they delight in the blood of victims, and in the smoke and odour of sacrifices, and that they feed their bodies on these, and that they take pleasure in such haunts as these, as though they sought in them the sustenance of their lives; in this resembling those depraved men who despise the purity of a life apart from the senses, and who have no inclination except for the pleasures of the body, and for that earthly and bodily life in which these pleasures are found. If the Delphian Apollo were a god, as the Greeks suppose, would he not rather have chosen as his prophet some wise man? or if such an one was not to be found, then one who was endeavouring to become wise? How came he not to prefer a man to a woman for the utterance of his prophesies? And if he preferred the latter sex, as though he could only find pleasure in the breast of a woman, why did he not choose among women a virgin to interpret his will?

CHAP. VI.

But no; the Pythian, so much admired among the Greeks, judged no wise man, nay, no man at

1 [See Dr. Lee on "the immemorial doctrine of the Church of God" as to the Divine influence upon the intellectual faculties of the prophets: *Inspiration of Holy Scripture: its Nature and Proof*, pp. 78, 79. S.].

all, worthy of the divine possession, as they call it. And among women he did not choose a virgin, or one recommended by her wisdom, or by her attainments in philosophy; but he selects a common woman. Perhaps the better class of men were too good to become the subjects of the inspiration. Besides, if he were a god, he should have employed his prophetic power as a bait, so to speak, with which he might draw men to a change of life, and to the practice of virtue. But history nowhere makes mention of anything of the kind. For if the oracle did call Socrates the wisest of all men, it takes from the value of that eulogy by what is said in regard to Euripides and Sophocles. The words are: —

"Sophocles is wise, and Euripides is wiser,
　But wiser than all men is Socrates." [1]

As, then, he gives the designation "wise" to the tragic poets, it is not on account of his philosophy that he holds up Socrates to veneration, or because of his love of truth and virtue. It is poor praise of Socrates to say that he prefers him to men who for a paltry reward compete upon the stage, and who by their representations excite the spectators at one time to tears and grief, and at another to unseemly laughter (for such is the intention of the satyric drama). And perhaps it was not so much in regard to his philosophy that he called Socrates the wisest of all men, as on account of the victims which he sacrificed to him and the other demons. For it seems that the demons pay more regard in distributing their favours to the sacrifices which are offered them than to deeds of virtue. Accordingly, Homer, the best of the poets, who describes what usually took place, when, wishing to show us what most influenced the demons to grant an answer to the wishes of their votaries, introduces Chryses, who, for a few garlands and the thighs of bulls and goats, obtained an answer to his prayers for his daughter Chryseis, so that the Greeks were driven by a pestilence to restore her back to him. And I remember reading in the book of a certain Pythagorean, when writing on the hidden meanings in that poet, that the prayer of Chryses to Apollo, and the plague which Apollo afterwards sent upon the Greeks, are proofs that Homer knew of certain evil demons who delight in the smoke of sacrifices, and who, to reward those who offer them, grant in answer to their prayers the destruction of others. "He," that is, Jupiter, "who rules over wintry Dodona, where his prophets have ever unwashed feet, and sleep upon the ground," [2] has rejected the male sex, and, as Celsus observes, employs the women of Dodona for the prophetic office. Granting that there are oracles

similar to these, as that at Clarus, another in Branchidæ, another in the temple of Jupiter Ammon, or anywhere else; yet how shall it be proved that these are gods, and not demons?

CHAP. VII.

In regard to the prophets among the Jews, some of them were wise men before they became divinely inspired prophets, while others became wise by the illumination which their minds received when divinely inspired. They were selected by Divine Providence to receive the Divine Spirit, and to be the depositaries of His holy oracles, on the ground of their leading a life of almost unapproachable excellence, intrepid, noble, unmoved by danger or death. For reason teaches that such ought to be the character of the prophets of the Most High, in comparison with which the firmness of Antisthenes, Crates, and Diogenes will seem but as child's play. It was therefore for their firm adherence to truth, and their faithfulness in the reproof of the wicked, that "they were stoned; they were sawn asunder, were tempted, were slain with the sword; they wandered about in sheepskins and goatskins; being destitute, afflicted, tormented; they wandered in deserts and in mountains, and in dens and caves of the earth, of whom the world was not worthy:" [3] for they looked always to God and to His blessings, which, being invisible, and not to be perceived by the senses, are eternal. We have the history of the life of each of the prophets; but it will be enough at present to direct attention to the life of Moses, whose prophecies are contained in the law; to that of Jeremiah, as it is given in the book which bears his name; to that of Isaiah, who with unexampled austerity walked naked and barefooted for the space of three years. [4] Read and consider the severe life of those children, Daniel and his companions, how they abstained from flesh, and lived on water and pulse. [5] Or if you will go back to more remote times, think of the life of Noah, who prophesied; [6] and of Isaac, who gave his son a prophetic blessing; or of Jacob, who addressed each of his twelve sons, beginning with "Come, that I may tell you what shall befall you in the last days." [7] These, and a multitude of others, prophesying on behalf of God, foretold events relating to Jesus Christ. We therefore for this reason set at nought the oracles of the Pythian priestess, or those delivered at Dodona, at Clarus, at Branchidæ, at the temple of Jupiter Ammon, or by a multitude of other so-called prophets;

---

[1] Suidas in Σοφός.
[2] Homer, *Iliad*, xvi. 234, etc.

[3] Heb. xi. 37, 38.
[4] [Isa. xx. 3. S.]
[5] [Dan. i. 16. S.]
[6] [Gen. ix. 25-27. S.]
[7] [Gen. xlix. 1. S.]

whilst we regard with reverent awe the Jewish prophets : for we see that the noble, earnest, and devout lives of these men were worthy of the inspiration of the Divine Spirit, whose wonderful effects were widely different from the divination of demons.

CHAP. VIII.

I do not know what led Celsus, when saying, " But what things were spoken or not spoken in the land of Judea, according to the custom of the country," to use the words " or not spoken," as though implying that he was incredulous, and that he suspected that those things which were written were never spoken. In fact, he is un-acquainted with these times ; and he does not know that those prophets who foretold the com-ing of Christ, predicted a multitude of other events many years beforehand. He adds, with the view of casting a slight upon the ancient prophets, that " they prophesied in the same way as we find them still doing among the in-habitants of Phœnicia and Palestine.' But he does not tell us whether he refers to persons who are of different principles from those of the Jews and Christians, or to persons whose prophecies are of the same character as those of the Jewish prophets. However it be, his statement is false, taken in either way. For never have any of those who have not embraced our faith done any thing approaching to what was done by the ancient prophets ; and in more recent times, since the coming of Christ, no prophets have arisen among the Jews, who have confessedly been abandoned by the Holy Spirit on account of their impiety towards God, and towards Him of whom their prophets spoke. Moreover, the Holy Spirit gave signs of His presence at the beginning of Christ's ministry, and after His ascension He gave still more ; but since that time these signs have di-minished, although there are still traces of His presence in a few who have had their souls puri-fied by the Gospel, and their actions regulated by its influence. " For the holy Spirit of disci-pline will flee deceit, and remove from thoughts that are without understanding." [1]

CHAP. IX.

But as Celsus promises to give an account of the manner in which prophecies are delivered in Phœnicia and Palestine, speaking as though it were a matter with which he had a full and per-sonal acquaintance, let us see what he has to say on the subject. First he lays it down that there are several kinds of prophecies, but he does not specify what they are ; indeed, he could not do so, and the statement is a piece of pure osten-tation. However, let us see what he considers

[1] Wisd of Sol. i. 5.

the most perfect kind of prophecy among these nations. " There are many," he says, " who, although of no name, with the greatest facility and on the slightest occasion, whether within or without temples, assume the motions and gestures of inspired persons ; while others do it in cities or among armies, for the purpose of attracting attention and exciting surprise. These are accus-tomed to say, each for himself, ' I am God ; I am the Son of God ; or, I am the Divine Spirit ; I have come because the world is perishing, and you, O men, are perishing for your iniquities. But I wish to save you, and you shall see me re-turning again with heavenly power. Blessed is he who now does me homage. On all the rest I will send down eternal fire, both on cities and on countries. And those who know not the punishments which await them shall repent and grieve in vain ; while those who are faithful to me I will preserve eternally.' " Then he goes on to say : " To these promises are added strange, fanatical, and quite unintelligible words, of which no rational person can find the meaning : for so dark are they, as to have no meaning at all ; but they give occasion to every fool or impostor to apply them to suit his own purposes."

CHAP. X.

But if he were dealing honestly in his accusa-tions, he ought to have given the exact terms of the prophecies, whether those in which the speaker is introduced as claiming to be God Almighty, or those in which the Son of God speaks, or finally those under the name of the Holy Spirit. For thus he might have endeav-oured to overthrow these assertions, and have shown that there was no divine inspiration in those words which urged men to forsake their sins, which condemned the past and foretold the future. For the prophecies were recorded and preserved by men living at the time, that those who came after might read and admire them as the oracles of God, and that they might profit not only by the warnings and admonitions, but also by the predictions, which, being shown by events to have proceeded from the Spirit of God, bind men to the practice of piety as set forth in the law and the prophets. The prophets have therefore, as God commanded them, declared with all plainness those things which it was de-sirable that the hearers should understand at once for the regulation of their conduct ; while in regard to deeper and more mysterious sub-jects, which lay beyond the reach of the common understanding, they set them forth in the form of enigmas and allegories, or of what are called dark sayings, parables, or similitudes. And this plan they have followed, that those who are ready to shun no labour and spare no pains in their endeavours after truth and virtue might search into their meaning, and having found it, might apply it as reason requires. But Celsus, ever vigorous in his denunciations, as though he were angry at his inability to understand the language of the prophets, scoffs at them thus : " To these grand promises are added strange, fanatical, and quite unintelligible words, of which no rational person can find the meaning ; for so dark are they as to have no meaning at all ; but they give occasion to every fool or impostor to apply them so as to suit his own purposes." This statement of Celsus seems ingeniously designed to dissuade readers from attempting any inquiry or careful search into their meaning. And in this he is not unlike certain persons, who said to a man whom a prophet had visited to announce future events, " Wherefore came this mad fellow to thee ? " [1]

CHAP. XI.

I am convinced, indeed, that much better arguments could be adduced than any I have been able to bring forward, to show the falsehood of these allegations of Celsus, and to set forth the divine inspiration of the prophecies ; but we have according to our ability, in our commentaries on Isaiah, Ezekiel, and some of the twelve minor prophets, explained literally and in detail what he calls " those fanatical and utterly unintelligible passages." [2] And if God give us grace in the time that He appoints for us, to advance in the knowledge of His word, we shall continue our investigation into the parts which remain, or into such at least as we are able to make plain. And other persons of intelligence who wish to study Scripture may also find out its meaning for themselves ; for although there are many places in which the meaning is not obvious, yet there are none where, as Celsus affirms, " there is no sense at all." Neither is it true that " any fool or impostor can explain the passages so as to make them suit his own purposes." For it belongs only to those who are wise in the truth of Christ (and to all them it does belong) to unfold the connection and meaning of even the obscure parts of prophecy, " comparing spiritual things with spiritual," and interpreting each passage according to the usage of Scripture writers. And Celsus is not to be believed when he says that he has heard such men prophesy ; for no prophets bearing any resemblance to the ancient prophets have appeared in the time of Celsus. If there had been any, those who heard and admired them would have followed the example of the ancients, and have recorded the prophecies in writing. And it seems quite clear that Celsus is speaking falsely, when he says that " those prophets whom he had heard, on being pressed by him, confessed their true motives, and acknowledged that the ambiguous words they used really meant nothing." He ought to have given the names of those whom he says he had heard, if he had any to give, so that those who were competent to judge might decide whether his allegations were true or false.

CHAP. XII.

He thinks, besides, that those who support the cause of Christ by a reference to the writings of the prophets can give no proper answer in regard to statements in them which attribute to God that which is wicked, shameful, or impure ; and assuming that no answer can be given, he proceeds to draw a whole train of inferences, none of which can be allowed. But he ought to know that those who wish to live according to the teaching of sacred Scripture understand the saying, " The knowledge of the unwise is as talk without sense," [3] and have learnt " to be ready always to give an answer to every one that asketh us a reason for the hope that is in us." [4] And they are not satisfied with affirming that such and such things have been predicted ; but they endeavour to remove any apparent inconsistencies, and to show that, so far from there being anything evil, shameful, or impure in these predictions, everything is worthy of being received by those who understand the sacred Scriptures. But Celsus ought to have adduced from the prophets examples of what he thought bad, or shameful, or impure, if he saw any such passages ; for then his argument would have had much more force, and would have furthered his purpose much better. He gives no instances, however, but contents himself with loudly asserting the false charge that these things are to be found in Scripture. There is no reason, then, for us to defend ourselves against groundless charges, which are but empty sounds, or to take the trouble of showing that in the writings of the prophets there is nothing evil, shameful, impure, or abominable.

CHAP. XIII.

And there is no truth in the statement of Celsus, that " God does the most shameless deeds, or suffers the most shameless sufferings," or that " He favours the commission of evil ; " for whatever he may say, no such things have ever been foretold. He ought to have cited from the prophets the passages in which God is represented as favouring evil, or as doing and enduring the most shameless deeds, and not to have sought without foundation to prejudice the minds of

---

[1] 2 Kings ix. 11.
[2] [See note *supra*, p. 612. S.]

[3] Ecclus. xxi. 18.
[4] 1 Pet. iii. 15.

his readers. The prophets, indeed, foretold what Christ should suffer, and set forth the reason why He should suffer. God therefore also knew what Christ would suffer; but where has he learnt that those things which the Christ of God should suffer were most base and dishonourable? He goes on to explain what those most shameful and degrading things were which Christ suffered, in these words: "For what better was it for God to eat the flesh of sheep, or to drink vinegar and gall, than to feed on filth?" But God, according to us, did not eat the flesh of sheep; and while it may seem that Jesus ate, He did so only as possessing a body. But in regard to the vinegar and gall mentioned in the prophecy, "They gave me also gall for my meat; and in my thirst they gave me vinegar to drink," [1] we have already referred [2] to this point; and as Celsus compels us to recur to it again, we would only say further, that those who resist the word of truth do ever offer to Christ the Son of God the gall of their own wickedness, and the vinegar of their evil inclinations; but though He tastes of it, yet He will not drink it.

CHAP. XIV.

In the next place, wishing to shake the faith of those who believe in Jesus on the ground of the prophecies which were delivered in regard to Him, Celsus says: "But pray, if the prophets foretold that the great God — not to put it more harshly — would become a slave, or become sick, or die; would there be therefore any necessity that God should die, or suffer sickness, or become a slave, simply because such things had been foretold? Must he die in order to prove his divinity? But the prophets never would utter predictions so wicked and impious. We need not therefore inquire whether a thing has been predicted or not, but whether the thing is honourable in itself, and worthy of God. In that which is evil and base, although it seemed that all men in the world had foretold it in a fit of madness, we must not believe. How then can the pious mind admit that those things which are said to have happened to him, could have happened to one who is God?" From this it is plain that Celsus feels the argument from prophecy to be very effective for convincing those to whom Christ is preached; but he seems to endeavour to overthrow it by an opposite probability, namely, "that the question is not whether the prophets uttered these predictions or not." But if he wished to reason justly and without evasion, he ought rather to have said, "We must show that these things were never predicted, or that those things which were predicted of Christ

have never been fulfilled in him," and in that way he would have established the position which he holds. In that way it would have been made plain what those prophecies are which we apply to Jesus, and how Celsus could justify himself in asserting that that application was false. And we should thus have seen whether he fairly disproved all that we bring from the prophets in behalf of Jesus, or whether he himself is convicted of a shameless endeavour to resist the plainest truths by violent assertions.

CHAP. XV.

After assuming that some things were foretold which are impossible in themselves, and inconsistent with the character of God, he says: "If these things were predicted of the Most High God, are we bound to believe them of God simply because they were predicted?" And thus he thinks he proves, that although the prophets may have foretold truly such things of the Son of God, yet it is impossible for us to believe in those prophecies declaring that He would do or suffer such things. To this our answer is that the supposition is absurd, for it combines two lines of reasoning which are opposed to each other, and therefore mutually destructive. This may be shown as follows. The one argument is: "If any true prophets of the Most High say that God will become a slave, or suffer sickness, or die, these things will come to God; for it is impossible that the prophets of the great God should utter lies." The other is: "If even true prophets of the Most High God say that these same things shall come to pass, seeing that these things foretold are by the nature of things impossible, the prophecies are not true, and therefore those things which have been foretold will not happen to God." When, then, we find two processes of reasoning in both of which the major premiss is the same, leading to two contradictory conclusions, we use the form of argument called "the theorem of two propositions," [3] to prove that the major premiss is false, which in the case before us is this, "that the prophets have foretold that the great God should become a slave, suffer sickness, or die." We conclude, then, that the prophets never foretold such things; and the argument is formally expressed as follows: 1st, Of two things, if the first is true, the second is true; 2d, if the first is [4] true, the second is not true, therefore the first is not true. The concrete example which the Stoics give to illustrate this form of argument is the following: 1st, If you know that you are dead, you are dead; 2d, if you know that you are dead, you are not dead. And the conclusion is — "you do not know that

---

[1] Ps. lxix. 21.
[2] Book ii. cap. xxxvii.

[3] διὰ δύο τροπικῶν θεωρήμα.
[4] We follow Bouhereau and Valesius, who expunge the negative particle in this clause.

you are dead." These propositions are worked out as follows : If you know that you are dead, that which you know is certain ; therefore you are dead. Again, if you know that you are dead, your death is an object of knowledge ; but as the dead know nothing, your knowing this proves that you are not dead. Accordingly, by joining the two arguments together, you arrive at the conclusion — "you do not know that you are dead." Now the hypothesis of Celsus which we have given above is much of the same kind.

CHAP. XVI.

But besides, the prophecies which he introduces into his argument are very different from what the prophets actually foretold of Jesus Christ. For the prophecies do not foretell that God will be crucified, when they say of Him who should suffer, "We beheld Him, and He had no form or comeliness ; but His form was dishonoured and marred more than the sons of men ; He was a man of sorrows, and acquainted with grief." [1] Observe, then, how distinctly they say that it was a man who should endure these human sufferings. And Jesus Himself, who knew perfectly that one who was to die must be a man, said to His accusers : " But now ye seek to kill Me, a man that hath spoken unto you the truth which I heard of God." [2] And if in that man as He appeared among men there was something divine, namely the only-begotten Son of God, the first-born of all creation, one who said of Himself, " I am the truth," " I am the life," " I am the door," "I am the way," "I am the living bread which came down from heaven," of this Being and His nature we must judge and reason in a way quite different from that in which we judge of the man who was seen in Jesus Christ. Accordingly, you will find no Christian, however simple he may be, and however little versed in critical studies, who would say that He who died was "the truth," "the life," "the way," "the living bread which came down from heaven," "the resurrection ; " for it was He who appeared to us in the form of the man Jesus, who taught us, saying, "I am the resurrection." There is no one amongst us, I say, so extravagant as to affirm "the Life died," "the Resurrection died." The supposition of Celsus would have some foundation if we were to say that it had been foretold by the prophets that death would befall God the Word, the Truth, the Life, the Resurrection, or any other name which is assumed by the Son of God.

CHAP. XVII.

In one point alone is Celsus correct in his statements on this subject. It is that in which

he says : " The prophets would not foretell this, because it involves that which is wicked and impious," — namely, that the great God should become a slave or suffer death. But that which is predicted by the prophets is worthy of God, that He who is the brightness and express image of the divine nature should come into the world with the holy human soul which was to animate the body of Jesus, to sow the seed of His word, which might bring all who received and cherished it into union with the Most High God, and which would lead to perfect blessedness all those who felt within them the power of God the Word, who was to be in the body and soul of a man. He was to be in it indeed, but not in such a way as to confine therein all the rays of His glôry ; and we are not to suppose that the light of Him who is God the Word is shed forth in no other way than in this. If, then, we consider Jesus in relation to the divinity that was in Him, the things which He did in this capacity present nothing to offend our ideas of God, nothing but what is holy ; and if we consider Him as man, distinguished beyond all other men by an intimate communion with the Eternal Word, with absolute Wisdom, He suffered as one who was wise and perfect, whatever it behoved Him to. suffer who did all for the good of the human race, yea, even for the good of all intelligent beings. And there is nothing absurd in a man having died, and in His death being not only an example of death endured for the sake of piety, but also the first blow in the conflict which is to overthrow the power of that evil spirit the devil, who had obtained dominion over the whole world.[3] For we have signs and pledges of the destruction of his empire, in those who through the coming of Christ are everywhere escaping from the power of demons, and who, after their deliverance from this bondage in which they were held, consecrate themselves to God, and earnestly devote themselves day by day to advancement in a life of piety.

CHAP. XVIII.

Celsus adds : "Will they not besides make this reflection? If the prophets of the God of the Jews foretold that he who should come into the world would be the Son of this same God, how could he command them through Moses to gather wealth, to extend their dominion, to fill the earth, to put their enemies of every age to the sword, and to destroy them utterly, which indeed he himself did — as Moses says — threatening them, moreover, that if they did not obey his commands, he would treat them as his avowed enemies ; whilst, on the other hand, his Son, the man of Nazareth, promulgated laws quite op-

---

posed to these, declaring that no one can come to the Father who loves power, or riches, or glory ; that men ought not to be more careful in providing food than the ravens ; that they were to be less concerned about their raiment than the lilies ; that to him who has given them one blow, they should offer to receive another ? Whether is it Moses or Jesus who teaches falsely? Did the Father, when he sent Jesus, forget the commands which he had given to Moses? Or did he change his mind, condemn his own laws, and send forth a messenger with counter instructions?" Celsus, with all his boasts of universal knowledge, has here fallen into the most vulgar of errors, in supposing that in the law and the prophets there is not a meaning deeper than that afforded by a literal rendering of the words. He does not see how manifestly incredible it is that worldly riches should be promised to those who lead upright lives, when it is a matter of common observation that the best of men have lived in extreme poverty. Indeed, the prophets themselves, who for the purity of their lives received the Divine Spirit, " wandered about in sheepskins and goatskins ; being destitute, afflicted, tormented : they wandered in deserts, and in mountains, and in dens and caves of the earth."[1] For, as the Psalmist says, " many are the afflictions of the righteous."[2] If Celsus had read the writings of Moses, he would, I daresay, have supposed that when it is said to him who kept the law, " Thou shalt lend unto many nations, and thou thyself shalt not borrow,"[3] the promise is made to the just man, that his temporal riches should be so abundant, that he would be able to lend not only to the Jews, not only to two or three nations, but " to many nations." What, then, must have been the wealth which the just man received according to the law for his righteousness, if he could lend to many nations? And must we not suppose also, in accordance with this interpretation, that the just man would never borrow anything? For it is written, " and thou shalt thyself borrow nothing." Did then that nation remain for so long a period attached to the religion which was taught by Moses, whilst, according to the supposition of Celsus, they saw themselves so grievously deceived by that lawgiver? For nowhere is it said of any one that he was so rich as to lend to many nations. It is not to be believed that they would have fought so zealously in defence of a law whose promises had proved glaringly false, if they understood them in the sense which Celsus gives to them. And if any one should say that the sins which are recorded to have been committed by the people are a

proof that they despised the law, doubtless from the feeling that they had been deceived by it, we may reply that we have only to read the history of the times in order to find it shown that the whole people, after having done that which was evil in the sight of the Lord, returned afterwards to their duty, and to the religion prescribed by the law.

CHAP. XIX.

Now if these words in the law, " Thou shalt have dominion over many nations, and no one shall rule over thee," were simply a promise to them of dominion, and if they contain no deeper meaning than this, then it is certain that the people would have had still stronger grounds for despising the promises of the law. Celsus brings forward another passage, although he changes the terms of it, where it is said that the whole earth shall be filled with the Hebrew race ; which indeed, according to the testimony of history, did actually happen after the coming of Christ, although rather as a result of God's anger, if I may so say, than of His blessing. As to the promise made to the Jews that they should slay their enemies, it may be answered that any one who examines carefully into the meaning of this passage will find himself unable to interpret it literally. It is sufficient at present to refer to the manner in which in the Psalms the just man is represented as saying, among other things, " Every morning will I destroy the wicked of the land ; that I may cut off all workers of iniquity from the city of Jehovah."[4] Judge, then, from the words and spirit of the speaker, whether it is conceivable that, after having in the preceding part of the Psalm, as any one may read for himself, uttered the noblest thoughts and purposes, he should in the sequel, according to the literal rendering of his words, say that in the morning, and at no other period of the day, he would destroy all sinners from the earth, and leave none of them alive, and that he would slay every one in Jerusalem who did iniquity. And there are many similar expressions to be found in the law, as this, for example : " We left not anything alive."[5]

CHAP. XX.

Celsus adds, that it was foretold to the Jews, that if they did not obey the law, they would be treated in the same way as they treated their enemies ; and then he quotes from the teaching of Christ some precepts which he considers contrary to those of the law, and uses that as an argument against us. But before proceeding to this point, we must speak of that which precedes. We hold, then, that the law has a twofold sense,

[1] Heb. xi. 37, 38.
[2] Ps. xxiv. 19.
[3] Deut. xxviii. 12.

[4] Ps. ci. 8.
[5] Deut. ii. 34.

— the one literal, the other spiritual, — as has been shown by some before us. Of the first or literal sense it is said, not by us, but by God, speaking in one of the prophets, that "the statutes are not good, and the judgments not good;"[1] whereas, taken in a spiritual sense, the same prophet makes God say that "His statutes are good, and His judgments good." Yet evidently the prophet is not saying things which are contradictory of each other. Paul in like manner says, that "the letter killeth, and the spirit giveth life,"[2] meaning by "the letter" the literal sense, and by "the spirit" the spiritual sense of Scripture. We may therefore find in Paul, as well as in the prophet, apparent contradictions. Indeed, if Ezekiel says in one place, "I gave them commandments which were not good, and judgments whereby they should not live," and in another, "I gave them good commandments and judgments, which if a man shall do, he shall live by them,"[3] Paul in like manner, when he wishes to disparage the law taken literally, says, "If the ministration of death, written and engraven in stones, was glorious, so that the children of Israel could not stedfastly behold the face of Moses for the glory of his countenance, which glory was to be done away; how shall not the ministration of the Spirit be rather glorious?"[4] But when in another place he wishes to praise and recommend the law, he calls it "spiritual," and says, "We know that the law is spiritual;" and, "Wherefore the law is holy, and the commandment holy, and just, and good."[5]

CHAP. XXI.

When, then, the letter of the law promises riches to the just, Celsus may follow the letter which killeth, and understand it of worldly riches, which blind men; but we say that it refers to those riches which enlighten the eyes, and which enrich a man "in all utterance and in all knowledge." And in this sense we "charge them that are rich in this world, that they be not high-minded, nor trust in uncertain riches, but in the living God, who giveth us richly all things to enjoy; that they do good, that they be rich in good works, ready to distribute, willing to communicate."[6] For, as Solomon says, "riches" are the true good, which "are the ransom of the life of a man;" but the poverty which is the opposite of these riches is destructive, for by it "the poor cannot bear rebuke."[7] And what has been said of riches applies to

dominion, in regard to which it is said, "The just man shall chase a thousand, and two put ten thousand to flight."[8] Now if riches are to be taken in the sense we have just explained, consider if it is not according to God's promise that he who is rich in all utterance, in all knowledge, in all wisdom, in all good works, may not out of these treasures of utterance, of wisdom, and of knowledge, lend to many nations. It was thus that Paul lent to all the nations that he visited, "carrying the Gospel of Christ from Jerusalem, and round about unto Illyricum."[9] And as the divine knowledge was given to him by revelation, and his mind was illumined by the Divine Word, he himself therefore needed to borrow from no one, and required not the ministry of any man to teach him the word of truth. Thus, as it had been written, "Thou shalt have dominion over many nations, and they shall not have dominion over thee," he ruled over the Gentiles whom he brought under the teaching of Jesus Christ; and he never "gave place by subjection to men, no, not for an hour,[10] as being himself mightier than they. And thus also he "filled the earth."

CHAP. XXII.

If I must now explain how the just man "slays his enemies," and prevails everywhere, it is to be observed that, when he says, "Every morning will I destroy the wicked of the land, that I may cut off all workers of iniquity from the city of Jehovah," by "the land" he means the flesh whose lusts are at enmity with God; and by "the city of Jehovah" he designates his own soul, in which was the temple of God, containing the true idea and conception of God, which makes it to be admired by all who look upon it. As soon, then, as the rays of the Sun of righteousness shine into his soul, feeling strengthened and invigorated by their influence, he sets himself to destroy all the lusts of the flesh, which are called "the wicked of the land," and drives out of that city of the Lord which is in his soul all thoughts which work iniquity, and all suggestions which are opposed to the truth. And in this way also the just give up to destruction all their enemies, which are their vices, so that they do not spare even the children, that is, the early beginnings and promptings of evil. In this sense also we understand the language of the 137th Psalm: "O daughter of Babylon, who art to be destroyed; happy shall he be that rewardeth thee as thou hast served us: happy shall he be that taketh and dasheth thy little ones against the stones."[11] For "the little ones" of Babylon

---

[1] Ezek. xx. 25.
[2] 2 Cor. iii. 6.
[3] [Ezek. xx. 21, 25. S.]
[4] 2 Cor. iii. 7, 8.
[5] Rom. vii. 12, 14.
[6] 1 Tim. vi. 17, 18.
[7] Prov. xiii. 8.

[8] Deut. xxxii. 30.
[9] Rom. xv. 19.
[10] Gal. ii. 5.
[11] Ps. cxxxvii. 8, 9. [An instance of Origen's characteristic spiritualizing.]

(which signifies confusion) are those trouble-some sinful thoughts which arise in the soul; and he who subdues them by striking, as it were, their heads against the firm and solid strength of reason and truth, is the man who "dasheth the little ones against the stones;" and he is therefore truly blessed. God may therefore have commanded men to destroy all their vices utterly, even at their birth, without having enjoined anything contrary to the teaching of Christ; and He may Himself have destroyed before the eyes of those who were "Jews inwardly"[1] all the offspring of evil as His enemies. And, in like manner, those who disobey the law and word of God may well be compared to His enemies led astray by sin; and they may well be said to suffer the same fate as they deserve who have proved traitors to the truth of God.

CHAP. XXIII.

From what has been said, it is clear then that Jesus, "the man of Nazareth," did not promulgate laws opposed to those just considered in regard to riches, when He said, "It is hard for the rich man to enter into the kingdom of God;"[2] whether we take the word "rich" in its simplest sense, as referring to the man whose mind is distracted by his wealth, and, as it were, entangled with thorns, so that he brings forth no spiritual fruit; or whether it is the man who is rich in the sense of abounding in false notions, of whom it is written in the Proverbs, "Better is the poor man who is just, than the rich man who is false."[3] Perhaps it is the following passages which have led Celsus to suppose that Jesus forbids ambition to His disciples: "Whoever of you will be the chiefest, shall be servant of all;"[4] "The princes of the Gentiles exercise dominion over them,"[5] and "they that exercise authority upon them are called benefactors."[6] But there is nothing here inconsistent with the promise, "Thou shalt rule over many nations, and they shall not rule over thee," especially after the explanation which we have given of these words. Celsus next throws in an expression in regard to wisdom, as though he thought that, according to the teaching of Christ, no wise man could come to the Father. But we would ask in what sense he speaks of a wise man. For if he means one who is wise in "the wisdom of this world," as it is called, "which is foolishness with God,"[7] then we would agree with him in saying that access to the Father is denied to one who is wise in that sense. But if by wisdom any one means

Christ, who is "the power and wisdom of God," far from such a wise man being refused access to the Father, we hold that he who is adorned by the Holy Spirit with that gift which is called "the word of wisdom," far excels all those who have not received the same grace.

CHAP. XXIV.

The pursuit of human glory, we maintain, is forbidden not only by the teaching of Jesus, but also by the Old Testament. Accordingly we find one of the prophets, when imprecating upon himself certain punishments for the commission of certain sins, includes among the punishments this one of earthly glory. He says, "O Lord my God, if I have done this; if there be iniquity in my hands; if I have rewarded evil unto him that was at peace with me; (yea, rather, I have delivered him that without cause is mine enemy;) let the enemy persecute my soul, and take it; yea, let him tread down my life upon the earth, and *set my glory up on high*."[8] And these precepts of our Lord, "Take no thought what ye shall eat, or what ye shall drink. Behold the fowls of the air, or behold the ravens: for they sow not, neither do they reap; yet your heavenly Father feedeth them. How much better are ye than they! And why take ye thought for raiment? Consider the lilies of the field;"[9] these precepts, and those which follow, are not inconsistent with the promised blessings of the law, which teaches that the just "shall eat their bread to the full;"[10] nor with that saying of Solomon, "The righteous eateth to the satisfying of his soul, but the belly of the wicked shall want."[11] For we must consider the food promised in the law as the food of the soul, which is to satisfy not both parts of man's nature, but the soul only. And the words of the Gospel, although probably containing a deeper meaning, may yet be taken in their more simple and obvious sense, as teaching us not to be disturbed with anxieties about our food and clothing, but, while living in plainness, and desiring only what is needful, to put our trust in the providence of God.

CHAP. XXV.

Celsus then extracts from the Gospel the precept, "To him who strikes thee once, thou shalt offer thyself to be struck again," although without giving any passage from the Old Testament which he considers opposed to it. On the one hand, we know that "it was said to them in old time, An eye for an eye, and a tooth for a

---

[1] Rom. ii. 29.
[2] Matt. xix. 23.
[3] Prov. xxviii. 6.
[4] Mark x. 44.
[5] Matt. xx. 25.
[6] Luke xxii. 25.
[7] 1 Cor. iii. 19.

[8] Ps. vii. 3–5. Origen follows the reading εἰς χοῦν (LXX.) instead of εἰς χνοῦν, "make my glory abide *in the dust*."
[9] Matt. vi. 25–28.
[10] Lev. xxvi. 5.
[11] Prov. xiii. 25.

tooth;"[1] and on the other, we have read, "I say unto you, Whoever shall smite thee on the one cheek, turn to him the other also."[2] But as there is reason to believe that Celsus produces the objections which he has heard from those who wish to make a difference between the God of the Gospel and the God of the law, we must say in reply, that this precept, "Whosoever shall strike thee on the one cheek, turn to him the other," is not unknown in the older Scriptures. For thus, in the Lamentations of Jeremiah, it is said, "It is good for a man that he bear the yoke in his youth : he sitteth alone, and keepeth silence, because he hath borne it upon him. He giveth his cheek to him that smiteth him ; he is filled full with reproach."[3] There is no discrepancy, then, between the God of the Gospel and the God of the law, even when we take literally the precept regarding the blow on the face. So, then, we infer that neither "Jesus nor Moses has taught falsely." The Father in sending Jesus did not "forget the commands which He had given to Moses:" He did not "change His mind, condemn His own laws, and send by His messenger counter instructions."

CHAP. XXVI.

However, if we must refer briefly to the difference between the constitution which was given to the Jews of old by Moses, and that which the Christians, under the direction of Christ's teaching, wish now to establish, we would observe that it must be impossible for the legislation of Moses, taken literally, to harmonize with the calling of the Gentiles, and with their subjection to the Roman government ; and on the other hand, it would be impossible for the Jews to preserve their civil economy unchanged, supposing that they should embrace the Gospel. For Christians could not slay their enemies, or condemn to be burned or stoned, as Moses commands, those who had broken the law, and were therefore condemned as deserving of these punishments ; since the Jews themselves, however desirous of carrying out their law, are not able to inflict these punishments. But in the case of the ancient Jews, who had a land and a form of government of their own, to take from them the right of making war upon their enemies, of fighting for their country, of putting to death or otherwise punishing adulterers, murderers, or others who were guilty of similar crimes, would be to subject them to sudden and utter destruction whenever the enemy fell upon them ; for their very laws would in that case restrain them, and prevent them from resisting the enemy.

And that same providence which of old gave the law, and has now given the Gospel of Jesus Christ, not wishing the Jewish state to continue longer, has destroyed their city and their temple : it has abolished the worship which was offered to God in that temple by the sacrifice of victims, and other ceremonies which He had prescribed. And as it has destroyed these things, not wishing that they should longer continue, in like manner it has extended day by day the Christian religion, so that it is now preached everywhere with boldness, and that in spite of the numerous obstacles which oppose the spread of Christ's teaching in the world. But since it was the purpose of God that the nations should receive the benefits of Christ's teaching, all the devices of men against Christians have been brought to nought ; for the more that kings, and rulers, and peoples have persecuted them everywhere, the more have they increased in number and grown in strength.

CHAP. XXVII.

After this Celsus relates at length opinions which he ascribes to us, but which we do not hold, regarding the Divine Being, to the effect that "he is corporeal in his nature, and possesses a body like a man." As he undertakes to refute opinions which are none of ours, it would be needless to give either the opinions themselves or their refutation. Indeed, if we did hold those views of God which he ascribes to us, and which he opposes, we would be bound to quote his words, to adduce our own arguments, and to refute his. But if he brings forward opinions which he has either heard from no one, or if it be assumed that he has heard them, it must have been from those who are very simple and ignorant of the meaning of Scripture, then we need not undertake so superfluous a task as that of refuting them. For the Scriptures plainly speak of God as of a being without body. Hence it is said, "No man hath seen God at any time ;"[4] and the First-born of all creation is called "the image of the invisible God,"[5] which is the same as if it were said that He is incorporeal. However, we have already said something on the nature of God while examining into the meaning of the words, "God is a Spirit, and they who worship Him must worship Him in spirit and in truth."

CHAP. XXVIII.

After thus misrepresenting our views of the nature of God, Celsus goes on to ask of us "where we hope to go after death ;" and he makes our answer to be, "to another land better than this." On this he comments as follows :

---

[1] Ex. xxi. 24.
[2] Matt. v. 39.
[3] Lam. iii. 27, 28, 30.

[4] John i. 18.
[5] Col. i. 15.

" The divine men of a former age have spoken of a happy life reserved for the souls of the blessed. Some designated it ' the isles of the blest,' and others ' the Elysian plain,' so called because they were there to be delivered from their present evils. Thus Homer says : ' But the gods shall send thee to the Elysian plain, on the borders of the earth, where they lead a most quiet life.' [1] Plato also, who believed in the immortality of the soul, distinctly gives the name ' land ' to the place where it is sent. ' The extent of it,' [2] says he, ' is immense, and we only occupy a small portion of it, from the Phasis to the Pillars of Hercules, where we dwell along the shores of the sea, as grasshoppers and frogs beside a marsh. But there are many other places inhabited in like manner by other men. For there are in different parts of the earth cavities, varying in form and in magnitude, into which run water, and clouds, and air. But that land which is pure lies in the pure region of heaven.' " Celsus therefore supposes that what we say of a land which is much better and more excellent than this, has been borrowed from certain ancient writers whom he styles " divine," and chiefly from Plato, who in his *Phædon* discourses on the pure land lying in a pure heaven. But he does not see that Moses, who is much older than the Greek literature, introduces God as promising to those who lived according to His law the holy land, which is " a good land and a large, a land flowing with milk and honey ; " [3] which promise is not to be understood to refer, as some suppose, to that part of the earth which we call Judea ; for it, however good it may be, still forms part of the earth, which was originally cursed for the transgression of Adam. For these words, " Cursed shall the ground be for what thou hast done ; with grief, that is, with labour, shalt thou eat of the fruit of it all the days of thy life," [4] were spoken of the whole earth, the fruit of which every man who died in Adam eats with sorrow or labour all the days of his life. And as all the earth has been cursed, it brings forth thorns and briers all the days of the life of those who in Adam were driven out of paradise ; and in the sweat of his face every man eats bread until he returns to the ground from which he was taken. For the full exposition of all that is contained in this passage much might be said ; but we have confined ourselves to these few words at present, which are intended to remove the idea, that what is said of the good land promised by God to the righteous, refers to the land of Judea.

CHAP. XXIX.

If, then, the whole earth has been cursed in the deeds of Adam and of those who died in him, it is plain that all parts of the earth share in the curse, and among others the land of Judea ; so that the words, " a good land and a large, a land flowing with milk and honey," cannot apply to it, although we may say of it, that both Judea and Jerusalem were the shadow and figure of that pure land, goodly and large, in the pure region of heaven, in which is the heavenly Jerusalem. And it is in reference to this Jerusalem that the apostle spoke, as one who, " being risen with Christ, and seeking those things which are above," had found a truth which formed no part of the Jewish mythology. " Ye are come," says he, " unto Mount Sion, and unto the city of the living God, the heavenly Jerusalem, and to an innumerable company of angels." [5] And in order to be assured that our explanation of " the good and large land " of Moses is not contrary to the intention of the Divine Spirit, we have only to read in all the prophets what they say of those who, after having left Jerusalem, and wandered astray from it, should afterwards return and be settled in the place which is called the habitation and city of God, as in the words, " His dwelling is in the holy place ; " [6] and, " Great is the LORD, and greatly to be praised in the city of our God, in the mountain of His holiness, beautiful for situation, the joy of the whole earth." [7] It is enough at present to quote the words of the thirty-seventh Psalm, which speaks thus of the land of the righteous, " Those that wait upon the LORD, they shall inherit the earth ; " and a little after, " But the meek shall inherit the earth, and shall delight themselves in the abundance of peace ; " and again, " Those who bless Him shall inherit the earth ; " and, " The righteous shall inherit the land, and dwell therein for ever." [8] And consider whether it is not evident to intelligent readers that the following words from this same Psalm refer to the pure land in the pure heaven : " Wait on the LORD, and keep His way ; and He shall exalt thee to inherit the land."

CHAP. XXX.

It seems to me also that the fancy of Plato, that those stones which we call precious stones derive their lustre from a reflection, as it were, of the stones in that better land, is taken from the words of Isaiah in describing the city of God, " I will make thy battlements of jasper, thy stones shall be crystal, and thy borders of

---

[1] *Odyss.*, iv. 563.
[2] *Phædo*, lviii. p. 109.
[3] Ex. iii. 8.
[4] Gen. iii. 17.

[5] Heb. xii. 22.
[6] Ps. lxxvi. 2; English version, " In Salem is His tabernacle."
[7] Ps. xlviii. 1, 2
[8] Ps. xxxvii. 9, 11, 22, 29, 34.

precious stones;"[1] and, "I will lay thy foundations with sapphires." Those who hold in greatest reverence the teaching of Plato, explain this myth of his as an allegory. And the prophecies from which, as we conjecture, Plato has borrowed, will be explained by those who, leading a godly life like that of the prophets, devote all their time to the study of the sacred Scriptures, to those who are qualified to learn by purity of life, and their desire to advance in divine knowledge. For our part, our purpose has been simply to say that what we affirm of that sacred land has not been taken from Plato or any of the Greeks, but that they rather — living as they did not only after Moses, who was the oldest, but even after most of the prophets — borrowed from them, and in so doing either misunderstood their obscure intimations on such subjects, or else endeavoured, in their allusions to the better land, to imitate those portions of Scripture which had fallen into their hands. Haggai expressly makes a distinction between the earth and the dry land, meaning by the latter the land in which we live. He says: "Yet once, and I will shake the heavens, and the earth, and the dry land, and the sea."[2]

CHAP. XXXI.

Referring to the passage in the *Phædon* of Plato, Celsus says: "It is not easy for every one to understand the meaning of Plato's words, when he says that on account of our weakness and slowness we are unable to reach the highest region of the air; but that if our nature were capable of so sublime a contemplation, we would then be able to understand that that is the true heaven, and that the true light." As Celsus has deferred to another opportunity the explanation of Plato's idea, we also think that it does not fall within our purpose at present to enter into any full description of that holy and good land, and of the city of God which is in it; but reserve the consideration of it for our Commentary on the Prophets, having already in part, according to our power, treated of the city of God in our remarks on the forty-sixth and forty-eighth Psalms. The writings of Moses and the prophets — the most ancient of all books — teach us that all things here on earth which are in common use among men, have other things corresponding to them in name which are alone real. Thus, for instance, there is the true light, and another heaven beyond the firmament, and a Sun of righteousness other than the sun we see. In a word, to distinguish those things from the objects of sense, which have no true reality, they say of God that "His works are truth;"[3] thus

making a distinction between the works of God and the works of God's hands, which latter are of an inferior sort. Accordingly, God in Isaiah complains of men, that "they regard not the works of the LORD, nor consider the operation of His hands."[4] But enough on this point.

CHAP. XXXII.

Celsus next assails the doctrine of the resurrection, which is a high and difficult doctrine, and one which more than others requires a high and advanced degree of wisdom to set forth how worthy it is of God; and how sublime a truth it is which teaches us that there is a seminal principle lodged in that which Scripture speaks of as the "tabernacle" of the soul, in which the righteous "do groan, being burdened, not for that they would be unclothed, but clothed upon."[5] Celsus ridicules this doctrine because he does not understand it, and because he has learnt it from ignorant persons, who were unable to support it on any reasonable grounds. It will be profitable, therefore, that in addition to what we have said above, we should make this one remark. Our teaching on the subject of the resurrection is not, as Celsus imagines, derived from anything that we have heard on the doctrine of metempsychosis; but we know that the soul, which is immaterial and invisible in its nature, exists in no material place, without having a body suited to the nature of that place. Accordingly, it at one time puts off one body which was necessary before, but which is no longer adequate in its changed state, and it exchanges it for a second; and at another time it assumes another in addition to the former, which is needed as a better covering, suited to the purer ethereal regions of heaven. When it comes into the world at birth, it casts off the integuments which it needed in the womb; and before doing this, it puts on another body suited for its life upon earth. Then, again, as there is "a tabernacle" and "an earthly house" which is in some sort necessary for this tabernacle, Scripture teaches us that "the earthly house of this tabernacle shall be dissolved," but that the tabernacle shall "be clothed upon with a house not made with hands, eternal in the heavens."[6] The men of God say also that "the corruptible shall put on incorruption,"[7] which is a different thing from "the incorruptible;" and "the mortal shall put on immortality," which is different from "the immortal." Indeed, what "wisdom" is to "the wise," and "justice" to "the just," and "peace" to "the peaceable," the same relation does "incorruption" hold to "the incorruptible," and "immortality" to "the immortal."

---

[1] Isa. liv. 12, 11.
[2] Hagg. ii. 6.
[3] Dan. iv. 37.

[4] Isa. v. 12.
[5] 2 Cor. v. 1, 4.
[6] 2 Cor. v. 1.
[7] 1 Cor. xv. 53.

Behold, then, to what a prospect Scripture encourages us to look, when it speaks to us of being clothed with incorruption and immortality, which are, as it were, vestments which will not suffer those who are covered with them to come to corruption or death. Thus far I have taken the liberty of referring to this subject, in answer to one who assails the doctrine of the resurrection without understanding it, and who, simply because he knew nothing about it, made it the object of contempt and ridicule.

CHAP. XXXIII.

As Celsus supposes that we uphold the doctrine of the resurrection in order that we may see and know God, he thus follows out his notions on the subject: "After they have been utterly refuted and vanquished, they still, as if regardless of all objections, come back again to the same question, 'How then shall we see and know God? how shall we go to Him?'" Let any, however, who are disposed to hear us observe, that if we have need of a body for other purposes, as for occupying a material locality to which this body must be adapted, and if on that account the "tabernacle" is clothed in the way we have shown, we have no need of a body in order to know God. For that which sees God is not the eye of the body; it is the mind which is made in the image of the Creator,[1] and which God has in His providence rendered capable of that knowledge. To see God belongs to the pure heart, out of which no longer proceed "evil thoughts, murders, adulteries, fornications, thefts, false witness, blasphemies, the evil eye,"[2] or any other evil thing. Wherefore it is said, "Blessed are the pure in heart, for they shall see God."[3] But as the strength of our will is not sufficient to procure the perfectly pure heart, and as we need that God should create it, he therefore who prays as he ought, offers this petition to God, "Create in me a clean heart, O God."[4]

CHAP. XXXIV.

And we do not ask the question, "How shall we go to God?" as though we thought that God existed in some place. God is of too excellent a nature for any place: He holds all things in His power, and is Himself not confined by anything whatever. The precept, therefore, "Thou shalt walk after the LORD thy God,"[5] does not command a bodily approach to God; neither does the prophet refer to physical nearness to God, when he says in his prayer, "My soul fol-

loweth hard after Thee."[6] Celsus therefore misrepresents us, when he says that we expect to see God with our bodily eyes, to hear Him with our ears, and to touch Him sensibly with our hands. We know that the holy Scriptures make mention of eyes, of ears, and of hands, which have nothing but the name in common with the bodily organs; and what is more wonderful, they speak of a diviner sense, which is very different from the senses as commonly spoken of. For when the prophet says, "Open Thou mine eyes, that I may behold wondrous things out of Thy law,"[7] or, "The commandment of the LORD is pure, enlightening the eyes,"[8] or, "Lighten mine eyes, lest I sleep the sleep of death,"[9] no one is so foolish as to suppose that the eyes of the body behold the wonders of the divine law, or that the law of the Lord gives light to the bodily eyes, or that the sleep of death falls on the eyes of the body. When our Saviour says, "He that hath ears to hear, let him hear,"[10] any one will understand that the ears spoken of are of a diviner kind. When it is said that the word of the Lord was "in the hand" of Jeremiah or of some other prophet; or when the expression is used, "the law by the hand of Moses," or, "I sought the Lord with my hands, and was not deceived,"[11] — no one is so foolish as not to see that the word "hands" is taken figuratively, as when John says, "Our hands have handled the Word of life."[12] And if you wish further to learn from the sacred writings that there is a diviner sense than the senses of the body, you have only to hear what Solomon says, "Thou shalt find a divine sense."[13]

CHAP. XXXV.

Seeking God, then, in this way, we have no need to visit the oracles of Trophonius, of Amphiaraus, and of Mopsus, to which Celsus would send us, assuring us that we would there "see the gods in human form, appearing to us with all distinctness, and without illusion." For we know that these are demons, feeding on the blood, and smoke, and odour of victims, and shut up by their base desires in prisons, which the Greeks call temples of the gods, but which we know are only the dwellings of deceitful demons. To this Celsus maliciously adds, in regard to these gods which, according to him, are in human form, "they do not show themselves for once, or at intervals, like him who has deceived men, but they are ever open to intercourse with those

---

[1] Bouhéreau follows the reading, "the mind which sees what is made in the image of the Creator."
[2] Matt. xv. 19 and vi. 23.
[3] Matt. v. 8.
[4] Ps. li. 10.
[5] Deut. xiii. 4.
[6] Ps. lxiii. 8.
[7] Ps. cxix. 18.
[8] Ps. xix. 8.
[9] Ps. xiii. 3.
[10] Matt. xiii. 9.
[11] Ps. lxxvii. 2, according to the LXX.
[12] 1 John i. 1.
[13] Prov. ii. 5. Eng. Vers. and LXX., "Thou shalt find the knowledge of God."

who desire it." From this remark, it would seem that Celsus supposes that the appearance of Christ to His disciples after His resurrection was like that of a spectre flitting before their eyes; whereas these gods, as he calls them, in human shape always present themselves to those who desire it. But how is it possible that a phantom which, as he describes it, flew past to deceive the beholders, could produce such effects after it had passed away, and could so turn the hearts of men as to lead them to regulate their actions according to the will of God, as in view of being hereafter judged by Him? And how could a phantom drive away demons, and show other indisputable evidences of power, and that not in any one place, like these so-called gods in human form, but making its divine power felt through the whole world, in drawing and congregating together all who are found disposed to lead a good and noble life?

CHAP. XXXVI.

After these remarks of Celsus, which we have endeavoured to answer as we could, he goes on to say, speaking of us: "Again they will ask, How can we know God, unless by the perception of the senses? for how otherwise than through the senses are we able to gain any knowledge?'" To this he replies: "This is not the language of a man; it comes not from the soul, but from the flesh. Let them hearken to us, if such a spiritless and carnal race are able to do so: if, instead of exercising the senses, you look upwards with the soul; if, turning away the eye of the body, you open the eye of the mind, thus and thus only will you be able to see God. And if you seek one to be your guide along this way, you must shun all deceivers and jugglers, who will introduce you to phantoms. Otherwise you will be acting the most ridiculous part, if, whilst you pronounce imprecations upon those others that are recognised as gods, treating them as idols, you yet do homage to a more wretched idol than any of these, which indeed is not even an idol or a phantom, but a dead man, and you seek a father like to him." The first remark which we have to make on this passage is in regard to his use of personification, by which he makes us defend in this way the doctrine of the resurrection. This figure of speech is properly employed when the character and sentiments of the person introduced are faithfully preserved; but it is an abuse of the figure when these do not agree with the character and opinions of the speaker. Thus we should justly condemn a man who put into the mouths of barbarians, slaves, or uneducated people the language of philosophy; because we know that the philosophy belonged to the author, and not to such persons, who could not know anything of philosophy. And in like manner we should condemn a man for introducing persons who are represented as wise and well versed in divine knowledge, and should make them give expression to language which could only come out of the mouths of those who are ignorant or under the influence of vulgar passions. Hence Homer is admired, among other things, for preserving a consistency of character in his heroes, as in Nestor, Ulysses, Diomede, Agamemnon, Telemachus, Penelope, and the rest. Euripides, on the contrary, was assailed in the comedies of Aristophanes as a frivolous talker, often putting into the mouth of a barbarian woman, a wretched slave, the wise maxims which he had learned from Anaxagoras or some other philosophers.

CHAP. XXXVII.

Now if this is a true account of what constitutes the right and the wrong use of personification, have we not grounds for holding Celsus up to ridicule for thus ascribing to Christians words which they never uttered? For if those whom he represents as speaking are the unlearned, how is it possible that such persons could distinguish between "sense" and "reason," between "objects of sense" and "objects of the reason?" To argue in this way, they would require to have studied under the Stoics, who deny all intellectual existences, and maintain that all that we apprehend is apprehended through the senses, and that all knowledge comes through the senses. But if, on the other hand, he puts these words into the mouth of philosophers who search carefully into the meaning of Christian doctrines, the statements in question do not agree with their character and principles. For no one who has learnt that God is invisible, and that certain of His works are invisible, that is to say, apprehended by the reason,[1] can say, as if to justify his faith in a resurrection, "How can they know God, except by the perception of the senses?" or, "How otherwise than through the senses can they gain any knowledge?" For it is not in any secret writings, perused only by a few wise men, but in such as are most widely diffused and most commonly known among the people, that these words are written: "The invisible things of God from the creation of the world are clearly seen, being understood by the things that are made."[2] From whence it is to be inferred, that though men who live upon the earth have to begin with the use of the senses upon sensible objects, in order to go on from them to a knowledge of the nature of things intellectual, yet their knowledge must not stop short with the objects of sense.

---

[1] νοητά, falling under the province of νοῦς, the reason. For convenience, we translate it elsewhere " intellectual."
[2] Rom. i. 20.

And thus, while Christians would not say that it is impossible to have a knowledge of intellectual objects without the senses, but rather that the senses supply the first means of obtaining knowledge, they might well ask the question, "Who can gain any knowledge without the senses?" without deserving the abuse of Celsus, when he adds, "This is not the language of a man; it comes not from the soul, but from the flesh."

CHAP. XXXVIII.

Since we hold that the great God is in essence simple, invisible, and incorporeal, Himself pure intelligence, or something transcending intelligence and existence, we can never say that God is apprehended by any other means than through the intelligence which is formed in His image, though now, in the words of Paul, "we see in a glass obscurely, but then face to face." [1] And if we use the expression "face to face," let no one pervert its meaning; but let it be explained by this passage, "Beholding with open face the glory of the Lord, we are changed into the same image, from glory to glory," which shows that we do not use the word in this connection to mean the visible face, but take it figuratively, in the same way as we have shown that the eyes, the ears, and the other parts of the body are employed. And it is certain that a man — I mean a soul using a body, otherwise called "the inner man," or simply "the soul" — would answer, not as Celsus makes us answer, but as the man of God himself teaches. It is certain also that a Christian will not make use of "the language of the flesh," having learnt as he has "to mortify the deeds of the body" [2] by the spirit, and "to bear about in his body the dying of Jesus;" [3] and "mortify your members which are on the earth," [4] and with a true knowledge of these words, "My spirit shall not always strive with man, for that he also is flesh," [5] and again, "They that are in the flesh cannot please God," [6] he strives in every way to live no longer according to the flesh, but only according to the Spirit.

CHAP. XXXIX.

Now let us hear what it is that he invites us to learn, that we may ascertain from him how we are to know God, although he thinks that his words are beyond the capacity of all Christians. "Let them hear," says he, "if they are able to do so." We have then to consider what the philosopher wishes us to hear from him. But instead of instructing us as he ought, he abuses us; and while he should have shown his goodwill to those whom he addresses at the outset of his discourse, he stigmatizes as "a cowardly race" men who would rather die than abjure Christianity even by a word, and who are ready to suffer every form of torture, or any kind of death. He also applies to us that epithet "carnal" or "flesh-indulging," "although," as we are wont to say, "we have known Christ after the flesh, yet now henceforth we know Him no more," and although we are so ready to lay down our lives for the cause of religion, that no philosopher could lay aside his robes more readily. He then addresses to us these words: "If, instead of exercising your senses, you look upwards with the soul; if, turning away the eye of the body, you open the eye of the mind, thus and thus only you will be able to see God." He is not aware that this reference to the two eyes, the eye of the body and the eye of the mind, which he has borrowed from the Greeks, was in use among our own writers; for Moses, in his account of the creation of the world, introduces man before his transgression as both seeing and not seeing; seeing, when it is said of the woman, "The woman saw that the tree was good for food, and that it was pleasant to the eyes, and a tree to be desired to make one wise;" [8] and again not seeing, as when he introduces the serpent saying to the woman, as if she and her husband had been blind, "God knows that on the day that ye eat thereof your eyes shall be opened;" [9] and also when it is said, "They did eat, and the eyes of both of them were opened." [10] The eyes of sense were then opened, which they had done well to keep shut, that they might not be distracted, and hindered from seeing with the eyes of the mind; and it was those eyes of the mind which in consequence of sin, as I imagine, were then closed, with which they had up to that time enjoyed the delight of beholding God and His paradise. This twofold kind of vision in us was familiar to our Saviour, who says, "For judgment I am come into this world, that they which see not, might see, and that they which see might be made blind," [11] — meaning, by the eyes that see not, the eyes of the mind, which are enlightened by His teaching; and the eyes which see are the eyes of sense, which His words do render blind, in order that the soul may look without distraction upon proper objects. All true Christians therefore have the eye of the mind sharpened, and the eye of sense closed; so that each one, according to the degree in which his better eye is quickened, and the eye of sense darkened, sees and knows the Supreme

---

[1] 1 Cor. xiii. 12.
[2] Rom. viii. 13.
[3] 2 Cor. iv. 10.
[4] Col. iii. 5.
[5] Gen. vi. 3.
[6] Rom. viii. 8.

[7] 2 Cor. v. 16.
[8] Gen. iii. 6.
[9] Gen. iii. 5.
[10] Gen. iii. 7.
[11] John ix. 39.

God, and His Son, who is the Word, Wisdom, and so forth.

CHAP. XL.

Next to the remarks of Celsus on which we have already commented, come others which he addresses to all Christians, but which, if applicable to any, ought to be addressed to persons whose doctrines differ entirely from those taught by Jesus. For it is the Ophians who, as we have before shown,[1] have utterly renounced Jesus, and perhaps some others of similar opinions who are " the impostors and jugglers, leading men away to idols and phantoms ; " and it is they who with miserable pains learn off the names of the heavenly doorkeepers. These words are therefore quite inappropriate as addressed to Christians : " If you seek one to be your guide along this way, you must shun all deceivers and jugglers, who will introduce you to phantoms." And, as though quite unaware that these impostors entirely agree with him, and are not behind him in speaking ill of Jesus and His religion, he thus continues, confounding us with them : "otherwise you will be acting the most ridiculous part, if, whilst you pronounce imprecations upon those other recognised gods, treating them as idols, you yet do homage to a more wretched idol than any of these, which indeed is not even an idol or a phantom, but a dead man, and you seek a father like to himself." That he is ignorant of the wide difference between our opinions and those of the inventors of these fables, and that he imagines the charges which he makes against them applicable to us, is evident from the following passage : " For the sake of such a monstrous delusion, and in support of those wonderful advisers, and those wonderful words which you address to the lion, to the amphibious creature, to the creature in the form of an ass, and to others, for the sake of those divine doorkeepers whose names you commit to memory with such pains, in such a cause as this you suffer cruel tortures, and perish at the stake." Surely, then, he is unaware that none of those who regard beings in the form of an ass, a lion, or an amphibious animal, as the doorkeepers or guides on the way to heaven, ever expose themselves to death in defence of that which they think the truth. That excess of zeal, if it may be so called, which leads us for the sake of religion to submit to every kind of death, and to perish at the stake, is ascribed by Celsus to those who endure no such sufferings ; and he reproaches us who suffer crucifixion for our faith, with believing in fabulous creatures — in the lion, the amphibious animal, and other such monsters. If we reject all these fables, it is not out of deference to Celsus, for we have never at any time held any such fancies ; but it is in accordance with the teaching of Jesus that we oppose all such notions, and will not allow to Michael, or to any others that have been referred to, a form and figure of that sort.

CHAP. XLI.

But let us consider who those persons are whose guidance Celsus would have us to follow, so that we may not be in want of guides who are recommended both by their antiquity and sanctity. He refers us to divinely inspired poets, as he calls them, to wise men and philosophers, without mentioning their names ; so that, after promising to point out those who should guide us, he simply hands us over in a general way to divinely inspired poets, wise men, and philosophers. If he had specified their names in particular, we should have felt ourselves bound to show him that he wished to give us as guides men who were blinded to the truth, and who must therefore lead us into error ; or that if not wholly blinded, yet they are in error in many matters of belief. But whether Orpheus, Parmenides, Empedocles, or even Homer himself, and Hesiod, are the persons whom he means by " inspired poets," let any one show how those who follow their guidance walk in a better way, or lead a more excellent life, than those who, being taught in the school of Jesus Christ, have rejected all images and statues, and even all Jewish superstition, that they may look upward through the Word of God to the one God, who is the Father of the Word. Who, then, are those wise men and philosophers from whom Celsus would have us to learn so many divine truths, and for whom we are to give up Moses the servant of God, the prophets of the Creator of the world, who have spoken so many things by a truly divine inspiration, and even Him who has given light and taught the way of piety to the whole human race, so that no one can reproach Him if he remains without a share in the knowledge of His mysteries? Such, indeed, was the abounding love which He had for men, that He gave to the more learned a theology capable of raising the soul far above all earthly things ; while with no less consideration He comes down to the weaker capacities of ignorant men, of simple women, of slaves, and, in short, of all those who from Jesus alone could have received that help for the better regulation of their lives which is supplied by his instructions in regard to the Divine Being, adapted to their wants and capacities.

CHAP. XLII.

Celsus next refers us to Plato as to a more effective teacher of theological truth, and quotes

---

[1] See book vi. cap. xxx., etc.

the following passage from the *Timæus:* " It is a hard matter to find out the Maker and Father of this universe ; and after having found Him, it is impossible to make Him known to all." To which he himself adds this remark : " You perceive, then, how divine men seek after the way of truth, and how well Plato knew that it was impossible for all men to walk in it. But as wise men have found it for the express purpose of being able to convey to us some notion of Him who is the first, the unspeakable Being, — a notion, namely, which may represent Him to us through the medium of other objects, — they endeavour either by synthesis, which is the combining of various qualities, or by analysis, which is the separation and setting aside of some qualities, or finally by analogy ; — in these ways, I say, they endeavour to set before us that which it is impossible to express in words. I should therefore be surprised if you could follow in that course, since you are so completely wedded to the flesh as to be incapable of seeing ought but what is impure." These words of Plato are noble and admirable ; but see if Scripture does not give us an example of a regard for mankind still greater in God the Word, who was " in the beginning with God," and " who was made flesh," in order that He might reveal to all men truths which, according to Plato, it would be impossible to make known to all men, even after he had found them himself. Plato may say that " it is a hard thing to find out the Creator and Father of this universe ; " by which language he implies that it is not wholly beyond the power of human nature to attain to such a knowledge as is either worthy of God, or if not, is far beyond that which is commonly attained (although if it were true that Plato or any other of the Greeks had found God, they would never have given homage and worship, or ascribed the name of God, to any other than to Him : they would have abandoned all others, and would not have associated with this great God objects which can have nothing in common with Him).[1] For ourselves, we maintain that human nature is in no way able to seek after God, or to attain a clear knowledge of Him without the help of Him whom it seeks. He makes Himself known to those who, after doing all that their powers will allow, confess that they need help from Him, who discovers Himself to those whom He approves, in so far as it is possible for man and the soul still dwelling in the body to know God.

CHAP. XLIII.

Observe that when Plato says, that "after having found out the Creator and Father of the universe, it is impossible to make Him known to

all men," he does not speak of Him as unspeakable, and as incapable of being expressed in words. On the contrary, he implies that He may be spoken of, and that there are a few to whom He may be made known. But Celsus, as if forgetting the language which he had just quoted from Plato, immediately gives God the name of " the unspeakable." He says : " since the wise men have found out this way, in order to be able to give us some idea of the First of Beings, who is unspeakable." For ourselves, we hold that not God alone is unspeakable, but other things also which are inferior to Him. Such are the things which Paul labours to express when he says, " I heard unspeakable words, which it is not lawful for a man to utter," [2] where the word " heard " is used in the sense of " understood ; " as in the passage, " He who hath ears to hear, let him hear." We also hold that it is a hard matter to see the Creator and Father of the universe ; but it is possible to see Him in the way thus referred to, " Blessed are the pure in heart, for they shall see God ; " [3] and not only so, but also in the sense of the words of Him " who is the image of the invisible God ; " " He who hath seen Me hath seen the Father who sent Me." [4] No sensible person could suppose that these last words were spoken in reference to His bodily presence, which was open to the view of all ; otherwise all those who said, " Crucify him, crucify him," and Pilate, who had power over the humanity of Jesus, were among those who saw God the Father, which is absurd. Moreover, that these words, " He that hath seen Me, hath seen the Father who sent Me," are not to be taken in their grosser sense, is plain from the answer which He gave to Philip, " Have I been so long time with you, and yet dost thou not know Me, Philip ? " after Philip had asked, " Show us the Father, and it sufficeth us." He, then, who perceives how these words, " The Word was made flesh," are to be understood of the only-begotten Son of God, the first-born of all creation, will also understand how, in seeing the image of the invisible God, we see " the Creator and Father of the universe."

CHAP. XLIV.

Celsus supposes that we may arrive at a knowledge of God either by combining or separating certain things after the methods which mathematicians call synthesis and analysis, or again by analogy, which is employed by them also, and that in this way we may as it were gain admission to the chief good. But when the Word of God says, " No man knoweth the Father but the Son,

---

[1] [See note *supra*, p. 573. S.]

[2] 2 Cor. xii. 4.
[3] Matt. v. 8.
[4] John xiv. 9.

and he to whomsoever the Son will reveal Him,"[1] He declares that no one can know God but by the help of divine grace coming from above, with a certain divine inspiration. Indeed, it is reasonable to suppose that the knowledge of God is beyond the reach of human nature, and hence the many errors into which men have fallen in their views of God. It is, then, through the goodness and love of God to mankind, and by a marvellous exercise of divine grace to those whom He saw in His foreknowledge, and knew that they would walk worthy of Him who had made Himself known to them, and that they would never swerve from a faithful attachment to His service, although they were condemned to death or held up to ridicule by those who, in ignorance of what true religion is, give that name to what deserves to be called anything rather than religion. God doubtless saw the pride and arrogance of those who, with contempt for all others, boast of their knowledge of God, and of their profound acquaintance with divine things obtained from philosophy, but who still, not less even than the most ignorant, run after their images, and temples, and famous mysteries; and seeing this, He " has chosen the foolish things of this world "[2] — the simplest of Christians, who lead, however, a life of greater moderation and purity than many philosophers — "to confound the wise," who are not ashamed to address inanimate things as gods or images of the gods. For what reasonable man can refrain from smiling when he sees that one who has learned from philosophy such profound and noble sentiments about God or the gods, turns straightway to images and offers to them his prayers, or imagines that by gazing upon these material things he can ascend from the visible symbol to that which is spiritual and immaterial.[3] But a Christian, even of the common people, is assured that every place forms part of the universe, and that the whole universe is God's temple. In whatever part of the world he is, he prays; but he rises above the universe, " shutting the eyes of sense, and raising upwards the eyes of the soul." And he stops not at the vault of heaven; but passing in thought beyond the heavens, under the guidance of the Spirit of God, and having thus as it were gone beyond the visible universe, he offers prayers to God. But he prays for no trivial blessings, for he has learnt from Jesus to seek for nothing small or mean, that is, sensible objects, but to ask only for what is great and truly divine; and these things God grants to us, to lead us to that blessedness which is found only with Him through His Son, the Word, who is God.

CHAP. XLV.

But let us see further what the things are which he proposes to teach us, if indeed we can comprehend them, since he speaks of us as being " utterly wedded to the flesh;" although if we live well, and in accordance with the teaching of Jesus, we hear this said of us: " Ye are not in the flesh, but in the Spirit, if the Spirit of God dwelleth in you."[4] He says also that we look upon nothing that is pure, although our endeavour is to keep even our thoughts free from all defilement of sin, and although in prayer we say, " Create in me a clean heart, O God, and renew a right spirit within me,"[5] so that we may behold Him with that "pure heart" to which alone is granted the privilege of seeing Him. This, then, is what he proposes for our instruction: " Things are either *intelligible*, which we call substance — being; or *visible*, which we call *becoming*:[6] with the former is truth; from the latter arises error. Truth is the object of knowledge; truth and error form opinion. Intelligible objects are known by the reason, visible objects by the eyes; the action of the reason is called intelligent perception, that of the eyes vision. As, then, among visible things the sun is neither the eye nor vision, but that which enables the eye to see, and renders vision possible, and in consequence of it visible things are seen, all sensible things exist, and itself is rendered visible; so among things intelligible, that which is neither reason, nor intelligent perception, nor knowledge, is yet the cause which enables the reason to know, which renders intelligent perception possible; and in consequence of it knowledge arises, all things intelligible, truth itself and substance have their existence; and itself, which is above all these things, becomes in some ineffable way intelligible. These things are offered to the consideration of the intelligent; and if even you can understand any of them, it is well. And if you think that a Divine Spirit has descended from God to announce divine things to men, it is doubtless this same Spirit that reveals these truths, and it was under the same influence that men of old made known many important truths. But if you cannot comprehend these things, then keep silence; do not expose your own ignorance, and do not accuse of blindness those who see, or of lameness those who run, while you yourselves are utterly lamed and mutilated in mind, and lead a merely animal life — the life of the body, which is the dead part of our nature."

---

[1] Matt. xi. 27.
[2] 1 Cor. i. 27.
[3] [Vol. ii. p. 186, this series.]

[4] Rom. viii. 9.
[5] Ps. li. 10.
[6] γένεσις. For the distinction between οὐσία and γένεσις, see Plato's *Sophista*, p. 246.

CHAP. XLVI.

We are careful not to oppose fair arguments even if they proceed from those who are not of our faith ; we strive not to be captious, or to seek to overthrow any sound reasonings. But here we have to reply to those who slander the character of persons wishing to do their best in the service of God, who accepts the faith which the meanest place in Him, as well as the more refined and intelligent piety of the learned ; seeing that both alike address to the Creator of the world their prayers and thanksgivings through the High Priest who has set before men the nature of pure religion. We say, then, that those who are stigmatized as "lamed and mutilated in spirit," as "living only for the sake of the body which is dead," are persons whose endeavour it is to say with sincerity : "For though we live¹ in the flesh, we do not war according to the flesh ; for the weapons of our warfare are not fleshly, but mighty through God." It is for those who throw out such vile accusations against men who desire to be God's servants, to beware lest, by the calumnies which they cast upon others who strive to live well, they "lame" their own souls, and "mutilate" the inner man, by severing from it that justice and moderation of mind which the Creator has planted in the nature of all His rational creatures. As for those, however, who, along with other lessons given by the Divine Word, have learned and practised this, "when reviled to bless, when persecuted to endure, when defamed to entreat,"² they may be said to be walking in spirit in the ways of uprightness, to be purifying and setting in order the whole soul. They distinguish — and to them the distinction is not one of words merely — between "substance," or that which is, and that which is "becoming ;" between things apprehended by reason, and things apprehended by sense ; and they connect truth with the one, and avoid the errors arising out of the other ; looking, as they have been taught, not at the things "becoming" or phenomenal, which are seen, and therefore temporary, but at better things than these, whether we call them "substance," or "spiritual" things, as being apprehended by reason, or "invisible," because they lie out of the reach of the senses. The disciples of Jesus regard these phenomenal things only that they may use them as steps to ascend to the knowledge of the things of reason. For "the invisible things of God," that is, the objects of the reason, "from the creation of the world are clearly seen" by the reason, "being understood by the things that are made." And when they have risen from the created things of this world to the invisible things of God, they do not stay there ; but after they have sufficiently exercised their minds upon these, and have understood their nature, they ascend to "the eternal power of God," in a word, to His divinity. For they know that God, in His love to men, has "manifested" His truth, and "that which is known of Him," not only to those who devote themselves to His service, but also to some who are far removed from the purity of worship and service which He requires ; and that some of those who by the providence of God had attained a knowledge of these truths, were yet doing things unworthy of that knowledge, and "holding the truth in unrighteousness," and who are unable to find any excuse before God after the knowledge of such great truths which He has given them.

CHAP. XLVII.

For Scripture testifies, in regard to those who have a knowledge of those things of which Celsus speaks, and who profess a philosophy founded on these principles, that they, "when they knew God, glorified Him not as God, neither were thankful, but became vain in their imaginations ;" and notwithstanding the bright light of knowledge with which God had enlightened them, "their foolish heart" was carried away, and became "darkened."³ Thus we may see how those who accounted themselves wise gave proofs of great folly, when, after such grand arguments delivered in the schools on God and on things apprehended by the reason, they "changed the glory of the incorruptible God into an image made like to corruptible man, and to birds, and four-footed beasts, and creeping things."⁴ As, then, they lived in a way unworthy of the knowledge which they had received from God, His providence leaving them to themselves, they were given "up to uncleanness, through the lusts of their own hearts to dishonour their own bodies,"⁵ in shamelessness and licentiousness, because they "changed the truth of God into a lie, and worshipped and served the creature more than the Creator."

CHAP. XLVIII.

But those who are despised for their ignorance, and set down as fools and abject slaves, no sooner commit themselves to God's guidance by accepting the teaching of Jesus, than, so far from defiling themselves by licentious indulgence or the gratification of shameless passion, they in many cases, like perfect priests, for whom such pleasures have no charm, keep themselves in act and in thought in a state of virgin purity. The Athenians have one hierophant, who, not having

---

¹ 2 Cor. x. 3, 4. The received text has "walk" instead of "live."
² 1 Cor. iv. 12, 13.

³ Rom. i. 21.
⁴ Rom. i. 23.
⁵ Rom. i. 24, 25.

confidence in his power to restrain his passions within the limits he prescribed for himself, determined to check them at their seat by the application of hemlock; and thus he was accounted pure, and fit for the celebration of religious worship among the Athenians. But among Christians may be found men who have no need of hemlock to fit them for the pure service of God, and for whom the Word in place of hemlock is able to drive all evil desires from their thoughts, so that they may present their prayers to the Divine Being. And attached to the other so-called gods are a select number of virgins, who are guarded by men, or it may be not guarded (for that is not the point in question at present), and who are supposed to live in purity for the honour of the god they serve. But among Christians, those who maintain a perpetual virginity do so for no human honours, for no fee or reward, from no motive of vainglory;[1] but "as they choose to retain God in their knowledge,"[2] they are preserved by God in a spirit well-pleasing to Him, and in the discharge of every duty, being filled with all righteousness and goodness.

CHAP. XLIX.

What I have now said, then, is offered not for the purpose of cavilling with any right opinions or sound doctrines held even by Greeks, but with the desire of showing that the same things, and indeed much better and diviner things than these, have been said by those divine men, the prophets of God and the apostles of Jesus. These truths are fully investigated by all who wish to attain a perfect knowledge of Christianity, and who know that " the mouth of the righteous speaketh wisdom, and his tongue talketh of judgment; the law of his God is in his heart."[3] But even in regard to those who, either from deficiency or knowledge or want of inclination, or from not having Jesus to lead them to a rational view of religion, have not gone into these deep questions, we find that they believe in the Most High God, and in His Only-begotten Son, the Word and God, and that they often exhibit in their character a high degree of gravity, of purity, and integrity; while those who call themselves wise have despised these virtues, and have wallowed in the filth of sodomy, in lawless lust, "men with men working that which is unseemly."[4]

CHAP. L.

Celsus has not explained how error accompanies the "becoming," or product of generation; nor has he expressed himself with suffi-

cient clearness to enable us to compare his ideas with ours, and to pass judgment on them. But the prophets, who have given some wise suggestions on the subject of things produced by generation, tell us that a sacrifice for sin was offered even for new-born infants, as not being free from sin.[5] They say, " I was shapen in iniquity, and in sin did my mother conceive me;"[6] also, "They are estranged from the womb;" which is followed by the singular expression, "They go astray as soon as they are born, speaking lies."[7] Besides, our wise men have such a contempt for all sensible objects, that sometimes they speak of all material things as vanity: thus, "For the creature was made subject to vanity, not willingly, but by reason of him that subjected the same in hope;"[8] at other times as vanity of vanities, "Vanity of vanities, saith the Preacher, all is vanity."[9] Who has given so severe an estimate of the life of the human soul here on earth, as he who says: "Verily every man at his best estate is altogether vanity?"[10] He does not hesitate at all as to the difference between the present life of the soul and that which it is to lead hereafter. He does not say, "Who knows if to die is not to live, and if to live is not death?"[11] But he boldly proclaims the truth, and says, "Our soul is bowed down to the dust;"[12] and, "Thou hast brought me into the dust of death;"[13] and similarly, "Who will deliver me from the body of this death?"[14] also, "Who will change the body of our humiliation."[15] It is a prophet also who says, "Thou hast brought us down in a place of affliction;"[16] meaning by the "place of affliction" this earthly region, to which Adam, that is to say, man, came after he was driven out of paradise for sin. Observe also how well the different life of the soul here and hereafter has been recognised by him who says, "Now we see in a glass, obscurely, but then face to face;"[17] and, "Whilst we are in our home in the body, we are away from our home in the Lord;" wherefore "we are well content to go from our home in the body, and to come to our home with the Lord."[18]

CHAP. LI.

But what need is there to quote any more passages against Celsus, in order to prove that

---

[5] [The noteworthy testimony of the Alexandrian school to the doctrine of birth-sin.]
[6] Ps. li. 5.
[7] Ps. lviii. 3.
[8] Rom. viii. 20.
[9] Eccles. i. 2.
[10] Ps. xxxix. 5.
[11] Euripides. [See De la Rue's note *ad loc.* in his edition of Origen's *Works.* S.]
[12] Ps. xliv. 25.
[13] Ps. xxii. 15.
[14] Rom. vii. 24.
[15] Phil. iii. 21.
[16] Ps. xliii. 20 (LXX.).
[17] 1 Cor. xiii. 12.
[18] 2 Cor. v. 6, 8.

---

[1] [See Robertson's *History of the Church,* vol. i. p. 145. S.]
[2] Rom. i. 28.
[3] Ps. xxxvii. 30, 31.
[4] Rom. i. 27.

his words contain nothing which was not said long before among themselves, since that has been sufficiently established by what we have said? It seems that what follows has some reference to this: "If you think that a Divine Spirit has descended from God to announce divine things to men, it is doubtless this same Spirit that reveals these truths; and it was under the same influence that men of old made known many important truths." But he does not know how great is the difference between those things and the clear and certain teaching of those who say to us, "Thine incorruptible spirit is in all things, wherefore God chasteneth them by little and little that offend;"[1] and of those who, among their other instructions, teach us that the words, "Receive ye the Holy Ghost,"[2] refer to a degree of spiritual influence higher than that in the passage, "Ye shall be baptized with the Holy Ghost not many days hence."[3] But it is a difficult matter, even after much careful consideration, to perceive the difference between those who have received a knowledge of the truth and a notion of God at different intervals and for short periods of time, and those who are more fully inspired by God, who have constant communion with Him, and are always led by His Spirit. Had Celsus set himself to understand this, he would not have reproached us with ignorance, or forbidden us to characterize as "blind" those who believe that religion shows itself in such products of man's mechanical art as images. For every one who sees with the eyes of his soul serves the Divine Being in no other way than in that which leads him ever to have regard to the Creator of all, to address his prayers to Him alone, and to do all things as in the sight of God, who sees us altogether, even to our thoughts. Our earnest desire then is both to see for ourselves, and to be leaders of the blind, to bring them to the Word of God, that He may take away from their minds the blindness of ignorance. And if our actions are worthy of Him who taught His disciples, "Ye are the light of the world,"[4] and of the Word, who says, "The light shineth in darkness,"[5] then we shall be light to those who are in darkness; we shall give wisdom to those who are without it, and we shall instruct the ignorant.

CHAP. LII.

And let not Celsus be angry if we describe as lame and mutilated in soul those who run to the temples as to places having a real sacredness, and who cannot see that no mere mechanical work of man can be truly sacred. Those whose piety is grounded on the teaching of Jesus also run until they come to the end of their course, when they can say in all truth and confidence: "I have fought a good fight, I have finished my course, I have kept the faith; henceforth there is laid up for me a crown of righteousness."[6] And each of us runs "not as uncertain," and he so fights with evil "not as one beating the air,"[7] but as against those who are subject to "the prince of the power of the air, the spirit that now worketh in the children of disobedience."[8] Celsus may indeed say of us that we "live with the body which is a dead thing;" but we have learnt, "If ye live after the flesh, ye shall die; but if ye by the Spirit do mortify the deeds of the body, ye shall live;"[9] and, "If we live in the Spirit, let us also walk in the Spirit."[10] Would that we might convince him by our actions that he did us wrong, when he said that we "live with the body which is dead!"

CHAP. LIII.

After these remarks of Celsus, which we have done our best to refute, he goes on to address us thus: "Seeing you are so eager for some novelty, how much better it would have been if you had chosen as the object of your zealous homage some one of those who died a glorious death, and whose divinity might have received the support of some myth to perpetuate his memory! Why, if you were not satisfied with Hercules or Æsculapius, and other heroes of antiquity, you had Orpheus, who was confessedly a divinely inspired man, who died a violent death. But perhaps some others have taken him up before you. You may then take Anaxarchus, who, when cast into a mortar, and beaten most barbarously, showed a noble contempt for his suffering, and said, 'Beat, beat the shell of Anaxarchus, for himself you do not beat,'—a speech surely of a spirit truly divine. But others were before you in following his interpretation of the laws of nature. Might you not, then, take Epictetus, who, when his master was twisting his leg, said smiling and unmoved, 'You will break my leg;' and when it was broken, he added, 'Did I not tell you that you would break it?' What saying equal to these did your god utter under suffering? If you had said even of the Sibyl, whose authority some of you acknowledge, that she was a child of God, you would have said something more reasonable. But you have had the presumption to include in her writings many impious things,[11] and set up as a god one who ended

---

[1] Wisd. xii. 1, 2.
[2] John xx. 22.
[3] Acts i. 5.
[4] Matt. v. 14.
[5] John i. 5.

[6] 2 Tim. iv. 7.
[7] 1 Cor. ix. 26.
[8] Eph. ii. 2.
[9] Rom. viii. 13.
[10] Gal. v. 25.
[11] [See vol. i. p. 169, note 9, and cap. lvi. *infra*.]

most infamous life by a most miserable death. How much more suitable than he would have been Jonah in the whale's belly, or Daniel delivered from the wild beasts, or any of a still more portentous kind!"

CHAP. LIV.

But since he sends us to Hercules, let him repeat to us any of his sayings, and let him justify his shameful subjection to Omphale. Let him show that divine honours should be paid to one who, like a highway robber, carries off a farmer's ox by force, and afterwards devours it, amusing himself meanwile with the curses of the owner; in memory of which even to this day sacrifices offered to the demon of Hercules are accompanied with curses. Again he proposes Æsculapius to us, as if to oblige us to repeat what we have said already; but we forbear. In regard to Orpheus, what does he admire in him to make him assert that, by common consent, he was regarded as a divinely inspired man, and lived a noble life? I am greatly deceived if it is not the desire which Celsus has to oppose us and put down Jesus that leads him to sound forth the praises of Orpheus; and whether, when he made himself acquainted with his impious fables about the gods, he did not cast them aside as deserving, even more than the poems of Homer, to be excluded from a well-ordered state. For, indeed, Orpheus says much worse things than Homer of those whom they call gods. Noble, indeed, it was in Anaxarchus to say to Aristocreon, tyrant of Cyprus, " Beat on, beat the shell of Anaxarchus," but it is the one admirable incident in the life of Anaxarchus known to the Greeks; and although, on the strength of that, some like Celsus might deservedly honour the man for his courage, yet to look up to Anaxarchus as a god is not consistent with reason. He also directs us to Epictetus, whose firmness is justly admired, although his saying when his leg was broken by his master is not to be compared with the marvellous acts and words of Jesus which Celsus refuses to believe; and these words were accompanied by such a divine power, that even to this day they convert not only some of the more ignorant and simple, but many also of the most enlightened of men.

CHAP. LV.

When, to his enumeration of those to whom he would send us, he adds, " What saying equal to these did your god utter under sufferings?" we would reply, that the silence of Jesus under scourgings, and amidst all His sufferings, spoke more for His firmness and submission than all that was said by the Greeks when beset by calamity. Perhaps Celsus may believe what was recorded with all sincerity by trustworthy men, who, while giving a truthful account of all the wonders performed by Jesus, specify among these the silence which He preserved when subjected to scourgings; showing the same singular meekness under the insults which were heaped upon Him, when they put upon Him the purple robe, and set the crown of thorns upon His head, and when they put in His hand a reed in place of a sceptre: no unworthy or angry word escaped Him against those who subjected Him to such outrages. Since, then, He received the scourgings with silent firmness, and bore with meekness all the insults of those who outraged Him, it cannot be said, as is said by some, that it was in cowardly weakness that He uttered the words: " Father, if it be possible, let this cup pass from Me: nevertheless, not as I will, but as Thou wilt." [1] The prayer which seems to be contained in these words for the removal of what He calls " the cup " bears a sense which we have elsewhere examined and set forth at large. But taking it in its more obvious sense, consider if it be not a prayer offered to God with all piety. For no man naturally regards anything which may befall him as necessary and inevitable; though he may submit to what is not inevitable, if occasion requires. Besides, these words, " nevertheless, not as I will, but as Thou wilt," are not the language of one who yielded to necessity, but of one who was contented with what was befalling Him, and who submitted with reverence to the arrangements of Providence.

CHAP. LVI.

Celsus then adds, for what reason I know not, that instead of calling Jesus the Son of God, we had better have given that honour to the Sibyl, in whose books he maintains we have interpolated many impious statements, though he does not mention what those interpolations are. [2] He might have proved his assertion by producing some older copies which are free from the interpolations which he attributes to us; but he does not do so even to justify his statement that these passages are of an impious character. Moreover, he again speaks of the life of Jesus as " a most infamous life," as he has done before, not once or twice, but many times, although he does not stay to specify any of the actions of His life which he thinks most infamous. He seems to think that he may in this way make assertions without proving them, and rail against one of whom he knows nothing. Had he set himself to show what sort of infamy he found in the actions of Jesus, we should have repelled the several charges brought against Him. Jesus did indeed meet with a most sad death; but the

---

[1] Matt. xxvi. 39.
[2] [Vol. i. pp. 280, 288, 289; vol. ii. pp. 192, 194, 346, and 622].

same might be said of Socrates, and of Anaxarchus, whom he had just mentioned, and a multitude of others. If the death of Jesus was a miserable one, was not that of the others so too? And if their death was not miserable, can it be said that the death of Jesus was? You see from this, then, that the object of Celsus is to vilify the character of Jesus; and I can only suppose that he is driven to it by some spirit akin to those whose power has been broken and vanquished by Jesus, and which now finds itself deprived of the smoke and blood on which it lived, whilst deceiving those who sought for God here upon earth in images, instead of looking up to the true God, the Governor of all things.

CHAP. LVII.

After this, as though his object was to swell the size of his book, he advises us "to choose Jonah rather than Jesus as our God;" thus setting Jonah, who preached repentance to the single city of Nineveh, before Jesus, who has preached repentance to the whole world, and with much greater results. He would have us to regard as God a man who, by a strange miracle, passed three days and three nights in the whale's belly; and he is unwilling that He who submitted to death for the sake of men, He to whom God bore testimony through the prophets, and who has done great things in heaven and earth, should receive on that ground honour second only to that which is given to the Most High God. Moreover, Jonah was swallowed by the whale for refusing to preach as God had commanded him; while Jesus suffered death for men after He had given the instructions which God wished Him to give. Still further, he adds that Daniel rescued from the lions is more worthy of our adoration than Jesus, who subdued the fierceness of every opposing power, and gave to us "authority to tread on serpents and scorpions, and over all the power of the enemy."[1] Finally, having no other names to offer us, he adds, "and others of a still more monstrous kind," thus casting a slight upon both Jonah and Daniel; for the spirit which is in Celsus cannot speak well of the righteous.

CHAP. LVIII.

Let us now consider what follows. "They have also," says he, "a precept to this effect, that we ought not to avenge ourselves on one who injures us, or, as he expresses it, 'Whosoever shall strike thee on the one cheek, turn to him the other also.' This is an ancient saying, which had been admirably expressed long before, and which they have only reported in a

coarser way. For Plato introduces Socrates conversing with Crito as follows: 'Must we never do injustice to any?' 'Certainly not.' 'And since we must never do injustice, must we not return injustice for an injustice that has been done to us, as most people think?' 'It seems to me that we should not.' 'But tell me, Crito, may we do evil to any one or not?' 'Certainly not, O Socrates.' 'Well, is it just, as is commonly said, for one who has suffered wrong to do wrong in return, or is it unjust?' 'It is unjust. Yes; for to do harm to a man is the same as to do him injustice.' 'You speak truly. We must then not do injustice in return for injustice, nor must we do evil to any one, whatever evil we may have suffered from him.' Thus Plato speaks; and he adds, 'Consider, then, whether you are at one with me, and whether, starting from this principle, we may not come to the conclusion that it is never right to do injustice, even in return for an injustice which has been received; or whether, on the other hand, you differ from me, and do not admit the principle from which we started. That has always been my opinion, and is so still.'[2] Such are the sentiments of Plato, and indeed they were held by divine men before his time. But let this suffice as one example of the way in which this and other truths have been borrowed and corrupted. Any one who wishes can easily by searching find more of them."

CHAP. LIX.

When Celsus here or elsewhere finds himself unable to dispute the truth of what we say, but avers that the same things were said by the Greeks, our answer is, that if the doctrine be sound, and the effect of it good, whether it was made known to the Greeks by Plato or any of the wise men of Greece, or whether it was delivered to the Jews by Moses or any of the prophets, or whether it was given to the Christians in the recorded teaching of Jesus Christ, or in the instructions of His apostles, that does not affect the value of the truth communicated. It is no objection to the principles of Jews or Christians, that the same things were also said by the Greeks, especially if it be proved that the writings of the Jews are older than those of the Greeks. And further, we are not to imagine that a truth adorned with the graces of Grecian speech is necessarily better than the same when expressed in the more humble and unpretending language used by Jews and Christians, although indeed the language of the Jews, in which the prophets wrote the books which have come down to us, has a grace of expression peculiar to the genius of the Hebrew tongue. And even if we

---

[1] Luke x. 19.   [2] Plato's *Crito*, p. 49.

were required to show that the same doctrines have been better expressed among the Jewish prophets or in Christian writings, however paradoxical it may seem, we are prepared to prove this by an illustration taken from different kinds of food, and from the different modes of preparing them. Suppose that a kind of food which is wholesome and nutritious has been prepared and seasoned in such a way as to be fit, not for the simple tastes of peasants and poor labourers, but for those only who are rich and dainty in their tastes. Suppose, again, that that same food is prepared not to suit the tastes of the more delicate, but for the peasants, the poor labourers, and the common people generally, in short, so that myriads of persons might eat of it. Now if, according to the supposition, the food prepared in the one way promotes the health of those only who are styled the better classes, while none of the others could taste it, whereas when prepared in the other way it promoted the health of great multitudes of men, which shall we esteem as most contributing to the public welfare, — those who prepare food for persons of mark, or those who prepare it for the multitudes? — taking for granted that in both cases the food is equally wholesome and nourishing; while it is evident that the welfare of mankind and the common good are promoted better by that physician who attends to the health of the many, than by one who confines his attention to a few.

CHAP. LX.

Now, after understanding this illustration, we have to apply it to the qualities of spiritual food with which the rational part of man is nourished. See, then, if Plato and the wise men among the Greeks, in the beautiful things they say, are not like those physicians who confine their attentions to what are called the better classes of society, and despise the multitude; whereas the prophets among the Jews, and the disciples of Jesus, who despise mere elegances of style, and what is called in Scripture "the wisdom of men," "the wisdom according to the flesh," which delights in what is obscure, resemble those who study to provide the most wholesome food for the largest number of persons. For this purpose they adapt their language and style to the capacities of the common people, and avoid whatever would seem foreign to them, lest by the introduction of strange forms of expression they should produce a distaste for their teaching. Indeed, if the true use of spiritual food, to keep up the figure, is to produce in him who partakes of it the virtues of patience and gentleness, must that discourse not be better prepared when it produces patience and gentleness in multitudes, or makes them grow in these virtues, than that which confines

its effects to a select few, supposing that it does really make them gentle and patient? If a Greek wished by wholesome instruction to benefit people who understood only Egyptian or Syriac, the first thing that he would do would be to learn their language; and he would rather pass for a Barbarian among the Greeks, by speaking as the Egyptians or Syrians, in order to be useful to them, than always remain Greek, and be without the means of helping them. In the same way the divine nature, having the purpose of instructing not only those who are reputed to be learned in the literature of Greece, but also the rest of mankind, accommodated itself to the capacities of the simple multitudes whom it addressed. It seeks to win the attention of the more ignorant by the use of language which is familiar to them, so that they may easily be induced, after their first introduction, to strive after an acquaintance with the deeper truths which lie hidden in Scripture. For even the ordinary reader of Scripture may see that it contains many things which are too deep to be apprehended at first; but these are understood by such as devote themselves to a careful study of the divine word, and they become plain to them in proportion to the pains and zeal which they expend upon its investigation.

CHAP. LXI.

From these remarks it is evident, that when Jesus said "coarsely," as Celsus terms it, "To him who shall strike thee on the one cheek, turn the other also; and if any man be minded to sue thee at the law, and take away thy coat, let him have thy cloak also,"[1] He expressed Himself in such a way as to make the precept have more practical effect than the words of Plato in the *Crito;* for the latter is so far from being intelligible to ordinary persons, that even those have a difficulty in understanding him, who have been brought up in the schools of learning, and have been initiated into the famous philosophy of Greece. It may also be observed, that the precept enjoining patience under injuries is in no way corrupted or degraded by the plain and simple language which our Lord employs, but that in this, as in other cases, it is a mere calumny against our religion which he utters when he says: "But let this suffice as one example of the way in which this and other truths have been borrowed and corrupted. Any one who wishes can easily by searching find more of them."

CHAP. LXII.

Let us now see what follows. "Let us pass on," says he, "to another point. They cannot

---

[1] Matt. v. 39, 40.

tolerate temples, altars, or images.[1] In this they are like the Scythians, the nomadic tribes of Libya, the Seres who worship no god, and some other of the most barbarous and impious nations in the world. That the Persians hold the same notions is shown by Herodotus in these words: 'I know that among the Persians it is considered unlawful to erect images, altars, or temples; but they charge those with folly who do so, because, as I conjecture, they do not, like the Greeks, suppose the gods to be of the nature of men.'[2] Heraclitus also says in one place: 'Persons who address prayers to these images act like those who speak to the walls, without knowing who the gods or the heroes are.' And what wiser lesson have they to teach us than Heraclitus? He certainly plainly enough implies that it is a foolish thing for a man to offer prayers to images, whilst he knows not who the gods and heroes are. This is the opinion of Heraclitus; but as for them, they go further, and despise without exception all images. If they merely mean that the stone, wood, brass, or gold which has been wrought by this or that workman cannot be a god, they are ridiculous with their wisdom. For who, unless he be utterly childish in his simplicity, can take these for gods, and not for offerings consecrated to the service of the gods, or images representing them? But if we are not to regard these as representing the Divine Being, seeing that God has a different form, as the Persians concur with them in saying, then let them take care that they do not contradict themselves; for they say that God made man His own image, and that He gave him a form like to Himself. However, they will admit that these images, whether they are like or not, are made and dedicated to the honour of certain beings. But they will hold that the beings to whom they are dedicated are not gods, but demons, and that a worshipper of God ought not to worship demons."

CHAP. LXIII.

To this our answer is, that if the Scythians, the nomadic tribes of Libya, the Seres, who according to Celsus have no god, if those other most barbarous and impious nations in the world, and if the Persians even cannot bear the sight of temples, altars, and images, it does not follow because we cannot suffer them any more than they, that the grounds on which we object to them are the same as theirs. We must inquire into the principles on which the objection to temples and images is founded, in order that we may approve of those who object on sound principles, and condemn those whose principles are false. For one and the same thing may be done for different reasons. For example, the philosophers who follow Zeno of Citium abstain from committing adultery, the followers of Epicurus do so too, as well as others again who do so on no philosophical principles; but observe what different reasons determine the conduct of these different classes. The first consider the interests of society, and hold it to be forbidden by nature that a man who is a reasonable being should corrupt a woman whom the laws have already given to another, and should thus break up the household of another man. The Epicureans do not reason in this way; but if they abstain from adultery, it is because, regarding pleasure as the chief end of man, they perceive that one who gives himself up to adultery, encounters for the sake of this one pleasure a multitude of obstacles to pleasure, such as imprisonment, exile, and death itself. They often, indeed, run considerable risk at the outset, while watching for the departure from the house of the master and those in his interest. So that, supposing it possible for a man to commit adultery, and escape the knowledge of the husband, of his servants, and of others whose esteem he would forfeit, then the Epicurean would yield to the commission of the crime for the sake of pleasure. The man of no philosophical system, again, who abstains from adultery when the opportunity comes to him, does so generally from dread of the law and its penalties, and not for the sake of enjoying a greater number of other pleasures. You see, then, that an act which passes for being one and the same — namely, abstinence from adultery — is not the same, but differs in different men according to the motives which actuate it: one man refraining for sound reasons, another for such bad and impious ones as those of the Epicurean, and the common person of whom we have spoken.

CHAP. LXIV.

As, then, this act of self-restraint, which in appearance is one and the same, is found in fact to be different in different persons, according to the principles and motives which lead to it; so in the same way with those who cannot allow in the worship of the Divine Being altars, or temples, or images. The Scythians, the Nomadic Libyans, the godless Seres, and the Persians, agree in this with the Christians and Jews, but they are actuated by very different principles. For none of these former abhor altars and images on the ground that they are afraid of degrading the worship of God, and reducing it to the worship of material things wrought by the hands of men.[3] Neither do

---

[1] [The temples here meant are such as enshrined images.]
[2] Herod., i. 131.

[3] [Note this wholesome fear of early Christians.]

they object to them from a belief that the demons choose certain forms and places, whether because they are detained there by virtue of certain charms, or because for some other possible reason they have selected these haunts, where they may pursue their criminal pleasures, in partaking of the smoke of sacrificial victims. But Christians and Jews have regard to this command, "Thou shalt fear the LORD thy God, and serve Him alone;"[1] and this other, "Thou shalt have no other gods before Me: thou shalt not make unto thee any graven image, or any likeness of anything that is in heaven above, or that is in the earth beneath, or that is in the water under the earth: thou shalt not bow down thyself to them, nor serve them;"[2] and again, "Thou shalt worship the LORD thy God, and Him only shalt thou serve."[3] It is in consideration of these and many other such commands, that they not only avoid temples, altars, and images, but are ready to suffer death when it is necessary, rather than debase by any such impiety the conception which they have of the Most High God.

CHAP. LXV.

In regard to the Persians, we have already said that though they do not build temples, yet they worship the sun and the other works of God. This is forbidden to us, for we have been taught not to worship the creature instead of the Creator, but to know that "the creation shall be delivered from the bondage of corruption into the liberty of the glory of the children of God;" and "the earnest expectation of the creation is waiting for the revelation of the sons of God;" and "the creation was made subject to vanity, not willingly, but by reason of him who made it subject, in hope."[4] We believe, therefore, that things "under the bondage of corruption," and "subject to vanity," which remain in this condition "in hope" of a better state, ought not in our worship to hold the place of God, the all-sufficient, and of His Son, the First-born of all creation. Let this suffice, in addition to what we have already said of the Persians, who abhor altars and images, but who serve the creature instead of the Creator. As to the passage quoted by Celsus from Heraclitus, the purport of which he represents as being, "that it is childish folly for one to offer prayers to images, whilst he knows not who the gods and heroes are," we may reply that it is easy to know that God and the Only-begotten Son of God, and those whom God has honoured with the title of God, and who partake of His divine nature, are very different from all

the gods of the nations which are demons; but it is not possible at the same time to know God and to address prayers to images.[5]

CHAP. LXVI.

And the charge of folly applies not only to those who offer prayers to images, but also to such as pretend to do so in compliance with the example of the multitude: and to this class belong the Peripatetic philosophers and the followers of Epicurus and Democritus. For there is no falsehood or pretence in the soul which is possessed with true piety towards God. Another reason also why we abstain from doing honour to images, is that we may give no support to the notion that the images are gods. It is on this ground that we condemn Celsus, and all others who, while admitting that they are not gods, yet, with the reputation of being wise men, render to them what passes for homage. In this way they lead into sin the multitude who follow their example, and who worship these images not simply out of deference to custom, but from a belief into which they have fallen that they are true gods, and that those are not to be listened to who hold that the objects of their worship are not true gods. Celsus, indeed, says that "they do not take them for gods, but only as offerings dedicated to the gods." But he does not prove that they are not rather dedicated to men than, as he says, to the honour of the gods themselves; for it is clear that they are the offerings of men who were in error in their views of the Divine Being. Moreover, we do not imagine that these images are representations of God, for they cannot represent a being who is invisible and incorporeal.[6] But as Celsus supposes that we fall into a contradiction, whilst on the one hand we say that God has not a human form, and on the other we profess to believe that God made man the image of Himself, and created man the image of God; our answer is the same as has been given already, that we hold the resemblance to God to be preserved in the reasonable soul, which is formed to virtue, although Celsus, who does not see the difference between "being the image of God," and "being created after the image of God," pretends that we said, "God made man His own image, and gave him a form like to His own." But this also has been examined before.

CHAP. LXVII.

His next remark upon the Christians is: "They will admit that these images, whether they are like or not, are made and dedicated to the honour of certain beings; but they will hold

---

[1] Deut. vi. 13.
[2] Ex. xx. 3, 4.
[3] Matt. iv. 10.
[4] Rom. viii. 19-21.

[5] [Let this be noted; and see book viii. 20, *infra*.]
[6] [Vol. ii. p. 186, note 1.]

that the beings to whom they are dedicated are not gods, but demons, and that a worshipper of God ought not to worship demons." If he had been acquainted with the nature of demons, and with their several operations, whether led on to them by the conjurations of those who are skilled in the art, or urged on by their own inclination to act according to their power and inclination; if, I say, he had thoroughly understood this subject, which is both wide in extent and difficult for human comprehension, he would not have condemned us for saying that those who worship the Supreme Being should not serve demons. For ourselves, so far are we from wishing to serve demons, that by the use of prayers and other means which we learn from Scripture, we drive them out of the souls of men, out of places where they have established themselves, and even sometimes from the bodies of animals; for even these creatures often suffer from injuries inflicted upon them by demons.

CHAP. LXVIII.

After all that we have already said concerning Jesus, it would be a useless repetition for us to answer these words of Celsus: "It is easy to convict them of worshipping not a god, not even demons, but a dead person." Leaving, then, this objection for the reason assigned, let us pass on to what follows: "In the first place, I would ask why we are not to serve demons? Is it not true that all things are ordered according to God's will, and that His providence governs all things? Is not everything which happens in the universe, whether it be the work of God, of angels, of other demons, or of heroes, regulated by the law of the Most High God? Have these not had assigned them various departments of which they were severally deemed worthy? Is it not just, therefore, that he who worships God should serve those also to whom God has assigned such power? Yet it is impossible, he says, for a man to serve many masters." Observe here again how he settles at once a number of questions which require considerable research, and a profound acquaintance with what is most mysterious in the government of the universe. For we must inquire into the meaning of the statement, that "all things are ordered according to God's will," and ascertain whether sins are or are not included among the things which God orders. For if God's government extends to sins not only in men, but also in demons and in any other spiritual beings who are capable of sin, it is for those who speak in this manner to see how inconvenient is the expression that "all things are ordered by the will of God." For it follows from it that all sins and all their consequences are ordered by the will of God, which is a different thing from saying that they come to

pass with God's permission. For if we take the word "ordered" in its proper signification, and say that "all the results of sin were ordered," then it is evident that all things are ordered according to God's will, and that all, therefore, who do evil do not offend against His government. And the same distinction holds in regard to "providence." When we say that "the providence of God regulates all things," we utter a great truth if we attribute to that providence nothing but what is just and right. But if we ascribe to the providence of God all things whatsoever, however unjust they may be, then it is no longer true that the providence of God regulates all things, unless we refer directly to God's providence things which flow as results from His arrangements. Celsus maintains also, that "whatever happens in the universe, whether it be the work of God, of angels, of other demons, or of heroes, is regulated by the law of the Most High God." But this also is incorrect; for we cannot say that transgressors follow the law of God when they transgress; and Scripture declares that it is not only wicked men who are transgressors, but also wicked demons and wicked angels.

CHAP. LXIX.

And it is not we alone who speak of wicked demons, but almost all who acknowledge the existence of demons. Thus, then, it is not true that all observe the law of the Most High; for all who fall away from the divine law, whether through heedlessness, or through depravity and vice, or through ignorance of what is right, all such do not keep the law of God, but, to use a new phrase which we find in Scripture, "the law of sin. I say, then, that in the opinion of most of those who believe in the existence of demons, some of them are wicked; and these, instead of keeping the law of God, offend against it. But, according to our belief, it is true of all demons, that they were not demons originally, but they became so in departing from the true way; so that the name "demons" is given to those beings who have fallen away from God. Accordingly, those who worship God must not serve demons. We may also learn the true nature of demons if we consider the practice of those who call upon them by charms to prevent certain things, or for many other purposes. For this is the method they adopt, in order by means of incantations and magical arts to invoke the demons, and induce them to further their wishes. Wherefore, the worship of all demons would be inconsistent in us who worship the Supreme God; and the service of demons is the service of so-called gods, for "all the gods of the heathen are demons."[1] The same thing also appears from

---

[1] Ps. xcv. 5 (LXX.); xcvi. 5 (Heb.)

the fact that the dedication of the most famous of the so-called sacred places, whether temples or statues, was accompanied by curious magical incantations, which were performed by those who zealously served the demons with magical arts. Hence we are determined to avoid the worship of demons even as we would avoid death; and we hold that the worship, which is supposed among the Greeks to be rendered to gods at the altars, and images, and temples, is in reality offered to demons.

CHAP. LXX.

His next remark was, "Have not these inferior powers had assigned to them by God different departments, according as each was deemed worthy?" But this is a question which requires a very profound knowledge. For we must determine whether the Word of God, who governs all things, has appointed wicked demons for certain employments, in the same way as in states executioners are appointed, and other officers with cruel but needful duties to discharge; or whether as among robbers, who infest desert places, it is customary for them to choose out of their number one who may be their leader, — so the demons, who are scattered as it were in troops in different parts of the earth, have chosen for themselves a chief under whose command they may plunder and pillage the souls of men. To explain this fully, and to justify the conduct of the Christians in refusing homage to any ob- ject except the Most High God, and the First- born of all creation, who is His Word and God, we must quote this from Scripture, " All that ever came before Me are thieves and robbers: but the sheep did not hear them;" and again, " The thief cometh not, but for to steal, and to kill, and to destroy;" [1] and other similar pas- sages, as, " Behold, I have given you authority to tread on serpents and scorpions, and over all the power of the enemy: and nothing shall by any means hurt you;" [2] and again, " Thou shalt tread upon the lion and adder: the young lion and the dragon shalt thou trample under feet." [3] But of these things Celsus knew nothing, or he would not have made use of language like this : " Is not everything which happens in the uni- verse, whether it be the work of God, of angels, of other demons, or of heroes, regulated by the law of the Most High God? Have these not had assigned to them various departments of which they were severally deemed worthy? Is it not just, therefore, that he who serves God should serve those also to whom God has as- signed such power?" To which he adds, " It is impossible, they say, for a man to serve many masters." This last point we must postpone to the next book; for this, which is the seventh book which we have written in answer to the treatise of Celsus, is already of sufficient length.

---

[1] John x. 8-10.
[2] Luke x. 19.
[3] Ps. xci. 13.

ORIGEN AGAINST CELSUS.

BOOK VIII.

CHAP. I.

HAVING completed seven books, I now propose to begin the eighth. And may God and His Only-begotten Son the Word be with us, to enable us effectively to refute the falsehoods which Celsus has published under the delusive title of *A True Discourse*, and at the same time to unfold the truths of Christianity with such fulness as our purpose requires. And as Paul said, "We are ambassadors for Christ, as though God did beseech you by us," [1] so would we in the same spirit and language earnestly desire to be ambassadors for Christ to men, even as the Word of God beseeches them to the love of Himself, seeking to win over to righteousness, truth, and the other virtues, those who, until they receive the doctrines of Jesus Christ, live in darkness about God and in ignorance of their Creator. Again, then, I would say, may God bestow upon us His pure and true Word, even "the LORD strong and mighty in battle" [2] against sin. We must now proceed to state the next objection of Celsus, and afterwards to answer it.

CHAP. II.

In a passage previously quoted Celsus asks us why we do not worship demons, and to his remarks on demons we gave such an answer as seemed to us in accordance with the divine word. After having put this question for the purpose of leading us to the worship of demons, he represents us as answering that it is impossible to serve many masters. "This," he goes on to say, "is the language of sedition, and is only used by those who separate themselves and stand aloof from all human society. Those who speak in this way ascribe," as he supposes, " their own feelings and passions to God. It does hold true among men, that he who is in the service of one master cannot well serve another, because the service which he renders to the one inter-feres with that which he owes to the other; and no one, therefore, who has already engaged himself to the service of one, must accept that of another. And, in like manner, it is impossible to serve at the same time heroes or demons of different natures. But in regard to God, who is subject to no suffering or loss, it is," he thinks, " absurd to be on our guard against serving more gods, as though we had to do with demi-gods, or other spirits of that sort." He says also, " He who serves many gods does that which is pleasing to the Most High, because he honours that which belongs to Him." And he adds, " It is indeed wrong to give honour to any to whom God has not given honour." "Wherefore," he says, " in honouring and worshipping all belonging to God, we will not displease Him to whom they all belong."

CHAP. III.

Before proceeding to the next point, it may be well for us to see whether we do not accept with approval the saying, " No man can serve two masters," with the addition, " for either he will hate the one, and love the other; or else he will hold to the one, and despise the other," and further, " Ye cannot serve God and mammon." [3] The defence of this passage will lead us to a deeper and more searching inquiry into the meaning and application of the words "gods" and "lords." Divine Scripture teaches us that there is " a great LORD above all gods." [4] And by this name " gods " we are not to understand the objects of heathen worship (for we know that " all the gods of the heathen are demons " [5]), but the gods mentioned by the prophets as forming an assembly, whom God " judges," and to each of whom He assigns his proper work. For " God standeth in the assembly of the gods: He judgeth among the gods." [6] For " God is Lord

[1] 2 Cor. v. 20.
[2] Ps. xxiv. 8.

[3] Matt. vi. 24.
[4] Ps. xcvii. 9.
[5] Ps. xcvi. 5.
[6] Ps. lxxxii. 1.

of gods," who by His Son "hath called the earth from the rising of the sun unto the going down thereof." [1] We are also commanded to "give thanks to the God of gods." [2] Moreover, we are taught that "God is not the God of the dead, but of the living." [3] Nor are these the only passages to this effect; but there are very many others.

CHAP. IV.

The sacred Scriptures teach us to think, in like manner, of the Lord of lords. For they say in one place, "Give thanks to the God of gods, for His mercy endureth for ever. Give thanks to the Lord of lords, for His mercy endureth for ever;" and in another, "God is King of kings, and Lord of lords." For Scripture distinguishes between those gods which are such only in name and those which are truly gods, whether they are called by that name or not; and the same is true in regard to the use of the word "lords." To this effect Paul says, "For though there be that are called gods, whether in heaven or in earth, as there are gods many, and lords many." [4] But as the God of gods calls whom He pleases through Jesus to his inheritance, "from the east and from the west," and the Christ of God thus shows His superiority to all rulers by entering into their several provinces, and summoning men out of them to be subject to Himself, Paul therefore, with this in view, goes on to say, "But to us there is but one God, the Father, of whom are all things, and one Lord Jesus Christ, by whom are all things, and we by Him;" adding, as if with a deep sense of the marvellous and mysterious nature of the doctrine, "Howbeit, there is not in every man that knowledge." When he says, "To us there is but one God, the Father, of whom are all things; and one Lord Jesus Christ, by whom are all things," by "us" he means himself and all those who have risen up to the supreme God of gods and to the supreme Lord of lords. Now he has risen to the supreme God who gives Him an entire and undivided worship through His Son — the word and wisdom of God made manifest in Jesus. For it is the Son alone who leads to God those who are striving, by the purity of their thoughts, words, and deeds, to come near to God the Creator of the universe. I think, therefore, that the prince of this world, who "transforms himself into an angel of light," [5] was referring to this and such like statements in the words, "Him follows a host of gods and demons, arranged in eleven bands." [6] Speaking of him-

self and the philosophers, he says, "We are of the party of Jupiter; others belong to other demons."

CHAP. V.

Whilst there are thus many gods and lords, whereof some are such in reality, and others are such only in name, we strive to rise not only above those whom the nations of the earth worship as gods, but also beyond those spoken of as gods in Scripture, of whom they are wholly ignorant who are strangers to the covenants of God given by Moses and by our Saviour Jesus, and who have no part in the promises which He has made to us through them. That man rises above all demon-worship who does nothing that is pleasing to demons; and he rises to a blessedness beyond that of those whom Paul calls "gods," if he is enabled, like them, or in any way he may, "to look not at the things which are seen, but at the things which are unseen." And he who considers that "the earnest expectation of the creature waiteth for the manifestation of the sons of God, not willingly, but by reason of him who subjected the same in hope," whilst he praises the creature, and sees how "it shall be freed altogether from the bondage of corruption, and restored to the glorious liberty of the children of God," [7] — such a one cannot be induced to combine with the service of God the service of any other, or to serve two masters. There is therefore nothing seditious or factious in the language of those who hold these views, and who refuse to serve more masters than one. To them Jesus Christ is an all-sufficient Lord, who Himself instructs them, in order that when fully instructed He may form them into a kingdom worthy of God, and present them to God the Father. But indeed they do in a sense separate themselves and stand aloof from those who are aliens from the commonwealth of God and strangers to His covenants, in order that they may live as citizens of heaven, "coming to the living God, and to the city of God, the heavenly Jerusalem, and to an innumerable company of angels, to the general assembly and Church of the first-born, which are written in heaven." [8]

CHAP. VI.

But when we refuse to serve any other than God through His word and wisdom, we do so, not as though we would thereby be doing any harm or injury to God, in the same way as injury would be done to a man by his servant entering into the service of another, but we fear that we ourselves should suffer harm by depriving ourselves of our portion in God, through which we live in the participation of the divine blessedness,

---

[1] Ps. l. 1.
[2] Ps. cxxxvi. 2.
[3] Matt. xxii. 32.
[4] 1 Cor. viii. 5, etc.
[5] 2 Cor. xi. 14.
[6] Plato, *Phædrus*, p. 246.

[7] Rom. viii. 19, 20.
[8] Heb. xii. 22, 23.

and are imbued with that excellent spirit of adoption which in the sons of the heavenly Father cries, not with words, but with deep effect in the inmost heart, "Abba, Father." The Lacedæmonian ambassadors, when brought before the king of Persia, refused to prostrate themselves before him, when the attendants endeavoured to compel them to do so, out of respect for that which alone had authority and lordship over them, namely, the law of Lycurgus.[1] But they who have a much greater and diviner embassy in "being ambassadors for Christ" should not worship any ruler among Persians, or Greeks, or Egyptians, or of any nation whatever, even although their officers and ministers, demons and angels of the devil, should seek to compel them to do so, and should urge them to set at nought a law which is mightier than all the laws upon earth. For the Lord of those who are "ambassadors for Christ" is Christ Himself, whose ambassadors they are, and who is "the Word, who was in the beginning, was with God, and was God."[2]

CHAP. VII.

But when Celsus speaks of heroes and demons, he starts a deeper question than he is aware of. For after the statement which he made in regard to service among men, that "the first master is injured when any of his servants wishes at the same time to serve another," he adds, that "the same holds true of heroes, and other demons of that kind." Now we must inquire of him what nature he thinks those heroes and demons possess of whom he affirms that he who serves one hero may not serve another, and he who serves one demon may not serve another, as though the former hero or demon would be injured in the same way as men are injured when they who serve them first afterwards give themselves to the service of others. Let him also state what loss he supposes those heroes or demons will suffer. For he will be driven either to plunge into endless absurdities, and first repeat, then retract his previous statements; or else to abandon his frivolous conjectures, and confess that he understands nothing of the nature of heroes and demons. And in regard to his statement, that men suffer injury when the servant of one man enters the service of a second master, the question arises: "What is the nature of the injury which is done to the former master by a servant who, while serving him, wishes at the same time to serve another?"

CHAP. VIII.

For if he answers, as one who is unlearned and ignorant of philosophy, that the injury sus-

tained is one which regards things that are outside of us, it will be plainly manifest that he knows nothing of that famous saying of Socrates, "Anytus and Melitus may kill me, but they cannot injure me; for it is impossible that the better should ever be injured by the worse." But if by injury he means a wicked impulse or an evil habit, it is plain that no injury of this kind would befall the wise, by one man serving two wise men in different places. If this sense does not suit his purpose, it is evident that his endeavours are vain to weaken the authority of the passage, "No man can serve two masters;" for these words can be perfectly true only when they refer to the service which we render to the Most High through His Son, who leadeth us to God. And we will not serve God as though He stood in need of our service, or as though He would be made unhappy if we ceased to serve Him; but we do it because we are ourselves benefited by the service of God, and because we are freed from griefs and troubles by serving the Most High God through His only-begotten Son, the Word and Wisdom.

CHAP. IX.

And observe the recklessness of that expression, "For if thou worship any other of the things in the universe," as though he would have us believe that we are led by our service of God to the worship of any other things which belong to God, without any injury to ourselves. But, as if feeling his error, he corrects the words, "If thou worship any other of the things in the universe," by adding, "We may honour none, however, except those to whom that right has been given by God." And we would put to Celsus this question in regard to those who are honoured as gods, as demons, or as heroes: "Now, sir, can you prove that the right to be honoured has been given to these by God, and that it has not arisen from the ignorance and folly of men who in their wanderings have fallen away from Him to whom alone worship and service are properly due? You said a little ago, O Celsus, that Antinous, the favourite of Adrian, is honoured; but surely you will not say that the right to be worshipped as a god was given to him by the God of the universe? And so of the others, we ask proof that the right to be worshipped was given to them by the Most High God." But if the same question is put to us in regard to the worship of Jesus, we will show that the right to be honoured was given to Him by God, "that all may honour the Son, even as they honour the Father."[3] For all the prophecies which preceded His birth were preparations for His worship. And the wonders which He wrought — through no magical art, as Celsus

---

[1] Herod., vii. 136.
[2] John i. 1.
[3] John v. 23.

supposes, but by a divine power, which was foretold by the prophets — have served as a testimony from God in behalf of the worship of Christ. He who honours the Son, who is the Word and Reason, acts in nowise contrary to reason, and gains for himself great good ; he who honours Him, who is the Truth, becomes better by honouring truth : and this we may say of honouring wisdom, righteousness, and all the other names by which the sacred Scriptures are wont to designate the Son of God.

CHAP. X.

But that the honour which we pay to the Son of God, as well as that which we render to God the Father, consists of an upright course of life, is plainly taught us by the passage, "Thou that makest thy boast of the law, through breaking the law dishonourest thou God?"[1] and also, "Of how much sorer punishment, suppose ye, shall he be thought worthy, who hath trodden under foot the Son of God, and hath counted the blood of the covenant, wherewith he was sanctified, an unholy thing, and hath done despite unto the Spirit of grace?"[2] For if he who transgresses the law dishonours God by his transgression, and he who treads under foot the word treads under foot the Son of God, it is evident that he who keeps the law honours God, and that the worshipper of God is he whose life is regulated by the principles and precepts of the divine word. Had Celsus known who they are who are God's people, and that they alone are wise, — and who they are who are strangers to God, and that these are all the wicked who have no desire to give themselves to virtue, — he would have considered before he gave expression to the words, "How can he who honours any of those whom God acknowledges as His own be displeasing to God, to whom they all belong?"

CHAP. XI.

He adds, "And indeed he who, when speaking of God, asserts that there is only one who may be called Lord, speaks impiously, for he divides the kingdom of God, and raises a sedition therein, implying that there are separate factions in the divine kingdom, and that there exists one who is His enemy." He might speak after this fashion, if he could prove by conclusive arguments that those who are worshipped as gods by the heathens are truly gods, and not merely evil spirits, which are supposed to haunt statues and temples and altars. But we desire not only to understand the nature of that divine kingdom of which we are continually speaking and writing, but also ourselves to be of those

who are under the rule of God alone, so that the kingdom of God may be ours. Celsus, however, who teaches us to worship many gods, ought in consistency not to speak of "the kingdom of God," but of "the kingdom of the gods." There are therefore no factions in the kingdom of God, nor is there any god who is an adversary to Him, although there are some who, like the Giants and Titans, in their wickedness wish to contend with God in company with Celsus, and those who declare war against Him who has by innumerable proofs established the claims of Jesus, and against Him who, as the Word, did, for the salvation of our race, show Himself before all the world in such a form as each was able to receive Him.

CHAP. XII.

In what follows, some may imagine that he says something plausible against us. "If," says he, "these people worshipped one God alone, and no other, they would perhaps have some valid argument against the worship of others. But they pay excessive reverence to one who has but lately appeared among men, and they think it no offence against God if they worship also His servant." To this we reply, that if Celsus had known that saying, "I and My Father are one,"[3] and the words used in prayer by the Son of God, "As Thou and I are one,"[4] he would not have supposed that we worship any other besides Him who is the Supreme God. "For," says He, "My Father is in Me, and I in Him."[5] And if any should from these words be afraid of our going over to the side of those who deny that the Father and the Son are two persons, let him weigh that passage, "And the multitude of them that believed were of one heart and of one soul,"[6] that he may understand the meaning of the saying, "I and My Father are one." We worship one God, the Father and the Son, therefore, as we have explained ; and our argument against the worship of other gods still continues valid. And we do not "reverence beyond measure one who has but lately appeared," as though He did not exist before ;[7] for we believe Himself when He says, "Before Abraham was, I am."[8] Again He says, "I am the truth ;"[9] and surely none of us is so simple as to suppose that truth did not exist before the time when Christ appeared.[10] We worship, therefore, the Father of truth, and the Son, who is the truth ; and these, while they are two, con-

---

[1] Rom. ii. 23.
[2] Heb. x. 29.

[3] John x. 30.
[4] John xvii. 22.
[5] John xiv. 11, and xvii. 21.
[6] Acts iv. 32.
[7] [See note *infra*, cap. xxvi. S.]
[8] John viii. 58.
[9] John xiv. 6.
[10] [ἡ τῆς ἀληθείας οὐσία: see Neander's *History of the Church*, vol. ii. pp. 282, 283; also note *supra*, book vi. cap. lxiv. p. 603. S.]

sidered as persons or subsistences, are one in unity of thought, in harmony and in identity of will. So entirely are they one, that he who has seen the Son, "who is the brightness of God's glory, and the express image of His person,"[1] has seen in Him who is the image of God, God Himself.

CHAP. XIII.

He further supposes, that "because we join along with the worship of God the worship of His Son, it follows that, in our view, not only God, but also the servants of God, are to be worshipped." If he had meant this to apply to those who are truly the servants of God, after His only-begotten Son, — to Gabriel and Michael, and the other angels and archangels, — and if he had said of these that they ought to be worshipped, — if also he had clearly defined the meaning of the word "worship," and the duties of the worshippers, — we might perhaps have brought forward such thoughts as have occurred to us on so important a subject. But as he reckons among the servants of God the demons which are worshipped by the heathen, he cannot induce us, on the plea of consistency, to worship such as are declared by the word to be servants of the evil one, the prince of this world, who leads astray from God as many as he can. We decline, therefore, altogether to worship and serve those whom other men worship, for the reason that they are not servants of God. For if we had been taught to regard them as servants of the Most High, we would not have called them demons. Accordingly, we worship with all our power the one God, and His only Son, the Word and the Image of God, by prayers and supplications; and we offer our petitions to the God of the universe through His only-begotten Son. To the Son we first present them, and beseech Him, as "the propitiation for our sins,"[2] and our High Priest, to offer our desires, and sacrifices, and prayers, to the Most High. Our faith, therefore, is directed to God through His Son, who strengthens it in us; and Celsus can never show that the Son of God is the cause of any sedition or disloyalty in the kingdom of God. We honour the Father when we admire His Son, the Word, and Wisdom, and Truth, and Righteousness, and all that He who is the Son of so great a Father is said in Scripture to be. So much on this point.

CHAP. XIV.

Again Celsus proceeds: "If you should tell them that Jesus is not the Son of God, but that God is the Father of all, and that He alone ought to be truly worshipped, they would not consent to discontinue their worship of him who is their leader in the sedition. And they call him Son of God, not out of any extreme reverence for God, but from an extreme desire to extol Jesus Christ." We, however, have learned who the Son of God is, and know that He is "the brightness of His glory, and the express image of His person," and "the breath of the power of God, and a pure influence flowing from the glory of the Almighty;" moreover, "the brightness of the everlasting light, the unspotted mirror of the power of God, and the image of His goodness."[3] We know, therefore, that He is the Son of God, and that God is His father. And there is nothing extravagant or unbecoming the character of God in the doctrine that He should have begotten such an only Son; and no one will persuade us that such a one is not a Son of the unbegotten God and Father. If Celsus has heard something of certain persons holding that the Son of God is not the Son of the Creator of the universe, that is a matter which lies between him and the supporters of such an opinion. Jesus is, then, not the leader of any seditious movement, but the promoter of peace. For He said to His disciples, "Peace I leave with you, My peace I give unto you;" and as He knew that it would be men of the world, and not men of God, who would wage war against us, he added, "Not as the world giveth peace, do I give peace unto you."[4] And even although we are oppressed in the world, we have confidence in Him who said, "In the world ye shall have tribulation; but be of good cheer, I have overcome the world." And it is He whom we call Son of God — Son of that God, namely, whom, to quote the words of Celsus, "we most highly reverence;" and He is the Son who has been most highly exalted by the Father. Grant that there may be some individuals among the multitudes of believers who are not in entire agreement with us, and who incautiously assert that the Saviour is the Most High God; however, we do not hold with them, but rather believe Him when He says, "The Father who sent Me is greater than I."[5] We would not therefore make Him whom we call Father inferior — as Celsus accuses us of doing — to the Son of God.

CHAP. XV.

Celsus goes on to say: "That I may give a true representation of their faith, I will use their own words, as given in what is called *A Heavenly Dialogue*: 'If the Son is mightier than God,

---

and the Son of man is Lord over Him, who else than the Son can be Lord over that God who is the ruler over all things? How comes it, that while so many go about the well, no one goes down into it? Why art thou afraid when thou hast gone so far on the way? Answer: Thou art mistaken, for I lack neither courage nor weapons.' Is it not evident, then, that their views are precisely such as I have described them to be? They suppose that another God, who is above the heavens, is the Father of him whom with one accord they honour, that they may honour this Son of man alone, whom they exalt under the form and name of the great God, and whom they assert to be stronger than God, who rules the world, and that he rules over Him. And hence that maxim of theirs, 'It is impossible to serve two masters,' is maintained for the purpose of keeping up the party who are on the side of this Lord." Here, again, Celsus quotes opinions from some most obscure sect of heretics, and ascribes them to all Christians. I call it "a most obscure sect;" for although we have often contended with heretics, yet we are unable to discover from what set of opinions he has taken this passage, if indeed he has quoted it from any author, and has not rather concocted it himself, or added it as an inference of his own. For we who say that the visible world is under the government of Him who created all things, do thereby declare that the Son is not mightier than the Father, but inferior to Him. And this belief we ground on the saying of Jesus Himself, "The Father who sent Me is greater than I." And none of us is so insane as to affirm that the Son of man is Lord over God. But when we regard the Saviour as God the Word, and Wisdom, and Righteousness, and Truth, we certainly do say that He has dominion over all things which have been subjected to Him in this capacity, but not that His dominion extends over the God and Father who is Ruler over all.[1] Besides, as the Word rules over none against their will, there are still wicked beings — not only men, but also angels, and all demons — over whom we say that in a sense He does not rule, since they do not yield Him a willing obedience; but, in another sense of the word, He rules even over them, in the same way as we say that man rules over the irrational animals, — not by persuasion, but as one who tames and subdues lions and beasts of burden. Nevertheless, he leaves no means untried to persuade even those who are still disobedient to submit to His authority. So far as we are concerned, therefore, we deny the truth of that which Celsus quotes as one of our sayings, "Who else than He can be Lord over Him who is God over all?"

CHAP. XVI.

The remaining part of the extract given by Celsus seems to have been taken from some other form of heresy, and the whole jumbled together in strange confusion: "How is it, that while so many go about the well, no one goes down into it? Why dost thou shrink with fear when thou hast gone so far on the way? Answer: Thou art mistaken, for I lack neither courage nor weapons." We who belong to the Church which takes its name from Christ, assert that none of these statements are true. For he seems to have made them simply that they might harmonize with what he had said before; but they have no reference to us. For it is a principle with us, not to worship any god whom we merely "suppose" to exist, but Him alone who is the Creator of this universe, and of all things besides which are unseen by the eye of sense. These remarks of Celsus may apply to those who go on another road and tread other paths from us, — men who deny the Creator, and make to themselves another god under a new form, having nothing but the name of God, whom they esteem higher than the Creator; and with these may be joined any that there may be who say that the Son is greater than the God who rules all things. In reference to the precept that we ought not to serve two masters, we have already shown what appears to us the principle contained in it, when we proved that no sedition or disloyalty could be charged against the followers of Jesus their Lord, who confess that they reject every other lord, and serve Him alone who is the Son and Word of God.

CHAP. XVII.

Celsus then proceeds to say that "we shrink from raising altars, statues, and temples; and this," he thinks, "has been agreed upon among us as the badge or distinctive mark of a secret and forbidden society." He does not perceive that we regard the spirit of every good man as an altar from which arises an incense which is truly and spiritually sweet-smelling, namely, the prayers ascending from a pure conscience. Therefore it is said by John in the Revelation, "The odours are the prayers of saints;"[2] and by the Psalmist, "Let my prayer come up before Thee as incense."[3] And the statues and gifts which are fit offerings to God are the work of no common mechanics, but are wrought and fashioned in us by the Word of God, to wit, the virtues in which we imitate "the First-born of all creation," who has set us an example of justice, of temperance, of courage, of wisdom, of piety, and of the other virtues. In all those,

---

[1] [See note, book ii. cap. ix. p. 433. S.]

[2] Rev. v. 8.
[3] Ps. cxli. 2.

then, who plant and cultivate within their souls, according to the divine word, temperance, justice, wisdom, piety, and other virtues, these excellences are their statues they raise, in which we are persuaded that it is becoming for us to honour the model and prototype of all statues : "the image of the invisible God," God the Only-begotten. And again, they who " put off the old man with his deeds, and put on the new man, which is renewed in knowledge after the image of Him that hath created him," in taking upon them the image of Him who hath created them, do raise within themselves a statue like to what the Most High God Himself desires. And as among statuaries there are some who are marvellously perfect in their art, as for example Pheidias and Polycleitus, and among painters, Zeuxis and Apelles, whilst others make inferior statues, and others, again, are inferior to the second-rate artists, — so that, taking all together, there is a wide difference in the execution of statues and pictures, — in the same way there are some who form images of the Most High in a better manner and with a more perfect skill ; so that there is no comparison even between the Olympian Jupiter of Pheidias and the man who has been fashioned according to the image of God the Creator. But by far the most excellent of all these throughout the whole creation is that image in our Saviour who said, " My Father is in Me."

CHAP. XVIII.

And every one who imitates Him according to his ability, does by this very endeavour raise a statue according to the image of the Creator, for in the contemplation of God with a pure heart they become imitators of Him. And, in general, we see that all Christians strive to raise altars and statues as we have described them, and these not of a lifeless and senseless kind, and not to receive greedy spirits intent upon lifeless things, but to be filled with the Spirit of God who dwells in the images of virtue of which we have spoken, and takes His abode in the soul which is conformed to the image of the Creator. Thus the Spirit of Christ dwells in those who bear, so to say, a resemblance in form and feature to Himself. And the Word of God, wishing to set this clearly before us, represents God as promising to the righteous, " I will dwell in them, and walk among them ; and I will be their God, and they shall be My people." [1] And the Saviour says, " If any man hear My words, and do them, I and My Father will come to him, and make Our abode with him." [2] Let any one, therefore, who chooses compare the altars which I have described with those spoken

of by Celsus, and the images in the souls of those who worship the Most High God with the statues of Pheidias, Polycleitus, and such like, and he will clearly perceive, that while the latter are lifeless things, and subject to the ravages of time, the former abide in the immortal spirit as long as the reasonable soul wishes to preserve them.

CHAP. XIX.

And if, further, temples are to be compared with temples, that we may prove to those who accept the opinions of Celsus that we do not object to the erection of temples suited to the images and altars of which we have spoken, but that we do refuse to build lifeless temples to the Giver of all life, let any one who chooses learn how we are taught, that our bodies are the temple of God, and that if any one by lust or sin defiles the temple of God, he will himself be destroyed, as acting impiously towards the true temple. Of all the temples spoken of in this sense, the best and most excellent was the pure and holy body of our Saviour Jesus Christ. When He knew that wicked men might aim at the destruction of the temple of God in Him, but that their purposes of destruction would not prevail against the divine power which had built that temple, He says to them, " Destroy this temple, and in three days I will raise it again. . . . This He said of the temple of His body." [3] And in other parts of holy Scripture where it speaks of the mystery of the resurrection to those whose ears are divinely opened, it says that the temple which has been destroyed shall be built up again of living and most precious stones, thereby giving us to understand that each of those who are led by the word of God to strive together in the duties of piety, will be a precious stone in the one great temple of God. Accordingly, Peter says, " Ye also, as lively stones, are built up a spiritual house, an holy priesthood, to offer up spiritual sacrifices, acceptable to God by Jesus Christ ; " [4] and Paul also says, " Being built upon the foundation of the apostles and prophets, Jesus Christ our Lord being the chief corner-stone." [5] And there is a similar hidden allusion in this passage in Isaiah, which is addressed to Jerusalem : " Behold, I will lay thy stones with carbuncles, and lay thy foundations with sapphires. And I will make thy battlements of jasper, and thy gates of crystal, and all thy borders of pleasant stones. And all thy children shall be taught of the Lord ; and great shall be the peace of thy children. In righteousness shalt thou be established." [6]

---

[1] 2 Cor. vi. 16.
[2] John xiv. 23.

[3] John ii. 19, 21.
[4] 1 Pet. ii. 5.
[5] Eph. ii. 20.
[6] Isa. liv. 11-14.

CHAP. XX.

There are, then, among the righteous some who are carbuncles, others sapphires, others jaspers, and others crystals, and thus there is among the righteous every kind of choice and precious stone. As to the spiritual meaning of the different stones, — what is their nature, and to what kind of soul the name of each precious stone especially applies, — we cannot at present stay to examine. We have only felt it necessary to show thus briefly what we understand by temples, and what the one Temple of God built of precious stones truly means. For as if in some cities a dispute should arise as to which had the finest temples, those who thought their own were the best would do their utmost to show the excellence of their own temples and the inferiority of the others, — in like manner, when they reproach us for not deeming it necessary to worship the Divine Being by raising lifeless temples, we set before them our temples, and show to such at least as are not blind and senseless, like their senseless gods, that there is no comparison between our statues and the statues of the heathen, nor between our altars, with what we may call the incense ascending from them, and the heathen altars, with the fat and blood of the victims; nor, finally, between the temples of senseless gods, admired by senseless men, who have no divine faculty for perceiving God, and the temples, statues, and altars which are worthy of God. It is not therefore true that we object to building altars, statues, and temples, because we have agreed to make this the badge of a secret and forbidden society; but we do so, because we have learnt from Jesus Christ the true way of serving God, and we shrink from whatever, under a pretence of piety, leads to utter impiety those who abandon the way marked out for us by Jesus Christ. For it is He who alone is the way of piety, as He truly said, "I am the way, the truth, the life."

CHAP. XXI.

Let us see what Celsus further says of God, and how he urges us to the use of those things which are properly called idol offerings, or, still better, offerings to demons, although, in his ignorance of what true sanctity is, and what sacrifices are well-pleasing to God, he call them "holy sacrifices." His words are, "God is the God of all alike; He is good, He stands in need of nothing, and He is without jealousy. What, then, is there to hinder those who are most devoted to His service from taking part in public feasts?" I cannot see the connection which he fancies between God's being good, and independent, and free from jealousy, and His devoted servants taking part in public feasts. I

confess, indeed, that from the fact that God is good, and without want of anything, and free from jealousy, it would follow as a consequence that we might take part in public feasts, if it were proved that the public feasts had nothing wrong in them, and were grounded upon true views of the character of God, so that they resulted naturally from a devout service of God. If, however, the so-called public festivals can in no way be shown to accord with the service of God, but may on the contrary be proved to have been devised by men when occasion offered to commemorate some human events, or to set forth certain qualities of water or earth, or the fruits of the earth, — in that case, it is clear that those who wish to offer an enlightened worship to the Divine Being will act according to sound reason, and not take part in the public feasts. For "to keep a feast," as one of the wise men of Greece has well said, "is nothing else than to do one's duty;"[1] and that man truly celebrates a feast who does his duty and prays always, offering up continually bloodless sacrifices in prayer to God. That therefore seems to me a most noble saying of Paul, "Ye observe days, and months, and times, and years. I am afraid of you, lest I have bestowed upon you labour in vain."[2]

CHAP. XXII.

If it be objected to us on this subject that we ourselves are accustomed to observe certain days, as for example the Lord's day, the Preparation, the Passover, or Pentecost, I have to answer, that to the perfect Christian, who is ever in his thoughts, words, and deeds serving his natural Lord, God the Word, all his days are the Lord's, and he is always keeping the Lord's day. He also who is unceasingly preparing himself for the true life, and abstaining from the pleasures of this life which lead astray so many, — who is not indulging the lust of the flesh, but "keeping under his body, and bringing it into subjection," — such a one is always keeping Preparation-day. Again, he who considers that "Christ our Passover was sacrificed for us," and that it is his duty to keep the feast by eating of the flesh of the Word, never ceases to keep the paschal feast; for the *pascha* means a "passover," and he is ever striving in all his thoughts, words, and deeds, to pass over from the things of this life to God, and is hastening towards the city of God. And, finally, he who can truly say, "We are risen with Christ," and "He hath exalted us, and made us to sit with Him in heavenly places in Christ," is always living in the season of Pentecost; and most of all, when going up to the upper chamber, like the apostles of Jesus,

---

[1] Thucyd., book i. sect. lxx.
[2] Gal. iv. 10, 11.

he gives himself to supplication and prayer, that he may become worthy of receiving "the mighty wind rushing from heaven," which is powerful to destroy sin and its fruits among men, and worthy of having some share of the tongue of fire which God sends.

CHAP. XXIII.

But the majority of those who are accounted believers are not of this advanced class; but from being either unable or unwilling to keep every day in this manner, they require some sensible memorials to prevent spiritual things from passing altogether away from their minds. It is to this practice of setting apart some days distinct from others, that Paul seems to me to refer in the expression, "part of the feast;"[1] and by these words he indicates that a life in accordance with the divine word consists not "in a part of the feast," but in one entire and never-ceasing festival.[2] Again, compare the festivals, observed among us as these have been described above, with the public feasts of Celsus and the heathen, and say if the former are not much more sacred observances than those feasts in which the lust of the flesh runs riot, and leads to drunkenness and debauchery. It would be too long for us at present to show why we are required by the law of God to keep its festivals by eating "the bread of affliction,"[3] or "unleavened with bitter herbs,"[4] or why it says, "Humble your souls,"[5] and such like. For it is impossible for man, who is a compound being, in which "the flesh lusteth against the Spirit, and the Spirit against the flesh,"[6] to keep the feast with his whole nature; for either he keeps the feast with his spirit and afflicts the body, which through the lust of the flesh is unfit to keep it along with the spirit, or else he keeps it with the body, and the spirit is unable to share in it. But we have for the present said enough on the subject of feasts.

CHAP. XXIV.

Let us now see on what grounds Celsus urges us to make use of the idol offerings and the public sacrifices in the public feasts. His words are, "If these idols are nothing, what harm will there be in taking part in the feast? On the other hand, if they are demons, it is certain that they too are God's creatures, and that we must believe in them, sacrifice to them according to the laws, and pray to them that they may be propitious."

In reference to this statement, it would be profitable for us to take up and clearly explain the whole passage of the first Epistle to the Corinthians, in which Paul treats of offerings to idols.[7] The apostle draws from the fact that "an idol is nothing in the world," the consequence that it is injurious to use things offered to idols; and he shows to those who have ears to hear on such subjects, that he who partakes of things offered to idols is worse than a murderer, for he destroys his own brethren, for whom Christ died. And further, he maintains that the sacrifices are made to demons; and from that he proceeds to show that those who join the table of demons become associated with the demons; and he concludes that a man cannot both be a partaker of the table of the Lord and of the table of demons. But since it would require a whole treatise to set forth fully all that is contained on this subject in the Epistle to the Corinthians, we shall content ourselves with this brief statement of the argument; for it will be evident to any one who carefully considers what has been said, that even if idols are nothing, nevertheless it is an awful thing to join in idol festivals. And even supposing that there are such beings as demons to whom the sacrifices are offered, it it has been clearly shown that we are forbidden to take part in these festivals, when we know the difference between the table of the Lord and the table of demons. And knowing this, we endeavour as much as we can to be always partakers of the Lord's table, and beware to the utmost of joining at any time the table of demons.

CHAP. XXV.

Celsus says that "the demons belong to God, and are therefore to be believed, to be sacrificed to according to laws, and to be prayed to that they may be propitious." Those who are disposed to learn, must know that the word of God nowhere says of evil things that they belong to God, for it judges them unworthy of such a Lord. Accordingly, it is not all men who bear the name of "men of God," but only those who are worthy of God, — such as Moses and Elias, and any others who are so called, or such as resemble those who are so called in Scripture. In the same way, all angels are not said to be angels of God, but only those that are blessed: those that have fallen away into sin are called "angels of the devil," just as bad men are called "men of sin," "sons of perdition," or "sons of iniquity." Since, then, among men some are good and others bad, and the former are said to be God's and the latter the devil's, so among angels some are angels of God, and others angels of the devil. But among demons there is no such dis-

---

[1] Col. ii. 16. The whole passage in the English version is, "Let no man judge you in meat, or in drink, or *in respect of an holyday*" (ἐν μέρει ἑορτῆς). Origen's interpretation is not followed by any modern expositors. It is adopted by Chrysostom and Theodoret.

[2] [Dr. Hessey notes this as "a curious comment" of Origen's on St. Paul's language: Bampton Lectures, *On Sunday: its Origin, History, and Present Obligation*, pp. 48, 286-289, 4th ed. S.]

[3] Deut. xvi. 3.

[4] Ex. xii. 8.

[5] Lev. xvi. 29.

[6] Gal. v. 17.

[7] I Cor viii. 4, 11.

tinction, for all are said to be wicked. We do not therefore hesitate to say that Celsus is false when he says, " If they are demons, it is evident that they must also belong to God." He must either show that this distinction of good and bad among angels and men has no foundation, or else that a similar distinction may be shown to hold among demons. If that is impossible, it is plain that demons do not belong to God; for their prince is not God, but, as holy Scripture says, " Beelzebub."

CHAP. XXVI.

And we are not to believe in demons, although Celsus urges us to do so; but if we are to obey God, we must die, or endure anything, sooner than obey demons. In the same way, we are not to propitiate demons; for it is impossible to propitiate beings that are wicked and that seek the injury of men. Besides, what are the laws in accordance with which Celsus would have us propitiate the demons? For if he means laws enacted in states, he must show that they are in agreement with the divine laws. But if that cannot be done, as the laws of many states are quite inconsistent with each other, these laws, therefore, must of necessity be no laws at all in the proper sense of the word, or else the enactments of wicked men; and these we must not obey, for "we must obey God rather than men." Away, then, with this counsel, which Celsus gives us, to offer prayer to demons: it is not to be listened to for a moment; for our duty is to pray to the Most High God alone, and to the Only-begotten, the First-born of the whole creation, and to ask Him as our High Priest to present the prayers which ascend to Him from us, to His God and our God, to His Father and the Father of those who direct their lives according to His word.[1] And as we would have no desire to enjoy the favour of those men who wish us to follow their wicked lives, and who give us their favour only on condition that we choose nothing opposed to their wishes, because their favour would make us enemies of God, who cannot be pleased with those who have such men for their friends, — in the same way those who are acquainted with the nature, the purposes, and the wickedness of demons, can never wish to obtain their favour.

CHAP. XXVII.

And Christians have nothing to fear, even if demons should not be well-disposed to them;

for they are protected by the Supreme God, who is well pleased with their piety, and who sets His divine angels to watch over those who are worthy of such guardianship, so that they can suffer nothing from demons. He who by his piety possesses the favour of the Most High, who has accepted the guidance of Jesus, the " Angel of the great counsel," [2] being well contented with the favour of God through Christ Jesus, may say with confidence that he has nothing to suffer from the whole host of demons. " The LORD is my light and my salvation; whom shall I fear? The LORD is the strength of my life; of whom shall I be afraid? Though an host should encamp against me, my heart shall not fear." [3] So much, then, in reply to those statements of Celsus: " If they are demons, they too evidently belong to God, and they are to be believed, to be sacrificed to according to the laws, and prayers are to be offered to them that they may he propitious."

CHAP. XXVIII.

We shall now proceed to the next statement of Celsus, and examine it with care : " If in obedience to the traditions of their fathers they abstain from such victims, they must also abstain from all animal food, in accordance with the opinions of Pythagoras, who thus showed his respect for the soul and its bodily organs. But if, as they say, they abstain that they may not eat along with demons, I admire their wisdom, in having at length discovered, that whenever they eat they eat with demons, although they only refuse to do so when they are looking upon a slain victim; for when they eat bread, or drink wine, or taste fruits, do they not receive these things, as well as the water they drink and the air they breathe, from certain demons, to whom have been assigned these different provinces of nature?" Here I would observe that I cannot see how those whom he speaks of as abstaining from certain victims, in accordance with the traditions of their fathers, are consequently bound to abstain from the flesh of all animals. We do not indeed deny that the divine word does seem to command something similar to this, when to raise us to a higher and purer life it says, " It is good neither to eat flesh, nor to drink wine, nor anything whereby thy brother stumbleth, or is offended, or is made weak ;" [4] and again, " Destroy not him with thy meat, for whom Christ died ; " [5] and again, " If meat make my brother to offend, I will eat no flesh while the world standeth, lest I make my brother to offend." [6]

---

[1] [See Liddon's Bampton Lectures on *The Divinity of our Lord and Saviour Jesus Christ*, p. 383, where it is pointed out that " Origen often insists upon the worship of Christ as being a Christian duty." S.]

[2] Isa. ix. 6 (LXX.).
[3] Ps. xxvii. 1, 3.
[4] Rom. xiv. 21.
[5] Rom. xiv. 15.
[6] 1 Cor. viii. 13.

CHAP. XXIX.

But it is to be observed that the Jews, who claim for themselves a correct understanding of the law of Moses, carefully restrict their food to such things as are accounted clean, and abstain from those that are unclean. They also do not use in their food the blood of an animal nor the flesh of an animal torn by wild beasts, and some other things which it would take too long for us at present to detail. But Jesus, wishing to lead all men by His teaching to the pure worship and service of God, and anxious not to throw any hindrance in the way of many who might be benefited by Christianity, through the imposition of a burdensome code of rules in regard to food, has laid it down, that "not that which goeth into the mouth defileth a man, but that which cometh out of the mouth; for whatsoever entereth in at the mouth goeth into the belly, and is cast out into the draught. But those things which proceed out of the mouth are evil thoughts when spoken, murders, adulteries, fornications, thefts, false witness, blasphemies."[1] Paul also says, "Meat commendeth us not to God: for neither, if we eat, are we the better; neither, if we eat not, are we the worse."[2] Wherefore, as there is some obscurity about this matter, without some explanation is given, it seemed good to the apostles of Jesus and the elders assembled together at Antioch,[3] and also, as they themselves say, to the Holy Spirit, to write a letter to the Gentile believers, forbidding them to partake of those things from which alone they say it is necessary to abstain, namely, "things offered to idols, things strangled, and blood."[3]

CHAP. XXX.

For that which is offered to idols is sacrificed to demons, and a man of God must not join the table of demons. As to things strangled, we are forbidden by Scripture to partake of them, because the blood is still in them; and blood, especially the odour arising from blood, is said to be the food of demons. Perhaps, then, if we were to eat of strangled animals, we might have such spirits feeding along with us. And the reason which forbids the use of strangled animals for food is also applicable to the use of blood. And it may not be amiss, as bearing on this point, to recall a beautiful saying in the writings of Sextus,[4] which is known to most Christians: "The eating of animals," says he, "is a matter of indifference; but to abstain from them is more agreeable to reason." It is not, therefore, simply on account of some traditions of our fathers that we refrain from eating victims offered to those called gods or heroes or demons, but for other reasons, some of which I have here mentioned. It is not to be supposed, however, that we are to abstain from the flesh of animals in the same way as we are bound to abstain from all vice and wickedness: we are indeed to abstain not only from the flesh of animals, but from all other kinds of food, if we cannot partake of them without incurring evil, and the consequences of evil. For we are to avoid eating for gluttony, or for the mere gratification of the appetite, without regard to the health and sustenance of the body. We do not believe that souls pass from one body to another, and that they may descend so low as to enter the bodies of the brutes. If we abstain at times from eating the flesh of animals, it is evidently, therefore, not for the same reason as Pythagoras; for it is the reasonable soul alone that we honour, and we commit its bodily organs with due honours to the grave. For it is not right that the dwelling-place of the rational soul should be cast aside anywhere without honour, like the carcases of brute beasts; and so much the more when we believe that the respect paid to the body redounds to the honour of the person who received from God a soul which has nobly employed the organs of the body in which it resided. In regard to the question, "How are the dead raised up, and with what body do they come?"[5] we have already answered it briefly, as our purpose required.

CHAP. XXXI.

Celsus afterwards states what is adduced by Jews and Christians alike in defence of abstinence from idol sacrifices, namely, that it is wrong for those who have dedicated themselves to the Most High God to eat with demons. What he brings forward against this view, we have already seen. In our opinion, a man can only be said to eat and drink with demons when he eats the flesh of what are called sacred victims, and when he drinks the wine poured out to the honour of the demons. But Celsus thinks that we cannot eat bread or drink wine in any way whatever, or taste fruits, or even take a draught of water, without eating and drinking with demons. He adds also, that the air which we breathe is received from demons, and that not an animal can breathe without receiving the air from the demons who are set over the air. If any one wishes to defend this statement of Celsus, let him show that it is not the divine angels of god, but demons, the whole race of whom are bad, that have been appointed to communicate all those blessings which have been mentioned. We indeed also maintain with re-

---

[1] Matt. xv. 11, 17-19.
[2] 1 Cor. viii. 8.
[3] Acts xv. 28, 29. It was at Jerusalem.
[4] [Sextus, or Xystus. See note of Spencer in Migne. S.]

[5] [1 Cor. xv. 35. S.]

gard not only to the fruits of the earth, but to every flowing stream and every breath of air, that the ground brings forth those things which are said to grow up naturally, — that the water springs in fountains, and refreshes the earth with running streams, — that the air is kept pure, and supports the life of those who breathe it, only in consequence of the agency and control of certain beings whom we may call invisible husbandmen and guardians; but we deny that those invisible agents are demons. And if we might speak boldly, we would say that if demons have any share at all in these things, to them belong famine, blasting of the vine and fruit trees, pestilence among men and beasts: all these are the proper occupations of demons, who in the capacity of public executioners receive power at certain times to carry out the divine judgments, for the restoration of those who have plunged headlong into wickedness, or for the trial and discipline of the souls of the wise. For those who through all their afflictions preserve their piety pure and unimpaired, show their true character to all spectators, whether visible or invisible, who behold them; while those who are otherwise minded, yet conceal their wickedness, when they have their true character exposed by misfortunes, become manifest to themselves as well as to those whom we may also call spectators.

CHAP. XXXII.

The Psalmist bears witness that divine justice employs certain evil angels to inflict calamities upon men: "He cast upon them the fierceness of His anger, wrath, and indignation, and trouble, sent by evil angels." [1] Whether demons ever go beyond this when they are suffered to do what they are ever ready, though through the restraint put upon them they are not always able to do, is a question to be solved by that man who can conceive, in so far as human nature will allow, how it accords with the divine justice, that such multitudes of human souls are separated from the body while walking in the paths which lead to certain death. "For the judgments of God are so great," that a soul which is still clothed with a mortal body cannot comprehend them; "and they cannot be expressed: therefore by unnurtured souls" [2] they are not in any measure to be understood. And hence, too, rash spirits, by their ignorance in these matters, and by recklessly setting themselves against the Divine Being, multiply impious objections against providence. It is not from demons, then, that men receive any of those things which meet the necessities of life, and least of all ourselves, who have been taught to

make a proper use of these things. And they who partake of corn and wine, and the fruits of trees, of water and of air, do not feed with demons, but rather do they feast with divine angels, who are appointed for this purpose, and who are as it were invited to the table of the pious man, who hearkens to the precept of the word, which says, "Whether ye eat or drink, or whatever ye do, do all to the glory of God." [3] And again, in another place it is written, "Do all things in the name of God." [4] When, therefore, we eat and drink and breathe to the glory of God, and act in all things according to what is right, we feast with no demons, but with divine angels: "For every creature is good, and nothing to be refused, if it be received with thanksgiving: for it is sanctified by the word of God and prayer." [5] But it could not be good, and it could not be sanctified, if these things were, as Celsus supposes, entrusted to the charge of demons.

CHAP. XXXIII.

From this it is evident that we have already met the next statement of Celsus, which is as follows: "We must either not live, and indeed not come into this life at all, or we must do so on condition that we give thanks and first-fruits and prayers to demons, who have been set over the things of this world: and that we must do as long as we live, that they may prove good and kind." We must surely live, and we must live according to the word of God, as far as we are enabled to do so. And we are thus enabled to live, when, "whether we eat or drink, we do all to the glory of God;" and we are not to refuse to enjoy those things which have been created for our use, but must receive them with thanksgiving to the Creator. And it is under these conditions, and not such as have been imagined by Celsus, that we have been brought into life by God; and we are not placed under demons, but we are under the government of the Most High God, through Him who hath brought us to God — Jesus Christ. It is not according to the law of God that any demon has had a share in worldly affairs, but it was by their own lawlessness that they perhaps sought out for themselves places destitute of the knowledge of God and of the divine life, or places where there are many enemies of God. Perhaps also, as being fit to rule over and punish them, they have been set by the Word, who governs all things, to rule over those who subjected themselves to evil and not to God. For this reason, then, let Celsus, as one who knows not God, give thank-offerings to demons. But we give thanks to the Creator of all, and, along with thanksgiving and prayer for the blessings we have received, we also eat the bread presented to us; and this bread becomes by prayer a sacred body, which sanctifies those who sincerely partake of it.

CHAP. XXXIV.

Celsus would also have us to offer first-fruits to demons. But we would offer them to Him who said, "Let the earth bring forth grass, the herb yielding seed, and the fruit tree yielding fruit after his kind, whose seed is in itself upon the earth."[1] And to Him to whom we offer first-fruits we also send up our prayers, "having a great high priest, that is passed into the heavens, Jesus the Son of God," and "we hold fast this profession"[2] as long as we live; for we find God and His only-begotten Son, manifested to us in Jesus, to be gracious and kind to us. And if we would wish to have besides a great number of beings who shall ever prove friendly to us, we are taught that "thousand thousands stood before Him, and ten thousand times ten thousand ministered unto Him."[3] And these, regarding all as their relations and friends who imitate their piety towards God, and in prayer call upon Him with sincerity, work along with them for their salvation, appear unto them, deem it their office and duty to attend to them, and as if by common agreement they visit with all manner of kindness and deliverance those who pray to God, to whom they themselves also pray: "For they are all ministering spirits, sent forth to minister for those who shall be heirs of salvation."[4] Let the learned Greeks say that the human soul at its birth is placed under the charge of demons: Jesus has taught us not to despise even the little ones in His Church, saying, "Their angels do always behold the face of My Father which is in heaven."[5] And the prophet says, "The angel of the LORD encampeth round about them that fear Him, and delivereth them."[6] We do not, then, deny that there are many demons upon earth, but we maintain that they exist and exercise power among the wicked, as a punishment of their wickedness. But they have no power over those who "have put on the whole armour of God," who have received strength to "withstand the wiles of the devil,"[7] and who are ever engaged in contests with them, knowing that "we wrestle not against flesh and blood, but against principalities, against powers, against the rulers of the darkness of this world, against spiritual wickedness in high places."[8]

CHAP. XXXV.

Now let us consider another saying of Celsus, which is as follows: "The satrap of a Persian or Roman monarch, or ruler or general or governor, yea, even those who fill lower offices of trust or service in the state, would be able to do great injury to those who despised them; and will the satraps and ministers of earth and air be insulted with impunity?" Observe now how he introduces servants of the Most High — rulers, generals, governors, and those filling lower offices of trust and service — as, after the manner of men, inflicting injury upon those who insult them. For he does not consider that a wise man would not wish to do harm to any, but would strive to the utmost of his power to change and amend them; unless, indeed, it be that those whom Celsus makes servants and rulers appointed by the Most High are behind Lycurgus, the lawgiver of the Lacedæmonians, or Zeno of Citium. For when Lycurgus had had his eye put out by a man, he got the offender into his power; but instead of taking revenge upon him, he ceased not to use all his arts of persuasion until he induced him to become a philosopher. And Zeno, on the occasion of some one saying, "Let me perish rather than not have my revenge on thee," answered him, "But rather let me perish if I do not make a friend of thee." And I am not yet speaking of those whose characters have been formed by the teaching of Jesus, and who have heard the words, "Love your enemies, and pray for them which despitefully use you, that ye may be the children of your Father which is in heaven; for He maketh His sun to rise on the evil and on the good, and sendeth rain on the just and on the unjust."[9] And in the prophetical writings the righteous man says, "O LORD my God, if I have done this; if there be iniquity in my hands; if I have returned evil to those who have done evil to me, let me fall helpless under mine enemies: let my enemy persecute my soul, and take it; yea, let him tread down my life upon the earth."[10]

CHAP. XXXVI.

But the angels, who are the true rulers and generals and ministers of God, do not, as Celsus supposes, "injure those who offend them;" and if certain demons, whom Celsus had in mind, do inflict evils, they show that they are wicked, and that they have received no office of the kind from God. And they even do injury to those who are under them, and who have acknowledged them as their masters; and accordingly, as it would seem that those who break through the regulations which prevail in any country in regard to matters of food, suffer for

---

[1] Gen. i. 11.
[2] Heb. iv. 14.
[3] Dan. vii. 10.
[4] Heb. i. 14.
[5] Matt. xviii. 10.
[6] Ps. xxxiv. 7.
[7] Eph. vi. 11.
[8] Eph. vi. 12.

[9] Matt. v. 44, 45.
[10] Ps. vii. 3-5.

it if they are under the demons of that place, while those who are not under them, and have not submitted to their power, are free from all harm, and bid defiance to such spirits ; although if, in ignorance of certain things, they have come under the power of other demons, they may suffer punishment from them. But the Christian — the true Christian, I mean — who has submitted to God alone and His Word, will suffer nothing from demons, for He is mightier than demons. And the Christian will suffer nothing, for " the angel of the LORD will encamp about them that fear Him, and will deliver them," [1] and his " angel," who " always beholds the face of his Father in heaven," [2] offers up his prayers through the one High Priest to the God of all, and also joins his own prayers with those of the man who is committed to his keeping. Let not, then, Celsus try to scare us with threats of mischief from demons, for we despise them. And the demons, when despised, can do no harm to those who are under the protection of Him who can alone help all who deserve His aid ; and He does no less than set His own angels over His devout servants, so that none of the hostile angels, nor even he who is called " the prince of this world," [3] can effect anything against those who have given themselves to God.

CHAP. XXXVII.

In the next place, Celsus forgets that he is addressing Christians, who pray to God alone through Jesus ; and mixing up other notions with theirs, he absurdly attributes them all to Christians. " If," says he, " they who are addressed are called upon by barbarous names, they will have power, but no longer will they have any if they are addressed in Greek or Latin." Let him, then, state plainly whom we call upon for help by barbarous names. Any one will be convinced that this is a false charge which Celsus brings against us, when he considers that Christians in prayer do not even use the precise names which divine Scripture applies to God ; but the Greeks use Greek names, the Romans Latin names, and every one prays and sings praises to God as he best can, in his mother tongue. For the Lord of all the languages of the earth hears those who pray to Him in each different tongue, hearing, if I may so say, but one voice, expressing itself in different dialects.[4] For the Most High is not as one of those who select one language, Barbarian or Greek, know-

ing nothing of any other, and caring nothing for those who speak in other tongues.

CHAP. XXXVIII.

He next represents Christians as saying what he never heard from any Christian ; or if he did, it must have been from one of the most ignorant and lawless of the people. " Behold," they are made to say, " I go up to a statue of Jupiter or Apollo, or some other god : I revile it, and beat it, yet it takes no vengeance on me." He is not aware that among the prohibitions of the divine law is this, " Thou shalt not revile the gods," [5] and this is intended to prevent the formation of the habit of reviling any one whatever ; for we have been taught, " Bless, and curse not," [6] and it is said that " revilers shall not inherit the kingdom of God." [7] And who amongst us is so foolish as to speak in the way Celsus describes, and to fail to see that such contemptuous language can be of no avail for removing prevailing notions about the gods? For it is matter of observation that there are men who utterly deny the existence of a God or of an overruling providence, and who by their impious and destructive teaching have founded sects among those who are called philosophers, and yet neither they themselves, nor those who have embraced their opinions, have suffered any of those things which mankind generally account evils : they are both strong in body and rich in possessions. And yet if we ask what loss they have sustained, we shall find that they have suffered the most certain injury. For what greater injury can befall a man than that he should be unable amidst the order of the world to see Him who has made it? and what sorer affliction can come to any one than that blindness of mind which prevents him from seeing the Creator and Father of every soul?

CHAP. XXXIX.

After putting such words into our mouth, and maliciously charging Christians with sentiments which they never held, he then proceeds to give to this supposed expression of Christian feeling an answer, which is indeed more a mockery than an answer, when he says, " Do you not see, good sir, that even your own demon is not only reviled, but banished from every land and sea, and you yourself, who are as it were an image dedicated to him, are bound and led to punishment, and fastened to the stake, whilst your demon — or, as you call him, ' the Son of God ' — takes no vengeance on the evil-doer?" This answer would be admissible if we employed such language as he ascribes to us ; although even then

---

he would have no right to call the Son of God a demon. For as we hold that all demons are evil, He who turns so many men to God is in our view no demon, but God the Word, and the Son of God. And I know not how Celsus has so far forgotten himself as to call Jesus Christ a demon, when he nowhere alludes to the existence of any evil demons. And finally, as to the punishments threatened against the ungodly, these will come upon them after they have refused all remedies, and have been, as we may say, visited with an incurable malady of sinfulness.

CHAP. XL.

Such is our doctrine of punishment; and the inculcation of this doctrine turns many from their sins. But let us see, on the other hand, what is the response given on this subject by the priest of Jupiter or Apollo of whom Celsus speaks. It is this: "The mills of the gods grind slowly." [1] Another describes punishment as reaching "to children's children, and to those who came after them." [2] How much better are those words of Scripture: "The fathers shall not be put to death for the children, nor the children for the fathers. Every man shall be put to death for his own sin." [3] And again, "Every man that eateth the sour grape, his teeth shall be set on edge." [4] And, "The son shall not bear the iniquity of the father, neither shall the father bear the iniquity of the son: the righteousness of the righteous shall be upon him, and the wickedness of the wicked shall be upon him." [5] If any shall say that the response, "To children's children, and to those who come after them," corresponds with that passage, "Who visits the iniquity of the fathers upon the children unto the third and fourth generation of them that hate Me," [6] let him learn from Ezekiel that this language is not to be taken literally; for he reproves those who say, "Our fathers have eaten sour grapes, and the children's teeth are set on edge," [7] and then he adds, "As I live, saith the Lord, every one shall die for his own sin." As to the proper meaning of the figurative language about sins being visited unto the third and fourth generation, we cannot at present stay to explain.

CHAP. XLI.

He then goes on to rail against us after the manner of old wives. "You," says he, "mock and revile the statues of our gods; but if you had reviled Bacchus or Hercules in person, you

would not perhaps have done so with impunity. But those who crucified your God when present among men, suffered nothing for it, either at the time or during the whole of their lives. And what new thing has there happened since then to make us believe that he was not an impostor, but the Son of God? And forsooth, he who sent his Son with certain instructions for mankind, allowed him to be thus cruelly treated, and his instructions to perish with him, without ever during all this long time showing the slightest concern. What father was ever so inhuman? Perhaps, indeed, you may say that he suffered so much, because it was his wish to bear what came to him. But it is open to those whom you maliciously revile, to adopt the same language, and say that they wish to be reviled, and therefore they bear it with patience; for it is best to deal equally with both sides, — although these (gods) severely punish the scorner, so that he must either flee and hide himself, or be taken and perish." Now to these statements I would answer that we revile no one, for we believe that "revilers will not inherit the kingdom of God." [8] And we read, "Bless them that curse you; bless, and curse not;" also, "Being reviled, we bless." And even although the abuse which we pour upon another may seem to have some excuse in the wrong which we have received from him, yet such abuse is not allowed by the word of God. And how much more ought we to abstain from reviling others, when we consider what a great folly it is! And it is equally foolish to apply abusive language to stone or gold or silver, turned into what is supposed to be the form of God by those who have no knowledge of God. Accordingly, we throw ridicule not upon lifeless images, but upon those only who worship them. Moreover, if certain demons reside in certain images, and one of them passes for Bacchus, another for Hercules, we do not vilify them: for, on the one hand, it would be useless; and, on the other, it does not become one who is meek, and peaceful, and gentle in spirit, and who has learnt that no one among men or demons is to be reviled, however wicked he may be.

CHAP. XLII.

There is an inconsistency into which, strangely enough, Celsus has fallen unawares. Those demons or gods whom he extolled a little before, he now shows to be in fact the vilest of creatures, punishing more for their own revenge than for the improvement of those who revile them. His words are, "If you had reviled Bacchus or Hercules when present in person, you would not have escaped with impunity." How any one can hear without being present in person, I leave

---

[1] "The mills of the gods grind slowly, but they grind to powder" (Plutarch): [De Sera Numinis Vindicta, sect. iii. S.].
[2] Hom., Il., xx. 308.
[3] Deut. xxiv. 16.
[4] Jer. xxxi. 30.
[5] Ezek. xviii. 20.
[6] Ex. xx. 5.
[7] Ezek. xviii. 2-4.

[8] 1 Cor. vi. 10.

any one who will to explain ; as also those other questions, "Why he is sometimes present, and sometimes absent?" and, "What is the business which takes demons away from place to place?" Again, when he says, "Those who crucified your God himself, suffered no harm for doing so," he supposes that it is the body of Jesus extended on the cross and slain, and not His divine nature, that we call God ; and that it was as God that Jesus was crucified and slain.   As we have already dwelt at length on the sufferings which Jesus suffered as a man, we shall purposely say no more here, that we may not repeat what we have said already.   But when he goes on to say that "those who inflicted death upon Jesus suffered nothing afterwards through so long a time," we must inform him, as well as all who are disposed to learn the truth, that the city in which the Jewish people called for the crucifixion of Jesus with shouts of "Crucify him, crucify him,"[1] preferring to have the robber set free, who had been cast into prison for sedition and murder, and Jesus, who had been delivered through envy, to be crucified, — that this city not long afterwards was attacked, and, after a long siege, was utterly overthrown and laid waste ; for God judged the inhabitants of that place unworthy of living together the life of citizens.   And yet, though it may seem an incredible thing to say, God spared this people in delivering them to their enemies ; for He saw that they were incurably averse to any amendment, and were daily sinking deeper and deeper into evil.   And all this befell them, because the blood of Jesus was shed at their instigation and on their land ; and the land was no longer able to bear those who were guilty of so fearful a crime against Jesus.

CHAP. XLIII.

Some new thing, then, has come to pass since the time that Jesus suffered, — that, I mean, which has happened to the city, to the whole nation, and in the sudden and general rise of a Christian community.   And that, too, is a new thing, that those who were strangers to the covenants of God, with no part in His promises, and far from the truth, have by a divine power been enabled to embrace the truth.   These things were not the work of an impostor, but were the work of God, who sent His Word, Jesus Christ, to make known His purposes.[2]   The sufferings and death which Jesus endured with such fortitude and meekness, show the cruelty and injustice of those who inflicted them, but they did not destroy the announcement of the purposes of God ; indeed, if we may so say, they served rather to make them known.   For Jesus Him-

self taught us this when He said, "Except a grain of wheat fall into the ground and die, it abideth by itself alone : but if it die, it bringeth forth much fruit."[3]   Jesus, then, who is this grain of wheat, died, and brought forth much fruit.   And the Father is ever looking forward for the results of the death of the grain of wheat, both those which are arising now, and those which shall arise hereafter.   The Father of Jesus is therefore a tender and loving Father, though "He spared not His own Son, but delivered Him up" as His lamb "for us all,"[4] that so "the Lamb of God," by dying for all men, might "take away the sin of the world."   It was not by compulsion, therefore, but willingly, that He bore the reproaches of those who reviled Him.   Then Celsus, returning to those who apply abusive language to images, says : "Of those whom you load with insults, you may in like manner say that they voluntarily submit to such treatment, and therefore they bear insults with patience ; for it is best to deal equally with both sides.   Yet these severely punish the scorner, so that he must either flee and hide himself, or be taken and perish."   It is not, then, because Christians cast insults upon demons that they incur their revenge, but because they drive them away out of the images, and from the bodies and souls of men.   And here, although Celsus perceives it not, he has on this subject spoken something like the truth ; for it is true that the souls of those who condemn Christians, and betray them, and rejoice in persecuting them, are filled with wicked demons.

CHAP. XLIV.

But when the souls of those who die for the Christian faith depart from the body with great glory, they destroy the power of the demons, and frustrate their designs against men.   Wherefore I imagine, that as the demons have learnt from experience that they are defeated and overpowered by the martyrs for the truth, they are afraid to have recourse again to violence.   And thus, until they forget the defeats they have sustained, it is probable that the world will be at peace with the Christians.   But when they recover their power, and, with eyes blinded by sin, wish again to take their revenge on Christians, and persecute them, then again they will be defeated, and then again the souls of the godly, who lay down their lives for the cause of godliness, shall utterly destroy the army of the wicked one.   And as the demons perceive that those who meet death victoriously for the sake of religion destroy their authority, while those who give way under their sufferings, and deny the faith, come under their power, I

---

[1] Luke xxiii. 21, 25.
[2] ἀγγελμάτων. Spencer reads ἀγαλμάτων in this and the following sentences.

[3] John xii. 24.
[4] Rom. viii. 32.

imagine that at times they feel a deep interest in Christians when on their trial, and keenly strive to gain them over to their side, feeling as they do that their confession is torture to them, and their denial is a relief and encouragement to them. And traces of the same feeling may be seen in the demeanour of the judges; for they are greatly distressed at seeing those who bear outrage and torture with patience, but are greatly elated when a Christian gives way under it. Yet it is from no feeling of humanity that this arises. They see well, that, while "the tongues" of those who are overpowered by the tortures "may take the oath, the mind has not sworn."[1] And this may serve as an answer to the remark of Celsus: "But they severely punish one who reviles them, so that he must either flee and hide himself, or be taken and perish." If a Christian ever flees away, it is not from fear, but in obedience to the command of his Master, that so he may preserve himself, and employ his strength for the benefit of others.

CHAP. XLV.

Let us see what Celsus next goes on to say. It is as follows: "What need is there to collect all the oracular responses, which have been delivered with a divine voice by priests and priestesses, as well as by others, whether men or women, who were under a divine influence?—all the wonderful things that have been heard issuing from the inner sanctuary?—all the revelations that have been made to those who consulted the sacrificial victims?—and all the knowledge that has been conveyed to men by other signs and prodigies? To some the gods have appeared in visible forms. The world is full of such instances. How many cities have been built in obedience to commands received from oracles; how often, in the same way, delivered from disease and famine! Or again, how many cities, from disregard or forgetfulness of these oracles, have perished miserably! How many colonies have been established and made to flourish by following their orders! How many princes and private persons have, from this cause, had prosperity or adversity! How many who mourned over their childlessness, have obtained the blessing they asked for! How many have turned away from themselves the anger of demons! How many who were maimed in their limbs, have had them restored! And again, how many have met with summary punishment for showing want of reverence to the temples—some being instantly seized with madness, others openly confessing their crimes, others having put an end to their lives, and others having become the victims of incurable

maladies! Yea, some have been slain by a terrible voice issuing from the inner sanctuary." I know not how it comes that Celsus brings forward these as undoubted facts, whilst at the same time he treats as mere fables the wonders which are recorded and handed down to us as having happened among the Jews, or as having been performed by Jesus and His disciples. For why may not our accounts be true, and those of Celsus fables and fictions? At least, these latter were not believed by the followers of Democritus, Epicurus, and Aristotle, although perhaps these Grecian sects would have been convinced by the evidence in support of our miracles, if Moses or any of the prophets who wrought these wonders, or Jesus Christ Himself, had come in their way.

CHAP. XLVI.

It is related of the priestess of Apollo, that she at times allowed herself to be influenced in her answers by bribes; but our prophets were admired for their plain truthfulness, not only by their contemporaries, but also by those who lived in later times. For through the commands pronounced by the prophets cities were founded, men were cured, and plagues were stayed. Indeed, the whole Jewish race went out as a colony from Egypt to Palestine, in accordance with the divine oracles. They also, when they followed the commands of God, were prosperous; when they departed from them, they suffered reverses. What need is there to quote all the princes and private persons in Scripture history who fared well or ill according as they obeyed or despised the words of the prophets? If we refer to those who were unhappy because they were childless, but who, after offering prayers to the Creator of all, became fathers and mothers, let any one read the accounts of Abraham and Sarah, to whom at an advanced age was born Isaac, the father of the whole Jewish nation: and there are other instances of the same thing. Let him also read the account of Hezekiah, who not only recovered from his sickness, according to the prediction of Isaiah, but was also bold enough to say, "Afterwards I shall beget children, who shall declare Thy righteousness."[2] And in the fourth book of Kings we read that the prophet Elisha made known to a woman who had received him hospitably, that by the grace of God she should have a son; and through the prayers of Elisha she became a mother.[3] The maimed were cured by Jesus in great numbers. And the books of the Maccabees relate what punishments were inflicted upon those who dared to profane the Jewish service in the temple at Jerusalem.

---

[1] Euripides, *Hippolytus*, 612.

[2] Isa. xxxviii. 19 (according to the LXX.).
[3] [2 Kings iv. 17. 4 Kings, Sept. and Vulg. S.]

CHAP. XLVII.

But the Greeks will say that these accounts are fabulous, although two whole nations are witnesses to their truth. But why may we not consider the accounts of the Greeks as fabulous rather than those? Perhaps some one, however, wishing not to appear blindly to accept his own statements and reject those of others, would conclude, after a close examination of the matter, that the wonders mentioned by the Greeks were performed by certain demons ; those among the Jews by prophets or by angels, or by God through the means of angels ; and those recorded by Christians by Jesus Himself, or by His power working in His apostles. Let us, then, compare all these accounts together ; let us examine into the aim and purpose of those who performed them ; and let us inquire what effect was produced upon the persons on whose account these acts of kindness were performed, whether beneficial or hurtful, or neither the one nor the other. The ancient Jewish people, before they sinned against God, and were for their great wickedness cast off by Him, must evidently have been a people of great wisdom.[1] But Christians, who have in so wonderful a manner formed themselves into a community, appear at first to have been more induced by miracles than by exhortations to forsake the institutions of their fathers, and to adopt others which were quite strange to them. And indeed, if we were to reason from what is probable as to the first formation of the Christian society, we should say that it is incredible that the apostles of Jesus Christ, who were unlettered men of humble life, could have been emboldened to preach Christian truth to men by anything else than the power which was conferred upon them, and the grace which accompanied their words and rendered them effective ; and those who heard them would not have renounced the old-established usages of their fathers, and been induced to adopt notions so different from those in which they had been brought up, unless they had been moved by some extraordinary power, and by the force of miraculous events.

CHAP. XLVIII.

In the next place, Celsus, after referring to the enthusiasm with which men will contend unto death rather than abjure Christianity, adds strangely enough some remarks, in which he wishes to show that our doctrines are similar to those delivered by the priests at the celebration of the heathen mysteries. He says, "Just as you, good sir, believe in eternal punishments, so also do the priests who interpret and initiate into the sacred mysteries. The same punish-ments with which you threaten others, they threaten you. Now it is worthy of examination, which of the two is more firmly established as true ; for both parties contend with equal assurance that the truth is on their side. But if we require proofs, the priests of the heathen gods produce many that are clear and convincing, partly from wonders performed by demons, and partly from the answers given by oracles, and various other modes of divination." He would, then, have us believe that we and the interpreters of the mysteries equally teach the doctrine of eternal punishment, and that it is a matter for inquiry on which side of the two the truth lies. Now I should say that the truth lies with those who are able to induce their hearers to live as men who are convinced of the truth of what they have heard. But Jews and Christians have been thus affected by the doctrines they hold about what we speak of as the world to come, and the rewards of the righteous, and the punishments of the wicked. Let Celsus then, or any one who will, show us who have been moved in this way in regard to eternal punishments by the teaching of heathen priests and mystagogues. For surely the purpose of him who brought to light this doctrine was not only to reason upon the subject of punishments, and to strike men with terror of them, but to induce those who heard the truth to strive with all their might against those sins which are the causes of punishment. And those who study the prophecies with care, and are not content with a cursory perusal of the predictions contained in them, will find them such as to convince the intelligent and sincere reader that the Spirit of God was in those men, and that with their writings there is nothing in all the works of demons, responses of oracles, or sayings of soothsayers, for one moment to be compared.

CHAP. XLIX.

Let us see in what terms Celsus next addresses us : "Besides, is it not most absurd and inconsistent in you, on the one hand, to make so much of the body as you do — to expect that the same body will rise again, as though it were the best and most precious part of us ; and yet, on the other, to expose it to such tortures as though it were worthless? But men who hold such notions, and are so attached to the body, are not worthy of being reasoned with ; for in this and in other respects they show themselves to be gross, impure, and bent upon revolting without any reason from the common belief. But I shall direct my discourse to those who hope for the enjoyment of eternal life with God by means of the soul or mind, whether they choose to call it a spiritual substance, an intelli-

---

[1] φιλόσοφον.

gent spirit, holy and blessed, or a living soul, or the heavenly and indestructible offspring of a divine and incorporeal nature, or by whatever name they designate the spiritual nature of man. And they are rightly persuaded that those who live well shall be blessed, and the unrighteous shall all suffer everlasting punishments. And from this doctrine neither they nor any other should ever swerve." Now, as he has often already reproached us for our opinions on the resurrection, and as we have on these occasions defended our opinions in what seemed to us a reasonable way, we do not intend, at each repetition of the one objection, to go into a repetition of our defence. Celsus makes an unfounded charge against us when he ascribes to us the opinion that "there is nothing in our complex nature better or more precious than the body;" for we hold that far beyond all bodies is the soul, and especially the reasonable soul; for it is the soul, and not the body, which bears the likeness of the Creator. For, according to us, God is not corporeal, unless we fall into the absurd errors of the followers of Zeno and Chrysippus.

CHAP. L.

But since he reproaches us with too great an anxiety about the body, let him know that when that feeling is a wrong one we do not share in it, and when it is indifferent we only long for that which God has promised to the righteous. But Celsus considers that we are inconsistent with ourselves when we count the body worthy of honour from God, and therefore hope for its resurrection, and yet at the same time expose it to tortures as though it were not worthy of honour. But surely it is not without honour for the body to suffer for the sake of godliness, and to choose afflictions on account of virtue: the dishonourable thing would be for it to waste its powers in vicious indulgence. For the divine word says: "What is an honourable seed? The seed of man. What is a dishonourable seed? The seed of man." [1] Moreover, Celsus thinks that he ought not to reason with those who hope for the good of the body, as they are unreasonably intent upon an object which can never satisfy their expectations. He also calls them gross and impure men, bent upon creating needless dissensions. But surely he ought, as one of superior humanity, to assist even the rude and depraved. For society does not exclude from its pale the coarse and uncultivated, as it does the irrational animals, but our Creator made us on the same common level with all mankind. It is not an undignified thing, therefore, to reason even with the coarse and unre-

fined, and to try to bring them as far as possible to a higher state of refinement — to bring the impure to the highest practicable degree of purity — to bring the unreasoning multitude to reason, and the diseased in mind to spiritual health.

CHAP. LI.

In the next place, he expresses his approval of those who "hope that eternal life shall be enjoyed with God by the soul or mind, or, as it is variously called, the spiritual nature, the reasonable soul, intelligent, holy, and blessed;" and he allows the soundness of the doctrine, "that those who had a good life shall be happy, and the unrighteous shall suffer eternal punishments." And yet I wonder at what follows, more than at anything that Celsus has ever said; for he adds, "And from this doctrine let not them or any one ever swerve." For certainly in writing against Christians, the very essence of whose faith is God, and the promises made by Christ to the righteous, and His warnings of punishment awaiting the wicked, he must see that, if a Christian were brought to renounce Christianity by his arguments against it, it is beyond doubt that, along with his Christian faith, he would cast off the very doctrine from which he says that no Christian and no man should ever swerve. But I think Celsus has been far surpassed in consideration for his fellow-men by Chrysippus in his treatise, *On the Subjugation of the Passions.* For when he sought to apply remedies to the affections and passions which oppress and distract the human spirit, after employing such arguments as seemed to himself to be strong, he did not shrink from using in the second and third place others which he did not himself approve of. "For," says he, "if it were held by any one that there are three kinds of good, we must seek to regulate the passions in accordance with that supposition; and we must not too curiously inquire into the opinions held by a person at the time that he is under the influence of passion, lest, if we delay too long for the purpose of overthrowing the opinions by which the mind is possessed, the opportunity for curing the passion may pass away." And he adds, "Thus, supposing that pleasure were the highest good, or that he was of that opinion whose mind was under the dominion of passion, we should not the less give him help, and show that, even on the principle that pleasure is the highest and final good of man, all passion is disallowed." And Celsus, in like manner, after having embraced the doctrine, "that the righteous shall be blessed, and the wicked shall suffer eternal punishments," should have followed out his subject; and, after having advanced what seemed to him the chief argu-

---

[1] Ecclus. x. 19. In the LXX. the last clause is, "What is a dishonourable seed? They that transgress the commandments."

ment, he should have proceeded to prove and enforce by further reasons the truth that the unjust shall surely suffer eternal punishment, and those who lead a good life shall be blessed.

CHAP. LII.

For we who have been persuaded by many, yea by innumerable, arguments to lead a Christian life, are especially anxious to bring all men as far as possible to receive the whole system of Christian truth ; but when we meet with persons who are prejudiced by the calumnies thrown out against Christians, and who, from a notion that Christians are an impious people, will not listen to any who offer to instruct them in the principles of the divine word, then, on the common principles of humanity, we endeavour to the best of our ability to convince them of the doctrine of the punishment of the wicked, and to induce even those who are unwilling to become Christians to accept that truth. And we are thus anxious to persuade them of the rewards of right living, when we see that many things which we teach about a healthy moral life are also taught by the enemies of our faith. For you will find that they have not entirely lost the common notions of right and wrong, of good and evil. Let all men, therefore, when they look upon the universe, observe the constant revolution of the unerring stars, the converse motion of the planets, the constitution of the atmosphere, and its adaptation to the necessities of the animals, and especially of man, with all the innumerable contrivances for the well-being of mankind ; and then, after thus considering the order of the universe, let them beware of doing ought which is displeasing to the Creator of this universe, of the soul and its intelligent principle ; and let them rest assured that punishment shall be inflicted on the wicked, and rewards shall be bestowed upon the righteous, by Him who deals with every one as he deserves, and who will proportion His rewards to the good that each has done, and to the account of himself that he is able to give.[1] And let all men know that the good shall be advanced to a higher state, and that the wicked shall be delivered over to sufferings and torments, in punishment of their licentiousness and depravity, their cowardice, timidity, and all their follies.

CHAP. LIII.

Having said so much on this subject, let us proceed to another statement of Celsus : "Since men are born united to a body, whether to suit the order of the universe, or that they may in that way suffer the punishment of sin ; or because the soul is oppressed by certain passions

until it is purged from these at the appointed period of time, — for, according to Empedocles, all mankind must be banished from the abodes of the blessed for 30,000 periods of time, — we must therefore believe that they are entrusted to certain beings as keepers of this prison-house." You will observe that Celsus, in these remarks, speaks of such weighty matters in the language of doubtful human conjecture. He adds also various opinions as to the origin of man, and shows considerable reluctance to set down any of these opinions as false. When he had once come to the conclusion neither indiscriminately to accept nor recklessly to reject the opinions held by the ancients, would it not have been in accordance with that same rule of judging, if, when he found himself not disposed to believe the doctrines taught by the Jewish prophets and by Jesus, at any rate to have held them as matters open to inquiry? And should he not have considered whether it is very probable that a people who faithfully served the Most High God, and who ofttimes encountered numberless dangers, and even death, rather than sacrifice the honour of God, and what they believed to be the revelations of His will, should have been wholly overlooked by God? Should it not rather be thought probable that people who despised the efforts of human art to represent the Divine Being, but strove rather to rise in thought to the knowledge of the Most High, should have been favoured with some revelation from Himself? Besides, he ought to have considered that the common Father and Creator of all, who sees and hears all things, and who duly esteems the intention of every man who seeks Him and desires to serve Him, will grant unto these also some of the benefits of His rule, and will give them an enlargement of that knowledge of Himself which He has once bestowed upon them. If this had been remembered by Celsus and the others who hate Moses and the Jewish prophets, and Jesus, and His faithful disciples, who endured so much for the sake of His word, they would not thus have reviled Moses, and the prophets, and Jesus, and His apostles ; and they would not have singled out for their contempt the Jews beyond all the nations of the earth, and said they were worse even than the Egyptians, — a people who, either from superstition or some other form of delusion, went as far as they could in degrading the Divine Being to the level of brute beasts. And we invite inquiry, not as though we wished to lead any to doubt regarding the truths of Christianity, but in order to show that it would be better for those who in every way revile the doctrines of Christianity, at any rate to suspend their judgment, and not so rashly to state about Jesus and His apostles such things as they do not know, and as they cannot prove, either by

---

[1] [Eccles. viii. 11. See cap. xl., *supra*. De Maistre has admirably annotated Plutarch's *Delay of the Divine Judgment*.]

what the Stoics call "apprehensive perception," [1] or by any other methods used by different sects of philosophers as criteria of truth.

CHAP. LIV.

When Celsus adds, "We must therefore believe that men are entrusted to certain beings who are the keepers of this prison-house," our answer is, that the souls of those who are called by Jeremiah "prisoners of the earth," [2] when eager in the pursuit of virtue, are even in this life delivered from the bondage of evil; for Jesus declared this, as was foretold long before His advent by the prophet Isaiah, when he said that "the prisoners would go forth, and they that were in darkness would show themselves." [3] And Jesus Himself, as Isaiah also foretold of Him, arose as "a light to them that sat in darkness and in the shadow of death," [4] so that we may therefore say, "Let us break their bands asunder, and cast their cords from us." [5] If Celsus, and those who like him are opposed to us, had been able to sound the depths of the Gospel narratives, they would not have counselled us to put our confidence in those beings whom they call "the keepers of the prison-house." It is written in the Gospel that a woman was bowed together, and could in no wise lift up herself. And when Jesus beheld her, and perceived from what cause she was bowed together, he said, "Ought not this daughter of Abraham, whom Satan has bound, lo, these eighteen years, to be loosed from this bond on the Sabbath day?" [6] And how many others are still bowed down and bound by Satan, who hinders them from looking up at all, and who would have us to look down also! And no one can raise them up, except the Word, that came by Jesus Christ, and that aforetime inspired the prophets. And Jesus came to release those who were under the dominion of the devil; and, speaking of him, He said with that depth of meaning which characterized His words, "Now is the prince of this world judged." We are, then, indulging in no baseless calumnies against demons, but are condemning their agency upon earth as destructive to mankind, and show that, under cover of oracles and bodily cures, and such other means, they are seeking to separate from God the soul which has descended to this "body of humiliation;" and those who feel this humiliation exclaim, "O wretched man that I am! who shall deliver me from the body of this death?" [7] It is not in vain, therefore, that we expose our

bodies to be beaten and tortured; for surely it is not in vain for a man to submit to such sufferings, if by that means he may avoid bestowing the name of gods on those earthly spirits that unite with their worshippers to bring him to destruction. Indeed, we think it both reasonable in itself and well-pleasing to God, to suffer pain for the sake of virtue, to undergo torture for the sake of piety, and even to suffer death for the sake of holiness; for "precious in the sight of God is the death of His saints;" [8] and we maintain that to overcome the love of life is to enjoy a great good. But when Celsus compares us to notorious criminals, who justly suffer punishment for their crimes, and does not shrink from placing so laudable a purpose as that which we set before us upon the same level with the obstinacy of criminals, he makes himself the brother and companion of those who accounted Jesus among criminals, fulfilling the Scripture, which saith, "He was numbered with transgressors." [9]

CHAP. LV.

Celsus goes on to say: "They must make their choice between two alternatives. If they refuse to render due service to the gods, and to respect those who are set over this service, let them not come to manhood, or marry wives, or have children, or indeed take any share in the affairs of life; but let them depart hence with all speed, and leave no posterity behind them, that such a race may become extinct from the face of the earth. Or, on the other hand, if they will take wives, and bring up children, and taste of the fruits of the earth, and partake of all the blessings of life, and bear its appointed sorrows (for nature herself hath allotted sorrows to all men; for sorrows must exist, and earth is the only place for them), then must they discharge the duties of life until they are released from its bonds, and render due honour to those beings who control the affairs of this life, if they would not show themselves ungrateful to them. For it would be unjust in them, after receiving the good things which they dispense, to pay them no tribute in return." To this we reply, that there appears to us to be no good reason for our leaving this world, except when piety and virtue require it; as when, for example, those who are set as judges, and think that they have power over our lives, place before us the alternative either to live in violation of the commands of Jesus, or to die if we continue obedient to them. But God has allowed us to marry, because all are not fit for the higher, that is, the perfectly pure life; and God would have us to bring up all our children, and not to destroy

---

[1] καταληπτικὴ φαντασία.
[2] Lam. iii. 34.
[3] Isa. xlix. 9.
[4] Isa. ix. 2.
[5] Ps. ii. 3.
[6] Luke xiii. 11, 16.
[7] Rom. vii. 24.

[8] Ps. cxvi. 15.
[9] Isa. liii. 12.

any of the offspring given us by His providence. And this does not conflict with our purpose not to obey the demons that are on the earth ; for, "being armed with the whole armour of God, we stand" [1] as athletes of piety against the race of demons that plot against us.

CHAP. LVI.

Although, therefore, Celsus would, in his own words, "drive us with all haste out of life," so that "such a race may become extinct from the earth ; " yet we, along with those who worship the Creator, will live according to the laws of God, never consenting to obey the laws of sin. We will marry if we wish, and bring up the children given to us in marriage ; and if need be, we will not only partake of the blessings of life, but bear its appointed sorrows as a trial to our souls. For in this way is divine Scripture accustomed to speak of human afflictions, by which, as gold is tried in the fire, so the spirit of man is tried, and is found to be worthy either of condemnation or of praise. For those things which Celsus calls evils we are therefore prepared, and are ready to say, "Try me, O Lord, and prove me ; purge my reins and my heart." [2] For "no one will be crowned," unless here upon earth, with this body of humiliation, "he strive lawfully." [3] Further, we do not pay honours supposed to be due to those whom Celsus speaks of as being set over the affairs of the world. For we worship the Lord our God, and Him only do we serve, and desire to be followers of Christ, who, when the devil said to Him, "All these things will I give thee if thou wilt fall down and worship me," answered him by the words, "Thou shalt worship the Lord thy God, and Him only shalt thou serve." [4] Wherefore we do not render the honour supposed to be due to those who, according to Celsus, are set over the affairs of this world ; for "no man can serve two masters," and we "cannot serve God and mammon," whether this name be applied to one or more. Moreover, if any one "by transgressing the law dishonours the lawgiver," it seems clear to us that if the two laws, the law of God and the law of mammon, are completely opposed to each other, it is better for us by transgressing the law of mammon to dishonour mammon, that we may honour God by keeping His law, than by transgressing the law of God to dishonour God, that by obeying the law of mammon we may honour mammon.

CHAP. LVII.

Celsus supposes that men "discharge the duties of life until they are loosened from its bonds," when, in accordance with commonly received customs, they offer sacrifices to each of the gods recognised in the state ; and he fails to perceive the true duty which is fulfilled by an earnest piety. For we say that he truly discharges the duties of life who is ever mindful who is his Creator, and what things are agreeable to Him, and who acts in all things so that he may please God. Again, Celsus wishes us to be thankful to these demons, imagining that we owe them thank-offerings. But we, while recognising the duty of thankfulness, maintain that we show no ingratitude by refusing to give thanks to beings who do us no good, but who rather set themselves against us when we neither sacrifice to them nor worship them. We are much more concerned lest we should be ungrateful to God, who has loaded us with His benefits, whose workmanship we are, who cares for us in whatever condition we may be, and who has given us hopes of things beyond this present life. And we have a symbol of gratitude to God in the bread which we call the Eucharist. Besides, as we have shown before, the demons have not the control of those things which have been created for our use ; we commit no wrong, therefore, when we partake of created things, and yet refuse to offer sacrifices to beings who have no concern with them. Moreover, as we know that it is not demons, but angels, who have been set over the fruits of the earth, and over the birth of animals, it is the latter that we praise and bless, as having been appointed by God over the things needful for our race ; yet even to them we will not give the honour which is due to God. For this would not be pleasing to God, nor would it be any pleasure to the angels themselves to whom these things have been committed. Indeed, they are much more pleased if we refrain from offering sacrifices to them than if we offer them ; for they have no desire for the sacrificial odours which rise from the earth.

CHAP. LVIII.

Celsus goes on to say : " Let any one inquire of the Egyptians, and he will find that everything, even to the most insignificant, is committed to the care of a certain demon. The body of man is divided into thirty-six parts, and as many demons of the air are appointed to the care of it, each having charge of a different part, although others make the number much larger. All these demons have in the language of that country distinct names ; as Chnoumen, Chnachoumen, Cnat, Sicat, Biou, Erou, Erebiou, Ramanor, Reianoor, and other such Egyptian names. Moreover, they call upon them, and are cured of diseases of particular parts of the body. What, then, is there to prevent a man from giving honour to these or to others, if he would

[1] Eph. vi. 11.
[2] Ps. xxvi. 2.
[3] 2 Tim. ii. 5.
[4] Matt. iv. 9, 10.

rather be in health than be sick, rather have prosperity than adversity, and be freed as much as possible from all plagues and troubles?" In this way, Celsus seeks to degrade our souls to the worship of demons, under the assumption that they have possession of our bodies, and that each one has power over a separate member. And he wishes us on this ground to put confidence in these demons of which he speaks, and to serve them, in order that we may be in health rather than be sick, have prosperity rather than adversity, and may as far as possible escape all plagues and troubles. The honour of the Most High God, which cannot be divided or shared with another, is so lightly esteemed by him, that he cannot believe in the ability of God, if called upon and highly honoured, to give to those who serve Him a power by which they may be defended from the assaults directed by demons against the righteous. For he has never beheld the efficacy of those words, "in the name of Jesus," when uttered by the truly faithful, to deliver not a few from demons and demoniacal possessions and other plagues.

CHAP. LIX.

Probably those who embrace the views of Celsus will smile at us when we say, "At the name of Jesus every knee shall bow, of things in heaven, of things on earth, and of things under the earth, and every tongue" is brought to "confess that Jesus Christ is Lord, to the glory of God the Father."[1] But although they may ridicule such a statement, yet they will receive much more convincing arguments in support of it than Celsus brings in behalf of Chnoumen, Chnachoumen, Cnat, Sicat, and the rest of the Egyptian catalogue, whom he mentions as being called upon, and as healing the diseases of different parts of the human body. And observe how, while seeking to turn us away from our faith in the God of all through Jesus Christ, he exhorts us for the welfare of our bodies to faith in six-and-thirty barbarous demons, whom the Egyptian magi alone call upon in some unknown way, and promise us in return great benefits. According to Celsus, then, it would be better for us now to give ourselves up to magic and sorcery than to embrace Christianity, and to put our faith in an innumerable multitude of demons than in the almighty, living, self-revealing God, who has manifested Himself by Him who by His great power has spread the true principles of holiness among all men throughout the world; yea, I may add without exaggeration, He has given this knowledge to all beings everywhere possessed of reason, and needing deliverance from the plague and corruption of sin.

CHAP. LX.

Celsus, however, suspecting that the tendency of such teaching as he here gives is to lead to magic, and dreading that harm may arise from these statements, adds: "Care, however, must be taken lest any one, by familiarizing his mind with these matters, should become too much engrossed with them, and lest, through an excessive regard for the body, he should have his mind turned away from higher things, and allow them to pass into oblivion. For perhaps we ought not to despise the opinion of those wise men who say that most of the earth-demons are taken up with carnal indulgence, blood, odours, sweet sounds, and other such sensual things; and therefore they are unable to do more than heal the body, or foretell the fortunes of men and cities, and do other such things as relate to this mortal life." If there is, then, such a dangerous tendency in this direction, as even the enemy of the truth of God confesses, how much better is it to avoid all danger of giving ourselves too much up to the power of such demons, and of becoming turned aside from higher things, and suffering them to pass into oblivion through an excessive attention to the body; by entrusting ourselves to the Supreme God through Jesus Christ, who has given us such instruction, and asking of Him all help, and the guardianship of holy and good angels, to defend us from the earth-spirits intent on lust, and blood, and sacrificial odours,[2] and strange sounds, and other sensual things! For even, by the confession of Celsus, they can do nothing more than cure the body. But, indeed, I would say that it is not clear that these demons, however much they are reverenced, can even cure the body. But in seeking recovery from disease, a man must either follow the more ordinary and simple method, and have recourse to medical art; or if he would go beyond the common methods adopted by men, he must rise to the higher and better way of seeking the blessing of Him who is God over all, through piety and prayers.

CHAP. LXI.

For consider with yourself which disposition of mind will be more acceptable to the Most High, whose power is supreme and universal, and who directs all for the welfare of mankind in body, and in mind, and in outward things,— whether that of the man who gives himself up to God in all things, or that of the man who is curiously inquisitive about the names of demons, their powers and agency, the incantations, the herbs proper to them, and the stones with the inscriptions graven on them, corresponding sym-

---

[1] Phil. ii. 10, 11.

[2] [Observe this traditional objection to incense. Comp. vol. ii. p. 532.]

bolically or otherwise to their traditional shapes? It is plain even to the least intelligent, that the disposition of the man who is simple-minded, and not given to curious inquiries, but in all things devoted to the divine will, will be most pleasing to God, and to all those who are like God; but that of the man who, for the sake of bodily health, of bodily enjoyment, and outward prosperity, busies himself about the names of demons, and inquires by what incantations he shall appease them, will be condemned by God as bad and impious, and more agreeable to the nature of demons than of men, and will be given over to be torn and otherwise tormented by demons. For it is probable that they, as being wicked creatures, and, as Celsus confesses, addicted to blood, sacrificial odours, sweet sounds, and such like, will not keep their most solemn promises to those who supply them with these things. For if others invoke their aid against the persons who have already called upon them, and purchase their favour with a larger supply of blood, and odours, and such offerings as they require, they will take part against those who yesterday sacrificed and presented pleasant offerings to them.

CHAP. LXII.

In a former passage, Celsus had spoken at length on the subject of oracles, and had referred us to their answers as being the voice of the gods; but now he makes amends, and confesses that "those who foretell the fortunes of men and cities, and concern themselves about mortal affairs, are earth-spirits, who are given up to fleshly lust, blood, odours, sweet sounds, and other such things, and who are unable to rise above these sensual objects." Perhaps, when we opposed the theological teaching of Celsus in regard to oracles, and the honour done to those called gods, some one might suspect us of impiety when we alleged that these were stratagems of demoniacal powers, to draw men away to carnal indulgence. But any who entertained this suspicion against us, may now believe that the statements put forth by Christians were well-founded, when they see the above passage from the writings of one who is a professed adversary of Christianity, but who now at length writes as one who has been overcome by the spirit of truth. Although, therefore, Celsus says that "we must offer sacrifices to them, in so far as they are profitable to us, for to offer them indiscriminately is not allowed by reason," yet we are not to offer sacrifices to demons addicted to blood and odours; nor is the Divine Being to be profaned in our minds, by being brought down to the level of wicked demons. If Celsus had carefully weighed the meaning of the word "profitable," and had considered that the truest profit lies in virtue and in virtuous action, he would not have applied the phrase "as far as it is profitable" to the service of such demons, as he has acknowledged them to be. If, then, health of body and success in life were to come to us on condition of our serving such demons, we should prefer sickness and misfortune accompanied with the consciousness of our being truly devoted to the will of God. For this is preferable to being mortally diseased in mind, and wretched through being separate and outcasts from God, though healthy in body and abounding in earthly prosperity. And we would rather go for help to one who seeks nothing whatever but the well-being of men and of all rational creatures, than to those who delight in blood and sacrificial odours.

CHAP. LXIII.

After having said so much of the demons, and of their fondness for blood and the odour of sacrifices, Celsus adds, as though wishing to retract the charge he had made: "The more just opinion is, that demons desire nothing and need nothing, but that they take pleasure in those who discharge towards them offices of piety." If Celsus believed this to be true, he should have said so, instead of making his previous statements. But, indeed, human nature is never utterly forsaken by God and His only-begotten Son, the Truth. Wherefore even Celsus spoke the truth when he made the demons take pleasure in the blood and smoke of victims; although, by the force of his own evil nature, he falls back into his errors, and compares demons with men who rigorously discharge every duty, even to those who show no gratitude; while to those who are grateful they abound in acts of kindness. Here Celsus appears to me to get into confusion. At one time his judgment is darkened by the influence of demons, and at another he recovers from their deluding power, and gets some glimpses of the truth. For again he adds: "We must never in any way lose our hold of God, whether by day or by night, whether in public or in secret, whether in word or in deed, but in whatever we do, or abstain from doing." That is, as I understand it, whatever we do in public, in all our actions, in all our words, "let the soul be constantly fixed upon God." And yet again, as though, after struggling in argument against the insane inspirations of demons, he were completely overcome by them, he adds: "If this is the case, what harm is there in gaining the favour of the rulers of the earth, whether of a nature different from ours, or human princes and kings? For these have gained their dignity through the instrumentality of demons." In a former part, Celsus did his utmost to debase our souls to the worship of demons; and now he wishes us to seek the favour of kings and princes, of whom, as the world and all history are full of them, I do not consider it necessary to quote examples.

CHAP. LXIV.

There is therefore One whose favour we should seek, and to whom we ought to pray that He would be gracious to us — the Most High God, whose favour is gained by piety and the practice of every virtue. And if he would have us to seek the favour of others after the Most High God, let him consider that, as the motion of the shadow follows that of the body which casts it, so in like manner it follows, that when we have the favour of God, we have also the good-will of all angels and spirits who are friends of God. For they know who are worthy of the divine approval, and they are not only well disposed to them, but they co-operate with them in their endeavours to please God : they seek His favour on their behalf; with their prayers they join their own prayers and intercessions for them. We may indeed boldly say, that men who aspire after better things have, when they pray to God, tens of thousands of sacred powers upon their side. These, even when not asked, pray with them, they bring succour to our mortal race, and if I may so say, take up arms alongside of it : for they see demons warring and fighting most keenly against the salvation of those who devote themselves to God, and despise the hostility of demons ; they see them savage in their hatred of the man who refuses to serve them with the blood and fumes of sacrifices, but rather strives in every way, by word and deed, to be in peace and union with the Most High through Jesus, who put to flight multitudes of demons when He went about " healing," and delivering " all who were oppressed by the devil." [1]

CHAP. LXV.

Moreover, we are to despise ingratiating ourselves with kings or any other men, not only if their favour is to be won by murders, licentiousness, or deeds of cruelty, but even if it involves impiety towards God, or any servile expressions of flattery and obsequiousness, which things are unworthy of brave and high-principled men, who aim at joining with their other virtues that highest of virtues, patience and fortitude. But whilst we do nothing which is contrary to the law and word of God, we are not so mad as to stir up against us the wrath of kings and princes, which will bring upon us sufferings and tortures, or even death. For we read : " Let every soul be subject unto the higher powers. For there is no power but of God : the powers that be are

ordained of God. Whosoever therefore resisteth the power, resisteth the ordinance of God." [2] These words we have in our exposition of the Epistle to the Romans, to the best of our ability, explained at length, and with various applications ; but for the present we have taken them in their more obvious and generally received acceptation, to meet the saying of Celsus, that "it is not without the power of demons that kings have been raised to their regal dignity." Here much might be said on the constitution of kings and rulers, for the subject is a wide one, embracing such rulers as reign cruelly and tyrannically, and such as make the kingly office the means of indulging in luxury and sinful pleasures. We shall therefore, for the present, pass over the full consideration of this subject. We will, however, never swear by " the fortune of the king," nor by ought else that is considered equivalent to God. For if the word " fortune " is nothing but an expression for the uncertain course of events, as some say, although they seem not to be agreed, we do not swear by that as God which has no existence, as though it did really exist and was able to do something, lest we should bind ourselves by an oath to things which have no existence. If, on the other hand (as is thought by others, who say that to swear by the fortune of the king of the Romans is to swear by his demon), what is called the fortune of the king is in the power of demons, then in that case we must die sooner than swear by a wicked and treacherous demon, that ofttimes sins along with the man of whom it gains possession, and sins even more than he.

CHAP. LXVI.

Then Celsus, following the example of those who are under the influence of demons — at one time recovering, at another relapsing, as though he were again becoming sensible — says : " If, however, any worshipper of God should be ordered to do anything impious, or to say anything base, such a command should in no wise be regarded ; but we must encounter all kinds of torment, or submit to any kind of death, rather than say or even think anything unworthy of God." Again, however, from ignorance of our principles, and in entire confusion of thought, he says : " But if any one commands you to celebrate the sun, or to sing a joyful triumphal song in praise of Minerva, you will by celebrating their praises seem to render the higher praise to God ; for piety, in extending to all things, becomes more perfect." To this our answer is, that we do not wait for any command to celebrate the praises of the sun ; for we have been

---

[1] Acts x. 38.

[2] Rom. xiii. 1, 2.

taught to speak well not only of those creatures that are obedient to the will of God, but even of our enemies. We therefore praise the sun as the glorious workmanship of God, which obeys His laws and hearkens to the call, " Praise the Lord, sun and moon," [1] and with all your powers show forth the praises of the Father and Creator of all. Minerva, however, whom Celsus classes with the sun, is the subject of various Grecian myths, whether these contain any hidden meaning or not. They say that Minerva sprang fully armed from the brain of Jupiter; that when she was pursued by Vulcan, she fled from him to preserve her honour; and that from the seed which fell to the ground in the heat of Vulcan's passion, there grew a child whom Minerva brought up and called Erichthonius,

> "That owed his nurture to the blue-eyed maid,
> But from the teeming furrow took his birth,
> The mighty offspring of the foodful earth." [2]

It is therefore evident, that if we admit Minerva the daughter of Jupiter, we must also admit many fables and fictions which can be allowed by no one who discards fables and seeks after truth.

CHAP. LXVII.

And to regard these myths in a figurative sense, and consider Minerva as representing prudence, let any one show what were the actual facts of her history, upon which this allegory is based. For, supposing honour was given to Minerva as having been a woman of ancient times, by those who instituted mysteries and ceremonies for their followers, and who wished her name to be celebrated as that of a goddess, much more are we forbidden to pay divine honours to Minerva, if we are not permitted to worship so glorious an object as the sun, although we may celebrate its glory. Celsus, indeed, says that " we seem to do the greater honour to the great God when we sing hymns in honour of the sun and Minerva;" but we know it to be the opposite of that. For we sing hymns to the Most High alone, and His Only-begotten, who is the Word and God; and we praise God and His Only-begotten, as do also the sun, the moon, the stars, and all the host of heaven. [3] For these all form a divine chorus, and unite with the just among men in celebrating the praises of the Most High God and His Only-begotten. We have already said that we must not swear by a human king, or by what is called " the fortune of the king." It is therefore unnecessary for us again to refute these statements : " If you are

commanded to swear by a human king, there is nothing wrong in that. For to him has been given whatever there is upon earth; and whatever you receive in this life, you receive from him." We deny, however, that all things which are on the earth have been given to the king, or that whatever we receive in this life we receive from him. For whatever we receive rightly and honourably we receive from God, and by His providence, as ripe fruits, and "corn which strengtheneth man's heart, and the pleasant vine, and wine which rejoiceth the heart of man." [4] And moreover, the fruit of the olive-tree, to make his face to shine, we have from the providence of God.

CHAP. LXVIII.

Celsus goes on to say : " We must not disobey the ancient writer, who said long ago,

> 'Let one be king, whom the son of crafty Saturn appointed;'" [5]

and adds : " If you set aside this maxim, you will deservedly suffer for it at the hands of the king. For if all were to do the same as you, there would be nothing to prevent his being left in utter solitude and desertion, and the affairs of the earth would fall into the hands of the wildest and most lawless barbarians; and then there would no longer remain among men any of the glory of your religion or of the true wisdom." If, then, " there shall be one lord, one king," he must be, not the man " whom the son of crafty Saturn appointed," but the man to whom He gave the power, who " removeth kings and setteth up kings," [6] and who " raiseth up the useful man in time of need upon earth." [7] For kings are not appointed by that son of Saturn, who, according to Grecian fable, hurled his father from his throne, and sent him down to Tartarus (whatever interpretation may be given to this allegory), but by God, who governs all things, and who wisely arranges whatever belongs to the appointment of kings. We therefore do set aside the maxim contained in the line,

> "Whom the son of crafty Saturn appointed;"

for we know that no god or father of a god ever devises anything crooked or crafty. But we are far from setting aside the notion of a providence, and of things happening directly or indirectly through the agency of providence. And the king will not " inflict deserved punishment " upon us, if we say that not the son of crafty Saturn gave him his kingdom, but He who " removeth and setteth up kings." And would that all were to follow my example in rejecting the maxim of Homer, maintaining the divine origin of the

---

[1] Ps. cxlviii. 3.
[2] Homer's *Iliad*, ii. 547, 548.
[3] [" Origen pointed out that hymns were addressed only to God and to His Only-begotten Word, who is also God. . . . The hymnody of the primitive Church protected and proclaimed the truths which she taught and cherished." — LIDDON's *Bampton Lectures, On the Divinity of our Lord and Saviour Jesus Christ*, pp. 385, 386. S.]

[4] Ps. civ. 15.
[5] Homer's *Iliad*, ii. 205.
[6] Dan. ii. 21.
[7] Ecclus. x. 4 (LXX.).

kingdom, and observing the precept to honour the king! In these circumstances the king will not "be left in utter solitude and desertion," neither will "the affairs of the world fall into the hands of the most impious and wild barbarians." For if, in the words of Celsus, "they do as I do," then it is evident that even the barbarians, when they yield obedience to the word of God, will become most obedient to the law, and most humane; and every form of worship will be destroyed except the religion of Christ, which will alone prevail. And indeed it will one day triumph, as its principles take possession of the minds of men more and more every day.

CHAP. LXIX.

Celsus, then, as if not observing that he was saying anything inconsistent with the words he had just used, "if all were to do the same as you," adds: "You surely do not say that if the Romans were, in compliance with your wish, to neglect their customary duties to gods and men, and were to worship the Most High, or whatever you please to call him, that he will come down and fight for them, so that they shall need no other help than his. For this same God, as yourselves say, promised of old this and much more to those who served him, and see in what way he has helped them and you! They, in place of being masters of the whole world, are left with not so much as a patch of ground or a home; and as for you, if any of you transgresses even in secret, he is sought out and punished with death." As the question started is, "What would happen if the Romans were persuaded to adopt the principles of the Christians, to despise the duties paid to the recognised gods and to men, and to worship the Most High?" this is my answer to the question. We say that "if two" of us "shall agree on earth as touching anything that they shall ask, it shall be done for them of the Father" of the just, "which is in heaven;"[1] for God rejoices in the agreement of rational beings, and turns away from discord. And what are we to expect, if not only a very few agree, as at present, but the whole of the empire of Rome? For they will pray to the Word, who of old said to the Hebrews, when they were pursued by the Egyptians, "The LORD shall fight for you, and ye shall hold your peace;"[2] and if they all unite in prayer with one accord, they will be able to put to flight far more enemies than those who were discomfited by the prayer of Moses when he cried to the Lord, and of those who prayed with him. Now, if what God promised to those who keep His law has not come to pass, the reason of its non-

fulfilment is not to be ascribed to the unfaithfulness of God. But He had made the fulfilment of His promises to depend on certain conditions, — namely, that they should observe and live according to His law; and if the Jews have not a plot of ground nor a habitation left to them, although they had received these conditional promises, the entire blame is to be laid upon their crimes, and especially upon their guilt in the treatment of Jesus.

CHAP. LXX.

But if all the Romans, according to the supposition of Celsus, embrace the Christian faith, they will, when they pray, overcome their enemies; or rather, they will not war at all, being guarded by that divine power which promised to save five entire cities for the sake of fifty just persons. For men of God are assuredly the salt of the earth: they preserve the order of the world;[3] and society is held together as long as the salt is uncorrupted: for "if the salt have lost its savour, it is neither fit for the land nor for the dunghill; but it shall be cast out, and trodden under foot of men. He that hath ears, let him hear"[4] the meaning of these words. When God gives to the tempter permission to persecute us, then we suffer persecution; and when God wishes us to be free from suffering, even in the midst of a world that hates us, we enjoy a wonderful peace, trusting in the protection of Him who said, "Be of good cheer, I have overcome the world."[5] And truly He has overcome the world. Wherefore the world prevails only so long as it is the pleasure of Him who received from the Father power to overcome the world; and from His victory we take courage. Should He even wish us again to contend and struggle for our religion, let the enemy come against us, and we will say to them, "I can do all things, through Christ Jesus our Lord, which strengtheneth me."[6] For of "two sparrows which are sold for a farthing," as the Scripture says, "not one of them falls on the ground without our Father in heaven."[7] And so completely does the Divine Providence embrace all things, that not even the hairs of our head fail to be numbered by Him.

CHAP. LXXI.

Celsus again, as is usual with him, gets confused, and attributes to us things which none of us have ever written. His words are: "Surely it is intolerable for you to say, that if our present rulers, on embracing your opinions, are taken by

---

[1] Matt. xviii. 19.
[2] Ex. xiv. 14.

[3] [Comp. Cowper, *Task*, book vi., *sub finem.*]
[4] Luke xiv. 34, 35; Matt. v. 13.
[5] John xvi. 33.
[6] Phil. iv. 13.
[7] Matt. x. 29, 30.

the enemy, you will still be able to persuade those who rule after them ; and after these have been taken you will persuade their successors, and so on, until at length, when all who have yielded to your persuasion have been taken, some prudent ruler shall arise, with a foresight of what is impending, and he will destroy you all utterly before he himself perishes." There is no need of any answer to these allegations : for none of us says of our present rulers, that if they embrace our opinions, and are taken by the enemy, we shall be able to persuade their successors ; and when these are taken, those who come after them, and so on in succession. But on what does he ground the assertion, that when a succession of those who have yielded to our persuasion have been taken because they did not drive back the enemy, some prudent ruler shall arise, with a foresight of what is impending, who shall utterly destroy us ? But here he seems to me to delight in inventing and uttering the wildest nonsense.

CHAP. LXXII.

Afterwards he says : " If it were possible," implying at the same time that he thought it most desirable, " that all the inhabitants of Asia, Europe, and Libya, Greeks and Barbarians, all to the uttermost ends of the earth, were to come under one law ; " but judging this quite impossible, he adds, " Any one who thinks this possible, knows nothing." It would require careful consideration and lengthened argument to prove that it is not only possible, but that it will surely come to pass, that all who are endowed with reason shall come under one law. However, if we must refer to this subject, it will be with great brevity. The Stoics, indeed, hold that, when the strongest of the elements prevails, all things shall be turned into fire. But our belief is, that the Word shall prevail over the entire rational creation, and change every soul into His own perfection ; in which state every one, by the mere exercise of his power, will choose what he desires, and obtain what he chooses. For although, in the diseases and wounds of the body, there are some which no medical skill can cure, yet we hold that in the mind there is no evil so strong that it may not be overcome by the Supreme Word and God. For stronger than all the evils in the soul is the Word, and the healing power that dwells in Him ; and this healing He applies, according to the will of God, to every man. The consummation of all things is the destruction of evil, although as to the question whether it shall be so destroyed that it can never anywhere arise again, it is beyond our present purpose to say. Many things are said obscurely in the prophecies on the total destruction of evil, and the restoration

to righteousness of every soul ; but it will be enough for our present purpose to quote the following passage from Zephaniah : " Prepare and rise early ; all the gleanings of their vineyards are destroyed. Therefore wait ye upon Me, saith the LORD, on the day that I rise up for a testimony ; for My determination is to gather the nations, that I may assemble the kings, to pour upon them Mine indignation, even all My fierce anger : for all the earth shall be devoured with the fire of My jealousy. For then will I turn to the people a pure language, that they may all call upon the name of the LORD, to serve Him with one consent. From beyond the rivers of Ethiopia My suppliants, even the daughter of My dispersed, shall bring My offering. In that day shalt thou not be ashamed for all thy doings, wherein thou hast transgressed against Me : for then I will take away out of the midst of thee them that rejoice in thy pride ; and thou shalt no more be haughty because of My holy mountain. I will also leave in the midst of thee an afflicted and poor people, and they shall trust in the name of the LORD. The remnant of Israel shall not do iniquity, nor speak lies ; neither shall a deceitful tongue be found in their mouth : for they shall feed and lie down, and none shall make them afraid." [1] I leave it to those who are able, after a careful study of the whole subject, to unfold the meaning of this prophecy, and especially to inquire into the signification of the words, " When the whole earth is destroyed, there will be turned upon the peoples a language according to their race," [2] as things were before the confusion of tongues. Let them also carefully consider the promise, that all shall call upon the name of the Lord, and serve Him with one consent ; also that all contemptuous reproach shall be taken away, and there shall be no longer any injustice, or vain speech, or a deceitful tongue. And thus much it seemed needful for me to say briefly, and without entering into elaborate details, in answer to the remark of Celsus, that he considered any agreement between the inhabitants of Asia, Europe, and Libya, as well Greeks as Barbarians, was impossible. And perhaps such a result would indeed be impossible to those who are still in the body, but not to those who are released from it.

CHAP. LXXIII.

In the next place, Celsus urges us " to help the king with all our might, and to labour with him in the maintenance of justice, to fight for him ; and if he requires it, to fight under him, or lead an army along with him." To this our answer is, that we do, when occasion requires,

---

[1] Zeph. iii. 7-13.
[2] " A language to last as long as the world." — BOUHÉREAU.

give help to kings, and that, so to say, a divine help, "putting on the whole armour of God."[1] And this we do in obedience to the injunction of the apostle, "I exhort, therefore, that first of all, supplications, prayers, intercessions, and giving of thanks, be made for all men; for kings, and for all that are in authority;"[2] and the more any one excels in piety, the more effective help does he render to kings, even more than is given by soldiers, who go forth to fight and slay as many of the enemy as they can. And to those enemies of our faith who require us to bear arms for the commonwealth, and to slay men, we can reply: "Do not those who are priests at certain shrines, and those who attend on certain gods, as you account them, keep their hands free from blood, that they may with hands unstained and free from human blood offer the appointed sacrifices to your gods; and even when war is upon you, you never enlist the priests in the army. If that, then, is a laudable custom, how much more so, that while others are engaged in battle, these too should engage as the priests and ministers of God, keeping their hands pure, and wrestling in prayers to God on behalf of those who are fighting in a righteous cause, and for the king who reigns righteously, that whatever is opposed to those who act righteously may be destroyed!" And as we by our prayers vanquish all demons who stir up war, and lead to the violation of oaths, and disturb the peace, we in this way are much more helpful to the kings than those who go into the field to fight for them. And we do take our part in public affairs, when along with righteous prayers we join self-denying exercises and meditations, which teach us to despise pleasures, and not to be led away by them. And none fight better for the king than we do. We do not indeed fight under him, although he require it; but we fight on his behalf, forming a special army — an army of piety — by offering our prayers to God.

CHAP. LXXIV.

And if Celsus would have us to lead armies in defence of our country, let him know that we do this too, and that not for the purpose of being seen by men, or of vainglory. For "in secret," and in our own hearts, there are prayers which ascend as from priests in behalf of our fellow-citizens. And Christians are benefactors of their country more than others. For they train up citizens, and inculcate piety to the Supreme Being; and they promote those whose lives in the smallest cities have been good and worthy, to a divine and heavenly city, to whom it may be said, "Thou hast been faithful in the smallest city, come into a great one,"[3] where "God standeth in the assembly of the gods, and judgeth the gods in the midst;" and He reckons thee among them, if thou no more "die as a man, or fall as one of the princes."[4]

CHAP. LXXV.

Celsus also urges us to "take office in the government of the country, if that is required for the maintenance of the laws and the support of religion." But we recognise in each state the existence of another national organization,[5] founded by the Word of God, and we exhort those who are mighty in word and of blameless life to rule over Churches. Those who are ambitious of ruling we reject; but we constrain those who, through excess of modesty, are not easily induced to take a public charge in the Church of God. And those who rule over us well are under the constraining influence of the great King, whom we believe to be the Son of God, God the Word. And if those who govern in the Church, and are called rulers of the divine nation — that is, the Church — rule well, they rule in accordance with the divine commands, and never suffer themselves to be led astray by worldly policy. And it is not for the purpose of escaping public duties that Christians decline public offices, but that they may reserve themselves for a diviner and more necessary service in the Church of God — for the salvation of men. And this service is at once necessary and right. They take charge of all — of those that are within, that they may day by day lead better lives, and of those that are without, that they may come to abound in holy words and in deeds of piety; and that, while thus worshipping God truly, and training up as many as they can in the same way, they may be filled with the word of God and the law of God, and thus be united with the Supreme God through His Son the Word, Wisdom, Truth, and Righteousness, who unites to God all who are resolved to conform their lives in all things to the law of God.

CHAP. LXXVI.

You have here, reverend Ambrosius, the conclusion of what we have been enabled to accomplish by the power given to us in obedience to your command. In eight books we have embraced all that we considered it proper to say in reply to that book of Celsus which he entitles *A True Discourse*. And now it remains for the readers of his discourse and of my reply to judge which of the two breathes most of the Spirit of

---

[1] Eph. vi. 11.
[2] 1 Tim. ii. 1, 2.
[3] Luke xix. 17.
[4] Ps. lxxxii. 1, 7.
[5] σύστημα πατρίδος. [A very notable passage as to the autonomy of the primitive Churches in their divers nations.]

the true God, of piety towards Him, and of that truth which leads men by sound doctrines to the noblest life. You must know, however, that Celsus had promised another treatise as a sequel to this one, in which he engaged to supply practical rules of living to those who felt disposed to embrace his opinions. If, then, he has not fulfilled his promise of writing a second book, we may well be contented with these eight books which we have written in answer to his discourse. But if he has begun and finished that second book, pray obtain it and send it to us, that we may answer it as the Father of truth may give us ability, and either overthrow the false teaching that may be in it, or, laying aside all jealousy, we may testify our approval of whatever truth it may contain.

GLORY BE TO THEE, OUR GOD; GLORY BE TO THEE.

INDEXES.

TERTULLIAN.

PART FOURTH.

INDEX OF SUBJECTS.

TERTULLIAN.

PART FOURTH.

INDEX OF TEXTS.

MINUCIUS FELIX.

INDEX OF SUBJECTS.

INDEX OF TEXTS.

COMMODIANUS.

INDEX OF SUBJECTS.

INDEX OF TEXTS.

ORIGEN AGAINST CELSUS.

ANALYSIS OF CONTENTS.

at all remarkable as compared with those attributed to Perseus and Amphion, and other mythological personages, but admits afterwards that some of them were remarkable, — such as His cures, and His resurrection, and the feeding of the multitude, — although he immediately afterwards compares them to the tricks of jugglers, and denies that they can furnish any proof of His being "Son of God:" Answer, cc. lxvii., lxviii. Objection of Celsus that the body of Jesus could not have been that of a god, nor could be nourished with such food as Jesus partook of: Answer, cc. lxix., lxx. Declares that opinions of Jesus were those of a wicked and God-hated sorcerer: Answer, c. lxxi.

This book contains Origen's answers to the charges which Celsus, in the person of a Jew, brings against the converts from Judaism to Christianity. Main charge is, that "they have forsaken the law of their fathers, in consequence of their minds being led captive by Jesus; that they have been most ridiculously deceived; and that they have become deserters to another name and to another mode of life." Answer to these charges, c. i. Digression upon certain declarations of Jesus in the Gospels, c. ii. Ignorance of Celsus evinced by the manner in which he represents the Jew as addressing the Israelitish converts, c. iii. Objection of Jew, that Christianity takes its origin from Judaism, and that after a certain point it discards Judaism: Answer, c. iv. Assertion of Celsus, that Jesus was punished by the Jews for His crimes, already answered, c. v. Observance by Jesus of Jewish usages and sacrificial observances, no argument against His recognition as the Son of God, c. vi Language of Jesus furnishes not the slightest evidence, but the reverse, of arrogance: Quotations, c. vii. Allegation, that when men are willing to be deceived, many persons like Jesus would find a friendly reception; inconsistency of this; various other charges disposed of, c. viii. Assertion of Celsus, that Jesus could not be deemed a god because He was currently reported to have performed none of His promises, and, after conviction and sentence, was found attempting to conceal Himself and endeavouring to escape, and was then betrayed by His disciples; impossibility of such things, according to Celsus, happening to a god: Answer to these calumnies and objections, cc. ix.-xi. Assertion of Celsus, that Jesus was inferior to a brigand chief, because He was betrayed by His disciples: Answer, c. xii. Celsus asserts that he omits mention of many things in the life of Christ which he could state to His disadvantage; challenged to produce such: Several predictions of Jesus quoted and commented on, c. xiii. Celsus makes light of the admission that future events were predicted by Jesus: Remarks of Origen in answer, c. xiv. Assertion of Celsus, that the disciples of Jesus devised the fiction that He foreknew everything before it happened: Answer, c xv. Asserts that the disciples wrote the accounts they have given by way of extenuating the charges against Him· Answer, c. xvi. Celsus alleges that a prudent man — much more a god or spirit — would have tried to escape dangers that were foreseen, whereas Jesus did the reverse: Answer, c. xvii. Objection of Celsus, that the announcements which Jesus made regarding those disciples who were to betray and deny Him had not the effect of deterring them from their treason and perjury, shown to be self-contradictory, c. xviii. Further statement of Celsus, that in such cases intending criminals abandon their intentions, shown to be untrue, c. xix. Objection, that if Jesus had been a god, His pre-

dictions must infallibly have come to pass; and assertion, that He plotted against the members of His own table: Refuted, cc. xx.-xxii. Assertion, that the things which He suffered could have been neither painful nor distressing, because He submitted to them voluntarily and as a god, c. xxiii. Misrepresentation of Celsus as to the language employed by Jesus during His sufferings, cc. xxiv., xxv. Celsus charges the disciples with having invented statements: Answer, c. xxvi. Alleges that Christian believers have corrupted the Gospel in order to be able to reply to objections: Answer, c. xxvii. The Jew of Celsus reproaches Christians with making use of the prophets: Answer, c. xxviii. Assertion of Celsus, that from such signs and misinterpretations, and from proofs so mean, no one could prove Jesus to be god and the Son of God: Answer, c. xxx. Charges Christians with sophistical reasoning in saying that the Son of God is the Logos Himself: Refutation, c. xxxi. Objection of Celsus to our Lord's genealogy: Refutation, c. xxxii. Celsus ridicules the actions of Jesus as unworthy of a god: Refutation, c. xxxiii. Inconsistency of Celsus in representing the Jew as conversant with Greek literature; various remarks of Celsus answered, c. xxxiv. Question of Celsus, why Jesus does not give some manifestation of His divinity by taking vengeance upon those who insult Him and His Father: Answered, c. xxxv. Celsus scoffingly inquires, What was the nature of the ichor in the body of Jesus? and asserts that Jesus rushed with open mouth to drink of the vinegar and gall: Answer, cc. xxxvi., xxxvii. Sneer of the Jew, that Christians find fault with Jews for not recognising Jesus as God: Answer, c. xxxviii. Falsehood of the assertion of this Jew of Celsus, that Jesus gained over to His cause no one during His life, not even His own disciples, c. xxxix. Jew goes on to assert that Jesus did not show Himself to be pure from all evil: Answer, cc. xli., xlii. Falsity of the statement, that Jesus, after failing to gain over those who were in this world, went to Hades to gain over those who were there, c. xliii. Celsus asserts further, that other individuals who have been condemned and died miserable deaths ought to be regarded as greater and more divine messengers of heaven than Jesus: Answer, c. xliv. Argument of Celsus against the truth of Christianity, from the different behaviour of the actual followers of Jesus during His life and that of Christians at the present day: Answer, c. xlv. Falsehood of the assertion, that Jesus when on earth gained over to Himself only sailors and tax-gatherers of the most worthless character, c. xlvi. Answer to the question, By what train of argument were Christians led to regard Jesus as the Son of God? c. xlvii. Assertion of Celsus, that Jesus is deemed by Christians to be the Son of God because He healed the lame and the blind and is asserted to have raised the dead: Answer, c. xlviii. Statement of Celsus, that Jesus convicted Himself of being a sorcerer: Refuted by His predictions regarding false prophets, etc., cc. xlix., l. No resemblance between the works of Jesus and those of a sorcerer, c. li. Inconsistency of the Jew in raising the objections which he does, seeing that the same objections might be raised against the divinity of Mosaism, cc. lii.-liv. Jew objects further, that the predictions, although actually uttered, prove nothing, because many have been deceived by juggling tricks; asserts also, that there is no satisfactory evidence of the resurrection of Jesus, the report of which can be explained in other ways: Answer, cc. lv.-lxii. Celsus proceeds to bring, as a serious charge against Jesus, that He did not appear after His resurrection to those who had ill-treated Him and condemned Him, and to

Celsus as to the meaning of such a descent: Answered, c. iii. Argument of Celsus turned against himself, c. iv. Celsus misrepresents Christians as saying that God Himself will come down to men, and that it follows that He has left His own abode, c. v. Celsus represents the object of God's descent to be a desire to make Himself known, and to make trial of men; and this, he alleges, testifies to an excessive and mortal ambition on the part of God: Answer, cc. vi.–ix. Celsus asserts, that Christians talk of God in a way that is neither holy nor reverential, and likens them to those who in the Bacchic mysteries introduce phantoms and objects of terror: Answer, c. x. Celsus endeavours to prove that the statements in the Christian records regarding floods and conflagrations are neither new nor wonderful, but may be paralleled and explained from the accounts of the Greeks: Answer, cc. xi.–xiii. Celsus returns to the subject of the descent of God, alleging that if He came down among men, He must have undergone a change from better to worse, which is impossible in the case of an immortal being: Answer, cc. xiv.–xvi. Superiority of the scriptural accounts of these matters over those of the Greek mythology, c. xvii. Celsus repeats his objections: Answer, cc. xviii., xix. Celsus' representation of the manner in which the Jews maintain that the advent of Jesus is still future, c. xx. Absurdity of the statement of Celsus that the overturning of the tower of Babel had the same object as the Deluge, viz., the purification of the earth, c. xxi. Proof that Jews brought on themselves the divine wrath, because of their treatment of Jesus, c. xxii. Celsus insolently compares Jews and Christians to bats, and ants, and frogs, and worms, etc., c. xxiii. Answer, cc. xxiv., xxv. Superiority of Christians in their opinions and practice to idolaters, cc. xxvi., xxvii. Celsus misrepresents the language of Christians as to God's descent among men, and His intercourse with them, cc. xxviii., xxix. Celsus, not understanding the words, "Let Us make man in Our image and likeness," has represented Christians as saying that they *resemble* God because created by Him: Answer, c. xxx. Celsus again asserts that the Jews were fugitives from Egypt, who never performed anything of note, and were never held in any account: Answer, cc. xxxi., xxxii. Celsus, in very ambiguous language, asserts that the Jews endeavoured to derive their origin from the first race of jugglers and deceivers, and appealed to the testimony of dark and ambiguous words: Answer, cc. xxxiii.–xxxv. Celsus adduces instances of alleged great antiquity put forth by other nations, and asserts that the Jews wove together some most incredible and stupid stories, regarding the creation of man, the formation of the woman, the issuing of certain commands by God, the opposition of the serpent, and the defeat of God, who is thus shown to have been weak at the very beginning of things, and unable to persuade a single individual to obey His will: Detailed answers to these misrepresentations, cc. xxxvi.–xl. Celsus next ridicules the accounts of the Deluge and the Ark: Answers, cc. xli., xlii. Goes on to carp at the histories of Abraham and Sarah, of Cain and Abel, of Esau and Jacob, of Laban and Jacob, c. xliii. Explanation of the statement that "God gave wells to the righteous;" other matters, also, to be allegorically understood, c. xliv. Celsus does not recognise the love of truth which characterizes the writers of Scripture; figurative signification of Sodom, and of Lot and his daughters; discussion on the nature of actions, c. xlv. Spirit of hostility which characterizes Celsus, in selecting from the narratives of Scripture whatever may serve as ground of accusation against Christians, while passing without notice whatever

may redound to their credit: Instances, c. xlvi. Celsus refers vaguely to the dreams of the butler and baker in the history of Joseph, and endeavours to find ground of objection in the history of Joseph's conduct towards his brethren, c. xlvii. Asserts that the more modest among Jews and Christians endeavour to give these things an allegorical meaning, because they are ashamed of them: Answer, c. xlviii. Falsity of his assertion that the scriptural writings are incapable of receiving an allegorical meaning, cc. xlix., l. The treatises which give allegorical explanations of the law of Moses evidently unknown to Celsus, otherwise he could not have said that these allegorical explanations were more shameful than the fables themselves: Illustrations, c. li. Celsus refers to the work entitled "Controversy between Papiscus and Jason," in support of his assertions, cc. lii., liii. Celsus conceals his real opinions, although he ought to have avowed them, when quoting from the *Timæus* of Plato, to the effect that God made immortal things alone, while mortal things are the work of others; that the soul is the work of God, while the body is different; that there is no difference between the body of a man and that of a bat: Examination of these statements, cc. liv.–lix. Asserts that a common nature pervades all bodies, and that no product of matter is immortal: Answers, cc. lx., lxi. Maintains that the amount of evil is a fixed quantity, which has never varied: Answers, cc. lxii.–lxiv. That it is difficult for any but a philosopher to ascertain the origin of evils, but that it is sufficient for the multitude to say that they do not proceed from God, but cleave to matter; and that, as the cause of mortal events never varies, the same things must always return, according to the appointed cycles: Answers, cc. lxv.–lxix. Assertion of Celsus that a thing which seems to be evil may not necessarily be so: Examined, c. lxx. Celsus misunderstands the anthropopathic language of Scripture: Explanation, cc. lxxi.–lxxiii. Celsus finds fault with Christians for asserting that God made all things for the sake of man, whereas they were made as much for the sake of the irrational animals: Answer, c. lxxiv. Celsus holds that thunders, and lightnings, and rains are not the works of God; that even if they were, they were brought into existence as much for the sake of plants, and trees, and herbs, as for that of human beings: Answer, cc. lxxv., lxxvi. Celsus maintains that the verse of Euripides, "The sun and night are to mortals slaves," is untrue, as these luminaries may be said to be created for the use of ants and flies as much as of man: Answer, c. lxxvii. Asserts that we may be said to be created as much on account of irrational animals as they on our account: Answer, cc. lxxviii.–lxxx. Celsus maintains that the superiority of man over irrational animals in building cities and founding political communities is only apparent: Examination of this assertion, cc. lxxxi.–lxxxiv. No great difference, according to Celsus, between the actions of men and those of ants and bees, c. lxxxv. Certain irrational animals, according to Celsus, possess the power of sorcery; instances: Examination of these, cc. lxxxvi., lxxxvii. Assertion that the thoughts entertained of God by irrational animals are not inferior to those of men; illustrations: Answer, cc. lxxxviii., lxxxix. Degrading views of Celsus, cc. xc.–xcix.

Continuation of the subject, c. i. Celsus repeats his denial that no God, or son of God, has either come, or will come, to earth; that if certain angels did come, by what name are they to be called? whether by that of gods or some other race of beings? in all probability such angels were demons: Refutation, cc. ii.–v. Celsus proceeds to express surprise that the Jews should worship heaven and angels, and yet pass by the heavenly bodies, as the sun and moon; which procedure is, according to his view, most unreasonable: Refutation, cc. vi.–x. Defence of Christians against the same charge, cc. x.–xiii. Celsus declares the Christian belief in the future conflagration of the world, in the salvation of the righteous, in the resurrection of the body, most foolish and irrational, alleging that this belief is not held by some of the Christian believers, and adducing certain considerations regarding the character of God and the nature of bodies which render such things impossible, c. xiv. Refutation in detail of these objections, cc. xv.–xxiv. Examination of Celsus' statement that the various quarters of the earth were from the beginning allotted to different superintending spirits, and that in this way the administration of the world is carried on, cc. xxv.–xxviii. Considerations of a profounder kind may be stated regarding the original distribution of the various quarters of the earth among different superintending spirits, which considerations may be shown to be free from the absurd consequences which would follow from the views of Celsus; enumeration of these, cc. xxix.–xxxiii. Statement of Celsus regarding the request of the people of Marea and Apis to the oracle of Ammon, as related by Herodotus, and the inference which he seems to draw from it and other similar instances adduced by him, examined and refuted, cc. xxxiv.–xxxix. Examination of Celsus' quotation from Pindar, that "Law is king of all things," c. xl. Celsus goes on to state objections which apply to Jews much more than to Christians, viz., that the Jewish doctrine regarding heaven is not peculiar to them, but has long ago been received by the Persians; and proceeds to observe that it makes no difference by what name the Supreme Being is called; nor are the Jews to be deemed holier than other nations because abstaining from swine's flesh, etc. Detailed examination and refutation of these statements, cc. xli.–xlix. Celsus denies that the Jews were regarded by God with greater favour than other nations: Answer, c. l. Statement of Celsus that, admitting Jesus to have been an angel, He was not the first who came to visit men, for the histories relate that there have been many instances, several of which he enumerates, c. lii. Refutation, cc. liii.–lviii. Conclusion of Celsus that Jews and Christians have the same God, and that the latter adopt the Jewish accounts regarding the six days; other points of agreement mentioned: Examination of these statements, as well as of his admission that certain Christians will admit the identity, while others will deny it, cc. lix.–lxii. Argument of Celsus against Christianity, founded upon the existence of those who have worshipped demons as their teacher, and of sects that have hated each other, examined and refuted, c. lxiii. Celsus has misunderstood the prediction of the apostle that deceivers will come in the last times, c. lxiv. Falsity of Celsus' statement that all who differ so widely may be heard saying, "The world is crucified to me, and I unto the world," c. lxv.

BOOK VI. . . . . . . pp. 573–610

Object of Sixth Book specially to refute those objections which *Celsus* brings against Christians, and not those derived from writers on philosophy, c. i. Explanation of the reasons which led the writers of Scripture to adopt a simple style of address, c. ii. Quotation from Plato regarding the "chief good," and remarks upon it, c. iii. Inconsistent conduct of those who can so express themselves pointed out,

c. iv. Comparison of the Platonic phraseology, regarding the kindling of a light in the soul, with the language of Scripture, c. v. Examination of the question whether Plato was acquainted with doctrines more profound than those which are contained in his writings, and demonstration of the fact that the prophets did know of greater things than any in Scripture, but did not commit them to writing, cc. vi.–x. Celsus inquires whether, amid the perplexity arising from the existence of different Christs, men are to cast the dice to divine which of them they ought to follow? Answer, c. xi. Perversion of the language of Paul regarding wisdom corrected, cc. xii., xiii. Examination of Celsus' charge that Christians are uninstructed, servile, and ignorant, c. xiv. Sneer of Celsus at the humility of Christians answered, c. xv. Celsus charges Jesus with having perverted the language of Plato in His saying regarding the impossibility of a rich man's entering the kingdom of heaven: Answer, c. xvi. Comparison of some points of Scripture doctrine with statements of Plato, cc. xvii., xviii. Charge of Celsus that Christians have misunderstood language of Plato, in boasting of a "super-celestial" God Answer, c. xix. Explanation of certain terms referring to heaven, cc. xx., xxi. Assertion of Celsus, that the Persian mysteries of Mithras contain many obscure allusions to those heavenly things mentioned in the Christian writings; absurdity of his statements, cc. xxii., xxiii. Celsus refers to a certain diagram, the statements regarding which he appears to have borrowed from the sect of the Ophites; which statements, however, are of no credibility, c. xxiv. Description of said diagram, and explanation of the names inscribed in it, cc. xxv., xxvi. Certain statements of Celsus regarding the "seal" examined, c. xxvii. Celsus asserts that Christians term the Creator an "accursed" divinity, and asks what could be more foolish or insane than such senseless wisdom? Examination of these statements, cc. xxviii., xxix. Celsus returns to the subject of the seven ruling demons, and makes reference to the diagram, c. xxx. Quotations illustrating the manner of invoking said demons, c. xxxi. Remarks on the procedure of Celsus, c. xxxii. Further statements of Celsus, c. xxxiii. Continuation of statements of Celsus, to the effect that Christians heap together one thing after another, — discourses of prophets, circles upon circles, effluents from an earthly church, and from circumcision; and a power flowing from one Prunicos, a virgin and living soul; and a heaven slain in order to live, etc., etc., c. xxxiv. Detailed examination and answer to these statements, cc. xxxv.–xxxvii. Celsus introduces other charges, stating that there are inscriptions in the diagram containing two words, "a greater and a less," which are referred to Father and Son: Answer, c. xxxviii. Statement of Celsus, that names of demons among the Greeks are different from what they are among the Scythians; gives illustrations: Answer, c. xxxix. Statement of Celsus, on the authority of Dionysius, an Egyptian magician, that magic arts have no power over philosophers, but only over uneducated men and persons of corrupt morals: Falsity of this shown, c. xli. Allegation of Celsus, that Christians have invented the fiction of the devil or Satan, as an adversary to God, who counterworks His plans and defeats them; that the Son of God, even, has been vanquished by the devil; and that the devil will exhibit great and marvellous works, and claim for himself the glory of God: Examination and refutation of these statements, cc. xlii.–xliv. Celsus has misunderstood the statements of Scripture regarding Antichrist: Explanation of these, cc. xlv., xlvi. Celsus perverts the language of Christians regarding the "Son of God:" Answer, c. xlvii. Mystical meaning of "Son of God" explained, c. xlviii. Celsus characterizes the Mosaic cosmogony as extremely silly, and alleges that Moses and the prophets, from ignorance, have woven together a web of sheer nonsense. Answers, cc. xlix.-li. Celsus will not decide whether the world was uncreated and indestructible, or created but not destructible, c. lii. Brings forward objections that were raised against Marcion, and after several disparaging observations on the manner of the divine procedure towards men, asks how it is that God created evil, etc., c. liii. Answer to the foregoing, cc. liv.-lix. Celsus repeats charges formerly made regarding the days of creation, cc. lx., lxi. Comments on the expression, "The mouth of the Lord hath spoken it:" Answer, c. lxii. Asserts that "the first-born of every creature" is the image of God, and that God did not make man in His image, because he is unlike to any other species of being; explanation of the expression, "Man is made after the image of God," c. lxiii. God partakes neither of form nor colour, nor can motion be predicated of Him; explanation of passages that seem to imply the reverse, c. lxiv. Inconsistency of Celsus with his declared opinions, in saying that God is the source of all things; asserts that He cannot be reached by word: Explanation and distinction, c. lxv. Celsus asks, in the person of another, how it is possible to know God, or to learn the way that leads to Him, because darkness is thrown before the eyes, and nothing distinctly seen: Answer to this query, and remark of Celsus retorted upon himself, cc. lxvi.-lxviii. Celsus represents our answer as being this: "Since God is great and difficult to see, He put His own Spirit into a body that resembled ours, and sent it down to us, that we might be enabled to hear Him, and become acquainted with Him:" Examination of this statement, cc. lxix., lxx According to Celsus, our doctrine regarding the spirit is the same as that of the Stoics, who maintain that "God is a spirit, diffused through all things, and containing all things within Himself:" Answer, c. lxxi. Assertion that the Son of God would not be immortal, because He was a spirit existing in a human body: Answer, c. lxxii. Criticises, in scoffing language, the Incarnation; exposure of his errors, c. lxxiii. Returns to the subject of Marcion's opinions; introduces "two sons of God," and speaks scoffingly of the supposed controversies between them, c. lxxiv. Maintains that the body of Jesus must have been different from that of other beings, in virtue of His divine qualities. Consideration of the prophecies regarding Jesus: Answers to his statements, cc. lxxv.-lxxvii. Celsus ridicules the sending of God's Spirit into *one* corner of the world alone, and compares God to Jupiter in the comedy, who sent Mercury to the Athenians and Lacedæmonians: Answer, cc. lxxviii., lxxix. Celsus terms the Chaldeans a divinely inspired nation; speaks of the Egyptian people as also inspired, although he condemned them formerly, and refuses this title to the Jews; inconsistency of all this, c. lxxx. Pretends not to understand how God could send His Son amongst wicked men, who were to inflict punishment upon Him: Answer, c. lxxxi.

BOOK VII. . . . . . . pp. 611-639

Celsus denies that the Jewish prophets predicted any of the events which occurred in the life of Christ, and asserts that those who believe in the existence of another God, besides that of the Jews, cannot refute his objections; while Christians, who recognise the God of the Jews, rely for their defence on the alleged predictions regarding Christ: Remarks, c. ii. Celsus declares Christians inconsistent in rejecting the ancient Grecian oracles of Delphi, Dodona, Clarus, Branchidæ, Jupiter Ammon, etc., which nevertheless were of high importance, while insisting that the sayings uttered in Judea are marvellous and unchangeably true : Detailed answer to this objection, cc. iii.-viii. Asserts that many individuals assume the attitude of inspiration, and claim to be God, or the Son of God, or the divine Spirit, and to have come down to save a perishing world, and promise rewards to those who do them homage, and threaten vengeance upon others; and, moreover, to these promises add strange and unintelligible words, which may be applied by any impostor to his own purposes, c. ix. Answer to these charges, cc. x.-xii. Falsity of Celsus' statement that God favours the commission of evil, c. xiii. Celsus objects, that even if the prophets foretold that the great God would become a slave, or die, there was no necessity that He should do so simply because such things had been predicted: Answers, cc. xiv.-xvii. Celsus objects further, that if the prophets of the God of the Jews foretold that Jesus was to be the Son of the same God, how could commands have been given through Moses that the Jews should accumulate wealth, extend their dominion, fill the earth, put their enemies to the sword, under threat of being treated by God as His enemies; whilst the man of Nazareth, His Son, delivered commands of a totally opposite kind? Errors of Celsus pointed out in detail, and the nature of the two dispensations explained, cc. xviii.-xxvi. Falsity of assertion that Christians believe the Divine Being to be corporeal in His nature, and to possess a body like a man, c. xxvii. Celsus alleges that the idea of a better land than this, to which Christians hope to go after death, has been borrowed from the divine men of a former age, and quotes from Homer and Plato in support of his assertion : Answers, cc. xxviii.-xxxi. Celsus next assails the doctrine of the resurrection, and asserts that we uphold this doctrine in order that we may see and know God : Answer, cc. xxxii.-xxxiv. The oracles of Trophonius, etc., to which Celsus would direct Christians, assuring them that there they would see God distinctly, shown to be demons, c. xxxv. Language of Christians as to the manner in which they see God misrepresented by Celsus, cc. xxxvi.-xxxix. Language of Celsus quite inappropriate as addressed to Christians, and applicable only to those whose doctrines differ widely from theirs, c. xl. Celsus recommends Christians to follow the guidance of divinely inspired poets, wise men, and philosophers, without mentioning their names : Remarks on this, c. xli. Proceeds to name Plato as an effective teacher of theological truth, quoting from the *Timæus* to the effect that it is a hard matter to find out the Maker and Father of the universe, and an impossibility to make Him known to all after having found Him; and remarking that Christians cannot follow the example of Plato and others, who proceed by analysis and synthesis, because they are wedded to the flesh: Answers, cc. xlii.-xlv. General remarks upon the tone in which Christians carry on controversy with their opponents, c. xlvi. Actions of those who, although seeming to be wise, did not yield themselves to the divine teaching, c. xlvii. Purity of life exhibited by Christians, c. xlviii. Even by those who are unable to investigate the deeper questions of theology, c. xlix. Explanation of certain scriptural expressions regarding "birth" or "generation," c. l. Difference between Christians and those who received a portion of the Divine Spirit before the dispensation of Christianity, c. li. Celsus proceeds to say to Christians that they would have done better to have selected as the object of their homage some one who had died a glorious death, whose divinity might have received the support of some myth to perpetuate his memory, and names Hercules, Æsculapius, Anaxarchus, and Epictetus, as instances, alleging that Jesus never uttered under suffering any words that could be compared to their utterances, c. liii. Answers, cc. liv.–lv. Sneering remark of Celsus that we might better have given the name of Son of God to the Sibyl than to Jesus, c. lvi. Scoffing advice of Celsus, that we had better choose Jonah than Jesus for our God: Answer, c. lvii. Celsus asserts that the Christian precept, " Whosoever shall strike thee on the one cheek, turn to him the other also," is an ancient saying, admirably expressed long ago, and reported by Christians in a coarser way, and quotes from Plato in support of his statement: Answer, cc. lviii.–lxi. Celsus goes on to say that Christians cannot tolerate temples, altars, or images, and that in this peculiarity they resemble Scythians and other barbarous nations, adducing quotations from Herodotus and Heraclitus in support of his opinion that none, save those who are utterly childish, can take these things for gods, c. lxii. · Detailed answer, cc. lxiii.–lxvi. Celsus remarks that Christians will not admit that these images are erected in honour of certain beings who are gods, but maintain that these are demons, and ought not to be worshipped: Remarks in answer, c. lxvii. Asks why demons are not to be worshipped, and asserts that everything, whether the work of angels, demons, or heroes, is part of the providential government of the Most High God. Answers, cc. lxviii.–lxx.

BOOK VIII. . . . . . . pp. 640–669

Celsus, after his question regarding the worship of demons, proceeds to represent us as saying that it is impossible to serve many masters, and remarks that this is the language of sedition, and used only by those who stand aloof from all human society, etc. Consideration of the true language of Scripture upon this and kindred points, in answer to this statement, cc. ii.–viii. Reckless language of Celsus, who would have us believe that we are led by our worship of God to that of other things which belong to God, without injury to ourselves, and who yet adds, "We may honour none except those to whom that right has been given by God:" Remarks, c. ix. Nature of the honour which Christians pay to the Son of God, c. x. Celsus asserts that those who uphold the unity of God are guilty of impiety: Answer, c. xi. That if Christians worshipped one God alone, they would have valid arguments against the worship of others, but they pay excessive reverence to one who is the servant of God: Refutation, cc. xii.–xiv. Celsus quotes from the opinions of some obscure heretical sect, contained in what is called a *Heavenly Dialogue*, to the effect that we suppose another God, who is above the heavens, to be the father of Him whom we honour, in order that we may honour the Son of Man alone; whom also we assert to be stronger than God, who rules the world and who rules over them: Answers, cc. xv.–xvi. Celsus goes on to say, that our shrinking from raising altars, statues, and temples, has been agreed upon among us as the badge of a secret society: Answer, cc. xvii.–xx. Assertion of Celsus, that those devoted to the service of God may take part in public feasts or idol offerings: Answer, c. xxi. Answer to objection that Christians themselves observe certain days, as the Preparation, the Passover, and Pentecost, cc. xxii., xxiii. Reasons alleged by Celsus why Christians may make use of idol offerings and public sacrifices at public feasts; examination of these, cc. xxiv.–xxvii. Celsus proceeds to state that if Christians abstain from idol offerings,

they ought. in consistency, to abstain from all animal food, like the Pythagoreans: Answer, cc. xxviii.–xxxii. Celsus alleges that if we come into the world at all, we must give thanks, and first-fruits, and prayers to demons, that they may prove good and kind: Answer, cc. xxxiii., xxxiv. Celsus remarks that the satraps of a Persian ,or Roman monarch could do great injury to those who despised them, and asks, will the satraps and ministers of air and earth be insulted with impunity? Answer, cc. xxxv., xxxvi. Asserts that if Christians invoke those whom they address by barbarous names they will have power, but not if invoked in Latin and Greek; falsity and absurdity of this statement, c. xxxvii. Misrepresents the language addressed by Christians to the Grecian statues, c. xxxviii. Scoffing language of Celsus to the Christians on the rejection of Jesus, whom he terms a demon, and on His inability to save His followers from being put to death, c. xxxix. Contrast between the Christian and heathen doctrine of punishment, c. xl. Railing address of Celsus, to the effect that although Christians may revile the statues of the gods, they would not have reviled the gods themselves with impunity; that nothing happened to those who crucified Jesus; that no father was ever so inhuman as was the Father of Jesus, etc., etc.: Answers, cc. xli.–xliv. Celsus asserts that it is of no use to collect all the oracular responses that have been delivered, for the world is full of them, and many remarkable events have happened in consequence of them, which establish their reality and divinity; general remark in answer, c. xlv. Contrast between conduct of Pythian priestess, who frequently allowed herself to be bribed, and that of the prophets, who were admired for their downright truthfulness, c. xlvi. Assertion of Greeks, that the Jewish history contains fabulous accounts, refuted, c. xlvii. Endeavour of Celsus to show that the doctrines delivered at the celebration of the pagan mysteries are the same as those of the Christians; absurdity of this, c. xlviii. Celsus reproaches Christians with inconsistency in their treatment of the body: Answer, cc. xlix., l. Celsus approves the Christian doctrine that the righteous shall enjoy everlasting life, and the wicked shall suffer everlasting punishment; inconsistency of this on the part of Celsus, c. li. Anxiety of Origen to bring all men to receive the whole system of Christian truth, c. lii. Doubtful manner in which Celsus speaks of certain weighty matters, and reluctance on his part to set down any of them as false; inconsistency of this with the manner in which he treats the doctrines of Christianity, which he regards with a hostile spirit, cc. liii., liv. Celsus asserts that Christians must make their choice between two alternatives; nature of these: Answer, cc. lv.–lvii. Seeks to degrade the souls of men to the worship of demons, by referring to certain practices and beliefs prevalent among the Egyptians: Answer, cc. lviii.–lix. Admits that there is a dangerous tendency in demon-worship: Remarks, cc. lx.–lxii. Yet adds that the more just opinion is that demons desire and need nothing, but that they take pleasure in those who discharge towards them offices of piety: Answer, cc. lxiii.–lxv. Celsus admits that no worshipper of God should submit to anything base, but should encounter any torments or death, rather than do anything unworthy of God; and yet to celebrate the sun, or the praises of Minerva, is only to render higher praise to God; inconsistency of this, cc. lxvi., lxvii. Maintains that the Homeric saying must be observed, " Let one be king, whom the son of crafty Saturn appointed;" sense in which this must be understood by Christians, c. lxviii. Inconsistency on the part of Celsus, after what he has said, in asking whether God would fight for the

Romans, if they were to become converts to the worship of the Most High, cc. lxix., lxx. Further misrepresentations of Celsus pointed out, c. lxxi. Time will come when the Word will change every soul into His own perfections, c. lxxii. Celsus enjoins us to help the king with all our might, and, if required, to fight under him, or lead an army along with him: Answer, c. lxxiii. Also to take office in the government of the country, if necessary for the maintenance of the laws and the support of religion: Answer, c. lxxv. Conclusion, in which Origen mentions that Celsus had announced his intention of writing a second treatise, which Origen requests Ambrose to send him if he should have carried his intentions into execution.

ORIGEN.

INDEX OF SUBJECTS.

ORIGEN.

PARTS FIRST AND SECOND.

INDEX OF TEXTS.